Cultural Studies

Cultural Studies

edited, and with an introduction, by

Lawrence Grossberg

Cary Nelson

Paula A. Treichler

with Linda Baughman
and assistance from John Macgregor Wise

Routledge
New York   London

Published in 1992 by

Routledge
An imprint of Routledge, Chapman and Hall, Inc.
29 West 35 Street
New York, NY 10001

Published in Great Britain by

Routledge
11 New Fetter Lane
London EC4P 4EE

Library of Congress Cataloging in Publication Data

Cultural studies / edited by Lawrence Grossberg, Cary Nelson, and
  Paula A. Treichler.
     p. cm.
  Includes bibliographical references.
  ISBM 0-415-90351-3   ISBN 0-415-90345-9 (PB)
  1. Culture—Methodology. 2. Culture—Study and teaching.
3. Popular culture. I. Grossberg, Lawrence. II. Nelson, Cary.
III. Treichler, Paula A.
GN357.C844 1991
306—dc20   91-30681
                                       CIP

British Library cataloguing in publication data also available.

Contents

Preface

This book grew out of a large international conference—"Cultural Studies Now and in the Future"—organized by the three editors through the Unit for Criticism and Interpretive Theory at the University of Illinois at Urbana-Champaign. The conference, attended by about nine hundred people, was held on the University of Illinois campus from April 4 through April 9, 1990. In addition to those presenting papers at the conference, a number of other people were invited to attend, participate in discussions, and submit papers to the book. Most of the papers have been substantially revised and expanded in the months since then, but several people worked to retain the style of a public presentation.

Something of the flavor of the original event can also be recovered in the discussion sessions, which were transcribed and edited both by us and by the contributors. Some responses remain unchanged; others have been revised or expanded. We have included the names of people asking questions or offering comments whenever they were willing to be identified; and we have cooperated with those who preferred to remain anonymous.

Neither the conference nor the book would have been possible without the help of a great many people. We have recognized on the title page the work of the two graduate assistants who worked longest on the project: Linda Baughman made many of the administrative arrangements for the conference, from scheduling travel for the speakers to contracting for the sound system that transmitted audience comments through the same speakers used by those presenting papers. John Macgregor Wise transcribed all the discussion sessions so that they could be sent to the contributors for revision. Other people employed during the conference were Aleka Akoyunoglou, Ali Anushirvanani, Ann Blanke, Tom Bosma, Traci Brown, Deanna Calvert, Marnie Coleman, Mitra Cowan, Sagri Dhairyam, Maureen Ebben, John Erni, Ian Fielding, Lee Furey, Kyle Grimes, Patrick Hawley, Timothy Jack, Amita Kachru, Linda Katner, Nely Keinanen, Gina Lacopulos, Laurie Lewis, Lynne Murphy, Gil Rodman, Marya Ryan, Stephanie Stavrakos, Taimur Sullivan, and Karine Verhoven. Special thanks goes to Peter Garrett, Director of the Unit for Criticism and Interpretive Theory, and to a number of other people on campus who helped with administrative arrangements: Trudi Gordon, Mona Friedman, Nick Natarella, Brenda Polk, and Sandy Roberts. Financial support within the University of Illinois came from the Afro-American Studies Program, the Center for Latin American and Caribbean Studies, the College of Communications, the College of Liberal Arts and Sciences, Department of English, Department of French, Department of Speech Communication, the Graduate College, the Institute for Communications Research, the Office of the Chancellor, the Program for the Study of Cultural Values and Ethics, the Research Board, Department of Anthropology, Department of Germanic Languages and Literatures, Department of History, Department of Philosophy, Department of Sociology, Graduage School of Library and Information Science, Medical Humanities and Social Science Program, Medical Scholars Program, Office for Women's Resources and Services, Program in Comparative Literature, Program for the Study of Religion, School of Music, Unit for Cinema Studies, and the Women's Studies Program. A grant from Illinois State University covered registration fees for their students and faculty. The Australian Film Commission and the Institute for Policy Studies (Griffith University) helped cover travel expenses from Australia. Finally, we would like to thank several other people for their assistance: Tony Bennett, David Colley, Charles Harris, Edward Sullivan. And we should point out that this book could not have made it into print so efficiently without the support of William Germano at Routledge.

1

Cultural Studies: An Introduction

CARY NELSON, PAULA A. TREICHLER, AND LAWRENCE GROSSBERG

The field of cultural studies is experiencing, as Meaghan Morris puts it, an unprecedented international boom. It remains to be seen how long this boom will last and what impact it will have on intellectual life. Certainly, within the fragmented institutional configuration of the academic left, cultural studies holds special intellectual promise because it explicitly attempts to cut across diverse social and political interests and address many of the struggles within the current scene. As Lata Mani notes in her essay in this volume, in its utopian moments cultural studies sometimes imagines "a location where the new politics of difference—racial, sexual, cultural, transnational—can combine and be articulated in all their dazzling plurality." At the same time, it is undoubtedly cultural studies' material and economic promise that contributes, as much as its intellectual achievement, to its current vogue. In the United States, where the boom is especially strong, many academic institutions—presses, journals, hiring committees, conferences, university curricula—have created significant investment opportunities in cultural studies, sometimes in ignorance of its history, its practitioners, its relation to traditional disciplines, and its life outside the academy.

The present book is partly occasioned by this explosion of interest in cultural studies. It seeks to identify the dimensions of cultural studies and its varied effects, to discuss cultural studies in relation to its intellectual history, its varying definitions, its current affiliations and affinities and diverse objects of study, and its possible futures. Here we introduce the field of cultural studies, describe the goals of the book, and offer a "user's guide" to the essays it includes. The section divisions in the user's guide themselves provide a rough map not only of the overlapping subject matter of the book but also of the major categories of current work in cultural studies: the history of cultural studies, gender and sexuality, nationhood and national identity, colonialism and post-colonialism, race and ethnicity, popular culture and its audiences, science and ecology, identity politics, pedagogy, the politics of aesthetics, cultural institutions, the politics of disciplinarity, discourse and textuality, history, and global culture in a postmodern age. But cultural studies can only partially and uneasily be identified by such domains of interest, since no list can constrain the topics cultural studies may address in the future.

One way to understand cultural studies is to employ the traditional strategies by which disciplines stake out their territories and theoretical paradigms mark their difference: by claiming a particular domain of objects, by developing a unique set of methodological practices, and by carrying forward a founding tradition and lexicon. In the following pages, we will suggest how domain, method, and intellectual legacy help us further understand cultural studies. Yet none of these elements makes cultural studies into a traditional discipline. Indeed, cultural studies is not merely interdisciplinary; it is

1

often, as others have written, actively and aggressively anti-disciplinary—a characteristic that more or less ensures a permanently uncomfortable relation to academic disciplines. As Graeme Turner writes in his essay, "motivated, at least in part, by a critique of the disciplines, cultural studies has been reluctant to become one."

Early in the history of cultural studies in Britain, Richard Hoggart (1969) stressed that cultural studies had no stable disciplinary base. "What was the bibliography of a cultural studies thesis?" Stuart Hall asks, looking back on his experience at the Centre for Contemporary Cultural Studies at Birmingham, "Nobody knew" (Hall, 1990a, p. 17). Cultural studies draws from whatever fields are necessary to produce the knowledge required for a particular project. In the course of its cross-national borrowings, some figures play different roles at different times and places. Richard Johnson (1986/7) suggests that in response to pressures to define cultural studies it be seen as a kind of process, an alchemy for producing useful knowledge about the broad domain of human culture. If it is an alchemy, he warns, codification might halt its ability to bring about reactions. As readers will also learn from this book, it is now an alchemy that draws from many of the major bodies of theory of the last several decades, from Marxism and feminism to psychoanalysis, poststructuralism, and postmodernism.

The methodology of cultural studies provides an equally uneasy marker, for cultural studies in fact has no distinct methodology, no unique statistical, ethnomethodological, or textual analysis to call its own. Its methodology, ambiguous from the beginning, could best be seen as a bricolage. Its choice of practice, that is, is pragmatic, strategic, and self-reflective. At Birmingham, a central goal was "to enable people to understand what [was] going on, and especially to provide ways of thinking, strategies for survival, and resources for resistance" (Hall, 1990a, p. 22). The choice of research practices depends upon the questions that are asked, and the questions depend on their context. It is problematic for cultural studies simply to adopt, uncritically, any of the formalized disciplinary practices of the academy, for those practices, as much as the distinctions they inscribe, carry with them a heritage of disciplinary investments and exclusions and a history of social effects that cultural studies would often be inclined to repudiate. Thus, for example, although there is no prohibition against close textual readings in cultural studies, they are also not required. Moreover, textual analysis in literary studies carries a history of convictions that texts are properly understood as wholly self-determined and independent objects as well as a bias about which kinds of texts are worthy of analysis. That burden of associations cannot be ignored.

Rearticulating to cultural studies the methods privileged by existing disciplines requires considerable work and reflection, work that can neither be done permanently or in advance. For cultural studies has no guarantees about what questions are important to ask within given contexts or how to answer them; hence no methodology can be privileged or even temporarily employed with total security and confidence, yet none can be eliminated out of hand. Textual analysis, semiotics, deconstruction, ethnography, interviews, phonemic analysis, psychoanalysis, rhizomatics, content analysis, survey research—all can provide important insights and knowledge. Some, though not all, of these are employed in the essays that follow; more still have been employed by our contributors in the course of their careers. But methodologies always bear the traces of their history, including methodologies that now have a history within cultural studies itself. This point is made repeatedly and decisively throughout this book: see, for example, Rosalind Brunt's critique of cultural studies' "simplified account of engagement with the media text," a critique taken up in related ways by Jody Berland, Simon Frith, Constance Penley, Janice Radway, William Warner, and others. Here and elsewhere, in individual essays and in discussion sessions, many contributors are acutely aware of the difficulty of providing accounts that draw on multiple methods simultaneously—meshing survey research with ethnography, for example, or information from modern marketing research with more utopian conceptions of empowered consumers. Much of this, for example in Berland's work, explicitly examines notions of what an audience is. As she suggests, the contemporary science of audience research, in which "the topography of consumption is increasingly identified as . . . the map of the social," can at least potentially be seen as a new form of colonialism; certainly its premises problematize the optimistic attribution of agency to consumers and also, perhaps, send a cautionary message about the tendency in cultural studies to celebrate fragmentation—for it is precisely fragmentation that audience research is increasingly able to capitalize. While the commitment of cultural studies is to take this sort of history and positioning into account, this rarely occurs without sustained interrogation or complicated effects. No intellectual practice, even the compelling images of collective effort and ongoing self-interrogation of the Centre for Contemporary Cultural Studies at Birmingham in the 1960s and 1970s, guarantees the practice of cultural studies in every context.

These introductory observations suggest that it is probably impossible to agree on any essential definition or unique narrative of cultural studies. "Cultural studies is not one thing," Stuart Hall has written, "it has never been one thing" (1990a, p. 11). Even when cultural studies is identified with a specific national tradition like British cultural studies, it remains a diverse and often contentious enterprise, encompassing different positions and trajectories in specific contexts, addressing many questions, drawing nourishment from multiple roots, and shaping itself within different institutions and locations. The passage of time, encounters with new historical events, and the very extension of cultural studies into new disciplines and national contexts will inevitably change its meanings and uses. Cultural studies needs to remain open to unexpected, unimagined, even uninvited possibilities. No one can hope to control these developments.

Yet we believe it matters how cultural studies is defined and conceptualized. While the question of "what cultural studies *really* is" may have become impossible to specify for all times and places, we believe that in any given context, cultural studies cannot be just anything. Even the most open definition of cultural studies here—Tony Bennett's "a term of convenience for a fairly dispersed array of theoretical and political positions"— is immediately qualified in a way that marks boundaries: "which, however widely divergent they might be in other respects, share a commitment to examining cultural practices from the point of view of their intrication with, and within, relations of power." To work even within that rather broad configuration, of course, requires an analysis of those relations of power and one's place within them. Moreover, the word "relations" opens out into cultural studies' long history of efforts to theorize and grasp the mutual determinations and interrelations of cultural forms and historical forces.

As Stuart Hall suggests in the discussion following his contribution to this collection, to arrive at such a situated definition requires a whole range of work. That work includes a "moment of self-clarification," which, as Hall emphasizes, has yet to be undertaken by many of us attempting to do cultural studies, particularly in the United States. For while the cultural studies boom is certainly international, its economic value is largely conditioned by its academic expansion in North America; this very success demands that it be closely watched. Will its vitality be compromised by the institutional pluralism of contemporary academic life? Will its rough edges be smoothed out to ease its fit within established disciplinary boundaries? Will the institutional norms of the American academy dissolve its crucial political challenges? What range of work is required to bring about an adequate understanding of what we are doing? What is it that our collective self-clarification must entail? Constructing a vision of cultural studies that can be fruitfully deployed in any particular set of circumstances requires a cultural studies analysis of those very circumstances. At the same time, to address or define the specificity of cultural studies is to ask why it matters. What is at stake in our efforts to practice cultural studies and to reflect on that practice?

As a first step, we can try to offer a very general, generic definition of cultural studies. Although it can be argued that cultural studies itself resists this kind of definition, we think it would be arrogant not to identify, as a starting point at least, some of the recurrent elements of the field. A number of efforts to define and delineate the cultural studies project help map the diversity of positions and traditions that may legitimately lay claim to the name.[1] Keeping those efforts in mind, one may begin by saying that cultural studies is an interdisciplinary, transdisciplinary, and sometimes counter-disciplinary field that operates in the tension between its tendencies to embrace both a broad, anthropological and a more narrowly humanistic conception of culture.[2] Unlike traditional anthropology, however, it has grown out of analyses of modern industrial societies. It is typically interpretive and evaluative in its methodologies, but unlike traditional humanism it rejects the exclusive equation of culture with high culture and argues that all forms of cultural production need to be studied in relation to other cultural practices and to social and historical structures. Cultural studies is thus committed to the study of the entire range of a society's arts, beliefs, institutions, and communicative practices.

Some of the tensions that constitute cultural studies in fact are built into the diverse history of meanings given the word culture itself. "Culture," Williams writes in *Keywords* (a book both Jan Zita Grover and Graeme Turner invoke in this volume rather differently), "is one of the two or three most complicated words in the English language." Its history includes not only static and elitist equations of culture with the achievements of civilization but also broader notions that encompass all symbolic activity, as well as references to culture as an active effort at nurturing and preservation. Moreover, as Williams was able to show through his researches on the "emergence of *culture* as an abstraction and an absolute," "the idea of culture is a general reaction to a general and major change in the condition of our common life. Its basic element is its effort at total qualitative assessment" (1958, pp. xvi, 295). The attempts to define culture thus each grew out of necessity, out of responses to historical change. Williams helps us locate the broad impetus that motivates not only the British tradition of cultural studies but all the traditions: to identify and articulate the relations between culture and society.

After his survey of the varied meanings associated with the word "culture," Williams concludes that it simultaneously invokes symbolic *and* material domains and that the study of culture involves not privileging one domain over the other but interrogating the relation between the two. Thus when Jody Berland discusses the paradoxical powers of technology—the "complex effects of emancipation and domination in the reformation of marginal political and cultural identities"—she focuses on how the music industry constructs potential audiences according to their spatial constitution—that is, the spaces through which music will circulate to them: cars, elevators, offices, malls, hotels, sidewalks, airplanes, buses, cities, small towns, northern settlements, satellite broadcasts, and so on. Fifteen years later, we can take her work as one of the many efforts to push further Williams's argument that culture in this context means "a whole way of life, material, intellectual, and spiritual" (1976, p. 16), including symbolic behavior in a community's everyday life. Writing shortly after Williams, Paul Willis declared that culture "is the very material of our daily lives, the bricks and mortar of our most commonplace understandings" (1977, p. 185). In his essay here John Fiske draws our attention to the most ordinary practices of daily life—how people select and arrange objects in their apartments, how they shop, what they eat. Following in a long cultural studies tradition, he argues that "the social order constrains and oppresses the people, but at the same time offers them resources to fight against those constraints." In cultural studies traditions, then, culture is understood *both* as a way of life—encompassing ideas, attitudes, languages, practices, institutions, and structures of power—and a whole range of cultural practices: artistic forms, texts, canons, architecture, mass-produced commodities, and so forth. Or as Hall puts it, *culture* means "the actual, grounded terrain of practices, representations, languages and customs of any specific historical society" as well as "the contradictory forms of 'common sense' which have taken root in and helped to shape popular life" (Hall, 1986a, p. 26).

As Johnson (1986) writes, cultural studies is both an intellectual and a political tradition. There is a kind of double articulation of culture in cultural studies, where "culture" is simultaneously the ground on which analysis proceeds, the object of study, and the site of political critique and intervention. But cultural studies has not embraced all political positions. As James Carey points out, resistance to cultural studies often reflects an uneasy awareness that its traditions "lead one to commit oneself in advance to a moral evaluation of modern society . . . to a revolutionary line of political action or, at the least, a major project of social reconstruction" (1989, p. 101). Of course the evaluations that cultural studies writers have offered differ considerably. In one of the founding texts of cultural studies, *The Uses of Literacy* (1958), Hoggart decries both contemporary popular culture and the very youth subcultures that subsequent cultural studies scholars have come to value. But it is nonetheless true that from the outset cultural studies' efforts to recover working-class culture and history and to synthesize progressive traditions in Western intellectual history have had both overt and implicit political aims.

These aims and necessities have always been situated historically. Different traditions of cultural studies, including British and American versions, have grown out of efforts to understand the processes that have shaped modern and postwar society and culture: industrialization, modernization, urbanization, the rise of mass communication, the disintegration of what Raymond Williams described as "knowable communities," the increasing commodification of cultural life, the collapse of the Western colonialist empires and the development of new forms of imperialism, the creation of a global economy and the worldwide dissemination of mass culture, the emergence of new forms of economically or ideologically motivated migration, and the re-emergence of nationalism and of racial and religious hostilities. These very general historical conditions manifest themselves differently in different national contexts, contexts that have resulted in several distinctive cultural studies traditions. Moreover, in each context these diverse forces have often produced significant social, political, and cultural disruption, dislocation, and struggle. Hence a continuing preoccupation within cultural studies is the notion of radical social and cultural transformation and how to study it. Yet in virtually all traditions of cultural studies, its practitioners see cultural studies not simply as a chronicle of cultural change but as an intervention in it, and see themselves not simply as scholars providing an account but as politically engaged participants.

Jan Zita Grover and Henry Giroux in their essays here both cite the classroom as one place where cultural studies can make a difference, but the variety of interventions aimed for in these essays eventually ranges through the culture as a whole. Angie Chabram-Dernersesian critiques the gender politics of traditional Chicano culture and offers an analysis of recent Chicana cultural interventions. Kobena Mercer seeks to open up new political alliances based on nonessentialist awareness of racial difference. Jennifer Daryl Slack and Laurie Anne Whitt believe cultural studies can help us to theorize the normative assumptions behind the environmental movement. Douglas Crimp presses us to recognize the effects of how people with AIDS are represented. Elspeth Probyn, talking about the fall 1990 massacre of women engineering students at the University of Montreal (where she teaches) and its impact on the feminist community, calls for greater generosity in our representations of identity and difference as well as in our everyday conduct toward each other. Meaghan Morris calls upon cultural analysts to engage more concretely with the details of contemporary world economic formations, specifically new configurations centering around the Pacific Rim. Tony Bennett argues that cultural studies needs to have an impact on public policy. Paul Gilroy urges us to loosen the hold of national identity on our cultural life and begin to think of the Atlantic community as both a fact of history and a potential field for future political activity. Cornel West gives a general talk on the political function of the intellectual at the present time. Finally, Donna Haraway attempts to lay out global principles for local politics in the postmodern age. She urges us to abandon a traditional politics of representation—which distances, objectifies, decontextualizes, and disempowers whatever it represents—and instead adopt local struggles for strategic collective articulations, articulations that are always contingent, contestable, and impermanent. As Michele Wallace demonstrates, the process of articulating alliances is never self-evident or guaranteed.

Cultural studies thus believes that its practice does matter, that its own intellectual work is supposed to—can—make a difference. But its interventions are not guaranteed; they are not meant to stand forever. The difference it seeks to make is necessarily relevant only for particular circumstances; when cultural studies work continues to be useful over time, it is often because it has been rearticulated to new conditions. Cultural studies is never merely a theoretical practice, even when that practice incorporates notions of politics, power, and context into its analysis. Indeed, the sense that cultural studies offers a bridge between theory and material culture—and has done so throughout its tradition— is an important reason for its appeal to contemporary scholars. In a period of waning enthusiasm for "pure" and implacably ahistorical theory, cultural studies demonstrates the social difference theory can make. In cultural studies, the politics of the analysis and the politics of intellectual work are inseparable. Analysis depends on intellectual work; for cultural studies, theory is a crucial part of that work. Yet intellectual work is, by itself, incomplete unless it enters back into the world of cultural and political power and struggle, unless it responds to the challenges of history. Cultural studies, then, is always partly driven by the political demands of its context and the exigencies of its institutional situation; critical practice is not only determined by, it is responsible to, its situation. Through the last two decades, when theory has sometimes seemed a decontextualized scene of philosophical speculation, cultural studies has regularly theorized in response to particular social, historical, and material conditions. Its theories have attempted to connect to real social and political problems. Now that "theory" is more broadly returning to material concerns and interrogating the social effects of its own discourses, it finds its enterprise clarified and facilitated by the cultural studies challenge.

Thus many of the contributors to this volume are concerned with the role of the intellectual in affecting social change, including Rosalind Brunt, John Fiske, Henry Giroux, Stuart Hall, bell hooks, Meaghan Morris, Andrew Ross, and Cornel West. In Ross's case, this was the primary subject of his 1989 book, *No Respect: Intellectuals and Popular Culture*. For many, this involves considerable self-interrogation. West, for example, calls for intellectuals to examine the academy's own self-sustaining practices and its role in the massive shift to an information and service economy. Hall points to the AIDS epidemic as "one of the questions which urgently brings before us our marginality as critical intellectuals in making real effects in the world . . . Against the urgency of people dying in the streets, what in God's name is the point of cultural studies . . . If you don't feel that as one tension in the work that you are doing, theory has let you off the hook." Yet, he continues, the question of AIDS is also "an extremely important terrain of struggle and contestation" in which the realities, now and in the future, of sexual politics, desire, and pleasure, who lives and dies, are bound up in metaphor and representation. What cultural studies must do, and has the capacity to do, is to articulate insights about "the constitutive and political nature of representation itself, about its complexities, about the effects of language, about textuality as a site of life and death." At the same time, AIDS "rivets us to the necessary modesty of theory, the necessary modesty of cultural studies as an intellectual project."

It is notable that even in a cultural studies collection as broad and international as this one, with a number of heavily theoretical essays, there is little attempt at the sort of grand theorizing that imagines it can define the politics and semiotics of representation, gender, race, or textuality for all time. You can draw much out of these essays for use in other contexts and to answer new challenges, but not, ideally, without asking how their theoretical work needs to be rethought. Douglas Crimp's essay on AIDS photographs can sensitize us to the effects of representation in other contexts. But since the power of his analysis grows partly out of its reflections on homophobia and its concern for the special cultural and psychic meanings of AIDS, we should properly rethink those contexts independently. Crimp argues that we should never analyze an object alone and out of context and then goes on to say that we should "formulate our activist demands, not in relation to the 'truth' of the image, but in relation to the conditions of its construction and to its social effects." Crimp's analysis is a strategic intervention; these same images could have different meanings and do diffrent cultural work in other contexts.

Similar strategies and contextual aims inform many of the other essays as well. Laura Kipnis's analysis of how class and gender are articulated together in the pages of *Hustler*—and her effort to grant it a certain oppositional force—is more a challenge to rethink the unconscious biases within the "tendency to locate resistance, agency, and micro-political struggle just about everywhere in mass cultural reception" than it is an effort simply to expand that tendency. And it would be risky to assume that Catherine Hall's reading of how nineteenth-century English national identity was grounded in race—"In 1833 the dominant definition of Englishness included the gratifying element of liberator of enslaved Africans"—could be easily applied to other national contexts, though her effort to understand how "English identity was constructed through the active silencing of the disruptive relations of ethnicity, of gender, and of class" gives us a model that deserves to be rethought for and articulated to other historical moments. Notably, it is partly the special character of the British experience—the alliances and tensions between different peoples of color in London, the historic specificity of the way immigration and racism have played themselves out in a British context—that have in part made possible the important advances among British cultural studies scholars in developing non-essentialist theories of race and ethnicity. The essays here by Kobena Mercer and Paul Gilroy take that work still further. These theories have been needed to account for social history in Britain and both to take advantage of and to open up new possibilities for political alliances. That work can be quite powerful in an American context, but this much larger, more dispersed, and historically distinctive country requires that we theorize different antagonisms and possibilities. Some of the difficulties and challenges involved in moving theory to new contexts are thought out in the essays on Australia by Meaghan Morris and Graeme Turner. Morris devotes part of her essay to an analysis of "the *social* conditions for inventing a critical practice" and Turner declares that his "paper has been about the cultural specificity of theory."

This kind of emphasis on contingencies is central to contemporary cultural studies, to a theory of articulation, and to models for carrying out conjunctural analysis—analysis, that is, which is embedded, descriptive, and historically and contextually specific. Only such an approach can hope to address the changing alliances within contemporary political movements and to sort out contingent intersections of social movements from longterm "organic" change. Hall (1986a, pp. 6–7), for example, writes that Gramsci's "most illuminating ideas and formulations are typically of this conjunctural kind. To make more general use of them, they have to be delicately disinterred from their concrete and specific historical embeddedness and transplanted to new soil with considerable care and patience." Some of the writers in this book, indeed, argue that theoretical transplants can be quite misleading. Thus Lata Mani warns us that poststructuralist readings of hegemony can be misleading when applied to a colonial state that achieved not hegemony but dominance.

This is not to say that every theoretical advance made within the cultural studies tradition requires the same level of disentanglement from prior uses before it is put to work in a markedly different cultural context. The concept of articulation—along with its companion terms, disarticulation and rearticulation—widely and successfully used in cultural studies in the 1980s—is an example of a concept sufficiently abstract and general that it can be moved to new contexts whenever it is helpful. It provides a way of describing the continual severing, realignment, and recombination of discourses, social groups, political interests, and structures of power in a society. It provides as well a way of describing the discursive processes by which objects and identities are formed or given meaning. In its application, therefore, it is anything but abstract. On the other hand, a concept like subcultures is much more historically entangled. It arose in cultural studies work in Britian as part of the effort to describe and understand youth cultures that—at a particular moment—had sufficient experiential and social depth and stylistic coherence to become a way of life. It has since sometimes been applied too casually, granting subcultural status to what are essentially American leisure activities. British subcultural work remains useful in other contexts, but it cannot simply be imitated unreflectively. Consider, for example, Graeme Turner's comments here on the effect of British theorizing about popular culture and its audiences when it is transported to the United States:

> The recovery of the audience, the new understandings of the strategies of resistance audiences employ, and the invocation of such strategies within definitions of popular culture, have all been important, corrective, developments within British cultural studies. Their export to the USA, however, to a context where the notion of the popular occupies a very different place within dominant cultural definitions, seems to have exacerbated an already significant expansion in the cultural optimism such explanations generate—an optimism that is ultimately about capitalism and its toleration of resistance.

On the other hand, to do research on working-class culture or youth subcultures, to examine the role of the media in producing consensus, to reflect on issues of class and gender in relation to popular culture, to deploy bodies of theory like Marxism, feminism, poststructuralism, or psychoanalysis in cultural studies projects *without* knowing the work done in Britain, Australia, and elsewhere is to willingly accept real incapacitation. There is, in short, a history of real achievements that is now part of the cultural studies tradition. The term *cultural studies* stands for, of course, the study of culture, but it is no more synonymous with that than the term *women's studies* is synonymous with the study of women. The broad rubric, involving the study of culture, has been loosely affixed to many kinds of enterprises, but it is the Centre for Contemporary Cultural Studies at Birmingham that adopted, constructed, and formalized the term cultural studies as a name for its own unique project. Some United States academics are willing to generalize about cultural studies in complete or virtually complete ignorance of the work that runs from Williams to many of the contributors in this book. It is hard to think of another body of work where that level of ignorance could be sustained unchallenged.

Yet in accounts of British cultural studies this history of investments and accomplishments is sometimes reconstructed in far too linear a fashion. It is not, however, the figures and institutions that are in doubt. Thus accounts of British cultural studies appropriately begin with Williams's efforts in *Culture and Society* (1958) and *The Long Revolution* (1961) to theorize the relations between culture and society; with Hoggart's two-part project in *The Uses of Literacy* (1958)—first, to track the connections between British working-class language, beliefs, values, family life, gender relations, and rituals and such working-class institutions as sporting events and pubs, and, second, to record the loss of that culture as American popular culture spread through Britain; and with E. P. Thompson's effort in *The Making of the English Working Class* (1963) to rescue "the poor stockinger, the Luddite cropper" and the rest of the working class from "the enormous condescension of posterity." The key institutional moment is the founding of the Centre for Contemporary Cultural Studies at Birmingham in 1964, with Hoggart as director. Hall succeeded him in 1969 and stayed on for a decade. The Centre's projects included the journal *Working Papers in Cultural Studies* and a series of important co-authored and co-edited books, among them the especially influential *Resistance Through Rituals: Youth Subcultures in Post-War Britain* (1976) and *Policing the Crisis: Mugging, the State, and Law and Order* (1978), the latter being a watershed example of a collaborative, contextural cultural analysis. Since then British cultural studies has also been associated with various Open University courses in ideology and popular culture, and with journals like *New Formations, Cultural Studies,* and *Screen.*

Through complex negotiations with Marxism and semiotics, and with various sociological and ethnographic traditions, the work of the Centre in fact culminates in several large bodies of work: subcultural theory (Hall and Jefferson, 1976; Willis, 1977; Clarke, Critcher, and Johnson, 1979; Hebdige, 1979) and media studies built upon a model of encoding and decoding (Morley, 1980; Hobson, 1982). Then, with a renewed interest in Gramsci, an interest that emphasized articulation and the struggle to make meanings, the Centre increasingly turned to questions of racism, hegemony, and Thatcherism (Hall, et al., 1978; CCCS, 1982; Hall, 1988; Gilroy 1987). This moved cultural studies away from both its earlier humanistic assumptions and the extreme deconstructive possibilities of some versions of poststructuralism. Meanwhile, feminism "interrrupted" this development, forcing cultural studies to rethink its notions of subjectivity, politics, gender, and desire (Women's Studies Group, 1978). And most recently, under the influence of studies of race, ethnicity, and postcolonialism, and in the face of the AIDS epidemic, cultural studies has become increasingly concerned with the complex ways in which identity itself is articulated, experienced, and deployed (ICA, 1987 and 1988; Rutherford, 1990; Parmar, 1989; Weeks, 1990; Watney, 1989). And all the time, cultural studies continues to produce important studies of the politics of popular culture (Chambers, 1986; Hebdige, 1988; Winship, 1987; Bennett and Woolacott, 1987; McRobbie, 1990; Fiske 1989). And the story continues.

But this narrative erases the complexity of the Centre's work, not only work in areas like education, leisure, welfare policy, and history (e.g., see Clarke and Critcher, 1985; CCCS Education Group, 1981; CCCS, 1982; Langan and Schwartz, 1985) but also the uncertainties, false starts, interruptions and detours, successes and failures, conflict. As Paul Gilroy points out in this collection, it is dangerous to fetishize an imaginary moment. British cultural theory is not, and never was, a homogenous body of work; it has always been characterized by disagreements, often contentious ones, by divergencies of direction and concern, by conflict among theoretical commitments and political agendas. As Carolyn Steedman points out in her essay here, the reification of its tradition obscures its real history and the complex relations of its institutional, historical, and intellectual development. No one paradigm can be taken, metonymically, as the exemplar of British cultural studies.

Nor is this, as we have suggested, a narrative into which we can now insert ourselves in any simple fashion, either at the beginning—as if we were required to relive the entire story—or at the end, as if, having mastered this imaginary narrative, we can comfortably claim its fruits. For in fact, cultural studies is continuously undermining canonical histories even as it reconstructs them for its own purposes. Constantly writing and rewriting its own history to make sense of itself, constructing and reconstructing itself in response to new challenges, rearticulating itself in new situations, discarding old assumptions and appropriating new positions, cultural studies is always contextual. As this collection demonstrates, even those who participated in this history regularly find the need to reevaluate it. Thus Hall rewrites the history of the Centre here as a series of ruptures and displacements, while Gilroy critiques cultural studies' early blindness toward issues of race and finds in its founding texts "an image of self-sustaining and absolute ethnicity lodged complacently between the concepts of people and nation." It is fair to say, then, that the *future* of cultural studies will include rereadings of its past that we cannot yet anticipate.

Of course, as Lidia Curti notes in her paper, we are theorizing about the status of cultural studies in the wake of poststructuralism and postmodernism, and the high degree of instability that we attribute to it is the result of two things: the state of theory at the moment, and our ability to look back on thirty years of cultural studies history and see it as "unstable"—more so than at many earlier points in its development. It is partly these historical and theoretical changes that enable Hall to revise his view of the history of cultural studies and see it as discontinuous and disrupted. More generally, James Clifford observes that we now work in the context of the "diverse, interconnected histories of travel and displacement in the late twentieth century"; as a result, we are inclined to question "the organic, naturalizing bias of the term culture—seen as a rooted body that grows, lives, dies, etc." No one could have foreseen where cultural studies would go; neither could anyone have anticipated the degree to which stability and fixity would be intellectually devalued. Further, several viable national cultural studies traditions now co-exist: in addition to spreading through academic disciplines and educational institutions, cultural studies will also proceed within these national traditions in partial autonomy.

It is the future of cultural studies in the United States that seems to us to present the greatest need for reflection and debate. The threat is not from institutionalization *per se,* for cultural studies has always had its institutionalized forms within and outside the academy. Nor is the issue where cultural studies should lead its disciplinary life, for practitioners of cultural studies have always carried on complex negotiations with the demands of different disciplines, and even in the United States no one discipline can now fully co-opt the cultural studies label. The issue for U.S. practitioners is what kind of work will be identified with cultural studies and what social effects it will have. If not every study of culture and politics is cultural studies, then people need to decide what difference it makes when they adopt the term "cultural studies" to describe their work. Too many people simply rename what they were already doing to take advantage of the cultural studies boom. Yet as this collection demonstrates, a number of people are doing inventive cultural studies work in the United States and elsewhere, including many countries not represented here.

One purpose of the book is to present cultural studies as a genuinely international phenomenon and to help people compare and contrast the work being done in different countries. Many of our contributors have long been associated with cultural studies; others, it is important to note, have not. Before we invited people to contribute to the book, we debated for some time about whose work, we believed, did or did not count as cultural studies. Sometimes we couldn't agree. In fact, some of the contributors were surprised when we invited them, because they were not sure they "belonged" in the field. In some instances, we felt their work represented a viable alternative tradition in cultural studies; in others, we felt their work had the potential for productive alliances with cultural studies. At the same time, we would argue that some of the scholarship now described or marketed as cultural studies does not actually fit within its traditions.

One common misconception about cultural studies is that it is primarily concerned with popular culture. Indeed, it is certainly to be expected that cultural studies will be used to legitimate the move of established disciplines like literary studies, history, and anthropology into the excluded domain of popular culture. But one may also note the presence here of such essays on high cultural topics as Peter Stallybrass on Shakespeare, Ian Hunter on aesthetics, and Janet Wolff on intellectual traditions in the study of art. Thus any familiarity with either the diverse history of cultural studies or the diverse contents of this book should persuade people that cultural studies' interests are much wider. Although popular culture has clearly been an important item on cultural studies' agenda for analysis, cultural studies is not simply "about" popular culture—though it is perhaps always, in part, about the rules of inclusion and exclusion that guide intellectual evaluations. Although cultural studies work is often occasioned by an examination of specific cultural practices, it should not be identified with any particular set of cultural practices. This is to say that a scholarly discipline, like literature, cannot begin to do cultural studies simply by expanding its dominion to encompass specific cultural forms (western novels, say, or TV sitcoms, or rock and roll), social groups (working class youth, for example, or communities "on the margins," or women's rugby teams), practices (wilding, quilting, hacking), or periods (contemporary culture, for example, as opposed to historical work). Cultural studies involves *how* and *why* such work is done, not just its content.

Cultural studies is, however, broadly concerned with the popular in other deeper and more challenging ways. First, because cultural studies is concerned with the inter-relationships between supposedly separate cultural domains, it necessarily interrogates the mutual determination of popular belief and other discursive formations. As Emily Martin and Andrew Ross show here, the dividing line between, for example, popular belief and science is more permeable that we are inclined to think. Second, cultural studies has long been concerned with the everyday terrain of people, and with all the ways that cultural practices speak to, of, and for their lives. In this sense, the significance of "the popular" in cultural studies involves the observation that struggles over power must increasingly touch base with and work through the cultural practices, languages, and logics of the people—yet "the people" cannot be defined ahead of time. There is no simple hierarchical binary system that can be taken for granted, as if "the people" are always absolutely subordinated to an elite minority and subordination can be defined along some single dimension of social difference. Indeed, cultural studies at its best is properly careful about invocations of "the people" in its own work and elsewhere. As Meaghan Morris observes, " 'culture' is one medium of a power struggle in which most participants, at some state or another, will passionately invoke on their own behalf the interests of 'Ordinary Australians.' "

Cultural studies does, to be sure, have a long history of commitment to disempowered populations. Some of its founding figures, like Williams and Hoggart, came from working-class families and indeed were among the first working-class students to gain access to the elite institutions of British higher education. Their need to make their own cultural heritage part of the culture universities study and remember helped motivate some of their early publications. Moreover, most of these people first taught not in universities but in adult education programs outside the university. Cultural studies was thus forged in the face of a sense of the margins versus the center. Hall writes that Hoggart, Thompson, Williams, and himself were all, in their different ways, distant from the center of British culture:

> We thus came from a tradition entirely marginal to the centers of English academic life, and our engagement in the questions of cultural change—how to understand them, how to describe them, and how to theorize them, what their impact and consequences were to be, socially—were first reckoned within the dirty outside world. The Centre for Cultural Studies was the locus to which we *retreated* when that conversation in the open world could no longer be continued: it was politics by other means. Some of us—me, especially—had always planned never to return to the university, indeed never to darken its doors again. But then, one always has to make pragmatic adjustments to where real work, important work, can be done. (Hall, 1990a, p. 12)

While it is important to honor that heritage, it is pointless for United States scholars either to assume they occupy the same marginalized positions or to struggle for that status, now that marginality has some currency in limited contexts. Nor can contemporary cultural studies across its varied institutional settings occupy any single position *vis à vis* the dominant culture. As Kobena Mercer argues in his paper, "no one has a monopoly on oppositional identity." Moreover, as we imply above, oppositional cultural analysis can have points of convergence with cultural studies without fulfilling the major imperatives of the cultural studies tradition. Indeed, it is incumbent on cultural studies scholars—as many of the contributors demonstrate here—to question both right and left scholarship from a cultural studies perspective.

It may, in fact, be useful to discuss in some detail an area of debate where neither cultural studies' contributions nor its positions will likely be those simplified ones the right has anticipated, especially since this is one area of left intellectual life now being given national publicity. We refer, of course, to the widespread efforts to redress the sexist, racist, and elitist biases of the traditional literary canon (the debate over which Glover and Kaplan's essay suggests may be peculiar to and perhaps even emblematic of American cultural studies). Given cultural studies' heritage of recovering or analyzing working-class culture and reconstructing left cultural traditions—and given as well the prominence of race and gender theory in cultural studies since the late 1970s—the shared commitments are clearly substantial. But these mutual interests do not in themselves make every "progressive" project of cultural recovery and transformation an integral part of cultural studies itself.

Current challenges to the traditional literary canon, for example, sometimes propose redrawing or eliminating the traditional line between elite and popular culture. Yet such proposals are not consistent with cultural studies unless they interrogate the cultural practices—within both academic and everyday life—that create, sustain, or suppress contestations over inclusion and exclusion. Certainly such contestations pervade many of our routine activities, often with limited theoretical reflection. At times such challenges may be used just as unreflectively—though perhaps to an end with which cultural studies scholars would feel sympathy—to unseat traditional works of the already legitimated canon. This, too, bears watching and reflection.

At a conference in 1990 on radical pedagogical practices, one speaker described his practice of using Milton's poem "Lycidas" to teach deconstruction and other theoretical reading strategies; another described using the Bible to explore a range of contemporary preoccupations in the classroom, including sexuality, gender, race, violence against women, incest, homosexuality, and so on. Both were vigorously attacked by some members of the audience who claimed that they were, in so many words, bludgeoning their students with instruments of patriarchal oppression and that, in the case of "Lycidas" at any rate, women students were quite possibly being irreversibly damaged. Cultural studies, we need note, has addressed these kind of unreflective arguments before, and has shown that a text's effects need to be established contextually. On the politics of the Bible one might, for example, read Stuart Hall's (1985c) work on Jamaica. As Anna Szemere shows here in her analysis of the contest over the Hungarian "uprising" of 1958, the meaning of texts, discourses, and political events is a continuing site of struggle.

But there are other appropriate contextual questions as well: Who decides? Who has power to decide? Are the views of the students important? What is the evidence for "damage"? Is any particular cultural product so powerful that it must be suppressed? Ultimately, we would argue, it is not only the content of the selection that must be examined—who ends up in the canon—the syllabus—the conference—the book—history. It is also the constitution and consequences of selection, by progressive as well as by conservative forces. And it is also the determinants that put the ideological indeterminacy of texts to work in particular ways. Cultural studies does not require us to repudiate elite cultural forms—or simply to acknowledge, with Bourdieu (1984), that distinctions between elite and popular cultural forms are themselves the products of relations of power. Rather, cultural studies requires us to identify the operation of specific practices, of how they continuously reinscribe the line between legitimate and popular culture, and of what they accomplish in specific contexts. At the same time, cultural studies must constantly interrogate its own connection to contemporary relations of power, its own stakes.

Every act of cultural struggle is thus not necessarily consistent with the politics of cultural studies, though cultural studies would agree with feminists, people of color, and those on the left that the canon presents a selective tradition that is deeply implicated in existing relations of power. Moreover, such projects can enrich cultural studies, make alliances with cultural studies, and themselves become cultural studies projects. Again, it is not selection alone that must be examined but rather its effects and the practices that constitute the selection—practices which implicate us, too, as intellectuals. What are the cultural conditions under which "Lycidas" can be called "damaging" and removed from the syllabus? At the very least, surely diverse resources should be available to any generation as it moves through history. And after a decade in which thousands of young men have died prematurely in the course of the AIDS epidemic and thousands of others have mourned them, "Lycidas" is quite probably a resource as rich and useful as many that could be named. We wrote earlier that the future of cultural studies cannot be wholly constrained by its own heritage of cultural investments. As Donna Haraway's essay suggests, cultural studies may yet need to consider objects of study we have not imagined. We may now add that cultural studies cannot be used to denigrate a whole class of cultural objects, though it can certainly indict the uses to which those objects have been put.

Finally, it is not only our acts of selection and recovery but also the cultural positioning of the objects and practices recovered that need scrutiny. It may be useful in this context to recall another lesson from Williams's early formulations of the project of cultural studies: his refusal to define culture in isolation from the rest of social life, a refusal that further distinguishes cultural studies from other enterprises and animates its central theoretical concepts, including articulation, conjuncture, hegemony, ideology, identity, and representation. Continually engaging with the political, economic, erotic, social, and ideological, cultural studies entails the study of all the relations between all the elements in a whole way of life. This is at once an impossible project and the necessary context of any objects or traditions rescued, to echo Thompson, from the enormous condescension of posterity. A recovery project that imagines the objects it recovers to exist as fully self-contained and independent entities, knowable apart from their own time and the time of their recovery, is, properly speaking, not part of cultural studies (Nelson, 1989). Academic disciplines often decontextualize both their methods and their objects of study; cultural studies properly conceives both relationally.

Somewhat different issues inform another visible tradition allied with cultural studies in the U.S.—the new ethnography, rooted primarily in anthropological theory and practice. Although the new ethnography does not, by itself, necessarily define an alternative tradition of cultural studies, it joins another body of work by feminist, black, and postcolonial theorists concerned with identity, history, and social relations. The tension between these traditions opens up new possibilities, not merely for a reformed practice of ethnography and anthropology, but for a cultural studies practice which can no longer be comfortably located within the discipline of anthropology, though Clifford points out that anthropologists "are in a much better position, now, to contribute to a genuinely comparative, and non-teleological, cultural studies." For the new work in feminism, racism, and postcolonialism has, after all, critiqued the normalizing and ex- oticizing construction of culture and otherness constitutive of traditional anthropology. In the present volume, the essays by Bhabha, Clifford, Haraway, and Martin give some sense of what a postdisciplinary anthropology might look like. At the same time, these alliances and collective challenges generate their own tensions. Some feminist anthro- pologists (including Martin) have noted how ironic it is that "the new ethnography" calls traditional representation into question at precisely the historical moment that that representation is taking place by, of, and on behalf of women and other subordinated groups more than ever before. At the moment that women's voices enter the anthro- pological literature as agents, in other words, "voices" are labeled inauthentic, contam- inated, and imperialist—and once again what comes to be most privileged in the scholarly literature are predominantly the voices of white male anthropologists speaking to each other.

This sensitivity to the politics of ethnography affects other cultural studies projects as well. Rosalind Brunt, taking issue with work in cultural studies that treats audiences as "imagined communities," suggests the time has come to bring research on constructed audiences and real audiences together. She observes that some of the most interesting work has been done by feminist researchers involved with communities of women who often form extraordinary audiences and who *want* to discuss and reflect on their particular cultural speciality (e.g., Constance Penley's work with Star Trek fanzine communities of women). They thus do not fit the conventional notion of "research subjects," and indeed, Brunt suggests, might better be described—together with the researchers, fans, fanatics, experts, critics, writers, and other interested participants—as part of "a com- munity of heightened consciousness" (the term is from Jacqueline Bobo). One can step back and note more generally that "the linguistic turn" in the humanities that Catherine

Hall, among others, addresses in this volume, need not inevitably lead away from the observation of experience; yet it has raised the value of linguistically dense, self-reflexive, and speculative work—often at the expense of other kinds of scholarship. The effect may not always be to empower women and others in an academic community newly diverse in its identities and cultural commitments: where they are concerned the effect may rather be that, as Sanchez-Tranquilino and Tagg write in the context of the *pachuco,* "There ceases to be an occupiable space in which to celebrate their arrival."

The productive tension surrounding models of culture and modernity defines the specific practice of cultural studies, shapes the constantly transformed relations of history, experience, and culture, and provides a place which makes judgment and even intervention possible.[3] This tension informs all traditions of cultural studies: the British and its rearticulation in other national contexts; the American pragmatic and anthropological traditions; work in America and elsewhere in media criticism, education, history, feminism, African-American studies, Latino studies, studies of indigenous and aboriginal cultures. And the tension itself is constantly being interrogated and challenged. As cultural studies confronts a changing historical world, new intellectual positions and knowledge, emergent political struggles, and its own institutional conditions, it must always contest its own sedimented practices by finding new ways to articulate its role. It must continue to spell out the relations between the theoretical and the empirical, and to rearticulate history in terms of specific material contexts. Even notions of context must be constructed contextually: as Meaghan Morris points out in the discussion following Steedman's paper in this collection, even history must be defined within the specificity of the place from which one speaks. If a crucial goal of cultural studies is, as Angela McRobbie says here, to understand social transformation and cultural change, it is a goal we need to approach with care and humility. We believe that the essays in this book represent a significant contribution.

Notes

1. Work that documents the evolution of cultural studies at Birmingham includes Stuart Hall (e.g., 1980a and 1980c), Raymond Williams (1958, 1976, 1989b), Richard Hoggart (1969), Richard Johnson (1986, 1987), Rosalind Coward (1977), Chambers et al. (1977), Women's Studies Group (1978), Angela McRobbie (1981 and 1991), John Fiske (1987), and Lawrence Grossberg (1989b). Other efforts to chart the terrain of cultural studies include Janice Radway (1986), Lana Rakow (1986), Paula A. Treichler and Ellen Wartella (1986), Fiske et al. (1987), Ernesto Laclau and Chantal Mouffe (1985), Patrick Brantlinger (1990), James Carey (1989), Graeme Turner (1990), Larry Grossberg (1988a, 1989a), Anne Balsamo and Paula A. Treichler (1990), bell hooks (1990), Anne Balsamo (1991), and Cary Nelson (1991).

2. Of course interdisciplinarity is often neither total nor intellectually burdensome—it's not hard to cite theoretical works, problems, and positions from outside our own field. Nor to make brief intellectual excursions into other domains, to cull good quotes or encapsulate the requisite background on history, economics, gender, or whatever. Cultural studies, however, involves taking other projects and questions seriously enough to do the work—theoretical and analytical—required to understand and position specific cultural practices. True interdisciplinarity thus poses difficult questions: what and how much must be learned from other fields to enable us sufficiently to contextualize our object of study for a given project?

3. We might plausibly place the emergence of the "culture and society tradition" at the intersection of modernization, modernity (as a structure of experience and identity), and modernism, each taken in its broadest sense. Modernization, then, can be understood not only as changing modes and relations of production but as a broad range of additional interrelated historical forces as well, including economic relations of production, distribution, and consumption (e.g., development of new commodity markets, expansion of cultural consumption), technology, co-

lonialism and imperialism, migration (whether necessitated by force, economic conditions, or ideology, the diaspora is now a dominant figure of contemporary experience), urbanization, democratization, and the rearticulation of normative systems based on race, class, nationality, sex, and sexuality. Modernity refers to the changing structures and lived realities that modernization responded to and in turn reshaped: contested and ritualized structures of experience, subjectivity, and identity. And modernism, finally, refers to the cultural forms, practices, and relations—elite and popular, commercial and folk—through which people attempted to make sense of, represent, judge, rail against, surrender, intervene in, navigate, or escape the worlds of modernization and modernity. Modernism extends far beyond the domain of academically valorized culture which, like modernity itself, was shaped by new forms of leisure and emergent cultural practices disparagingly called *mass culture.* Modernism can rather be represented as the whole complex of responses to the changing historical landscape of the modern.

We can use this redefined terrain to understand how diverse traditions have laid claim to, or contributed to, the shape and work of cultural studies. And it may also help us understand the peculiar relationship that exists between cultural studies and communications: why for example it was largely in the field of communications that cultural studies initially found a home in the United States. For communication, too, has been marked by the ambivalences of the mass society debates of the nineteenth and early twentieth centuries and the mass culture debates that took place in America, largely in defense of American society, after World War II—and marked, too, by the major communication research programs the two debates produced: the paranoid vision of the masses embodied in so-called propaganda research, and the more ambiguous and sympathetic perspectives of subsequent studies.

Different intellectual and political traditions can be seen as responding to a perceived crisis and coding it in terms of a vision of the modern or of the mass: as a structure and crisis of relations of production (Marx), or of social norms (Durkheim), or of subjective consciousness (Husserl), or of technological-bureaucratic rationalization (Weber, Frankfurt School), or of reification (Lukács) or of a technological mode of being (Heidegger), or of social relations (Dewey), or as a totalizing structure of domination and power which acts upon the masses as the new subject of history (totalitarianism in Arendt, fascism in Benjamin). In each case, the modern implied an alienation from some—imaginary—past (or future) which was, in fact, the projection of a position and measure of judgment. This temporal displacement, projected as a standard, is what Williams calls culture, and in the various meanings Williams identified, we can locate the values that were, in a variety of ways, held up against the modern: the tending of natural growth, organic community, a particular class vision of the proper social standards of behavior, the imaginative creativity of the romantic (individual or) artist, the body of intellectual and imaginative work privileged as the embodiment of "the best that has been thought and said," or, as Williams himself eventually argues, "the long revolution" (of democracy, literacy, and socialism) of a whole way of life.

But not all these visions of the modern have equally informed cultural studies, although all have at some point been taken up by and brought into its specific articulations. Some have provided an essential component for a particular tradition of cultural studies, while others provided key arguments that are more specifically relevant. Many have been taken up and bent to the specific strategic demands of cultural studies at a particular moment. Others have forced themselves upon cultural studies, interrupting its illusions of its own progress. Still others emerged in the context of postwar society, the context in which the project of cultural studies itself was formulated, as critics attempted to make sense of the increasingly rapid reconstruction of the modern. These considerations have continued into the debates around the various "posts": post-Marxism, postcolonialism, postfeminism, and, of course, postmodernism.

Cultural studies is formed at the intersection of these various visions of the modern. For example, Dewey's sense of the modern as a threat to community was triggered but also potentially remedied by the new forms of social communication. American cultural studies, often inflected toward sociology and anthropology, and readily visible in the work of people like James Carey, in many respects parallels Williams's image of the community of process in which forms of communications embody structures of social relationships and from which the modern can itself be judged.

Cultural Studies: **A User's Guide to This Book**

As we have worked through the essays in the book, it has become increasingly clear that no conventional table of contents could represent their multiple investments and interventions and the many alternative ways they could be grouped together. We solved that problem with an earlier collection (Nelson and Grossberg, 1988) by adopting fairly abstract division headings that would cut across some of the established categories of theoretical work. With cultural studies, however, that option proves rather unhelpful. The mix of theoretical and material investments needs to be registered in its specificity. Moreover, the necessarily relational character of cultural studies—its concern with how different discourses and social and cultural domains are articulated together, how they can both restrict and stimulate one another—inevitably means that cultural studies projects often contribute to more than one area of research and debate. Thus we decided to print the essays in alphabetical order (according to their author's last name) and provide a user's guide here that would allow us to place essays in multiple categories as appropriate. In combination with our commentary this should help people to see relationships between the essays more clearly and help them as well to use the book effectively to pursue their own interests. We are confident that the user's guide groups essays together in ways that make for productive comparisons and contrasts.

Beginning with one or two of the categories that match your current interests is one workable way to read the book. Some topics, however, are so pervasive that the only way to get at them is to read the book and make your own map of its contents. The two most obvious examples of this are the issue of representation—which is probably the theoretical category mentioned most often—and the concern with the current and future status of cultural studies, which recurs throughout the essays and the discussion sections. Merely tracking your own disciplinary and theoretical interests through the topics suggested in the user's guide will not take you to all the places where representation is analyzed and theorized nor to all the polemical interventions in the field as a whole. Thus someone who decides not to read, say, the David Glover and Cora Kaplan essay because they aren't interested in crime fiction will miss their long concluding section on cultural studies and its potential in English departments.

Our user's guide includes an essay in a category when we feel it is one of the essay's major points of focus, but the dividing line between major and minor is far from precise. Thus the series of essays listed under "gender," already relatively long, would be still longer if we noted every essay that explicitly or implicitly takes up gender issues. The section on nationhood and national identity will not tell you, for example, that the relation between race and national identity is also at issue in the essays by Kobena Mercer and Cornel West. The section on pedagogy will not alert you to West's brief but useful passage on teaching as cultural activism. Neither a table of contents nor anything less than a book-length introduction, moreover, could track all the important points of correspondence and difference in the book. In reading the book, you may note that Paul Gilroy calls for an analysis of how Britain's colonial role in Jamaica contributed to Britain's sense of national identity. Catherine Hall's analysis of the mutual articulation of race, class, and gender in Jamaica substantially answers Gilroy's call. Conversely, nothing short of a full reading of the book will allow a reader the chance to test all of the book's claims and counter-claims against one another. Lata Mani, for example, critiques the tendency to take the concept of the subaltern out of the specific context of Indian historiography and use it as a general figure for all oppressed peoples. John Fiske, Kobena Mercer, and others, however, deliberately use it in just that way. It is also worth noting that cultural studies titles often cannot really signal all the kinds of objects and issues addressed in an essay. One would not know from their titles, therefore, that Lidia Curti's essay includes detailed analysis of several television series, that Constance Penley analyzes the slash fandom that has grown up around the *Star Trek* series, that Meaghan Morris uses two poems to ground her analysis of Australian culture, that Angie Chabram-Dernersisian analyzes several recent paintings, that not only William Warner but also Michele Wallace comments on the *Rambo* films, or that Angela McRobbie ends her essay with an analysis of a recent film. For all these reasons it is impossible to know in advance which essays will prove most relevant to your own work.

Finally, the user's guide can be a first step toward recognizing the theoretical and political commitments that underlie the important interrelations between these major areas of cultural studies research. If one takes, for example, the sections on gender, nationhood, postcolonialism, race, and identity politics, and then if one tracks the connections signaled by the essays that appear in more than one of these sections, certain shared interests become apparent. A conjunction of historical changes—the collapse of the colonial empires, the effects in Britain of the modern diaspora of peoples of color, the fragmentation of gender identities and the complexities of identity politics in the postmodern world—have led cultural studies writers to combine Gramscian politics with poststructuralist notions of subjectivity in a search at once for ways of explaining and intervening in the contemporary world. Across inquiries into gender, race, and national identity, then, cultural studies shows how the so-called "self" that underpins ideological formations is not a unified but a contradictory subject and a social construction.

Identities, too, then, are relational and contextual. An ongoing effect of cultural studies research has been to destabilize and de-essentialize standard categories of identity—race, class, nationality, gender, sexuality, ethnicity. But such a deconstructive effect is not an end in itself for cultural studies, for its goal is not to arrive at fractures, fragments, and differences which can themselves in turn be fetishized. Cultural studies undertakes the much more difficult project of holding identities in the foreground, acknowledging their necessity and potency, examining their articulation and rearticulation, and seeking a better understanding of their function. For some, identities would be seen as fundamentally harmonious and unitary, threatened only by large-scale social schisms; for others, identities entail continuous antagonism at every site of difference. For some, identities are the inevitable product of history; for others, the illusory product of history, or even individual psychic history; for still others, the site of real struggles, real attempts to forge historical unity out of pervasive fragmentation and difference. But none of these perspectives, if located within cultural studies, would take any given identity for granted. Cultural studies proposes neither a "mantra of subordination," in Kobena Mercer's phrase, nor a politics of an ever-expanding list of subordinate positions based on such identities as class, race, sex, etc. Instead it looks for the relations that exist among these positions in specific contexts, and the ways these positions are themselves produced by context.

1. The History of Cultural Studies
Paul Gilroy, Cultural Studies and Ethnic Absolutism
Stuart Hall, Cultural Studies and Its Theoretical Legacies
Jennifer Daryl Slack and Laurie Anne Whitt, Ethics and Cultural Studies
Carolyn Steedman, Culture, Cultural Studies, and the Historians
Graeme Turner, "It Works for Me": British Cultural Studies, Australian
    Cultural Studies, Australian Film

2. Gender and Sexuality
Angie Chabram-Dernersesian, I Throw Punches for My Race, but I Don't Want
    to be a Man: Writing Us—Chica-nos (Girl/Us)/ Chicanas—Into the
    Movement Script

Paul Gilroy, Cultural Studies and Ethnic Absolutism
Donna Haraway, The Promises of Monsters: A Regenerative Politics for
    Inappropriate/d Others
Meaghan Morris, "On the Beach"

2

Putting Policy into Cultural Studies

Tony Bennett

There is a calculated ambiguity in my title. For it might seem, in one reading, that I want merely to argue that policy considerations should be accorded a more central place within the concerns of cultural studies. Another reading, however, might suggest that my purpose in proposing that we put "policy" into "cultural studies" is to advocate that the latter be displaced by, or transformed into, something else: namely cultural policy studies. Let me, then, lessen the ambiguity a little: my argument does not have the kind of modesty implied by the first reading. But nor is its ambit quite described by the second, and for the good reason that the currency of "cultural studies" is presently so unsettled that the perspectives I shall advocate could either come to comprise essential components of future work which falls under this heading or, alternatively, require the establishment of a separate field of study with its own nomenclature to distinguish its concerns from those of cultural studies. Which of these proves to be necessary will depend on how the kinds of debates this conference was arranged to engage with are conducted and resolved over the next few years.

For the present, however, I see little alternative but to recognize the elasticity of usage that the term "cultural studies" has acquired. It now functions largely as a term of convenience for a fairly dispersed array of theoretical and political positions which, however widely divergent they might be in other respects, share a commitment to examining cultural practices from the point of view of their intrication with, and within, relations of power.[1] Assuming, then, that how future work in this area might develop is open to bids, I want to advance four claims regarding the conditions that are necessary for any satisfactory form of engagement, both theoretical and practical, with the relations between culture and power. These are: *first,* the need to include policy considerations in the definition of culture in viewing it as a particular field of government; *second,* the need to distinguish different regions of culture within this overall field in terms of the objects, targets, and techniques of government peculiar to them; *third,* the need to identify the political relations specific to different regions of culture so defined and to develop appropriately specific ways of engaging with and within them; and, *fourth,* the need for intellectual work to be conducted in a manner such that, in both its substance and its style, it can be calculated to influence or service the conduct of identifiable agents within the region of culture concerned.

If this is to stake out a possible future for cultural studies, however, it is clearly one that will require a break with many aspects of its past. Rather than mapping out such a possible future in greater detail, therefore, I shall try to identify the kinds of political and theoretical reorientations that I think are called for to redirect cultural studies down the road I have suggested. I shall do so by engaging critically with some of the trajectories—past and present—which have emerged out of British cultural studies with a view to identifying the respects in which they constitute an impediment to the formation of the kinds of positions I have outlined. Focusing particularly on the Gramscian moment of this tradition and the subsequent politics of difference which has flowed out of its engagements with postmodernism, I shall suggest that it now needs to be viewed as deficient in three crucial respects: its definition of culture; its commitment, however qualified, to the theoretical and political terms of reference supplied by the Gramscian concept of hegemony; and its theory of agency.

A brief biographical note might be appropriate at this point inasmuch as, in criticizing these aspects of British cultural studies, I shall be taking to task arguments and positions which have informed some components of my own earlier work. Indeed, what follows is, in some senses, a formalized working through of some of the disentanglings from earlier positions that have accompanied my more recent concern, in establishing an Institute for Cultural Policy Studies at Griffith University, to put "policy" into "cultural studies" theoretically, practically, and institutionally.[2] This has, however, been a fully collaborative project and, in that sense, my paper has been collectively authored by the many conversations and debates which have fueled the development of this work.[3]

Culture, Policy, Government

Let me come first, then, to the question of culture's definition. But let me do so indirectly by considering its bearing on the manner in which questions of cultural politics have typically been posed and conceived within cultural studies. Two main concerns can be distinguished here. In the first, the emphasis falls on modifying the relationship between persons—whether as readers, members of a subculture, or the devotees of a fashion system—and those cultural forms which have borne consequentially on their formation. The key instrument of politics here is criticism and its primary object is to modify the relationship between, for example, text and reader in such a way as to allow the texts in question to serve as the means for a politically transformative practice of the self into which the reader is inducted. Where such practices of the self are supposed to lead, of course, varies in accordance with the specific ways in which they aim to equip or empower the reader culturally. They might lead from the delusions of ideology to true consciousness and hence revolution, or from the critique of patriarchy to the search for a feminine position in discourse. Whichever the case, however, such critical politics usually have two things in common. First, they always map out a direction, chart an itinerary, for the subject. Second, they produce, as an artifact of their own procedures, a text that is capable of serving as both a resource and a landscape for the itinerary they propose. The course which Althusserian Marxism criticism charts for the reader is thus one plotted across the epistemologized landscape of the literary text. Poised midway between the misrecognition effect of ideology and scientific knowledge, the literary text is so fashioned as to assist the subject's transition from ideology to science in providing a means through which—by constantly measuring the difference between the literary and the ideological—the reader can scrape away the clouded visions of ideology and hence embark upon the royal road which leads to scientific knowledge.[4]

Precisely how such journeys are mapped, and precisely how the field of texts is laid out to support them, varies with different accounts of the relations between culture and power. How such relations are viewed also affects the second kind of cultural politics associated with cultural studies. This consists in the type of connections that are made between, on the one hand, the different transformative trajectories for the self that are plotted through the conduct of critical politics, and, on the other, the kinds of political subjects or constituencies it is envisaged might be organized and mobilized in support of specific collective political projects. Although there is more than one version of the argument, the Gramscian tradition in cultural studies is thus distinguished by its concern, first, to produce subjects opposed to the manifold and varied forms of power in which they find themselves and, second, through its commitment to a politics of articulation, to organize those subjects—however loosely, precariously, and provisionally—into a collective political force which acts in opposition to a power bloc.

Of course, these rough summaries cut more than a corner or two. The point I want to make, however, concerns the respects in which both kinds of politics rest upon a view of culture which sees it as, chiefly, the domain of signifying practices. Moreover, the central tasks of cultural politics are, in both cases, to be pursued by cultural—in the sense of signifying or discursive—means: by means of specific technologizations of the text/reader relationship in the first case and, in the second, via the discursive organization of a chain of equivalences between different forms of oppression and the struggles against them. And both are, in this respect, liable to the criticism that they pay insufficient attention to the institutional conditions which regulate different fields of culture. This leads, in turn, to a tendency to neglect the ways in which such conditions give rise to specific types of political issues and relations whose particularities need to be taken into account in the development of appropriately focused and practicable forms of political engagement.

To argue that institutional and, more broadly, policy and governmental conditions and processes should be thought of as constitutive of different forms and fields of culture, however, requires that the currency of the term "culture" as it has figured in the main problematics of cultural studies be reviewed. The most important single influence here, of course, has been Raymond Williams's work, especially in the distinction it proposes between culture as "a particular way of life, whether of a people, a period or a group" and culture, in its more restricted sense, as "works and practices of intellectual and especially artistic activity" (R. Williams, 1976, p. 80). While the value of this distinction has been enormous, it has tended to distract attention—including, I would say, Williams's own attention—from the fact that he identifies a third modern usage of culture as "the independent and abstract noun which describes a general process of intellectual, spiritual and aesthetic development" (p. 80). Arguing that this usage first became regular in the late eighteenth century, Williams notes that its currency in this period was not unheralded. Indeed, when illustrating this usage, he dwells most on a late seventeenth-century example from Milton's *The Readie and Easie Way to Establish a Free Commonwealth* (1660) in which Milton urges the need to

> spread much more Knowledg and Civility, yea, Religion, through all parts of the Land, by communicating the natural heat of Government and Culture more distributively to all extreme parts, which now lie num and neglected. (cited p. 78)

Here, Williams goes on to observe, we can "read government and culture in a quite modern sense." Unfortunately, he does not say what he means by this. Clearly, however, he sees no contradiction in government and culture being placed on the same side of the equation. For, in Milton's passage, culture is neither the object of government nor, assuredly, its subversive opposite; rather, it is its *instrument* and—with residues of its earlier horticultural uses surviving but also qualified by its conception as a social and political process—is to be applied in *the service of government* to all those parts which "lie num and neglected." Yet, having noted this usage, Williams almost immediately takes his eye off it as his discussion takes another, more familiar tack as he traces, first, the processes whereby "culture" and "civilization" (still working together in the passage from Milton) come to be separated from one another and, subsequently, the contradictory nineteenth-century passage of "culture" as its usage becomes at once both more restricted (in aesthetics) and more extended (the route from Herder to, ultimately, Williams's own "whole ways of life").

A good deal of the history of British cultural studies can be written in terms of the ways in which the relations between these two senses of "culture" have been read and redefined: the use of the extended definition to legitimize and ground the study of subcultures, popular culture, and ways of life; the construction of culture, in this extended sense, as the forcing ground for forms of symbolic opposition to culture in its more restricted dominant and aesthetic forms.[5] However, in spite of the considerable weight placed on it, there has been little critical examination of the methodological assumptions which underlie Williams's genealogical account of these modern uses of "culture." Yet there are grounds for caution here. As Ken Ruthven (1989) has carefully argued, much of this aspect of Williams's work remains in the orbit of Cambridge English in its "conviction that the hidden processes of history are somehow sedimented in a handful of so-called key-words" (p. 112). While, as Ruthven goes on to note, Williams's particular variant of this argument is useful in "reuniting the diachronic warps undergone by an individual word with the synchronic wefts produced by the company it keeps" (p. 116), it remains the case that Williams offers us more a snapshot of the shifting semantic horizons of words as traced by the lexicographer than an analysis of the conditions regulating their functioning as parts of a field of discourse.

This limitation is underscored by the system of references which organizes the relations between Williams's keywords. For in acknowledging that the history and meaning of each keyword is writable only in terms of its relations to other keywords, these references also make it abundantly clear that Williams's judgment as to the semantic field in which each keyword is to be located is, to a degree, arbitrary; it rests on a choice in favor of some semantic coordinates at the expense of others. For Williams, the history and meaning of "culture" is thus conceived as being writable in terms of its relations to "aesthetic," "art," "civilization," "humanity," and "science." While not disputing the relevance of these choices, their incompletness is equally evident: quite different consequences—pointing the analysis toward quite different fields of discourse—would follow from considering "culture" in relation to "morals" and "manners," for instance.

It is, indeed, in not pursuing considerations of this kind that Williams—and, consequently, a good deal of the subsequent definitional discussion within English cultural studies—misses one of the most distinctive aspects of the late eighteenth- and nineteenth-century transformations in which the changing and conflicting semantic destinies of "culture" are implicated. This consists in the emergence of new fields of social management in which culture is figured forth as both the *object* and the *instrument* of government: its object or target insofar as the term refers to the morals, manners, and ways of life of subordinate social strata; its instrument insofar as it is culture in its more restricted sense—the domain of artistic and intellectual activities—that is to supply the means of a governmental intervention in and regulation of culture as the domain of morals, manners, codes of conduct, etc.

In arguing for the anthropological plentitude of Williams's extended definition of culture versus its aesthetically restrictive sense in defining its object, then, cultural studies has misperceived at least some aspects of the organization of its field of study. Culture is more cogently conceived, I want to suggest, when thought of as a historically specific set of institutionally embedded relations of government in which the forms of thought and conduct of extended populations are targeted for transformation—in part via the extension through the social body of the forms, techniques, and regimens of aesthetic and intellectual culture. As such, its emergence is perhaps best thought of as a part of that process of the increasing governmentalization of social life characteristic of the early modern period which Foucault and others have referred to by the notion of *police.*

While this concept has many aspects, I shall mention only two here. The first consists in the contrast it organizes between feudal and modern forms of power. The former, as Foucault puts it, was concerned only with "the relations between juridical subjects insofar as they were engaged in juridical relations by birth, status, or personal engagement" (Foucault, 1988, p. 156). *Police,* by contrast, relates to individuals "not only according to their juridical status but as men, as working, trading, living beings" (p. 156), forming a network of more or less permanent, constantly enlarging and positive mechanisms for intervening within the lives and conditions of existence of both individuals and specific populations. The aim of *police,* to cite Foucault again, "is the permanently increasing production of something new, which is supposed to foster the citizen's life and the state's strength" (p. 159). Moreover—and this brings me to my second point—culture, in the sense in which I have defined the term, was clearly thought of as integral to the concerns of *police* from the very earliest elaborations of the conception. In Delamare's *Traite de la police* (1705) theater, literature, and entertainment were as much a matter of concern as public health and safety while, in the English context, Patrick Colquhoun, in his *Treatise on the Police of the Metropolis* (1806), advocated forms of cultural regulation which, a half century later, might well have been penned by an advocate of rational recreations:

> And it is no inconsiderable feature in the science of Police to encourage, protect, and controul such as tend to innocent recreation, to preserve the good humour of the Public, and to *give the minds of the People a right bias.* . . . Since recreation is necessary to Civilised Society, all Public Exhibitions should be rendered subservient to the improvement of morals, and to the means of infusing into the mind a love of the Constitution, and a reverance and respect for the Laws . . . How superior this to the odious practice of besotting themselves in the Ale-houses, hatching seditious and treasonable designs, or engaging in pursuits of the vilest profligacy, destructive to health and morals. (cited in Philipp, 1980, p. 175)

Viewed in the light of these considerations, then, culture might be thought of, and its emergence accounted for, in terms analogous to those associated with Donzelot's (1979) conception of the constitution and development of "the social" as a particular surface of social management. This would involve a theoretical procedure different from those which seek to arrive at some transhistorical construction of the specificity of culture: as a particular level of social formations, for example, or as the domain of signifying practices, or as both lived cultures and textual practices and their interrelations. In their stead it would enjoin the need to think of culture as a historically produced surface of social regulation whose distinctiveness is to be identified and accounted for in terms of (i) the specific types of attributes and forms of conduct that are established as its targets, (ii) the techniques that are proposed for the maintenance or transformation of such attributes or forms of conduct, (iii) the assembly of such techniques into particular programs of government, and (iv) the inscription of such programs into the operative procedures of specific cultural technologies.

While this is not a task I propose to undertake here, some brief comments on the historical aspects of the argument and its methodological and political consequences will help contextualize my later arguments. First, then, let me simply stress the historical peculiarity of that process—traceable to the eighteenth century—through which artistic and intellectual practices come to be inscribed into the processes of government. This is not to say that, in the pre-modern period, such practices had no role in the organization of the relations between rulers and ruled. They manifestly did but more by way, for example, of establishing circuits of inter-elite communication from which the vast mass of the populace was both excluded and meant to feel the symbolic weight of that exclusion—as was the case with the various precursors of the public museum—or, if we recall the Elizabethan theater, as a vehicle for publicly staging and broadcasting the lessons of monarchical power. It is only with the Enlightenment and its aftermath that artistic and intellectual practices come to be thought of as instruments capable of being utilized, in a positive and productive manner, to improve specific mental or behavioral attributes of the general population—usually as parts of programs of citizen formation.

Yet it is never in themselves or solely by virtue of their own properties that such practices are integrated into programs of this kind. To so suppose would be to take the strictures of culture's advocates—like Coleridge and Arnold—at their word in accepting that art and culture, in their restrictive senses, are intrinsically endowed with improving qualities.[6] Rather, it is by virtue of the ways in which such practices function as components of particular cultural technologies—and, consequently, of the fields of use and effect that are thus established for them—that they are able to be harnessed to particular types or regions of citizen or person formation. Ian Hunter (1988a) has offered one of the most fully developed arguments of this kind in his analysis of the processes through which modern literary education has so fashioned the literary text as to allow it to play a facilitative role in the development of capacities of ethical self-monitoring. The argument, however, can be generalized. The civilizing function attributed to the visual arts in the nineteenth century depended directly on that new cultural technology, the public art museum. Of especial importance in this respect was the new contextualization of artistic practices organized by the art museum in offering, as Carol Duncan and Alan Wallach (1980) have put it, a programmed experience in which the visitor is addressed not, as in earlier princely collections, as a subject but "in the role of an ideal citizen—a member of an idealized 'public' and heir to an ideal, civilised past" (pp. 451–52).

If this is a historical argument, however, it is also a methodological one. For it points to the more general consideration that the programmatic, institutional, and governmental conditions in which cultural practices are inscribed—in short, the network of relations that fall under a properly theoretical understanding of policy—have a substantive priority over the semiotic properties of such practices. For it is the "overdetermination" of such properties by these conditions that establishes, in any particular set of circumstances, the regions of person or citizen formation to which specific types of cultural practice are connected and the manner in which, as parts of developed technologies, they function to achieve specific kinds of effects. It is, therefore, only by according a methodological priority to considerations of this kind—rather than to the more immediately perceptible qualities of texts or lived cultures—that cultural studies can, as Marx suggested we should, appropriate the "real concrete" in thought.

And what is accorded a substantive and methodological priority should be similarly treated at the level of practical reasoning. Where culture is viewed as primarily the domain of signification, the critique of cultural practices conducted in a manner intended to empower or culturally resource their participants or users in new ways often seems to be both the starting and the end point of cultural politics. If my analysis holds, however, this is not so. The field of policy relations, as I have outlined it, poses political issues an exclusively critical politics cannot address. Equally, one cannot calculate what the politics of a particular type of criticism are without taking into account the field of policy relations in which it is likely to surface and have effects. The key question to ask of any literary work, Walter Benjamin (1973a) once argued, is not how it stands *vis-à-vis* the productive relations of its time—does it underwrite them or aspire to their revolutionary overthrow?—but how it stands *within* them (p. 87). To bend this to my own purpose, my contention is that the key questions to pose of any cultural politics are: how does it stand within a particular cultural technology? what difference will its pursuit make to the functioning of that cultural technology? in what new directions will it point it? And to say that is also to begin to think the possibility of a politics which might take the form of an administrative program, and so to think also of a type of cultural studies that will aim to produce knowledges that can assist in the development of such programs rather than endlessly contrive to organize subjects which exist only as the phantom effects of its own rhetorics.

Beyond Hegemony

I shall return to this last matter later. Before doing so, however, I want to relate the points raised so far to my opening remarks regarding the limitations of the Gramscian moment in cultural studies. It will be clear that the general tenor of my argument so far displays a leaning toward Foucauldian forms of analysis.[7] Yet I might have made some of my historical points equally well by drawing on Gramsci's conception of the historical distinctiveness of the educative and moral functions of the bourgeois state. That I have not drawn on a Gramscian lineage in making these arguments, however, is by way of signaling that—undeniably important and productive though the Gramscian moment in cultural studies has been—it has also now to be recognized that there are real limitations to the work that can be done from within the Gramscian tradition.

This is in part because of the ways in which the Gramscian problematic has been warrened out by the various attempts that have been made to establish some form of accommodation between, on the one hand, the Gramscian theory and project of hegemony, and, on the other, aspects of postmodernism and discourse theory. While, in my view, the resulting formulations are often deeply contradictory and, particularly in their libertarian leanings, politically harmful, the kind of theoretical excavations of Gramsci's work undertaken by Ernesto Laclau and Chantal Mouffe make it clear that many of the assumptions which underlie the Gramscian conception of hegemony—the role accorded class as the coordinating center of social and political life—can neither be sustained theoretically nor, anymore, be of much service politically.[8]

There is to my mind, however, a more compelling difficulty associated with the Gramscian problematic: namely, that it commits us to too automatic a politics, one which—since it contends that all cultural activities are bound into a struggle for hegemony—is essentially the same no matter what the region of its application. The Gramscian moment in cultural studies, in consequence, has tended to be institutionally indifferent and, accordingly, has paid insufficient attention to those considerations which, in differentiating cultural technologies one from another, give rise to specific sets of political relations and forms of calculation.

Let me give an example. Much—but not all—of what I have said concerning the relations between culture and government could be loosely accommodated within Gramsci's conception of the modern state as an educator. There are, moreover, many respects in which this perspective usefully illuminates those cultural technologies—I have in mind the public museum—whose formation has been intimately associated with that of modern conceptions of state-people relations. Duncan and Wallach (1980) have thus usefully noted the respects in which, as an instrument for the display of power, the public museum is governed by different principles from those regulating earlier royal collections. For the museum is characterized by its rhetorical incorporation of the public—conceived as a citizenry—into the form of power which the museum itself displays. Whereas the iconographic program of royal collections served to validate the splendor and power of the prince, thus placing the visitor in a relationship of vassalage to a superior power, the public museum inscribes the visitor in a new relation to power in addressing him/her as "a citizen and therefore a shareholder in the state" (p. 457). The public museum, that is, serves as an instrument for relaying to the citizens of modern democratic polities a power that is re-presented to them as their own.

In thus inscribing the visitor in a relation of complicity with the power it makes manifest, the museum might be regarded as a textbook instance of the relations between people and state Gramsci had in mind when, distinguishing modern forms of hegemony from mere domination, he referred to the rhetorical enlistment of "the people" in support of programs of moral, cultural, and intellectual leadership.[9] While I have no wish to gainsay these arguments, it is equally important to note their limitations. Here I will focus on two, although both are aspects of the same argument: that however useful it may be, in a general kind of way, to view museums as hegemonic apparatuses, this perspective is no more able to theorize the specific forms of politics peculiar to the museum than it is able to engage practically and productively with the actual agents that are operative within the field of museum politics.

So far as the first matter is concerned, the two types of political demand which have most typically, and most distinctively, been brought to bear on museums derive from two contradictions which have been inscribed in the institutional form of the public museum from the moment of its inception.[10] The first of these contradictions is that between, on the one hand, the museum's conception as an instrument for the collective ownership of cultural property charged with the responsibility for making its resources equally and freely available to all who might be counted among its public, and, on the other, the fact that, in actuality, museums have functioned rather as instruments for differentiating populations. While theoretically democratic and open to everyone, that is to say, museums have proved in practice to be a remarkably productive technology for the development of those practices of social distinction whereby, in the nineteenth century, the bourgeoisie and, in the contemporary context, Bourdieu's "dominated fraction of the dominant class" have sought to display those principles of taste and forms of demeanor which symbolically police the boundary lines between themselves and the unrulier members of the popular classes.[11] It is the tension thus produced between what the museum is in theory and what it is in practice that accounts for the emergence of a politics of access vis-à-vis the museum—that is, for the unending and, I would argue, unendable demand that museums develop more democratic profiles of public use and access.

This, clearly, is a political demand peculiar to the public museum. The conditions which make it intelligible and fuel it are lacking in the case of private museums or other exhibitionary institutions. The same is true of what might be called the principle of representational proportionality which governs the political demands placed on representational practices within museums—that the cultures of different groups should be equally represented within the museum, and represented on their own terms or not at all (as with the "include us out" perspective which governs Aboriginal demands for the restitution of cultural property from Australian museum).[12] This is generated by the contradiction between the space of representation shaped into being in association with the formation of the public museum—one which, in purporting to tell the story of Man, embodied a principle of general human universality—and the fact that, viewed from this perspective, any particular museum display can be regarded as lacking because of the gendered, racist, class, or national patterns of its exclusions and biases. It is in thus having fashioned a representational norm—Man—which cannot be met that the museum itself fuels the incessant critique to which it is subject. For since no actual representation can be judged adequate in relation to this norm, every museum display can be held to be in need in some form of supplementation or other, thus giving rise to an unstoppable representational politics which, in earlier collections not based on a principle of general human universality—royal collections, for example, or cabinets of curiosities—would have been unintelligible.

These are, of course, no more than brief pointers to the kind of light which appropriately focused genealogies of different cultural technologies might throw on the political rationalities which characterize their present constitution and functioning. Nonetheless, enough has been said to sustain my general argument here. For the types of politics suggested by the perspective of hegemony—restructuring the representational practices of the museum to facilitate the emergence of the oppositional subject of a counter-hegemony, for example—offer no means of connecting with those specific institutional and discursive conditions which, subtending the political pressures brought to bear on museums both from within and without, determine the forms of calculation of those agents with an identifiable capacity to influence museum practices.

Talking to the ISAs

This leads me to the final prong of my argument: that if Gramscian perspectives are limited in their capacity to theorize the forms of political conflict and relations specific to the functioning of particular cultural technologies, they are equally limited in the assistance they can lend to the development of practicable forms of politics capable of affecting the actions of agents within those cultural technologies. This, finally then, raises the question of agency I referred to earlier, a question that might usefully be introduced by way of Brecht's remark that it is no use just to write "the truth"; one has, he argued, "to write it *for* and *to* somebody, somebody who can do something with it" (Brecht, cited in Slater, 1977). For Brecht, of course, this meant the proletariat. For Gramsci it meant "the people" conceived as an ensemble of subordinate social forces fused into a provisional unity that is nucleated around the proletariat by means of a politics of articulation whose primary means are rhetorical or discursive. For the post-Gramscian phase in cultural studies, Brecht's "somebody" would refer to the totality of all subordinate social forces who, *not* nucleated around the proletariat or any other definite social force, rhetorically hegemonize themselves in relation to the equally rhetorically constructed power bloc they suppose themselves to be opposing.

Yet if, as Barry Hindess (1988) has argued, not even social classes can be construed as agents—that is, as he defines them, as entities capable of arriving at decisions and putting them into effect—it is clear that neither the Gramscian nor the post-Gramscian constructions of "the people" would meet this test either. And one would find neither classes nor "the people"—or, for that matter, races or genders—active as identifiable agents in the sphere of museum politics. What one *would* find, of course, would be claims to *represent* class or popular interests, claims which might be advanced by a whole range of effective social agents—museum critics, sectional pressure groups like WHAM,[13] committees of management, teams of designers, curators, sometimes even boards of trustees. One would also be able to point to respects in which the calculations of such agents might have classes, or races, or genders as their targets in the sense that they are intended to give rise to actions envisaged as affecting—benignly or malevolently—the conditions of existence of the occupants of specific class, race, or gender positions. Nonetheless, while "class" and "the people" and similar constructs undoubtedly have a real existence as both the targets of specific political programs and as representations which inform the suasive strategies of social agents, they cannot themselves be such agents.

This is not, assuredly, to argue against those rhetorical aspects of political processes which seek to promote shared perspectives among the occupants of the same social positions or to organize alliances between the political struggles of different subordinate social groups. Nor is it to argue against forms of political action which target classes, or women, or blacks, or specific combinations of these, in aiming for specific forms of betterment of their life circumstances. What it *is* to argue against are ways of conducting both of these aspects of political processes, and of connecting them to one another, in ways which anticipate—and are envisaged as paving the way for—the production of a unified class, gender, people, or race as a social agent likely to take decisive action in a moment of terminal political fulfillment of a process assigned the task of bringing that agent into being.[14] And it is to do so precisely because of the degree to which such political projects and the constructions which fuel them hinder the development of more specific and immediate forms of political calculation and action likely to improve the social circumstances and possibilities of the constituencies in question. The road which beckons toward the phantom agents of much cultural theory is littered with missed political opportunities.

My purpose in recalling Brecht's pragmatic maxim, then, is to suggest the need for more circumspect and circumstantial calculations about how and where knowledge needs to surface and emerge in order to be consequential. Foucault (1981) has identified his concerns as being with the ways in which we are governed, and govern ourselves, by means of the production and circulation of specific regimes of truth—regimes which organize the relations between knowledge and action in specific ways in different fields of social regulation. To apply Brecht's maxim in the light of this contention and in the light of my earlier argument that the field of culture needs to be thought of as constitutively governmental is to suggest the need for forms of cultural theory and politics that will concern themselves with the production and placing of forms of knowledge—of functioning truths—that can concretely influence the agendas, calculations, and procedures of those entities which can be thought of as agents operating within, or in relation to, the fields of culture concerned.

This might mean many things. It might mean careful and focused work in the service of specific cultural action groups. It might mean intellectual work calculated to make more strategic interventions within the operating procedures and policy agendas of specific cultural institutions. It might mean hard statistical work calculated to make certain problems visible in a manner that will allow them to surface at the level of political debate or to impinge on policy-making processes in ways which facilitate the development of administrative programs capable of addressing them. It might mean providing private corporations with such information. One thing is for sure, however: it will mean talking to and working with what used to be called the ISAs rather than writing them off from the outset and then, in a self-fulfilling prophecy, criticizing them again when they seem to affirm one's direst functionalist predictions.

These are not, I must admit, intoxicating prospects compared with the other clarion calls which might rally us in support of different futures for cultural studies: perhaps a few more years of heady skirmishing with postmodernism before it goes out of style or a little more sleuth-like searching for subversive practices just where you'd least expect to find them. Yet, I am arguing here, it is only by using the kinds of correctives that would come from putting "policy" into cultural studies that cultural studies may be deflected from precisely those forms of banality which, in some quarters, have already claimed it while also resisting the lure of those debates whose contrived appearance of ineffable complexity makes them a death trap for practical thinking.

Notes

I should make it clear that I do not think cultural studies is or ever has been definable as a specifically national tradition or as a school of thought anchored in a particular institutional locale. In particular, it is not possible to make sense of what was, even in the British context, a much more dispersed and varied set of initiatives than myths of origin usually allow for if it is pretended that cultural studies was somehow spawned at Birmingham. Nor can such a genealogy help us understand the range of debates which are now brought under the heading of "cultural studies." This term has now to be recognized as largely a convenient label for a whole range of approaches which, however divergent they might be in other respects, share a commitment to examining cultural practices from the point of view of their intrication with, and within, relations of power. This, in turn, accounts for further shared attributes in differentiating the concerns of these approaches from those of aestheticizing, moralizing, or formalist kinds of cultural analysis.

Viewed in this light, cultural studies comprises less a specific theoretical and political tradition or discipline than a gravitational field in which a number of intellectual traditions have found a provisional *rendez-vous*. It designates an area of debate in which, certain things being taken for granted, the dialogue can be more focused. As such, the only matter of substance at issue in these debates concerns the development of ways of theorizing the relations between culture and power that will be of service to practical engagements with, and within, those relations.

Now that cultural studies is attracting its historians, thought needs to be given to the type of histories that will best serve this end. So far as accounts of British cultural studies are concerned, it seems likely that, at least for a time, such histories will echo too closely those purely theoretical accounts of cultural studies' formation which trace its shifts from paradigm to paradigm—from culturalism through structuralism to hegemony. (See, for the most influential account of this type, Stuart Hall [1980a], plus his contribution to this volume.) Apart from their tendency to a heroic mode of telling which transforms cultural studies into a full subject capable, it seems, of entering into battles on its own behalf, the most signal weakness of such accounts consists in their neglect of the position of cultural studies within the academy. More interesting and more serviceable accounts will be produced only when attention shifts from such histories of thought to concern itself with the institutional conditions of cultural studies, and especially the changing social composition of tertiary students and teachers. For some interesting reflections on the problems and possibilities for a more critical history of cultural studies, see Grossberg (1988a).

2. The Institute for Cultural Policy Studies was established in 1987 for the purpose of organizing research, publications, and conference programs capable of playing a positive role within the processes of Australian cultural policy formation. Its work to date has resulted in the development of a variety of collaborative or consultative relationships with a range of local and national governmental or quasi-governmental agencies operative within the spheres of museum, arts, film, language, and education policies.

3. The paper was first presented at an Institute for Cultural Policy Studies seminar and has been revised in the light of the comments made by those who attended this occasion. I am especially grateful to the suggestions made by Peter Anderson, Jennifer Craik, and David Saunders in this regard.

4. For a fuller elaboration of this argument, see chapter 6 of Bennett (1990a).

5. It is necessary, however, to apply a gender as well as a class perspective to the relations between culture in its elite and extended definitions. See, for an especially telling consideration of the gendered aspects of artistic and aesthetic hierarchies, Parker and Pollock (1983).

6. Yet perhaps this is to malign Arnold who, in a passage in *Culture and Anarchy,* clearly envisages that culture must undergo a process of transformation in order to function effectively as an instrument of government when he argues that "the great men of culture" are those "who have laboured to divest knowledge of all that was harsh, uncouth, difficult, abstract, professional, exclusive; to humanise it, to make it efficient outside the clique of the cultivated and learned yet

still remaining the *best* knowledge and thought of the time, and a true source, therefore, of sweetness and light" (Arnold, 1965, p. 113).

7. Not, however, one without reservations. The tendency to stress the plurality and dispersal of power relations, while a useful corrective to the conception of all power emanating from the state, often leans to a premature dismissal of state theory. The resulting neglect of the respects in which, through the state, attempts are made to coordinate the functioning of different fields of power relations often leads to different fields of governmentality being granted wildly exaggerated degrees of autonomy from one another: the error of moving from the position of no necessary coordination to no coordination at all. Such views are also often at odds with Foucault's (1980) own formulations, and in particular his contention that, although not all power relations may arise from the state, the state "consists in the codification of a whole number of power relations which render its functioning possible" (p. 122).

8. See Laclau and Mouffe (1985). Where, as in Stuart Hall (1986b) and Dick Hebdige (1988a), selected aspects of postmodernism are integrated into a Gramscian framework, the resulting incoherences—while of a different political hue from Laclau and Mouffe's libertarianism—are equally serious. I have discussed these elsewhere: see the penultimate chapter of Bennett (1990a).

9. I have, indeed, drawn fully on Gramsci in drawing attention to this aspect of the museum's historical specificity. See Bennett (1988a).

10. For a fuller attempt to identify and outline the consequences of the museum's political rationality, see Bennett (1990b).

11. See Bourdieu (1984).

12. See Fourmile (1989) for a clear and influential statement of present Aboriginal demands on these matters.

13. Women Heritage and Museums. For details of its work, see G. Porter (1988).

14. My position is, therefore, in contention with Stuart Hall's view, expressed in his presentation to the conference from which these proceedings derive, that Cultural Studies should commit itself to the production of organic intellectuals in the mode of the "as if"—that is, as if the social movements, of class, race, or gender existed in the forms that would make the function of organic intellectuals intelligible. This, it seems to me, is a way of relating to "new times" which makes little concession to their newness since it belies too clearly a wistfulness for the political logic of old times in its aspiration to conjure back into being full subjects whose fullness is the product, precisely, of the historical process of their begetting. That apart, to attribute such a function to an intellectual project which has and continues to be based primarily in the academy suggests a degree of misrecognition of its relations to the real conditions of its existence that can only be described as ideological.

DISCUSSION: TONY BENNETT

BILL BUXTON: I understand that Australia, like Canada, has a protective policy specifying a minimal amount of "Australian content" in cultural media. What is your perspective on such questions? In Canada, the issue has arisen recently both in terms of the acquisition of art works and the distribution of Canadian films within Canada itself.
BENNETT: I welcome your question because I think it illustrates just how important it is for us to engage effectively in the policy arena, because the consequences can be hugely important. I'll limit my comments, however, to the area of broadcasting. There has been quite a long debate in Australian television regarding content regulations, and there currently exist quota requirements specifying that commercial broadcasters must devote so much program time per week to Australian material. Yet this poses huge problems of definition. In a recent review of its control regulations, for example, the Australian Broadcasting Tribunal has proposed that it would be useful, in the area of television, to say that Australianness should be defined in terms of a particular, distinctive "Australian look" or visual style. One of my colleagues at Griffith University, Albert Moran, has published a critique of this position which has helped to prevent it acquiring

too much policy momentum. Moran argues that such a content policy would mean that you would get more programs dealing with outback Australia than ones placed in an urban setting simply because the "Australian look" is traditionally defined in terms of the land and landscape. This would, in turn, lead to the "Australian character" being portrayed as the outback type and, in so doing, ignore the cultural needs of a mainly urban audience. Moran thus suggests that the more important question is to define Australianness in terms of the programs being produced in Australia, or their employment of so many Australian actors, and so on. This suggests a quite different cultural policy agenda simply by making the definition of content a pragmatic matter rather than an essentialist definition of Australianness.

SANDRA BRAMAN: Do you think that linking political economy and cultural studies is necessary in order to frame arguments that will make sense in the policy context?
BENNETT: The political economy approach to the functioning of cultural institutions and cultural policy is absolutely vital. Let me give just one example. Increasingly, governmental calculations about how vast amounts of public money will be spent in the cultural sphere are made on the basis of performance indicators. Determining the parameters within which performance indicators are defined and interpreted is thus of considerable importance. If we let them be defined through the operation of crude economic rationalist criteria, the cultural consequences for specific communities in Australia would be devastating. So the political need to intervene, very directly and centrally, in the forms of statistical calculation the major cultural bureaucracies make, and are obliged to make, is thus vital. In this regard, people with the capacity to do sophisticated statistical and economic work have a major contribution to make to work at the cultural studies/policy interface—perhaps more than those who engage solely in cultural critique.

TOM STREETER: How are you using the words "government" and "agency"? In the U.S., the words "government" and "government action" are part of a larger ideological problematic in which we're told that we're a democracy—we can influence government and how government controls things—because we can vote. Yet, in the case of culture, the government doesn't have any control over culture to speak of because our culture is corporate, in what the law calls "private hands." Sometimes, of course, the government takes up the funding slack. So liberal policy activists advocate practical research at the FCC that tell lawyers and bureaucrats what to do. This is clearly not what you're saying, but there's something about the way you're using "government" and "agency" which seems to stray close to these other definitions. Can you clarify your position on these matters?
BENNETT: I understand your confusion, because I do think I've been using the word "government" in two different ways. In the theoretical parts of my paper, it refers to the development of fairly extended apparatuses of social regulation which might be defined as government: the museum might be an instance, so might popular schooling or statistical apparatuses. However, toward the end of my paper, I've referred to government in a more identifiable sense, as, if you like, the state. In that sense, I've reproduced a semantic confusion that's part of the problem of the word "government."

With regard to what you see as the marginality of the forms of cultural activity that could be influenced by the decisions of government (in the second sense I've just identified) in the American context: I think this is an area in which questions of national specificity are particularly important. I remember a little while ago Larry Grossberg came to Griffith University and gave a seminar in which he was speaking on rock music side by side with a lawyer from the Australian Broadcasting Tribunal, the major regulatory authority of media in Australia, one of what we used to wrongly call, the "ideological state apparatuses." There are three points I'd like to make here. First, government probably influences a larger sphere of culture in Australia and Canada than it does in the United States. Second, societies on the wrong end of colonial or imperialist relationships have more urgent needs for culture to be a sphere of policy than do dominant powers. Third, while Britain and the United States have been suffering under the blight of Reaganite and Thatcherite administrations, Australia has been under a Labour administration—admittedly a right-wing one—but a Labour administration all the same for the last six or seven years. That makes a very considerable difference to what can be done politically in the cultural policy sphere. I should add that the Australian public service is also presently a reasonably progressive bureaucracy.

TOM PRASCH: Does the fact that we're working under Reaganite and Thatcherite regimes limit the extent to which we can talk to and with the representatives of the State apparatus? Specifically consider the situation in England where heritage as a notion increasingly embodies a Thatcherite vision of the past. How do you deal with that in practical terms?

BENNETT: It does limit what might be done, that's true, but it doesn't make useful work in the policy sphere impossible. The work that the Institute for Cultural Policy Studies at Griffith is trying to do is not, I think, unique. There are other Centers in Australia, there are Centers in Britain that try to engage, at whatever level they can, with particular regions of culture and to make policy contributions of a theoretical and practical kind. The spaces may be more limited, but even where the government—in the sense of the party in power—is conservative, it does not follow that the bureaucracies that they superintend function like seamless webs and that there are no contradictions within them. This is simply far from being the case. One of the most instructive aspects of the experience of working with government cultural agencies is to realize that— whilst Althusser says they function via the category of the subject—some of them just don't seem to function at all! There's a real lack of coordination between different branches of government and this makes many openings that can be utilized. The political complexion of the party in power clearly makes a difference as do national political traditions; but neither of these is a reason for giving the game away.

COMMENT: I disagree with your statement that cultural politics and policy are more important for those on the wrong end of the hegemonic relationship. Those who are in dominant positions can wind up culturally impoverished (as in the U.S.A.) and then the effects of that cultural impoverishment are exported with multiplying effects. Those on the receiving end may be more conscious of it. The current battle over the treatment of cultural products under international trade agreements is a case in point: for example, the long-standing Canadian tradition of supporting Canadian novelists who can actually live off their work is now considered an unfair trade practice.

BENNETT: I didn't mean to say that questions of cultural policy *ought* to be thought of as more important in the one case than in the other. I was simply saying that, as a matter of fact, it seems to me that they're not accorded as much importance within the political debates of major metropolitan powers as they tend to assume within countries like Australia. I was simply recording a personal impression.

COMMENTOR: I think it's a matter of politics. What the office of the U.S. Trade Representative says in response to cultural complaints about the U.S.-Canada free trade agreement is that we have no culture. It's a facade for economic arguments and so a strategy to deny the importance of any cultural values or roles.

TERRY COMITO: The cultural policy of the Reagan-Bush Administration has been to whip up populist sentiment against what they characterize as the elitism of the fine arts and the elitism of people like us who are theorizing the possibilities of social change. Conversely a return to the classics and to tradition is presented as a democratic project. Where does that leave our rhetoric?

BENNETT: This is not unique to the United States, and I don't think it's particularly unique to conservative parties and governments at the moment. There have been similar moves against the Humanities in Australia over the last couple of years, a period of a Labour Administration. Rather than answer your question directly then—for I don't know much about the American context—I'll focus on the Australian context. In the Australian case, the so-called attack on the Humanities has not been made on the grounds of their elitism but their lack of perceived relevance. The Humanities, consequently, are being asked to make themselves more directly relevant to Australian needs: cultural, economic, and political. The reaction of the academy toward these pressures has been interesting, ambivalent, and I'm not entirely sure where I stand on them. A lot of people in the Humanities—and those who would see themselves on the left as much as those on the right—have responded in a traditional kind of way to say that such demands are an attack on culture, high art, everything that we hold valuable, and so no more than a form of governmental philistinism. I've really not wanted to go along with this line of argument because it seems to me that there are considerable sectors of the Humanities which *do* function as privileged sites for the reproduction of elite knowledges that are not particularly useful—except, of course, for helping organize relations of cultural power. I really don't mind such examples of the Humanities getting a hard time. Rather than a blanket defense, then, a more productive task is to argue that the Humanities need to be reoriented in ways that will allow them to make practicable and useful contributions to existing social, intellectual, and political debates and processes. We ought not to let ourselves be bought into a general defense of the Humanities. That is my response, to the situation in Australia at any rate.

MEAGHAN MORRIS: What I wanted to say follows on from that exchange. I want to thank you for your paper, Tony, and also for the work that your Institute does in a context—I really want to point out to people—which has almost no academic home for the sort of work we've been all talking about. It's very interesting, coming from a culture where someone who wants to be what was called in another discussion an "intellectual freedom fighter," that one is now virtually forced to work in the media or in the bureaucracy or increasingly in the private sector because there are no academic homes left. But I wanted to push on from what you'd said, which is why I care about real estate, to point out that when you work on policy in a national context, you're forced to look at the global economy and the necessity for the very difficult task of making international alliances across spaces where you don't even have a language in common. So, for example, with tourism and tourism policy, you have to ask who's the ideal consumer, and for lots of other countries it's usually America or Japan, and your kind of work gives us ways into this bigger problem of international alliances.

BENNETT: Thanks for the words of appreciation; they're appreciated!

3

Angels Dancing: Cultural Technologies and the Production of Space

Jody Berland

For geography matters. The fact that processes take place over space, the facts of distance or closeness, of geographical variation between areas, of the individual character and meaning of specific places and regions—all these are essential to the operation of social processes themselves. Just as there are no purely spatial processes, neither are there any non-spatial processes. Nothing much happens, bar angels dancing, on the head of a pin. (Massey, 1984, p. 52)

Capitalism perpetually strives, therefore, to create a social and physical landscape in its own image and requisite to its own needs at a particular point in time, only just as certainly to undermine, disrupt and even destroy that landscape at a latter point in time. The inner contradictions of capitalism are expressed through the restless formation and reformation of geographical landscapes. This is the tune to which the historical geography of capitalism must dance without cease. (Harvey, 1985, p. 150)

In a recent study of activity and interaction within a French recording studio, Antoine Hennion (1990) notes how producers, authors, musicians, and technicians are united by "the permanent and organized quest for what holds meaning for the public." The successful assimilation of this knowledge into the collective creative process is the basis for what Hennion calls the "art of pleasing." Under the direction of the producer, they learn to "preserve and develop artistic methods that act as veritable mediators of public taste" (p. 186). It is the producer, Hennion writes, "who must try to 'draw out' of the singer what the public wants and conversely to pave the way for the special emotional ties that bind the singer to his public, by himself embodying for the singer an audience that is as yet only potential" (pp. 186–87). None of the elements of the song are above negotiation, Hennion finds; what we should look for in trying to understand a song's success therefore is not musical form, but the self-consumption of "real audiences, in the form of consumers."

This account of the "art of pleasing" arises from a long-standing dilemma in the sociological literature on cultural production, concerning the nature of the popular as an ideological, economic, and/or aesthetic construction. While each of these modes of inquiry presents its own tangible problematics, I wish to approach the constitutive nature of cultural production from a different perspective: that of the constitution of space. For the "real audience," which is from the singer's or engineer's, or the cameraman's, DJ's, or director's point of view, "only potential," has become more and more spatially dispersed, yet more and more spatially defined. The process that produces these audiences is in fact indissoluble from the process that produces the spaces which they inhabit. As a sound mixer in the 1970s put it, dismissing the mix preferred by a musician: "Well, that won't sound good on a car radio . . ." (Kealy, 1990, p. 216).

In theoretical terms, we need to situate cultural forms within the production and reproduction of capitalist spatiality. How does one produce the other: the song, the car, the radio station, the road, the radio, the town, the listener? What does it mean to conceive of producing a listening audience this way, to imagine it as mainly not temporal, not really subjective, not simply the expression of something called taste? Why is the literature on pop music, like that on other genres, other media, so often empty of cars, not to mention elevators, offices, shopping malls, hotels, sidewalks, airplanes, buses, urban landscapes, small towns, northern settlements, or satellite broadcasts? Music is now heard mainly in technologically communicated form, not live, and its circulation through these spaces (in connection with that of its listeners), along with its assimilation to and appropriation of previous contexts for music performance, is part of the elaboration of its forms and meanings (Rosing, 1984). Yet little writing about music addresses the meanings that might be produced in these spaces, or by them, or for them, or between them. Why is music so rarely conceived spatially, not as meaningful text or meaningful event (both still dominantly temporal constructs), but in relation to the changing production of spaces for listeners, and thus as an extension of the changing technologies that follow or draw their subjects into these spaces?

This bias towards the temporal (which is also clearly and differentially audible in the sound of pop music itself, not just in writing about it) is an instance of what Soja (1989) has termed "the suppression of space in social theory." As he demonstrates, both positivist and Marxist historians and sociologists—with the exception of Canadian economic historian and communication theorist Harold Innis, who is not mentioned in his account, and subsequent thinkers influenced by him—have tended to privilege historical determinations in the interpretation of society and culture, and to render spatial determinants as both static and secondary. This historicism of the theoretical imagination has permeated accounts of every type of social and cultural phenomenon in the Anglo-American and European mainstreams of academic thought. For a number of reasons which are both historical and geographic in scope, this "bias" is now being challenged in social theory and contemporary theoretical geography. Yet Canadian communication theory has been exploring the spatio-temporal dimensions of contemporary media for some four decades. As yet rarely applied to the study of popular culture, its legacy to that project might be to insist that the production of texts cannot be conceived outside of the production of diverse and exacting spaces: that much of the time we are not simply listeners to sound, or watchers of images, but occupants of spaces for listening who, by being *there*, help to produce definite meanings and effects. The mediation between these processes—producing texts, producing spaces, producing listeners—is what I wish to emphasize through the term "cultural technologies." The term points us beyond seeing musical or audio-visual communication as a diachronic event, whether as text or as expression, even one that has already absorbed, in order to be absorbed by, its listener. Rather, it draws our attention to the ways that pop culture represents a mediation between technologies, economics, spaces, and listeners: or in other words, to the often paradoxical dynamics of contemporary culture as it is technologically articulated with the changing spatiality of social production.

Cultural Technologies

Writing about the rise of popular literature, Colin Mercer (1988) reminds us that Dickens was read aloud in households organized around specific dispositions of morality and power. Mercer argues that "reading is the product of a specific cultural technology organizing the work that these texts are doing in relation to the family, the hearth, the home, and the household. Such texts employ quite specific techniques—as their counterparts do today—in order to establish their appropriateness in the place where they are read . . . and therefore need to be understood as invoking particular audiences with specific trainings and dispositions. They are emininently targeted forms of writing" (p. 63).

Crucially, such conditions of power and location are materialized not only in the reception of these stories, but in their production itself: "The household scenario of reading had a decisive effect in obliging the writer to formulate a specific address to this domestic sphere, and to provide an appropriate range of characters" (C. Mercer, 1988, p. 63). Thus reading, and subsequent modes of reception constituting the activity of culture, are not practices independent of the strategies of authors and publishers. On the contrary: constituted as a relation as much as an identity, the reader is, as Teresa de Lauretis says of gender, "both the product and the process of its representation" (1987, p. 5).

The insertion of a targeted public into the heart of the production of popular culture marks the beginning of the industrial revolution within the realm of culture. From the early industrialization of popular entertainment in the 1800s, the profitable dissemination of entertainment commodities has relied on the ability of producers to make reception—requiring more refined knowledge of audiences' situation and location as well as their taste and interpretive response—part of the productive apparatus.[1]

In contemporary broadcasting this pursuit and motivated mediation of listeners' "self-consumption" has led to increasingly rationalized methods for identifying the situations and subjectivities of its audiences, and for formulating a specific address designed thereto. The major networks test new products *before* they are aired, hoping to "take the guesswork out of TV production" (J. Nelson, 1987, p. 88). Test-audiences push buttons or switch dials so that technicians can trace overall audience response to each moment of a previewed program. "Response is broken down into categories such as: men under thirty-five, women, college graduates, fans of Dukes of Hazzard (or whatever program provides the desired comparison) or professional level" (J. Nelson, 1987, p. 87). Programs are then refined in response to these encounters, whose subjects have been chosen to help elaborate the shared physiognomy of marketable audiences, whether to be won from other buyers, or to form an audience which previously didn't exist, at least with equal combinatory precision, from an exchange point of view. For radio and TV producers, then, to find the audience—which for the electronic media is collectively always present, and always absent—is also to create it. The programs offer a vehicle for this potential audience's self-consumption, whether or not actually consumed; since domestic viewing can not be counted on to embody the physiological responses monitored in this way, more technically advanced modes of testing are being developed to observe viewing behavior in the home.[2]

This escalation of observational science challenges traditional analytic distinctions between production and consumption. It has also helped to make television production more expensive, more hierarchical in internal production relationships, more dependent on the integration and concentration of production and distribution, and more international in distribution. It is the structural integration of continuously refined audience observation with serial production which has allowed American dramatic television to assume its role as "telegenic entertainment incarnate" in so many other countries (H.-D. Fischer, 1979, p. 13). Radio programming has also been been taken over by the increasingly technologically sophisticated administration of audience research and selection management. This process contributes to the economic, technological, spatial, and musical centralization of radio programming; in Canada, whose music industry remains a dependent branch of the American industry and market, its effect has been to localize an audience for internationally popular music and to permit distribution and airplay for Canadian music only when it is deemed exportable, discouraging the commercial circulation of music that is too specifically indigenous to communities and tastes of a particular region.

This seeking out and continuous economic/symbolic recentralizing of viewers and listeners is a necessary feature of producing entertainment through what Innis (1950) calls the space-biased media: that which favors dissemination across space over continuity in time, and therefore enhances the spatial extension and hierarchical differentiation of its administrative structures, the centralization of its economic structure, and the wide and rapid dissemination of its supply. This has consequences beyond limiting the availability of local or marginal commodities, a grievance which would seem to call only for a better distribution system, as though distribution were not, in a sense, the determinant process. It also facilitates the continuous and expansionary (re)structuration of centers and margins, first by drawing new types of listeners (or listening contexts) into the market through new types of technologies, more generally in connection with this by creating monopolies that perpetuate and legitimate bureaucratic relations of production and expand their political and economic territory in a continuous process of "pervasive recentralization" (J. Carey, 1975, p. 33). It is in this context that every new medium introduces a specific relationship, strengthening one type of interaction at the expense of others, and again in this context that every mediated relationship exists in space and changes its configurations. Like any text, any discursive apparatus, cultural technologies work to set the terms, possibilities, and effects of their negotiation.

Since McLuhan, studies in communication have tended to emphasize the technological components of this process. However, the complex dynamic of discursive rationalization and spatial dissemination I have described was already formative in drawing popular entertainment into a commodity market. In concerts, exhibitions, and music halls of the nineteenth century, "the crowd were as much producers as consumers of a form of social drama" (Bailey, 1986, p. xvii). That sense of "making the scene" drew people to them and made them meaningful as spaces and as events, not only as performances or displays. Through the evolution of such spaces, commercial entertainment emerged both as an industry and as a focal site for the expression and policing of urban popular culture.

It was the music halls, prototype of nineteenth-century popular culture, that first made it an industrial practice to "reconcile an invitation to indulgence with the newer norms of orderly consumption" (Bailey, 1986, p. viii). Previously, the largest entertainment institutions were traveling fairs, complete with melodramas, menageries, tricksters, ballad hawkers, and peddlers of food and drink. The fairs were above all occasions for social and sexual transgression, for dramatic lapses of the taboos of everyday life. By the mid-1850s, fairs were perceived as "out of date": "too rowdy," Briggs (1960, p. 6) observes, "for the respectable mid-Victorians." The 1851 Crystal Palace Exhibition signaled the new impetus towards moral improvement, accomplished through the increasing commercialization and regulation of music, sport, publishing, and spectacle in general.

The music halls' reconciliation of order and indulgence was indissoluble from their changing production of entertainment as a social space. The emergence of music halls took place through the differentiation of specific types of entertainment territories (new licensing regulations of the 1860s were introduced to distinguish pubs from theaters, thereby disallowing paid entertainment in pubs, not to mention drinking in theaters), the commercialization of their operation, the professionalization of their labor force, the standardization of entertainments offered, the fixing and stratification of the physical and social position of their audiences (seats were gradually fixed to face the stage, and the architecture was renovated to permit clearer stratification between the pits and the boxes), and the syndicalization and integration of their ownership structures. They subsequently spread outwards to suburbs and provincial towns whose own entertainments had gone into decline as a consequence of these innovations. Then, of course, with this structure in place, cinema was introduced; it both appropriated and displaced the earlier structures in order to extend the logic of their production (Bailey, 1986; Crump, 1986).

Throughout this transformation, the noisy dynamics of music-hall reception remained a crucial element, semantically and organizationally, in the production and style of performance. A sensitivity to the situation and disposition of audiences (who started as crowds, and ended, due to these architectural, economic, and regulatory actions, as audiences) made music-hall performers successful, but in the end it also made them obsolete. The concept of "cultural technology" helps us to understand this process. As part of a spatial production which is both determinant and problematic, shaped by both disciplinary and antidisciplinary practices, cultural technologies encompass simultaneously the articulated discourses of professionalization, territoriality, and diversion. These are the necessary three-dimensional facets of analysis of a popular culture produced in the shadow of American imperialism. In locating their "audiences" in an increasingly wider and more diverse range of dispositions, locations, and contexts, contemporary cultural technologies contribute to and seek to legitimate their own spatial and discursive expansion. This is another way of saying that the production of texts cannot be conceived outside of the production of spaces. Whether or not one conceives of the expansion of such spaces as a form of colonialism remains to be seen. The question is central, however, to arriving at an understanding of entertainment that locates its practices in spatial terms.

The Space of Entertainment and the Colonization of Space

Perhaps the political conditions surrounding this question (more on this later) justify my challenge to what Lefebvre (1983) has called "The propagandist character, superficial and artificial, of optimism (socialist or American)" (p.6) which has embraced Anglo-American cultural studies in recent years. It has become commonplace to approach cultural consumption as a central agency for popular social empowerment, and thus as a locus for questions of agency and practice, especially with reference to the production of collective or expressive difference. As the production of meaning is located in the activities and agencies of audiences, *the topography of consumption is increasingly identified as (and thus expanded to stand in for) the map of the social.* This reproduces in theory what is occurring in practice: just as the spaces of reception expand in proportion to the number of texts in circulation, so the time accorded to reception expands in proportion to (and through appropriation of) other modes of interaction. For the most part, however, cultural studies has not comprehended the spatio-temporal dimensionality of this process. Aside from some work in pop music studies and feminist television criticism, which traces performative interaction through three-dimensional, non-homogenous audio-visual social space, the flat two-dimensionality of the film and televisual text has been largely reproduced in the analysis of reception as a cognitive activity (cf Berland, 1991). Thus we have achieved a complex semiotics of the visual and of the temporal, without addressing the productivity of space upon which capital now equally relies. The increasing social, symbolic, economic, and physiological territory occupied by the technologies of cultural consumption needs (as recent discourse on the body testifies) to be investigated in terms of the dynamics of spatial production within which such audience activity is situated, and by which it is constituted, and not only in terms of the linguistic or semantic renegotiation of representational meanings.

In situating the production of audiences in the context of technological-administrative developments, Canadian communication theory differs from mainstream communications research, which has tended to approach the audience as an aggregate of individual moods, dispositions, intentions, and choices, spontaneous or otherwise. McLuhan argued that "It is the formal characteristics of the medium, recurring in a variety of material situations, and not in any particular 'message', which constitutes the efficacy of its historical action" (Czitrom, 1982, p. 172). What he means is that media produce not only texts and textual receptions, but also a continuous sensory and spatial reorganization of social life. Each technical innovation in the communication media has helped to produce new domestic, urban, industrial, regional, and national patterns of social and spatial relationships. In Lefebvre's (1979) terms, such innovation has continuously "produced a space" (p. 285) to be filled by new capital relations.

Consequently consumption practices produce more than "meaning" in symbolic or representational terms, just as media technologies produce more than "messages" in two-dimensional or linear space. As Canadian history makes clear, media consumption has been inseparable from very tangible processes of economic and political transformation which make the concept of consumption as social empowerment (outside of the circumscribed parameters of consumer choice, upon whose privileging they rely) problematic. If pleasure is a determinative process, it remains to determine what exactly is being produced by the "art of pleasing," in the social sphere as well as in the life of the individual, outside the realm of entertainment as well as within its own morphologies. The particular socio-political conditions surrounding this question are variously inscribed in the movement between the space of entertainment and the colonization of space.

Like many features of commercial media, the capacities of new media for "occupying a space, producing a space" have been more readily recognized by their marketers; already in the 1920s, American advertisers understood radio as an ideal extension of their trade with "extraordinary power to carry them into the intimate circle of family life at home ..." As the chairman of Westinghouse put it: "Broadcast advertising is modernity's medium of business expression. It made industry articulate" (Czitrom, 1982, p. 77). Both radio's triumphant domestic diffusion, integration, and economic concentration, *and* its subsequent demographic, technical, spatial, and economic fragmentation as its listeners abandoned the domestic scene after television, are consistent with this prognosis.

McLuhan (1964) contends that each new medium adopts the "content" of its predecessor and thereby disguises its real historical efficacy. Another way of putting this is that cultural hardware precedes the software that will constitute its content. As Brecht said of radio, it finds a market, and then looks for a reason to exist.[3] The hardware is initially promoted through software appealing to a targeted market on the basis of already-established tastes: early gramophone records, for instance, were mainly recordings of classical music, because it was the middle class who could afford the gramophones, and classical music made gramophones respectable (Frith, 1988). Similarly early CDs were either classical music or re-releases from the 1960s. As the hardware becomes more widely available, new software (radio programs, video games, CDs) emerges for a larger, more fragmented market. By the time that market is exhausted, there is a new invention on the horizon.

This dynamic changes everything but preserves two structural components: constant technical innovation, and stratification of access to the technologies available at any given time. This pattern also has spatial consequences. Just as music halls initially combined pub and theater, but gradually introduced new styles of professional variety performance, thereby facilitating the creation of a newly capitalized and centralized entertainment industry and the birth of cinema, so television started with live variety and film, but consolidated the dramatic series once the industry had been thoroughly capitalized by the purchase of sets. American television production now relies mainly on the dramatic series, whose centrality in television's highly integrated structure of financing facilitates international export and the dominance of American productive relations as well as programs abroad. The intensification of international competition and privatization, and the increasing dominance of entertainment programming in many countries, ensure that "successful international formulas tend to be reproduced nationally . . . [and] series are seen as unique solutions with a universal appeal."[4] The series also forms a direct link with television's rhetorical and physical centrality in the home. Both industrial structure and narrative form, as John Ellis (1982) has observed, privilege the domestic consumer. This privileging is both refined and disrupted in the financing and design of new cultural technologies.

This rhetorical and technological emphasis on domesticity is what Raymond Williams (1975) had in mind when he described the "mobile privatization" of twentieth-century media technologies, thereby distinguishing them from the more public orientation of nineteenth-century innovations such as the railroad, the streetlamp, and I might add, the music hall. Whether people later chose to stay home and were followed there by technological invention, or whether this preference was formed in more direct and/or more complex response to the force of technological imperatives, the complexity of the contemporary mobilization/privatization process recalls Poulantzas's incisive description (1978, p. 107; Soja, 1989, p. 215) of capitalist spatiality: "Social atomization and splintering . . . separation and division in order to unify . . . atomization in order to encompass; segmentation in order to totalize; individualization in order to obliterate differences and otherness." This spatial dynamic of isolation and reunification has been touched on in recent studies exploring daytime or women's television in relation to domestic time and space. Such studies address but often remain circumscribed by the paradigmatic situation of the suburban family, whose postwar emergence as a physically atomized and ideologically reunified unit of consumption provided the economic cornerstone and discursive subject for the marketing and subsequent generic consolidation of American television. That is, such studies successfully demonstrate that the economic, architectural, and gender relations of the suburban family provided the context for the emergence of television. It is equally true, however, that the emergence of television was instrumental in producing such economic, architectural, and gender relations constituting the postwar suburban family.[5] The consequence of the latter proposition is substantial. Aside from problematizing the complex dependency of the modern family on television (studies of families voluntarily deprived of their TV sets describe depression, violence, adultery, and/or separation, and inevitable requests for their early return, eg.

Huther, 1979), this proposition emphasizes family viewing not only as *context* but also, equally crucially, as (targeted) *product* of commercial television as a cultural technology.

This formulation reminds us that cultural technologies produce not only content and thus something called ideology, to be negotiated by already-located viewers, but also material practices with their own structural effects and tensions. How complicated such effects can be is evident with the transistorization of radio after the advent of television. Tracing this development, which was contemporaneous with that of television, and which was formative in the creation of urban youth and other subcultures, reveals that social change is as much a product and necessity of contemporary cultural technologies as is social stability; for this reason their analysis challenges the duality of stability/subversion as a cognitive paradigm for the analysis of texts, as de Lauretis (1987) has observed in connection with debates about postmodernism (p. 73). While network television remains the dominant expression of "mobile privatization," it is not its final expression, but rather the articulation of a particular historic conjuncture of family and economic-urban structuration which is already being transformed by the proliferation of different kinds of families and residential units, by working women, new information technologies, and the continuous transformation of urban landscapes (re-separation in order to reunify) in the wake of transnational movements of people and capital.

And is this even a controversial claim? Capitalist modernity is after all founded in the necessity of dismembering what capital processes have already produced. As David Harvey (1978) has written,

> Capitalist development has therefore to negotiate a knife-edge path between pre-serving the exchange values of past capital investments in the built environment and destroying the value of these investments in order to open up fresh room for accu-mulation. Under capitalism, there is then a perpetual struggle in which capital builds a physical landscape appropriate to its own condition at a particular moment in time, only to have to destroy it, usually in the course of crises, at a subsequent point in time. The temporal and geographical ebb and flow of investment in the built envi-ronment can be understood only in terms of such a process. (p. 124; cited in Soja 1989, p. 102)

This depicts graphically the "pervasive and problem filled spatialization process" de-scribed by Lefebvre (1979) and warns us against a depiction of television or any other technology that endows space with the static quality once attributed to ideology. There is no necessary or lasting homogeneity in the production of those social spaces into which we are so efficiently pursued. Nuclear families with women at home are no longer the dominant family form, and are thus not necessarily television's primary consumption unit. TV itself now potentially includes VCRs, various film, music, and other narrow-casting cable services, videotapes, instructional and other software, games, and so forth. Its viewers may be in pubs, shops, bus stations, corner stores, and dance clubs. Music-based youth cultures hanging out in live clubs are no longer the primary consumers (though they remain the elite) of popular music, which is disseminated through tapes, radio, and video in homes, cars, walkmans, telephones, and watches, in television ad-vertising, films, and an explosion of radio and other musical soundtracks in stores and offices. The traditional family household, the metropolitan-suburban domestic residence, and the urban core are all declining as dominant configurations in the contemporary production of cultural technologies. Given its proliferation and fragmentation, being fixed to the TV screen at home is now the effect of economic disadvantage as much as sexual or ideological conformity. Television doesn't "mean" the hegemony of the nuclear family any more than popular music "means" or works to reproduce the oppositional identity of a youth culture that erupted in opposition to the nuclear family, though both may still "represent" them in terms of narrative and myth.

Indeed both television and music-based media remain dominated by referential treatment of these now mythic origins, of the gendered architecture of family life on the one hand and the quasi-defiant collectively defined autonomy of youth culture on the other (cf. Berland, 1991). Meanwhile *we* are consumed by the desire for new hardware, and it is no longer common or desirable to confine oneself to ownership of television sets and vinyl. Like their myths of origin, these now carry the traces of the obsolete which, as McLuhan observed, separate the older media and turn their language into art, reinvested with aura and newly desirable as content for the newer technologies, which exactly in this way remain invisible to us in terms of their real or potential meaning, their social physiognomy, their "historical efficacy." Thus cable services offer mainly more network television, films, and music videos; music videos remain defined by the parameters of the 3-minute song; *I Love Lucy* is available on videocassette; CDs have filled the stores with re-releases. We are both subjects and carriers of a wide dissemination of consumer technologies that have been shaped with the same economic and discursive rationality and, paradoxically, disruptive social logic as their contents to conform to the spatio-temporal practices of individual everyday life, whether in the home or at work, en route or at play among these spaces.

This plenitude of pleasures maintains a hierarchy of access to new technologies in conjunction with the continuing marginalization or suppression of less profitable social uses currently facilitated by the combined and interdependent processes of privatization and technological innovation. Broadcasting and the cultural industries are increasingly privatized in Canada, a process which has helped to create an expanded market for newer technologies in the form of consumer durables, not literally of course, as they are more and more—and in equal measure—widely available and rapidly obsolete. These consumer technologies function as distribution systems for entertainment and consumable information which enables their producers to "occupy and produce a space" that is newly capitalized in both national and individual terms. Such technologies are becoming more and more refined in their ability to adapt to increasingly individuated uses, parts of the body, parts of the home, parts of the city, to separate and reunite their users in differentiated and expanded space. Their functional precision offers another expression of entertainment's mode of address, a kind of liberating fabulosity, a mode of possible excess superimposed upon the normal. Yet there are other technologies and other uses that won't flourish in or help to expand the market in the same way. Judging from their situation, an unregulated market in communications and information which treats these as pure commodity forms would resemble that of medicine, in which a private system distributes care based on the ability to pay, offering no control of costs, or equity of access; no non-commercially motivated research; and an array of brilliant technological innovations that reproduce and even intensify hierarchies of access to medicine and health. So it is in perfect harmony with the still ascendant conservative political agenda, currently promoting a pro-consumer model of privatized broadcasting internationally, that funds for Native broadcasting were eradicated in the recent budget. Obviously there is no adequate consumer market for new communications hardware to be found in the Canadian north.

These issues reaffirm the paradoxical powers of technology, whose complex effects of emancipation and domination in the (re)formation of marginal political and cultural identities have formed the principle critical object of Canadian communication theory (Kroker, 1984). From this perspective they also confront the limits of content analysis, which cannot adequately account for the complexities of media relations or effects, and audience ethnography, whose authors have become so adept at rendering assurance that power rests with the viewer (cf. H. Schiller, 1989, p. 152). Rather than concerning themselves with individual texts, responses, or practices contextualized in a social-environment-as-given, the problematics of new cultural technologies forces us to confront questions addressed specifically to their place in the technological proliferation, cumulative privatization, and spatial expansion of global capitalization.

Entertainment and the New Rhetoric of International Trade

"At last!," begins a recent feature in a Toronto TV listings magazine. "A home-grown family that not only admits to watching television—and lots of it—but also is upfront about why. 'It's good entertainment,' " explains the father.

Why this article, why "at last," and why now?

The constellation of meanings associated with the term "entertainment" dates from the late nineteenth century, by which time, as we have seen with music halls, it combined a number of opposing meanings. Entertainment provided the space in which people didn't have to keep their place; many of its conventional modes of address originated in variety and vaudeville performance styles, which worked to elaborate a discursive pact with audiences against defenders of the social order. The perceived need to "improve" such entertainment in the interest of a more hygienic "common life" extended to later furors among the respectable over popular responses to movies, television, and popular music. The emergence of these later technologies traces entertainment's move from a particular space to a non-particular space. Entertainment has been continuously transformed by technological mediation from "medium of the special" to "medium of the everyday" (Rosing, 1984, p. 125). Yet its value is determined by (and calculated on the basis of) its claim to autonomy from the constraints of work, philosophy, politics, effort, discipline, boredom, history, and the "normal" confines of everyday life, of which it remains, in fact, an integral part.

Situated as a spatial-technological discourse, this is its central and most productive paradox. The programmatic exclusion of other claims echoes the modernist teleology of the purification of form: "entertainment" in its more hygienic forms offers the promise of a similar exclusion. At the same time the triumph of entertainment values finds its alibi in the restitution of dangerous pleasures to the discipline of the everyday, and thus in the reunification of dispersed audiences, the "common culture" of Springsteen or *Family Ties* representing both posited value and the economic and political expansion of perfect commodity production.

Rhetorically this posited value conflates two concepts: pleasure and democracy. Fun is fun, and has nothing to do with power (or is power's sole and adequate source). This is why women are told so often they have no sense of humor. The implicit complement of this is that good entertainment is "what people want," which means if you don't like it, you aren't people. This suggests that entertainment value arises from a classless, genderless, raceless popular desire, rather than, as part of the productive process, seeking incessantly to produce such desire in its own image, to make its space a universal space, which would make a critique of entertainment values a critique of popular right, an assault on the progressive universalization of pleasure by which "the popular" is now dominantly understood.

This expression of entertainment value has historical roots in the industrialization of culture, as we've seen with music halls; it valorizes at one and the same time the high production values attendant upon the professionalization of cultural production, and the assault on traditional bourgeois culture and morality requisite to its popular success. In the current period it also represents an important mechanism whereby populist discourse is appropriated by the right. The conflation of pleasure and democracy under the rubric of entertainment constitutes, among other things, a central instrument in the neo-conservative deproblematization of democracy: it's analogous to saying, for instance, "I'm not a woman, I'm a person."

This concept of entertainment has provided the central rationale for the socio-economic structure of American broadcasting, with its refusal of public ownership or regulation, its rhetoric of responsiveness to consumer demand in an open market, its economic and structural integration with the electronics manufacturing industry, and its permissive/intolerant affection for the products of massive economies of scale. For apologists of this system, "Democratic control of programs implies control by the listening majority," as an American writer put it in 1935. When the author concludes that "It is only to be expected that the majority of listeners would rather be entertained than edified" (Peers, 1969, pp. 444–45), he is reiterating the central rationale for the economic structuring of U.S. network-dominated broadcasting practices, while, in a more prescriptive sense, indicating the rhetorical strategies that would propel their international expansion.[6]

Canadians have been less likely to evade the implications of this formulation, with its continentalist reach, its liberal rhetoric, and its valorization of the market as preferred arbiter of social values. In 1935 there were already sharp conflicts between Canada and the U.S. over control of the airwaves. Since then it has been increasingly evident that the discursive apparatus of "entertainment" functions not only as a depoliticization of "the popular," but also as a central vehicle for introducing new economic and industrial policies in both Western and "developing" countries. In the last decade Canadians have witnessed a dramatic reversal of public and governmental language to the extent that for the first time a similar rhetoric is now being used to justify the "de-regulation" of radio and television and the strategic capitalization of the cultural industries. From this vantage point it seems ironic that the pro-market "liberalization" of entertainment and audience production is being successfully imported simultaneously from the Hollywood/Washington communication and information lobbies and their representatives within Canadian commerce and government, and the new academic mainstream of Anglo-American cultural studies.

In *No Respect,* to take a recent example from the field of cultural studies, Andrew Ross (1989a) asserts that Quebec's Radio-Canada has been creatively diverse in its preservation of indigenous culture because it is not part of Canada's public broadcasting system. This is meant to substantiate the claim that "independent" broadcasting better serves local, innovative, or complex facets of popular culture than any national public system. But Radio-Canada is the French section of the Canadian Broadcasting Corporation, and what has made it what it is is not free enterprise but public broadcasting further protected and enhanced by French language and culture. Ross's celebration of the international collapse of the public sector reinforces the concept of public broadcasting as an intrusive apparatus of the state (or at best as the moralizing pedagogy of the upper middle class) incapable of mobilizing or articulating popular sentiments or symbols.

But few Canadians support the demise of the public sector, or believe that cultural diversity would benefit from the eradication of the CBC. For it is not only postmodern cultural studies to which public broadcasting falls victim. The battle between public and private interests has a long history culminating in recent negotiations for the Free Trade

Agreement between our two countries, wherein American government-industry spokesmen repeatedly threatened a "scorched earth policy" (Cahill, 1985) should measures be taken to reclaim control over Canadian cultural industries. The negotiation process revealed and consolidated the pivotal position of U.S. communication and information corporations in the creation of what Reagan hailed as "a new economic constitution for North America" (Mosco, 1990, p. 46).

Consider the ramifications of this Agreement, which was signed in 1989 despite widespread popular opposition. Just as the pleasurable experience, and the personality which produces (and is produced by) it, have come to be formulated as a corporate entity, so the corporate entity has acquired personality in the most material sense of legal construction. The acquisition of "personal rights" by corporations now extends beyond the growth of "corporate speech" and First Amendment rights in the U.S., and is for the first time consolidated in international law (Patrick, 1989). The U.S. government succeeded in extending the exclusive right of corporations to organize, process, store, retrieve, and disseminate information, currently entrenched in corporate economic structures, to an internationally ratified, legally guaranteed right of corporations to override government policies and political rights.

This is a major victory for the transnational corporate sector currently seeking international deregulation. As Herb Schiller writes of the influential U.S. "Business Roundtable," "The sovereign right of nations to determine their own telecommunications policies is not the issue; rather it is the international consequences of these national policies that may be subject to legitimate challenge by other countries whose interests are adversely affected" (Schiller, 1989, p. 119). By interpreting culture, telecommunications, information, and consumer services as legal commodities, the Free Trade Agreement establishes in law the right to challenge any national policy directed to their protection. Thus it sets a precedent in international agreements (the EEC, frequently cited as precedent to the FTA, does not supercede public policies of national governments; thus it represents international trade, where the FTA represents transnational integration and the successful corporate suppression of public policies). It establishes the legal power of transnational corporations to override policies seeking to defend various political and economic rights of national sovereignty, policies which until now were commonly justified in the name of culture. Its effects extend therefore beyond the redefinition of culture as a marketable commodity to encompass an entire political concept of the relationship between marketplace and state. It stands as "a model that the U.S. is offering to the world as its way of forging and managing the global economy" (Mosco, 1990 p. 47), because it guarantees U.S. rights to commercial retaliation against any policy which it interprets as "unfair competition." This is what industry lobbyists mean by the term "scorched earth policy." Such retaliation can prohibit economic or regulatory measures taken to retain control of telecommunications, information, or indeed any form of manufacturing, services, or information which might still be conceived by government in terms of social policy rather than as exchangeable commodity. Thus the Agreement promotes major changes in Canadian political culture. "Public interest" no longer refers to cultural agencies or representative processes, or guarantees the state's right or obligation to intervene in defense of civil (as opposed to corporate) rights. Rather, it now refers to unrestricted commercial control of the information and cultural marketplace and the ostensibly improved provision of a wider range of preferred commodities which results from a freer market and from corporate economies of scale.

The vulnerability of the industry's interpretation of "public interest" on which this depends (which, like American law, conflates democracy and the open market) can be found in the fact that corporate expansion in the broadcast marketplace does not bring a parallel expansion of "choice"; thirty-three cable stations bring more network television, and eighteen radio stations bring more contemporary hit radio. This is countered incessantly by the rhetoric of the "entertainment" discourse itself: we have what we please, and what we have pleases us.

By situating Canada as a country with the dependencies of the third world and the information and cultural needs of the first, the Free Trade Agreement is a culmination of the history which produced Innis's theorization of the center/margin dialectic of modern communications technologies. All cultural studies is both conjunctural and motivated. Our environment is being powerfully reshaped by the globalization of cultural production; the increasing economic and political status of its major corporations; the continuing battle between privatization and the public sector; the revision of the Canadian Broadcasting Act; the Free Trade Agreement with the United States and consequent transmogrification of Canada's economic, legislative, and social structures and policies. The effects of these changes are evident already in the erosion of social services, medicare, unionized jobs, native communications, funding for womens' organizations and services, cultural and educational subsidies, public broadcasting, public transportation, public hospitals, public control of natural resources, and other services previously conceived as unprofitable rights; in a whole range of measures designed to expand the political and spatial reach and legitimation of corporate interests and initiatives in conjunction with growing improverishment and disenfranchisement of much of the population. These effects are also visible in the concerns and practices of musicians, journalists, cultural producers, and community activists. This context has exacerbated tensions in the political sphere which have consequences for the social and institutional production of culture, suggesting that what is being displaced is now arguably as important as what is being received, and reproblematizing such tensions (one hopes, at least) in the sphere of academic commentary on culture.

NOTES

For comments and critical feedback at various stages of writing this, thanks to David Tomas, Larry Grossberg, the Cultural Studies Programme at Trent University, and participants in the Canadian Sociology and Anthropology Association/Canadian Communication Association annual conferences, June 1990.

1. Adorno commented on this development with great acuity in his essay on "Mediation" (1976 p. 208):

> For the first time composers [of the mid-eighteenth century] were confronted with the anonymous marketplace. Without the protection of a guild or of a prince's favor they had to sense a demand instead of following transparent orders. They had to turn themselves, their very core, into organs of the market; this was what placed the desiderates of the market at the heart of their production. The leveling that resulted—in comparison with Bach, for instance—is unmistakable. Not unmistakable, although just as true: that by virtue of such internalization the need for entertainment turned into one for diversity in the compositions, as distinct from the relatively unbroken unity of what is falsely called the musical Baroque . . . It was the source of a way to pose musical problems that has survived to this day. The customary invectives against commercial mischief in music are superficial. They delude regarding the extent to which phenomena that presuppose commerce, the appeal to an audience already viewed as customers, can turn into compositorial qualities unleashing and enhancing a composer's productive force. We may phrase this in the form of a more comprehensive legality: *social compulsions under which music seems to be placed from*

without are absorbed by its autonomous logic and the need for compositorial expression, and are transformed into an artistic necessity: into steps of the right consciousness. (emphasis added)

2. The most recent Nielson ratings technologies introduced in the U.S. do not require that home audiences participate in the tests. They have photographic images of the residents entered into the monitoring equipment, and are able to observe and analyze individuals coming and going from the room without the observed audience having to push buttons or otherwise control their surveillance by their own voluntary actions.

3. "In our society one can invent and perfect discoveries that still have to conquer their market and justify their existence; in other words discoveries that have not been called for. Thus there was a moment when technology was advanced enough to produce the radio and society was not yet advanced enough to accept it. The radio was then in its first phase of being a substitute: a substitute for theatre, opera, concerts, lectures, cafe music, local newspapers and so forth. This was the patient's period of halcyon youth. I am not sure if it is finished yet, but if so then this stripling who needed no certificate of competence to be born will have to start looking retrospectively for an object in life." "The radio as an apparatus of communication," Brecht, (1964, p. 51).

4. Mattelart, Delcourt, and Mattelart (1984, pp. 102–3). Patrick Crawley makes a comparable argument about Canadian television and film, whose different value systems are continuously undermined by enforced technological and economic adaptation to changing conditions in the American industry. This enforced adaptation leads to the production of TV series which are intended to compete with American series without the advantage of the American production infrastructure (Crawley, 1986, p. 22).

5. Lynn Spigel has argued that "television's arrival in domestic space [was] marked by a vast production of discourses which spoke to the relationship between television, the home and the family" (1988, p. 11). Such discourses emphasized at one and the same time the newly theatrical privacy of suburban domesticity, and the technological conquering of space bringing instant connections with the wider world. By being preferred as providing a utopian technological link with the globe, televisualized domestic space was depicted as the ideal site for participation in the public sphere; "This interest in bringing an illusion of the world into the home can be seen as part of a larger historical process in which the home was designed to incorporate social space" (p. 20). Spigel's analysis of these discourses also emphasizes the degree to which "the domestic gaze" moved in both directions.

6. The passage was cited negatively as justification for the Massey Commission's defense of the public broadcasting system in the context of the introduction of television in Canada. "It was [private broadcasters'] view, the Massey Report said, that radio was primarily a means of entertainment, a by-product of the advertising business. The United States, according to the Massey Commission, follows the view that radio broadcasting is primarily an industry; there radio has been treated primarily as a means of entertainment open to commercial exploitation, limited only by the public controls found necessary in all countries . . . ." (Peers, 1969, p. 446).

DISCUSSION: JODY BERLAND

TIMOTHY DUGDALE: Communications systems are a part of Canadian identity and the way that we represent ourselves through communication is certainly a lot different than being part of this American free trade system. We're certainly not part of that.
BERLAND: Well, we are and we aren't. But what I was talking about was the way that a particular kind of thinking about culture works in different kinds of political contexts, not wanting to generalize from one into an other. I was using this particular instance of the free trade negotiations to draw out the implications of discourses around culture in the current period.
DUGDALE: But understanding Canada is understanding our culture, it is understanding it on its own terms and the way that it develops within itself. It's not a product of hegemony.

BERLAND: Whether or not that is the case, I'm not talking here about Canadian identities, which raises a whole set of issues which I haven't touched on at all. These issues have been a kind of focal point for a number of historical alliances between different groups in Canadian history. Issues around culture and the media, around ownership or control of the apparatus of cultural production have brought together quite broad alliances of different groups within Canadian society. I think that the whole problematic of identity is complex and I've stayed away from it completely.

DAVE DOUGLAS: In your discussion of the introduction of new media, you referred to new media finding a market and then finding a reason to exist within that market, which I took to imply a disempowerment of the individual, moving from a form to a content. Do you agree?

BERLAND: I don't see it only as a disempowerment. The point I was trying to make was that the use of technologies is a conditional one related to all kinds of other social situations and possibilities which it both addresses and shapes but isn't completely determined by. I think that there have been some very empowering uses of radio, for instance, and of course being a Canadian I could talk about public broadcasting in Canada and its heroic history and the way it is endangered at the present; in general radio has had many diverse empowering uses. But I am talking about an historical process in which various kinds of technology are introduced into a market and culture already shaped by the current media field, and then get negotiated in terms of how they're going to be used, what kinds of content, if you like, or what kinds of institutional structures are going to shape them, and also how they change and then are changed by other media. Radio as a technology emerged with the possibility of many different kinds of uses, and the broadcasting that we know today is one possibility which is variously empowering and disempowering. There were others that disappeared and are now re-emerging. The challenge is to widen the frame of reference for conceptualizing empowerment to extend beyond problems of content.

IOAN DAVIES: You seem to be talking about the relationship between how a country identifies itself against the whole process of communication which is imposed on it. It seems to me that one of the questions about Canada and the United States is that Canadians can come into and leave this country. Americans don't think they exist. And yet in the sense they're defined by the Americans.

BERLAND: The reason I refused the idea of identity in terms of a historical tradition in the struggle around communications was that, in Canada, it's both impossible and compulsory to talk about the problem of identity. It's a complete double-bind: one has to talk about it constantly because it's a problem, but you can't talk about it because as soon as you start you're in danger of imposing a singular definition on something which isn't singular at all; Canada has no singular language, ethnicity, or culture. All you're talking about in that sense is a set of historical processes of which we are the result. One of the central historical processes and one that informs me is this whole problematic and history of crises around the shape and structure and uses of communications media. It's a very central and very paradoxical and very problematic issue in our history and public discourse, just as the issues surrounding race are in other contexts. It's not so much a question of identity *per se,* it's a question of various sites on which struggle take place and change from one period to another.

QUESTION: You talk about media space needing to be filled with new relations, and the transformation of daytime television from being women's television in a domestic time and space. Women have gone out of the home to come up with a new space. Could you describe the new relationship with the media which had developed for women?

BERLAND: I think that the point I was trying to make is that you can see a set of representations now on television having to do with women in family situations, but the fact that such images continue to be produced doesn't necessarily mean that there is a direct referential relationship to women who are actually like that watching the television at home: one is not a representation of the other. Where women are located now and how they are produced in or by television is far more complicated than what is suggested by saying that women are in the home and in front of and inside of TV as a domestic technology. There's been some excellent historical work on television in the home in the 1950s. Unfortunately this seems to be used as a paradigm for the present, when women are being located quite differently. That's one of the things I had to deal with when I started to look at radio, as well, since a lot of the people listening to radio are women at work. So, I just was trying to complicate it a little bit. I watch television when I'm at home. I mean everybody watches television at home, and if you go into a school cafeteria there are people watching soap operas, while other people go to work and tape the soaps and watch them when they get home. And of course TVs are on at a lot of workplaces. At the same time, other technological changes have made the whole distinction between workplace and home much more complicated: with computers and so on, the home has become a workplace for many women, not just for raising children but for performing many other jobs. I was just trying to say that the issue of media in the home is a much more complicated one than we once thought. And I think that fracturing and complication is also evident within TV programming, as well as in spatial terms, but that's another matter.

PETER BLOOM: I'd like to ask you why you were using the metaphor of space and why you find it to be an apt metaphor. I wonder if you could clarify it and what kind of possibilities you see in it?

BERLAND: That's a hard question to answer because I don't think I have a singular use of it, or even a singular preoccupation with it. Nor do I consider it a metaphor. So to answer that simply, a lot of the writing about radio and television and in fact music generally is dealing with them in terms of meanings but not in terms of how they change or how they situate people in terms of space. Yet this is very important both in changing everyday life and in terms of economics. So that's part of the way that I'm using it. I suppose I find it an interesting preoccupation, maybe because I'm a Canadian and Canadian writing about media always talks about space, as both a problem and a product. It's a problem because of geography and colonial economics; it's also a product of these. I come out of a theoretical tradition which is a response to both geographical accident and political history. Innis's work connects the spatial bias of modern electronic media to the material and cultural foundations of imperialism, and this has certainly shaped much of my own thinking about media. And then I think also that I became preoccupied because I see it so absent everywhere else. How can the spatial implications of that history have been so invisible? If you find a black hole you jump in and it tends to get larger, it becomes more and more important the more you see it as an absence elsewhere. So I think part of it is that I've been interested in trying to find out why there's so much of an absence. I was interested in a political deconstruction of where that absence comes from.

MEAGHAN MORRIS: It occurred to me if I had, in Australia, given a similar talk to yours I too would have been hit with questions of identity, nationalism, etc. almost immediately. Because the formation of intellectuals in English-speaking countries produces the peculiar assumption that Europeans talking about their own countries without including any parameters can be forgiven for their eurocentrism because the knowledge they produce is automatically useful and interesting to people all over the world. Whereas when an Australian, even in Australia, mentions the Australian parameters of the problem, he or she is necessarily seen as advocating some kind of aggressive nationalism, instead of what I would call a normal everyday materialist approach to the shape of problems in a space within which one can effectively act—which, on my scale of things, is not the world. It seems to me, and I think this is a comment on the discussion rather than a question to you, that people become mystified by what is then called the metaphor of space. There is a problem in, for example, Soja's way of discussing things: the affirmation of space as a metonym of geography is read against time which becomes the metonym of historicism. But more importantly, the question should not be why is Jody Berland talking about space? It should be why has cultural studies been so unutterably slow to talk about the fact that the whole power structure in this world is changing and changing so fast that a lot of the traditional protocols of eurocentric intellectual discourse simply don't make sense of anything? So the real question is not why is Jody Berland talking about space, but why don't we know?

JOLIE COLLIER: I was thinking about your use of historical models, the music hall and before that the fair, to talk about popular entertainment in general as a kind of locus for, as you put it, social and sexual transgression, the Dionysian aspect of things. How important are the differences in spaces between the fair and the music hall as sites of social and sexual aggression? Might the transformation be to attempt to gain greater control over that locus of transgression? And is the transformation a matter of space, not just of forms of entertainment?

BERLAND: The contradiction is that if you go into something like a music hall, or into a similar social situation today, you're entering into that kind of promise of emancipation from all the boring or disciplinary practices of your everyday life. You're escaping it and also entering into it. I think that's a very central contradiction which takes utterly different forms. So that, if you were to look at something like walkmans or shopping malls, the same contradiction is there, but it takes completely different shapes. It's that same kind of situation. You could say that the whole history of the privatization and atomization of the media on the one hand as people trying to escape these disciplinary apparatuses and trying to form a much more autonomous kind of pleasure, and at the same time getting bound into another kind of disciplinary situation in which they are being atomized and drawn into some other kind of social disciplinary apparatus. There are a lot of different and changing locations for this dynamic to take place, but it takes very very different forms depending on the particular cultural technologies which are following us as we move out of these situations when they become overly disciplined and try and find other kinds of situations.

BILL WARNER: My question has to do with the degree to which you see media as at least a single decisive causal factor in shaping the transformations of culture. In your talk you seemed to leave that question open but you also offered a valuable corrective to theories of audience empowerment through pleasure by arguing that they reinscribe within theory what the media marketers are saying: come to the media, be entertained, take pleasure, and you will be empowered. So, my question is: was the free trade agreement the inevitable culmination of technological factors or was it a contingent historical event?

BERLAND: In terms of looking at the particular kinds of effects of particular kinds of media and the way that they can be shaped by different kinds of practices in different kinds of situations, I think that's an historically specific question. I also think that how one looks at it is motivated, depending on the particular situation and the particular kind of mood that you're in. I would never say that television, or even Jack Valente and the Motion Picture Export Association is solely responsible for free trade, or that it is an inevitable result of Hollywood exports. It would never have happened without a Conservative government, at least in its present form. Of course this is a more general shift in governmentality with the expansion of global capital, and technology is very instrumental in this larger dynamic. This has played a very strong role in the evolution of these political events which have therefore motivated me to be much more critical about particular discourses around entertainment. In terms of the process of technological histories, I don't believe in a technological determinism about media any more than I do about transportation. You can say, our whole society's been utterly changed by the existence of cars, but the car wasn't just a new technology, it was the emergence of a particular invention into a particular kind of political economy which required that the government build lots and lots of roads and the oil companies make lots and lots of money. And then this even changes, because what does it mean when they decide to get rid of public transportation and build even more roads? This is not a technologically determined history, but there are technological shapes in which different things take place.

WARNER: But, it seemed at certain points in your talk that it was media that determined the spaces as the framing context for various social practices. And that seemed to imply a kind of cause and effect sequence that had a deterministic resonance.

BERLAND: I guess I don't know what you mean by deterministic. I think things have shapes and forms and that those forms have effects. I think that if you're far away from somebody it's different than if you're next to them. And I think that if you communicate with somebody by telephone it's different and so forth. And I think also these have institutional structures that have shapes. So that, for instance, I think that you can't talk about music now without talking about the structure of the recording industry. But it doesn't follow that our whole horizon of existence is determined by the structure or the technological shape of those things. I think that they're there, and that they set certain kinds of patterns and certain kinds of limits and certain kinds of shapes in space, and that they put in place certain kinds of processes which are themselves shaped by what we do. But again my whole outlook on that is determined by what I would call a determining political situation at the present time which makes me emphasize certain things more than others.

4

Postcolonial Authority and Postmodern Guilt

Homi K. Bhabha

Sliding off his banquette in a gay bar in Tangiers, Roland Barthes, the semiotic pedagogue, attempts "to enumerate the stereophony of languages within earshot": music, conversations, the sound of chairs, glasses, Arabic, French, the high notes of the English expatriates, when suddenly the inner speech of the writer turns into the exorbitant space of the Moroccan sook. "Through me passed words, tiny syntagms, bits of formulae and *no sentence formed* . . . It set up in me a definitive discontinuity: this *non-sentence* was in no way something that could not have acceded to the sentence, that might have been *before* the sentence: it was: *outside the sentence*" (1975, p. 49). At the point at which the hierarchy and the subordinations of the sentence are replaced by the definitive discontinuity of the text, at that point, the subject of discourse spatializes and moves beyond the sententious. It turns "outside" the sentence to inscribe the boundaries of meaning (not its depths) but in the affective language of cultural difference. This speech, Barthes writes, "of which Tangiers was the exemplary site, was at once very cultural and very savage"; being drunk in Tangiers reminds him, *après-coup,* of dreaming in Paris. The dream-work "makes *everything in me which is not strange, foreign,* speak: the dream is an uncivil anecdote made up of very civilized sentiments" (1975, p. 60).

From the unconscious of cultural difference and sexual difference, Barthes enacts a kind of affectivity that is outside the "sentence," completely social and sentient, but not sentientious. Barthes derives a language of performativity to contest the pedagogical. Writing aloud is the hybrid he proposes in language lined with flesh, the metonymic art of the articulation of the body not as pure presence of Voice, but as a kind of affective writing, after the sumptuousness or suffering of the signifier. And it is, coincidentally, this very passage that André Green, the psychoanalyst, uses to demonstrate the affectivity of the relation of transference in psychoanalysis. This affectivity exceeds the linearity of the written or spoken transference and allows us to grasp the space of the body in writing as a kind of present-absence or absent-presence: a "word-thing and affect presentation, acting-out affects of writing which undermine and compete with the affects of life" (1987, pp. 321–22).

It is one of the salutary features of postmodern theory to suggest that it is the disjunctive, fragmented, displaced agency of those who have suffered the sentence of history—subjugation, domination, diaspora, displacement—that forces one to think outside the certainty of the sentientious. It is from the affective experience of social marginality that we must conceive of a political strategy of empowerment and articulation, a strategy outside the liberatory rhetoric of idealism and beyond the sovereign subject that haunts the "civil" sentence of the law. To speak Outside the sentence, or the sentientious, is to disturb the causality of what Ranajit Guha (1989) of the subaltern

56

studies project calls "tertiary discourse that rationalizes the ambiguities of rebel politics by placing it on a continuum of context—event—perspective"; in doing this the self-alienation of insurgency, with its polyphonic discourses of myth, ritual, and rumor, are laid to waste and regularized in a barren prose. The strategic objective of being "outside" is not to be outside theory but to be its exorbitant object, to overcome the pedagogical predictability of the sententious professor and the politician: "The sentence is hierarchical: it implies subjections, subordinations, internal reactions . . . How can a hierarchy remain open? The professor finishes his sentence . . . The politician clearly takes a great deal of trouble to imagine an ending to his sentence."

Now the purpose of this Barthesian anecdote on discursive closure is to point to a growing tradition of the importance of "affective writing" in theoretical discourses that attempt to construct modes of political and cultural agency that are commensurate with historical conjunctures where populations are culturally diverse, racially and ethnically divided—the objects of social, racial, and sexual discrimination. In other words, what is at issue is the question of cultural diversity. In that sense, this talk is itself non-sententious because it speaks from a moment *in medias res,* from in-between unequal and often antagonistic sites without the certainty of imagining what happens or emerges at the end. From that perspective, the perspective of the "edge" rather than the end, it is no longer adequate to think or write culture from the point of view of the liberal "ethic" of tolerance, or within the pluralistic time frame of multiculturalism. My focus today is on the moment of culture caught in an aporetic, contingent position, in-between a plurality of practices that are different and yet must occupy the same space of adjudication and articulation. It is this liminal form of cultural identification that Charles Taylor proposes as the basis for non-ethnocentric, transcultural judgments in his thesis of minimal rationality emerging from the problem of cultural incommensurability which "takes us beyond merely formal criteria of rationality . . . [towards] the *human activity of articulation;* this gives the value of rationality its sense" (1985, p. 151)—a position Satya Mohanty (1989) has nicely adopted in a reading of Us and Them in critical discourses concerned with the representation of cultural difference.

This shift from the positivistic sense of rationality, as the possession of an *a priori* subject, to a mode of minimal rationality as the process of the activity of articulation, not only changes the concept of cultural value as pleasure and instruction but also alters the very subject of culture. It shifts the focus from the validity of judgment as causality, or the negative dialectics of the "symptomatic reading," to an attention to the place and time of the enunciative agency. There is an emphasis on the relation between temporality and meaning in the *present* of utterance, in the performativity of a history of the present; in the political struggle around the "true" (in the Foucauldian sense) rather than its pedagogical authenticity secured as an epistemological "outside," on the problematic level of a "*General* Ideology." Our attention is occupied with the relations of authority which secure professional, political, and pedagogical status through the strategy of speaking in a particular time and from a specific space. That is part of what is entailed in being a strategic intellectual.

The epistemological distance between subject and object, inside and outside, that is part of the cultural binarism that emerges from relativism is now replaced by a social process of enunciation. If the former focuses on function and intention, the latter focuses on signification and institutionalization. If the epistemological tends toward a "representation" of its referent, prior to performativity, the enunciative attempts repeatedly to "reinscribe" and relocate that claim to cultural and anthropological priority (High/Low; Ours/Theirs) in the act of revising and hybridizing the settled, sententious hierarchies, the locale and the locutions of the cultural. If the former is always locked into the hermeneutic circle, in the *description* of cultural elements as they tend towards a totality, the latter is a more *dialogic* process that attempts to track the processes of displacement and realignment that are already at work, constructing something different and hybrid from the encounter: a third space that does not simply revise or invert the dualities, but *revalues* the ideological bases of division and difference. For instance, the definitive discontinuity in Barthes's anecdote is reinscribed in the enunciative present. From a splitting of the psychic enunciative subject of desire into its naming in the savage/civil metaphor, we witness the possibility of a reading of cultural difference in which Tangiers simultaneously becomes the space for the writing of sexual difference. "Writing aloud," which is the hybrid articulation of such relocation, is the place of the Name of the Father and the sign of savagery-culture; alterity.

Why is the metaphor of the *articulation of language* so central to contemporary cultural theorists concerned with the problem of ambivalence and contingency in the construction of political identities within what is loosely called, a "politics of difference"—twinning the notion of "the unconscious like a language" with "the political as a language"? Listen to Cornel West enacting "a measure of synechdochical thinking"— his phrase—as he attempts to talk of the problems of address and identification in the context of a black, radical "practicalist" culture: "When it comes to speaking with the black masses, I use Christian narratives and stories, a language meaningful to them but filtered with intellectual developments from de Tocqueville to Derrida .... A tremendous articulateness is syncopated with the African drumbeat into an American postmodernist product: there is no subject expressing originary anguish here but a fragmented subject, pulling from past and present, innovatively producing a heterogeneous product .... it is part and parcel of the subversive energies of black underclass youth, energies that are forced to take cultural *mode of articulation* ..." (1988, p. 281). Or take Stuart Hall, writing from the perspective of those fragmented, marginalized, racially discriminated, populations of a Thatcherite underclass, unskilled, unwaged, unemployed, the homeless for whom, as he says, material interests on their own have no class belonging. Hall questions the sententiousness of Left orthodoxy where "we go on thinking a unilinear and irreversible political logic, driven by some abstract entity that we call the economic or capital, whereas ... *politics works actually more like the logic of language* ... The ideological sign is always multi-accentual and Janus-faced ... Ideology does not obey the logic of rational discourse. Its unity is always in quotation marks and always complex, a suturing together of elements which have no necessary or eternal belongingness. It is always in that sense articulated around arbitrary and not natural closures" (1988b).

The address of the ideological formation must be thought in that "temporality" that gives the practice of language symbolic access to the social movement of the political imaginary. There is a continual tension between the spatial incommensurability of the articulation of cultural differences and the temporal non-synchronicity of signification as they attempt to speak, quite literally, in terms of each other. As you will see in a moment, for Stuart Hall the multi-accentual sign of discursive ideology (as he calls it) becomes in another site—in the contemporary politics of communities and race—the multivalent subject of the enunciation of what Stuart Hall calls "new ethnicities," or what *Marxism Today,* the CPGB journal, calls "New Times." It is the ambivalence and liminality enacted in the enunciative present of human articulation (C. Taylor, 1985) that results in the signs and symbols of cultural difference being conjugated (not conjoined or complemented) through the interactive temporality of signification. This produces that object of contemporary, postmodern political desire, what Hall calls "arbitrary closure," like the signifier. But this arbitrary closure is also the cultural space for opening up *new* forms of agency and identification that confuse historical temporalities, confound sententious, continuist meanings, traumatize tradition, and may even render communities contingent: The African drumbeat syncopating heterogenous American postmodernism, the arbitrary, but strategic logic of politics, the material space of the body—these moments contest the linearity of pedagogy and the sententiousness of rationalist agency. Why does the linguistic metaphor speak the affectivity of the politics of cultural difference? What form of cultural agency is accessible to heterogeneity and arbitrary closure? What lesson of the writing of culture is spoken through affective inscription at the point of human enunciation?

The linguistic metaphor opens up a movement of contingency and ambivalence in the positioning of cultural and political identity that is neither teleological or dialectical. What is crucial is to work out a notion of arbitrary closure for cultural judgment and political agency that leads neither to "relative autonomy" nor to an open-ended liberal pluralism where, in Rortyesque style, we must always be on the "look out for marginalization," without necessarily shifting the finitude of our final vocabularies, unless of course the "other" is in pain or humiliated. Difficult though it is, we cannot understand what is being proposed for new times—politics at the site of cultural enunciation; culture in the place of political affiliation—if we do not see that the discourse of the language-metaphor suggests that in each achieved symbol of cultural/political identity or synchronicity there is always the repetition of the sign that represents the place of psychic ambivalence and social contingency.

This opens us a spatial movement of cultural representation which I shall call a "time-lag": an iterative, interrogative space produced in the interruptive overlap between symbol and sign, between synchronicity and caesura or seizure (not diachronicity). In each symbolic structure of a "homogeneous empty time" there is the repetition of the iterative stoppage or caesura of the sign which is not so much arbitrary as "interruptive," not so much a closure as a liminal interrogation "without" words of the culturally given, traditional boundaries of knowledge. This distinction between sign/symbol has a familiar Hjelmslevian history. But for my emphasis on cultural temporality, the enunciative displacement of *sign-n-symbol,* I prefer the Lacanian hybrid, because it places that linguistic distinction in the Unconscious as writing and knowledge, and, with a certain laconic irony, it also speaks of the discursive, cultural, "world of truth" at one and the same time. In "What is Speech? What is Language?" Lacan writes:

> It is the temporal element . . . or the temporal break . . . the intervention of a scansion permitting the intervention of something which can take on meaning for a subject. . . . There is in fact a reality of signs within which there exists a world of truth entirely deprived of subjectivity, and that on the other hand there has been a historical development of subjectivity manifestly directed towards the rediscovery of truth which lies in the order of symbols. (1988, p. 285)

What is interesting here, is that the temporal break or intervention, associated with the activity of the sign, happens in the liminal moment of the ego-deprived of subjectivity—but that is precisely where something happens which can take on a new and differential meaning for the subject in synchronic order of symbols. Nowhere is a better illustration of this complex argument to be found than in Fanon's famous caesura: "The Black man is not. Any more than the White Man" (1967). In this non-sententious, ungrammatical break, where the cut of the sign is the dereliction of semantic and symbolic synchrony, there opens up the site of another discourse, a reinscription and relocation—an affective writing as interrogation. Fanon goes on to say: "O my body, make of me a man who questions!"

What are the cultural dimensions of the time-lag? What conditions of narrative does it empower to reinscribe cultural differences, to relocate cultural strategies, as they emerge from the displacements and derelictions of social marginality? This conflictual articulation of meaning and place, the partial—and—double identifications of race, gender, class, generation at their point of unfamiliarity, even incommensurability, does not simply conform to the slippage of desire or jouissance. That would be a poetics of "time-lack" not time-lag—a sententious, knowing nullity in the refiguring of the subject that Borch-Jacobsen nicely describes as the "auto-enunciative even though the auto has been reduced to nothing."

The time-lag that I want to inscribe for the analysis of postcolonial discourse as a productive, hybrid "betweenness," relocation and reinscription, has, for instance, a descriptive history in the writings of the Guyanian novelist Wilson Harris when he conceives of the complexities of social transformation as the dialectic of, what he calls, "material advance and a concurrent void": "What does Russian American détente mean for the particular peoples on either side of the fence? If indeed any real sense is to be made of material change it can only occur with a concurrent void . . . wherein one may begin to come into confrontation with a spectre of invocation whose freedom to participate in an alien territory has become a necessity for one's reason or salvation." The cultural void—with its discursive "time-lag"—is part of a strategy of cultural survival in conditions of political contestation which necessitates a relocation of the specificity of difference or the incommensurable. The temporal break in cultural synchronicity that I have attempted to describe produces in the "scansion of the sign" (Lacan, 1988) a truth outside the knowledge of the subject, the sentence, or the sententious. In a reinscription of Lacan's time of the sign—"truth deprived of the subject"—Harris describes this process as the breakdown of the "self-righteous moral privilege."

Nothing locates this moment of enunciatory "void" as the necessity of survival with greater force than Toni Morrison's *Beloved* (1987). The time-lag in *Beloved* is nothing less than the haunting of slavery in the very act of its "re-memoration" and reinscription as the death of Culture as continuum, historicism, linear narration, discursive generality premised on the synchronous symbolic structure of the Social Imaginary. What narrative figure could speak more compellingly of the enunciative time-lag than Morrison's repetition of the number 124, with which the book starts? For in the "presentness" of that sign, 124, whose presence is the habitus of death and slave memory, there is the concurrent void of a history that emerges outside the sententious, synchronous narrative of historical naming. The number as sign—124—can add to without adding up but may disturb the calculation. No nouns or proper names, no cozy claims to instant history and legend, Morrison writes: Numbers constitute an address, a thrilling enough prospect for slaves who owned nothing, least of all an address (in both senses of the word). The address is therefore personalized but personalized by its own activity, not the pasted on desire for personality: "124 was spiteful. Full of baby's venom. The women in the house knew it and so did the children."

The unknowing which is inscribed in the break of the number—the sign 124— constitutes in the narrative "present" the social conditions of slave history now relocated in the address of language. No native informant here, no lobby, no door, no entrance, Morrison writes, "snatched just as the slaves were from one place to the other . . . The reader is snatched, yanked, thrown into an environment completely foreign." It is this temporality of caesura and seizure—124 is "the first stroke" of the shared experience— that challenges what Morrison considers to be the synchrony of Western chronology and community. The community that she envisages is represented in the subliminal, underground life of the novel whose progress of solidarity lies in a metonymic process of getting, as she says, from the "first to the next and next . . ." This is no sign of linearity or totality. In Morrison's truth "without pasted on personality," a time deprived of subjectivity, there is, as she puts it, "especially no time because memory, pre-historic memory, has no time. There is just a little music because that is all (the slaves) had . . . a little music . . . for that work, the work of language has to get out of the way," revealing the necessity of the sign, the address of 124.

The literary figure of time-lag as the temporality of the reinscription of difference and the relocation of cultural meaning has a tragic history in Salman Rushdie's *The Satanic Verses.* The scandal of the book focuses on the chapter called "The return of Jahilia" which, according to Mashriq Ibn Ally, a Bradford spokesman, gives offense because of the obscene and derogatory remarks made by Rushdie "on the person of the prophet . . . and the insinuations about the wives of the prophet." What is the "person" of the prophet in the book? What is the guilt of the author? What is the source of the secular as it inscribes the literary?

These are not questions posed either by the London literary fundamentalists too busy defending liberal freedom in the name of the author, nor by the Bradford fundamentalists too zealously guarding the person of the prophet which becomes the totem of their cultural migration. To turn to the book, they both miss the moment when the migrant, exilic "sign" splits the synchronicity of the symbol of authority: God, Father, Author. The discourse of the controversy, it has recently struck me, is profoundly masculinist, even as it is racist. The Oriental despot contending the modernist, secular author; the liberal author protecting the rights of public man; the Eastern male protecting the honor of those behind the veil. As if to collude with this reading, the major political issue that has accompanied the controversy has been the setting up of muslim schools, within the state sector, to provide special education to muslim girls.

But can zealous Jahilia be read without lackadaisical Bombay being staged retroactively in its midst, *in medias res?* Can the prophet who presides over the later chapter be read without the Father who appears in the earlier one in Bombay? It is the primal scene enacted in the return to Bombay that is neither the source nor the cause of the row in Jahilia, but a kind of time-lag suggests that the one is relocated in terms of the other. That retroactive space of meaning belongs neither to author or father or God; it moves beyond the sphere of these authorities who gain their power in the presence of the phallus, possessors and protectors of the Letter and the Law. For it is the return to Bombay which turns Chamcha into a secular person and the return to Bombay is the scenario of the encounter with his dead mother—the mother's absence—which the Father attempts to cover up by marrying the maid servant, who becomes the mother's simulacrum, at once the symbol of her presence and the sign of her absence. The mother as enunciation is the place where, in the act of death and doubling, Bombay and Jahilia become partial and conflictual doubles of each other.

The body of the mother becomes the writing of cultural difference herself. For it is the death of the mother that makes possible the process of renaming in the book that opens up the void in the act of cultural naming that allows cultures to be translated, reinscribed, relocated. The servant as mother is named Kasturba, the wife of Mahatma Gandhi, the Mother of the Independent Indian nation; the irony here, of course, reflects on the empty promises of nationalist renaming where the untouchables were renamed harijans—the people of God—by Gandhi. It is the splitting that becomes the sign of the mother in the text—totally ignored by mullahs and the literati—that enables the act of secular narration. For it is only through the difference that the mother's place enables— at once sign and symbol, death and the double—that the act of secular discourse becomes possible. Chamcha discovers that he can talk in many voices, that he is constituted in

partial and incommensurable times. Salman, the wandering Persian scribe who interpolates the Koranic text with the Satanic Verses, loses his belief not out of conviction,
not because he espouses another set of beliefs, but because in the act of inscription he
is able to change words without Mohammed knowing—it is the act of performativity
that unseats the authority of Koranic pedagogy. What we begin to see, forming in the
present moment of this act of writing, is the ascendancy of a historical, perspectival
secular text that has its own temporality. If we look beyond the conflict of belief to the
temporality of writing we also find that it is Ayesha who represents the Muse of History.
It is Ayesha who is locked in battle with the Imam who stands for the death of History,
the end of the timeless and the totally synchronous. Ayesha's time of history, in contrast
goes, we are told, tick-tock, tick-tock. . . .

Blasphemy is the most public and legal sign of the Rushdie affair. He is being
charged for blasphemy in the High Courts; the major political initiative has been to
suggest widening the blasphemy laws. The first use of the word blasphemy in the text
occurs when Chamcha is confused between the image of his mother and the simulacrum
of the servant. "Can you tell a living ayah from your departed Ma" asked his father?
In that *trompe l'oeil* moment, the England-returned exile exclaims, "Oh God," and
another servant Vallabh exclaims, "Excuse, baba, but you should not blaspheme." Blasphemy is the migrant's shame at returning home; it is the time-lag effected through
the absent-presence of the mother; it is the indistinguishability of being God and human
in a confusion of sign and symbol without which it is difficult to speak historically, or
of history: A man who invents himself needs someone to believe in him. Playing God
again, you could say . . . how like a man.

How like a man, precisely. For if the masculinist discourse of the controversy stops
here, in this double-bind, it is an interesting historical fact that it has been feminist
groups in England that have done most to move on this controversy, which otherwise
remains one between authors and priests with their horns locked, fighting for authority.
The wider social and cultural implications of this issue, as it affects questions of education,
schooling, domestic politics, and public policy have only really been elaborated by feminists and women's groups.

The notions of reinscription and relocation emerging out of cultural difference must
not be confused with Richard Rorty's highly influential figure of the "white body in
pain," which is at the bleeding heart of his concern with non-fundationalist contingent
languages of solidarity and community. Rorty's language-metaphor of political culture
is the consensual overlapping of "final languages" which allow "imaginative identification" with the Other, so long as certain words—kindness, decency, dignity are held
in common. However, as he says, the liberal ironist can never elaborate an empowering
strategy, unless you happen to be a novelist in the liberal, Western literary tradition.
Just how disempowering his views are, how steeped in a Western, ethnocentric, liberal
universalism is best seen, appropriately for a non-foundationalist, in a footnote.

"Liberal society already contains the institutions for its own improvement. Western
social and political thought may have had the last conceptual revolution it needs in J. S.
Mill's suggestion that governments should optimize the balance between leaving private
lives alone and minimizing suffering." Appended to this statement is the footnote where
suddenly the liberal ironist loses his powers of redescription: "This is not to say that
the world has had the last political revolution it needs. . . . But in such countries (as
South Africa, Albania, Paraguay) raw courage (like that of the leader of COSATU) is
the relevant virtue, not the sort of reflective acumen which makes contributions to social
theory" (1989, p. 63).

This is where Rorty's conversation stops, but we must force him to dialogue in order to teach him the social theory of pain and suffering. From the limits of liberalism emerges the subaltern perspective. "Liberal bourgeois culture hits its historical limits in colonialism," says Ranajit Guha (1989) sententiously, and almost as if to speak "outside the sentence" Veena Das reinscribes it into the affective language of metaphor and the body: Subaltern rebellions can only provide a nighttime of love . . .

In her excellent essay "Subaltern as Perspective" (1989), commissioned by the subaltern scholars, the Indian historian Veena Das demands a historiography of the subaltern that displaces the paradigm of social action as defined primarily by rational action, and seeks a form of discourse where affective writing develops its own language. History as a writing that constructs the moment of defiance emerges in the "magma of significations," for the "representational closure of . . . thought in objectified forms is now ripped open." In an argument that demands an enunciative temporality remarkably close to my notion of the "time-lag" that circulates at the point of the sign's seizure/caesura of symbolic synchronicity, Das locates the moment of transgression in the splitting of the discursive "present": a greater attention is required to transgressive agency in "the splitting of the various types of speech produced into statements of referential truth in the indicative present. . . ." This emphasis on the disjunctive present of utterance enables the historian to get away from defining subaltern consciousness as binary, as having positive or negative dimensions. It allows the articulation of subaltern agency as relocation and reinscription. In the seizure of the sign, as I've said, there is neither dialectical sublimation nor the "empty" signifier; there is a contestation of the given symbols of authority that shifts the terrain of antagonism; the synchronous is challenged on its own terms, but the grounds of engagement have been displaced in a "supplementary" movement. This is the historical movement of hybridity as camouflage, as a contesting, antagonistic agency functioning in the time-lag of sign/symbol which is a space in-between the rules of engagement. And this form of political agency is beautifully described by Das:

> It is the nature of the conflict within which a caste or tribe is locked which may provide the characteristics of the historical moment; to assume that we may know a priori the mentalities of castes or communities is to take an essentialist perspective which the evidence produced in the very volumes of *Subaltern Studies* would not support.

Is this not similar to what Fanon describes as the knowledge of the practice of action? The primitive Manicheanism of the settler—Black and White, Arabs and Christians—breaks down in the struggle for independence and comes to be replaced with truths that are only partial, limited, and unstable. Each local ebb of the tide reviews the political question from the standpoint of all political networks. The leaders should stand firmly against those within the movement who tend to think that shades of meaning will drive wedges into the solid block of popular opinion.

Does this affective knowledge of the practice of action—Stuart Hall, Andrew Ross, Cornel West, Frantz Fanon, Veena Das, the subalterns—constitute the elements of a social theory? Is its emphasis on the enunciative present, splitting, disjunctive temporalities, affective writing, and contingency immediately appropriatable by the poststructuralist critique of liberal humanism?

In the form of agency that I've attempted to describe—the ebb and flow of sign and symbol, affective action—the nighttime of love returns, I believe, to interrogate the major dialectic of Foucault, the doubling of "Man" and the finitude of modernity. His great influence on postcolonial and subaltern scholars cannot excuse his sanctioned ignorance (Gayatri Spivak) of the colonial and postcolonial moment. His own text betrays him at the magisterial end of *The Order of Things,* when the rationale of modernity is dispersed in the sciences of the Unconscious—Psychoanalysis and Anthropology. The time-lag of cultural difference, neither symbol nor sign, intervenes in Foucault's description of the "slenderness of the narrative" of nineteenth-century historicism. It is the moment when the rationalist and universalist claims of history—which were also the technologies of colonial governance: Evolutionism, Evangelism, Utilitarianism—are attenuated in their encounter with the question of cultural difference. An incommensurability ensues when history constitutes the "homeland" of the human sciences—its cultural area, chronological or geographical boundaries—and yet in making its claims to Universalism, "the subject of knowledge becomes the nexus of different times, foreign to it and heterogeneous in respect to one another" (1970, p. 369). As a result, the Western subject that arises in the nineteenth century is *heimlich,* "organicist," and dehistoricized, but at the same time, cannot stop constituting the knowledge of itself by compulsively relating one cultural episode to another in an infinitely repetitious series.

It is in this time-lag—"History now takes place on the outer limits of subject and object"—that we must relocate Foucault's modernity by turning to the "post-modern" position that he gives anthropology. There is a "certain position in the western ratio," Foucault writes, "that was constituted in its history and provides the foundation it can have with all other societies." Foucault fails to name that position or the moment of Constitution. By disavowing it, however, he names it in the next sentence by negating it: "Obviously this does not mean that the colonizing situation is indispensable to ethnology" (1970).

From the subaltern perspective, are we demanding that Foucault should historicize "imperialism" as the origin of modernity, so that he may "complete" the argument? Definitely not. I want to suggest that the colonial and postcolonial is, metaleptically, partially present in the text, in a spirit of subaltern resistance that will turn it toward other things. In talking of psychoanalysis Foucault is able to see how knowledge and power come together in the enunciative "present" of transference, the "calm violence" of a relationship that constitutes psychoanalytic discourse. By disavowing "the colonial moment" as an enunciative, transferential discursive relation, Foucault can say nothing of the power and knowledge that constitutes the position of the Western ratio, in its moment of modernity, as a dialogic "colonial" relation, a colonial/postcolonial discourse. Read from this perspective, we can see clearly that in insistently spatializing the "time" of history Foucault constitutes a doubling that is strangely collusive with its dispersal, equivalent to its equivocation, strangely self-constituting despite its play with the double. If we insert, in the finitude of Foucault, the time-lag where the sign and the symbol contend, the synchronous and the iterative that create the necessity for relocation, then Foucault would have had to radically reinscribe his perspective. His description of the dehistoricized emergence of the human sciences in the nineteenth century would have to be seen in relation to those "objects" of that disciplinary gaze, who, at that historical moment, in the supplementary spaces of the colonial and slave world, were tragically becoming the peoples without a history.

If I started "outside the sentence" in Morocco, with Barthes, whose semiology has had such a profound influence on cultural studies, I want to end in Algeria, with a challenge to liberal humanist sententiousness from that revolutionary psychoanalyst Frantz Fanon, whose moment in cultural studies has yet to come:

> Under the colonial regime anything may be done for a loaf of bread of a miserable sheep. . . . For a colonized man . . . living does not mean embodying moral values or

taking his place in the coherent world. To live means to keep on existing. Every stolen date or sheep is a victory; not the result of work but the triumph of life. Thus to steal dates . . . is not the negation of the property of others, nor the transgression of the Law . . . You are forced to come up against yourself. Here we discover the kernel of that hatred against the self which is characteristic of racial conflicts in segregated societies. (1965, p. 249)

In the colonial condition, the dictates of the Law, and the authority of the supergo—embodying moral values, taking a coherent place in the world—become forms of cultural knowledge constituted of guilt and doubt. Fanon's colonial subject constitutes its identity and authority, not in relation to the "content" of the Law or its transgression of its edicts. His existence is defined in a perpetual performativity that intervenes in that syntax or grammar of the superego, in order to disarticulate it. "The native's guilt," Fanon writes, "is never a guilt which he accepts; it is rather a kind of curse, a sword of Damocles . . . he is overpowered but not tamed" (1965). This is the guilt that sonorously resists the symbolic organization of the paternal metaphor that will lead us to the narrative of melancholia.

For the installation of the phallic Damoclean sword as a Social Ideal evokes an ambivalent social identification embodied in the muscular tension of the borderline native. His "disincorporation" in paranoia and melancholia are attempts to break the marginality of the social and political limits of space; to redraw the boundaries in a psychic, fantasmatic space. The Damoclean sword installs an ambivalence in the symbolic order, where it is itself the immobile Sign of an authority whose meaning is continually contested by the fantasmatic, fragmented, motility of the signifiers of revolt. The Law is entombed as loss at the point of its ideal authority. But as the dominating force of symbolic ordering it also "mummifies" the authority of the native social order. The colonial sword is constituted in an indeterminate doubling; the native "superego" is itself displaced in the colonial contention. Here, in this order signifying a double loss, we encounter what may be a symbolic space of cultural survival—a melancholia in revolt.

It is the shadow that guilt casts on the "object" of identification that is the origin of melancholia, according to Freud. Fanon's "guilt" is intriguingly different. Patterns of avoidance amongst the oppressed are those of the death reflex that, at the same time, never cease to drive the oppressed to resist the authority of the oppressor, to usurp his place and to transform the very basis of authority. The sword of Damocles is double-edged, striking a seizure like the temporal edge of the sign, opening up the time-lag between sign and symbol. For "the symbols of social order—the police, the bugle calls, the waving flags—are at once inhibitory and stimulating; for they do not convey the message 'Don't dare to budge'; rather they cry out 'Get ready to attack' " (1965, p. 41).

The melancholic discourse, Freud says, is a plaint in the oldfashioned sense; the insistent self—exposure and the repetition of loss must not be taken at face value for its apparent victimage and passivity. Its narrative metonymy, the repetition of the piecemeal, outside the sentence, bit by bit, its insistent self-exposure, comes also from a mental constellation of revolt: "The melancholic are not ashamed and do not hide themselves, since everything derogatory they say about themselves is at bottom said about somebody else" (1917). This inversion of meaning and address in the melancholic discourse—when it "incorporates" the loss or lack in its own body, displaying its own weeping wounds—is also an act of "disincorporating" the authority of the Master. Fanon, again, comes close to saying something similar when he suggests that the native wears his psychic wounds on the surface of his skin like an open sore—an eyesore to the colonizer.

Let us call the melancholic revolt the "projective disincorporation" by the marginal of the Master. This narrative speaks from the elision between the synchronous symbol of loss and its non-referential, fragmented, phantasmatic narratives. It says: All these bits and pieces in which my history is fragmented, my culture piecemeal, my identifications fantasmatic and displaced; these splittings of wounds of my body are also a form of revolt. And they speak a terrible truth. In their ellipses and silences they dismantle your authority: the vanity of your mimetic narratives and your monumental history; the metaphoric emblems in which you inscribe The Great Book of Life. My revolt is to face the Life of literature and history with the scraps and fragments that constitute its double, which is living as surviving, meaning as melancholia.

Remember the lesson of the violent ingestion, or "incorporation," of the stolen, murderous Algerian date!

DISCUSSION: HOMI BHABHA

RUTH TOMASELLI: I want to draw upon your discussion of the concept of constituting subaltern groups, and your recognition that people can formulate critical and/or social theory both through courageous action and through thought. I was wondering how you see those of us who function in the area of cultural studies coming to terms with the fact that we are not the instigators of theory but must make sense of theory which will happen despite us.

BHABHA: I was attempting to think that in relation to the critique of various traditions where a certain kind of sententious and over-rationalist notion of agency and historical transformation doesn't produce a kind of time both for the description and for eliciting such forms of subversive or subaltern agency that I tried to describe through the paper. I think that, in some sense, we *are* the instigators or the institutionalizers of theory. But I think I also take your sense that we may not be the instigators because I don't think we can describe the world with a set of binary oppositions: things out there and theory in here, or institutions here and actions there. That's what I was trying to do with the notion of inactive enunciation. Any pedagogical position, in actually trying to construct its authority, is always the internally alienated. It is always being erased in that very process, and in that sense, then, I think that the lesson we have to learn is that we cannot and must not imagine that we know exactly where the opposition is or where the interrogation is coming from. If we do, then we're only shoring up a kind of authority. My way of looking at this edge or boundary of the construction of any pedagogical position is actually to construct its authority in a position of being challenged. Now there are obviously conditions under which this can happen and there are conditions under which this doesn't happen. But I'm just trying to suggest that the inevitability of the tension between the institutionalization and the instigation is something I would like to stay with, and something I would like to develop.

TOM PRASCH: I want to ask a question about the paucity of the debates over Rushdie. It seems that Rushdie's book is not being read by either side. In light of this, one approach is obviously yours of giving the book a very close textual reading; another might be to look at its status as an unread book itself, its status as unreadable to these particular groups.

BHABHA: I have never taken the line that somehow, because the book had not been read, that made it less culturally symptomatic or interesting. Yet, I also agree with you: the fact that an unread book, and a book of this kind, has generated the sort of situation it has, is in fact very important. This idea of the individual reader and the individual book, which is a kind of paradigm of a certain kind of literary history has, for me, very questionable cultural, philosophical, and political assumptions. The unreadness of the book raises the question of authorship in a displaced and much more interesting way than, Who is writing the book, or How is the book being written now? Instead—Where is the book being authored from?—which is not a simple question. I think that we must look at the many disseminated authors of the book, groups of people who felt, not only that they were not being listened to but that they were unheard. So in that sense, one of the authors of the unread book is the whole racial situation. An other, of course, has been both the political and the international situation in and around Iran. The third set has been (the uncomprehending response on the part of) the English, London and international literati who seem to be, in one sense, in a very important position because they have preserved, through their activities, the life of Salman Rushdie. But, on the other hand, the literati has totally disavowed the changing status of Britain as a multi-ethnic community. This is very clear if you read recent responses which recuperate a romantic nineteenth-century notion of the writer, even Rushdie's work. I'll just give you one example of the inappropriateness of this. At the end of Rushdie's Herbert Reeve Memorial Lecture, he wrote a passage which clearly moved away from any form of intentionality. It's a very complex image of living in a house: you hear voices, you see people, and then you go into a room, and all these voices start speaking from your own head. I think he was enacting, without knowing it himself, the whole problem of paranoia about cultural dissemination, incommensurability, the kinds of texts that that produces, literature in a way almost out of control, and so forth. In the newspapers the next day, the headline was, "Rushdie pleads for the little room of literature to be preserved."

FRED PFEIL: I confess that I found your paper of forbidding difficulty, as I think many people here did. What I want to ask about is your emphasis on and what seemed to me your valorization of: splitting; disjunctive; enunciation; affective strategies; and the night of love. Perhaps I can locate my problem in your reading of Beloved. The silence, the prehistoric time without language, around which the book draws its circle, is precisely a time that must be gotten through so that historic time can begin. That space is represented as the space of catastrophe, not a valorized place, but the place where a catastrophe happens and a dilemma asserts itself that must be resolved. Another way of putting this, is that you seem to be offering an aesthetic of the fragment, not a politics.
BHABHA: I can't apologize for the fact that you found my paper completely impenetrable. I did it quite consciously, I had a problem, I worked it out. And if a few people got what I was saying or some of what I am saying, I'm happy. If not, obviously it's a disaster. So that's something that I shall face when I step down from here and meet a few people and see what has happened. My reading of Beloved was in fact inspired in some ways by Toni Morrison's Tanner lecture where she actually talks about the openings of her books. Although our objects were different, for me there was a real project there in trying to work out the kind of temporality she's talking about. Toni Morrison's Beloved is in fact a re-historicization, as she calls it, a "re-memoration." She is producing precisely this temporality now, not because she wants us to move out of it into what she calls a kind of Western chronology; I think she's constructing a kind of cultural temporality, emerging from certain experiences of suffering which she is not valorizing in any kind of politically indulgent way. She's saying, just as indeed Fanon is saying, if you start with a different time and in a different space and from a different point, you do not construct the kind of history that I think she's arguing against in the book. So I actually do take very positively the kinds of temporality she's opening up in the book, for it allows a different kind of construction of the political. That's precisely what was signaled in the work of the subaltern studies writers: yet the totalizing moment is not

the moment. For a lot of the people within *Beloved* or indeed within the annals and archives of colonial polity and policy, the attempt at totalization was in fact the attempt at a kind of absolutism and the consequence of the whole problem of oppression. So I want to learn from those disjunctive temporalities; I do not see them as small scale, and I do not see them as the aestheticization of the fragment, I see them precisely as other points from which to start.

CARY NELSON: I wonder whether the kind of general theorizing that people do is constrained and conditioned by the material circumstances and historical moments that they are also focusing on. My sense is that your mapping of the linguisticality of the fragment was partly shaped by the situation of the postcolonial subject. I wonder if you would say something about the way in which the theorizing was prompted by the historical situations you're talking about.

BHABHA: Yes, but that is something I marked at every step in my talk. That's where I started and those are the conditions I wanted to address. Why, at a particular time, do people who want to construct the question of agency use a linguistic metaphor? My suggestion was that it was not to do with some formal linguistics; it was actually to do with introducing a new time into meaning. And that I represented and then again located in developments of Afro-American literary criticism and indeed in black theory with very specific examples. I could go on like this, at that point I looked at two texts where the whole question of cultural difference, reinscription, and relocation have actually produced political issues. My reading of Rushdie located it very much both in what the row was on the ground, so to speak, and in the text. Subaltern studies may be unfamiliar to some people, but I think it's a very important historical development in the history of South Asia. Fanon is also unfamiliar, but I think very important; psychoanalysis is certainly a moment of placing of that kind, particularly in the work and use of it by Fanon. So I think I ranged from what you could call the language and the discourse of postmodern linguistic metaphors in metropolitan countries to questions of colonial agency. And at each point I was not speaking out some private thoughts for a private meditative moment. I was trying to at least face texts which have been very influential.

5

Engaging with the Popular: Audiences for Mass Culture and What to Say about Them

ROSALIND BRUNT

What I want to do in this paper is pick up on some of the conference discussion around cultural studies as a radical practice. In particular I want to focus on the issue that's bubbled up in a number of sessions concerning the relationship of the researcher to various formulations of "the people" researched upon. My own angle on the question is an interest in media audience studies and what cultural studies does or could do in this area—including rendering the notion of "audience" itself more problematic.

My remarks are reduced to a number of schematic "points" as I'm assuming some familiarity with the issues outlined, but more importantly they're offered in the spirit of continuing a debate which anyone could fill out with their own experience, their own concrete detail.

At the same time, it's all a bit sketchy because there's still not much audience research taking perspectives from cultural studies to talk *about*. There are some pragmatic/political reasons for this. Like any ethnographic project, audience studies are inordinately time consuming and labor-intensive, and certainly in Britain unlikely to attract funding unless there's an obvious social policy pay-off or corporate enterprise function.

But at a theoretical level, researchers in cultural studies have tended to construct audiences as "imagined communities" (B. Anderson, 1983) to which theories about other aspects of the mass communication process, in particular, media messages, could be referred, rather than concern themselves with actual beings living in a material world. The many "imagined" audiences that emanated as theoretical projections from cultural studies provided an important route out of the impasse of "effects" research in conventional mass communication theory. In 1970 the British media sociologist, James Halloran, whose early research was funded by the Home Office and examined the relationship between juvenile delinquency and exposure to television violence, summed up the extent of the problem in a book he edited, *The Effects of Television*. Reviewing the main postwar trends in media research, he noted that these had not demonstrated, let alone proved, anything of significance about the actual relationship between dominant forms of mass media and their audiences. So he came to the conclusion, was it because we "weren't asking the right questions in the first place?"

In framing the problem thus, Halloran symbolically passed the baton of media analysis to cultural studies. Acknowledging that orthodox audience research had taken the media message for granted, merely grading it into lumps of *a priori* dangerous influence for categorization purposes, he announced the end of an era of untheorized, unquestioning empiricism and proclaimed a new beginning: the study of content from the perspective of "pictures of the world." The terminology actually derived from one of the earliest studies of mass communication, Walter Lippman's liberal classic, *Public Opinion* (1922). But it's also not that remote from *Weltanschauungen* and a seventies' concern with "critical theory," reexamining, *inter alia,* sociologies of knowledge and Marxism. So, cutting a longer story very short, "pictures of the world" got inflected by cultural studies into an engagement with "the ideological effectivity" of the message, how the media serve "to perform the critical ideological work of 'classifying out the world' in terms of the dominant ideologies" (S. Hall, 1977).

But in the process, "message" itself, and "content," got absorbed, along with all other cultural artifacts, by the huge semiotic embrace of "the text" and subjected to a battery of critical procedures. The sheer productivity of textual analysis often rendered any reference to actual audiences redundant as the audience-text relationship became unproblematically inferred from a particular "reading" of the by now extremely problematized text. Interpreted only as "textual subjects," audiences became primarily positioned, produced by, inscribed in, *the* text. So for media studies, what started as a useful way out of a research deadend caused by a failure to analyze exactly how media encodings operated often resulted in a theoretical detour that inhibited any concrete engagement with audiences.

It was partly in response to the extreme formalism of this position that, in the context of British cultural studies, Stuart Hall (1980s) developed his model of encoding and decoding whereby media codes were analyzed, not in terms of complete ideological closure, but according to "preferred" or "dominant" meanings which could be decoded by viewers from within similar frameworks or, along lines suggested by the sociologist Frank Parkin's (1972) schema of "value systems," "negotiated" or "opposed" in various ways. Stuart Hall's theoretical intervention was paralleled at an empirical level by David Morley's (1980) pioneering audience study, *The "Nationwide" Audience,* a sequel to his earlier textual examination of a British current affairs program, *Nationwide* (Brunsdon and Morley, 1978) and conducted by his showing a particular episode of the program about the annual Budget Day to a wide variety of audience groups whose discussion was analyzed in terms of "dominant," "negotiated," and "oppositional" readings of the text.

This simplified account of "engagement" with the media text is by way of prefacing what I think is now involved in any return by cultural studies to an interest in actual audiences. I also want to identify some problems around both the encoding-decoding model and other paradigms, such as the reader-reception theory which informs that other pioneering audience study of the eighties, Janice Radway's *Reading the Romance* (1984). In considering these problems, I'll refer to some of the few other empirical audience studies of the last decade, including some research I participated in.

In the same spirit as Constance Penley (who has described embarking on her study of fanzines and their writers and readers with the model of Radway in mind), my colleague, M. Jordin, and I set out to do "another David Morley" for the mid-eighties in Britain. Or more accurately, we didn't "set out," so much as "fall into," and much of what follows arises from *post hoc* reflecting, rationalizing, and wishing we could find both time and occasion to do it all again "properly."

I won't go into the substantive detail of what we did and what we found because it's been written up in other contexts (Brunt and Jordin, 1987; Jordin and Brunt, 1988). But to explain the situation briefly: a group of us in Sheffield won a research grant to do a case study entitled, "Media, the Polls and the Public" based on a local parliamentary election in a nearby town. We aimed to examine the processes of political opinion formation in relation to the media's coverage of politics and in particular, what had been the hot issue of previous elections, the dissemination of poll data (but which promptly sank without trace this time). A peculiarity of British local elections is that a particular community that's often quite obscure in terms of regular national media coverage suddenly finds itself in the spotlight as an exemplar, a barometer, of the political "state of the nation". This election in the mid-eighties was particularly overdetermined because it consolidated a set of national issues around the current position of the political parties, particularly the emergence of centrist "third force" politics and their threat to the "official opposition" Labour Party. But it also focused on the much talked-about "North-South divide"—the increasing polarity perceived between the Tory-voting prosperous South of England, and the much poorer anti-Tory regions of Northern England and the nations of Wales and Scotland. Finally, in linking with current campaigns around local hospital and pit closures, this election highlighted national concern with the future of the Health Service, unemployment, and the impending Miners' Strike, the most devastating industrial battle of the period.

The only type of fieldwork our research proposal had specified was a detailed survey of the electorate based on random sampling methods. Because M. Jordin and I were not involved in this work but—such are the contingencies of research—had drawn the short straw of tape recording TV broadcasts to analyze and newspapers to collect and cut up and so were missing out on the excitement of "being there," we decided, given the already available ideological cover of the opinion survey, that we could afford something more experimental on the lines of David Morley's Nationwide study: to show a current affairs program that introduced the town and outlined the election issues to a variety of groups for discussion. Since we hadn't written this into the original research specification, we decided to use it for comparative purposes, to debate the merits of group discussion versus individual questionnaire.

And I suppose I should honestly record, as a sort of corrective to some of the objections raised to the way John Fiske characterized the distinction between academics and the people in his paper, just what a wonderfully liberating experience "doing a Morley" was like for us. It felt like playing truant, escaping from academia: here we are, in the field; we've arrived with The Real People at last—the academic equivalent of the worst kind of workerism, if not entryism. But our excitement was also to do with what Paul Willis (1980) has characterized as ethnography's "profoundly important methodological possibility—that of *being surprised,* of reaching knowledge not prefigured in one's starting paradigms."

I want to mention some of the "surprises" which then contributed to our questioning of the model we'd brought with us. What struck us most forcibly in the discussions we had with thirteen different community groups over one- to three-hour sessions was their blanket distrust of all forms of mass communication of politics. None of our reading of media research had prepared us for the strength of feeling about the general unreliability of "the media"—whether from groups who described themselves as "not really interested in politics" or "apolitical" or from those who saw themselves as activists in their union or Labour Party branch. On the basis of survey evidence, we had expected people to differentiate between forms of communication, with television and public service broadcasting being seen as more credible than the press. While some groups did distinguish between press and broadcasting and between national and local forms of communication, the overwhelming sense was of a massive cynicism and suspicion about "the media" as some total system.

This feeling registered as a strong resistance to media coverage of current affairs. Discussion in the groups was conducted within the generally available vocabularies for criticizing the media, those of "bias" and "distortion." From an assumed standard baseline of truth, discussion focused on providing textual examples of deviations from it. But precisely because these were groups in discussion, they were enabled to work through some of the problems associated with an essentialist notion of bias as an *a priori* given of all media and to challenge some of their own overly conspiratorial views of media production. In the process what became clear was that "bias" operated as a kind of codeword for all the varied ways the media were perceived to belong to "them" and not to "us"—and in the case of the particular election program: although it was about "our" town, it was presented through "their" eyes in ways which prevented any identification with the media "world" of current affairs.

Attributions of bias as "them" versus "us" took specific forms in different groups. For instance, contrary to Morley's finding that some of the most rejectionist groups espouse a radical value system, the groups who were most hostile to the program we showed and found it boring, uninvolving, and "a waste of time" were also those most implicated in media images of politics. They rejected current affairs television on precisely the same grounds as the media's own definitions of "politics": it was all a cynical electoral game played by "the politicians," astute manipulators of the public realm. Whereas those groups who had some other knowledge of politics derived from their own participation and experience voiced their resistance to the media in terms of personal involvement in arenas of conflict highlighted by the media. For groups like the miners who had been involved in key struggles for union recognition by other groups of workers in the seventies and eighties, actually "being there" on the picket line contrasted markedly with media interpretations of events. There was more to this view than naive realism. It involved a recognition of different perspectives: that actual participation or practical knowledge produced a different interpretation from a media standpoint of "outside observer," operating on the sidelines or somewhere "above it all." At the same time it was this group of miners who most frequently cited as evidence in arguments examples taken from specific television programs and who went furthest in differentiating types of media. For them, "the media" could be both important sources of knowledge about national and international politics as well as routine distorters of political events.

One further example of "resistance": for a group of unemployed people who met regularly at a community center specifically to study the media in sessions called "Behind the News," arguing about media bias and distortion constituted an important way of maintaining a sense of self-worth. The views of group members about the media's defining powers were quite divergent and their common situation *as* unemployed did not produce the homogeneous voice of "*the* unemployed." But what gave the group a degree of solidarity and coherence was that, on the basis of a shared experience of recently losing work and consequently both material resources and social status, everyone from very different class, gender, and race locations, placed a high priority on the one "entitlement" that cost nothing and kept up pride: every individual's right to hold a strong opinion. "We enjoy a good argument," they said, interrupting, all speaking at once, in unabashed "fighting talk" in which "the media" were constantly and triumphantly caught in the act of bias and fortunately revealed as part of an all-embracing "they" intent on doing "us" down.

From these brief examples of quite different sorts of resistance to current affairs television, I hope there's sufficient context to go on to indicate where we, reflecting on what we'd not at all predicted or prepared for, began to see some of the problems with the model we'd been using.

In the first place, through working with these groups (which it's probably relevant to say here were not constituted by us but already had some independent social existence and included, in addition to those mentioned, another group of people receiving benefits who met to discuss welfare rights, friends in an old people's home, women shop stewards, trainee caterers, a keep fit group of women . . .) we had gone beyond our starting point of the text-audience relationship, and in a way that the original encoding-decoding paradigm didn't seem to envisage. The aim of the *Nationwide* audience study, and indeed, what we had intended in attempting to replicate it, was that it returned the analyst to the text. The metaphors of "encoding"/"decoding" are those of a loop, a circuit or a chain with "ends," and there seems to be a methodological sequence to the model. It starts with the analyst's own textual examination of "preferred readings," then goes to the audience to test out degrees of textual fit or variation, then checks off these "responses" with the original text. So that the moment of "return to the audience" is one that is actually only completed by a return to the *text*. It is the text, still, rather than the audience, that remains the privileged location.

But an immediate caveat: in making this point I certainly don't want to counterpose audience studies to textual studies. Rather I want to start thinking of the text-audience relationship in a less self-enclosing way. Most particularly, I don't want to suggest that any new focus on the audience means we can casually junk the best sort of rigorous patient work on the effectivity of the text developed in the last twenty years. There is after all no shortage of audience studies which ignore the text but also eschew mean-minded empiricism, proclaim the benefits of "qualitative" research, and adopt the "unfocused discussion group" as a major technique. They too celebrate the "active" audience and its resistances and appear to take similar approaches to cultural studies.

Most recently there has been the study of "television talk," examining how television has become a taken-for-granted topic of everyday conversation. In *Uninvited Guests: Intimate Secrets of Television and Radio* (Taylor and Mullan, 1986) British sociologist and broadcaster Laurie Taylor reproduces the talk of a number of discussion groups he and co-author Bob Mullan set up to comment on their daily experience of popular television. The book is most persuasive, breezily accessible, cheerily demotic, and takes the audience's part in sharing their "sheer delight" in popular television.

But in the absence of any interpretive theory or textual reading, the notion of "discussion" is misleading. The audience groups whose comments are reproduced function as the exotic natives who furnish quirky quotations for the experts. So, for instance, in the section on current affairs television, the groups obligingly provide "irreverent" copy about the atrocious ties and nice jumpers worn by newsreaders, and the bags under their eyes.

The effect of this type of audience research is that it valorizes the kind of spontaneous, casual, off-the-cuff remarks that everyone makes when watching television in precisely the same way as the random sample questionnaire does. Far from promoting an active audience, viewers are confirmed and confined in the ordinariness of their common sense. They say fascinating, quotable, indeed, surprising things, but their function is merely to act as a bit of local color, to enliven what is actually a return to an individualized "uses-and-gratifications" account of television. In the absence of any theoretical understanding of the relationship between text and audience, this type of research remains at the level of description and is neither about groups nor about discussion.

But although, by contrast, Morley is both theoretically committed to examining the link between text and audience and to the importance of using groups rather than individuals on the grounds that communication is social, much of *his* actual method itself appears to be pulled towards the paradigm of the survey. He quotes from the groups as if they're a decontextualized aggregate of individual responses. And as we've argued elsewhere in more detail (Jordin and Brunt, 1988), Morley's references to "demographic variables" and valid "samples" indicate that his rejection of theoretical individualism and the absence of statistics are themselves no guarantee that the formalism of a survey approach has been replaced with the materialist analysis he requires. But more important for this argument, it is not clear in what sense Morley's research actually analyzes how exactly *groups* decode television, and similar findings could well have come out of working with individuals.

This is also because while Morley presents the groups he researches as real social entities with an unstructured empirical mix of gender, age, and ethnic identity, he also insists on formally categorizing each group for the purposes of analysis in terms of one homogeneous class identity—with the result that the real complexity of each group and its collective decodings of the television text is not an object to be investigated, but a problem to be circumvented in order to discover "consistency and similarity of perspective within groups."

It was particularly at this point that we departed from Morley's procedures in our work with groups. We felt that Morley's groups were not so much real participants operating in a specific context, but had been reduced to "research respondents" who were formally treated as merely "standing for" and "illustrating" larger segments of society, classes, that were existing somewhere else.

What we wanted to do was to try not to think of class as some inert, outside, macro-level "thing" that operates on another "thing," the small group. Rather, we wanted to think of class, along with other social determinations, as *also* internal to the group. In this sense, what the group does as a group, how it defines itself *as* a group (and in relation to, or against us as researchers), how it works to produce collective decodings of a text, what discourses it mobilizes, what disagreements arise among members of the group, how these are resolved in the group—were all issues that interested us. So that "decoding" represented not a finished mechanical product, but a process, a collective engagement working with and through a text.

Hence also the importance of the process as a *discussion*—where there is something actually "in it" for the group itself. They are not simply acting as "informants" helping out the researcher by purveying spontaneous untouched and uninterfered-with common sense. Instead, possibilities are opened up for the group to *reflect* on their own concerns, to, in Gramsci's terms, work with the rational kernel of "good sense" within common sense. This is how I think Janice Radway's groups, who had not met before to discuss their common interest in romance, expressed their pleasure in the group sessions because they had "never been stimulated before into thinking why we like the novels," and enjoyed the attempt to take seriously and to analyze systematically and extensively something that they knew others regarded as trivial.

Radway, too, though, like Morley, is still haunted by the paradigm of the survey and is at pains to point out that *although* the network of readers is selected for extensive knowledge and interest in romance and can discuss it in ways that the majority of women would not, nevertheless, they could still amount to an average demographic random sample.

But this is to downplay precisely what is the value of this kind of ethnographic work. Whether it is researching with groups or with individuals, it is working not in the realm of "the average" but of "the typical" in the sense that Lukács or Weber meant the term. "The typical" engages with often heightened circumstances, special conditions, exceptional cases, extreme positions, precisely in order to highlight tendencies that may in "normal circumstances" be merely incipient—and hence the concern in that tradition that carries on with Lucien Goldmann, not with the immediate, but with "the maximum possible consciousness of the group." And that is because something is perceived, both by researcher and by the community researched, to be at stake.

As I've indicated, previous theorists of "the typical" have been in the tradition of high art and great men, but maybe it's time to claim the notion in the name of the popular and women. For "it's no accident" that much of the most interesting work on audiences that's informed by cultural studies has been by feminist researchers involved with different communities of women. Besides Radway herself and Constance Penley, I am thinking of Ien Ang's (1985) work, *Watching Dallas,* which develops a textual theory around the "melodramatic imagination," Helen Taylor's (1989) on *Gone with the Wind, Scarlett's Women,* which analyzes the appeal for women of an overtly racist text and like Ang's uses letters from fans; and Jacqueline Bobo's (1988) work on black women as cultural readers in the light of controversy about Steven Spielberg's film of Alice Walker's *The Color Purple.*

Now such interest in women is not primarily because, demographically speaking, it's just been discovered there are a lot of women in the world. It is based on a recognition that something, or a lot of things, is stirring "down among the women" that needs analysis and detailed attention. Furthermore, none of the audience groups in the studies just mentioned is "typical" in the average Mrs. Normal sense. Their interest in the text is by definition extreme or extra-ordinary: they are fans, they are experts, they have special knowledges, competences, enthusiasms, which they themselves want to reflect on and analyze. In this sense, they are far more than just "informants," "respondents," or "receivers" of research procedures, even if they are unfortunately so-named in some of the write-ups. Perhaps they're not that far removed from Gramsci's idea of "organic intellectuals." Where then are we, the researchers, as "traditional intellectuals" to be placed? The best kind of cultural studies has always taken an explicitly partisan position, developing the work of clarification, codification, and analysis in order not only to interpret, but to change things—as all the feminist researchers I've just mentioned clearly state. And, to paraphrase a bit more of *The Theses on Feuerbach,* there's an acknowledgment that partisanship includes a willingness on our part as educators to be educated precisely by listening to the kernel of very good sense among those in our audience communities who are telling us precisely why they can't or don't want change on our terms—as, for instance, when they disclaim our sense of what "feminism" itself is about.

In clarifying their own partisanship, feminist researchers concerned with texts and audiences have proposed different strategies for social change. For Ien Ang, for instance, there is a danger of overpoliticizing the pleasurable fantasy of soap opera. In the end she would rather accept that the politics of radical change is often deeply unpleasurable, involving anger and pain. Her decision is to get on with the unpleasurable politics, but make her life a little more pleasurable in the here and now with the utopian possibilities she envisages in soap opera.

For Radway, while she wants to insist on the incipient feminism of many of the readers of romance and the possibilities of resistance that are opened up by reading romance, at the end of the day she sees romance as a form that "manages" readers in favor of the social order. So she is left wishing that readers may find *other* channels than romance in order that their potential for resistance can lead in the direction of real social change.

Via different routes, then, both Ang and Radway end up counterposing textual reading to some notion of "real politics." But, I wonder, why does there have to be such a choice? Why can't movements for social change also continue to work with and through texts *and* in relation to the real world?

And this, the question of a "cultural politics," is the one I think Bobo's work on *The Color Purple* addresses in considering the *use* to which a group puts "discourse." She considers why audiences of black women, whilst recognizing real problems with the film version of *The Color Purple* nevertheless, against what many black male critics said about it, took overwhelming delight in the picture. She relates the answer in terms of pride in the acting "by black brothers and sisters" in a mainstream film, but also because, through their identification with the women characters, they became not merely audiences, but were addressed as "significant political beings"—because "finally someone has said something about us."

Bobo goes on to suggest ways in which feelings of pride and self-esteem engendered by a film representing black women's everyday experience articulate with a new impetus in black women's writing in a way that creates a community of black women as writers/ critics/scholars/knowledgeable audiences and readers. This is a dynamic process that constitutes a new social force, what she calls, with reference to the notion of the typical as the extraordinary, "a community of heightened consciousness," involved in the process of creating new self-images and thereby forming a force for change.

What this position suggests, then, is that there is no need to counterpose text and real-world politics. But that it may be more productive for cultural studies research to view the text as, to paraphrase again, "in short, one of the key ideological forms in which women and men become conscious of the conflict (that involves determining material circumstances) and fight it out" (see Marx, 1968 [1859]).

So where, finally, do these points leave the earlier encoding-decoding model? Not, I would suggest, abandoned, but possibly rethought in a way that breaks out of the circuit that seems to require a return to the privileged text. By not asking merely, What do people do with the text? (stop) but, What do they do with the text *in the real world?*, a way is offered for "audience" to mean more than merely receiver or reader of others' encodings.

I want to conclude by returning to our own work in the area of electoral current affairs television. In the process of discussions that mostly remained within the dominant framework of "bias," the question community groups were starting to address was not only the issue of whether bias resided in the media and if so where. They also began to conceptualize bias in terms of *a politics of representation,* asking who of "them" is speaking for "us," and in whose language? All the groups, including those who perceived themselves as most "apolitical" saw the media using definitions of politics that ignored their own experience. "Ordinary" or "working" people, as they described themselves, were not only excluded from access to television, they were, in all senses, "not in the picture." Nor did they appear to have any entitlement to representation; they were invited to remain onlookers, television spectators, with no visual or verbal recognition of what they regarded as their interests.

In attempting to hammer out a different construction of political images in discussion, the groups suggested notions of representation that would be contextualized, empirical, and based on a belief in "seeing and hearing it for yourself" with minimal professional mediation. They suggested that concrete evidence of support for political parties should be demonstrated on the streets or in public meetings so that viewers could "make up their own minds" about what political constituencies were made of. They wanted partisan positions declared so "everyone knew where they stood"; they imagined a politics that could be both practical and popular. From this perspective, the vocabulary of "bias" was renegotiated to express all those instances where the media had somehow failed to "represent the people" while arrogantly proclaiming their unique ability to do so. By unpacking and repacking the notion of "bias" in this way to suggest what other media representations it might be possible to make on behalf of "us," I think these groups were also showing examples of how the encoding-decoding circuit could be broken out of and how maybe decoders would always be encoders too.

DISCUSSION: ROSALIND BRUNT

E. ANN KAPLAN: I am very interested in the national differences between the kinds of work you can do given the British situation and what might be possible here. I feel, in the U.S., we need to address more directly the issues and theories of processes of identification, of the text-spectator relationship, as at least one part of which is how texts construct communities or groups. You had already politically constituted groups; that's hard to find in America.

BRUNT: In the specific work we did looking at the specific current affairs program, identification was the main issue we raised. The program was saying, "this is your town," and so we asked them, "do you think this is your town?" And, overwhelmingly, they couldn't identify, they felt it was a spectator's town. They seemed to say: This particular represented place is an industrial, working-class town, and that's partly ours. But it was constructed for the spectator. They very clearly saw it as a quaint, touristy place which, they also wanted to say, "we helped make. The Labour council did that. They redesigned the market and we're all so proud of that. But it also denies any sense of us. Where are we in this?" So there was a lot of discussion around how they felt their town had been constructed and their place in it. And also around how they felt, as the voters, that in presenting the issues for a national audience, they were precisely the ones excluded from the discussion. So they were turned into the passive spectators of their own constituency. So, certainly, in those terms, identification was very important.

JENNIFER SLACK: I was really interested in the categories you developed in the early part of your paper about the different kinds of resistance. I was particularly interested in the first kind, and would like to ask you to expand a little on this. You said that some of the most resistant groups were the most cynical in the media's own terms? I'm not clear what you mean by "the media's own terms," particularly given the context of your paper.

BRUNT: Perhaps I should have given some more substantial examples. For instance, the group that defined itself as the most apolitical, which was the women in the Keep Fit group, thought this whole election was a waste of time. They were looking for a coalition, which would be led, interestingly, by a woman, Shirley Williams (a centrist), or by Mrs. Thatcher or somebody. There was an idea of all the parties coming together, if only they could all agree. There was a sense of that position represented in the media, because one of the ways the media represents politics, precisely because it has to be balanced, is in that sort of moderate, "why can't they all come together?" way. And so often those terms were adapted in rejecting the media: "this is all boring and a waste of time and we don't want anything to do with it and Labour's going to get in anyway and we hate them." Another example was the Labour candidate, who was stigmatized by the media as mad. What was interesting was that we couldn't find anyone in this Labour voting town who didn't think the candidate was absolutely wonderful, until we came across these women. There were good reasons why they disliked this guy because he had patronized them. He'd come into their class and compared them to a character—the Green Goddess—on British television. So they talked about him in precisely the way in which the media had constructed him. We found that those groups who were most bored and alienated by the media and felt most rejected, who weren't interested and would never dream of watching current affairs programs, were also those who had the immediate images in all sorts of ways of politics.

CATHERINE HALL: You talked about the importance of the new ways in which feminist research has tried to open up different kinds of relationships with the groups with which they're working. And I think you were suggesting at the end something about the specificity of women's relationships to what one might call textual politics. And I was wondering if you could say a bit more about the gender differentiation between the groups and within the groups as to the ways in which men and women talked about the issues that you were dealing with.

BRUNT: It was very striking in the original research that I didn't bother to quote, when we commented on the style of talk. It confirmed all the linguistic research for instance about the way women encourage each other, as in the Keep Fit class. Whereas in men's groups, the miners for instance, it was very much, there was a sort of pecking order; they were all in the Labour Party but there were enormous differences being fought out, like the Labour Party in microcosm. They had a very formal way of talking to each other, very much in explicit class conscious terms. We contrasted them with a group of women shop stewards who were more critical, in some ways, of the Labour party. A very interesting group of women, some who felt their duty was to uphold the official discourse of the Labour party, older women who had been in the Labour party a very long time, and young ones like a woman telling the story about how she had actually voted Tory because her father said, when the canvassers came, "This is a Labour household!" And she said she went out to vote conservative because Margaret Thatcher is a woman. And then she felt embarrassed telling this story, and also said, "of course my father was right, but I wasn't having him take . . ." So the women, interestingly, did raise those issues about the problems around the Labour party in a way that the men, much more obviously class conscious, didn't. So there were all sorts of differences between modes of speech within the groups, what was allowed to be said. The men were much more conscious about not letting their guard down, and it was very important that you didn't betray the Labour party, for instance, or you didn't betray your sense of action and point to problems. The women were much more tentative about their politics.

JAN RADWAY: I agree with virtually everything you said about my own work. I only want to say one thing in defense. I think you minimized how much Reading the Romance actually does talk about how those women to whom I talked used the text. But I agree that finally at the end it comes back to that distinction between the political and the text. I myself have written about this and critiqued my earlier work about the romance. I'm more interested in the distinction between fantasy and the real and argue that there's a break in romance work with Cora Kaplan's and others' work that suggests that we're beginning to deconstruct this binary between fantasy and the real and no longer place ourselves as the people who aren't duped by fantasy. My question has to do with your argument that Bobo's work suggests that their textual engagement shows that that text is a form in which they come to consciousness, that it's a work, it's a process, it's an activity. I agree with that entirely. What I'm worried about is that I'm not sure you posed the most difficult questions. If that's the case, and if the audiences that we construct through our own discursive practices in fact are coming to their own political consciousness through their own engagement with the text, why do they then need us? What's the point of our kind of activity as intellectuals in this kind of arena?

BRUNT: I think sometimes they don't. And some of the groups that we visited clearly did not. But I think there is a responsibility of intellectuals because we have the time and the resources to analyze. I don't think that's being elitist, I think there is something about a clarifying and codifying procedure. I just wanted much more of you and them in that book and I felt it was really sad you went back to talk about the text, because without you, the group wouldn't have come together. Now there's all sorts of possibilities then opened by that. Now, I'm not sure what you do after that. I thought the questions you raised—you wanted to know about their marriages, their work outside—were right, I wanted to too. I didn't want to go into the text, because I was so excited by the beginning and where I thought that was leading, and then, oh dear, you returned to the text. So I think that work is still to be done, and we need to fight for the resources to do it.

RADWAY: I don't want to defend that return to the text at all. I think you're exactly right, the business of articulation is what's on the agenda. But the way we articulate with "them" is something that is extremely difficult to work out. There simply are not the institutions, the arenas. We still are in many ways isolated by our practices and discourses. Romance writing has been profoundly affected by the feminist critique, and there are writers and readers who know very well not only that there is a feminist critique, but they know the details of that and they've responded to it. So I don't want to suggest that there isn't a role for the intellectual, but what I do want to suggest is that the material nature of that role has yet to be worked out.

MARTIN ALLOR: Over the last several years I've become increasingly distrustful of the utility of the concept "audience" in itself as the founding position for the study of the range of social relations and power relations in relationship to media or leisure or political practices. "Audience" is an abstract conception of a totality like population or the people. When we study audience relations, we constitute a particular audience relationship in our research practice itself. So I quite agree with your criticism of earlier traditions of work. So you reconstituted groups that existed for other purposes, for their own purposes, and then for your purposes invited them in to constitute a different kind of formation for discussion, in which you included yourself. And I find all that laudable. But it seems to me there's still a danger in holding on to the concept of audience as the organizing principle because it doesn't get at the subtending social relations that we're after. Because I think the danger in holding on to audience as the organizing conception is that it still pulls us into text-audience interrelationships. And even if we can break away from returning to the text, it still focuses us very tightly around doing research that has commitments to a bias that thinks broadcasting is the dominant model of audience relations, that sees the relations of decoding or activating by individuals or groups of diagetic texts as the dominant mode. This cuts off other ways of cutting into other levels of the real, for example looking at dancing in discos, or listening to music in different ways, or looking at the relationships between other leisure practices like commodity consumption and those practices that might more traditionally be conceptualized as audience relations. So it seems to me that one of the challenges for all of us who are returning to questions of audience is precisely to find lines of connecting them to other practices so we don't get locked into a circuit.

BRUNT: I agree.

CORA KAPLAN: I've been trying to negotiate some of these romance texts together with the feminist texts that comment on them, in a classroom of undergraduates. I wondered whether you would like to comment on what that particular occasion does to this relationship between politics, fantasy, intellectuals, and the public?

BRUNT: As an educator, I'm always insisting on the text because a lot of students, particularly mature students, who discuss popular culture deeply resent it. They say, "we have come here to get away from that stuff, this is what we ordinarily read, you know we want to do other things that we think universities and polytechnics are for, and you're making us study this stuff and we're grown up now." So there is a problem about getting that recognized as a valid area of study from working-class women who feel they're making some move into education. And I think that's very important to understand. Another response is the one I mentioned in terms of one of the groups we observed: the idea that "we see through it all. We know this is crap, this oppresses women. Again, why are you making us read it?" And I constantly say, "yes it does oppress women but we need to know specifically in the text the ways in which it oppresses women." And so, in terms of strategies, it is quite complicated. It depends very much on the sort of teaching groups you're with.

ANITA SHETH: I was wondering about your own location, how do you locate yourself as researcher and as a consumer of popular culture? If watching television is all of what televiewing is all about, then how is a researcher and a non-televiewer competent to make interpretations of what people are saying about their assumed or imagined political consciousness?

BRUNT: There is a danger of saying, "I'm just the same as these people." I think actually that's a sort of elitism because it denies the way in which you're different and you're also going to do some other sort of work. I think one has to honestly say there's a contradiction and a problem there and not deny it. And what worries me more are academics who go on about being fans. I'm deeply suspicious of that, and I think it's more honest to say that yes I'm a fan but also I am differently located, and that has certain implications and responsibilities.

SHERI PARKS: One way that I've found to deal with the problem of research is to become a participant with the group because often groups have their own agenda with which we can be very helpful. Poor black women in Baltimore, for instance, who really are very concerned with the effect of cartoons upon their children. So that I have an agenda, they have an agenda, we both know each other's agenda, and we work together. That way we don't replicate the traditional power relationship between researcher and subject.

BRUNT: I just think you can't be prescriptive, you can't say there's one thing that researchers do with audiences, because it always depends on what the question is you're looking at. And obviously in my case, I wasn't dealing with fans. And the interest wasn't helping them to develop their interest in the media so much. It was more that I was interested in how do people come to inhabit certain political discourses.

6

*I Throw Punches for My Race,
but I Don't Want to Be a Man:
Writing Us—Chica-nos (Girl, Us)/
Chicanas—into the Movement Script*

ANGIE CHABRAM-DERNERSESIAN[1]

I. From You: The Manifest ChicanO to us: La Nueva/The New ChicanA

Spring 1972, an unspecified university, Aztlán EEUU, U.S.A. A Chicano critic prepares to labor, desk replete with now widely recognizable instruments of literary production: "I am Joaquín" (1967), *Pocho* (1959), *With His Pistol in His Hand* (1958), *Barrio Boy* (1971), *The Autobiography of a Brown Buffalo* (1972), . . . *And the Earth Did Not Part* (1971), *The Chicano Manifesto* (1971). Walls are lined, on the one side with brave Aztec Chicano warriors who scout the cultural horizon accompanied by shapely Aztec Chicana princesses sporting the national denomination, Aztlán, on their reproductive organs, and on the other side, with revolutionary posters imaging Ché's angry admonition: You are not a minority! In the background, inspirational music, that much loved movement song, resounds:

> I am a Chicano, brownskinned, an American but with honor. When they tell me that the revolution has started, I will defend my people with all my courage.

> I have my pride and manliness, my culture and love, I have my faith, I'm different, my skin is brown. I have a culture, I have a heart. And no one can take them from me, no not any bastard.[2]

For those Chicanos involved in this historic endeavor, denied to their parents for generations, criticism is both a liberating and a troubling act. As a paid profession, it offers an escape from a legacy of work in the fields, the canneries, the railroads, and the service sector. As a creative act, it enables us to explore forgotten community narratives, unwritten literary dialogues, and censured indigenous presences. Yet for all its material and ideological benefits, practicing criticism in the alternative ethnic sector has its drawbacks. Publicly sanctioned histories of culture fail to legitimate the object of one's labor: Chicano literature. And institutions of criticism are not forthcoming in welcoming unconventional bicultural critics who converse in various traditions and idioms, subjecting the sanctity of critical language to the unsaintly rhythms of the Chicano vernacular.

Yes, within the halls of the Academy, the position of the Chicano critic is still precarious. Nevertheless this precariousness is dissolved at the symbolic, imaginary level by a nationalist aesthetic which offers the marginalized Chicano critic an escape from subjection to another ethnicity, even if this escape often falls short of its intended function. The appeal of this aesthetic is captured by one of the popular anthologies of the period, *El Espejo* (1969), which marked out a new Chicano literary sensibility with the proposal "that they were those who needed no other reflection other than themselves, thus *The Mirror*." Four decades of critical life and a plethora of Chicana voices, which draw inspiration in the construction of yet another politics of representation, have instructed us well as to the identity of those who have only required their own reflection in order to know themselves and are privileged enough to encounter that image in a seemingly unmediated, transparent fashion.

Who is this subject so empowered with literary capital as to know itself, not once, but many times, doubling incessantly within the tasty banquet of alternative literary production? Pivotal texts which map out significant passages toward culturalist and universalist discourses in Chicano criticism foreground the answer. At the heart of nationalism's preferred revolutionary narrative, *With His Pistol* (Paredes, 1982 [1958]), looms the commanding hero of the ballad of border conflict, *Gregorio Cortez,* "pistol in hand" and defiantly proclaiming his right to aggressive self-defense in the face of Anglo encroachment.

And, at the heart of Bruce-Novoa's (1975, pp. 22–42) "The Space of Chicano Literature," which references cultural domination from the lens of abstract idealism, lies the generic, twentieth-century anti-hero, *Occidental Man*—a Man whose existential problematic of literary salvation becomes a Chicano writer's dilemma at the hand of Juan Bruce-Novoa's philosophical *mestizaje*. Criticism's partner in dialogue faithfully delivers this cultural subject through a myriad of male literary identities: el pachucho, el vato loco, el cholo, the Aztec, the militant Chicano, the existential Chicano, the political Chicano, the precocious Chicano, the Jungian Chicano-o-o-o, and mostly authoritarian fathers.

| Antonio | Adan | Juan |
| Joaquín | Miguel | Louie |

Literary subjects such as these mark an alternative national cultural border, dividing Chicanos/Chicanas in the company of Mexican brothers to the South: Villa, Zapata, Paz, selectively recruited into the pantheon of La Raza by authoritative discourse for their crusades against domination under the unifying impulse of Aztlán—the imaginary geography claimed as the true site of Chicano subjectivity. The cultural border encircling Chicano subjects is, in turn, etched by productions that visualize new racial subjects inspired by José Vasconcelos, a Mexican scholar/politician/essayist from whose philosophical spirit and imaginary cosmic body the *entire* Mexican Race was said to speak. In this vein, José Medina's "The Chicano has emerged from Indo-Hispanic Roots" (1970, p. 217) inscribes the three-headed mestizo as the essential subject for Chicano identity, figuring *him* as a combined genealogy of Spanish conquistadores and Aztec Warriors without a trace of a Chicana/Mexicana authenticating root.

Textually within the very same Chicano vernacular which challenged the Euro-lingocentrism of English and Spanish by crossing their borders in illegal codes that would elicit charges of "illiteracy," Chicano identity is written with linguistic qualifiers—*o/os*—which subsume the Chicana into a universal ethnic subject that speaks with the masculine instead of the feminine and embodies itself in a Chicano male. Except, of course, in those cases where the embodied Chicana is overwritten with "Chicanos"— a collective denomination referencing an other subject. A case in point is the now familiar *We are Chicanos* (Ortego, 1973), which opens the gate to Mexican American Literature with the image of a young Chicana representing the passage to modern Chicano expression.

The Chicano Manifesto (Rendón, 1972), acclaimed by politicians of reputable stature for its insights into the militancy and origins of the Chicano Movement, furnishes ideological support for this transcription of the Chicano/a subject. While contesting racism, economic exploitation, and political domination, the author, Armando Rendón, reinforces dominant ideology by identifying "machismo" as the symbolic principle of the Chicano revolt and adopting machismo as the guideline for Chicano family life. Thus, nationalism's preferred male subject is imbued with a masculine, patriarchal ideology that resists the apologetic sympathies ascribed to it by Chicano cultural practitioners seeking to erase male domination from the semantic orbit of machismo.[3]

For those inclined to minimize the specific gender connotations of this imaginary postcolonial(?) representation, Rendón clarifies that his tendency to view the Chicano revolt as a male-dominated phenomenon can be attributed to his gender status: his being "macho." Thus he grounds his symbolic treatment of machismo in a specific male body: his, equating macho with Chicano, a term generalized to embrace the nationalist objective: nationhood. Rendón elaborates: "macho in other words can no longer merely relate to manhood but to nationhood as well" (1972, p. 105).

With this gender objectification, the silenced Other, Chicanas/hembras, are thus removed from full-scale participation in the Chicano movement as fully embodied, fully empowered U.S. Mexican female subjects. They are not only engendered under machismo but their gender is disfigured at the symbolic level under malinchismo, an ideological construct signifying betrayal which draws inspiration from the generic Malinche.[4] (According to official Mexican histories, she is the Mexican Eve who delivered her people to Cortez.) Thus, within the subtext of Rendón's essay, the forces of revolutionary contention are drawn around the equation of male power with machismo and female betrayal with malinchismo. The former, Chicano power, represents revolutionary fervor, while the latter, female power, malinchismo, represents betrayal and conquest.

Like la llorona (the female weeping woman), who was condemned to limbo as punishment for breaking with socially prescribed female norms, these engendered Chicanas are confined to a state of permanent exile and distanced from the political struggle that they waged daily alongside heroines of the likes of Dolores Huerta. But these Chicanas are not only displaced, they are disowned, arbitrarily cast over to the other side, lumped together with the likes of Miss JiM-enez, a character who is significantly the daughter of Jim not Juan and the most ridiculed antagonist in Luis Valdez's drama of Chicana/o assimilation: "Los Vendidos/The Sell-Outs" (El Teatro Campesino, 1967, pp. 35–49).[5] Within this logic, if Chicanas wished to receive the authorizing signature of predominant movement discourses and figure within the record of Mexican practices of resistance in the U.S., then they had to embody themselves as males, adopt traditional family relations, and dwell only on their racial and/or ethnic oppression.

Yet even this type of definition, which implies affirming oneself through the symbolic construction of an other, was deceptive, since Chicano nationalism was also predicated on the necessity of mimesis: a one-to-one correspondence between the subject and its reflection in a mirror-like duplication. Without the possibility of uninterrupted self-duplication, without the possibility of inscribing viable Mexicana/Chicana female subjects with which to identify at the center of Chicana/o practices of resistance, Chicanas were denied cultural authenticity and independent self-affirmation. And both these elements were central to a movement dedicated to altering the negative figurations of Chicanas/os at the hands of others who had for centuries blocked any possibility of legitimate self-representation to Americanas/os of Mexican descent.

In retrospect, it can be said that at some level Rendón's gendered account of the Chicano revolt represents an extreme variant of Movement thinking—extreme in honesty and in its Manichean treatment of social relations. Nevertheless, like many other Raza manifestos of the period *The Chicano Manifesto* only served to reinforce the saliency of the Chicano male subject within authoritative Chicano/a cultural production. Ironically, this cultural production came into representation by foregrounding "difference" and the right of all Mexicans (here brown people) to battle aggressively for cultural proprietorship and definition as fully empowered ethnic beings against the nullifying desire of any "bastard." It was precisely nationalism's failure to inscribe gender differences and the struggle of Chicanas at *the center* of political resistance, that rendered the now famous national anthem, "Yo soy Chicano," problematic.[6]

For if this affirmation of ethnic subjectivity constituted an impassioned moment of truthful self-revelation in which for the first time we admitted publicly that, indeed, we were Brown and not beige or off-white *and* Chicanos—against the imperatives not only of the dominant regimes of representation but also of the instruction of our parents— this affirmation of Chicano identity also signified a betrayal and deception. This was the case because the "us" of cultural nationalist discourse was more often than not a "he" and not a s/he. Thus the necessity of altering the collective subject of Chicano movement discourse, of giving it a Chicana female presence. It was precisely this necessity that inspired a young generation of Chicanas who, protesting their figuration as Chicano males, retorted: "I don't want to be a man."

Ironically, the discourse of exclusion and betrayal, which assisted in displacing Chicanas such as these from the nationalist script of Chicano identity, flourished in a period when Chicanas were questioning their traditional roles, increasing their participation within the political arena, and inscribing a budding Chicana feminist discourse and practice. As Anna Nieto-Gómez (1976, p. 9) pointed out, the discourse of betrayal flourished among Chicano nationalists and their natural allies: Chicana "loyalists," both of whom aimed at containing the woman question within the Cause by availing themselves of a number of male-centered Chicano ideologies.

It is not surprising that the targets of the discourse of exclusion were precisely those Chicana activists/feminists who met themselves and others on the other side of the page, shunned traditional roles and/or actively pursued Chicana-centered practices of resistance. These were the Chicanas who replaced the discourses of compadres and carnalismo with the discourses of comadres (sisters) and feminismo (feminists), macho with hembra, and fiercely combated male domination in the leadership of the Chicano Movement and the political life of the community.[7] These were the Chicanas who were often targeted as the objects of the newly revised malinche narrative, authored under the prerequisites of a dogmatic nationalism which was irreverent toward the shaping influences of the heterogeneous experiences of conquest and regionalism on Chicanas/ os.

These were the Chicanas who would go on to rename the much misunderstood Malinche, Malintzin, figuring her as a precursor to Chicana nationalism *and* feminism, and opening up another alternative space of cultural production: ChicanA studies. Like Rendón's imaginary malinches, who were made to personify betrayal, these Chicanas were routinely told that they were dividing and weakening the Chicano Movement. It was not uncommon that they were labeled "vendidas" and reminded of a purported complicity with White hegemonic frameworks which sought to dominate, not liberate the Cause.

To echo a young Chicana activist/feminist for whom being a woman and being a *ChicanA* were equally important, no one likes being called a traitor in a movement one would die for. Particularly not the newly constructed, newly vindicated Women of the Race—those Women who broke their shackles and stabbed the spirit of injustice when confronted in the fields by a shotgun, when bloodied on the streets of Whittier Boulevard, or when constructed under the violent disfigurement of Anglo/a chauvinism or Chicano machismo. Those Women of the Race contested Bakke, Farah, and the War in Vietnam, protesting with pickets in hands under the ethnic denomination Chicano. And this was a self-denomination which they assumed as Villanueva (1970 p. 189) had intended it: "as a challenge for those who stereotype and as an act of defiance," not submission to another. "Other" here means the Chicano male, a figure also reified within the ideological equation Chicano=machismo.

Margarita Virgina Sánchez, a thirteen-year-old from California, outlined this passionate spirit of Chicano consciousness in her poetic narrative of ethnic identity ("Escape") which moves its speaking subject from the complacency of meltingpotism to militant, ethnic self-awareness and separatism. Rather than constituting Chicano identity as an immutable given, a once and for all to be recovered arbitrarily through mutually exclusive gender categories, Sánchez constructs it as a shifting positionality, variously enlisting competing interests and alliances throughout time and space. And she emphasizes the process leading up to Chicano identity rather than its product, versing:

Last week,
I had been white
     . . . we were friends
Yesterday
I was Spanish
     . . . we talked . . .
          once in a while.

The poet follows with the affirmation: "Today, I am Chicano . . . and you do not know me," thereby addressing the other ethnic exclusion to which Chicanas were subjected within dominant society when they assumed their identities as self-directed agents of change. And the poem ends with the promise of contestation—separatism and political struggle:

Tomorrow,
     I rise to fight
. . . and we are enemies. (Sánchez, 1973, p. 208)

Viewed from the exclusive boundaries of the manifest ChicanO, this affirmation, which offers a limited social analysis based on racial oppositions, is transgressive because it reappropriates for its female speaking subject the basic principles of nationalist discourse and places her at the frontline of ethnic contestation. While this poem successfully "escapes" the ethnic subjection of Chicanas within discourse, it does not, however, foreground gender within its contestation. This oppositional spirit of the Women of the Race would be figured through "a" of ChicanA cultural practices and ChicanA feminist discourse.

Viola Correa exemplifies this oppositional spirit with "La Nueva Chicana," which introduces a new subject for political identity by taking us from the Manifest ChicanO to the New ChicanA. Significantly, this nueva Chicana is figured by multiple female subjects who are linked together by a common history of work and protest. Yet these female subjects are located with different roles that confirm their allegiance to the movement and they are spoken in multiple expressions of gender that simultaneously reference family relations and political commitments. This practice of representation celebrates the comraderie between Chicanas/os and creates an intimate bond between these women and their public. This bond, in turn, disclaims the negative figurations of Chicanas within discourse, encouraging others to hear what they have to say. To those who might be inclined to dismiss these Chicanas and their significant role in the movement for social reform, Correa's message is look around, look at our women. Thus, the poem "calls" its spectator, you, to attention:

> ¡Hey!
> See that lady protesting against injustice,
> es mi mamá [she's my mother]
> That girl in the brown beret,
>   The one teaching the children
>   she's my hermana [sister]
> Over there fasting with the migrants
>   es mi tía [she's my aunt]
> . . . .
> The lady with the forgiving eyes
> . . . .
> listen to her shout. (Correa, 1970)

This Chicana identity is itself the site of multiple contestations, for not only does la nueva Chicana contest ignorance, but she, herself, is the object of another contestation: the establishment condemns her in the poem as a "militant Chicana," the newspapers name her a "dangerous subversive," and the FBI, classifies her as "a big problem." Once having convinced her readers of the valuable role of this new Chicana within the movement, Correa celebrates this new subject of political identity, overriding these external constructions with another one: ours. She states: "In Aztlán, we call her la Nueva Chicana." Thus, the new Chicana at last receives the authorizing signature of her peers. And she enters movement discourse with her own name, a name which constructs her both as a Chican-a and a woman and subverts the twin myths of malinchismo and assimilation.

II: Writing Another Story/Manifest-ación—Hers: Yo Soy ChicanA or Answering Joaquín and José

Writing "us" Chicanas into the movement script took more than just referencing a largely essential Chicana subject into the narrative of Chicana/o liberation. As Margarita Cota-Cárdenas pointed out, the Chicana had to give herself her own value and definition, avoiding the trendy overtures of the men and mainstream feminists, both of whom only promised to deliver a life in the service of others. For Chicanas to alter this course, we had to construct another political category: Chicanas, marking a female presence within the ethnic discourse of Chicanos in the playful fashion of Chica-nos (Girl, Us), Chicana/as, Chicana/o, and Chicano/a. We had to write another story: a mujer story, another discourse from the perspective of the foregrounded Chicana.

As Cota-Cárdenas suggested, writing "us" into the movement script meant more than substituting an A for an O at the end of Chican. We Chicanas had to create our own word, our own cosmos, constructed by "Chicana"—here, sister, woman. While Cota-Cárdenas's (1980) formula for writing Chicana liberation inscribes a universal female subject which suffers from many of the limitations of essentialism, her "Late Declaration/Manifesto" (pp. 37–38) signals an important passageway toward a new subjectivity and aesthetics, located in Chicana women's experiences and expressive forms. "Manifestación" thus facilitates the inscription of a belated alternative mujer-centered discourse of Chicana expression, opening the way for the jump to nationalist feminism and Chicana socialist feminism. "Manifestación" also textualizes Chicana militancy—already in full swing—with the title "manifestación," signifying in Español not only "declaration" or "new phenomenon," but "protest" as well.

Finally Cota-Cárdenas rewrites the nationalist discourse that equated female practices of resistance with betrayal of the Race. Rather than alienate the Chicana from "La Causa," she suggests that by speaking her female names: Chicana, Sister Woman, and imagining a universe which constructs her experiences and rallies on her behalf, the Chicana will be a "homage to her race." In proposing that the Chicana's self-affirmation will be of collective benefit, Cota-Cárdenas enacts a strategy of reversal typical of early Chicana movement writings that generalized the interest of the Chicana to the entire group and isolated "machismo" as antithetical to the Cause.

With this practice, Cota-Cárdenas implies that for Chicana liberation to be written, Chicanas had to avail themselves not only of different semantic markers, from which to imagine new subjectivities and intersected social relations, but also of new forms and strategies of representation. In the seventies, these alternative forms of representation would surface largely from the pens of young Chicana cultural practitioners who inscribed their own independent ethnic identities within poetic narratives. Raquel Rodríguez and Sara Estrella were among these Chicanas who responded to the male-centered texts in such terms as these:

> Yo soy mujer [I am a woman]
> I don't want to be a man
> El hombre, the man is my brother
> . . . .
> but always a man
> Yo soy una mujer [I am a woman]
> I wish to be one
> . . . I no longer like being none.
>   ("Yo soy mujer," Rodríguez, 1978, p. 18)[8]

> Yo soy india. [I am an Indian woman]
> Yo soy morena. [I am a brown woman]
> Yo soy la mestiza. [I am a mixed blooded woman]
> Yo soy la Chicana de Aztlán. [I am a Chicana from Aztlán.]
> (Untitled, Sara Estrella, c. 1972, p. 10)[9]

These declarations represent a step toward Chicana representation within new expressive forms. They alter Chicano movement discourse with their absented presences and modify nationalism's existential formula. "Yo soy"/"I am" with a female subject: a Chicana mujer. Yet these narratives tell a different, though related, story of la mujer. Rodríguez replaces the male subject of Chicano identity with a female subject, emphasizing not her ethnicity but silenced gender and repressed desire to be figured as someone: a mujer/woman.

In contrast, Estrella's "Yo soy la Chicana de Aztlán" inscribes a Chicana as the subject of an alternative narrative of ethnic ancestry. This narrative writes mestizaje—that prized nationalist ideal and symbol of ethnicity—with the multiple evocations of a female speaking subject who affirms various racial identities to configure the Chicana from Aztlán. Thus the poet gives the Chicana the color and mixed parentage formerly restricted to the preferred Chicano male subject. But this poem also establishes a distance from universal feminism, for the speaker goes on to elaborate that she is not just any woman—not a generic woman"—but a woman "of the" movement. Thus, Estrella outlines the path taken by many early Chicana feminists and together with Rodríguez opens the way towards other types of Chicana identity narratives that speak Chicana subjectivity within more complex figurations. These unknowingly carry the mark of Noemí Lorenzana (1974, p. 39), a sister who anticipated many of us by stating: "There is no one Chicana, but different women who call themselves Chicanas."

Writing this plural "Us"—the multiplicity of Chicana subjectivity—is an endeavor which currently occupies the attention of many writers and critics who seek to establish a distance between the old politics of cultural representation, based on similarity, and the new politics, based on difference as described by Stuart Hall.[10] In the seventies, the so-called essential Chicana subject was a common figure on the Chicana cultural horizon, featuring herself with the Aztec woman, the three-headed Mestiza, the Adelita, and the earth Mother. Yet, even within this early period, the essential singularity commonly attributed to Chicana nationalist discourse was already subject to question. First of all, this Mujer spoke in multiple idioms that short-circuited a one-to-one correspondence between herself and her representation. This subversion was flaunted by Chicanas in phrases like "bilingual says twice as much." And second, already in the essential Chicana subject, there was *a multiplicity of us's* which threatened to cross the borders of the singular A of ChicanA.

Such was the case, for example with Martha Cotera's (1978, pp. 5–9) "La Loca de La Raza Cósmica"/"The Crazy Woman/Queen of La Raza Cósmica," which greets its readers throughout different stanzas with Chicana subjects such as these:

> Soy la Mujer Chicana [I am the Chicana Woman]
> Soy mujer [I am a woman]
> . . . .
> Soy la India Maria [I am the Indian, María]
> . . . .
> Soy la revolucionaria [I am the revolutionary]
> . . . .
> Soy la que hecha chingazos por su Raza [I am the one who throws punches for
> her Race] (1978, p. 5)

Following the essentialist critique, it can be said that "Crazy Queen of the Cosmic Race" seeks to inscribe an all-knowing, ever-present universal Chicana subject for ethnic identity: one Mujer/Queen, without concern for difference or contradiction between mujeres who disagree or compete from different positions. And, certainly, "Crazy Queen" does not engage those Chicana materialists who would contest the idealism which introduces the poem. Yet within this poem the tensions between the singular and the collective do surface. It is, after all, dedicated to the Chicana women and Crazy Queens of the Race. "Crazy Queen" offers multiple innovations and strategies that speak to its creation of an alternative identity narrative which both contests and foregrounds significant differences. And these "differences" are not necessarily available to the reader at first sight—they surface once the poem is examined within its context.

Cotera achieves this shift in Chicana identity, from similarity to difference, by altering the formula popularized within the most famous nationalist identity narrative, "I am Joaquín" (Rodolfo González, 1967).[11] Whereas "I am Joaquín" constructed an essential identity for cultural affirmation through an epic which moved through five and a half centuries of Mexican and Chicano history and linked the common Chicano hero to legendary Mexican and Chicano male figures, this Chicana-centered text roots itself in the present and the contrary experiences of a variety of Chicana prototypes. These subjects of Chicana identity are not the heroines of an uncharted binational counter-her/story. Unlike Phyllis López's poem "La Chicana" (1978)—which honors those Chicana/Mexicana heroines neglected by González (a neglect underlined by the photograph of a male child/adult protagonist that opens the text of "I am Joaquín")—these Chicanas inhabit the script of everyday life. They include the one who heats up the TV dinner, the lovemaker, the streetwalker, the political prisoner, the community organizer, the Avon Lady, the factory worker, the Brown Beret, the drop-out, and the college graduate. In the fashion of the seventies this multiplicity is brought together under the unifying voice of the poetic subject, yet her imaginary female/mestiza body spans interpersonal and geographic spaces versing in a twin bilingual and bicultural discourse that says "twice as much."

From another perspective "Crazy Queen" offers more than just another invitation for Chicanas to rewrite the Cause/La Causa by incorporating difference, here gender, into the prevailing discourses of oppression and resistance. "Crazy Queen" offers a complex elaboration of Chicana identity, drawing from the familiar categories of national origin, beliefs, political affiliation, and economic status, all of which make possible the entry of Chicanos into representation. Yet "Crazy Queen" subverts limits of nationalist discourse by substituting the male *vato loco* for a "crazy woman," a Chicana prototype of the sixties who intruded into previously restricted spaces within politics, the academy, and sexuality. If this were not enough, "Crazy Queen" parodies classical identity narratives such as those which modified "La Raza Cósmica," originally written by José Vasconcelos.

Thus "Crazy Queen" begins playfully rather than with the somber existential attitude of Chicano identity narratives. It trades the historical, social, and ethnic movements of binational history for a local female journey through civil states, political movements, linguistic dialects, sexual politics, cultural practices, and urban locales. "Crazy Queen" trades the singularity of passive and idealized women for Chicanas who are defined by their disparate practices of everyday life and who are engendered with multiple names: mujer, señorita, ms. These Queens maintain different political affiliations. They "throw punches for la Raza," screaming "Chicano power" or they assimilate by anglification. They embody different types of labor: work in the cannery, the Silicone Valley, the fields, and the service sector. And they transform English with their Spanish accents: often saying "tank you" instead of thank you; "chooz" instead of "shoes."

Unlike the calendar Aztec princess, who hung like ornaments on the laps of their mates in an untouched paradisiacal landscape, these Chicana "Queens" are not foreign to the downside of contemporary life: the unemployment office, prison, and drug rehabilitation centers. Rather than personifying singular aspects of traditional Mexican high culture in the example of "Joaquín," they are linked to a barrage of mixed popular cultural practices, including Guadalupe, holy-rollers, lowriding, styling, and sarape sandals; Mariachis, Salsa, Freddy Fender, Vicki Carr; spray painting, True Confessions, and revolutionary literature.

These Chicanas also embody multiple ethnic denominations. Unlike Joaquín, their ethnicity is written in the feminine and incorporates political identities not listed by such Census bureau designations as American of Spanish surname—here, "a.s.s.," and "coconut." And while "Crazy Queen" rejects assimilation, the poem ends by paying tribute to raza women, crediting them for their perseverance, creativity, and struggle in the face of racism, machismo, economic exploitation, and the combined pressures of everyday life. Finally, the poem celebrates the practice of affirming Chicana women in counter-discourses which recognize the Chicana for "achieving a higher status in the cause of Chicana women and men equally, both together, as well as apart" (Cotera, 1978 p. 8).

Unlike most Chicano movement productions, which often generalized from the speaker's condition to the interests of the group without recognizing the partiality of the representation, the poet acknowledges the limitations of her own female narrative by prefacing her poem with the disclaimer: "If you don't see yourself here, sister, I can only tell you I'm sorry." Thus she mimics a good number of Chicana-centered texts of the period which solicited feedback from a mixed public, favoring open-ended productions, or addressing the possibility of multiple subjects in their figurations of Chicanas/os and/or feminism(s).

Another—more classical—type of Chicana her/story, "La Chicana" by Phyllis López (1978), registers its pluralities and contains its multiplicities within a nationalist discourse. In this poem López enlists some of the conventions of the Chicano cultural identity narrative, including the story of race and class oppression. This is presented from the perspective of a Chicana prototype who, embodying all aspects of her heritage and imaginative ancestral geography, achieves the monumental stature reserved for Chicano males. What is most significant, perhaps, is that while the speaker entitles her poem "La Chicana," speaking the silence of Chicano cultural nationalism, she also alternates between a male and female identity, invoking Chicanas/os under a new identity: La Chicana.

The identity of this speaking subject and her entitlement within Chicano movement discourse is disclosed at the beginning of the poem with the words "La Chicana," and at the end with the familiar self-affirmation "I am a Chicana/Yo soy una Chicana." This belated assertion of Chicana identity at once underscores her omission from classical movement narratives at the same time that it identifies the common interests that link Chicano men and women.

Like Cotera, López avoids the grand narratives of his/her-stories which recount singular historic deeds of remarkable individuals. She reenacts a collective struggle of group survival, constructing her identity with a barrage of affirmations that variously link her to the "weary campesina" (female farm worker) who "stoops," "sweats," and "toils," and to the farm worker who has been denied the right to live like other human beings. Her identification with the socially dispossessed links her to key movement texts like "El Plan Espiritual de Aztlán/The Spiritual Manifesto of Aztlán" which specifies that "Aztlán belongs to those who plant the seeds, water the fields, and gather the crops" (Denver Conference, March 1969). Thus, "La Chicana" progressively outlines the multiple burdens which Chicanas/os encounter by interlacing the accumulated negative impact of racism and classism with her identity.

This dual burden introduces the poem which commences with the testimony of the speaking subject who admits that "she has fought and survived the pains of racial hatred" but has yet to free herself of the "bondage of poverty." Her identification with the farm worker in turn affirms this burden, for in the states of California and Texas, this figure is synonymous with national minority identity and lower social class, and again with indio and the mestizo. The link between race, class, and gender is thus made available through the embodied female speaking subject who establishes herself at the center of the struggle for survival and resistance through the liberating power of her newly found discourse.

"La Chicana" also celebrates difference by its final affirmation of "una mujer valiente," extending to the Chicana access to the traditional values associated with bravery, strength, and effectiveness. The poem recalls the cultural axiom "hacerse valer" (to make oneself worthy) but breaks the link between valentía and hombría (bravery and manhood) through the use of the generic "mujer valiente"—a brave woman. La Chicana thus references a new subject for political identity: a forceful, long-suffering, and effective source of strength and resistance.

"Look at Our Women: The Strength Upon Which Our Culture Builds," Dolores Huerta. UFW

From other artistic quarters la mujer valiente was widely featured in alternative artistic representations referencing political identity. By far the most forceful representation of this figure was the militant Chicana who embodied a number of struggles, including the famous Farah Strike, the Farm Worker's Boycott, and the struggle against male domination voiced under "Abajo Con Los Machos!" (Down with the machos!). Within art this was the Chicana who raised her clenched fist in defiance, opened her mouth wide in protest, and reveled in her long black hair which boldly defied the Señorita bun or the Twiggy Look. More so than any other female image, this Chicana referenced liberation, and for this reason, she was commonly represented as towering or remaking Lady Liberty. Often the militant Chicana embraced the cause of the Women of the Brown Beret or the Mujeres who visualized their escape from the prison of poverty, racism, and unsympathetic husbands with extensive triptychs featuring their multiple passages to liberation.

Nowhere was this *mujer valiente* more forcefully captured than in the series of portraits built on images of the Chicana Guadalupe, all of them radical revisions of the brown Virgin, patroness of México. A traditional portrait of the Virgin of Guadalupe (Fig. 1) shows the iconography that is adapted and transformed in the later paintings, from Ester Hernández's "The Virgin of Guadalupe Defending the Rights of Chicanos" (1975, fig. 2) to three paintings (fig. 3–5) by Yolanda López: "Margaret Stewart: Our Lady of Guadalupe" (1978), "Victoria F. Franco: Our Lady of Guadalupe" (1978), and "Portrait of the Artist as the Virgin of Guadalupe" (1978). In the portrait by Hernández, which frequently carries the name "The Militant Guadalupe," a Chicana breaks out of tradition with a karate kick, shedding the oppressive cloak and motionless stance of the Catholic Virgin whose hands and legs are bound by the dictates of religious rituals. In her portrait of the abuelita seamstress, Yolanda López shows a grandmother, dressed in street clothes and centered within the frame of the Guadalupe sun. From this centered position, she gains recognition for her work and calls upon the spectator to look at her, the new heroine producer of the race.[12] The transformation of Guadalupe into "Our Lady of Guadalupe" is complete with Lopez's portrait of her grandmother, Victoria F. Franco, whose dignity, strength, and endurance are captured in a full length reproduction of an abuelita, proudly sitting on top of the Guadalupe cloak. Unlike the singular Chicana, these subjects represent at least two Chicana identities simultaneously: the old and the new, us and them.

Within these Guadalupe texts the nationalist and feminist discourses of Chicana liberation are cross-referenced in the cultural metaphor of the artist as producer, a theme of another portrait by López in which the painter herself, running from the Guadalupe space, snake in hand, legs fully uncovered, displays her own energy and control.

Together these Guadalupe texts echo the resolution of many Chicana activists who clarified, once and for all, that "the issue of freedom and self-determination of the Chicana—like the right of self-determination, equality, and liberation of the Mexican

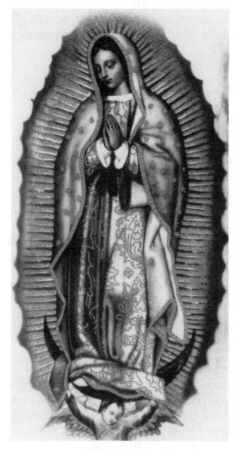

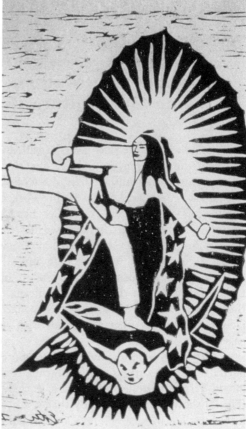

FIGURE 1. Virgin of Guadalupe
(traditional portrait).

FIGURE 2. Ester Hernández, "The
Virgin of Guadalupe Defending the
Rights of Chicanos" (1975).

community—is not negotiable" (F. Flores, 1971, p. 1). This resolution was echoed from
various quarters by Chicanas seeking to combat sexism within Chicano studies, to develop supportive services, foment sisterhood, and explore the linkages between sexism,
racism, patriarchy, and economic exploitation. Then, as now, Chicana feminism embraced multiple contestations and practices of resistance.

Writing Us into the movement script documents one such contestation: the challenge to the Manifest ChicanO, but this is only one part of the story. The Mujer story
is prefaced by another narrative of struggle in which we (brown people) challenge the
you of dominant discourse in an effort to alter the relations of cultural production with
alternative ethnic subjects. The mujer story is punctuated by a challenge to mainstream
feminist discourse for its shadowing of race and class under an ideal universal (white)
woman and the upper-class text milieus of her texts—someone who has been more easily
assimilated within dominant discourse than her sisters across the linguistic tracks. These
are sisters/hermanas who speak in different barrios of literary production and incorporate
multiple histories of feminism within the continental Americas. They have given the
universal woman a brown body, a Spanish accent, codes to switch, a history of domination
and cultural suppression, and a contentious dialogue with the Manifest ChicanO.

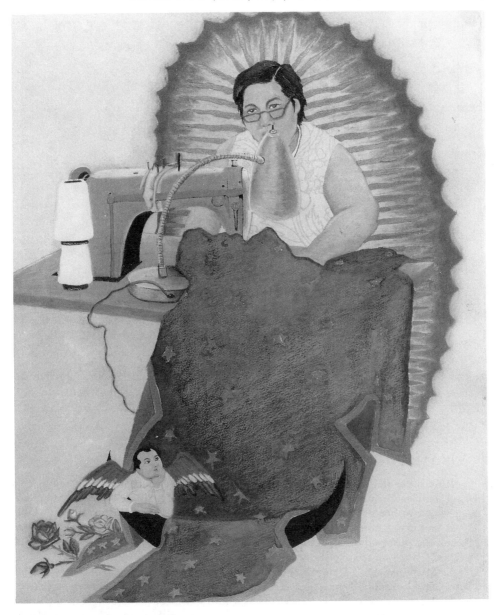

FIGURE 3.   Yolanda López, "Margaret F. Stewart: Our Lady of Guadalupe" (1978).

These Chicana sisters have also contested the nationalist tendency to remove sex from politics and vice versa. Following their footsteps, contemporary Chicana writers and poets have opened up the gate to human sexuality, giving Chicana subjects back their desire (both heterosexual and gay), and they have interrogated the sexual privilege of Chicano males within increasingly complex formulations that democratize cultural discourse from various positions of similarity and difference. These stories are also her/ stories—the stories of Chicana activists, feminists, mujeres—and they merit further consideration by you (feminists, nationalists, and Marxists) who follow the paths of alternative discourses of identity as they resist and transform subjectivity from the multiple borders of ethnic subjection and domination.

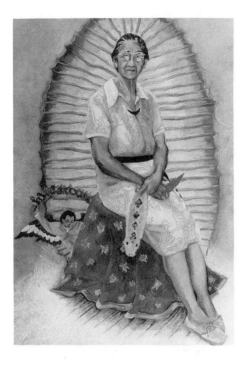
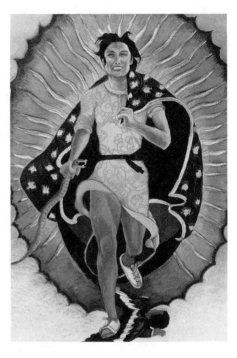

FIGURE 4.   Yolanda López, "Victoria F. Franco: Our Lady of Guadalupe" (1978).

FIGURE 5.   Yolanda López, "Portrait of the Artist as the Virgin of Guadalupe" (1978).

NOTES

1. I dedicate this essay to Zare Dernersesian for his encouragement and editorial support. I would also like to remember my aunt, Myrtha Chabrán, an early Chicana-Riqueña Mujer who struggled on two fronts.

2. This song is attributed by Armando Rendón to Juanita Domínguez although there have not been any studies confirming this fact. Rpt. in *The Chicano Manifesto,* Armando Rendón (1971) p. 182, from where this excerpt is taken.

3. "Machismo" was a highly disputed term in the sixties and seventies. For some Chicanas/ os it was linked to ethnic stereotyping of Chicano males by the dominant culture; for others it signified courage. Chicana feminists tended to link it with sexism. For an account of these positions see Alma García (1990), "The Development of Chicana Feminist Discourse." Also see Marcela Trujillo's "The Terminology of Machismo," *De Colores.* Whatever the positive connotations associated with the word, I take the position that it promoted male privilege and the male-centered nationalist text of Chicano liberation. The ethnic defense of machismo against Anglo prototypes has functioned to the detriment of Chicanas, who were already marginalized within the Chicano movement. As a sign of their loyalty they were often expected to engage in a war of positions for machismo that privileged cultural pride and race and class differences over gender differences. Naturally these problems are aggravated by the linkage of machismo to the malinche narrative.

4. Rendón (1971) notes: "We Chicanos have our share of malinches, which is what we call traitors to la raza who are of la raza, after the example of an Aztec woman of that name who became Cortez's concubine under the name of Doña Marina, and served him also as an interpreter and informer against her own people" (pp. 96–97). While Rendón is willing to admit that Chicanas are "half of the Movement," within his account of the Chicano revolt, their half is cancelled out through the male gender and the link between the Mexican Eve and contemporary Chicanas.

5. It is interesting that for Rendón (1971) the malinches are "worse characters and more dangerous than the Tio Tacos, the Chicanismo euphemism for an Uncle Tom." Male betrayal is excused while female betrayal is not tolerated. Rendón explains: "The Tio Taco may stand in the way of progress only out of fear or misplaced self-importance. In the service of the gringo, malinches attack their own brothers, betray our dignity and manhood, cause jealousies and misunderstandings among us, and actually seek to retard the advance of the Chicanos, if it benefits themselves—while the gringo watches" (pp. 96–97).

6. For a discussion of some of the problematic aspects of Chicano identity as constructed under the nationalist project, see the introduction of "Chicana/o cultural representations" edited by myself and Rosa Linda Fregoso (1990).

7. For an account of some of these early Chicana activist or feminist writings, see the following newspapers and journals: *Women Struggle, El Popo Femenil, Hijas de Cuahtemoc, La Comision Femenil, La Razón Mestiza II, Comadre,* and *Hembra.* Many of the best examples of Chicana feminist writings appeared in student newspapers and alternative presses. For an example of the variants of Chicana feminism see: Martha Cotera (1980) "Feminism: The Chicana and the Anglo Versions"; Anna Nieto Gómez (1975) "La Chicana"; and Mirta Vidal's (1971) "New Voices of La Raza: Chicanas Speak Out" An overview of themes in the evolution of Chicana poetry can be found in Tey Diana Rebolledo (1985), "The maturing of Chicana poetry: The quiet revolution of the 1980s," in *For Alma Mater: Theory and Practice in Feminist Scholarship,* ed. Paula A. Treichler, Cheris Kramarae, and Beth Stafford. An anthology referencing Chicana women's writings in culture and history, *Building With Our Hands,* by Adela de la Torre and Beatriz Pesquera (1992), offers a contemporary review of Chicana scholarship.

8. This is a modified excerpt of the text which appears in full form in Comadre (1978) p. 18.

9. Sara Estrella's entire poem can be found in *Hijas de Cuahtemoc,* published in Long Beach, California. The newspaper is not dated, but probably is from 1972. Here and elsewhere, translations are mine.

10. See Stuart Hall (1989), "Cultural Identity and Cinematographic Representation."

11. I am referring to the full length version of "I am Joaquín" published by Rodolfo Gonzáles (1967).

12. The majority of the works associated with the Guadalupe Series of Yolanda López were produced from 1975–1978.

7

Traveling Cultures

James Clifford

To begin with, a quotation from C. L. R. James's *Beyond a Boundary* (1984): "Time would pass, old empires would fall and new ones take their place. The relations of classes had to change before I discovered that it's not quality of goods and utility that matter, but movement, not where you are or what you have, but where you come from, where you are going and the rate at which you are getting there."

Or begin again with hotels. Conrad, (1957) in the first pages of *Victory:* "The age in which we are encamped like bewildered travelers in a garish, unrestful hotel." In *Tristes Tropiques*, Lévi-Strauss (1977a) evokes an out-of-scale concrete cube siting in the midst of the new Brazilian city of Goiania in 1937. It's his symbol of civilization's barbarity, "a place of transit, not of residence." The hotel as station, airport terminal, hospital, and so on: somewhere you pass through, where the encounters are fleeting, arbitrary.

Its most recent avatar: the hotel as chronotope of the modern in the new Los Angeles "downtown," Portman's Bonaventure Hotel evoked by Fredric Jameson (1984) in an influential essay, "Postmodernism: or, the Cultural Logic of Late Capitalism." The Bonaventure's glass cliffs refuse to interact, merely reflecting back the surroundings; there's no opening, no apparent main entrance; inside a confusing maze of levels frustrates all continuity—the narrative stroll of any modernist *flâneur.*

Or begin with June Jordan's "Report from the Bahamas"—her stay in something called the Sheraton British Colonial Hotel. A black woman from the United States on vacation . . . confronting her inescapable privilege and wealth, uncomfortable encounters with people who make the bed and serve food in the hotel . . . reflections on concrete conditions for human connections and alliance cross-cutting class, race, gender, and national locations.

Begin again with a London boarding house. The setting for Naipaul's *Mimic Men* (1976), a different place of inauthenticity, exile, transience, rootlessness.

Or again the Parisian hotels, homes away from home for the Surrealists, launching points for strange and wonderful urban voyages: *Nadia, Paysan de Paris*—places of collection, juxtaposition, passionate encounter—"l'Hôtel des Grands Hommes."

Begin with the hotel stationery and restaurant menus lining (along with star charts) Joseph Cornell's magical boxes. Untitled: Hôtel du Midi, Hôtel du Sud, Hôtel de l'Etoile, English Hotel, Grand Hôtel de l'Univers. Enclosed beauty of chance encounters—a feather, some ball bearings, Lauren Bacall. Hotel/*autel,* reminiscent of, but *not the same as*—no equal sign—marvelous-real altars improvised from collected objects in Latin American popular healing cults, or the home "altars" constructed by contemporary Chicano artists. A local global fault line opening in Cornell's Queens basement, filled with souvenirs of Paris, the place he never visited. Paris, the Universe, Queens N.Y., basement of an ordinary house, 3708 Utopia Parkway.

This, as we often say, is "work in progress," work *entering* a very large domain of comparative cultural studies: the diverse, interconnected histories of travel and displacement in the late twentieth century.¹ This entry is marked, empowered, and constrained, by previous work—my own, among others—which needs to be displaced. And so I'll be working, today, *out of* my historical research on ethnographic practice in its twentieth-century exoticist, anthropological forms. I find the work I'm *going towards* does not so much build on my previous work as locate and displace it.

Perhaps I could start with a travel conjuncture that has, to my thinking at least, come to occupy a paradigmatic place. Call it the "Squanto effect." Squanto was, of course, the Indian who greeted the pilgrims in 1620 in Plymouth, Massachusetts, who helped them through a hard winter and who spoke good English. To imagine the full effect, you have to remember what the "New World" was like in 1620; you could smell the pines fifty miles out to sea. Think of coming into a new place like that and having the uncanny experience of running into a Patuxet just back from Europe.

A disconcertingly hybrid "native" met at the ends of the earth: strangely familiar, and different precisely in that unprocessed familiarity. The trope is increasingly common in travel writing: it virtually organizes "postmodern" reports like Pico Iyer's *Video Night in Kathmandu* (1988). And it's reminiscent for me of my own historical research into specifically anthropological encounters, always running up against a problematic figure, the "informant." A great many of these interlocutors, complex individuals routinely made to speak for "cultural" knowledge, turn out to have their own "ethnographic" proclivities and interesting histories of travel. Insider-outsiders, good translators and explicators, they've been around. The people studied by anthropologists have seldom been homebodies. Some of them, at least, have been travelers: workers, pilgrims, explorers, religious converts, or other traditional "long distance specialists" (Helms, 1988). In the history of twentieth-century anthropology, "informants" first appear as natives; they emerge as travelers. In fact, as I will suggest soon, they are specific mixtures of the two roles.

Twentieth-century ethnography—an evolving practice of modern travel—has become increasingly wary of certain localizing strategies in the construction and representation of "cultures." I'm going to dwell on some of these localizing moves in the first part of my talk. But I should say right away that I'll be speaking here of an ideal type of mid-twentieth-century disciplinary anthropology. There have been exceptions, and these normative strategies have always been contested. My goal in criticizing a certain set of somewhat oversimplified practices is not primarily to say that they have been wrong, untruthful, or politically incorrect. Every focus excludes; there is no politically innocent methodology for intercultural interpretation. Some strategy of localization is inevitable if significantly different ways of life are to be represented. But "local" in whose terms? How is significant difference politically articulated, and challenged? Who determines where (and when) a community draws its lines, names its insiders and outsiders? These are far reaching issues. My aim in the first half of my talk today is simply to open up the question of how cultural analysis constitutes its objects—societies, traditions, communities, identities—in spatial terms and through specific spatial practices of research.²

Let's focus for a moment on two photographs near the beginning of Malinowski's *Argonauts of the Western Pacific* (1922), arguably one of a few crucial texts that established the modern disciplinary norm of a certain kind of participant observation. This fieldwork, you'll recall, rejected a certain style of research: living among fellow whites, calling up "informants" to talk culture in an encampment or on a verandah, sallying forth to "do the village." The fieldwork Malinowski dramatized required one to live full time in the village, learn the language, and be a seriously involved participant observer. The photographs at the beginning of *Argonauts,* Plates I and II, feature "the Ethnographer's tent" among Trobriand dwellings. One shows a small beach settlement, setting for the seafaring Kula activities the book chronicles. The other shows the chief's personal hut in Omarakana village, with the researcher's tent pitched nearby. In the text, Malinowski defends this style of dwelling/research as a (relatively) unobtrusive way of sharing the life of those under study. "In fact, as they knew I would thrust my nose into everything, even where a well-mannered native would not dream of intruding, they finished by regarding me as part and parcel of their life, a necessary evil or nuisance, mitigated by donations of tobacco." He also claimed a kind of panopticism. There was no need to search out the important events in Trobriand life, rituals, rifts, cures, spells, deaths, etc. "They took place under my very eyes, at my own doorstep, so to speak" (Malinowski, 1922, p. 8). (And in this regard, it would be interesting to discuss the image/technology of the research *tent:* its mobility, thin flaps, providing an "inside" where notebooks, special foods, a typewriter, could be kept, a base of operations minimally separated from "the action.")[3]

Nowadays when we see these pictures of tents in villages we may find ourselves asking different questions: Who, exactly, is being observed? Who is localized when the ethnographer's tent is permitted in the center of a village? Cultural observers, anthropologists, are often themselves in the fishbowl, under surveillance (for example, by the omnipresent kids who won't leave them alone). Who is being observed when that tent is pitched in the middle of the village? What are the political locations involved? It matters that Malinowski's tent is next to a chief's house. Which chief? What are the relations of power? What reverse appropriations may be going on? All of these are "postcolonial" questions that, we may assume, were not evoked by the photo in 1921. Then, the image represented a powerful localizing strategy: centering "the culture" around a particular locus, "the village," and a certain spatial practice of dwelling/research which itself, as I'll argue in a moment, depended on a complementary localization—that of "the field."

"Villages," inhabited by "natives," are bounded sites particularly suitable for intensive visiting by anthropologists. They have long served as habitable, mappable centers for the community, and by extension, the "culture." After Malinowski, fieldwork among "natives" tended to be construed as a practice of co-residence rather than of travel, or even of visiting. And what more natural place to live with people than in their village? (The village localization was, I might add, a portable one. You'll remember in the great world's fairs—St. Louis, Paris, Chicago, San Francisco—native populations were exhibited as native villages, with live inhabitants.) The village was a manageable unit. It offered a way to centralize a research practice, and at the same time it served as synecdoche, as point of focus, or part, through which one could represent the "cultural" whole.[4]

Simple village/culture synecdoches have largely gone out of style in current anthropology. Anthropologists, as Geertz has written, don't study villages, they study *in* villages. And increasingly, I might add, they don't study in villages either, but rather in hospitals, labs, urban neighborhoods, tourist hotels, the Getty Center. This trend challenges a modernist/urban configuration of the "primitive" object of study as romantic, pure, threatened, archaic, simple, and so forth. But despite the move out of literal villages, the notion of fieldwork as a special kind of localized *dwelling* remains.

Of course, one can only be a participant-observer some *where.* How is this place of work bounded in space and time? The question brings into view a more persistent localization: "the field." I'm concerned with how this specific set of disciplinary practices (spatial and temporal constraints) has tended to become confused with "the culture."

How are complex, interactive, cultural conjunctures temporally and spatially bounded? In Boas's generation, the field was talked about with some seriousness as a "laboratory," a place of controlled observation and experiment. This sounds crudely positivistic now. And contradictory: the field has also—since Boas's time—been seen as a "rite of passage," a place of personal/professional initiation, learning, growth, ordeal, and the like. One is struck by the powerfully ambiguous ways in which the field experience/experiment has been prefigured. (The French *experience* would serve us better here.) And one wonders, what specific kinds of travel and dwelling (where? how long?), and interaction (with whom? in what languages?) have made a certain range of experiences count as *fieldwork?* The disciplinary criteria have changed since Malinowski's time, and are changing.

It may help to view "the field" as both a methodological ideal and a concrete *place* of professional activity. The anthropologist's field is defined as a site of displaced dwelling and productive work. Since the 1920s, a certain kind of research experience, participant observation, has been normatively conceived as a sort of mini-immigration. The fieldworker is "adopted," "learns" the culture and the language. The field is a home away from home, a place of dwelling. This dwelling includes work and growth, the development of both personal and "cultural" competence. Ethnographers, typically, are travelers who like to stay and dig in (for a time), who like to make a second home/workplace. Unlike other travelers who prefer to pass through a series of locations, most anthropologists are homebodies abroad. The field as spatial practice is thus a specific style, quality, and duration of dwelling.[5]

The field is also a set of discursive practices. Dwelling implies a kind of communicative competence. One no longer relies on translators, but speaks and listens for oneself. After Malinowski's generation, the discipline prescribed "learning the language" or at least "working in the local language." This opens a rather large can of worms: *the* language, singular, as if there were only one? What does it mean to learn or use a language? How well can one learn a language in a few years? What about stranger talk, the specific kind of discourse used with outsiders? What about many anthropologists' continuing reliance on translators and explicators for complex events, idioms, and texts? The subject deserves a full study which I am not yet able to offer. It's worth pointing out, however, the fallacy, culture (singular) equals language (singular). This equation, implicit in nationalist culture ideas, has been thoroughly unraveled by Bakhtin for whom a language is a diverging, contesting, dialoguing set of discourses that no "native"—let alone visitor—can ever learn. An ethnographer thus works in or learns some part of "the language." And this does not even broach the question of multilingual/intercultural situations.[6]

I've been arguing that ethnography (in the normative practices of twentieth-century anthropology) has privileged relations of dwelling over relations of travel. I don't think I need to linger on the advantages, in focused "depth" of understanding, that can accrue to these fieldwork practices. Intensive participant-observation is probably anthropology's most enduring contribution to humanistic study, and it is, I think, adequately appreciated, even by those like me who find it deeply problematic, while urging its reform and dissemination. Let me continue, then, to worry about the dangers of construing ethnography as *field*work.

Localizations of the anthropologist's objects of study in terms of a "field" tend to marginalize or erase several blurred boundary areas, historical realities that slip out of the ethnographic frame. Here is a partial list. 1) The means of transport is largely erased—the boat, the land rover, the mission airplane, etc. These technologies suggest systematic prior and ongoing contacts and commerce with exterior places and forces which are not part of the field/object. The discourse of ethnography ("being there") is too sharply separated from that of travel ("getting there"). 2) The capital city, the national context is erased. This is what Georges Condominas has called the "préterrain," all those places you have to go through and be in relation with just to get to your village or to that place of work you will call your field. 3) Also erased: the university home of the researcher. Especially now that travel is easier to even the most remote sites and now that all sorts of places in the "first world" can be fields (churches, labs, offices, schools, and so forth), the coming and going in and out of the field by both natives and anthropologists may be very frequent. 4) The sites and relations of *translation* are minimized. When the field is a dwelling, a home away from home where one speaks the language and has a kind of vernacular competence, the cosmopolitan intermediaries—and complex, often political, negotiations involved—tend to disappear. We are left with participant observation, a kind of hermeneutic freedom to circle inside and outside social situations.

Generally speaking, what's elided is the wider global world of intercultural import-export in which the ethnographic encounter is always already enmeshed. I've said things are changing. I'll mention some recent ethnographic work in a moment. And in various critiques of anthropology—responding in part to anticolonial upheavals—we see the emergence of the informant as a complex, historical subject, neither a cultural "type" nor a unique "individual." For example, in my own work, among others, there has been an attempt to question the oral-to-literate narrative, hidden in the very word "informant" (Clifford, 1986). The native speaks, the anthropologist writes. "Writing" or "inscribing" functions controlled by indigenous collaborators are elided. My own attempt to multiply the hands and discourses involved in "writing culture" is not to assert a naive democracy of plural authorship, but to loosen at least somewhat the monological control of the executive writer/anthropologist and to open for discussion ethnography's hierarchy and negotiation of discourses in power-changed, unequal situations.

If thinking of the so-called informant as writer/inscriber shakes things up a bit, so does thinking of her or him as *traveler*. In several recent articles, Arjun Appadurai (1988) has challenged anthropological strategies for localizing non-Western people as "natives." He writes of their "confinement," even "imprisonment," through a process of representational essentializing, what he calls a "metonymic freezing," in which one part or aspect of peoples' lives come to epitomize them as a whole, constituting their theoretical niche in an anthropological taxonomy. India equals hierarchy, Melanesia equals exchange, and so forth. "Natives, people confined to and by the places to which they belong, groups unsullied by contact with a larger world have probably never existed" (Appadurai, 1988, p. 39).[7]

In much traditional ethnography, I've been arguing, the ethnographer has localized what is actually a regional/national/global nexus, relegating to the margins a "culture's" external relations and displacements. This is now increasingly questioned. The title of Greg Dening's superb ethnographic history of the Marquesas is indicative: *Islands and Beaches* (1980). Beaches, sites of travel interaction, are half the story. Eric Wolf's *Europe and the People Without History* (1982), though it may tip the local/global cultural dialectic a little too strongly toward "external" (global) determinations, is a dramatic and influential step away from notions of separate, integral cultures. "Rather than thinking of social alignments as self-determining," Wolf writes, "we need—from the start of our inquiries—to visualize them in their multiple external connections" (1982, p. 387). Or, in another current anthropological vein, consider an opening sentence from James Boon's intricate work of ethnological "crisscrossing," *Affinities and Extremes*: "What has come to be called Balinese culture is a multiply authored invention, a historical formation, an enactment, a political construct, a shifting paradox, an ongoing translation, an emblem, a trademark, a nonconsensual negotiation of contrastive identity, and more" (Boon, 1990,

p. ix). Anthropological "culture" is not what it used to be. And once the representational challenge is seen to be the portrayal and understanding of local/global historical encounters, co-productions, dominations, and resistances, then one needs to focus on hybrid, cosmopolitan experiences as much as on rooted, native ones. In my current problematic, the goal is not to *replace* the cultural figure "native" with the intercultural figure "traveler." Rather the task is to focus on concrete mediations of the two, in specific cases of historical tension and relationship. In varying degrees, both are constitutive of what will count as cultural experience. I am not recommending that we make the margin a new center (e.g. "we" are all travelers) but rather that specific dynamics of dwelling/traveling be comparatively analyzed.

In tipping the balance toward traveling as I am doing here, the "chronotope" of culture (a setting or scene organizing time and space in representable whole form) comes to resemble as much a site of travel encounters as of residence, less a tent in a village or a controlled laboratory or a site of initiation and inhabitation, and more like a hotel lobby, ship, or bus. If we rethink culture and its science, anthropology, in terms of travel, then the organic, naturalizing bias of the term culture—seen as a rooted body that grows, lives, dies, etc—is questioned. Constructed and disputed *historicities,* sites of displacement, interference, and interaction, come more sharply into view.[8]

To press the point: why not focus on any culture's farthest range of travel while *also* looking at its centers, its villages, its intensive field sites? How do groups negotiate themselves in external relationship, and how is a culture also a site of travel for others? How are spaces traversed from outside? How is one group's core another's periphery? Looked at this way, there would be no question of relegating to the margins a long list: missionaries, converts, literate or educated informants, mixed bloods, translators, government officers, police, merchants, explorers, prospectors, tourists, travelers, ethnographers, pilgrims, servants, entertainers, migrant laborers, recent immigrants, etc. New representational strategies are needed, and are, under pressure, emerging. I just want to evoke quickly several examples—notes for ways of looking at culture (along with tradition and identity) in terms of travel relations.

Ex-centric natives. The most extreme case I know of traveling "indigenous" culture-makers is a story I learned about quite recently through Bob Brosman, a musician and non-academic historian of music, who for some years now has been bringing traditional Hawaiian music into the Continental United States. Brosman became very involved with the Moe (pronounced "Moay") family, a veteran performing group, playing Hawaiian guitar, singing, and dancing. Their work represents the most authentic version of early-century Hawaiian slide guitar and singing styles. But to approach "traditional" Hawaiian music through the Moes brings some unexpected results, because their experience has been one of almost uninterrupted travel. For various reasons the Moes spent something like fifty-six years on the road, almost never going back to Hawaii. They played Hawaiian music in "exoticist" shows all over the East and South Asia, the Middle East, North Africa, Eastern and Western Europe, and the United States. And they performed, too, the gamut of hotel-circuit pop music. Now in their eighties, the Moes have recently returned to Hawaii where, encouraged by revivalists like Brosman, they are making "authentic" music from the teens and twenties.

Bob Brosman is working on a film about the Moes which promises to be quite remarkable, in part because Tal Moe made his own films, home movies, everywhere he went. Thus the film can present a traveling Hawaiian view of the world, while posing the question of how the Moe family maintained a sense of identity in Calcutta, Istanbul, Alexandria, Bucharest, Berlin, Paris, Hong Kong. How did they compartmentalize their Hawaiianness in constant interaction with different cultures, musics, and dance traditions—influences they worked into their act, as needed? How, for fifty-six years in transient, hybrid environments, did they preserve and invent a sense of Hawaiian "home?" And how, currently, is their music being recycled in the continuing invention of Hawaiian authenticity? This story of dwelling-in-travel is an extreme case, no doubt. But the Moes' experience is strangely resonant. (By the way, I also learned from Brosman's research that the National Steel Guitar, an instrument immensely popular across the U.S. in the twenties and thirties, often called the "Hawaiian Guitar," was actually invented by a Czech immigrant living in California.)

Several more examples, glimpses only, of an emergent culture-as-travel-relations ethnography. *Joe Leahy's Neighbors,* a recent film by Bob Connolly and Robin Anderson is a good example. (You may know its predecessor, *First Contact,* set in early twentieth-century New Guinea.) Joe Leahy, a mixed-blood colonial product, is a successful entrepreneur—kids in Australian schools, satellite dish behind his house in the New Guinea highlands. Connolly and Anderson include Leahy's own travels to Port Moresby and to Australia while focusing on his ambiguous relation with the locals, his relatives. The entrepreneur seems to be exploiting his "neighbors," who resent his wealth. Sometimes he appears as an uncontrolled individualist impervious to their demands, while on other occasions he distributes gifts, acting as a "big man" within a traditional economy. Joe Leahy seems to move in and out of a recognizably Melanesian culture. This sort of focus simply could not have been entertained by Malinowski. Not only is the "native" here a traveler in the world system, but the focus is on an atypical character, a person out of place, but not entirely—a person *in history.* Joe Leahy is the sort of figure who turns up in travel books, but seldom in ethnographies. And yet, he is not simply an eccentric or acculturated individual. In Connolly and Anderson's film, it remains uncertain whether Joe Leahy is a Melanesian capitalist or a capitalist Melanesian—a *new* kind of Big Man, still bound in complex ways to his jealous, more traditional neighbors. He is, and is not, of the local culture.

While I'm still discussing films, I might just mention Jean Rouch as a precursor. I'm sure many of you know his film *Jaguar,* a marvelous (real) travel story set in West Africa of the early 1950s. Rouch follows three young men as they walk from Mali to the cities of what was then called Gold Coast—in search of adventure, fun, prestige, bride-wealth. In a kind of "ethnographie vérité" the three act themselves for the camera; and their recorded commentary/travel story/myth of the journey ends up as the film's soundtrack. Much could be said about *Jaguar's* peculiarly seductive, and problematic, dialogic realism. Suffice it to say that the cultural "performance" of the film is an encounter among travelers, Rouch included. And the characters in this home movie "play" themselves, for the camera, as individuals *and* allegorical types.

Other examples: Michael Taussig's (1987) very complex localization in his recent book *Shamanism, Colonialism, and the Wild Man.* His "field" includes: the Putumayo region of Columbia and Amazonia, the contiguous Andean Highlands, migrant Indian shamans, traveling mestizos in search of healing, a meandering anthropologist, the violent inroads of world commerce in the 1890s rubber boom and currently in the World Bank's development policies. Taussig's sprawling ethnography (of almost Melvillean ambitions) portrays a region in historical relations of travel—involving conquest, curing, commerce, and mutual ideological appropriation. As George Marcus and Michael Fischer (1986) have stressed, innovative forms of multi-locale ethnography may be necessary to do justice to transnational political, economic, and cultural forces that traverse and constitute local or regional worlds (pp. 94–95). So too, specific histories of population movement, exile, and labor migration require new approaches to the representation of "diaspora cultures." Michael Fischer and Mehdi Abedi's multiply centered work of ethnographic cultural critique, *Debating Muslims* (1990), is a powerful case in point. Subtitled "cultural dialogues in postmodernity and tradition," the work (dis)locates Iranian Islamic culture in a history of national and transnational relations. One chapter is set in Houston, Texas.

Culture *as* travel. Many more examples could be cited, opening up an intricate comparative field. So far, I have been talking about the ways people leave home and return, enacting differently centered worlds, interconnected cosmopolitanisms. I should add: cultures as sites traversed—by tourists, by oil pipelines, by Western commodities, by radio and television signals. I think of Hugh Brody's (1982) ethnography, *Maps and Dreams,* which focuses on conflicting spatial practices—ways of occupying, moving through, using, mapping—by Athapascan hunters and the oil companies driving pipelines across their lands. But here, as I'll develop in a moment, a certain normative concept and history of travel begins to weigh heavily. (Can I, without serious hesitations, assimilate Athapascan hunting to travel? Even to dwelling-in-traveling? With what violence and loss of specificity?)

Christina Turner, who teaches anthropology at UCSD, pressed me on this point recently. Squanto as emerging norm? Ethnographic informants as travelers? But informants are not all travelers, and they're not "natives" either. People may choose to limit their mobility, and people may be kept "in their place" by repressive forces. Turner did ethnographic work among female Japanese factory workers, women who have not traveled, by any standard definition. They do watch TV; they do have a local/global sense; they do contradict the anthropologist's typifications; and they don't simply enact a culture. But it's a mistake, she told me, to insist on literal "travel." It begs too many questions and overly restricts the important issue of how subjects are culturally "located." Stress rather, different modalities of inside-outside connection, that the travel, or displacement, can involve forces that pass powerfully *through*—television, radio, tourists, commodities, armies.[9]

Turner's point leads me to my last ethnographic example, Smadar Lavie's *The Poetics of Military Occupation* (1990). Lavie's ethnography of Bedouins is set in the southern Sinai, a land long traversed by all sorts of people, most recently by an Israeli occupation immediately followed by Egyptian occupation. The ethnography shows Bedouins in their tents telling stories, joking, making fun of tourists, complaining about military rule, praying, and doing all sorts of "traditional" things . . . but with the radio on, the BBC World Service (Arabic version) coming in. In Lavie's ethnography you hear the crackle of that radio.

> "Shgetef, could you pour some tea?" the Galid nonchalantly requests the local Fool. Shgetef enters the mag'ad and for the umpteenth time pours us yet more cups of hot sweet tea.
>
> "So what did the news say?" the Galid asks the man with his ear glued to the transistor radio, but doesn't wait for an answer. "I'll tell you," he says with a half-bemused, half-serious expression. "No one will solve the problems between Russia and America. Only the Chinese will ever figure a way out. And when the day comes that they conquer the Sinai, that will be the end of that."
>
> It's a good pun—the Arabic for "Sinai" is *Sina,* for "Chinese" is *Sini*—and we laugh heartily. But Shgetef, perhaps betraying his deep fool's wisdom, stares at us with eyes wide open.
>
> The Galid continues, "The Greeks were here and left behind the Monastery [Santa Katarina], the Turks were here and left behind the Castle [in Nuweb'at Tarabin], and the British drew up maps, and the Egyptians brought the Russian army (and a few oil wells), and the Israelis brought the Americans who made the mountains into movies, and tourists from France and Japan, and scuba divers from Sweden and

Australia, and, trust Allah to save you from the devil, we Mzeina are nothing but pawns in the hands of them all. We are like pebbles and the droppings of the shiza."

Everyone but Shgetef again roars with laughter. The Coordinator points to me with his long index finger, saying in a commanding voice, "Write it all down, The One Who Writes Us!" *(Di Illi Tuktubna*—one of my two Mzeini nicknames). (Lavie, 1990, p. 291)

Before moving to the second part of my talk, I should say that I have deliberately restricted this discussion to examples of exotic ethnography/anthropology. I'm sure it will be clear to all of you that the field of "ethnographic" practice is much wider and more diverse. The recent return of anthropology to the metropoles, the increasing practice of what's called in the trade "studying up" (studying elite institutions), these and other developments have forged and re-forged many connections—with sociological ethnography, with socio-cultural history, with communications, and with cultural criticism. Anthropologists are in a much better position, now, to contribute to a genuinely comparative, and non-teleological, cultural studies, a field no longer limited to "advanced," "late capitalist" societies. Diverse ethnographic/historical approaches need to be able to work together on the complexities of cultural localization in post- or neo-colonial situations, on migration, immigration, and diaspora, on different paths through "modernity." These are some of the domains in which a reconstructed anthropological ethnography can participate, bringing to bear its inherently bifocal approach, its intensive research practices, its distinctive and changing forms of travel and enunciation.[10]

In the time remaining, I'd like to start in again with that odd invocation of hotels. It was written in the course of returning to some work I'd done on Paris and Surrealism during the 1920s and 30s. I'd been struck by how many of the Surrealists lived in hotels, or hotel-like transient digs, and were moving in and out of Paris. And I was beginning to see that the movement was not necessarily *centered* in Paris, or even in Europe. (Paris may have been Walter Benjamin's "capital of the 19th century"—but of the twentieth?) It all depended on how (and where) one saw the historical *outcomes* of the modernist moment.

Rereading that earlier essay, "On Ethnographic Surrealism" (1981), which was reprinted in my book the *Predicament of Culture* (1988), I came, with some embrassment, on a footnote that ended with a throwaway: "and Alejo Carpentier, who was a collaborator on the Journal *Documents.*" The loose thread suddenly seemed crucial. I wanted to revise my account of Paris, pulling out and reweaving that thread, and many others like it. I began to imagine rewriting Paris of the twenties and thirties as travel encounters—including New World detours through the Old—a place of departures, arrivals, transits (Clifford, 1990b). The great urban centers could be understood as specific, powerful sites of dwelling/traveling.

I found myself working with intersecting histories—discrepant detours and returns. The notions of *détour* and *retour* have been proposed by Edouard Glissant, in *Le Discours Antillais* (1981) and developed productively in a theory of "post-colonial habitus" by Vivek Dhareshwar (1989a, b). Paris as a site of cultural creation included the detour and return of people like Carpentier. He moved from Cuba to Paris and then back to the Caribbean and South American, to name "Lo real maravilloso," Surrealism with a difference. Surrealism traveled, and was changed in travel. Paris included also the detour and return of Leopold Senghor, Aimé Césaire, and Ousmane Socé, meeting at the Lycée Louis Le Grand, returning to different places with the cultural politics of "Negritude." Paris was the Chilean Vincente Huidobro challenging modernist genealogies, proclaiming, "Contemporary poetry begins with me." In the thirties it was Luis Buñuel traveling, somehow, between Montparnasse Surrealist meetings, civil war Spain, Mexico, and . . . Hollywood. Paris included the Salon of the Martiniquan Paulette Nardal and her sisters. Nardal founded the *Revue du Monde Noir,* a place of contact between the Harlem Renaissance and the negritude writers.

In my invocation of different hotels the relevant sites of cultural encounter and imagination began to slip away from Paris. At the same time, levels of ambivalence appeared in the hotel chronotope. At first I saw my task as finding a frame for negative and positive visions of travel: travel, negatively viewed as transience, superficiality, tourism, exile, and rootlessness (Lévi-Strauss's invocation of Goiania's ugly structure, Naipaul's London boarding house); travel positively conceived as exploration, research, escape, transforming encounter (Breton's Hôtel des Grands Hommes, June Jordan's tourist epiphany). The exercise also pointed toward the broader agenda I've been getting at here: to rethink cultures as sites of dwelling *and* travel, to take travel knowledges seriously. Thus the ambivalent setting of the hotel suggested itself as a supplement to the field (the tent and the village). It framed, at least, encounters between people to some degree away from home.

But almost immediately the organizing image, the chronotope, began to break up. And I now find myself embarked on a research project where any condensed epitome or place of survey is questionable. The comparative scope I'm struggling toward here is not a form of overview. Rather I'm working with a notion of comparative knowledge produced through an *itinerary,* always marked by a "way in," a history of locations and a location of histories: "partial and composite traveling theories," to borrow a phrase from Mary John (1989, 1990). The metaphor of travel, for me, has been a serious dream of mapping without going "off earth."

As recycled in this talk, then, the hotel epitomizes a specific *way into* complex histories of traveling cultures (and cultures of travel) in the late twentieth century. As I've said, it has become seriously problematic, in several major ways involving class, gender, race, cultural/historical location and privilege. The hotel image suggests an older form of gentlemanly Occidental travel, when home and abroad, city and country, East and West, metropole and antipodes, were more clearly fixed. Indeed, the marking of "travel" by gender, class, race, and culture is all too clear.

"Good travel" (heroic, educational, scientific, adventurous, ennobling) is something men (should) do. Women are impeded from serious travel. Some of them go to distant places, but largely as companions or as "exceptions"—figures like Mary Kingsley, Freya Stark, or Flora Tristan, women now rediscovered in volumes with titles like *The Blessings of a Good Thick Skirt,* or *Victorian Lady Travellers* (Russell, 1986; Middleton, 1982). "Lady" travelers (bourgeois, white) are unusual, marked as special in the dominant discourses and practices. While recent research is showing that there were more of them than formerly recognized, women travelers were forced to conform, masquerade, or rebel discreetly within a set of normatively male definitions and experiences.[11] One thinks of George Sand's famous account of dressing as a man in order to move freely in the city, to experience the gendered freedom of the *flâneur.* Or Lady Mary Montague's envy of the anonymous mobility of veiled women in Istabul. And what forms of displacement, closely associated with women's lives, do *not* count as proper "travel"? Visiting? Pilgrimage? We need to know a great deal more about how women have traveled and currently travel, in different traditions and histories. This is a very large comparative topic that's only beginning to be opened up: for example in the work of Sara Mills (1990 and forthcoming), Caren Kaplan (1986 and forthcoming), and Mary Louise Pratt (forthcoming, esp. chapters 5 and 7). The discursive/imaginary topographies of Western travel are being revealed as systematically gendered: symbolic stagings of self and other that are powerfully institutionalized, from scientific research work (Haraway, 1989a) to transnational tourism (Enloe, 1990). While there are certainly exceptions, particularly in the area of pilgrimage, a wide predominance of male experiences in the institutions and discourses of "travel" is clear—certainly in the West and, in differing degrees, elsewhere.

But it is hard to generalize with much confidence, since the serious, *cross-cultural* study of travel is not well developed. What I'm proposing here are research questions, not conclusions. I might note, in passing, two recent sources: *Ulysses' Sail* (1988), by Mary Helms, a broadly comparative study of the cultural uses of geographical distance and the power/knowledge gained in travel (a study focused on male experiences); and *Muslim Travelers* (1990), edited by Dale Eickelman and James Piscatori, an interdisciplinary collection designed to bring out the complexity and diversity of religious/economic spatial practices.

Another problem with the hotel image: its nostalgic inclination. For in those *parts* of contemporary society we can legitimately call postmodern (I do not think, pace Jameson, that postmodernism is yet a cultural dominant, even in the "first world") the *motel* would surely offer a better chronotope. The motel has no real lobby, it's tied into a highway network—a relay or node rather than a site of encounter between coherent cultural subjects. Meaghan Morris (1988a) has used the motel chronotope effectively to organize her essay, "At Henry Parkes Motel," recently published in *Cultural Studies*. I can't do justice to its suggestive discussions of nationality, gender, spaces, and possible narratives. I merely cite it as a displacement of the hotel chronotope of travel, for, as Morris says, "Motels, unlike hotels, demolish sense regimes of place, locale, and history. They memorialize only movement, speed, and perpetual circulation" (1988a, p. 3).

Other major ways in which the hotel chronotope—and with it the whole travel metaphor—becomes problematic have to do with class, race, and socio-cultural "location." What about all the travel that largely avoids the hotel, or motel, circuits? The travel encounters of someone moving from rural Guatemala or Mexico across the United States border are of a quite different order. A West African can get to a Paris *banlieu* without ever staying in a hotel. What are the settings that could realistically configure the cultural relations of these "travelers"? As I abandon the bourgeois hotel setting for travel encounters, sites of intercultural knowledge, I struggle, never quite successfully, to free the related term "travel" from a history of European, literary, male, bourgeois, scientific, heroic, recreational, meanings and practices.

Victorian bourgeois travelers, men and women, were usually accompanied by servants, many of whom were people of color. These individuals have never achieved the status of "travelers." Their experiences, the cross-cultural links they made, their different access to the society visited, such encounters seldom find serious representation in the literature of travel. Racism certainly has a great deal to do with this. For in the dominant discourses of travel, a non-white person cannot figure as a heroic explorer, aesthetic interpreter, or scientific authority. A good example is provided by the long struggle to bring Matthew Henson, the Black American explorer who reached the North Pole with Robert Peary, equally into the picture of this famous feat of discovery (as it was constructed by Peary, a host of historians, newspaper writers, statesmen, bureaucrats, and interested institutions such as *National Geographic* magazine) (Counter, 1988). And this is still to say nothing of the Eskimo travelers who made the trip possible![12] A host of servants, helpers, companions, guides, bearers, etc. have been discursively excluded from the role of proper travelers because of their race and class, and because theirs seemed to be a dependent status in relation to the supposed independence of the individualistic, bourgeois voyager. The independence was, in varying degrees, a myth. As Europeans moved through unfamiliar places their relative comfort and safety were insured by a well-developed infrastructure of guides, assistants, suppliers, translators, carriers, etc. (Fabian, 1986).

Does the labor of these people count as "travel"? Clearly, a comparative cultural studies account would want to include them and their specific cosmopolitan viewpoints. But to do so it would have to thoroughly criticize travel as a discourse and genre. Obviously, many different kinds of people travel, acquiring complex knowledges, stories, political and intercultural understandings, without producing "travel writing." Some accounts of these experiences have found their way to publication in Western languages, for example, the nineteenth-century travel journals of the Rarotongan missionary Ta'unga or the fourteenth-century records of Ibn Battouta (Crocombe and Crocombe, 1968; Ibn Battouta, 1972). But they are tips of lost icebergs.

Working in a historical vein, some of this diverse travel experience may be accessible through letters, diaries, oral history, music and performance traditions. A fine example of reconstructing a working-class traveling culture is provided by Marcus Rediker (1987) in his history of eighteenth-century Anglo-American merchant seamen (and pirates), *Between the Devil and the Deep Blue Sea*. A cosmopolitan, radical, political culture is revealed, fully justifying the several resonances of Rediker's final chapter title, "The Seaman as Worker of the World." Ongoing research by Rediker and Peter Linebaugh (1990) is now bringing more sharply into view the role of African laborers and travelers in this North Atlantic maritime (often insurrectionary) capitalist world. The resonances with Paul Gilroy's current research on the Black Atlantic Diaspora are clear.[13]

To call the mobile, maritime workers described by Rediker and Linebaugh "travelers" ascribes to their experience a certain autonomy and cosmopolitanness. It risks, however, downplaying the extent to which the mobility is coerced, organized within regimes of dependent, highly disciplined labor. In a contemporary register, to think of cosmopolitan workers, and especially migrant labor, in metaphors of "travel" raises a complex set of problems. The political disciplines and economic pressures that control migrant labor regimes pull very strongly against any overly sanguine view of the mobility of poor, usually non-white, people who *must* leave home in order to survive. The traveler, by definition, is someone who has the security and privilege to move about in relatively unconstrained ways. This, at any rate, is the travel myth. In fact, as recent studies like those of Mary Louise Pratt are showing, most bourgeois, scientific, commercial, aesthetic, travelers moved within highly determined circuits. But even if these bourgeois travelers can be "located" on specific itineraries dictated by political, economic, and intercultural global relations (often colonial, postcolonial, or neo-colonial in nature) such constraints do not offer any simple equivalence with other immigrant and migrant laborers. Alexander von Humboldt obviously did not arrive on the Orinoco coast for the same reasons as an Asian indentured laborer.

I want to argue, nonetheless, that while there is no ground of equivalence between the two "travelers," there is at least a basis for comparison and (problematic) translation. Von Humboldt became a canonical travel writer. The knowledge (predominantly scientific and aesthetic) produced in his American explorations has been enormously influential. The Asian laborer's view of "The New World," knowledge derived from displacement, was certainly quite different. I do not now, and may never, have access to it. But a comparative cultural studies would be very interested in such knowledge and in the ways it could potentially complement or critique Von Humboldt's. Given the prestige of travel experiences as sources of power and knowledge in a wide range of societies, Western and non-Western (Helms, 1988), the project of comparing and translating different traveling cultures need not be class- or ethno-centric. For example, a modern African traveling culture is detailed in Justin-Daniel Gandoulou's *Entre Paris et Bacongo* (1984), a fascinating study of Congolese "Aventuriers," migrant workers in Paris. Their specific culture (focused on the goal of being "well dressed") is compared with the European tradition of the dandy as well as with that of the "Rastas," different black visitors to Paris.

The project of comparison would have to grapple with the evident fact that travelers move about under strong cultural, political, and economic compulsions and that certain travelers are materially privileged, others oppressed. These different circumstances are crucial determinations of the travel at issue—movements in specific colonial, neo-colonial, and postcolonial circuits, different diasporas, borderlands, exiles, detours and returns. Travel, in this view, denotes a range of material, spatial practices that produce knowledges, stories, traditions, comportments, musics, books, diaries, and other cultural expressions. Even the harshest conditions of travel, the most exploitative regimes, do not entirely quell resistance or the emergence of diasporic and migrant cultures. The history of trans-Atlantic enslavement, to mention only a particularly violent example, an experience including deportation, uprooting, marronnage, transplantation, and revival, has resulted in a range of interconnected black cultures—African-American, Afro-Caribbean, British, and South American.

We need a better comparative awareness of these, and a growing number of other, "diaspora cultures" (Mercer, 1988). As Stuart Hall has argued in a provocative series of recent articles, diasporic conjunctures invite a reconception—both theoretical and political—of familiar notions of ethnicity and identity (Hall 1987b, 1988a, 1990b). Unresolved historical dialogues between continuity and disruption, essence and positionality, homogeneity and differences (cross-cutting "us" and "them") characterize diasporic articulations. Such cultures of displacement and transplantation are inseparable from specific, often violent, histories of economic, political, and cultural interaction, histories that generate what might be called *discrepant cosmopolitanisms*. In this emphasis we avoid, at least, the excessive localism of particularist cultural relativism, as well as the overly global vision of a capitalist or technocratic monoculture. And in this perspective the notion that certain classes of people are cosmopolitan (travelers) while the rest are local (natives) appears as the ideology of one (very powerful) traveling culture. The point of my exercise today, I'd like to stress again, is not simply to invert the strategies of cultural localization, the making of "natives" I criticized at the outset. I'm not saying there are no locales or homes, that everyone is—or should be—traveling, or cosmopolitan, or deterritorialized. This is not nomadology. Rather, I'm trying to sketch a comparative cultural studies approach to specific histories, tactics, everyday practices of dwelling *and* traveling: traveling-in-dwelling, dwelling-in-traveling.

I'll end with a series of exhortations.

We need to think comparatively about the distinct routes/roots of tribes, barrios, favellas, immigrant neighborhoods—embattled histories with crucial community "insides" and regulated traveling "outsides." What does it take to define and defend a homeland? What are the political stakes in claiming (or sometimes being relegated to) a "home"? As I've said, we need to know about places traveled through, kept small, local, and powerless by forces of domination. Jamaica Kincaid's trenchant portrayal of tourism and economic dependency in Antigua, *A Small Place* (1988), criticizes a local neo-colonial history in ways that resonate globally. (An Antiguan critique written from Vermont!) How are national, ethnic, community "insides" and "outsides" maintained, policed, subverted, crossed—by distinct historical subjects, for their own ends, with different degrees of power and freedom? (Riding, at times, on the same planes . . .)

We need to conjure with new localizations like "the border." A specific place of hybridity and struggle, policing and transgression, the U.S./Mexico frontier, has recently attained "theoretical" status, thanks to the work of Chicano writers, activists, and scholars: Americo Paredes, Renato Rosaldo, Teresa McKenna, José David Saldívar, Gloria Anzaldúa, Guillermo Gomez-Peña, and the Border Arts Project of San Diego/Tijuana. The border experience is made to produce powerful political visions: the subversion of all binarisms, the projection of a "multicultural public sphere (versus hegemonic pluralism)" (Flores and Yudice, 1990). How translatable is this place-metaphor of crossing? How are historical borderlands (sites of regulated and subversive travel, natural and social landscapes) like and unlike diasporas?

We need to conjure with "cultures," such as Haiti, that can now be ethnographically studied both in the Caribbean and in Brooklyn. The need to think of at least *two* places, when thinking of "Haiti!"[14] Or some of you may know an exuberant short story by Luis Rafael Sánchez (1984), "The Airbus" (beautifully translated by Diana Vélez). Something like Puerto Rican "culture" erupts in a riot of laughter and overflowing conversation during a routine night flight, San Juan—New York. Everyone more or less permanently in transit . . . Not so much "where are you from?" but "where are you between?" (The intercultural identity question.) Puerto Ricans who can't bear to think of staying in New York. Who treasure their return ticket. Puerto Ricans stifled "down there," newly alive "up here." "Puerto Ricans who are permanently installed in the wanderground between here and there and who must therefore informalize the trip, making it little more than a hop on a bus, though airborne, that floats over the creek to which the Atlantic Ocean has been reduced by the Puerto Ricans" (1984 p. 43).

In dealing with migration and immigration, serious attention to gender and race complicates a variety of classic approaches, particularly overly linear models of assimilation. Aiwa Ong, an anthropologist at Berkeley is currently studying Cambodian immigrants in Northern California. Her research is attentive to different, and incomplete, ways of belonging in America, different ways Cambodian men and women negotiate identities in the new national culture. Sherri Grasmuck and Patricia Pessar's (1991) new study of Dominican international migration, *Between Two Islands* is concerned, among other things, with differences between male and female attitudes toward settlement, return, and workplace struggle. Julie Matthaeli and Teresa Amott (1990) have written perceptively on specific struggles and barriers, relating to race, gender, and work, facing Asian and Asian-American women in the United States.

I've already mentioned the crucial role of political-economic push and pull in such movements of populations. (It's prominent in the Cambodian, Dominican, and Asian-American studies just cited.) A comprehensive theory of migration and capitalist labor regimes is proposed by Robin Cohen's *The New Helots: Migrants in the International Division of Labor* (1987), a work that leaves room for political/cultural resistance within a strongly deterministic global account.

In a regionally centered analysis, "The Emerging West Atlantic System" (1987), Orlando Patterson tracks the development of a "postnational" environment, centered on Miami, Florida. "Three powerful currents," he writes, "are undermining the integrity of national boundaries." The first is a long history of United States military, economic, and political intervention beyond its frontiers. The second is the growing transnational character of capitalism, its need to organize markets at a regional level. "The third current undermining the nation state is that of migration."

> . . . Having spent the last century and a half violating, militarily, economically, politically, and culturally the national boundaries of the region, the center now finds

itself incapable of defending the violation of its own national borders. The costs of doing so are administratively, politically, and, most important, economically, too high. Trade, and the international division of labor, follows the flag. But they also set in motion winds that tear it down." (p. 260)

The cultural consequences of a "Latinization" of significant regions within the political-economic "center" are, according to Patterson, likely to be unprecedented. They will certainly differ from more classic immigrant patterns (European and Asian) which do not build upon "geographic proximity and co-historical intimacy" (p. 259). We are seeing the emergence of new maps: borderland culture areas, populated by strong, diasporic ethnicities unevenly assimilated to dominant nation states.

And if contemporary migrant populations are not to appear as mute, passive straws in the political-economic winds, we need to listen to a wide range of "travel stories" (not "travel literature" in the bourgeois sense). I'm thinking, among others, of the oral histories of immigrant women that have been gathered and analyzed at the Centro de Estudios Puertoriquenos in New York City (Benmayor, et al., 1987). And, of course, we cannot ignore the full range of expressive culture, particularly music—a rich history of traveling culture-makers and transnational influences (e.g. Gilroy, 1987, and this volume).

Enough. Too much. The notion of "travel," as I've been using it, cannot possibly cover all the different displacements and interactions I've just invoked. Yet it has brought me into these borderlands.

I hang onto "travel" as a term of cultural comparison, precisely because of its historical taintedness, its associations with gendered, racial bodies, class privilege, specific means of conveyance, beaten paths, agents, frontiers, documents, and the like. I prefer it to more apparently neutral, and "theoretical," terms, such as "displacement," which can make the drawing of equivalences across different historical experiences too easy. (The postcolonial/postmodern equation, for example). And I prefer it to terms such as "nomadism," often generalized without apparent resistance from non-Western experiences. (Nomadology: a form of postmodern primitivism?) "Pilgrimage" seems to me a more interesting comparative term to work with. It includes a broad range of Western and non-Western experiences and is less class and gender-biased than "travel." Moreover, it has a nice way of subverting the constitutive modern opposition: traveler/tourist. But its "sacred" meanings tend to predominate—even though people go on pilgrimages for secular as well as religious reasons. And in the end, for whatever reasons of cultural bias, I find it harder to make "pilgrimage" stretch to include "travel" than the reverse. (The same is true of other terms such as "migration.") There are, in any event, no neutral, uncontaminated, terms or concepts. A comparative cultural studies needs to work, self-critically, with compromised, historically encumbered tools.

Today I've been working, overworking, "travel" as a *translation term*. By translation term I mean a word of apparently general application used for comparison in a strategic and contingent way. "Travel" has an inextinguishable taint of location by class, gender, race, and a certain literariness. It offers a good reminder that all translation terms used in global comparisons—terms like culture, art, society, peasant, mode of production, man, woman, modernity, ethnography—get us some distance *and* fall apart. Tradittore, traduttore. In the kind of translation that interests me most, you learn a lot about peoples, cultures, and histories different from your own, enough to begin to know what you're missing.

NOTES

1. I would like specially to acknowledge the stimulation I have received from the work of four people: Daniel Defert, Mary Louise Pratt, Lee Drummond, and Caren Kaplan. Their form-

ative influence is not adequately reflected in the paper's citations, which record a variety of other specific debts. I'm grateful, also, to participants in the Fall 1990 Luce Faculty Seminar at Yale University where I was able to develop these preliminary ideas in an atmosphere of friendly rigor. I shall always associate that productive atmosphere with my host at the Whitney Humanities Center, Peter Brooks.

2. "Spatial practice" is derived from Michel De Certeau (1984a). My overriding emphasis will, to some degree, obscure the fact that these are always spatio-*temporal* localizations. In the words of Adrienne Rich (1986), "A Place on the map is also a place in history." The temporal dimensions elided in this paper have been fully explored by Johannes Fabian in *Time and the Other* (1983). Also Clifford, (1986).

3. For a glimpse of the tent flap as threshold for certain practices of writing, see Clifford (1990a, p. 67).

4. Of course, the relevant populations did not always come clustered in stable villages. See Clifford (1988, pp 230–33) for Margaret Mead's difficulties "locating" the Mountain Arapesh in highland New Guinea.

5. Of course fieldworkers also pass through. Their departure is a crucial moment, articulating separate "places" of empirical research and theoretical elaboration, fieldnotes and writing up (Clifford, 1990a, pp. 63–66). Ethnographies have classically given some prominence to arrivals, little to departures. But seeing fieldwork as a form of travel, a multi-locale spatial practice, brings the end (and loose ends) of "dwelling" into the picture.

6. In this regard, before moving on, I might just mention Homi Bhabha's recent reminders about the discrepant temporalities and histories that do not add up to a homogeneous language/ time/culture, or nation (Bhabha, 1990). We need a critical genealogy of the connection between holistic concepts of culture, language, and nation. See Wolf (1982, p. 387) and Handler (1987) for some strands implicating anthropology.

7. For archaeological evidence in support of this conclusion see Irving Rouse (1986), *Migrations in Prehistory.*

8. In this connection, I cannot resist mentioning what may be a sign of the changing interpretive times. "Ancient Tribes That Didn't Vanish, They Just Moved" proclaims the headline of a recent article (Barringer, 1990). Archaeologists of the U.S. Southwest believe they have solved a long-standing mystery: what happened to the Anasazi? Cliff dwellers, builders of impressive permanent settlements and road networks, the Anasazi simply "vanished" when at certain moments (1150 AD at Chaco Canyon; 1300 AD at Mesa Verde, . . . their sites were abandoned. Given strong evolutionist assumptions about the development of agriculture and cities, the end of these and other developed settlements could only be interpreted as a terminus, a cultural "disappearance" or "death." Thus no continuous connection could be established between the Anasazi (a kind of catch-all name, actually Navajo in origin, for "the old ones") and contemporary cultures with deep historical roots in the region: Hopi, Zuni, Acoma. But in the new interpretive approach, cliff *dwellers* turn into cliff *travelers*. "Accumulated evidence" now suggests that the Anasazi moved around in the region, building and leaving settlements of varying complexity right up until European settlers began to invade and contain them in drastic ways. Their recent names are: Hopi, Zuni, Acoma. No mysterious absence or death separates the vanished old ones from the current populations, only a complex history of dwelling *and* traveling. While I am certainly not an expert, I cannot help wondering whether the new conclusion is adequately accounted for by what authorities call an "accumulation of new evidence." Assumptions about spatial continuity and cultural localization are currently being challenged in a wide variety of fields. The global developments that underlie my remarks today may have something to do with this mood.

9. I am grateful to Christina Turner for her very helpful comment. This is its gist, at least as I understood it.

10. The rather limited role that academic anthropology/ethnography has played, so far, in cultural studies (particularly in Britain) is a subject that deserves a discussion of its own. Specific disciplinary and imperial histories would need to be explored. My impression, for what it's worth, is that current possibilities of interaction are greater in the Americas—although cultural studies is still felt as a threat in many anthropology departments, and an (inexpungable?) taint of colonialism makes anthropology untouchable in some progressive and "third world" milieus.

11. How rare the experience of Alice Fletcher, sent as special government agent in 1889 to survey and allot the lands of the Nez Perce Indians. Fletcher was leader of her expedition, with real power over white men and Indians. Her considerable personal authority was recognized by the nickname, "Queen Victoria." For a generous and lucidly ironic account of women on the frontier doing "men's work" in their own way see the recently published letters by Fletcher's companion E. Jane Gay, *With the Nez Perce* (1981).

12. Lisa Bloom (1990) has written insightfully on Peary, Henson, Eskimos, and the various efforts by *National Geographic* to retell a deeply contested story of discovery.

13. See his contribution to this volume. I am grateful to Paul Gilroy for bringing the work of Rediker and Linebaugh to my attention during several very stimulating conversations on commuter trains.

14. See the recent experiment in feminist ethnographic writing by Karen McCarthy Brown, *Mama Lola: A Vodou Priestess in Brooklyn* (1991). Also, the bifocal study of Grasmuck and Pessar (1991).

DISCUSSION: JAMES CLIFFORD

JENNY SHARPE: I'm sympathetic to what you say about the field of anthropology being a fiction constituted only as exclusions of movements of both the anthropologist and of cultures. But, I'm wondering if that notion of the field itself exists in anthropology any longer. I'm thinking of the fact that anthropologists can no longer go out to the field in the way that they used to because of political upheavals. I'm thinking also of the recent shifts in the notion of the field itself (to include, for example, the work of anthropologists in Philadelphia's inner-city ghettos, work which constructs those ghettos as transplanted migrant communities from "third world" countries), so that we no longer have a field that looks like what Malinowski and the others you mentioned were talking about.

CLIFFORD: These are very important political issues connected to current attempts to redefine anthropology's "fields." As you said, a whole series of political upheavals have made it more and more difficult to do fieldwork in the way Malinowski, Mead, and Co. did. And, as you know, it's not that things have suddenly gotten "political," whereas previously the research was somehow neutral. One of the advantages of looking at ethnography as a form of travel is that you can't avoid certain concerns that always come up in travel accounts, but seldom in social scientific ones. I mentioned some of them. But one I didn't go into is the issue of physical safety. Here the gender and race of the traveler in foreign lands matter a lot. Ethnographers "in the field" have, of course, taken risks. Some have died from disease and accidents. But few, to my knowledge, have actually been killed by their "hosts." Why, to take a rather stark case, was Evans-Pritchard not killed, or at least hurt, by the Nuer when he set up his tent in their village on the heels of a military expedition? (He makes it perfectly clear in his book, *The Nuer,* that they didn't want him there.) Underlying his safety, and that of a host of other anthropologists, missionaries, and travelers, was a prior history of violent conflict. All over the world "natives" learned, the hard way, not to kill whites. The cost, often a punitive expedition against your people, was too high. Most anthropologists, certainly by Malinowski's time, came into their "field sites" *after* some version of this violent history. To be sure, a few daring researchers worked in unpacified areas becoming, as they did so, part of the contact and pacification process. But by the twentieth century there were relatively few of these. My point is simply that the safety of the field as a place of dwelling and work, a place for neutral, unpolitical social science, was itself a historical and political creation.

Your question presupposes this, because the recent lack of safety (at least of political safety) for fieldworkers in many places marks the collapse of a historical "world" containing inhabitable research "fields." I'd just want to add that the collapse is a very uneven one, with a lot of room for local variation and negotiation. There are still many places anthropologists can go with impunity. In other places they can do fieldwork, sometimes, with restrictions. In others, it's basically off limits. Since I'm not among those who think postcolonial ethnographers should simply stay home (wherever that is!), I'm particularly interested in the situations where an ethnography of initiation is giving way to one of negotiation, where rapport is recast as alliance. Of course this only makes explicitly political something that was going on already in the social relations of ethnographic "dwelling." (I touched on it in the questions about Malinowski's tent next to the chief's house, the matter of reverse appropriations.) But there *is* a new context, and the balance of power has shifted, in many places. Today, if ethnographers want to work among Native American communities, or in many regions of Latin America, the question "What's in it for us?" is right up front. The researcher may be required to hire, or train, local students. He or she may have to testify in a land-claims case, or work on a pedagogical grammar of the language, or help with local history projects, or support the repatriation of ancestral objects from metropolitan museums, etc. Not all communities can make this kind of demand, of course. And there's a danger that an anthropology that wants to preserve its political neutrality (also its objectivity and authority) will simply turn away from such places and toward populations where fieldwork is less "compromised," where people can be construed in the old exoticist ways.

The issue of reconstituting disciplinary practices around a new "primitive," no longer in the so-called "third world," is very suggestive. You mentioned the transplanted "third world" immigrant communities in Philadelphia. I don't think there's any question of going back to, say, the pre-1950 "primitive." But aspects of that figure are being reinvented in new conditions. For example, I said that we need to be very wary of a "postmodern primitivism" which, in an affirmative mode, discovers non-Western travelers ("nomads"), with hybrid, syncretic, cultures, and in the process projects onto their different histories of culture contact, migration, and inequality a homogeneous (historically "avant-garde") predicament.

I do think "postmodernism" can serve as a translation term, to help make visible and valid something strange (as modernism did for the early twentieth-century primitivists discovering African and Oceanian "art"), but I want to insist on the crucial *traduttore* in the traditore, the lack of an equals sign, the reality of what's missed and distorted in the very act of understanding, appreciating, describing. One keeps getting closer *and* farther away from the truth of different cultural/historical predicaments. This reflects a historical process by which the global is always localized, its range of equivalences cut down to size. It's a process that can be contained—temporarily, violently— but not stopped. New political subjects will, I assume, continue to emerge, demanding that their excluded history be recognized.

How the inescapably political dialectic of understanding and contestation is being played out in the Philadelphia neighborhoods you mentioned I don't know. You suggested that the new immigrant "third-world" people there are being objectified. A taste of otherness, without having to travel very far? Anthropology might here be seen as rejoining one of its forgotten roots: the study of "primitive" communities in the urban centers of capitalism. I'm thinking of the nineteenth-century precursors, Mayhew, Booth and company, doing research in "darkest England." The equivalence of savages "out there" and "in our midst," of travel out to the Empire and travel in to the city, was explicit in their work. You suggest we may be rearticulating that equivalence in a new historical moment. I'd want to know exactly how the ethnographers in question are working in the immigrant neighborhoods, how their "fields" are politically negotiated.

HOMI BHABHA: I really want you to talk about the place of a lack of movement and fixity in a politics of movement and a theory of travel. Refugees and exiles, are of course a part of this economy of displacement and travel but also, once they are in a particular place, then almost for their survival they need to fix upon certain symbols. The process of hybridization which goes on can often represent itself by a kind of impossibility to move and by a kind of survival identified in the holding on to something which actually then doesn't allow that circulation and movement to take place. Another site for this, which actually is not dealt with enough, are the proletariat and the lower middle classes in what is called the "third world," who are the recipients of kind of Urbana, Illinois or Harvard T-shirts which you see on the streets of Bombay, or of particular kinds of sunglasses, or particular kinds of television programs, or indeed, particular kinds of music. There is another problem of travel and fixity when they then, in something like Fanon's sense, hold on to certain symbols of the elsewhere, of travel, and elaborate around it a text which has not to do with movement and displacement, but with a kind of fetish-ization of other cultures, of the elsewhere, or of the image and figure of travel. And it's just that element of people caught in that margin of non-movement within an economy of movement that I would like you to address.

CLIFFORD: What you've said is very interesting, and I must confess I haven't got a lot to say about it, at this stage. I suppose I've steered away from a focus on "exile" because of the privilege it enjoys in a certain modernist culture: Joyce, Beckett, Pound, Conrad, Auerbach, etc., their special uprootedness, pain, authority. And for me, Conrad is the prime example of the sort of "fixing" you mention: his deliberate limitation of horizons, the labored fiction of his "Englishness," that persona of "everyone's favorite old English author" he produced in the Author's notes to his books (as Edward Said has shown), the fixation on certain symbols of Englishness because he needed to stay put, there was nowhere else for him. And paradoxically, as you know, Conrad's ex-traordinary experience of travel, of cosmopolitanness, finds expression only when it is limited, tied down to a language, a place, an audience—however violent and arbitrary the process. But perhaps this is the paradox you're getting at in foregrounding the exile's desire and need for fixity. Because in your question dwelling seems the artificial, achieved, hybrid "figure" against the "ground" of traveling, movement, and circulation. This reverses, it seems to me, the usual relation of stasis to movement, and it presupposes the problematic I was working my way into through a critique of exoticist anthropology and its culture ideas. A focus on comparative travel raises the question of dwelling, seen not as a ground or starting place, but as an artificial, constrained practice of fixation. Is that what you're getting at?

In that optique, we could compare, for example, the experience/practice of "exile" with that of "diaspora," and with that of people fixing themselves in Bombay by means of University of Illinois T-shirts. But I'd want to ask, what dialectic, or mediation (I don't know how to theorize the relation) of fixation and movement, of dwelling and traveling, of local and global, is articulated on those T-shirts? I recall, over a decade ago, seeing "UCLA" T-shirts all over the Pacific. What did they mean? I don't know. Or the New Caledonian Kanak militant in a Tarzan T-shirt I also saw, or the Lebanese militiamen wearing Rambo I recently heard about? Is this a fetishization of other cultures, of the elsewhere, as you suggest, or is it a way of localizing global symbols, for the purposes of action? Again, I don't know. Both processes must somehow be at work. (And of course T-shirts are made in virtually every locale to advertise festivals, local bands, all manner of institutions and productions.) I'm eager for a comparative cultural studies account of the T-shirt, that blank sheet, mystic writing pad, so close to the body

. . .

STUART HALL: One of the things that I appreciated in your paper was that you took the traveling metaphor as far as it could go, and then showed us where it couldn't go. In that way, you separated yourself from the fashionable postmodernist notion of nomadology—the breakdown of everything into everything. But if you don't want it simply to be "everybody now goes everywhere," then you also have to conceptualize what dwelling means. Hence, the T-shirt is not a good example because the T-shirt is something which travels well. The question is, what stays the same even when you travel? And you gave us a wonderful illustration of that in the Hawaiian musicians who were never at home for most of their lives, who traveled round the world. But you said they carried something Hawaiian with them. What?

CLIFFORD: I agree very strongly with what I hear you saying and with what I only half heard in Homi's question. Once traveling is foregrounded as a cultural practice then dwelling, too, needs to be reconceived—no longer simply the ground from which traveling departs, and to which it returns. I've not gone far enough yet in reconceptualizing the varieties, different histories, cultures, constraints, and practices of dwelling in the transnational contexts I've been sketching here. So far I've been better on traveling-in-dwelling than on dwelling-in-travel. You ask, what stays the same even when you travel? A lot. But its significance may differ with each new conjuncture. How was the Moes' Hawaiianness maintained for fifty-six years on the road? (And how was it reconstituted as "authenticity" on their return?) Are we to think of a kind of kernel or core of identity they carried everywhere with them? Or is it a question of something more polythetic, something more like a habitus, a set of practices and dispositions, parts of which could be remembered, articulated in specific contexts? I lean toward the latter view, but I have to say I don't really know enough about the Moes to be at all sure. I've just begun to learn about them.

Obviously the issue is a crucial one in discussing diaspora cultures. What is brought from a prior place? And how is it both maintained and transformed by the new environment? Memory becomes a crucial element in the maintenance of a sense of integrity—memory which is always constructive. But one would not want to go too far along the invention of tradition tack, certainly not in all cases. Oral tradition can be very precise, transmitting a relatively continuous, if rearticulated, cultural substance over many generations. This is particularly true when there is a land base to organize recollection, as with Native American societies, Melanesians, Aboriginals, etc. But African-American and Afro-Caribbean, and other diasporic experiences also show varying degrees of continuity, of something like a collective memory (which is not, of course, individual memory writ large). But you, especially, could tell me a lot more about this! I just want to affirm what I take to be the general direction of your question and repeat that, in my terms, cultural dwelling cannot be considered except in specific historical relations with cultural traveling, and vice versa.

KEYA GANGULY: I'd like to preface by saying I find your idea of bifocality very interesting and I think it sort of resembles in some ways, I hope, Stuart Hall's notion of the contrastive double vision of a familiar stranger of sorts. When you extend the metaphor of bifocality to call for a comparative study of, e.g., Haitians in Haiti and Haitians in Brooklyn, New York, don't you make the kind of reifying move that Appadurai critiques, as the othering of others? By locating them as Haitians in a continuous space between Haiti and New York, Indian in India and Indian in New York, are you reinscribing an ideology of cultural difference? Being a child of Indian immigrants I find it very difficult to identify myself with that sort of ideology of difference especially since the identification may occur at another level. For instance, I choose to be identified with Philadelphians rather than with Indians from Bombay.

CLIFFORD: A very far-reaching question. I can say a few things. First, the sort of comparative account I'm proposing would want to be sensitive to the differences between, say, Indians in New York and Haitians in New York, while claiming their comparability. The proximity, patterns of immigration and return, the sheer political-economic weight of the relationship between the two places may make it more useful to talk of a kind of intercultural axis in the Haitian case than in the Indian one. I'm not sure. But I do want to hesitate before generalizing (what I first heard Vivek Dhareshwar call) "immigritude." And having said that, I will admit to a specific localizing of "Haitian" difference when I speak of Haiti simultaneously in Brooklyn and the Caribbean. I would hope that this does not reinscribe an ideology of absolute cultural difference. I would also want to hold onto the notion that there are different cultures that are some where(s), not all over the map. It's a fine line to walk, as you suggest. Why Haiti/Brooklyn, and not Haiti/Paris, or other places Haitians travel and emigrate? Here I would return to the research of Orlando Patterson. Patterson sees the Caribbean as enmeshed in political-economic relations of "peripheral dualism," destructively tied to a United States "center." This dualism would account for why the transnational relationship with the North overrides other possible historical connections, with France for example. And it might justify localizing an intercultural "Haiti" along that axis. I would certainly not want to exoticize Haitians in this cultural space by pinning their identity on some sort of essence (Vodou, for example, important though it is).

But your question nicely opens up the whole question of identity as a politics rather than an inheritance—the tense interaction between these two sources. When you speak about possibly choosing to be identified with Philadelphians rather than with Bombay Indians I hear you rejecting all-or-nothing ethnic agendas. And I certainly agree with this questioning of a kind of automatic cultural or racial inscription as a diasporic "Indian." (Inscriptions made in hostile as well as friendly ways.) I would only add, as I'm sure you'd agree, that the "choice"—not voluntaristic, but historically constrained— is *neither* a binary one (in assimilationist scenarios, a before/after), *nor* is it an open set of alternatives. Rather, cultural/political identity is a processual configuration of historically given elements—including race, culture, class, gender, and sexuality—different combinations of which may be featured in different conjunctures. These elements may, in some conjunctures, cross cut and bring each other to crisis. What components of identity are "deep" and what "superficial"? What "central" and what "peripheral"? What elements are good for traveling, what for dwelling? What will be articulated within "the community"? What in coalition work? How do these elements interact historically, in tension and dialogue? Questions like these do not lend themselves to systematic or definitive answers; they are what cultural politics is all about.

8

Portraits of People with AIDS

DOUGLAS CRIMP

In the fall of 1988, the Museum of Modern Art in New York presented an exhibition of Nicholas Nixon's photographs called "Pictures of People." Among the people pictured by Nixon are people with AIDS (PWAs), each portrayed in a series of images taken at intervals of about a week or a month. The photographs form part of a larger work-in-progress, undertaken by Nixon and his wife, a science journalist, to, as they explain it, "tell the story of AIDS: to show what this disease truly is, how it affects those who have it, their lovers, families and friends, and that it is both the most devastating and the most important social and medical issue of our time."[1] These photographs were highly praised by reviewers, who saw in them an unsentimental, honest, and committed portrayal of the effects of this devastating illness. One photography critic wrote:

> Nixon literally and figuratively moves in so close we're convinced that his subjects hold nothing back. The viewer marvels at the trust between photographer and subject. Gradually one's own feelings about AIDS melt away and one feels both vulnerable and privileged to share the life and (impending) death of a few individuals. (Atkins, 1988)

Andy Grundberg, photography critic of the *New York Times,* concurred:

> The result is overwhelming, since one sees not only the wasting away of the flesh (in photographs, emaciation has become emblematic of AIDS) but also the gradual dimming of the subjects' ability to compose themselves for the camera. What each series begins as a conventional effort to pose for a picture ends in a kind of abandon; as the subjects' self-consciousness disappears, the camera seems to become invisible, and consequently there is almost no boundary between the image and ourselves. (1988, p. H37)

In his catalogue introduction for the show, MOMA curator Peter Galassi also mentions the relationship between Nixon and his sitters:

> Any portrait is a collaboration between subject and photographer. Extended over time, the relationship can become richer and more intimate. Nixon has said that most of the people with AIDS he has photographed are, perhaps because stripped of so many of their hopes, less masked than others, more open to collaboration. (Galassi, 1988, p. 26)

And, after explaining that there can be no representative portrait of a person with AIDS, given the diversity of those affected, he concludes, "Beside and against this fact is the irreducible fact of the individual, made present to us in body and spirit. The life and death of Tom Moran [one of Nixon's subjects] were his own" (p. 27).

I quote this standard mainstream photography criticism to draw attention to its curious contradictions. All these writers agree that there is a consensual relationship

117

between photographer and subject that results in the portraits' effects on the viewer. But is this relationship one of growing intimacy? or is it one of the subjects' gradual tuning out, their abandonment of a sense of self? And is the result one of according the subjects the individuality of their lives and deaths? or do their lives and deaths become, through some process of identification, ours?

For those of us who have paid careful attention to media representations of AIDS, none of this would appear to matter, because what we see first and foremost in Nixon's photographs is their reiteration of what we have already been told or shown about people with AIDS: that they are ravaged, disfigured, and debilitated by the syndrome; they are generally alone, desperate, but resigned to their "inevitable" deaths.

During the time of the MOMA exhibition, a small group from ACT UP, the AIDS Coalition to Unleash Power, staged an uncharacteristically quiet protest of Nixon's portraits. Sitting on a bench in the gallery where the photographs of PWAs were hung, a young lesbian held a snapshot of a smiling middle-aged man. It bore the caption, "This is a picture of my father taken when he'd been living with AIDS for three years." Another woman held a photograph of PWA Coalition cofounder David Summers, shown speaking into a bank of microphones. Its caption read, "My friend David Summers living with AIDS." They and a small support group spoke with museum visitors about pictures of PWAs and handed out a flier which read, in part:

NO MORE PICTURES WITHOUT CONTEXT

We believe that the representation of people with AIDS affects not only how viewers will perceive PWAs outside the museum, but, ultimately, crucial issues of AIDS funding, legislation, and education.

In portraying PWAs as people to be pitied or feared, as people alone and lonely, we believe that this show perpetuates general misconceptions about AIDS without addressing the realities of those of us living every day with this crisis as PWAs and people who love PWAs.

FACT: Many PWAs now live longer after diagnosis due to experimental drug treatments, better information about nutrition and health care, and due to the efforts of PWAs engaged in a continuing battle to define and save their lives.

FACT: The majority of AIDS cases in New York City are among people of color, including women. Typically, women do not live long after diagnosis because of lack of access to affordable health care, a primary care physician, or even basic information about what to do if you have AIDS.

The PWA is a human being whose health has deteriorated not simply due to a virus, but due to government inaction, the inaccessibility of affordable health care, and institutionalized neglect in the forms of heterosexism, racism, and sexism.

We demand the visibility of PWAs who are vibrant, angry, loving, sexy, beautiful, acting up and fighting back.

STOP LOOKING AT US; START LISTENING TO US.

As against this demand—stop looking at us—the typical liberal position has held, from very early in the epidemic, that one of the central problems of AIDS, one of the things we needed to combat, was bureaucratic abstraction. What was needed was to "give AIDS a face," to "bring AIDS home." And thus the portrait of the person with AIDS had become something of a genre long before a famous photographer like Nicholas Nixon entered the field. In the catalogue for an exhibition of another well-known photographer's efforts to give AIDS a human face—Rosalind Solomon's *Portraits in the Time of AIDS* (1988)—Grey Art Gallery director Thomas Sokolowski wrote of their perceived necessity: "As our awareness of [AIDS] grew through the accumulation of vast amounts of numerically derived evidence, we still had not seen its face. We could count it, but not truly describe it. Our picture of AIDS was a totally conceptual one ...." (1988a, n.p.). Sokolowski's catalogue essay is entitled "Looking in a Mirror," and it begins with an epigraph quoted from the late George Whitmore, which reads, "I see Jim—and that could be me. It's a mirror. It's not a victim-savior relationship. We're the same person. We're just on different sides of the fence." With Sokolowski's appropriation of these sentences from a man who himself had AIDS, we are confronted once again—as with the texts written in response to the Nixon photographs—with a defense mechanism, which denies the difference, the obvious sense of otherness, shown in the photographs by insisting that what we really see is ourselves.

A remarkably similar statement begins a CBS *Sixty Minutes* newsmagazine devoted to AIDS, in which a service organization director says, "We know the individuals, and they look a lot like you, they look a lot like me." The program, narrated by CBS news anchor Dan Rather, is titled "AIDS Hits Home." Resonating with the assertion that PWAs look like you and me, the "home" of the show's title is intended to stand in for other designations: white, middle class, middle American, but primarily *heterosexual*. For this program was made in 1986, when, as Paula Treichler (1988) has written, "the big news—what the major U.S. news magazines were running cover stories on—was the grave danger of AIDS to heterosexuals" (p. 39).

"AIDS Hits Home" nevertheless consists of a veritable catalogue of broadcast television's by-then typical portraits of people with AIDS, for example, the generic or collective portraits, portraits of so-called risk groups: gay men in their tight 501s walking arm in arm in the Castro district of San Francisco; impoverished Africans; prostitutes, who apparently always work on streets; and drug addicts, generally shown only metonymically as an arm with a spike seeking its vein. Also included in this category of the generically portrayed in "AIDS Hits Home," however, are "ordinary" heterosexuals—ordinary in the sense that they are white and don't shoot drugs—since they are the ostensible subject of the show. But the heterosexual in AIDS reportage is not quite you and me. Since television routinely assumes its audience as heterosexual and therefore unnecessary to define or explain, it had to invent what we might call the heterosexual of AIDS. As seen on *Sixty Minutes,* the heterosexual of AIDS appears to inhabit only aerobics classes, discos, and singles bars, and is understood, like *all* gay men are understood, as always ready for, or readying for, sex. In addition, in spite of the proportionately much higher rate of heterosexually transmitted AIDS among people of color, the heterosexuals portrayed on *Sixty Minutes* are, with one exception, white.

"AIDS Hits Home"'s gallery of portraits also includes individuals, of course. These are the portraits that Dan Rather warns us of in the beginning of the program, when he says, "The images we have found are brutal and heartbreaking, but if America is to come to terms with this killer, they must be seen." For the most part, though, they are not seen, or only partially seen, for these are portraits of the ashamed and dying. As they are subjected to callous interviews and voice-overs about the particularities of their illnesses and their emotions, they are obscured by television's inventive techniques. Most often they appear, like terrorists, drug kingpins, and child molesters, in shadowy silhouette, backlit with light from their hospital room windows. Sometimes the PWA is partially revealed, as doctors and nurses manipulate his body while his face remains off-camera, although in some cases, we see *only* the face, but in such extreme close-up that we cannot perceive the whole visage. And in the most technologically dehumanizing instance, the portrait of the PWA is digitized. This is the case of the feared and loathed bisexual, whose unsuspecting suburbanite wife has died of AIDS. He is shown—or rather not shown—responding to an interlocutor who says, "Forgive me asking you this question, it's not easy, but do you feel in some way as if you murdered your wife?"

As we continue to move through the *Sixty Minutes* portrait gallery, we come eventually to those whose faces can see the light of day. Among these are a few gay men, but most are women. They are less ashamed, for they are "innocent." They or the narrator explain how it is that these perfectly normal women came to be infected with HIV: one had a boyfriend who used drugs, another had a brief affair with a bisexual, and another had a bisexual husband; none of them suspected the sins of their partners. And finally there are the most innocent of all, the white, middle-class hemophiliac children. They are so innocent that they can even be shown being comforted, hugged, and played with.

Among the gay men who dare to show their faces, one is particularly useful for the purposes of *Sixty Minutes,* and interestingly he has a counterpart in an ABC *20/20* segment of a few years earlier. He is the identical twin whose brother is straight. The double portrait of the sick gay man and his healthy straight brother makes its moral lesson so clear that it needs no elaboration.[2]

Indeed, the intended messages of "AIDS Hits Home" are so obvious that I don't want to belabor them, but only to make two further points about the program. First, there is the reinforcement of hopelessness. Whenever a person with AIDS is allowed to utter words of optimism, a voice-over adds a caveat such as: "Six weeks after she said this, she was dead." Following this logic, the program ends with a standard device. Dan Rather mentions the "little victories and the *inevitable* defeats," and then proceeds to tell us what has happened to each PWA since the taping of the show. This coda ends with a sequence showing a priest—his hand on the KS-lesion-covered head of a PWA—administering last rights. Rather interrupts to say, "Bill died last Sunday," and the voice of the priest returns: "Amen."

My second point is that the privacy of the people portrayed is both brutally invaded and brutally maintained. Invaded, in the obvious sense that these people's difficult personal circumstances have been exploited for public spectacle, their most private thoughts and emotions exposed. But at the same time, maintained: The portrayal of these people's personal circumstances never includes an articulation of the public dimension of the crisis, the social conditions that made AIDS a crisis and continue to perpetuate it as a crisis. People with AIDS are kept safely within the boundaries of their private tragedies. No one utters a word about the politics of AIDS, the mostly deliberate failure of public policy at every level of government to stem the course of the epidemic, to fund biomedical research into effective treatments, provide adequate health care and housing, and conduct massive and ongoing preventive education campaigns. Even when the issue of discrimination is raised—in the case of children expelled from school—this too is presented as a problem of individual fears, prejudices, and misunderstandings. The role of broadcast television in creating and maintaining those fears, prejudices, and misunderstandings is, needless to say, not addressed.

It is, then, not merely faceless statistics that have prevented a sympathetic response to people with AIDS. The media has, from very early in the epidemic, provided us with faces. Sokolowski acknowledges this fact in his preface to the Rosalind Solomon catalogue:

> Popular representations of AIDS have been devoid of depictions of people living with AIDS, save for the lurid journalistic images of patients *in extremis,* published in the popular press where the subjects are depicted as decidedly *not* persons *living* with AIDS, but as victims. The portraits in this exhibition have a different focus. They are, by definition, portraits of individuals with AIDS, not archetypes of some abstract notion of the syndrome. Rosalind Solomon's photographs are portraits of the human condition; vignettes of the intense personal encounters she had with over seventy-

five people over a ten-month period. "I photographed everyone who would let me, who was HIV-positive, or had ARC, or AIDS . . . they talked to me about their lives."

The resulting seventy-five images that comprise this exhibition provide a unique portrait gallery of the faces of AIDS. (1988a, n.p.)

The brute contradiction in this statement, in which "portraits of individuals with AIDS, not archetypes of some abstract notion" is immediately conflated with "portraits of the human condition"—as if that were not an abstract notion—is exacerbated in So-kolowski's introductory text, where he applies to the photographs interpretations that read as if they were contrived as parodies of the art historian's formal descriptions and source mongering. In one image, which reminds Sokolowski of Watteau's *Gilles,* we are asked to "contemplate the formal differences between the haphazard pattern of facial lesions and the thoughtful placement of buttons fastened to the man's pullover" (1988b). He completes his analysis of this photograph by comparing it with an "early fifteenth-century *Imago Peitatis* of the scourged Christ." Other photographs suggest to him the medieval *Ostentatio Vulneris,* the *Momento Mori,* the *Imago Clipeata,* and the image of the *Maja* or Venus.

Clearly when viewing Solomon's photographs most of us will not seek to place them within art historical categories. Nor will we be struck by their formal or com-positional interest. Rather, many of us will see in these images, once again, and in spite of Sokolowski's insistence to the contrary, the very representations we have grown accustomed to in the mass media. William Olander, a curator at New York's New Museum of Contemporary Art who died of AIDS on March 18, 1989, saw precisely what I saw:

> The majority of the sitters are shown alone; many are in the hospital; or at home, sick, in bed. Over 90% are men. Some are photographed with their parents, or at least their mothers. Only four are shown with male lovers or friends. For the pho-tographer, "The thing that became very compelling was knowing the people—know-ing them as individuals. . . ." For the viewer, however, there is little to know other than their illness. The majority of sitters are clearly ravaged by the disease. (No fewer than half of those portrayed bear the most visible signs of AIDS—the skin lesions associated with Kaposi's Sacroma. Not one is shown in a work environment; only a fraction are depicted outside. None of the sitters is identified. They have no identities other than as victims of AIDS. (1988, p. 5)[3]

But giving the person with AIDS an identity as well as a face can also be a dangerous enterprise, as is clear from the most extended, and the most vicious, story of a person with AIDS that American television has thus far presented: the notorious episode of PBS *Frontline,* "AIDS: A National Inquiry." "This is Fabian's story," host Judy Woodruff informs us, "and I must warn you it contains graphic descriptions of sexual behavior." One curious aspect of this program, given its ruthlessness, is its unabashed self-reflexivity. It begins with the TV crew narrating about itself, apparently roaming the country in search of a good AIDS story: "When we came to Houston, we didn't know Fabian Bridges. He was just one of the faceless victims." After seeing the show, we might conclude that Fabian would have been better off it he'd remained so. "AIDS: A National Inquiry" is the story of the degradation of a homeless black gay man with AIDS at the hands of virtually every institution he encountered, certainly including PBS. Fabian Bridges was first diagnosed with AIDS in a public hospital in Houston, treated, released, and given a one-way ticket out of town—to Indianapolis, where his sister and brother-in-law live. They refuse to take him in, because they're afraid for their young child, about whom the brother-in-law says, "He doesn't know what AIDS is. He doesn't know what homosexuality is. He's innocent." Arrested for stealing a bicycle, Fabian is harassed and humiliated by the local police, who are also under the illusion that they might "catch" AIDS from him. After a prosecutor drops the charges against him, Fabian is once again provided with a one-way ticket out of town, this time to Cleveland, where his mother lives. But in Indianapolis, a police reporter has picked up the story, and, as the *Frontline* crew informs us, "It was Kyle Niederpreun's story that first led us to Fabian. It was a story about the alienation and rejection that many AIDS victims suffer"—an alienation and rejection that the crew seemed all too happy to perpetuate.

Frontline finally locates its "AIDS victim" in a cheap hotel room in Cleveland. "We spent several days with Fabian," the narrator reports, "and he agreed to let us tell his story." Cut to Fabian phoning his mother in order that her refusal to let him come home can be reenacted for the video camera. "He said he had no money," the crew goes on, "so sometimes we bought him meals, and we had his laundry done. One day Fabian saw a small portable radio he liked, so we bought it for him." The narration continues, "He spent time in adult bookstores and movie houses, and he admitted it was a way he helped support himself." Then, in what is surely the most degrading invasion of privacy ever shown on TV, Fabian describes, on camera, one of his tricks, ending with the confession, "I came inside him . . . accident . . . as I was pulling out, I was coming." "After Fabian told us he was having unsafe sex, we faced a dilemma," the narrator explains. "Should we report him to authorities or keep his story confidential, knowing that he could be infecting others? We decided to tell health officials what we knew."

At this point begins the story *Frontline* has really set out to tell, that of the supposed conflict between individual rights and the public welfare.[4] It is a story of the futile attempts of health officials, policemen, and the vice squad to lock Fabian up, protected as he is by troublesome civil rights. A city council member in Cleveland poses the problem: "The bottom line is we've got a guy on the street here. The guy's got a gun and he's out shootin' people. . . . What do we say collectively as a group of people representing this society?" But while the city council contemplates its draconian options, the disability benefits Fabian had applied for several months earlier arrive, and after a nasty sequence involving his sadly ill-counseled mother, who has momentarily confiscated the money in order to put it aside for Fabian's funeral, Fabian takes the money and runs.

By now *Time* magazine has published a story on what it calls this "pitiful nomad," and the local media in Houston, where Fabian has reappeared, have a sensational story for the evening news. The *Frontline* crew finds him, homeless and still supporting himself as a hustler, so, they report, "We gave him $15 a night for three nights to buy a cheap hotel room. We gave him the money on the condition that he not practice unsafe sex and that he stay away from the bathhouses." Pocketing the generous gift of $45, Fabian continues to hustle, and the vice squad moves in to enforce an order by the Houston health department, issued in a letter to Fabian, that he refrain from exchanging bodily fluids. But now the vice squad, too, faces a dilemma. "Catch 22," one of the officers says. How do you entrap someone into exchanging bodily fluids without endangering yourself? They decide to get Fabian on a simple solicitation charge instead, to "get him to hit on one of us," as they put it, but Fabian doesn't take the bait.

Ultimately a leader of the gay community decides on his own to try to help Fabian, and a lawyer from the Houston AIDS Foundation offers him a home, developments about which the Houston health commissioner blandly remarks, "It would never have occurred to me to turn to the gay community for help." But *Frontline* has now lost its story. As the narrator admits, "The gay community was protecting him from the local press and from us." There is, nevertheless, the usual coda: "The inevitable happened. Fabian's AIDS symptoms returned. Just one week after he moved into his new home, he went back into the hospital. This time, he stayed just over a month. Fabian died on November 17. His family had no money to bury him, so after a week he was given a pauper's funeral and buried in a county grave."

Judy Woodruff had introduced this program by saying, "The film you are about to see is controversial; that's because it's a portrait of a man with AIDS who continued to be promiscuous. In San Francisco and other cities, the organized gay community is protesting the film, because they say it is unfair to persons with AIDS." This strikes me as a very ambiguous reason to protest, and I have no doubt that the organized gay community's position against the film was articulated more broadly. How is it unfair to person with AIDS? What persons with AIDS? Isn't the film unfair, first and foremost, to Fabian Bridges? The true grounds on which I imagine the gay community protested are the dangerous insinuations of the film: that the public health is endangered by the free movement within society of people with AIDS; that gay people with AIDS irresponsibly spread HIV to unsuspecting victims. They might also have protested the film's racist presumptions and class biases, its exploitation not only of Fabian Bridges but of his entire family. In addition, it seems hard to imagine a knowledgeable person seeing the film who would not be appalled at the failure of PBS to inform its audience of the extraordinary misinformation about AIDS conveyed by virtually every bureaucratic official in the film. And finally I imagine the gay community protested the film because it is so clear that the filmmakers were more interested in getting their footage than in the psychological and physical welfare of their protagonist, that instead of leading him to social service agencies or AIDS service organizations that could have helped him and his family, they lured him with small bribes, made him dependent upon them, and then betrayed him to various authorities. A particularly revealing sequence intercut toward the end of the film takes us back to Fabian's hotel room in Cleveland. "We remembered something he'd said to us earlier," the narrator says, and Fabian then intones in his affectless voice, "Let me go down in history as being . . . I am somebody, you know, somebody that'll be respected, somebody who's appreciated, and somebody who can be related to, because a whole lot of people just go, they're not even on the map, they just go."

Here we have explicitly the terms of the contract between the *Frontline* crew and Fabian Bridges. *Frontline* found in Fabian, indeed, the "alienation and rejection" that many people with AIDS suffer, and offered him the false means by which our society sometimes pretends to grant transcendence of that condition, a moment of glory in the mass media. They said to this lonely, ill, and scared young man, in effect, "We're gonna make you a star."

After witnessing this contract, we may wish to reconsider the various claims made for photographers Nicholas Nixon and Rosalind Solomon that the difference of their work from ordinary photojournalism's exploitation of people with AIDS resides in the pact they have made with their sitters. "The rather unique situation of Rosalind Solomon's portraits, done in the time of AIDS," writes Thomas Sokolowski, "is that the subjects have been asked" (1988a). The claim for Nixon is made less directly by his curatorial apologist. When introducing Nixon for a lecture at the Museum of Modern Art, Peter Galassi said,

> Mr. Nixon was born in Detroit in 1947. It seems to me that's all you really need to know, and the part about Detroit isn't absolutely essential. What is relevant is that Nixon has been on the planet for about forty years and has been a photographer for about half of that time. It's also relevant that for about the past fifteen years he has

124   DOUGLAS CRIMP

worked with a large, old-fashioned view camera which stands on a tripod and makes negatives measuring eight by ten inches.[5]

The point about the size of Nixon's equipment, of course, is that it is so obtrusive that we can never accuse him of catching his subjects unawares; he has to win their confidence. According to a friend of Nixon quoted in the *Boston Globe,* "The reason people trust him is that he has no misgivings about his own motivations or actions" (N. Miller, 1989, p. 36). Or, as Nixon himself put it in his talk at MOMA, "I know how cruel I am, and I'm comfortable with it."

My initial reaction upon seeing both the Nixon and Solomon exhibitions was incredulity. I had naively assumed that the critique of this sort of photography, articulated over and again during the past decade, might have had some effect. I will cite just one paragraph from a founding text of this criticism as an indication of the lessons not learned. It comes from Allan Sekula's "Dismantling Modernism, Reinventing Documentary (Notes on the Politics of Representation)," written in 1976:

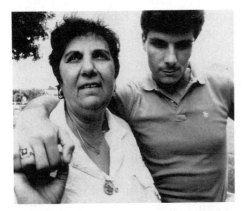

FIGURE 1.   Nicholas Nixon, "Tony and Anna Mastrorilli" (Mansfield, MA, July 1987).

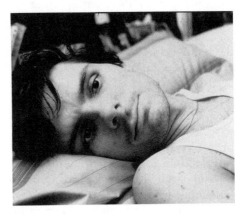

FIGURE 2.   Nicholas Nixon, "Tony Mastrorilli" (Mansfield, MA, December 1987).

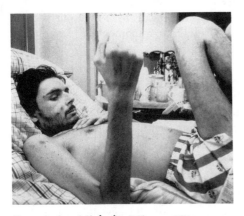

FIGURE 3.   Nicholas Nixon, "Tony Mastrorilli" (Mansfield, MA, April 1988).

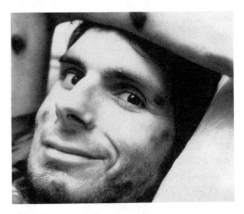

FIGURE 4.   Nicholas Nixon, "Tony Mastrorilli" (Mansfield, MA, May 1988).

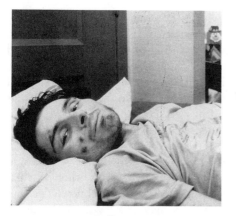

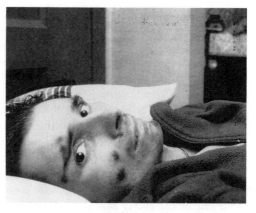

FIGURE 5.   Nicholas Nixon, "Tony
Mastrorilli" (Mansfield, MA, June
1988).

FIGURE 6.   Nicholas Nixon, "Tony
Mastrorilli" (Mansfield, MA, June
1988).

> At the heart of [the] fetishistic cultivation and promotion of the artist's humanity is
> a certain disdain for the "ordinary" humanity of those who have been photographed.
> They become the "other," exotic creatures, objects of contemplation. . . . The most
> intimate, human-scale relationship to suffer mystification in all this is the specific
> social engagement that results in the image; the negotiation between photographer
> and subject in the making of a portrait, the seduction, coercion, collaboration, or rip
> off. (Sekula, 1984, p. 59)

Here is one indication of the photographer's disdain while negotiating with his sitter:
Showing one of his serial PWA portraits (of Tony Mastrorilli), Nixon explained,

> I started taking his picture in June of '87, and he was so resistant to the process—
> even though he kept saying "Oh no, I love it, I want to do it"—every other part of
> him was so resistant that after three times I kind of kicked him out and said, "When
> you really want to do this, call me up, you don't really want to do this." Then one
> day in December he called me up and said, "I'm ready now," and so I went, of course,
> and this picture doesn't kill me, but, I'll tell you, it's miles better than anything I'd
> gotten from him before. I really felt like he *was* ready when I saw it. He was paralyzed
> from the waist down. That was part of the challenge, I guess.

An audience member asked Nixon to explain what he meant when he said the
subject was resistant, and he replied,

> He wasn't interested. He was giving me a blank wall. He was saying, "Yes, I think
> this is something I'm interested in, but I don't like this process, I don't like this big
> camera, I don't like it close to me, I don't like cooperating with you, I don't like the
> fact that your being here reminds me of my illness, I'm uncomfortable." But at the
> same time he kept on going through the motions. I had to drive forty minutes to his
> house. I'm not interested in somebody just going through the motions. Life's too
> short.

How, then, might this intimate, human-scale relationship that Sekula cautions us
about be constructed differently?

We can perhaps agree that images of people with AIDS created by the media and
art photographers alike are demeaning, and that they are overdetermined by a number
of prejudices that precede them about the majority of the people who have AIDS—about
gay men, IV drug users, people of color, poor people. Not only do journalism's (and

art's) images create false stereotypes of people with AIDS, they depend upon already existing false stereotypes about the groups most significantly affected by AIDS. Much of the PBS discussion with "experts" that followed its airing of Fabian's story involved the fear that Fabian would be seen as the stereotype of the homosexual with AIDS. The reaction of many of us when we see homosexuality portrayed in the media is to respond by saying, "That's not true. We're not like that" or "I'm not like that" or "we're not all like that." But what *are* we like? What portrait of a gay person, or of a PWA, would be feel comfortable with? Which one would be representative? How could it be? and why should it be? One problem of opposing a stereotype, a stereotype which Fabian Bridges was indeed intended to convey, is that we tacitly side with those who would distance themselves from the image portrayed, we tacitly agree that it is other, whereas our foremost responsibility in this case is to *defend* Fabian Bridges, to acknowledge that he is one of us. To say that it is unfair to represent a gay man or a PWA as a hustler is tacitly to collaborate in the media's ready condemnation of hustlers, to pretend along with the media that prostitution is a moral failing rather than a choice based on economic and other factors limiting autonomy. Or, to take another example, do we really wish to claim that the photographs by Nicholas Nixon are untrue? Do we want to find ourselves in the position of denying the horrible suffering of people with AIDS, the fact that very many PWAs become disfigured and helpless, and that they die? Certainly we can say that these representations do not help us, and that they probably hinder us, in our struggle, because the best they can do is elicit pity, and pity is not solidarity. We must continue to demand and create our own counter-images, images of PWA self-empowerment, of the organized PWA movement and of the larger AIDS activist movement, as the ACT UP demonstrators insisted at MOMA. But we must also recognize that every image of a PWA is a *representation,* and formulate our activist demands not in relation to the "truth" of the image, but in relation to the conditions of its construction and to its social effects.

I want to conclude this discussion, therefore, with a work that does not seek to displace negative images with positive ones, that does not substitute the good PWA for the bad, the apparently healthy for the visibly ill, the active for the passive, the exceptional for the ordinary. My interest in the videotape *Danny* (1987), made by Stashu Kybartas,[6] does not derive from its creation of a counter-type, but rather from its insistence upon a particular stereotype, one which is referred to among gay men, whether endearingly or deprecatingly, as the clone.

Without, I think, setting out deliberately or programmatically to articulate a critique of media images of PWAs, *Danny* nevertheless constitutes one of the most powerful critiques that exists to date. This is in part because it duplicates, in so many of its features, the stereotypes of PWA portraiture, but at the same time reclaims the portrait for the community from which it emerges, the community of gay men, who have thus far been the population most drastically affected by AIDS in the United States. *Danny* accomplishes this through one overriding difference: the formulation of the relationship between artist and subject not as one of empathy or identification, but as one of explicit sexual desire, a desire that simultaneously accounts for Kybartas's subjective investment in the project and celebrates Danny's own sense of gay identity and hard-won sexual freedom.

A great many of the conventions of media portraits of the PWA appear in *Danny,* but their meanings are reinvested or reversed. *Danny* begins, for example, where virtually every other television portrait ends: with the information about the death of the video's subject, here matter-of-factly announced in a rolling text before we have even seen an image. Thus, although the video ends at the second recounting of Danny's death, it does not come as a coda to tell us what has happened to the subject after the tape was made. Indeed, as we discern from the apostrophizing voice-over, the tape was made as a work of mourning, the artist's working through of his loss of a friend in the AIDS movement. The retrospective voice is reinforced by a refusal of the live video image's movement. Using videotape that he shot with Danny during their brief friendship, Kybartas compiled it as a series of stills, which also serves to make it equivalent to the still photographs taken of Danny prior to his illness, when he lived in Miami.

The first words uttered by Danny, in his somewhat difficult-to-understand voice, are the following: "He doesn't refer to me as his son. Instead of saying, 'My son'll be up to get it,' 'The boy'll be up to get it.' Whadaya mean the boy? It makes me feel like Tarzan and the jungle. Me boy." The statement remains somewhat opaque until we come to those fragments of dialogue in which Kybartas queries Danny further about his father. When Danny talks of his decision to return to his parents' home in Steubenville, Ohio, at the moment when he learned he'd have to begin chemotherapy for his Kaposi's sarcoma, he mentions the difficulty of telling his mother, who nevertheless accepted the fact. Kybartas asks, "Were you worried about your dad?" "Yeah," says Danny, "I was wondering how he was going to take having a gay son, and one with AIDS on top of it, but she never told him. I have to watch what I say around him, or if anything about AIDS is on television, my mom flicks it off. She doesn't want him to hear about it."

We are left to imagine Danny's home life, as his father watches his son die and never bothers to ask why. Then, in the final conversation between the two friends before the tape ends, Danny says, "What I should have done this week was to have contacted the funeral home, because I would like to feel secure knowing that I could be buried there, instead of their getting the body and saying, 'No, we can't handle that body,' and my father saying, 'Why?' 'Because he has AIDS.' That's not a time that he needs to be faced with that, not after my dying." Kybartas probes, "Why are you concerned about his reaction to that?," and Danny answers, "Trying to spare his feelings, I guess." "Why?," Kybartas persists. "I guess as much as I dislike him, I don't want to hurt him either." "Why not?," Kybartas chides, and the dialogue fades out.

It is this gruesome family scene, so typical—perhaps even stereotypical—of gay men's relations with their fathers, that is denied in sentimental media stories of gay men going home to die in the caring fold of the family, something they often do as a last resort when medical insurance has run out or disability benefits won't cover the rent.

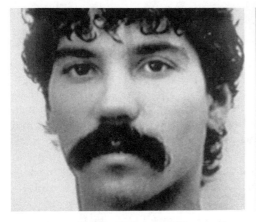

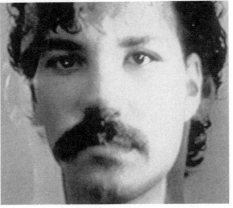

FIGURE 7. Stashu Kybartas, "Danny." FIGURE 8. Stashu Kybartas, "Danny."

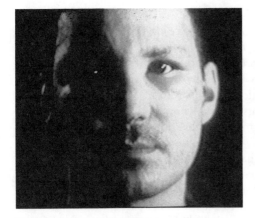

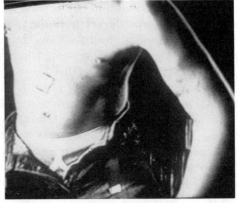

FIGURE 9.   Stashu Kybartas, "Danny."   FIGURE 10.   Stashu Kybartas, "Danny."

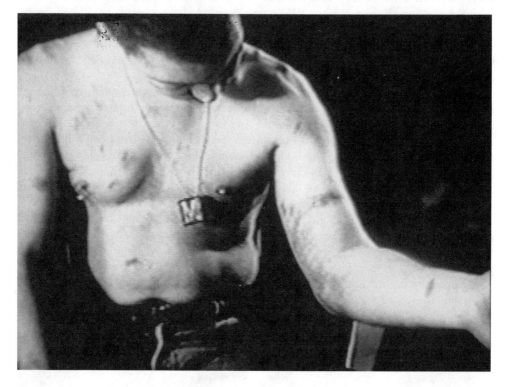

FIGURE 11.   Stashu Kybartas, "Danny."

In the mainstream media, though, this scenario tells of the abandonment of gay men by their friends in the dark and sinful cities they inhabit, and the return to comfort and normality in some small town in the Midwest. But in Kybartas's tape it is the small hometown, a steel town near Pittsburgh, that is dark and sinister, "slowly dying," as Danny puts it, whereas the metropolis to which Danny fled to find his sexual freedom is the very opposite of dark, though it may, in conventional moralizing terms, be sinful—that, of course, is its appeal.

This reversal of mainstream media pieties about hometown USA and the biological family serves to delimit the space of the sexual for gay men, for if Danny's father has not discerned that his son is gay and dying of AIDS, it is because Danny's identity as a sexual being must be disavowed. Kybartas articulates this in the tape by saying, "I wanted you to come and live with us. We'd take care of you. We could go to the gay bars in Pittsburgh, dance, and watch the go-go boys."

Danny's image as a kid who lived for sex is complicated in the video by another subtle reversal. Mainstream coverage of AIDS is padded with portentous pictures of medical procedures—IV needles being inserted, doctors listening through stethoscopes, tinkering in laboratories. Parallel imagery in *Danny* refers not to Danny's disease, but to his profession as a medical technician, showing the procedure of the carotid angiogram that he performed. But just because Danny is a full human being with a respectable profession doesn't mean he's heroicized by Kybartas. Immediately following Danny's reminiscence about his job is the "Miami Vice" sequence, in which Kybartas uses footage from that program's credits as Danny talks about shooting cocaine with shared needles back in 1981, before anyone knew the transmission risks. The result is that still another media myth is interfered with: the one that makes gay men (always presumed to be white and middle class) and IV drug users (presumed to be poor people of color) separate "risk groups."

A standard media device for constructing AIDS as a morality tale uses before-and-after images of people with AIDS. Stuart Marshall's *Bright Eyes,* made for Britain's Channel 4 in 1984, performed a brilliant analysis on the British tabloid *Sunday People*'s use of PWA Kenny Ramsaur to that end. In 1983, ABC's 20/20 also used Kenny Ramsaur to show the effects of AIDS in one of the earliest and most lurid television newsmagazine stories on the subject, narrated by none other than Geraldo Rivera. ABC's camera first shows Ramsaur's face, horribly swollen and disfigured; then snapshots of the handsome, healthy Kenny as hedonistic homosexual appear, after which we return to the live image as the camera pans down to Kenny's arm to see him pull up his sleeve to reveal his KS lesions. Kybartas reworks this ploy in *Danny.* We see snapshots of a young and healthy hedonist in Miami as Danny talks with relish of his life, of how he would spend the day on the beach, return home and let the suntan oil sink in, and then shower. After douching in the shower, he tells us, he would shave his balls and the side of his cock, put on his tight 501s, and go out and cruise. Close-ups of Danny putting in his nipple ring are intercut with a close-up of the nipple surrounded by KS lesions, taken in Kybartas's studio in Pittsburgh during Danny's illness. And when we move from a second series of early snapshots of Danny to the video images of his face, shot after he has returned to Steubenville, it is bloated from chemotherapy. He is nevertheless still fully sexualized. Kybartas, narrating over the image of the face, laments, "Danny, when I look at all these pictures of you, I can see that the chemotherapy caused your appearance to change from week to week. One day when you walked into the studio, I thought you looked like a longshoreman who had just been in a fight.[7] [pause] The only time I saw you cry was on Christmas Eve, when your doctor told you that the chemotherapy was no longer working." This movement back and forth from the tough to the tender, from desiring to grieving in relation to the whole series of images constitutes the major text of the tape, and it may be said to encompass something of the range of gay men's sexuality as well as our present condition. The thematic is most often shown in the revelation of the KS lesions, as time and again we see stop-motion footage of Danny removing his shirt, or as still images show fragments of his chest and arms covered with lesions. But, like scars or tatoos, the lesions are always seen as marking the body as sexually attractive, a sexiness that is indicated by Kybartas in the following way: "Danny, do you remember the first night we were shooting the film at my studio? You'd taken off your shirt and we were looking at all your lesions. Later, as I was rubbing your back and you were telling me about the problems you were having with relationships and sex, something happened. It was suddenly very quiet in the studio, and my heart was beating fast. I don't know what it was . . . the heat, your body. The only sound was the steam hissing out of the radiator. . . ."

After seeing *Danny,* it occurred to me that there is a deeper explanation for portrayals of PWAs, and especially of gay male PWAs, as desperately ill, as either grotesquely disfigured or as having wasted to fleshless, ethereal bodies. These are not images that are intended to overcome our fear of disease and death, as is sometimes claimed. Nor are they meant only to reinforce the status of the PWA as victim or pariah, as we often charge. Rather, they are, precisely, *phobic* images, images of the terror at imagining the person with AIDS as still sexual. In the *Frontline* special the Houston public health commissioner says, with patent fear and loathing, "Fabian was only diagnosed last April. He might live another two years, and furthermore this person is in remission now. He's not demonstrating any *signs* of illness!" The unwillingness to show PWAs as active, as in control of their lives, as acting up and fighting back, is the fear that they might also still be sexual, or as Judy Woodruff said of Fabian Bridges, that "he was a man with AIDS who continued to be promiscuous."

The comfortable fantasy that AIDS would spell the end of gay promiscuity, or perhaps of gay sex altogether, has pervaded American and Western European culture for a decade now. But we will fail to understand its pervasiveness and its representational effects if we think it only occupies the minds of the likes of Jesse Helms and Patrick Buchanan. I want to end, therefore, with a quotation that will bring this phobic fantasy closer to home in the context of cultural studies. In an interview published in the German art magazine *Kunstforum,* Jean Baudrillard appears sanguine about William Burroughs's (and Laurie Anderson's) dictum that "language is a virus."

> Language, particularly in all areas of information, is used in a more and more formulaic way, and thereby gets sicker and sicker from its own formulas. One should no longer speak of sickness, however, but of virality, which is a form of mutation. . . . Perhaps the new pathology of virality is the last remedy against the total disintegration of language and of the body. I don't know, for example, whether a stock market crash such as that of 1987 should be understood as a terrorist process of economy or as a form of viral catharsis of the economic system. Possibly, though, it is like AIDS, if we understand AIDS as a remedy against total sexual liberation, which is sometimes more dangerous than an epidemic, because the latter always ends. Thus AIDS could be understood as a counterforce against the total elimination of structure and the total unfolding of sexuality. (Rötzer, 1990, p. 266)[8]

NOTES

1. Nick and Bebe Nixon, "AIDS Portrait Project Update," January 1, 1988, quoted in the press release for "People with AIDS: Work in Progress," New York, Zabriskie Gallery, 1988 (this exhibition was shown at the same time as the MOMA show).

2. For both *Sixty Minutes* and *20/20,* the ostensible reason for showing the twins is to discuss an experimental bone marrow transplant therapy, which requires an identical twin donor. It does not, of course, require that the donor twin be straight.

3. William Olander (1988), " 'I Undertook this Project as a Personal Exploration of the Human Components of an *Alarming Situation*' 3 Vignettes (2)." The quote used as a title is Rosalind Solomon's.

4. The fascination of the media with the supposed threat of "AIDS carriers" was most dramatically revealed in the response to Randy Shilts's *And the Band Played On,* which focused almost exclusively on Shilts's story of the so-called Patient Zero (see my essay "How to Have

Promiscuity in an Epidemic," in *AIDS: Cultural Analysis/Cultural Activism,* esp. pp. 237–46). The fascination has clearly not abated. At the Sixth International Conference on AIDS in San Francisco, June 20–24, 1990, members of the media took part in a panel addressing "AIDS and the Media: A Hypothetical Case Study." The hypothetical case was that of an American soldier stationed in the Philippines accused of infecting 40 prostitutes. The soldier's "past" had him frequenting prostitutes in Uganda and bathhouses in the Castro district of San Francisco.

5. This introduction by Peter Galassi and the following statements by Nicholas Nixon are transcribed from Nixon's talk at the Museum of Modern Art, October 11, 1988.

6. *Danny,* 1987, is distributed by Video Data Bank, Chicago.

7. The sexual attractiveness of the gay clone was constructed through stylistic reference to clichéd hyper-masculine professions such as the cowboy, policeman, sailor, and, indeed, the longshoreman.

8. Thanks to Hans Haacke for bringing this interview to my attention.

DISCUSSION: Douglas Crimp

MARTIN ALLOR: I would like to invite you to go back to your opening comments and talk about the resources that you drew on from gay culture, gay politics, gay theory for your analysis.

CRIMP: Since 1987, when I got involved with ACT UP, the cultural and political questions I've wanted to address, and the analysis I've wanted to provide, have arisen from within the movement. ACT UP has been, among other things, an extraordinary resource, a reservoir of knowledge about every aspect of AIDS in the United States. The strength of the AIDS activist movement derives in part from the many various skills and kinds of expertise members of ACT UP are able to bring to the movement or to develop while working within it. After producing the special issue of *October* on AIDS in 1987, it became clear to me that my own expertise involved problems of representation and that this was the area I wanted to focus on.

When Nicholas Nixon's PWA portraits were shown at the Museum of Modern Art and a group from ACT UP decided to protest, the discussion at the weekly ACT UP meeting was divided. Many people still think of artists and museums as somehow sacred, as above politics. For them, a demonstration in a museum is tantamount to censorship of "free expression." When some members of ACT UP did demonstrate, they produced a handout with which I generally agreed, insofar as it was able to detail the effects of these representations through their effacement of the social and political context of AIDS. But in the end, that flier resorted to the demand for "positive images." That was a demand I wanted to rethink. On the one hand, I wanted to show the similarity of Nixon's and Rosalind Solomon's fine-art PWA portraits to the stereotypical "negative images" produced by broadcast television. But I also wanted to suggest a different, more critical "solution" than the call for positive images. The videotape *Danny,* which I'd seen a year earlier and had wanted to write about, provided the example of a more complex representation and at the same time suggested the less conscious agenda of the stereotype.

My hope is that the work I do will have direct effects on the cultural analyses that take place all the time within the AIDS activist movement. At the same time, I know that my primary audience is an academic one. I've taught courses on the representation of AIDS in universities and art schools, and I lecture mostly within academic and art-world institutions. I find that it is very useful to bring the example and the lessons of a direct-action movement into these contexts. It provides a concrete grounding for theoretical work and it puts the politics of AIDS on the agenda where it is otherwise largely absent.

LAURA KIPNIS: I have a question for you about the way that consent functions in your argument in regard to the relations of production of the images that you talked about. The question is prompted partly because of the way the issue of consent comes up so similarly in the feminist anti-pornography movement and the work of people like Dworkin and MacKinnon, who have the problem of how to deal with the fact of women in the porn industry, and deal with it by obliterating the notion of consent. Particularly MacKinnon, who I remember here at the Marxism Conference in 1983, explicitly said that there is no possibility of consent for women in patriarchal social relations. And the problem with this politically is that it creates a vanguard party out of that branch of the women's movement which claims to speak for all women. I'm certain that that's not the position you would take, or that ACT UP takes in regard to speaking for people with AIDS.

CRIMP: I wanted to deal with the question of consent in Nixon's and Solomon's photographs because it's been the means by which their apologists distinguish these representations from those of photo-journalism or TV. And I hoped, through the example of Fabian Bridges, to show both how similar the representations in different cultural contexts are and just how manipulated the notion of consent can be. But you're right, I certainly don't want to find myself in the position of suggesting anything like diminished capacity or even special vulnerability of people with AIDS who participate in these projects. I do think that there is an aura that attaches to art (and to art photography) that is very seductive to people, especially people whose lives are underrepresented. And I think many artists traffic in that aura. For me, the more important question would be, what is the stake of the *artist* in such a project? As representations, these photographs are themselves productive of social relations; but they are also the product of a social relation, one which is obscured in the photograph itself. Without any indication of the subjective investment of the photographer, as Allan Sekula said, that "intimate, human-scale relationship suffers mystification." In addition, photography is a very impoverished medium for representing anything so complex as AIDS, as *living* with AIDS.

QUESTION: Would you elaborate on your comments about the remark that the difficulty cultural studies—and virtually every other field within the academy—has in addressing directly questions of sexual identity. Has the equation of gay identity with AIDS in academia provided a cover for people to interrogate questions about their own sexuality?

CRIMP: What I wanted to make clear, first of all, was that the inclusion of discussions of AIDS within a cultural studies conference must not be taken as an inclusion of queer sexuality. The tendency to collapse AIDS and homosexuality has had murderous effects for both people with AIDS and gay men and lesbians since the beginning of the epidemic. Not only is there an important, mostly suppressed, history of gay and lesbian culture that is prior to and separate from the catastrophe of AIDS, but any attempt to understand AIDS apart from that history will be unable to comprehend the kinds of contributions to fighting AIDS that gay men and lesbians have made.

The other obvious point—one that anti-homophobic work has attempted to make for some time now—is that any area of study will be insufficient to the extent that it omits sexuality. Sexuality, or queer culture, is no more a narrow special interest than is gender, or race, or class. There now begins to be significant pressure within the academy to address issues of gay and lesbian sexuality. It comes from a generation of scholars and activists who grew up in the post-Stonewall era, were able to be "out" in university settings, and through such programs as women's studies were able to produce openly gay work. This leads almost inevitably to a demand for gay studies courses and programs, which I think, given the homophobic climate we live in, are absolutely necessary. But such academic ghettoization is a short-term solution. I think it would be much more productive for a broader area of study, such as cultural studies, to include work on sexuality within its purview. And this means, just has it has for feminism and anti-racist struggles, that everyone will have to take account of sexuality, of gay and lesbian sexuality specifically. We must all learn to recognize how structurally pervasive homophobia is in our culture, often even within progressive discourses.

9

What is Real and What is Not:
Female Fabulations in Cultural Analysis

LIDIA CURTI

Cultural Studies at Champaign

"Cultural studies now and in the future" is a very optimistic title, but this optimism can only be based on the awareness of a deep crisis. *Crisis* has been the password of the field from Hoggart to Williams, from Hall to Jameson and Hebdige; the crisis in English, to use Hoggart's words, fostered its start. Today this word could be replaced by another more apocalyptic term: Baudrillard, speaking of the "transpolitical," says that "it is the site of catastrophe, not of crisis any more" (cf. Baudrillard 1983a, p. 23). This discourse of crisis touches intellectual work as well—our work, our research, our role. Thus we are here to find a sort of anchorage, to utter a temporary "truth" on the state of affairs, while being aware, more than in the past, of the loss of that centrality which our role as intellectuals had conferred on us, and with it of the break up of former methodological, literary, philosophical guarantees.

The previous decades, in spite of all, have given us some strong narratives: structuralism, semiotics, psychoanalysis, Marxism. Today, in front of them, we experience a sense of confusion and indecision. As Barthes says in his autobiography, speaking of himself in the third person, "His relation with psychoanalysis is not a strict one (though he cannot take the resolution of contestation, or refusal). It is an undecided relation" (1980, p. 170). As researchers, teachers, interpreters of art, and sometime prophets of reality, we remain on the margins. Yet our prophecies and our readings are now subjected to rhetorical analysis, like the poems on which we are commenting.

This sense of margins comes first of all from the experience of being women and feminists. With its reference to a divided and plural subjectivity, feminism has inspired and informed much of this contemporary sense of crisis; at the same time, some see feminism itself—with its belief in social progress, transformation, and the binary structure of sexual difference—as one of the great metanarratives in decline. Derrida has advocated replacing the dualistic opposition with an indefinite series of differences, in an anti-dialectic movement: "When we speak here of sexual difference, we must distinguish between opposition and difference. Opposition is two, opposition is man/woman. Difference, on the other hand, can be an indefinite number of sexes . . . All that you can call 'gift'—love, jouissance—is absolutely forbidden, is forbidden by the dual opposition" (1987, p. 198). In *In Other Worlds,* Gayatri Spivak refers to margins in speaking of literary criticism. According to her, every privileged explanation must be questioned even while it is being expressed: "That is the question I will put on the agenda: the pedagogy of the humanities as the arena of cultural explanations that question the explanations of culture" (Spivak, 1987, p. 117). Spivak's book concludes by stating that a textual gap inevitably exceeds the knowledge of the textual critic: "In the mise-en-scène where the text persistently rehearses itself, writer and reader are both upstaged. If the reader clandestinely carves out a piece of action by using the text as a tool, it's only in celebration of the text's apartness *(être-à-l'écart)* . . . in that scene of writing, the authority of the author (writer, reader, teacher) . . . must be content to stand in the wings" (1987, p. 268). In fact, the explanation of a text or a phenomenon, though necessary and, I would say, unavoidable, also establishes the marginality of the critic or observer.

Stuart Hall, too, speaks of margins in his essay "Minimal Selves": "Thinking about my own sense of identity, I realize that it has always depended on the fact of being a migrant, on the difference from the rest of you . . . Now that, in the postmodern age, you all feel so dispersed, I become centered. What I've thought of as dispersed and fragmented comes . . . to be the representative postmodern experience! Welcome to migranthood" (1987a, p. 44). This centrality of "marginalization" is a paradox and carries the risk that once more we become prophets, the prophets of margins. But it is not simply a question of moving the terms around (black instead of white, women instead of men, and so on); rather, it is a substantial change deriving directly from decentralization. Hall himself, speaking about black youth in contemporary London, deprived of rights, fragmented and dispersed, observes that in spite of all that "they look as if they own the territory" (1987b, p. 44). I have had a similar experience with my students: they might be defined as people who have come from the province to the town—and the town is Naples, a very particular reality—if we had not just said that dualistic terms like province and city, center and periphery, do not make much sense any longer. They live the conflict between the originary cultural traditions back there and this metropolitan, chaotic, post-earthquake experience. The crisis is there, but it is part of their territory, the substance of their experience in all its aspects—life, study, entertainment, daily choices. The crisis is an essential part, "a way, however weak, of experiencing reality, not as an object that we own and pass on, but as a horizon, a background against which we modestly move," as Gianni Vattimo says (1985, p. 21).

Cultural studies has from the start given attention to margins; we could say that it was born on the margins, and is now at the center, in the formulation of this conference. We are going to have our say, while aware of speaking on the margins—but are we? That is our contradiction here—the awareness of "undecidability" and the necessity of deciding: deciding means "determining" but also "cutting the knots" or "putting an end to," as it comes from *de* (thoroughly) + *caedere* (cut). Every choice involves an affirmation and a negation. "By doing we forgo," says Nietzsche in *The Gay Science*.

Gramsci at Disneyland; Brecht at the Bonaventure Hotel

This contradiction has been at the center of the eighties debate between modernism and postmodernism; on the one hand, we know there can be no clear dividing line between the vague and ever-shifting meanings of these two terms; the *post,* along with the absence of a new definition, asserts that vagueness as well as the impossibility of uttering a new name. On the other hand, the debate is heated and has by now become an autonomous discourse, a sort of genre in itself, like the *"querelle des anciens et des modernes"* and the dispute between classics and romantics (cf. Ferraris, 1983, pp. 7–8). Everybody speaks of its futility before launching headlong into it.

Like all polemics, the debate has created artificial and rarefied scenery in which structuralism goes out and hermeneutics enters, scientism exists and ethics enters, and so on. Rightly enough, Jim Collins observes that "distinctions between the two move-ments/moments have tended towards the hyperbolic" (1989, p. 113). It can be linked with the oppositional discourse that has traversed cultural studies for the previous two decades, starting with structuralism and culturalism and proceeding to psychoanalysis and Marxism. These theories offered different contexts for such oppositions as inside versus outside, individual psyche versus social reality, and personal feelings versus col-lective political action. The debates of the last decade maintain some of the old terms and add new ones, such as meaning and surface, political commitment and individual hedonism. The correspondences may be inverted: feelings may be identified with social reality or with evasion and fantasy. Eventually each term seems to be claimed by all sides. In this debate, which has been mostly defensive, people like Baudrillard and Jameson have been treated as prophets of postmodernism—Baudrillard, in spite of his apocalyptic vision; Jameson of his defense of modernism.[1]

The British debate has been marked by a familiar suspicion toward definitions or labels, toward the -isms. The development of cultural studies has been fraught with such oppositions—Thompson's argument on the "poverty of theory" and his pragmatic attack on foreign-ness come to mind, but there have been other turns in earlier decades.[2] Once more, as in the past, an atmosphere of suspicion and guilt, sin and repentance, has surrounded theory and in particular the theory that comes from elsewhere. The geo-graphical and theoretical elsewhere is often France, sometimes Italy, sometimes Ger-many. The debate coincides with a difficult time of transition for the left in general, and for Marxist critical discourse in particular. Whether right or wrong, postmodernism is associated with the end of ideology and the decline of master narratives. And Marxism has certainly been the latter if not the former.

In the beginning postmodernism was seen as a pluralist, capitalist discourse op-posing Marxism (and what it stood for). Things have been moving rapidly: with the great changes within socialism, oppositions are not so easily established any longer. Similarly in that first phase of the debate, the connection between aesthetics and politics was presented as quite unmediated and simple. I am referring in particular to an exchange of the early eighties among Anderson, Eagleton, Jameson, and Latimer in *New Left Review*. Perry Anderson, in "Modernity and Revolution," took his start from Marshall Berman's *All that is Solid Melts into Air* (1982). Anderson, though admiring its rigorously Marxist inspiration, criticized its reading of the dialectics of modernism as a revolutionary process. In the name of a strictly Leninist concept of revolution, he condemned both modernism and postmodernism as empty terms, "one void chasing another, in a serial regression of self-congratulatory chronology" (1984, p. 113). He placed both among those "morbid symptoms" that, according to Gramsci, appear in the interregnum be-tween the old and the new, when the new is not yet here (1984, p. 112).

Gramsci appears here in the debate and will be invoked again on the strength of the concrete character of his analysis, which keeps him safe from hated theory and underlines his political purity. Bill Schwartz more recently sees him as the last bulwark of a totalizing theory of knowledge as opposed to the informal, fragmentary world of the spectacle ("Gramsci goes to Disneyland" is the title of his essay), forgetting that Gramsci had developed the art of the fragment to perfection. The brilliant intuitions of *Americanism and Fordism* and all his work on popular culture make it difficult to view him in an anti-American and anti-popular frame.[3] As Dick Hebdige writes, "It would be foolish to present a polar opposition between the Gramscian line(s) and the (heter-ogeneous) Posts. There is too much shared historical and intellectual ground . . . from the perspectives heavily influenced by the Gramscian approach, nothing is anchored to the *grand récits,* to master narratives, to stable (positive) identities, to fixed and certain meanings: all social and semantic relations are contestable, hence mutable" (1988a, p. 206). Gramsci, however, is not the only name standing for nostalgia. Lukács, Brecht, and Benjamin are invoked both in Jameson's famous essay (1984) and in Terry Eagleton's reply to it (1985).[4] Reviewing Jameson's essay, Franco Rella, though no fan of post-modernity, criticizes Jameson's generic and constant reference to socio-economic reality motivated, in his opinion, by the nostalgia "of Brechtian art and by Lukács' marxist theory: once more the two stumbling blocks of modernity" (1989, p. 19). Rella sees such nostalgia as the "sickness" marring the whole debate.

Jameson's essay cannot be discussed in detail here. His vision is too complex to squeeze into any simple dualistic opposition. He carries on a sustained critique of post-modernity while underlining that it is no longer possible to ignore this new map of knowledge. He himself speaks of the decline of the dialectics between substance and appearance, the latent and the manifest, the authentic and the inauthentic. Instead there are surfaces made of textual practices, discourses, games as in *pastiche,* in the past revisited, in the metropolitan collage. The Bonaventure Hotel is the object replacing the work of art. Like the Beaubourg and other buildings of the kind, it is a miniaturized city, a self-referential space where movement is the emblem of movement and the roads are predetermined narrative paths for visitors to follow. "Here the narrative stroll has been underscored, symbolized, reified, and replaced by a transportation machine, which becomes the allegorical signifier of that older promenade we are no longer allowed to conduct on our own" (Jameson, 1984, p. 82). This limitation to individual creativity and lack of distance in critical discourse are the features of postmodernism that he most severely criticizes, along with its links to late capitalism. He confirms his mixed feelings in a recent conversation with Stuart Hall. Speaking of the "plebianization of culture," he says: "That's a crucial part of postmodernism, which underscores its ambiguity. One cannot object to the democratization of culture, but one must object to other features of it. Those mixed feelings have to be preserved in any analysis of the postmodern" (Hall and Jameson, 1990, p. 29). In spite of some shift in his recent positions, Jameson still regrets the absence of "reflexive, critical distance" (p. 30).

Baudrillard is much more critical, even in his more recent and less pessimistic *America,* where he extends his *"j'accuse"* to all the appliances of this postmodern world:

> Is this still architecture, this pure illusionism, this mere box of spatio-temporal tricks? Ludic and hallucinogenic, is this post-modern architecture? . . . Everywhere the transparency of interfaces ends in internal refraction. Everything pretentiously termed "communication" and "interaction"—walkman, dark glasses, automatic household appliances, hi-tech cars, even the perpetual dialogue with the computer—ends up with each monad retreating into the shade of its own formula, into its self-regulating little corner and its artificial immunity. (1989, pp. 59–60)

Brecht and Benjamin are the main constellations of a lost planet, the lost planet that is at the center of an essay written by Dick Hebdige in 1987, "The Bottom Line on Planet One." This successful science-fiction metaphor introduces the planet of modernism (one) as opposed to that of surfaces, simulacra, and simulations (two). Three is the planet of reality, of politics, of the underdeveloped and hungry third world. The first is the place of nostalgia, the second of escape and evasion. The magazine *The Face,* considered by Hebdige's students, to his dismay, "the Ur Text for Magazine Construction" (Hebdige 1987a, p. 29), is the emblem of this escapism. The essay concludes with a call for a world in which passions still have a place.

However, this essay, not very dissimilar from Jameson's, gives a picture of post-modernism that is pervaded by an involuntary fascination. It is superfluous to recall here that Hebdige is by many considered one component of the postmodern vogue, with his *Subculture: The Meaning of Style* (1979), an analysis of the importance of style and appearance both in representations and in reality, in the arts not less than in popular culture.[5]

There have increasingly been contrasting voices speaking for the "New Times," or for less rigid oppositions. Some are coming from the "historical" group that had lived the preeminence of the Marxist-historicist stress of the seventies at the Birmingham Centre: Angela McRobbie, Iain Chambers, and Ian Connell have spoken in favor of the potentialities of this cultural pluralism.[6] They were all working on popular culture, and the shift that took the argument out of the strictures of a debate came precisely from that field.[7]

Andreas Huyssen, though not through adhesion to the new sensibility, was the first to point out more consciously that postmodernity had the merit of overcoming the modernist division between high and popular art. An interesting aspect of his study is his denial of the identification between the avant-garde and modernism, an identification that in the debate to which I have just referred was taken for granted: "Despite its ultimate and perhaps inevitable failure, the historical avant garde aimed at developing an alternative relationship between high art and mass culture and thus should be distinguished from modernism, which for the most part insisted on the inherent hostility between the high and the low" (Huyssen, 1986a, p. viii). His book *After the Great Divide* marks a revival of interest in the avant-garde and the post-avant-garde that has influenced the subsequent debate for the better, pushing it beyond the generic tones of polemical writings.

The magazine *Marxism Today* exemplifies the increasing attention to the debate within British Marxism and the British Communist Party (which by now must be one of the few parties left in the world with this name). Its special issue called *New Times* (October 1988) was a bold attempt to bring together Marxism and postmodernism.

Dick Hebdige himself, in his recent book *Hiding In the Light,* though unchanging in his suspicion and caution, moves away from that Marxist "religion" that is today under attack and proposes a Marxism without guarantees—"a marxism more prone perhaps to listen, learn, adapt and to appreciate, for instance, that words like 'emergency' and 'struggle' don't just mean fight, conflict, war, and death but birthing, the prospect of new life emerging: a struggling to the light" (1988a, p. 207). These accents and contributions go beyond simple mediation; rather they indicate a shift, a move forward that cancels any simple oppositional paradigm.

Difference deconstructed, or Feminism "a St. Germain-de-Près"

The place that feminist criticism occupies in the debate is rather controversial, though the existence of a growing critical literature explores the relation between feminism and postmodernism and suggests generally that there are many affinities between the two. Patricia Waugh, for example, sees common concerns in their developments since the 1960s. "Both are concerned to disrupt traditional boundaries: between 'art' and 'life,' masculine and feminine, high and popular culture, the dominant and the marginal. Both examine the cultural consequences of the decline of a consensus aesthetics, of an effective 'literary' voice, or the absence of a strong sense of stable subjectivity" (1989, p. 6). At the same time, a strong anti-theoretical component within the Women's Liberation Movement has created some suspicion of postmodernism as well as resistance to the anti-social emphasis of poststructuralism. The latter seems a stumbling block to Chris Weedon, one more voice from the Centre for Contemporary Cultural Studies. Although her *Feminist Practice and Poststructuralist Theory* (1987) actually commences with the assumption that postructuralism offers a useful framework for feminist struggle, she goes on to note that "deconstructionist" approaches to textual analysis, which share a disregard for the wider historically specific discursive context of reading and writing and the power relations which structure the literary field itself, do not meet feminist needs" (p. 165).

The feminist delay in entering the debate is underlined by Andreas Huyssen, whose "Mapping the Postmodern" emphasizes the affinities between postmodernism and feminism (stress on the hidden and the marginal, denial of canonized forms, fragmentation of the subject) and expresses regret that feminist criticism has kept out of the postmodernist debate (Huyssen, 1990, p. 250). Craig Owens, in "The Discourse of Others: Feminists and Postmodernism," observes that the "absence of discussions of sexual difference in writings about postmodernism, as well as the fact that few women have engaged in the modernism/postmodernism debate, suggest that postmodernism may be another masculine invention to exclude women" (Owens, 1985, p. 61). Waugh herself devotes attention to this absence, at least before the eighties: "During the 1960s, as Vonnegut waves a fond goodbye to character in fiction, women writers are beginning, *for the first time in history,* to construct an identity . . . As male writers lament its demise, women writers have not yet experienced that subjectivity which will give them a sense of personal autonomy, continuous identity, a history and agency in the world" (Waugh, 1989, p. 6). Such identity construction, however, runs the risk of reviving the ghost of the old dichotomy between emancipation and liberation, with the latter always denying the value of recuperating male ground.

I would add that one must not forget that, however slowly, feminism was developing its own creative voice, whether one wants to call it postmodern or not, and that in the early eighties, once it enters the debate, it has the task of disentangling itself from too mechanical an identification with the male seers. The association of French and American thought has been fruitful in the critical writings of Gayatri Spivak, Alice Jardine, Teresa de Lauretis, and others, but their work can in no way be simply identified with that of Derrida or Barthes. The same is true of their French counterparts, with thinkers such as Michelle Montrelay, Luce Irigaray, and Hélène Cixous. As to Julia Kristeva, she occupies a space of her own, outside specific trends or movements.

It is also true, as Waugh rightly notices, that discussions of and attempts to define postmodernism have long ignored gender or denied its relevance: "The deconstructionist tenet that the ego must be eradicated or dismembered, that the text is all that counts, and that discourse must be at the level of language alone would be a form of death for the female experience" (Frederick Karl, quoted by Waugh, 1989 p. 27). On the whole, the debate has been, as Owens notes (1985, p. 59), "scandalously in-different" to feminist issues.

On the other hand, some see in feminism one of the main components of postmodernism, the weakening of a unitary, universal subject. Linda Nicholson, for example, gives a long list of points of overlap in her introduction to *Feminism/Postmodernism:* the opposition to "the supposed neutrality and objectivity of the academy," to reason, to the autonomous self and other Enlightenment ideals that have reflected male Western values. "On such grounds," she concludes, disagreeing with critics who emphasize the transitional character of postmodernism, "postmodernism would appear to be a cultural ally of feminism" (1990, p. 5).

The female character of postmodernism has been asserted by quite a few male critics. In *Les stratégies fatales* (1983a), Baudrillard announces that in entering the world of "models, fashion, simulation," the world of the "event without consequences," we enter the universe of seduction and metamorphosis (cf. p. 9 and ff). As his argument becomes more and more apocalyptic, it becomes apparent that this is the universe of the woman, being deprived of all subjectivity: "What gives her power is . . . her triumphant in-difference, her triumphant lack of subjectivity" (p. 113). Craig Owens, in more positive tones, deals with the intersection between the feminist critique of patriarchy and the postmodernist critique of representation: "If one of the most salient aspects of our postmodern culture is the presence of an insistent feminist voice, theories of postmodernism have tended either to neglect or to repress that voice . . . I would like to propose, however, that women's insistence on difference and incommensurability may not only be compatible with, but also an instance of postmodern thought" (1985, p. 61). More cautiously, Huyssen writes in "Mass Culture as Woman: Modernism's Other": "Whether one uses the term 'postmodernism' or not, there cannot be any question about the fact that the position of women in contemporary culture and society, and their effect on that culture, is fundamentally different from what it used to be in the period of high modernism and the historical avant garde" (1986b, p. 202).

As to Derrida himself, quite clearly his thought owes much to women, as they occupy a crucial space in his work and in his metaphorical web of terms: *undecidability, différance, border, hymen, invagination,* and others. The concept of woman has inspired his consistent critique of the European phallogocentric structure, as he himself says in an interview given to *subjects/objects* in 1984 and republished in *Men in Feminism.* He immediately proceeds to say (even people like Derrida "proceed," and it is uncanny how the idea of progress insinuates itself in the following quotation) that his first position must be superseded: "We need to find some way to progress strategically. Starting with deconstruction of phallogocentrism, and using the feminine force, so to speak, in this move and then—and this would be the second stage or second level—to give up the opposition between men and women" (1987, p. 194). Cary Nelson speaks of Derrida's contradictory and hesitant relation to feminism as "a totalizing cultural project" in his "Men, Feminism: The Materiality of Discourse." Derrida's difficulties are with its notion of progress and its simplistic dichotomy between the sexes, which make feminism, according to Derrida, another version of "phallocentric mastery" (cf. Nelson, 1987, p. 168).

The deconstructionist position has been criticized by Teresa de Lauretis in *Technologies of Gender.* She points out that Derrida, in his critique of phallogocentrism, uses women as mere instruments for theoretical discourse. Just as Nietzsche positioned woman as the symbol of Truth, the discourse of woman becomes the discourse of male philosophers, her problem becomes man's problem. Philosophers speak about woman, never about real women. In spite of her "deconstructive" positions, Spivak in "Displacement and the Discourse of Woman," similarly observes that deconstruction defines its own "displacement" through woman, and woman becomes its figuration: "The discourse of man is the metaphor of woman" (1983, p. 169). And Rosi Braidotti, though defining herself as a "follower of Nietzsche and of contemporary neonietzschian thought" (1987, p. 189), refuses woman as metaphor of the unrepresentable and of the undecidable: " 'The praise of the feminine' is confused with the apology of shadow, dispersion, silence, mystery, of the eternal wandering" (pp. 198–99).

The issue of difference has brought about what could be called a postmodern shift within feminism. Bringing forward previous oppositions between culturalism and essentialism, it has seen the opposing fronts of those who, like Irigaray and Wittig, see difference as an unrenounceable difference, and those who defend the existence of multiple differences.[8] In *This Sex Which Is Not One,* Luce Irigaray speaks of the "apartness" of being a woman, apartness even from language: "I am a woman, I am a female sexed being. The motive of my work lies in the impossibility of articulating such a proposition; in fact its utterance is in many ways nonsensical, unsuitable (unseemly), indecent . . . In other words, to articulate the reality of my sex is impossible in discourse" (1978, p. 123). Gayatri Spivak polemically declares that essentialism is a trap and, following the deconstructive lesson, that "no rigorous definition of anything is ultimately possible, so that if one wants to, one could go on deconstructing the opposition between man and woman, and finally show that it is a binary opposition that displaces itself" (1987, p. 77). Teresa de Lauretis stresses that the paradigm of a universal sexual opposition keeps feminist thought anchored to Western patriarchal thought and makes it impossible to articulate the difference among women: "I see a shift, a development . . . in the feminist understanding of female subjectivity: a shift from the earlier view of woman defined purely by sexual difference (i.e., in relation to man) to the more difficult and complex notion that the female subject is a site of differences" (1986, p. 14).

This extension does not only include economic, racial, and cultural differences but also those existing among women. Julia Kristeva insists on the importance of not creating a new totalitarism in which the female universe is considered to be made of "equals": it would only be a mechanical and useless substitution of one universal for another. She refers to women's writing in particular: "Who is interested in asking a woman to write like (all) other women? That there is such a generalization as woman's condition should be the lever to allow each woman to utter her singularity" (1979, p. 88). After sameness, it is necessary to deny the love of sameness, to look for difference.[9] The difference between one woman and another is a discourse that has been neglected in the first triumphal phase of the discovery of woman as the same, and has become necessary in the reflections on the *post.* The difficult play between sameness and difference is a crucial element in the formation of women's identity. Braidotti, though accepting the experience of separateness, has emphasized the importance of the "infinite richness of our singular differing the one from the other" (1987, p. 192). She uses the example of the inequality between herself as a teacher in women's studies and her pupils to underline the complexity of the female symbolic world. In *In Other Worlds,* Spivak perceptively deals with the problem as a feminist teacher relating to her pupils, a problem that is an important part of my life and work as well. The relation to the other woman, according to Nadia Fusini, implies "dis-symmetry, dis-parity, dis-tance, dis-equality." She recommends that we "adopt a pattern of subtler, finer oppositions than those used up to now . . . in order to avoid returning to positions dictated, imposed, by the thought we wish to deconstruct" (1987, 259–60). She thus recommends praising that very identification—woman/undecidability—that causes so much disagreement among feminists.

The refusal of a binary opposition comes not only from feminists allied with deconstruction but also from those allied with psychoanalysis, working with and sometimes against Freud and Lacan. In addition to the French feminists, Jacqueline Rose represents an important voice: "Feminism, through its foregrounding of sexuality (site of fantasies, impasses, conflict and desire) and of sexual difference (the structure towards which all of this constantly tends but against which it just as constantly breaks) is in a privileged position to challenge the dualities (inside/outside, victim/aggressor, real event/fantasy, and even good/evil) on which so much traditional politics has so often relied" (1986 p. 15). The challenge to those dualities seems to involve an important convergence between feminism and postmodernism; the challenge to the opposition between reality and fantasy, history and stories, has been particularly strong within cultural studies.

In recasting these terms into more extensive narratives, both historical and imaginary, a complex construction—fabulation as the mark of the "feminine"—becomes central. Though fabulation has in the past often been contrasted with the concrete lives of women and men, a new interest in the issues of pleasure, fantasy, and the body has encouraged a new focus on fiction, art, and creativity, and has weakened the barrier between what is fiction and what is not. I would like to argue that fact and fiction are different but both crucial aspects of the same reality. Here the debate within history studies suggests that there are histories and not one history; hidden histories emerge that parallel official ones. Michel Foucault's *Moi Pierre Riviére* is at one time the documentation of a criminal case, the study of the power relations between psychiatry and law at the beginning of the nineteenth century, and a personal memoir whose "stupefying" beauty is underlined by the author in what has become one of the great novels of our century. Fantasy becomes another way to connect with reality and history.

Female Fabulations

Fiction flows between life and imagination, between history and everyday life, between anthropological and novelistic orderings of meaning. As de Certeau says, "Our stories order our world, providing the mimetic and mythical structures for experience" (1984, p. 87).

Fables and myth have a longstanding link to gender, to the feminine. Scheherazade, in the active role of story teller, provided the means to sustain life. Laura Mulvey links the Sphinx and her riddles to the enigma of sexual difference and connects women to the narrative drive: "Curiosity describes a desire to know something secret so strongly that it is experienced like a drive. It is a source of danger and pleasure and knowledge . . . In the myths of Eve and Pandora, curiosity lay behind the first woman's desire to penetrate a forbidden secret that precipitated the fall of man. These myths associate female curiosity with an active narrative function" (1989, p. x). Mythical stories are fabulations of women. Probably not created by women, they are narratives, like other dominant discourses, that are used as metaphors. Yet women have been important motors of these mythical (his)tories in which history comes from discord, and discord comes from women.[10] Helen, Medea, Europa, Arianna, Io, and Phaedra were objects of rape, kidnapping, abandonment, and betrayal. At the same time, they were also subjects—of pleasure, movement, revenge, and betrayal in their own turn. As Eco has commented, "The novel as a genre may disappear, but not narrative, as it has a biological function" (Umberto Eco, interviewed by J. Le Goff in the *Nouvel Observateur*, reprinted in *las Repubblica—Mercurio*, February 24, 1990). Stephen Heath has similarly observed that there are "fictions everywhere, all pervasive, with consumption obligatory by virtue of this omnipresence, a veritable requirement of our social existence. We cannot live today without contact with this fictional continuum" (1982, p. 85). For the remainder of this paper I will be considering this age old centrality of narrative and its intimate linkage to the idea of the feminine in terms of a particular contemporary genre (and technology)—one called "women's television." Women's television, that is, soap opera, is filled with invention rather than information, phantasy rather than facts, tales rather than events; that endless flow of narratives crossing the screen both horizontally and vertically, in parallel lines or in close succession. Its form is one of suspension, both because soap operas are serial and because they move from one interrogation to another, one enigma to another. It is as if they reproduce even outside the single narrative the structure of narrative itself.

The Space of the Female Eye

Do such "female" narratives as soap opera establish the existence of women's subjectivity on the small screen? What is the dialectic between woman as subject and object, as spectator and as character? It would be easier just watching and liking it; but liking soap opera is still quite a suspect activity. Dorothy Hobson, writing about the English soap opera *Crossroads* notes the contradiction between disparaging critical judgments and its enormous popularity among women viewers: "*Crossroads* would seem to be the most maligned program on British television. Alone among the few soap operas currently appearing on our screens, it is at the same time enormously popular and yet devastatingly criticized" (1982, p. 36).

Romance and love are also suspect, though it may be slightly more fashionable for women to find pleasure in them. The positions range from contempt for "silly novels by lady novelists" and the "sentimental rubbish" that is produced for women to the scientifically argued thesis that women "seek to escape from reality."[11] This moralistic attitude carries over to the analysis of women as objects of the look; the existence of women's gaze has at times been forgotten on the assumption that our guilty pleasures derive from watching other women or ourselves through men's eyes.

The advantages of psychoanalytic theory in analyzing the conscious and unconscious pleasure of the viewer are partially offset by a limited view of woman as subject who, if she exists at all, is seen largely as sharer and accomplice of the voyeuristic and fetishistic look. In the strict division of labor established within a heterosexual economy, the space left for the woman viewer is minimal.

This is one reason why closer attention is now paid to the complex and contradictory patterns of women's "ways of looking," most notably in feminist film criticism. Thus Jackie Stacey, in "Desperately Seeking Difference," poses the following question: "If these pleasures have been organized in accordance with the needs, desires and fears of heterosexual masculinity, then what is the place of women's desire towards women within this analysis of narrative cinema?" (1988, p. 112). And Julia Lesage, in her analysis of D. W. Griffith's *Broken Blossoms,* says: "The critical question that remains unresolved as a feminist viewer is this: where does Lucy's pathos, which affects me so strongly, derive from? Are my eyes constantly on Lucy in the way that a male viewer's would be, insofar as traditional feature films constantly have us look at women as objects in stories told through men's eyes?" (1987, p. 250).

Stacey, speaking of "difference and desire among women," points out that the relation between identification and desire is one of complex interplay rather than reciprocal elision (1988, p. 129). The look of women at other women is not mechanically divided between identification or (by analogy with male looking) objectification. Women's pleasure has many complex components, among which there is a strong autonomous element. In the most banal of these female narratives women are present in multiple roles: viewers, actresses, characters, writers, producers. This diffused subject works against the singular universality assumed by common sense. The passage from a centered subject to a dispersed one seems to be a feature of women's space on the small screen. Neither the singular subject nor the displacement into a third person, but the multiple points of a voyage of the "I" along the narrative path.

Bodies, Stories, Identities

There is much to be said on the use and abuse of stereotypes in television narratives, in which everything is stated and counterstated, everything can be read in a different way. We can refer to the Gramscian difference between common sense and good sense: in spite of all, television narratives often demystify the very commonsensical situations they are presenting. Any story can be inscribed in the text through contradictory images, denials, constant erasures, but infinite variations come above all from the decoding: the possibility of reading stereotypes against the grain, of playing between sense and senses. Cultural ambiguities, for instance, influence how the charm of the dark woman operates in different contexts, how the clichés of masculinity and femininity are perceived, and how they can be deflated by kitsch or irony.

Character, this solid structural whole of much great literature, loses all coherence and undergoes a deconstructive process usually found only in experimental narrative. The search for identity is reflected in the play on identities that is at the center of these narratives: split and change of identities, loss of memory (this one is insistent, and its variations are infinite), the reduplication of characters and actors. The change of actors in fact intersects with this complex play, bringing the reality out there into the fantasy world. Identity becomes a shifting concept and moves from one body to another; bodies oscillate between one identity and another. Only a surface naming is maintained. Whatever the reasons, it produces an aesthetics of flux, splits, and fragmentation.

As in all melodrama, the play between the loss and the finding of identity (and/or memory) is a recurrent motif. It is a device used to complicate and enrich the narrative, make adventurous and surprising what would otherwise be predictable and linear, lengthen what would be too short. In serial narrative, and particularly in soap opera, all this seems particularly necessary since the economy of narration is one of lingering, delaying, staying, as an end in itself rather than as an instrument for suspense.[12]

The game of identity has a further twist, since what is one of the most ancient narrative devices gets entangled with a production process, that, due to the length of series and serials, can span several years. The characters are unavoidably influenced by the changes undergone by the actors, and change face and voice, because the actors go away or die; for the same extradiegetic reasons, they disappear and sometime reappear as "other." Well-known examples have been Miss Ellie, Jock Ewing, and Pamela in *Dallas;* Fallon and Stephen in *Dynasty:* in all these cases there is a conscious interplay between the character and the actor, between fact and fiction, a device used by the popular press, and not only in Britain.[13]

The reduplication of a character is more complex and usually justified by diegetic reasons. The use of a double has been widespread in great novels (Dostoevski and Conrad are two outstanding examples) and also in Hollywood cinema: a classic of the kind is *The Dark Mirror* with Olivia de Havilland. The most recent variation is *Dead Ringers* by David Cronenberg. In television narrative the double is a recurrent motif in contexts and languages otherwise defined as naturalistic.

The "case" of Crystal Carrington occupied a whole season of *Dynasty* episodes, with the real Crystal imprisoned down in a dungeon, without ever losing her shoulder pads, while the double was upstairs in Crystal's place beside her husband Blake. In the bedroom, the false Crystal put up the excuse of constant headaches in order to avoid paying her conjugal duties: is it the usual malicious skirting with sexual matters that is typical of mainstream soap opera? Or would Blake's incapacity to realize there is an other in his bed have been too much even for the large suspension of disbelief of the viewer? The situation here is perversely upturned in relation to Freudian theory and its echoing in literature and cinema, where the double is usually hidden in the depths.

The use of the same actress for the two characters is yet another variation, mostly inexplicable as it is difficult to find a basis for it in the narrative. The parallel agonies of Julie Clegg and Jenny Diamond, both played by Catherine Hickland, have occupied an important part of *Capitol*. The necessity to make a better use of a good and popular actress, once her first role had been fully exploited, is a possible motive. But the physical juxtaposition of an open and simple character such as Julie with the complex, dark personality of Jenny, troubled by amnesia and a dangerous instability, has had an uncanny effect in this soap.

In spite of any practical explanations, this movement between actor and character, mind and body, wavers over the diegetic edge and blurs the line between the inside and the outside of narrative, fact and fiction, subject and object. It becomes an important component of a metanarrative that is not infrequent in popular fiction, though it is usually encountered in avant-garde art. When the game is pushed too far, effects of excess and parody are decisive, as in Crystal Carrington's case. There is rarely a resolution to these cases of lost or split identity, creating an area of uncertainty and suspense around the character's personality. Women are the most frequent cases: the movement between the two Crystals and the two Fallons (here a second actress replaced the role's original one), or between Jenny and Julie, becomes a transit and a passage between one woman and another, between one and the same.

This passage can take place within one (and un-split) character who then becomes a palimpsest of female attitudes. There are many characters in *Capitol* who drastically change roles during the long life of the serial: Sloane herself from the competitive schemer of the beginning, opposed to the angelic Julie, becomes the truly good heroine of this soap. But the matriarch Myrna Clegg, director of all intrigues, shows a coexistence of opposites: ruthless in her hate for the other family, the MacCandles, a bad and tyrannical mother (especially to her daughters), competitive business woman (to the point of stealing her husband's job and position), an envious plotting friend, she can be at the very same time a protective wife and mother, and an affectionate friend. In all these contradictory aspects, she is always excessive. This is a recurrent pattern in quite a few other daytime soaps: Stephanie in *The Bold and the Beautiful* and Gwyneth in *Loving* are two more intriguing examples.

Gore Vidal has given an elitist ironic vision of popular culture and its fictions in *Duluth,* a metanarrative saga crowded with characters moving freely from one plot to another, among different media, in a void deprived of temporal, spatial, or syntactical limits. He makes one of them declare: "We are simply formulations of words. We do not live. We are interchangeable. We go on, and we go on, from narrative to narrative, whether in serial form or in those abstract verbal constructions so admired by the French and boolaboola Yale! It is all the same" (Vidal, 1983, p. 280). Though not belonging to either of these two categories (but undoubtedly influenced by them), I must say that this differing of the I, this moving back and forward of identities, bodies, and stories is one of the seductive elements—for me—of such disparaged tales.

Women's Space

In a recent essay Catherine Stimpson quotes "Attacks," a fragment from Gertrude Stein's *Bee Time Vine:*

> She is.
>> She is the best way.
>> She is the best way from here to there.

These lines are arrayed so as to suggest a female expansion into space; they are certainly a "tribute to women's being, and being in space," as Stimpson says (Stimpson, 1986, p. 3). As Jessica Benjamin puts it, "what is experientially female is the association of desire with a space, a place within the self" (1986, p. 97). She states that from this comes the strength to own one's own desire in the presence of the other.

Those who fall into the temptation of thinking of women's television, of the screen space materially occupied by women, as a space *for* women, have been accused of falling into "the seductive trap of the image," of taking its sheer presence as triumph or at least as a mark of presence, of a subjective position, of the independence of desire. This has been widely argued for cinema. Thus Julia Lesage wonders about the fascination she feels for the heroine in *Broken Blossoms* by Griffith and for Lillian Gish, the actress performing the role: "As a woman I must ask how the media can so seduce me that I enjoy, either as entertainment or as art, works that take as one of their essential ingredients the victimization of women" (1987, p. 235). She also notes that identification with the heroine places the viewer in a passive role (p. 242). Identification is seen as the real problem; Mary Ann Doane, in a fascinating analysis of *Rebecca* and *Caught,* and of the scenes focusing on women's relation to the image, speaks of the lack of a gap between the female gaze and the image, and of how this effects a confusion between subjectivity and objectivity, between the internal and the external: "the most disturbing images of the two films are those which evoke the absence of the woman. In both films these images follow projection scenes which delineate the impossibility of female spectatorship" (1987, pp. 174–75).

In television it is easy to be fascinated by the crowd of women moving from one plot to another in the uninterrupted flow of daytime soap operas. It is nearly unavoidable to be seduced by "presence" when, for example, in *Capitol* Clarissa McCandles and Myrna Clegg, representing the two rival families at the center of the story, occupy the scene.[14] The first of their many dramatic confrontations reveals that behind the political plot, and the plot itself, there is an old personal rivalry over the same man. The men are mostly absent, like Sam Clegg or the presumed dead Barry MacCandles, or puppets, like Trey in Myrna's hands; politics becomes a subordinate province without it being noticed. It is true that this female power in the last instance lies in men's love (the limit of romance?), but how can one resist the fascination of the triumph of such "limit," or feeling, female desire, the body?

It can occur in the female collective scenes in *Gabriela,* the telenovela based on Jorge Amado's novel, often rigidly structured in a symmetrical view of sexual and class differences in the village that provides the choral background of the tale. One of the episodes opens with a series of alternate shots of the notables' wives rebelling against their husbands and of the dressmakers in revolt against the boss. In both scenes, female bodies, first seen together in medium shot and then individually in successive close shots, are a strong statement of an alternative strength. In another episode, the sequence of Gabriela herself (the beautiful Sonia Braga) dominating with her phallus-like body the men around her—who are literally on their knees—demonstrates the lure of the image.

It has been said many times that the language of women's cinema can be a Lacanian trap, pushing women to lose themselves as subjects, to be reified in the image. Popular narrative has been criticized for its uncritical emphasis on the female image, in contrast to the "resistance to the image" that can be found in avant-garde cinema, or in any language that refuses obvious readings and prevents easy and dangerous identifications. Some film critics have claimed feminist experimental cinema as the only legitimate discourse for women, in opposition to the "classic realist text," which has been identified with Hollywood cinema. As to television, its danger would be confirmed by the dominance of the image over other languages, by the absence of distancing elements, by the open-endedness of the narrative—and, of course, by the total absence of a dividing line between avant-garde and popular.

The Claustrophobic Space

Mary Ann Doane has spoken of filmic visual space as "continually being outlined, territorialized, divided along sexual lines" (1987, p. 17). In television narratives the split is between open spaces, mainly metropolitan scenes specific to male narratives, and closed claustrophobic spaces allotted to women, mainly in soap opera or in such feminizations of male genres as female police series.

The room is the one dominating space in most daytime soap operas and telenovelas. It is important even when the main space is a public place used as a meeting point and a common background. Hospitals, courts, police headquarters, squares, a housing estate (corresponding to a smaller "palazzo" in Italy) are some of these choral spots, but they all end up among four walls. In more expensive soaps, mostly moving from the United States to imaginary exotic places and back, the room is often unmoved and unmoving.

This is usually the site of romantic love, where the "I" faces a "you"; the natural space for the heterosexual couple, speaking, flirting, scheming, confronting one another but mostly making love. The female spectator's gaze is split in a double fascination: she is looking at a woman looking at love, and at a man as fetishistic object. The heterosexual couple is a recurrent icon, a sort of linguistic constant of sentimental and domestic narrative, from novel to film and television. As we have seen, both Jessica Benjamin and Luce Irigaray have defined this as the space not for oneself but for the other.

But there is also another space, that of the woman alone, the space of lack and desire. Often represented as a prison, it is a topos of melodrama, for cinema and television. Thanks to a succession of metonymic passages, we go from the home to the room, from the room to parts of it, mainly to the markers of its boundaries such as doors and windows, arches and angels, as Julia Lesage had already observed in *Broken Blossoms*. Melodrama is the favorite arena for the many links between cinema and television.

The motif of the woman at home lonely and desperate is taken up in the recurrent image of Kelly Harper in *Capitol*, anxious and distressed, looking for comfort in alcohol and drugs. She is seen in the large downstairs room in her flat, a space exhibiting the elements of her paranoia: the staircase leading up to her son's room (she is a single parent and all her problems—mainly the loss of love—are tied to this difficult maternity); the tools of her work as a painter; the drugs to which she becomes slowly addicted, hidden in drawers, pots, bags; the door as object of her obsessive gaze torn between fear and need of the other, the outside, freedom; finally the famous window, a fundamental icon of melodrama, with its obvious reference to prison, closure, victimization. The comparison with the woman's film is obvious but the elements are blurred, repeated, parodied, in a jarring reworking of those themes. There is the conscious memory of classical *topoi* of Hollywood cinema, but these images come *after;* they are quotes, over-lappings; they unite past and present, underline and deny the similarity.

The link is particularly evident in the epilogue to one of *Capitol's* last episodes. As Trey goes out of the door, Kelly rushes to the window, and the camera from outside frames her crying behind the window panes, while she looks at him abandoning her. We cannot but think in this particular instance of the recurring image in *Madame X* (Rich, 1966, with Lana Turner), of the heroine looking at the rain behind the window of the mansion in which her husband's long absences leave her alone; or also of the final scene of the much analyzed *Stella Dallas*. This famous window scene, in King Vidor's version (1937), is shot from behind Stella's shoulders, with Stella (Barbara Stanwyck) outside the room and not prisoner in it. In spite of this, the window is again a screen, a barrier, through which she observes her beloved daughter's marriage.

Stella's final position is identifiable with the spectator's look. Kelly instead is a passive object of the camera, a prisoner behind the window panes. The objective shot is tied to the neutral language of television "realism" and to the instrumental diegetic hook; the sentimental leading tune of the serial brings the emotions to a climax at command and stops them to defer the closure to the next program. The still of Kelly's face in tears freezes the viewer's emotions in a metanarrative twist that at the same time assures that the emotions can continue. It suggests a gallery of similar images built on the long memory of this icon: the tragedy of the loss of love in the life of a woman.

Towards the (provisional?) end of *Dynasty,* there is a long sequence intended to recall Fallon's memory of a distant dramatic episode in her childhood. The allusion to a similar sequence in Hitchcock's *Marnie* cannot be mistaken, with the dramatic use of the flashback to reach the same hidden truth: the mother's lover has been killed by the child herself rather than by her mother, as was suspected. A close comparison between these two texts, apart from signaling the change in genre toward the end of this soap and paying an homage to one of its forerunners, is useful in studying similarities and differences between the two languages.

There are similar icons in other soaps. *Eastenders* found a leitmotif in Angie's despair over her failed marriage, and the failure coursed through many programs and quite a few narrative twists. The numerous close shots of Angie in the upstairs room above the pub, crying with a glass in her hand, or hoarding pills for her planned suicide, were a contrast with the pub full of people and animation, where Angie appeared smiling and controlled. In the same serial, Michelle, a young unmarried mother, after agonizing (with the whole of the British audience) over whether she should make a convenience marriage with Lofty, decides not to do it in a memorable scene at the church. Even more memorable is the scene in which, having to meet him to explain her behavior, she arranges the empty room carefully and maniacally for the site of rejection.

The paranoid state in soap is nearly always linked to the loss of love (for Kelly and Angie, the impossibility to accept it for Michelle), and its subsequent displacement in alcohol or drugs. Single parenthood is its variation, as we can see in the case of Mary and Michelle in *Eastenders,* Kelly and Julie in *Capitol.* These are some of the conditions for which the enclosed room becomes the space of paranoia. This is the non-place for the self, the space for the other: the other (invariably a he) is not there; the room is the setting for his absence.

The Other Woman

As important, and interesting, in this discourse is the space of two women together. The recurrence of the image of two women—mothers and daughters, sisters, friends, colleagues or assistants, enemies and rivals—is specific of television domestic drama, more so than of other kinds of popular fiction. If we were trying to trace the woman's gaze in the televisual text and its pleasure, we could examine the space between women on the screen as the narrative inscription of this gaze. The movement between sameness and difference is particularly explored in the pair of confronting females; in all its nuances, from solidarity to tenderness and protection; from tension and rebellion to hostility and hatred.

The privileged liaison is mother and daughter, or anyway women belonging to generations. In a crucial scene in *Eastenders,* the chain extends to three and even four, when Michelle is discussing with her grandmother and mother her right to choose the way to give birth to her child. Here women's presence is expressed in a relatedness that varies from tenderness to tension, or even opposition, or simply to their bodies and voices held together by the camera. There is a varied spectrum in *Capitol:* tender between Clarissa and her daughters or daughters-in-law, and between Sloane and Paula, at least after her father's death; antagonistic in the case of Myrna and Brenda, or Julie. It is often supportive in British soap opera, and scenes of mutual solidarity between mothers and daughters have a regular cadence in *Brookside* and *Eastenders,* underlining the crises in each of the heroines' lives.

The relation between women, usually in the same age group, can also be marked by rivalry, opposition, hostility. The traditional motif of the opposition between the good and the bad woman reappears here. This trait, present in mythical narration and fables, has become the mark of the variegated genre literature that is behind soap opera, from melodrama and sentimental novels to the gothic and noir, right up to the popular women's romance of recent years. Enmity is mostly expressed through the gaze; it could be said that the gaze is certainly female in *Dynasty* due to the recurrent "duels" in gazing between Alexis and Crystal, Alexis and Dominique, Alexis and every other woman in the serial, including her own daughter and rival Amanda; *Dallas* is only a modest follower, but one must not forget Sue Ellen and J.R.'s successive mistresses, or Pamela and Jenny. Love and ambition are the most frequent motives for the hostility.

Telenovelas occupy a remarkable place with their strong, fierce women expressing their strength above all when confronted with another woman. Veronica Castro has played many roles as the great opposer of the wicked woman, in a line transcending the barriers of this or that novela. Daytime soap opera is not far behind: often, as with the relationship between Nina and her mother in *All My Children,* the hostility between two women is not necessarily tied to the opposition good-bad. Sometimes it is a sort of necessary syntactical twist defying the narrative logic, as for instance in the case of *The Rich also Cry,* where the fierce enmity between two women in the first part of the novela melts into friendship.

Cherríe Moraga speaks of the sense of betrayal between women and again relates it to the mother-daughter relationship. She speaks of her desperate and impossible need for the exclusive love of her mother, who always put her husband and brother first. Any Chicano woman is a betrayer to her race if she does not put the man first of all; and in doing so, she betrays her own daughter, the other woman. It is a sort of perverse chain that is present even in mythical history. *"Traitor begets traitor.* Malinche betrayed her own race by aiding Cortez as she had been betrayed by her own mother" (Moraga, 1986, p. 176). It is this myth of the inherent unreliability of women, our natural propensity for treachery, which has been carved into the very bone of Mexican/Chicano collective psychology.

The movement between sameness and difference is essential also in the solidarity that we find more frequently in another genre, the female police series. The best example comes from *Cagney and Lacey,* constantly expressing reciprocal support through looks and words in the most unlikely moments, but also through bodily touch. But other examples in the genre come from *Cassie and Company* and even in *Charlie's Angels,* where the solidarity among the "angels" is no less important than their subordination to Charlie, the absent male.

This confrontation and closeness between women—whether it is hostility or solidarity—shows the complexity of a relationship that in an earlier moment had seemed clear and "natural." The complexity is there, inside and outside fiction. It also involves the relation of the woman spectator to the woman on the screen through a series of mirror images: the gaze recreates the difficult relationship to the other woman, in the recurrence of the images of mothers and daughters, sisters and friends, enemies and rivals. The relation to the other becomes relation to the self, autobiography becomes vision and fantasy. The same as other is known and familiar, yet at the same time hidden, mysterious, unknown, "uncanny."

Are Feelings Real?

Women watching fiction are an accepted stereotype. This stereotype imposes a rigid specialization: women watch or read fiction but, within that and differently from Scheherazade, who had a very wide repertory, specialize in tales of love, hate, passion; in one word, in feeling.

There is an ad for a British beer portraying a couple sitting in the cinema and watching a famous film of the twenties; it's all in black and white, the iconography and atmosphere inspired by the silent movie which is the object of the gaze; she is so absorbed by the screen, while weeping profusely, as not to notice that her husband disappears through the floor to go and drink a beer (Courage, of course) at the pub opposite with a pal of his in the same situation. Then he comes back, without her noticing, her gaze still riveted to the screen. Later on, both—back to reality—drink beer in the very same bar with the other reconstituted couple. Fiction as the mark of sexual difference.

The association between women and narrative has quickly moved from the active role indicated by Mulvey to the passive one. Women reading novels, women watching series, in the passive ghetto of the home, the "wedge-shaped core of darkness" of their privacy and loneliness, when and where they are not replying to other people's needs and desires, have been the object of critical analysis that has not always been negative.

As we have seen, the fables women watch are also a fabulation of the female, an exploration of the space as "desire for the self." Thus these improbable tales are often a minute relentless exploration of the self. The similarity of soap operas to the repetitive, continuous rhythms of everyday life has been already noted by many critics working on television fiction. The restricted space of the home—of the eye, of the mind as evasion into boundless worlds, as the scene of escape into fantasy—can be considered a female ghetto, a solipsistic world that is outside action, outside history, outside . . . pubs? Feminists have given different replies to this question. The women of Diotima see in this— the space of the lack, of the negative, of being a non-man—their ontological existence, their being there, with themselves, in a voiceless intimacy (cf. A. A. W., 1987, p. 33). Virginia Woolf in *To the Lighthouse* saw it in this way: "This core of darkness could go anywhere, for no one saw it. They could not stop it, she thought, exulting. There was freedom, there was peace, there was, most welcome of all, a summoning together, a resting on the platform of stability" (p. 73).

At this point let us return to the wider debate. First of all we may have noticed that here the equation presented by those who regret the absence of feeling and passions in postmodernism is reversed. In the media, particularly the visual media, the eighties have been crossed by the horizontal flow of love and hate, passion and revenge. [15] Some of the nostalgic essays I have quoted above ended on the importance of feelings for the reality principle: hate and love, or the Gramscian political passion. In different ways they were expressing the desperate nostalgia for a world in which naming means signifying with transparent and unidirectional correspondence, where feeling and unreason can be defined within the paradigms of rationality.

I have spoken of a version of love, passion, hate, revenge that is far from being obviously real, though it is real enough for people watching soap opera. In Italy there is the habit of announcing the death of a member of small communities by putting up mourning notices on the streets. This happens mostly in villages but survives in large cities as well, at least in the South; it recalls a rural economy, a time before the press and other media. Two small towns in Sicily, Recalmuto and Grotte, have recently put up mourning notices all over the place announcing the death of a foreigner, a certain Steve Sowolski. Not many here will know who this man is but there was no need to explain down there, since everybody had been watching his agony, death, and funeral for over a week at 2 o'clock on RAI.2, in the American series *Loving*. It has been said that Sicily has been left out of history; indeed racist posters in Northern Italy have very pictorially (since the mainland has the shape of a boot) suggested that it should definitely be kicked out of Europe; in this way we could easily expel them with these fabled versions of love, passion, sorrow. [16] Once more, as with women, my impression is that this episode proves that there might be a new way of asserting feelings that, in spite of its humble and scarcely literate contexts, speaks of new paradigms for old feelings, extends frontiers, and proposes a way out of the old rigid dichotomy between basic elementary needs and superfluous shadows and dreams.

NOTES

1. In *Les stratégies fatales,* he calls the new regime of the transpolitical "this historical collapse, this coma, this disappearance of the real" (1983a, p. 14). Iain Chambers, in *Border Dialogues,* observes: "Behind this science-fiction scenario I think we can hear the dying echo of the call for a now apparently impossible 'authenticity'. . . . We are left to wander alone, without direction, in the desert among the semiotic debris of dead meanings. Jean Baudrillard . . . remains faithful to his wild rationalism—the universe is finally revealed to be alien, ruled over by the meaningless power of The Thing" (Chambers, 1990, p. 89).

2. See, among others, Stuart Hall, "Cultural Studies and the Centre: some problematics and problems" (1980c).

3. A reductive reading of Gramsci has been partly responsible for his neglect during the eighties, further accentuated during the recent events that are transforming the Italian Communist Party. However, there is a strong alternative view of Gramsci both in Italy and in Britain, where he is still very much in fashion. I was thinking of the interesting work of people like Biagio De Giovanni in Italy, or Stuart Hall, Ernesto Laclau, Chantal Mouffe, and others in England. Stuart Hall has developed his recent critique of Thatcherism using the concept of articulation and showing that the terrain of struggle shifts ad must be constantly dismantled and upturned; the many resulting and possible new political alliances make it impossible to go back to that static notion of class that was ours for many years (cf. Hall, 1988b).

4. Eagleton sees postmodernism as the betrayal of the revolutionary values implied by the historical avant-garde and of the political project of the struggle for human emancipation. He invokes Brecht and Benjamin, who were isolated in modernism as well, as it was crossed by "antipolitical impulses" (1985, p. 72). The neglect of ethical values ("The postmodernism which celebrates kitsch and camp caricatures the Brechtian slogan by proclaiming not that the bad contains the good, but that the bad is good," 1985, p. 68) and the commodification of the work of art ("In a sardonic commentary on the avant-garde work, postmodernist culture will dissolve its own boundaries and become coextensive with ordinary commodified life itself," 1985) are among what he sees as the most dangerous features of the post-metaphysical moment.

5. He later defends himself against this imputation, indirectly emphasizing the guilty halo that has surrounded postmodernism in England. He does it in a subsequent essay, by recalling a personal crisis (cf. Hebdige, 1985), and this again places him in an ambiguous position as the collapse of the barrier between public and private, theory and praxis, is often seen as a central feature of postmodernism. He also underlines the emotional character with which this intellectual *querelle* is curiously charged.

6. In an essay written in the mid-eighties ("Postmodernism and Popular Culture"), Angela McRobbie speaks of the breath of fresh air that this new sensibility has brought to Great Britain: its attention to the importance of representation, to the "instantaneity of communication," to the fragmentation of experience, seems to her closer to the lived experience of women and young people than the unitary vision that is viewed so nostalgically by many. She refers to de Beauvoir and Sontag, who have spoken of a dimension where public and private are joined and where pastiche, parody, and camp show a subversive potential (cf. McRobbie, 1986).

7. The crucial role that popular culture has played in postmodernism is often mentioned in the debate, more often in the positive views of it, though it is not totally absent on the other side. Jameson and Hebdige have used it as the main basis for contention, using as their main examples such urban temples as shopping centers, hotels, and youth magazines. In his *Uncommon Cultures*, Collins has spoken at length of the important convergence of culturalists and feminists with the postmodernist vision of a non-monolothic concept of mass culture (cf. 1989, p. xiv and p. 20).

8. I would also like to recall the Italian feminist group of philosophers called Diotima, originally constituted within the University of Verona. Moving from Luce Irigaray's statement that "sexual difference is one of the problems or the problem that our epoch must think of," they set out to elaborate new concepts and epistemological categories within the thought of difference. "By essential and originary differing I mean that for women to be sexed in difference is unre-nounceable; for anybody who happens to be born as a woman, it is an already given and not otherwise.... As sexual difference is in this sense an originary, it must be kept as a difference that is not preceded by any category of previous understanding" (Cavarero, 1987, pp. 180–81).

9. The relations between women of different generations and different power groups has been the object of feminist reflection in Italy in the eighties; in particular the group *Sottosopra* based in Milan has written on the difficulty and the importance of relating to the "woman with more power."

10. Motors is not the right word perhaps, as one conveying passivity would probably be more exact. Sacrificed, victimized, raped, and kidnapped—in these roles they still constitute the main motives of all the wars between Asia and Europe.

11. Elisabetta Rasy, in *La lingua della nutrice,* has spoken of the devaluation and the censorship to which romantic novels have been submitted and of the refusal to acknowledge their symbolic value (Rasy, 1978, p. 78). As Tania Modleski has underlined, this contempt has been expressed by women critics in particular, starting from George Eliot (1984, p. 14). More than a century later, Germaine Greer, in *The Female Eunuch,* sees in love a "cheap ideology" (1971, p. 170). More recently, romance is judged by Teresa Stratford as decreasing women's power, though in a context offering a positive open attitude towards it (Davies, 1987, p. 140). In the same section on romance, Charlotte Brunsdon, who had started denouncing how risky it is to like soap opera, gives this final judgment: "The problem—of the lack of credibility of alternative and oppositional representations—is particularly pronounced in a form like soap opera which is mainly pleasurable in its predictable, conservative, repetitive elements, and its necessary commitment to realism" (Davies, 1987, p. 149). See also my "Genre and Gender" (1988).

12. A very good example is given in the first part of *Capitol,* all devoted to describing the obstacles created by Julie's family to her marriage with Tyler. Once they seem to have been overcome, she loses her memory after the first of many accidents in the serial, and the plots against the couple (together with the plot) can start all over again.

13. Cf. Hobson (1982, pp. 23–4). She quotes a journalist of the Birmingham *Evening Mail* on the uproar caused in the press and among the viewers by the sacking of the actress interpreting the role of Megin in *Crossroads:*"... Nolly Gordon, as Meg, is for them a typical, hard-working, decent, clean-living woman. Her sacking—and the decision to remove Meg from the motel—is a human story"; the equivalence of soap opera and real life is underlined repeatedly both by Coward and Hobson. Rosalind Coward has referred to the construction of parallel lives (of characters and actors) as the main element conferring an effect of immediacy and reality on otherwise highly conventionalized narratives (1986, p. 173).

14. The serial deals with Washington political intrigues, and has been followed by others in this vein, like *Top of the Hill.* Its whole action is centered on men's competitions and struggles

for the White House, spanning three generations (the grandfather in flashback), with constant references to McCarthyism and to more recent events of the Kennedy and post-Kennedy era.

15. In the mid-eighties in Italy they were kept in special "pink" slots: "afternoon with feelings," with the icon of a heart in the introduction titles. Today things are less specialized and, as we all know, very often soap operas have men among their viewers. But there still are networks, mostly private, totally devoted to the broadcasting of soap operas and telenovelas. Even RAI, the public network, has been giving increasing attention to fiction. "Love is a wonderful thing" has been the title of a long afternoon slot on RAI.2 in 1989–90. See my "Imported Utopias" (1990).

10

Cultural Studies and the Culture of Everyday Life

John Fiske

I want to start this paper from the premise that both academics in cultural and media studies, and left-wing political theorists and activists have found the everyday culture of the people in capitalist societies particularly difficult to study either empirically or theoretically. In this paper I wish, then, to interweave two lines of theoretical inquiry: one into the culture of everyday life within subordinated social formations and the other into our own academic practices involved in such an inquiry.

I would like to start with the concept of "distance" in cultural theory. Elsewhere (Fiske, 1989a) I have argued that "distance" is a key marker of difference between high and low culture, between the meanings, practices, and pleasures characteristic of empowered and disempowered social formations. Cultural distance is a multidimensional concept. In the culture of the socially advantaged and empowered it may take the form of a distance between the art object and reader/spectator: such distance devalues socially and historically specific reading practices in favor of a transcendent appreciation or aesthetic sensibility with claims to universality. It encourages reverence or respect for the text as an art object endowed with authenticity and requiring preservation. "Distance" may also function to create a difference between the experience of the art work and everyday life. Such "distance" produces ahistorical meanings of art works and allows the members of its social formation the pleasures of allying themselves with a set of humane values that in the extreme versions of aesthetic theory, are argued to be universal values which transcend their historical conditions. This distance from the historical is also a distance from the bodily sensations, for it is our bodies that finally bind us to our historical and social specificities. As the mundanities of our social conditions are set aside, or distanced, by this view of art, so, too, are the so-called sensuous, cheap, and easy pleasures of the body distanced from the more comtemplative, aesthetic pleasures of the mind. And finally this distance takes the form of distance from economic necessity: the separation of the aesthetic from the social is a practice of the elite who can afford to ignore the constraints of material necessity, and who thus construct an aesthetic which not only refuses to assign any value at all to material conditions, but validates only those art forms which transcend them. This critical and aesthetic distance is thus, finally, a marker of distinction between those able to separate their culture from the social and economic conditions of the everyday and those who cannot.

There is no "distancing," however, in the culture of everyday life. Both Bakhtin and Bourdieu show how the culture of the people denies categorical boundaries between art and life: popular art is part of the everyday, not distanced from it. The culture of everyday life works only to the extent that it is imbricated into its immediate historical and social setting. This materiality of popular culture is directly related to the economic materiality of the conditions of oppression. Under these conditions, social experience and, therefore, culture is inescapably material: distantiation is an unattainable luxury. The culture of everyday life is concrete, contextualized, and lived, just as deprivation is concrete, contextualized, and lived. It is, therefore, a particularly difficult object of academic investigation.

I wish to turn to Bourdieu's (1977, 1984) theory of the "habitus" as a way to think through both the material practices of everyday culture and our difficulty in studying them. The concept "habitus" contains the meanings of habitat, habitant, the processes of habitation and habit, particularly habits of thought. A habitat is a social environment in which we live: it is a product of both its position in the social space and of the practices of the social beings who inhabit it. The social space is, for Bourdieu, a multidimensional map of the social order in which the main axes are economic capital, cultural capital, education, class, and historical trajectories; in it, the material, the symbolic, and the historical are not separate categories but interactive lines of force whose operations structure the macro-social order, the practices of those who inhabit different positions and moments of it, and their cultural tastes, ways of thinking, of "dispositions." The habitus, then, is at one and the same time, a position in the social and a historical trajectory through it: it is the practice of hiring within that position and trajectory, and the social identity, the habits of thoughts, tastes and dispositions that are formed in and by those practices. The position in social space, the practices and the identities are not separate categories in a hierarchical or deterministic relation to each other, but mutually inform each other to the extent that their significance lies in their transgression of the categorical boundaries that produced the words I have to use to explain them and which are therefore perpetuated by that explanation.

The point I wish to make at this stage of my argument is that the taste for "distance" in art is part of inhabiting a definable habitus, one characterized by high educational levels, high cultural but low economic capital that has been acquired rather than inherited. And within this same habitus we may find the taste for congruent social and academic theories, a taste expressed in the dispositions for macro–theories that transcend the mundanities of the everyday through distantiation, that move towards generalized, abstracted understandings rather than concrete specificities and that try to construct academic or political theories that are as distanced, detached, and self-contained as any idealized art object. This is, needless to say, the habitus in which most of us academics feel most at home.

But it is a habitus at odds with those through which the various formations of the people live their everyday lives. An explanation is necessarily of a different ontological order from that which it explains, but this difference should not be absolute: the gap should be both crossable and crossed. Bourdieu's theory of the habitus allows the possibility of such movement—we can, after all, visit and live in habitats other than the one in which we are most at home. But though such tourist excursions can give us *some* inside experience they can never provide the same experience of these conditions as those who live or have lived there. Brett Williams (1988) gives a good example of both living in a mainly black, working class culture, and providing an academic account of it. She moves between the two habituses in a way I believe to be exemplary.

Her study details some of the key features of a habitus whose culture is of the material density of embodied practices. One of these she calls "texture." By "texture" she refers to dense, vivid, detailed interwoven narratives, relationships, and experiences. The materially constrained narrowness of the conditions of everyday life are compensated for and contradicted by the density and intensity of the experiences, practices, and objects packed into them. She finds this density as she follows a man down his neighborhood main street, when every store, every encounter, every piece of gossip exchanged is packed with concrete meanings in its minutiae. The density of apartment life is part of the conditions of oppression, yet it is also available to be turned by popular creativity and struggle, into a textured culture: "The Manor's dense living, in combination with the poverty of its families is battering. Using a small space intensively, cleaning it defensively, and lacking the resources to expand or transform it, families need to work out ways to make that density bearable."

Williams goes on to describe how Lucy and Robert, as typical renters, cope with their material conditions by "texturing domestic density by weaving through it varied sights, sounds and rhythms" (p. 102). To middle class taste their apartment would seem intolerably cluttered with knickknacks and decorations yet Robert still feels a need to fill what seems to him to be a glaringly empty space. It is as though a density which is chosen by Lucy and Robert becomes a way of negotiating and coping with a density that is imposed upon them: constructing a bottom-up density is a tactic of popular culture for "turning" the constraints of a top-down density. It is an instance of the creative use of the conditions of constraint.

Television is used to increase, enrich and further densify the texture. It is typically left on all the time, adding color, sound and action to apartment life: it is used to frame and cause conversations, to fill gaps and silences. It can provide both a means of entering and intensifying this dense everyday culture and a way of escaping it, for it is also used to dilute "the concentration of crowded families, whose members can tune into television, establish a well of privacy, and yet remain part of the domestic group" (102–3).

Television not only enriches and enters the interwoven texture of everyday life, it re-presents it, too. Programs like *Dallas,* with its "vivid historically interwoven concreteness" offered renters "the same kind of texture that is so valued on the street." The women in the apartments lived in and with *Dallas* over a number of years, growing to know each character in "painstaking detail." Williams concludes: "As renters texture an already dense domestic situation by weaving in more density, shows like these favorites are appropriate vehicles" (Williams, 1988, p. 106)

Leal (1990; Leal and Oliver, 1988) too, has shown how certain formations of the people (in her case first generation urbanized Brazilian peasants) weave a densely textured symbolic environment through which they live. She analyzes in detail one such environment, or rather a mini–environment or *"entourage"* constructed from objects placed around the TV set. Around the TV set were plastic flowers, a religious picture, a false gold vase, family photographs, a broken laboratory glass and an old broken radio. Williams finds the culture in the density itself, but Leal interprets this texture. Her analysis shows how these people live meaningfully within the contradictions between the city and the country, urban sophistication and rural peasantry, science and magic, the future and the past. In the suburbs they are placed on the spatial boundary between the city and the country, as first generation migrants they are on the equivalent historical boundary between the past and the future.

Their use of photographs was an instance of this cultural process. On the TV set were large pictures of dead or absent family members, typically ones left behind in the country, and stuck into their frames were small I.D. pictures of those who had moved to the city: The I.D. photos were not only signs of family, but also signs of modern, urban life. As Leal comments "The social system that broke these kinship webs is reproduced in the symbolic system within the photograph frames" (p. 23) and these lost kinship webs are reasserted, reformed through bricolage. So, too, the plastic flowers were considered more beautiful than natural ones because they bore meaning of the urban, the manufactured, the new; and also because they cost money. They were validated by their origins in the "better" life the people hoped to find by their move to the city. Natural flowers, on the other hand, were from the life they were fleeing. Leal also shows how class specific these meanings are—in the middle-class homes, for instance, there was a reversal of values so that peasant art would be displayed as bearers of valid meanings of the country and an escape from the urban. In those homes, of course, plastic flowers would never raise their cheap, manufactured, urbanized heads. Her interpretation of this dense texture of objects continues, including the TV set which is seen as "a vehicle of a knowledgeable and modern speech" (p. 24). Her readings reveal a popular culture in process by which the people live within the larger social order not in a reactive, but a proactive way. The entourage of objects around the TV set comprises

> a symbolic system, including an ethos of modernity, that is itself part of a larger symbolic universe that has as its principal focus of significance the city and industry. This system of meanings seeks to "conquer" the urban power space (that of capitalistic relations), while insistently trying to differentiate and delimit urban cultural space from the rural space that is still very close to the actors, by manipulating signs that are shared by their group as indicators of social prestige. (Leal, 1990, p. 25)

Studies such as Leal's and Williams's show how the material, densely lived culture of everyday life is a contradictory mixture of creativity and constraint. This is a way of embodying and living the contradictory relations between the dominant social order and the variety of subaltern formations within it. Williams comments somewhat sardonically that "A passion for texture is not always rewarded in American society, and more middle-class strategies for urban living aim at breadth instead" (1988, p. 48). It is a comment that I wish to extend to cover academic theory as part of middle-class strategies for living.

The social order constrains and oppresses the people, but at the same time offers them resources to fight against those constraints. The constraints are, in the first instance, material, economic ones which determine in an oppressive, disempowering way, the limits of the social experience of the poor. Oppression is always economic. Yet the everyday culture of the oppressed takes the signs of that which oppresses them and uses them for its own purposes. The signs of money are taken out of the economic system of the dominant and inserted into the culture of the subaltern and their social force is thus complicated. The plastic flowers are for Leal's newly suburbanized peasants, deeply contradictory. They have a mystique because of the "mystery" of their production (unlike natural flowers)—they are fetishes, syntheses of symbolic meanings, of modernity: but they are also commodity fetishes. They require money, another fetish, and transform that money into an object of cultural display. Real money is not an appropriate decoration or cultural object, but transformed money is; its transformation occurs not just in its form, coin to plastic flower, but in the social formation, theirs to ours. The commodity fetish is deeply conflicted: it bears the forces of both the power bloc and the people. It produces and reproduces the economic system, yet simultaneously can serve the symbolic interests of those subordinated by it. The plastic flowers, Leal argues, because they cannot be produced within the domestic space but must be bought, bring with them the "social legitimacy, prestige and power" that, in an urban capitalist society can most readily be gained, in however transformed a manner, from the order of oppression.

So, too, the accumulation of objects in Lucy and Robert's apartment is not a sign of their having bought into the system by accumulating a literal, if devalued, cultural capital. It is rather their way of filling their constrained lives with a variety of multiplicity of experiences that the more affluent can achieve by their greater mobility through physical and social space.

Of course the desire for the expectation of variety and richness of experience is a produce of capitalism, and serves to maintain the system—for such variety whether of objects or experience—must usually be bought and paid for. But producing that variety, richness, density is also the work of popular creativity; it is the people's art of making do with what they have (de Certeau, 1984), and what they have is almost exclusively what the social order that oppresses them offers them.

Many of Williams's subjects were African-Americans who had moved from rural North Carolina to Washington, D.C. and thus shared important social determinants with Leal's. It is not surprising then, that both Williams and Leal find traces of a rural folk culture of previous generations within the urban popular culture of contemporary capitalism. Our thinking about such a rural or folk culture should not be nostalgically romantic—it was a culture of deprivation, oppression, or slavery, which is why its popular creativities of making do with limited resources transfer so readily to contemporary conditions. The argument that some of those resources, at least, came from nature rather than the oppressor is hardly convincing—in both agrarian capitalism and feudalism nature was transformed into land owned by the elite, its resources had to be "poached"—a constant cultural and material activity of the oppressed which de Certeau (1984) uses as a metaphor for popular practices in general. The material and cultural resources were limited, they were the resources of the other, and they always worked, in part at least, to constrain or oppress. The "continuing interplay of constraint and creativity," which Williams (1988, p. 47) identifies as characteristic of popular culture is a condition of oppression, and thus transfers readily from rural to urban, from a slave or serf-based rural capitalism to its urban industrial equivalent.

Williams describes how this creativity works in, for instance, the culture of collard greens—the fertilizing, nurturing, and harvesting of them in urban backyards, and the multitude of ways of chopping, cooking, seasoning, and serving them. Collard greens are used to negotiate the differences and similarities between Carolina and Washington, and also between individual creativities within a common set of constraints. Barbecue sauce is another, equally important, opportunity for popular creativity. Because the ingredients for the sauce, as the conditions for growing the greens, were different in Washington from Carolina, both greens and sauce were consciously used to make comparative sense of the difference: but the difference lay in the constraints, in the resources available, not in the creativity of their use.

Popular creativity is concretely contextual. It exists not as an abstract ability as the bourgeois habitus conceives of artistic creativity: it is a creativity of practice, a bricolage. It is a creativity which both produces objects such as quilts, diaries, or furniture arrangements but which is equally if not more productive in the practices of daily life, in the ways of dwelling, of walking, of making do. Objects are comparatively easy for the investigator to describe and transcribe from one habitus to another, but the specificities of their context and the practiced ways of living are much more resistant; they constitute a culture which is best experienced from the inside and difficult to study from without.

Ethnographers attempting to get access to this culture frequently come up against what Levine (1972, p. 140) calls "sacred inarticulateness," by which he refers to people's inability to explain their most sacred institutions in an objective discourse: instead they resort to responses like "It's hard to explain this one, but if you were one of us and did it, then you would understand" (Levine, in Brett Williams, 1988, p. 104). Williams argues that this inarticulateness, this reluctance to transform a contextualized experience into decontextualized discourse, extends beyond the sacred to the mundane; *Dallas* fans constantly "explained" their experience of the program with remarks like "if you watch it, you'll see."

As Bourdieu (1977) points out, practices can circulate and reproduce culture without their meanings passing through discourse or consciousness. He distinguishes between practice and discourse, and notes somewhat sadly that to study practice we need to bring it to the level of discourse, but in doing so we change its ontological status, for a defining feature of practice is that it is *not* discourse (pp. 110, 120). It is hard to find a final answer to this problem, and indeed there may not be one, but a partial solution may well involve a discursive and social flexibility, the development of the ability to experience as far as possible from the inside other peoples' ways of living that must be theorized from the outside. This may well require cultural theorists to follow the example of some feminists, for example, in using their personal experience of living and practicing culture as a key element in the production of a theoretical discourse and its more distanced and generalized explanations of the world.

It is not a coincidence that the devaluation of mundane culture in many academic theories goes hand in hand with the epistemological, methodological, and ethical problems of studying it, or even of describing it or identifying it as an object of study. A science of the particular is alien to our academic habitus. This problem is not confined to social and cultural theory, it is also addressed in contemporary cognitive theory. Like traditional cultural theory, cognitive psychology has tended to focus its attention upon generalizable laws that transcend the immediate contexts of their uses. Cognitive theory has tended to devalue the contextual in favor of the universal.

Jean Lave (1988), however, in her account of the Adult Math Project and subsequent investigations into mathematics in everyday life argues against these attempts to explain calculation as a universal, non-contextualized process:

> "Cognition" observed in everyday practice is distributed—stretched over, not divided among—mind, body, activity and culturally organized settings. . . . Math "activity" (to propose a term for a distributed form of cognition) takes form differently in different situations. (p. 1)

The main thrust of Lave's rhetoric is to challenge traditional cognitive theory and its pedagogic application. She gives numerous examples from her own and from others' studies of successful contextualized math opposed to "failures" in the decontextualized math performed in the classroom. A young scorer for a local bowling team performed complex, rapid error-free calculations in practice, but when asked to perform what the researchers thought were the same cognitive operations out of context (i.e. in the classroom under test conditions) he was utterly unable to. Similarly, women in supermarkets never made a mistake when comparing comparative values of different-sized, differently priced cans that they held in their hands, but were far less accurate when asked to perform the same calculations out of their social context.

Lave cites an example of contextualized math. A women shopper was faced with the problem of how many apples to buy. She picked up the apples one at a time and put them into her cart as she verbalized her math processes to the researchers:

> There's only about three or four [apples] at home, and I have four kids, so you figure at least two apiece in the next three days. These are the kind of things I have to resupply. I only have a certain amount of storage space in the refrigerator, so I can't load it up totally . . . Now that I'm home in the summertime, this is a good snack food. And I like an apple sometimes at lunchtime when I come home. (Lave, 1988, p. 2)

Lave comments that there are a number of acceptable solutions, 9, 13, 21. It also seems significant that the calculations are performed through the actions of picking up apples, the matching of the actions to the idea of her children eating them, and, I assume, a visualization of the amount of space in her fridge at that time, not as an abstract capacity but as a concrete specificity. Lave observes that this woman is not interested in a generalizable answer that relates to the problem in terms of a universalized criterion of right-wrong, but that problem and answer shaped each other in action in a specific setting. In this material setting the shopper's cognitive processes are part of her physical relationship with the goods on display. The supermarket is a densely woven texture of commodity information and display, but through her routine practices the experienced shopper transforms information overload into an information-specific setting. As she selects the commodities she wants, so she selects the information she wants. Her selections from *their* repertoire constitutes her setting which is both produced by her cognitive processes and plays a part in producing them. The "setting" is a coming together of the material specificity of the context and the mental processes by which that context is lived.

Lave's concept of the setting reminds us, in many respects of Bourdieu's habitus. Settings are constructed within the larger arenas which are the products of the social order. The supermarket is an arena full of the goods and information produced by the political economy of capitalism, but within it, shoppers construct for the period and purposes of shopping their own settings. A setting is, in Lave's definition, a "repeatedly experienced, personally ordered and edited version of the arena" (p. 151).

A setting is generated out of the practice of grocery shopping but at the same time generates that practice:

> [A setting's] articulatory nature is to be stressed; a setting is not simple a mental map in the mind of the shopper. Instead it has simultaneously an independent, physical character and a potential for realization only in relation to shoppers' activity. (Lave, 1988, p. 152–53)

The setting-arena relationship also relates to the difference between place and space as theorized by de Certeau (1984). For him place is an ordered structure provided by the dominant order through which its power to organize and control is exerted. It is often physical. So cities are places built to organize and control the lives and movements of their "city subjects" in the interests of the dominant. So, too, supermarkets, apartment blocks, and universities are places. But within and against them, the various formations of the people construct their spaces by the practices of living. So renters make the apartment, the place of the landlord, into their space by the practices of living; the textures of objects, relationships, and behaviors with which they occupy and possess it for the period of their renting. Space is practiced place, and space is produced by the creativity of the people using the resources of the other. De Certeau stresses the political conflict involved, the confrontation of opposing social interests that is central to the construction of space out of place. Lave focuses more on the functional creativity of the activities involved in constructing a setting out of an arena. But her argument shows that a setting is a material and cognitive space where the inhabitant or shopper is in control, is able to cope successfully.

The construction, occupation, and ownership of one's own space/setting within their place/arena, the weaving of one's own richly textured life within the constraints of economic deprivation and oppression, are not just ways of controlling some of the conditions of social existence; they are also ways of constructing, and therefore exerting some control over, social identities and social relations. The practices of everyday life within and against the determinate conditions of the social order construct the identities of difference of the social actors amongst the various formations of the subaltern.

Theories of subjectivity, even when elaborated into ones of split or nomadic subjectivities, still stress the top-down construction of social identity or social consciousness.

Theories of split or multiple subjectivity, in particular, try to encompass the contradictions that produce differences, but these contradictions are traced back to the complex elaborations of late capitalist societies: splits in subjectivities are produced by splits in the system. Theories of the nomadic subject so move more towards the idea of social agents who exert some control over their trajectories through the social space, but their emphasis is still more upon the determining, if loosely determining, structures through which they move, rather than the practices by which those movements are put in effect and made material.

I want to help develop a cultural theory that can both account for and validate popular social difference, for it is in these differences that we find what the people bring to the social order. In promoting this perspective, I am not devaluing those studies which focus on the pervasive and determining effectivities of the power bloc, but I am asserting that accounts of the social and cultural systems which neglect the positive input of the people are not yet complete. The differences that I call popular are produced by and for the various formations of the people: they oppose and disrupt the organized disciplined individualities produced by the mechanisms of surveillance, examination, and information which Foucault has shown are the technologies of the mechanism of power. Popular differences exceed the differences required by elaborated white patriarchal capitalism. They are bottom-up differences which are socially and historically specific, so they cannot be explained by psychologically based theories of individual difference, nor by idealist visions of free will. Popular differences are not the product of biological individualism nor of any ultimate freedom of the human spirit. The embodied, concrete, context-specific culture of everyday life is the terrain in which these differences are practiced, and the practice is not just a performance of difference, but producer of it.

The Body of Difference

Foucault argues that the mechanisms which organize us into the disciplined subjects required by capitalism work ultimately through the body. He shares with ideology theorists the attempt to account for the crucial social paradox of our epoch—that our highly elaborated social system of late capitalism is at once deeply riven with inequalities and conflicts of interest yet still manages to operate smoothly enough to avoid the crises of antagonism that might spark revolution. He differs from them in disarticulating power and its attendant disciplinary mechanisms from a direct correlation with the class system, and in focusing less upon the forces that produce subjects in ideology, than upon the micro-technologies of power which produce, organize, and control social differences.

Within his enterprise the body replaces the subject. It is through the body and its behaviors that medicine, psychiatry, and the law define and impose our social norms and work to cure or punish those that exceed them. Within these norms the organization of bodily behavior in space and time forms the basis of the social order. For the system to work, we must occupy certain "work stations" at certain times in the office or factory, the classroom or family home, the shipping mall or holiday beach. These "work stations" must be individualized so that any *body* not occupying them properly can be identified and disciplined. Similarly, every *body's* individual history, his or her accumulation of behaviors, is recorded and rated in school records and grade sheets, work records, credit ratings, criminal records, driving records—our society works on a highly elaborated system of surveying, and recording, ranking, and individuating our everyday behaviors. Individuality of this sort is a top-down product: individuals are differentiated according to the demands of the system, and individuation becomes a disciplinary mechanism. Its technologies of differentiation do not measure individual differences that pre-exist them, but actively produce those differences as part of the operation of its power. This continuous process of individuation is power-in-practice, is discipline-in-practice. It is not the power of one class over another, nor the discipline of officers over subalterns; it is a social technology of control that organizes the behaviors of everyone within it, the big cogs as much as the little cogs. The social order, as Foucault analyzes it, depends upon the control of people's bodies and behaviors: it couldn't give a damn about their subjectivities.

The body and its specific behavior is where the power system stops being abstract and becomes material. The body is where it succeeds or fails, where it is acceded to or struggled against. The struggle for control, top-down vs. bottom-up, is waged on the material terrain of the body and its immediate context.

The culture of everyday life is a culture of concrete practices which embody and perform differences. These embodied differences are a site of struggle between the measured individuations that constitute social discipline, and the popularity-produced differences that fill and extend the spaces and power of the people.

The body enters into immediate, performed relationship with the different settings or spaces it inhabits. The shopper who picks up the apples as she calculates the relationship between the number of her kids, the days till the next shopping trip, and the room in her refrigerator is not performing an abstract calculation that any *body* could but is living a concrete relationship specific to her and thus different from every *body* else's. So, too, the memorabilia that fill Lucy and Robert's apartment are not commodities that any *body* could have bought; they are embodiments of unique, personal histories that are different from every *body* else's, and they are part of the texture of everyday culture *only* because they carry this difference, because they bring the absent but unique past into the concreteness of the present where it is apprehensible by the senses of the body.

My argument's focus upon the particularity of the body and its setting does not mean that I wish to ignore or marginalize the relationship of the body of the person to the body politic, the social body. For the body is necessarily a socially situated body. Our bodies' behaviors in time and space, our practices of habitation, extend the body into the habitat and relate it to other similarly but differently habituated bodies. In this body-habitat, social space becomes geographical place, structural social relations become lived personal relationships. The body-habitat is the materializing process of habitus not a subset of it, but an embodying performance of it. The body-habitat incarnates the habitus; the habitus informs the body-habitat, and, at the same time, inscribes the larger social order into its incarnated, practiced forms. This relationship of the concrete body-habitat through the habitus to the historical social order is a synecdochal, contingent one, not a metaphorical, transformed one.

The body in this account differs theoretically though not politically from Bakhtin's account of the relationship between the body politic, the body of the people, and the licensed, excessive bodies, the grotesque bodies of carnival. For Bakhtin, the relationship between the carnivalesque bodies and the body politic is one of metaphoric transformation: the social antagonisms in the body politic are given expressive, material form in the inversions and disorder of bodies in the carnival. For him, the body becomes the expressive site of the life of the people only at moments when the oppressive order is transformed into a liberatory disorder. These moments are historically produced by the differences within the body politic between the official order and the life of the people, so the carnival body is the materialization of social difference: but the carnival body is a transformation of the mundane body. The theory I am exploring proposes the mundane body as the synecdochal embodiment of the social order, and therefore of the social differences within that order.

Without social difference there can be no social change. The control of social difference is therefore always a strategic objective of the power bloc. A progressive theory of social difference needs to include, but must go beyond, the analysis of differences produced and controlled by the dominant social order.

I am turned, then, towards an attempt to account for the origin of progressive or popular social difference in the inescapable differences of the body's physical, geographical, and historical specificities. The fact that we have different bodies, and that no two of those bodies can occupy the same place at the same time seems a reasonable starting point. But the body, its geography and history, are not empiricist facts in a Newtonian nature. Their natural essences are semiotically inert: they become epistemologically interesting only when they enter a social order, for only then do their differences become structured rather than essential; only a social order, therefore, can make differences signify. The concrete practices of everyday life are the insertion of the body into the social order, and, de Certeau would argue, the inscription of the social order upon that body.

It is here that I find Bourdieu's theory of the habitus most helpful even if I push it somewhat further than he does. The habitus is located within a social space which has both spatial and temporal dimensions; the spatial dimension models the social space as a dynamic relationship among the major determining forces within our social order—economic, class, education, culture—and their materialization in the behavior, tastes, and dispositions of those who, because of their differential positioning within the social space, embody and enact those forces differently. The temporal dimension is where we can trace the trajectories by which social formations or individuals within them, change their geographical positioning through historical movements.

The theory of the habitus collapses many of our conventional distinctions between the individual and the social, between the interior and the exterior, between the micro and the macro, between practices and structures, between time and place. The habitus is not just a pre-given environment into which we are born, it lives in us just as much as we live in it, we embody it just as it informs us. It admits of no categorical distinctions between the inhabitants, the habitat, and the practices of habitation.

Similarly, the habitus does not relate to the social space as does a social category—class, gender, race, age, or whatever. A habitus is not distinguished from others by a categorical boundary; rather, it is a conjunctural process by which we experience and enact the forces that form (and potentially transform) the social space and the locatable practices of habitation within it. It is a process with historical and social specificity, not a generalized category. But because the habitus disallows traditional categorical distinctions does not mean that its conceptual movement is towards a polymorphous homogeneity: far from it. The whole thrust of Bourdieu's work shows that the habitus is a factor of social difference. The "habitus" offers a theoretical framework within which physical difference and social difference can be related contingently, not metaphorically, and within which social processes can be analyzed in terms of concrete practices intersecting with the structuring forces of a particular social order. Because the habitus is not circumscribed by categorical boundaries it admits of greater mobility than Bourdieu himself gives it credit for. His theory focuses on the homogenizing factors that enable him to specify more precisely where each habitus is centered in the map of social space; the corollary of this is that he tends to ignore the contradictory forces that make it difficult for some people to "settle" comfortably and make one habituated position their home. All of us, I believe, experience enough of the contradictory forces of elaborated capitalist societies to have developed a degree of familiarity with more than one position in the social space. And some, particularly those who experience most acutely the crucial contradictions that are often set up when class, gender, and race intersect, can have multiple "homes" or habitats, often quite distant from each other. The habitus, then, describes the ways of living within a social space rather than its inhabitants, and though these ways of living are constitutive of social identity they do not constitute it totally.

As I argued at the start of this paper, most academics are most comfortable in the same region in the map of social space, that of high education, relatively high-class, high-cultural, but low economic capital, most of it acquired rather than inherited. The habitus of this position disposes our habits of thought towards the generalizable and abstract; the equivalent disposition in the academic sphere to that which validates aesthetic distance in the sphere of art. We are habituatedly disposed to find the greatest significance, as the greatest beauty, in structures that seek to explain the concrete by distancing themselves from it. We therefore, as historical products, find a science of the particular particularly difficult to envisage.

Academic theory, no less than cultural taste, is produced within and for a habitus in order to draw social distinction between it and other, differently located, habituses. From this point of view, we can usefully extend the politics of Jean Lave's work on cognition in practice. Her rhetoric is intended to challenge first the traditional orthodoxy of cognitive psychology and its universalizing tendency, and then to challenge its adoption by the educational system so that the universalized "laws" of arithmetic are used to make and measure individuated differences of mathematical competence. These laws, however, are the product of a particular academic habitus—ours—which not only produces them, but universalizes them in a way that obscures their social production—just as the traditional theory of aesthetics universalizes and obscures its own social and historical specificity. It is more useful, then, to situate her argument more broadly and to see it as not just a marshalling of counter-evidence that orthodox cognitive theory has failed to accommodate but as symptomatic of a larger problem within academia in general. Understanding the disposition or practices of habituses that are alien to our own faces us directly with the need to recognize the socially produced dimensions of our habits of thinking. I believe that the theoretical and empirical exploration of the relationships between practice, the body, and place will prove to be one of the more fruitful directions that the field will take. In taking this direction, though, I hope that cultural studies never loses its political edge.

Politics have never been far below the surface in my attempt to think critically about the relationships between dominant and subordinated habituses in cultural theory. I hope we can narrow the gap and increase the travel between them because by doing so I believe we can help change the relationship between the academy and other social formations, in particular those of the subordinate. Many of those living within such subordinated formations find little pertinence between the conditions of their everyday lives and academic ways of explaining the world. It is in none of our interests to allow this gap to grow any wider, particularly when we consider that many of the most effective recent movements for social change have involved allegiances between universities and members of repressed or subordinated social formations.

Cultural studies has always been concerned to examine critically and to restructure the relationship between dominant and subordinated cultures; it has always been concerned to interrogate the relationship between the academy and the rest of the social order, and I hope that the development whose outline is sketched in this paper will offer one way of continuing these traditions. Feminism, for example, has achieved much in making us recognize how patriarchy has shaped and informed what once appeared to be "disinterested" academic thought. Similarly, those working in the cultural politics of ethnicity are exposing the whiteness of traditional Western theory. These movements are so valuable because they do more than explain and validate the experiences of women and people of color within a white patriarchy; they also refuse to admit that their ways of knowing and experiencing the world are in any way subordinate or inferior: instead they position them as powerful challenges to the dominant epistemological frameworks. I think there are signs that these challenges are being reproduced along other axes of domination, particularly those of class, age, educational attainment, and cultural prestige.

In this paper I have focused on one formulation of such a challenge and the problems it poses. This conference invites us to peer into the future of cultural studies, and one direction that I hope the field will continue in, and one that I intend to contribute to, is the development of ways of theorizing culture that grant the concrete practices of subordinated ways of living a degree of importance in theory which is the equivalent to that which they have in their own habitus, even though this is distanced from, and socially subordinated to, the habitus whose discourses are necessary to produce theory. Such a cultural theory will, hopefully, not position itself too singularly and securely within the academic habitus, and will thus try to avoid the risk of implicitly granting its theoretical discourse a position of privilege which would reproduce in academic terms the process of subordination which is characteristic of the social order that we wish to criticize and change. Practice may have to be changed into discourse in order to be analyzed; specificities may have to be subjected to generalization for their significances to be understood and communicated, however incompletely: but, equally, practice should be allowed to expose the incompleteness of theory, to reveal the limits of its adequacy, and specificity should be able to assert the value of that which generalization overlooks or excludes.

It should be possible to grant to the dispositions, tastes, and ways of knowing that are germane to the habituses subordinated by our current social hierarchy a legitimacy equivalent to those of a more dominant habitus. In achieving this, we should be able to set up relatively more reciprocal relationships between the habituses involved so that the critical and explanatory perspective by which one views the other can work in a bottom-up direction as well as a top-down.

Such a way of theorizing culture may well produce insights into how social differences can be produced and maintained by the people in their own interests. This bottom-up production of difference is likely to be found, *inter alia,* in the specificities of everyday life, and I think there are three movements in cultural studies which are addressing this area with different but related foci of interest. These are the ethnography of contextualized cultural practices, the theorizations of the cultural politics of the body, and the development of a cultural geography through which to analyze the meanings of place and environment at a particular historical conjuncture. In following these through I hope we can minimize the problems of establishing productive, rather than reductive, relationships between practice and discourse, and between more dominant and more subordinated ways of living in and explaining our social world.

DISCUSSION: JOHN FISKE

MEAGHAN MORRIS: I have a real problem with the notion of the habitus and with your deployment of it, and with the dichotomies that flow from it: the abstract vs the concrete, the dominant vs the popular, the cool vs the warm (in Bourdieu). You began your talk with a description of the academic position and at the end of your talk you came back again to an academic position from which it's possible to talk about habituses alien to us. Now, it seems to me that if I had a habitus—and I'm not sure that I do—it wouldn't be the kind of high-bourgeois grounded space that you described. My habitus would be much more like a cyberpunk novel, in which this room is not the grounding of a tradition but just another knot in the net, and after a while it's no different from some grubby little concrete bunker in Sydney. The people in these spaces, are not very different, the discussions are not very different. Saying that is not an occasion for cynicism about the situation of contemporary knowledge production, but rather a question about the politics of movement which are at stake in the current redeployment and redefinition of economic oppression. These Bourdieuian oppositions have been extensively criticized by de Certeau and by John Frow (in *Textual Practice*) as coming, in the end, from an impossible perspective which is that of the disciplinary self-affirmation of a sociological knowledge which can discriminate between the abstract and the concrete. When you use these oppositions (e.g. concrete/abstract), do you believe they have an ontological status of some kind? Do you think that they emerge from your history as an English academic, or do you have some kind of strategic purpose in mind in maintaining what seems to me an increasingly difficult rhetoric to generalize in the modern world? This seems particularly true in cultural studies where people whose everyday life is constructed by gender, racial, national, and in some cases economic marginalization from the wider society are funded to theorize their lived concrete specificity. I don't think we can maintain this distance which is specific to the old European bourgeois academic class.

FISKE: Yes, I do. I find Bourdieu's work very productive and useful provided that we don't buy into what I think he often invites us to, which is a fairly rigidly deterministic framework. It seems to me his own account of his own theories is much too Marxistly deterministic and doesn't allow enough room for ideas of the social agent having to negotiate these multiple contradictions that elaborated capitalism faces us with. So, when I push Bourdieu a bit further, what I want to do is to break his class determination, his strong polarity of thought between the bourgeois and the proletariat, and to increase the theoretical and conceptual opportunities for movement within the social space as he maps it.

And I think we need to understand that you and I inflect Bourdieu somewhat differently. Your example of a cyberpunk novel shows that you emphasize the cultural and textual dimension of habitus over the social and economic. I find his theory useful because it relates cultural and textual differences to social and economic ones and that is why, I think, I find him more useful than you do. You look for similarities, if I heard you correctly, between the people in this room and people in a concrete bunker in Sydney. I find Bourdieu useful because he helps me clarify the differences in a way that does not privilege those in this room.

Having said that, I think you have correctly pointed out that my paper may have done him a disservice. I did argue from a polarized position in a way that his map of social space does not require. The differences he charts are much more mobile and multiple than I may have implied in my paper. In particular, I think I underemphasized the space for movement both within the habitus and between habituses. We are agents active in the process of structuration, and while we are very much part of the product of our own social history, and his theory gives us some attempt to account for how we may not be totally imprisoned by that history. I find this bit of his work particularly useful, because it gives me a way of understanding, as I review my own academic development, why it is that I've not in the past been very good at seeing where my thinking has come from socially. I've not in the past been very good at seeing where my thinking has come from socially. I've tended to assume that in some way my theory has freed me from my social history, enabling me to produce frameworks of reference and ways of thinking that I appear to have chosen and developed myself in some oddly asocial, ahistorical way. So Bourdieu's theory of the habitus gives me at least a purchase upon a way of trying to think through the production of my own thought: that is where I find Bourdieu most useful for myself. In terms of your larger question, I've got some real doubts about the traditional role of the intellectual as the provider of theory for the people that will enable the people to politicize their own experience in a way that they could not were the intellectual not to give them this new ability. It seems to me that historically we've not been very good at doing it, anyway, particularly in recent social conditions and formations. And that part of the reason we've not been good at it is because some intellectuals assume that when experience is not theorized, is not made explicitly political, the cause of this is an imagined deficiency in the people and their ways of knowing the world, a deficiency that in some way academic theory, academic intellect, can correct. I do have some real problems with this, particularly as we're getting more and more evidence to show that there are very real and valuable insights, ways of knowing, ways of thinking, in subordinate social formations. And I suppose that at the back of my mind, and sometimes at the front, is the belief that I have at least as much to learn from people who experience the world in ways that differ from my own as I have to teach them. In other words, I want to try to exploit the mobility in the habitus theory to see if I can't move my habitus closer to theirs, to narrow the gap between social differences without denying the validity and vitality of those differences. So what I'm trying to explore is how we, with our disposition towards discourse and our problem of understanding practice in concrete specificities, might be able to narrow the gap. I'm asking if it is possible to develop a two-way traffic between these different ways of experiencing social conditions and their different ways of knowing, different ways of thinking, different ways of producing culture. Because I value these differences, I think they're a source of terrific vitality in our culture, and may, under certain conditions, be a source of social change. But for us to be able to tap into this vitality, we have to try to understand it in its own terms, and in order to do that I believe we have to critically examine the limitations of our own socially produced thought processes.

PAULA TREICHLER: This is actually a mundane version of what Meaghan Morris just asked. Several years ago a colleague and I wrote a paper which required us to review the literature on actual everyday life in academic institutions. We were shocked at how pitiful and poverty-stricken this literature was. There are a lot of terrible quantitative studies about classrooms and such, but almost nothing interpretive of any depth. There are novels, like *The Mind-Body Problem,* that begin to get at the practices of academic life. There are conservative studies, like *The Academic Tribes.* There are hundreds of first-person testimonials from women, black people, gay people, postcolonial people, who are in academic institutions. But there are few real ethnographies of what universities are about or what academics do. And it seemed obvious to us that academics found the mundane activities of their own lives extremely uncomfortable and difficult to write about, perhaps ethically problematic, certainly uninteresting and unproductive. We also felt that a certain kind of leftist politics prevented academics from writing about themselves, as though it were too bourgeois, too professional, too narcissistic, too self-indulgent. Now aren't you reproducing this rather conventional received view of academic life? Isn't it possible that, like language, every habitus—including an academic habitus—is equally complex although maybe in different ways, and that the academy has as dense a culture of everyday life as that of the Brazilian peasants that you talked about? Isn't some of this already suggested in feminist work of the last twenty years?

FISKE: I think the point you make is an excellent one—there is an everyday life in academic institutions which, as you rightly point out, is disparaged by the lack of attention paid to it. I hadn't thought of it in quite that way before, but it still seems to me that we can trace the dominant tendencies in the academic habitus at work in the way certain ways of living and knowing in academia are highly rewarded and encouraged while others are suppressed. If one implication of your question is that the study of the silenced, concrete ways of living in our own institutions is as valuable an object of study as those of other social formations, and that in addition, it is one which I am better equipped to carry out, then I take that very much to heart—it's something to think about. The question within your comment is a difficult one. I take your point that in describing the academic habitus in this way I run the risk of reproducing it, but I hope my description is critical enough to minimize that risk. My intention is certainly not to reproduce it, but rather to reveal and disqualify some of its most highly self-regarded attributes. Whether, in attempting to do this, I have oversimplified the academic habitus, homogenized it and minimized its internal contradictions, is, I think, the core of your question. I don't know. I don't know if a habitus can have the internal heterogeneity and complexity of a language, and thus be as productive or generative, but I think in Bourdieu's account of it, it does not. I think that in his model the contradictions and complexities arise between different positions in the map of social space. A habitus, for him, is relatively coherent and homogeneous. Those who are relatively immobile, who inhabit a limited terrain are thus likely to experience their world and themselves in relatively coherent and homogeneous ways: the more mobile, which means the less habituated, will experience more contradictions and complexities. This sort of generative complexity may well derive from the experience, or very often the necessity, of living in different social habitats and the habituses that go with them. What your question has made me think of, perhaps more explicitly than before, is that I may well have generalized too much from my own relative immobility and homogeneity to academia in general. I am very conscious that as a white educated male I live and work in institutions that reward precisely those social characteristics, and that therefore encourage the ways of thinking, writing, and knowing that go with them, epistemologies which both produce and are the products of the current academic habitus. The theory of the habitus helps me understand how such a social position is made interior and lived from the inside, not in terms of a subjectivity produced in domination, but through positionality within a hierarchized, but not monodimensional power structure. And, if I may continue in a confessional and self-reflexive mode for a moment, I am deeply aware that my own social trajectory has not required me to inhabit widely different terrains and thus to develop the mobility of habitus that I am trying to understand. But I offer this self-reflexivity in public only because the characteristics which dominate my habitus— whiteness, middle-classness, also dominate the academic habitus.

And this brings me to another point in your question, one that contains, I believe, an implicit rebuke which I accept. I agree with you that feminism has revealed and validated aspects of women's culture within and against patriarchy, which patriarchy systematically ignores or disparages. One aspect of this culture, not the only one by any means, but one important aspect, is that it is to be found in the specificities and practices of everyday life. My own thinking has been immensely influenced by this sort of feminist scholarship, which I hope I have acknowledged more fully in my other work that I did in this particular paper. What I did not do in this paper, and I should have done, is to make explicit in my theorizing and interpretation the fact that all three of my chosen paradigm case studies were produced by women, and that one of them was African-American, one Brazilian, and one of unspecified race. Gender and race are clearly pertinent here: I believe they not only struggle against the dominant tendencies of the academic habitus, but also produce knowledges that these dominant ways of knowing overlook. I think these studies evidence a mobility between habituses which, if we understand it better, may lead us towards a synthesizing of theory and practice. You are quite right to make explicit, in a way that I did not, the contribution to this that can only come by knowledge crossing gender, race, and, I would add, class, differences. So, as I hear myself responding to your question, I think I am concluding that the habitus does not have the internal complexity and generativity of a language, but that mobility between or among habituses may.

BILL WARNER: What concerned me was the discrepancy or tension between what your talk sought to promote—valuing the concrete everyday life of the people in the hopes of eliding the distance between academia and academic space and the space of the people—and what your talk actually *does,* which is to produce a very abstract and ultimately aesthetic image of the life of the people. You start with a critique, by now very familiar, of a liberal humanist aesthetic stance which valorizes the aesthetic distance between the knower and the known. But in your representation of the culture of everyday life, you compose an aesthetic object with all of the classical elements of that composition. You have, for the frame, a neutral space behind everyday life which is the unspecified oppression of the people. Then you have the heroic artist, the people, where individual figures of the people are recruited to act the role of the artistic agent, the individual family that moves from North Carolina to Washington. Then you have certain specific vivid images, a flower on the television set, the apples carried into the cart by the canny English housewife. And finally you have a series of aesthetic judgments: unity, convergence, density, richness, and so on. My concern with this series of aesthetic judgments is that you are conferring upon these artists of everyday life, the people, the kind of freedom that is classically conferred upon the consumers of great art. So finally it seemed to me that you do exactly what you accuse postmodernism of doing: reducing experience to a series of images.

FISKE: In many ways of course you have reiterated the problem I was addressing in the paper, a problem which we inevitably face when we attempt to change the practices of others into our discourse—which we have to if we are to talk about them in our professional lives. I agree with you that I cannot talk about an entourage of objects around a television set without changing their ontological status by putting them into my discourse. But maybe my discourse does not have to erase their particularity entirely and does not have to set its own way of knowing as inherently superior, but tries to account for the value of concrete cultural practices in the process of putting them into discourse.

I disagree with you completely, however, in your two final points. The culture of everyday life is absolutely different from that of the heroic artist, precisely because everyone produces it, not the privileged artist. Robert and Lucy are significant because they are typical and ordinary rather than special. And far from conferring freedom upon these artists of everyday life, I emphasized how constrained they are and how this constraint makes aesthetic distance impossible.

Equally, these densely signifying objects and practices are very different from the fragmentary images of postmodernism. These practices and objects are not empty signifiers, they are not just a shiny surface, despite the shininess of many of their surfaces. They are deeply significant and firmly anchored in their users' ways of living: there is not infinite deferral or senselessness about them; they are coherent, signifying, and fixed in the particular culture of their practitioners.

HOMI BHABHA: I think, John, by setting up this habitus, that is you who are actually producing the distance between the habitus and everyday life. In a sense, in trying to overcome the distance, you reproduce it. Perhaps there's another way of thinking that any institutional or pedagogical site, in constructing its own authority as a discourse, is always being internally distanciated, is actually getting into a very chancy area where it is always going to be erased in some sense. So perhaps, instead of looking at it in a binary way, we should look (and I think Claude Lefort is quite interesting here) at the way that every pedagogical site is always having to become the exorbitant site of its own practice. Then we don't have a division between everyday life and the institution. We begin to see a much more hybrid, in-between area of contestation developing. Then questions of consensual culture and totalization don't always tend to be the horizons towards which we work. We are able then to construct differences—the differences of gender, of class, of race—in new, hybrid, unrecognizable, and perhaps even incommensurable figurations and prefigurations.

ROSALIND BRUNT: I disagree with your comment that the problem with Marxism, is that it wasn't good at looking at particularities and specificities of everyday life. I would like to reverse that and say that Marxism is only good as a practice if it does start by looking at the specificities and particularities of everyday life. But I think that it doesn't stop there. And, at the risk of being old fashioned in my Marxism, I would remind you of Lenin's description of Marxism as the science of the concrete against those who reified Marxism. He insisted that it was a concrete analysis of current situations. And nobody examined that better than Gramsci in looking at popular culture, at how common sense articulated with hegemony and so on. But Gramsci didn't just look at the particularities of popular culture; he looked at them precisely in order to move to macro-analysis and link up civil society with political society. What worries me is that if you stick with everyday life you can end up being purely descriptive and reifying theory, leaving it as a middle-class and academic practice in a way I think that Gramsci at least attempts to overcome. Thus although you constantly mentioned capitalism and patriarchy, you leave them inert and not dynamic.

FISKE: Certainly, the first part of that, Ros, I take as a well-deserved rebuke and a warning not to throw in a quick handwritten comment at the start of a paper. Of course, we should not think of Marxism, as you rightly point out, in a singular mode. There are as many different Marxisms as almost there are practitioners. And, yes, I agree with you entirely, that Gramsci's emphasis on historical specificity and the concrete is very productive. The Marxism I was referring to was more that Althusserian, Barthesian type that is much better at tracing the way that the flow of meanings and ideologies around society serves the interests of those with social power. The debate is within Marxism for sure, and certainly a very interesting one.

This leads me on to your other point, which is, I think part of an equally crucial debate over the relationship between the politics of everyday life and the politics of theory or between micro-practices and macro-political action. I think that most brands of Marxism, including many of the developments of Gramsci, though not Gramsci's work itself, have tended to underestimate the politics of everyday life, and, indeed have sometimes identified them as reactionary and have disqualified everyday life as a site of significant political activity at all. What would be more productive would be an attempt to find and build links between progressive elements at all levels of activity and culture, and this may involve favoring progressive change over radical or revolutionary change. I think James Scott's work on peasant culture may be helpful here. He starts his book on peasant culture in Malaysia with a broad survey of peasant rebellions throughout history and concludes that the peasant lot in general has not been improved by rebellion—actually the reverse for rebellion often calls down extremely repressive measures. What has improved the lot of peasants is the everyday tactical dissembling, the working to find the weak spots in the system and to exploit them, the evasion of authority so as to create spaces for promoting, as far as practicable, their own interests; that is, he concludes it is the politics of concrete practice which have had greater practical effect than the politics of macro-social action. Now I'm not saying that the politics of everyday life are enough on their own, but I am saying that everyday life is political, that its politics can be and often are progressive (though not radical), and that political theorists on the left have not been very good at understanding these politics nor at tapping into them.

ELSPETH PROBYN: I'd just like to remind you that there are also questions of actual, real danger to people, to women who walk on the street. And I would also like to recall at this moment, in the United States, in Canada, and in Britain, we have a growing popular discourse on the home, women returning to the home, the new traditionalism, the new family. And this is not about genders; this is *one* gender that is being representationally repositioned in the home with all the ideological problems that poses, as well as the problems of the violence that occurs to women in the house.

BELL HOOKS: I am frustrated by the binary opposition you make between the intellectual and the underclass, because I feel myself to be both working in the underclass in many ways and an intellectual. So that I feel all the more like an outsider here, at this conference that seems to me to be so much a mirroring of the very kinds of hierarchies that terrorize and violate.

The problem is we can't even dialogue in this space. The challenge to us here *is* to try and disrupt and subvert and change that and not just to sit here and be passively terrorized. We need to actualize the politics that we are trying to evoke as being that radical moment in cultural studies.

LINDA CHARNES: I appreciate the cookery in your paper, your efforts to fold de Certeau and his theory of the practice of everyday life into Bourdieu. But I think that there's an important distinction that de Certeau himself makes between strategy and tactics. What distinguishes tactics from strategies is that tactics are the practices that are deployed by people who don't own property. They're what renters do when they operate in a space that is owned by somebody else. People who operate tactically cannot keep what they produce. What I want to ask you is, how is anything produced by a renter keepable? And what would keep your practice and project from simply becoming a more "caring" way to keep the disempowered in the position where they remain simply objects of study and can't keep what you produce for them through your theory of practices?

FISKE: Yes, that's a very good question. In other of my writings, I spent much more time on the de Certeauian difference between tactics and strategy than I did here. And I do agree, it's a big problem, that, as you say, what is won by tactics cannot be stored, cannot be accumulated, cannot be kept. The victories of tactics exist only in their moments of performance. That is similar to the problem I was trying to address in this paper: tactics are practice. It is not a comfortable problem to address, but at least I am sure that we should not take one obvious way out which is to say that because tactics or because the practices of culture don't produce anything that can be accumulated and stored, they are therefore inherently less valuable objects of study or less valuable social practices than those that accumulate. I definitely want to oppose that assumption, and I'm sure you do too. And I think we ought to make something explicit which de Certeau doesn't make quite explicit enough in his writing, but I think it's there at the back of it, and this is the idea that there is something that is kept, there is something that is maintained, and that is what he calls a popular intransigence, an ultimate refusal to be subjugated.

CHARNES: There's a difference between subverting and refusing to be subjugated and actually materially benefiting from one's own practices. Every guerrilla fighter knows that it's possible to destabilize the power plot, but that doesn't necessarily transfer any of that real power, real property, or real capital into the hands of the people.

FISKE: Again, I think there's a difference that we haven't gone very far in understanding in between micro-politics of everyday life and micro-politics at the social level. I think we've got some evidence at least that in micro-politics of everyday life some of the gains may be kept, some of the terrain may be held. At what stage and under what conditions this can be translated to macro-social politics, I certainly have no answer. I agree with you, it's a very important question. And it's certainly one I'm going to think a lot about in the future.

TARA MCPHERSON: First I wanted to say that I agree with your assessment of Constance Penley's paper yesterday, and that it did provide a movement in and out of fandom and that culture, and I'm not convinced that your work bridges that gap between formulations within the academy and those in the proletariat. It seems to me that you're talking less about formulations within the proletariat, than about simultaneously universal and isolated individuals. The examples you provided us with today—a single woman grocery shopping, and the textured knickknacks of one apartment—lack the tension which was crucial in the contributions by Constance Penley, Donna Haraway, or Andrew Ross. All of them seemed to be addressing social formations more than specific individuals, and all were incorporating theory, be it psychoanalytic, Marxist, feminist, or ecological, with the practices of the everyday. Your examples and your specificities seem to replace what you call the divine habitus of the academy with a single habitant, so that it is just an act of reversal of the grand narrative you accuse the academy of producing.

FISKE: I agree with you that the problem of how to deal with the individual is crucial in contemporary cultural theory and you may well be right in pointing out that I haven't theorized it adequately either today or in the rest of my work. But I must disagree with you when you suggest that I talk about simultaneously universal and isolated individuals: I most emphatically do not, and the fact that you think I do is, I suspect, symptomatic of part of the main argument of my paper today—that is our difficulty in understanding the significance of the particular. The densely textured apartment, packed with particular and singular meanings for its renters, was related to the dense texturing of their walks down the neighborhood main street and their preference for densely textured television programs. And this cultural pattern was shown to be characteristic of others living in similar conditions of material deprivation and was shown to be a direct response to those conditions. Similarly, the woman shopping for apples was an example of situated cognition that could also be found in the young scorer for the bowling team and in other women shoppers, but could *not* be found in academic classrooms or most traditional academic cognitive theory. It was a particular instance of a situated, not generalized, knowledge in practice, just as the apartment was an instance of situated, not textualized, culture in practice. The way I am trying to work with the concept of the individual is first of all not to use the word because it brings with it all the baggage of ahistoricism, free will, enlightenment rationalism and so on which I reject entirely.

I suppose there are two main dimensions to my current thinking about the individual, which I might call particularity and agency. The individual body has a particularity in space and time which does differentiate it from other bodies and their spaces and their times. The socio-historical conditions that are shared by members of similar social formations are experienced in one important way, not the only way but a very important one, on the level of particularity: Particular experiences belonging to socially situated individuals are where macro-social conditions are made material, become part of people's lives and consciousness and where, in the culture of practice, they really start to *matter*. The dimension of people's lives and social identities which often seems most important to people themselves is this particularity. In arguing this I don't want to be seen to be arguing against theories which stress the importance of class consciousness, of solidarity, and so on, but I do want to argue against the possible inflections of those theories which discount the particular and which therefore, in my opinion, misstate the main problem. For I believe that our main problem is not how we can make individuals conscious of their class (or gender or ethnic) affiliations, but rather how we can understand the links between particular experiences of subordination and the more general and historical conditions which produce that subordination.

I also believe that we need to think of the person not as an individual, nor as a subject or embodied subjectivity, but as a socially interested agent. It seems to me that there are so many contradictory forces at work within the multiple elaborations of late capitalist societies that we have to develop the notion of a social agent who is capable of negotiating his or her particular trajectory through them. The contradictions in these forces are so many that we cannot be simply subject to them, for as soon as we become subject to one set of determination, we meet another set which clash with or deflect them. Complexly elaborated societies produce social agents, not social subjects. I call these agents "socially interested" because I believe that under certain conditions, though maybe not all the time, people can both be aware of their social interests and be capable of acting to promote them. Again, I don't want this agency to appear like a revised rationalism, for there is nothing ahistorical about it. It is a situated agency which is concerned to negotiate those specific conditions with which it is faced and in this negotiation to use the resources which those historical conditions have made available.

Throughout my more recent work I have given numerous examples of people exercising this agency: nowhere do I suggest that they are free-floating individuals, but I take pains to situate them as clearly as possible at this interface between macro–social forces and micro–histories and -experiences. They are not individuals in the way that you characterize them but neither are they embodied subjectivities; I believe the most productive way of thinking about them is as socially interested agents negotiating their particular trajectories through the historical conditions into which they were born.

11

The Cultural Study of Popular Music

Simon Frith

The Practice of Music

In her systematic, obsessive survey of musical life in Milton Keynes in the 1980s, the social anthropologist Ruth Finnegan (1989) comments that

> Milton Keynes was swarming with rock and pop bands. They were performing in the pubs and clubs, practising in garages, youth clubs, church halls and school classrooms, advertising for new members in the local papers and lugging their instruments around by car or on foot. There were probably around 100 groups, each with their own colourful names and brands of music. (p. 123)

Sara Cohen's (1987) recent ethnographic study of young music-makers in Liverpool begins similarly, by noting that a 1980 survey had found more than a thousand bands on Merseyside; there was no reason for her to think that there were any fewer groups by the mid-1980s. And both Finnegan and Cohen comment that these "creative amateurs" make a nonsense of residual suggestions either that people's involvement with pop is essentially parasitic or, alternatively, that playing rock music is somehow a spontaneous, folk-like activity.

Finnegan makes three general points about young people's pop involvement:

First, it rests on a substantial body of knowledge and an active sense of choice—musicians and audiences alike have a clear understanding of genre rules and histories, can hear and place sounds in terms of influence and source, have no hesitation about making and justifying judgments of musical meaning and value.

Second, (and this point is brought out even more strikingly by Cohen), young rock bands and musicians put the highest value on originality and self-expression, on music as a means of defining one's individual identity. "Most of the many rock bands in Milton Keynes composed their own music," notes Finnegan, defining the "rock mode" of musical creation as "collective prior composition through practice."

> Perhaps the most prominent single characteristic of the proccupations of rock players in Milton Keynes—apart from their variety—was their interest in expressing their own views and personality through music-making: a stress on individuality and artistic creation which accords ill with the mass cultural theorists' delineations of popular music. (1989, p. 129)

Cohen's young Liverpool groups saw themselves similarly as romantic artists, doing something personal and new, setting their work against the commercial formulas of the charts (holding such music, indeed, in a positively Adornoesque contempt). Such creativity isn't just seen as a matter of writing words and tunes; it involves the instrumental arrangement of songs, an understanding of sound, an ability to "compose" a performance and get an effect.

Third, following on from this, live performance is, for virtually all young rock bands, still the focal point of their work, "the epitome of musical enactment," in Finnegan's words. Performance is the central *ritual* of local rock, a special setting for music for which the audience is as important as the performers. It is in performance, as the musicians of Liverpool and Milton Keynes explain, that they experience the most intense feelings of achievement. To be on stage, the object of public attention, is to have confirmed the *glamor* of their chosen musical role.

One reason why pop music-making is deemed somehow less "cultured" than classical music-making (by low as well as high cultural theorists) is because it is described by the wrong criteria—pop musicians are taken to be a counter-form of classical musicians, proudly untaught and semi-skilled. The great strength of Finnegan's exhaustive account of every facet of a local music scene is that she is able to compare different music practices systematically, and thus show how both the differences and the similarities work. The pedagogical difference between rock and classical music, for example, is not that one group of musicians is taught, one untaught, but that they are taught differently, in different institutions, though often according to the same values. Most pop and rock musicians *are,* in formal terms, self-taught, which means by ear and hand (rather than by score and teacher), and it is true that in the pop world there is a remarkably short period between deciding to play an instrument and having the nerve and confidence to join a group and play in public. But such an apparently "spontaneous" process is still time-consuming, dependent on dedication, a rigorous rehearsal routine, and very hard work, and, indeed, a clear sense of "master" performers, the guitarists, drummers, and producers whose recordings the learner musician endlessly tries to copy. If popular musicians don't pass courses by satisfying examiners or teachers, if they, are, in Finnegan's words, "self-reliant and outside the formal organization pattern typical of many other musical groupings," they still do have to "pass" the practical tests set by fellow musicians and audiences; they are still perfectly capable of judging good and bad players, knowing whether their own work is hopeless, adequate, or improving.

To learn by copying is by necessity to be inventive—guitarists and drummers and home producers have to work out for themselves how to sound like their models, usually with quite different (and much cheaper) sound equipment. This means developing manual skills, a discriminating ear, and an ad hoc understanding of sound amplification (even singers have to learn to use the mike). And it brings into play, just as importantly, musical taste, a series of personal judgments as to what sounds right. The rock mode of music learning, in short, unlike the classical mode of apprenticeship and slow progress through fixed grades of performing difficulty, is by its nature *individualizing* (which is why even the lowliest performers believe they have something special to say). At the same time (at least as soon as performers move out of their bedrooms—and even there learning is often shared with friends) it is also essentially *collective.* Because many rock musicians don't read music, they have to learn to play together in endless collective experiments (this is what Finnegan means by "collective prior composition through practice"). As she notes, "among musical groups in Milton Keynes it was quite striking how many hours were spent in practices." And such collective work is also a consequence of the emphasis on performance: the basic musical skill rock and pop musicians want to learn is how to play to an audience.

Two additional points follow from this:

first, even at the most local level, playing music is only one role in a more elaborate set of tasks and relationships that define the musical world. The simplest school or garage group becomes "a band" by developing a support network of promoters and publicists, drivers and carriers, dedicated fans and followers. A performing pop band depends on a lot of people doing a lot of tasks, and the rock worlds of Liverpool and Milton Keynes are peopled by men and women teaching each other organizational and entrepreneurial as well as musical skills.

second, the tension in this world is less that between amateurs and professionals (labels which describe positions in the continuity of a performing career) than between local and national reference groups. Finnegan and Cohen both show that almost all young rock musicians do fantasize about "making it" nationally and becoming rich and famous. They almost all take the initial steps to achieve this—making demo tapes for radio play and A&R attention, for example. At the same time, though, these musicians can't really be said to be "in it for the money." Whatever the dreams of global stardom, the immediate pleasure of music-making, the reasons bands keep going, are local performances and support. The stress on originality among Cohen's Liverpool groups was thus used not only to feed the fantasy that the groups would be big (because they were "different") but also to explain the lack of record company response (because they were *too* different). And while almost all bands in both samples (whatever type of music they played) made a working distinction between "serious" pop (with meaningful lyrics, a personal approach) and commercial entertainment (made to formula), they also all depended on some sort of show of local appreciation. The aim of even "serious" rock musicians (unlike maybe the art world avant-garde) is, in short, to be "popular," but popularity is taken to mean occupying a particular place in the community rather than just accumulating large record sales. The tensions emerge when these two goals are thought, for whatever reasons, to be incompatible.

Finnegan suggests that while local pop and rock is, then, quite clearly, a form of cultural expression, it is not necessarily a form of youth or subcultural expression. She's arguing this partly as an empirical point: if the majority of pop and rock band members in her sample were young (half aged between 18 and 21, a fifth in their early 20s), it was also true that musical interests cut across age (and social class) categories, for both players and audiences. One reason why rock is valued, indeed, is precisely because it can be used to create a world in which such categories don't matter. And even if, in general, rock and pop musicians (unlike their classical contemporaries) were doing something independent of both family and school, both institutions also provided significant support for them in terms of material resources and personal encouragement.

This is not to say that rock isn't (especially in genres like punk) oppositional to mainstream adult/bourgeois values, but, rather, that such ideological sounds are a matter of conscious decision, not immediate "street" expression. Musicians whose own social and educational backgrounds can be quite varied thus come together in their use of an oppositional voice, but the commitment is as much aesthetic as political. Even in Cohen's Liverpool, "drop out" middle-class and college-educated musicians were as important to the shaping of local musical anger as straight "dole queue rockers," and in Milton Keynes, although musicians talked determinedly about expressing their own views (which often meant challenging convention), they did not describe their reason for making music as anything to do with "protest." Rather,

> Again and again they stressed the comradeship of playing together in a band, the great feel of being on stage, "giving people pleasure and excitement," self-expression, an outlet for their energy and expertise, making people think about their views and music, getting some public recognition and, for some but not all, one day becoming professional musicians. (p. 127)

It follows that through their engagement with music young people are actually placing themselves culturally in the *adult* world, managing a particularly important form of social transition by choosing from, operating with (and perhaps subverting) musical practices that carry wider cultural messages. This is most obvious in the use of so-called "ethnic" musics—Irish and Indian musics in Finnegan's Milton Keynes, Afro-Caribbean music in Liverpool. As Simon Jones (1988) has noted, young people use music to situate themselves historically, culturally, and politically in a much more complex system of symbolic meaning than is available locally, and Finnegan usefully describes different genres as "pathways" to the wider world—the wider world of taste and identity, commerce and expertise.

It also follows that music-making is, perhaps above all, an expression and celebration of *sociability*. Whatever the individual egos and "musical differences" involved in a band, musicians know that personal fulfilment depends on the ability to do things together. As Finnegan points out, for most young groups, the band's name (emblazoned on equipment, clothes, and posters) matters much more than any individual billing or attention. And in describing performance as their most satisfying musical experience, these musicians were describing a kind of collective experience which involved the audience too— when a rock show works it is because in speaking to the crowd the musicians come to speak for them; the music both creates and articulates the very idea of community.

It is interesting that in Milton Keynes, as elsewhere, youth clubs discourage live performance and prefer discos, on the grounds that the latter are less divisive—a band represents a single taste group only, discos can cater for everyone. Pubs, on the other hand, prefer live groups (even though discos make more money) precisely because the former bring in customers who have something in common and understand the rules of an event, whether it be punk or country or metal. Pub discos almost always mean trouble, as quite different taste groups converge. The point is that for young people, at least, music probably has the most important role in the mapping of social networks, determining how and where they meet and court and party.

Both Finnegan and Cohen describe the remarkable energy and creativity of people who would, in other circumstances, be described as uncultured, idle, and unskilled. The young musicians of Milton Keynes, Liverpool, and every other British town are, in fact, capable of deploying complex and subtle means of both individual and collective expression, and they create around themselves a system of symbolic action which is essential to the ways in which young people come to make sense of the social world and their place in it, come to terms with (and perhaps oppose) dominant media and educational discourses, come to define their own aesthetic and ideological values. Music, in short, is not just something young people like and do. It is in many respects the model for their involvement in culture, for their ability to see beyond the immediate requirements of work and family and dole.

One of Finnegan's most suggestive findings is music's central importance locally in charity work. Every type of sound, from opera to punk, is used to raise money for every kind of cause, from a wheelchair for a handicapped school to CND or a black arts center. In all such events music is taken both to represent a particular community and its values and to transcend them, to add something sublimely altruistic to the routine pursuit of political and social self-interest. It is impossible to reach the end of Finnegan's study without thinking that as long as people make music, Britain won't be in thrall to Thatcherite values. There is such a thing as society and it is through music more than any other cultural activity that people become part of it.

It follows that musical practice, like any other social activity, is shaped (and distorted) by the inequalities of class, gender, and racial power. The most striking statistic of Milton Keynes' rock and pop scene is, then, that its musicians are "almost always male": of the 125 players in Finnegan's 1982–83 interview sample, only 8 were women. And whereas other musical worlds were sexually mixed, even if there was usually a clear gender division of labor, the rock world was primarily male even in its support structures. Cohen suggests that Liverpool's young rock world is so essentially male that women are seen as a positive threat to it. Their presence as wives or girlfriends, let alone as performers or band members, was blamed for the break up of groups, for their lack of success, bad performances, etc. If musical practice is as important an aspect of youth culture as Finnegan and Cohen suggest, then young women are not just being denied a means of self-expression and pleasure; the music is also working directly to keep them in their domestic place.

A second thing to note is that the aspirations of young male bands are often thwarted too—not because they lack talent or determination but because they lack material resources. If different musical genres represent different cultural pathways, then some of these pathways have gates across that are hard to push aside or climb over. The most obvious frustration for young musicians in both Milton Keynes and Liverpool was the lack of suitable public performance spaces—Finnegan notes that while all the bands she spoke to described public performance as their reason for being, in fact about a quarter of them had made no public appearance in the previous year. And if most bands can, one way or another, get hold of basic sound equipment, to move up the career ladder does mean, at some stage, sounding good enough to attract promoters, agents, managers, and A&R people—rich friends, backers, or parents do help!

Most performed music in Britain is, in fact, subsidized, whether by the state through arts councils and education departments, by record companies promoting new releases, or by broadcasters, churches, patrons, and sponsors. Local pop and rock bands depend on subsidy too, but in a more erratic and much poorer guise—youth clubs which provide rehearsal space (and "indirect" audiences), local radio and music businesses (instrument, equipment, and record shops), pubs. But access to local college rooms and funds probably makes the most difference to bands' chances of continuing success. Students have the means (rehearsal space, equipment, experimental self-confidence, audiences, *time*) to learn and change at the moment in their careers when young non-college groups often find themselves stalled in a local pub routine or obliged to refine and retain only their most crowd-pleasing routines to get other work. These days pop and rock music are less ways out of the dead ends of no jobs, bad jobs, and a lifetime's grind than orderly careers, in which middle-class children, as ever, have all the advantages.

The Theory of Music

Now what I've been talking about up to now is an approach to popular music which, in British terms, comes not from cultural studies but from social anthropology and sociology (and I could cite other examples, like Mavis Bayton's [1990] work on how women become rock musicians). One reason I find this work important is because it focuses on an area and issue systematically (and remarkably) neglected by cultural studies: the rationale of cultural production itself, the place and thought of cultural producers. But what interests me here (which is why this paper is now going to be a different narrative altogether) is something else: compared to the flashy, imaginative, impressionistic, unlikely pop writing of a cultural studies academic like, say, Iain Chambers, the dogged ethnographic attention to detail and accuracy is, as Dick Hebdige once remarked of my sociological approach in contrast to Chamber's, kind of dull (Nelson and Grossberg, 1988, p. 612).

To put it more plainly, social anthropology, on the one hand, and cultural studies, on the other, construct popular music as a different kind of object: for the anthropologists it is a particularly *ordered* kind of social and symbolic structure; for cultural studies it is a particularly *disruptive* kind of myth, a myth of resistance through rituals, the politics of style, etc. etc. And if, as I hope my earlier section made clear, I believe that we sociologists and anthropologists do present a more accurate empirical account of popular music as a cultural process than the subcultural theorists, then I am also sure that the subcultural pop music myth contains its own much more powerful and much more materially effective truth. The point, though, and this is what I want to explore in the rest of this paper, is that from my sociological perspective, popular music is a solution, a ritualized resistance, not to the problems of being young and poor and proletarian but to the problems of being an intellectual. And the paradox is that in making pop music a site for the play of their fantasies and anxieties, intellectuals (and I think this process has a rather longer history than that of cultural studies)[1] have enriched this site for everyone else too. To take a simple example: the meaning of punk in Britain was, for all its participants, whether they knew it or not, made more exciting by Dick Hebdige's transformation of a disparate, noisy set of people and events into the fantastic theoretical narrative of *Subculture*.

Hebdige is, indeed, the key to understanding the cultural study of popular music and this paper is, in a sense, my personal tribute to (and argument with) his work. Last summer I read, back to back, his latest collection of essays, *Hiding in the Light (1988a)*, and one of the posthumous Raymond Williams (1989e) collections, a gathering of his occasional pieces on politics and culture. I found the combined reading unexpectedly moving—mostly, I think, for what Hebdige and Williams turned out to have in common: a commitment to a particular sort of humanistic, communal, *lived* politics. But what I want to describe here are the even more obvious differences.

Many of these are embodied in their respective tones of voice. Williams always defined himself as occupying a border country—between Wales and England, between the rural and the metropolitan, between the working and the intellectual class. But he was always—or seemed always—sure of his place in these borderlands. He seemed rooted as a man (a son, a husband, a father), as a thinker (in the tradition of radical Welsh and English thought), and as a political activist (in a broadly defined Labour politics). Williams's prose had a measuredness, an authority, that reflected such rootedness.

Hebdige's writing, by contrast, is jittery, unwilling to take itself seriously, punctuated by puns. If *Hiding in the Light* contains Hebdige's most personal essays (and the book, among other things, announces his conversion, or, rather, his deconversion from postmodernism—we see him decide here that he does not want to live the rest of his life in quotation marks); if these are his most personal essays it is because they reveal so clearly his anxieties about his *lack of roots*. We don't get any sense from Hebdige (as we do from Williams) of family or class or place; we do get from Hebdige (which we don't from Williams) a sense of the problems now of being an English, white, middle-class male. It is, again, a question of authority; if Williams has no doubt about the need to speak, Hebdige wonders why anyone should listen.

In terms of cultural studies, Williams's and Hebdige's volumes are most revealing in terms of their contrasting cultural references. In defining himself and clarifying his political positions Williams draws easily, unconsciously, from so-called high culture, on the one hand (the usual canonical texts of literature, art, and music), and from the practices of working-class culture, on the other (whether trade unionism or domesticity). Commercial popular culture—films, TV programs, pop records—may interest Williams, but they never seem to be part of his life. Hebdige's references are, by contrast, almost exclusively pop; even the intellectuals he refers to are intellectuals-as-commodities, the latest French theorists packaged as fashion goods.

In short, if Williams is clearly placed in a tradition (literary culture), a geography (the border country), a kinship system (his family), and a political collectivity (the Labour movement), which, in combination, give him the confidence to speak, Hebdige is placed simply (and as if from nowhere) *as a consumer,* a place defined, in Iain Chambers's words, by a sense of homelessness.

Now what I want to argue next is that for Hebdige (as for other cultural studies commentators) the solution to the anxieties of consumption, to the problem of having no place from which to speak (in which to rest) is music. I haven't got the space here to go into the question of why pop music is so important in giving people a sense of place (though this is a question for which the sociological work I cited earlier is obviously relevant)[2] nor to examine why, for this reason, pop consumption or, rather, the imagined community of the pop fan seems to be becoming the model for "active" popular cultural consumption in general.[3] I'll simply assert, then, that the cultural study of popular music has been, in effect, an anxiety-driven search by radical intellectuals and rootless academics for a model of consumption—for the perfect consumer, the subcultural idol, the mod, the punk, the cool commodity fetishist, the organic intellectual of the high street who can *stand in for them.*

There is much to be said about this but here I just want to address three points which serve to emphasize that what we're dealing with in cultural studies of popular music, from Paul Willis's (1990) to Lawrence Grossberg's (1990), are academic not working-class fantasies, that what's at stake in such writings are what it means to be male, to be white, to be middle class.

I'll deal with the last issue—class anxiety—briefly because its analytic consequences have already been summarized concisely in Meaghan Morris's (1990a) elegant dissection of the "banality" of cultural studies. For me, this has meant the relentless politicizing of consumption, the deployment of vacuous sociological terms (resistance, empowerment) at the expense of aesthetic categories, the constant misreading of the mainstream as the margins. The resulting politics of style, as developed, for example, by *The Face* magazine in the 1980s, has had dire effects on left approaches to cultural politics generally in Britain. But these are too parochial to discuss here so I will use the rest of this paper to address two questions that have been raised at this conference—first, Kobena Mercer's "What is it about white people that makes them want to be black?"; second, Douglas Crimp's "Why are cultural studies shy of sexuality?"

Race

The point I want to make here is that the academic myth of popular culture is still haunted by, even determined by, terms drawn from high cultural theory. Writing on popular music, in particular, still rests on the way in which the high cultural distinction between "seriousness" (the aesthetic) and "fun" (the hedonistic) is read as a distinction between mind and body.

This sort of romanticism, still deeply implicated in the production and consumption of Anglo-American pop music, has always been tied up historically and ideologically with the figure of the African, a figure not just of white fear but also of white desire, for two sorts of reasons:

first, as the shocking, exotic, primitive *other* of bourgeois respectability (hence the long history of white bohemian fascination with black music, a fascination which could easily be coded as rebellion, symbolized by the weirdly racist idea of the White Negro).

second, as "nature" as opposed to "culture," a means of access to the pre-social, to "innocence" (defined against the civilized, the sophisticated, the rational, the controlled—this is a recurring theme of white pop criticism).

My argument, in short, is not that African or Afro-American or Afro-Caribbean music is "naturally" or essentially physical and hedonistic but that the myth of the "natural" African is read *onto* African and Afro-American and Afro-Caribbean musical expression. The white pop, cultural studies obsession with black music (particularly noticeable in Britain) is thus an expression of a yearning for a "natural" (unbourgeois, uncivilized) state of grace. The answer to Kobena Mercer's question is literally pathetic: *white boys just want to have fun!*

Sex

My use of the word "boys" here is deliberate and moves me onto the second question, concerning sexuality. There's a line in the best book I've read about being a British pop fan in the 1980s, *The Shoe,* by the young Scottish novelist Gordon Legge (1989), which sums up the situation:

> Richard says when you cease to spend most of your time in the bedroom you become a boring bastard.

The bedroom described here is not a place of sexual activity but a site of consumption, the place for listening to records and the John Peel Show, for filing back numbers of *The Face* and the *New Musical Express,* for dressing up and posing, for practicing the guitar and messing around with a tape-deck. And what cultural studies mythology does is take this space and move it into the streets, to collectivize it while retaining its air of male narcissism.

Angela McRobbie (1990) was the first of many feminist theorists to point out that subcultural theory rendered young women invisible. My point is that women are excluded from the subcultural myth not structurally but discursively; what's actually at issue is the denial not of gender as such but of sexuality itself (which explains, for example, the *disgust,* with which Cohen's young Liverpool groups treated women). There are ironies in this, as the figure of "the fan" conventionally and empirically female, is translated into the "feminized" man, the mod, the ideal male consumer, subject to the confirming gaze of *other men!* But what is most startling about this subcultural text is not the absence from it of women, but the suppression of its obvious homosexual implications.

This is even more startling if one considers the historical contribution of gay culture to British pop culture. As Jon Savage (1990) has shown, British subcultural style from Teddy Boy to punk and Acid House can only be understood with reference to the gay scene, and male gay sensibility has had a determinative influence on two aspects of British pop culture in particular:

first, how men can have fun together (the model of the gay club and the gay disco).

second, how desire can be expressed across class lines, in bourgeois fantasies of the proletarian body, in working-class fantasies of the good life.

The absence of gays from the subcultural pop myth reflects, then, the fantasy involved: what academic commentators long to do is place themselves in a utopia of innocence, whether in terms of the "natural" African body or the "non-sexualized" community of boys. The cultural study of popular music has, after all, always rested on a valorization of *youth*—youth not as a sociological category but as a state of being.

Conclusion

I'll end with two more general points about cultural studies now and in the future:

first, it seems to me that one important strand of cultural studies, rarely discussed explicitly but implicitly in much that is written and said (in this collection, for example), is nostalgia, expressed in pop music studies as a fond look back at adolescence but suggesting more resonantly the deep desire of intellectuals not to be intellectual.

second, the question that most interests me now (a question posed more clearly by pop music studies than in other research areas) is not why certain forms of popular culture are so resonant for intellectuals, but why (and under what circumstances) do intellectuals' myths become so resonant for popular culture itself? There is no doubt in my mind that what we do as intellectuals has material, cultural effects. This is obvious not just in the old anthropological discussion of the effects of the watchers on the watched, but also, for example, in the role of academic rock mythology in the youth and student movements of Eastern Europe. But the point I want to end with here is this: if, as is variously suggested in this book, fans are "popular" (or organic) intellectuals, then they may well have the same anxieties about being fans (and take comfort from the same myths) as the rest of us.

NOTES

1. For the history of intellectual attitudes to popular culture see Morag Shiach (1989), *Discourse on Popular Culture.*

2. And for a schematic theoretical attempt to address this issue see Simon Frith (1987), "The Aesthetics of Popular Music."

3. This was a recurring suggestion at this conference, for example.

DISCUSSION: SIMON FRITH

MARTIN ALLOR: I wasn't quite sure whether you think it's good or bad that Dick Hebdige and other pop music writers have had material effects on musical formations.
FRITH: I think it's both good and bad. I think it's good that intellectual work has a popular cultural resonance, that popular culture takes meaning from the way it's being interpreted and that those interpretations are read back. And I certainly think it would be impossible to understand punk without realizing how many of the punks had done cultural studies courses, and understood semiotics for example. At least some of the politics of punk was about trying to put into mass media terms some of the arguments and ideas that had been discussed in, say, Griselda Pollock's classes in Leeds University Art Department (by the Gang of Four). On the other hand, rock music remains an astonishingly male preserve, and I think that the mythology of subcultural theory fed into that, in some ways more explicitly than others. There hasn't been an effective countermyth, and as Mavis Bayton shows in her work on becoming a female rock musician, the rock world depends on a whole series of discursive practices which are, in gender terms, constantly exclusionary.

QUESTION: When is myth empowering, when is myth something that in fact is useful?
FRITH: I don't think you could answer that question outside the specific circumstances of where the myth is operating. For example, it is said, and I don't know how true this is, that American sixties rock ideology was a significant organizing aspect of the continuing opposition (particularly within youth and student groups) in 1970s and 1980s

Czechoslovakia. And certainly when I went there a year before recent events, when it still felt like an incredibly repressed country, the significance of punk interpreted as a political movement was extremely important. And I could see well how music was empowering in the sense of giving people a sense of collectivity, community, something that was against the establishment and so on. In those circumstances rock is an empowering myth. Whether it's an empowering myth in the circumstances in Czechoslovakia now is a different question. Cultural politics are only significant in the circumstances in which they're being made. And I suppose what I was trying to argue was that one can't make a clear separation between the "reality" of how music is actually made and the "mythical" interpretation of what it means. That mythical interpretation has its own real effects, and the constant task is to decide whether it is empowering at a particular moment and under what circumstances it ceases to be helpful.

MICHAEL BERUBE: The question has often been asked: Why, if fans of slash zines, readers of romance, etc., can theorize and articulate themselves, do they need us? I'd like to ask you to elaborate on the opposite question: Why do we need them?
FRITH: I think we need them to satisfy our own desire to feel that we're part of a real world. Intellectuals spend a lot of time anxious that what they're working on doesn't have any significance for anyone else. They constantly need (speaking for myself) to *feel* that they have a place.

IAIN CHAMBERS: I'd like to open up the discussion a bit on the question of romanticism. Romanticism in pop music and popular culture is quite clearly the site of the imaginary, the site of an excess of sound and bodies and desires. And these are dimensions which are persistently repressed in classical sociological accounts of popular culture and in many cases even in accounts of pop music. Accounts that intend to "reveal" the so-called real relations of cultural production often avoid altogether the tissues and textures of their lived relationships and how their meanings are actually embodied in everyday life. And that seems to me to open up a problem about how to deal with the real counter-space which does exist within the sounds of popular music, a counter-space that exceeds and snaps the chains of rational explanation. That is the space of the imaginary, the unexpected, the not wholly, however historically determined, foreseeable. I agree there is an ambiguity in projecting intellectual fantasies and desires on to "the popular." But the analysis of empirical reality is also a narrative, a way of telling, a way of constructing the world, which is itself deeply indebted to a romantic sense of the authentic, of a particular sense of truth which is presented in the so-called transparent language of sociological analysis. And perhaps that would then open up a space that would talk about diverse ways of telling, the dialogics of diverse ways of telling, and which would no longer posit an antithesis or black-and-white relationship between the imaginary and the empirical sociological analysis, between intellectuals and fans, but bring them together in a set of dialogics.
FRITH: I agree. You're describing a move in my own approach, put in that way.

QUESTION: I would like to see if you could further address the issue of exploding the binary between the fan and the intellectual.
FRITH: I used the word "intellectuals" most of the time rather than "academics" because I think that for a lot of reasons many fans of pop music who are not academics are certainly intellectuals. And that's why I was saying they're involved in the same sort of fantasizing that academics or a particular sort of intellectual are also involved in. So in that sense I don't see there being a clear binary division between fans and academics. I mean academics can be fans and fans can be academics. The relationship between

musicians and fans is, though, a second and more interesting and difficult question. As I said, one of the things that has been astonishingly neglected in cultural studies is the processes of cultural production, not with reference to its political economy but with reference to the actual people who write songs (or write romantic fiction) who are symbolic creators. What is their relationship to their work? How does it relate to consumption? After all, both fans and intellectuals are consumers. Now, shifting in to sociological gear, it's clear that people become pop musicians because they're pop fans. But only some fans make this move. Other fans, like me, have no desire to become pop musicians whatsoever. What pushes people into wanting to be performers or wanting to create? This can't be answered in terms of their wanting to make money, it involves too a desired social experience. How does that differ from the social experience of being a fan? I can't think of a study in any area which addresses this.

CONSTANCE PENLEY: I think that your description of the desire of intellectuals when they go to subcultural groups to try to find a picture of themselves and their own intellectual activity there is very good. The only part of your formulation that I have a problem with is the characterization of the University as not the real world. The last thing that you've said about this is that we need fans to make us to feel that we are part of a real world, that we have a place. That feeds into that dichotomy between the University and what goes on out there in the real world. I think that you're absolutely right to draw our attention to that work of fantasy on the part of intellectuals. But I think that there's also a real desire there to try to see what these two worlds, which are both real worlds, might have to say to each other.

FRITH: I agree very much with that. I believe with you that the University is a real world, but there does seem to be a peculiar way in which academics don't believe it is the real world. I've felt this for as long as I can remember being an academic! I mean, this goes back to very different sorts of settings, to, say, radical 1960s' meetings in which somehow, by declaring oneself as a graduate student, one was defining oneself as no longer part of the real world. This was a feeling that was commonly expressed and led to endless debates about how one should "relate" to the real world. And so I suppose the question that now interests me is this: What is it about academic life that makes academics believe that somehow they're living un-really? And that's the question I can't answer.

I'd only add that the other thing about academic work, particularly cultural studies work for those of us who are lucky enough to be paid to do it, is that it makes for a very complicated relationship between work and pleasure.

MARY ELLEN BROWN: Could you comment on the need in studying any kind of musical phenomenon to look at it across the whole spectrum of music that's available, as Ruth Finnegan did? You commented that rock is a highly gender-exclusive environment. I was thinking where in Britain do I see women, and one of the places is in the folk song revival. But why? It might be because in a folk song revival there are more collaborative environments for performance, it's not as individuated and specific a kind of performative activity.

FRITH: Yes, I think Finnegan's work is exemplary precisely in this respect. It makes you realize with how narrow a definition of popular music cultural studies operates. One additional comment: Finnegan makes the point that rock was by far the most exclusively male of the musical worlds in Milton Keynes, although if you go into the other worlds there are other questions raised about the gender division of who does what. But just to add to your comment on folk, the one world that was exclusive in class terms was the folk music world, which was exclusively middle class, unlike all the other worlds she looked at.

QUESTION: I'm not sure I understood it correctly, but my impression was that the music scene in Milton Keynes is a very self-contained world, an idealized world of musicians at the grass roots level of music-making. And I just wonder if this is because these musicians regard their music-making activities as only a transitory part of their life that they abandon as they enter adulthood. Are there tensions between this world and the professional world of music-making? I would like you to expand on this tension a little bit more.

FRITH: Two points. The first is that one of my criticisms of Finnegan's work is that she doesn't address thoroughly enough the relationship of the local music scene to wider music scenes. You don't really get a sense of how either social mobility or musical mobility works. One of the absences in the book is a description of the music media, through which people get a sense of what music is and how it works. But, secondly, one of the points Finnegan would still want to argue is that although it might sound idealized, this is a quite self-contained world. For most of the people involved, making music is simply one of the things they do in their locality. This is one of the reasons why any straightforward connection between age and rock music is breaking down. There are now people who have been playing rock music in the same locality for thirty years; there are punk bands who have been together for fifteen years. Punk is what they do, it's a hobby. There might once have been a dream of making it and moving away, but the fact that one is still an amateur local musician doesn't stop one from going on making music and enjoying that sort of sociability. So, I agree with you, there is more that could be said about the relationship between the local music scene and wider music scenes; but the worlds Finnegan is describing are not transitory. Most of the groups she describes will go on making music locally, making music that won't change much.

BARRY SHANK: The question of originality is very important as a process of individuation. It's a technology of individuation that is a product among other things of the basic commodity nature of the form and the fact that even bands that claim not to be interested in being stars but in only being able to continue making their music have to differentiate their music from all other musicians within this very narrow generic form. This process of commodification and individuation is very easily ascribed into or works very neatly with the nature of the romantic artist that you referred to earlier and provides a neat set of means to elide contradictions when it comes time for bands to make decisions about working within the major label industries and in other alternative forms of expression.
FRITH: To stress the commodity part of the equation is important. Romantic ideology is central to the organization of the capitalist record industry.

QUESTION: Do you think cultural studies should look at academic culture? Why hasn't it?
FRITH: Well, I could give you a glib answer, which is that I'd always rather study pop musicians than academics! This goes back to Constance Penley's point, and it's worth stressing (because it sometimes seems to be forgotten here) that the reason most of us study popular cultures is because we've got some sort of engagement with or commitment to them. They continue to nag away at us. One of the things that happens when you become an intellectual is that you start thinking about your obsessions in more analytic ways but they remain obsessions in ways that don't have academic equivalents. My involvement in pop music thus long pre-dated my involvement with the academy,

and while I still brood endlessly about this I don't wake up in the morning thinking about academic issues. On the other hand, I think you're absolutely right: it is important to study academic culture, and there probably are now people around who find the academy fascinating. With cultural studies, though, I suspect there will be less interest in the academy as an institution than in trying to make sense of the teaching process.

12

Cultural Studies and Ethnic Absolutism[1]

Paul Gilroy

The starting point of critical elaboration is the consciousness of what one really is, and is "knowing thyself" as a product of the historical process to date which has deposited in you an infinity of traces, without leaving an inventory. Antonio Gramsci (1971, p. 324)

Now one of the chief errors of thought is to continue to think in one set of forms, categories, ideas etc., when the object, the content, has moved on, has created or laid premises for an extension, a development of thought. C. L. R. James (1981, p. 15)

Sitting in the Viktoria Cafe, on the Unter den Linden, Berlin, Matthew looked again at the white leviathan—at the mighty organisation of white folk against which he felt himself so bitterly in revolt. It was the same vast, remorseless machine in Berlin as in New York. Of course there were differences—differences which he felt like a tingling pain. W. E. B. Du Bois (1975, p. 7)

The institutionalization of cultural studies is easier to talk about than its problems with racism, ethnocentrism, and nationalism, let alone the ways in which ethnicity has been mobilized as part of its distinctive hermeneutics. However, these two conversations ought to be continuous with one another not least because the marketing and reification of cultural studies as a discrete academic subject also has what might be called an ethnic aspect. Cultural studies may be a more or less attractive candidate for institutionalization according to the ethnic garb in which it appears—the question of whose culture is being studied is a pressing one, as is the issue of where the instruments which will make that study possible are going to come from. It is impossible not to wonder how much American enthusiasm for cultural studies is generated by its association with England and Englishness. This question can be used as a threshold into consideration of the ethno-historical specificity of the discourse of cultural studies itself.

Looking at cultural studies from an ethno-historical perspective requires more than just noting its association with "English." It necessitates questioning the adaptation of the distinctively English heritage to the very different situation of American intellectual and academic life where, as several writers have recently pointed out, commodification and institutionalization may have already led to the recuperation of cultural studies by the academic and disciplinary conventions against which it was once provocatively defined (O'Connor, 1989). It is very hard to combine thinking about these issues with consideration of the pressing need to get black cultural traditions, analyses, and histories taken seriously in events like this. The two conversations pull in different directions and often threaten to cancel each other out. The struggle to have blacks perceived as agents with cognitive capacity, and historicity, even an intellectual history—attributes that modern racism has denied us—is for me, the primary reason for being here. It also provides my warrant for questioning some of the ways in which ethnicity is appealed to both in English cultural theory and history, and in the scholarly legacy of black America. Both these traditions contribute to the political culture of blacks in Britain.

If the radical interventionist tradition in cultural studies scholarship is to be preserved and extended, then the "war of position" involved in getting black cultural history and theory recognized as serious fields of inquiry will have to contribute a great deal to it. This is true not just because successive generations of black intellectuals have pursued a distinct mode of cultural and political critique—urged on by the brutal absurdity of racial classification. It is also important because the situation of blacks in the West, within what I propose to call the black Atlantic world, points to some new intermediate concepts, between the local and the global, which have a wider applicability.

These intermediate concepts are exemplary because they break the dogmatic focus on *national* cultures and traditions which has characterized so much Euro-American cultural thought. Getting beyond this national and nationalistic perspective is essential for two principal reasons: one is to do with the postmodern eclipse of the modern nation-state as a political, economic, and cultural unit. Neither political nor economic structures of domination are still co-extensive with the borders of nation-states. This, of course, has a special significance in contemporary Europe where new political and economic relations are being created seemingly day by day, but it is a worldwide phenomenon. Its most salient features are changes in the relationship between information and accumulation and the growing centrality of ecological movements that, through their insistence on the association of sustainability and justice, shift the moral and scientific precepts on which the modern separation of politics and ethics was built. The second concerns the integrity of cultures and in particular the relationship between nationality and ethnicity. This, too, currently has a special force in Europe, but it reflects much more directly the hybrid postcolonial histories and distinctive political locations of Britain's black settlers.

Black Britain's specific condition—what might be called the peculiarity of the black English, requires attention to a variety of distinct cultural forms, political and intellectual traditions which converge and, in their coming together, overdetermine the process of our social and historical formation. This confrontation is misunderstood if it is conceived in simple ethnic terms, but right and left, racist and anti-racist, black and white share a view of it as little more than a collision between mutually exclusive cultural communities. This has become the dominant view where black history and culture are seen, like black settlers themselves, as an illegitimate intrusion into a vision of authentic British national life that, prior to their arrival, was as stable and as peaceful as it was ethnically homogenous.

Considering this history points to issues of power and knowledge that are beyond the scope of this paper and this event. Though it arises from present rather than past conditions, contemporary British racism bears the imprint of the past in many ways. The especially crude and reductive notions of culture that form the substance of racial politics are clearly associated with an older discourse of racial and ethnic difference which is entangled with the history of the idea of culture in the modern West.

It is significant that prior to the consolidation of scientific racism, the term race was used very much in the way that the word culture is used today. But in the attempts to differentiate the true, the good, and the beautiful which characterize the junction point of capitalism, industrialization, and political democracy and give substance to the discourse of Western modernity, scientists did not monopolize either the image of the black or the emergent concept of biologically based racial difference. As far as cultural studies is concerned, it is equally significant that both were centrally employed in those European attempts to think through beauty, taste, and aesthetic judgment that are the precursors of contemporary cultural criticism.

Tracing these "racial" signs and their conditions of existence in relation to European aesthetics and philosophy can contribute much to an ethno-historical reading of the discourse and aspirations of Western modernity as a whole. It would appear, that "race," ethnicity, and nationality form an important seam of continuity linking English cultural studies with one of its foreparents—the doctrines of classical (that is European) aesthetics. There isn't time to go deeply into the broader dimensions of this intellectual inheritance. Valuable work has already been done by Sander Gilman (1982) and others on the history and role of the image of the black in the discussions which found modern aesthetics. The figure of the black appears in different forms in the aesthetics of Hegel, Schopenhauer, and Nietzsche (among others) as a marker for moments of cultural relativism and to support the production of aesthetic judgments of a supposedly universal character (for example, to say what is authentic music and what is, as Hegel puts it, "the most detestable noise").

This is doubly important because it has been purged from more recent orthodox histories of aesthetic judgment. Precisely how the residue of these discussions was imported into cultural studies also requires elaboration. The use of the concept of fetishism in Marxism and psychoanalytic studies is one issue that needs further exploration. Hegel uses it as part of his argument that blacks are incapable of producing properly abstract art. The emphatically national character ascribed to the concept of modes of production is another fundamental question which demands further work.

These general issues appear in rather specific form in the distinctive English idiom in cultural reflection. Here too, the moral and political problem of slavery was once recognized as *internal* to the structure of Western civilization and appears as a central political and philosophical concept. The primitive and the civilized become fundamental cognitive markers. It is impossible not to be struck, for example, when reading Burke's 1756 discussion of the sublime, which has achieved a certain currency lately, by the use he makes of the association of darkness with blackness and the skin of a real live black woman. Seeing her produces a "sublime" feeling of terror in the boy whose sight has been restored to him by Mr. Cheselden's operation:

> Perhaps it may appear on enquiry, that blackness and darkness are in some degree painful by their natural operation, independent of any associations whatever. I must observe that the ideas of blackness and darkness are much the same; and they differ only in this, that blackness is a more confined idea.
>
> Mr. Cheselden has given us a very curious story of a boy who had been born blind, and continued so until he was thirteen or fourteen years old; he was then couched for a cataract, by which operation he received his sight. . . . Cheselden tells us that the first time the boy saw a black object, it gave him great uneasiness; and that some time after, upon accidentally seeing a negro woman, he was struck with great horror at the sight.

These words came into mind while I was listening to Meaghan Morris's casual remarks about "the menacing nature of semi-darkness" yesterday. Burke who, as I'm sure you all know, opposed slavery and argued for its gradual abolition, stands at the doorway of the tradition of enquiry mapped by Raymond Williams—which is also the structure on which much of English cultural studies came to rest. This origin is part of the explanation of how some of the contemporary manifestations of this tradition lapse into what can only be called a morbid celebration of England and Englishness—two modes of subjectivity and identification that acquire a special political charge in the post-imperial, postwar history that sees black settlers from Britain's colonies take up their citizenship rights as subjects in the United Kingdom. The entry of blacks into national life is itself a powerful factor in the formation of cultural studies.

Fragments of this history may have recently become known to you through the sequence of events you identify as "The Rushdie Affair." These conflicts are, in a sense, the culmination of a distinct historical period in which a new, ethnically absolute, and culturalist racism explains the burning of books on English streets as manifestations of irreducible cultural difference. This new racism was produced in part, by the move towards a political discourse which aligns "race" closely with the idea of national belonging and stresses cultural difference rather than biological hierarchy. Last week the name of Allah was discovered magically written in seeds inside aubergines. This was the latest proof of the backwardness and cultural incompatibility of Asian Britons with the real thing. The ironies in Rushdie's own position—not least how a novel that claims to celebrate rootlessness, hybridity, marginality, and migration is allied to an aesthetic that endows the writing of novels with an absolute and non-negotiable privilege—need not detain us here.

These are some of the strange conflicts that have emerged in circumstances where blackness and Englishness appear as mutually exclusive attributes and where the conspicuous antagonism between them proceeds on cultural terrain. Whatever view you have of Rushdie, his fate offers another small, but significant, omen of the extent to which England and Englishness are currently being contested. His experiences are a reminder of the difficulties involved in attempts to construct a more pluralistic, postcolonial sense of British culture and national identity. In this context, locating and answering the nationalism, if not the racism and ethnocentrism, of English cultural studies becomes a directly political issue. Returning to the imperial figures who supply Williams with the raw material for his own critical reconstruction of English intellectual life is therefore instructive. I have already mentioned Edmund Burke. Revisiting him, Thomas Carlyle, John Ruskin, Charles Kingsley, and the rest of Williams's cast of worthy characters, can become valuable not simply in purging cultural studies of its doggedly ethnocentric focus but in actively reshaping contemporary England by reinterpreting the cultural core of its supposedly authentic national life. In the work of reinterpretation and reconstruction, reinscription and relocation, required to transform England and Englishness, discussion of 1865 and the cleavage in the Victorian intelligentsia around the response to Governor Eyre's handling of the Morant Bay Rebellion in Jamaica is likely to be prominent. Like English responses to the 1857 uprising in India, it may well turn out to be a much more formative moment than has, so far, been suspected. Morant Bay represents a mode of conflict that emanates directly from the slave experience and that, too, may be recognized as a much more powerful element in the historical, social, and cultural memory of our glorious nation than has previously been supposed.

I am suggesting, then, that even the radical varieties of English cultural sensibility examined by Williams, were not produced spontaneously from their own internal and intrinsic dynamics but generated in a complex pattern of antagonistic relationships with the *external,* supra-national, and imperial world for which the ideas of "race," nationality, and national culture are the primary indices. Charting the involvement of black slaves and their descendants in the radical history of our country in general, and the working-class movement in particular, is also part of this work. Oluadah Equiano, whose involvement in the beginnings of the working-class movement is now widely recognized; the anarchist, Jacobin, ultra-radical, Methodist heretic Robert Wedderburn; William Davidson, son of Jamaica's attorney general, hanged for his role in the Cato Street conspiracy to blow up the British cabinet in 1819 (Fryer, 1984, p. 219); and the Chartist William Cuffay are only the most obvious candidates for rehabilitation. It is also a matter of seeing how thinking with and through the discourses, and the imagery of "race" appears in English political and cultural life. Davidson's speech from the gallows is one moving appropriation of the rights of freeborn Englishmen that is not widely read today. Of these, Wedderburn is perhaps the most interesting. The child of a slaveholder and a slave woman, he was brought up by a Kingston magic woman who acted as an agent for smugglers. He migrated to London where, as part of his subversive political labors, he presented himself as a living embodiment of the horrors of slavery in a disreputable, Spencean debating chapel in the Haymarket. There he preached a variety of chiliastic anarchism infused with deliberate blasphemy. In one of the debates held in his "ruinous hayloft with 200 persons of the lowest description" Wedderburn defended the inherent rights of the Caribbean slave to slay his master and promised to write home and "tell them to murder their masters as soon as they please." On this occasion he got off a charge of blasphemy by persuading the jury that he had not been uttering sedition but merely practicing the "true and infallible genius of prophetic skill" (MacCallman, 1986).

Both Wedderburn and Davidson had been sailors, and in the shift from a nationalist to a hemispheric or diasporic perspective this may turn out to be especially significant both for the politics and for the poetics of the black Atlantic world. Wedderburn served in the Royal Navy and as a privateer (Wedderburn, 1824). It has been estimated that at the end of the eighteenth century a quarter of the British navy was composed of Africans. Looking for similar patterns in America, one thinks also of Crispus Attucks at the head of his "motley rabble of saucy boys, negroes, molattoes, Irish teagues and outlandish jack tars" (John Adams, quoted in Linebaugh, 1982); of Denmark Vesey sailing the Caribbean and picking up stories of the Haitian revolution (one of his co-conspirators testified that he had said they would "not spare one white skin alive for this was the plan they pursued in San Domingo"); and of Frederick Douglass learning of freedom in the North from Irish sailors while working as a ship's caulker in Baltimore (producing there, ironically, "Baltimore Clippers"—the fastest ships in the world, and the only vessels capable of outrunning the British blockade). Douglass escaped from bondage disguised as a sailor and put his success down to the ability to "talk sailor like an old salt."[2] These are nineteenth-century examples. The involvement of Marcus Garvey, George Padmore, Claude McKay, and Langston Hughes with ships and sailors lends additional support to Peter Linebaugh's suggestion that "the ship remained perhaps the most important conduit of Pan-African communication before the appearance of the long-playing record."

J. M. W. Turner is an artist whose pictures represent, in the view of many contemporary critics, the pinnacle of achievement in the English school in painting. Any visitor to London will testify to the importance of the Clore Gallery as a national institution and of the place of Turner's art as an enduring embodiment of British civilization. Turner was secured on the summit of critical appreciation by John Ruskin who occupies a special place in Williams's constellation of great men. Turner painted this picture of a slave ship[3] throwing its dead and dying overboard as a storm comes on. The picture was exhibited at the Royal Academy at the same time as the World Anti-Slavery Convention was held in London in 1840. The picture, which Ruskin owned for 28 years, was much more than an answer to the absentee Caribbean landlords who had commissioned its creator to record the tainted splendor of their country houses (which have incidentally become an important contemporary signifier of the inner, ruralist essence of national life). It offered an open protest against the direction and moral tone of English politics. This was made explicit in the epigraph Turner took from his own poetry: "Hope, hope, fallacious hope where is thy market now?" Three years after his involvement in the campaign to defend Governor Eyre (Semmel, 1976; see also Workman 1974), Ruskin put the painting up for sale at Christie's. It is said that he had begun to find its subject matter too painful to live with. No buyer was found at that time and he eventually sold the picture to an American three years later. The painting has remained here ever since. Its exile in this country is itself worth delving into, but here I want to draw your attention to the fact that Ruskin was only able to discuss it in terms of what it has to tell us about the aesthetics of painting water, relegating the information that it was a slave ship to a footnote in the first volume of *Modern Painters*.[4]

The New Left heirs to this aesthetic and cultural tradition compounded and reproduced its nationalism and therefore its racism (the former entails the latter) by denying its external referents. Their political affiliations and their cultural preferences amplify these problems still further. This is most visible in the historiography that supplies a counterpart to Williams's subtle literary reflections. Despite their enthusiasm for the work of C. L. R. James, the British Communist Party's historians group (Hobsbawm, 1979) are culpable here, for the symbiotic legacies of the freeborn Englishman and of socialism in one country, legacies which frame their work, are both found to be wanting. This pairing can be traced through the work of Edward Thompson and Eric Hobsbawm, who contribute much to the foundations of cultural studies and who share an approach to economic, social, and cultural history in which the nation—understood as a stable receptacle for the class struggle—is the primary focus. Thompson's and Hobsbawm's nationalism is articulated in different ways to their political practice. Both favor left flag-waving as a means to reanimate the vital traditions English popular nationalism vulgarized by conservative populism but somehow transmitted from the Glorious Revolution to the present with only minor interruptions. Both stand foursquare in the tradition of English nationalist socialism that would, for example, claim William Blake's utopian vision as an English "national" phenomenon rather than an Atlantic one (Erdman, 1977).

These problems within English cultural studies form at its junction point with practical politics and instanciate wider difficulties with nationalism and with the discursive slippage or connotative resonance between race, ethnicity, and nation. Similar problems appear in rather different form in black America, where an equally volkish popular cultural nationalism is again registered powerfully in the work of several generations of radical black scholars and an equal number of not-so-radical ones. Absolutist conceptions of cultural difference allied to a culturalist understanding of "race" and ethnicity can be found here too.

In opposition to these nationalist or ethnically absolute approaches, I want to support the idea that cultural historians should take the Atlantic (Linebaugh, 1982) as a unit of analysis in their discussions of the modern world to produce an explicitly transnational perspective. I want to suggest that much of the precious political, cultural, and intellectual legacy claimed by Afro-American intellectuals is in fact only partly their "ethnic" property. There are other claims to it which can be based on the structure of the Atlantic diaspora itself. A concern with the Atlantic as a cultural and political system has been forced on black historiography and intellectual history by the economic and historical matrix in which plantation slavery ("capitalism with its clothes off") was one special moment. The fractal patterns of cultural and political exchange and transformation that we try to specify through manifestly inadequate theoretical terms like creolization and syncretism indicate how both ethnicities and political cultures have been made anew in ways that are significant not simply for Caribbean peoples but for Europe, for Africa (especially for Liberia and Sierra Leone), and of course, for Afro-America.

Britain's black settler communities have forged their compound culture from various sources. Elements of political tradition and cultural expression transmitted by Afro-America have been reaccentuated by black Britain, and are central though not dominant within the increasingly novel configurations that characterize our vernacular culture—no longer either dependant upon or simply imitative of the cultures of black America or the Caribbean. The rise of black British groups such as Jazzy B and Soul II Soul constitutes one valuable sign of this new assertive mood. With the Funki Dreds they have projected the distinct culture and rhythm of life of black Britain outwards into the world. One enormously popular version of "Keep On Moving," a song produced in England by the children of Caribbean settlers and re-mixed in a dub format here in the U.S. by Teddy Riley, an Afro-American, includes segments or samples of music taken from American and Jamaican records by The JBs and Mikey Dread respectively. This formal unity of diverse cultural elements encapsulates the diasporic intimacy that has been a marked feature of transnational black Atlantic creativity. The record and its extraordinary popularity enact the ties of affiliation and affect which articulate the discontinuous histories of black settlers in the new world. "Keep On Moving" expresses the restlessness of spirit which makes that diaspora culture vital. It is part of a black arts movement in film, visual arts, and theater, as well as music, which has created a new topography of loyalty and identity in which the structures and presuppositions of the nation-state have been left behind because they are seen to be outmoded. Sitting in London watching a video tape of Jazzy receiving an award from the NAACP simply underscored this point and the new complex of opportunities which it pre-figures.

These Atlantic phenomena may not be as novel as their digital encoding via Soul II Soul suggests. Remember when 1992 comes around, that Columbus's pilot, Pedro Nino, was an African. The history of the black Atlantic since then, continually criss-crossed by the movement of black people—not only as a commodities—but engaged in various struggles towards emancipation, autonomy, and citizenship, is a means to re-examine the problems of nationality, location, identity, and historical memory. They all emerge from it with special clarity when we contrast the national, nationalistic, and ethnically absolute paradigms of cultural criticism to be found on both sides of the Atlantic, with those hidden traditions both residual and emergent, that are global or at least transnational and international in nature. These traditions have supported countercultures of modernity that touch the workers' movement but are not reducible to it.

Turner's extraordinary painting of the slaveship throwing overboard the dead and the dying is a useful image not only for its self-conscious moral power and the striking way that it aims directly for the sublime in its invocation of racial terror, commerce, and England's ethico-political degeneration. It bears repetition that ships were the living means by which the points within that Atlantic world were joined. Accordingly they need to be thought of as complex cultural and political units rather than abstract embodiments of the triangular trade. Of course they are machines, but the writings and experiences of black intellectuals suggests that they are something more—a means to conduct political dissent and, possibly, a distinct mode of cultural production. The link with abolitionism is significant here. Surely this could be viewed as an exemplary international movement that pre-figures the imperative of postmodern political sensibility—namely that we should strive to act locally and think globally.

I want to move on now and suggest something of the impact which this extranational reconceptualization might have on the cultural history of Afro-America. In the long term, this will mean reevaluating Garvey and Garveyism as Atlantic phenomena and thinking freshly about the importance of Haiti and its revolution for the development of Afro-American political culture. From the European side, it will be important to reconsider Frederick Douglass's relationship to English and Scottish radicalisms; to meditate on William Wells Brown's five years in Europe as a fugitive slave; on Alexander Crummell living and studying in Cambridge; and to comprehend such difficult and complex questions as Du Bois's childhood interest in Bismarck, his likely thoughts sitting in Heinrich Von Treitschke's (Winzen, 1981) seminars, or the use his messianic heroes make of European culture. The 1928 novel *Dark Princess*, which Du Bois tells us was his favorite book, opens with a transatlantic crossing. Its medical student hero, Matthew Towns, is fleeing to Europe having been unable, like Martin Delany, Du Bois's predecessor at Harvard, to complete his training at a white institution. He becomes the prototypical black *flâneur* sipping his tea on the Unter den Linden. Du Bois's relationship to Europe in general and Germany in particular defies summary here. Suffice to say that I have grown fascinated by the way that "Of The Coming of John" in *The Souls of Black Folk*—a cautionary tale for aspiring organic intellectuals if ever there was one—is a reworking of the Lohengrin myth. John turns towards the ocean as death closes in, having sung the song of the bride *in German*.

Black American travelers from Phyllis Wheatley onwards came to Europe and had their perceptions of America and racial domination shifted as a result of their experiences there. This experience of European travel is not an exclusively male preserve. In this counterculture of modernity, the *flâneuse* is also visible. Ida B Wells is typical in describing her experiences in England as like "being born again in a new condition." Lucy Parsons is a more problematic figure in the political history of Afro-America, but what *did* she and William Morris say to each other? What of Nella Larsen's relationship to Denmark? How was the course of jazz changed by Donald Byrd's life in Paris? What indeed, of Richard Wright's life in exile written off by black critics of the left, right, and center as a betrayal of his Afro-American authenticity and as a process of seduction by philosophical traditions supposedly outside his narrow ethnic compass?[5] It is interesting that Wright gets routinely counterposed with Hurston (also in my view an Atlantic figure). She is claimed as a representative of the folk, while his personality and career become evidence of the corrosive power of Jews and communists on black political sensibility. He describes his move thus:

> The break from the U.S. was more than a geographical change. It was a break with my former attitudes as a Negro and a Communist—an attempt to think over and re-define my attitudes and my thinking. I was trying to grapple with the big problem— the problem and meaning of Western civilization as a whole and the relation of Negroes and other minority groups to it. (W. Smith, 1953)

I have not chosen these figures at random. All of them are potential candidates for inclusion in the latest Afro-American canon, a canon that is conditional on or required by the academic packaging of black cultural studies. *Dark Princess* will no doubt be excluded from that canon, precisely because it articulates Afro-American ethnicity with a wider set of global concerns. What version of Du Bois will that canon construct from the rich transnational textures of his long and nomadic life? All these figures begin as Afro-Americans, but are changed into something else which evades that label. Whether their experience of exile is enforced or chosen, temporary or, like Wright's, permanent, time and again they articulate their desire to escape the bonds of ethnicity, national identification, and even "race" itself. Some speak, like Wells and Wright, in terms of the rebirth that Europe offers. Whether or not they dissolve their Afro-American sensibility into an explicitly pan-Africanist discourse or political commitment, their relationship to the land of their birth and their ethnic political constituency is absolutely transformed. The specificity of the black Atlantic can be defined on one level through this desire to transcend both the structures of the nation-state and the constraints of ethnicity and national particularity. These desires are relevant to understanding political organizing and cultural criticism. They have always sat uneasily alongside the strategic choices of national political life in America, the Caribbean, and in Europe.

We can examine this pattern of "double consciousness" in more detail through the figure and work of Martin Delany—journalist, doctor, scientist, judge, soldier, inventor, customs inspector, orator, and novelist. Once hailed as the progenitor of American black nationalism, Delany is a figure of extraordinary complexity. He visits England (Blackett, 1978) and has important adventures there. He also organizes the first scientific expedition to Africa from the Western hemisphere: the Niger Valley Exploring Party was marshaled by Delany and Robert Campbell, a Jamaican naturalist, who had been head of the science department at the Institute for Coloured Youth in Philadelphia. Delany was born in 1812 of a slave father and a free mother who both apparently enjoyed the benefits of royal African blood. I think he is especially interesting for several reasons. First, the proximity to Africa revealed in his family life. Second, as a doctor at the time when the slaves' desire to run away was still being rationalized as a medical condition—*drapetomania* or *dysaesthesia Aetheopis* (Szasz, 1971; Guillory, 1969). (Delany's work initiates some interesting inquiries into the relationship between scientific reason and racial domination. For example, he takes up phrenology in pursuit of answers to the arguments of racist ethnology.) Third, his aspirations as a man of science are further entwined with his political radicalization which developed partly through a bitter reaction to being denied the right to patent his invention for transporting locomotives over mountainous terrain (Sterling, 1971). He becomes a leader of the emigrationist movement but doesn't emigrate to Africa, going instead to Chatham in Western Canada in 1856 (Ripley, 1986). In later life, Delany blended his nationalism anew with American patriotism-after the Civil War had rekindled his enthusiasm for an American future. His eventual retreat into the shell of that patriotism was joined to a resolutely elitist view of black nationalism that stressed the obligation of blacks to elevate themselves through the values of thrift, temperance, and hard work.

I want to offer another perspective on Delany as an Atlantic figure by looking very briefly at his book *Blake; or, The Huts of America*, among the first novels written by a black American and certainly a more radical work than comparable early attempts at fiction. The book took its epigraph from *Uncle Tom's Cabin* and was, as Delany's title implies, an explicit response to that book. *Blake* was serialized in the *Anglo-African Magazine* (1859) and in *Weekly Anglo-African* (1861–62), a magazine which would eventually sell 25 cent pictures of Delany in his uniform as a Major in the Union Army. Written in Canada by an Afro-American of recent African descent, the book concerns a West Indian enslaved in the United States who escapes to Canada, returns to the United States to lead slave resistance there, and then visits Africa as a crewman on a slave ship as part of his grand plan to lead a slave revolt in Cuba. The topography of the black Atlantic world is thus directly incorporated into the narrative. The hero, Blake, assumes various names in each of these locations, but his English appellation which gives the book its title is significant. It offers an echo of an earlier, explicitly Atlanticist radicalism. Ships occupy a primary symbolic and political place in the work. One chapter is called "Transatlantic" and another, chapter 52 entitled "The Middle Passage," includes a harrowing scene of a slaver throwing overboard the dead and dying just as Turner depicts it—amidst the rage of nature itself.

It is particularly strange that this book is not widely read today. Its use of music is extraordinary complex and bold. It includes some strikingly sympathetic portraits of black women and it offers one of the few presentations of the middle passage and life in the barracoons to be found in nineteenth-century black writing. I believe it remains overlooked for similar reasons to those which dictate the marginal status of *Dark Princess*. *Blake* makes Afro-American experience continuous with a hemispheric order that, like Du Bois's globalism, is explicitly anti-ethnic; blackness is here a matter of politics rather than a purely cultural condition. While the horror of slavery is invoked from within the conventions of abolitionist literature, particularly a fascination with divided families, slavery itself is primarily presented as an exploitative economic system of an international nature. Delany was a member of the African Methodist Episcopal Church, but uses his hero Blake to articulate criticisms of religion in general and Christianity in particular. It is this representation of religious belief which supplies the key to the book's anti-ethnic, pan-African stance. Blake refuses to "stand still and see salvation" in the rituals of the white church on the plantation, the Catholic Church, or the conjurers in the dismal swamp. His scepticism and strictly instrumental orientation towards religion as a tool for the political project he seeks to advance is important because Afro-American religion is often the central sign for the folk-cultural, narrowly ethnic definition of authenticity that I'm trying to query. Delany's position recalls Douglass's insistence that his most religious master was also his worst. Delany and his hero boast of their rational principles: stealing from the master is rationalized in terms derived from the labor theory of value. From this rationalist stance, blacks are rebuked for confusing spiritual means with moral ends. Black Americans are not uniquely oppressed, and if they are to be free, they must contribute to the establishment of a strong and completely synthetic nation-state that is crucial to the ongoing struggle to defeat racial oppression everywhere in the new world. Delany's rationalism also requires that blacks of all shades, classes, and ethnic groups give up the ethnic and religious differences that symbolize intraracial division. Black survival depends upon forging a new means to build alliances. The best way to create this new metacultural identity is provided by the condition of slavery and ironically by the transnational structure of the slave trade itself. Abyssa, a Sudanese slave and ex-textile merchant; Placido, a Cuban revolutionary poet; Gofer Gondolier, a West Indian cook who has attended a Spanish grandee in Genoa; the wealthy quadroons and octoroons of Cuba, Blake himself, and, indeed, their white revolutionary supporters constitute a rainbow army for the emancipation of oppressed men and women of the new world. Because religion marks their ethnic differences, its overcoming signifies the move beyond ethnicity and the establishment of a new basis for community, mutuality, and reciprocity:

> I first a catholic and my wife bred as such are both Baptists; Abyssa Soudan once a pagan was in her own native land converted to the Methodist or Wesleyan belief; Madame Sabastina and family are Episcopalians; Camina from long residence in the colony a Presbyterian and Placido is a believer in the Swedenborgian doctrines. We have all agreed to know no sects, no denomination and but one religion for the sake of our redemption from Bondage and degradation. . . . No religion but that which brings us liberty will we know; no God but he who owns us as his children will we serve. The whites accept nothing but that which promotes their interests and happiness, socially politically and religiously. They would discard a religion, tear down a church, overthrow a government or desert a country which did not enhance their freedom. In God's great and righteous name are we not willing to do the same? (Delany, 1970, part II, chapter 61)

There is lots more to say about *Blake*. It is useful here because it moves beyond a binary opposition between national and diaspora perspectives. The suggestive way that it locates the black Atlantic world between the local and the global challenges the coherence of all national perspectives and points to the spurious invocation of ethnic particularity to enforce them and to ensure the tidy flow of cultural output into neat, symmetrical units. This applies whether this impulse comes from the oppressors or the oppressed.

I want to ask now, where do the culturally protectionist stance and the aspiration to ethnic totality come from? They reached something of a peak in the sixties, but they still lead black Americans to write about Rap as if it sprang automatically from the spirit of the blues—the definitive ethnic and authentic folk from—without recognizing the decisive input of Caribbean migrants to New York? There is here, no less than in the work of Williams and Thompson, an image of self-sustaining and absolute ethnicity lodged complacently between the concepts of people and nation. The example of Rap enables us to draw out the unfinished, recombinant qualities of black culture and to focus on the implications of this struggle against those Afro-American ethnicists who want to confine the Atlantic legacy within their own particular set of local, national, or nationalist concerns. Sometimes this is an overt and assertive cultural nationalism. At other times it is a simpler, more straightforwardly conservative impulse recognizable as the work of those self-appointed custodians of an already embattled tradition which the diaspora critique of ethnicity and consequent dissolution of the essential black subject appears to jeopardize. Isaac Julien's controversial appropriation of the memory of Langston Hughes (Gilroy, 1990b) and Hazel Carby's (1987) re-evaluation of the significance of Nella Larsen are two additional, recent examples that are best understood in this context.

By way of an ending I want to briefly mention Du Bois again. The Emersonian resonance of Du Bois's "double consciousness" idea is beyond dispute. I have no objection to Cornel West seeking to situate him as part of an argument about the scope and history of American pragmatism (West, 1990a). He belongs there. But he also belongs elsewhere, and I am dubious about what is gained by that invocation of America and American national identity to ground his analyses of black cultural, philosphical, and political practice. How can we settle the conflict between these competing claims to Du Bois's legacy? This is not a criticism of West, who would surely concede that what he has called kinetic orality is a black Atlantic rather than an Afro-American ethnic phenomenon. I must say, though, that I always found his assignment of Larsen, Wright, Morrison, and others to a "marginalist" option within the tradition of Afro-American responses to modern racism rather puzzling. If their writing is marginal, where would the center be?

What can be called the ethnic tendency is a much more serious problem in the ascendent anti-political configuration which seems to dominate Afro-American literary scholarship at the moment and which is laying significant claims to the idea of cultural studies. The recent debate, if one can call it that, in *New Literary History* typified this. There was no escape there from the hermeneutic claims of ethnicity and nationality, only an argument over the precise ethnic recipe involved in being able to walk that walk and talk that talk. I understand these impulses. The invocation of nationality and ethnicity corresponds to real political choices and to the wider field of political struggle. Yielding to them makes the world a simpler place but if the political tradition of cultural studies scholarship teaches us anything at all, then it is surely that the drive towards simplicity should be distrusted.

NOTES

1. I wish to thank Vron Ware, Lawrence Marlow, and Yvonne Ocampo all of whom helped me in the preparation of this essay.

2. Douglass's own account of this is best set out in Frederick Douglass (1962), *Life and Times,* p. 199. See also Phillip Hamer (1935b), "Great Britain, the United States and the Negro Seaman's Acts"; (1935a), "British Consuls and the Negro Seaman's Acts 1850–1860." Introduced after Denmark Vesey's rebellion, these interesting pieces of legislation required free black sailors to be jailed while their ships were in dock as a way of minimizing the forms of political contagion their presence in the ports was bound to transmit.

3. Paul Gilroy (1990a), "Art of Darkness, Black Art and the Problem of Belonging to England." A very different interpretation of Turner's painting is given in Albert Boime's (1990), *The Art of Exclusion: Representing Blacks in the Nineteenth Century.*

4. Vol. 1, section 5, chapter III, section 39. Du Bois reprinted this commentary while he was editor of *The Crisis,* see vol. 15, p. 239, 1918.

5. I have challenged this view in "Richard Wright and the Metaphysics of Modernity," an introduction to the reissue of Wright's novel *The Outsider* (forthcoming).

13

Resisting Difference: Cultural Studies and the Discourse of Critical Pedagogy

HENRY A. GIROUX

All those men and women in South Africa, Namibia, Zaire, Ivory Coast, El Salvador, Chile, Philippines, South Korea, Indonesia, Grenada, Fanon's "Wretched of the Earth," who have declared loud and clear that they do not sleep to dream, "but dream to change the world." (Thiong'o, 1986, p. 3)

American public education is in crisis. It is not an isolated crisis affecting a specific aspect of American society, it is a crisis that is implicated in and produced by a transformation in the very nature of democracy itself. This is not without a certain irony. As a number of countries in Eastern Europe move toward greater forms of democraticization, the United States presents itself as the prototype for such reforms and leads the American people to believe that democracy in the United States has reached its penultimate form. The emptiness of this type of analysis is best revealed by the failure of the American public to participate actively in the election of its own government officials, to address the growing illiteracy rates among the general population, and to challenge the increasing view that social criticism and social change are irrelevant to the meaning of American democracy. In part, this is an illiteracy built on the refusal of a large segment of the American public to "dream to change the world." But the failure of formal democracy is most evident in the refusal of the American government and the general population to view public schooling as fundamental to the life of a critical democracy. At stake here is the refusal to grant public schooling a significant role in the ongoing process of educating people to be active and critical citizens capable of fighting for and reconstructing democratic public life.

The struggle over public schools cannot be separated from the social problems currently facing this society. These problems are not only political in nature but are pedagogical as well. That is, whenever power and knowledge come together, politics not only functions to position people differently with respect to the access of wealth and power, it also provides the conditions for the production and acquisition of learning; put another way, it offers people opportunities to take up and reflect on the conditions that shape themselves and their relationship with others. The pedagogical in this sense is about the production of meaning and the primacy of the ethical and the political as a fundamental part of this process. This means that any discussion of public schooling has to address the political, economic, and social realities that construct the contexts that shape it as an institution and the conditions that produce the diverse populations of students who constitute its constituencies. This perspective suggests making visible the social problems and conditions that affect those students who are at risk in our society while recognizing that such problems need to be addressed in both pedagogical and political terms, inside and outside of the schools. The problems that are emerging do not augur well for either the fate of public schooling or the credibility of the discourse of democracy itself as it is currently practiced in the United States. For example, it has been estimated that nearly 20% of all children under the age of 18 live below the poverty line. In fact, the United States ranks first among the industrialized nations in child poverty; similarly, besides South Africa, the United States is the only industrialized country that does not provide universal health care for children and pregnant women. Moreover, the division of wealth is getting worse, with the poor getting poorer while the rich are getting richer. In fact, the division of wealth was wider in 1988 than at any other time since 1947. As Sally Reed and Craig Sautter (1990) have recently pointed out: "the poorest 20% of families received less than 5% of the national income, while the wealthiest 20% received 44% . . . 1% of families own 42% of the net wealth of all U.S.families" (p. k6). At the same time, it is important to note that neo-conservative attempts to dismantle public schooling in this country during the last decade have manifested themselves not only in the call for vouchers and the development of school policy based on the market logic of choice, but also in the ruthless cutbacks that have affected those most dependent on the public schools, i.e., the poor, people of color, minorities, the working class, and other subordinate groups. The Reagan "commitment" to education and the underprivileged manifested itself shamefully in policies noted for slashing federal funds to important programs such as Aid to Families with Dependent Children, drastically reducing federal funding for low income housing and, in general, cutting over 10 million dollars from programs designed to aid the poor, homeless, and the hungry. At the same time the Reagan government pushed the cost of military spending up to $1.9 trillion dollars.

Within this perspective, the discourse of democracy was reduced to conflating patriotism with the Cold War ideology of military preparedness, and the notion of the public good was abstracted from the principles of justice and equality in favor of an infatuation with individual achievement. Greed became respectable in the 1980s while notions of community and democratic struggle were either ignored or seen as subversive. Absent from the neo-conservative public philosophy of the 1980s was any notion of democracy that took seriously the importance of developing a citizenry which could think critically, struggle against social injustices, and develop relations of community based on the principles of equality, freedom, and justice. This should not suggest that as educational and cultural workers we have nothing to do but to offer a language of critique. On the contrary, we need a new language of educational and cultural criticism that provides the basis for understanding how different social formations are structured in dominance within specific pedagogical and cultural practices. At the same time, cultural workers need to rupture the relationship between difference and exploitation through a vision and a social movement that transform the material and ideological conditions in which difference, structured in the principles of justice, equality, and freedom, becomes central to a postmodern conception of citizenship and radical democracy.[1]

In what follows, I want to argue that cultural studies needs to be reconstructed as part of a broader discourse of difference and pedagogical transformation, one that is forged in the dialectic of critique and possibility. In effect, I want to argue that cultural studies offers a theoretical discourse for a new cultural politics of difference, pedagogy, and public life. Central to this task is the need to develop a discourse that accentuates the organic connections between cultural workers and everyday life, on the one hand, and schooling and the reconstruction of democratic public culture on the other. In effect, I develop the proposition that cultural studies provides the opportunity for educators and other cultural workers to rethink and transform how schools, teachers, and students define themselves as political subjects capable of exhibiting critical sensibilities, civic courage, and forms of solidarity rooted in a strong commitment to freedom and democracy.

Cultural Studies as Pedagogical Practice

When I moved into internal University Teaching . . . we started teaching in ways that. . . . [related] history to art and literature, including contemporary culture, and suddenly so strange was this to the Universities that they said "My God, here is a new subject called Cultural Studies." . . . The true position. . . . was not only a matter of remedying deficit, making up for inadequate educational resources in the wider society, nor only a case of meeting new needs of the society, though those things contributed. The deepest impulse was the desire to make learning part of the process of social change itself (Williams, 1989d, pp. 162, 158)

Raymond Williams reminds us that the relationship between cultural studies and education has a long history, it is a history that appears to have been forgotten in the United States. More specifically, the theoretical and historical legacy of cultural studies has largely been ignored by progressive American educators. In part, this is because radical educational theory has never adequately escaped from an overly orthodox concern with the relationship between schooling and political economy and as such has refused to engage the complex and changing traditions that have informed the diverse formations and projects in which cultural studies has developed.[2]

While it is not my intention to reconstruct either the history of cultural studies or to present an analyses of its ever-changing theoretical strengths and weaknesses, I do want to focus on some of the implications it has for providing a set of categories that deepens the radical democratic project of schooling while theoretically advancing the discourse and practice of critical pedagogy as a form of cultural politics. In what follows, I want to cast cultural studies as a political and pedagogical project that provides a convergence between a species of modernism that takes up questions of agency, voice, and possibility with those aspects of a postmodern discourse that have critically deconstructed issues of subjectivity, language, and difference. In effect, I will argue that cultural studies offers a theoretical terrain for rethinking schooling as a form of cultural politics while at the same time providing a discourse of intervention and possibility.

Cultural studies is important to critical educators because it provides the grounds for making a number of issues central to a radical theory of schooling. First, it offers the basis for creating new forms of knowledge by making language constitutive of the conditions for producing meaning as part of the knowledge/power relationship. Knowledge and power are reconceptualized in this context by reasserting not merely the indeterminacy of language but also the historical and social construction of knowledge itself. In this case, the cultural studies strategy of interrogation points to an evaluation of the disciplines within which intellectual knowledge is configured. Holding these disciplines to be constructed under historically specific circumstances leads to the discovery that as these conditions have been surpassed the legitimacy of dominant forms of knowledge are in doubt. Therefore, efforts to preserve the distinctions between natural, social, and human sciences and between the "arts" can be viewed as exemplars of the politics and historicity of the academic disciplines. Rather than holding knowledge in some kind of correspondence with a self-enclosed objective reality, a critical cultural studies views the production of knowledge in the context of power. The consequences of these moves are: to reshape knowledge according to the strategy of transgression; to define the traditional disciplines as much by their exclusions as by their inclusions; and to reject the distinctions between high and low culture. At issue here are not merely aesthetic standards or how they emerge, but the question of how educators address the relationship between difference and democracy, the creation of social and political spaces that speak to the needs of a broader popular culture. This suggests more than a politics of discourse and difference, it also points to a politics of social and cultural forms in which new possibilities open up for naming in concrete terms what struggles are worth taking up, what alliances are to be formed as a result of these struggles, and how a discourse of difference can deepen the political and pedagogical struggle for justice, equality, and freedom.

Second, by defining culture as a contested terrain, a site of struggle and transformation, cultural studies offers critical educators the opportunity for going beyond cultural analyses that romanticize everyday life or take up culture as merely the reflex of the logic of domination.[3] A more critical version of cultural studies raises questions about the margins and the center, especially around the categories of race, class, and gender. In doing so, it offers educators the opportunity to read history oppositionally, that is, cultural studies deconstructs historical knowledge as a way of reclaiming an identity for subordinate groups. In this case, culture is taken up not merely as a marker for the specificity of different cultural identities but as a theoretical construct for calling into question not only forms of subordination that create inequities among different groups as they live out their lives, but also as a basis for challenging those institutional and ideological boundaries that have historically masked their own relations of power behind complex forms of distinction and privilege. This points to the need to analyze the relationship between culture and power as historical differences that manifest themselves in public struggles.

Third, cultural studies offers the opportunity to rethink the relationship between the issue of difference as it is constituted within subjectivities and between social groups. This suggests understanding more clearly how questions of subjectivity can be taken up so as not to erase the possibility for individual and social agency. As such subjectivities are seen as contradictory and multiple, produced rather than given, and are both taken up and received within particular social and historical circumstances. What is important to note is developing a pedagogical practice based on what Larry Grossberg (1989b) calls a theory of articulation. He writes:

> A theory of articulation denies an essential human subject without giving up the active individual who is never entirely and simply "stitched" into its place in social organizations of power. . . . There are always a multiplicity of positions, not only available but occupied, and a multiplicity of ways in which different meanings, experiences, powers, interests and identities can be articulated together (p. 137)

Finally, cultural studies provides the basis for understanding pedagogy as a form of cultural production rather than as the transmission of a particular skill, body of knowledge, or set of values. In this context, critical pedagogy is understood as a cultural practice engaged in the production of knowledge, identities, and desires. As a form of cultural production, critical pedagogy becomes a critical referent for understanding how various practices in the circuit of power inscribe institutions, texts, and lived cultures in particular forms of social and moral regulation which presuppose particular visions of the past, present, and future. In what follows, I want to analyze the above issues as part of a broader debate on language, difference, voice, and pedagogy.

Schooling and the Politics of Language

Education may well be, as of right now, the instrument whereby every individual, in a society like our own, can gain access to any kind of discourse. But we all know that in its distribution, in what it permits and prevents, it follows the well-trodden battle lines of social conflict. Every educational system is a political means of maintaining or modifying the appropriation of discourse with the knowledge and powers it carries with it. (Foucault, 1972b, p. 227)

There is a long tradition in the United States of viewing schools as relatively neutral institutions whose language and social relations mirror the principles of equal opportunity. For example, liberal theories of education are grounded upon the belief that students have open access to the language and knowledge that schools provide as part of their public responsibility to educate. More recently, radical educators have drawn on a number of theoretical traditions that link language and power to disprove this assumption.[4] Not only do they expose the naivete of such views by revealing the social and political constraints that operate upon language, they provide an intricate reading of how school language functions through a web of hierarchies, prohibitions, and denials to reward some students and deny others access to both what can be learned and spoken within the confines of dominant schooling.[5] For radical educators, schools are sites where knowledge and power enter into relations that articulate with conflicts being fought out in the wider society. Central to this thesis is the assumption that the language of schooling is implicated in forms of racism that attempt to silence the voices of subordinate groups whose primary language is not English and whose cultural capital is either marginalized or denigrated by the dominant culture of schooling.

Language, therefore, cannot be abstracted from the forces and conflicts of social history. In other words, the historicity of the relationship between dominant and subordinate forms of language offers insights into countering the assumption that the dominant language at any given time is simply the result of a naturally given process rather than the result of specific historical struggles and conflicts. In effect, this work provides an important lesson in refusing to analyze the language/power relationship in simply synchronic and structural terms. While radical educators are acutely concerned with taking up the ideologies that structure dominant language paradigms and the ways of life they legitimate, they do not abstract this type of inquiry from particular forms of historical and social analyses. That is, rather than developing an analysis that is simply concerned with the codes, classifications, orderings, and distribution of discourse they are also attentive to the historical contexts and conflicts that are central to its purpose and meaning.[6] In effect, this work builds upon Bakhtin's insight that specific languages cannot be uprooted from the historical struggles and conflicts that make them heteroglossic rather than unitary. Bakhtin (1981) is clear on this issue and argues that

> at any given moment of its historical existence, language is heteroglot from top to bottom: it represents the co-existence of socio-ideological contradictions between the present and the past, between differing epochs of the past, between different socio-ideological groups in the present, between tendencies, schools, circles and so forth, all given a bodily form. These "languages" of heteroglossia intersect each other in a variety of ways, forming new socially typifying "languages." (p. 291)

More recent analyses have argued that any claim to a totalizing and unitary language is the result of forms of social, moral, and political regulation that attempt to erase their own histories (Aronowitz and Giroux, 1991). At stake here is the need to make clear that language is always implicated in power relationships expressed, in part, through particular historical struggles over how established institutions such as education, law, medicine, social welfare, and the mass media produce, support, and legitimate particular ways of life that characterize a society at a given time in history. Language makes possible both the subject positions that people use to negotiate their sense of self and the ideologies and social practices that give meaning and legitimacy to institutions that form the basis of a given society.

More recently, radical educators have not been content simply to situate the analysis of language in the discourse of domination and subjugation. They are also concerned with developing a "language of possibility" (Giroux, 1988a, 1988b). In this case, the emphasis is on perceiving language as both an oppositional and affirmative force. That is, discursive practices are viewed as deconstructing and reclaiming not only new forms of knowledge but also providing new ways of reading history through the reconstruction of suppressed memories that offer identities with which to challenge and contest the very conditions through which history, desire, voice, and place are experienced and lived. It is within this context that radical education offers educators a critical approach to pedagogy forged in the discourse of difference and voice.

The Politics of Voice and Difference

So, if you want to really hurt me, talk badly about my language. Ethnic identity is twin skin to linguistic identity—I am my language. Until I can accept as legitimate Chicano Texas Spanish, Tex-Mex and all the other languages I speak, I cannot accept the legitimacy of myself. . . . and as long as I have to accommodate . . . English speakers rather than having them accommodate me, my tongue will be illegitimate. I will no longer be made to feel ashamed of existing. I will have my voice: Indian, Spanish, white. I will have my serpent's tongue—my woman's voice, my sexual voice, my poet's voice. I will overcome the tradition of silence (Anzaldúa, 1987, p. 59)

Difference must be not merely tolerated, but seen as a fund of necessary polarities between which our creativity can spark like a dialectic. Only then does the necessity for interdependency become unthreatening. . . . Within the interdependence of mutual (nondominant) differences lies that security which enables us to descend into the chaos of knowledge and return with true visions of our future, along with the concomitant power to effect those changes which can bring that future into being. . . . As women, we have been taught either to ignore our differences, or to view them as causes for separation and suspicion rather than as forces for change. Without community there is no liberation, only the most vulnerable and temporary armistice between an individual and her oppression. But community must not mean a shedding of our differences, nor the pathetic pretense that these differences do not exist (Lorde, 1984, pp. 111–12)

The discourse of difference as used by both Gloria Anzaldúa and Audre Lorde provides a glimpse of the multiple and shifting ground which the term suggests. Defined in opposition to hegemonic codes of culture, subjectivity, and history, a number of social theorists have begun recently to use a discourse of difference to challenge some of the most fundamental dominant assertions that characterize mainstream social science. For example, theorists writing in anthropology, feminism, liberation theology, critical education, literary theory, and a host of other areas firmly reject mainstream assumptions regarding culture as a field of shared experiences defined in Western ethnocentric terms; in addition, critical theorists have rejected the mainstream humanist assumption that the individual is both the source of all human action and the most important unit of social analysis; and, moreover, many critical theorists reject the view that objectivity and consensus are the privileged and innocent concerns of dominant social science research. Reading in opposition to these assumptions, the notion of difference has played an important role in making visible how power is inscribed differently in and between zones of culture; how cultural borderlands raise important questions regarding relations of inequality, struggle, and history; and how differences are expressed in multiple and contradictory ways within individuals and between different groups.

While theories of difference have made important contributions to a discourse of progressive politics and pedagogy, they have also exhibited tendencies that have been theoretically flawed and politically regressive. In the first instance, the most important insights have emerged primarily from feminist women of color. These include: "the recognition of a self that is multiplicitous, not unitary; the recognition that differences are always relational rather than inherent; and the recognition that wholeness and commonality are acts of will and creativity, rather than passive discovery" (Harris, 1990, p. 581).[7] In the second instance, the discourse of difference has contributed to paralyzing forms of essentialism, ahistoricism, and a politics of separatism. In what follows, I first want to explore the dialectical nature of the relationship between difference and voice that informs a discourse of critical pedagogy. I conclude by pointing to some of the broader implications that a discourse of difference and voice might have for what I call a liberatory border pedagogy.

It is important for critical educators to take up culture as a vital source for developing a politics of identity, community, and pedagogy. In this perspective, culture is not seen as monolithic or unchanging, but as a site of multiple and heterogeneous borders where different histories, languages, experiences, and voices intermingle amidst diverse relations of power and privilege. Within this pedagogical cultural borderland known as school, subordinate cultures push against and permeate the alleged unproblematic and homogeneous borders of dominant cultural forms and practices. It is important to note that critical educators cannot be content merely to map how ideologies are inscribed in the various relations of schooling, whether they be the curriculum, forms of school organization, or in teacher-student relations. While these should be important concerns for critical educators, a more viable critical pedagogy needs to go beyond them by analyzing how ideologies are actually taken up in the voices and lived experiences of students as they give meaning to the dreams, desires, and subject positions that they inhabit. In this sense, radical educators need to provide the conditions for students to speak so that their narratives can be affirmed and engaged along with the consistencies and contradictions that characterize such experiences. More specifically, the issue of student experiences has to be analyzed as part of a broader politics of voice and difference.

As bell hooks (1989) points out, coming to voice means "moving from silence into speech as a revolutionary gesture. . . . the idea of finding one's voice or having a voice assumes a primacy in talk discourse, writing, and action. . . . Only as subjects can we speak. As objects, we remain voiceless—our beings defined and interpreted by others. . . . Awareness of the need to speak, to give voice to the varied dimensions of our lives, is one way [to begin] the process of education for critical consciousness" (p. 12). This suggests that educators need to approach learning not merely as the acquisition of knowledge but as the production of cultural practices that offer students a sense of identity, place, and hope. To speak of voice is to address the wider issue of how people become either agents in the process of making history or how they function as subjects under the weight of oppression and exploitation within the various linguistic and institutional boundaries that produce dominant and subordinate cultures in any given society. In this case, voice provides a critical referent for analyzing how students are made voiceless in particular settings by not being allowed to speak, or how students silence themselves out of either fear or ignorance regarding the strength and possibilities that exist in the multiple languages and experience that connect them to a sense of agency and self-formation. At the same time, voices forged in opposition and struggle provide the crucial conditions by which subordinate individuals and groups can reclaim their own memories, stories, and histories as part of an ongoing collective struggle to challenge those power structures that attempt to silence them.

By being able to listen critically to the voices of their students, teachers become border-crossers through their ability to not only make different narratives available to themselves and other students but also by legitimating difference as a basic condition for understanding the limits of one's own voice. By viewing schooling as a form of cultural politics, radical educators can bring the concepts of culture, voice, and difference together to create a borderland where multiple subjectivities and identities exist as part of a pedagogical practice that provides the potential to expand the politics of democratic community and solidarity. Critical pedagogy serves to make visible those marginal cultures that have been traditionally suppressed in American schooling. Moreover, it provides students with a range of identities and human possibilities that emerge among, within, and between different zones of culture. Of course, educators cannot approach this task by merely giving equal weight to all zones of cultural differences; on the contrary, they must link the creation, sustenance, and formation of cultural difference as a fundamental part of the discourse of inequality, power, struggle, and possibility. Difference in this sense is not about merely registering or asserting spatial, racial, ethnic, or cultural differences but about historical differences that manifest themselves in public and pedagogical struggles. The possibilities for making difference and voice a central aspect of critical pedagogy can be further elaborated around a number of concerns that are integral to a politics of border pedagogy.

Resisting Difference: Toward a Liberatory Theory of Border Pedagogy

To take up the issue of difference is to recognize that the concept cannot be analyzed unproblematically. In effect, the concept has to be used to resist those aspects of its ideological legacy used in the service of exploitation and subordination as well as to develop a critical reference for engaging the limits and strengths of difference as a central aspect of a critical theory of education. In what follows, I want to look briefly at how the concept of difference has been used by conservatives, liberals, and radicals in ways which either produce relations of subordination or undermine its possibility for developing a radical politics of democracy.

Conservatives have often used the term in a variety of ways to justify relations of racism, patriarchy, and class exploitation by associating difference with the notion of deviance while simultaneously justifying such assumptions through an appeal to science, biology, nature, or culture. In many instances, difference functions as a marker of power to name, label, and exclude particular groups while simultaneously being legitimated within a reactionary discourse and politics of public life, i.e., nationalism, patriotism, and "democracy."[8] What needs to be noted here is that there is more at stake than the production of particular ideologies based on negative definitions of identity. Difference when defined and used in the interests of inequality and repression is "enacted in violence against its own citizens as much as it is against foreigners" (Cubitt, 1989, p. 5).

Liberals generally take up a dual approach to the issue of difference. This can be illuminated around the issue of race. On the one hand, liberals embrace the issue of difference through a notion of cultural diversity in which it is argued that race is simply one more form of cultural difference among many that make up the population of a country like the United States. The problem with this approach is that "by denying both the centrality and uniqueness of race as a principle of socio-economic organization, it redefines difference in a way that denies the history of racism in the United States and thus denies white responsibility for the present and past oppression and exploitation of people of color" (Rothenberg, 1990, p. 47). In this view, the systems of inequalities, subordination, and terror that inform the dominant culture's structuring of difference around issues of race, gender, and class are simply mapped out of existence. On the other hand, liberals often attempt both to appropriate and dissolve cultural differences into the melting pot theory of culture. In this position, the history, language, experiences, and narratives of the Other are relegated to invisible zones of culture, borderlands where the dominant culture refuses to hear the voice of the Other while celebrating a "white, male, middle-class, European, heterosexuality [as] the standard of and the criteria for rationality and morality" (Rothenberg, 1990, p. 43). Under the rubric of equality and freedom, the liberal version of assimilation wages "war" against particularity, lived differences, and imagined futures that challenge culture as unitary, sacred, and unchanging and the identity, as unified, static, and natural.

On the other hand, radical educational theorists have taken up the issue of difference around two basic considerations. First, difference has been elaborated as part of an attempt to understand subjectivity as fractured and multiple rather than unified and static (Henriques, et al., 1984). Central to this approach is the notion that subjectivities and identities are constructed in multi-layered and contradictory ways. Identity in this sense is seen not only as a historical and social construction, but is also viewed as part of a continual process of transformation and change. This position is of enormous significance for undermining the humanist notion of the subject as both unified and as the determinate source of human will and action. As significant as this position is, it is fraught with some theoretical problems.

By arguing that human subjectivities are constructed in language through the production and availability of diverse subject positions, many radical theorists have developed a theory of subjectivity that erases any viable notion of human agency. In effect, subjectivity becomes an effect of language and human agency disappears into the discredited terrain of humanist will. Lost here is any understanding of how agency works within the interface of subject positions made available by a society and the weight of choices constructed out of specific desires, forms of self-reflection, and concrete social practices. In this case, there is little sense of how people actually take up particular subject positions, what individuals and groups are privileged in having access to particular positions, and what the conditions are that make it impossible for some groups to take up, live, and speak particular discourses (Grossberg, 1989a, p. 29).

The second approach to difference that radical educational theorists have taken up centers around the differences between groups. In this sense, a number of theorists, particularly feminists, have developed what can be called a discourse of identity politics.[9] In the most general sense, identity politics refers to "the tendency to base one's politics on a sense of personal identity—as gay, as Jewish, as Black, as female" (Fuss, 1989b, p. 97). This is a politics of identity that celebrates differences as they are constructed around the categories of race, class, gender, and sexual preference. Again, I will first point to the limitations that have emerged around this position only to later highlight the importance of identity politics within a broader notion of difference, politics, and culture.

Initially, identity politics offered a powerful challenge to the hegemonic notion that Eurocentric culture is superior to other cultures and traditions by offering political and cultural vocabularies to subordinate groups by which they could reconstruct their own histories and give voice to their individual and collective identities. This was especially true for the early stages of the feminist movement when the slogan "the personal is the political" gave rise to the assumption that lived experience offered women the opportunity to insert themselves back into history and everyday life by naming the injustices they had suffered within a society constructed in patriarchal social relations. A number of problems emerged from the conception of difference that informed this view of identity politics. A number of theorists argued that there was a direct correlation between one's social location and one's political position. At stake here was the assumption that one's identity was rooted in a particular set of experiences that led rather unproblematically to a particular form of politics. This position is questionable on a number of grounds. To accept the authority of experience uncritically is to forget that identity itself is complex, contradictory, and shifting and does not unproblematically reveal itself in a specific politics. Second, the emphasis on the personal as a fundamental aspect of the political often results in highlighting the personal through a form of confessional politics that all but forgets how the political is constituted in social and cultural forms outside of one's own experiences. Bell hooks (1989) puts the issue well.

> While stating "the personal is the political" did highlight feminist concern with the self, it did not insist on a connection between politicization and the transformation of consciousness. It spoke most immediately to the concerns women have about self and identity. . . . Feminist focus on self was then easily linked not to a process of radical politicization, but to a process of de-politicization. Popularly, the important quest was not to radically change our relationship to self and identity, to educate for critical consciousness, to become politically engaged and committed, but to explore one's identity, to affirm and assert the primacy of the self as it already existed. (p. 106)

Another problem with the radical notion of difference is that it sometimes produces a politics of assertion that is both essentialist and separatist. By ignoring the notion that "the politics of any social position is not guaranteed in advance" (Grossberg, 1989a, p. 28), identity politics often reproduced the very problems it thought it was attacking. The essentialism at work in particular constructions of feminism has been made clear by Audre Lorde, Angela Harris, bell hooks, and others who have criticized white women for not only privileging patriarchy over issues of race, class, sexual preference, and other forms of oppression, but also for defining patriarchy and the construction of women's experiences in terms that excluded the particular narratives and stories of women of color.[10] In this case, racial and class differences among women are ignored in favor of an essentializing notion of voice that romanticizes and valorizes the unitary experience of white, middle-class women, who assumed the position of being able to speak for all women. Moreover, forms of identity politics that forgo the potential for creating alliances among different subordinate groups run the risk of reproducing a series of hierarchies of identities and experiences which serves to privilege their own form of oppression and struggle. All too often this position results in totalizing narratives that fail to recognize the limits of their own discourse in explaining the complexity of social life and the power such a discourse wields in silencing those who are not considered part of the insider group. June Jordan (1989) captures this sentiment well in her comment that "Traditional calls to 'unity' on the base of only one of these factors—race or class or gender—will fail, finally, and again and again, I believe, because no simple one of these components provides for a valid fathoming of the complete individual" (p. 16).[11]

Far from suggesting that critical educators should dispense with either the notion of difference or an identity politics, I believe that we need to learn from the theoretical shortcomings analyzed above and begin to rethink the relationship among difference, voice, and politics. What does this suggest for a liberatory theory of Border Pedagogy? I want to end by pointing briefly to a number of suggestions.

First, the notion of difference must be seen in relational terms that link it to a broader politics, one which deepens the possibility for reconstructing democracy and schools as democratic public spheres. This means organizing schools and pedagogy around a sense of purpose and meaning that makes difference central to a critical notion of citizenship and democratic public life. Rather than merely celebrating specific forms of difference, a politics of difference must provide the basis for extending the struggle for equality and justice to broader spheres of everyday life. This suggests that the discourse of difference and voice be elaborated within rather than against a politics of solidarity. By refusing to create a hierarchy of struggles, it becomes possible for critical educators to take up notions of political community in which particularity, voice, and difference provide the foundation for democracy. Chantal Mouffe (1988a) persuasively argues that this view of difference is central to developing a postmodern notion of citizenship.

> An adequate conception of citizenship today should be "postmodern" if we understand by that the need to acknowledge the particular, the heterogeneous and the multiple . . . Only a pluralistic conception of citizenship can accommodate the specificity and multiplicity of democratic demands and provide a pole of identification for a wide range of democratic forces. The political community has to be viewed, then, as a diverse collection of communities, as a forum for creating unity without denying specificity. (p. 30)

Second, critical educators must provide the conditions for students to engage in cultural remapping as a form of resistance. That is, they should be given the opportunity to engage in systematic analyses of the ways in which the dominant culture creates borders saturated in terror, inequality, and forced exclusions. At the same time, students should be allowed to rewrite difference through the process of crossing over into cultural borders that offer narratives, languages, and experiences that provide a resource for rethinking the relationship between the center and margins of power as well as between themselves and others. In part, this means giving voice to those who have been normally excluded and silenced. It means creating a politics of remembrance in which different stories and narratives are heard and taken up as lived experiences. Most importantly, it means constructing new pedagogical borders where difference becomes the intersection of new forms of culture and identity.

Third, the concept of border pedagogy suggests not simply opening diverse cultural histories and spaces to students, it also means understanding how fragile identity is as it moves into borderlands crisscrossed with a variety of languages, experiences, and voices. There are no unified subjects here, only students whose voices and experiences intermingle with the weight of particular histories that will not fit into the master narrative of a monolithic culture. Such borderlands should be seen as sites for both critical analysis and as a potential source of experimentation, creativity, and possibility. This is not a call to romanticize such voices. It is instead to suggest that educators construct pedagogical practices in which the ideologies that inform student experiences be both heard and interrogated (Rosaldo, 1988). Moreover, these pedagogical borderlands, where blacks, whites, latinos, and others meet, demonstrate the importance of a multicentric perspective that allows students not only to recognize the multilayered and contradictory ideologies that construct their own identities but also to analyze how the differences within and between various groups can expand the potential of human life and democratic possibilities.

Fourth, the notion of border pedagogy needs to highlight the issue of power in a dual sense. Not only does power have to be made central to understanding the discourse of difference from the perspective of historically and socially constructed forms of domination, but also from the perspective of how teachers can use power through a politics of authority that provides them with a basis for reading differences critically. Difference cannot be merely experienced or asserted by students. It must also be read critically by teachers who can speak for those not available to speak; moreover, teacher authority can be used to provide the conditions for students to engage their own views through critical dialogue. Teachers need to construct pedagogical practices that neither position students defensively nor allow them to speak by simply asserting their voices and experiences. A pedagogy of affirmation is no excuse for refusing students the obligation to interrogate the claims or consequences their assertions have for the social relationships they legitimate. Larry Grossberg (1989a) is correct in arguing that teachers who refuse to assert their authority or take up the issue of political responsibility as social critics and committed intellectuals often end up "erasing themselves in favor of the uncritical reproduction of the audience [students]" (p. 30).

Fifth, border pedagogy also points to the importance of offering students the opportunity to engage the multiple references and codes that position them within various structures of meaning and practice. In part, this means educating students to become media literate in a world of changing representations. It also means teaching them to read critically not only how cultural texts are regulated by various discursive codes but also how such texts express and represent different ideological interests and how they might be taken up differently by students. More generally, border pedagogy points to the need to establish conditions of learning that define literacy inside rather than outside of the categories of power and authority. This suggests providing students with the opportunities to read texts as social and historical constructions, to engage texts in terms of their presences and absences, and to read texts oppositionally. This means teaching students to resist particular readings while simultaneously learning how to write their own narratives. At issue here is not merely the need for students to develop a healthy skepticism towards all discourses of authority, but also to recognize how authority and power can be transformed in the interest of creating a democratic society.

Finally, border pedagogy points to the need for educators to rethink the syntax of learning and behavior outside of the geography of rationality and reason. For example, racist, sexist, and class discriminatory narratives cannot be dealt with in a purely limited, analytical way. As a form of cultural politics, border pedagogy must engage how and why students make particular ideological and affective investments in these narratives. Moreover, this should not suggest that educators merely expand their theoretical and pedagogical understanding of how meaning and pleasure interact to produce particular forms of investment and student experience; it points to a pedagogical practice that takes seriously how ideologies are lived, experienced, and felt at the level of everyday life as a basis for student experience and knowledge (Grossberg, 1986b; Giroux and Simon, 1989). It means restructuring the curriculum so as to redefine the everyday as an important resource for linking schools to the traditions, communities, and histories that provide students with a sense of voice and relationship to others.

All of these concerns are relevant to the discourses of cultural studies. While it is true that cultural studies cannot be characterized by a particular ideology or position, it does offer a terrain through which cultural borders can be refigured, new social relations constructed, and the role of teachers as engaged critics rethought within the parameters of a politics of resistance and possibility. It is within this shifting and radical terrain that schooling as a form of cultural politics can be reconstructed as part of a discourse of opposition and hope.

NOTES

1. The issue here is to develop a politics of difference that would allow various cultural workers to rethink and deepen the purpose and meaning of a radical democracy. Chantal Mouffe (1988b) is useful on this issue.

> If the task of radical democracy is indeed to deepen the democratic revolution and to link together diverse democratic struggles, such a task requires the creation of new subject-positions that would allow the common articulation, for example, of antiracism, antisexism, and anticapitalism. These struggles do not spontaneously converge, and in order to establish democratic equivalences, a new "common sense" is necessary, which would transform the identity of different groups so that the demands of each group could be articulated with those of others according to the principle of democratic equivalence. For it is not a matter of establishing a mere alliance between given interests but of actually modifying the very identity of these forces. In order that the defense of workers' interests is not pursued at the cost of the rights of women, immigrants, or consumers, it is necessary to establish an equivalence between these different struggles. It is only under these circumstances that struggles against power becomes truly democratic. (p. 42)

2. Three of the best commentaries on both the history and central assumptions that informed cultural studies, at least in its British versions, since the fifties can be found in: Lawrence Grossberg (1989b), "The Formations of Cultural Studies: An American in Birmingham"; Lawrence Grossberg, et al. (1988) *It's a Sin;* Richard Johnson (1986), "The Story So Far: and Further Transformations?"

3. For an excellent analyses of some of the theoretical pitfalls various forms of cultural studies have fallen into, see Meaghan Morris (1990a), "Banality in Cultural Studies."

4. For a summary of the various discourses now being taken up by radical educators, see Diane Macdonell (1986), *Theories of Discourse.*

5. I take this issue up in my *Schooling and the Struggle for Public Life* (1988a).

6. See for instance, Noelle Bisseret (1979), *Education, Class Language, and Ideology*; Cleo Cherryholmes (1988), *Power and Criticism: Poststructural Investigations in Education;* Tony Crowley (1989), *Standard English and the Politics of Language.*

7. For an analysis of women of color who have contributed significantly to a theory of difference, see Henry Giroux (forthcoming, a), "Postmodernism as Border Pedagogy: Redefining the Boundaries of Race and Ethnicity." Not included in the article are important contributions by feminist women of color in critical legal studies. A very partial list would include: Kimberle Crenshaw (1989), "Demarginalizing the Intersection of Race and Sex: A Black Feminist Critique of Antidiscrimination Doctrine, Feminist Theory and Antiracist Politics" and Regina Austin (1989), "Sapphire Bound!" I am deeply indebted to Linda Brodkey for bringing this literature to my attention. Also see her excellent (1990) piece, "Towards a Feminist Rhetoric of Difference."

8. Of course, we have a vast literature of anti-colonialism that points this out very clearly. For example, see Frantz Fanon (1967), *Black Skin, White Masks;* Albert Memmi 1965), *The Colonizer and the Colonized.* For a particularly powerful example with respect to the use of language in the production of difference as a marker of colonialism, see Ngugi Wa Thiong'o (1986) *Decdonizing the Mind;* see also, Edward Said (1978). *Orientalism.* Of course, most of the anti-colonial literature constructs difference through the modernist dichotomies of colonized versus colonizer, enemy versus foe. More recently, especially in the racist discourse being developed by the French Right, the concept of difference is being affirmed through themes that appear to eschew racism (the right to be different), while they actually are used to reproduce its effects. On this issue, see Alain Policar (1990), "Racism and Its Mirror Images"; Pierre-André Taguieff (1990), "The New Cultural Racism in France."

9. For some insightful comments on this issue, see bell hooks (1989), *Talking Back;* Linda Brodkey (1990), "Towards a Feminist Rhetoric of Difference"; Regina Austin (1989), "Sapphire Bound!", Henry Giroux (forthcoming, b), "Rethinking the Boundaries of Educational Discourse: Modernism, Postmodernism, and Feminism."

10. The literature on this issue is much too extensive to list here, but three excellent examples can be found in Angela Harris (1990), Audre Lorde (1984), and bell hooks (1989).

11. Of course, the call to move beyond a politics of difference and identity that reproduces totalizing narratives should not be mistaken as a criticism of all theorists and social movements that take up particular issues in order to promote specific struggles against racism, sexism, or class exploitation. Such a criticism is warranted only when these issues are developed as part of a politics of assertion and separatism that functions to silence other progressive voices and oppressed groups. In this case, identity politics and the discourse of difference collapse into a hegemonic narrative. The complexity of the issues surrounding the relationship between a politics of location, difference, and essentialism are taken up in Teresa de Lauretis (1989), "The Essence of the Triangle or, Taking the Risk of Essentialism Seriously: Feminist Theory in Italy, the U.S., and Britain"; Cornel West (1990b), "The New Cultural Politics of Difference"; Rita Felski (1989), "Feminism, Postmodernism, and the Critique of Modernity."

14

Guns in the House of Culture?
Crime Fiction and the
Politics of the Popular[1]

DAVID GLOVER AND CORA KAPLAN

Since the nineteenth century great political institutions and great political parties have confiscated the process of political creation; that is, they have tried to give to political creation the form of a political program in order to take over power. I think what happened in the 1960s and early 1970s is something to be preserved; that there has been political innovation, political creation and political experimentation outside the great political parties, and outside the normal or ordinary program. It's a fact that people's everyday lives have changed from the early 1960s to now, and certainly within my own life. And surely, that is not due to political parties but is the result of many movements. These social movements have really changed our whole lives, our mentality, our attitudes, *and* the attitudes and mentality of other people—people who do not belong to these movements. And that is something very important and positive. (Michel Foucault)

I

Writing to his British publisher Hamish Hamilton in 1950, Raymond Chandler reconstructed the origins of his career in crime fiction, locating them in the Depression years:

> Wandering up and down the Pacific Coast in an automobile, I began to read pulp magazines, because they were cheap enough to throw away and because I never had at any time any taste for the kind of thing which is known as women's magazines. This was in the great days of the *Black Mask* (if I may call them great days) and it struck me that some of the writing was pretty forceful and honest, even though it had its crude aspect. I decided that this might be a good way to try to learn to write fiction and get paid a small amount of money at the same time. (Chandler, 1973, p. 26)

At once history and credo, this picaresque cameo of author-to-be as discriminating masculine consumer at large in the landscape he would invent and people, maps genre, gender, and geography together in an aggressively revised aesthetic of the popular.

Here as elsewhere, images of fiction's commodity forms haunt Chandler's critical writing—male pulps and women's magazines, publications "cheap enough to throw away." The popular provides both the ground for his own self-consciously beleaguered work—"crude" but "pretty forceful and honest"—and the greatest threat to it (Chandler 1973, p. 26). Good work "can exist in a savage and dirty age," he once wrote, "but it cannot exist in the Coca-Cola age . . . the age of the Book-of-the-Month and the Hearst

Press." For the disposable is threatening precisely because it is endlessly mass-produced: "efficient vulgarity." Hence, too, it is only the "semi-literate educated people one meets nowadays"—themselves the products of a kind of social and educational mass production—who "deprecate the mystery story as literature" (p. 58).

In "The Simple Art of Murder," an essay tailored for the upmarket literary periodical *Atlantic Monthly* in 1944, Chandler cleverly constructed an apologia for his own work which again resorted to a cultural hierarchy divided between high and low, but which explicitly used gender as a device for turning this binary inside out, inverting and displacing many of its key elements. There "the great days of *Black Mask*" are given canonical roots and an ethical/aesthetic imprimatur in the fictions of Fielding and Smollett which he judged "realistic in the modern sense because they dealt largely with uninhibited characters many of whom were about two jumps ahead of the police." By contrast, the "classic detective story" is doubly feminized. Its debased literary genealogy is first traced back to "Jane Austen's chronicles of highly inhibited people against a background of rural gentility," and then read forwards, re-discovering "the social and emotional hypocrisy" so central to Austen's domestic novels alive and well amongst the tastes and interests that underwrite the modern publishing industry. For its best-sellers are the ultimate literary commodities, made and promoted by a feminized and effeminate critical fraternity playing upon "a sort of indirect snob appeal" under the pretense of "fostering culture." The dismal result is that "rather second-rate items outlast most of the high velocity fiction" and "old ladies jostle each other at the mystery shelf" in search of "the traditional . . . novel of detection," whether native English or American MGM imitation, recycling upper-class deportment and style via "the right kind of luxury goods"—"glasses of crusty old port" or new "clothes by *Vogue.*"

Within and across genres, then, the "high" reaches a new "low" insofar as it endlessly circulates an artificial and feminine version of the literary, advertising a culture of consumption and manners, the preserve of "flustered old ladies—of both sexes (or no sex) and almost all ages." Chandler's predictable antidote to this sorry state of affairs was an upgraded and firmly heterosexual masculinity, critically modeled on Dashiell Hammett. Its ethics and aesthetics valued "a sharp, aggressive attitude to life," readers, writers, and texts unafraid "of the seamy side of things; they lived there. Violence did not dismay them; it was right down their street." Yet this explicitly male crime fiction necessarily required a "spirit of detachment" if it was to avoid contamination from the vulgar and violent demotic of the streets: "otherwise nobody but a psychopath would want to write it or read it" (Chandler, 1944, p. 173–90). Masculinity itself can slip or split into dangerously carnivalesque modes which Chandler negatively figured as a kind of proletarian satyriasis. For every Dashiell Hammett there is a James M. Cain, "a Proust in greasy overalls," smelling "like a billygoat," "a brothel with a smell of cheap scent in the front parlor and a bucket of slops at the back door" (Chandler, 1942, p. 169). Where the language and landscape of art is all-encoded in this de-feminized vernacular, it becomes more important than ever to distinguish the good from the bad *within* the popular.

It's easy enough to see Chandler's stance as paradigmatically intellectual, operating *on* the popular, seeking to elevate and transform it, to defend it from itself. In Chandler's eyes a sound "public taste" could only be founded on "a sense of style and quality throughout the whole structure"—already for him virtually an impossibility—and his aesthetic preference was for writing that was "hard and clean and cold and ventilated" (Chandler, 1973, p. 58; 1942, p. 169). And we might view this as one more version of what Pierre Bourdieu has called "the pure gaze" implying "a break with the ordinary attitude towards the world which, as such, is a social break" (Bourdieu, 1984, p. 31).

Pure taste requires that sense of distance from the commodity form and control over it that are the modern intellectual's stock-in-trade. Hence the interminable desire to discriminate, to set up divisions, to draw boundaries and install categories and classifications—moves which seek to fix and confine the popular, simultaneously devaluing and revaluing its characteristic narrative formulas and strategies. Thus P. D. James is today rescued as "good writing," and her work is used as an essential valorization of the continuing vitality of "the English novel." These veritable genre wars are indeed what a good deal of the response to crime fiction in the last sixty years has been about, from Dorothy L. Sayers's attempt to sift out "the uncritical" from "the modern educated public" to Chandler's "The Simple Art of Murder" (Sayers, 1929, pp. 63–73).

However, there is more here than simply a bloodless war between "bloody" categories and labels. For Chandler was also attacking academicism and sometimes the intellectual function itself. This is why he diagnoses "Hammett's style at its worst" as a kind of formalism (Chandler, 1944, p. 186). And it is also why he criticizes "the traditional novel of detection" for being at once precious and abstruse, deriding its typical author as someone "living psychologically in the age of the hoop skirt," someone whose books ostentatiously hinge upon displaying a mastery "of rare knowledge" in such recondite and implicitly feminine subjects as "ceramics and Egyptian needlework." When Chandler makes the counter-claim that "the realist in murder writes of a world in which gangsters can rule nations and almost rule cities" and "where the mayor of your town may have condoned murder as an instrument of money-making," what is being contested is more than simply a definition of the popular; it is also, and more importantly, a move in the contest over the possibilities of the public sphere and its domain (pp. 176–89). We can read Chandler's reworking of these gendered and generic codes and frameworks as an attempt to moralize an amoral or lawless public world, keeping intact its genealogies of masculine privilege through a trans-generic, trans-class heroism, but always discriminating *within* the hyper-masculine demotic, weeding out the degenerates and the truly vicious underclass. This is, of course, a strategy with echoes and parallels in other branches of literary naturalism and realism, and most recently and urgently restated by Tom Wolfe's *Bonfire of the Vanities* (1987), an urban blockbuster with a panoramic social sweep and strong narrative debts to crime and thriller writing, whose misogyny and racism energetically update Chandler's own. As all these claims to realism make plain, what's at stake in both the old and the new hard-boiled is who the people are, and what their relationship to the public spaces of speech and action may be. In this, as in so much else, Chandler is merely making explicit the inner rationale of the many modern permutations of the genre.

But crime genres and their fellow travelers, the many novels and films which now make up the broad border country where "high" and "low" narrative traditions now mix and mingle do not simply reproduce the map of the public sphere that was shaped by earlier postwar cultural development. This older representation of the public terrain and the civic relations that are engaged there have been sharply challenged on several fronts. One thinks immediately of the tactically important "entryism" of feminist crime writers, creatively opening up the discursive landscape for women cops and 'tecs, gay as well as straight, black and white. Never utopian, feminist crime fiction at the very least invents an urban imaginary at odds with the sentimental homosocial populism and competitive individualism condensed in those "mean streets" that continue to provide the most durable set of social fantasies for the genre. More surprisingly, there has been a major challenge to these deeply entrenched scenarios from leading male practitioners, many of them middle-aged or even older, whose socio-political imaginations have been stirred, if not wholly shaken up by feminism—the late Charles Willeford, Elmore Leonard, George V. Higgins, K. C. Constantine, Joseph Hansen, Robert B. Parker in the U.S. are leading examples; Reginald Hill and Dan Kavanagh (Julian Barnes) in England. Across the board, it is probably fair to say that the intersection of sexual politics with other pressing social concerns has been the site of the most significant ideological shifts within the genre. One result has been a positive revaluation of those popular practices typically designated as low or middlebrow. The culture of the everyday, particularly those aspects associated with women or the feminine—what we might call the domestic popular, running from soap opera to astrology—are treated with less contempt, as are the social identities called up by them. In a deliberately low-key, unsentimental, and unprogrammatic way, trivial pursuits and their pursuers have come to signify possible productive and self-improving patterns of life, a valorization instead of a debasement à la Chandler of the "feminine" ordinary. In this revision the categories of "masculine" and "feminine" are not quite left in place. Popular versions of psychoanalysis, for example, tend to surface in a critique of masculinity rather than of a perverse or transgressive femininity. Almost ritually, it is now solely the male villains and *not* the male heroes who are inscribed through their sadistic fantasies and practices. And in the police stations, law courts, seedy bars and clubs, or nouveau riche interiors that these male protagonists still frequent, there are more women as civic actors, but hardly a fatal femme to be found. Women in urban public spaces are no longer simply matter out of place, to be disciplined and punished. The forms, conditions, and limits of female agency are now among the most troubling of all the working assumptions a crime narrative has to make, and can no longer be kept quietly under surveillance.

Given the continued male dominance of the hard-boiled, this may still seem a merely superficial change in the manners of these fictions, an instrumental response to a much greater self-consciousness or a surface reformation among readers and writers about sexism and male sadism. But we would argue that this redeployment of sexual difference as an arbiter of cultural difference goes deeper. The "new man" that these texts collectively produce through what Bourdieu has called "a process of 'deculturation' and 'reculturation' " which "set such store on the seemingly most insignificant details of *dress, bearing,* physical and verbal *manners*" does use the semiotics of sexual difference as a "mnemonic . . . form" of "the fundamental principles of the arbitrary content of the culture" (Bourdieu, 1977, pp. 94–95).

But if the new soft hard-boiled does genuinely democratize public space, highlighting its dangers *to* women instead of symbolizing its dangers *from* women, too often it does so by effacing the origins of that ideological transformation. Directly or indirectly these novels disavow the ethical force of the collective social movements behind their "reculturation" of present and future social relations.

II

The move which rewrites sixties and seventies radicalism as the thinly disguised criminality of the children of the idle white rich or lumpen black poor is part of a general struggle in the eighties as to what should constitute the public memory of popular politics. Though searching for an objective truth about this past against which to measure present deformations is no longer a viable political or theoretical project, thinking politically and historically about the many versions of it now in circulation certainly is. This contestation has been taking place across best-selling fictions and serious documentaries alike, from public television series like *Eyes on the Prize* to Hollywood cinema's *Mississippi Burning* and *Born on the Fourth of July.* The late eighties saw Elmore Leonard and George V. Higgins both trashing the student movements and the counterculture generally in two well-received novels, *Freaky Deaky* (1988) and *Outlaws* (1987). And in each case we see a kind of eighties popular feminism, a diffused consciousness already a part of an enlightened, if not hegemonic, common sense being deployed as a weapon with which to unmask both the radical pretensions of the political past, and its present mnemonic, the aging ex-agitators themselves.

Freaky Deaky is the more shocking example of the two, if only because Leonard has good credentials as a liberal writer who in his fictions and in his commentaries on them has attempted to revise his own earlier and more conservative representations of gender and race. Risking his reputation as the most "writerly" of mainstream authors, he has used his late-blooming success to bend his entertainments to political critique. *Bandits* (1987), the novel immediately before *Freaky Deaky,* was a winning, funny scam story about American policies in Nicaragua in which Jack, an ex-jewel thief and Lucy, an ex-nun, and a few ex-cons, conspire to outwit a Noriega figure. Consistently in all his eighties novels, Leonard's characters—both working class and bourgeois—are seen as produced through the popular cultural fantasies of their youth: in *Bandits,* for example, the protagonists re-imagine themselves and their mission in terms of Catholic iconographies materialized in denominational schooling and sexualized by Hollywood cinema. Fantasy in Leonard can be frightening, especially when it gets stuck in the compulsion to repeat sexual or violent scenarios. It can also, interestingly, be the stuff of which the agency and productive emotional relations of "ordinary" people are made in an otherwise anomic, dehistoricized social topography where neither "community" nor "culture," as traditionally and Eurocentrically understood, can endow subjects with ethical identities. The progressive positions which Jack and Lucy come to occupy *vis-à-vis* Nicaragua in *Bandits* have no ideological links to New or Old Left radicalism. Instead they are forged in the eighties by a process of identification which mobilizes the libidinal and the humanist remnants of their Catholic childhoods against the sadistic terrorism of contra colonels.

Freaky Deaky continues this exploration of fantasy, politics, and the everyday, but also turns it around in order to stigmatize a generation of radicals. The novel's criminal anti-heroes are Robin and Skip, two ex-Weatherpeople, and Donnell, an ex-Black Panther, all of whom have been jailed for adventurist or terrorist activities; their victims, Woody and Mark Ricks, are two rich brothers who were caught up in the student movement too. (Indeed, it is remarkable that the activism of the sixties and seventies in which terrorism and personal violence played such a minor part, and was explicitly rejected by so many in the social movements during this period, has come in fiction—even in some feminist fictions like *The Women's Room* (1977) and *Vida* (1979)—to stand as a politically skewed synecdoche for the practices and ideologies of those movements as a whole.)

In *Freaky Deaky* these variously degenerate subjects bear the historical traces of the inauthentic political and cultural populisms they supported:

> "Man, we let it rip, didn't we? Dope, sex, and rock and roll. Ol Mao and Karl Marx tried to keep up but didn't stand a chance against Jimi Hendrix, man, the Doors, the Dead, Big Brother and Janis . . . and my all-time favorite outlaw band—you know the one it was?" (Leonard, 1988, p. 19)

Significantly, given these past priorities, all of them are now connected to the culture industries and their places within them index the relative levels of their moral and political degradation. The middle-class ex-con ex-lovers became real criminals during their spell underground: Robin shoplifted, Skip robbed banks and worked as a hit man. In the eighties Skip and Robin have found legit "professions": Robin writes historical

"bodice-rippers" under the pseudonym of Nicole Robinette for "the great silent majority" who "don't have a fucking thing to say" (p. 13). Skip is a skilled stuntman and
technician for the movies, blowing up cars and bridges for male adventure flicks rather
than the revolution. Woody Ricks, the fat alcoholic heir to an automobile parts fortune,
and Mark his younger brother—a "media freak" in his protest days—now own a regional
theater. Woody's mainstream tastes dominate the running of the theater which showcases
musicals like *Oklahoma, Fiddler on the Roof,* and *Seesaw.* Meanwhile Mark, who has been
featured in *People* magazine as a "Yippie turned yuppie," can only dream nostalgically
of putting on rock concerts (p. 40). Donnell the ex-Panther has a more passive, yet no
less perverse connection to this order of cultural survivals. As the all-purpose "minder"
of the "wet-brained" Woody, one of Donnell's main tasks is to play him his favorite
videos—either Arnold Schwarzenegger or classical Hollywood song and dance.

For the old lefties in *Freaky Deaky* collective cultural memories have the negative
function of hysterical reminiscence: they reveal the dark side of the political unconscious
symptomatically expressing "outlawed," outdated, and repressed social pleasures as individual pathology—greed, vengeance, violence. The different cultural/political "histories" represented in the text are made to converge: Robin is a compulsive diarist,
keeping extensive and self-incriminating notebooks on her past, and her bookshelf contains Genet, Bukowski, Ginsberg, Hoffman, *Soledad Brother, Sisterhood is Powerful, The
Politics of Protest* as well as "old copies of underground newspapers" (p. 197). She is the
true *auteur* of the criminal plot to kill Woody. Snake-like, Robin's motives are slippery,
sliding between revenge, greed, and an Iago-ish pleasure in controlling the action, her
reasons so overdetermined that they become pure "motiveless malignity." Unlike most
of Leonard's recent female figures, Robin is a caricature *femme fatale* complete with phallic
femininity. This spider woman is able to draw her ex-lovers Skip and Mark, and even
the more aloof Donnell, into her web by offering them their own brand of cultural
nostalgia through the talisman of her aging body and her teasing remembrance of the
precise scenarios where these particular actors had it all: sex, drugs, politics, and rock
'n' roll.

This political melodrama of repetition is intensified through its performance in
the imploding, asocial Detroit of the eighties—the book's opening chapter sets the scene
with the blowing up of a twenty-four-year-old black drug czar by his sidekick and
girlfriend. The only relief Leonard offers from this entropic scenario is a redemptive
mini-romance. The antidotes to anomie and pathology in *Freaky Deaky* are Chris, a
bomb squad cop—a Vietnam vet who was a classmate but no friend of the baddies—and
Greta, a young would-be film actress who has been raped by Woody the drunk. Amusing
and likable, sexual democrats, commonsense feminists—Chris and Greta function in the
novel as a kind of postmodern "folk," mobile but humane and harmless subjectivities.
They stay afloat—and continue to swim—ethical survivors in the slimy shark-ridden
waters of the urban sublime, while Skip and Robin blow themselves up in a predictably
suitable sticky end.

"Just don't tell me you've become a women's lib vegetarian lesbian," Skip pleads
with Robin in *Freaky Deaky,* before he is made only too aware that he has teamed up
with an unreformed, heterosexual carnivore (p. 15). Robin, it is implied, compulsively
plays out her role as old style *film noir* villainess, because she has remained immune to
the lessons of the women's movement. Conversely, the younger Greta is saved because
she has absorbed that ethical consciousness through cultural osmosis as part of the popular
of her generation—without ever having to embrace either its collective practices or
confront its alternative sexualities. The women's movement is simultaneously the sup-

pressed and invoked political text of *Freaky Deaky*, a conservative, populist appropriation—feminism without struggle.

An even more conservative appropriation of radical history and sexual politics can be found in George V. Higgins's *Outlaws*. Here, in a more reactionary and offensive reworking of the rich kid radicals-as-terrorists mythology, transgressive female sexuality becomes the primary meaning that feminism is allowed to have. Higgins's outlaw adventurists are a gang of Weatherpeople, robbers whose personnel and politics squeeze a bizarre selection of political bedfellows into a condensed and paranoid vision of postwar radicalism. Its charismatic white male leader is a figure of Mansonesque proportions who disciplines his followers through sexual humiliation, graphically and grotesquely detailed in the novel. As well as weak heterosexual women, two members of his gang are sadistic lesbians, who have somehow come under his sway, and another is a partly black male, a "natural follower." This is a ragbag coalition who are ready to commit *and* submit to sadomasochistic violence, but the group's revolutionary rationales are too thinly present in the book for it to persuasively hold their historically dissonant racial and sexual politics together. As in Leonard, there is a kind of essentialist teleology of countercultural movements here, and the spectacle of their libidinized violence is made to substitute for a coherent account of their aims, principles, and practices.

The moral ground of *Outlaws* is sited in Higgins's regionalism, his celebration of Boston and its environs, those historically rooted, ethnically various (white) communities of cops, lawyers, politicians, and "ordinary" criminals. Higgins's Boston is a lovingly evoked world of men, rendered linguistically through a rich, stylized vernacular. Their unreformed but basically benevolent masculinity is ideologically more egalitarian, less abusive of women than that of the terrorists. But it is resistant to programmatic feminism: "What Miss Gloria Steinem and that gang say about how you got equal rights—none of that applies here. Doesn't matter if it's right" (Higgins, 1987, p. 68). Modern, moderate patriarchy that affirms the "right" of women to be cops, of betrayed wives to leave stale marriages, is part of the ethical facelift given to the traditional values of the male community. And, like the commonsense conscience so frequently invoked in Higgins by representatives of the law, they are passed down from father to son—feminism without women. This extension of male integrity is so confident that it can generously include a qualified final page apologia for the gang, spoken by one of the cops: "Whatever else you want to say about that pack of animals, at least they had strong beliefs. And so did Fred, and so did you, and I had them too. Theirs meant they could do things that the law said they could not. Ours said that the law came first, and that's how we all behaved" (p. 359). In this masculine stand-off between "beliefs," outlaw sexuality—sexuality rendered at once as violent and homosexual—tips the scales in favor of the traditional community and its regulators. That society can stand as a positive cultural agent, bearably corrupt, because of the absence of a stark misogyny in the representation of its heterosexual norms. As in *Freaky Deaky*, feminism serves as a shadow text responsible for its everyday idealism, its claims for a good-enough social order. In Higgins's fiction, however, this feminism is also figured as anarchic sexuality and must be suppressed and delegitimized.

In a sense, both Leonard and Higgins are using the past in order to settle accounts with the present—as well as, in Higgins's case at least, using the present in order to settle accounts with the past. But what of the future? Is it possible to shift this gendered and generational politics of the popular into a future conditional tense? Writing against the background of Thatcherism's third successive electoral victory, J. G. Ballard (1981) has recently made such an attempt by combining the male adventure with the police procedural to effect what he has elsewhere called "an oblique and open fiction in the cautionary mode" (Ballard, 1981, p. 19). His bleak novella *Running Wild* (1988) is an exercise in imaginary horror—the story of "the Pangbourne Massacre, as it is now known in the popular press throughout the world"—the gruesome murder of ten professional and business families, together with their servants and employees, in an English village guarded by a private security firm, and the mysterious disappearance of their thirteen children (Ballard, 1988, p. 5). But this murderous imaginary is also deliberately placed in close juxtaposition to the murderously real. For the text is offered up as "the Forensic Diaries of Dr. Richard Greville, Deputy Psychiatric Adviser" to the London Metropolitan Police, and the author of an "unpopular minority report on the Hungerford killings" of August 1987, a reference to an actual incident in which a lone gunman named Michael Ryan randomly shot down sixteen people in a small English town, in what was widely reported as a Rambo-style bloodbath (p. 6).

It is this tabloid version of Ryan's criminal persona that Ballard places in the foreground of his novella. Since the Pangbourne Massacre brings "the Hungerford tragedy . . . immediately to mind," Michael Ryan's name is used to dramatize the possibility that these fictional crimes might be the work of a "solitary assassin." "A group of Michael Ryans" may even be hypothesized, "perhaps five or six deranged members of a local rifle club" (pp. 18–19). These speculative conclusions are narrative red herrings and are briskly dismissed. However, once the real killers have been correctly identified, Michael Ryan as signifier of contemporary histories of violence makes another, even more sinister appearance.

Running Wild points an accusing finger at the least likely suspects—the thirteen children of the victims. In choosing this solution, Ballard effectively re-mythologizes the Hungerford murders and presents a new political fable in its place. Just as Michael Ryan's actions targeted his mother, neighbors, school, and high street, so the Pangbourne children target *their* families and homes, wreaking a terrible vengeance upon the heartland of the affluent English South. A true "return of the repressed," this is also a possibility that official discourse finds unthinkable and must therefore continue to repress. All evidence to the contrary, the Home Office persists in believing "to this day . . . that the children were abducted by their parents' murderers" (p. 78). What is completely inadmissable is that these eight boys and five girls should actually *be* their parents' murderers.

By contrast, Greville argues for a direct parallel between Ryan's state of mind and that of the Pangbourne children. "As with the Hungerford killer, Michael Ryan, or the numerous American examples of crazed gunmen opening fire on passers-by," he writes, "the identity of the victims probably had no special significance for them." These acts of violence are only possible because of their "comparative unimportance," bleached of "any meaning" whatsoever. Greville believes that this extreme state of alienation was brought about by "the devoted and caring regime" of childrearing practiced in the village, in which the children were "suffocated under a mantle of praise and encouragement" ("whether earned or not") and completely "denied any self-expression." Ironically, what seemed like a progressive and humane upbringing induced "a state closely akin to sensory deprivation," turning the children into "prisoners in their own homes" with the aid of closed-circuit TV, computer-assisted learning, and "crowded recreation schedules" (p. 63). As a result, they spontaneously and surreptitiously began to disengage themselves from that world, seeking to remove themselves from it by any means necessary, in effect by violent insurrection. Inevitably, this means that in the future "all authority and parental figures" will become "their special target." And Ballard's cautionary tale closes with a "1993 Postscript" which tells of an unsuccessful attempt on the life of an unnamed retired British prime minister in *her* high-security estate in south-east London, a figure still popularly known as "Mother England" (pp. 78–80).

"Mother England" is however more than simply an appropriate Oedipal substitute. She is also emblematic of all those forces of conservative Puritanism which have spent the past decade trying to roll back the sixties. More broadly, Ballard's animus is directed against the encroaching moralisms of the New Left and of feminism as much as those of the New Right. And this position is implicit in the book's treatment of popular culture which points precisely to what has been suppressed from the children's apparently impeccably "unrepressed" lives. In a vivid replay of the day of the massacre we are shown one of the eldest boys reading "a lurid American horror comic" which "he has smuggled into the estate" (pp. 71–75). It is this seventeen-year-old adolescent who hides what Greville's assistant calls "the real porn"—special weapons and tactics magazines like *Guns and Ammo* and *Commando Small Arms*—underneath the "well-thumbed copies of *Playboy* and *Penthouse*" which are tacitly condoned by his liberal psychiatrist parents with their bookshelves "an A–Z of once-modish names from Althusser and Barthes to Husserl and Perls" (pp. 29–31). The illicit activities of the girls are equally appropriately true to type, putting an originary sexual difference back in place. Like Robin in *Freaky Deaky,* two of them write "Robinettes"—sentimental, historical novels "reminiscent of Jane Austen," "*Pride and Prejudice* with its missing pornographic passages restored," scenes of "sexual passion" important primarily for "the powerful emotions" they elicit. Hopelessly "over-civilized," youthful terrorism is the only way in which these "inhabitants . . . can make their escape into a more brutal and more real world of the senses" (p. 54). Greville's final comment on this bizarre narrative strikes a curiously unforensic, even anarchic note that could almost be borrowed from the late R. D. Laing's anti-psychiatric writings of the sixties: "in a totally sane society, madness is the only freedom" (p. 64).

Recalling a bestiary of revolutionary cells that included the Baader Meinhof group and the Angry Brigade, *Running Wild* exploits the conventionalized demonology of European terrorism by picturing the Pangbourne children's violence as a form of collective madness, an unholy and unnatural alliance which recruits women to its overridingly masculine fantasy. But in Ballard's aggressive counter-myth of Hungerford it is censorship, not the proliferation of popular culture that sets the terrifying social imaginary of paramilitary violence in motion. A complex signifier, Ballard's image of trashy American pulp fiction denotes both the shadowier side of the psyche and a kind of untameable raw energy; it also gestures towards a formative period in Ballard's own career when the pop art of the earlier sixties took up the icons of popular culture as a vehicle for the critique of an effete high art. Thus in Ballard—unlike Leonard or Higgins—there is a profound nostalgia for a precise historical moment, a libertarian and expansive sixties innocent of left politics and the women's movement.

III

In this essay we have been looking at some of the ways in which popular culture has been pressed into service politically by popular fiction. Our examples have been chosen from male crime fiction of the last fifty years, because these texts deliberately foreground questions of sexual politics. In each case, from Chandler to Ballard, the popular has been taken up, even celebrated, as a reservoir of cultural dynamism and virility. Whether implicitly or explicitly, this meaning of the popular is always secured by a contrast with an enfeebled world of high culture, a polarity which is always constructed in gendered terms. And in the recent fictions we have examined, there is also a process of consolidation going on in which the popular is subdivided, split into its good and bad components, with the text performing a kind of exorcism of its most intimately related Other in a work of denial and disavowal. If the popular is being defended *externally* from the condescension of traditional cultural hierarchies, it is at the same time defending itself *internally* from its own competitors, and these defense mechanisms give the books their narrative momentum as well as their particular political complexion. There is an intricate cultural politics being deployed in these and many other popular texts, and it is part of its task to retrieve the vulgar and defend it from its own political history. Sexual politics—and feminism in particular—serves as a point of attraction and repulsion in these narratives, permitting a reformed masculinity to shore up the law and protect it from the possibilities of collective action. As a consequence, everyday corruption becomes preferred, normalized, the least worst system in the world.

These novels by Leonard, Higgins, and Ballard from the late eighties are typical of a spectrum of recent narratives which see the political past as vitally at stake in the present. Today the fate of the sixties-within-the-eighties is a notoriously important issue in the struggle for cultural and political meaning, an instance of the way the conflicting forces in every conjuncture attempt to write uncontestable histories for themselves. The hegemony of the New Right has involved a sustained attempt to monopolize the complex terrain of the popular, and in particular to drastically overhaul the social significance of the sixties. Its relative success in doing so has made it especially urgent that we understand how the new and constantly shifting hierarchies of taste within the popular are articulated with the political, for these are often the effective points at which political history and aesthetics meet and condense. Any analysis of these shifts must of course involve us in a reflexive critique, for intellectual and political movements on the left are just as implicated in the selective reinterpretation of their histories as other political currents. Part of the value of cultural studies has lain precisely in the space it has opened up for such a reflexive political critique. In fact, its early history in Britain was marked by painful but successful internal struggles to make both gender and race central to its concerns. Now more than twenty-five-years-old, cultural studies is ironically undergoing a kind of crisis generated by its own longevity and success as traveling theory, one that demands an historically informed self-analysis. Because the sixties-in-the-eighties links the two key moments of cultural studies' institutionalization, that symbolic temporality unavoidably defines the ground on which it operates, at least in Britain, Australia, and North America. Negotiating this tricky ground without rejecting cultural studies' earlier formations or embracing them uncritically has become both a substantive and a strategic problem for intellectuals on the left who have located their political analysis of culture in its name.

Each constituency is dealing with this crisis in different ways, but its effects seem especially acute in the United States, where the most recent attempts to fashion a version of cultural studies are currently taking place. There are a number of reasons for this. The size and funding of American higher education has meant that cultural studies has had to become heavily embroiled in a bewildering variety of local and institutional politics within the academy, involving issues which also have their correlates at the national level. For there already exist defenders of the study of popular culture as well as a plurality of new disciplinary or sub-disciplinary affiliations occupying some of the same ground to which cultural studies lays claim: communications, media studies, film and television studies, as well as the many refurbished literature departments still reeling under the impact of the various poststructuralisms. Fighting for a place for cultural studies has often meant engaging with debates whose governing assumptions are very different from those which inform its own paradigms. The heated controversies over endeavors to revise and extend the literary canon in English studies are a case in point. Questions of canonicity abut on to cultural studies insofar as the latter takes a keen interest in the social conditions underpinning the production and consumption of popular literature, the social relations of taste and evaluation that are embedded in everyday culture. At the same time, however, cultural studies concerns itself with a wide range of popular practices—sport, music, and factory floor work-cultures for example—that are not easily accommodated by revamping the literary canon. As Raymond Williams (1981) once argued: "What is now often called 'cultural studies' " is better understood as "a distinctive mode of entry into general sociological questions than . . . a reserved or specialized area" (p. 14).

Williams's emphasis on the "general" and the "sociological" may sound a distinctly unfashionable note amidst requiems for the social and calls for an end to grand narratives, but one of the real strengths of cultural studies has been its insistence on the need to link biographies, structures, and cultures, to explore the fully social articulation of subjectivity, representation, and cultural power. Although concepts of subjectivity and representation have been the site of fruitful exchanges between literary and cultural theory, when cultural studies has been incorporated in literary studies the analysis of social processes often becomes a very silent partner in the resulting merger. There are two convergent aspects to this narrowing down of cultural studies. The first is purely practical and professional: cultural studies initiatives must unavoidably make compromises with the already existing canonical curricula and must not be seen either to dilute or to grossly inflate the disciplinary expertise of English. The second is a suspicion, well developed by the disciplinary training itself, of any attempt to move beyond the specificity of systems of representation, moves that inevitably arouse fears of vulgar reductionism, sociologism, or essentialism. The danger in simply adding more culturally varied and demotic texts to English department curricula under this thinner cultural studies rubric is that it risks effacing the provenance of those texts in social movements and political struggles. The emergent cultural studies in the United States now urgently needs to settle the question of its relationship to the bodies of intellectual work that have grown out of the overlapping political movements of the last three decades: to African-American studies, women's studies, and gay and lesbian studies, and the wider critiques of Eurocentrism in the academy. Only if cultural studies can serve as an umbrella that respects the discrete developments and possible conflicts between these various interventions and, what is harder, can regard them as potentially productive differences, will it retain its political edge.

Enhanced by the turn to theory, a turn that sometimes includes a turn to cultural studies, English often styles itself the avant-grade of the humanities. Institutionally speaking, however, English departments are not solely the elite preservers of the canon or the new guardians of high theory, but the most densely populated disciplinary area within the academy, raising the standards of literacy in the whole student body through the writing and composition programs and distribution requirements that give English, especially in the public sector, its numerical strength and economic clout. These humbler service functions are of course performed by the most poorly paid and institutionally powerless teachers within the university, a casualized and feminized workforce of visiting part-time lecturers and teaching assistants, whose role is played down in the preferred self-image of these departments. Nevertheless, both structurally and intellectually gender is a critical variable in the changing shape of English studies. The high profile and rising market value of feminist criticism and theory nationally, a very recent legitimation, has challenged the masculine hegemony of senior scholars still overwhelmingly dominant in the professoriat. Where cultural studies has ridden into English partly on the crest of that surprising success it has also suffered from the considerable backlash feminism has provoked. For English is both a highly contentious and heavily stratified discipline, whose social being is rife with structural tensions; these conflicts have inevitably affected the ways its internal struggles over the uses of literacy are conducted. Seen in this light, the anxieties of English *vis-à-vis* cultural studies, as well as those of cultural studies inside English, articulate the contradictions in the discipline and closely resemble the dynamic of the popular within the popular we have been describing.

Institutionalizing cultural studies today often seems to court the danger of making mass art forms and everyday culture into an idealized popular—a new good object whose problems and pleasures replace those of purer texts. Yet, as we have argued, an idealized popular can have its own dubious purity, seeking to stay uncontaminated by the dirty world of politics and washing its hands of messy mundane versions of the popular. If what we have been saying about texts, disciplines, and institutions is characteristic of a more general move to obscure the sources of "political innovation, political creation, and political experimentation" in our era, then keeping both cultural politics and political histories as living parts of nineties cultural studies may prove to be its greatest challenge.

NOTES

1. We would like to thank John Barrell, Larry Grossberg, and Jacqueline Rose for helpful comments on an earlier draft of this essay. Our title was inspired by a chapter heading in Nancy Armstrong's (1987) *Desire and Domestic Fiction.*

DISCUSSION: CORA KAPLAN AND DAVID GLOVER

JOHN FISKE: I'd like to focus on your model of the agency ascribed to the text and the critic. I think you positioned the text as the prime agent in the circulation of meaning, ignoring the cultural activity of fans and audiences. Your paper demonstrated a traditional view of the critic as the privileged revealer of the hidden ideological political meaning of the text, with the danger that they may be producing those meanings as they actually reveal them.

KAPLAN: I don't think that John Fiske's way of problematizing the role of the critic in terms of a Manichean distinction between sympathetic populist fan-niks, and sinister, snooty Privileged Revealers is a helpful one for understanding the very real differences between Constance Penley's project and our work on crime fiction. In any case we're interested in things that this binary doesn't really capture. First of all, we are trying to place the emergence of new themes and narrative twists in the genre historically. We want to know why they appear when they do, and with what other sorts of public discourses they are in dialogue. Second, we are focusing on the way in which such tropes and stories circulate. Crime fiction seems to us lately to have taken a surprising narrative lead in the reworking and interweaving of the political legacies of postwar social movements. Why should these diverse strands get condensed in this particular popular genre? What debates and currents do these fictions intersect and interact with? Lastly, we are exploring what Manthia Diawara has called the "sociology of narrative elements"—the way in which certain recurrent motifs, parts of larger cultural myths which have a long duree as well as more immediately conjunctural fragments, move around from text to text. As to the relative agency of text, critic, and audience, I would want to displace the implied power relations in John Fiske's question. Popular fiction, its very active readerships, cultural criticism all produce political meanings—texts and audiences have a hell of a lot more agency in this production than academic critics, but no one of these activities is politically illegitimate, nor should it be a question of locating a superior politics in any one of them.

GLOVER: In the question, there is an implicit contrast which crops up an awful lot these days. It's a contrast that's drawn between a kind of theoreticism of the text and an empiricism of the audience, and it's also a contrast that readily gets transcoded into charges of elitism, on the one hand, and rank populism on the other. One reason why it's especially important to break with the false alternative this offers is precisely because of the difficulty involved in tracking the impact of popular texts across highly dispersed and heavily diversified publics. There simply are no easy empirical procedures ready to hand to help you out here, particularly since people's reading practices and discussions of their reading are so casual and informally situated most of the time. We've spent a lot of time at crime fiction conferences and talking to organized fan groups, and one thing you quickly realize is that these are very specific gatherings with very specific ideologies. It's important to understand and make sense of them, sure. But finding out what makes these sorts of fans tick isn't necessarily going to help you to get a hold on why a novel like *Presumed Innocent* has been such a runaway success and how it has become a public narrative at the widest possible level. To do that you need to look at what Meaghan Morris has recently called "popular theories"—"the theoretical debates that circulate in and as popular culture."

To return to our own paper for a moment, I think that what we were trying to do in the paper was really two things. One was to look at the politics of a set of texts— and I want to insist that we weren't looking at this politics purely in the dark. If you look at the history of *Bandits,* Leonard's novel immediately prior to *Freaky Deaky,* for example, you'll see that it came in for a lot of criticism precisely on the basis of the political position it seemed to be imaginatively adopting—a left-liberal position on Nicaragua, criticism of aid to the contras, and so on. There's nothing "hidden" or mysterious about this, just as there's nothing mysterious about the fact that these otherwise very different texts converge in their rewriting of the sixties and seventies. It's a part of the way this field of popular culture is now structured. So we wanted to underline that fact, and, secondly, to try to link it to a more general argument about cultural studies. Because very often when you get into questions about what cultural studies is and what it should be, one version that you often get is that it is some kind of interdisciplinarity, and that that's what we need. But, to the contrary, we wanted to argue that cultural studies ought to be conceived instead as an approach to the politics of culture.

KAPLAN: If we were to take that point forward into our particular project we would be looking at the slippery relationship between the libidinal economies the texts offer, and the political contexts in which their value can be realized. For example Turow, Leonard, Higgins, Parker—all the soft hard-boiled male writers have a lot more to say about restructured masculinity than femininity. They go on at length about a less macho, less misogynist homosociality, but they have a horror of both male and female homosexuality. That is exactly the place where their fantasies cannot go. And this implies that they are obliquely involved in a negative engagement with the newest social movement, with gay and lesbian politics. How their diverse readers relate to their implicit and explicit homophobia is another question, and it doesn't have a simple answer. Are gay and lesbian readers completely alienated by these texts?—not always, or not quite in our experience, for the books have other pleasures, and they aren't read to provide a politically correct experience. However, it is arguable but by no means certain that for some heterosexual readers a world which excludes the positive possibilities of same-sex love is somehow a "safer" space for fantasy. In any case these are the kinds of textual conditions that the hooked but discontented reader must work on, work over.

LIDIA CURTI: You were speaking about the importance of women's readership for this new kind of crime story. I think there's a lot to be said for women's readership and for the other older kinds as well. I don't know whether you exclude that or whether you think it is more women-specific, this second rewriting.

GLOVER: That's a very good point about the question of women's readership of the hard-boiled. What I'd want to be concerned with is to see where the points of identification would be for those women readers. And also whether boundaries would be set, for example comparing Chandler vs. Spillane, whether Spillane would be out of bounds for women readers whereas Chandler might not be, and how that actually could be constructed in terms of subjectivity. One of the things that we're interested in is precisely this question of moving across the gender divide in popular fiction where ostentatiously masculine texts are recruiting women readers too.

KAPLAN: We are not saying that older reading relationships were pre- or a-political, but I think that there is a difference that has everything to do with the intervention of feminism, though for both writing and readers there is no absolute "before and after," and no simple set of effects. The broad dissemination of feminist ideas has produced a diaspora of effects; it can make readers aware of the crude misogyny of certain texts by both men and women, a recognition that may turn them off and/or it can empower more "transgressive" gender-bending identifications. It can trigger a reaction against what is seen as its politically correct agendas at the same time as it appropriates aspects of them. I think at the very least that feminism has developed new social and psychic languages through which both women and men are able to imagine their fantasy relations to these and other narratives, and that gift has been empowering, a term which seems to me more ethically neutral than most American uses of it would claim. New crime subgenres give overt form to a utopian desire for the restructuring of masculinity and femininity, a desire widely if unevenly shared by men and women. These themes are often located in very violent narratives, and in the case of the female readership of soft hard-boiled male fiction and some of the feminist crime fiction that violence seems part of the reading pleasure, not a drawback to it. That is in itself worth speculating about; perhaps there is something about the imbrication of violence, both social and psychic in these desires, and to the immanent violence of the social world in which utopian identities must invariably be imagined.

In relation to female readers before and after second wave feminism, I would want to emphasize most of all that there isn't a radical opposition between something called feminism and the unsettling ambiguities of its everyday effects. And that ought to lead us to explore the interdependence of these seemingly segmented readerships; the complex ways in which men and women, men and men, women and women, can use such social texts to negotiate and mediate their understanding of sexual politics. For instance our romance with each other, Dave's and mine, involved a very libidinal, semi-serious identification with a series of romances in Elmore Leonard's novels, with the scenarios more than with the gendered subjects in them, an identification weakened or at least cut across, when we read *Freaky Deaky,* by a conflicting investment in our own political histories. We haven't abandoned our interest or pleasure in Leonard as a writer; we still find his romance grabs us. At the same time we're moved to protest against their political logic, their psychic *realpolitik,* their false binaries—feminism or fantasy, socialism or new subjectivity, and their insistence on the framing of romance as heterosexual.

15

AIDS, Keywords, and Cultural Work

Jan Zita Grover

I never met or heard Raymond Williams speak: I know him only through his published writing. His importance for me is probably quite different than it is for those of you who knew and worked with him. His greatest gifts to me were his convictions that culture is the lived experience of all of us, constantly and actively produced, and that scholarship that ignored this fact, that didn't acknowledge and explore the seamless interplay between culture and society, was bloodless. My paper today is partly an homage to Williams, partly a description of work on AIDS that I have undertaken—I hope in the spirit of his good scholarship—and partly an application of Williams's criticism of British cultural studies to an American situation. To get to these, I must begin with my own experience.

Like some others here today, I came up through a state university system in which literature was studied formally, one in which all other considerations—who *wrote* the literature, where they lived, how they earned a living, what they thought and did about the great issues of their day—were relegated to a separate field called literary history. Our job as students of literature was to understand the internal arrangements of works of literature, to absorb, as if we were blotters, the slow sweating-out of whatever meaning resided in the formal configurations of metaphor, repetition, oxymoron. Without being able to identify at age 21 just what was wrong with this approach *for me,* I felt dissatisfied and frustrated with it, and my solution was to remove myself as much as possible to the university's history department. There, however, though I found my studies on the whole more rounded than they had been in English, I found that literature was treated merely as *illustration* to themes and issues better embodied by other sorts of documents— public records, diaries, journalism, memoirs. Had I encountered Raymond Williams's work at this time—this was the late 1960s—I think I could have solved my dilemma quite handily. Unfortunately for me, *Culture and Society* wasn't reprinted in this country for another decade, and I had already left my formal schooling before Williams's other books saw print in the U.S.

After taking my doctorate in 1973, I taught American literature at Arizona State University for three years. This experience was a revelation to me. Because while there had been little distinction between me and my students while I was a graduate student at the University of California—I too had to worry about the cost of books and supplies, the cost of hamburgers, what I would do for a living after graduate school—the distinctions between students and faculty in Arizona were profound. It was there that I discovered—and I am still batting .500 with this—that faculty members do not know how much tuition their students pay or how much the textbooks they require students to buy cost. I saw that most of my students were going to take whatever they learned at the university and go out to work in a world in which I had never supported myself

and that the terms on which they would continue their study of literature would necessarily be very different from my own. *And I did not know how to help them with that:* I
didn't even know what that world outside the university was like.

Moreover, I suspected that I couldn't even make a living in that world or even,
perhaps, maintain my own interests in literature and history without the support of a
university. Feeling as hemmed in by teaching in a program stressing literary form as I
did while studying it, I began working on the side for a community newspaper and a
community radio station. I realized that I could survive after all outside the academy.
So three years later, I quit full-time teaching. Except for a three-year stint at an open
admissions college of applied arts in the early eighties and a lot of part-time night school
teaching, I have worked outside the academy ever since. Since 1986, I have worked full-
time against the AIDS crisis, first as a typist, then as a medical editor and a writer, and
always as a volunteer with AIDS agencies.

There are three things I want to say about what I've learned outside the academy
that have a bearing on cultural studies: first, how difficult and heroic it is for people
who work conventional jobs in business and government to go home afterward and
choose to do brainwork in the evenings and on weekends—*but how much of this gets done
despite the obstacles,* and how little evidence I can find that academic training prepares
students for this transition; second, how different a "discipline" looks to someone working its applications on a daily basis—and I do not mean how different it looks to a
theorizer and a worker, because both are theorizers; and third, how much resentment
there is in the majority of workplaces towards academics. It is the last two points that
I'll talk about here.

Meaghan Morris (1990a) has shrewdly observed that ethnographic approaches to
cultural studies hinge on a narcissistic structure: "What takes place is firstly a citing of
popular voices (the informants), an act of translation and commentary, and then a play
of *identification* between the knowing subject of cultural studies, and a collective subject,
'the people.'" She goes on. "In the end they are not simply the cultural student's object
of study, and his native informants. The people are also the textually delegated, allegorical emblem of the critic's own activity. . . . Once 'the people' are both a source of
authority for a text and a figure of its own critical activity, the populist enterprise is not
only circular but (like most empirical sociology) narcissistic in structure" (p. 20). I would
add, and bluntly: For writers who profess to have an interest in what "the people" think
and do, academic critics seem remarkably uninterested in addressing their remarks *to*
those same people. Quite simply, the bulk of writing on culture in this country that
acknowledges culture as being produced by people other than artists, intellectuals, and
academics seems directed to other academics rather than to the people whom they
describe as producing it.

This is an error that I wish to avoid as much as possible, for two reasons: first of
all, I *am* "those people," working customarily in an office, a not-for-profit agency, or
a community newspaper; second, I know that it is not the concepts but the vocabulary
and style of writing that make most academic writing in the U.S. so tedious and difficult
for non-academics to follow. People outside the academy read and use many of the same
materials that scholars do, although often their style of dealing with them is more direct,
blunt, and emotional. These, I think, are virtues rather than defects at any level of
discourse.

Let me give you some examples. I noticed three very interesting data about culture
the day I sat down to begin this paper last fall. The Giants had won the National League
pennant from the Cubs, and when I opened the *San Francisco Chronicle* that morning,
the cover story quoted Giants pitcher Mike Krukow describing Will Clark's pivotal

two-run single as like a "script by Bernard Malamud"—not a writer that many intellectuals would expect a baseball pitcher to quote.

Later on in the *Chronicle* story, a department-store electronics salesman commented that most of his department's one hundred-plus television sets had been tuned to the game and drew a crowd of 150 people. " 'Normally,' " he said, "We have the TVs tuned to KQED, the educational station, because we don't want the subject matter to absorb people.' "

Pondering all this, at noon I went to my favorite dive, the 524 Club, for lunch. The waitress had her nose in a book, a Sidney Sheldon. Two burly men came in in work clothes and talked with her while they waited for their lunch. One of them asked her if she read a lot and if she wanted suggestions for a good read. She said *Sure.* As he got up to leave, he slapped some change on the counter, put on his CAT cap and said, "You want a good read, read anything by Carlos Fuentes. Anything. Can that guy write!"

I know the dangers of using anecdotes as the basis for producing inductive arguments. I think they're best used as indexes of widely distributed practices. In this case, there's nothing marvelous in finding that workingmen read Carlos Fuentes and that PBS can be matter-of-factly described as cultural Muzak by a department store clerk. What *is* marvelous, however, is that surprise about such matters should exist, for as the late Raymond Williams emphasized, "Culture is ordinary." It is both made and consumed by ordinary people under ordinary circumstances. *That so much* academic cultural criticism—and here I must apologize for universalizing a term that takes in so much, from the mistrust of Stuart Ewen on the left to the mistrust of Allan Bloom on the right—proceeds in willed ignorance of non-academics' ability to use and critique the materials of what academics like to believe is their own—and exclusive—toolbox has nurtured an understandable amount of resentment among its putative subjects.

Most of us concede that the notion of high and low culture is an heuristic device of little value in understanding what actually goes on in American culture. The furthest we have got in most cases is the gee-whizism of conceding the "complexity and contradiction" in ordinary culture. Generous and open-minded as such a formulation may initially sound, it is—in addition to being sentimental—a loving but dismissive admission that the critic finds no theory at work in ordinary culture save his or her own. *They're loveable, they're contradictory, what can I say?—They're the people.*

My essay "AIDS: *Keywords*" (in Crimp, ed., 1988) was an attempt to deal with some materials of contemporary culture in the terms of the communities most affected by these materials—rather than in the terms of, say, Ewen's or Bloom's approaches, with their general mistrust of non-intellectuals' ability to make and interpret culture. It is also, obviously, an homage to Raymond Williams's *Keywords,* though with a significant difference. Because while Williams was interested in tracing the shifts in meaning of key terms throughout the pre-industrial and modern periods, I was tracking terms as they first erupted into public discourse.

My aim was to record the usages that I heard and read in the several AIDS-connected worlds that I moved through: the gay activist community in San Francisco; the student community at California Institute of the Arts near Los Angeles; the academic medical community of physicians for whom I edited an AIDS textbook at San Francisco General Hospital; the healthcare workers—social workers, nurses, orderlies, ward clerks, protocol managers—with whom I worked at the hospital; the volunteers and staff of San Francisco's Shanti Project and Hospice and New York's Gay Men's Health Crisis; and other writers for gay community newspapers.

I undertook this guide to how language shapes reality as someone who swims near the bottom. Like a catfish, I feed off others' castoffs; I am less interested in cultural forms as something *for me* to interpret than I am in listening as other people offer their interpretations of them. My sense of language and photographs, the two media with which I am most practiced and comfortable, is that their meaning is seldom very fixed; it is the act of so many other people attributing meaning that stimulates my own interest. Simply by watching and listening, I am situated to observe culture-in-the-making. River-bottom feeding, I swallow their proffered meanings and try to figure out what sorts of sense they make.

There's another sense in which I am a bottom-feeder: my thinking and writing about AIDS has been done, to invoke one of the only metaphors by which AIDS can be understood, at the level of everyday involvement. AIDS has been my job, in one way or another, for five years, so I am subject to the same pressures of anger, sorrow, numbness, burn-out, and sexual dysfunction that most other people working in hospitals, test-sites, prevention programs, and voluntary agencies, are. Like other activists, I have found that AIDS is a 360° sense-surround, and there is no door out of it leading back to a faculty office for me. I think this is crucial to the anger that informs the writing of AIDS activists as opposed to most scholars writing about AIDS.

Things change very fast within the communities primarily affected by AIDS: new drugs enter clinical trials; statutes affecting discrimination and insurance are enacted; physicians develop new ways of treating opportunistic infections; people get antibody-tested much earlier now than they did five years ago; most hospital staff are less inclined now to avoid ward duties involving HIV-infected people; volunteers are less inclined to idealize people living with AIDS; and everyone involved over time is more burned-out. So although there's no comparison to the richness and texture with which Williams discussed changes in the meanings attributed to terms like "industry" or "culture" over the eighteenth and nineteenth centuries, it is nonetheless true that terms like "AIDS" and "safer sex" and "general population" have changed quite dramatically over the nine years that the epidemic has been tracked and written about.

These changes, I believe, are for the most part traceable principally at the level of everyday practices. They cannot be traced alone, as Susan Sontag obviously chose to do in her research, by clipping articles from the *New York Times,* by reading previously published studies, by consulting the etymology of "plague" and "epidemic." To use only published resources in tracing shifts within this epidemic is to be fooled both by the centralization of American media, which makes the epidemic in this country syn-onymous with the epidemic in New York and San Francisco—a patent falsehood—and by the superficiality of most AIDS reporting, which takes at face-value the words of a narrow range of research directors, government policy makers, and selected experts like Randy Shilts. Meanwhile, the significant shifts occur elsewhere, down, if I may employ a military metaphor—*pace,* Susan Sontag—in the trenches.

I wrote "AIDS: *Keywords*" on the airplane week after week as I commuted between San Francisco and Los Angeles, and it grew as I saw more clearly the dimensions of the problems language created about AIDS. Media, medical, and government formulations about AIDS made life more complicated or stressful to my friends who were ill, to my students and my fellow activists. My aim was to produce something that would resonate with the experience my readers already had and help them make sense of it through what others had made out of it. More: make them angrier about it. I wanted to write for and help make some sense of the experience of people who, like me, had mopped up shit, changed adult diapers, cooked for people who couldn't eat, cried inappropriately, sat numb and thoughtless in empty rooms, called parents to say their sons had died. It was a very tendentious piece of writing; it was not speculative or balanced and judicious, and it certainly didn't pretend to any degree of objectivity.

I do not have the remove that most of the authors, for example, of *AIDS: The Burdens of History* (Fee and Fox, eds., 1988) had. I found that a very unsettling book, with the exception of Paula Treichler's and Dennis Altman's articles. Unlike mass-media work on AIDS, unlike letters-to-the-editor and the words of people at public forums, this book lacked a sense of anger and loss, those sentiments so easily masked or cut loose in the academicizing of a subject in order to look at it in a "scholarly fashion." When anger and loss are gone, replaced by evasion and historical parallels, as they so largely are in a book like *AIDS: The Burdens of History,* then living culture becomes an abstraction, an object of speculation, just as the language used to describe it becomes filled with agentless processes, abstractions acting as agents, passive constructions, latinate phrases. I don't know how many of you are familiar with this book, but in its twelve articles on AIDS as an object of historical inquiry, only six essays actually deal directly *with* AIDS: the rest creep up on the subject by analyzing a (perhaps) comparable historical episode in detail and then noting, in brief epilogues, that the conclusions drawn there may or may not be applicable to the situation of AIDS. Of the remaining six essays, only two—Treichler's and Altman's—deal with AIDS at other than public policy level. To me, this is dissimulation: whether from caution, diffidence, resistance, terror—who knows what motives, conscious and unconscious?—the authors and editors have produced a book putatively about AIDS but which manages for half the book to avoid discussing it directly.

The introduction makes clear that the editors think historians have been shunted aside from involvement in public policy-making because they have too often directed their work only at their fellow historians. Their book is offered as evidence of the role that historians *could* play in public policy debates if their work were less discipline-directed. But then the editors conclude, "In emphasizing the contributions of historians, we hope to bring new voices into the discussion of public policy and to share some insights of historians with colleagues, students, and general readers." You will notice that "general readers" are the last to be acknowledged; colleagues are still the primary audience, followed by students. But what if, instead of "sharing insights" with first colleagues, then students, then "general readers," an historian were to write *for* the people who played the most significant part in the production of those "insights"—the people who could make the most immediate use of those insights, in this case people who were actively dealing with AIDS, whether they were healthcare workers, AIDS volunteers, school teachers, people with HIV infection? Why the prevailing assumption that these people, "the informants" of so much sociological and historical writing, do not also constitute *an audience* for it?

This, it seems to me, is a central dilemma in much American writing and broadcasting on AIDS: it ignores the communities with the greatest stake in AIDS as *subjects,* as viewers or readers, and uses them only as *objects* of its discourses. This is also a dilemma for cultural studies as a whole—when academic and publishing conventions codify what could be of immediate and long-term use to the subjects in question and instead becomes material for an analysis aimed at other communities: those of other scholars and intellectuals. As Raymond Williams (1989a) remarked of cultural studies, people's interests are not bounded by course outlines; they will consistently "refuse to limit their questions to the boundaries of the set course" (p. 160). Certainly the thousands of articles and books and radio/television broadcasts on AIDS in the past nine years have done what they could to bound the outlines of discourses on AIDS; what is so remarkable is that they have not succeeded.

Books and articles on AIDS have sold well in the U.S.; particularly in the period of great panic in 1986–1987. There has clearly been widespread interest in AIDS for a variety of reasons. But consider what has been on offer to the public; it is much like Williams's description of academic cultural studies: a matter of interest narrowed to a range set by scholarly and commercial discourses.

Virtually all of the books and articles published in this country on AIDS fall into several categories: books and papers on public policy, which are aimed at government officials and other academic policy people; medical, biological, and epidemiological papers; analyses of representations of AIDS contributed by art and culture critics; broadcast media's *what if* . . . hysteria pieces and heartwarming human-interest stories; safersex advice; and memoirs, diaries, and fiction. It is significant to me that in none of these genres is the interrelatedness of social formations and cultural practices regularly acknowledged and explored.

Public policy and scientific papers with disheartening consistency assume the worst about human behavior, advocating HIV-testing and surveillance where ample evidence exists of human restraint and willingness to sacrifice. Public policy-makers consistently conflate *acknowledging* social formations with *condoning* or *encouraging* their continuation—witness the federal and state resistance to providing intravenous drug-users with clean needles and gay men with safer-sex guidelines. Guidelines are laid out with little knowledge or interest in the actual cultural practices of the target populations.

Medical and epidemiological researchers build extraordinary biases into their studies—witness the many flawed projects on prostitutes as vectors of HIV infection, which have ignored the fact of intravenous drug use as the primary risk practice for prostitutes, just as it is for everyone else, and which have ignored the abundant evidence that prostitutes constitute a population of motivated, active AIDS prevention workers.

Too many culture critics see AIDS only in terms of its representations, analyzing the films, television programs, and outpourings of the press as an index to "what AIDS means," "how AIDS means," while ignoring the relationship between these representations and the lived experience of people coping with AIDS. The political and economic structures of our culture that mark so many media and public responses to AIDS as extensions of already-existing beliefs and practices are surely at least as important as their representation.

Broadcast media's willingness to pursue the singular story, the unique angle, has resulted in an overemphasis on the horrific—the family burnt out of their home in Florida, the infected gay hustler continuing to turn tricks for income—at the expense of understanding—and honoring—everyday decencies in the epidemic. When was the last time you saw a prime-time television show profiling one of the voluntary AIDS service agencies—the only organizations that *to this day* coordinate and provide services for the people with AIDS and HIV infection? There is what amounts to a virtual media blackout on the difficult and heroic work these largely gay organizations have done since 1982 for over five years without the help of public funds, unless they are counted a "troubled" organization. Yet we can all name or recall the AIDS *victims* (as media persists in terming them) that television has chosen to personalize and render real: the Ryan Whites, the *innocent victims* who contracted their disease through transfusions or hemophiliac fractions. Here again, no explicit connections are ever drawn in the media between its own already-existing practices of excluding gays, prominently featuring whites, and using blacks and Latinos as undifferentiated *minorities* and these practices' place in American economic and political life as a whole.

The safer-sex guidelines that most people encounter are those appearing on television, in wide-circulation magazines, and as mass-marketed paperbacks. These too fail to draw connections between individual practices and the social formations against and within which they arise. Books like Art Ulene's *Safe Sex in a Dangerous World* and Helen Singer Kaplan's *The Real Truth About Women and AIDS* focus on the technofix of antibody testing each time a person—always presumed in these texts to be a heterosexual female—becomes involved with a new sexual partner. Such advice ignores the failures of our government to provide clear public health guidelines on HIV prevention for everyone. It barely acknowledges the uneven distribution of power between men and women; its stress is on each person's isolation and relative helplessness in grappling with AIDS. In this, such works are similar to the so-called "prevention" programs for many other American health problems, such as smoking, drinking, and heart disease: they focus exclusively on the individual and his or her weakness, leaving unacknowledged the social relationships between individuals and their positioning by class, occupation, religion, politics, education, region. All responsibility, they propose, rests with the individual.

Now, despite the conscious and unconscious attempts in all these publications and broadcasts to constrain the terms of discourse on AIDS, what I find so heartening in all this is that people nonetheless slip through the cracks, make their own discoveries, see the lie in these threadbare formulations. At the level of public opinion, for example, for three years in a row, from 1986 through 1988, Californians rejected initiatives on the state ballot that would have made HIV disease a reportable illness and AIDS a condition meriting quarantine. This despite tremendous lobbying efforts on the part of conservative public-health and political figures. There was not a single county in California in any of the three years, including conservative Orange, San Diego, and rural counties that did not vote down these initiatives by a margin of 2–to–1 or greater. And recent Gallop polls and L.A. *Times* polls indicate that there has been a major reversal in Americans' attitudes toward people with AIDS—from forcibly retiring them from the workforce to working alongside them. At the level of everyday involvement, an increasing percentage of AIDS service volunteers are heterosexual women with no prior involvement in gay communities and no personal acquaintances who are ill with HIV disease. Their reasons for involving themselves in AIDS work are of a piece with their other volunteer work, which suggests to me that AIDS is taking its place as another disease among chronic diseases for a significant part of the population—the pool of middle-class volunteers who have always been the backbone of chronic care in a country lacking in a national health care service.

Finally, I would like to comment on AIDS as a subject of study in the academy. The classroom is at least as remote a place to work on the relationship between culture and society as the scholar's or writer's study. When I decided to teach a course on AIDS at California Institute of the Arts in the fall of 1987, my first idea was to ask students to spend at least two hours a week working for an AIDS service group or hot line as part of the course requirement. I hoped in this way to make the subject matter less abstract, less a matter solely of dealing with representations, which art students at colleges like Cal Arts are usually quite good at doing. I wanted students to have the experience of dealing with AIDS *on the ground,* not solely as a structure made up of media images and texts. But no AIDS service groups were active in the extreme north end of the San Fernando Valley in 1987, so I reluctantly had to give up that idea.

We began the course, then, by examining the medical papers that had initially defined AIDS and so firmly bound it in physicians' and the media's minds with homosexuality. And as so often happens, the students' own experience outside the classroom introduced the pieces of living culture that the representations we were handling both mirrored and shaped: one student's brother taught at a prep school where a teacher was fired after developing AIDS and the entire faculty, staff, and student body were polarized by the experience; another student got into a row with a social worker over the term *AIDS victim,* which the social worker insisted on using when he called her agency for information on North Valley services; another student had a friend who was diagnosed with HIV infection. AIDS was not so very far from these students' lives at all. It took on additional meaning when several became involved with organizing the Los Angeles ACT UP chapter. Eventually the class became more of an organizing unit than a scholarly one—a place each of us brought the materials that had particularly infuriated us that week, or pieces that we planned to incorporate into our own work. I ceased thinking of our group as a class and I believe the students did, too: we were a collective resource that used what we made together *to act, to change things* as best we could outside the classroom.

I can conceive of no better role for cultural studies inside the classroom or out of it than to enable people to act, to change things that they think need changing more effectively than they feel they could have if they hadn't taken that class or read that book or paper. There is real anger among AIDS activists at the way their—our—efforts have been used in broadcast media productions, the way they have been ignored in favor of the speculative fancies of government policy theorists and feature writers. This is simply a local example of a widespread practice, in which informants see their ways of framing the world appropriated and distorted by framers with greater social authority.

I should like to end by quoting one of the few American books on AIDS that displays an admirable balance between the contributions of individual men and women in forging a cultural response to AIDS and the social formations that make this so difficult. It is by the anthropologist and literary scholar Mary Catherine Bateson and the biologist Richard Goldsby (1988). They write in their book, *Thinking AIDS:*

> . . . it is possible to respond to the epidemic by reaching for a more open, just, and intercommunicating society and world in which no one is disenfranchised and individuals have the information to make appropriate decisions. Thus if we were able, as a society, to talk openly about matters related to sex and to feel compassion equally for all our neighbors, the AIDS epidemic would probably be under control by now. Instead, we are in a situation where help has been withheld because of unstated ideas about who is and is not deserving, where essential information is not imparted to those who need it, and where many lack the trust and self-esteem needed to use the information available to them. The perennial problems of our society and of the world, which we have not had the resolution or imagination to address, are the principal sources of vulnerability. (p. 122)

I wish that AIDS work, aimed as it is at imagining and creating a better society for all of us, were not fueled by so much anger. But it is; it must be, until changes in healthcare, government responsibility, and widespread beliefs about social collectivity occur. Until then, cultural criticism on AIDS will remain significantly over-adversarial, an advocate's criticism.

DISCUSSION: Jan Zita Grover

SCOTT COOPER: I'm interested in the fact of your presentation as much as the content of it, given the fact that you have left, or left as a career, the academy. Has cultural studies, or is cultural studies, working successfully toward breaking through those con-tradictions of the institution, the very institution within which it exists in terms of academia? What further needs to happen for that to occur so that in fact the activism could be successful? What is it we are attempting to do, and does the institution allow it to do that? Or, do you still feel now, Jan, that really you had to leave because once you got to a sense of what you wanted to accomplish it just couldn't be done in academia? *GROVER:* I'd have to begin by saying that I don't feel like I can do what I need to do inside the academy. That's why I am no longer there. And what I said at the beginning and lost as I got angrier (as I always do about the AIDS crisis in particular) is that students are not being in any sense prepared for what happens after they leave the university—unless they stay there on different grounds, as a teacher or fellow rather than as a student. I'm in contact with a lot of my old students. And what seems clearest to me from their experience is just how hard it has been for them to find a way to keep some kind of an intellectual edge when they're doing draining work. And where do you find an intellectual community if you're not attached to a university or a college, where do you find a place that does not leave you alone with your own ideas? Those are very difficult questions, especially if you're not in a very, very large city where there's a tradition and network of readings groups. I never heard those sorts of problems articulated in the time I spent inside the academy, so it goes without saying that I never heard any really viable ideas about solving them. I taught so many extension courses, and that's clearly one way people try to keep going that part of themselves that values critical reading. Besides the problem of sustaining critical thinking of the type learned in the academy outside the academy, there is the larger question of integrating theory applicable to everyday life into the academy in the first place. I question whether it can be done. The academy excels in theorizing systems, and no actual system on earth is as clean, works as clean, as the models that get theorized. Activism in every community, including academic communities, is heavily weighted in favor of empiricism. Theory very often gets in the way of effective activism. Activism is instrumental; theory is customarily quite detached. Perhaps the two are incompatible. But again, course outlines tend to be much narrower than people's inquiries actually are. There's one further thing I might mention. The junior colleges in California have their budgets set by head counts, so they're incredibly aggressive at finding every last living soul that they can sign up for classes. One of the things they've started to do, which I think would be an absolutely fabulous way of connecting with post-college people, is teaching courses at work sites. They're devising all these contract courses that actually take place on lunch hours or from four to five in the afternoon in big offices, hospitals, or factories so that people can take on-site courses. It works very well for the corporations that they go into, too, because instead of having to do costly in-services with their own permanent staff and the overhead that comes with that, they just hire feckless J.C. teachers, who get paid $25/hour for classroom hours only. Anybody who has some degree of latitude teaching inside of a four-year college or a university might propose an idea like that to local businesses and be able to bring what she or he can do into settings where an equitable exchange can take place with other adults whose experience and skills are very unlike one's own.

JENNIFER SLACK: I'm a little saddened and frustrated by the distinction that you're making between "the people" and "the academics." I feel like I am one of the people, too; and finding ways within the academy to struggle with the same kinds of issues that are in fact connected to the issues that you're dealing with. You have posited academics or cultural theorists as seeing AIDS merely in terms of its representations, as though they are only concerned with representations of representations, and not about things in the real world. And I think it's absolutely fundamental for us to teach our students and one another to understand the power of those representations for people as well as how to use them. I acknowledge that that is a tremendous struggle to learn how to make those connections, but that is what most of us are in cultural studies struggling with. And I'm shaking because I feel like you've sort of inadvertently trivialized the real struggles that we live with as the people.

GROVER: First, let me dispose of the term "the people" because as I mentioned, I don't see any kind of "the people" at all. I think of people as historically specific, and the people whom I talked about, as I hope I indicated, are people who are working inside of AIDS communities; those are the specific people whom I deal with. I know cultural studies on AIDS from the texts that come out of cultural studies. I know nothing about their author's motivations, but neither do I think motivations are a defense or justification for one's work. Based on the work itself, by and large I don't find it very helpful and I don't think it goes very far. I have no idea what the authors do in their personal life—they may spend another fifteen hours a day working on AIDS or education for disadvantaged children. But that wasn't my point. The study of representations can more easily occur outside the contexts that initially gave rise to those representations than can the study of other kinds of actions. The study of representations can be, often is, perilously close to a formalism because it is disconnected from the messy exigencies of, for example, budgets, schedules, board approvals, political events immediately preceding the production of an image, a poster, a television program. Studies that do not factor in all these variables—and unhappily most of the papers on AIDS that I have seen coming from universities do not—are relatively worthless. They are misleading, they are ahistorical. And they overprivilege the power and autonomy of images in many of the same ways that advertisers do. As far as the topic of AIDS and the academy goes, I don't think it's a coincidence that the only two papers presented here on AIDS and by self-identified gay people are by two out of the conference's four invited non-academics.

SLACK: Can I follow up by asking what you think valid academic work on AIDS would be?

GROVER: I would start by putting both myself and my students in the trenches—one semester in some variety of AIDS service. We'd be better equipped to know, in all humility, how bad, how complicated, things are. Then perhaps I could theorize something, perhaps know how much I didn't know.

LINDA CHARNES: What's intriguing to me about what you've said is that a certain kind of theoretical approach to cultural studies runs the risk of itself functioning like an opportunistic infection, to the extent that it isolates a host culture, moves in, and injects its own theoretical RNA, and then replicates its own structures from the inside out. And in particular it tends to look for host cultures and host communities that have typically been immune to these kinds of analysis, if only by virtue of their marginality. That is not to suggest that we shouldn't engage in a certain kind of theoretical approach to cultural studies but that we should be aware of our own potential for parasitism.

GROVER: That's a very elegant conceit, but no, I wouldn't want to say that. Quite frankly, I don't think anybody here is as crass and opportunistic as that metaphor would imply. I don't know what the answer is: one of the reasons I left the academy was because I did not know how to do the kind of work I wanted to from my situation in the classroom.

JOHN ERNI: Please comment on the relationship between the academic attempts to struggle with AIDS and the attempts made by artists, many of whom are also academics.

GROVER: The thing about young artists who were also either in school or had recently left it that I think is most salient is that it was precisely AIDS that made them decide that there were enormous limitations to what they had learned to do, or what they were authorized to do, inside of an academic art discipline. AIDS was what provided them with the moral escape velocity to blast outside of the restrictions imposed on them by school. What made those restrictions so vivid and visible was their involvement with AIDS through groups like ACT UP and other activist groups or the work they did inside of voluntary organizations. They discovered that their academic training had given them neither the theory nor the practice they needed to do the work that was prompted by the experiences they had of AIDS. I assume that a comparable realization would occur among people in other academic disciplines. In the case of both arts and writing that come not out of community experience but out of an isolated sense of one's own vulnerability, the results seem to me very different; self-contained and self-reflexive, as if their makers' own sense of horror over AIDS should be sufficient to carry them right into a profound understanding of it. Well, it just doesn't work that way. It's a matter instead of getting in contact with the actual lived experience of people who are dealing with the extraordinary complications of this—that is what entitles, empowers, somebody to have something profound to say about AIDS. Now, Arthur Kroker is probably an extreme case, but he's a fine example of what I mean. Because if you're only dealing out of your own sense of horror, and limitations, and mortality, there's no place to take that reaction—just an endless loop of hopelessness. But experience shared in common with other people in the organizations, the political actions, the support groups, the affinity groups, the opportunities for hospital service, that are out there—those are the things that allow you to go through the horror and come out to some earned place where you know you've really both learned and experienced something you can do. We don't need lessons in helplessness and abjection—we need instead to learn how to tackle huge, complicated questions of social import, socially. These things can't be solved in isolation—scholarly, artistic, literary.

PAULA TREICHLER: I wanted first to make a comment that I think relates to what has been said already. It has to do with our work as academics, attempting to address different people. There is actually a technical problem of audiences: of where to publish, who to write to, and who to speak to. If you are in a speaking circuit where you can address people living with AIDS then it is possible to begin to work out a vocabulary and a way of speaking that includes many different groups and speaks to particular kinds of problems. But publications are either academic or they're not. There are very few publications right now that actually bridge the two domains. I think probably all of us who do AIDS cultural work have had articles rejected by the journals that are read by the populations we feel are most in need of cultural analysis. In my case, I don't necessarily feel that that's people with HIV but rather physicians. Like I was cautioned by medical colleagues when I came up for tenure in the medical school that the first AIDS article I wrote, "An Epidemic of Signification," had too many big words—if you can imagine physicians thinking "signification" is too big a word! But I got fan letters from people with AIDS or people with HIV infection who had read it, and found it a very practical guide on how to read newspaper articles about AIDS and how to deconstruct the kind of contradictory television images. Of course when I saw Jan's first article, it signalled to me that cultural theory about AIDS *could* be written in a different way and physicians would read it—because Jan's stuff is actually read by physicians. Also, Douglas Crimp's issue of *October* which was then republished as a book, *AIDS: Cultural Analysis, Cultural Activism,* really stands as a model of a publication that has gone out to many more people than probably the journal *October* was originally intended for.

That was just a preface, about voice and audiences, and two questions that have to do with the real world and with realism. First could you comment on the construction of medical images and the way they construct particular kinds of realities, particularly in terms of viruses, like Gallo's famous images of the HIV virus? Second, knowing as we do that reality is culturally constructed in so many different ways and at so many different levels, how would you then work with someone who knows that he or she is HIV-infected and is trying to decide whether and at what point to, let's say, take AZT? How would you go about using their personal experience, their lived experience, and the various realities that are constructed in medical and scientific discourse to help them make a practical real-life decision in the real world?

My question has to do with a kind of duality which as cultural critics we have to face: on the one hand we see reality constantly constructed in a variety of ways, and it is our job in part to identify these constructions and articulate their implications; on the other hand, so crucially in the case of AIDS, we are dealing with people who are making real-life decisions, and you really can't say to people with HIV that "the virus is just a discursive construction." There are limits to that discourse. But how do you make that bridge? Donna Haraway said that these kinds of dilemmas sometimes bring out the real positivist in her: empirical research does suggest that some of these drugs work better than others; some of them will kill you, some of them won't; some of them will prolong your life, some of them won't. And yet there's a tremendous resistance within both the academic community and the communities with HIV to those truths that are constructed by medical science. So I guess what I'm asking is a totally impossible question: What could our role be in making such decisions more understandable? Personal decisions about how to find your own way through all these different, negotiated, partial, constructed, unacceptable "truths"?

GROVER: I worked with physicians for three years and I have a million stories about them. To give you one example, I edited a physician-author who was writing about the problem of infants born to HIV-infected mothers who were IV drug-users. He persistently referred to the fathers of these infants as intravenous drug-users and the mothers as intravenous drug-*abusers*. That kind of thing happens all the time—we drag around our cultural baggage like dead horses on our backs all the time. It all gets dumped right into AIDS, just as it does, for example, into reproductive rights and sex education. I think that is one of the reasons AIDS is such an enormously fascinating field to a fair number of people who regard themselves as cultural critics: the things that we handle all the time are just sitting on the surface waiting to be snatched off and applied to AIDS.

Now, viruses, images of them? As to viruses, I know that both Paula and I have vast collections of virus ideographs. Viruses are part of that wonderful world of the almost purely imaginary in the sense that in order to personalize them for readers, medical illustrators must come up with quite amazing stylizations. Robert Gallo's virus is the one that has Africa inscribed inside it. There's one virus whose core proteins look like the moon shot of Earthrise. There's another one where the DNA and the RNA strands of the virus look like two little baby corns on a nouveau cuisine plate. There is one with a coiled serpent in the middle, representing the viral protein. In a sense, these are wonderfully projective devices. The thing I don't know about them though, is whether these are demons in the minds of medical illustrators or in the minds of physicians who actually say, "Give me a dragon in the middle of that." But there's a whole world of these kinds of imaginary universes beyond the HIV—the HIV is just the "hottest" virus we have to deal with right now. None of these, of course, bears any resemblance to what you see if you actually see an electron micrograph of an HIV.

A significant number of people I've known with AIDS and HIV infection have talked about their very jarring sense of no longer feeling themselves as an integrated self, but instead as a container for the virus. I've sat with people who just stare at their arm and say, "I know what's going on in there, it looks just the same but there's this thing in there, this universe in me, that's eating me out from the inside"—this really jarring, disorienting sense that you are now merely an encasement—you are inhabited by a world, by a universe, the swarm.

As to your question about the possible usefulness of theory in helping someone make very difficult real-life decisions about treatment or, for example, deciding whether or not to attribute AIDS as a bodily disease to the HIV: that's a very complicated question. I've noticed among friends who are suffering from other very serious illnesses, most particularly breast cancer, that people who would otherwise describe themselves and be described by most around them as extremely rational, thoughtful, linear, left-brain people develop an irrational, absolutely visceral attachment to whatever treatment protocol they have decided to embrace. In the case of AIDS, that has surfaced most visibly and frequently around the issue of AZT, between those who have chosen to take it and those who have not. The choices somebody makes seem to kick in a need to patrol the perimeters of that choice—they want to enforce the same choice among other people, too. Perhaps that is because winning other people's agreement and compliance validates the particular choice that one has made. For me, standing on the periphery of those choices, I have never been able to arrive at any behavior more appropriate than asking the person in question what he or she needed in order to feel supported in and then trying to give that to him or her. There are many very potent factors in the kinds of decisions people make around issues like treatment: positioning by class; how interested they are in being very active about dealing with their infection; what kind of doctors they have; what city they live in, whether they live in a small city or a city like San Francisco or New York where a lot of physicians have a lot of experience; whether they still have insurance or whether they are now an SDI/SSI person on Medicaid. But I can honestly say that sophistication around critical discourse, theories of representation, power and knowledge, appear to have played *no* role in the ways that people I know have arrived at personal treatment decisions. I know writers, artists, critics who have made such decisions after writing, filming, ACTing UP about AIDS, and it is my impression that theoretical sophistication is no help at all when people come to make decisions about their mortality. There is a large element of magical thinking in people's treatment decisions; these are *Yes, but* . . . decisions made *despite,* not because of, their theoretical knowledge.

16

Missionary Stories: Gender and Ethnicity in England in the 1830s and 1840s

Catherine Hall

In the 1990s nationalisms and national identities have become key political issues.[1] The collapse of the Cold War, the reunification of Germany, the re-mapping of Europe, and the planned increased economic and political integration of EEC member countries in 1992 all raise critical questions about the nation-state, national sovereignty, national "belonging," and forms of citizenship. In this context national identity has emerged as a crucial issue in British politics.

But what does it mean to be British? National communities are, as Benedict Anderson (1983) has argued, "imagined communities." Whilst sometimes appearing natural they have always been constructed through elaborate ideological and political work which produces a sense of nation and national identity, but a sense which can always be challenged. For there is no one national identity—rather competing national identities jostle with each other in a struggle for dominance. "Britishness" and "Englishness" are continually contested terrains in which meaning is not given but discursively constructed and reconstructed in conditions of historical specificity.

English national identity is a subject which has received relatively little attention.[2] In England the recognition that Englishness is an ethnicity, just like any other, demands a decentering of the English imagination. For ethnicities have been constructed as belonging to "others," not to the norm which is English. A recognition that Englishness *is* an ethnicity, just like any other, necessitates, therefore, its own relativization of the West.[3] This paper is about English ethnicity—but it is centrally preoccupied with exposing the relations of power involved in that ethnicity and problematizing the relation between center and margin. Ethnicities do not only belong to those on the margins—every culture has its own forms of ethnic identity. How then has Englishness been constructed as a national identity and what have been its historical specificities? What white ethnic identities were available and what dominant in the England of the mid-nineteenth century?

I use *English* advisedly rather than British but I would argue that Englishness marginalizes other identities, those from the peripheries, the Welsh, the Scottish, and the Irish. In constructing what it meant to be English a further claim was constantly being made—that Englishness was British, whereas those on the margins could never claim the right to speak for the whole. A Welsh identity could never be anything other than distinctively Welsh: an English identity could claim to provide the norm for the whole of the United Kingdom, and indeed the Empire.

In writing about the construction of white English ethnicity, the trap of participating in the "morbid celebration of Englishness" castigated by Paul Gilroy recently,
has to be avoided.[4] In recent decades a celebration of Englishness, of England's heritage
in her rich history, her country houses, her empire, her once assured place as the first
industrial nation, has provided one response to postcolonialism, the collapse of Britain
as a world empire and the challenge to white British identity constituted in the emergence of black British identities within the urban communities of the 1980s and 1990s.

In working on the English middle class in the period from the 1830s to the 1860s,
the time when England could securely claim to lead the world in industrial and economic
development, in empire building and the development of democratic political forms,
and when the English middle class was effectively challenging aristocratic power not
only within the bastions of the national and local state but also within the hearts and
minds of the English people, I aim not to celebrate those stories which we have been
told and have told ourselves about nation, empire, and civilization. Rather, I aim to
deconstruct those English identities which were constructed in the mid-nineteenth century, to unpack the stories which gave meaning to the national and the imperial project,
and to understand the ways in which English identity was constructed through the active
silencing of the disruptive relations of ethnicity, of gender, and of class. My project is
not to reconstitute Englishness but to uncover the contingency of that construction in
its historical specificity—to look at the dependencies, inequalities, and oppressions which
it hid in its celebration of national identity.

That national identity was powerfully articulated by middle-class men in this
period. Men who claimed to speak for the nation and on behalf of others. Those men,
however, lived in a society cross-cut by complex social and political antagonisms, not
only the antagonism of class which they thought, spoke, and wrote about most forcibly,
but also those of gender (which they silenced) and of race and ethnicity. Their search
for a masculine independence, for a secure identity, was built on their assertion of their
superiority over the decadent aristocracy; over dependent females; over children, servants,
and employees; over the peoples of the Empire, whether in Ireland, India, or Jamaica;
over all *others* who were not English, male, and middle class. But this identity was rooted
in an ever-shifting and historically specific cultural and political world, where the search
for certainty and stability, "I know who I am and I know how and why I have power
over you," masked conflict, insecurity, and resistance. In attempting to open up the
contradictions within this middle-class identity, to demonstrate the shifting sands upon
which an apparently secure sense of nationality was constructed, I hope to investigate
a complex set of articulations in which class, gender, and ethnicity are all axes of power,
sometimes mutually reinforcing each other, sometimes contradicting each other. Cultural
identity is always complexly constituted within a field of power and never depends upon
any single dimension. To understand the construction of a national identity we need an
analysis of the interrelations between class, gender, and ethnicity as axes of power.

In the England of the 1830s and 40s religion provided one of the key discursive
terrains for the articulation of these axes and thus for the construction of a national
identity.[5] The evangelical revival of the late eighteenth century provided middle-class
men and women with a language redolent with certainty—the certainty of religious
conviction. The experience of conversion, so central to evangelical belief, and the consequent commitment to a new life governed by faith, gave men the confidence to insist
on their truths, even when this meant fundamental challenges to received wisdoms.
Religious belief provided a vocabulary of right—the right to know and to speak that
knowledge, with the moral power that was attached to the speaking of God's word.
One of the issues on which they spoke was what it meant to be English.

My investigation of national identity is based on the argument that the English can only recognize themselves in relation to others. My project, therefore, is concerned with English representations of Jamaica and its peoples between the 1830s and the 1860s. For in characterizing, defining, and identifying those others they characterized, defined, and identified themselves. "Englishness" was what the planters did not possess and what the freed slaves might possess but never did. In the turbulent decades between emancipation (1833) and the rising at Morant Bay in 1865 the changes in English perceptions of Jamaican blacks and the debates about those perceptions not only revealed changing attitudes to blacks but also to "whiteness" itself and what it meant to be English. By the early 1830s an emancipationist position was effectively an orthodoxy within respectable middle-class society in England—only the paid lackeys of the planters would publicly defend slavery. The famous anti-slavery slogans, "Am I not a man and a brother? Am I not a woman and a sister?," and the icon of the kneeling slave seeking British help represented the belief in the civilizational equality of the negro, the potential of the negro to be raised from the state of savagery, through childhood to manhood, which characterized the cultural racism of the anti-slavery movement. That cultural racism, with its paradoxical conviction that slaves were brothers and sisters, all God's children, but younger brothers and sisters who must be educated and led by their older white siblings, was most clearly articulated by the middle-class vanguard of the anti-slavery movement, in the forefront of whom in the crucial years of 1831–33 were a group of Baptist missionaries from Jamaica (M. Turner, 1982). These men organized the public campaign, the petitions, the pamphlets, the lecture tours, the questioning of parliamentary candidates, which ensured that the first substantial piece of legislation from the reformed Parliament of 1832, elected by large numbers of middle-class voters who were exercising their right for the first time, was the emancipation of the slaves. Behind the men, never in the public forefront but absolutely central to the organization of the struggle, were large numbers of women whose activities until very recently have been seen as unimportant.[6] In 1833 the dominant definition of Englishness included the gratifying element of liberator of enslaved Africans.

By 1865, when in the wake of Morant Bay Jamaica once again occupied center stage in English politics, the situation had changed. English middle-class discourses on Jamaican blacks had by this time become much more explicitly racist. The failure of the public campaign spearheaded by John Stuart Mill and a group of liberal intellectuals, to censure Governor Eyre for his brutal acts of suppression in the wake of the events at Morant Bay, and the success of the oppositional campaign, led by Thomas Carlyle, in celebrating Eyre's actions and narrating him as an English hero, revealed the extent to which the cultural racism of the 1830s with its liberal and progressive attachments, had been displaced by a more aggressive biological racism, rooted in the assumption that blacks were not brothers and sisters but a different species, born to be mastered.[7] This biological racism with its conservative structures of thought encoded an Englishness which celebrated hierarchy and difference, and relied on military power to enforce its superiority.

In the debates over slaves or freed blacks English men and women were as much concerned with constructing their own identities as with defining those of others, and those identities were always classed and gendered as well as ethnically specific. Furthermore, their capacity to define those others was an important aspect of their own authority and power. English national identity, in other words, cannot be understood outside of England's colonial dependencies. Jamaica, a small island in the Caribbean, may never have been seen by the majority of the English population yet it occupied a place in their imaginary. Their ethnic identity as *English* was rooted in a series of assumptions about others.

This paper is concerned, then, with examining a particular colonial discourse, not primarily to extricate the history of those "others" who the missionaries and their allies aimed to contain in their narrative strategies, but rather to investigate those English ethnicities which were in play. The regime of knowledge constructed by the abolitionists was to fix the relations of dominant and subordinate—the construction of the dominant "gaze" was as central a preoccupation as the suppression of resistant "others." In their public interventions the missionaries and their allies were constructing their own identities and writing their own histories. Their mutual celebration of their effectivity in Jamaica was important in confirming and sustaining English middle-class confidence in their capacity to check "Old Corruption" in whatever form it took—whether English aristocrats or Jamaican planters.

The missionary story that this paper is concerned with deals with a particular group of Baptist missionaries in Jamaica in the 1830s and 40s. It has been widely argued that British missionaries of all persuasions were a powerful force in defining the imperial project in the nineteenth century and that anti-slavery discourse, which informed much of their practice and to which they made an important contribution, played a significant role in generating and consolidating British imperialist discourse.[8] But missionaries from varying denominations are characterized as much by difference as by their similarities. Different racist discourses jostled for power amongst different missionary groups, and between those groups, and missionaries were themselves positioned very differently in different colonized societies. Some missionaries relied on a close partnership with the elite of the society in which they worked, others had a more contentious and marginal position.

This small group of Baptist missionaries in Jamaica in the 1830s and 40s, radicalized by their encounter with slavery, allied themselves with the slaves and put themselves in the forefront of the struggle for emancipation in England in the 1830s. Through their public speaking and writing on the anti-slavery and missionary circuits they were able to claim that their special knowledge of Jamaican society and of the institution of slavery gave them a right to be heard. In the most immediate and dramatic ways they evoked the horrors of the plantations: the whips, the cries, the instruments of torture, and worst sin of all, the denial of revealed religion. They represented themselves as the conscience of England, and indeed Britain.

Between the 1830s and the late 1840s they were able to build on this heritage and significantly intervene in public debate in England on questions of race and ethnicity. They articulated gendered representations of the "other," of Jamaican black men and women, which significantly reduced the distance between themselves and their subjects, though that distance was never obliterated.[9] As colonizing subjects they privileged themselves as narrators, those who represented others, the leaders, the guides, the parents of the universal imperial Christian family. In constituting their own subjectivity they also constituted their subjects as manly men and domesticated and virtuous women rather than suffering and victimized slaves; the characteristics which they sought to clothe them with were a version of those which they sought for themselves and which expressed their national identity.

Jamaica provided the test case for the great British experiment with emancipation, since it was the largest and the richest of the British West India islands. For the anti-slavery movement, and especially for the missionaries, it was vital that the experiment should work. Missionary dependence on the British public did not end with emancipation. It soon became clear that apprenticeship was in effect slavery by another name and that the historic work was unfinished. Furthermore, once apprenticeship was abolished, the planters tried other means to secure an unfree labor force. The missionaries engaged in unceasing efforts to secure the success of what they defined as the project of a free Jamaica, to make the island into a Christian, civilized, capitalist, free labor economy with democratic institutions; in other words into a country on their version of the British model. This task occupied them without rest until the late 1840s when their optimism began to weaken, their faith in their own power become more limited. Between the public campaign of 1832–33 and the late 1840s there was a never-ending flow of words and people between England and Jamaica, attempting to secure the ongoing politics of emancipation. Reports in the missionary press and in the anti-slavery press, public meetings, lecture tours, fund-raising campaigns, books, pamphlets, private letters designed to be read in part at missionary prayer meetings or abolitionist gatherings, all fueled the fires of the emancipatory public and kept the issue of Jamaica at the forefront of the public conscience.

A series of substantial reports and memoirs were published between 1837–49 which together marked a strategic intervention in this politics.[10] Their authors were those who claimed authority to write on Jamaica and the Jamaicans, missionaries such as Thomas Burchell and James Mursell Phillippo who had lived there for many years; established British middle-class figures including the well-known Birmingham philanthropist and businessman, Joseph Sturge, and the eminent Quaker banker and public man, Joseph John Gurney, who visited the island in order to inquire for themselves and the British public what the *true* state of the island was. These texts referred to and relied upon each other, established what Said (1978, p. 20) calls a "strategic formation" within the culture at large through their density and referential power. Their particular version of colonial discourse, their strategic creation of a space for subject peoples through the production of knowledge and exercise of power and surveillance, was abolitionist discourse, organized around the notion of negroes as younger brothers and sisters. These texts explicitly concerned the category black, what it had meant and what it could mean; implicitly they masked a preoccupation with whiteness, a category which was masked because it was seen as normal (Dyer, 1988). Whiteness, in the discourse of the Baptist missionaries and their allies, should mean order, civilization, Christianity, separate spheres, and domesticity, rationality, modernity, and industry. Those moments when whiteness meant something quite other were terrifying, as, for example, when white Anglican clergymen and planters allied to burn down chapels and mission stations and lynch, tar, and feather missionaries themselves. Whites then became "savages," with all the characteristics of the planter stereotype of the black. As Thomas Burchell wrote of his experiences in 1831 on his return to Jamaica in the wake of Sam Sharpe's rebellion:

> the most furious and savage spirit was manifested by some of (what were called) the most respectable white inhabitants, that ever could have been discovered amongst civilized society. They began to throng around me, hissing, groaning and gnashing at me with their teeth. Had I never been at Montego Bay before, I must have supposed myself among cannibals, or in the midst of the savage hordes of Siberia, or the uncultivated and uncivilized tribes of central Africa . . . I am fully persuaded, had it not been for the protection afforded me by the coloured part of the population—natives of Jamaica—I should have been barbarously murdered—yea, torn limb from limb, by my countrymen—by so-called *enlightened*, RESPECTABLE! CHRISTIAN BRITONS! (Clark, et al., 1865, p. 204)

In writing and publishing these texts, and in their lecture tours and campaigns in Britain, the missionaries and their friends were empowering themselves, deriving authority from their capacity to speak for others. Slaves spoke through and by virtue of a particular male, middle-class, English imagination (to paraphrase and adapt Said [1978]). In that process the slaves themselves were partially silenced. William Knibb (1832), in his most famous speech on abolition delivered at Exeter Hall, that Jerusalem of evangelicals (a speech that was printed and widely circulated), to a packed audience whose response was tumultuous, opened with these words:

> Next to the heartfelt satisfaction of being instrumental to the conversion of the ignorant to the knowledge of the truth as it is in Christ Jesus, there is nothing more delightful than to stand forward as the advocate of the innocent and persecuted; and, when I consider that on the present occasion I appear before an assembly of my countrymen on behalf of the persecuted African, I find in the fact a reward for all the sufferings in character and person which I have endured in the cause, as a missionary, for the last eight years. (p. 9)

At a public meeting in Newcastle he opened in similar vein:

> There is nothing more delightful and interesting than to plead the cause of the injured, the degraded and the oppressed. This, under any circumstances, is peculiarly delightful; but it is especially so when the speaker finds himself surrounded by so large a number of his fellow-Christians, who he feels assured never hear of misery but they endeavour to remove it; who never hear of sorrow, but they are anxious to dry the mourner's tears; and who never hear of oppression, but every feeling of their heart rises up in just and holy indignation against the person who inflicts it. (Knibb, 1833, p. 13)

Here the pleasure which Knibb incited, to use Homi Bhabha's (1983) definition of colonial discourse, was the pleasure of speaking for the oppressed, than which there was nothing "more delightful." Especially pleasurable was the capacity to speak for those who were doubly oppressed—female slaves:

> I ask, in the presence of ladies, what Englishman could stand by, what Englishman could even contemplate the flogging of females without a flush of indignation? . . . Must I not therefore plead for women? . . . if I must speak at all, I must speak the real sentiments of my mind, and those sentiments must, to my latest moment, be uttered against slavery—slavery of every kind—but, above all, slavery of woman. (Knibb, 1832, pp. 15, 16)

Whiteness at this moment meant pity and care for lesser peoples, the authority through public campaigns to exercise that power, to challenge existing power relations in Britain, challenge the West India interest, and insist on emancipation as a moral and political imperative. That definition of whiteness, however, was subject to constant attack itself. When planters behaved like savages and freed coloreds saved whites from their fury, what did it mean to be white and what distinctions could be made between black and white?

Such denunciations of the planters and the doubts their conduct cast on the nature of a supposedly English and Christian brethren were taken up with vigor by the rhetoricians of the anti-slavery movement. Sir Thomas Fowell Buxton, the Parliamentary leader of the movement after the retirement of William Wilberforce, relied heavily on missionary information for his speeches and reports. Horrified by the tales of missionary persecution in the aftermath of the 1831 rebellion, he contrasted the "savage" behavior of the Jamaican planters with the expectations as to how a supposedly Christian grouping should conduct themselves.

> Hereafter we must make selection among our missionaries. Is there a man whose timid or tender spirit is unequal to the storm of persecution? Send him to the savage,

expose him to the cannibal, save his life by directing his steps to the rude haunts of the barbarian. But, if there is a man of a stiffer, sterner nature, a man willing to encounter obloquy, torture and death, let him be reserved for the tender mercies of our Christian brethren and fellow countrymen, the planters of Jamaica. (Buxton, 1848, p. 295)

Emancipation meant that the politics of racial equality came closer. As the reality of blacks as brothers and sisters loomed larger it became increasingly important to denote the differences between black and white. At the heart of the Baptist missionary enterprise was a profound ambivalence—a belief in brotherhood and spiritual equality combined with an assumption of white superiority. This contradiction, which so closely echoed the fraught ambivalence of evangelical discourses on gender, destabilizes missionary discourse and ensures that there is never a single utterance. Rather they are complex and ambivalent, with gender and racial contradictions erupting from the text, carrying the uncertainties and confusions of a particular definition of white identity, whilst attempting to present certainty and confidence, maintaining a fiction. By the late 1840s the fiction of the Englishman as defender of grateful Africans, which had continued to dominate respectable British middle-class opinion from the early 1830s was much less secure. Conflicting colonial discourses with different rhetorical strategies were increasingly displacing and challenging the abolitionist voice, and the ambivalence of the missionaries themselves threatening to blow apart their dream.

As part of the British Empire Jamaica was nominally a Christian country and had an established Anglican presence. No attempts were made to christianize the slaves, however, until the mid-eighteenth century when Moravian missionaries settled in the island.[11] The planters were extremely suspicious of missionary activity and many of them were actively hostile to it. The Moravians were followed by some Wesleyans in 1791 and then by black Baptists in the wake of the American Revolution. In 1813 the Baptist Missionary Society (BMS) finally decided to send a missionary to Jamaica and established their first white station there. All the missionary societies insisted on political neutrality and instructed their employees not to involve themselves with political questions. This, however, as Mary Turner has documented so well, proved impossible, since the "serious" religion of the evangelical enterprise was inevitably at odds with slavery. Planter toleration for missionary activity was at best uneasy and in periods of political tension broke down. The missionaries depended for their survival on the protection of the imperial government. This in turn meant that the imperial government had to be constantly petitioned and pressured to defend non-conformist missionaries, hardly a likely group for the Colonial Office to concern themselves with. Inevitably, therefore, the missionaries depended on public support in England and the activities of their Societies, not only to fund their work but to be able to do it at all.

The BMS had its roots in the evangelical revival of the late eighteenth century, that re-emergence of vital, serious, or real Christianity as compared with the nominal and empty forms which had come to dominate Christian worship and experience. Both non-conformists and Anglicans were inspired by the revival and shared a common body of doctrine which at times allowed them to overcome the division between church and chapel and work together on missionary endeavors both at home and abroad. They shared a common insistence on the centrality of individual sin and the conversion experience, on the individual's capacity to be born anew and to construct a new Christian identity, whether as man or woman, built around their particular relation to the Christian household, and on a close monitoring both by the individual and by his/her pastor and his/her congregation of each soul and its progress towards salvation.[12]

Many non-conformists shared the conviction of William Wilberforce and Hannah More, key ideologues of the Anglican evangelical revival and leaders of the movement to abolish the slave trade and slavery on the grounds that they were deeply immoral and irreligious, that the real struggle which Christians must engage with in the wake of the French Revolution and the growth of English radicalism, was the struggle for the hearts and minds of those heathens at home and abroad who did not understand that the fight was with the devil and with sin, the army that was required was the army of God. The BMS, in the words of its contemporary historian the Rev. F. A. Cox (1842), was born of this conviction. The French Revolution had had disastrous effects,

> infidelity eclipsed the glory of truth, and spread its pestilential atmosphere amidst the moral darkness and confusion. The nation became warm in politics and cold in religion. (vol. 1, p. 2)

Disturbed by this state of affairs a small group of Baptist ministers met for an anniversary meeting in Kettering, Northamptonshire and decided, under the inspiration of William Carey, to "act together in society for the purpose of propagating the gospel among the heathen (Cox, 1843 vol. 1, p. 2). Carey, a Baptist minister in Northamptonshire, had been preoccupied for some time with the importance of this work and wrote his *Enquiry into the Obligations of Christians to use means for the Conversion of the Heathens* (1792) to convince others of the importance of this project and of the desperate need abroad. "It has been objected," he wrote,

> that there are multitudes in our own nation . . . who are as ignorant as the South-Sea savages, and that therefore we have work enough at home, without going into other countries . . . (but) . . . Our own countrymen have the means of grace, and may attend on the word preached if they chuse it . . . faithful ministers are placed in almost every part of the land, whose spheres of action might be much extended if their congregations were but more hearty and active in the cause: but with them the case is widely different, who have no Bible, no written language . . . no ministers, no good civil government, nor any of those advantages which we have. Pity therefore, humanity, and much more Christianity, call loudly for every possible exertion to introduce the gospel amongst them.

The first field of activity for the BMS was in India and Carey ("this new Columbus [who] beheld a yet undiscovered world of heathenism") established with Ward and Marshman the station at Serampore which was to dominate Baptist missionary endeavors for the first years (Cox, 1842, p. 11). In 1814, after pleas from the black Baptists established in Jamaica for support, and correspondence between Dr. Ryland, the Baptist divine, and William Wilberforce, the BMS sent John Rowe out as their first emissary to the West Indies. His instructions from the Committee, secure in their ethnocentric assumption of British superiority, impressed on him that he must not despise the slaves on account of "their ignorance, their color, their country, or their enslaved condition" (quoted in Payne, 1933 p. 21). The first years in Jamaica were dogged by ill health, death, and political problems for the missionaries but in the early 1820s the general revival of British interest in anti-slavery affected the Baptists too and they committed more resources to Jamaica. Three of the men who were to be most influential both in the island and at home went to Jamaica at this time—William Knibb, Thomas Burchell, and James Phillippo.

The BMS venture remained on a relatively modest scale. By 1827 there were 8 Baptist churches with approximately 5,000 members; by 1831 there were 24 churches with 10,000 members and 17,000 inquirers (that is people who were seeking membership), by 1835 this had increased to 52 stations with 13,795 members and for some years these figures were to rise steadily as the missionaries benefitted from the conviction amongst blacks that they had been crucial to the ending of slavery and apprenticeship.[13] Most Baptist missionaries came from artisanal families, some from the borders of the middle class. Baptists in England tended to occupy these class positions and had much less solid middle-class support than the Independents or Anglican Evangelicals, nothing like the wealth and status of Quakers or Unitarians. From the very beginning the missionaries had to contend with planter contempt, derision, and harassment, but they were used to being laughed at for their faith, used to a society in which they were discriminated against and in which they had to fight to make their voices heard; they were used to being part of the army of God, outfacing sin in whatever manifestations it appeared. Their struggle both at home and abroad as they conceptualized it was with the forces of evil, reaction, "dark savagery," heathenism, and superstition—all of which could be met in the back streets of Birmingham, in the markets of Calcutta, or the plantations of Jamaica. Jamaica, however, had its own special horror. As William Knibb described it to a friend soon after his arrival in Jamaica in 1823,

> I have now reached the land of sin, disease, and death, where Satan reigns with awful power, and carries multitudes captive at his will. True religion is scoffed at, and those who profess it are ridiculed and insulted. . . . The poor, oppressed, benighted, and despised sons of Africa, form a pleasing contrast to the debauched white population. (Hinton, 1847, p. 45)

Thomas Burchell, who came from a solidly middle-class mercantile background and was used to being treated with respect at least for his status if not for his religion, was shocked, despite all preparation, at the contempt with which he was treated by planters and officials in Jamaica. On one occasion he was summoned to court with a verbal message from a "common constable." "Thus a slave would be called to appear before a court of magistrates," he commented in a letter to England, "but no Englishman, except a missionary, would be treated with so much contempt (Burchell, 1849, pp. 68–69). Similarly, Phillippo noted that even an invitation from the Governor to meet him did not save him from the disdain of Jamaican whites. He found himself, "in a large room filled with planters and others of the ruling class, including the rector and curate of the parish. I was treated with superciliousness and contempt" (Underhill 1881, p. 181). As many have noted the missionaries were placed in a highly ambivalent position— white, yet allies of the slaves and freed blacks, white yet for the most part of a very different class background from that of the planters and the Anglican clergy.

The contempt which they faced could be offset, however, with the influence which they established with the black population. Missionaries were consistently impressed with the "hunger" which they found for Christianity amongst the blacks, which contrasted so sharply with the situation in England. Lee Compere, one of the earliest missionaries on the island, was much quoted in later years for his depiction of eager blacks seeking British Christian guidance:

> here are many souls continually heaving a sigh to England, and in their broken language continually crying out, "O buckra, buckra, no one care for poor black man's soul! Buckra know God in England. O buckra, come over that great big water, and instruct me, poor black negro." (quoted in Clark, et al., 1865, p. 147)

Mary Ann Hutchins, the wife of a missionary, wrote to her brother in similar vein in 1834:

> The thirst for knowledge amongst the blacks and coloured people is very great; many of them are asking for books to read, and the anxiety they evince, is very pleasing.

> I was much pleased one of the Sabbaths I was at Montego Bay, to see a Chapel pretty well filled with communicants, and instead of two—*fourteen bottles of wine* were used at the Sacrament. Oh! when in my dear native land will a scene like this be witnessed? (Middleditch, 1840, p. 99)

The missionaries delighted in sending home computations of the numbers they had baptized, the numbers of their members and inquirers—a scientific demonstration of the power of the Word amongst the heathen.

Since real religion depended on a conversion experience, all missionaries had gone through this watershed (not always experienced as a blinding moment, but always as a fundamental turning point), usually in their late adolescence or early manhood. For Thomas Burchell, the son of a wool stapler, conversion meant freedom from sin, the only true freedom there was; "his captivity was exchanged for freedom, and his mourning turned into joy" (1849, p. 7). William Knibb, the son of a tradesman, described the growth of his conviction to the congregation at his baptism:

> Having enjoyed the unspeakable advantages of a religious education, and of being trained under the care of a pious and affectionate mother, I was early taught my state as a sinner, and the necessity of flying to Jesus Christ as the only hope of escape from that punishment which my sins had deserved. (Hinton, 1847, p. 7)

Conversion brought with it the need for action, for Christian manliness was defined through action. As the Rev. Isaac Taylor, a popular evangelical preacher and writer of manuals on Christian practice, put it, "A man must act."[14] It was through his action in the world, his assertion of his independence, that he recognized himself as a man and was recognized by others. For evangelical Christians the action of combatting sin, of enlisting in the army of God provided a worthy arena within which they could prove their manhood. For aspirant artisans or lower middle-class men missionary work abroad offered an exciting opportunity; indeed it proved to be a great deal more exciting than working as a minister in England where congregations were pitifully small and the word went mainly unheeded. In Jamaica, for those who survived (for the assault of ill health and death meant that the average length of service was less than three years), converts came in the thousands and the influence of the missionaries appeared to be profound.

The desire to become a missionary often closely followed conversion. Joshua Tinson was inspired by an overwhelming pity for those who were "ignorant and wretched" (Quoted in Clark, et al., 1865, p. 172). Thomas Knibb, William's brother who preceded him to Jamaica and whose death determined William to go, looked forward with delight to missionary work:

> I thought that, however Christians were separated during the short time allotted to human life, they all reached the same home; and that it would be far more delightful, more honourable, to go to heaven from a heathen country than a Christian one. (Hinton, 1847, p. 9)

Some of the missionaries recorded that they had been preoccupied since childhood with stories of heathens as, for example, Thomas Burchell, who then as a young man loved to read conversion stories in the missionary press. This was a peculiarly dissenting version of Martin Green's (1980) argument about the place of empire in the British imaginary. Imperial adventure stories were, he argues,

> collectively the story England told itself as it went to sleep at night; and in the form of its dreams, they charged England's will with the energy to go out into the world and explore, conquer and rule. (p. 3)

For missionaries their stories were those of the glories of the conversion of the heathen against all odds, their dreams concerned sin and its defeat rather than money or conquest. After some years in Jamaica William Knibb, amongst others, became preoccupied with the idea of a mission to Africa. He was especially enthusiastic that this should be the first task of native missionaries. When this happened he wrote in great excitement to a friend in England, "a beloved brother, one of the despised, traduced, black christians, an African by birth, has left this island . . . has worked his passage to Africa, and . . . is now on the spot from whence he was stolen as a boy, telling his fellow-countrymen the name of Jesus." He implored his friend to plead for Africa,

> think of Africa, her wrongs, her sins, her openings. O my heavenly Father! work by whom thou wilt work, but save poor, poor, benighted, degraded, Europe-cursed Africa! my affection for Africa may seem extravagant. I cannot help it. I dream of it nearly every night, nor can I think of anything else. (Hinton, 1847, p. 276)

Such dreams inspired Bernard Barton, the Quaker poet, when he was invited to write some introductory verses for Cox's *History of the Baptist Missionary Society* (1842). Barton celebrated the men who went to the colonies not for the more traditional prizes of wealth, or land, not for excitement or because they wanted to be tourists enjoying the wonders of nature; rather their noble task, commanded from above, was to save sinners, they were the tools of the living God;

> For they went forth as followers of the Lamb,
> To spread his gospel-message far and wide,
> In the dread power of Him, the great I AM,
> In the meek spirit of the Crucified,—
> With unction from the Holy Ghost supplied,
> To war with error, ignorance and sin,
> To exalt humility, to humble pride,
> To still the passion's stormy strife within,
> Through wisdom from above immortal souls to win. (Vol. 1, p. vi)

Burchell's (1849) reading of the missionary press made him long "to tread their shores, to mingle with their swarthy people, and to unfurl in their midst the banners of salvation." As he became "more acquainted with their barbarous atrocities and superstitious rites, together with their sanguinary and obscene abominations" he was increasingly convinced that he could find the strength to give up home. As he declared at his ordination, "all my thoughts were occupied on missionary themes, and my chief happiness was associated with solicitude for the heathen." His dreams were of India, for this was where Baptist missionaries were active. "India," he wrote in a letter in 1820, "I long to place my foot on thy polluted shores. I long to enter the field of action as an ensign in the army of the Saviour, bearing the banner of his cross. I long to exert myself in the glorious revolution now taking place" (pp. 26, 27, 29, 33). James Phillippo, meanwhile, the son of a master builder who was converted in young adulthood, felt an increasing desire to be useful, "especially among the far-off nations lying in darkness and in the shadow of death." He read missionary publications with avidity and trained himself in skills which he thought would stand him in good stead: medicine, brick-making, house-building, cabinet work, agriculture, and the production of food and clothes. As he expressed his philosophy to his parents, "This world is not a place of repose for a faithful soldier of the Cross" (Underhill, 1881, pp. 8, 17).

Entry into missionary work meant applying to the BMS committee as a suitable candidate. Once accepted the young men would undergo some training either at one of the dissenting academies or in the home of a Baptist minister, who would be deemed suitable to take in a small group for preparation. Most of the trainees had a very limited educational background, having left school to go into trade at age twelve to thirteen. The lack of a "proper" education provided another source of derision from their class superiors both at home and abroad. Ordination followed the training and the ritual of "setting apart" the missionaries for their work, usually performed by a group of established ministers, some of whom would have personal connections with the ordinand. Many of the Baptist missionaries in Jamaica were trained together and "set apart" together, often with senior missionaries officiating, thus ritually affirming the existence of a "mission family," which it was a primary object to sustain. The BMS committee decided where missionaries were to go and each missionary was responsible to the committee for his actions. In the hostile circumstances into which so many of them went support from home was a necessary part of survival, and there was a constant flow of letters between England and Jamaica. Missionaries were always at least partially dependent for money from home to finance their activities as well as needing committee intervention with the Colonial Office at times of acute tension.

The final "necessary preparation" before sailing was marriage, for it was assumed that a married missionary would be more use than a single one.[15] Furthermore, evangelical horror at the debauchery, as they saw it, of planter society, with its acceptance of concubinage, made Jamaica a dangerous place to be a man alone. Time and again in missionary biographies, their marriages are seen as entirely secondary to their act of faith. For women this was rather different; those women who were seized with the missionary spirit could not themselves become preachers in the early nineteenth century. Indeed, the claim that women should be engaged in missionary work at all was one that had to be contested and won just as the right to do philanthropic work was continually fought over. Women were needed to accompany men, it was argued. Furthermore, women's missionary work was crucial to the heathen, for it would be impossible to have access to many heathen women without workers of their own sex. It was widely believed in early nineteenth-century England that Western women owed their superior position to Christianity; it was Christianity which had raised society from its superstitions and freed women from the degradations associated in the English mind with heathenism, in particular the practice of "sati" in India. It was proper, argued the protagonists of a special missionary sphere for women, that the daughters of Eve, first in transgression, should be the first in restoration (J. Thompson, 1841). There was no question, however, of accepting women as trainees or granting them equal access with men. Marriage, therefore, offered a possible route into the work for those women who wanted to do it. Similarly, accompanying an unmarried brother was occasionally possible, and by the 1830s a small number of women were going out as teachers.

Mary Ann Chambers, for example, experienced conversion at age 20 while her brother was training to be a missionary. "What a noble cause," she wrote to him, "to be employed in teaching Jesus to the poor heathen . . . My soul does indeed long to be with the poor heathen." She longed to go abroad with him, "I do indeed love the missionary cause; it is nearer my heart than anything else; my soul seems in the work." She was terrified that he would leave her behind. Through a friend she then met the Rev. James Coultart who was about to go to Jamaica as a missionary. Her contemporary biographer explains that:

> Her elegant person and accomplished mind at once engaged his heart; while she regarded the whole affair as the gracious leadings of Providence. (J. Thompson, 1841, pp. 10, 13)

Mary Ann Middleditch, the daughter of a Baptist minister, also suffered from envy of a brother who trained to be a minister and who, under her influence, eventually became a missionary for a short time. Baptized in 1830 she became heavily involved with the struggle for emancipation and fascinated by Jamaica. On first leaving home to work in a school, she greatly missed the missionary news that she had had access to at home. "Let me know all that you can about the missionary meetings," she wrote to her parents in 1833. "Is Mr. Knibb to be there? Oh! that I had the wings of a dove." In a pious correspondence with a woman friend she discussed the hardship of not being able to be missionaries abroad but argued that they must do all that they could in the mission field at home. "I long to go as a missionary, more and more," she wrote to her friend. "I think I speak advisedly, when I say, that I would rather go to Jamaica than dwell in England." She attended missionary prayer meetings, read missionary books ("I have had a great treat this week, in reading Stathams's *Indian Recollections.* I have almost fancied myself there"), longed for the day when schoolmasters and schoolmistresses would be sent out to teach the "emancipated negroes." Eventually her route was through marriage, but in her letter to her parents explaining her decision to go it was love of Christ which was emphasized, not of her husband-to-be.

> Could your Mary Ann be happy, think you, if she refused to devote herself to Missionary work? Dare I, then, indulge the hope that I love Christ more than Father or Mother, if I refused to relinquish the pleasure of their society for His sake? No, my dear parents, duty calls, and great as is the sacrifice, your child must go . . . (Middleditch, 1840, pp. 41, 45, 49, 60, 70)

In the discourse of evangelical Christianity there was plenty of space for imagination and adventure but little for the idea of romantic love as the key to marital choice.

Faith was at the heart of the missionary endeavor. In his letter of application to the BMS James Phillippo made a brief statement of his faith:

> I believe in the total depravity of all mankind; in the absolute necessity of a change of heart; in man's inability to accomplish this work; that it is effected by the Holy Spirit, through the use of means; that Christ is the only way of salvation; the necessity of personal holiness. I recognize also two Ordinances: Baptism, administered to adults on a profession of faith in Christ; and the Lord's Supper. I believe in the final salvation of believers, and the final destruction of unbelievers. (Underhill, 1881, p. 12)

This statement would have been heartily endorsed by most Baptists. The sect was marked off by the belief in adult baptism but in all other respects was very close to other evangelical dissenters. Individual sin and the conversion experience were at the heart of their Christianity, the loss of self and the being born anew in Christ. This rebirth of the Christian man and Christian woman, embedded in the Christian household, the finding of a new sense of self in Christ, was central to the evangelical project. The abandonment of self, the conviction that men and women were but "worms" in God's service, the most abject creatures at his command, has to be held together, however, with the powerful sense of self which both sexes derived from their beliefs. Thus, William Knibb, writing to his wife during a very successful visit to England in 1840 when he achieved all that he had hoped and was being celebrated at large public meetings all over the country, commented,

> When I look at the results of my mission to England, I am both thankful and humbled. O what a condescending creature God must be, to employ such an instrument in his service. (Hinton, 1847, p. 371)

He then went on to document his achievements concluding with, "O this is a mercy and God shall have all the glory." Similarly, Thomas Burchell, described by many visitors as a patriarch, a gentleman, dispensing hospitality from his very comfortable country residence in ample style, wrote to the Secretary of the BMS committee after establishing successfully a series of new stations, "I do not wish to mention anything boastingly, I feel my own nothingness, and my anxious desire is to be found at the foot of the cross" (Burchell, 1849, pp 305–36).

The strength of the missionaries was in their righteousness combined with their weakness ("worms" in the face of God), their isolation, their persecution, their oft-invoked spirit of Protestant martyrdom, their commitment to the voluntary principle, and, therefore, their conviction that it was only through the agency of men and women such as themselves that the new moral world would be created. The savagery and barbarism, as they constructed it, of the societies they went to justified their intervention. In bringing Christianity they were bringing civilization, for the two were equated in their discourse. The contest over slavery was a contest with Christianity—freedom meant the light of the word of God, the chains of bondage were infidelity and ignorance. In the "contest for empire" between Christianity and slavery, the light had triumphed and Satan was defeated.[16] The missionaries were the "messengers of mercy" as Phillippo (1843) described it:

> (They) have gone forth singly and at intervals, almost unperceived, while by their seeming weakness they have excited the pity and contempt rather than roused the opposition of foes . . . By residing among cruel savages and effeminate idolaters till, by their blameless lives and disinterested efforts, they have conciliated their respect, by introducing the useful arts of civilized society, or imperceptibly infusing the spirit of Christian truth . . . they have prepared the way for the Lord. (p. 470)

The missionaries seem to have suffered little from doubts as to the absolutism of their faith. This absolutism was built on a faith rooted in an ethnic superiority; by virtue of being white and European they "knew" and had the right to teach others. Whatever the inadequacies of their own education as perceived in England, for Baptist missionaries were denounced as low mechanics and tradesmen, they had no problems in scoffing at their rivals in Jamaica. They were possessed of the one truth, the one correct reading of the gospel. Those first missionaries who had to establish themselves on the basis of the work done by black Baptists found much to contend with. James Coultart often had to deal with those who thought they were Baptists but had been, in his view, very badly taught. His task was "to separate the precious from the vile, to correct what was erroneous, to instruct the ignorant, to humble without offending the conceit and pride of the self-sufficient and out of these elements to form a Church according to the New Testament of our Lord Jesus Christ" (Clark, et al., 1865, p. 4). Thomas Knibb was shocked at the presence of "pretend preachers" in the island who claimed to teach the gospel:

> There are many persons who profess to be teachers, who are as ignorant of the gospel as a Hindoo or Hottentot. They preach to, and live upon the people, and tell them tales that are as ridiculous as they are irreligious . . . Some of the black people go about the island *preaching* and baptizing. They generally have a book to preach out of, but sometimes mistake a spelling-book, or a dictionary, for a Testament, and sometimes preach with it upside down.

It did not apparently occur to him that his own difficulties in understanding "the negroes" when he first arrived might be to do not with their inadequacies, but his own. "Their understandings are very limited," he wrote in a patronizing vein to an English friend, "exceedingly so with field negroes, so that we find the greatest difficulty in understanding what they mean" (pp. 89–90). James Coultart noted with satisfaction that "abundant evidences appear both of the power and progress of religion" amongst the blacks. The "sublime character and the sanctifying energy of the gospel flash," he observed, "like brilliant beams of sunshine amidst parting clouds, through the broken forms of negro language" (Cox, 1842, Vol. 2, p. 39). The truth would out, even with these broken forms.

The construction of a new Jerusalem depended on the ceaseless industry and activity of the little band of missionaries who had set themselves the task of converting the heathen. Their enterprise was rooted in the "mission family," which they worked hard to create and sustain. The Baptist missionaries came from a society in which family enterprises were at the heart of economic, social, and cultural life."[17] They were used to a world which was physically organized around the family enterprise, in which men, women, and children all contributed to that enterprise in the "properly" gendered ways—men as the public and legal front, women as the informal partners. In the world of tradesmen, small proprietors and merchants, artisans and ministers from which they came, it would have been unthinkable for women not to have contributed to the family enterprise in innumerable ways. Men provided the driving force and the public face but women were the source of capital, labor, and contacts, they were the mothers who bore children to carry on the family business and to reproduce it in its daily life. Missionary wives, it was assumed, needed no training to know how to do any of this, it was their vocation.

But the family enterprise was only the starting point for the mission family. Mission stations provided the basis for what became an extended family stretching across the island. The family was defined not only by blood but also by religious brotherhood: "friend," "brother," and "sister" were all terms whose meanings crossed blood relations and ties of friendship. Stations might begin with only one couple but would hope to bring in others as their work extended and the numbers of chapels under their care grew. When new stations were established they kept in close touch with their "parent" stations and relied on them for succor and support. A Jamaica Baptist Association was formed in 1824 to link the missions across the island. Family was indeed a many-layered concept in this context, for there was the family of origin, the family of marriage, the family of the chapel, the mission family, the family of Baptists at home; and the family-to-be in the skies—this last providing the key to the overarching spiritual nature of the Christian family. Without a religious family individuals would be hard-pressed to maintain their faith—the family was a bulwark, a defense against the immorality of "the world," a haven in which Christian morality was practiced. The overlapping family networks provided a series of settings in which people could live their daily lives and enjoy a promise for the future to come. As Mary Ann Hutchins (née Middleditch) put it in the last letter that she wrote to her parents before she left England, the pain of parting was lessened by her great desire that they might "form a family anew, unbroken in the skies" (Middleditch, 1840, p. 86). Once in Jamaica she found that the mission family treated her just like a daughter and that Thomas Burchell and his wife took her into their home as if she were their child. Indeed, the months of her last illness and early death were spent with them. For these Baptists, like their evangelical counterparts in England, the terrible pain of the loss of children was alleviated by the presence of the family in heaven. William Knibb wrote to his wife Mary while she was in England in 1843, telling her that he had preached from,

> "the whole family in heaven." It is a delightful subject, and I hope I feel it to be so. In that family *there are an innumerable company of children* . . . our five sweet cherubs are there; but Oh! the loneliness they have left. (Hinton, 1847, p. 488)

The mission family was literally tied by a web of cross-cutting relationships. Many of the missionaries came from Baptist families and carried their father's and grandfather's activities into another field. They married into Baptist families, named their children after Baptist luminaries and friends, saw their children marry missionaries or become missionaries themselves. Thomas Burchell's grandfather was a Baptist minister; his wife's sister married another Jamaican Baptist missionary, Samuel Oughton; his daughter married a missionary, Edward Hewett.[18] William Knibb's brother was a missionary, his nephew, left orphaned, was cared for by him and returned to Jamaica to work as a schoolteacher in the new village of Kettering which he had established, named after his hometown in Northamptonshire; one of his daughters married a minister who took over the church in Kettering and their son was a minister. Knibb's sister's son also became a missionary. Two sisters, the Misses Drayton, who came to Jamaica in the 1840s as teachers, both married missionaries. Missionaries who were widowed married relatives of their extended mission family, widows often remarried other missionaries or ministers. Naming patterns confirmed these connections and friendships. Two of William Knibb's sons were named after missionary friends, James Coultart and Thomas Burchell—the latter was originally to have been named Augustus Africanus but they changed their minds, a significant indicator of where primary identifications lay. His first son was named Andrew Fuller, after the celebrated Baptist divine from Kettering, with whose chapel he had been connected and to whose son he had been apprenticed. James Phillippo sealed a friendship for life with a Baptist brother when they were both undergoing their missionary training—they exchanged names and each took the other's surname as a middle name, James Mursell Phillippo.

Like all families, this extended mission family was subject to acute tensions and conflicts, as well as providing support for each other. There were tensions between London and Jamaica over many issues; most notably over slavery and open political commitment in 1831–32 when the BMS committee was reluctant to abandon its insistence on political neutrality and was propelled into this by the weight of Baptist opinion mobilized by Knibb and his friends, and in 1841 over issues about Baptist missionary conduct in Jamaica which some saw as smacking dangerously of Africanisms. This debate was to push the missionaries in Jamaica into the decision to become entirely self-supporting, a decision taken in even more contentious circumstances at Serampore in 1837, and a decision which several of the Jamaican missionaries, including James Phillippo, were not happy with.[19] The subject of the development of a native ministry was also divisive. Both in India and Jamaica many Baptist missionaries were convinced that one of their most important tasks was to educate and train a native ministry who would be able in time to take on the work. What period of training and apprenticeship was necessary was, however, a matter of dispute in both places. In 1837 Burchell had serious reservations about native agency. He argued that:

> It is not to the men, but to their present want of fitness that I feel compelled to object. So far as the free coloured people are concerned, in consequence of their very defective and partial education, they were till lately deemed ineligible to the office of clerks or book-keepers. With respect to the slaves, they could be instructed only by stealth or in the Sunday school. Their acquirements, therefore, are very, very meagre indeed. Yet, this is no reflection upon them, but rather upon that accursed system under which they have so long laboured and suffered . . . This is not the age of miracles; and it is scarcely reasonable to expect that the negro churches can grow from infancy to manhood in a day.

His cautious words, however, went unheeded; a decision that was to be regretted by the BMS later, when they admitted that in utilizing the example of the East Indies they

had not taken "into full consideration the difference which existed in the mental development of the partially educated Hindoos and the utterly untutored children of Ham"
(Burchell, 1849, pp. 324–325).

A very serious division occurred within the family in Jamaica when Phillippo
visited England for a lengthy period because of ill-health and on his return found that
Dowson, the "native agent" who had been looking after his congregation in Spanish
Town, now claimed the chapel as his own. On the death of one of Dowson's followers,
Phillipo refused permission for a burial in the chapel cemetery. Enraged by this, Dowson's supporters stormed the cemetery at night and were attacked by a group of Phillippo's allies. Only the calling out of the militia quelled the violence.[20] Several years of
dispute and litigation followed which severely taxed all concerned (Underhill, 1881 pp.
231–232). On the whole, however, the beleaguered position of the missionaries and
their need for mutual support ensured the cohesiveness of the little community, whatever
the untold costs. "We have been a happy and united family," wrote Burchell (1849),
"we have generally consulted each other in our concerns" (p. 150).

The structure of the mission family, as with the early nineteenth-century English
family from which it was derived, was strictly patriarchal. It was the missionary who
was appointed by the BMS and who had all formal responsibilities. It was most unusual
for there to be any direct correspondence, for example, between the BMS and a missionary's wife. All dealings with the authorities in Jamaica went through the missionary
and his wife was understood as helpmeet and junior partner, covered by him in law.
The missionary's part in the family enterprise was in part defined by his fatherhood,
head of household, father of the family, father of the congregation, father of the children
in his schools. The range of his activities was immense, his working hours extensive.
James Phillippo described his working day, and indirectly the ways in which it intersected
with that of his wife, to his mother in 1828:

> I rise every morning at five o'clock, spend an hour in my study, pass another hour
> in my garden, or walking about to inhale the freshness of the morning air. I then
> return to my study, and remain there till eight. Breakfast; conduct family worship,
> including any persons who may happen to be on the premises. We afterwards go
> down into the school, which is on the floor beneath us, and which we superintend,
> and there remain until other engagements require attention. At two o'clock, when
> at home, I again visit the school, and remain till it is over for the day, concluding as
> it was begun, with singing and prayer.
>
>   About half-past four we dine, then get ready for chapel, class-meetings, singing
> classes, leaders' meetings, evening adult school, or meetings of some kind or another
> in town or country every day of the week. They usually commence at six o'clock
> and continue for an hour and a half. We then take tea, have family prayers, and at
> nine or half-past retire for the night.

On Sundays there were of course the services and the Sunday schools, there were
visits to the sick, monthly meetings with members and inquirers, "experience meetings,"
church meetings, the settlement of disputes, marriages, burials, baptisms, meetings with
other missionaries, encounters with officials and all the other myriad responsibilities of
the pastor. By 1841, Phillippo had been taking care of the district of Spanish Town
"alone," as he put it, for seventeen years. He was responsible for eight stations, some
of them 20 miles away from his base, all of which required services and meetings. He
superintended 8 schools, was building 3 new chapels and enlarging another. His congregations were between 2,000 and 3,000, and as father of his churches he kept a sharp
eye, or as sharp as he could given the numbers, on their practices. He managed the
budget of this entire enterprise, receiving some money from England but raising much

of it from his members (Underhill, 1881, pp. 82–83, 174). In his conception of his duties Phillippo was typical of the missionaries. As William Knibb pointed out in a letter to the treasurer of the BMS, discussing the differences between England and Jamaica:

> Here we are obliged to be everything—everything religiously, politically, civilly, and (if I may coin a word) buildingly. While our brethren at home have deacons who can manage the temporal affairs of the church, and collect the necessary moneys, we must be responsible for all, and manage all. While there are laymen to whom the poor can go for advice, and even for legal advice, here ours is the only appeal. Every disagreement, domestic or civil, comes before us; by our advice they go to law, or by our advice abstain. It is just the same in political matters; not a step will they take, nor an agreement will they sign, without asking us. (Hinton, 1847, p. 470)

Phillippo and his brothers all relied heavily on their wives to support them in whatever ways were appropriate. Mrs. Phillippo lived above the school in which she worked alongside her husband. She taught the girls while he taught the boys—a division of labor firmly established in evangelical schools, whether Sunday or day schools, from the late eighteenth century. In addition, she ran the household, bore nine children, five of whom died, and suffered extreme ill-health. As a missionary's wife she would be expected to run a household in which hospitality was always available, receive callers and visitors on all the occasions when her husband was not there, visit sick and poor women and children, question female applicants for church membership.

This last activity became a source of serious attack from some quarters in the early 1840s. At a time when the influence of the Baptist missionaries was at its height, there was considerable envy from the missionaries of other denominations who resented their success. Accusations were published in the press which included a critique of the practice whereby female inquirers, who sought baptism and membership, were dealt with by missionary wives rather than the pastors themselves. This was seen as a dangerous dereliction of duty, for how could untrained and unordained women treat inquirers with the proper rectitude? Knibb was sent to England by the Jamaica Baptists to defend the record both to the BMS and to the British public. He was aggressive in his defense, linking it to the propriety of women working with women, a favored discourse amongst evangelicals and one that was widely used to justify women's intervention in spheres that might have been deemed unsuitable:

> I know that a great deal of the examination of females for church-fellowship devolves upon our wives; but it is not necessary for me to state the reasons why females should be thus employed, when we think of the former state of Jamaica. It is right that this should be done by females who, though unobtrusive, are well qualified to form a judgment, and who know what the female mind of Jamaica is; who in their humble walk never slacken, though seldom praised, but are doing a work which angels will admire, and Jesus approve. I say, if we are wrong to take the testimony of our wives to the competency of those in scriptural knowledge who wish to come into our churches, being females, then we are wrong and shall be wrong still (Knibb, 1842, p. 25)

He added that he always spoke to them afterwards himself, thus confirming the female judgment.

The appalling relations of men and women under slavery, in the eyes of the missionaries, made the task of raising women to a Christian state a particularly crucial one. "Like the inhabitants of all uncivilized nations, the men treated the women as inferior in the scale of being to themselves," every woman was a prostitute, every man a libertine (Phillippo, 1843, p. 218). Even after the abolition of apprenticeship Knibb saw the young girls on the estates as prey to seduction. "I wish I could interest the females of Birmingham" (where there was a very strong women's anti-slavery society), he wrote to an English correspondent, no doubt hoping that the hint would be passed on, "in the situation of the young girls on the estates, most of whom are the prey of the seducer. I want to establish separate schools for them, under female teachers. . . . I know full well, that until the female character is raised, we shall never far advance in civilization and virtue." He welcomed signs of domesticity amongst his congregations and measured civilization and freedom by "the cottager's comfortable home, by the wife's proper release from toil, by the instructed child"—by the English middle-class family model in other words (Hinton, 1847, pp. 273–274, 310). One of the missionaries' proudest claims was of the thousands that they had married in the years after emancipation, a claim that gave them the opportunity both to count numbers, a favorite early Victorian activity, and to concretely illustrate an improvement in morality; for "those who are married," wrote Phillippo, when going to church on Sundays, exhibit "the truly civilized and social spectacle of walking arm in arm" (Phillippo, 1843, p. 284).

Missionary wives got none of the public praise which was heaped on their successful husbands in the heady years of the 1830s and 40s. The public funerals, the public meetings, the obituaries, the memorials and biographies were not for them. They had to be satisfied with a quieter form of praise. "I assure you, my dear girls," wrote Knibb to his daughters, "that I attribute most of my success in my missionary career to your excellent mother, while we are mutually impressed with the truth that we owe all to sovereign mercy, and feel that we have been unprofitable servants" (Hinton, 1847, p. 480). If wives died before husbands, their daughters took on the task of providing help and support. The family enterprise was defined by being a family—the family under God the father and the father/head of household. The pressure to conform with this was immense. Sons or daughters who did not move in a clear line towards adult baptism and a life of service were pressured, prayed for, publicly urged to identify themselves with Christ. Those children who died young were sometimes mythologized for their love of freedom and of the Savior, as in the case of young William Knibb, the only son left in the family:

> The destroyer of our race had left him but one son, a noble boy of twelve years of age, intelligent, pious, and enthusiastically interested in the negro's welfare. No sooner was the manumission of the apprentices in his father's church determined, than the heart of William leaped for joy; and, hastily bounding away, he sketched a British ship in full sail, with the word liberty on her flag, chasing two slavers, who were in the act of striking their colours. On the pendant was written, slavery must fall. The excitement brought on a fever in the night, in the delirium of which, his rambling words showed a mind filled with ideas of negro emancipation, and the triumphs of humanity, law, and religion (Burchell, 1849, p. 332).

Since during slavery the plantation provided the major community to which the slaves belonged, one of the essential tasks of the missionaries, both before and after emancipation, was to build an alternative community around the chapel. The chapel could potentially provide a place of belonging, a source of identity, a social life. Much of the strength of dissenting congregations in England derived from this sense of community, the cohesion of the chapel world, with its voluntary principles and its clear rules of conduct. The missionaries worked to develop equivalent structures in Jamaica. In order to extend their supervision and build up a band of responsible helpers outside the immediate family but within the family of the church, missionaries made use of the pattern of leaders established within the Wesleyan church and of the appointment of deacons, a feature of all non-conformist churches in England. Teachers, deacons, helpers, all were trained by the missionary and delegated by him. He sat at the center of this web of surveillance, managing and organizing. "The characteristics of this organization," wrote Phillippo, "are union, division of labour, and classification, combined with the most vigilant pastoral direction and supervision." Each church was divided into classes, each class superintended and fueled with the "holy ambition" to excel their brothers in duty. Each individual was encouraged to see himself as part of the whole and there were frequent social meetings to foster a sense of union and mutual effort. The agents, "instructed inquirers, visited the sick, sought after backsliders, superintended funerals, and reported cases of poverty and distress throughout their respective districts." Each member of the church thought of himself as his brother's keeper; together they were one family. "Bound closely to each other by mutual knowledge, intercourse, and love, there is neither Jew nor Greek, there is neither male nor female, there is neither bond nor free, but all are one in Christ Jesus," wrote Phillippo (1843), quoting St. Paul and failing to recognize the ways in which equality was hardly the central characteristic of this system, for at the center, "planning, improving and directing all its movements" was the pastor himself, the patriarch (pp. 432, 437).

If gender hierarchy was inscribed at the heart of the missionary enterprise so was that of race. Missionaries arrived in the island with their heads full of images of "poor Africans," "savages," "heathens." The welcome they met softened the notions of savagery and heathenism, which are, indeed, increasingly found attached to the planters in missionary discourse, and intensified the emphasis on pity. As Mary Ann Middleditch (1840) put it to a friend, "I wish you could hear the artless way in which we are welcomed by the Negroes.—poor things!—they are interesting creatures" (p. 97). Here the language of chatteldom, "poor things," and of difference, "interesting creatures," specimens to be observed, are clearly in play. Mary Ann increasingly identified herself with these "poor things," however, and in her letters home probably designed to be read at the missionary prayer meetings that she had so missed when she first left the parental nest, she tried to identify her parents with the project of brotherhood. After her husband's first baptismal service she wrote to her mother, describing the glorious scene, "a song of praise, a fervent prayer, and then nine of *our*—yes *your* black brethren and sisters buried in the stream." Similarly, she described to them the immensely moving scene when Burchell returned to the island after the 1831 rebellion and his persecution. One of those who welcomed him was "a fine looking black man" who was completely overcome:

> Big tears rolled down his manly face, and he was obliged to retire to give vent to his feelings. He lifted up his hands, and could thank God only with tears!—*This is a specimen of that tribe between the monkey and the human species, who are quite destitute of feeling.*

In closing his book on his daughter and articulating her last thoughts on race and difference, her father thought it appropriate to quote these lines, celebrating brotherhood across cultures:

> Afric's emancipated sons
> Shall join with Europe's polish'd race,
> To celebrate in different tongues
> The triumphs of Redeeming grace. (Middleditch, 1840, pp. 104, 110, 171)

Poetic effusions on the brotherhood of man were a favored form for the missionaries. In Phillippo's discussion of the race question in his book on Jamaica, written for an English audience, he quoted approvingly these lines:

Children we are all
Of one great Father, in whatever clime
His Providence hath cast the seeds of life,—
All tongues, all colours! Neither after death
Shall we be sorted into languages
And tints—white, black, and tawny, Greek and Goth,
Northmen and offspring of hot Africa;
Th' all-seeing Father—he in whom we live and move—
He, th' indifferent Judge of all—regards
Nations, and hues, and dialects alike;
According to their works shall they be judged.

Phillippo undoubtedly believed with one part of himself that all nations and hues were equal under God, just as he thought that "neither male nor female, we are all one in Christ Jesus." Slaves, he argued, were the hapless victims of a revolting system; they were

> men of the same common origin with ourselves,—of the same form and delineation of feature, though with a darker skin,—men endowed with minds equal in dignity, equal in capacity, and equal in duration of experience—men of the same social dispositions and affections, and destined to occupy the same rank with ourselves in the great family of man.

This family of man, however, was, like all families, internally ordered. Jostling with the language of equality in Phillippo's mind was the language of hierarchy, undercutting that very equality he claimed to espouse. There was an evolutionary ladder, he believed, at the top of which were Europeans and up which, when things were going well, freed blacks would climb. As the free coloreds rose there was a "corresponding improvement" amongst the more respectable blacks:

> The latter have advanced to that degree in the scale of civilization and intelligence, formerly occupied by the people of colour, and the former to that previously held by their more favoured white brethren. In no respect do these now differ from the middling and lower classes of tradesmen and others in England. Their eyes have long been open to the disgrace and sin of concubinage, and marriage among them has become common. The eye of the Christian is now delighted, especially on the Sabbath, by the spectacle of multitudes of these classes with their families walking to and fro from the house of God in company. (Phillippo, 1843, pp. 151–152, 154)

Blacks, in other words, proved that they were the same as whites by aspiring to behave like them.

Phillippo declared in his preface that he had tried to make his book more interesting for English readers by the inclusion of anecdotes and dialect. The black voices, both male and female, which were encoded in his text told a story of accommodation, piety, and respectability. Few disruptive moments surfaced in his stories of negro gratitude and affection. Similarly Cox, in his account of missionary activities in Jamaica, was at pains to quote the testimony of negroes to demonstrate their loyalty and affection to the English. Negroes were thus constructed by the missionaries and their friends, both for themselves and for an English audience, through the filter of a set of assumptions as to what post-emancipation society should be like—a set of assumptions which seesawed on the ambivalence of racial difference, blacks were, and were not, equal.

Black inferiority was further encoded in the language of the family. Blacks were the "sons of Africa," "babes in Christ," children who must be led to freedom, which meant adulthood. The missionaries were the parents who would act as their guides, teaching them, admonishing and reproving them, congratulating them when they did right. "They are willing to be taught," wrote Knibb, "and where there is sympathy with them, they love those who instruct them." At the same time he balked at including them in his own immediate family. He disliked, for example, having to employ a black wet-nurse when his wife was too ill to feed one of their children: "I feel at having a black person for this purpose, but there is no remedy." He was also entirely comfortable, on occasion, with using the epithet "blackey" and with stereotyping negro characteristics. "The little dears leaped for joy when I entered," he wrote to a friend about a visit to a school, "and many could not refrain from dancing, for a negro must express his joy" (Hinton, 1847, pp. 50, 75, 210, 306).

Emancipation, for the missionaries, meant black entry into manhood, for masculinity in their world meant freedom from dependence on the will of another (Davidoff, 1990). To be subject meant a loss of male identity, whereas for women one form of subjectivity, that of the female slave dependent on her master, was ideally exchanged for another, that of the freed woman on her husband. Marriage and domesticity was the desired status for women. "Emancipation," wrote Knibb in 1839, "is a glorious triumph of Christianity. The insulted African has, by his calm propriety of conduct, fully vindicated his claim to be a man" (Hinton, 1847, p. 310). Once again this hierarchical conception of racial difference was cross-cut with a more egalitarian rhetoric. "The same God that made the white made the black man," Knibb preached on the anniversary of the end of apprenticeship, "the same blood that runs in the white man's veins, flows in yours" (p. 313). The old characteristics of "the negro," it was concluded, were disappearing as the legacy of slavery was destroyed by a Christian culture and Christian education:

> That cunning, craft, and suspicion—those dark passions and savage dispositions before described as characteristics of the negro, if ever possessed in the degree in which they are attributed to him,—are now giving place to a noble, manly, and independent, yet patient and submissive spirit. (Phillippo, 1843, p. 253)

Those respectable English visitors who came to the island in the wake of abolition to inquire into apprenticeship and its aftermath and write their definitive and authoritative reports on "the negro," shared these sets of assumptions. They came to Jamaica to look at a species, were impressed by the potential which they saw, but, in the words of Joseph John Gurney (1840, p. x), "raising the native mind" to European standards was the key to their project. Joseph Sturge and Thomas Harvey (1838) put great stress on the promise of their objects of study; "their conduct and their character are full of promise for the future," they wrote, "full of tokens of their capacity to become, when free, a well-ordered, industrious and prosperous community" (p. 346). "The negroes," John Candler (1840–41) thought three years later in 1840, were like children:

> The Negroes now they have got freedom like to show that they have it, and cannot bear to be told that if they want a day to themselves they must ask their master to let them have it. They wish to work, and to intermit work as they please, and think they have a right to do so. This we know is perplexing to the master; but the Negroes, with all their shrewdness, have much of the child about them, and need to be humoured. (p. 2)

Gurney, while attempting to convince both himself and his readers throughout his text of the respectability and seriousness of blacks, ended on a hopelessly optimistic note as to the rapid disappearence of distinctions of color in the West Indies—an argument which his own writing belied.

For these visitors, subaltern voices in the text are occasionally disruptive in ways which suggest their deep uncertainties as to the relations of black and white. Candler and Gurney both tell the story of an encounter with a myalman. In Candler's (1840–41, pp. 28–29) account:

> The doctor, a black young man of about twenty, very fashionably attired, came in with the easy manners of a perfect gentleman, and taking his seat, called for a glass of water, which was brought him with haste and reverence by one of the company. At first he only professed to cure diseases by the administration of simple medicines, suited to the disease complained of; but, on being pressed further, told us that he was qualified to hold discourse with good spirits of the dead, who intimated to him all the secret and hidden evils of the human body, such as no human eye could penetrate, and that by this means he could effect cures which no white man could perform. We asked the people whether they believed this; they said with one voice, We do believe it, and seemed astonished at our incredulity. J. J. Gurney spoke to them on the folly of such superstition; and some of them, in return, before we went away, hoped that God would open our eyes and make us see clearer.

In Gurney's (1840, p. 98) account he concludes optimistically, "We were sorry to observe the obstinacy of their delusions, but such things will be gradually corrected by Christian instruction." The unspoken worry was that they would not be. For anxious readers he adds the rational note that it was because the negroes were deprived of medical help that they inevitably resorted to quacks.

Part of what was in play here was an articulation of class difference as well as racial difference. If men such as Phillippo and Knibb had stayed in England as Baptist ministers, their professional status would have secured them positions within the middle class. With modest stipends they would have occupied the lower end of that class economically, whilst deriving status from their profession. They would never, however, have been able to compete with an Anglican clergyman. Some non-conformist ministers in England were able to achieve solid middle-class positions by virtue of the success of their chapels and attached ventures in taking in pupils or writing books. The most comfortable often owed that comfort to a well-made marriage once they had achieved status as preachers. In Jamaica their prospects were much better. As George Bridges (1968 [1828]), Anglican clergyman, scourge of all dissenters and founder of the Colonial Church Union, acidly commented in his *Annals of Jamaica,* "a cloud of itinerant preachers," had "hastened to exchange a parish pittance in England, for a lucrative profession in the West Indies" (Vol. 2, p. 294).

In Jamaica, despite the contempt of the established white population, white missionary skins gave authority, an authority confirming that derived from faith, an authority to command. The Baptist missionaries saw it as a part of their historic task to create an industrious, respectable, free working class in Jamaica. In class terms, as well as in racial terms, they only partially believed in equality. Spiritual equality might be one thing. Economic and cultural equality were entirely another. Despite the suspicions of the planters, less blinkered contemporaries were convinced of the missionaries' commitment to the construction of a genuinely free labor market and their tirelessness in their efforts to convince the blacks that they must fulfill their side of the bargain. "A fair day's work for a fair day's wage" was their maxim (Wilmot, 1982). In line with this, they were delighted to see women becoming respectable domestic servants as the terrible vestiges of slavery were abandoned, for if women had to work outside the home they believed that the best possible work was that of a domestic kind. For respectable English middle-class men, the spectacle of women working in someone else's home was far less damaging to their concept of femininity than to see them working, sometimes in mixed gangs, on the estates. Conveniently forgetting the complaints about servants which were part of the stock-in-trade of the English middle class, Phillippo (1843) wrote with great smugness:

> Domestic servants are beginning to be eminently trustworthy; and, when properly treated and confided in, do not suffer by a comparison with the great bulk of the same class in England.

This was indeed a sign of "society advancing to that high moral standard which is fixed in the great Christian code" (p. 265).

There were complicated issues at play, however, in the class relations of missionary and church member, for the missionaries became increasingly financially dependent, as were their counterparts in England, on their congregations. Some money came from the BMS, but after the abolition of apprenticeship an increasing proportion of the income came from the membership. This necessarily meant a shift in power. Missionaries might be the fathers of their children, their guides and leaders; yet their physical comfort and security rested on those children. Take the case of the building of a new home for William Knibb, a story which was widely reported in England because of the attack in 1841 on the luxurious way of life of some of the Baptists. In a public speech at Exeter Hall Knibb told the tale and defended his actions:

> When I laid a report before the members of my church, and read the title deeds of the chapels—that all those chapels that are out of debt were vested in trustees—and when they found that the house in which I lived, the bed on which I reposed, and the furniture which I used, was not my property, but theirs, and belonged entirely to the church, they said, Minister, have you took care and got a house for your wife? I said, No: do you think that I would take your money without your leave, and buy a house for Mrs. Knibb? They replied, If you have not got one, it is time you had. You go to Kettering, to the land left that belongs to you, and you build a good house there, and we will pay for it. I took them at their word . . . for Edward Barrett (a deacon) said, set about it soon, minister; you may cut—that is, you might die—and we cannot bear the thought that your wife should go home; let her stop here. I built the house and it cost 1,000 sterling; and as soon as it was completed, I assigned it over to Mrs. Knibb and our dear children, determined not to hold property there. In Kettering House she is now . . .

Knibb claimed that none of the Baptists that he knew in Jamaica lived in houses that were more "costly or commodious, or better furnished, than any individual with a family, who has been used to move in respectable life, is fairly entitled to" (1842, pp. 34–35). There was a certain naivety in this; it is unlikely that any Baptist minister in England had had a thousand-pound house built for him by his congregation, furnished, furthermore, with a £200 library. Knibb's status and power were secure in post-emancipation Jamaica, but in the end depended, as he put it himself, on the generosity of the blacks. Building a large house for your minister was one way of showing him his dependence on you—a reversal which figures little in missionary discourse.

In the wake of the abolition of apprenticeship it soon became clear to the missionaries that the planters would do everything in their power to drive down wages and construct new forms of unfree labor. The missionary response to this proved to be their most ambitious venture in Jamaica—the establishment of free villages (Mintz, 1974; Tyrrell, 1987). Yet in those villages racial, class, and gender hierarchies were literally built in. Faced with the planters' refusal to rent houses and provision grounds at a reasonable rate a group of missionaries, in the forefront of whom were Knibb, Phillippo, and Burchell, started to raise money to buy land themselves, establish new villages and then sell the plots mainly to their trusted church members. Joseph Sturge was a key figure in supporting this in England. He had established close friendships with several of the Baptist missionaries during his visit to Jamaica and in his efforts to bring the apprenticeship issue to the front of the public conscience in England, and was the driving force behind the Jamaica Education Society which provided money for new schools. He was entirely in favor of a project which he saw as promoting negro welfare and set up the West India Land Investment Company to buy up bankrupt plantations. As the prospectus put it, the point of the Company was "to transfer the control of West India property gradually from those who have systematically opposed the advancement of the Negroes in civilization, knowledge and christianity, to such men as would really promote their moral and religious welfare . . ." (quoted in Tyrrell 1987). Between 1838–44, 19,000 freedmen and their families settled in these free villages, possibly 100,000 people in all (Mintz, 1974, p. 160).

These villages were imagined as missionary utopias; designed and planned by them, they were built around the church, mission house, and school. Free peasants could buy their plot of land, sometimes paying it off in installments, and thus securing their manhood, not only with the possession of property but also the vote that it carried. The lots sold were designed to contribute to a family enterprise in which men would continue to work on the estates but the family would be able to grow provisions, both to sell on the local market and to feed themselves. Phillippo hoped through the establishment of these villages to give "his" people "a relish for the comforts and conveniences of civilized life," to improve their domestic economy, and to "convince these simple-minded people that their *own* prosperity, as well as that of the island at large, depended on their willingness to work for moderate wages, on the different properties around them." He had personally first purchased the land, then,

> surveyed and laid out the allotments, superintended the construction of the roads and streets, directed the settlers in the building of their cottages, and cultivation of their grounds, supplied them with their deeds of conveyance, formed societies among them for the improvement of agricultural operations. . . . (1843, pp. 430–431)

Phillipo's early estimation of the multiple skills necessary for the missionary had indeed come to fruition! The towns were named after the heroes of the anti-slavery movement, Sligoville; Clarkson Town; Wilberforce Ville; Sturge Town, later to be renamed Birmingham after Sturge's hometown; Buxton; Gurney; Albert; and Macaulay. Even one heroine of the movement, a Quaker feminist Anne Knight, had a village named after her, and Victoria, of course, also figured.[21] Knibb named one village in his area Kettering after his birthplace, and it was here that the commodious Kettering House was built and legally placed in the names of his wife and children so that, in his eyes, his position as pastor was not impugned.

In Sligoville, named after the Marquis of Sligo, onetime Governor of Jamaica who had been supportive of missionary efforts, the houses were named too; Victoria, Happy Home, Content, Comfort Castle, Industry, Happy Hut, Happy Grove, Content My Own, Paradise, Liberty Content, Comfortable Garden, Happy Retreat, the names expressing both the meaning for freed slaves of owning a place of their own and the definitions of home and domesticity which were inscribed in these properties. Phillippo proudly described a typical cottage in Sligoville, where he himself had "a neat but commodious country house" (Gurney, 1840, p. 116); they were thatched or shingled, plastered or built in stone or wood, some had a porch with shutters or glass and there was a sitting-room in the middle, a bedroom at each end:

many of the latter contain good mahogany bedsteads, a wash-handstand, a looking glass, and chairs. The middle apartment is usually furnished with a sideboard, displaying sundry articles of crockery-ware, some decent-looking chairs, and not unfrequently with a few broad-sheets of the Tract society hung round the walls in neat frames of cedar.

There was a kitchen at the back and a place for stock. Sometimes the gardens at the front were decorated in European style with rose bushes and other flowering shrubs. All in all, they were a perfect setting for a domesticated family life. As Phillippo (1843) commented, "On returning from their daily labor the men almost uniformly employ themselves in cultivating their own grounds or in improving their own little freeholds, and the women in culinary and other domestic purposes" (p. 235). Visitors to the villages were impressed, though Gurney was concerned about the evidence of too much love of luxury amongst the negroes and hoped they would soon learn to be more frugal. In Sligoville he was delighted that, "The people settled there were all married pairs, mostly with families, and the men employed the bulk of their time in working for wages on the neighboring estates." Overall the scene was one of contentment, industry, and piety; all under the eye of James Mursell Phillippo (Gurney, 1840, pp. 115–16).

These villages represented the perfect society for the Baptist missionaries: Knibb in Kettering and Hoby Town, named after another Baptist minister and friend in England; Burchell in Bethel Town and Mount Carey, after William Carey; Phillippo in Sligoville, Sturge Town, Clarkson Town; Clark in Wilberforce and Buxton, all had the opportunity to create a new moral and material world in which Christianity and freedom reigned, where the chief benefactor was the missionary and the very structure of the town embodied his beliefs about the right ordering of the races, the classes, the sexes. This potentially perfect dream, of model villages, of more-ordered Englands in the Caribbean, offset the fears and anxieties of the missionaries themselves as they tried to live their lives between two cultures. Of course, the missionary stories give us very limited access to the meanings which the black residents made of those communities—to uncover that would require a different kind of research. What the missionary tales do tell us about, however, is the ways in which English dreams and aspirations were expressed through the construction of these Jamaican villages.

The missionaries suffered from troubling uncertainties as to where they really belonged—uncertainties that are highly evocative in the 1990s. They always thought of themselves as English, British, and saw England and the abolitionist public as their ultimate source of support. But they also suffered from feelings of shame about their "race," as they constructed it, and were engaged in a constant polemic to ensure that their definition of what it meant to be English should be the dominant one. When contemplating slavery Knibb felt, "ashamed that I belong to a race that can indulge in such atrocities" (Hinton, 1847, p. 48). In his campaign in 1832–33 he constantly called upon his audiences to be "patriots," which in his terms meant to be opposed to slavery—this was the true nature of the English, and, therefore, to his mind, British, love of freedom. After abolition, when apprenticeship became the issue, Knibb despaired of Jamaican whites and declared that, "from English patriots must come, if it come at all, the Magna Charta of Africa's rights" (p. 245). Similarly, Phillippo bemoaned the ways in which the planters' behavior impugned the national honor; it was not English to persecute blacks and despise other races, and he was particularly ashamed on one occasion when a French official visitor observed the planters' vituperations (Underhill, 1881, p. 159). Abolitionist activists all assumed that it was up to England. Since the whites in Jamaica would not take their responsibilities to their race seriously and the prospect of the blacks taking decisions into their own hands was too horrifying to think of except at moments of extreme stress, it was up to the *right kinds* of English people to assert *their* conception of what it meant to be English and ensure that appropriate legislation was passed for "our colony."[22]

In England the missionaries spoke for the afflicted, whether as slaves or freed men being denied their proper opportunities, and begged the English, primarily the middle class, since these were the people they addressed at their meetings and in their writings, to show their kindness, their generosity, their pity for those less fortunate than themselves, to exercise their power and influence and free the slaves, give money for their education, raise them to full personhood through the building of proper villages, with proper homes, schools, churches, and jobs.

In a series of grand celebrations of abolition, of the ending of apprenticeship, of the succeeding anniversaries of these historic events, of the BMS Jubilee, of the Jamaican missionary Jubilee, England and the English were ritually constructed as the benefactors, those who had given the slaves freedom, those to whom the freed slaves must demonstrate their worthiness, their manhood, their domesticated femininity. In renderings of "God save the Queen" and "Rule Britannia," in the banners which celebrated the English heroes of the anti-slavery movement, just as the names of the villages did, in their portraits which were hung in the chapels, in the "Freedom Flag" with the Union Jack in the corner, in the posters proclaiming "England, land of liberty, of light, of life" and "Philanthropy, Patriotism and Religion have under God achieved for us this glorious triumph," in the marble memorial in Knibb's chapel at Falmouth celebrating the death of slavery, in the English hymns which were sung, England was celebrated as the land of the free and the giver of freedom.[23] Listen to the reported witness which was invited from respectable black (male) deacons in Knibb's church in Falmouth at the ending of apprenticeship and then reported in the British missionary press with all the accompanying insignia of proper forms of address and English names:

> Mr. Andrew Dickson: I do truly thank God for the light of the everlasting gospel. I present my thanks to the people of England for the gospel."

> Mr. William Kerr: "We bless God, we bless the queen, we bless the governor, we bless the people of England for the joy we have."

> Mr. Edward Barrett: "My good friends, we are meet together here to show our gratitude to a certain gentleman and the people of England, who felt for us when we did not feel for ourselves. We have been made to stand up and see our wives flogged, and we could not help them. The people of England did not see us, but God see us, and God stir up their hearts to get us freedom, and now we are all free people! (Cox, 1842, pp. 252–283)

Meanwhile in England celebrations were held, also to celebrate England's greatness and magnanimity, as, for example, in Birmingham in 1838 to mark the end of apprenticeship and the contribution which Joseph Sturge, their renowned citizen, had made to this. There was a large meeting in the Town Hall, addressed by Baptist ministers and other dignitaries and attended by Daniel O'Connell, that emancipator of another British colony, followed by a meal of British bread and beef and a procession through the town with thousands of schoolchildren to the site of a new school, the Negro Emancipations School Rooms, the foundation stone of which was laid by Sturge himself. An inscription hailed Sturge as "the friend of the negro, the friend of the children, and the friend of man," thus definitively distinguishing between negroes and men. The children, who would undoubtedly have been predominantly working class, sang "Rejoice the Saviour Reigns" and "The Trump of Freedom Sounds," thus in theory at least, rejoicing that their Savior reigned in the colonies as well as at home and that their betters had given freedom to their inferiors in Jamaica (Payne, 1933, p.54; Tyrrell, 1987, p. 82).

Thus one England, the middle-class, non-conformist-influenced, patriarchal England, identified herself for herself and her multiple "others." As the greatly loved abolitionist poet Montgomery put it,

> Thy chains are broken: Africa be free!
> Thus saith the Island-Empress of the sea;
> Thus saith Britannia—Oh, ye winds and waves!
> Waft the glad tidings to the land of slaves! (quoted in Clark, et al., 1865, p. 76)

In 1840 the considered opinion of James Stephen, the powerful Permanent Undersecretary at the Colonial Office with an unrivaled knowledge of colonial affairs, was that the influence of the Baptist missionaries would steadily increase and "make them masters at no very distant time of the fortunes of Jamaica." "The tendency of things in Jamaica," he wrote, "appears to be towards the Establishment of a sacerdotal Government, exercised by narrow-minded men over a Body of docile, grateful, and affectionate Disciples. All things considered I doubt whether this is a just subject of regret" (quoted in Knapland, 1953, p. 171). His judgment, however, on this matter was substantially wrong. Missionary influence was to be steadily weakened in the subsequent years.

In June and July 1842 the jubilee of the BMS was celebrated in Kettering, England and Kettering, Jamaica. In England Knibb joined in the services, at which five-to-six thousand people were present. One of the texts was, "The Lord hath done great things for us, whereof we are glad" (Cox, 1842, Vol. 2, p. 384). In Jamaica there were huge celebrations with thousands of people. Knibb addressed 500 deacons and leaders "on the important position they occupied" (Hinton, 1847, p. 452). On the second day, after a prayer meeting, he spoke to the assembled multitudes and pressed them to do a fair day's work for a fair day's pay. "The eyes of the world are upon you," he warned them,

> and every slave who moaning clanks his chain, expects by your conduct to have it smitten from his manacled body. By the woes of bleeding Africa, by you to be hushed; by the hopes of the American slaves, by you to be realized; by all the great and eternal principles of justice; by all the past mercies you have received; by the present momentous position in which you stand!—do, I implore you, use the influence you so justly possess, to maintain on fair and equitable principles, Jamaica's welfare. (Clark, et al., 1865, p. 128)

Now it was Knibb's turn to "implore" the negroes to behave as England thought they should, to show their gratitude for all that England had done for them by being good wage laborers and responsible citizens and fathers. But the times were becoming less auspicious for missionary dreams.

In September 1842 an alarming irruption took place at Salter's Hill Baptist chapel in Jamaica, where Walter Dendy had been the missionary for more than ten years. At that time,

> a fearful spirit of delusions came over many persons who resided on estates near Ironside-by-the-Sea . . . Some of the members and inquirers became affected with it, and seemed fascinated as by a spell. On the 25th December they entered the chapel at Salter's Hill, in the time of Divine Service. They ran about like mad persons, jumped on the benches, began to speak wildly, and interrupted the worship. [Mr. Dendy asked the congregation to keep calm, the Myal men and women were removed

and the deacons guarded the doors.] Mr. Dendy preached from Ephesians vii: Have no fellowship with the unfruitful works of darkness, but rather reprove them. Towards the close a woman came in, and ran wildly about the chapel with pictures in her hands. She exhibited one, which was intended to represent the crucifixion of the Saviour, and lifting up her eyes in a peculiar manner, curtsied to it. At the end of the service a scene of confusion took place. The myalists rushed into the chapel, with frantic gesticulations. They tore away ornaments from the females, and the watch-guards of the men. In the chapel-yard several people were seized and thrown down and had water poured on them. Some were considerably injured by these fanatics, who threatened violence to all.

The magistrate was applied to and the police arrived who arrested and charged the offenders, but the "bad effects" of these superstitious practices were felt by the members of the chapel for a long time to come (Clarke, 1869, pp. 162–63). Similar events occurred in other places and the hold of the missionaries over the popular imagination seemed to be waning.

In 1844 James Phillippo returned to the island after a lengthy stay in England on account of ill health. While he was away, his major chapel in Spanish Town had been looked after by a "native agent," a Mr. Dowson. When he returned, Dowson, as has been seen, refused to give up the chapel and claimed it was his, with the support of large sections of the congregation. Phillippo was deeply wounded and only succeeded in regaining the premises after seven years of litigation, supported with financial help from England. This dispute, in the words of his biographer, "greatly affected Mr. Phillippo's judgement of the negro character." It became clear to him that his bright hopes had been too bright, his expectations too high:

> If the people were free, it was also evident that long years of patient labour were yet needed to bring to maturity the seeds of truth and righteousness, purity and order, which it had been his aim and that of many other benevolent men to sow. (Underhill, 1881, p. 231)

The ascent to manhood was clearly going to be a very long business indeed. Phillippo's gloom was increased by the collapse of the prosperity of the immediate post-emancipation period and the increase in poverty and unemployment. After 1846, wages fell, sugar production declined, and between 1844–54 49% of plantations were abandoned, while provision prices also fell (D. Hall, 1859). It was impossible to assert with such confidence any longer the superiority of free over slave labor (Curtin, 1955).

Meanwhile in England, anti-slavery support was lagging after the fiasco of the Niger expedition and the intense division amongst the abolitionists as to whether the preferential duties on West Indian sugar should be maintained. Phillippo wrote anxiously in his diary, "the future is dark and gloomy. The country is increasing in poverty, and religious feeling is rapidly declining. But the Lord reigneth, therefore will I hope in Him" (Underhill, 1881, p. 245).

Phillippo's own sense of a flawed dream must have been sharply intensified by the publication in 1847 of *Jane Eyre,* with its particular and different articulation of all that was made and bad in Jamaica, soon to be followed by Thomas Carlyle's *Occasional Discourse on the Negro Question,* later retitled *Nigger* in a symptomatic sign of the times, which launched a powerful and vitriolic attack on the experiment of emancipation. New voices were coming to the fore, a new colonial discourse with its own form of racism and its own polemic on England and Englishness was emerging. The missionary struggle to define blackness as both equal and not equal, whiteness as superior, but with patronage, kindness, and generosity to the fore, was collapsing under the combined weight of its own contradictions, its own refusal to face the uncomfortable reality that black people might choose to be different, and a new assault from elsewhere on the mutability of racial difference. The moment of the "poor negro" was over.

NOTES

1. A version of this paper was first presented at the Cultural Studies Conference in Champaign-Urbana in April 1990. Since then it has been substantially revised. The revised version was presented to the Atlantic Center Seminar at Johns Hopkins University and to a Women's History seminar at New York University in October 1990, with most helpful discussions in both places. In addition, I would like to thank Stuart Hall, Sally Alexander, and David Albury for their comments. The paper is part of a larger project on English national identity in the mid-nineteenth century, currently funded by the Economic and Social Research Council.

2. The most helpful introduction to the history of "Englishness" can be found in Robert Colls and Phillip Dodd, eds. (1987), *Englishness: Politics and Culture 1880–1920.*

3. For a discussion of black British identities and their implications see Stuart Hall (1987b), "Minimal Selves"; (1988a), "New Ethnicities."

4. Paul Gilroy, "Cultural Studies and Ethnic Absolutism," Paper presented to the International Cultural Studies Conference, University of Illinois at Urbana-Champaign, 1990; and printed in this volume.

5. On the centrality of religion to the formation of the English middle class see Leonore Davidoff and Catherine Hall (1987), *Family Fortunes: Men and Women of the English Middle Class 1780–1850.*

6. For a thorough survey of women's anti-slavery activities in England see Clare Midgeley (1989), "Women and the Anti-Slavery Movement 1780s–1860s."

7. For an analysis of some of the gender aspects of this debate see Catherine Hall (1989), "The Economy of Intellectual Prestige: Thomas Carlyle, John Stuart Mill and the Case of Governor Eyre."

8. On the place of religion in the anti-slavery debates about the construction of a free labor, capitalist world, see, for example, David Brion Davis (1975), *The Problem of Slavery in the Age of Revolution 1770–1823;* Robin Blackburn (1988), *The Overthrow of Colonial Slavery.*

9. In conceptualizing the specificity of the Baptist missionary discourse I have benefitted greatly from discussions with Moira Ferguson and from reading her forthcoming book, *Subject to Others: British Women Writers and Colonial Slavery 1670–1834.*

10. They are in order of dates of publication: Joseph Sturge and Thomas Harvey (1838), *The West Indies in 1837 being the journal of a visit to Antigua, Montserrat, Dominica, St. Lucia, Barbadoes, and Jamaica; undertaken for the purpose of ascertaining the actual condition of the negro population of those islands;* Joseph John Gurney (1840), *A Winter in the West Indies described in familiar letters to Henry Clay of Kentucky;* John Candler (1840–1841), *Extracts from the Journal of John Candler whilst travelling in Jamaica,* 2 parts; T. Middleditch (1840), *The Youthful Female Missionary: A Memoir of Mary Ann Hutchins, wife of the Rev. John Hutchins, Baptist missionary, Savanna-la-mar, Jamaica; and daughter of the Rev. T. Middleditch of Ipswitch: compiled chiefly from her own correspondence by her father;* Rev. F. A. Cox (1842), *History of the Baptist Missionary society from 1792–1842,* 2 vols; James M. Phillippo (1843), *Jamaica; its past and present state;* John Howard Hinton (1847), *Memoir of William Knibb, Missionary in Jamaica;* William Fitzer Burchell (1849), *Memoir of Thomas Burchell, 22 years a Missionary in Jamaica.*

11. A number of works deal with the missionary presence in Jamaica: see particularly, Mary Turner (1982), *Slaves and Missionaries;* Ernest A. Payne (1933), *Freedom in Jamaica;* Philip D. Curtin (1955), *Two Jamaicas: The Role of Ideas in a Tropical Colony 1830–1865;* C. Duncan Rice (1982), "The missionary context of the anti-slavery movement"; and Michael Craton (1982), "Slave culture, resistance and the achievement of emancipation in the British West Indies 1783–1838."

12. On the centrality of gender definitions to the evangelical revival, see Davidoff and Hall (1987), especially Part 1.

13. The figures are from Payne (1933), p. 26 and Cox (1842), Vol. 2, p. 231.

14. For a discussion of the evangelical concept of manliness, see Davidoff and Hall (1987).

15. The phrase is Underhill's, for many years the Secretary of the BMS, in relation to Phillippo (1843), p. 28.

16. The phrase is Cox's (1842), Vol. 2, p. 193.

17. On the family enterprise, its place in middle-class culture and the development of capitalism, see Davidoff and Hall (1987), esp. Part 2.

18. Name cards have been compiled for the missionaries, using a wide variety of sources. This data is derived from the name cards.

19. On the debates between the BMS and the missionaries in Jamaica, see Cox (1842); Underhill (1881) on Phillippo's doubts about independence; on the Serampore controversy, see Cox (1842), Vol. 1 and Potts (1967).

20. See the account of this episode in William A. Green (1976), p. 342.

21. The information about Anne Knight came from Clare Midgely (1989), fn. p. 249.

22. In one of his speeches in England at the height of the contest "between slavery and Christianity," Knibb referred to the danger that if the British did not act, the slaves would. Knibb (1833), p. 20.

23. There are rich descriptions of the end of apprenticeship celebrations in Phillippo (1843) and Cox (1842), of the marble memorial and the BMS Jubilee in Hinton (1847), of the Jamaica Jubilee in Clark, et al. (1865).

DISCUSSION: CATHERINE HALL

TOM PRASCH: I was wondering if you could talk a bit more about the status of the Baptist Church in England at this time and its place in the history you're telling.

HALL: The evangelical revival at the end of the eighteenth century, the rebirth of a new faith which swept across the British Isles, affected the Baptists as well as the Anglicans and other dissenting groups. In 1751 there were only 200 Baptist congregations in England, by 1830 there were 1,025. The impact of the French Revolution in the 1770s, with its powerful critique of the church and its celebration of reason, produced a sense of crisis amongst many of the faithful. "God's army" had to go to work whether at home or abroad. At the same time, as I have pointed out, the opportunities abroad made the idea of missionary work a compelling dream, particularly for those whose ambitions could not be met in England. In the 1820s the political struggle with the state which non-conformists where engaged in to establish their equal rights with members of the established church may well have increased their sense of collective agency and power, which was then in part expressed through the anti-slavery campaign, with its closely associated activity, missionary work.

CARY NELSON: We have heard that it is time for cultural studies to move beyond the "mantra of race, class, and gender." It seems to me that in at least two respects your work can help us to do that: first, by carefully working through the ways in which race, class, and gender are complexly articulated to one another and, second, by taking up these issues in precise historical contexts. Do you see your work as having this general methodological relevance?

HALL: Yes, I do indeed. I don't think that we have, as yet, a theory as to the articulation of race, class, and gender and the ways in which these articulations might generally operate. The terms are often produced as a litany, to prove political correctness, but that does not necessarily mean that the forms of analysis which follow are really shaped by a grasp of the workings of each axis of power in relation to the others. Indeed, it is extremely difficult to do such work because the level of analysis is necessarily extremely complex with many variables in play at any one time. Case studies, therefore, whether historical or contemporary, which carefully trace the contradictory ways in which these articulations take place both in historically specific moments and over time, seem to me to be very important. This is not to suggest that the theoretical developments which we need can only come through this kind of work, far from it. But I certainly think that rigorous historical analysis can contribute to the development of new theoretical insights and, indeed, are not only to be confined to the methodological sphere.

There is another point which I would make about your comment. The popular litany is clearly "race, class, and gender" but it is vital to take on the argument as to the problems with the category "race" and to recognize that we are frequently talking about ethnicity when we use the term "race."

CARY NELSON: Obviously work by historians has had a sort of double life, both within the discipline and within cultural studies, feminism, and Marxism. Can you talk about that double history and your own place in it?

Could you comment more broadly on how being a historian has shaped your understanding of cultural studies?

Some cultural studies people believe that cultural studies becomes increasingly difficult to do as one moves back in time and eventually becomes impossible. Do you agree? Is there something like a dividing line?

HALL: That double history has had its own particular complexities for me. In the early days of the women's movement in the 1970s, when feminist history was in its infancy, I was living with Stuart in Birmingham, but saw no obvious connections between what was going on at the Centre for Contemporary Cultural Studies and what I was beginning to try and do as a feminist historian. At that stage the two projects seemed to me to have little connection. My early work on the history of the housewife, for example, came directly from my engagement with feminist politics, rooted in my experience as a mother with two small children. In retrospect, of course, thinking historically, I can see many connections between the work that was being done at the Centre, for example around the critique of economism, the engagement with structuralism, the preoccupation with Gramsci, the attempts to theorize culture and ideology, the celebration of resistance—these were intimately linked with some of the issues which women talked about in another way.

At the same time, Thompson's The Making of the English Working Class was always described as one of the three founding texts for cultural studies and Williams's Culture and Society is also, of course, a rereading of a nineteenth-century tradition of cultural analysis. So history both was, and wasn't, at the heart of cultural studies in its Birmingham manifestations; relatively little of the published work from the Centre has been historical, and one of the most public debates of the late 1970s with which members of the Centre engaged was the somewhat vitriolic debate with Thompson over structuralism. Theory, with a big "T," was always privileged over history, which ought to have been spelt with an "e" for the dreaded empiricism.

As a feminist historian my own involvement with the rich tradition of Marxist historiography in Britain has been that of a rebellious daughter. The patriarchs were both formative and had to be rejected; "history from below" was a major inspiration for women's history but the oppressed in that version of "below" never included women.

Unfortunately I think that in general the encounter between mainstream history and cultural studies in Britain has been extremely limited. Interdisciplinary work is still the exception rather than the rule and historians have not for the most part felt it necessary to engage with a body of work which does not appear to them to relate to their concerns. Of course there are expectations as, for example, in the work that has been done on the history of popular culture in the past. But it is very striking how many historians do not feel obliged to investigate work which would relate to their own across a disciplinary boundary. A recent major reinterpretation of the history of the British Empire in the early nineteenth century, for example, does not cite Said's *Orientalism,* a book which could broadly be described as connected with cultural studies. Similarly, many practitioners of cultural studies have little interest in history and rely for their "background" on secondary sources which they do not scrutinize with the textual eagle eye that is in use for their own objects of study. Furthermore, the discourse of post-modernity in the 1990s means that it's particularly easy at the moment to discuss history when all meaning has been replaced with style—as Dick Hebdige puts it "No Classes. No history. Just a ceaseless procession of simulacra."

I imagine that many others suffer from the same quandary that I find myself in. I love the imagined certainty of being "an historian"—I know what history is and what historians do, in my dreams at least. But teaching in a Department of Cultural Studies (one, it should be said that regards cultural history as an integral part of cultural studies), and being surrounded by people who do all kinds of cultural analysis both contemporary and historical, I am aware how artificial the disciplinary boundaries are, and indeed how damaging they are. I don't really think that there should be one kind of work which historians do, one which literary theorists and critics do, and one which students of culture (which is after all what cultural studies means) do. Our objects of study are of course different, but our theoretical frameworks and methods should be complementary. The great strength of cultural studies is that it was driven by a spirit of critical inquiry which meant being voracious in looking for ways of analyzing cultural forms. It would be very sad if that challenge to disciplinary boundaries was lost and the project became rooted in a narrow definition, based on a new orthodoxy—the "discipline" of "cultural studies."

QUESTION: My question is this: What was specifically "cultural studies" about your work? And I want to put that in context. I can see where it was very good history, and very anthropological.

HALL: I'd say it was cultural history, and if cultural history isn't a part of cultural studies, then I think there's a serious problem. So if anybody wants to say that you can't do this work because it is not a part of cultural studies, go away and be a historian, then I'd better just pack up my books and despair, because I think that a lot of cultural studies is saying that, actually. And I think there's an enormous neglect of history within cultural studies. But teaching in a cultural studies department has made me think differently about history. The impact of poststructuralism would be one example of this and though I think there are dangers in what might be described as the excesses of textuality, I also think historians can learn a great deal from poststructuralism and deconstructive work. For example, in the book that I did with Leonore Davidoff on the English middle class, *Family Fortunes,* we were not sufficiently attentive, as we now realize, to the multiple meanings in the texts which we used. Indeed, I remember Cora Kaplan saying that to me before we published it, but by then it was too late; we would have had to reconsider our whole methodology. But that's one of the ways in which I now realize I could do different kinds of work on texts, without abandoning all the archival minutiae which I think is so important to the historical enterprise. I'd say that the best of English social history has always been informed by political questions and political commitments, but English social history needed both feminism and some of the questions that have been raised around cultural studies, particularly around the theorization of culture, ideology, and discourse, and the black movement and the challenging of racism to rethink and reconceptualize what the critical issues were. As a child of Thompson, which I am in terms of my formation as a historian, it's been a long engagement of many years to think about and work out the absences in *The Making of the English Working Class.* So that whole process of rethinking class and rethinking sexual antagonisms, and rethinking race and ethnicity, has had many rich sources. But I do think that cultural studies has contributed to rethinking what historians should be doing.

CAROLYN STEEDMAN: This is not in answer to your question at all, but I was thinking of my own massive transferential relationship to *The Making of the English Working Class.* Imagine making a twenty-five-year response to one particular text, which one cannot leave alone, and which will not leave one alone. The absences within it are really what one goes on trying to deal with.

HALL: British History has been traditionally committed to empiricism and extremely suspicious of theory, and the engagement of cultural studies with theoretical questions has been important for me, the conceptualizations. Because what I'm interested in is culture; I can't do without the work that thinks about how to theorize and understand culture.

QUESTION: In the contrast that you made between history and textual studies which we've heard previously, in Janet Wolff's talk, I feel peculiarly positioned as an art historian for whom textual studies are always implicated in historicity. Could you comment on this difference and on the way interpreting specific texts—monuments, town plans—may interrupt the flow of that historiographical narrative?

HALL: Well, if I understand correctly what you're asking me, that's a very difficult question because I think of what that would require to deal with it properly—that is, research into the ground plans and the commemorative monument and so on. There are histories to those, to what monuments in Jamaica look like, to where those plans come from, to what artistic conventions they were working within, to who the designers were. You could do a whole piece on that, which would require me to know a set of things about design and monumental architecture and so on, which I don't at this moment know. But I think that is the way cultural history ought to be; I don't think it's an interruption—maybe it is an interruption but it's an interruption that needs to be there, similarly with the town plans. I precisely want to be able to use those kinds of evidence, those kinds of texts that are of a different sort from the published ones. But I think that properly done cultural history requires one to enter so many different domains, and that's very taxing in terms of the kinds of, the amount, that you have to understand and grasp. That isn't a very good answer, but it makes me think about what the tensions are for me between doing history and being a feminist, which is the productive political tension out of which my work comes. And then the tensions between being a historian, being trained as a historian, and then trying to learn new kinds of methods through the development of cultural studies and associated activities. And all the time there's just *so much;* being a pilgrim is nothing on what we've got somehow to grasp and deal with and try and do properly and develop collaborative connections to help us do those things, because you can never know all those things yourself, you need other people to work with. It goes back to the point Janet was making yesterday, about the possible productive collaborations between historians, art historians, sociologists, etc. We just need each others' skills so much. Is that any help?

QUESTION: It's not just a question of an intellectual division of labor however. Your distinction between textual and historical has to be problematized by a notion of discourse as the historical enactment of meaning, what Homi Bhabha called the notion of enunciation. By disturbing those categories, don't we interrupt the history as narration?

STEEDMAN: You're talking about one answer or solution: the particular form of writing in which you present what it is you've done. You're talking about the particular organization and form of a book, in the end, aren't you? A particular way of telling which will include visual representation and commentary on visual representation. What history might do is find other ways of telling, different modes of narrative that will include the things you are talking about. So we are very profoundly talking about written forms or literary forms, textual forms, and how we produce them as historians. That's the thing that you hand over to people in the end, is a book. At least you do in historical practice.

SIOBHAN KILFEATHER: I have a question about gender and ethnicity and the deconstruction of English identity. During your talk I was thinking particularly about three texts about Empire; *Jane Eyre*—in terms of gender and voluntariness of a kind of participation in missionary activity; Aphra Behn's *Oroonoko,* in which we see the wild Irish who have been deported as criminals and slaves to Surinam and themselves become the instruments of putting down the slave rebellion; *Black Narcissus,* the Powell/Pressburger film about a nun coming to terms with being a missionary in India. She has flashbacks to her own adolescence in Ireland and the emigration of the male population that left her with the feeling that becoming a missionary was the only choice she had. And I wondered if you could say something about the ethnic makeup of missionaries and what you feel might be the equivalent today of the missionary population?

HALL: I think the first point that I'd make is that the three texts that you're drawing on are from very different periods, and since I'm arguing that English national identity, and indeed any national identity, can only be understood in terms of its historical specificities you would need to think about the particularities. In early nineteenth-century Britain, missionaries tended to come from the lower to middle middle class and were exclusively men. Gradually missionary work became a realm of opportunity for women; they were able to go out as school teachers, assistants, and later full-blown missionaries. The point you raise about the importance of the "minority" ethnic groups in missionary work is very interesting. Scot missionaries were certainly very important, and it would be fascinating to look at what kinds of ethnic identities they established for themselves and how that related to their ideas about Britain. There are crucial differences in the ways in which missionaries are situated in different societies even in the period I'm looking at. In New Zealand, for example, missionaries were well established there before New Zealand was claimed by the British crown. Some of them had established good relationships with the Maori chiefs and played a vital part in persuading them to sign the treaty of Watangi in 1840, in which the chiefs ceded New Zealand to the crown. Those missionaries were in a totally different situation from the Baptist missionaries in Jamaica, who had a complex and tortured relationship with the colonial authorities and who were in 1831–33 engaged in a political struggle with successive British governments to bring an end to slavery. On *Jane Eyre,* I think it would be better if Cora Kaplan said something because that's what she's working on.

CORA KAPLAN: Well, *Jane Eyre,* as Catherine said, is part of the debate in this period and it is not just emblematic. Like Carlyle's discourse, it helps to construct, to reconstruct, and to thematize and combine new elements of the discussion about Jamaican missionaries abroad, and it does so in a very roundabout way. If you'll remember, St. John Rivers goes off to India, and why he's chosen as an Indian missionary I think is extremely interesting. In relation to the demonized Jamaica of the text, the text also has a huge metaphorical association of slavery with Jane, but also disassociated powerfully from the question of race. So slavery is a metaphor that both joins Jane together with any other rebel slave and that works to distinguish her from them. It's also a book which joins those debates about free labor and free villages in Jamaica, with the whole question of peasantry, riot, and revolt in England and on the Continent. And the role of missionaries both as regulators and enforcers of Englishness and as rebels against the more authoritarian and masculine forms of that Englishness are textualized in *Jane Eyre* in very interesting and contradictory ways. So, that's just a taste of the kind of things you get into when you start to look at the productive ways in which an imaginative text tries to combine and recombine and restate the arguments that are going on in the public sphere at this time.

HALL: Historians are always terribly anxious about talking about anything that's not in "their period." But I know with *Oroonoko* that there are whole sets of discourses around race which are reorganized, reformulated, rearticulated again and again in the history of British discourses on race and racism. So I could be sure, if I was to do the work, that I would be able to find traces in those texts of previous conceptions which would be rearticulations of ideas which had been worked through in previous periods. I think that's happening all the time, that we're looking at reformulations, rearticulations, reworkings of old ideas, as well as positively new ideas entering discourses. But positively new ideas don't enter all that often. So when you think about the new racism of the 1980s being defined as new because this is a form of cultural racism rather than biological racism, what I'm saying is look here, in the 1830s and 40s we also have cultural racism not biological racism, and that runs right against progressive notions of history which assume that everything always gets better, that people always get more civilized. What I'm pointing out is that there are very serious forms of regression in this area.

QUESTION: I have a question more about clarification because I'm getting a little bit confused. I get the impression that I'm seeing two different kinds of story being told between both your and Carolyn Steedman's presentations. On the one hand I see both of you somehow speaking about that which escapes the text, roles which are incompletely signified in the kinds of texts that we use for historical research—I think those were your words, Catherine. And I'm somehow getting different worlds that are escaping the text from both of your kinds of research. And I wonder if I'm sensing the difference between what would constitute a case study and what is left out of texts, and what constitutes a narrative—as I see it in your telling of history, Catherine—which seems to signify something different which is escaping the text. And my temptation right now is to pose a question around the politics, the different politics, that I see at play here. In other words, my question to Catherine would be that even though I understand how the kind of history you are doing illuminates how there are reconstitutions and reconstructions of the same sorts of stories in the contemporary around race, I'm missing a sense of the politics of that which I think perhaps relates back to the earlier question of cultural studies. I'm tempted to ask Carolyn to speak to Catherine's history in terms of the question of the case study. Perhaps I've got that all wrong, but that's how I'm seeing it right now.

HAROLD HINES: There was one important group left out of your analysis, which struck me must have offered some sort of model for freedom from slavery, and that was the marooned societies in the interior of Jamaica. I was wondering if you've done any work with them and thought about their relationship with the missionary movement and the island and so on.

HALL: That's a very interesting point, but as yet I have done very little work on the Maroons. At the time of the Morant Bay rebellion in 1865 the black leadership attempted to win Maroon support. Their failure was critical to the collapse and suppression of the rebellion. The Maroons were actively involved with the British troops in hunting down the rebels. Since the Maroon wars of the eighteenth century, the Maroons had made a deal with the whites in Jamaica that in return for living in peace and freedom they would refuse quarter to runaway slaves and indeed assist in their capture. So there was a terrible fracturing of the relations between blacks and Maroons which had disastrous consequences for black resistance.

17

Cultural Studies and its Theoretical Legacies

Stuart Hall

This Conference provides us with an opportunity for a moment of self-reflection on cultural studies as a practice, on its institutional positioning, and what Lidia Curti so effectively reminds us is both the marginality and the centrality of its practitioners as critical intellectuals. Inevitably, this involves reflecting on, and intervening in, the project of cultural studies itself.

My title, "Cultural Studies and its Theoretical Legacies," suggests a look back to the past, to consult and think about the Now and the Future of cultural studies by way of a retrospective glance. It does seem necessary to do some genealogical and archaeological work on the archive. Now the question of the archives is extremely difficult for me because, where cultural studies is concerned, I sometimes feel like a *tableau vivant,* a spirit of the past resurrected, laying claim to the authority of an origin. After all, didn't cultural studies emerge somewhere at that moment when I first met Raymond Williams, or in the glance I exchanged with Richard Hoggart? In that moment, cultural studies was born; it emerged full grown from the head! I do want to talk about the past, but definitely not in that way. I don't want to talk about British cultural studies (which is in any case a pretty awkward signifier for me) in a patriarchal way, as the keeper of the conscience of cultural studies, hoping to police you back into line with what it really was if only you knew. That is to say, I want to absolve myself of the many burdens of representation which people carry around—I carry around at least three: I'm expected to speak for the entire black race on all questions theoretical, critical, etc., and sometimes for British politics, as well as for cultural studies. This is what is known as the black person's burden, and I would like to absolve myself of it at this moment.

That means, paradoxically, speaking autobiographically. Autobiography is usually thought of as seizing the authority of authenticity. But in order not to be authoritative, I've got to speak autobiographically. I'm going to tell you about my own take on certain theoretical legacies and moments in cultural studies, not because it is the truth or the only way of telling the history. I myself have told it many other ways before; and I intend to tell it in a different way later. But just at this moment, for this conjuncture, I want to take a position in relation to the "grand narrative" of cultural studies for the purposes of opening up some reflections on cultural studies as a practice, on our institutional position, and on its project. I want to do that by referring to some theoretical legacies or theoretical moments, but in a very particular way. This is not a commentary on the success or effectiveness of different theoretical positions in cultural studies (that is for some other occasion). It is an attempt to say something about what certain theoretical moments in cultural studies have been like for me, and from that position, to take some bearings about the general question of the politics of theory.

Cultural studies is a discursive formation, in Foucault's sense. It has no simple origins, though some of us were present at some point when it first named itself in that way. Much of the work out of which it grew, in my own experience, was already present in the work of other people. Raymond Williams has made the same point, charting the roots of cultural studies in the early adult education movement in his essay on "The Future of Cultural Studies" (1989b). "The relation between a project and a formation is always decisive," he says, because they are "different ways of materializing . . . then of describing a common disposition of energy and direction." Cultural studies has multiple discourses; it has a number of different histories. It is a whole set of formations; it has its own different conjunctures and moments in the past. It included many different kinds of work. I want to insist on that! It always was a set of unstable formations. It was "centered" only in quotation marks, in a particular kind of way which I want to define in a moment. It had many trajectories; many people had and have different trajectories through it; it was constructed by a number of different methodologies and theoretical positions, all of them in contention. Theoretical work in the Centre for Contemporary Cultural Studies was more appropriately called theoretical noise. It was accompanied by a great deal of bad feeling, argument, unstable anxieties, and angry silences.

Now, does it follow that cultural studies is not a policed disciplinary area? That it is whatever people do, if they choose to call or locate themselves within the project and practice of cultural studies? I am not happy with that formulation either. Although cultural studies as a project is open-ended, it can't be simply pluralist in that way. Yes, it refuses to be a master discourse or a meta-discourse of any kind. Yes, it is a project that is always open to that which it doesn't yet know, to that which it can't yet name. But it does have some will to connect; it does have some stake in the choices it makes. It does matter whether cultural studies is this or that. It can't be just any old thing which chooses to march under a particular banner. It is a serious enterprise, or project, and that is inscribed in what is sometimes called the "political" aspect of cultural studies. Not that there's one politics already inscribed in it. But there is something *at stake* in cultural studies, in a way that I think, and hope, is not exactly true of many other very important intellectual and critical practices. Here one registers the tension between a refusal to close the field, to police it and, at the same time, a determination to stake out some positions within it and argue for them. That is the tension—the dialogic approach to theory—that I want to try to speak to in a number of different ways in the course of this paper. I don't believe knowledge is closed, but I do believe that politics is impossible without what I have called "the arbitrary closure"; without what Homi Bhabha called social agency as an arbitrary closure. That is to say, I don't understand a practice which aims to make a difference in the world, which doesn't have some points of difference or distinction which it has to stake out, which really matter. It is a question of positionalities. Now, it is true that those positionalities are never final, they're never absolute. They can't be translated intact from one conjuncture to another; they cannot be depended on to remain in the same place. I want to go back to that moment of "staking out a wager" in cultural studies, to those moments in which the positions began to matter.

This is a way of opening the question of the "worldliness" of cultural studies, to borrow a term from Edward Said. I am not dwelling on the secular connotations of the metaphor of worldliness here, but on the worldliness of cultural studies. I'm dwelling on the "dirtiness" of it: the dirtiness of the semiotic game, if I can put it that way. I'm trying to return the project of cultural studies from the clean air of meaning and textuality and theory to the something nasty down below. This involves the difficult exercise of examining some of the key theoretical turns or moments in cultural studies.

The first trace that I want to deconstruct has to do with a view of British cultural studies which often distinguishes it by the fact that, at a certain moment, it became a Marxist critical practice. What exactly does that assignation of cultural studies as a Marxist critical theory mean? How can we think cultural studies at that moment? What moment is it we are speaking of? What does that mean for the theoretical legacies, traces, and aftereffects which Marxism continues to have in cultural studies? There are a number of ways of telling that history, and let me remind you that I'm not proposing this as the only story. But I do want to set it up in what I think may be a slightly surprising way to you.

I entered cultural studies from the New Left, and the New Left always regarded Marxism as a problem, as trouble, as danger, not as a solution. Why? It had nothing to do with theoretical questions as such or in isolation. It had to do with the fact that my own (and its own) political formation occurred in a moment historically very much like the one we are in now—which I am astonished that so few people have addressed—the moment of the disintegration of a certain kind of Marxism. In fact, the first British New Left emerged in 1956 at the moment of the disintegration of an entire historical/political project. In that sense I came into Marxism backwards: against the Soviet tanks in Budapest, as it were. What I mean by that is certainly not that I wasn't profoundly, and that cultural studies then wasn't from the beginning, profoundly influenced by the questions that Marxism as a theoretical project put on the agenda: the power, the global reach and history-making capacities of capital; the question of class; the complex relationships between power, which is an easier term to establish in the discourses of culture than exploitation, and exploitation; the question of a general theory which could, in a critical way, connect together in a critical reflection different domains of life, politics and theory, theory and practice, economic, political, ideological questions, and so on; the notion of critical knowledge itself and the production of critical knowledge as a practice. These important, central questions are what one meant by working within shouting distance of Marxism, working on Marxism, working against Marxism, working with it, working to try to develop Marxism.

There never was a prior moment when cultural studies and Marxism represented a perfect theoretical fit. From the beginning (to use this way of speaking for a moment) there was always-already the question of the great inadequacies, theoretically and politically, the resounding silences, the great evasions of Marxism—the things that Marx did not talk about or seem to understand which were our privileged object of study: culture, ideology, language, the symbolic. These were always-already, instead, the things which had imprisoned Marxism as a mode of thought, as an activity of critical practice—its orthodoxy, its doctrinal character, its determinism, its reductionism, its immutable law of history, its status as a metanarrative. That is to say, the encounter between British cultural studies and Marxism has first to be understood as the engagement with a problem—not a theory, not even a problematic. It begins, and develops through the critique of a certain reductionism and economism, which I think is not extrinsic but intrinsic to Marxism; a contestation with the model of base and superstructure, through which sophisticated and vulgar Marxism alike had tried to think the relationships between society, economy, and culture. It was located and sited in a necessary and prolonged and as yet unending contestation with the question of false consciousness. In my own case, it required a not-yet-completed contestation with the profound Eurocentrism of Marxist theory. I want to make this very precise. It is not just a matter of where Marx happened to be born, and of what he talked about, but of the model at the center of the most developed parts of Marxist theory, which suggested that capitalism evolved organically from within its own transformations. Whereas I came from a society where the profound integument of capitalist society, economy, and culture had been imposed by conquest and colonization. This is a theoretical, not a vulgar critique. I don't blame Marx because of where he was born; I'm questioning the theory for the model around which it is articulated: its Eurocentrism.

I want to suggest a different metaphor for theoretical work: the metaphor of struggle, of wrestling with the angels. The only theory worth having is that which you have to fight off, not that which you speak with profound fluency. I mean to say something later about the astonishing theoretical fluency of cultural studies now. But my own experience of theory—and Marxism is certainly a case in point—is of wrestling with the angels—a metaphor you can take as literally as you like. I remember wrestling with Althusser. I remember looking at the idea of "theoretical practice" in *Reading Capital* and thinking, "I've gone as far in this book as it is proper to go." I felt, I will not give an inch to this profound misreading, this super-structuralist mistranslation, of classical Marxism, unless he beats me down, unless he defeats me in the spirit. He'll have to march over me to convince me. I warred with him, to the death. A long, rambling piece I wrote (Hall, 1974) on Marx's 1857 Introduction to *The Grundrisse,* in which I tried to stake out the difference between structuralism in Marx's epistemology and Althusser's, was only the tip of the iceberg of this long engagement. And that is not simply a personal question. In the Centre for Contemporary Cultural Studies, for five or six years, long after the anti-theoreticism or resistance to theory of cultural studies had been overcome, and we decided, in a very un-British way, we had to take the plunge into theory, we walked right around the entire circumference of European thought, in order not to be, in any simple capitulation to the *zeitgeist,* Marxists. We read German idealism, we read Weber upside down, we read Hegelian idealism, we read idealistic art criticism. (I've written about this in the article called "The Hinterland of Science: Sociology of Knowledge" [1980d] as well as in "Cultural Studies and the Centre: Some Problems and Problematics" [1980c].)

So the notion that Marxism and cultural studies slipped into place, recognized an immediate affinity, joined hands in some teleological or Hegelian moment of synthesis, and there was the founding moment of cultural studies, is entirely mistaken. It couldn't have been more different from that. And when, eventually, in the seventies, British cultural studies did advance—in many different ways, it must be said—within the problematic of Marxism, you should hear the term problematic in a genuine way, not just in a formalist-theoretical way: as a problem; as much about struggling against the constraints and limits of that model as about the necessary questions it required us to address. And when, in the end, in my own work, I tried to learn from and work with the theoretical gains of Gramsci, it was only because certain strategies of evasion had forced Gramsci's work, in a number of different ways, to respond to what I can only call (here's another metaphor for theoretical work) the conundrums of theory, the things which Marxist theory couldn't answer, the things about the modern world which Gramsci discovered remained unresolved within the theoretical framework of grand theory— Marxism—in which he continued to work. At a certain point, the questions I still wanted to address in short were inaccessible to me except via a detour through Gramsci. Not because Gramsci resolved them but because he at least addressed many of them. I don't want to go through what it is I personally think cultural studies in the British context, in a certain period, learned from Gramsci: immense amounts about the nature of culture itself, about the discipline of the conjunctural, about the importance of historical specificity, about the enormously productive metaphor of hegemony, about the way in which one can think questions of class relations only by using the displaced notion of ensemble and blocs. These are the particular gains of the "detour" via Gramsci, but I'm not trying to talk about that. I want to say, in this context, about Gramsci, that while Gramsci belonged and belongs to the problematic of Marxism, his importance for this moment of British cultural studies is precisely the degree to which he radically *displaced* some of the inheritances of Marxism in cultural studies. The radical character of Gramsci's "displacement" of Marxism has not yet been understood and probably won't ever be reckoned with, now we are entering the era of post-Marxism. Such is the nature of the movement of history and of intellectual fashion. But Gramsci also did something else for cultural studies, and I want to say a little bit about that because it refers to what I call the need to reflect on our institutional position, and our intellectual practice.

I tried on many occasions, and other people in British cultural studies and at the Centre especially have tried, to describe what it is we thought we were doing with the kind of intellectual work we set in place in the Centre. I have to confess that, though I've read many, more elaborated and sophisticated, accounts, Gramsci's account still seems to me to come closest to expressing what it is I think we were trying to do. Admittedly, there's a problem about his phrase "the production of organic intellectuals." But there is no doubt in my mind that we were trying to find an institutional practice in cultural studies that might produce an organic intellectual. We didn't know previously what that would mean, in the context of Britain in the 1970s, and we weren't sure we would recognize him or her if we managed to produce it. The problem about the concept of an organic intellectual is that it appears to align intellectuals with an emerging historic movement and we couldn't tell then, and can hardly tell now, where that emerging historical movement was to be found. We were organic intellectuals without any organic point of reference; organic intellectuals with a nostalgia or will or hope (to use Gramsci's phrase from another context) that at some point we would be prepared in intellectual work for that kind of relationship, if such a conjuncture ever appeared. More truthfully, we were prepared to imagine or model or simulate such a relationship in its absence: "pessimism of the intellect, optimism of the will."

But I think it is very important that Gramsci's thinking around these questions certainly captures part of what we were about. Because a second aspect of Gramsci's definition of intellectual work, which I think has always been lodged somewhere close to the notion of cultural studies as a project, has been his requirement that the "organic intellectual" must work on two fronts at one and the same time. On the one hand, we had to be at the very forefront of intellectual theoretical work because, as Gramsci says, it is the job of the organic intellectual to know more than the traditional intellectuals do: really know, not just pretend to know, not just to have the facility of knowledge, but to know deeply and profoundly. So often knowledge for Marxism is pure recognition—the production again of what we have always known! If you are in the game of hegemony you have to be smarter than "them." Hence, there are no theoretical limits from which cultural studies can turn back. But the second aspect is just as crucial: that the organic intellectual cannot absolve himself or herself from the responsibility of transmitting those ideas, that knowledge, through the intellectual function, to those who do not belong, professionally, in the intellectual class. And unless those two fronts are operating at the same time, or at least unless those two ambitions are part of the project of cultural studies, you can get enormous theoretical advance without any engagement at the level of the political project.

I'm extremely anxious that you should not decode what I'm saying as an anti-theoretical discourse. It is not anti-theory, but it does have something to do with the conditions and problems of developing intellectual and theoretical work as a political practice. It is an extremely difficult road, not resolving the tensions between those two requirements, but living with them. Gramsci never asked us to resolve them, but he gave us a practical example of how to live with them. We never produced organic intellectuals (would that we had) at the Centre. We never connected with that rising historic movement; it was a metaphoric exercise. Nevertheless, metaphors are serious things. They affect one's practice. I'm trying to redescribe cultural studies as theoretical work which must go on and on living with that tension.

I want to look at two other theoretical moments in cultural studies which interrupted the already-interrupted history of its formation. Some of these developments came as it were from outer space: they were not at all generated from the inside, they were not part of an inner-unfolding general theory of culture. Again and again, the so-called unfolding of cultural studies was interrupted by a break, by real ruptures, by exterior forces; the interruption, as it were, of new ideas, which decentered what looked like the accumulating practice of the work. There's another metaphor for theoretical work: theoretical work as interruption.

There were at least two interruptions in the work of the Centre for Contemporary Cultural Studies: The first around feminism, and the second around questions of race. This is not an attempt to sum up the theoretical and political advances and consequences for British cultural studies of the feminist intervention; that is for another time, another place. But I don't want, either, to invoke that moment in an open-ended and casual way. For cultural studies (in addition to many other theoretical projects), the intervention of feminism was specific and decisive. It was ruptural. It reorganized the field in quite concrete ways. First, the opening of the question of the personal as political, and its consequences for changing the object of study in cultural studies, was completely revolutionary in a theoretical and practical way. Second, the radical expansion of the notion of power, which had hitherto been very much developed within the framework of the notion of the public, the public domain, with the effect that we could not use the term power—so key to the earlier problematic of hegemony—in the same way. Third, the centrality of questions of gender and sexuality to the understanding of power itself. Fourth, the opening of many of the questions that we thought we had abolished around the dangerous area of the subjective and the subject, which lodged those questions at the center of cultural studies as a theoretical practice. Fifth, the "re-opening" of the closed frontier between social theory and the theory of the unconscious—psychoanalysis. It's hard to describe the import of the opening of that new continent in cultural studies, marked out by the relationship—or rather, what Jacqueline Rose has called the as yet "unsettled relations"—between feminism, psychoanalysis, and cultural studies, or indeed how it was accomplished.

We know it was, but it's not known generally how and where feminism first broke in. I use the metaphor deliberately: As the thief in the night, it broke in; interrupted, made an unseemly noise, seized the time, crapped on the table of cultural studies. The title of the volume in which this dawn-raid was first accomplished—*Women Take Issue*— is instructive: for they "took issue" in both senses—took over that year's book and initiated a quarrel. But I want to tell you something else about it. Because of the growing importance of feminist work and the early beginnings of the feminist movement outside in the very early 1970s, many of us in the Centre—mainly, of course, men—thought it was time there was good feminist work in cultural studies. And we indeed tried to buy it in, to import it, to attract good feminist scholars. As you might expect, many of the women in cultural studies weren't terribly interested in this benign project. We were opening the door to feminist studies, being good, transformed men. And yet, when it broke in through the window, every single unsuspected resistance rose to the surface— fully installed patriarchal power, which believed it had disavowed itself. There are no leaders here, we used to say; we are all graduate students and members of staff together, learning how to practice cultural studies. You can decide whatever you want to decide, etc. And yet, when it came to the question of the reading list . . . Now that's where I really discovered about the gendered nature of power. Long, long after I was able to pronounce the words, I encountered the reality of Foucault's profound insight into the individual reciprocity of knowledge and power. Talking about giving up power is a radically different experience from being silenced. That is another way of thinking, and another metaphor for theory: the way feminism broke, and broke into, cultural studies.

Then there is the question of race in cultural studies. I've talked about the important "extrinsic" sources of the formation of cultural studies—for example, in what I called the moment of the New Left, and its original quarrel with Marxism—out of which cultural studies grew. And yet, of course, that was a profoundly English or British moment. Actually getting cultural studies to put on its own agenda the critical questions of race, the politics of race, the resistance to racism, the critical questions of cultural politics, was itself a profound theoretical struggle, a struggle of which *Policing the Crisis*, was, curiously, the first and very late example. It represented a decisive turn in my own theoretical and intellectual work, as well as in that of the Centre. Again, it was only accomplished as the result of a long, and sometimes bitter—certainly bitterly contested—internal struggle against a resounding but unconscious silence. A struggle which continued in what has since come to be known, but only in the rewritten history, as one of the great seminal books of the Centre for Cultural Studies, *The Empire Strikes Back*. In actuality, Paul Gilroy and the group of people who produced the book found it extremely difficult to create the necessary theoretical and political space in the Centre in which to work on the project.

I want to hold to the notion, implicit in both these examples, that movements provoke theoretical moments. And historical conjunctures insist on theories: they are real moments in the evolution of theory. But here I have to stop and retrace my steps. Because I think you could hear, once again, in what I'm saying a kind of invocation of a simple-minded anti-theoretical populism, which does not respect and acknowledge the crucial importance, at each point in the moves I'm trying to renarrativize, of what I would call the necessary delay or detour through theory. I want to talk about that "necessary detour" for a moment. What decentered and dislocated the settled path of the Centre for Contemporary Cultural Studies certainly, and British cultural studies to some extent in general, is what is sometimes called "the linguistic turn": the discovery of discursivity, of textuality. There are casualties in the Centre around those names as well. They were wrestled with, in exactly the same way I've tried to describe earlier. But the gains which were made through an engagement with them are crucially important in understanding how theory came to be advanced in that work. And yet, in my view, such theoretical "gains" can never be a self-sufficient moment.

Again, there is no space here to do more than begin to list the theoretical advances which were made by the encounters with structuralist, semiotic, and poststructuralist work: the crucial importance of language and of the linguistic metaphor to *any* study of culture; the expansion of the notion of text and textuality, both as a source of meaning, and as that which escapes and postpones meaning; the recognition of the heterogeneity, of the multiplicity, of meanings, of the struggle to close arbitrarily the infinite semiosis beyond meaning; the acknowledgment of textuality and cultural power, of representation itself, as a site of power and regulation; of the symbolic as a source of identity. These are enormous theoretical advances, though of course, it had always attended to questions of language (Raymond Williams's work, long before the semiotic revolution, is central there). Nevertheless, the refiguring of theory, made as a result of having to think questions of culture through the metaphors of language and textuality, represents a point beyond which cultural studies must now always necessarily locate itself. The metaphor of the discursive, of textuality, instantiates a necessary delay, a displacement, which I think is *always* implied in the concept of culture. If you work on culture, or if you've tried to work on some other really important things and you find yourself driven back to culture, if culture happens to be what seizes hold of your soul, you have to recognize that you will always be working in an area of displacement. There's always something decentered about the medium of culture, about language, textuality, and signification, which always escapes and evades the attempt to link it, directly and immediately, with other structures. And yet, at the same time, the shadow, the imprint, the trace, of those other formations, of the intertextuality of texts in their institutional positions, of texts as sources of power, of textuality as a site of representation and resistance, all of those questions can never be erased from cultural studies.

The question is what happens when a field, which I've been trying to describe in a very punctuated, dispersed, and interrupted way, as constantly changing directions, and which is defined as a political project, tries to develop itself as some kind of coherent theoretical intervention? Or, to put the same question in reverse, what happens when an academic and theoretical enterprise tries to engage in pedagogies which enlist the active engagement of individuals and groups, tries to make a difference in the institutional world in which it is located? These are extremely difficult issues to resolve, because what is asked of us is to say "yes" and "no" at one and the same time. It asks us to assume that culture will always work through its textualities—and at the same time that textuality is never enough. But never enough of what? Never enough for what? That is an extremely difficult question to answer because, philosophically, it has always been impossible in the theoretical field of cultural studies—whether it is conceived either in terms of texts and contexts, of intertextuality, or of the historical formations in which cultural practices are lodged—to get anything like an adequate theoretical account of culture's relations and its effects. Nevertheless I want to insist that until and unless cultural studies learns to live with this tension, a tension that all textual practices must assume—a tension which Said describes as the study of the text in its affiliations with "institutions, offices, agencies, classes, academies, corporations, groups, ideologically defined parties and professions, nations, races, and genders"—it will have renounced its "worldly" vocation. That is to say, unless and until one respects the necessary displacement of culture, and yet is always irritated by its failure to reconcile itself with other questions that matter, with other questions that cannot and can never be fully covered by critical textuality in its elaborations, cultural studies as a project, an intervention, remains incomplete. If you lose hold of the tension, you can do extremely fine intellectual work, but you will have lost intellectual practice as a politics. I offer this to you, not because that's what cultural studies ought to be, or because that's what the Centre managed to do well, but simply because I think that, overall, is what defines cultural studies as a project. Both in the British and the American context, cultural studies has drawn the attention itself, not just because of its sometimes dazzling internal theoretical development, but because it holds theoretical and political questions in an ever irresolvable but permanent tension. It constantly allows the one to irritate, bother, and disturb the other, without insisting on some final theoretical closure.

I've been talking very much in terms of a previous history. But I have been reminded of this tension very forcefully in the discussions on AIDS. AIDS is one of the questions which urgently brings before us our marginality as critical intellectuals in making real effects in the world. And yet it has often been represented for us in contradictory ways. Against the urgency of people dying in the streets, what in God's name is the point of cultural studies? What is the point of the study of representations, if there is no response to the question of what you say to someone who wants to know if they should take a drug and if that means they'll die two days later or a few months earlier? At that point, I think anybody who is into cultural studies seriously as an intellectual practice, must feel, on their pulse, its ephemerality, its insubstantiality, how little it registers, how little we've been able to change anything or get anybody to do anything. If you don't feel that as one tension in the work that you are doing, theory has let you off the hook. On the other hand, in the end, I don't agree with the way in which this dilemma is often posed for us, for it is indeed a more complex and displaced question than just people dying out there. The question of AIDS is an extremely important terrain of struggle and contestation. In addition to the people we know who are dying, or have died, or will, there are the many people dying who are never spoken of. How could we say that the question of AIDS is not also a question of who gets represented and who does not? AIDS is the site at which the advance of sexual politics is being rolled back. It's a site at which not only people will die, but desire and pleasure will also die if certain metaphors do not survive, or survive in the wrong way. Unless we operate in this tension, we don't know what cultural studies can do, can't, can never do; but also, what it has to do, what it alone has a privileged capacity to do. It has to analyze certain things about the constitutive and political nature of representation itself, about its complexities, about the effects of language, about textuality as a site of life and death. Those are the things cultural studies can address.

I've used that example, not because it's a perfect example, but because it's a specific example, because it has a concrete meaning, because it challenges us in its complexity, and in so doing has things to teach us about the future of serious theoretical work. It preserves the essential nature of intellectual work and critical reflection, the irreducibility of the insights which theory can bring to political practice, insights which cannot be arrived at in any other way. And at the same time, it rivets us to the necessary modesty of theory, the necessary modesty of cultural studies as an intellectual project.

I want to end in two ways. First I want to address the problem of the institutionalization of these two constructions: British cultural studies and American cultural studies. And then, drawing on the metaphors about theoretical work which I tried to launch (not I hope by claiming authority or authenticity but in what inevitably has to be a polemical, positional, political way), to say something about how the field of cultural studies has to be defined.

I don't know what to say about American cultural studies. I am completely dumfounded by it. I think of the struggles to get cultural studies into the institution in the British context, to squeeze three or four jobs for anybody under some heavy disguise, compared with the rapid institutionalization which is going on in the U.S. The comparison is not only valid for cultural studies. If you think of the important work which has been done in feminist history or theory in Britian and ask how many of those women have ever had full-time academic jobs in their lives or are likely to, you get a sense of what marginality is really about. So the enormous explosion of cultural studies in the U.S., its rapid professionalization and institutionalization, is not a moment which any of us who tried to set up a marginalized Centre in a university like Birmingham could, in any simple way, regret. And yet I have to say, in the strongest sense, that it reminds me of the ways in which, in Britian, we are always aware of institutionalization as a moment of profound danger. Now, I've been saying that dangers are not places you run away from but places that you go towards. So I simply want you to know that my own feeling is that the explosion of cultural studies along with other forms of critical theory in the academy represents a moment of extraordinarily profound danger. Why? Well, it would be excessively vulgar to talk about such things as how many jobs there are, how much money there is around, and how much pressure that puts on people to do what they think of as critical political work and intellectual work of a critical kind, while also looking over their shoulders at the promotions stakes and the publication stakes, and so on. Let me instead return to the point that I made before: my astonishment at what I called the theoretical fluency of cultural studies in the United States.

Now, the question of theoretical fluency is a difficult and provoking metaphor, and I want only to say one word about it. Some time ago, looking at what one can only call the deconstructive deluge (as opposed to deconstructive turn) which had overtaken American literary studies, in its formalist mode, I tried to distinguish the extremely important theoretical and intellectual work which it had made possible in cultural studies from a mere repetition, a sort of mimicry or deconstructive ventriloquism which sometimes passes as a serious intellectual exercise. My fear at that moment was that if cultural studies gained an equivalent institutionalization in the American context, it would, in rather the same way, formalize out of existence the critical questions of power, history, and politics. Paradoxically, what I mean by theoretical fluency is exactly the reverse. There is no moment now, in American cultural studies, where we are *not* able, extensively and without end, to theorize power—politics, race, class, and gender, subjugation, domination, exclusion, marginality, Otherness, etc. There is hardly anything in cultural studies which isn't so theorized. And yet, there is the nagging doubt that this overwhelming textualization of cultural studies' own discourses somehow constitutes power and politics as exclusively matters of language and textuality itself. Now, this is not to say that I don't think that questions of power and the political have to be and are always lodged within representations, that they are always discursive questions. Nevertheless, there are ways of constituting power as an easy floating signifier which just leaves the crude exercise and connections of power and culture altogether emptied of any signification. That is what I take to be the moment of danger in the institutionalization of cultural studies in this highly rarified and enormously elaborated and well-funded professional world of American academic life. It has nothing whatever to do with cultural studies making itself more like British cultural studies, which is, I think, an entirely false and empty cause to try to propound. I have specifically tried not to speak of the past in an attempt to police the present and the future. But I do want to extract, finally, from the narrative I have constructed of the past some guidelines for my own work and perhaps for some of yours.

I come back to the deadly seriousness of intellectual work. It is a deadly serious matter. I come back to the critical distinction between intellectual work and academic work: they overlap, they abut with one another, they feed off one another, the one provides you with the means to do the other. But they are not the same thing. I come back to the difficulty of instituting a genuine cultural and critical practice, which is intended to produce some kind of organic intellectual political work, which does not try to inscribe itself in the overarching metanarrative of achieved knowledges, within the institutions. I come back to theory and politics, the politics of theory. Not theory as the will to truth, but theory as a set of contested, localized, conjunctural knowledges, which have to be debated in a dialogical way. But also as a practice which always thinks about its intervention in a world in which it would make some difference, in which it would have some effect. Finally, a practice which understands the need for intellectual modesty. I do think there is all the difference in the world between understanding the politics of intellectual work and substituting intellectual work for politics.

DISCUSSION: STUART HALL

TOM PRASCH: I wonder if you could talk a bit about *New Times* as an ongoing struggle within and around English Marxism and cultural studies?

HALL: *New Times* is the name of an intervention which a number of people made in the journal *Marxism Today* in a series of essays, partly on economic questions, partly on cultural questions. It could be read as an intersection between a radical political project and a selective number of themes in postmodernism. It takes on certain debates about the nature of the advanced capitalist economy, and about the nature and effect of globalization on that. More than that, it metaphorically renders the enormous breaks and caesuras going on around us in the political life of the world. It registers a series of "New Times" as the conjuncture in which we are living, and in which many of the guides and metaphors of the past, many of the theoretical paradigms that have come to be held in a rather doctrinal way, many of the political programs and strategies of reform are thrown open to inspection. Not tossed away, necessarily, but thrown open to inspection in a kind of critical reflection which, as it were, confesses that most of the time most of the people don't quite know where they are or where they are going.

In this context, there are many different arguments, which I won't go into, around whether "New Times" is only a sort of hint of the future, an attempt to read off from certain leading developments in some advanced societies what might be important underlying historical trends. I say that only because the book and the interventions around it and the subsequent debates have often been read as if they were staking out a new position, but it is trying to open new debates. Though it's perfectly clear from the book that people don't agree with one another, from one page to another, such are the habits of critical and theoretical orthodoxy. It's assumed that if you write a book you must know what you are talking about; you must already have a position which you are trying to impose on someone else. So we keep saying, "What I've just said may not be true. I would like to discuss with other people whether this might be true because we are in 'New Times.'" Now, it has a bearing, obviously, on cultural studies. Although it doesn't call itself "cultural studies," many of the people who are contributing to it are people who have been formed within cultural studies in Britain, which by now is a house of many mansions, but a lot of people who are in it don't know one end of cultural studies from another. It is, obviously, in some ways an attempt to translate some of the modes of work and insights of cultural studies into a wider terrain. Nevertheless, it figures as part of my ongoing responsibility for a debate which is wider, which cannot be contained simply in an academic debate. That's not to say it doesn't draw on academic research: there's a whole literature around flexible specialization and global integration on which the "New Times" debate is drawing. But it is drawing on it in a way which suggests that these are questions that need to be debated in a political as well as an intellectual and cultural-critical-theoretical arena. Those different overlapping arenas of debate do exist; they can be found. And intellectuals who believe in intellectual work as a serious project must try to address those questions to those audiences as part of *what they do,* as part of a responsibility that is laid on them in trying to be critical intellectuals and to do critical intellectual work.

ROSALIND BRUNT: I'd like you to say a bit more about Gramsci's notion of the organic intellectual. I think there's another point that Gramsci makes which relates to another moment in the Centre which you didn't raise. This involves my favorite metaphor for the organic intellectual: the whalebone in the corset. This is not only a rather feminized metaphor, but it has that notion that you were suggesting about real rigorous seriousness. I liked that sort of iron discipline of the corset. Also, of course, as a metaphor, it is about being supportive. But where Gramsci used it, what he actually meant it for was talking about contact with the people. I think the point that you didn't mention in defining the organic intellectual is the way in which you not only transmit to the people but you learn from them in Gramsci's sense. I can understand why you didn't mention it because of all the sentimental populism that it can lead to. But it connects to a very important moment in the Centre For Contemporary Cultural Studies around ethnography. I wondered if you'd care to comment on that.

HALL: I think you not only sussed out my silence, if I might put it that way, but sussed out the reason for my silence as well. I've heard all of the metaphors of the organic intellectual used in ways which simplify the notion and which aren't critical of their vanguardist implications, or which suggest that it is perfectly easy to find those outside voices and take responsibility for them. The question is how to do it without vulgar popularization, which is not at all what Gramsci means by the mutually educative relationship. I can't respond in a very adequate way to the question about how one takes that responsibility, partly because it is conjunctural to specific cultures. Indeed, I think that part of the way in which new forms of cultural studies rid themselves of the possible shadow of earlier forms is precisely to go through that argument: how on earth can we make those connections without absolving ourselves of the need for reflection and theoretical work? I think that discussion, difficult as it is, has to be engaged. And certainly the Centre, as you know, did not find it easy. And there isn't some movement out there waiting for it to be done. So I am very anxious not to suggest that this is an easy evangelical call to arms, as if you could just go out and do it. What I want to say is something more like what I meant by the notion of modesty. You have to work under the pressure to find that moment, that connection. And with the sense that when you don't, even though it may not have been possible, something is missing, some voices which ought to be in your head are not in your head. You have to recognize that the theory is going to run away with you. You're going to end up at some point with the illusion that you can cover, in the textuality of the critical debate, the whole of the world, not recognizing the worldliness of the object you are trying to analyze and place theoretically.

But let me also say that I think it can be made more often than we think it can. While certain institutional conditions block its being made, being institutionalized also means struggling against the institutional constraints which make it impossible to make those kinds of links, and to write in that kind of way. And the language with which we communicate with one another and do our intellectual work is also part of that struggle to be overheard, if not today, then sometime. That's what I mean by living with the possibility that there *could* be, sometime, a movement which would be larger than the movement of petit-bourgeois intellectuals, if you will forgive my using a vulgar phrase. That's what I mean by our modesty. Who would imagine that from within those circles alone the world can be changed, or the power that we talk about in such a wonderfully articulate way could be shifted? It cannot be. I'm not trying to deny the difficulties posed by the political disconnections and fragmentations as the political context in which this work is done. Nevertheless, I think we have to work in the "as if" of the organic possibility.

I know there are lots of objections to the metaphor of the organic intellectual, I have lots of them myself. We have to take seriously Foucault's suggestion that perhaps the moment of the organic intellectual is over; now we are in another historical moment, that of the specific intellectual. I understand exactly what he means by that because, of course, I don't propose the organic intellectual as the source of another grand metanarrative or as producing the theory for the movement from outside. Nevertheless, I hold on to the notion of the organic intellectual because I think it puts a shadow across intellectual work. If it's done with the realization of that worldliness of our object and of our own situation—of the location and constraints of our own institutional position—

it comes out differently. I think it is different when you genuinely feel the pressure on our language, to show its workings, to open itself to accessibility, to open a window, not to disable, not to close out, etc. But this cannot be done at the expense of serious thinking, because the last thing that we want is a rousing populist work that doesn't tell us anything. My main problem with a great deal of work in cultural studies is that it didn't tell us anything new. It was a circular exercise and the wonderful thing was that you could arrive back at the beginning by a very long and intellectually rewarding route: The bourgeoisie produces bourgeois culture which exercises bourgeois hegemony. Hooray! That is the last thing that anybody out there needs: to be told what they already know. They need the production of new knowledges. We won't always be able to control the ways in which that's appropriated or the political conditions in which it's appropriated, but we need to work as if our work would be better if we could; we need to work with the pressure of that behind us. And that is what I think constitutes what I called our modesty.

ANDREW ROSS: I have a query about a term which you invoked throughout your history of cultural studies—"theoretical gains." Exactly how does one recognize what theoretical gains are? The term seems to appeal to a narrative of progress which was almost completely problematized by those moments which you described in vivid detail, when gender and race came crashing in through that window.

HALL: I think your criticism is quite right; it does have a sort of narrative of progress smuggled into it. I don't think I meant theoretical gains in that way but it may be that I did, and that it was part of the unconsciousness of what I was saying, that I meant more than I said, or said more than I meant. What I meant by theoretical gains was that the next kind of work that you feel able to do is done in a profoundly different way because you've had to wrestle with a new set of what I call conundra. You move within a different set of positions and with a set of conceptual insights which have emerged through what I metaphorically called struggling with the angels. I don't know if that new work has any built-in guarantee that it's better than the work you did before, quite often it's not. I'm trying to represent the movement of theory, not from theorist to theorist or problematic to problematic, but from problem to . . . I don't want to say solution because as soon as you get something which resolves a particular theoretical problem, you have instantly to recognize what it doesn't do.

Let me put it in a concrete way. As I tried to say, I entered Marxism as a problem; I wrestled with Althusser and finally was able to do some work within the framework of a Marxian problematic radically revised by Gramsci. Now, is that a gain? Well, it's a gain in the sense that I could get something said that I couldn't get said before. And I could say some different things. But if you think by that that we are now in the Gramscian problematic, we're also in the problems of the Gramscian problematic. There are problems that Gramsci's gains present to one, and then you have to look elsewhere, which forces you to wrestle on a different terrain. So I'm trying to describe what I talked about as interruptions in cultural studies, the periods in which work was done, though it was never done in a guaranteed theoretical space, and the movements, a set of theoretical movements, that drove it on.

To be quite honest about your criticism, I guess I do think that some terrain is gained, otherwise I won't make those moves. I don't think those gains are guaranteed, but I do think the work is better when someone understands those complexities that one wrestles to gain insight into. Sometimes, they are actually reversals; some of those gains take one into terrains where the work is too facile, very good but empty. There are lots of blind alleys. I don't think that there's any simple notion of linear progress in theoretical work, as I see it. But I do think that one moves from one detotalized or deconstructed problematic to the gains of another, recognizing its limitations. That, I think, is the infinite open-endedness of critical work, why critical work is always dialogical. It does have the capacity to establish some important conversations on some ground. That's what I mean by the gain; it gains some ground where thinking can go on around a particular set of problems. It's almost never stable; it will be punctuated and interrupted by some new thing, not necessarily by a new book or by a new theory but by some new turn of events which requires one to address a problem which shows the underside of the positive ground you've gained. Suddenly, it doesn't explain that stuff, suddenly you've got to start again, perhaps from the bad side of the gains that you've made. In these ways I'm trying to describe what a critical practice is like which isn't just circular and repetitious and which has no guaranteed advances or progress written into it but which continues to be open-ended. In these ways I'm trying to use the term "gains" without looking at an infinite series of interconnected, well-ordered theoretical progressions from position to position.

RUTH TOMASELLI: The question I'm going to ask is an extremely presumptuous one, but I think somebody must voice it and I've decided to. I wonder how you would place your notion of the organic intellectual into the world which is made up of our colleagues and our students, because that after all is our world.

HALL: When I said that part of what the Centre was about was trying to produce organic intellectual work, I of course had the question of pedagogy essentially in mind. I don't think we can divorce theoretical work and pedagogy. At the Centre for Contemporary Cultural Studies there were only three academics, so the organic intellectuals we were trying to produce were not only ourselves but our students. So the question of pedagogy as a form of intellectual production is crucial. I agree with what I take to be an underlying criticism in your comment, namely that when we talk about the institutional position of cultural studies, we often fail to talk about questions of teaching and pedagogy. We talk about intellectual practice as if it is the practice of intellectuals in the library reading the right canonical texts or consulting other intellectuals at conferences or something like that. But the ongoing work of an intellectual practice for most of us, insofar as we get our material sustenance, our modes of reproduction, from doing our academic work, is indeed to teach. And I suppose my real silence was in not responding to Ros Brunt by saying that the first people we might make some connection with are our students. Before we invoke the great mass ranks out there, it might be quite important that our students are with us in the project and that we are helping them to conduct a little intellectual work. I'm sorry if I appeared to take that for granted.

JENNY SHARPE: I wonder if you might elaborate upon the notion of "irritable tension" with which you organized your narrative (as opposed to solution and resolution). I was also wondering if this irritable tension could be productive in alliance politics.

HALL: I'll say just three brief things about the tensions. One of the most important examples for me of a tension which has been enormously theoretically productive for my own work and which I'm damned if I know how to resolve, and which I therefore have to live with, is exactly that triangle that I referred to earlier, which has been put on the agenda by the interruption of feminism. The interrelations between feminism, psychoanalysis, and cultural studies defines a completely and permanently unsettled terrain for me. The gains of understanding cultural questions in and through the insights of psychoanalytic work, especially as those have been reread through the political practices of feminism, opened up enormous insights for me—that's what I mean by gain. I just feel I know something after that moment that I didn't know before that I now have to work with. But every attempt to translate the one smoothly into the other doesn't work; no attempt to do so can work. Culture is neither just the processes of the unconscious writ large nor is the unconscious simply the internalization of cultural processes through the subjective domain. The latter just doesn't work. Psychoanalysis completely breaks that sociological notion of socialization; I'll never use it again. That's what I mean by interruption: the term falls out the bottom. I cannot explain how social individuals are constituted and reconstituted through the concept of socialization. It just had to go. But I cannot translate the one onto the other. I have to live with the tension of the two vocabularies, of the two unsettled objects of analysis and try to read the one through the other without falling into psychoanalytic readings of everything. It's the reason why, of many books on the subject, I like Jacquelyn Rose's *Sexuality and the Field of Vision* so much because I think it is a very political book. It's also a deeply Lacanian book, and the arguments between those two things are unsettled and she just has to say: I know these two things are important, and I know that they're conjoined in a number of extremely complex ways, and I can't tell you how the translation is effected. That's what I mean by living in and with tension.

Let me say, secondly, I agree that this is not a question of theoretical practice alone, far from it. I think that just as we have to understand politics as a language we have to understand politics as living with the tension. The notion of a political practice where criticism is postponed until the day after the barricades precisely defines the politics which I always refused. And if you don't go that way you go into politics of contention, of continuous argument, of continuous debate. Because what is at stake really matters.

Finally, then, the question of the manner in which our tensions are worked through matters a great deal. I don't want to prescribe but I want to draw your attention to the problem of courtesy, of living with a tension that matters without eating each other. Because there is a kind of competitive way in which intellectuals live with their tensions in which they can only do so by climbing on the backs of those people whose positions they're trying to contest. We have a great deal to learn about respecting the positions being advanced while contesting them because something important is at stake. I don't think we're very good at that. We have a lot to learn about the manners of a genuinely dialogically critical engagement.

MEAGHAN MORRIS: I am not a pluralist but I actually like both those models—organic and specific intellectuals—because I think they describe different kinds of possibility that exist for people in the present, certainly in my country. But one thing that bothers me about the rhetoric of the organic intellectual is the way the problem of theory/practice/politics can get posed. At one moment, you said that if you don't feel the tensions in your work, it's because theory has let you off the hook. But sometimes it's not that theory lets you off the hook, it's that the academy or the forms of academic institutionalization can drive tension out of people's work, can absolutely kill the angels in a sense. And this, I suppose, is a question about how you see the resilience of cultural studies in the face of that. I've seen a moment in another time and place with feminist theory, for example, where a whole group of women who had wrestled with angels for many years suddenly found themselves teaching a curriculum which most of their students found boring and oppressive and irrelevant. And totally unangelic. But because of the nature of the structural political problems that feminism responds to, that moment passed. More people came in, infused by their criticism, to displace the work we had done, and renewed the whole project of feminist theory. I wonder whether cultural studies has a sufficient identity to do that. The reason I'm not a pluralist is that I don't think pluralism is an option, I think it's the problem. I think that when the academy institutionalizes the fact of pluralism, it makes it hard for people to care about the difference between various arbitrary closures. So what I would want to see is a definition against pluralism.

HALL: There are really a number of important questions there, and I can't respond to them adequately. But just let me say that I too like both the model of the specific intellectual and of the organic intellectual. I was not trying to ditch one in favor of the other. I tried to represent the second by talking about cultural studies as not having an aspiration to an overall metalanguage, as always having to recognize its positioning, as a set of contested localized knowledges, etc. Also, contrary to the promise that in the Gramscian discourse clinches the organic intellectual, namely that there is a party out there to deliver, the party isn't there. So it's the organic intellectual, metaphorically, as the hope, and it's the specific intellectual as the mode of operation. I also agree with what you said about pluralism. And I think that one of the difficulties for us results because cultural studies has always been interdisciplinary, for very good and, I think, very important reasons. Some of the subversive force of cultural studies, along with a number of other forms of critical work, results from its having contested the institutionalized spaces of knowledge as disciplines and regulators. And so even in its rather loose way, it's surging across the boundaries and taking a number of vocabularies from different places in order to explain a problem. This is one of the most important things about it. But obviously in the moment of institutionalization that can become just an extremely slack form of pluralism.

But the moment of institutionalization has more dangers written into it from the outside as it were. And sometimes this can push people who are trying to do cultural studies in that pluralistic direction. For instance, one of the places where cultural studies is growing is in institutes of humanities which have emerged, out of the enormous good will and funding generosity of universities and institutions, but partly as places where the specific educational attack on the humanities, on the politicization of the humanities, on the destruction of a canon, can be contested. There are places of resistance which have been thrown up around some of that, so that critical intellectual work can get done. Not all the institutes are like that, but I know some where that is one of the reasons why they appear to be very pluralistic, because a number of people are coming under the umbrella of cultural studies as a mode of defense. So let us not fail to recognize that these institutional spaces have really quite specific conditions and constraints and that the work which can be done requires a much more careful job of trying to define what that project is, not in an empty pluralistic way that we've understood before. However, at that point I come to halt because, when pressed to say what cultural studies is and what it isn't, something in me stops short. I have a stake, and cultural studies isn't every damn thing. But I think, for one thing, that in the American context it needs a whole range of work to say what it is in this context. What it is in relation to this culture that would genuinely separate it from earlier work or work done elsewhere. I'm not sure that cultural studies in the United States has actually been through that moment of self-clarification. So I don't want to, as it were, impose another set of definitions on it. But I do think it matters what it is in particular situations. I don't think it can be simply a pluralistic umbrella. I think that sort of pluralism is the effect of certain political conditions which are constraints on intellectual work in the academy here. So I'm agreeing with your point—it's not theory that's let you off the hook, it's the precise insertion of a certain kind of critical practice at an institutional moment, and that moment is precisely the moment of academic institutional life in this country, which is a big enterprise to crack.

ALEXANDRA CHASIN: I have been anonymous up til now. Until, I suppose, the moment of speaking. I mean to be both courteous and constructive but I'm also quite serious and I think this stuff really matters. My comment is not addressed to the speaker, although I take profound encouragement from what he has said. I speak now because there is no scheduled place for a participant in this conference to say anything which is not to or from the podium. I take encouragement, too, from previous attempts at intervention, like the remark on Friday by a participant that she felt terrorized. She asserted that there was no room for dialogue among all participants, an assertion which has also been made in the spatial margins of this conference: halls, bathrooms, motel rooms, etc. She said out loud what many others have whispered. I am responding in part to the invitation implicit in the literature of the conference itself, which says, among other things: "increasingly visible, increasingly influential, Cultural Studies is also in the process of being more widely institutionalized and commodified. This conference is designed not only to reflect on these events, but also to intervene in them." It says later, "we welcome substantive comments and questions from all attendants," and I hope that's still true. In its structure, the conference most definitely privileges certain people, empowering them to speak while disempowering others. It also duplicates the traditional structures of power which practitioners of cultural studies almost uniformly claim to be committed to subverting. One or two rounds of applause for graduate student labor and for staff helping with conference "mechanics" does not go very far towards changing a familiar and oppressive division of labor. Allowing people who can afford two dinners in one evening to slough off their extras in the general direction of those who cannot afford the meal pass, or don't want to buy it for health-related reasons, or any other reasons, does not go very far towards reconsidering exclusionary practices. The presentation of a solution is mystified by concealing the problem. My friend and I gathered from this that we were not the only ones with a problem, more than this we could only guess. Yet, this issue might have been an opportunity for self-criticism, for reflexivity, for asking the questions of ourselves that we ask theoretically about other institutions, organizations, groups, and even about academia as a whole. Or is it just too embarrassing to talk about meal passes, or child care? Where is our feminism? I do not just level these charges at the organizers, or the speakers, many of whom have made gestures at intervention. I address myself to everybody here, because although in this context silence is not exactly or immediately death, it is frustration and complicity. In order that my words might not be covered over, I come forward with concrete proposals. I hope that the bureaucracy of the conference is not too entrenched to deal with them. It might be useful to organize caucuses for lesbians and gays and for people of color whose work and livelihoods are often more marginalized and threatened than those of practitioners of cultural studies even where those categories overlap. How about small discussions, or workshops? How about some formal treatment or discussion of pedagogy, a subject whose absence here, until a minute ago, surprises and alarms me, since I have personally considered the classroom the place where I might integrate my, of course, politically correct intellectual politics with political action. Since I assume my dissertation will either be read in typescript by four people, or in hardback by twice as many. What about taking a few minutes to open up the floor to suggestions for more constructive interventions than these?

BELL HOOKS: I feel very bad, because one of the things Gayatri Spivak says in *Marxism and the Interpretation of Culture* is that things in this country always come down to the question of how the room is arranged. When I talk about being terrorized, I wasn't talking about the room, or the microphones; I was talking about how the discourse of cultural studies as it was being constructed here was silencing certain kinds of people. And I didn't like the fact that it took this personal form of people coming up to me, white people coming up to me, and making very negative comments about me: "bell hooks, come off it, how could you ever be terrorized?" That shows a lack of understanding of the issues of race, gender, and class that I was trying to raise. I wanted to come to this conference because I am excited about cultural studies. I am excited about it as a critical intervention, as a critical political intervention. And when I felt that I was being marginalized and silenced, I felt that as terror. I felt that as terror about the danger of cultural studies appropriating issues of race, gender, and sexual practice, and then continuing to hurt and wound in that politics of domination. And I felt bad because I felt my comments got reduced to this question of the room and the microphones and things like that, which are important but which are not what I was trying to talk about. I was trying to talk about what kind of discourse was being produced here and its implications for political practice. I would much rather have been able to say, around the question of pedagogy, that I thought a lot about the fact that cultural critique for me has been about really responding to students. Really responding to students who go see *Do the Right Thing* and come back and say "Look, we took your class, we understand this feminist standpoint, but we also think Spike Lee is a down brother so how do we deal with what we feel we saw in this particular cultural production?" To me, that's the exciting dimension of cultural studies, that it can take place, not as me writing a privatized article, but as a response to students asking what type of critical thinking allows them to engage this cultural production in a way that informs our political practice. I hope that clarifies some what I meant by the use of the word "terrorism."

SCOTT COOPER: Stuart, I just wanted to say that I attended your class at the Institute that took place here at Illinois in 1983 and I share the concerns that were addressed here. But my concerns have more to do with what cultural studies is becoming in the American context. My fear is that cultural studies will be just another listing in the college catalog under the letter "C," near Ethnic studies and World Arts and Culture. In other words, it's going to be denied its political meaning. American institutions of education are far more powerful than even all the people in this room. What I find lacking in this conference is any sense of the strategies by which we're going to intervene in those institutions. I don't mind listening to people I admire, but it seems to me we need four days of discussion about how we can intervene in the institutions in which we work, rather than four days reproducing the same kind of hierarchy we already have.

18

The Promises of Monsters: A Regenerative Politics for Inappropriate/d Others

DONNA HARAWAY

If primates have a sense of humor, there is no reason why intellectuals may not share in it. (Plank, 1989)

A Biopolitics of Artifactual Reproduction

"The Promises of Monsters" will be a mapping exercise and travelogue through mind-scapes and landscapes of what may count as nature in certain local/global struggles. These contests are situated in a strange, allochronic time—the time of myself and my readers in the last decade of the second Christian millenium—and in a foreign, allotopic place—the womb of a pregnant monster, here, where we are reading and writing. The purpose of this excursion is to write theory, i.e., to produce a patterned vision of how to move and what to fear in the topography of an impossible but all-too-real present, in order to find an absent, but perhaps possible, other present. I do not seek the address of some full presence; reluctantly, I know better. Like Christian in *Pilgrim's Progress*, however, I am committed to skirting the slough of despond and the parasite-infested swamps of nowhere to reach more salubrious environs.[1] The theory is meant to orient, to provide the roughest sketch for travel, by means of moving within and through a relentless artifactualism, which forbids any direct si(gh)tings of nature, to a science fictional, speculative factual, SF place called, simply, elsewhere. At least for those whom this essay addresses, "nature" outside artifactualism is not so much elsewhere as nowhere, a different matter altogether. Indeed, a reflexive artifactualism offers serious political and analytical hope. This essay's theory is modest. Not a systematic overview, it is a little siting device in a long line of such craft tools. Such sighting devices have been known to reposition worlds for their devotees—and for their opponents. Optical instruments are subject-shifters. Goddess knows, the subject is being changed relentlessly in the late twentieth century.

My diminutive theory's optical features are set to produce not effects of distance, but effects of connection, of embodiment, and of responsibility for an imagined elsewhere that we may yet learn to see and build here. I have high stakes in reclaiming vision from the technopornographers, those theorists of minds, bodies, and planets who insist effectively—i.e., in practice—that sight is the sense made to realize the fantasies of the phallocrats.[2] I think sight can be remade for the activists and advocates engaged in fitting political filters to see the world in the hues of red, green, and ultraviolet, i.e., from the perspectives of a still possible socialism, feminist and anti-racist environmentalism, and science for the people. I take as a self-evident premise that "science is culture."[3] Rooted in that premise, this essay is a contribution to the heterogeneous and very lively contemporary discourse of science studies *as* cultural studies. Of course, what science, culture, or nature—and their "studies"—might mean is far less self-evident.

Nature is for me, and I venture for many of us who are planetary fetuses gestating in the amniotic effluvia of terminal industrialism,[4] one of those impossible things characterized by Gayatri Spivak as that which we cannot not desire. Excruciatingly conscious of nature's discursive constitution as "other" in the histories of colonialism, racism, sexism, and class domination of many kinds, we nonetheless find in this problematic, ethno-specific, long-lived, and mobile concept something we cannot do without, but can never "have." We must find another relationship to nature besides reification and possession. Perhaps to give confidence in its essential reality, immense resources have been expended to stabilize and materialize nature, to police its/her boundaries. Such expenditures have had disappointing results. Efforts to travel into "nature" become tourist excursions that remind the voyager of the price of such displacements—one pays to see fun-house reflections of oneself. Efforts to preserve "nature" in parks remain fatally troubled by the ineradicable mark of the founding explusion of those who used to live there, not as innocents in a garden, but as people for whom the categories of nature and culture were not the salient ones. Expensive projects to collect "nature's" diversity and bank it seem to produce debased coin, impoverished seed, and dusty relics. As the banks hypertrophy, the nature that feeds the storehouses "disappears." The World Bank's record on environmental destruction is exemplary in this regard. Finally, the projects for representing and enforcing human "nature" are famous for their imperializing essences, most recently reincarnated in the Human Genome Project.

So, nature is not a physical place to which one can go, nor a treasure to fence in or bank, nor as essence to be saved or violated. Nature is not hidden and so does not need to be unveiled. Nature is not a text to be read in the codes of mathematics and biomedicine. It is not the "other" who offers origin, replenishment, and service. Neither mother, nurse, nor slave, nature is not matrix, resource, or tool for the reproduction of man.

Nature is, however, a *topos,* a place, in the sense of a rhetorician's place or topic for consideration of common themes; nature is, strictly, a commonplace. We turn to this topic to order our discourse, to compose our memory. As a topic in this sense, nature also reminds us that in seventeenth-century English the "topick gods" were the local gods, the gods specific to places and peoples. We need these spirits, rhetorically if we can't have them any other way. We need them in order to reinhabit, precisely, *common* places—locations that are widely shared, inescapably local, worldly, enspirited; i.e., topical. In this sense, nature is the place to rebuild public culture.[5] Nature is also a *trópos,* a trope. It is figure, construction, artifact, movement, displacement. Nature cannot pre-exist its construction. This construction is based on a particular kind of move— a *trópos* or "turn." Faithful to the Greek, as *trópos* nature is about turning. Troping, we turn to nature as if to the earth, to the primal stuff—geotropic, physiotropic. Topically, we travel toward the earth, a commonplace. In discoursing on nature, we turn from Plato and his heliotropic son's blinding star to see something else, another kind of figure. I do not turn from vision, but I do seek something other than enlightenment in these sightings of science studies as cultural studies. Nature is a topic of public discourse on which much turns, even the earth.

In this essay's journey toward elsewhere, I have promised to trope nature through a relentless artifactualism, but what does artifactualism mean here? First, it means that nature for us is *made,* as both fiction and fact. If organisms are natural objects, it is crucial to remember that organisms are not born; they are made in world-changing techno-scientific practices by particular collective actors in particular times and places. In the belly of the local/global monster in which I am gestating, often called the postmodern world,[6] global technology appears to *denature* everything, to make everything a malleable matter of strategic decisions and mobile production and reproduction processes (Hayles, 1990). Technological decontextualization is ordinary experience for hundreds of millions if not billions of human beings, as well as other organisms. I suggest that this is not a *denaturing* so much as a *particular production* of nature. The preoccupation with productionism that has characterized so much parochial Western discourse and practice seems to have hypertrophied into something quite marvelous: the whole world is remade in the image of commodity production.[7]

How, in the face of this marvel, can I seriously insist that to see nature as artifactual is an *oppositional,* or better, a *differential* siting?[8] Is the insistence that nature *is* artifactual not more evidence of the extremity of the violation of a nature outside and other to the arrogant ravages of our technophilic civilization, which, after all, we were taught began with the heliotropisms of enlightenment projects to dominate nature with blinding light focused by optical technology?[9] Haven't eco-feminists and other multicultural and intercultural radicals begun to convince us that nature is precisely *not* to be seen in the guise of the Eurocentric productionism and anthropocentrism that have threatened to reproduce, literally, all the world in the deadly image of the Same?

I think the answer to this serious political and analytical question lies in two related turns: 1) unblinding ourselves from the sun-worshiping stories about the history of science and technology as paradigms of rationalism; and 2) refiguring the actors in the construction of the ethno-specific categories of nature *and* culture. The actors are not all "us." If the world exists for us as "nature," this designates a kind of relationship, an achievement among many actors, not all of them human, not all of them organic, not all of them technological.[10] In its scientific embodiments as well as in other forms, nature is made, but not entirely by humans; it is a co-construction among humans and non-humans. This is a very different vision from the postmodernist observation that all the world is denatured and reproduced in images or replicated in copies. That specific kind of violent and reductive artifactualism, in the form of a hyper-productionism actually practiced widely throughout the planet, becomes *contestable* in theory and other kinds of praxis, without recourse to a resurgent transcendental naturalism. Hyper-productionism refuses the witty agency of all the actors but One; that is a dangerous strategy—for everybody. But transcendental naturalism also refuses a world full of cacophonous agencies and settles for a mirror image sameness that only pretends to difference. The commonplace nature I seek, a public culture, has many houses with many inhabitants which/who can refigure the earth. Perhaps those other actors/actants, the ones who are not human, are our topick gods, organic and inorganic.[11]

It is this barely admissible recognition of the odd sorts of agents and actors which/whom we must admit to the narrative of collective life, including nature, that simultaneously, first, turns us decisively away from enlightenment-derived modern and post-modern premises about nature and culture, the social and technical, science and society and, second, saves us from the deadly point of view of productionism. Productionism and its corollary, humanism, come down to the story line that "man makes everything, including himself, out of the world that can only be resource and potency to his project and active agency."[12] This productionism is about man the tool-maker and -user, whose highest technical production is himself; i.e., the story line of phallogocentrism. He gains access to this wondrous technology with a subject-constituting, self-deferring, and self-splitting entry into language, light, and law. Blinded by the sun, in thrall to the father, reproduced in the sacred image of the same, his reward is that he is self-born, an autotelic copy. That is the mythos of enlightenment transcendence.

Let us return briefly to my remark above that organisms are not born, but they are made. Besides troping on Simone de Beauvoir's observation that one is not born a woman, what work is this statement doing in this essay's effort to articulate a relentless differential/oppositional artifactualism? I wrote that organisms are made as objects of knowledge in world-changing practices of scientific discourse by particular and always collective actors in specific times and places. Let us look more closely at this claim with the aid of the concept of the apparatus of bodily production.[13] Organisms are *biological* embodiments; as natural-technical entities, they are not pre-existing plants, animals, protistes, etc., with boundaries already established and awaiting the right kind of instrument to note them correctly. Organisms emerge from a discursive process. Biology is a discourse, not the living world itself. But humans are not the only actors in the construction of the entities of any scientific discourse; machines (delegates that can produce surprises) and other partners (not "pre- or extra-discursive objects," but partners) are active constructors of natural scientific objects. Like other scientific bodies, organisms are not *ideological* constructions. The whole point about discursive construction has been that it is *not* about ideology. Always radically historically specific, always lively, bodies have a different kind of specificity and effectivity; and so they invite a different kind of engagement and intervention.

Elsewhere, I have used the term "material-semiotic actor" to highlight the object of knowledge as an active part of the apparatus of bodily production, without *ever* implying immediate presence of such objects or, what is the same thing, their final or unique determination of what can count as objective knowledge of a biological body at a particular historical juncture. Like Katie King's objects called "poems," sites of literary production where language also is an actor, bodies as objects of knowledge are material-semiotic generative nodes. Their boundaries materialize in social interaction among humans and non-humans, including the machines and other instruments that mediate exchanges at crucial interfaces and that function as delegates for other actors' functions and purposes. "Objects" like bodies do not pre-exist as such. Similarly, "nature" cannot pre-exist as such, but neither is its existence ideological. Nature is a commonplace and a powerful discursive construction, effected in the interactions among material-semiotic actors, human and not. The siting/sighting of such entities is not about disengaged discovery, but about mutual and usually unequal structuring, about taking risks, about delegating competences.[14]

The various contending biological bodies emerge at the intersection of biological research, writing, and publishing; medical and other business practices; cultural productions of all kinds, including available metaphors and narratives; and technology, such as the visualization technologies that bring color-enhanced killer T cells and intimate photographs of the developing fetus into high-gloss art books, as well as scientific reports. But also invited into that node of intersection is the analogue to the lively languages that actively intertwine in the production of literary value: the coyote and protean embodiments of a world as witty agent and actor. Perhaps our hopes for accountability for techno-biopolitics in the belly of the monster turn on revisioning the world as coding trickster with whom we must learn to converse. So while the late twentieth-century immune system, for example, is a construct of an elaborate apparatus of bodily production, neither the immune system nor any other of biology's world-changing bodies—like a virus or an ecosystem—is a ghostly fantasy. Coyote is not a ghost, merely a protean trickster.

This sketch of the artifactuality of nature and the apparatus of bodily production helps us toward another important point: the corporeality of theory. Overwhelmingly, theory is bodily, and theory is literal. Theory is not about matters distant from the lived body; quite the opposite. Theory is *anything* but disembodied. The fanciest statements about radical decontextualization as the historical form of nature in late capitalism are tropes for the embodiment, the production, the literalization of experience in that specific mode. This is not a question of reflection or correspondences, but of technology, where the social and the technical implode into each other. Experience is a semiotic process— a semiosis (de Lauretis, 1984). Lives are built; so we had best become good craftspeople with the other worldly actants in the story. There is a great deal of rebuilding to do, beginning with a little more surveying with the aid of optical devices fitted with red, green, and ultraviolet filters.

Repeatedly, this essay turns on figures of pregnancy and gestation. Zoe Sofia (1984) taught me that every technology is a reproductive technology. She and I have meant that literally; ways of life are at stake in the culture of science. I would, however, like to displace the terminology of reproduction with that of generation. Very rarely does anything really get *reproduced;* what's going on is much more polymorphous than that. Certainly people don't reproduce, unless they get themselves cloned, which will always be very expensive and risky, not to mention boring. Even technoscience must be made into the paradigmatic model not of closure, but of that which is contestable and contested. That involves knowing how the world's agents and actants work; how they/we/it come into the world, and how they/we/it are reformed. Science becomes the myth not of what escapes agency and responsibility in a realm above the fray, but rather of account- ability and responsibility for translations and solidarities linking the cacophonous visions and visionary voices that characterize the knowledges of the marked bodies of history. Actors, as well as actants, come in many and wonderful forms. And best of all, "repro- duction"—or less inaccurately, the generation of novel forms—need not be imagined in the stodgy bipolar terms of hominids.[15]

If the stories of hyper-productionism and enlightenment have been about the reproduction of the sacred image of the same, of the one true copy, mediated by the luminous technologies of compulsory heterosexuality and masculinist self-birthing, then the differential artifactualism I am trying to envision might issue in something else. Artifactualism is askew of productionism; the rays from my optical device diffract rather than reflect. These diffracting rays compose *interference* patterns, not reflecting images. The "issue" from this generative technology, the result of a monstrous[16] pregnancy, might be kin to Vietnamese-American filmmaker and feminist theorist Trinh Minh- ha's (1986/7b; 1989) "inappropriate/d others."[17] Designating the networks of multi- cultural, ethnic, racial, national, and sexual actors emerging since World War II, Trinh's phrase referred to the historical positioning of those who cannot adopt the mask of either "self" or "other" offered by previously dominant, modern Western narratives of identity and politics. To be "inappropriate/d" does not mean "not to be in relation with"—i.e., to be in a special reservation, with the status of the authentic, the untouched, in the allochronic and allotopic condition of innocence. Rather to be an "inappropriate/ d other" means to be in critical, deconstructive relationality, in a diffracting rather than reflecting (ratio)nality—as the means of making potent connection that exceeds domi- nation. To be inappropriate/d is not to fit in the *taxon,* to be dislocated from the available maps specifying kinds of actors and kinds of narratives, not to be originally fixed by difference. To be inappropriate/d is to be neither modern nor postmodern, but to insist on the amodern. Trinh was looking for a way to figure "difference" as a "critical difference within," and not as special taxonomic marks grounding difference as apartheid.

She was writing about people; I wonder if the same observations might apply to humans and to both organic and technological non-humans.

The term "inappropriate/d others" can provoke rethinking social relationality within artifactual nature—which is, arguably, global nature in the 1990s. Trinh Minh-ha's metaphors suggest another geometry and optics for considering the relations of difference among people and among humans, other organims, and machines than hierarchical domination, incorporation of parts into wholes, paternalistic and colonialist protection, symbiotic fusion, antagonistic opposition, or instrumental production from resource. Her metaphors also suggest the hard intellectual, cultural, and political work these new geometries will require. If Western patriarchal narratives have told that the physical body issued from the first birth, while man was the product of the heliotropic second birth, perhaps a differential, diffracted feminist allegory might have the "inappropriate/d others" emerge from a third birth into an SF world called elsewhere—a place composed from interference patterns. Diffraction does not produce "the same" displaced, as reflection and refraction do. Diffraction is a mapping of interference, not of replication, reflection, or reproduction. A diffraction pattern does not map where differences appear, but rather maps where the *effects* of difference appear. Tropically, for the promises of monsters, the first invites the illusion of essential, fixed position, while the second trains us to more subtle vision. Science fiction is generically concerned with the interpenetration of boundaries between problematic selves and unexpected others and with the exploration of possible worlds in a context structured by transnational technoscience. The emerging social subjects called "inappropriate/d others" inhabit such worlds. SF—science fiction, speculative futures, science fantasy, speculative fiction—is an especially apt sign under which to conduct an inquiry into the artifactual as a reproductive technology that might issue in something other than the sacred image of the same, something inappropriate, unfitting, and so, maybe, inappropriated.

Within the belly of the monster, even inappropriate/d others seem to be interpellated—called through interruption—into a particular location that I have learned to call a cyborg subject position.[18] Let me continue this travelogue and inquiry into artifactualism with an illustrated lecture on the nature of cyborgs as they appear in recent advertisements in *Science,* the journal of the American Association for the Advancement of Science. These ad figures remind us of the corporeality, the mundane materiality, and literality of theory. These commercial cyborg figures tell us what may count as nature in technoscience worlds. Above all, they show us the implosion of the technical, textual, organic, mythic, and political in the gravity wells of science in action. These figures are our companion monsters in the *Pilgrim's Progress* of this essay's travelogue.

Consider Figure 1, "A Few Words about Reproduction from a Leader in the Field," the advertising slogan for Logic General Corporation's software duplication system. The immediate visual and verbal impact insists on the absurdity of separating the technical, organic, mythic, textual, and political threads in the semiotic fabric of the ad and of the world in which this ad makes sense. Under the unliving, orange-to-yellow rainbow colors of the earth-sun logo of Logic General, the biological white rabbit has its (her? yet, sex and gender are not so settled in this reproductive system) back to us. It has its paws on a keyboard, that inertial, old-fashioned residue of the typewriter that lets our computers feel natural to us, user-friendly, as it were.[19] But the keyboard is misleading; no letters are transferred by a mechical key to a waiting solid surface. The computer-user interface works differently. Even if she doesn't understand the implications of her lying keyboard, the white rabbit is in her natural home; she is fully artifactual in the most literal sense. Like fruit flies, yeast, transgenic mice, and the humble nematode worm, *Caenorhabditis elegans,*[20] this rabbit's evolutionary story transpires in the lab; the lab is its proper niche, its true habitat. Both material system and symbol for the measure of fecundity, this kind of rabbit occurs in no other nature than the lab, that preeminent scene of replication practices.

With Logic General, plainly, we are not in a biological laboratory. The organic rabbit peers at its image, but the image is not her reflection, indeed, *especially* not her reflection. This is not Lacan's world of mirrors; primary identification and maturing metaphoric substitution will be produced with other techniques, other writing technologies.[21] The white rabbit will be translated, her potencies and competences relocated radically. The guts of the computer produce another kind of visual product than distorted, self-birthing reflections. The simulated bunny peers out at us face first. It is she who locks her/its gaze with us. She, also, has her paws on a grid, one just barely reminiscent of a typewriter, but even more reminiscent of an older icon of technoscience—the Cartesian coordinate system that locates the world in the imaginary spaces of rational modernity. In her natural habitat, the virtual rabbit is on a grid that insists on the world as a game played on a chess-like board. This rabbit insists that the truly rational actors will replicate themselves in a virtual world where the best players will not be Man, though he may linger like the horse-drawn carriage that gave its form to the railroad car or the typewriter that gave its illusory shape to the computer interface. The functional privileged signifier in this system will not be so easily mistaken for any primate male's urinary and copulative organ. Metaphoric substitution and other circulations in the very material symbolic domain will be more likely to be effected by a competent mouse. The if-y femaleness of both of the rabbits, of course, gives no confidence that the new players other to Man will be women. More likely, the rabbit that is interpellated into the world in this non-mirror stage, this diffracting moment of subject constitution, will be literate in a quite different grammar of gender. *Both* the rabbits here are cyborgs—compounds of the organic, technical, mythic, textual, and political—and they call us into a world in which we may not wish to take shape, but through whose "Miry Slough" we might have to travel to get elsewhere. Logic General is into a very particular kind of *écriture*. The reproductive stakes in this text are future life forms and ways of life for humans and unhumans. "Call toll free" for "a few words about reproduction from an acknowledged leader in the field."

Ortho-mune*™'s monoclonal antibodies expand our understanding of a cyborg subject's relation to the inscription technology that is the laboratory (Figure 2). In only two years, these fine monoclonals generated more than 100 published papers—higher than any rate of literary production by myself or any of my human colleagues in the human sciences. But this alarming rate of publication was achieved in 1982, and has surely been wholly surpassed by new generations of biotech mediators of literary replication. Never has theory been more literal, more bodily, more technically adept. Never has the collapse of the "modern" distinctions between the mythic, organic, technical, political, and textual into the gravity well, where the unlamented enlightenment transcendentals of Nature and Society also disappeared, been more evident.

LKB Electrophoresis Division has an evolutionary story to tell, a better, more complete one than has yet been told by physical anthropologists, paleontologists, or naturalists about the entities/actors/actants that structure niche space in an extra-laboratory world: "There are no missing links in MacroGene Workstation" (Figure 3). Full of promises, breaching the first of the ever-multiplying final frontiers, the prehistoric monster *Ichthyostega* crawls from the amniotic ocean into the future, onto the dangerous but enticing dry land. Our no-longer-fish, not-yet-salamander will end up fully identified and separated, as man-in-space, finally disembodied, as did the hero of J. D. Bernal's fantasy in *The World, the Flesh, and the Devil*. But for now, occupying the zone between

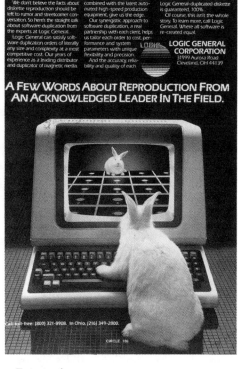
FIGURE 1.

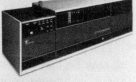
FIGURE 2.

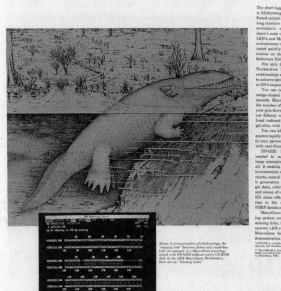
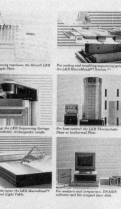

FIGURE 3.

fishes and amphibians, *Ichthyostega* is firmly on the margins, those potent places where theory is best cultured. It behooves us, then, to join this heroic reconstructed beast with LKB, in order to trace out the transferences of competences—the metaphoric-material chain of substitutions—in this quite literal apparatus of bodily production. We are presented with a travel story, a *Pilgrim's Progress,* where there are no gaps, no "missing links." From the first non-original actor—the reconstructed *Ichthyostega*—to the final printout of the DNA homology search mediated by LKB's software and the many separating and writing machines pictured on the right side of the advertisement, the text promises to meet the fundamental desire of phallologocentrism for fullness and presence. From the crawling body in the Miry Sloughs of the narrative to the printed code, we are assured of full success—the compression of time into instantaneous and full access "to the complete GenBank . . . on one laser disk." Like Christian, we have conquered time and space, moving from entrapment in body to fulfillment in spirit, all in the everyday workspaces of the Electrophoresis Division, whose Hong Kong, Moscow, Antwerp, and Washington phone numbers are all provided. Electrophoresis: *pherein*—to bear or carry us relentlessly on.

Bio-Response, innovators in many facets of life's culture, interpellates the cyborg subject into the barely secularized, evangelical, Protestant Christianity that pervades American techno-culture: "Realize the potential of your cell line" (Figure 4). This ad addresses us directly. We are called into a salvation narrative, into history, into biotechnology, into our true natures: our cell line, ourselves, our successful product. We will testify to the efficacy of this culture system. Colored in the blues, purples, and ultraviolets of the sterilizing commercial rainbow—in which art, science, and business arch in lucrative grace—the virus-like crystalline shape mirrors the luminous crystals of New Age promises. Religion, science, and mysticism join easily in the facets of modern and postmodern commercial bio-response. The simultaneously promising and threatening crystal/virus unwinds its tail to reveal the language-like icon of the Central Dogma, the code structures of DNA that underlie all possible bodily response, all semiosis, all culture. Gem-like, the frozen, spiraling crystals of Bio-Response promise life itself. This is a jewel of great price—available from the Production Services office in Hayward, California. The imbrications of layered signifiers and signifieds forming cascading hierarchies of signs guide us through this mythic, organic, textual, technical, political icon.[22]

Finally, the advertisement from Vega Biotechnologies graphically shows us the final promise, "the link between science and tomorrow: Guaranteed. Pure" (Figure 5). The graph reiterates the ubiquitous grid system that is the signature and matrix, father and mother, of the modern world. The sharp peak is the climax of the search for certainty and utter clarity. But the diffracting apparatus of a monstrous artifactualism can perhaps interfere in this little family drama, reminding us that the modern world never existed and its fantastic guarantees are void. Both the organic and computer rabbits of Logic General might re-enter at this point to challenge all the passive voices of productionism. The oddly duplicated bunnies might resist their logical interpellation and instead hint at a neo-natalogy of inappropriate/d others, where the child will not be in the sacred image of the same. Shape-shifting, these interfering cyborgs might craft a diffracted logic of sameness and difference and utter a different word about reproduction, about the link between science and tomorrow, from collective actors in the field.

II. The Four-Square Cyborg: Through Artifactualism to Elsewhere

It is time to travel, therefore, with a particular subset of shifted subjects, Cyborgs for Earthly Survival,[23] into the mindscapes and landscapes indicated at the beginning of this

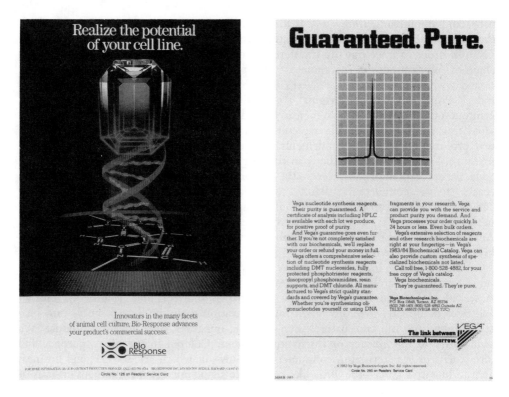

FIGURE 4.   FIGURE 5.

essay. To get through the artifactual to elsewhere, it would help to have a little travel machine that also functions as a map. Consequently, the rest of the "Promises of Monsters" will rely on an artificial device that generates meanings very noisily: A. J. Greimas's infamous semiotic square. The regions mapped by this clackety, structuralist meaning-making machine could never be mistaken for the transcendental realms of Nature or Society. Allied with Bruno Latour, I will put my structuralist engine to amodern purposes: this will not be a tale of the rational progress of science, in potential league with progressive politics, patiently unveiling a grounding nature, nor will it be a demonstration of the social construction of science and nature that locates all agency firmly on the side of humanity. Nor will the modern be superceded or infiltrated by the postmodern, because belief in something called the modern has itself been a mistake. Instead, the amodern refers to a view of the history of science as culture that insists on the absence of beginnings, enlightenments, and endings: the world has always been in the middle of things, in unruly and practical conversation, full of action and structured by a startling array of actants and of networking and unequal collectives. The much-criticized inability of structuralist devices to provide the narrative of diachronic history, of progress through time, will be my semiotic square's greatest virtue. The shape of my amodern history will have a different geometry, not of progress, but of permanent and multi-patterned interaction through which lives and worlds get built, human and unhuman. This Pilgrim's Progress is taking a monstrous turn.

I like my analytical technologies, which are unruly partners in discursive construction, delegates who have gotten into doing things on their own, to make a lot of noise, so that I don't forget all the circuits of competences, inherited conversations, and coalitions of human and unhuman actors that go into any semiotic excursions. The semiotic square, so subtle in the hands of a Fredric Jameson, will be rather more rigid and literal here (Greimas, 1966; Jameson, 1972). I only want it to keep four spaces in differential, relational separation, while I explore how certain local/global struggles for meanings and embodiments of nature are occurring within them. Almost a joke on "elementary structures of signification" ("Guaranteed. Pure."), the semiotic square in this essay nonetheless allows a contestable collective world to take shape for us out of structures of difference. The four regions through which we will move are A, Real Space or Earth; B, Outer Space or the Extraterrestrial; not–B, Inner Space or the Body; and finally, not–A, Virtual Space or the SF world oblique to the domains of the imaginary, the symbolic, and the real (Figure 6).

Somewhat unconventionally, we will move through the square clockwise to see what kinds of figures inhabit this exercise in science studies as cultural studies. In each of the first three quadrants of the square, I will begin with a popular image of nature and science that initially appears both compelling and friendly, but quickly becomes a sign of deep structures of domination. Then I will switch to a differential/oppositional

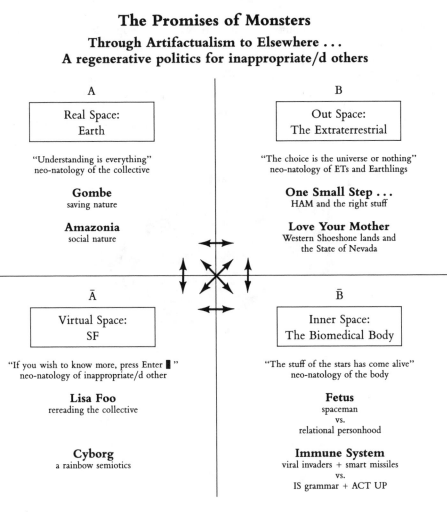

The Promises of Monsters
Through Artifactualism to Elsewhere . . .
A regenerative politics for inappropriate/d others

A	B
Real Space: Earth	**Out Space:** The Extraterrestrial
"Understanding is everything" neo-natology of the collective	"The choice is the universe or nothing" neo-natology of ETs and Earthlings
Gombe saving nature	**One Small Step . . .** HAM and the right stuff
Amazonia social nature	**Love Your Mother** Western Shoshone lands and the State of Nevada

Ā	B̄
Virtual Space: SF	**Inner Space:** The Biomedical Body
"If you wish to know more, press Enter ▌" neo-natology of inappropriate/d other	"The stuff of the stars has come alive" neo-natology of the body
Lisa Foo rereading the collective	**Fetus** spaceman vs. relational personhood
Cyborg a rainbow semiotics	**Immune System** viral invaders + smart missiles vs. IS grammar + ACT UP

FIGURE 6

image and practice that might promise something else. In the final quadrant, in virtual space at the end of the journey, we will meet a disturbing guide figure who promises information about psychic, historical, and bodily formations that issue, perhaps, from some other semiotic processes than the psychoanalytic in modern and postmodern guise. Directed by John Varley's (1986) story of that name, all we will have to do to follow this disquieting, amodern Beatrice will be to "Press Enter." Her job will be to instruct us in the neo-natology of inappropriate/d others. The goal of this journey is to show in each quadrant, and in the passage through the machine that generates them, metamorphoses and boundary shifts that give grounds for a scholarship and politics of hope in truly monstrous times. The pleasures promised here are not those libertarian masculinist fantasmics of the infinitely regressive practice of boundary violation and the accompanying *frisson* of brotherhood, but just maybe the pleasure of regeneration in less deadly, chiasmatic borderlands.[24] Without grounding origins and without history's illuminating and progressive tropisms, how might we map some semiotic possibilities for other topick gods and common places?

A. Real Space: Earth

In 1984, to mark nine years of underwriting the National Geographic Society's television specials, the Gulf Oil Corporation ran an advertisement entitled "Understanding Is Everything" (Figure 7). The ad referred to some of the most watched programs in the history of public television—the nature specials about Jane Goodall and the wild chimpanzees in Tanzania's Gombe National Park. Initially, the gently clasped hands of the ape and the young white woman seem to auger what the text proclaims—communication, trust, responsibility, and understanding across the gaps that have defined human existence

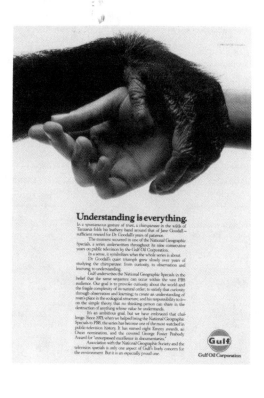

FIGURE 7.

in Nature and Society in "modern" Western narratives. Made ready by a scientific practice coded in terms of "years of patience," through a "spontaneous gesture of trust" *initiated by the animal,* Goodall metamorphoses in the ad copy from "Jane" to "Dr. Goodall." Here is a natural science, coded unmistakenly feminine, to counter the instrumentalist excesses of a military-industrial-technoscience complex, where the code of science is stereotypically anthropocentric and masculine. The ad invites the viewer to forget Gulf's status as one of the Seven Sisters of big oil, ranking eighth among the Forbes 500 in 1980 (but acquired by Chevron by the end of the decade's transnational capitalist restructuring). In response to the financial and political challenges mounted in the early 1970s by the Organization of Oil Exporting Countries (OPEC) and by ecological activism around the globe, by the late 1970s the scandal-ridden giant oil corporations had developed advertising strategies that presented themselves as the world's leading environmentalists—indeed, practically as the mothers of eco-feminism. There could be no better story than that of Jane Goodall and the chimpanzees for narrating the healing touch between nature and society, mediated by a science that produces full communication in a chain that leads innocently "from curiosity, to observation, to learning, to understanding."[25] Here is a story of blissful incorporation.

There is another repressed set of codes in the ad as well, that of race and imperialism, mediated by the dramas of gender and species, science and nature. In the National Geographic narrative, "Jane" entered the garden "alone" in 1960 to seek out "man's" closest relatives, to establish a knowing touch across gulfs of time. A natural family is at stake; the PBS specials document a kind of inter-species family therapy. Closing the distance between species through a patient discipline, where first the animals could only be known by their spoor and their calls, then by fleeting sightings, then finally by the animal's direct inviting touch, after which she could name them, "Jane" was admitted as "humanity's" delegate back into Eden. Society and nature had made peace; "modern science" and "nature" could co-exist. Jane/Dr. Goodall was represented almost as a new Adam, authorized to name not by God's creative hand, but by the animal's transformative touch. The people of Tanzania disappear in a story in which the actors are the anthropoid apes and a young British white woman engaged in a thoroughly modern sacred secular drama. The chimpanzees and Goodall are both enmeshed in stories of endangerment and salvation. In the post-World War II era the apes face biological extinction; the planet faces nuclear and ecological annihilation; and the West faces expulsion from its former colonial possessions. If only communication can be established, destruction can be averted. As Gulf Oil insists, "Our goal is to provoke curiosity about the world and the fragile complexity of its natural order; to satisfy that curiosity through observation and learning; to create an understanding of man's place in the ecological structure, and his responsibility to it—on the simple theory that no thinking person can share in the destruction of anything whose value he understands." Progress, rationality, and nature join in the great myth of modernity, which is so thoroughly threatened by a dozen looming apocalypses. A cross-species family romance promises to avert the threatened destruction.

Inaudible in the Gulf and National Geographic version, communication and understanding are to emerge in the communion between Jane/Dr. Goodall and the spontaneously trusting chimpanzee at just the historical moment when dozens of African nations are achieving their national independence, 15 in 1960 alone, the year Goodall set out for Gombe. Missing from the family romance are such beings as Tanzanians. African peoples seek to establish hegemony over the lands in which they live; to do that the stories of the natural presence of white colonists must be displaced, usually by extremely complex and dangerous nationalist stories. But in "Understanding Is Everything," the metonymic "spontaneous gesture of trust" from the animal hand to the white hand obliterates once again the invisible bodies of people of color who have never counted as able to represent humanity in Western iconography. The white hand will be the instrument for saving nature—and in the process be saved from a rupture with nature. Closing great gaps, the transcendentals of nature and society meet here in the metonymic figure of softly embracing hands from two worlds, whose innocent touch depends on the absence of the "other world," the "third world," where the drama actually transpires.

In the history of the life sciences, the great chain of being leading from "lower" to "higher" life forms has played a crucial part in the discursive construction of race as an object of knowledge and of racism as a living force. After World War II and the partial removal of explicit racism from evolutionary biology and physical anthropology, a good deal of racist and colonialist discourse remained projected onto the screen of "man's closest relatives," the anthropoid apes.[26] It is impossible to picture the entwined hands of a white woman and an African ape without evoking the history of racist inconography in biology and in European and American popular culture. The animal hand is metonymically the individual chimpanzee, all threatened species, the third world, peoples of color, Africa, the ecologically endangered earth—all firmly in the realm of Nature, all represented in the leathery hand folding around that of the white girl-woman under the Gulf sun logo shining on the Seven Sisters' commitment to science and nature. The spontaneous gesture of touch in the wilds of Tanzania authorizes a whole doctrine of representation. Jane, as Dr. Goodall, is empowered to speak for the chimpanzees. Science speaks for nature. Authorized by unforced touch, the dynamics of representation take over, ushering in the reign of freedom and communication. This is the structure of depoliticizing expert discourse, so critical to the mythic political structures of the "modern" world and to the mythic political despair of much "post-modernism," so undermined by fears about the breakdown of representation.[27] Unfortunately, representation, fraudulent or not, is a very resilient practice.

The clasping hands of the Gulf ad are semiotically similar to the elution peak in the Vega ad of Figure 5: "Guaranteed. Pure."; "Understanding Is Everything." There is no interruption in these stories of communication, progress, and salvation through science and technology. The story of Jane Goodall in Gombe, however, can be made to show its conditions of possibility; even in the footage of the National Geographic specials we see the young woman on a mountain top at night eating from a can of pork and beans, that sign of industrial civilization so crucial to the history of colonialism in Africa, as Orson Welles's voice-over speaks of the lonely quest for contact with nature! In one of Goodall's published accounts of the early days at Gombe, we learn that she and her mother, enroute to the chimpanzee preserve, were stopped on the shores of Lake Tanganyika in the town of Kigoma, across from the no-longer-Belgian Congo, as *uhuru,* freedom, sounded across Africa. Goodall and her mother made 2000 spam sandwiches for fleeing Belgians before embarking for the "wilds of Tanzania" (Goodall, 1971, p. 27). It is also possible to reconstruct a history of Gombe as a research site in the 1970s. One of the points that stands out in this reconstruction is that people—research staff and their families, African, European, and North American—considerably outnumbered chimpanzees during the years of most intense scientific work. Nature and Society met in one story; in another story, the structure of action and the actants take a different shape.

It is hard, however, to make the story of Jane Goodall and the wild chimpanzees shed its "modern" message about "saving nature," in both senses of nature as salvific and of the scientist speaking for and preserving nature in a drama of representation. Let us, therefore, leave this narrative for another colonized tropical spot in the Real/Earth quadrant in the semiotic square—Amazonia. Remembering that all colonized spots have, euphemistically stated, a special relation to nature, let us structure this story to tell something amodern about nature and society—and perhaps something more compatible with the survival of all the networked actants, human and unhuman. To tell this story we must disbelieve in both nature and society and resist their associated imperatives to represent, to reflect, to echo, to act as a ventriloquist for "the other." The main point is there will be no Adam—and no Jane—who gets to name all the beings in the garden. The reason is simple: there is no garden and never has been. No name and no touch is original. The question animating this diffracted narrative, this story based on little differences, is also simple: is there a consequential difference between a political semiotics of articulation and a political semiotics of representation?

The August 1990 issue of *Discover* magazine has a story entitled "Tech in the Jungle." A one and one-half page color photo of a Kayapó Indian, in indigenous dress and using a videocamera, dramatically accompanies the opening paragraphs. The caption tells us the man is "tap[ing] his tribesmen, who had gathered in the central Brazilian town of Altamira to protest plans for a hydroelectric dam on their territory" (Zimmer, 1990, 42-5). All the cues in the *Discover* article invite us to read this photo as the drama of the meeting of the "traditional" and the "modern," staged in this popular North American scientific publication for audiences who have a stake in maintaining belief in those categories. We have, however, as disbelieving members of those audiences, a different political, semiotic responsibility, one made easier by another publication, Susanna Hecht and Alexander Cockburn's *The Fate of the Forest* (1989; see also T. Turner, 1990) through which I propose to suggest articulations and solidarities with the *filming practice* of the Kayapó man, rather than to read the *photograph of him,* which will not be reproduced in this essay.[28]

In their book, which was deliberately packaged, published, and marketed in a format and in time for the 1989 December gift-giving season, a modest act of cultural politics not to be despised, Hecht and Cockburn have a central agenda. They insist on deconstructing the image of the tropical rain forest, especially Amazonia, as "Eden under glass." They do this in order to insist on locations of responsibility and empowerment in current conservation struggles, on the outcome of which the lives and ways of life for people and many other species depend. In particular, they support a politics not of "saving nature" but of "social nature," not of national parks and walled-off reserves, responding with a technical fix to whatever particular danger to survival seems most inescapable, but of a different organization of land and people, where the practice of justice restructures the concept of nature.

The authors tell a relentless story of a "social nature" over many hundreds of years, at every turn co-inhabited and co-constituted by humans, land, and other organisms. For example, the diversity and patterns of tree species in the forest cannot be explained without the deliberate, long-term practices of the Kayapó and other groups, whom Hecht and Cockburn describe, miraculously avoiding romanticizing, as "accomplished environmental scientists." Hecht and Cockburn avoid romanticizing because they do not invoke the category of the modern as the special zone of science. Thus, they do not have to navigate the shoals threatening comparisons of, according to taste, mere or wonderful "ethnoscience" with real or disgusting "modern science." The authors insist on visualizing the forest as the dynamic outcome of human as well as biological history. Only after the dense indigenous populations—numbering from six to twelve million in 1492—had been sickened, enslaved, killed, and otherwise displaced from along the rivers could Europeans represent Amazonia as "empty" of culture, as "nature," or, in later terms, as a purely "biological" entity.

But, of course, the Amazon was not and did not become "empty," although "nature" (like "man") is one of those discursive constructions that operates as a technology for making the world over into its image. First, there are indigenous people in the forest, many of whom have organized themselves in recent years into a regionally grounded, world-historical subject prepared for local/global interactions, or, in other terms, for building new and powerful collectives out of humans and unhumans, technological and organic. With all of the power to reconstitute the real implied in discursive construction, they have become a new discursive subject/object, the Indigenous Peoples of the Amazon, made up of national and tribal groups from Colombia, Ecuador, Brazil, and Peru, numbering about one million persons, who in turn articulate themselves with other organized groups of the indigenous peoples of the Americas. Also, in the forest are about 200,000 people of mixed ancestry, partly overlapping with the indigenous people. Making their living as petty extractors—of gold, nuts, rubber, and other forest products—they have a history of many generations in the Amazon. It is a complex history of dire exploitation. These people are also threatened by the latest schemes of world banks or national capitals from Brasília to Washington.[29] They have for many decades been in conflict with indigenous peoples over resources and ways of life. Their presence in the forest might be the fruit of the colonial fantasies of the *bandeirantes,* romantics, curators, politicians, or speculators; but their fate is entwined intimately with that of the other always historical inhabitants of this sharply contested world. It is from these desperately poor people, specifically the rubber tappers union, that Chico Mendes, the world-changing activist murdered on December 22, 1988, came.[30]

A crucial part of Mendes's vision for which he was killed was the union of the extractors and the indigenous peoples of the forest into, as Hecht and Cockburn argue, the "true defenders of the forest." Their position as defenders derives not from a concept of "nature under threat," but rather from a *relationship* with "the forest as the integument in their own elemental struggle to survive" (p. 196).[31] In other words, their authority derives *not* from the power to represent from a distance, *nor* from an ontological natural status, but from a constitutive social relationality in which the forest is an integral partner, part of natural/social embodiment. In their claims for authority over the fate of the forest, the resident peoples are articulating a social collective entity among humans, other organisms, and other kinds of non-human actors.

Indigenous people are resisting a long history of forced "tutelage," in order to confront the powerful representations of the national and international environmentalists, bankers, developers, and technocrats. The extractors, for example, the rubber tappers, are also independently articulating their collective viewpoint. Neither group is willing to see the Amazon "saved" by their exclusion and permanent subjection to historically dominating political and economic forces. As Hecht and Cockburn put it, "The rubber tappers have not risked their lives for extractive reserves so they could live on them as debt peons" (p. 202). "Any program for the Amazon begins with basic human rights: an end to debt bondage, violence, enslavement, and killings practiced by those who would seize the lands these forest people have occupied for generations. Forest people seek legal recognition of native lands and extractive reserves held under the principle of collective property, worked as individual holdings with individual returns" (p. 207).

At the second Brazilian national meeting of the Forest People's Alliance at Rio Branco in 1989, shortly after Mendes's murder raised the stakes and catapulted the issues into the international media, a program was formulated in tension with the latest Brazilian state policy called *Nossa Natureza.* Articulating quite a different notion of the first person plural relation to nature or natural surroundings, the basis of the program of the Forest People's Alliance is control by and for the peoples of the forest. The core matters are direct control of indigenous lands by native peoples; agrarian reform joined to an environmental program; economic and technical development; health posts; raised incomes; locally controlled marketing systems; an end to fiscal incentives for cattle ranchers, agribusiness, and unsustainable logging; an end to debt peonage; and police and legal protection. Hecht and Cockburn call this an "ecology of justice" that rejects a technicist solution, in whatever benign or malignant form, to environmental destruction. The Forest People's Alliance does not reject scientific or technical know-how, their own and others'; instead, they reject the "modern" political epistemology that bestows jurisdiction on the basis of technoscientific discourse. The fundamental point is that the Amazonian Biosphere is an irreducibly human/non-human collective entity.[32] There *will be* no nature without justice. Nature and justice, contested discursive objects embodied in the material world, will become extinct or survive together.

Theory here is exceedingly corporeal, and the body is a collective; it is an historical artifact constituted by human as well as organic and technological unhuman actors. Actors are entities which do things, have effects, build worlds in concatenation with other *unlike* actors.[33] Some actors, for example specific human ones, can try to reduce other actors to resources—to mere ground and matrix for their action; but such a move is contestable, not the necessary relation of "human nature" to the rest of the world. Other actors, human and unhuman, regularly resist reductionisms. The powers of domination do fail sometimes in their projects to pin other actors down; people can work to enhance the relevant failure rates. Social nature is the nexus I have called artifactual nature. The human "defenders of the forest" do not and have not lived in a garden; it is from a knot in the always historical and heterogeneous nexus of social nature that they articulate their claims. Or perhaps, it is within such a nexus that I and people like me narrate a possible politics of articulation rather than representation. It is our responsibility to learn whether such a fiction is one with which the Amazonians might wish to connect in the interests of an alliance to defend the rain forest and its human and non-human ways of life—because assuredly North Americans, Europeans, and the Japanese, among others, cannot watch from afar as if we were not actors, willing or not, in the life and death struggles in the Amazon.

In a review of *Fate of the Forest*, Joe Kane, author of another book on the tropical rain forest marketed in time for Christmas in 1989, the adventure trek *Running the Amazon (1989)*,[34] raised this last issue in a way that will sharpen and clarify my stakes in arguing against a politics of representation generally, and in relation to questions of environmentalism and conservation specifically. In the context of worrying about ways that social nature or socialist ecology sounded too much like the multi-use policies in national forests in the United States, which have resulted in rapacious exploitation of the land and of other organisms, Kane asked a simple question: "[W]ho speaks for the jaguar?" Now, I care about the survival of the jaguar—and the chimpanzee, and the Hawaiian land snails, and the spotted owl, and a lot of other earthlings. I care a great deal; in fact, I think I and my social groups are particularly, but not uniquely, *responsible* if jaguars, and many other non-human, as well as human, ways of life should perish. But Kane's question seemed wrong on a fundamental level. Then I understood why. His question was precisely like that asked by some pro-life groups in the abortion debates: Who speaks for the fetus? What is wrong with both questions? And how does this matter relate to science studies as cultural studies?

Who speaks for the jaguar? Who speaks for the fetus? Both questions rely on a political semiotics of representation.[35] Permanently speechless, forever requiring the services of a ventriloquist, never forcing a recall vote, in each case the object or ground of representation is the realization of the representative's fondest dream. As Marx said in a somewhat different context, "They cannot represent themselves; they must be represented."[36] But for a political semiology of representation, nature and the unborn fetus are even better, epistemologically, than subjugated human adults. The effectiveness of such representation depends on distancing operations. The represented must be disengaged from surrounding and constituting discursive and non-discursive nexuses and relocated in the authorial domain of the representative. Indeed, the effect of this magical operation is to disempower precisely those—in our case, the pregnant woman and the peoples of the forest—who are "close" to the now-represented "natural" object. Both the jaguar and the fetus are carved out of one collective entity and relocated in another, where they are reconstituted as objects of a particular kind—as the ground of a representational practice that *forever* authorizes the ventriloquist. Tutelage will be eternal. The represented is reduced to the permanent status of the recipient of action, never to be a co-actor in an articulated practice among unlike, but joined, social partners.

Everything that used to surround and sustain the represented object, such as pregnant women and local people, simply disappears or re-enters the drama as an agonist. For example, the pregnant woman becomes *juridically* and *medically,* two very powerful discursive realms, the "maternal environment" (Hubbard, 1990). Pregnant women and local people are the *least* able to "speak for" objects like jaguars or fetuses because they get discursively reconstituted as beings with opposing "interests." Neither woman nor fetus, jaguar nor Kayapó Indian is an actor in the drama of representation. One set of entities becomes the represented, the other becomes the environment, often threatening, of the represented object. The *only* actor left is the spokesperson, the one who represents. The forest is no longer the integument in a co-constituted social nature; the woman is in no way a partner in an intricate and intimate dialectic of social relationality crucial to her own personhood, as well as to the possible personhood of her social—*but unlike*—internal co-actor.[37] In the liberal logic of representation, the fetus and the jaguar must be protected precisely from those closest to them, from their "surround." The power of life and death must be delegated to the epistemologically most disinterested ventriloquist, and it is crucial to remember that all of this *is* about the power of life and death.

Who, within the myth of modernity, is less biased by competing interests or polluted by excessive closeness than the expert, especially the scientist? Indeed, even better than the lawyer, judge, or national legislator, the scientist is the perfect representative of nature, that is, of the permanently and constitutively speechless objective world. Whether he be a male or a female, his passionless distance is his greatest virtue; this discursively constituted, structurally gendered distance legitimates his professional privilege, which in these cases, again, is the power to testify about the right to life and death. After Edward Said quoted Marx on representation in his epigraph to *Orientalism,* he quoted Benjamin Disraeli's *Tancred,* "The East is a career." The separate, objective world—non-social nature—is a career. Nature legitimates the scientist's career, as the Orient justifies the representational practices of the Orientalist, even as precisely "Nature" and the "Orient" are the *products* of the constitutive practice of scientists and orientalists.

These are the inversions that have been the object of so much attention in science studies. Bruno Latour sketches the double structure of representation through which scientists establish the objective status of their knowledge. First, operations shape and enroll new objects or allies through visual displays or other means called inscription devices. Second, scientists speak as if they were the mouthpiece for the speechless objects that they have just shaped and enrolled as allies in an agonistic field called science. Latour defines the actant as that which is represented; the objective world *appears* to be the actant solely by virtue of the operations of representation (Latour, 1987, pp. 70–74, 90).

The authorship rests with the representor, even as he claims independent object status for the represented. In this doubled structure, the simultaneously semiotic and political ambiguity of representation is glaring. First, a chain of substitutions, operating through inscription devices, relocates power and action in "objects" divorced from polluting contextualizations and named by formal abstractions ("the fetus"). Then, the reader of inscriptions speaks for his docile constituencies, the objects. This is not a very lively world, and it does not finally offer much to jaguars, in whose interests the whole apparatus supposedly operates.

In this essay I have been arguing for another way of seeing actors and actants—and consequently another way of working to position scientists and science in important struggles in the world. I have stressed actants as collective entities doing things in a structured and structuring field of action; I have framed the issue in terms of articulation rather than representation. Human beings use names to point to themselves and other actors and easily mistake the names for the things. These same humans also think the traces of inscription devices are like names—pointers to things, such that the inscriptions and the things can be enrolled in dramas of substitution and inversion. But the things, in my view, do not pre-exist as ever-elusive, but fully pre-packaged, referents for the names. Other actors are more like tricksters than that. Boundaries take provisional, never-finished shape in articulatory practices. The potential for the unexpected from unstripped human and unhuman actants enrolled in articulations—i.e., the potential for generation—remains both to trouble and to empower technoscience. Western philosophers sometimes take account of the inadequacy of names by stressing the "negativity" inherent in all representations. This takes us back to Spivak's remark cited early in this paper about the important things that we cannot not desire, but can never possess—or represent, because representation depends on possession of a passive resource, namely, the silent object, the *stripped* actant. Perhaps we can, however, "articulate" with humans and unhumans in a social relationship, which for us is always language-mediated (among other semiotic, i.e., "meaningful," mediations). But, for our unlike partners, well, the action is "different," perhaps "negative" from our linguistic point of view, but crucial to the generativity of the collective. It is the empty space, the undecidability, the wiliness of other actors, the "negativity," that give me confidence in the *reality* and therefore ultimate *unrepresentability* of social nature and that make me suspect doctrines of representation and objectivity.

My crude characterization does not end up with an "objective world" or "nature," but it certainly does insist on the *world*. This world must always be articulated, from people's points of view, through "situated knowledges" (Haraway, 1988; 1991). These knowledges are friendly to science, but do not provide any grounds for history-escaping inversions and amnesia about how articulations get made, about their political semiotics, if you will. I think the world is precisely what gets lost in doctrines of representation and scientific objectivity. It is *because* I care about jaguars, among other actors, including the overlapping but non-identical groups called forest peoples and ecologists, that I reject Joe Kane's question. Some science studies scholars have been terrified to criticize their constructivist formulations because the only alternative seems to be some retrograde kind of "going back" to nature and to philosophical realism.[38] But above all people, these scholars should know that "nature" and "realism" are precisely the consequences of representational practices. Where we need to move is not "back" to nature, but *elsewhere*, through and within an artifactual social nature, which these very scholars have helped to make expressable in current Western scholarly practice. That knowledge-building practice might be articulated to other practices in "pro-life" ways that aren't about the fetus or the jaguar as nature fetishes and the expert as their ventriloquist.

Prepared by this long detour, we can return to the Kayapó man videotaping his tribesmen as they protest a new hydroelectric dam on their territory. The National Geographic Society, *Discover* magazine, and Gulf Oil—and much philosophy and social science—would have us see his practice as a double boundary crossing between the primitive and the modern. His representational practice, signified by his use of the latest technology, places him in the realm of the modern. He is, then, engaged in an entertaining contradiction—the preservation of an unmodern way of life with the aid of incongruous modern technology. But, from the perspective of a political semiotics of articulation, the man might well be forging a recent collective of humans and unhumans, in this case made up of the Kayapó, videocams, land, plants, animals, near and distant audiences, and other constituents; but no boundary violation is involved. The way of life is not unmodern (closer to nature); the camera is not modern or postmodern (in society). Those categories should no longer make sense. Where there is no nature and no society, there is no pleasure, no entertainment to be had in representing the violation of the boundary between them. Too bad for nature magazines, but a gain for inappropriate/d others.

The videotaping practice does not thereby become innocent or uninteresting; but its meanings have to be approached differently, in terms of the kinds of collective action taking place and the claims they make on others—such as ourselves, people who do not live in the Amazon. We *are all* in chiasmatic borderlands, liminal areas where new shapes, new kinds of action and responsibility, are gestating in the world. The man using that camera is forging a practical claim on us, morally and epistemologically, as well as on the other forest people to whom he will show the tape to consolidate defense of the forest. His practice invites further articulation—on terms shaped by the forest people. They will no longer be represented as Objects, not because they cross a line to represent themselves in "modern" terms as Subjects, but because they powerfully form articulated collectives.

In May of 1990, a week-long meeting took place in Iquitos, a formerly prosperous rubber boom-town in the Peruvian Amazon. COICA, the Coordinating Body for the Indigenous Peoples of the Amazon, had assembled forest people (from all the nations constituting Amazonia), environmental groups from around the world (Greenpeace, Friends of the Earth, the Rain Forest Action Network, etc.), and media organizations (*Time* magazine, CNN, NBC, etc.) in order "to find a common path on which we can work to preserve the Amazon forest" (Arena-De Rosa, 1990, pp. 1–2). Rain forest protection was formulated as a necessarily joint human rights-ecological issue. The fundamental demand by indigenous people was that they must be part of *all* international negotiations involving their territories. "Debt for nature" swaps were particular foci of controversy, especially where indigenous groups end up worse off than in previous agreements with their governments as a result of bargaining between banks, external conservation groups, and national states. The controversy generated a proposal: instead of a swap of debt-for-nature, forest people would support swaps of debt-for-indigenous-controlled territory, in which non-indigenous environmentalists would have a "redefined role in helping to develop the plan for conservation management of the particular region of the rain forest" (Arena-De Rosa, 1990). Indigenous environmentalists would also be recognized not for their quaint "ethnoscience," but for their *knowledge*.

Nothing in this structure of action rules out articulations by scientists or other North Americans who care about jaguars and other actors; but the patterns, flows, and intensities of power are most certainly changed. That is what articulation does; it is always a non-innocent, contestable practice; the partners are never set once and for all. There is no ventriloquism here. Articulation is work, and it may fail. All the people who care, cognitively, emotionally, and politically, must articulate their position in a field constrained by a new collective entity, made up of indigenous people and other human and unhuman actors. Commitment and engagement, not their invalidation, in an emerging collective are the conditions of joining knowledge-producing and world-building practices. This is situated knowledge in the New World; it builds on common places, and it takes unexpected turns. So far, such knowledge has not been sponsored by the major oil corporations, banks, and logging interests. That is precisely one of the reasons why there is so much work for North Americans, Europeans, and Japanese, among others, to do in articulation with those humans and non-humans who live in rain forests and in many other places in the semiotic space called earth.

B. Outer Space: The Extraterrestrial

Since we have spent so much time on earth, a prophylactic exercise for residents of the alien "First World," we will rush through the remaining three quadrants of the semiotic square. We move from one topical commonplace to another, from earth to space, to see what turns our journeys to elsewhere might take.

An ecosystem is always of a particular type, for example, a temperate grassland or a tropical rain forest. In the iconography of late capitalism, Jane Goodall did not go to that kind of ecosystem. She went to the "wilds of Tanzania," a mythic "ecosystem" reminiscent of the original garden from which her kind had been expelled and to which she returned to commune with the wilderness's present inhabitants to learn how to survive. This wilderness was close in its dream quality to "space," but the wilderness of Africa was coded as dense, damp, bodily, full of sensuous creatures who touch intimately and intensely. In contrast, the extraterrestrial is coded to be fully general; it is about escape from the bounded globe into an anti-ecosystem called, simply, space. Space is not about "man's" origins on earth but about "his" future, the two key allochronic times of salvation history. Space and the tropics are both utopian topical figures in Western imaginations, and their opposed properties dialectically signify origins and ends for the creature whose mundane life is supposedly outside both: modern or postmodern man.

The first primates to approach that abstract place called "space" were monkeys and apes. A rhesus monkey survived an 83 mile-high flight in 1949. Jane Goodall arrived in "the wilds of Tanzania" in 1960 to encounter and name the famous Gombe Stream chimpanzees introduced to the National Geographic television audience in 1965. However, other chimpanzees were vying for the spotlight in the early 1960s. On January 31, 1961, as part of the United States man-in-space program, the chimpanzee HAM, trained for his task at Holloman Air Force Base, 20 minutes by car from Alamogordo, New Mexico, near the site of the first atom bomb explosion in July 1945, was shot into suborbital flight (Figure 8). HAM's name inevitably recalls Noah's youngest and only black son. But this chimpanzee's name was from a different kind of text. His name was an acronym for the scientific-military institution that launched him, *H*olloman *A*ero-*M*edical; and he rode an arc that traced the birth path of modern science—the parabola, the conic section. HAM's parabolic path is rich with evocations of the history of Western science. The path of a projectile that does not escape gravity, the parabola is the shape considered so deeply by Galileo, at the first mythic moment of origins of modernity, when the unquantifiable sensuous and countable mathematical properties of bodies were separated from each other in scientific knowledge. It describes the path of ballistic weapons, and it is the trope for "man's" doomed projects in the writings of the existentialists in the 1950s. The parabola traces the path of Rocket Man at the end of World

War II in Thomas Pynchon's *Gravity's Rainbow* (1973). An understudy for man, HAM went only to the boundary of space, in suborbital flight. On his return to earth, he was named. He had been known only as #65 before his successful flight. If, in the official birth-mocking language of the Cold War, the mission had to be "aborted," the authorities did not want the public worrying about the death of a famous and named, even if not quite human, astronaut. In fact, #65 did have a name among his handlers, Chop Chop Chang, recalling the stunning racism in which the other primates have been made to participate.[39] The space race's surrogate child was an "understudy for man in the conquest of space" (Eimerl and De Vore, 1965, p. 173). His hominid cousins would transcend that closed parabolic figure, first in the ellipse of orbital flight, then in the open trajectories of escape from earth's gravity.

HAM, his human cousins and simian colleagues, and their englobing and interfacing technology were implicated in a reconstitution of masculinity in Cold War and space race idioms. The movie *The Right Stuff* (1985) shows the first crop of human astronau(gh)ts struggling with their affronted pride when they realize their tasks were competently performed by their simian cousins. They and the chimps were caught in the same theater of the Cold War, where the masculinist, death-defying, and skill-requiring heroics of the old jet aircraft test pilots became obsolete, to be replaced by the media-hype routines of projects Mercury, Apollo, and their sequelae. After chimpanzee Enos completed a fully automated orbital flight on November 29, 1961, John Glenn, who would be the first human American astronaut to orbit earth, defensively "looked toward the future by affirming his belief in the superiority of astronauts over chimponauts." *Newsweek* announced Glenn's orbital flight of February 20, 1962, with the headline, "John Glenn: One Machine That Worked Without Flaw."[40] Soviet primates on both sides of the line of hominization raced their U.S. siblings into extraterrestrial orbit. The space ships, the recording and tracking technologies, animals, and human beings were joined as cyborgs in a theater of war, science, and popular culture.

Henry Burroughs's famous photograph of an interested and intelligent, actively participating HAM, watching the hands of a white, laboratory-coated, human man release him from his contour couch, illuminated the system of meanings that binds humans and apes together in the late twentieth century (Weaver, 1961). HAM is the perfect child, reborn in the cold matrix of space. *Time* described chimponaut Enos in his "fitted contour couch that looked like a cradle trimmed with electronics.[41] Enos and HAM were cyborg neonates, born of the interface of the dreams about a technicist automaton and masculinist autonomy. There could be no more iconic cyborg than a telemetrically implanted chimpanzee, understudy for man, launched from earth in the space program, while his conspecific in the jungle, "in a spontaneous gesture of trust," embraced the hand of a woman scientist named Jane in a Gulf Oil ad showing "man's place in the ecological structure." On one end of time and space, the chimpanzee in the wilderness modeled communication for the stressed, ecologically threatened and threatening, modern human. On the other end, the ET chimpanzee modeled social and technical cybernetic communication systems, which permit postmodern man to escape both the jungle and the city, in a thrust into the future made possible by the social-technical systems of the "information age" in a global context of threatened nuclear war. The closing image of a human fetus hurtling through space in Stanley Kubrick's *2001: A Space Odyssey* (1968) completed the voyage of discovery begun by the weapon-wielding apes at the film's gripping opening. It was the project(ile) of self-made, reborn man, in the process of being raptured out of history. The Cold War was simulated ultimate war; the media and advertising industries of nuclear culture produced in the bodies of animals—paradigmatic natives and aliens—the reassuring images appropriate to this state of pure war (Virilio and Lotringer, 1983).[42]

In the aftermath of the Cold War, we face not the end of nuclearism, but its dissemination. Even without our knowing his ultimate fate as an adult caged chimpanzee, the photograph of HAM rapidly ceases to entertain, much less to edify. Therefore, let us look to another cyborg image to figure possible emergencies of inappropriate/d others to challenge our rapturous mythic brothers, the postmodern spacemen.

At first sight, the T-shirt worn by anti-nuclear demonstrators at the Mother's and Others' Day Action in 1987 at the United States's Nevada nuclear test site seems in simple opposition to HAM in his electronic cradle (Figure 9). But a little unpacking shows the promising semiotic and political complexity of the image and of the action. When the T-shirt was sent to the printer, the name of the event was still the "Mother's Day Action," but not long after some planning participants objected. For many, Mother's Day was, at best, an ambivalent time for a women's action. The overdetermined gender coding of patriarchal nuclear culture all too easily makes women responsible for peace while men fiddle with their dangerous war toys without semiotic dissonance. With its commercialism and multi-leveled reinforcement of compulsory heterosexual reproduction, Mother's Day is also not everybody's favorite feminist holiday. For others, intent

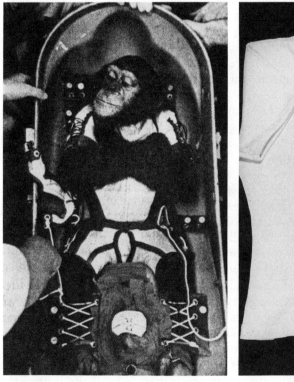

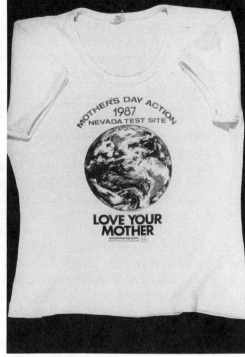

FIGURE 8. Ham awaits release in his couch aboard the recovery vessel LSD *Donner* after his successful Mercury Project launch. Photograph by Henry Borroughs.

FIGURE 9. Mother's Day 1987 Nevada Test Site Action T-shirt.

on reclaiming the holiday for other meanings, mothers, and by extension women in general, do have a special obligation to preserve children, and so the earth, from military destruction. For them, the earth is metaphorically mother and child, and in both figurations, a subject of nurturing and birthing. However, this was not an all-women's (much less all-mothers') action, although women organized and shaped it. From discussion, the designation "Mother's and Others' Day Action" emerged. But then, some thought that meant mothers and men. It took memory exercises in feminist analysis to rekindle shared consciousness that mother does not equal woman and vice versa. Part of the day's purpose was to recode Mother's Day to signify men's obligations to nurture the earth and all its children. In the spirit of this set of issues, at a time when Baby M and her many debatable—and unequally positioned—parents were in the news and the courts, the all-female affinity group which I joined took as its name the Surrogate Others. These surrogates were not understudies for man, but were gestating for another kind of emergence.

From the start, the event was conceived as an action that linked social justice and human rights, environmentalism, anti-militarism, and anti-nuclearism. On the T-shirt, there is, indeed, the perfect icon of the union of all issues under environmentalism's rubric: the "whole earth," the lovely, cloud-wrapped, blue, planet earth is simultaneously a kind of fetus floating in the amniotic cosmos and a mother to all its own inhabitants, germ of the future, matrix of the past and present. It is a perfect globe, joining the changeling matter of mortal bodies and the ideal eternal sphere of the philosophers. This snapshot resolves the dilemma of modernity, the separation of Subject and Object, Mind and Body. There is, however, a jarring note in all this, even for the most devout. That particular image of the earth, of Nature, could only exist if a camera on a satellite had taken the picture, which is, of course, precisely the case. Who speaks for the earth? Firmly in the object world called nature, this bourgeois, family-affirming snapshot of mother earth is about as uplifting as a loving commercial Mother's Day card. And yet, it *is* beautiful, and it is ours; it must be brought into a different focus. The T-shirt is part of a complex collective entity, involving many circuits, delegations, and displacements of competencies. Only in the context of the space race in the first place, and the militarization and commodification of the whole earth, does it make sense to relocate that image as the special sign of an anti-nuclear, anti-militaristic, earth-focused politics. The relocation does not cancel its other resonances; it contests for their outcome.

I read Environmental Action's "whole earth" as a sign of an irreducible artifactual social nature, like the Gaia of SF writer John Varley and biologist Lynn Margulis. Relocated on this particular T-shirt, the satellite's eye view of planet earth provokes an ironic version of the question, who speaks for the earth (for the fetus, the mother, the jaguar, the object world of nature, all those who must be represented)? For many of us, the irony made it possible to participate—indeed, to participate as fully committed, if semiotically unruly, eco-feminists. Not everybody in the Mother's and Others' Day Action would agree; for many, the T-shirt image meant what it said, love your mother who is the earth. Nuclearism is misogyny. The field of readings in tension with each other is also part of the point. Eco-feminism and the non-violent direct action movement have been based on struggles over differences, not on identity. There is hardly a need for affinity groups and their endless process if sameness prevailed. Affinity is precisely *not* identity; the sacred image of the same is not gestating on this Mother's and Others' Day. Literally, enrolling the satellite's camera and the peace action in Nevada into a new collective, this Love Your Mother image is based on diffraction, on the processing of small but consequential differences. The processing of differences, semiotic action, is about ways of life.

The Surrogate Others planned a birthing ceremony in Nevada, and so they made a birth canal—a sixteen-foot long, three-foot diameter, floral polyester-covered worm with lovely dragon eyes. It was a pleasingly artifactual beast, ready for connection. The worm-dragon was laid under the barbed-wire boundary between the land on which the demonstrators could stand legally and the land on which they would be arrested as they emerged. Some of the Surrogate Others conceived of crawling through the worm to the forbidden side as an act of solidarity with the tunneling creatures of the desert, who had to share their subsurface niches with the test site's chambers. This surrogate birthing was definitely not about the obligatory heterosexual nuclear family compulsively reproducing itself in the womb of the state, with or without the underpaid services of the wombs of "surrogate mothers." Mother's and Others' Day was looking up.

It wasn't only the desert's non-human organisms with whom the activists were in solidarity as they emerged onto the proscribed territory. From the point of view of the demonstrators, they were quite legally on the test-site land. This was so not out of some "abstract" sense that the land was the people's and had been usurped by the war state, but for more "concrete" reasons: all the demonstrators had written permits to be on the land signed by the Western Shoshone National Council. The 1863 Treaty of Ruby Valley recognized the Western Shoshone title to ancestral territory, including the land illegally invaded by the U.S. government to build its nuclear facility. The treaty has never been modified or abrogated, and U.S. efforts to buy the land (at 15 cents per acre) in 1979 was refused by the only body authorized to decide, the Western Shoshone National Council. The county sheriff and his deputies, surrogates for the federal government, were, in "discursive" and "embodied" fact, trespassing. In 1986 the Western Shoshone began to issue permits to the anti-nuclear demonstrators as part of a coalition that joined anti-nuclearism and indigenous land rights. It is, of course, hard to make citizens' arrests of the police when they have you handcuffed and when the courts are on their side. But it is quite possible to join this ongoing struggle, which is very much "at home," and to articulate it with the defense of the Amazon. That articulation requires collectives of human and unhuman actors of many kinds.

There were many other kinds of "symbolic action" at the test site that day in 1987. The costumes of the sheriff's deputies and their nasty plastic handcuffs were also symbolic action—highly embodied symbolic action. The "symbolic action" of brief, safe arrest is also quite a different matter from the "semiotic" conditions under which most people in the U.S., especially people of color and the poor, are jailed. The difference is not the presence or absence of "symbolism," but the force of the respective collectives made up of humans and unhumans, of people, other organisms, technologies, institutions. I am not unduly impressed with the power of the drama of the Surrogate Others and the other affinity groups, nor, unfortunately, of the whole action. But I do take seriously the work to relocate, to diffract, embodied meanings as crucial work to be done in gestating a new world.[43] It is cultural politics, and it is technoscience politics. The task is to build more powerful collectives in dangerously unpromising times.

Not–B. Inner Space: The Biomedical Body

The limitless reaches of outer space, joined to Cold War and post-Cold War nuclear technoscience, seem vastly distant from their negation, the enclosed and dark regions of the inside of the human body, domain of the apparatuses of biomedical visualization. But these two quadrants of our semiotic square are multiply tied together in technoscience's heterogeneous apparatuses of bodily production. As Sarah Franklin noted, "The two new investment frontiers, outer space and inner space, vie for the futures market."

In this "futures market," two entities are especially interesting for this essay: the fetus and the immune system, both of which are embroiled in determinations of what may count as nature and as human, as separate natural object and as juridical subject. We have already looked briefly at some of the matrices of discourse about the fetus in the discussion of earth (who speaks for the fetus?) and outer space (the planet floating free as cosmic germ). Here, I will concentrate on contestations for what counts as a self and an actor in contemporary immune system discourse.

The equation of Outer Space and Inner Space, and of their conjoined discourses of extraterrestrialism, ultimate frontiers, and high technology war, is literal in the official history celebrating 100 years of the National Geographic Society (Bryan, 1987). The chapter that recounts the magazine's coverage of the Mercury, Gemini, Apollo, and Mariner voyages is called "Space" and introduced with the epigraph, "The Choice Is the Universe—or Nothing." The final chapter, full of stunning biomedical images, is titled "Inner Space" and introduced with the epigraph, "The Stuff of the Stars Has Come Alive."[44] The photography convinces the viewer of the fraternal relation of inner and outer space. But, curiously, in outer space, we see spacemen fitted into explorer craft or floating about as individuated cosmic fetuses, while in the supposed earthy space of our own interiors, we see non-humanoid strangers who are the means by which our bodies sustain our integrity and individuality, indeed our humanity in the face of a world of others. We seem invaded not just by the threatening "non-selves" that the immune system guards against, but more fundamentally by our own strange parts.

Lennart Nilsson's photographs, in the coffee table art book *The Body Victorious* (1987), as well as in many medical texts, are landmarks in the photography of the alien inhabitants of inner space[45] (Figure 10). The blasted scenes, sumptuous textures, evocative colors, and ET monsters of the immune landscape are simply *there*, inside *us*. A white extruding tendril of a pseudopodinous macrophage ensnares bacteria; the hillocks of chromosomes lie flattened on a blue-hued moonscape of some other planet; an infected cell buds myriads of deadly virus particles into the reaches of inner space where more cells will be victimized; the auto-immune disease-ravaged head of a femur glows against a sunset on a dead world; cancer cells are surrounded by the lethal mobil squads of killer T-cells that throw chemical poisons into the self's malignant traitor cells.

A diagram of the "Evolution of Recognition Systems" in a recent immunology textbook makes clear the intersection of the themes of literally "wonderful" diversity, escalating complexity, the self as a defended stronghold, and extraterrestrialism in inner space (Figure 11). Under a diagram culminating in the evolution of the mammals, represented without comment by a mouse and a *fully-suited spaceman*, is this explanation: "From the humble amoeba searching for food (top left) to the mammal with its so-phisticated humoral and cellular immune mechanisms (bottom right), the process of 'self versus non-self recognition' shows a steady development, keeping pace with the in-creasing need of animals to maintain their integrity in a hostile environment. The decision at which point 'immunity' appeared is thus a purely semantic one" (Playfair, 1984, emphasis in the original). These are the "semantics" of defense and invasion. The perfection of the fully defended, "victorious" self is a chilling fantasy, linking phago-cytotic amoeba and space-voyaging man cannibalizing the earth in an evolutionary te-leology of post-apocalypse extraterrestrialism. When is a self enough of a self that its boundaries become central to institutionalized discourses in biomedicine, war, and business?

Images of the immune system as a battlefield abound in science sections of daily newspapers and in popular magazines, e.g., *Time* magazine's 1984 graphic for the AIDS virus's "invasion" of the cell-as-factory. The virus is a tank, and the viruses ready for

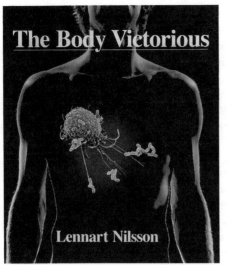

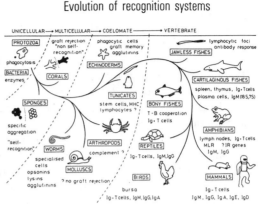

FIGURE 10. Design for Lennart Nilsson book.

FIGURE 11. From a recent immunology textbook.

export from the expropriated cells are lined up ready to continue their advance on the body as a productive force. The *National Geographic* explicitly punned on Star Wars in its graphic called "Cell Wars" (Jaret, 1986). The militarized, automated factory is a favorite convention among immune system technical illustrators and photographic processors. The specific historical markings of a Star Wars-maintained individuality are enabled by high-technology visualization technologies, which are also basic to conducting war and commerce, such as computer-aided graphics, artificial intelligence software, and specialized scanning systems.

It is not just imagers of the immune system who learn from military cultures; military cultures draw symbiotically on immune system discourse, just as strategic planners draw directly from and contribute to video game practices and science fiction. For example, arguing for an elite special force within the parameters of "low-intensity conflict" doctrine, a U.S. army officer wrote: "The most appropriate example to describe how this system would work is the most complex biological model we know—the body's immune system. Within the body there exists a remarkably complex corps of internal bodyguards. In absolute numbers they are small—only about one percent of the body's cells. Yet they consist of reconnaissance specialists, killers, reconstitution specialists, and communicators that can seek out invaders, sound the alarm, reproduce rapidly, and swarm to the attack to repel the enemy.... In this regard, the June 1986 issue of *National Geographic* contains a detailed account of how the body's immune system functions" (Timmerman, 1987).

The circuits of competencies sustaining the body as a defended self—personally, culturally, and nationally—spiral through the fantasy entertainment industry, a branch of the apparatus of bodily production fundamental to crafting the important consensual hallucinations about "possible" worlds that go into building "real" ones. In Epcot Center of Walt Disney World, we may be interpellated as subjects in the new Met Life Pavilion, which is "devoted to dramatizing the intricacies of the human body." A special thrill ride, called "Body Wars," promises that we will "experience the wonders of life," such as encountering "the attack of the platelets."[46] This lively battle simulator is promoted as "family entertainment." The technology for this journey through the human body uses a motion-based simulator to produce three-dimensional images for a stationary observer. As in other forms of high-tech tourism, we can go everywhere, see everything and leave no trace. The apparatus has been adopted to teach medical anatomy at the University of Colorado Health Sciences Center. Finally, we should not forget that more Americans travel to the combined Disney worlds than voyage in most other myth-realizing machines, like Washington, D.C.[47] Met Life cautions those who journey on "Body Wars" that they may experience extreme vertigo from the simulated motion. Is that merely "symbolic action" too?

In the embodied semiotic zones of earth and outer space, we saw the diffraction patterns made possible by recomposed visualizing technologies, relocated circuits of competencies that promise to be more user-friendly for inappropriate/d others. So also, the inner spaces of the biomedical body are central zones of technoscientific contestation, i.e., of science as culture in the amodern frame of social nature. Extremely interesting new collectives of human and unhuman allies and actors are emerging from these processes. I will briefly sketch two zones where promising monsters are undergoing symbiogenesis in the nutrient media of technoscientific work: 1) theories of immune function based on laboratory research, and 2) new apparatuses of knowledge production being crafted by Persons with AIDS (PWAs) and their heterogeneous allies. Both sets of monsters generate distinctly diffracted views of the self, evident in beliefs and practices in relation to vulnerability and mortality.

Like non-violent direct action and environmentalism, immune system discourse is about the unequally distributed chances of life and death. Since sickness and mortality are at the heart of immunology, it is hardly surprising that conditions of battle prevail. Dying is not an easy matter crying out for "friendly" visualization. But battle is not the only way to figure the process of mortal living. Persons coping with the life-threatening consequences of infection with the HIV virus have insisted that they are *living* with AIDS, rather than accepting the status of *victims* (or prisoners of war?). Similarly, laboratory scientists also have built research programs based on non-militaristic, relational embodiments, rather than on the capabilities of the defended self of atomic individuals. They do this in order to construct IS articulations more effectively, not in order to be nice folks with pacifist metaphors.

Let me attempt to convey the flavor of the artifactual bodily object called the human immune system, culled from major textbooks and research reports published in the 1980s. These characterizations are part of working systems for interacting with the immune system in many areas of practice, including business decisions, clinical medicine, and lab experiments. With about 10 to the 12th cells, the IS has two orders of magnitude more cells than the nervous system. IS cells are regenerated throughout life from pluripotent stem cells. From embryonic life through adulthood, the immune system is sited in several morphologically dispersed tissues and organs, including the thymus, bone marrow, spleen, and lymph nodes; but a large fraction of its cells are in the blood and lymph circulatory systems and in body fluids and spaces. If ever there were a "distributed system," this is one! It is also a highly adaptable communication system with many interfaces.

There are two major cell lineages to the system: (1) The first is the *lymphocytes,* which include the several types of T cells (helper, suppressor, killer, and variations of all these) and the B cells (each type of which can produce only one sort of the vast array of potential circulating antibodies). T and B cells have particular specificities capable of recognizing almost any molecular array of the right size that can ever exist, no matter how clever industrial chemistry gets. This specificity is enabled by a baroque somatic mutation mechanism, clonal selection, and a polygenic receptor or marker system. (2) The second immune cell lineage is the *mononuclear phagocyte system,* including the multi-talented macrophages, which, in addition to their other recognition skills and connections, also appear to share receptors and some hormonal peptide products with neural cells. Besides the cellular compartment, the immune system comprises a vast array of circulating acellular products, such as antibodies, lymphokines, and complement components. These molecules mediate communication among components of the immune system, but also between the immune system and the nervous and endocrine systems, thus linking the body's multiple control and coordination sites and functions. The genetics of the immune system cells, with their high rates of somatic mutation and gene product splicings and rearrangings to make finished surface receptors and antibodies, makes a mockery of the notion of a constant genome even within "one" body. The hierarchical body of old has given way to a network-body of amazing complexity and specificity. The immune system is everywhere and nowhere. Its specificities are indefinite if not infinite, and they arise randomly; yet these extraordinary variations are the critical means of maintaining bodily coherence.

In the early 1970s, winning a Nobel Prize for the work, Niels Jerne proposed a theory of immune system self-regulation, called the network theory, which deviates radically from notions of the body victorious and the defended self. "The network theory differs from other immunological thinking because it endows the immune system with the ability to regulate itself using only itself" (Golub, 1987; Jerne, 1985).[48] Jerne proposed that any antibody molecule must be able to act functionally as both antibody to some antigen *and* as antigen for the production of an antibody to itself, at another region of "itself." These sites have acquired a nomenclature sufficiently daunting to thwart popular understanding of the theory, but the basic conception is simple. The concatenation of internal recognitions and responses would go on indefinitely, in a series of interior mirrorings of sites on immunoglobulin molecules, such that the immune system would always be in a state of dynamic internal responding. It would never be passive, "at rest," awaiting an activating stimulus from a hostile outside. In a sense, there could be no *exterior* antigenic structure, no "invader," that the immune system had not already "seen" and mirrored internally. Replaced by subtle plays of partially mirrored readings and responses, self and other lose their rationalistic oppositional quality. A radical conception of *connection* emerges unexpectedly at the core of the defended self. Nothing in the model prevents therapeutic action, but the entities in the drama have different kinds of interfaces with the world. The therapeutic logics are unlikely to be etched into living flesh in patterns of DARPA's latest high-tech tanks and smart missiles.

Some of those logics are being worked out in and by the bodies of persons with AIDS and ARC. In their work to sustain life and alleviate pain in the context of mortal illness, PWAs engage in many processes of knowledge-building. These processes demand intricate code switching, language bridging, and alliances among worlds previously held apart. These "generative grammars" are matters of life and death. As one activist put it, "ACT UP's humor is no joke" (Crimp and Rolston, 1990, p. 20; see also Crimp, 1983). The AIDS Coalition to Unleash Power (ACT UP) is a collective built from many articulations among unlike kinds of actors—for example, activists, biomedical machines, government bureaucracies, gay and lesbian worlds, communities of color, scientific conferences, experimental organisms, mayors, international information and action networks, condoms and dental dams, computers, doctors, IV drug-users, pharmaceutical companies, publishers, virus components, counselors, innovative sexual practices, dancers, media technologies, buying clubs, graphic artists, scientists, lovers, lawyers, and more. The actors, however, are not all equal. ACT UP has an animating center—PWAs, who are to the damage wrought by AIDS and the work for restored health around the world as the indigenous peoples of the Amazon are to forest destruction and environmentalism. These are the actors with whom others must articulate. That structure of action is a fundamental consequence of learning to visualize the heterogeneous, artifactual body that is our "social nature," instead of narrowing our vision that "saving nature" and repelling alien invaders from an unspoiled organic eden called the autonomous self. Saving nature is, finally, a deadly project. It relies on perpetuating the structure of boundary violation and the falsely liberating *frisson* of transgression. What happened in the first Eden should have made that clear.

So, if the tree of knowledge cannot be forbidden, we had all better learn how to eat and feed each other with a little more savvy. That is the difficult process being engaged by PWAs, Project Inform, ACT UP, NIH, clinical practitioners, and many more actors trying to build responsible mechanisms for producing effective knowledge in the AIDS epidemic.[49] Unable to police the same boundaries separating insiders and outsiders, the world of biomedical research will never be the same again. The changes range across the epistemological, the commercial, the juridical, and the spiritual domains. For example, what is the status of knowledge produced through the new combinations of decision-making in experimental design that are challenging previous research conventions? What are the consequences of the *simultaneous* challenges to expert monopoly of knowledge *and* insistence on both the rapid improvement of the biomedical knowledge base and the equitable mass distribution of its fruits? How will the patently amodern hybrids of healing practices cohabit in the emerging social body? And, who will live and die as a result of these very non-innocent practices?

Not–A. Virtual Space: SF[50]

Articulation is not a simple matter. Language is the effect of articulation, and so are bodies. The articulata are jointed animals; they are not smooth like the perfect spherical animals of Plato's origin fantasy in the *Timaeus*. The articulata are cobbled together. It is the condition of being articulate. I rely on the articulata to breathe life into the artifactual cosmos of monsters that this essay inhabits. Nature may be speechless, without language, in the human sense; but nature is highly articulate. Discourse is only one process of articulation. An articulated world has an undecidable number of modes and sites where connections can be made. The surfaces of this kind of world are not frictionless curved planes. Unlike things can be joined—and like things can be broken apart—and vice versa. Full of sensory hairs, evaginations, invaginations, and indentations, the surfaces which interest me are dissected by joints. Segmented invertebrates, the articulata are insectoid and worm-like, and they inform the inflamed imaginations of SF filmmakers and biologists. In obsolete English, to articulate meant to make terms of agreement. Perhaps we should live in such an "obsolete," amodern world again. To articulate is to signify. It is to put things together, scary things, risky things, contingent things. I want to live in an articulate world. We articulate; therefore, we are. Who "I" am is a very limited, in the endless perfection of (clear and distinct) Self-contemplation. Unfair as always, I think of it as the paradigmatic psychoanalytic question. "Who am I?" is about (always unrealizable) identity; always wobbling, it still pivots on the law of the father, the sacred image of the same. Since I am a moralist, the real question must have more virtue: who are "we"? That is an inherently more open question, one always ready for contingent, friction-generating articulations. It is a remonstrative question.

In optics, the virtual image is formed by the apparent, but not actual, convergence of rays. The virtual seems to be the counterfeit of the real; the virtual has effects by seeming, not being. Perhaps that is why "virtue" is still given in dictionaries to refer to women's chastity, which must always remain doubtful in patriarchal optical law. But then, "virtue" used to mean manly spirit and valor too, and God even named an order of angels the Virtues, though they were of only middling rank. Still, no matter how big the effects of the virtual are, they seem somehow to lack a proper ontology. Angels, manly valor, and women's chastity certainly constitute, at best, a virtual image from the point of view of late twentieth-century "postmoderns." For them, the virtual is precisely *not* the real; that's why "postmoderns" *like* "virtual reality." It seems transgressive. Yet, I can't forget that an obsolete meaning of "virtual" was having virtue, i.e., the inherent power to produce effects. "Virtu," after all, is excellence or merit, and it is still a common meaning of virtue to refer to having efficacy. The "virtue" of something is its "capacity." The virtue of (some) food is that it nourishes the body. Virtual space *seems* to be the negation of real space; the domains of SF *seem* the negation of earthly regions. But perhaps this negation is the real illusion.

"Cyberspace, absent its high-tech glitz, is the idea of virtual consensual community. . . . A virtual community is first and foremost a community of belief."[51] For William Gibson (1986), cyberspace is "consensual hallucination experienced daily by billions. . . . Unthinkable complexity." Cyberspace seems to be the consensual hallucination of too much complexity, too much articulation. It is the virtual reality of paranoia, a well-populated region in the last quarter of the Second Christian Millenium. Paranoia is the belief in the unrelieved density of connection, requiring, if one is to survive, withdrawal and defense unto death. The defended self re-emerges at the heart of relationality. Paradoxically, paranoia is the condition of the impossibility of remaining articulate. In virtual space, the virtue of articulation—i.e., the power to produce connection—threatens to overwhelm and finally to engulf all possibility of effective action to change the world.

So, in our travels into virtual space, if we are to emerge from our encounter with the artifactual articulata into a livable elsewhere, we need a guide figure to navigate around the slough of despond. Lisa Foo, the principal character in a Hugo and Nebula award-winning short story by John Varley (1986), will be our unlikely Beatrice through the System.

"If you wish to know more, press enter" (p. 286).[52]

With that fatal invitation, Varley's profoundly paranoid story begins and ends. The Tree of Knowledge is a Web, a vast system of computer connections generating, as an emergent property, a new and terrifyingly unhuman collective entity. The forbidden fruit is knowledge of the workings of this powerful Entity, whose deadly essence is extravagant connection. All of the human characters are named after computers, programs, practices, or concepts—Victor Apfel, Detective Osborne, and the hackers Lisa Foo and Charles Kluge. The story is a murder mystery. With a dubious suicide note, called up by responding to the command "press enter" on the screen of one of the dozens of personal computers in his house, which is also full of barrels of illicit drugs, Kluge has been found dead by his neighbor, Apfel. Apfel is a reclusive middle-aged epileptic, who had been a badly treated prisoner-of-war in Korea, leaving him with layers of psychological terror, including a fear and hatred of "orientals." When Los Angeles homicide Detective Osborne's men prove totally inept at deciphering the elaborate software running Kluge's machines, Lisa Foo, a young Vietnamese immigrant, now a U.S. citizen, is called in from Cal Tech; and she proceeds to play Sherlock Holmes to Osborne's Lestrade. The story is narrated from Apfel's point of view, but Foo is the tale's center and, I insist, its pivotal actor.

Insisting, I wish to exercise the license that is built into the anti-elitist reading conventions of SF popular cultures. SF conventions invite—or at least permit more readily than do the academically propagated, respectful consumption protocols for literature—rewriting as one reads. The books are cheap; they don't stay in print long; why not rewrite them as one goes? Most of the SF I like motivates me to engage actively with images, plots, figures, devices, linguistic moves, in short, with worlds, not so much to make them come out "right," as to make them move "differently." These worlds motivate me to test their virtue, to see if their articulations work—and what they work for. Because SF makes identification with a principal character, comfort within the patently constructed world, or a relaxed attitude toward language, especially risky reading strategies, the reader is likely to be more generous and more suspicious—*both* generous and suspicious, exactly the receptive posture I seek in political semiosis generally. It is a strategy closely alligned with the oppositional and differential consciousness theorized by Chela Sandoval and by other feminists insistent on navigating mined discursive waters.

Our first view of Lisa Foo is through Apfel's eyes; and for him, "[l]eaving out only the moustache, she was a dead ringer for a cartoon Tojo. She had the glasses, ears, and the teeth. But her teeth had braces, like piano keys wrapped in barbed wire. And she was five-eight or five-nine and couldn't have weighed more than a hundred and ten. I'd have said a hundred, but added five pounds for each of her breasts, so improbably large on her scrawny frame that all I could read of the message on her T-shirt was 'POCK LIVE.' It was only when she turned sideways that I saw the esses before and after" (pp. 241–42). Using such messages among the many other languages accessed by this intensely literate figure, Foo communicated constantly through her endless supply of T-shirts. Her breasts turned out to be silicone implants, and as Foo said, "I don't think I've ever been so happy with anything I ever bought. Not even the car [her Ferrari]" (p. 263). From Foo's childhood perspective, "the West . . . [is] the place where you buy tits" (p. 263).

When Foo and Apfel became lovers, in one of the most sensitively structured heterosexual, cross-racial relationships in print anywhere, we also learn that Foo's body was multiply composed by the history of Southeast Asia. Varley gave her a name that is an "orientalized" version of the computer term "fu bar"—"fucked up beyond all recognition." Her Chinese grandmother had been raped in Hanoi by an occupying Japanese soldier in 1942. In Foo's mother's Vietnam, "Being Chinese was bad enough, but being half Chinese and half Japanese was worse . . . My father was half French and half Annamese. Another bad combination" (p. 275). Her mother was killed in the Tet offensive when Foo was ten. The girl became a street hustler and child prostitute in Saigon, where she was "protected" by a pedophilic white U.S. major. Refusing to leave Saigon with him, after Saigon "fell," Foo ended up in Pol Pot's Cambodia, where she barely survived the Khmer Rouge work camps. She escaped to Thailand, and "when I finally got the Americans to notice me, my Major was still looking for me" (p. 276). Dying of a cancer that might have been the result of his witnessing the atom bomb tests in Nevada early in his career, he sponsored her to the U.S. Her intelligence and hustling got her "tits by Goodyear" (p. 275), a Ferrari, and a Cal Tech education. Foo and Apfel struggle together within their respective legacies of multiple abuse, sexual and otherwise, and criss-crossing racisms. They are both multi-talented, but scarred, survivors. This story, its core figure and its narrator, will not let us dodge the scary issues of race/racism, gender/sexism, historical tragedy, and technoscience within the region of time we politely call "the late twentieth century." There is no safe place here; there are, however, many maps of possibility.

But, there is entirely *too much* connection in "Press Enter," and it is only the beginning. Foo is deeply in love with the power-knowledge systems to which her skills give her access. "This is money, Yank, she said, and her eyes glittered" (p. 267). As she traces the fascinating webs and security locks, which began in military computer projects but which have taken on a vastly unhuman life of their own, her love and her skills bring her too deep into the infinitely dense connections of the System, where she, like Kluge before her, is noticed. Too late, she tries to withdraw. Soon after, a clearly fake suicide note appears on her T-shirt on her ruined body. Investigation showed that she had rewired the microwave oven in Kluge's house to circumvent its security checks. She put her head in the oven, and she died shortly after in the hospital, her eyes and brain congealed and her breasts horribly melted. The promise of her name, "fu bar," was all-too-literally fulfilled—fucked up beyond all recognition. Apfel, who had been brought back into articulation with life in his love with Lisa Foo, retreated totally, stripping his house of all its wiring and any other means of connecting with the techno-webs of a world he now saw totally within the paranoid terms of infinite and alien connection. At the end, the defended self, alone, permanently hides from the alien Other.

It is possible to read "Press Enter" as a conventional heterosexual romance, bourgeois detective fiction, technophobic-technophilic fantasy, dragon-lady story, and, finally, white masculinist narrative whose condition of possibility is access to the body and mind of a woman, especially a "Third World" woman, who, here as elsewhere in misogynist and racist culture, is violently destroyed. Not just violently—superabundantly, without limit. I think such a reading does serious violence to the subtle tissues of the story's writing. Nonetheless, "Press Enter" induces in me, and in other women and men who have read the story with me, an irreconcilable pain and anger: Lisa Foo should not have been killed that way. It really is not alright. The text and the body lose all distinction. I fall out of the semiotic square and into the viciously circular thing-in-itself. More than anything else, that pornographic, gendered and colored death, that excessive destruction of her body, that total undoing of her being—that extravagant final connection—surpasses the limits of pleasure in the conventions of paranoid fiction and provokes the necessity of active rewriting as reading. I cannot read this story without rewriting it; that is one of the lessons of transnational, intercultural, feminist literacy. And the conclusion forces rewriting not just of itself, but of the whole human and unhuman collective that is Lisa Foo. The point of the differential/oppositional rewriting is not to make the story come out "right," whatever that would be. The point is to rearticulate the figure of Lisa Foo to unsettle the closed logics of a deadly racist misogyny. Articulation must remain open, its densities accessible to action and intervention. When the system of connections closes in on itself, when symbolic action becomes perfect, the world is frozen in a dance of death. The cosmos is finished, and it is One. Paranoia is the only possible posture; generous suspicion is foreclosed. To "press enter" is, in that world, a terrible mistake.

The whole argument of "The Promises of Monsters" has been that to "press enter" is not a fatal error, but an inescapable possibility for changing maps of the world, for building new collectives out of what is not quite a plethora of human and unhuman actors. My stakes in the textual figure of Lisa Foo, and of many of the actors in Varley's SF, are high. Built from multiple interfaces, Foo can be a guide through the terrains of virtual space, but only if the fine lines of tension in the articulated webs that constitute her being remain in play, open to the unexpected realization of an unlikely hope. It's not a "happy ending" we need, but a non-ending. That's why none of the narratives of masculinist, patriarchal apocalypses will do. The System is not closed; the sacred image of the same is not coming. The world is not full.

The final image of this excessive essay is *Cyborg,* a 1989 painting by Lynn Randolph, in which the boundaries of a fatally transgressive world, ruled by the Subject and the Object, give way to the borderlands, inhabited by human and unhuman collectives (Figure 12).[53] These borderlands suggest a rich topography of combinatorial possibility. That possibility is called the Earth, here, now, this elsewhere, where real, outer, inner, and virtual space implode. The painting maps the articulations among cosmos, animal, human, machine, and landscape in their recursive sidereal, bony, electronic, and geological skeletons. Their combinatorial logic is embodied; theory is corporeal; social nature is articulate. The stylized DIP switches of the integrated circuit board on the human figure's chest are devices that set the defaults in a form intermediate between hardwiring and software control—not unlike the mediating structural-functional anatomy of the feline and hominid forelimbs, especially the flexible, homologous hands and paws. The painting is replete with organs of touch and mediation, as well as with organs of vision. Direct in their gaze at the viewer, the eyes of the woman and the cat center the whole composition. The spiraling skeleton of the Milky Way, our galaxy, appears behind the cyborg figure in three different graphic displays made possible by high-technology visualizing apparatuses. In the place of virtual space in my semiotic square, the fourth square is an imaging of the gravity well of a black hole. Notice the tic-tac-toe game, played with the European male and female astrological signs (Venus won this game); just to their right are some calculations that might appear in the mathematics of chaos. Both sets of symbols are just below a calculation found in the Einstein papers. The mathematics and games are like logical skeletons. The keyboard is jointed to the skeleton of the planet Earth, on which a pyramid rises in the left mid-foreground. The whole painting has the quality of a meditation device. The large cat is like a spirit animal, a white tiger perhaps. The woman, a young Chinese student in the United States, figures that which is human, the universal, the generic. The "woman of color," a very particular, problematic, recent collective identity, resonates with local and global conversations.[54] In this painting, she embodies the still oxymoronic simultaneous statuses

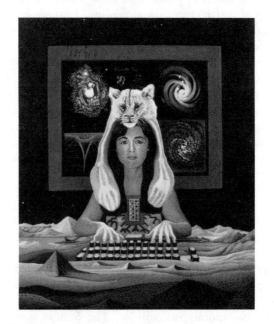

FIGURE 12.   Lynn Randolph, "Cyborg" (1989).

of woman, "Third World" person, human, organism, communications technology, mathematician, writer, worker, engineer, scientist, spiritual guide, lover of the Earth. This is the kind of "symbolic action" transnational feminisms have made legible. S/he is not finished.

We have come full circle in the noisy mechanism of the semiotic square, back to the beginning, where we met the commercial cyborg figures inhabiting technoscience worlds. Logic General's oddly recursive rabbits, forepaws on the keyboards that promise to mediate replication and communication, have given way to different circuits of competencies. If the cyborg has changed, so might the world. Randolph's cyborg is in conversation with Trinh Minh-ha's inappropriate/d other, the personal and collective being to whom history has forbidden the strategic illusion of self-identity. This cyborg does not have an Aristotelian structure; and there is no master-slave dialectic resolving the struggles of resource and product, passion and action. S/he is not utopian nor imaginary; s/he is virtual. Generated, along with other cyborgs, by the collapse into each other of the technical, organic, mythic, textual, and political, s/he is constituted by articulations of critical differences within and without each figure. The painting might be headed, "A few words about articulation from the actors in the field." Privileging the hues of red, green, and ultraviolet, I want to read Randolph's *Cyborg* within a rainbow political semiology, for wily transnational technoscience studies as cultural studies.

NOTES

1. "They drew near to a very Miry Slough . . . The name of this Slow was Dispond" (John Bunyan, *Pilgrim's Progress,* 1678; quoted in the Oxford English Dictionary). The non-standardization of spelling here should also mark, at the beginning of the "Promises of Monsters," the suggestiveness of words at the edge of the regulatory technologies of writing.

2. Sally Hacker, in a paper written just before her death ("The Eye of the Beholder: An Essay on Technology and Eroticism," manuscript, 1989), suggested the term "pornotechnics" to refer to the embodiment of perverse power relations in the artifactual body. Hacker insisted that the heart of pornotechnics is the military as an institution, with its deep roots and wide reach into science, technology, and erotics. "Technical exhilaration" is profoundly erotic; joining sex and power is the designer's touch. Technics and erotics are the cross hairs in the focusing device for scanning fields of skill and desire. See also Hacker (1989). Drawing from Hacker's arguments, I believe that control over technics is the enabling practice for class, gender, and race supremacy. Realigning the join of technics and erotics must be at the heart of anti-racist feminist practice. (cf. Haraway, 1989b; Cohn, 1987).

3. See the provocative publication that replaced *Radical Science Journal, Science as Culture,* Free Association Books, 26 Freegrove Rd., London N7 9RQ, England.

4. This incubation of ourselves as planetary fetuses is not quite the same thing as pregnancy and reproductive politics in post-industrial, post-modern, or other posted locations, but the similarities will become more evident as this essay proceeds. The struggles over the outcomes are linked.

5. Here I borrow from the wonderful project of the Journal, *Public Culture,* Bulletin of the Center for Transnational Cultural Studies, The University Museum, University of Pennsylvania, Philadelphia, PA 19104. In my opinion, this journal embodies the best impulses of cultural studies.

6. I demure on the label "postmodern" because I am persuaded by Bruno Latour that within the historical domains where science has been constructed, the "modern" never existed, if by modern we mean the rational, enlightened mentality (the subject, mind, etc.) actually proceeding with an objective method toward adequate representations, in mathematical equations if possible, of the object—i.e., "natural"—world. Latour argues that Kant's *Critique,* which set off at extreme poles Things–in–Themselves from the Transcendental Ego, is what made us believe ourselves to be "modern," with escalating and dire consequences for the repertoire of explanatory possibilities

of "nature" and "society" for Western scholars. The separation of the two transcendances, the object pole and subject pole, structures " 'the political Constitution of Truth.' I call it 'modern,' defining modernity as the complete separation of the representation of things—science and technology—from the representation of humans—politics and justice." (Latour, forthcoming, a).

Debilitating though such a picture of scientific activity should seem, it has guided research in the disciplines (history, philosophy, sociology, anthropology), studying science with a pedagogical and prophylactic vengeance, making culture seem other to science; science alone could get the goods on nature by unveiling and policing her unruly embodiments. Thus, science studies, focused on the edifying object of "modern" scientific practice, has seemed immune from the polluting infections of cultural studies—but surely no more. To rebel against or to lose faith in rationalism and enlightenment, the infidel state of respectively modernists and postmodernists, is not the same thing as to show that rationalism was the emperor that had no clothes, that never was, and so there never was its other either. (There is a nearly inevitable terminological confusion here among modernity, the modern, and modernism. I use modernism to refer to a cultural movement that rebelled against the premises of modernity, while postmodernism refers less to rebellion than loss of faith, leaving nothing to rebel against.) Latour calls his position *a*modern and argues that scientific practice is and has been amodern, a sighting that makes the line between real scientific (West's) and ethnoscience and other cultural expressions (everything else) disappear. The difference reappears, but with a significantly different geometry—that of scales and volumes, i.e., the size differences among "collective" entities made of humans and non-humans—rather than in terms of a line between rational science and ethnoscience.

This modest turn or tropic change does not remove the study of scientific practice from the agenda of cultural studies and political intervention, but places it decisively on the list. Best of all, the focus gets fixed clearly on inequality, right where it belongs in science studies. Further, the addition of science to cultural studies does not leave the notions of culture, society, and politics untouched, far from it. In particular, we cannot make a critique of science and its constructions of nature based on an ongoing belief in culture or society. In the form of social constructionism, that belief has grounded the major strategy of left, feminist, and anti-racist science radicals. To remain with that strategy, however, is to remain bedazzled by the ideology of enlightenment. It will not do to approach science as cultural or social construction, as if culture and society were transcendent categories, any more than nature or the object is. Outside the premises of enlightenment—i.e., of the modern—the binary pairs of culture and nature, science and society, the technical and the social all lose their co-constitutive, oppositional quality. Neither can explain the other. "But instead of providing the explanation, Nature and Society are now accounted for as the historical consequences of the movement of collective things. All the interesting realities are no longer captured by the two extremes but are to be found in the substitution, cross over, translations, through which actants shift their competences" (Latour, 1990, p. 170). When the pieties of belief in the modern are dismissed, both members of the binary pairs collapse into each other as into a black hole. But what happens to them in the black hole is, by definition, not visible from the shared terrain of modernity, modernism, or postmodernism. It will take a superluminal SF journey into elsewhere to find the interesting new vantage points. Where Latour and I fundamentally agree is that in that gravity well, into which Nature and Society as transcedentals disappeared, are to be found actors/actants of many and wonderful kinds. Their relationships constitute the artifactualism I am trying to sketch.

7. For quite another view of "production" and "reproduction" than that enshrined in so much Western political and economic (and feminist) theory, see Marilyn Strathern (1988, pp. 290–308).

8. Chela Sandoval develops the distinctions between oppositional and differential consciousness in her forthcoming doctoral dissertation, University of California at Santa Cruz. See also Sandoval (1990).

9. My debt is extensive in these paragraphs to Luce Irigaray's wonderful critique of the allegory of the cave in *Spæculum de l'autre femme* (1974). Unfortunately, Irigaray, like almost all white Europeans and Americans after the mid-nineteenth-century consolidation of the myth that the "West" originated in a classical Greece unsullied by Semitic and African roots, transplants, colonizations, and loans, never questioned the "original" status of Plato's fathership of philosophy,

enlightenment, and rationality. If Europe was colonized first by Africans, that historical narrative element would change the story of the birth of Western philosophy and science. Martin Bernal's extraordinarily important book, *Black Athena,* Vol. 1, *The Fabrication of Ancient Greece, 1785–1985* (1987), initiates a groundbreaking re-evaluation of the founding premises of the myth of the uniquences and self-generation of Western culture, most certainly including those pinnacles of Man's self-birthing, science and philosophy. Bernal's is an account of the determinative role of racism and Romanticism in the fabrication of the story of Western rationality. Perhaps ironically, Martin Bernal is the son of J. D. Bernal, the major pre-World War II British biochemist and Marxist whose four-volume *Science in History* movingly argued the superior rationality of a science freed from the chains of capitalism. Science, freedom, and socialism were to be, finally, the legacy of the West. For all its warts, that surely would have been better than Reagan's and Thatcher's version! See Gary Wersky, *The Invisible College: The Collective Biography of British Socialist Scientists in the 1930s (1978).*

Famous in his own generation for his passionate heterosexual affairs, J. D. Bernal, in the image of enlightenment second birthing so wryly exposed by Irigaray, wrote his own vision of the future in *The Word, the Flesh, and the Devil* as a science-based speculation that had human beings evolving into disembodied intelligences. In her manuscript (May, 1990) "Talking about Science in Three Colors: Bernal and Gender Politics in the Social Studies of Science," Hilary Rose discusses this fantasy and its importance for "science, politics, and silences." J. D. Bernal was also actively supportive of independent women scientists. Rosalind Franklin moved to his laboratory after her nucleic acid crystallographic work was stolen by the flamboyantly sexist and heroic James Watson on his way to the immortalizing, luminous fame of the *Double Helix* of the 1950s and 60s and its replicant of the 1980s and 90s, the Human Genome Project. The *story* of DNA has been an archetypical tale of blinding modern enlightenment and untrammeled, disembodied, autochthonous origins. See Ann Sayre (1975); Mary Jacobus (1982); Evelyn Fox Keller (1990).

10. For an argument that nature is a *social* actor, see Elizabeth Bird (1987).

11. Actants are not the same as actors. As Terence Hawkes (1977, p. 89) put it in his introduction to Greimas, actants operate at the level of function, not of character. Several characters in a narrative may make up a single actant. The structure of the narrative generates its actants. In considering what kind of entity "nature" might be, I am looking for a coyote and historical grammar of the world, where deep structure can be quite a surprise, indeed, a veritable trickster. Non-humans are not necessarily "actors" in the human sense, but they are part of the functional collective that makes up an actant. Action is not so much an ontological as a semiotic problem. This is perhaps as true for humans as non-humans, a way of looking at things that may provide exits from the methodological individualism inherent in concentrating constantly on who the agents and actors are in the sense of liberal theories of agency.

12. In this productionist story, women make babies, but this is a poor if necessary substitute for the real action in reproduction—the second birth through self-birthing, which requires the obstetrical technology of optics. One's relation to the phallus determines whether one gives birth to oneself, at quite a price, or serves, at an even greater price, as the conduit or passage for those who will enter the light of self-birthing. For a refreshing demonstration that women do not make babies everywhere, see Marilyn Strathern (1988), pp. 314–18.

13. I borrow here from Katie King's notion of the apparatus of literary production, in which the poem congeals at the intersection of business, art, and technology. See King (1990). See also Donna Haraway (1991), chaps. 8–10.

14. Latour has developed the concept of delegation to refer to the translations and exchanges between and among people doing science and their machines, which act as "delegates" in a wide array of ways. Marx considered machines to be "dead labor," but that notion, while still necessary for some crucial aspects of forced and reified delegation, is too unlively to get at the many ways that machines are part of *social* relations "through which actants shift competences" Latour (1990, p. 170). See also Bruno Latour (forthcoming, b). Latour, however, as well as most of the established scholars in the social studies of science, ends up with too narrow a concept of the "collective," one built up out of only machines and scientists, who are considered in a very narrow time and space frame. But circulations of skills turn out to take some stranger turns. First, with the important

exception of his writing and teaching in collaboration with the primatologist Shirley Strum, who has fought hard in her profession for recognition of primates as savvy social actors, Latour pays too little attention to the non-machine, *other* non-humans in the interactions. See Strum (1987).

The "collective," of which "nature" in any form is one example from my point of view, is always an artifact, always social, not because of some transcendental Social that explains science or vice versa, but because of its heterogeneous actants/actors. Not only are not all of those actors/ actants people; I agree there *is* a sociology of machines. But that is not enough; not all of the other actors/actants were *built* by people. The artifactual "collective" includes a witty actor that I have sometimes called coyote. The interfaces that constitute the "collective" must include those between humans and artifacts in the form of instruments and machines, a genuinely *social* landscape. But the interface between machines and *other* non-humans, as well as the interface between humans and *non-machine* non-humans must also be counted in. Animals are fairly obvious actors, and their interfaces with people and machines are easier to admit and theorize. See Donna Haraway (1989a); Barbara Noske (1989); Paradoxically, from the perspective of the kind of artifactualism I am trying to sketch, animals lose their *object* status that has reduced them to things in so much Western philosophy and practice. They inhabit neither nature (as object) nor culture (as surrogate human), but instead inhabit a place called elsewhere. In Noske's terms (p. xi), they are other "worlds, whose otherworldliness must not be disenchanted and cut to our size but respected for what it is." Animals, however, do not exhaust the coyote world of non-machine non-humans. The domain of machine and non-machine non-humans (the unhuman, in my terminology) joins people in the building of the artifactual collective called nature. None of these actants can be considered as simply resource, ground, matrix, object, material, instrument, frozen labor; they are all more unsettling than that. Perhaps my suggestions here come down to re-inventing an old option within a non-Eurocentric Western tradition indebted to Egyptian Hermeticism that insists on the active quality of the world and on "animate" matter. See Martin Bernal (1987, pp. 121–60); Frances Yates (1964). Worldly and enspirited, coyote nature is a collective, cosmopolitan artifact crafted in stories with heterogeneous actants.

But there is a second way in which Latour and other major figures in science studies work with an impoverished "collective." Correctly working to resist a "social" explanation of "technical" practice by exploding the binary, these scholars have a tendency covertly to reintroduce the binary by worshipping only one term—the "technical." Especially, *any* consideration of matters like masculine supremacy or racism or imperialism or class structures are inadmissible because they are the old "social" ghosts that blocked real explanation of science in action. See Latour (1987). As Latour noted, Michael Lynch is the most radical proponent of the premise that there is no social explanation of a science but the technical content itself, which assuredly includes the interactions of people with each other in the lab and with their machines, but excludes a great deal that I would include in the "technical" content of science if one really doesn't want to evade a binary by worshipping one of its old poles. Lynch (1985); Latour (1990, p. 169n). I agree with Latour and Lynch that practice creates its own context, but they draw a suspicious line around what gets to count as "practice." They *never* ask how the *practices* of masculine supremacy, or many other systems of structured inequality, get *built* into and out of working machines. How and in what directions these transferences of "competences" work should be a focus of rapt attention. Systems of exploitation might be crucial parts of the "technical content" of science. But the SSS scholars tend to dismiss such questions with the assertion that they lead to the bad old days when science was asserted by radicals simply to "reflect" social relations. But in my view, such transferences of competences, or delegations, have nothing to do with reflections or harmonies of social organization and cosmologies, like "modern science." Their unexamined, consistent, and defensive prejudice seems part of Latour's (1990, pp. 164–69) stunning misreading of several moves in Sharon Traweek's *Beam Times and Life Times: The World of High Energy Physicists* (1988). See also Hilary Rose, "Science in Three Colours: Bernal and Gender Politics in the Social Studies of Science," unpublished manuscript, May 2, 1990.

The same blind spot, a retinal lesion from the old phallogocentric heliotropism that Latour *did* know how to avoid in other contexts, for example in his trenchant critique of the modern and postmodern, seems responsible for the abject failure of the social studies of science as an organized discourse to take account of the last twenty years of feminist inquiry. What counts as "technical" and what counts as "practice" should remain far from self-evident in science in action. For all of their extraordinary creativity, so far the mappings from most SSS scholars have stopped dead at the fearful seas where the worldly practices of inequality lap at the shores, infiltrate the estuaries, and set the parameters of reproduction of scientific practice, artifacts, and knowledge. If only it were a question of reflections between social relations and scientific constructions, how easy it would be to conduct "political" inquiry into science! Perhaps the tenacious prejudice of the SSS professionals is the punishment for the enlightenment transcendental, the social, that did inform the rationalism of earlier generations of radical science critique and is still all too common. May the topick gods save us from both the reified technical and the transcendental social!

15. See Lynn Margulis and Dorion Sagan (1986). This wonderful book does the cell biology and evolution for a host of inappropriate/d others. In its dedication, the text affirms "the combinations, sexual and parasexual, that bring us out of ourselves and make us more than we are alone" (p. v). That should be what science studies as cultural studies do, by showing how to visualize the curious collectives of humans and unhumans that make up naturalsocial (one word) life. To stress the point that all the actors in these generative, dispersed, and layered collectives do not have human form and function—and should not be anthropomorphized—recall that the Gaia hypothesis with which Margulis is associated is about the tissue of the planet as a living entity, whose metabolism and genetic exchange are effected through webs of prokaryotes. Gaia is a society; Gaia is nature; Gaia did not read the *Critique*. Neither, probably, did John Varley. See his Gaea hypothesis in the SF book, *Titan* (1979). Titan is an alien that is a world.

16. Remember that *monsters* have the same root as *to demonstrate*; monsters signify.

17. Trinh T. Minh-ha, ed., 1986/7b, *She, the Inappropriate/d Other*. See also her *Woman, Native, Other: Writing Postcoloniality and Feminism* (1989).

18. Interpellate: I play on Althusser's account of the call which constitutes the production of the subject in ideology. Althusser is, of course, playing on Lacan, not to mention on God's interruption that calls Man, his servant, into being. Do we have a vocation to be cyborgs? Interpellate: *Interpellatus*, past participle for "interrupted in speaking"—effecting transformations like Saul into Paul. Interpellation is a special kind of interruption, to say the least. Its key meaning concerns a procedure in a parliament for asking a speaker who is a member of the government to provide an explanation of an act or policy, usually leading to a vote of confidence. The following ads interrupt us. They insist on an explanation in a confidence game; they force recognition of how transfers of competences are made. A cyborg subject position results from and leads to interruption, diffraction, reinvention. It is dangerous and replete with the promises of monsters.

19. In *King Solomon's Ring*, Konrad Lorenz pointed out how the railroad car kept the appearance of the horse drawn carriage, despite the different functional requirements and possibilities of the new technology. He meant to illustrate that biological evolution is similarly conservative, almost nostalgic for the old, familiar forms, which are reworked to new purposes. Gaia was the first serious bricoleuse.

20. For a view of the manufacture of particular organisms as flexible model systems for a universe of research practice, see Barbara R. Jasny and Daniel Koshland, Jr., eds., *Biological Systems* (1990). As the advertising for the book states, "The information presented will be especially useful to graduate students and to all researchers interested in learning the limitations and assets of biological systems currently in use," *Science* 248 (1990), p. 1024. Like all forms of protoplasm collected in the extra-laboratory world and brought into a technoscientific niche, the organic rabbit (not to mention the simulated one) and its tissues have a probable future of a particular sort—as a commodity. Who should "own" such evolutionary products? If seed protoplasm is collected in peasants' fields in Peru and then used to breed valuable commercial seed in a "first world" lab, does a peasant cooperative or the Peruvian state have a claim on the profits? A related problem about proprietary interest in "nature" besets the biotechnology industry's development of cell lines and other products derived from removed human tissue, e.g., as a result of cancer surgery. The California Supreme Court recently reassured the biotechnology industry that a patient, whose cancerous spleen was the source of a product, Colony Stimulating Factor, that led to a patent that brought its scientist-developer stock in a company worth about $3 million, did not have a right to a share of the bonanza. Property in the self, that lynchpin of liberal existence, does not seem to be the same thing as proprietary rights in one's body or its products—like fetuses

or other cell lines in which the courts take a regulatory interest. See Marcia Barinaga (1990, p. 239).

21. Here and throughout this essay, I play on Katie King's play on Jacques Derrida's *Of Grammatology*, (1976). See King (1990), and King (in progress), where she develops her description, which is also a persuasive enabling construction, of a discursive field called "feminism and writing technologies."

22. Roland Barthes, *Mythologies* (1972a) is my guide here and elsewhere.

23. Peace-activist and scholar in science studies, Elizabeth Bird came up with the slogan and put it on a political button in 1986 in Santa Cruz, California.

24. I am indebted to another guide figure throughout this essay, Gloria Anzaldúa, *Borderlands, La Frontera: The New Mestiza* (1987) and to at least wo other travelers in embodied virtual spaces, Ramona Fernandez, "Trickster Literacy: Multiculturalism and the (Re) Invention of Learning," Qualifying Essay, History of Consciousness, University of California at Santa Cruz, 1990, and Allucquére R. Stone, "Following Virtual Communities," unpublished essay, History of Consciousness, University of California at Santa Cruz. The ramifying "virtual consensual community" (Sandy Stone's term in another context) of feminist theory that incubates at UCSC densely infiltrates my writing.

25. For an extended reading of National Geographic's Jane Goodall stories, *always to be held in tension with other versions of Goodall and the chimpanzees at Gombe,* see Haraway, "Apes in Eden, Apes in Space," in *Primate Visions* (1989a, pp. 133–95). Nothing in my analysis should be taken as grounds to oppose primate conservation or to make claims about the other Jane Goodalls; those are complex matters that deserve their own careful, materially specific consideration. My point is about the semiotic and political frames within which survival work might be approached by geopolitically differentiated actors.

26. My files are replete with recent images of cross-species ape-human family romance that fail to paper over the underlying racist iconography. The most viciously racist image was shown to me by Paula Treichler: an ad directed to physicians by the HMO, Premed, in Minneapolis, from the *American Medical News,* August 7, 1987. A white-coated white man, stethoscope around his neck, is putting a wedding ring on the hand of an ugly, very black, gorilla-suited female dressed in a white wedding gown. White clothing does not mean the same thing for the different races, species, and genders! The ad proclaims, "If you've made an unholy HMO alliance, perhaps we can help." The white male physician (man) tied to the black female patient (animal) in the inner cities by HMO marketing practices in relation to medicaid policies must be freed. There is no woman in this ad; there is a hidden threat disguised as an ape female, dressed as the vampirish bride of scientific medicine (a single white tooth gleams menacingly against the black lips of the ugly bride)—another illustration, if we needed one, that black women do not have the *discursive* status of woman/human in white culture. "All across the country, physicians who once had visions of a beautiful marriage to an HMO have discovered the honeymoon is over. Instead of quality care and a fiscally sound patient-base, they end up accepting reduced fees and increased risks." The codes are transparent. Scientific medicine has been tricked into a union with vampirish poor black female patients. Which risks are borne by whom goes unexamined. The clasped hands in this ad carry a different surface message from the Gulf ad's, but their enabling semiotic structures share too much.

27. At the oral presentation of this paper at the conference on "Cultural Studies Now and in the Future," Gloria Watklins/bell hooks pointed out the painful current U.S. discourse on African—American men as "an endangered species." Built into that awful metaphor is a relentless history of animalization and political infantilization. Like other "endangered species," such people cannot speak for themselves, but must be spoken for. They must be represented. Who speaks for the African-American man as "an endangered species"? Note also how the metaphor applied to black *men* justifies anti-feminist and misogynist rhetoric about and policy toward black women. They actually become one of the forces, if not the chief threat, endangering African-American men.

28. Committing only a neo-imperialist venial sin in a footnote, I yield to voyeuristic temptation just a little: in *Discover* the videocam and the "native" have a relation symmetrical to that of Goodall's and the chimpanzee's hands. Each photo represents a touch across time and space,

and across politics and history, to tell a story of salvation, of saving man and nature. In this version of cyborg narrative, the touch that joins portable high technology and "primitive" human parallels the touch that joins animal and "civilized" human.

29. It is, however, important to note that the present man in charge of environmental affairs in the Amazon in the Brazilian government has taken strong, progressive stands on conservation, human rights, destruction of indigenous peoples, and the links of ecology and justice. Further, current proposals and policies, like the government's plan called *Nossa Natureza* and some international aid and conservations organizations' activities and ecologists' understandings, have much to recommend them. In addition, unless arrogance exceeds all bounds, *I* can hardly claim to adjudicate these complex matters. The point of my argument is not that whatever comes from Brasília or Washington is bad and whatever from the forest residents is good—a patently untrue position. Nor is it my point that nobody who doesn't come from a family that has lived in the forest for generations has any place in the "collectives, human and unhuman," crucial to the survival of lives and ways of life in Amazonia and elsewhere. Rather, the point is about the self-constitution of the indigenous peoples as *principal* actors and agents, with whom others must interact—in coalition and in conflict—not the reverse.

30. For the story of Mendes's life work and his murder by opponents of an extractive reserve off limits to logging, see Andrew Revkin (1990).

31. Further references are parenthetical in the text.

32. Similar issues confront Amazonians in countries other than Brazil. For example, there are national parks in Colombia from which native peoples are banned from their historical territory, but to which loggers and oil companies have access under park multi-use policy. This should sound very familiar to North Americans, as well.

33. Revising and displacing his statements, I am again in conversation with Bruno Latour here, who has insisted on the social status of both human and non-human actors. "We use actor to mean anything that is made by some other actor the source of an action. It is in no way limited to humans. It does not imply will, voice, self-consciousness or desire." Latour makes the crucial point that "figuring" (in words or in other matter) non-human actors as if they were like people is a semiotic operation; non-figural characterizations are quite possible. The likeness or unlikeness of actors is an interesting problem opened up by placing them firmly in the shared domain of social interaction. Bruno Latour (forthcoming, b).

34. Kane's review appeared in the *Voice Literary Supplement,* February 1990, and Hecht and Cockburn replied under the title "Getting Historical," *Voice Literary Supplement,* March 1990, p. 26.

35. My discussion of the politics of representation of the fetus depends on twenty years of feminist discourse about the location of responsibility in pregnancy and about reproductive freedom and constraint generally. For particularly crucial arguments for this essay, see Jennifer Terry (1989); Valerie Hartouni (1991); and Rosalind Pollock Petchesky (1987).

36. *The Eighteenth Brumaire of Louis Bonaparte.* Quoted in Edward Said (1978, p. xiii), as his opening epigraph.

37. Marilyn Strathern describes Melanesian notions of a child as the "finished repository of the actions of multiple others," and not, as among Westerners, a resource to be constructed into a fully human being through socialization by others. Marilyn Strathern, "Between Things: A Melanesianist's Comment on Deconstructive Feminism," unpublished manuscript. Western feminists have been struggling to articulate a phenomenology of pregnancy that rejects the dominant cultural framework of productionism/reproductionism, with its logic of passive resource and active technologist. In these efforts the woman-fetus nexus is refigured as a knot of relationality within a wider web, where liberal individuals are not the actors, but where complex collectives, including non-liberal social persons (singular and plural), are. Similar refigurings appear in eco-feminist discourse.

38. See the fall 1990 newsletter of the Society for the Social Study of Science, *Technoscience* 3, no. 3, pp. 20, 22, for language about "going back to nature." A session of the 4S October meetings is titled "Back to Nature." Malcolm Ashmore's abstract, "With a Reflexive Sociology of Actants, There Is No Going Back," offers "fully comprehensive insurance against going back," instead of other competitors' less good "ways of not going back to Nature (or Society or Self)."

All of this occurs in the context of a crisis of confidence among many 4S scholars that their very fruitful research programs of the last 10 years are running into dead ends. They are. I will refrain from commenting on the blatant misogyny in the Western scholar's textualized terror of "going back" to a phantastic nature (figured by science critics as "objective" nature. Literary academicians figure the same terrible dangers slightly differently; for both groups such a nature is definitively pre-social, monstrously not-human, and a threat to their careers). Mother nature always waits, in these adolescent boys' narratives, to smother the newly individuated hero. He forgets this weird mother is his creation; the forgetting, or the inversion, is basic to ideologies of scientific objectivity and of nature as "eden under glass." It also plays a yet-to-be-examined role in some of the best (most reflexive) science studies. A theoretical gender analysis is indispensible to the reflexive task.

39. *Time,* February 10, 1961, p. 58. The caption under HAM's photograph read "from Chop Chop Chang to No. 65 to a pioneering role." For HAM's flight and the Holloman chimps' training see Weaver (1961) and *Life Magazine,* February 10, 1961. *Life* headlined, "From Jungles to the Lab: The Astrochimps." All were captured from Africa; that means many other chimps died in the "harvest" of babies. The astrochimps were chosen over other chimps for, among other things, "high IQ." Good scientists all.

40. *Time,* December 8, 1961, p. 50; *Newsweek,* March 5, 1962, p. 19.

41. *Time,* December 8, 1961, p. 50.

42. See also Chris Gray, "Postmodern War," Qualifying Exam, History of Consciousness, UCSC, 1988.

43. For indispensable theoretical and participant-observation writings on eco-feminism, social movements, and non-violent direct action, see Barbara Epstein (1991).

44. For a fuller discussion of the immune system, see Haraway, "The Biopolitics of Post-modern Bodies," in *Simians, Cyborgs, and Women* (1991).

45. Recall that Nilsson shot the famous and discourse-changing photographs of fetuses (really abortuses) as glowing back-lit universes floating free of the "maternal environment." Nilsson (1977).

46. Advertising copy for the Met Life Pavilion. The exhibit is sponsored by the Metropolitan Life and Affiliated Companies. In the campground resort at Florida's Walt Disney World, we may also view the "endangered species island," in order to learn the conventions for "speaking for the jaguar" in an eden under glass.

47. Ramona Fernandez, "Trickster Literacy," Qualifying Exam, History of Consciousness, UCSC, 1990, wrote extensively on Walt Disney World and the multiple cultural literacies required and taught on-site for successfully traveling there. Her essay described the visualizing technology and medical school collaboration in its development and use. See the *Journal of the American Medical Association* 260, no. 18 (November 18, 1988), pp. 2776–83.

48. Building an unexpected collective, Jerne (1985) drew directly from Noam Chomsky's theories of structural linguistics. The "textualized" semiotic body is not news by the late twentieth century, but what kind of textuality is put into play still matters!

49. See, for example, the recent merger of Project Inform with the Community Research Alliance to speed the community-based testing of promising drugs—and the NIH's efforts to deal with these developments: *PI Perspective,* May 1990. Note also the differences between President Bush's Secretary of Health and Human Services, Lewis Sullivan, and Director of the National Institute of Allergy and Infectious Diseases, Anthony Fauci, on dealing with activists and PWAs. After ACT UP demonstrations against his and Bush's policies during the secretary's speech at the AIDS conference in San Francisco in June 1990, Sullivan said he would have no more to do with ACT UP and instructed government officials to limit their contacts. (Bush had been invited to address the international San Francisco conference, but his schedule did not permit it. He was in North Carolina raising money for the ultra-reactionary senator Jesse Helms at the time of the conference.) In July 1990, at the ninth meeting of the AIDS Clinical Trials Group (ACTG), at which patient activists participated for the first time, Fauci said that he would work to include the AIDS constituency at every level of the NIAID process of clinical trials. He urged scientists to develop the skills to discuss freely in those contexts ("Fauci," 1990). Why is constructing this kind of scientific articulation "softer"? I leave the answer to readers' imaginations informed by decades of feminist theory.

50. This quadrant of the semiotic square is dedicated to A. E. Van Vogt's Players of Null-A (1974), for their non-Aristotelian adventures. An earlier version of "The Promises of Monsters" had the imagination, not SF, in virtual space. I am indebted to a questioner who insisted that the imagination was a nineteenth-century faculty that is in political and epistemological opposition to the arguments I am trying to formulate. As I am trying vainly to skirt psychoanalysis, I must also skirt the slough of the romantic imagination.

51. Allucquére R. Stone, "Following Virtual Communities," unpublished manuscript, History of Consciousness, UCSC, 1990.

52. Thanks to Barbara Ige, graduate student in the Literature Board, UCSC, for conversations about our stakes in the figure of Lisa Foo.

53. Oil on canvas, 36" by 28", photo by D. Caras. In conversation with the 1985 essay "A Manifesto for Cyborgs" (in Haraway, 1991), Randolph painted her Cyborg while at the Bunting Institute and exhibited it there in a spring 1990 solo exhibition, titled "A Return to Alien Roots." The show incorporated, from many sources, "traditional religious imagery with a postmodern secularized context." Randolph paints "images that empower women, magnify dreams, and cross racial, class, gender, and age barriers" (exhibition brochure). Living and painting in Texas, Randolph was an organizer of the Houston Area Artists' Call Against U.S. Intervention in Central America. The human model for Cyborg was Grace Li, from Beijing, who was at the Bunting Institute in the fateful year of 1989.

54. I borrow this use of "conversation" and the notion of transnational feminist literacy from Katie King's (in progress) concept of women and writing technologies.

19

Representing Whiteness in the Black Imagination

BELL HOOKS

Although there has never been any official body of black people in the United States who have gathered as anthropologists and/or enthnographers whose central critical project is the study of whiteness, black folks have, from slavery on, shared with one another in conversations "special" knowledge of whiteness gleaned from close scrutiny of white people. Deemed special because it was not a way of knowing that has been recorded fully in written material, its purpose was to help black folks cope and survive in a white supremacist society. For years black domestic servants, working in white homes, acted as informants who brought knowledge back to segregated communities—details, facts, observations, psychoanalytic readings of the white "Other."

Sharing, in a similar way, the fascination with difference and the different that white people have collectively expressed openly (and at times vulgarly) as they have traveled around the world in pursuit of the other and otherness, black people, especially those living during the historical period of racial apartheid and legal segregation, have maintained steadfast and ongoing curiosity about the "ghosts," "the barbarians," these strange apparitions they were forced to serve. In the chapter on "Wildness" in *Shamanism, Colonialism, and The Wild Man,* Michael Taussig urges a stretching of our imagination and understanding of the Other to include inscriptions "on the edge of official history." Naming his critical project, identifying the passion he brings to the quest to know more deeply *you who are not ourselves,* Taussig explains:

> I am trying to reproduce a mode of perception—a way of seeing through a way of talking—figuring the world through dialogue that comes alive with sudden transformative force in the crannies of everyday life's pauses and juxtapositions, as in the kitchens of the Putumayo or in the streets around the church in the Nina Maria. It is always a way of representing the world in the roundabout "speech" of the collage of things . . . It is a mode of perception that catches on the debris of history . . .

I, too, am in search of the debris of history, am wiping the dust from past conversations, to remember some of what was shared in the old days, when black folks had little intimate contact with whites, when we were much more open about the way we connected whiteness with the mysterious, the strange, the terrible. Of course, everything has changed. Now many black people live in the "bush of ghosts" and do not know themselves separate from whiteness, do not know this thing we call "difference." Though systems of domination, imperialism, colonialism, racism, actively coerce black folks to internalize negative perceptions of blackness, to be self-hating, and many of us succumb, blacks who imitate whites (adopting their values, speech, habits of being, etc.) continue to regard whiteness with suspicion, fear, and even hatred. This contradictory longing to possess the reality of the Other, even though that reality is one that wounds and negates, is expressive of the desire to understand the mystery, to know intimately through imitation, as though such knowing worn like an amulet, a mask, will ward away the evil, the terror.

Searching the critical work of postcolonial critics, I found much writing that bespeaks the continued fascination with the way white minds, particularly the colonial imperialist traveler, perceive blackness, and very little expressed interest in representations of whiteness in the black imagination. Black cultural and social critics allude to such representations in their writing, yet only a few have dared to make explicit those perceptions of whiteness that they think will discomfort or antagonize readers. James Baldwin's collection of essays *Notes of A Native Son* (1955) explores these issues with a clarity and frankness that is no longer fashionable in a world where evocations of pluralism and diversity act to obscure differences arbitrarily imposed and maintained by white racist domination. Writing about being the first black person to visit a Swiss village with only white inhabitants, who had a yearly ritual of painting individuals black who were then positioned as slaves and bought, so that the villagers could celebrate their concern with converting the souls of the "natives," Baldwin responded:

> I thought of white men arriving for the first time in an African village, strangers there, as I am a stranger here, and tried to imagine the astounded populace touching their hair and marveling at the color of their skin. But there is a great difference between being the first white man to be seen by Africans and being the first black man to be seen by whites. The white man takes the astonishment as tribute, for he arrives to conquer and to convert the natives, whose inferiority in relation to himself is not even to be questioned, whereas I, without a thought of conquest, find myself among a people whose culture controls me, has even in a sense, created me, people who have cost me more in anguish and rage than they will ever know, who yet do not even know of my existence. The astonishment with which I might have greeted them, should they have stumbled into my African village a few hundred years ago, might have rejoiced their hearts. But the astonishment with which they greet me today can only poison mine. ("Stranger in the Village")

Addressing the way in which whiteness exists without knowledge of blackness even as it collectively asserts control, Baldwin links issues of recognition to the practice of imperialist racial domination.

My thinking about representations of whiteness in the black imagination has been stimulated by classroom discussions about the way in which the absence of recognition is a strategy that facilitates making a group "the Other." In these classrooms there have been heated debates among students when white students respond with disbelief, shock, and rage, as they listen to black students talk about whiteness, when they are compelled to hear observations, stereotypes, etc., that are offered as "data" gleaned from close scrutiny and study. Usually, white students respond with naive amazement that black people critically assess white people from a standpoint where "whiteness" is the privileged signifier. Their amazement that black people watch white people with a critical "ethnographic" gaze, is itself an expression of racism. Often their rage erupts because they believe that all ways of looking that highlight difference subvert the liberal conviction that it is the assertion of universal subjectivity (we are all just people) that will make racism disappear. They have a deep emotional investment in the myth of "sameness" even as their actions reflect the primacy of whiteness as a sign informing who they are and how they think. Many of them are shocked that black people think critically about whiteness because racist thinking perpetuates the fantasy that the Other who is subjugated, who is subhuman, lacks the ability to comprehend, to understand, to see the working of the powerful. Even though the majority of these students politically consider themselves liberals, who are anti-racist, they too unwittingly invest in the sense of whiteness as mystery.

In white supremacist society, white people can "safely" imagine that they are invisible to black people since the power they have historically asserted, and even now collectively assert over black people accorded them the right to control the black gaze. As fantastic as it may seem, racist white people find it easy to imagine that black people cannot see them if within their desire they do not want to be seen by the dark Other. One mark of oppression was that black folks were compelled to assume the mantle of invisibility, to erase all traces of their subjectivity during slavery and the long years of racial apartheid, so that they could be better—less threatening—servants. An effective strategy of white supremacist terror and dehumanization during slavery centered around white control of the black gaze. Black slaves, and later manumitted servants, could be brutally punished for looking, for appearing to observe the whites they were serving as only a subject can observe, or see. To be fully an object then was to lack the capacity to see or recognize reality. These looking relations were reinforced as whites cultivated the practice of denying the subjectivity of blacks (the better to dehumanize and oppress), of relegating them to the realm of the invisible. Growing up in a Kentucky household where black servants lived in the same dwelling with her white family who employed them, newspaper heiress Sallie Bingham recalls, in her autobiography *Passion and Prejudice* (1989), "Blacks, I realized, were simply invisible to most white people, except as a pair of hands offering a drink on a silver tray." Reduced to the machinery of bodily physical labor, black people learned to appear before whites as though they were zombies, cultivating the habit of casting the gaze downward so as not to appear uppity. To look directly was an assertion of subjectivity, equality. Safety resided in the pretense of invisibility.

Even though legal racial apartheid no longer is a norm in the United States, the habits of being cultivated to uphold and maintain institutionalized white supremacy linger. Since most white people do not have to "see" black people (constantly appearing on billboards, television, movies, in magazines, etc.) and they do not need to be ever on guard, observing black people, to be "safe," they can live as though black people are invisible and can imagine that they are also invisible to blacks. Some white people may even imagine there is no representation of whiteness in the black imagination, especially one that is based on concrete observation or mythic conjecture; they think they are seen by black folks only as they want to appear. Ideologically, the rhetoric of white supremacy supplies a fantasy of whiteness. Described in Richard Dyer's (1988) essay "White" this fantasy makes whiteness synonymous with goodness:

> Power in contemporary society habitually passes itself off as embodied in the normal as opposed to the superior. This is common to all forms of power, but it works in a peculiarly seductive way with whiteness, because of the way it seems rooted, in common-sense thought, in things other than ethnic difference.... Thus it is said (even in liberal textbooks) that there are inevitable associations of white with light and therefore safety, and black with dark and therefore danger, and that this explains racism (whereas one might well argue about the safety of the cover of darkness, and the danger of exposure to the light); again, and with more justice, people point to the Judaeo-Christian use of white and black to symbolize good and evil, as carried still in such expressions as "a black mark," "white magic," "to blacken the character" and so on.

Socialized to believe the fantasy, that whiteness represents goodness and all that is benign and non-threatening, many white people assume this is the way black people conceptualize whiteness. They do not imagine that the way whiteness makes its presence felt in black life, most often as terrorizing imposition, a power that wounds, hurts, tortures, is a reality that disrupts the fantasy of whiteness as representing goodness.

Collectively, black people remain rather silent about representations of whiteness in the black imagination. As in the old days of racial segregation where black folks learned to "wear the mask," many of us pretend to be comfortable in the face of whiteness only to turn our backs and give expression to intense levels of discomfort. Especially talked about is the representation of whiteness as terrorizing. Without evoking a simplistic, essentialist "us and them" dichotomy that suggests black folks merely invert stereotypical racist interpretations, so that black becomes synonomous with goodness and white with evil, I want to focus on that representation of whiteness that is not formed in reaction to stereotypes but emerges as a response to the traumatic pain and anguish that remains a consequence of white racist domination, a psychic state that informs and shapes the way black folks "see" whiteness. Stereotypes black folks maintain about white folks, are not the only representations of whiteness in the black imagination. They emerge primarily as responses to white stereotypes of blackness. Speaking about white stereotypes of blackness as engendering a trickle-down process, where there is the projection onto an Other of all that we deny about ourselves, Lorraine Hansberry in *To Be Young, Gifted, and Black* (1969) identifies particular stereotypes about white people that are commonly cited in black communities and urges us not to "celebrate this madness in any direction":

> Is it not "known" in the ghetto that white people, as an entity, are "dirty" (especially white women—who never seem to do their own cleaning); inherently "cruel" (the cold, fierce roots of Europe; who else could put all those people into ovens *scientifically*); "smart" (you really have to hand it to the m.f.'s); and anything *but* cold and passionless (because look who has had to live with little else than their passions in the guise of love and hatred all these centuries)? And so on.

Stereotypes, however inaccurate, are one form of representation. Like fictions, they are created to serve as substitutions, standing in for what is real. They are there not to tell it like it is but to invite and encourage pretense. They are a fantasy, a projection onto the Other that makes them less threatening. Stereotypes abound when there is distance. They are an invention, a pretense that one knows when the steps that would make real knowing possible cannot be taken—are not allowed.

Looking past stereotypes to consider various representations of whiteness in the black imagination, I appeal to memory, to my earliest recollections of ways these issues were raised in black life. Returning to memories of growing up in the social circumstances created by racial apartheid, to all black spaces on the edges of town, I re-inhabit a location where black folks associated whiteness with the terrible, the terrifying, the terrorizing. White people were regarded as terrorists, especially those who dared to enter that segregated space of blackness. As a child I did not know any white people. They were strangers, rarely seen in our neighborhoods. The "official" white men who came across the tracks were there to sell products, Bibles, insurance. They terrorized by economic exploitation. What did I see in the gazes of those white men who crossed our thresholds that made me afraid, that made black children unable to speak? Did they understand at all how strange their whiteness appeared in our living rooms, how threatening? Did they journey across the tracks with the same "adventurous" spirit that other white men carried to Africa, Asia, to those mysterious places they would one day call the third world? Did they come to our houses to meet the Other face to face and enact the colonizer role, dominating us on our own turf? Their presence terrified me. Whatever their mission they looked too much like the unofficial white men who came to enact rituals of terror and torture. As a child, I did not know how to tell them apart, how to ask the "real white people to please stand up." The terror that I felt is one black people have shared. Whites learn about it secondhand. Confessing in *Soul Sister* (1969) that she too began to feel this terror after changing her skin to appear "black" and going to live in the South, Grace Halsell described her altered sense of whiteness:

> Caught in this climate of hate, I am totally terror-stricken, and I search my mind to know why I am fearful of my own people. Yet they no longer seem my people, but rather the "enemy" arrayed in large numbers against me in some hostile territory.... My wild heartbeat is a secondhand kind of terror. I know that I cannot possibly experience what *they*, the black people experience....

Black folks raised in the North do not escape this sense of terror. In her autobiography, *Every Good-bye Ain't Gone* (1990), Itabari Njeri begins the narrative of her northern childhood with a memory of southern roots. Traveling south as an adult to investigate the murder of her grandfather by white youth who were drag racing and ran him down in the streets, killing him, Njeri recalls that for many years "the distant and accidental violence that took my grandfather's life could not compete with the psychological terror that begun to engulf my own." Ultimately, she begins to link that terror with the history of black people in the United States, seeing it as an imprint carried from the past to the present:

> As I grew older, my grandfather assumed mythic proportions in my imagination. Even in absence, he filled my room like music and watched over me when I was fearful. His fantasized presence diverted thoughts of my father's drunken rages. With age, my fantasizing ceased, the image of my grandfather faded. What lingered was the memory of his caress, the pain of something missing in my life, wrenched away by reckless white youths. I had a growing sense—the beginning of an inevitable comprehension—that this society deals blacks a disproportionate share of pain and denial.

Njeri's journey takes her through the pain and terror of the past, only the memories do not fade. They linger, as does the pain and bitterness: "Against a backdrop of personal loss, against the evidence of history that fills me with a knowledge of the hateful behavior of whites toward blacks, I see the people of Bainbridge. And I cannot trust them. I cannot absolve them." If it is possible to conquer terror through ritual reenactment, that is what Njeri does. She goes back to the scene of the crime, dares to face the enemy. It is this confrontation that forces the terror of history to loosen its grip.

To name that whiteness in the black imagination is often a representation of terror: one must face a palimpsest of written histories that erase and deny, that reinvent the past to make the present vision of racial harmony and pluralism more plausible. To bear the burden of memory one must willingly journey to places long uninhabited, searching the debris of history for traces of the unforgettable, all knowledge of which has been suppressed. Njeri laments in her Prelude that "nobody really knows us"; "So institutionalized is the ignorance of our history, our culture, our everyday existence that, often, we do not even know ourselves." Theorizing black experience, we seek to uncover, restore, as well as to deconstruct, so that new paths, different journeys are possible. Indeed, Edward Said (1983) in "Traveling Theory" argues that theory can "threaten reification, as well as the entire bourgeoise system on which reification depends, with destruction." The call to theorize black experience is constantly challenged and subverted by conservative voices reluctant to move from fixed locations. Said reminds us:

> Theory, in fine, is won as the result of a process that begins when consciousness first experiences its own terrible ossification in the general reification of all things under

capitalism; then when consciousness generalizes (or classes) itself as something opposed to other objects, and feels itself as contradiction to (or crisis within) objectification, there emerges a consciousness of change in the status quo; finally, moving toward freedom and fulfillment, consciousness looks ahead to complete self-realization, which is of course the revolutionary process stretching forward in time, perceivable now only as theory or projection.

Traveling, moving into the past, Njeri pieces together fragments. Who does she see staring into the face of a southern white man who was said to be the one? Does the terror in his face mirror the look of the unsuspected black man whose dying history does not name or record? Baldwin wrote that "people are trapped in history and history is trapped in them." There is then only the fantasy of escape, or the promise that what is lost will be found, rediscovered, returned. For black folks, reconstructing an archaeology of memory makes return possible, the journey to a place we can never call home even as we reinhabit it to make sense of present locations. Such journeying cannot be fully encompassed by conventional notions of travel.

Spinning off from Said's essay, James Clifford in "Notes on Travel and Theory" celebrates the idea of journeying, asserting that

> This sense of worldly, "mapped" movement is also why it may be worth holding on to the term "travel," despite its connotations of middle-class "literary," or recreational, journeying, spatial practices long associated with male experiences and virtues. "Travel" suggests, at least, profane activity, following public routes and beaten tracks, How do different populations, classes, and genders travel? What kinds of knowledges, stories, and theories do they produce? A crucial research agenda opens up.

Reading this piece and listening to Clifford talk about theory and travel, I appreciated his efforts to expand the travel/theoretical frontier so that it might be more inclusive, even as I considered that to answer the questions he poses is to propose a deconstruction of the conventional sense of travel, and put alongside it or in its place a theory of the journey that would expose the extent to which holding on to the concept of "travel" as we know it is also a way to hold on to imperialism. For some individuals, clinging to the conventional sense of travel allows them to remain fascinated with imperialism, to write about it seductively, evoking what Renato Rosaldo (1988) aptly calls in *Culture and Truth* "imperialist nostalgia." Significantly, he reminds readers that "even politically progressive North American audiences have enjoyed the elegance of manners governing relations of dominance and subordination between the 'races.' " Theories of travel produced outside conventional borders might want the Journey to become the rubric within which travel as a starting point for discourse is associated with different headings—rites of passage, immigration, enforced migration, relocation, enslavement, homelessness. Travel is not a word that can be easily evoked to talk about the Middle Passage, the Trail of Tears, the landing of Chinese immigrants at Ellis Island, the forced relocation of Japanese-Americans, the plight of the homeless. Theorizing diverse journeying is crucial to our understanding of any politics of location. As Clifford asserts at the end of his essay: "Theory is always written from some 'where,' and that 'where' is less a place than itineraries: different, concrete histories of dwelling, immigration, exile, migration. These include the migration of third world intellectuals into the metropolitan universities, to pass through or to remain, changed by their travel but marked by places of origin, by peculiar allegiances and alienations."

Listening to Clifford "playfully" evoke a sense of travel, I felt such an evocation would always make it difficult for there to be recognition of an experience of travel that is not about play but is an encounter with terrorism. And it is crucial that we recognize that the hegemony of one experience of travel can make it impossible to articulate another experience and be heard. From certain standpoints, to travel is to encounter the terrorizing force of white supremacy. To tell my "travel" stories, I must name the movement from a racially segregated southern community, from a rural black Baptist origin, to prestigious white university settings, etc. I must be able to speak about what it is like to be leaving Italy after I have given a talk on racism and feminism, hosted by the parliament, only to stand for hours while I am interrogated by white officials who do not have to respond when I inquire as to why the questions they ask me are different from those asked the white people in line before me. Thinking only that I must endure this public questioning, the stares of those around me, because my skin is black, I am startled when I am asked if I speak Arabic, when I am told that women like me receive presents from men without knowing what those presents are. Reminded of another time when I was strip-searched by French officials, who were stopping black people to make sure we were not illegal immigrants and/or terrorists, I think that one fantasy of whiteness is that the threatening Other is always a terrorist. This projection enables many white people to imagine there is no representation of whiteness as terror, as terrorizing. Yet it is this representation of whiteness in the black imagination, first learned in the narrow confines of the poor black rural community, that is sustained by my travels to many different locations.

To travel, I must always move through fear, confront terror. It helps to be able to link this individual experience to the collective journeying of black people, to the Middle Passage, to the mass migration of southern black folks to northern cities in the early part of the twentieth century. Michel Foucault posits memory as a site of resistance suggesting (as Jonathan Arac puts it in his introduction to *Postmodernism and Politics*) that the process of remembering can be a practice which "transforms history from a judgment on the past in the name of a present truth to a 'counter-memory' that combats our current modes of truth and justice, helping us to understand and change the present by placing it in a new relation to the past." It is useful when theorizing black experience to examine the way the concept of "terror" is linked to representations of whiteness.

In the absence of the reality of whiteness, I learned as a child that to be "safe" it was important to recognize the power of whiteness, even to fear it, and to avoid encountering it. There was nothing terrifying about the sharing of this knowledge as survival strategy; the terror was made real only when I journeyed from the black side of town to a predominately white area near my grandmother's house. I had to pass through this area to reach her place. Describing these journeys "across town" in the essay "Homeplace: A Site of Resistance" I remembered:

> It was a movement away from the segregated blackness of our community into a poor white neighborhood. I remember the fear, being scared to walk to Baba's, our grandmother's house, because we would have to pass that terrifying whiteness—those white faces on the porches staring us down with hate. Even when empty or vacant those porches seemed to say *danger,* you do not belong here, you are not safe.
>
> Oh! that feeling of safety, of arrival, of homecoming when we finally reached the edges of her yard, when we could see the soot black face of our grandfather, Daddy Gus, sitting in his chair on the porch, smell his cigar, and rest on his lap. Such a contrast, that feeling of arrival, of homecoming—this sweetness and the bitterness of that journey, that constant reminder of white power and control.

Even though it was a long time ago that I made this journey, associations of whiteness with terror and the terrorizing remain. Even though I live and move in spaces where I am surrounded by whiteness, surrounded, there is no comfort that makes the terrorism disappear. All black people in the United States, irrespective of their class status or politics, live with the possibility that they will be terrorized by whiteness.

This terror is most vividly described in fiction writing by black authors, particularly the recent novel by Toni Morrison (1987), *Beloved.* Baby Suggs, the black prophet, who is most vocal about representations of whiteness, dies because she suffers an absence of color. Surrounded by a lack, an empty space, taken over by whiteness, she remembers: "Those white things have taken all I had or dreamed and broke my heartstrings too. There is no bad luck in the world but white folks." If the mask of whiteness, the pretense, represents it as always benign, benevolent, then what this representation obscures is the representation of danger, the sense of threat. During the period of racial apartheid, still known by many folks as Jim Crow, it was more difficult for black people to internalize this pretense, hard for us not to know that the shapes under white sheets had a mission to threaten, to terrorize. That representation of whiteness, and its association with innocence, which engulfed and murdered Emmett Till was a sign; it was meant to torture with the reminder of possible future terror. In Morrison's *Beloved* the memory of terror is so deeply inscribed on the body of Sethe and in her consciousness, and the association of terror with whiteness is so intense, that she kills her young so that they will never know the terror. Explaining her actions to Paul D. she tells him that it is her job "to keep them away from what I know is terrible." Of course Sethe's attempt to end the historical anguish of black people only reproduces it in a different form. She conquers the terror through perverse reenactment, through resistance, using violence as a means of fleeing from a history that is a burden too great to bear. It is the telling of that history that makes possible political self-recovery.

In contemporary society, white and black people alike believe that racism no longer exists. This erasure, however mythic, diffuses the representation of whiteness as terror in the black imagination. It allows for assimilation and forgetfulness. The eagerness with which contemporary society does away with racism, replacing this recognition with evocations of pluralism and diversity that further mask reality, is a response to the terror, but it has also become a way to perpetuate the terror by providing a cover, a hiding place. Black people still feel the terror, still associate it with whiteness, but are rarely able to articulate the varied ways we are terrorized because it is easy to silence by accusations of reverse racism or by suggesting that black folks who talk about the ways we are terrorized by whites are merely evoking victimization to demand special treatment.

Attending a recent conference on cultural studies, I was reminded of the way in which the discourse of race is increasingly divorced from any recognition of the politics of racism. I went there because I was confident that I would be in the company of likeminded, progressive, "aware" intellectuals; instead, I was disturbed when the usual arrangements of white supremacist hierarchy were mirrored both in terms of who was speaking, of how bodies were arranged on the stage, of who was in the audience, of what voices were deemed worthy to speak and be heard. As the conference progressed I began to feel afraid. If progressive people, most of whom were white, could so blindly reproduce a version of the status quo and not "see" it, the thought of how racial politics would be played out "outside" this arena was horrifying. That feeling of terror that I had known so intimately in my childhood surfaced. Without even considering whether the audience was able to shift from the prevailing standpoint and hear another perspective, I talked openly about that sense of terror. Later, I heard stories of white women joking about how ludicrous it was for me (in their eyes I suppose I represent the "bad" tough black woman) to say I felt terrorized. Their inability to conceive that my terror, like that of Sethe's, is a response to the legacy of white domination and the contemporary

expressions of white supremacy is an indication of how little this culture really understands the profound psychological impact of white racist domination.

At this same conference I bonded with a progressive black woman and white man
who, like me, were troubled by the extent to which folks chose to ignore the way white
supremacy was informing the structure of the conference. Talking with the black
woman, I asked her: "What do you do, when you are tired of confronting white racism,
tired of the day-to-day incidental acts of racial terrorism? I mean, how do you deal with
coming home to a white person?" Laughing, she said, "Oh, you mean when I am
suffering from White People Fatigue Syndrome. He gets that more than I do." After
we finished our laughter, we talked about the way white people who shift locations, as
her companion has done, begin to see the world differently. Understanding how racism
works, he can see the way in which whiteness acts to terrorize without seeing himself
as bad, or all white people as bad, and black people as good. Repudiating "us and them"
dichotomies does not mean that we should *never* speak the ways observing the world
from the standpoint of "whiteness" may indeed distort perception, impede understanding
of the way racism works both in the larger world as well as the world of our intimate
interactions. Calling for a shift in locations in "the intervention interview" published
with the collection *The Post-Colonial Critic* (1990), Gayatri Spivak clarifies the radical
possibilities that surface when positionality is problematized, explaining that "what we
are asking for is that the hegemonic discourses, the holders of hegemonic discourse
should de-hegemonize their position and themselves learn how to occupy the subject
position of the other." Generally, this process of repositioning has the power to deconstruct practices of racism and make possible the disassociation of whiteness with terror
in the black imagination. As critical intervention, it allows for the recognition that
progressive white people who are anti-racist might be able to understand the way in
which their cultural practice reinscribes white supremacy without promoting paralyzing
guilt or denial. Without the capacity to inspire terror, whiteness no longer signifies the
right to dominate. It truly becomes a benevolent absence. Baldwin ends his essay
"Stranger in the Village" with the declaration: "This world is white no longer, and it
will never be white again." Critically examining the association of whiteness as terror
in the black imagination, deconstructing it, we both name racism's impact and help to
break its hold. We decolonize our minds and our imaginations.

20

Aesthetics and Cultural Studies

IAN HUNTER

The cultural studies movement conceives of itself as a critique of aesthetics. It construes its history in terms of the need to transcend the limited conception of culture handed down by nineteenth-century aesthetics. And it formulates its project in terms of the expansion of this conception to include other departments of existence—the political, the economic, the popular—perhaps even "the way of life as a whole."[1] The slogan of this project is the proposal to "politicize aesthetics."

In these remarks I raise some questions about this understanding of the relation between aesthetics and cultural studies. In particular, I ask whether aesthetics is open to a critique of the proposed kind. And I ask whether aesthetic cultivation can indeed be subsumed within a more general culture, diffused throughout society. Further, I question whether cultural studies has traveled as far beyond the domain of aesthetics as it thinks. My reason for posing these questions is not that I am out of sympathy with the project to politicize aesthetics *per se*. I do so because it seems to me that this project entails a significant misunderstanding of the historical mode of existence of aesthetics and, more importantly, a misconstruction of the ways in which we relate to the domain of aesthetics in the present. These problems are highlighted by the way in which cultural studies construes the limits of aesthetics.

I. The Question of Limits

For cultural studies the limits of the aesthetic domain are set by its place in a more general process of historical and cultural development. The aesthetic is seen as partial in relation to the spheres of labor and politics, where humanity takes shape in the processes of securing its material existence and governing itself. This partial and incomplete character of the aesthetic is formulated in the exemplary histories of the cultural studies movement. According to one such history, it was the division of labor that led to the appearance of a specialized aesthetic sphere, splitting it from a culture in which art had been, or would be, integrated more broadly in social and economic life. Thus divorced from culture as "the way of life as a whole" aesthetics declined into the purely ethical pursuit of a deracinated elite (R. Williams, 1958, chap. 2). Alternatively, ejected from the "public sphere," in which bourgeois cultural institutions had temporarily integrated the promise of aesthetic self-realization in a politics based on rational communication, aesthetics emerged as a purely subjective minority pastime (for examples, see Hohendahl, 1982; Eagleton, 1984). In either case, the limits of the aesthetic domain are held to be established by the manner in which it is detached from and related to the processes of human completion. And if this detachment impoverishes these processes by depriving labor and politics of the archetype of self-realizing activity, aesthetics is simultaneously impoverished in being uprooted from the soil of real human development and left to wither in the thin air of ethics and taste.

In short, the limits that cultural studies establishes for aesthetics are those of a knowledge or practice of cultivation segregated from the driving forces of human development—labor and politics—and retarding further development by diverting culture into the ideal realm of ethics and taste. Given this specification, the way to transcend these limits is clear. The narrowly ethical practice of culture associated with aesthetics must be subsumed within culture as the whole way of life. Then it will be possible to actualize the promise of self-realization by harnessing aesthetics to the processes of economic and political development.

Today, however, this way of establishing the limits of aesthetics and formulating the project of cultural studies is becoming increasingly difficult to sustain. Two distinct but converging lines of reflection have brought it into question. First, a reconstruction is underway in our understanding of the ethical sphere itself. This is associated with the revival of interest in Weber's classic studies of particular ethical orders (e.g. Lash and Whimster, 1987; Hennis, 1988; Tribe, 1989) and with Foucault's last investigations of late antique and early Christian sexual ethics (1985, 1986). At the heart of this reconstruction lies an analysis of the ethical sphere that does not view it as an ideal or subjective domain; that is, one consisting of ideas and values in some sort of general relation to a counterposed sphere of material existence. Instead, the ethical sphere is held to consist of ways of conducting one's life—specific means for establishing the consistency of conduct and outlook that we associate with having a personality, to speak in a Weberian manner. Or, to borrow from Foucault's lexicon: technologies for problematizing conduct and events that permit individuals to compose themselves as "subjects" of their actions and experiences. So, while I shall indeed argue that aesthetics belongs to the ethical domain, this is not to imply that it consists simply of values, ideas, and doctrines. Nor is it to testify to the subjective character of aesthetics—its alleged separation from the sphere of our real existence. To the contrary, it means that we shall describe the aesthetic as a distinctive way of actually conducting one's life—as a self-supporting ensemble of techniques and practices for problematizing conduct and events and bringing oneself into being as the subject of an aesthetic existence. If this view can be sustained then it will not be possible to identify the limits of the aesthetic with the limits of the domain of ideas, values, or the subjective.

The second line of reflection has its roots in recent critiques of Hegelian and Marxian theories of politics and economics. From a burgeoning literature let me make two selections. Barry Hindess (1986) has provided a distinctive formulation of the argument that political interests cannot be derived from economic positions. Hindess shows that such interests are formed within specific institutions of political calculation, assessment, and decision—trade unions, bureaucracies, parties, lobby groups. Hence the distribution of political interests cannot be read off from the distribution of "subject-positions" in the relations of production. Peter Miller and Nikolas Rose (1990), arguing in a similar vein, have discussed the role of "intellectual and political technologies" in bringing economic and political life within the sphere of calculation and intervention. The burden of these arguments is that the *means* by which human beings govern themselves and organize their economic lives do not arise from their political and economic existences, in the manner of ideologies. Rather, these means are contingent inventions and developments, emerging from the most diverse historical circumstances—like those, for example, in which Puritanism unexpectedly gave birth to forms of conduct and calculation conducive to capitalist economic activity. Such circumstantial technologies lead in no particular direction and realize no general form of "man" as a "species being."

From this perspective, then, political, ideological, and cultural interests must be analyzed in terms of the available institutions of their formation and deployment; and they must be analyzed without recourse to the notion of a privileged set of interests, such as that ascribed to the working class as the universalized subject of a totalizing system of production. It seems unlikely, therefore, that we can determine the limits of the aesthetic domain by treating it as an "instance" or "moment" of a more general "material" formation of "man" or the universal class.

At the risk of seeming apocalyptic, let us say that the convergence of these two trajectories of analysis signals the close of the era of political and cultural theory inaugurated by late eighteenth-century German criticism and philosophy. This was the period in which it seemed possible to subsume ethics, politics, and economics within a philosophical anthropology purporting to be a general theory of the making of "man" in "society." The end of this period calls into question all attempts to establish transcendable limits for the aesthetic domain by incorporating it within a general theory of "culture and society." If aesthetics as an ethic is neither a subjective phenomenon, nor related in any principled manner to more general or "real" processes of humanity's social formation, then there can be no question of showing its intrinsic partiality or of subsuming it within culture as "the way of life as a whole."

Such an outcome is by no means wholly negative, however. To the contrary, it has potential for inaugurating a new and fruitful mode of reflection on aesthetics. By virtue of its inheritance of nineteenth-century philosophical anthropology, cultural studies has conceived of the limits of the aesthetic as those of a "moment" in the developmental dialectic of the ideal and the real, culture and society. Theorized in this way, aesthetics appears both to embody and forestall the *unfolding of all that we might become*. In abandoning this profoundly aesthetic critique of aesthetics we free ourselves for a quite different reflection on the limits of the aesthetic domain, by beginning to treat it as one of the *"contingencies that make us what we are."*[2] This mode of reflection may lack the guarantees of transcendence provided by structural theories of our future development, but it holds out the prospect of delivering into our hands one of the technologies of our present existence.

II. Aesthetics as a Practice of the Self

In the course of his discussion of Protestantism Weber (1930) distinguishes between the theologico-moral doctrines of the Puritan churches and their "practical ethics." The doctrine of predestination may have been astonishingly destructive of the certitude of salvation—once guaranteed by sacramental ritual—but it did not by itself, argues Weber, equip individuals to conduct their lives in the absence of such a guarantee (pp. 95–128). This equipment involved the practical deployment of definite ethical techniques and practices; in particular, the techniques and practices of self-watchfulness and self-control, spiritual record-keeping and stock-taking, through which individuals transformed everyday events into "signs of grace" and their own conduct into a sign of election. Far from deriving directly from Protestant theological doctrine, the ethic or ethos of the Puritan sects stands in an unexpected, even paradoxical, relation to the former: its intense "this-worldly" activity contrasting with the resigned other-worldly character of predestinarian doctrine.

Foucault draws a similar distinction and makes a similar point regarding the autonomy of practical ethics when discussing the moral injunction of conjugal fidelity (1985, pp. 25–26). This injunction is one thing, says Foucault, but the means by which one relates to oneself as a faithful person and lives a faithful life—these are quite another.

These have changed over time and between cultural milieus even while the moral code has remained deceptively constant. So it is not at all the same thing to practice fidelity as a means of conserving one's semen on health grounds; as a way of demonstrating one's self-restraint to one's political subordinates; or in order to approximate the true sexual mutuality of the romantic couple. To study the history of these different ways of conducting oneself with regard to morality is to study the history of forms of ethical problematization and "practices of the self."

In what way might aesthetics fall within this type of history? Clearly, to answer this question we must distinguish between aesthetic doctrine or ideas and the means by which individuals have formed themselves as subjects of such doctrine. More particularly, the doctrine that literature is a source of delight and moral instruction is, we know, of classical origin; but the means by which individuals have formed themselves as subjects of literary instruction and delight have not been constant. Take, for example, the techniques permitting the sixteenth-century grammar-school boy to comb the classical canon for wise sayings, elegant turns of phrase, and ethical maxims, to store these as the commonplaces of his memory and copy book, and to retrieve them in times of oratorical and ethical need.[3] These techniques only faintly resemble the ones that we use today to compose ourselves as literary subjects. Let us say that the ethic of our aesthetic—the means by which we form ourselves as subjects of aesthetic experience—first emerged in German philosophical and religious circles at the end of the eighteenth century and that it differed significantly from the rhetorical ethos of the classical tradition. We can isolate four central features of this new ethic.[4]

First, there is the form in which individuals problematize themselves as potential subjects of aesthetic experience; that is, the means by which they come to know what it is about themselves that calls for aesthetic concern and attention. At this level the distinctive thing about the aesthetic approach is the manner in which it *denies* the individual immediate instructional or pleasurable access to literature. Individuals learn to call themselves into aesthetic question by learning that true literary art is not immediately open to them, owing to a series of fundamental internal oppositions. Such are the famous divisions between form and content, intellect and imagination, morality and the senses.

The crucial role of this schema lies not in its theoretical relation to literature but in its practical role as a means of problematizing the intellectual conduct of the individual who reads literature. That this is so immediately becomes clear once we observe that any judgment regarding the content of work, its moral bearing, its "lack of form," and so on can be immediately converted into a symptom of aesthetic imbalance in the reader. This is the burden of a remarkable comment by Schiller (1968), on the work that seems to lack formal structure and is inclined towards didacticism: "But it is by no means always proof of formlessness in the work of art if it makes its effect solely through its contents; *this may just as often be evidence of a lack of form in him who judges*" (p. 158, my emphasis). The inner divisions of the aesthetic object provide a means for individuals to concern themselves with the disintegration of their own sensibilities. Thus Schiller continues:

> If he [who judges the work of art] is either too tensed or too relaxed, if he is used to apprehending either exclusively with the intellect or exclusively with the senses, he will, even in the case of the most successfully realized whole, attend only to the parts, and in the presence of the most beauteous form respond only to the matter . . . The interest he takes in it is quite simply either a moral or a material interest; but what precisely it ought to be, namely aesthetic, that it certainly is not. (pp. 158–159)

What must be observed here is that the work of art is essentially a device in a practice of self-problematization. Its instituted incomprehensibility provides a convenient site for individuals to begin to relate to themselves as subjects of aesthetic experience. This is achieved through the successive counterpointed destruction of one's "ordinary" responses as sentimental or naive, as "too tensed" or "too relaxed," as moralistic or rhapsodic, and so on. We must take immediate note, however, that from the outset the work of art has not been the only site of experience for this practice of problematization. Already for Schiller politics and economics provide similarly "dialectical" domains:

> This disorganization, which was first started within man by civilization and learning, was made complete and universal by the new spirit of government . . . That polypoid character of the Greek states, in which every individual enjoyed an independent existence but could, when the need arose, grow into the whole organism, now made way for an ingenious clock-work, in which, out of the piecing together of innumerable but lifeless parts, a mechanical kind of collective life ensued. State and Church, laws and customs, were now torn asunder; enjoyment was divorced from labour, the means from the end, the effort from the reward. Everlastingly chained to a single little fragment of the Whole, man develops into nothing but a fragment . . . instead of putting the stamp of humanity on his own nature, he becomes nothing more than the imprint of his occupation or of his specialized knowledge. (p. 35)

Here the division of labor and classes is deployed as an exemplary occasion for Schiller to problematize and diagnose humanity's lack of integral being or "wholeness." The dialectical schema of aesthetic problematization is thus not determined by a particular sphere of existence, art. Rather, its character derives from its use as an ethical technique— as a means of putting into question the individual's "ordinary" relation to *all* spheres of existence, and of reconstituting them as sites of aesthetic incompletion.

The second feature of aesthetic ethos consists of the means by which individuals subject themselves to its peculiar demands, or, the means by which they come to relate to themselves as aesthetic subjects. The central devices of these means of "subjectification" can be found in the distinct but interlocking figures of the dissociated sensibility and the divided or alienated society. Through the figure of the dissociated sensibility certain individuals learn to relate to themselves as bearers of an imbalanced, fragmented— hence incomplete—inner being. And through that of the alienated society it becomes possible for them to relate their personal incompletion to a fundamental social fragmentation—the division of labor and classes—which plays the roles of both symptom and cause of the inner division.

We can see both figures at work, in the context of highly characteristic historical narrative, in Schiller's comments on why modern life fails to produce synthetic personalities that compare with the Greeks:

> At that first fair awakening of the powers of the mind [i.e., in classical Greece], sense and intellect did not as yet rule over strictly separate domains; for no dissension had as yet provoked them into hostile partition and mutual demarcation of their frontiers. Poetry had not as yet coquetted with wit, nor speculation prostituted itself to sophistry. Both of them could, when need arose, exchange functions, since each in its own fashion paid honour to truth. However high the mind might soar, it always drew matter lovingly along with it; and however fine and sharp the distinctions it might make, it never proceeded to mutilate. It did indeed divide human nature into its several aspects, and project these in magnified form into the divinities of its glorious pantheon; but not by tearing it to pieces; rather by combining its aspects in different proportions, for in no single one of their deities was humanity in its entirety ever lacking. How different with us Moderns! With us too the image of the human species is projected

in magnified form into separate individuals—but as fragments, not in different combinations, with the result that one has to go the rounds from one individual to another
in order to be able to piece together a complete image of the species. With us, one
might almost be tempted to assert, the various faculties appear as separate in practice
as they are distinguished by the psychologist in theory, and we see not merely individuals, but whole classes of men, developing but one part of their potentialities,
while of the rest, as in stunted growths, only vestigial traces remain ...

Whence this disadvantage among individuals when the species as a whole is
at such an advantage? Why was the individual Greek qualified to be the representative
of his age, and why can no single Modern venture as much? Because it was from all-
unifying Nature that the former, and from the all-dividing Intellect that the latter,
received their respective forms. (pp. 31–33)

Of course, this apparently pessimistic comparison does not in fact inhibit Schiller from
representing his age. To the contrary: just as the statement that we live in an age in
which it is impossible to talk about sex is invariably followed by a highly verbose
discourse on sex, so the statement that we live in an age whose fragmentation precludes
its synthetic representation is typically a preface to totalizing cultural diagnoses. These
statements are not descriptions of the age but devices inciting us to adopt a certain
attitude towards ourselves. Schiller's invocation of the dissociated sensibility allows the
aesthetic polarities—intellect and emotion, philosophy and poetry, form and content,
morality and sensuousness—to surface in the individual as antagonistic drives or impulses.
And his model of the divided society offers an objective manifestation of these oppositions
in the "social contradictions" between law and desire, labor and fulfillment, rulers and
ruled. It is in this way that individuals come to accept the reconciliatory tasks of the
aesthetic ethos as ineluctable consequences of the kind of being they are and of the
history that has formed them.

The third component of this ethic comprises a particular means of carrying out
work on the self and its experiences. The preceding exercises, through which individuals
come to relate to themselves as aesthetically incomplete beings, are in fact inseparable
from a highly distinctive "practice of the self." This practice is the means by which
individuals shape themselves as subjects of aesthetic experience and conduct their lives
as aesthetic beings. We are most familiar with this practice in the form of *Bildung* or
aesthetic self-cultivation. No doubt we have good reason to be skeptical of *Bildung*, so
much has been claimed for it. It has long been proclaimed as the key to realizing our
full humanity through the harmonizing of our internal divisions or the overcoming of
social contradictions.[5] However, once we deprive these divisions and contradictions of
universality, by treating their imputation as a contingent means by which individuals
call themselves into aesthetic question, then *Bildung* can be accepted as a specific form
of self-discipline, analogous—perhaps—to the yogas.

The *techne* of this discipline is provided by a dialectical practice. The opposed sides
of the divided self are successively played off against each other in a process of "mutual
modification." We have already noted that Schiller provides a foundation for this practice
via the story of the historical "wounding" of the human sensibility. This event left the
sensibility riven by antagonistic drives, or warring factions of the soul, but it also gave
birth to culture as the process of their reconciliation:

To watch over these, and secure for each of these two drives [the form and sense
drives] its proper frontiers, is the task of culture [*Kultur*], which is, therefore, in duty
bound to do justice to both drives equally: not simply to maintain the rational against
the sensuous, but the sensuous against the rational too. Hence its business is twofold:
first to preserve the life of the sense against the encroachments of freedom; and second,

to secure the Personality against the forces of Sensation. The former it achieves by developing our capacity for feeling, the latter by developing our capacity for reason. (Schiller, 1968, pp. 86–87)

But even in Schiller's universalizing history of culture the essentially voluntary and practical character of the practice of cultivation breaks through. Culture is above all something that must be undertaken by the individual. We can see this in Schiller's comment that: "the relaxing of the sense-drive must in no wise be the result of physical impotence or blunted feeling, which never merits anything but contempt. It must be an act of free choice, an activity of the Person . . ." and in his complementary remark that: "In the same way the relaxing of the formal drive must not be the result of spiritual impotence or flabbiness of thought or will . . . It must, if it is to be at all praiseworthy, spring from abundance of feeling and sensation . . ." (p. 93).

Let us say that aesthetic culture is the means by which individuals undertake a special kind of ethical work on the being whose incompleteness they have accepted as their own. The distinctive character of this work is visible in the "practical criticism" of literature first developed by the Romantics. In this exercise one can see a peculiarly intense version of the practice of "mutual modification." Literature provides a surface on which events from the most diverse spheres of existence are made available as objects of identification and experience. The vicarious affirmation of oneself as the subject of experience—the identification with fictions, the confirmation of feelings—is not, however, the defining characteristic of practical criticism. Indeed, this affirmation is elicited only that it may be canceled by the counter-movement of the critical dialectic: the recourse to "formal" judgments that systematically problematize one's existing experience and feelings by revealing their moral naivety or unconscious dependence on the formal organization of the literary universe. Such formal judgments are, however, also only made in order to be called into question in their turn. A counter-affirmation of "feeling"—of openness to experience, emotion, desire, "excess"—reveals and mortifies the abstract, didactic, or moralistic character of the formal moment. And so the process continues as an intellectual gymnastic in which individuals achieve aesthetic virtuosity— shaping a distinctively aesthetic self through the successive intensification and neutralization of capacities for feeling and thought. In this manner true *virtuosi* conduct their aesthetic lives by incorporating literature in a practice of self-formation. The reciprocating mortifications of the dual self mean that, unlike the rhetorical ethos, this practice is one that suspends conclusions and conclusiveness. Hence it is always able to compel its practitioners to begin again. The ethical intensity and minuteness of practical criticism testify to the remorseless character of this practice of reading, which is in fact a technique of writing deployed as a practice of the self.

As we have already noted, however, literature is not the only or essential source of materials for this practice of ethical labor. From the beginning, the political, economic, and social spheres have been constituted as repositories for variant forms of the same practice. These forms operate by construing society as a domain in which humanity is alienated from its true being, or rendered incomplete, through objective analogues of the aesthetic divisions: analogues such as the divisions between law and inclination, labor and self-actualization, dominating and dominated classes, utility and desire. Through this schema political, economic, and social events are transformed into "occasions" for the practice of aesthetic problematization.[6] Hence, for example, government is routinely found wanting for its failure to reconcile utility and desire, law and inclination, social norms and individual will, and so on.

In this manner individuals constitute themselves as subjects of political experience by construing political events as symptoms of the same fundamental divisions of the "ethical substance" that afflict them personally. Official, governmental, and professional forms of political activity are rejected precisely as symptomatic of the stalled dialectic— as signs of the tyranny of utility, law, and social normativity at the expense of desire, inclination, and individual will. At the same time an alternative "oppositional" mode of political life emerges as a variant form of the aesthetic practice of the self. This occurs when political activity is engaged in as the key site of self-problematization and when the shaping of the incomplete self is made conditional on the dialectical overcoming of political and social contradiction. The literary and political versions of the aesthetic practice of the self thus represent variant technologies for conducting one's intellectual life, or, conducting one's life as an intellectual.

The final component of this ethos is its ethical telos, or, the kind of being that individuals aspire to as the goal of their ethical activity. From Schiller's time onwards, individuals aspiring to an aesthetic existence have taken as their twin goals the many-sided personality and the organic or "non-alienated" society. The personality whose harmonious culture of its discordant drives permits a complete development of the human faculties, and the state or people in which social antagonism and class division have been overcome in self-realizing labor and self-governing politics—these are the abiding emblems of the aesthetic ethos.

These goals, however, are organized by a feature that is not immediately apparent: namely, their unreachable character. Schiller formulates the elusiveness of the completely balanced aesthetic personality in the following way:

> Since in actuality no purely aesthetic effect is ever to be met with (for man can never escape his dependence on conditioning forces), the excellence of a work of art can never consist in anything more than a high approximation to that ideal of aesthetic purity; and whatever the degree of freedom to which it may have been sublimated, we still leave it in a particular mood and with some definite bias. (1968, p. 153)

But, in light of the preceding analysis, we can provide a more immediate understanding of the elusiveness of the ideal of aesthetic purity. This quality belongs not to the ideal itself but to the ascetic practice which supports it: a practice that as it were moves on only by problematizing its current state and promises only the problematization of its next state, in a series of contrapuntal cancellations. Indeed, its practitioners take the fact that this process has no end—in either sense of the word—as a sign of its ethical superiority. To have an end would reduce the aesthetic existence to the status of an instrument wielded for certain rational purposes, hence depriving it of completeness. But neither is it quite true to say that aesthetic cultivation is endless and its goals unreachable. It is simply a practice for neutralizing ends and for moving on from whatever point one happens to have reached.

Let us say, then, that the objectives of the aesthetic ethos are not to be found in its official goals but in the entrance to a state of permanent "readiness" or ethical preparation. At the center of this ethic lies a powerful technology for *withdrawing* from the world as a sphere of mundane knowledge and action. In fact the aesthete does not pursue knowledge or "worldly" activity as such, having subjected them to a problematization that makes them ethically worthless. Instead, he or she seeks to prepare or cultivate the kind of self that will be worthy of enlightened knowledge and action in an indefinitely deferred future.

One gets a glimpse of this "non-rational" conception of enlightenment in Schiller's insistence on the training *(Ausbildung)* of the capacity for feeling as the prior condition for access of understanding:

> It is not, then, enough to say that all enlightenment of the understanding is worthy of respect only inasmuch as it reacts upon character. To a certain extent it also proceeds from character, since the way to the head must be opened through the heart. The development of man's capacity for feeling is, therefore, the more urgent need of our age, not merely because it can be a means of making better insights effective for living but precisely because it provides the impulse for bettering our insights. (p. 53)

We should not, however, pay too much attention to the language of feeling and understanding, head and heart. The non-rational character of aesthetic cultivation stems not from any emotionalism but from its dialectical withdrawal from "ordinary" understanding. Hence it is better termed "supra-rational." And this same practice of withdrawal finds expression in the political version of the ethic also; specifically, in the imperative to abstain from direct political activity until the reconciliatory movement of the dialectic brings the time to ripeness. Terry Eagleton (1990) provides us with a symptomatic statement of the need for such abstention.

> Certainly the content of [communist] society cannot be "read off" from the institutions set in place to produce it. "We have to ensure the means of life, and the means of community," writes Raymond Williams in *Culture and Society 1780–1950*. "But what will then, by these means, be lived, we cannot know or say." Marxism is not a theory of the future, but a theory and practice of how to make a future possible . . . its role is simply to resolve those contradictions that currently prevent us from moving beyond [pre-history] to history proper. About that history proper, Marxism has little to say. . . . (p. 215)

The notion that the work of art cannot be known directly and definitively finds its correlate in the idea that society cannot be immediately subjected to administrative reason and intervention. Both ideas are symptomatic of a practice of the self that displaces the objectives of existing knowledge and politics with the objective of the permanent preparation of a self worthy to know and to act.

This, then, in schematic outline is what the aesthetic looks like as an ethic or form of life conduct. In the means by which individuals achieve the aesthetic problematization of experience and come to recognize themselves as its subjects, in the means by which they master the practice of the aesthetic self and thereby aspire to a heightened mode of being, we come face to face with a powerful and sophisticated technology of existence. No doubt any embarrassment we feel at this moment springs from the chasm separating this technology from all existing models of formal rationality, excepting of course the model developed by Hegel. At the same time it is clear that aesthetics is highly rational in the substantive sense; that is, in giving rise to an ascetic or systematized mode of existence. In its remorseless problematization of non-aesthetic life, in the state of permanent self-critique and self-modification induced in its practitioners, and in the remarkable consistency of outlook and conduct that results, we can recognize a full-blown rationalization of existence in the Weberian sense.

What are we to make of the aesthetic ethos, analyzed in this manner? In particular—keeping in mind our initial argument that the limits of the aesthetic are not those of an "instance" or "moment" of a totality—how are we to chart its limits in relation to other departments of existence?

III. Aesthetics and Politics

We can begin to answer this question by drawing out the negative lessons of the preceding description. In the first place, we can observe that the limits of the aesthetic ethos are not those of an ideology or failed knowledge. Aesthetics is not an ideology in the straightforward sense of promoting false consciousness at the behest of a political or otherwise sectional interest. Neither is it an ideology in the more ramified sense of failing to represent the "structural relations" that present its object to its subject. Aesthetics is not a failed knowledge because it is not a knowledge at all, at least not in the sense required by these critiques.

We have seen that its objects—whether the dissociated sensibility or alienated society, the organic poem or integral "public sphere"—are not objects of knowledge presented to a putative subject of consciousness. Rather, they are the instruments and objects of a special practice of the self, deployed for essentially ethical purposes. They are phenomena whose systematically polarized structure is symptomatic of their systematic use as reflexive instruments of self-problematization and self-modification. The notion, common in the literature of cultural studies, that the subject of aesthetics sits spellbound in a specular relation to the object of its own reified consciousness is false, and in a decidedly ironic way. False, because the subject of aesthetics is brought into being only as the result of a highly athletic exercise in the problematization of experience; that is, the practice in which "vision" of the object is perpetually deferred in the successive reciprocal cancellations of its meaning and form, its content and structure. Ironically false, because the notion that in a fixed view of the object the subject is only contemplating the "dead" form of its own prior activity—this notion so central to the cultural studies' critique of aesthetics—is itself thoroughly aesthetic. It is neither more nor less than the accusation that the subject has not completed the process of self-problematization and cultivation and has lapsed into a premature knowledge of the object.

Next, we can observe that—despite its ethical character—the limits of the aesthetic sphere are not those of a specific ethical content, morality, or set of value judgments. One of the most damaging charges that the cultural studies movement has leveled against aesthetics is that it is wedded to a ("high cultural") canon of works expressing the taste and values of a particular class. Additionally it is alleged that the value judgments to which aesthetics itself gives rise—specifically those in favor of the organic work of art— serve the moral interests of the bourgeoisie. Here the argument is that by privileging the organic unity of form and content such judgments serve only to naturalize tendentious values by presenting them as experience. Our description of the aesthetic as an ethos, however, suggests that neither of these charges can be sustained.

With regard to the question of privileged canons, we have noted that the aesthetic is not identified with a particular kind of literary object but with an attitude individuals can adopt in relation to all kinds of objects, literary or not. This aesthetic attitude is the "critical" outlook arising from the inclusion of these objects in the practice of aesthetic problematization. The fact that this practice is carried out using autonomous ethical techniques means that it is not dependent on particular aesthetic objects nor, indeed, on aesthetic objects in particular. We have seen that from Schiller onwards a diverse array of political, economic, and social phenomena have been constituted as objects of this kind of critical attention. For this reason it is impossible to expand or "dilute" the aesthetic—for example, by including the non-valorized artifacts of popular culture— because to do so expands the sphere of aesthetic valorization.

This is not to deny that the practice of aesthetics has given rise to canons as privileged bodies of worked materials. Leavis's "great tradition" and Lukács's great realists are clearly cases in point. Such canons are, however, intrinsically fissile. The specific configuration and disposition of the works they contain is neither more nor less than the shaping of the aesthetic field produced by a particular virtuoso practice of the self. The inherent instability of such acts of canon formation derives from the fact that any judgment of inclusion or exclusion—for example, Lukács's (1977) argument that the modernists lacked the formal prerequisites for realism; Leavis's (1969, pp. 133–57) claim that Eliot's formal virtuosity divorced his poetry from the sensuous dimension of life found in Lawrence; Blackmur's (1957) diagnosis that Lawrence's work lacked the form to universalize his expressive energy—all such judgments can be and have been routinely inverted and read as symptoms of failings in the sensibilities of the judges. The fates of Lukács, Leavis, and Blackmur were already sealed in Schiller's comment that the judgment that a work lacks form "may just as often be evidence of a lack of form in him who judges." The period since the Romantics is noteworthy not for its stable canons but for the remorseless destabilization of canons through the practice of aesthetic problematization. In fact it is possible to suggest that the text that lies at the heart of the aesthetic ethos is not canonical but anonymous; for example, the unsigned poems that I. A. Richards administered to his students when diagnosing their "lack of form."

As far as the second charge is concerned, it is undoubtedly true that the aesthetic ethic valorizes works whose "organic" character neutralizes the normative expression of values. This is not done, however, as means of slipping such expressions past the censor wrapt in the immediacy of "experience." The organic character of aesthetic objects and experiences belongs not to them but to the ethos whose instruments they are. It derives from the practice in which all normative judgments are neutralized—placed on one side of the divided self as signs of "moralism" and "didacticism," to be canceled by a countervailing affirmation of sensuousness, desire, pleasure, "excess," and the unpredictability of the "event." Once again this is not to say that critics like Lukács, Leavis, and Blackmur do not in fact valorize as "organic" works expressive of particular normative tendencies. It is simply to say that in doing so, far from securely transmitting the disguised values of their class positions, they routinely expose themselves to the practice that excoriates them for, precisely, their moralism and didacticism! So, while we may well want to say that the ceaseless problematization of and withdrawal from all normative judgment itself has ethical problems, these cannot be problems arising from the covert endorsement of particular moral values. We will return to this point below.

The final conception of limits that we can call into question on the basis of our description is the notion that the limits of the aesthetic coincide with the limits of a particular politico-economic class or its intellectual elite. The most vivid forms of this conception are those that invest the aesthetic, in its original historical incarnation, with a limited form of universality and organic integration in society. Its present "merely" aesthetic and elite character are then derived from a history of social fragmentation and cultural division.

We have already noted Raymond Williams's version of this story. Peter Hohendahl (1982) provides a variant form. In his account the aesthetic was universalized to the level that was historically possible in the institutions of the eighteenth-century "bourgeois public sphere." Apparently this sphere integrated aesthetic discussion with the general political and economic activities that formed the material life of the middle class. The historical fracturing of this organic domain divorced aesthetics from political and economic life and confined it, on the one hand, to the elite institutions of academia (where it faded into literary criticism) and, on the other, to the media of mass communication (where it degenerated into commodity and spectacle) (pp. 72–73).

Despite its attractive "just so" quality this attempt to specify the contemporary political limits of the aesthetic fails on a number of grounds. As an historical account it is empirically implausible. The idea that the aesthetic ethos, in whatever form, was more widespread in the early eighteenth century than it is today is, to say the least, improbable. The development of systems of popular education from the beginning of the nineteenth century, the achievement of near complete literacy by the end, and the intensive deployment of the aesthetic disciplines in these systems in our own century—suggest a quite different historical conclusion. It seems far more plausible to say that more individuals have access to the aesthetic ethic today than ever before. What is surely remarkable about the Anglo-Saxon education systems is the manner in which, through the teaching of "English," they equip large numbers of children, of diverse social origin, with an extremely exacting way of constituting a self through literary reading and writing. Indeed, it is necessary to invert the usual history: What was once an esoteric discipline through which a minority constituted itself as an ethical elite within its own class is now a discipline of self-formation for a large cross-section of the educated population.

But Hohendahl's account of the limits of aesthetics is no more plausible as political theory. Its working assumption in this regard is that the elite character of the aesthetic signifies the degeneration of a formerly more democratic and organic embodiment of this ethos. It is held that the ethical hierarchy formed by the aesthetic ethos is the disguised expression of a political hierarchy. Apparently this political hierarchy and its ethical double were formed when the rising middle class passed its organic moment—that moment in which the aesthetic could still authentically express the interests of the subordinate classes as a whole—and emerged as the new dominant class. Under these circumstances the aesthetic lost its socially expressive power and democratic potential and declined into an auxiliary (ethical) means of domination in the hands of an elite.

If only this were true, one almost wants to say, for the actual character of the aesthetic hierarchy is far less comforting and far less escapable than this account allows for. The ethical hierarchy of aesthetics is not the expression of a political hierarchy at one remove. It is the direct and autonomous creation of the techniques and functions of the ethic itself. We have seen that this ethic provides the means for some individuals to distinguish themselves from others by problematizing "ordinary" experience and conducting themselves as subjects of a superior mode of being. The aesthetic practice of the self is a set of techniques for investing the self with ethical value and for placing true experience beyond the reach of all who do not undergo the rigors of the discipline. In this respect it is directly comparable with the techniques of monastic discipline, which Peter Brown (1978) describes as responsible for the emergence of an elite of holy men in late antiquity (esp. pp. 79–101). On the one hand, the hierarchy formed by the aesthetic ethos is directly and positively ethical; it is not an indirect expression of political and economic power. On the other hand, it is also clear that today this ethos is widely disseminated and that the ethical hierarchy fulfills significant political and social functions. The task confronting the political analysis of aesthetics, therefore, is not to unmask it as the disguised expression of political domination. It is to describe the contingent circumstances in which a distinctively ethical hierarchy could find a place in the political sphere. We will return to this problem below.

Let us say, then, that aesthetics does not have epistemological, ethical, and political limits of the sort attributed to it by cultural studies. This is because, I have argued, aesthetics is neither a knowledge, a morality, nor a politics. It is, rather, an ethic: an autonomous set of techniques and practices by which individuals continuously problematize their experience and conduct themselves as the subjects of an aesthetic existence. This is not to argue, of course, that the aesthetic ethos is without epistemological, moral, and political consequences—some of which I have pointed to in an anticipatory way. Neither is it to argue that this ethical technology is unrelated to the mechanisms of our political, economic, and social existence. It is to say, however, that there is no general model for the relation between the aesthetic and these other departments of existence; for example, the model in which the aesthetic represents part of a larger whole, a moment in a pattern of development whose ethical character is that which must be transcended on the way to complete being. This is the model that we must put behind us. In its place we must learn to describe the aesthetic ethic as an historical invention; a device for living, made up of autonomous components, self-supporting, and entering into relationships with other spheres of existence of the most contingent and unpredictable kind. The description of such contingent and circumstantial historical configurations has been called genealogy. And to capture the contingency of the aesthetic—as one of the "contingencies that make us what we are"—we need to give some indication, necessarily brief, of its genealogy.

IV. Genealogical Notes

Here I wish to make note of four factors that we must take into account if we are to understand the emergence of the aesthetic sphere and the manner in which it informs the present. I should stress, however, that this schema is not meant to be exhaustive and represents the beginning of historical research on the topic, not its conclusion.

In the first place we need to locate the aesthetic in a history of "practices of the self"; that is, a history of the means by which individuals have come to form themselves as the subjects of various kinds of experience and action and to endow their lives with particular kinds of significance and shape. These are the practices that Weber identifies with *Lebensführung* or the conduct of life and that Foucault describes as ethical technologies. And we have already singled out Weber's analysis of Puritan ethical conduct and Foucault's account of late-classical sexual ethics as showing us the broad sphere of historical reality in which the aesthetic ethos is to be found. The differences between Calvinist practices for monitoring the self for signs of election and the classical arts for shaping the self as the subject of a stylized sexual conduct give some sense of the diversity of this field. Emerging in a variety of milieus—religious, political, domestic, literary, medical, pedagogic—these "arts of living" represent a kind of subterranean historical current, undergoing perpetual mutation but not without maintaining certain continuities in the means by which individuals invent themselves.

We can identify Shaftesbury's (1900) *Philosophical Regimen* as indicative of a current in the arts of living that flows directly into the aesthetic ethos. Shaftesbury used his knowledge of the classics not as a source for public oratory but as a repository of techniques for constituting the self as an object of ethical attention. The following remarks on how to conceive of the self as in need of ethical improvement are representative of his method:

> Improvement. Advancement.—In what? whither? as how? Is there such a thing belonging in this place? is there study or art here? Bethink thyself. Is there really such a science? And is the faculty, mystery, skill real? If so, how is it in other arts, where improvement is looked for, advancement aimed at? How if a mathematician? how if an accountant? how if a student of language, in rhetoric, aiming at mastery in writing or in speaking; a manner; a style? . . .
>
> [For as the material of the carpenter is wood—so the material of the art of living is each man's own life. —*Epictetus, Discourse,* Bk. I, ch. XV]. This is the subject, and accordingly in this must be the improvement. Begin, therefore, and work upon this subject—collect, digest, methodise, abstract . . .
>
> Know thy work, know thy subject, matter, instruments, rules. Has the carpenter so many? is there so much closet-work, paper-work, so much study, writing, figuring,

practising here? Why writing? why this flourishing, drawing, figuring, over and over, the same still? what for?—What, but for the art? Not for show; but for exercise, practice, improvement.—Writing and then burning. Drawing and then rubbing out . . .

Go on, then: exercise and write, but remember . . . [for yourself and not for others. —*Epictetus, Enchiridion,* ch. xlvii]. (pp. 240–42)

What the philosophers and critics of late eighteenth-century Germany found in Shaftesbury's regimen was an exemplary set of exercises for taking the self as an object of ethical concern and labor. They found a means of turning away from the courtly culture of the self—centered on the public civility and bodily grace of the courtier (see Elias, 1982, pp. 258–319)—and reconstituting nobility on inward co-ordinates, in the relation of the self to the self. And they found a set of techniques for perfecting this self, including a prototype of the dialectic—here explicitly introduced as an exercise in self-recognition and self-problematization. Authors who aspire to moral insight, says Shaftesbury, must first clarify and modify their own passions and opinions. The exercise begins with the imperative to "Recognize yourself: which was as much to say, *Divide* your-self, or Be Two":

And here it is that our Sovereign Remedy and *Gymnastick* Method of Soliloquy takes its Rise: when by a certain powerful figure of inward Rhetorick, the Mind *apostrophizes* its own Fancys. . . . (Shaftesbury, n.d., vol. 1., p. 84)

Thus apostrophized through the "inward rhetoric" of "self-conversation" the passions could be modified and the opinions clarified.

In this light it is possible to reconsider a number of leading features of the modern aesthetic ethos: inwardness, attentiveness to subjective states, intensification of imaginative experience, disregard for "public" appearances, the identification of nobility with self–cultivation, dialectical thinking. We can suggest that these derive not from the epochal discovery of subjective experience but from the dissemination of an ethical regimen in which individuals compose themselves as the subjects of their experience.

The second factor bearing on the emergence of the aesthetic sphere lies in the manner in which this eighteenth-century "art of living" was transformed by German critical philosophy. We know that this philosophy, far from regarding itself as a practical knowledge or ethic, aspired to reveal the transcendental conditions underlying all knowledge and judgment. But, whatever we might say about the Kantian aspiration as such, we can say that in the works of writers like Fichte, Schiller, and Hegel it resulted in something quite other than formal metaphysics. It issued in a hybrid discourse in which an ethical regimen of the same type as Shaftesbury's is "transcendentalized" while nonetheless retaining an irreducibly practical core.

The constitutional ambivalence of the new discourse is readily visible in Schiller's *On the Aesthetic Education of Man.* On the one hand, we seem to have moved a long way from the sphere of voluntary practical ethics: the sphere in which Shaftesbury could recommend the dialectic—"Recognize your-self: which was as much to say, *Divide* your-self, or Be Two"—as a technique of ethical self-attentiveness. In Schiller the dialectic has been universalized and rendered absolute. It appears not in the form of a practice of the self that certain individuals might choose to master in pursuit of inner nobility, but as the underived ground of all thought, judgment, and action. Hence Schiller outlines a fundamental dialectic between "person" and "condition." The former is understood as the "unrealized" infinity of possible forms of human being and is identified with the principle of freedom. The latter is construed in terms of "matter," sensation, and the laws of the physical universe and is the locus of the principle of determination (1968, pp. 73–77). In the mediating agencies of culture and labor, art and play, Schiller sees not practical technologies through which a few men choose to perfect themselves, but the universal agency of the "World Spirit" which realizes man as a collective subject in the play between the ideal and the real.

On the other hand, for all this, it remains the case that the dialectic retains a voluntary and practical character. We have already quoted Schiller's comment that the intellectual pacification of the senses must not be regarded as the inevitable outcome of the latter's weakness, that "It must be an act of free choice, an activity of the Person which, by its moral intensity, moderates that of the senses . . . " The partnering remark from the other side of the dialectic can also be recalled: "In the same way the relaxing of the formal drive must not be the result of spiritual impotence or flabbiness of thought or will . . . It must . . . spring from abundance of feeling and sensation" (p. 93). In this context, Schiller's specification of *Kultur* as the dual cultivation of reason and feeling in a process of "mutual modification" retains—despite his attempt to identify it with mankind's universal development—the character of ethical technique and advice.

It is possible to propose that the central *figura* of the aesthetic ethos—man's divided ethical substance, the dissociated sensibility, the alienated society, the internally divided work of art, history as the process of humanity's dialectical development—emerge in this space between a transcendentalized ethic and its use as a voluntary practice of the self. Their task is to present a highly specialized practice of ethical problematization in a universal and binding form—to present it as the form in which individuals must conduct themselves as subjects in all walks of life and spheres of existence, if they are to be true to their inner being, their history, and their future. This remark applies with equal force to the "idealist" and "materialist" versions of the dialectic.

This philosophical reconstruction of the discursive space surrounding the art of living—this redisposition of the ethical practice in a distinctively aesthetic cosmography—was not the only change that took place in Germany. The third factor in the emergence of the aesthetic ethic concerns parallel changes in the milieu in which this ethic was articulated and in the milieu or "world" against which it was articulated. Above all, we must not lose sight of the fact that we are dealing with an ethic of withdrawal; that is, with a means by which individuals set themselves apart from "ordinary" existence and conduct themselves as subjects of a heightened form of being.

Of course, the nature of the world from which such individuals withdraw varies with the targets of the problematization and the sites from which it is carried out. For Shaftesbury the world to be problematized was that of courtly and aristocratic life and he carried this out from the position of a private gentleman aspiring to a purely inner nobility. The targets of the German problematization, however, lay elsewhere—let us say in the image of the instrumentally administered state as a political, economic, and cultural totality. And the site from which this problematization was carried out now shifted to the intellectual milieu centered in the university system and the "republic of letters." It was in this new space of problematization, organized by the newly transcendentalized dialectic, that the topography of an aesthetic life conduct was formed.

If individuals are in need of ethical attention, says Schiller, if they are "too tensed" or "too relaxed," torn between narrow morality and irresistible sensuousness, forced to develop only their mental or only their physical sides, unable to reconcile social norms and personal desires, incapable of appreciating literature unless they are drawing lessons or titillating themselves—if these are "modern man's" ethical failings, says Schiller, then they derive from a society whose political structure fails to express individual will, whose division of labor prevents the harmonious development of all man's sides, whose laws enforce norms with no regard to human inclinations, and whose sciences specialize and objectify man's cognitive faculties in a manner that defeats their synthesis in human feeling and organic insight (pp. 33–40).

Conversely, if society is prone to economic, political, and cultural failure this is not because it cannot achieve an appropriate balance of trade or solve the problem of unemployment; nor is it because it has difficulties in developing an appropriate electoral machinery or system of decision and administration; neither is it because the school, health, and welfare systems are inadequate to their appointed tasks. No, society fails in a different and higher modality in the eyes of its aesthetic critics. Indeed, it fails in this higher way even if—perhaps even because—it succeeds in all these particular economic, political, and cultural endeavors. It fails because its economic, political, and cultural organization fails to reconcile the fundamental ethical contradictions, by forming society as the organic expression of human self-actualization and self-government (pp. 41–43).

It is necessary, then, to invert the standard accounts. It is not the signs of a prescient and exemplary engagement with modern forms of social organization that we find in Schiller's diagnosis, but the figures formed by an exemplary practice of problematization and withdrawal. It must be observed that such aesthetic topographies appeared first not in countries with the most backward forms of social and political organization but in those with the most most sophisticated and advanced. Scholars from Albion Small (1909) to Gerhard Oestreich (1982) have characterized the system of small German states between the sixteenth and nineteenth centuries as a forcing house for the development of a network of administrative institution, techniques, calculations, and concepts. This network, which Foucault (1979) describes under the heading of "governmentality," was responsible for transforming politics into a "rational art." It made it possible for societies to be constituted as objects of knowledge and intervention whose security could be strengthened, civilization advanced, and wealth increased. This could be achieved through the managed optimilization of their trade, industries, social infrastructure, and of the "moral and physical condition" of their populations.

It is precisely this new "governmentalized" form of society that the aesthetic ethos constitutes as the "mechanical," "alienated," "ordinary," and "mundane" world to be transcended. And it does so not by engaging with the governmental organization of this world but by constituting it as the site on which the self must call itself into question; that is, by using it as a domain of experience to be subjected to continuous ethical problematization as the means of constituing oneself as the subject of a higher mode of being.

The result of this practice of critique through exemplary withdrawal can be seen in the ambivalent figure of Schiller's "statesman-artist." Like Shelley's poet, the states-man-artist is society's unacknowledged legistor, yet he governs only by turning inwards where, in his life and art, he embodies and reconciles the great contradictions of society. He abstains from direct political intervention in society, treating this as the hallmark of ethical failure, and instead asppires to lead it to completeness only through his ex-emplary completion of himself (pp. 19–21). Some have seen in this figure a telling symptom of the political weakness of aesthetics. I would rather see it as the emblem of a singular ethical and social potency. The practice of exemplary aesthetic withdrawal is in fact widely accepted as the condition of access to a level of ethical being from where the whole of society can be judged and found wanting. The incandescent figure of the stateman-artist—lighting the political spectrum from Matthew Arnold to William Morris, from Coleridge to Lukács—is charged with the remarkable voltages of ethical regard and authority that flow to the social persona of the aesthete, currents generated solely by the latter's ascetic distance from "society."

At the same time, no "social logic" dictated that this ethical power would reach beyond the academic milieus and literary circles that supported the practice of aesthetic virtuosity. To understand how the aesthetic ethos came to make the transition from cult to culture we need to take note of a set of historical circumstances that form the fourth and final component of our genealogical sketch. These were the circumstances in which, towards the end of the nineteenth century, the aesthetic discipline was itself attached to the technologies of the governmental sphere, specifically, to the emergent system of popular education. As I have described these circumstances in detail elsewhere (Hunter, 1988a), I will select only two features of particular relevance to the present discussion.

In the first place, the new education system was not itself an invention of the aesthetic personage. It was not brought into being by the likes of Schiller, Coleridge, Carlyle, or Arnold as a device for man's cultural realization or ideological anaesthesis. (Schiller's *On the Aesthetic Education of Man* contains no references to educational *institutions*.) Instead, its designers were administrative intellectuals acting as agents of the political and intellectual technologies of government. These were the technologies that had constituted the "moral and physical condition" of the population (health, literacy, manners, forms of consumption) as a governmental objective. They were also responsible for a new conception of the school—as a purpose-built space for the moral supervision of large numbers of children—that provided the key to realizing this objective. Hence, when the aesthetic personage eventually found a place in the school system it was not what he *knew* that permitted him to occupy a position in the new space of moral supervision, but what he *was;* that is, an ethically exemplary personality. It was his ethical standing as the subject of a higher life that allowed this figure to take the place of teacher in a system where discipline was to be based on ethical regard rather than coercion. And this is entirely representative of the unexpected circumstances in which the ethical hierarchy formed by the aesthetic ethos found a place in the governmental sphere.

Second, the effectiveness of the aesthetic personage in this new role did not derive from his or her custodianship of the riches of art, literature, play, or *Bildung.* Rather, it lay in the manner in which the aesthetic as a practice of the self permitted the teacher to occupy the position of ethical regard built into the architecture of the classroom and into the teacher-student couple. The full flowering of these developments occurs of course in the discipline of "English" or popular literary education. In the teaching of English the techniques for relating to the self as the subject of aesthetic experience are integrated with the techniques of supervision and emulation forming the relation of teacher to student. The new school provided the space in which the virtuso techniques of self-problematization and self-modification would be administered as pedagogical techniques—techniques through which the children of the popular classes would come to problematize and modify the conduct of their own lives.

Let those who see in this event the purely negative spectacle of one class depriving another of its culture say what they will. I would rather see it as a remarkable and unpredictable occurrence—one in which the exigencies of government led to the massive social dissemination of a sophisticated and powerful means for constituting the self as an object of ethical concern and labor. Still, the historical irony is inescapable. It was not through its own inner logic, of dialectical advancement towards human completion, that the aesthetic ethos achieved its modern spread and importance. Instead, this occurred when the aesthetic as an ethical technology was incorporated into the governmental sphere that it had taken—and continues to take—as the focus for ascetic withdrawal and transcendence.

V. Contingency Planning

Let me conclude by offering a few comments on how we should conceive of the limits of the aesthetic ethos on the basis of this genealogy. I have argued that we should not locate these limits in the way the aesthetic stands in the path of all that we might become; we should look for them instead in the means by which it enables us to become what we happen to be. I have indicated that these limits are to be found not in the structural relations that divide society into incomplete fragments, but in the entirely contingent and circumstantial relations through which an ethic has been incorporated in the social sphere. If this is the case then the limits of the aesthetic are not to be transcended through the exemplary movement in which critique overcomes its inherent contradictions, subsuming it within a theory of culture as "the way of life as a whole." Instead, it is possible to suggest that we can specify and modify the limits of the aesthetic only when and where its contingency—and the contingency of its relations to other departments of existence—gives us reasons to do so. Clearly it is impossible to provide a general account of how and under what circumstances such reasons arise. We can, however, exemplify them, taking three cases as representative.

The first case concerns the problematic relations linking aesthetics as an ethical work performed with literary texts to literary philology as an empirical knowledge of such texts. In a typical recent instance a philologist has shown that a text being read by literary critics as a lyric poem was something else altogether (Wenzel, 1985). This text, which one critic had praised for its "special quality of vision" and described as "a dramatic achievement of an extremely high order" (Wenzel, 1985, p. 344), turns out to have been a rhymed mnemonic device; an *aide memoire*, written in English but used as a compositional formula for the production of Latin sermons. This might seem an extreme case but it typifies an important pattern of interaction. We can find similar empirical demonstrations of the fallacy of aesthetic form in Rosemund Tuve's (1947) historical analysis of metaphysical poetry, T. W. Baldwin's (1944) reconstruction of Shakespeare's oratory, and Albert Lord's (1960) archaeology of oral epic poetry.

We are equally familiar of course with the counter-attack mounted from the aesthetic side: literature cannot be known empirically and objectively, is known anew and differently each time it is responded to by a different reader, and is therefore inexhaustible.[7] Our genealogy, however, would allow us to withdraw our allegiance from both sides of this apparently interminable combat. The philologist is mistaken in charging the aesthetic reading with a failure to know the poem because the aesthetic reading is not a knowledge of the poem at all. It is, as we have seen, a use of the poem in a practice of problematizing and heightening the reader's sensibility. But for the same reason critics are equally mistaken in treating such a practice as a special or higher kind of knowledge of the poem. What is elevated by this practice is not knowledge but the ethical standing of the subject of aesthetic experience.

Let me be clear that I am not drawing on a philosophical distinction between knowledge and ethics or facts and values to establish the difference in question. Philology is a knowledge not because it is somehow infallibly in touch with literary facts but simply because it employs techniques of description, evidential accumulation, and confirmation that brings its objects into the sphere of the true and the false. In short, it deploys what Foucault calls "techniques of veridiction" and constitutes a particular "regime of truth." Aesthetic criticism on the other hand does not employ such techniques, except incidentally, and forms a different kind of domain. To recall Schiller's dictum, as long as an aesthetic judgment can be treated not as a description of the object but as a symptom of the aesthetic condition of the person who judges then we are not dealing with a knowledge. We are dealing instead with a practice of self-problematization and self-modification in which literature functions as a device—an object for a practice of comtemplation targeted on the self. The reason that a poem can always be read again in aesthetic criticism is not that it cannot be exhaustively known; it is because individuals do not exhaust the practice in which each reading of the poem is the means by which they open themselves to further ethical problematization and labor. It is not that literature is open-ended but that we open its ends, subjecting it to permanent aesthetic surgery as a means of operating on ourselves.

In the relations between criticism and philology, then, we find one set of reasons for limiting and modifying the aesthetic ethic. The character of these relations suggests that we should declare our neutrality in the war between criticism and philology. They indicate that we should indeed accept philology as a positive knowledge of literature, though not of course of literature with any redemptive ethical powers. And they suggest that we should cease treating aesthetic criticism as a higher knowledge of literature and begin to treat it as a technology for the ethical heightening of subjectivity. By force of the circumstances in which the aesthetic ethos entered modern education systems it was yoked to philology inside academic departments of literature. Perhaps it is time to consider what it would mean to sever this alliance and to conceive of the aesthetic as an autonomous ethical practice that happens to utilize literary, among other, materials.

This proposal, however, only serves to identify a second set of relations in which limits to the aesthetic ethos become apparent. It highlights the problematic relations between the aesthetic ethic and an array of other ethical practices and domains. Clearly the aesthetic is not the only means by which individuals come to problematize their experience and relate to themselves as subjects of various kinds of ethical conduct. Apart from specifically religious ethics like Protestantism, there is the whole field of social ethics in which individuals learn to conduct themselves as subjects of their domestic, legal, conjugal, professional, sexual, and medical existences.

Like the aesthetic ethos, these social ethics also comprise distinctive techniques and practices through which individuals problematize and modify their perceptions and conduct in particular domains. Unlike the aesthetic, however, the field of social ethics deploys explicit norms as part of the means by which individuals conduct themselves, for example, as caring parents, effective professionals, good teachers, faithful spouses, balanced personalities, healthy bodies, and so on. As we have seen, not only does the aesthetic ethos refuse to deploy an explicit norm for the aesthetic personality, it forms this being through a practice of problematizing all normative commitments—as signs of moralism, instrumentalism, didacticism. Now, while this practice was relatively inconsequential as the esoteric ethos of the aesthetic cults, this is no longer the case once it has been widely deployed inside the domain of social ethics as a pedagogical discipline. In these changed circumstances the aesthetic leads to what might be called the "hyper-problematization" of neighboring ethical domains.

A typical example can be drawn from the writings of Jürgen Habermas. Taking as his framework "the shift from what hitherto had been a socially integrated sphere of life to the imperatives of an economic system regulated by law, formally organized, and steered through the medium of exchange," Habermas (1983b) proceeds to problematize whole domains of ethical regulation:

> Many "modernist" reforms lead to an ambiguous legal regulation of life conditions. The ambiguity involved in reform-oriented intrusions into relations between parents and children, teachers and students, colleagues, or neighbours lies in the fact that these signify a detachment from traditionally established norms and, at the same time, also from value orientations per se. This detachment can and should promote an

> emancipation from encrusted power relations. But it carries the danger of a bureau-
> cratic dessication of communicative relations, the danger of a deadening, as opposed
> to a liberating, formalization of relations that in essence are not formalizable. (p. 19)

In the light of our preceding remarks, the character of this critque—which can be applied
as easily to rape-in-marriage legislation as to the use of academic performance measures,
as readily to sexual harassement statutes as to the disciplinary norms used in school
systems—should be clear enough. The charge that the domains of pratical ethical regulation represent a "formalization of relations that in essence are not formalizable" is
an instance of aesthetic "hyper-problematization." Behind it lies the image of a sphere
of being in which norms had been (or will be) incorporated with feelings, inclinations,
and customs in an integrated or complete existence. The formal ethical regulation of
specific departments of existence is interpreted as a sign of the fragmentation of this
organic "life world." And it is assumed that only the aesthetic, through its eschewal of
formal norms, is able to transcend the spheres of normative regulation and realize a
fully human conduct of life.

Perhaps now we are in a position to turn our backs on this sort of critique, in
which the aesthetic presents itself as the subsumption and universalization of the field
of social ethics. After all, we have seen that the aesthetic is in no sense more complete
than the various domains of social ethics. It is simply the domain opened up when these
other spheres are transformed into occasions for the practice of aesthetic self-problematization. This practice presents itself as a process of critique through which individuals
can commit themselves to a universal "human" ethic. But it is neither more nor less
than a practice through which they can withdraw their commitment to any particular
normative ethic, by treating each as a symptom of the alienation of reason and custom,
morality and feeling, law and desire; that is, by treating each as a symptom of the
aesthetic self. We can propose, then, to disengage from this practice of ethical hyper-
critique that leads to no actionable outcomes, this practice that proposes a "higher"
ethical commitment as a means of withdrawing from the available forms of ethical
engagement. In short, it is possible to propose more "wordly" forms of ethical investigation and activity, carried out *within* the normative domains of existing social ethics.[8]

Perhaps it will please some to see in this proposal a sign of "neo-conservatism,"
a loss of nerve and vision resulting from the failure to grasp the deeper "political"
character of these issues. After all, the sort of ethical critique practiced by Habermas is
founded in a political theory of society. And the proposal to abandon such general
problematization, or reconstitute it within the existing spheres of normative social regulation, must run the risk of depoliticizing critique and turning it into a species of
reformism or worse. But this sort of response seems to me symptomatic of the third
area where the limits of the aesthetic become visible. I will conclude, then, with some
remarks on the relations between the aesthetic and the governmental.

In fact, what is striking about the social and political theorizing in Habermas's
work is how completely it is carried along by currents that first surfaced in writers like
Schiller and Hegel. The idea that our political and social predicament results from the
fragmentation of an integral mode of being; the analysis of the division of labor as the
disintegration of a fully realized humanity; the critique of a "mechanical," "alienated,"
or "administered" society, characterized by contradictions between law and desire, labor
and self-expression, the governmental and the personal, utility and culture; and the
prospect of a dialectical overcoming of these contradictions in a movement toward true
community and complete being—we have noted the presence of all of these themes in
Schiller's aesthetic. Moreover, we noted them in the context of a specific genealogical
description. These themes first emerged when, at the end of the eighteenth century,

the aesthetic as a specialized practice of the self took as its "domain of problematization" the sphere of government. "Government," it will be recalled, is used to name the historical emergence of politics as a rational art through the deployment of governmental technologies. These technologies—everything from techniques of statistical survey to forms of bureaucratic administration, from tax systems to school systems—aspired to transform the security and wealth of the state, and the health and well-being of its citizens, into objects of rational calculation and control.

In constituting this domain as its primary site of ethical problematization, the aesthetic ethos did two things. It located the site for "true" politics beyond the governmental sphere, in the dialectical overcoming of fundamental social (i.e., aesthetic) contradictions. And it sought to "politicize" any and all of the myriad occurrences taking place inside the governmental sphere by reading them as symptoms of contradictions lying at this higher or deeper level. Both tendencies are plainly displayed in the passage from Habermas cited above.

The limits to this way of construing the political field should be already apparent. In transforming political events into occasions for attending to the ethical incompleteness of "man" it divorces itself from the governmental technologies which bring such events within the reach of political knowledge and action. And in taking the governmental as the reflexive target of a practice of self-problematization it produces a critique whose deepest significance lies in its ascetic withdrawal from practical politics. This practice is, of course, by no means incompatible with individuals engaging in a "higher" politics, where their *own* actions become exemplary dramatizations of the contradictions between law and desire, social norms and personal will. Perhaps this is all the more reason for envisaging a form of a political activity that no longer problematizes events as symptoms of humanity's deepest divisions and alienations. All the more reason, in other words, to begin to cultivate our political selves by mastering the available arts of government.

NOTES

1. The phrase comes, of course, from Raymond Williams's (1958) *Cultural and Society 1780–1950,* which is the *locus classicus* of this conception of cultural studies.

2. The formulation is taken from Michel Foucault (1984), p. 46.

3. Shakespeare's training in these techniques is described in T. W. Baldwin (1944).

4. This four-part schema is freely adapted from Foucault (1985), *The Use of Pleasure,* pp. 26–28.

5. For a recent reaffirmation of these claims, see J. Chytry (1989).

6. On the "occasional" character of aesthetic politics, see Carl Schmitt (1986), pp. 78–108.

7. For representative statements see Jane Tompkins (ed.) (1980), *Reader Response Criticism.*

8. I have found Jeffrey Minson's work particularly helpful in this regard. See, for example, Minson (1989).

DISCUSSION: IAN HUNTER

BILL WARNER: I value your effort to weave aesthetics into cultural practices so as to find a political dimension to those aesthetic practices. But it seems to me that you suppress two dimensions of the aesthetic. First, its performative dimension. There is always a kind of social and communal dimension to the aesthetic, however isolated its particular practices may appear to be. Second, the motives and effects of this aesthetic performance are not merely to be good—which the yogic analogy emphasizes—or even to appear to be good, but also to be bad and to appear to be bad for others in view of forging a community that has a critical relation with some other practice. I'm thinking here of

Alice Echols's *Daring to Be Bad,* and Andrew Ross's *No Respect,* both of which seem to point to "being bad" as a dimension of popular culture that is not so privatizing as your image of an aesthetic ethos.

HUNTER: I'll take your second criticism first. The problem with the way you make this criticism is that you continue to assume the equivalence of morality and ethos, and this equation is one of the things that the paper calls into question. Both Weber and Foucault show that the ethos or ethic of a particular way of living cannot be simply read-off from the moral code associated with it. The latter indeed consists of doctrines, beliefs, rules, prohibitions that determine certain ideas of good and bad, godly and ungodly, thought and behavior. The ethic, on the other hand, consists of all the techniques and practices that individuals apply to themselves in order to compose themselves as subjects of moral conduct; that is, to make themselves into the kind of person capable of sustaining moral thought and action. These ethical techniques and practices are not an ideology; they are historical devices and inventions—"techniques for living"—in no sense prescribed by the moral code and often resulting in conducts of life quite at variance with it. (Most famously, of course, in Weber's account of the unexpected relation between the other-worldly morality of Puritanism and its intensely "this-worldly" ethic.) This relative autonomy of the ethos is especially marked in the case of aesthetics which employs, as one of its techniques of self-questioning and modification, the voluntary problematization of moral norms and codes (as didactic, repressive, etc.). It is for this reason that aesthetes have been able to make an ethical career out of being bad. (How else could one understand a phenomenon like the "life of Oscar Wilde"?) Of course, in seeking aesthetic stylization and insight through the systematic problematization of "imposed" normativities the aesthete is engaged in an intensely ethical conduct of life. So, no, describing aesthetics as an ethic or ethos in no way implies that it is about being morally good; it quite easily encompasses what is, after all, the entirely familiar aesthetic striving after moral extremes. In this light I find your remarks on the political significance of "daring to be bad" a little over-optimistic. Literary intellectuals can make good careers out of this kind of daring and are in little danger of becoming politically significant. As for your first point, of course the achievement of aesthetic withdrawal and transcendence is a public performance that only makes sense in a particular historical and social setting. My paper is an attempt at an historical sketch of that performance and setting.

KEYA GANGULY: I am concerned at the way in which a certain Eurocentrism creeps into your argument, through your analogy to yoga. Because in the Vedantic tradition in which yoga is theorized, there is no rigid distinction between yoga and Rasa or the theory of aesthetics. They're both integral to a theory of Tattvagnana which is a sort of material and political philosophy of life. So in fact in the Vedantic and in other Hindu traditions, aesthetics is not separated from culture or politics or any material philosophy of life. And your casual throwaway gesture to yoga appears very Orientalist, if you will, a kind of condescension towards an alternative tradition.

HUNTER: Speakers should be warned against adding last-minute analogies to their papers! At the same time I should respond to your use of the terms "Eurocentrist," "Orientalist," and "condescending" to characterize my remarks—terms of moral condemnation which slip easily from the remarks to their author. What strikes me as problematic in your comments is the way in which you seek to give them moral force by situating yourself as a representative of a number of marginalized or repressed constituencies. This is not, of course, to say that individuals shouldn't speak for socially or politically disadvantaged groups. It is to suggest, however, that this may be undesirable when used as a way of scoring points at a cultural studies conference. This risks trivializing important political problems by turning them into settings for a certain kind of self-presentation. It also threatens a comical over-inflation of the importance of question time at cultural studies conferences by turning participants into exemplary representatives of global political antagonisms. As for the point of my comparison of aesthetics and the yogic tradition, it was simply this: that if aesthetics is not a set of ideas (in a relation of representation/misrepresentation to "society") then it may be likened to a set of techniques for problematizing and augmenting the self, perhaps with a view to achieving a "higher" level of being and insight. Far from being Eurocentric this analysis is in fact an attempt to achieve a kind of anthropological distance on a particular component of European culture—to match the ethical and geopolitical limits of a particular conduct of life. This is why it is radically anti-universalist and quite skeptical of the claims of the aesthetic mode to represent a "complete" development of the person and a "higher" insight into politics and society.

GANGULY: Unlike you, I believe it is important to face squarely the relationship between speaking position and that which is spoken. Those of us put in the position of being interlocutors need to keep in mind that any "response" is likely to get subsumed under the authority of the speaker's narrative. Regardless of how hackneyed it sounds today, the personal is *still* political and it is more important than ever that we not disavow accountability in the name of the "last-minute" additions, "cultural studies conferences," or whatever. In fact, cultural studies—if it is done well—represents a fairly unique opportunity to interrogate the connections between the intellectual and her "object" of analysis. In this connection, I am struck by your seeming desire to reinscribe distance between speaker and audience ("comical over-inflation of the importance of question time . . . "). The "over-inflation" in this case might very well reside in the attempt to rescue aesthetics as a category, but that is a discussion for another time and place.

More importantly, I want to point to your continuing inattention to substance, consonant with your initial analogy between aesthetics and *yoga*. In addressing the matter of your Eurocentric and careless analogizing, I did not seek to construct myself "as the representative of a number of marginalized or repressed constituencies," because I did not need to. The traditions and practices I was referring to have a long, vigorous, and quite fully theorized intellectual history, despite your characterization of them as "marginalized or repressed." Moreover, it is important to distinguish between an epistemological tradition *(tattvagnana)*, a philosophical practice *(yoga)*, and political *constituencies*. The attempt to conflate them in the name of critiquing me for "situating myself as representative" reflects, above all, a profound misunderstanding of the problematic of representation, and Marx's distinction between *Vertretung* and *Darstellung*.

Finally, I am completely in favor of your recommendation that aesthetics re-orient itself towards a concern with "achieving a higher level of being and insight." However, this is not likely to be achieved by making mystifying analogies *or* by seeking to elide one's own interests and subject position. Might I remind you, even as I remind myself, that we are all complicit in systems of domination and subordination and that cultural studies cannot provide us with an alibi for that?

BOB MORGAN: One of the claims of your work is that concepts like culture itself were handed down, in some sense born within, pedagogical form. Could you comment on the ways in which the absence of theorizing about pedagogy has affected cultural studies at the present?

HUNTER: I'm not sure whether it's that cultural studies doesn't pay enough attention to the educational sphere or that it pays the wrong kind of attention. In either case this is a symptom of a larger problem; that is, the dependence of cultural studies on what might be called "meta-institutional" theories of culture derived from the Hegelian and Marxian traditions. It is striking for example that, despite its title, Schiller's *On the Aesthetic Education of Man* makes absolutely no reference to educational institutions. Yet it was written at a time when school systems were being organized on a massive scale, in the context of governmental programs to lift the cultural levels of entire populations. The reason for this absence is of course that Schiller sees "man's" development as flowing from historical forces far more "fundamental" than mere school systems: from the division of labor, the antagonism of opposed classes, the opposition of intellect and materiality, and so on. Where cultural studies does look at school systems and other governmental mechanisms (health and welfare systems, social insurance) it typically treats them as "expressions" of these supposedly deeper dialectical forces. This is especially the case in the "culture and society" tradition—in work by Raymond Williams, Chris Baldick, Terry Eagleton—which imagines that school systems were inventions of the "prophets of culture" (Carlyle, Arnold) and treats them as a sorry compromise between the ideal of culture and the reality of capitalist society. I have argued elsewhere that school systems were designed by administrative rather than aesthetic intellectuals and that they were acting as agents of specific political and intellectual technologies associated with the "governmentalizing" of society. One of the ironies of this history is that it was through the new school system that the dialectical understanding of culture—which had previously been the esoteric accomplishment of a small intellectual stratum—achieved a broader dissemination, initially in the ethical formation of teachers. I say "irony" because this means that the current importance of dialectical theory—including in cultural studies—is the result of its deployment as a discipline in an education system whose normativity it despises and whose history it cannot comprehend.

ELSPETH PROBYN: Since Foucault based his discussion of the technologies of the self in the homosexual practices of Greek antiquity, I wonder if you could elaborate on the implications of your concepts for contemporary sexual politics.

HUNTER: The short answer is that the use I make of Foucault's late work on ethics in this paper has no direct bearing on contemporary sexual politics. This is not to say of course that this work can't be used productively in this regard. And it is true that in volumes 2 and 3 of the *History of Sexuality* Foucault elaborates the morality-ethic distinction in order to pursue an historical account of the problematization of homosexual conduct in antiquity. Nonetheless, what I have done here is to take this framework—particularly the insight that subjectivity (or the way one relates to oneself) is an artifact of special ethical techniques—and apply it to a quite different department of existence: aesthetics. In other words, on this occasion I draw on Foucault not as historian of sexuality but as ethical anthropologist. What Foucault offers in this regard is an account of subjectivity that doesn't universalize it, for example, by treating it as the ever-present foundation or effect of language, the categories, labor, or history—as in Kantian and Hegelian *philosophical* anthropology. In this respect I have found Weber's sociology of ethical orders and Mauss's anthropological history of the category of "person" just as useful as Foucault's work. Each of these writers teaches us how to detach the domain of subject-formation from the putative universals of history, language, etc., and to describe it as a definite and limited department of existence. Not that this move is without political implications. Far from it! As Foucault has argued, if there is no single point from which our historical existence and future can be comprehended—that is, no point at which history both brings subjectivity into being and is rendered transparent to it—then politics can have no Archimedian fulcrum, least of all the sexual liberation of the subject.

MEAGHAN MORRIS: Your history of your idea of the aesthetic is fascinating because it shows how it comes about that people keep posing problems at a level of generality where you simply can't solve them. I appreciate your effort to produce a less fraught space of debate about the possibility of action in relation to the culture/politics issue. But I have two questions. Firstly, do you think that the history of the structure of thinking you trace actually changes the meaning of the invocation of all of those dichotomies? In other words, is the situation of Raymond Williams sufficiently different from that of Schiller for us to be able to say that the structure derived from that tradition in Williams is producing a completely different outcome? And secondly, would the emergence of what I would call institutions (perhaps you would see them as patchworks and motleys in your sense) like the mass media and international banking, which keep producing notions of an unlimitedness of culture, also need explaining? Where would you put the media in your genealogical method, because you tend to stick to the Foucauldian repertoire: the prison, the army, the factory? Do you think that twentieth-century institutions change the shape of your problem?

HUNTER: I appreciate both questions Meaghan, which push at the limits of the case I have presented, though in slightly different ways. The first issue is difficult as there are both continuities and discontinuities between the Romantics and modern cultural critics like Williams and, for that matter, Jaspers, Marcuse, and Habermas. The continuity is profound, though, and I think that the story goes something like this: The Romantics mark the point at which a stratum of intellectuals detaches itself from the emergent technologies of government and, in this regard at least, renders itself powerless by founding itself in a higher realm—morality, aesthetic completeness. It needn't have been this way, of course. Weber points out that the *literati* were the single most powerful intellectual stratum in China, regulating the rituals of state and staffing the Confucian bureaucracy. And if we look at the European "humanists" of the sixteenth and seventeenth centuries we can see another powerful and significant group of "literary" intellectuals; their philological and pedagogical work played a key role in rationalizing the new legal, military, administrative, fiscal, and cultural systems of the early-modern state. Of course these intellectuals were "literary" in a broader sense than the aesthetic. They were severe and pragmatic, often exponents of neo-stoical ethical discipline, and they dedicated their classical learning and literacy to creating political and intellectual technologies of unprecedented reach and sophistication. The Romantic contraction of the literary field to the aesthetic might be seen as the mark of a specialized subgroup within this intellectual stratum: a subgroup whose elaboration of the ethic of aesthetic problematization, withdrawal, and transcendence can be treated analogously to a religious exercise. From this point on, aesthetic intellectuals relate to the sphere of government largely through a practice of "critique by withdrawal"; and the profundity of their criticism in fact reflects their lack of familiarity with the sophisticated technologies that compose this sphere. These remain in the hands of legal, medical, administrative, and fiscal intellectuals, not to mention welfare and human-relations technologists. It is anything but accidental then that an intellectual like Marcuse would go back to Schiller's image of aesthetic fulfillment in order to problematize "modern society" and project its future. As far as your second point is concerned I think it's perfectly correct. It's not that difficult to limit and differentiate the field of culture by going to well-defined institutions like armies, bureaucracies, and schools. Dispersed institutions like communications media are not so easily dealt with in this way and yet are no less important. On the other hand, important lessons can be learnt from the historians of communications technologies, in particular the historians of print, Eisenstein, Davis, Chartier. They also de-universalize culture, by reminding us that ideas circulate not in conscious-

ness but in books; hence the significance of their concerns with distribution and dissemination, specific literate milieus and audience formation. The "Republic of Letters"
to which the Romantics belonged was initially a media republic, occupying a micro-
niche at the top end of the book market. This milieu was independent of the new
popular school system, although the demographic distribution of the aesthetic ethos
remained insignificant until it was relayed through this system. You are quite right to
point out that the media can disseminate non-aesthetic conceptions of culture: the culture
of office work, for example, or the culture of banking. It can also construct senses
(cultures) of the self and invest them in commodities, life styles and styles of consumption.
What must be said about these more dispersed zones of culture is that they can't be
understood via the aesthetic model. This model is simply too "profound" (withdrawn).
It can't help but transform these zones into sites of aesthetic self-problematization
through, for example, the critique of "instrumentalism" or the "commodification of
pleasure." The problem with aesthetic critique—and with cultural studies to the degree
that it is still caught in its slipstream—is that it presumes to comprehend and judge these
other cultural regions from a single metropolitan point, typically the university arts
faculty. To travel to these other regions though—to law offices, media institutions, government bureaus, corporations, advertising agencies—is to make a sobering discovery:
They are already replete with their own intellectuals. And they just look up and say,
"Well, what exactly is it that you can do for us?"

21

(Male) Desire and (Female) Disgust: Reading Hustler

Laura Kipnis

Let's begin with two images. The first is of feminist author-poet Robin Morgan as she appears in the anti-pornography documentary *Not a Love Story*. Posed in her large book-lined living room, poet-husband Kenneth Pitchford at her side, she inveighs against a number of sexualities and sexual practices: masturbation—on the grounds that it promotes political quietism—as well as "superficial sex, kinky sex, appurtenances and [sex] toys" for benumbing "normal human sensuality." She then breaks into tears as she describes the experience of living in a society where pornographic media thrives.[1] The second image is the one conjured by a recent letter to *Hustler* magazine from E.C., a reader who introduces an account of an erotic experience involving a cruel-eyed, high-heeled dominatrix with this vivid vocational self-description: "One night, trudging home from work—I gut chickens, put their guts in a plastic bag and stuff them back in the chicken's asshole—I varied my routine by stopping at a small pub . . . ."[2] Let's say that these two images, however hyperbolically (the insistent tears, the insistent vulgarity), however inadvertently, offer a route toward a consideration of the relation between discourses on sexuality and the social division of labor, between sexual representation and class. On one side we have Morgan, laboring for the filmmakers and audience as a feminist in-tellectual, who constructs, from a particular social locus, a normative theory of sexuality. And while "feminist intellectual" is not necessarily the highest paying job category, it is a markedly different class location—and one definitively up the social hierarchy—from that of E.C., whose work is of a character which tends to be relegated to the lower rungs within a social division of labor that categorizes jobs dealing with things that smell, or that for other reasons we prefer to hide from view—garbage, sewerage, dirt, animal corpses—as of low status, both monetarily and socially. E.C.'s letter, carefully (certainly more carefully than Morgan) framing his sexuality in relation to his material circumstances and to actual conditions of production, is fairly typical of the discourse of *Hustler*—in its vulgarity, its explicitness about "kinky" sex, and in its imbrication of sexuality and class. So as opposed to the set of norms Morgan attempts to put into circulation (a "normal human sensuality" far removed from E.C.'s night of bliss with his Mistress, who incidentally, "mans" herself with just the kind of appurtenances Morgan seems to be referring to), *Hustler* also offers a theory of sexuality—a "low theory." Like Morgan's radical feminism, it too offers an explicitly political and counter-hege-monic analysis of power and the body; unlike Morgan it is also explicit about its own class location.

The feminist anti-porn movement has achieved at least temporary hegemony over the terms in which debates on pornography take place: current discourses on porn on the left and within feminism are faced with the task of framing themselves in relation

373

to a set of arguments now firmly established as discursive landmarks: pornography is defined as a discourse about male domination, is theorized as the determining instance in gender oppression—if not a direct cause of rape—and its pleasures, to the extent that pleasure is not simply conflated with misogyny, are confined to the male sphere of activity. "Pro-sex" feminists have developed arguments against these positions on a number of grounds, but invariably in response to the terms set by their opponents: those classed by the discourse as sexual deviants (or worse, as "not feminists")—S/M lesbians, women who enjoy porn—have countered on the basis of experience, often in first person, asserting both that women *do* "look" and arguing the compatibility of feminism and alternative sexual practices—while condemning anti-porn forces for their universalizing abandon in claiming to speak for all women. There have been numerous arguments about the use and misuse of data from media effects research by the anti-porn movement and charges of misinterpretation and misrepresentation of data made by pro-porn feminists (as well as some of the researchers). On the gendered pleasure front, psychoanalytic feminists have argued that identification and pleasure don't necessarily immediately follow assigned gender: for instance, straight women may get turned on by gay male porn or may identify with the male in a heterosexual coupling. Others have protested the abrogation of hard-won sexual liberties implicit in any restrictions on sexual expression, further questioning the politics of the alliance of the anti-porn movement and the radical right.[3] Gayle Rubin (1984) has come closest to undermining the terms of the anti-porn discourse itself: she points out, heretically, that feminism, a discourse whose object is the organization of gendered oppression, may in fact not be the most appropriate or adequate discourse to analyze sexuality, in relation to which it becomes "irrelevant and often misleading." Rubin paves the way for a re-examination of received truths about porn: is pornography, in fact, so obviously and so simply a discourse about gender? Has feminism, in arrogating porn as its own privileged object, foreclosed on other questions? If feminism, as Rubin goes on, "lacks angles of vision which can encompass the social organization of sexuality," it seems clear that at least one of these angles of vision is a theory of class, which has been routinely undertheorized and undetermined within the anti-porn movement in favor of a totalizing theory of misogyny. While class stratification, and the economic and profit motives of those in the porn industry have been exhaustively covered, we have no theory of how class plays itself out in nuances of representation.

The extent of misogyny is certainly monumental, so monumental as to be not only tragic, but banal in its everyday omnipresence. If it appears as superficially more evident in the heightened and exaggerated realms of fantasy, pleasure, and projection—the world of pornography—then this is certainly only a localized appearance, and an appearance which may be operating under other codes than those of gender alone. So if the question of misogyny is momentarily displaced here to allow consideration of questions of class, it isn't because one supersedes the other but because bringing issues of class into the porn debates may offer a way of breaking down the theoretical monolith of misogyny—and in a manner that doesn't involve jumping on the reassuring bandwagon of repression and policing the image world or the false catharsis of taking symptoms for causes. The recent tradition of cultural studies work on the body might pose some difficult questions for feminism (and thus might contribute to the kind of revamped critical discourse on sexuality that Rubin calls for): questions such as whether anti-porn feminists, in abjuring questions of class in analyzing representation, are constructing (and attempting to enforce) a theory and politics of the body on the wrong side of struggles against bourgeois hegemony, and ultimately complicit in its enforcement. But at the same time, in taking on porn as an object, U.S. cultural studies—or at least that tendency to locate resistance, agency, and micro-political struggle just about everywhere in mass cultural reception—might have difficulty finding good news as it takes on the fixity of sexuality and power.

Hustler is certainly the most reviled instance of mass circulation porn, and at the same time probably one of the most explicitly class-antagonistic mass circulation periodicals of any genre. Although it's been the tendency among writers on porn to lump it together into an unholy triad with *Penthouse* and *Playboy,* the other two top circulating men's magazines, *Hustler* is a different beast in any number of respects, even in conventional men's magazine terms. *Hustler* set itself apart from its inception through its explicitness, and its crusade *for* explicitness, accusing *Playboy* and *Penthouse* of hypocrisy, veiling the body, and basically not delivering the goods. The strategy paid off—*Hustler* captured a third of the men's market with its entree into the field in 1974 by being the first to reveal pubic hair—with *Penthouse* swiftly following suit (in response to which a *Hustler* pictorial presented its model shaved),[4] then upping the explicitness ante and creating a publishing scandal by displaying a glimpse of pubic hair on its cover in July 1976 (this a typically *Hustler* commemoration of the Bicentennial: the model wore stars and stripes, although not enough of them). Throughout these early years *Hustler*'s pictorials persisted in showing more and more of the forbidden zone (the "pink" in *Hustler*-speak) with *Penthouse* struggling to keep up and *Playboy*—whose focus was always above the waist anyway—keeping a discreet distance. *Hustler* then introduced penises, first limp ones, currently hefty erect-appearing ones, a sight verboten in traditional men's magazines where the strict prohibition on the erect male sexual organ impels the question of what traumas it might provoke in the male viewer. *Hustler,* from its inception, made it its mission to disturb and unsettle its readers, both psycho-sexually and socio-sexually, interrogating, as it were, the typical men's magazine codes and conventions of sexual representation: *Hustler*'s early pictorials included pregnant women, middle-aged women (horrified news commentaries referred to "geriatric pictorials"), overweight women, hermaphrodites, amputees, and in a moment of true frisson for your typical heterosexual male, a photo spread of a pre-operative transsexual, doubly well-endowed. *Hustler* continued to provoke reader outrage with a 1975 interracial pictorial (black male, white female) which according to *Hustler* was protested by both the KKK and the NAACP. It's been known to picture explicit photo spreads on the consequences of venereal disease, the most graphic war carnage . . . None of these your typical, unproblematic turn-on.

And even more so than in its explicitness, *Hustler*'s difference from *Playboy* and *Penthouse* is in the sort of body it produces. Its pictorials, far more than other magazines, emphasize gaping orifices, as well as a consistent sharp focus on *other* orifices. *Hustler* sexuality is far from normative. It speaks openly of sexual preferences as "fetishes" and its letters and columns are full of the most specific and wide-ranging practices and sexualities, which don't appear to be hierarchized, and many of which have little to do with the standard heterosexual telos of penetration. (Male-male sexuality is sometimes raised as a possibility as well, along with the men's magazine standard woman-woman scenario.) The *Hustler* body is an unromanticized body—no vaselined lenses or soft focus: this is neither the airbrushed top-heavy fantasy body of *Playboy,* nor the ersatz opulence, the lingeried and sensitive crotch shots of *Penthouse,* transforming female genitals into *objets d'art.* It's a body, not a surface or a suntan: insistently material, defiantly vulgar, corporeal. In fact, the *Hustler* body is often a gaseous, fluid-emitting, *embarrassing* body, one continually defying the strictures of bourgeois manners and mores and instead governed by its lower intestinal tract—a body threatening to erupt at any moment. *Hustler*'s favorite joke is someone accidentally defecating in church.

Particularly in its cartoons, but also in its editorials and political humor, *Hustler* devotes itself to what tends to be called "grossness": an obsessive focus on the lower stratum, humor animated by a downward movement, representational techniques of exaggeration and inversion. *Hustler*'s bodily topography is straight out of Rabelais, as even a partial inventory of the subjects it finds of interest indicates: fat women, assholes, monstrous and gigantic sexual organs, body odors (the notorious Scratch and Sniff centerfold, which due to "the limits of the technology," publisher Larry Flynt apologized, smelled definitively of lilacs); and anything that exudes from the body: piss, shit, semen, menstrual blood, particularly when it sullies a sanitary or public site; and most especially, farts: farting in public, farting loudly, Barbara Bush farting, priests and nuns farting, politicians farting, the professional classes farting, the rich farting . . . (see Bakhtin, 1984). Certainly a far remove from your sleek, overlaminated *Playboy/Penthouse* body. As *Newsweek* complained, "The contents of an average issue read like something Krafft-Ebing might have whispered to the Marquis de Sade . . . *Hustler* is into erotic fantasies involving excrement, dismemberment, and the sexual longings of rodents . . . where other skin slicks are merely kinky, *Hustler* can be downright frightful . . . The net effect is to transform the erotic into the emetic."[5]

It's not clear if what sets *Newsweek* to crabbing is that *Hustler* transgresses bourgeois mores of the proper or that *Hustler* violates men's magazine conventions of sexuality. On both fronts its discourse is transgressive—in fact on *every* front *Hustler* devotes itself to producing generalized transgression. Given that control over the body has long been associated with the bourgeois political project, with both the "ability and the right to control and dominate others" (Davidoff, 1979, p. 97), *Hustler*'s insistent and repetitious return to the iconography of the body out of control, rampantly transgressing bourgeois norms and sullying bourgeois property and proprieties, raises certain political questions. On the politics of such social transgressions, for example, Peter Stallybrass and Allon White (1986), following Bakhtin, write of a transcoding between bodily and social topography, a transcoding which sets up an homology between the lower bodily stratum and the lower social classes—the reference to the body being invariably a reference to the social.

Here perhaps is a clue to *Newsweek*'s pique, as well as a way to think about why it is that the repressive apparatuses of the dominant social order return so invariably to the body and to somatic symbols. (And I should say that I write this during the Cincinnati Mapplethorpe obscenity trial, so this tactic is excessively visible at this particular conjuncture.) It's not only because these bodily symbols "are the ultimate elements of social classification itself" but because the transcoding between the body and the social sets up the mechanisms through which the body is a privileged political trope of lower social classes, and through which bodily grossness operates as a critique of dominant ideology. The power of grossness is predicated on its opposition from *and to* high discourses, themselves prophylactic against the debasements of the low (the lower classes, vernacular discourses, low culture, shit . . .). And it is dominant ideology itself that works to enforce and reproduce this opposition—whether in producing class differences, somatic symbols, or culture. The very highness of high culture is structured through the obsessive banishment of the low, and through the labor of suppressing the grotesque body (which is, in fact, simply the material body, gross as that can be) in favor of what Bakhtin refers to as "the classical body." This classical body—a refined, orifice-less, laminated surface— is homologous to the forms of official high culture which legitimate their authority by reference to the values—the highness—inherent in this classical body. According to low-theoretician Larry Flynt: "Tastelessness is a necessary tool in challenging preconceived notions in an uptight world where people are afraid to discuss their attitudes, prejudices and misconceptions." This is not so far from Bakhtin on Rabelais:

Things are tested and reevaluated in the dimensions of laughter, which has defeated fear and all gloomy seriousness. This is why the material bodily lower stratum is needed, for it gaily and simultaneously materializes and unburdens. It liberates objects from the snares of false seriousness, from illusions and sublimations inspired by fear. (p. 376)

So in mapping social topography against bodily topography, it becomes apparent how the unsettling effects of grossness and erupting bodies condense all the unsettling effects (to those in power) of a class hierarchy tenuously held in place through symbolic (and less symbolic) policing of the threats posed by bodies, by lower classes, by angry mobs.

Bakhtin and others have noted that the invention of the classical body and the formation of this new bodily canon have their inception in the sixteenth-century rise of individualism and the attendant formation and consolidation of bourgeois subjectivity and bourgeois political hegemony, setting off, at the representational level, the struggle of grotesque and classical concepts (Bakhtin, 1984, p. 320; see also F. Barker, 1984). A similar historical argument is made by Norbert Elias (1978) in his study *The History of Manners,* which traces the effects of this social process on the structure of individual affect. The invention of Bakhtin's classical body entails and is part of a social transformation within which thresholds of sensitivity and refinement in the individual psyche become heightened. Initially this reform of affect takes place in the upper classes, within whom increasingly refined manners and habits—initially a mechanism of class distinction—are progressively restructuring standards of privacy, disgust, shame, and embarrassment. These affect-reforms are gradually, although incompletely, disseminated downward through the social hierarchy (and finally to other nations whose lack of "civilization" might reasonably necessitate colonial etiquette lessons). These new standards of delicacy and refinement become the very substance of bourgeois subjectivity: constraints that were originally socially generated gradually become reproduced in individuals as habits, reflexes, as the structure of the modern psyche. And as Elias reminds us, the foundational Freudian distinction between id and ego corresponds to historically specific demands placed on public behavior in which certain instinctual behaviors and impulses—primarily bodily ones like sex and elimination—are relegated to the private sphere, behind closed doors, or in the case of the most shameful and most socially prohibited drives and desires, warehoused as the contents of the unconscious.

So we can see, returning to our two opening images, how Morgan's tears, her sentiment, might be constructed *against* E.C.'s vulgarity, how her desire to distance herself from and if possible banish from existence the cause of her distress—the sexual expression of people unlike herself—has a sort of structural imperative: as Stallybrass and White (1986) put it, the bourgeois subject has "continuously defined and redefined itself through the exclusion of what it marked out as low—as dirty, repulsive, noisy, contaminating . . . [the] very act of exclusion was constitutive of its identity" (p. 191). So disgust has a long and complicated history, the context within which should be placed the increasingly strong tendency of the bourgeois to want to remove the distasteful from the sight of society (including, of course, dead animals, which might interest E.C.—as "people in the course of the civilizing process seek to suppress in themselves every characteristic they feel to be animal . . ." [Elias, 1978, p. 120]). These gestures of disgust are crucial in the production of the bourgeois body, now so rigidly split into higher and lower stratum that tears will become the only publicly permissible display of bodily fluid. So the bodies and bodily effluences start to stack up into neat oppositions: on the one side upper bodily productions, a heightened sense of delicacy, and the project of removing the distasteful from sight (and sight, of course, at the top of the hierarchization of the senses central to bourgeois identity and rationality); and on the other hand, the lower body and *its* productions, the insistence on vulgarity and violations of the bourgeois body. To the extent that, in Morgan's project, discourse and tears are devoted to concealing the counter-bourgeois body from view by regulating its representation and reforming its pleasures into ones more consequent with refined sensibilities, they can be understood, at least in part, as the product of a centuries-long socio-historical process, a process that has been a primary mechanism of class distinction, and one that has played an important role as an ongoing tool in class hegemony. So perhaps it becomes a bit more difficult to see feminist disgust in isolation, and disgust at pornography as strictly a gender issue, for any gesture of disgust is not without a history and not without a class character. And whatever else we may say about feminist arguments about the proper or improper representation of women's bodies—and I don't intend to imply that my discussion is exhaustive of the issue—bourgeois disgust, even as mobilized against a sense of violation and violence to the female body, is not without a function in relation to class hegemony, and more than problematic in the context of what purports to be a radical social movement.

Perhaps this is the moment to say that a large part of what impels me to write this essay is my own disgust in reading *Hustler*. In fact, I have wanted to write this essay for several years, but every time I trudge out and buy the latest issue, open it and begin to try to bring analytical powers to bear upon it, I'm just so disgusted that I give up, never quite sure whether this almost automatic response is one of feminist disgust or bourgeois disgust. Of course, whether as feminist, bourgeois, or academic, I and most likely you, are what could be called *Hustler*'s implied target, rather than its implied reader. The discourse of *Hustler* is quite specifically *constructed against*—not only the classical body, a bourgeois hold-over of the aristocracy, but against all the paraphernalia of petit-bourgeoisiehood as well. At the most manifest level *Hustler* is simply against any form of social or intellectual pretention: it is against the pretensions (and the social power) of the professional classes—doctors, optometrists, dentists are favored targets; it is against liberals, and particularly cruel to academics who are invariably prissy and uptight. (An academic to his wife: "Eat your pussy? You forget Gladys, I have a Ph.D.") It is against the power of government—which is by definition corrupt, as are elected officials, the permanent government, even foreign governments. Of course, it is against the rich, particularly rich women, down on the Chicago Cubs, and devotes many pages to the hypocrisy of organized religion—with a multiplication of jokes on the sexual instincts of the clergy, the sexual possibilities of the crucifixion, the scam of the virgin birth—and, as mentioned previously, the plethora of jokes involving farting/shitting/fucking in church and the bodily functions of nuns, priests, and ministers. In *Hustler* any form of social power is fundamentally crooked and illegitimate.

These are just *Hustler*'s more manifest targets. Reading a bit deeper, its offenses provide a detailed road map of a cultural psyche. Its favored tactic is to zero in on a subject, an issue, which the bourgeois imagination prefers to be unknowing about, which a culture has founded itself upon suppressing, and prohibits irreverent speech about. Things we would call "tasteless" at best, or might even become physically revulsed by: the materiality of aborted fetuses,[6] where homeless people go to the bathroom, cancer, the proximity of sexual organs to those of elimination—any aspect of the material body, in fact. A case in point, one which again subjected *Hustler* to national outrage: its two cartoons about Betty Ford's mastectomy. If one can distance oneself from one's automatic indignation for a moment, *Hustler* might be seen as posing, through the strategy of transgression, an interesting metadiscursive question: which are the subjects that are taboo ones for even sick humor? Consider for a moment that while, for example, it was not uncommon, following the Challenger explosion, to hear the sickest jokes about scattered body parts, while jokes about amputees and paraplegics are not entirely unknown even on broadcast TV (and, of course, abound on the pages of *Hustler*), while jokes about blindness are considered so benign that one involving Ray Charles features in a current "blind taste test" soda pop commercial, mastectomy is one subject that appears to be completely off limits as a humorous topic. But back to amputees for a moment, perhaps a better comparison: apparently a man without a limb is considered less tragic by the culture at large, less mutilated, and less of a cultural problem it seems, than a woman without a breast. A mastectomy more of a tragedy than the deaths of the seven astronauts. This, as I say, provides some clues into the deep structure of a cultural psyche—as does our outrage. After all, what *is* a woman without a breast in a culture that measures breasts as the measure of the woman? Not a fit subject for comment. It's a subject so veiled that it's not even available to the "working through" of the joke. (And again a case where *Hustler* seems to be deconstructing the codes of the men's magazine: where *Playboy* creates a fetish of the breast, and whose *raison d'être* is, in fact, very much the cultural obsession with them, *Hustler* perversely points out that they are, after all, materially, merely tissue—another limb.)[7]

Hustler's uncanny knack for finding and attacking the jugular of a culture's sensitivity might more aptly be regarded as intellectual work on the order of the classic anthropological studies which translate a culture into a set of structural oppositions (obsession with the breast/prohibition of mastectomy jokes), laying bare the structure of its taboos and arcane superstitions. (Or do only "primitive" cultures have irrational taboos?) *Hustler,* in fact, performs a similar cultural mapping to that of anthropologist Mary Douglas, whose study *Purity and Danger* (1966) produces a very similar social blueprint. The vast majority of *Hustler* humor seems to be animated by the desire to violate what Douglas describes as "pollution" taboos and rituals—these being a society's set of beliefs, rituals, and practices having to do with dirt, order, and hygiene (and by extension, the pornographic). As to the pleasure produced by such cultural violations as *Hustler*'s, Douglas cheerily informs us, "It is not always an unpleasant experience to confront ambiguity," and while it is clearly more tolerable in some areas than in others, "there is a whole gradient on which laughter, revulsion and shock belong at different points and intensities" (p. 37).

The sense of both pleasure and danger that violation of pollution taboos can invoke is clearly dependent on the existence of symbolic codes, codes that are for the most part only semi-conscious. Defilement can't be an isolated event, it can only engage our interest or provoke our anxiety to the extent that our ideas about such things are systematically ordered, and that this ordering matters deeply—in our culture, in our subjectivity. As Freud (1963a) notes, "Only jokes that have a purpose run the risk of meeting with people who do not want to listen to them."

Of course, a confrontation with ambiguity and violation can be profoundly displeasurable as well, as the many opponents of *Hustler* might attest. And for Freud this displeasure has to do with both gender and class (p. 9a).[8] One of the most interesting things about Freud's discussion of jokes is the theory of humor and gender he elaborates in the course of his discussion of them, with class almost inadvertently intervening as a third term. He first endeavors to produce a typology of jokes according to their gender effects. For example, in regard to excremental jokes (a staple of *Hustler* humor) Freud tells us that this is material *common to both sexes,* as both experience a common sense of shame surrounding bodily functions. And it's true that *Hustler*'s numerous jokes on the proximity of the sexual organs to elimination functions, the confusion of assholes and vaginas, turds and penises, shit and sex—i.e., a couple fucking in a hospital room while someone in the next bed is getting an enema, all get covered with shit—can't really be said to have a gender basis or target (unless, that is, we women put ourselves, more so than men, in the position of upholders of "good taste").

But obscene humor, whose purpose is to expose sexual facts and relations verbally, is, for Freud, a consequence of male and female sexual incommensurability, and the dirty joke is something like a seduction gone awry. The motive for (men's) dirty jokes is "in reality nothing more than women's incapacity to tolerate undisguised sexuality, an incapacity correspondingly increased with a rise in the educational and social level." Whereas both men and women are subject to sexual inhibition or repression, apparently upper-class women are the more seriously afflicted in the Freudian world, and dirty jokes thus function as a sign for both sexual difference ("smut is like an exposure of the sexually different person to whom it is directed . . . it compels the person who is assailed to imagine the part of the body or the procedure in question"), and class difference. So apparently, if it weren't for women's lack of sexual willingness and class refinement the joke would be not a joke, but a proposition: "If the woman's readiness emerges quickly the obscene speech has a short life; it yields at once to a sexual action," hypothesizes Freud. While there are some fairly crude gender and class stereotypes in circulation here—the figure of the lusty barmaid standing in for the lower-class woman—it's also true that obscene jokes and pornographic images *are* perceived by *some* women as an act of aggression against women. But these images and jokes are aggressive only insofar as they're capable of causing the woman discomfort, and they're capable of causing discomfort *only* insofar as there *are* differing levels of sexual inhibition between at least some men and some women. So Freud's view would seem to hold out: the obscene joke is directed originally toward women; it presupposes not only the presence of a woman, but that women are sexually constituted differently than men; and upper classness or upper-class identification—as Morgan's discourse also indicates—exacerbates this difference.

But if there are differing levels of inhibition, displeasure, or interest between some men and some women (although *Hustler*'s readership is primarily male, it's not exclusively male), the origins of this pleasure/displeasure disjunction are also a site of controversy in the porn debates. For Freud it's part of the process of *differentiation* between the sexes, not originative—little girls are just as "interested" as little boys. Anti-porn forces tend to reject a constructionist argument such as Freud's in favor of a description of female sexuality as inborn and biologically based—something akin to the "normal human sensuality" Morgan refers to.[9] Women's discomfiture at the dirty joke, from this vantage point, would appear to be twofold. There is the discomfort at the intended violation—at being assailed "with the part of the body or the procedure in question." But there is the further discomfort at being addressed as a subject of repression—as a subject with a history—and the rejection of porn can be seen as a defense erected against representations which mean to unsettle her in her subjectivity. In other words, there is a violation of the *idea* of the "naturalness" of female sexuality and subjectivity, which is exacerbated by the social fact that not all women *do* experience male pornography in the same way. That "pro-sex" feminists, who tend to follow some version of a constructionist position on female sexuality, seem to feel less violated by porn is some indication that these questions of subjectivity are central to porn's address, misaddress, and violations. To the extent that pornography's discourse engages in setting up disturbances around questions of subjectivity and sexual difference—after all, what does *Hustler*-variety porn consist of but the male fantasy of women whose sexual desires are in concert with men's—and that this fantasy of undifferentiation is perceived as doing violence to female subjectivity by some women but not others, the perception of this violence is an issue of difference between women.[10] But the violence here is that of misaddress, of having one's desire misfigured as the male's desire. It is the violence of being absent from the scene. The differentiation between female spectators as to how this address or misaddress is perceived appears to be bound up with the degree to which a certain version of female sexuality is hypostatized as natural, versus a sense of mobility of sexuality, at least at the level of fantasy. But hypostatizing female sexuality and assigning it to all women involves universalizing an historically specific class position as well, not as something acquired and constructed through difference, privilege, and hierarchy, but as also somehow inborn—as identical to this natural female sexuality. Insisting that all women are violated by pornography insists that class or class identi-fication doesn't figure as a difference between women, that "normal human sensuality" erases all difference between women.

For Freud, even the form of the joke is classed, with a focus on joke technique associated with higher social classes and education levels. In this light it's interesting to note how little *Hustler* actually engages in the technique of the joke—even to find a pun is rare. But then as far as obscene humor, we're subject to glaring errors of judgment about the "goodness" of jokes insofar as we judge them on formal terms, according to Freud—the technique of these jokes is often "quite wretched, but they have immense success in provoking laughter." Particularly in regard to obscene jokes, we aren't "in a position to distinguish by our feelings what part of the pleasure arises from the sources of their technique and what part from those of their purpose. Thus, strictly speaking, we do not know what we are laughing at" (p. 102). And so too with displeasure—it would seem we can't be entirely sure what we're *not* laughing at either, and this would be particularly true of both the bourgeois and the anti-pornography feminist, to the extent that both seem likely to displace or disavow pleasure or interest in smut, one in favor of technique—like disgust, a mechanism of class distinction—and the other against perceived violations against female subjectivity. So for both, the act of rejection takes on far more significance than the terrains of pleasure; for both, the nuances and micro-logics of *displeasure* are defining practices.

Yet at the same time, there does seem to be an awful lot of interest in porn among both, albeit a negative sort of interest. It's something of a Freudian cliche that shame, disgust, and morality are reaction-formations to an original interest in what is not "clean." One defining characteristic of a classic reaction-formation is that the subject actually comes close to "satisfying the demands of the opposing instinct while actually engaged in the pursuit of the virtue which he affects," the classic example being the housewife obsessed with cleanliness who ends up "concentrating her whole existence on dust and dirt (Laplanchs and Pontalis, 1973, pp. 376–278). And it does seem to be the case that a crusader against porn will end up making pornography the center of her existence. Theorizing it as central to women's oppression means, in practical terms, devoting one's time to reading it, thinking about it, and talking about it. It also means simultaneously conferring this *interest,* this subject-effect, onto others—predicting tragic consequences arising from such dirty pursuits, unvaryingly dire and uniform effects, as if the will and individuality of consumers of porn are suddenly seized by some (projected) all-controlling force, a force which becomes—or already is—the substance of a monotonic male sexuality. Thusly summing up male sexuality, Andrea Dworkin (1987) writes: "Any violation of a woman's body can become sex for men; this is the essential truth of pornography" (p. 138).

The belief in these sorts of essential truths seem close to what Mary Douglas (1966) calls "danger-beliefs"—

[A] strong language of mutual exhortation. At this level the laws of nature are dragged in to sanction the moral code: this kind of disease is caused by adultery, that by incest . . . the whole universe is harnessed to men's attempts to force one another into good citizenship. Thus we find that certain moral values are upheld and certain social rules defined by beliefs in dangerous contagion. (p. 3)

And Douglas, like Freud, also speaks directly about the relation of gender to the "gradient" where laughter, revulsion, and shock collide: her discussion of danger beliefs also opens onto questions of class and hierarchy as well. For her, gender is something of a trope in the realm of purity rituals and pollution violations: it functions as a displacement from issues of social hierarchy.

I believe that some pollutions are used as analogies for expressing a general view of the social order. For example, there are beliefs that each sex is a danger to the other . . . Such patterns of sexual danger can be seen to express symmetry or hierarchy. It is implausible to interpret them as expressing something about the actual relation of the sexes. I suggest that many ideas about sexual dangers are better interpreted as symbols of the relation between parts of society, as mirroring designs of hierarchy or symmetry which apply in the larger social system. (p. 3)[11]

To put a feminist spin on Douglas's pre-feminist passage, while men do certainly pose actual sexual danger to women, the content of pollution beliefs expresses that danger symbolically at best: it would be implausible to take the content of these beliefs literally. So while, for Douglas, gender is a trope for social hierarchy, a feminist might interpret the above passage to mean that *danger* is a trope for gender hierarchy. Douglas's observations on the series of displacements between defilement, danger, gender, and class puts an interesting cast on female displeasure in pornography in relation to class hierarchies and "the larger social system"—in relation to *Hustler*'s low-class tendentiousness and its production of bourgeois displeasure, and why it might happen that the feminist response to pornography ends up reinscribing the feminist into the position of enforcer of class distinctions.

But historically, female reformism aimed at bettering the position of women has often had an unfortunately conservative social thrust, as in the case of the temperance movement. The local interests of women in reforming male behavior can easily dovetail with the interests of capital in producing and reproducing an orderly, obedient, and sober workforce. In social history terms we might note that *Hustler* galumphs onto the social stage at the height of the feminist second wave, and while the usual way to phrase this relation would be the term "backlash," it can also be seen as a retort—even a political response—to feminist calls for reform of the male imagination. There's no doubt that *Hustler* sees itself as doing battle with feminists: ur-feminist Gloria Steinem makes frequent appearances in the pages of the magazine as an uptight, and predictably, upper-class, bitch. It's fairly clear that from *Hustler*'s point of view, feminism is a class-based discourse. So *Hustler*'s production of sexual differences are also the production of a form of class consciousness—to accede to feminist reforms would be to identify upward on the social hierarchy.

But any automatic assumptions about *Hustler*-variety porn aiding and abetting the entrenchment of male power might be put into question by actually reading the magazine. Whereas Freud's observations on dirty jokes are phallocentric in the precise sense of the word—phallic sexuality is made central—*Hustler* itself seems much less certain about the place of the phallus, much more wry and often troubled about male and female sexual incommensurability. On the one hand it offers the standard men's magazine fantasy babe—always ready, always horny, willing to do anything, and who finds the

Hustler male inexplicably irresistible. But just as often there is her flip side: the woman who is disgusted by the *Hustler* male's desires and sexuality, a superior, rejecting, often upper-class woman. It becomes clear how class resentment is modulated through resentment of what is seen as the power of women to humiliate and reject: "Beauty isn't everything, except to the bitch who's got it. You see her stalking the aisles of Cartier, stuffing her perfect face at exorbitant cuisineries, tooling her Jag along private-access coastline roads. . . ." Doesn't this reek of a sense of disenfranchisement rather than any sort of certainty about male power over women? The fantasy life here is animated by cultural disempowerment in relation to a sexual caste system and a social class system. This magazine is tinged with frustrated desire and rejection: *Hustler* gives vent to a vision of sex in which sex is an arena for failure and humiliation rather than domination and power. There are numerous ads addressed to male anxieties and sense of inadequacy: various sorts of penis enlargers ("Here is your chance to overcome the problems and insecurities of a penis that is too small. Gain self-confidence and your ability to satisfy women will sky rocket" reads a typical ad), penis extenders, and erection aids (Stay-Up, Stay-Hard . . .).[12] One of the problems with most porn from even a pro–porn feminist point of view is that men seize the power and privilege to have public fantasies about women's bodies, to imagine and represent women's bodies without any risk, without any concomitant problematization of the male body—which is invariably produced as powerful and inviolable. But *Hustler* does put the male body at risk, representing and never completely alleviating male anxiety (and for what it's worth, there is a surprising amount of castration humor in *Hustler* as well). Rejecting the sort of compensatory fantasy life mobilized by *Playboy* and *Penthouse* in which all women are willing and all men are studs—as long as its readers fantasize and identify upward, with money, power, good looks, and consumer durables—*Hustler* pulls the window dressing off the market/exchange nature of sexual romance: the market in attractiveness, the exchange basis of male-female relations in patriarchy. Sexual exchange is a frequent subject of humor: women students are coerced into having sex with professors for grades, women are fooled into having sex by various ruses, lies, or barters usually engineered by males in power positions: bosses, doctors, and the like. All this is probably truer than not true, but problematic from the standpoint of male fantasy: power, money, and prestige are represented as essential to sexual success, but the magazine works to disparage and counter identification with these sorts of class attributes on every other front. The intersections of sex, gender, class, and power here are complex, contradictory, and political.

Much of *Hustler*'s humor *is,* in fact, manifestly political, and much of it would even get a warm welcome in left-leaning circles, although its strategies of conveying those sentiments might give some of the flock pause. A 1989 satirical photo feature titled "Farewell to Reagan: Ronnie's Last Bash" demonstrates how the magazine's standard repertoire of aesthetic techniques—nudity, grossness, and offensiveness—can be directly translated into scathingly effective political language. It further shows how the pornographic idiom can work as a form of political speech that refuses to buy into the pompously serious and highminded language in which official culture conducts its political discourse: *Hustler* refuses the language of high culture along with its political forms. The photospread, laid out like a series of black and white surveillance photos, begins with this no-words-minced introduction:

> It's been a great eight years—for the power elite, that is. You can bet Nancy planned long and hard how to celebrate Ron Reagan's successful term of filling special-interest coffers while fucking John Q. Citizen right up the yazoo. A radical tax plan that more than halved taxes for the rich while doubling the working man's load; detaxation

of industries, who trickled down their windfalls into mergers, takeovers, and investments in foreign lands; crooked deals with enemies of U.S. allies in return for dirty
money for right wing killers to reclaim former U.S. business territories overseas; more
than 100 appointees who resigned in disgrace over ethics or outright criminal charges
. . . are all the legacies of the Reagan years . . . and we'll still get whiffs of bullyboy
Ed Meese's sexual intimidation policies for years to come, particularly with conservative whores posing as Supreme Court justices.

The photos that follow are of an elaborately staged orgiastic White House farewell
party as imagined by the *Hustler* editors, with the appropriate motley faces of the political
elite photomontaged onto naked and semi-naked bodies doing fairly obscene and polymorphously perverse things to each other. (The warning "Parody: Not to be taken
seriously. Celebrity heads stripped onto our model's bodies," accompanies each and every
photo—more about *Hustler*'s legal travails further on.) That more of the naked bodies
are female and that many are in what could be described as a service relation to male
bodies clearly opens up the possibility of a reading limited to its misogynistic tendencies.
But what becomes problematic for such a singular reading is that within these parodic
representations, this staging of the rituals of male hegemony also works in favor of an
overtly counter-hegemonic political treatise. The style is something like a *Mad* magazine
cartoon come to life with a multiplication of detail in every shot (the Ted Kennedy
dartboard in one corner, in another stickers that exhort "Invest in South Africa," the
plaque over Reagan's bed announcing "Joseph McCarthy slept here"). The main room
of the party: various half-naked women cavort, Edwin Meese is glimpsed filching a
candelabra. Reagan greets a hooded Ku Klux Klanner at the door, and a helpful caption
translates the action: "Ron tells an embarrassed Jesse Helms it wasn't a come-as-you-
are party," while in the background the corpse of Bill Casey watches benignly over the
proceedings (his gaping mouth doubles as an ashtray), as does former press secretary
James Brady—the victim of John Hinkley's attempted assassination and Reagan's no-
gun control policy—who, propped in a wheelchair, wears a sign bluntly announcing
"Vegetable Dip" around his neck. In the next room Ollie North as a well-built male
stripper gyrates on top of a table while a fawning Poindexter, Secord, and Weinberger
gathered at his feet stuff dollar bills into his holster/g-string in homoerotic reverie. In
the next room Jerry Falwell's masturbating to a copy of *Hustler* concealed in the Bible,
a bottle of Campari at his bedside and an "I love Mom" button pinned to his jacket
(this a triumphant *Hustler* pouring salt on the wound—more on the Falwell Supreme
Court case further on). In another room "former Democrat and supreme skagbait Jeanne
Kirkpatrick demonstrates why she switched to the Republican Party," as, grinning and
topless, we find her on the verge of anally penetrating a bespectacled George Bush with
the dildo attached to her ammunition belt. A whiny Elliott Abrams, pants around his
ankles and dick in hand, tries unsuccessfully to pay off a prostitute who won't have him;
and a naked Pat Robertson, doggie style on the bed, is being disciplined by a naked
angel with a cat-o-nine–tails. And on the last page the invoice to the American Citizens:
$283,000,000.

While the anti-establishment politics of the photospread are fairly clear, *Hustler*
can also be maddeningly incoherent, all over what we usually think of as the political
spectrum. Its incoherence as well as its low-rent tendentiousness can be laid at the door
of publisher Larry Flynt as much as anywhere, as Flynt, in the early days of the magazine,
maintained such iron control over the day-to-day operations that he had to approve even
the pull quotes. Flynt is a man apparently both determined and destined to play out the
content of his obsessions as psychodrama on our public stage; if he weren't so widely
considered such a disgusting pariah, his life could probably supply the material for many

epic dramas. The very public nature of Flynt's blazing trail through the civil and criminal justice system and his one-man campaign for the first amendment justify a brief descent into the murkiness of the biographical, not to make a case for singular authorship, but because Flynt himself has had a decisive historical and political impact in the realpolitik of state power. In the end it has been porn king Larry Flynt—not the left, not the avant-garde—who has decisively expanded the perimeters of political speech.

Larry Flynt is very much of the class he appears to address—his story is like a pornographic Horatio Alger. He was born in Magoffin County, Kentucky, in the Appalachians—the poorest county in America. The son of a pipe welder, he quit school in the eighth grade, joined the Navy at fourteen with a forged birth certificate, got out, worked in a G.M. auto assembly plant, and turned $1,500 in savings into a chain of go-go bars in Ohio named the Hustler Clubs. The magazine originated as a 2-page newsletter for the bars, and the rest was rags to riches: Flynt's income was as high as $30 million a year when *Hustler* was at its peak circulation of over 2 million (he then built himself a scale replica of the cabin he grew up in in the basement of his mansion to, he says, remind him where he came from, one replete with chickenwire and hay, and a three-foot lifelike statue of the chicken he claims to have lost his virginity to at age eight).

Since the magazine's inception Flynt has spent much of his time in and out of the nations courtrooms on various obscenity and libel charges as well as an array of contempt charges and other bizarre legal entanglements—notably his somehow becoming entangled in the government's prosecution of automaker John DeLorean. All proceeded as normal (for Flynt) until his well-publicized 1978 conversion to evangelical Christianity at the hands of presidential sister Ruth Carter Stapleton. The two were pictured chastely hand in hand as Flynt announced plans to turn *Hustler* into a *religious* skin magazine and told a Pentecostal congregation in Houston (where he was attending the National Women's Conference) "I owe every woman in America an apology." Ironically, it was this religious conversion that led to the notorious *Hustler* cover of a woman being ground up in a meat grinder, which was, in fact, another sheepish and flat-footed attempt at apologia by Flynt. "We will no longer hang women up as pieces of meat," was actually the widely ignored caption to the photo. (Recall here Freud's observation on the sophistication of the joke form as a class trait.)[13]

In 1978, shortly after the religious conversion, during another of his obscenity trials in Lawrenceville, Georgia, Flynt was shot three times by an unknown assassin with a 44 magnum. His spinal nerves were severed, leaving him paralyzed from the waist down and in constant pain. He became a recluse, barricading himself in his Bel Air mansion, surrounded by bodyguards. His wife Althea, then 27, a former go-go dancer in the Hustler clubs, took over control of the corporation and the magazine, and returned the magazine to its former focus. Flynt became addicted to morphine and Dilaudid, finally detoxing to methadone. (He repudiated the religious conversion after the shooting.) Now confined to a wheelchair, he continued to be hauled into court by the government for obscenity and in various civil suits. He was sued by *Penthouse* publisher Bob Guccione and a female *Penthouse* executive who claimed *Hustler* had libeled her by printing that she had contracted VD from Guccione. He was sued by author Jackie Collins after the magazine published nude photos it incorrectly identified as the nude author. He was fined $10,000 a day—increased to $20,000 a day—when he refused to turn over to the feds tapes he claimed he possessed documenting a government frame of DeLorean. Flynt's public behavior was becoming increasingly bizarre. He appeared in court wearing an American flag as a diaper and was arrested. At another 1984 Los Angeles trial, described by a local paper as "legal surrealism," his own attorney asked for permission to gag his client and after an "obscene outburst" Flynt, like Black Panther Bobby Seale, was bound and gagged at his own trial.

The same year the FCC was forced to issue an opinion on Flynt's threat to force television stations to show his X-rated presidential campaign commercials. Flynt, whose compulsion it was to find loopholes in the nation's obscenity laws, vowed to use his presidential campaign(!) to test those laws by insisting that TV stations show his campaign commercials featuring hard core sex acts. (The equal time provision of the Federal Communications Act prohibits censorship of any ad in which a candidate's voice or picture appears—while the U.S. Criminal Code prohibited dissemination of obscene material.) He had begun to make it his one-man mission to exploit every loophole in the first amendment as well. In 1986 a federal judge ruled that the U.S. Postal Service could not constitutionally prohibit *Hustler* and Flynt from sending free copies of the magazine to members of Congress, a ruling stemming from Flynt's decision to mail free copies of *Hustler* to members of Congress, so they could be "well informed on all social issues and trends." Flynt's next appearance, ensconced in a gold-plated wheelchair, was at the $45 million federal libel suit brought by the Reverend Jerry Falwell over the notorious Campari ad parody, in which the head of the Moral Majority describes his "first time" as having occurred with his mother behind an outhouse. A Virginia jury dismissed the libel charge but awarded Falwell $200,000 for intentional infliction of emotional distress. A federal district court upheld the verdict, but when it landed in the Rehnquist Supreme Court the judgment was reversed by a unanimous Rehnquist-written decision that the Falwell parody was not reasonably believable, and thus fell into category of satire—an art form often "slashing and one-sided." This Supreme Court decision significantly extended the freedom of the press won in the 1964 New York Times vs. Sullivan ruling (which mandated that libel could only be founded in cases of "reckless disregard"), and "handed the press one of its most significant legal triumphs in recent years," was "an endorsement of robust political debate," and ended the influx of "pseudo-libel suits" by celebrities with hurt feelings, crowed the grateful national press, amidst stories generally concluding that the existence of excrescences like *Hustler* are the price of freedom of the press.

Flynt and wife Althea had over the years elaborated various charges and conspiracy theories about the shooting, including charges of a CIA-sponsored plot (Flynt claimed to have been about to publish the names of JFK's assassins—conspiracy theories being another repeating feature of the *Hustler mentalité*). Further speculation about the shooting focused on the mob, magazine distribution wars, and even various disgruntled family members. The shooting was finally acknowledged by white supremacist Joseph Paul Franklin, currently serving two life sentences for racially motivated killings. No charges were ever brought in the Flynt shooting. That Flynt, who has been regularly accused of racism, should be shot by a white supremacist is only one of the many ironies of his story. In another—one which would seem absurd in the most hackneyed morality tale—this man who made millions on the fantasy of endlessly available fucking is now left impotent. And in 1982, after four years of constant and reportedly unbearable pain, the nerves leading to his legs were cauterized to stop all sensation—Flynt, who built an empire on offending bourgeois sensibilities with their horror of errant bodily functions, is now left with no bowel or urinary control.

Flynt, in his obsessional one-man war against state power's viselike grip on the body of its citizenry, seized as his *matériel* the very pornographic idioms from which he had constructed his *Hustler* empire. The exhibitionism, the desire to shock, the deployment of the body—these are the very affronts that have made him the personification of evil to both the state and anti-porn feminists. Yet willingly or not, Flynt's own body has been very much on the line as well—the pornographer's body has borne the violence of the political and private enforcement of the norms of the bourgeois body. If *Hustler's* development of the pornographic idiom as a political form seems—as with other new cultural political forms—politically incoherent to traditional political readings based on traditional political alliances and political oppositions—right-left, misogynist-feminist— then it is those very political meanings that *Hustler* throws into question. It is *Hustler's* very political incoherence—in conventional political terms—that makes it so available to counter-hegemonic readings, to opening up new political alliances and strategies. And this is where I want to return to the question of *Hustler's* misogyny, another political category *Hustler* puts into question. Do I feel assaulted and affronted by *Hustler's* images, as do so many other women? Yes. Is that a necessary and sufficient condition on which to base the charge of its misogyny? Given my own gender and class position I'm not sure that I'm exactly in a position to trust my immediate response.

Take, for example, *Hustler's* clearly political use of nudity. It's unmistakable from the "Reagan's Farewell Party" photospread that *Hustler* uses nudity as a leveling device, a deflating technique following in a long tradition of political satire. And perhaps this is the subversive force behind another of *Hustler's* scandals (or publishing coups from its point of view), its notorious nude photospread of Jackie Onassis, captured sunbathing on her Greek island, Skorpios. Was this simply another case of misogyny? The strategic uses of nudity we've seen elsewhere in the magazine might provoke a conceptual tran- sition in thinking through the Onassis photos: from Onassis as unwilling sexual object to Onassis as political target. Given that nudity is used throughout the magazine as an offensive against the rich and powerful—Reagan, North, Falwell, Abrams, as well as Kirkpatrick, and in another feature, Thatcher, all, unfortunately for the squeamish, through the magic of photomontage, nude—it would be difficult to argue that the nudity of Onassis functions strictly in relation to her sex, exploiting women's vulnerability as a class, or that its message can be reduced to a genericizing one like "you may be rich but you're just a cunt like any other cunt." Onassis's appearance on the pages of *Hustler* does raise questions of sex and gender insofar as we're willing to recognize what might be referred to as a sexual caste system, and the ways in which the imbrication of sex and caste make it difficult to come to any easy moral conclusions about *Hustler's* violation of Onassis and her right to control and restrict how her body is portrayed. As recent pulp biographies inform us, the Bouvier sisters, Jacqueline and Princess Lee, were more or less bred to take up positions as consorts of rich and powerful men, to, one could put it bluntly, professionally deploy their femininity. This is not so entirely dissimilar from *Hustler's* quotidian and consenting models, who while engaged in a similar activity are confined to very different social sites. Such social sites as those pictured in a regular *Hustler* feature, "The Beaver Hunt," a photo gallery of snapshots of non-professional models sent in by readers.[14] Posed in paneled rec rooms, on plaid Sears sofas or chenille bedspreads, amidst the kind of matching bedroom suites seen on late night easy credit furniture ads, nude or in polyester lingerie, they are identified as secretaries, waitresses, housewives, nurses, bank tellers, cosmetology students, cashiers, factory workers, sales- women, data processors, nurse's aides. . . . Without generalizing from this insufficiency of data about any kind of *typical* class-based notions about the body and its appropriate display,[15] we can simply ask, where are the doctors, lawyers, corporate execs, and college professors? Or moving up the hierarchy, where are the socialites, the jet-setters, the wives of the chairmen of the board? Absent because of their fervent feminism? Or merely because they've struck a better deal? Simply placing the snapshots of Onassis in the place of the cashier, the secretary, the waitress, violates the rigid social distinctions of place and hardened spatial boundaries (boundaries most often purchased precisely as protection from the hordes) intrinsic to class hierarchy. These are precisely the distinctions that would make us code differently the deployment of femininity that achieves marriage to a billionaire shipping magnate from those that land you a spot in this month's Beaver Hunt. These political implications of the Onassis photospread indicate, I believe, the necessity of a more nuanced theory of misogyny than those currently in circulation. If any symbolic exposure or violation of *any* woman's body is automatically aggregated to the transhistorical misogyny machine that is the male imagination, it overlooks the fact that *all* women, simply by virtue of being women, are not necessarily political allies, that women can both symbolize and exercise class power and privilege, not to mention oppressive political power.

Feminist anti-pornography arguments, attempting to reify the feminine as an a priori privileged vantage point against pornographic male desires work on two fronts: apotropaic against the reality of male violence they simultaneously work to construct a singular version of (a politically correct) femininity against other "unreconstructed" versions. Their reification of femininity defends against any position that might suggest that femininity is not an inherent virtue, an inborn condition, or in itself a moral position from which to speak—positions such as those held by pro-sex feminists, psychoanalytic theory, and the discourse of pornography itself. But among the myriad theoretical problems which the reification of femininity gives rise to,[16] there are the contradictions of utilizing class disgust as a vehicle of the truly feminine. A theory of representation that automatically conflates bodily representations with real women's bodies, and symbolic or staged sex or violence as equivalent to real sex or violence, clearly acts to restrict political expression and narrow the forms of political struggle by ignoring differences between women—and the class nature of feminist reformism. The fact that real violence against women is so pervasive as to be almost unlocalizable may lead us to want to localize it within something so easily at hand as representation; but the political consequences for feminism—to reduce it to another variety of bourgeois reformism—make this not a sufficient tactic.

However, having said this, I must add that *Hustler* is certainly not politically unproblematic. If *Hustler* is counter-hegemonic in its refusal of bourgeois proprieties, its transgressiveness has real limits. It is often only incoherent and banal where it means to be alarming and confrontational. Its banality can be seen in its politics of race, an area where its refusal of polite speech has little countercultural force. *Hustler* has been frequently accused of racism, but *Hustler* basically just wants to offend—anyone, of any race, any ethnic group. Not content merely to offend the right, it makes doubly sure to offend liberal and left sensibilities too, not content merely to taunt whites, it hectors blacks. Its favored tactic in regard to race is to simply reproduce the stupidest stereotype it can think of—the subject of any *Hustler* cartoon featuring blacks will invariably be huge sexual organs which every women lusts after, or alternately, black watermelon-eating lawbreakers. *Hustler*'s letter columns carry out a raging debate on the subject of race, with black readers writing both that they find *Hustler*'s irreverence funny or resent its stereotypes, whites both applauding and protesting. It should also be noted that in the area of ugly stereotypes *Hustler* is hardly alone these days. The most explicitly political forms of popular culture recently are ones which also refuse to have proper representations—as any number of examples from the world of rap, which has also been widely accused of misogyny, as well as anti-Semitism, would attest. What this seems to imply is that there is no guarantee that counter-hegemonic or even specifically anti-bourgeois cultural forms are necessarily also going to be progressive. And as one of the suppositions in recent American cultural studies seems to have been that there is something hopeful to find in popular culture this might demand some rethinking.[17] *Hustler* is against government, against authority, against the bourgeoisie, diffident on male power—but its anti-liberalism, anti-feminism, anti-communism, and anti-progressivism leave little space for envisioning any alternative kind of political organization.

Hustler does powerfully articulate class resentment, and to the extent that anti-porn feminism lapses into bourgeois reformism, and that we devote ourselves to sanitizing representation, we are legitimately a target of that resentment. Leninism is on the wane around the world. The model of a vanguard party who will lead the rest of us to true consciousness holds little appeal these days. The policing of popular representation seems like only a path to more domination, and I despair for the future of a feminist politics that seems dedicated to following other vanguard parties into dogma and domination.

NOTES

I'd like to thank Lauren Berlant for her extensive and exhaustive aid and comfort on this paper, and Lynn Spigel for many helpful suggestions.

1. For an interesting and far more extensive analysis of the politics of *Not a Love Story* see B. Ruby Rich (1986), "Anti-Porn: Soft Issue, Hard World" in *Films For Women,* ed. Charlotte Brunsdon, pp. 31–43.

2. Several writers who have visited the *Hustler* offices testify that to their surprise these letters *are* sent by actual readers, and *Hustler* receives well over 1000 letters a month. As to whether this particular letter is genuine in its authorship I have no way of knowing, but I'm happy enough to simply consider it as part of the overall discourse of *Hustler.*

3. Central anti-anti-porn texts are *Pleasure and Danger,* ed. Carole S. Vance (1984); *Caught Looking: Feminism, Pornography and Censorship,* ed. Kate Ellis, et al. (1988); *Powers of Desire: The Politics of Sexuality,* ed. Ann Snitow, Christine Stansell, and Sharon Thompson (1983), especially section VI on "Current Controversies." Also see Linda Williams (1989), *Hard Core: Power, Pleasure and the Frenzy of the Visible,* and Andrew Ross (1989b), "The Popularity of Pornography" in *No Respect: Intellectuals and Popular Culture* (1989), pp. 171–208 for a thorough summation of anti-pornography arguments.

4. This corresponds to Linda Williams's analysis of pornography as a "machine of the visible" devoted to intensifying the visibility of all aspects of sexuality, but most particularly, to conducting detailed investigations of female bodies. Williams (1989), pp. 34–57.

5. *Newsweek* (February 16, 1976), p. 69.

6. And there are ongoing attempts to regulate this sort of imagery. In the current NEA controversies, a Republican representative plans to introduce amendments that would prohibit funding of art that depicts aborted fetuses, the *New York Times* reports (October 10, 1990, p. B6). This would seem to be something of a shortsighted strategy for anti-abortion forces, as the aborted fetus has been the favored incendiary image of anti-abortion forces, including anti-abortion artists. See Laura Kipnis (1986), "Refunctioning Reconsidered: Toward a Left Popular Culture," *High Culture/Low Theory,* ed. Colin MacCabe, pp. 29–31.

7. Of course, the counter-argument could be made that such a cartoon really indicates the murderous male desire to see a woman mutilated, and that the cartoon thus stands in for the actual male desire to do violence to women. This was, of course, a widespread interpretation of the infamous *Hustler* "woman in the meat grinder" cover, about which more later. This sort of interpretation would hinge on essentializing the male imagination and male sexuality as, a priori, violent and murderous, and on a fairly literal view of humor and representation, one that envisions a straight leap from the image to the social practice rather than the series of mediations between the two I'm describing here.

8. Freud's observations on jokes, particularly on obscene humor, might be extended to the entirety of *Hustler* as so much of its discourse, even aside from its cartoons and humor, is couched in the joke form.

9. For an interesting deconstruction of the essentialist/anti-essentialism debate see Diana Fuss (1989a), *Essentially Speaking: Feminism, Nature and Difference.*

10. By violence here I mean specifically violence to subjectivity. On the issue of representations of actual physical violence to women's bodies that is represented as non-consensual—as opposed to the sort of tame consensual S/M ocassionally found in *Hustler*—my view is that this sort of representation should be analyzed as a subgenre of mainstream violent imagery, not only in relation to pornography. I find the continual conflation of sexual pornography and violence a deliberate roadblock to thinking through issues of porn—only abetted by a theorist like Andrea Dworkin for whom *all* heterosexuality is violence. The vast majority of porn represents sex, not physical violence, and while sexuality generally undoubtedly contains elements of aggression and violence, it's important to make these distinctions.

11. The passage in the ellipsis reads "For example, there are beliefs that each sex is a danger to the other through contact with sexual fluids." Compare Douglas to this passage by Andrea Dworkin, "... in literary pornography, to ejaculate is to *pollute* the woman" [her emphasis]. Dworkin goes on to discuss, in a lengthy excursus on semen, the collaboration of women-hating women's magazines, which "sometimes recommend spreading semen on the face to enhance the complexion" and pornography, where ejaculation often occurs on the woman's body or face [see Linda Williams, pp. 93–119, on another reading of the "money shot"], to accept semen and eroticize it. Her point seems to be is that men prefer that semen be a violation of the woman by the man, as the only way they can get sexual pleasure is through violation. Thus semen is "driven into [the woman] to dirty her or make her more dirty or make her dirty by him." But at the same time semen has to be eroticized to get the woman to comply in her own violation. Andrea Dworkin (1987), p. 187. In any case, that Dworkin sees contact with male "sexual fluids" as harmful to women seems clear, as does the relation of this pollution (Dworkin's word) danger to Douglas's analysis.

12. *Hustler*'s advertising consists almost entirely of ads for sex toys, sex aids, porn movies, and phone sex services, as the automobile makers, liquor companies and manufacturers of other upscale items that comprise the financial backbone of *Playboy* and *Penthouse* refuse to hawk their wares in the pages of *Hustler*. In order to survive financially, *Hustler* began, among other enterprises, a successful and extensive magazine distribution company which distributes, among other periodicals, the *New York Review of Books.*

13. The story of the cover was related by Paul Krassner (1984) who worked for *Hustler* in 1978. Recall also that this cover was instrumental in the founding the following year of Women Against Pornography. The meat grinder joke seems to encapsulate many of the aforementioned issues of class, humor, vulgarity, and gender.

14. Recently *Hustler,* after yet another legal entanglement, began threatening in its model release form to prosecute anyone who sent in a photo without the model's release. They now demand photocopies of two forms of ID for both age and identity purposes; they also stopped paying the photographer and began paying only the model (currently $250 and the promise of consideration for higher paying photospreads).

15. Throughout this essay, my intent has not been to associate a particular class with particular or typical standards of the body, but rather to discuss how *Hustler* opposes hegemonic, historically bourgeois, conceptions of the body. Whether the *Hustler* bodily idiom represents a particular class or class fraction is not readily ascertainable without extensive audience studies of the sort difficult to carry out with a privatized form like porn magazines. The demographics that are available aren't current (because the magazine doesn't subsist on advertising, its demographics aren't made public, and *Hustler* is notoriously unwilling to release even circulation figures). The only readership demographics I've been able to find were published in *Mother Jones* magazine in 1976, and were made available to them because publisher Larry Flynt desired, for some reason, to add *Mother Jones* to his distribution roster. Jeffrey Klein (1978) writes: "Originally it was thought that *Hustler* appealed to a blue collar audience yet ... demographics indicate that except for their gender (85 percent male), *Hustler* readers can't be so easily categorized. About 40 percent attended college; 23 percent are professionals; 59 percent have household incomes of $15,000 or more a year [about $29,000 in 1989 dollars], which is above the national mean, given the median reader

age of 30." His analysis of these figures is: "Probably it's more accurate to say that *Hustler* appeals to what people would like to label a blue-collar urge, an urge most American men seem to share."

16. For an analysis of the structuring contradictions in the discourse of Catharine Mac-Kinnon, who along with Dworkin, is the leading theorist of the anti-pronography movement, see William Beatty Warner (1989), "Treating Me Like an Object: Reading Catharine MacKinnon's Feminism."

17. For a critique of this tendency see Mike Budd, Robert M. Entman, and Clay Steinman (1990), "The Affirmative Character of U.S. Cultural Studies."

22

Cultural Theory, Colonial Texts: Reading Eyewitness Accounts of Widow Burning

LATA MANI

Introduction: Cultural Studies Now; And in the Future?[1]

Cultural studies in the U.S.A. is being reconfigured. Explicitly interdisciplinary as a field, its institutionalization, we are promised, will bring respite to those weary from disciplinarily inflected ideological skirmishes. It will offer hospitality, if not centrality, to practitioners of postmodern, postcolonial, transnational historiography and ethnography, and provide a location where the new politics of difference—racial, sexual, cultural, transnational—can combine and be articulated in all their dazzling plurality. While I may be faulted for caricaturing the situation somewhat, there can be little question that these are indeed the ambitions of cultural studies in a postmodern and diasporic world.

The grounds for the emergence of a cultural studies so defined are related by most analysts to global socio-economic and political changes in the post-World War II period. These developments, it is claimed, confound, complicate, and increasingly render irrelevant earlier mappings of the world, whether in terms of binary divisions or discrete units. Thus is inaugurated "postmodernity," characterized by Arjun Appadurai (1990) as a new global cultural economy criss-crossed by complex, overlapping, and disjunctive transnational flows. It is to an analysis adequate to this "new" moment that cultural critics are urged to turn.

The sheer scope of the project thus constituted and the global shifts on which it is said to be founded, prompt careful consideration of claims being made. Chief among problems already discernible are the dangers of homogenization and hasty globalization. One consequence of this is that such analysis can frequently leave in place Western ethnocentrism and white-centeredness, the very edifices it supposedly challenges. As Kum Kum Sangari (1987), Aijaz Ahmad (1987 and 1989), bell hooks (1990, esp. chaps. 3, 13), Angie Chabram and Rosa Linda Fregoso (Chabram and Fergoso, 1990; see also Chabram, 1990) among others have pointed out, despite its critique of universalisms and essentialisms, there are ways in which certain forms of Euro-American poststructuralism continue to reproduce both. Sangari criticizes the selectivity of the valorization of García Márquez as "postmodern." Ahmed challenges Fredric Jameson's reductive reading of third world literatures as allegories of nationalism, and problematizes the very concept of "third world." Hooks, and Chabram and Fregoso, oppose "poststructuralism's reappropriation of the decentered conditions of marginal people of color" (Chabram and Fregoso, 1990, p. 207) into an abstract, depoliticized, and internally undifferentiated notion of "difference." Collectively, these practitioners of cultural critique warn against the dangers of conflating different orders of historical experience and underscore the importance of taking into account historical and cultural specificities.

It is important to note at the outset that cultural studies is no homogeneous terrain and that there exist competing ways of conceiving the field, even its "origins" in the Birmingham Centre for Contemporary Cultural Studies.[2] What I am concerned with here are problems with one, particularly common, narrative about contemporary cultural theory and the conditions of its emergence. A series of developments, in technology, global trade flows and finances, media, migration, anti-colonial struggles, decolonization, sixties protest movements, are invoked to explain the logic of postmodern or postcolonial cultural theory. The precise relation of these events to each other is, however, frequently unexamined. Instead, the argument appears to proceed through a cut-and-paste mode of juxtaposition, as if the cumulative pressure of these developments is in itself sufficient to explain the postmodern condition.

Not only does this narrative imply a spontaneous combustion model of historical change, but it sets up problematic chains of equivalences, between, say, women, people of color in the U.S., people from the third world, lesbians, gay men. It implies that these groups are caught in the webs of postmodernity in analogous ways. The thrust of this story about contemporary theory glosses over very real differences.[3] As Norma Alarcon (1990) and Chela Sandoval (forthcoming) have argued in relation to white feminism, it is not as though difference is not acknowledged, for an inventory of difference is crucial to this narrative; rather it is that difference is insufficiently engaged. The result is a lost opportunity. Tensions and disjunctions central to the present moment are evaded in favor of ultimately unrealistic, utopian conceptions of collectivity, however multi-layered or complexly conceived. This makes a mockery of the escalating racial, class, and social tensions which characterize the U.S. today. The problem, once again, is one of inadequate specification: inattention to differences, even contradictions, in our locations and aspirations in the present moment. The problems with this narrative multiply exponentially when one extends its application from the U.S. to the rest of the globe.

Curiously, despite disavowal of theorizing as disembodied activity, the history of cultural analysis in the past forty years can often sound like a bloodless tale of theoretical innovation and reformulation. This effectively banishes to the margins people whose collective hopes and struggles have ruptured hitherto dominant fictions. They are refigured as "evidence" in a story that is partly of their own making; their practices serving to corroborate, or refine, not produce theory. As such they come to represent the "nature" (raw material) out of which (Western) "cultural analysis" is produced.[4] Alternately, one encounters metalepsis: the multiple subjects of black and Chicana feminist theory are interpreted as another version of the decentered bourgeois subject when, in fact, it could be argued that it is black and Chicana feminists among others who have been active in decentering this bourgeois subject. Such moves leave the Anglo/West at the center, conflating vastly different histories.

To note the issue of differences—whether of historical experience or location—is not, however, to suggest that they are the effect of autonomous histories. As Satya Mohanty (1989) and Hazel Carby (1990) among others have pointed out, it is precisely the co-implication and interconnectedness of these histories within "societies structured in dominance" that we need to engage (Hall, 1980b). Failing that, we will be left with a pluralist, "separate but equal" notion of difference[5] which will preclude analysis of the crucible of power relations within which such differences emerge and are sustained. One instance of this apparently benign, but actually hierarchal, conception of difference may be found in feminist typologies (frequently manifest in syllabi) that identify a "woman of color feminism." This category homogenizes the varieties of socialist, nationalist, and poststructuralist feminisms articulated by U.S. women of color. And when contrasted with categories like "Marxist feminist" or "poststructuralist" the essentialist and naturalizing premises of this classification become evident.[6]

I would now like to turn to a field whose development overlaps with cultural studies in its current incarnation: the critical study of colonial discourse. Although critique of colonialist knowledge and representation of subject populations has been integral to anti-colonial struggle from the start, the past ten years have brought fresh and sustained attention to the discursive dimensions of colonial expansion and rule. Among other things, this literature has documented complicities between colonialism and anthropology,[7] between colonialist and nationalist historiography,[8] and between colonial and postcolonial discourses.[9]

The analysis of colonial discourse has drawn some of its tools from structuralist and poststructuralist theory, specifically textual strategies for reading against the grain of colonial representations. However, such work often applies these tools to texts produced in radically different socio-historical conditions from that which poststructuralist theory in particular has sought to address. While poststructuralist theory emerged in context of mass capitalist societies with highly developed superstructures, the colonial state, as Ranajit Guha (1989; see also Canclini, 1988), has argued forcefully in the case of India, achieved not hegemony but dominance. In other words, its reach into society was extremely uneven. Given this, the question of the effects of colonial discourse on colonized societies must be broached with a great deal of care. Analysts of colonial discourse may begin with the assumption that representations matter, but the issue of *how* they matter or *to whom* they matter is an open question in need of demonstration.[10] For example, to take at face value the self-aggrandizing claims of colonial or missionary texts is, to borrow Guha's phrase, to endow dominance with hegemony. Unlike in postmodern, late capitalist societies one must, in colonial contexts, concede the possibility of a radical disjuncture between particular cultural texts and the wider social text.

In short, we need to exercise analytic caution at every step, adequately localizing concepts both spatially and temporally before they are either exported or extended. A few examples from current academic practice will suffice to illustrate what I mean. There is, for instance, a problematic logic of substitution in many academic conferences whereby people of color from the U.S. and of the third world diaspora are assumed to occupy identical locations and to be interchangeable. This posits an equivalence which must be resisted, eliding as it does differences in the relationships, both historically and in the present, between different third world groups and the U.S. power structure.[11] In the same vein, we need to think critically about currently fashionable terms like postcoloniality, asking for whom this term most resonates, and who would resist it and why. Finally, there is the attempt to transpose the notion of the subaltern which emerged to address particular analytical problems in Indian historiography (Guha, 1982), into a more generalized subject position or political location. What losses of specificity—of class, power, and histories of oppression—does this transposition entail? In what ways is it similar to the troubling attempts to metaphorize the concepts of "borderlands" and *mestizaje,* moves which have recently come under criticism (Yarbro-Bejarano, forthcoming).

The plea here is not for a return to empiricism. It is not as though there is only one way to read or locate texts. Neither is it that theoretical concepts developed in one context are by definition unavailable for use elsewhere. But if theory as tool kit is not to degenerate into theory as grab bag, if theory is to address the present in any meaningful way, what is necessary is a rigorous politics of translation in the widest sense of the term: transcoding that is scrupulously alert to specificities, avoiding the triple pitfalls of conflation, erasure, and elision.

Problems of Reading:
The Female Subject, The Colonial Gaze

To track . . . through the colonial representations of Algerian women—the figures of a phantasm—is to attempt a double operation: first to uncover the nature and meaning of the colonialist gaze; then, to subvert the stereotype that is so tenaciously attached to the bodies of women.
Malek Alloula, *The Colonial Harem* (1986, p. 5)

One never encounters the testimony of the women's voice-consciousness. Such a testimony would not be ideology-transparent or "fully" subjective, of course, but it would have constituted the ingredients for producing a counter-sentence. As one goes down the grotesquely mistranscribed names of these women, the sacrificed widows, in the police reports included in the records of the East India Company, one cannot put together a "voice." The most one can sense is the immense heterogeneity breaking through even such a skeletal and ignorant account. Gayatri C. Spivak, "Can the Subaltern Speak?" (1988, p. 297)

In this section I turn to problems of interpretation generated by a specific set of colonial texts: eyewitness accounts of *sati,* the predominantly high caste Hindu practice of the burning of widows on the funeral pyres of their husbands. In reading these descriptions, I attempt to navigate between European accounts of women's words and actions at the funeral pyre and dominant representations of women. Both Alloula and Spivak provide excellent maps for such a task although, as we shall see, eyewitness accounts of *sati* also raise issues distinct from those addressed by them.

Alloula's *Colonial Harem* is a brilliant critique of semi-pornographic French colonial postcards of Algerian women. He demonstrates how such postcards staged the wished-for encounters with Algerian women not available to European men. According to Alloula, they represent the art of simulacrum in both the theatrical and compensatory senses of the term. Such postcards, he argues, say more about the vivisecting and libidinal investments of the colonial gaze than about the women hired by the studio photographer. Analyzing them is, for Alloula, a form of exorcism. He attempts, as he puts it, "to return this immense postcard to its sender" (1986, p. 5).

As a woman, as a feminist, it is impossible for me to read descriptions of *sati* in this way, simply turning the glare of analytic scrutiny back on the colonizer. It is the burning of women's bodies that is being described. The violence of this practice is in constant tension with what Spivak (1985, p. 131) has called the epistemic violence of colonialism, even if European descriptions are themselves exemplary instances of colonial discourse. This tension is not merely an intellectual one, but also emotional and visceral. Keeping it central to my reading has been my strategy for developing a critique of the discourse on *sati* that is simultaneously anti-imperialist and feminist.[12] Finally, unlike Alloula's, my own project is not merely concerned with what such sources might say about Europeans but with what their value and limitations might be as sources for an understanding of widow burning.

Gayatri Spivak's position, reiterated through the text of "Can the Subaltern Speak?," that the "female subaltern *cannot* speak" (Spivak, 1988, emphasis mine), is to be read in context of her important critique of the multiple determinations of archival sources, and her well-founded rejection of any simplistic desire to counter discourses of domination by "letting the native speak," a position that, as she points out, renders the analyst transparent. As she herself has noted, her argument in the essay has provoked controversy (Patai 1988),[13] and she has been repeatedly asked to clarify her position (Harasym, 1990; Winant, 1990; Koundoura 1989). In her responses Spivak has been at pains to restate the points noted above. Read in context of liberal neo-colonialism, her intervention is an important one. Here, however, I will examine the issues of evidence and voice condensed in the question "Can the subaltern speak?," specifically in relation to eyewitness accounts of *sati* in early nineteenth-century Bengal. Rather than treat Spivak's statement regarding the female subaltern as conclusions about colonial discourse in general, I shall use them as a starting point for exploring colonial representations of widows' words and actions at the funeral pyres of their deceased husbands.

Eyewitness accounts of widow immolation bring to crisis the complexities of reading against the grain. Almost exclusively the product of European male observers,[14] they are, as we shall see, simultaneously rich sources for the illumination of certain aspects of *sati* and frustratingly limited in their representation of others.

Eyewitness descriptions of *sati* are generally organized around four moments: the narrator hastening to the spot on receiving information that a burning is about to occur; the monitoring of the widow's demeanor and the attempts to dissuade her; details of the practices that precede the burning; the setting alight of the pyre and the death of the widow. Most of the narrative is given over to a scrutiny of the widow. Accounts frequently include conversations between the narrator and the widow. Some observers also described the practices that preceded the burning.

The focus on the widow's actions and subjective state is related to the ambivalence towards *sati* that fundamentally shaped colonial attitude to the practice. As I have argued elsewhere, despite the canonical place that the prohibition of *sati* occupies in the list of British colonial accomplishments, ambivalence towards widow burning had led to its legalization by the East India Company in 1813 as long as it was based on the widow's "consent"[15] not coercion. It was precisely to ascertain "consent" that widows were cross-examined at the pyre. Reports of such exchanges, although minimal and overdetermined, give us some sense of the subjectivity of the widow and of the logic of her actions.

Colonial discourse on *sati* also shaped other aspects of these accounts, for instance their representation of human activity at the pyre as ritualistic.[16] In this essay, however, I shall focus on the discursive and ideological consequences of the way eyewitness accounts construct the widow and her relationship to widow burning. Before I turn to the accounts I would like to draw attention to the partiality of these descriptions in one important respect. Whilst we may read these narratives for a more nuanced (although of course by no means exhaustive) understanding of the widow and the European observer, their representation of the widow's relatives and of pundits officiating at the burning are without complexity. Both groups emerge in these descriptions as entirely devoted to the widow's destruction. No doubt pundits and relatives stood to gain materially from burning the widow, and by the same token, there is insurmountable evidence that women were coerced, drugged and tied to the pyre. But such accounts suggest a uniformity of purpose shared by all those around the widow. With some exceptions, there is little hint of disagreement, or of competing interests over her fate. This is the limit of these texts. Even while we may, for example, press them for a richer conception of the widow's agency, we must be mindful of the accounts' homogenization of the collective agency of those around her. The gains, however, are neither minimal nor insignificant.

Within the discourse on *sati*, women are represented in two mutually exclusive ways: either as heroines able to withstand the raging blaze of the funeral pyre, or else as pathetic victims coerced against their will into the flames. These poles preclude the possibility of a female subjectivity that is shifting, contradictory, inconsistent. Such a constrained and reductive notion of agency discursively positions women as objects to be saved—never as subjects who act, even if within extremely constraining social conditions. This representation of Indian women has been fertile ground for the elaboration of discourses of salvation, in context of colonialism, nationalism, and, more recently, Western feminism. For the most part, all three have constructed the Indian woman not as someone who acts, but as someone to be acted upon.

This view of women is contestable through reading eyewitness accounts of incidents in which the widow escapes or is successfully dissuaded from burning. Even when such descriptions are squarely within a colonialist framework, they provide a sense of the complex forces that converge in bringing the widow to the pyre. The following account appeared in the *India Gazette* on October 23, 1828.[17] Receiving information that an incident was about to occur, the narrator states that he

> with several Gentlemen proceeded to the Ghaut, in order to expostulate with the infatuated creature, where the Police Darogah was in attendance. . . . Every argument that could be thought of was now urged by him to dissuade her from her purpose . . . and the remonstrances of her own relations, also, not proving successful after many persevering efforts, the Magistrate reluctantly retired and the other Gentlemen also withdrew to a distance. (p. 4)

They wait there till the immolation is about to begin, at which point they "placed themselves nearer the scene of action." The widow's movements are then described in detail.

> With most inimitable composure the *Suttee* went through the performance of various preparatory rites. Having conversed with the *Goroo,* washed her hands in the *Gunga* water, and been decked out according to established forms by kinswomen, she slowly and calmly raised herself from the ground, poured some rice into her lap, and scattering the grain as she marched in a direction contrary to the sun's course, encircled the pile three times, and [at] last unassisted, with unblenched lip, mounted the structure, and threw herself on the remains of her husband. (p. 4)

Her son then sets the pile alight and the cry, "Hari Bol," is raised by the spectators. The narrator continues to watch the widow who, he says, acknowledges the spectators:

> by waving her hand until the flames began to envelop her, when her courage, which had been wrought to the highest pitch, failed, and she sprung from amid the devouring fire in a state of extreme agitation from pain and terror. (p. 4)

The relatives are described as disappointed by this turn of events while the widow is said to have been "scarce[ly] sensible of what was taking place." The widow is then conveyed to the house of the British Resident, given medication and questioned "into the motives that had led her to ascend the funeral pyre." Her responses are reported in indirect speech.

> Her determination to become a *Suttee* had been the result *not of choice, or of any notion that by so doing she would escape some undefined misery in some future state*; but fear of personal obloquy and neglect from her friends, and of bringing disgrace on them and her son; indeed her apprehensions that her want of firmness would prejudice the boy's interests and success in life were with great difficulty quieted by repeated assurances of *protection.* (p. 4, emphasis in original)

The narrator speculates that "she had sprung from the pile from an instinctive impulse," continuing that the attempted dissuasions and the presence of persons "who would shield her from immediate injury or insult," should she renege, no doubt influenced the widow's actions. The account ends with the return home of a now "tranquil" widow with her relatives "who also appeared quite reconciled to the course that the affair had taken" (p. 4).

This incident is interesting for the light it throws on the question of the widow's subjectivity. An apparently "voluntary" act (note her reported resistance to dissuasion, her ostensible composure, her being unassisted at every stage) turns out to be the effect of fear of disgracing family and friends and of jeopardizing her son's future prospects. By her own account, it is such material pressures that have brought the widow to the pyre of her deceased husband. The family are noted as discouraging her from burning, then being disappointed by her escape and eventually as reconciled to it, an account which undercuts the claim for any unilateral familial stance. The ideology of *sati,* as an act undertaken by a devoted wife with a view to future spiritual reward, is nowhere alluded to by the widow. The narrator emphasizes this, possibly because Europeans remained drawn, however ambivalently, to the possibility and legitimacy of "voluntary" *sati,* and persisted in evaluating incidents they observed against this idealized notion. This move was, of course, entirely consonant with the colonial assumption that all social practices derived from scriptural texts and were therefore to be measured against them.

The narrator describes the widow first as "infatuated creature," then in terms of her composure and finally, in the aftermath of her escape, as "scarce[ly] sensible of what was taking place." Whilst the shock of her narrow escape might indeed have made her appear barely conscious of her surroundings, the logic of her decision-making process hardly warrants the adjective "infatuated." In this, the narrator is firmly within a colonial discourse on women which conceives them as dreamily enacting "tradition" (*sati,* for example), being woken from their misguided reverie primarily by European dissuasion and the shock of physical pain, whereupon they are saved by their, usually Western, protectors.[18] While this version of events, may contain some element of truth—the presence of the police and European spectators could well have ensured, for instance, that the widow was not thrown back on the pyre—it occludes the agency of the widow, both in her decision, albeit overdetermined, to submit to destruction, and in her leaping off the pyre. It fails, in other words, to acknowledge her as capable of evaluating the conditions of her life, and overlooks her part in her own rescue, not to mention the rationality of her response to fear and pain.

It is not merely women's words that serve as testimonials to their condition. Women also spoke through their actions. Sometimes, as in the cases below, their actions contradicted the expectations generated by their speech. In an account published in the *Bengal Hurkaru* of July 1, 1828 the narrator writes that the widow rejected every effort at dissuasion and, "obstinately bent on self-destruction," mounted the pile.

> The brushwood was soon set fire to in several places, and soon rose into an awful and majestic blaze . . . As the flames reached her I observed her move, as if about to lay down, that the conflict might the sooner be over, but what was my astonishment and delight to see her make a jump from the pile, throwing the body of her husband from her lap with a strong convulsive start. (p. 2)

The narrator continues that she sank to "the ground in a state of exhaustion . . . we had the proud satisfaction of conducting this infatuated devotee to Brahminical influence, from the ground to her village, where she now is, and I believe thankful for her rescue" (p. 2). He goes on to note that, given the exhaustion and hunger caused by three days of awaiting official permission to burn, and the badly burnt state of her back and arms, her survival had been miraculous.

Having said that, however, the narrator cannot refrain from claiming that the act had been, until her escape, a "voluntary" affair.

> No intoxicating drugs were administered to stupefy her, so far as I could ascertain, and the determined heroic fortitude she displayed throughout the whole of the ceremony, till the moment of pain and trial, was worthy [of] a better cause, and would have done honor to a Christian Martyr. (p. 2)

What kind of "voluntary" act is this that is undertaken in a state of exhaustion and hunger? And on the part of the narrator, what else is this if not the fascination for *sati* that is the underside of horror? The narrator remains transfixed by her so-called fortitude, even as he laments what he believes accounts for it. Indeed, it is her apparent willingness to attempt immolation, not her courage in rescuing herself, that is seen as heroic. Drawn as he is to the idea of "voluntary" *sati,* the widow's escape is intelligible to him primarily as a failure of nerve. Meanwhile her escape is rewritten as "rescue." The language used to describe her jump from the pyre is instructive. The widow is said to have made the jump "with a strong convulsive start." In another account of a widow's escape, the narrator states that she had "sprung from the pile from an instinctive impulse." Both descriptions imply a primarily physical process, not one that involves both mind and body. They represent the widow's escape not as a decisive act but as a bodily reflex. As a consequence, even after such a dramatic act of self-affirmation as escape from the burning funeral pyre, she remains the "deluded young widow" and "infatuated devotee to Brahminical influence." It must be, however, noted that not all widows were as fortunate in surviving the burns they sustained before jumping off the pyre. Many died in hospital or soon after their attempted escape.

The accounts of *sati* incidents available to us suggest many of the external pressures on the widow. These include fear of future economic insecurity and the absence of protection by family. Indeed, financial insecurity is the recurring reason given by women questioned at the pyre. Such statements confirm the argument made by Rammohun Roy (symbol of the indigenous lobby against *sati*), the missionaries and some anti-*sati* EIC officials that access to the property due to the widow on her husband's decease was a key factor in relatives' investment in the widow's destruction.

The widow's life was sometimes determined by a power struggle between contending parties. The following report is unusual in not representing those around the widow as united in their purpose. A widow, said to be under sixteen, the age below which *sati* was not permissible under East India Company law, was prevented from burning. Her prevention was reportedly not the result of concern for her, but the outcome of a contest between her in-laws, anxious to promote her destruction for control over the property that would fall to her, and her deceased husband's spiritual mentor, equally anxious to prevent it, since she was a minor and "in all probability, the expenditure of her property will principally pass through his [the mentor's] hands."[19] Another woman who had been successfully dissuaded confessed that her older brothers had pressured her to commit *sati* to get hold of the money due to her.[20]

Women were not merely persuaded to commit *sati.* They were also physically coerced into immolating themselves. There are numerous examples of women being tied to the pyre,[21] held down with bamboo poles,[22] or else weighted down with wood.[23] Women were also drugged. One widow, who managed to escape from the pyre testified to having been given large quantities of opium and *bang.*[24] Other women were observed to have been barely sensible and to have been physically assisted onto the pyre. There was, then, sufficient evidence to severely undermine the persistent notion of "voluntary" *sati*. Yet this conception endured even in accounts of women whose deaths were secured by coercion. Thus a newspaper item which goes on to detail an incident in which the widow was weighted down with wood begins, "The Cholera Morbus has put the *fidelity* of many a Hindoo Widow to the test.[25]

Colonialists' fascination for *sati* was most clearly expressed in accounts of apparently voluntary burnings. It is clear from the numerous instances of coercion and from the testimonials of widows who escaped that this is a problematic and pernicious concept. One can only wonder at how many other stories, other details of coercion overt and subtle, perished untold in the pyres of those so-called voluntary *satis*.

The valorization of the apparently voluntary *sati* shaped eyewitness accounts of widow immolation in important ways. Firstly there is the hastening to the pyre on the news of a *sati*. Something in excess of the hope of dissuading the widow is often expressed in the desire to witness widow burning.

> I beheld a sight I long felt to see, but a more horrible one I never witnessed. It was an immolation of a human creature in the prime of life, with health and youth blooming in the countenance.[26]

Or, having reached the spot, there is the desire to stay:

> I had almost determined to leave the spot, when observing that the magistrate went and stood close to the pile, I felt a wild and impatient desire to remain.[27]

Then there is the admiration of women who burnt in incidents deemed to be "voluntary," but whose real nature we can guess at, given what we know of *sati*. Such admiration is frequently expressed in relation to women described as unusually beautiful.

> I stood close to her, she observed me attentively. . . . She might be about twenty-four or five years of age, a time of life when the bloom of beauty had fled the cheek in India; but she still preserved a sufficient share to prove that she must have been handsome. Her figure was small, but elegantly turned; and the form of her hands and arms was peculiarly beautiful. (William Hodges, quoted in Johns, 1816, pp. 21–22)

Such "tender" descriptions of the personal appearance and beauty of widows suggests the voyeuristic pleasure of a specifically male gaze, contemplating what it constructs as the wife devoted to her husband in death as in life. Malek Alloula (1986) is helpful here.

> It is the nature of pleasure to scrutinize its object detail by detail, to take possession of it in both a total and fragmented fashion. It is an intoxication, a loss of oneself in the other through sight. (p. 49)

This phallocentric reverie, by mystifying coercion as the devotion and free will of the widow, enacts a discursive violence that is every bit as cruel and indefensible as the practice that is its referent.

One effect of such a valorizing of the beautiful widow engaged in apparently voluntary *sati* was that "sympathy" was reserved for such women. Such women's deaths are rendered empathetically. However, the pathos expressed here is not for the widow's predicament but for the imminent loss of one so attractive. In an account from the *Calcutta Journal* reprinted in the *Asiatic Journal,* the narrator writes thus of a widow who he says was so drugged that she had to be lifted onto the pyre.

> She was twenty-one years of age, beautiful to my conception, by far the most so of any native female I have ever seen; combined with the beauty of face, the figure was

perfect, which heightened the distress, if possible, in the minds of those who were witnesses of the sacrifice, and felt their inability to prevent it.[28]

The qualifier, "if possible," is unconvincing. It is her beauty, not her coercion, that provokes his sympathy. Could it be that, in a repetition of the masculinist gaze noted earlier, this observer is distressed for himself, not for the widow?

Eyewitness accounts have relatively few kind words for women who struggled, escaped, were badly burnt, or were, in the eyes of the observer, not beautiful to behold. Such women are invariably described as "miserable wretches," "suffering wretches," "unfortunate women," or "unfortunate victims."[29] The descriptive repertoire in such cases is neither rich nor elaborate. The struggles of women against their coercion are not imposing or admirable. As we shall see, they merely inspire horror and distaste.

There is strikingly little description of suffering in most eyewitness accounts of *sati.*[30] As already noted, much of the narrative is taken up with the efforts at dissuasion and in describing the practices leading up to the burning. The widow's death itself occupies very little of the account. The following are typical descriptions: the bodies were "quickly enveloped in flames,"[31] or "she fell on the fire and was soon burnt to ashes,"[32] "a load of hemp . . . was thrown on her, and a blaze kindled, which in a few minutes consumed the living and the dead."[33] This abrupt conclusion to narratives that otherwise closely detail the widow's demeanor and track her desires, is surprising indeed. It forecloses discussion of the widow's suffering. Some accounts suggest that the flames, and the fact that widows were tied down, made it difficult to see whether they struggled, while the cries of "hari bol," drowned the screams of widows, if such were issued.

This difficulty of actually knowing how the widow experienced burning does not seem entirely satisfactory as an explanation for the absence, in general, of an explicit thematization of her suffering. After all, her motivations and subjective state in relation to *sati* were equally difficult of access. Yet observers frequently made the widow ground for their own speculations in the matter. Why then this reticence in the matter of her pain and distress?

Sometimes observers reported having seen a little of the widow's struggle.

> Surely none that saw the convulsed twitching of the hand and sinews could hesitate for an instant in thinking, that if they had not been prevented by the weight of wood, they would have endeavoured to escape from the excruciating death.[34]

Such fragments give us some sense, however minimal, of the torture of *sati.* The few descriptions we have of women's suffering are of women who escaped from the pyre.

> I arrived at the ground as they were bringing her . . . from the river [to which the widow had escaped from the pyre] . . . I cannot describe to you the horror I felt on seeing the mangled condition she was in, almost every inch of skin on her body had been burnt off, her legs and thighs, her arms and back were completely raw, her breasts were dreadfully torn and the skin hanging from them in shreds, the skins and nails of her fingers had peeled wholly off and were hanging.[35]

The widow was taken to hospital where she lingered "in the most excruciating pain for about 20 hours and then died" (p. 348).

Such accounts are exceptional in their attention to the palpable, visceral effects of *sati.* They are also unusual in representing the woman as "subject of/in pain" (Rajan, 1990, p. 19). In most descriptions of *sati,* however, as the widow ascends the pyre, details vanish almost as magically, it would seem, as the narrator would have us believe that the widow herself evaporates.[36] Accounts conclude cryptically, we might say, evasively:

"the widow was soon consumed." Or worse, they positively romanticized the widows' experience on the pyre: "in a moment the souls of the devoted girls fled in shrieks to the world of spirits."[37] Such metaphoric excesses achieved full expression in poems on widow burning.

Anguish or sorrow for the widow is not commonplace in such descriptions. Grief, when expressed, was frequently articulated as horror. Horror distances the observer, objectifies the practice, and excludes, by definition, even empathy for victims of horrible acts. Within such a framework, anguish for the victim can frequently be displaced by anguish for the observing self:

God forbid I should ever witness such another horrid scene.[38]

I would willingly endure a week's gout, rather than suffer again what I did on this day, in the vain hope of saving a life.[39]

There were accounts in which a more genuine concern was expressed for the widow. One such example was an item carried by the missionary *Friend of India* in July 1820. The report concludes with a discussion of the ridiculousness of the concept of "voluntary" *sati* that conveys pathos without sensationalism. It would seem the reader is being directed to the facts themselves, and not, as is more typical of evangelical fundraising materials, to what such facts may imply about Indian society.

[O]n whom had these two young persons to lean for counsel at this awful moment which was to decide their fate? Their own father and mother? These were far away as is generally the case. Their husband's uncle, and his sons! It is probable that these felt quite as much for them as is felt for widows in general; but could they be ignorant that if they chose to live they must remain a perpetual burden on them, of which nothing could rid them but death itself? These two young widows, in their husband's death had indeed *lost their all*. . . . Can we contemplate all these circumstances without feeling that no one amidst them *could act freely?* (emphasis in original)[40]

In general, missionaries were least likely to produce fascinated accounts of *sati*, although they also persisted, the above report notwithstanding, in lending credence to the notion of "voluntary" *sati*. On a pragmatic level, this notion was useful since it confirmed the all-powerful influence of Hinduism, or, as William Ward (1822) put it, "the amazing power which this superstition has over the mind of its votaries." Compare also the preceding discussion of the material forces underpinning *sati* with the following fictional testimonial written by Ward, stating his view of what the widow might have said at the pyre:

Such a widow reflects thus: "It is right that the wife leave the world with her husband; a son can never be to the mother what a husband is to a wife; the extinction of life is the work of a minute; by strangling, by drowning, how soon does the soul leave the body: there are no terrors then in the funeral pile, and I shall at once enter on happiness! What multitudes have died in this manner before me; and if I live, I have nothing but sorrow to expect." (p. 327)

These words, of which the pro-*sati* lobby would have been proud, are at variance with what most women were reported as having said at the pyre. They suggest that even missionaries were not entirely immune to that troubling and tenacious concept, the apparently voluntary *sati*. Like the question at the heart of twentieth-century patriarchal discourse on rape—"did she want it?"—the refrain—"did she go willingly?"—centrally structured debate on *sati*, mystifying the practice and delaying its prohibition.

Conclusion

Eyewitness accounts of widow burning have been read here with the double purpose of mapping one dimension of "the obsessive scheme that regulates the totality of the output . . . and endows it with meaning" (Alloula, 1986, p.4) and of foregrounding the marginalizations and inflections that sustain particular aspects of these narratives. In other words, in rereading observers' accounts of widow burning, I have attempted to engage the disjunctions between their construction of women's words and actions at the funeral pyre, and the evidence to the contrary that they themselves contain. Several fictions about *sati* and Hindu widows are compromised by this reading. The testimonials of widows challenge the dominant represenation of *sati* as a religiously inspired act of devotion to the deceased husband. Similarly, the binary and static conception of the widow as either entirely self-determining or totally victimized emerges as simplistic, giving way to a more complex scenario in which the widow can be seen to be actively negotiating her circumstances at every point and till the very end. Further, the obsessive fascination with voluntary *sati* in the face of blatant coercion demonstrates the hollowness of colonial horror regarding the practice and, more importantly, clarifies the intimate relationship between horror and fascination.

If, as I have argued elsewhere (Mani, 1987), women were ground for the discourse on *sati* in the official debate on widow burning, here they move between being object and ground. At times women are the object of description, at other times, ground for the projections of a distinctively male, voyeuristic gaze. In reading against the grain, contrary to "the obsessive scheme," I have attempted to reconstruct woman as subject and to restore to the center elements that are marginalized and elided by these accounts: the violence of *sati,* the active suffering of widows, and women's resistance to, and coercion in, widow burning.[41]

At the same time, the limits of these accounts of widow burning, and thus the specificities of this reading, must be borne in mind. While there is sufficient evidence here to unsettle the image of the widow as passive, willing, or silent, these descriptions of widow burning do not yield elaborate representations of women's subjectivity. Questions of female subject formation, of the place of the ideology of widow burning in the socialization of Hindu women, for instance, are not "answerable" on the basis of these texts alone. Similarly, the reductive representations of the widow's relatives and of Brahmin pundits undercuts their value for fleshing out, except in the most preliminary way that I have attempted here, familial pressures on the widow and the broader social context of widow burning. This is not to propose that a social history of widow burning in the nineteenth century is entirely discontinuous with an analysis of colonial discourse on *sati.* A social history that fails to interrogate the ideology of any of its sources is doomed to reproduce it. Furthermore, social historians can hardly claim that they are exempt from engaging questions of representation. What I am urging, rather, is care in the conclusions drawn from an analysis of colonial texts, a reminder that one's conclusions are constrained by the nature of one's sources.

The question "Can the subaltern speak?," then, is perhaps better posed as a series of questions: Which groups constitute the subalterns in any text? What is their relationship to each other? How can they be heard to be speaking or not speaking in a given set of materials? With what effects? Rephrasing the questions in this way enables us to retain Spivak's insight regarding the positioning of woman in colonial discourse without conceding to colonial discourse what it, in fact, did not achieve—the erasure of women.

NOTES

1. I would like to thank Yvonne Yarbro-Bejarano, Ted Swedenburg, and especially Ruth Frankenberg for their critical comments and editorial assistance.

2. This was quite evident at the "Cultural Studies Now and in the Future" conference in, for instance, the contrast between accounts of the history of cultural studies presented by Lidia Curti and Stuart Hall. See also, Hall (1990a), "The Emergence of Cultural Studies and the Crisis of the Humanities." For some idea of the range of current conceptions of cultural studies in the U.S., see, in addition to work already cited, Andrew Ross (1988a), Renato Rosaldo (1989), James Clifford and Vivek Dhareshwar (1989), Cornel West (1990b).

3. Accounts which place a politicized notion of difference at the center of their framework include West (1989, 1990b) and Appadurai (1990).

4. On this point see hooks (1990), pp. 21, 23–31.

5. For a critique of this conception of difference, see Trinh T. Minh-ha (1986/7a) "Difference: A Special Third World Women's Issue."

6. For complex representations of third world feminisms, see Alarcon (1990) and Sandoval (forthcoming *Genders,* 1991).

7. Among others, James Clifford and George Marcus (1986), James Clifford (1988), Trinh T. Minh-ha (1989), Ruth Frankenberg (forthcoming).

8. Among others, Partha Chatterjee (1986); Ranajit Guha (ed.) (1982/9), *Subaltern Studies,* vols. 1–6; Kum Kum Sangari and Sudesh Vaid (1989).

9. Chandra Mohanty (1988), Minh-ha (1989), among others. It should be noted that although for my purposes here I am locating this body of work under the synthetic rubric "critique of colonial discourse," I am well aware that there are compelling reasons for situating them in other traditions. For instance, the rethinking in anthropology may equally be placed within an earlier history of autocritique within the discipline. See for instance, Talal Asad (1973). Similarly, the work of the Subaltern Studies Collective or the volume *Recasting Women* (Sangari and Vaid, 1989) needs to be understood as part of the third wave in Indian historiography. My designation of them as instances of a critique of colonial discourse is then ultimately a local gesture and at best a partial one.

10. On this point see Kum Kum Sangari (1989).

11. For a fine discussion of questions of location, history, and intellectual formation see Mary John (1989), "Postcolonial feminists in the intellectual field: Anthropologists *and* Native Informants?"

12. Although this essay focuses on colonial discourse, elsewhere (forthcoming) I also examine indigenous discourses on widow burning.

13. For a broader critique, Benita Parry (1987), "Problems in current theories of colonial discourse."

14. Indigenous papers like *Sambad Kaumudi, Samachar Darpan,* and *Samachar Chundrika* did not carry descriptions like the English press, only information of incidents which included such details as date, location, and persons involved. For a general account of Western responses to widow burning see Arvind Sharma (1979).

15. Throughout this text the terms consent and voluntary will be set off by quotation marks since they are, as we shall see, dubious concepts.

16. See, for an extended analysis of accounts of widow burning including their representation of human activity, and accounts by white women, Mani (forthcoming).

17. "Suttee," *India Gazette,* October 23, 1828, p. 4.

18. Part of what sustains this discourse are colonial conceptions of culture and the representation as "ritual" of the practices that precede the burning.

19. "Suttee Prevented," *Asiatic Journal,* May 1821, p. 508.

20. *Bengal Hurkaru,* September 16, 1828, p. 2.

21. See for instance, "Immolation of a Widow," *Bengal Hurkaru,* August 12, 1823; "Suttee," *Bengal Hurkaru,* June 20, 1829, p. 2.

22. Letter to the Editor, *Calcutta Journal,* May 2, 1819, p. 357; Letter to the Editor, *Bengal Hurkaru,* February 6, 1824, p. 3; *Quarterly Papers of the Baptist Missionary Society,* October 13, 1824, p. 47. Among others.

23. "Suttee," *Bengal Hurkaru,* September 15, 1825, p. 2; "Horrible Suttee," *Bengal Hurkaru,* January 4, 1826, p. 2; "Immolation of Widows," *Bengal Hurkaru,* April 19, 1826, p. 2; *Bengal Hurkaru,* July 27, 1826, p. 2.

24. *Missionary Register,* 1821, p. 115; "Concremation," *Bengal Hurkaru,* February 2, 1828, p. 2; "Suttee at Cuttack," *Bengal Hurkaru,* August 22, 1828, p. 2. In this last case, the magistrate, on finding that the widow had been intoxicated by her brothers-in-law conspiring to be rid of her, refuses permission for her immolation. The relatives appeal his decision, are successful and the widow was burnt some sixteen days later.

25. "Suttee," *Bengal Hurkaru,* September 15, 1825, p. 2, emphasis mine.

26. "Horrible Suttee," *Bengal Hurkaru,* January 4, 1826, p. 2.

27. *Calcutta Journal,* April 23, 1822, p. 586.

28. "Suttee," *Asiatic Journal,* March 1823, p. 292.

29. For instance, in arguing that *sati* was coerced, an article in *Bengal Hurkaru,* April 2, 1823, p. 232, describes the widows as "wretched and deluded . . . harrassed and goaded into assent[ing] to . . . they know not what."

30. I have found very useful here Rajeswari Sunder Rajan's (1990) analysis of the absence of a discussion of pain in contemporary discourse on *sati* sparked off by Roop Kanwar's burning in Deorala, Rajasthan, on September 22, 1987.

31. *Bengal Hurkaru,* February 6, 1824, p. 3.

32. "Another Woman Burnt Alive," *Circular Letters of the Baptist Missionary Society,* September 1814, p. 178.

33. "Immolation of Widows," *Bengal Hurkaru,* August 12, 1823.

34. *Bengal Hurkaru,* July 27, 1826, p. 2.

35. "Burning of Widows," *Friend of India,* Monthly, November 1823, p. 348.

36. In the contemporary debate on *sati* in India, in lieu of details of suffering are stories of the miraculous ascent of the unscathed, untouched widow to celestial regions. The widow here is said to *literally* evaporate.

37. Letter to the Editor, *Asiatic Journal,* March 1818, p. 222.

38. "Female Immolations," *Friend of India,* Monthly, March 1822, p. 94.

39. Letter to the Editor, *Calcutta Journal,* May 2, 1819, p. 357.

40. "The Burning of Two Widows on One Pile," *Friend of India,* Monthly, July 1820, p. 208.

41. There are not simply historiographical, but also contemporary, stakes in this reading. In the aftermath of Roop Kanwar's coerced burning in September 1987, Hindu fundamentalists and their nativist, anti-Western ideologues have been involved in a concerted effort to romanticize *sati.* Analysis of nineteenth-century eyewitness accounts of *sati* provides the groundwork for exploring complicities between colonial discourse and that of its self-proclaimed Other, contemporary Hindu fundamentalism. See Mani (1990) and Rajan (1990).

DISCUSSION: LATA MANI

QUESTION: Did you have any access to eyewitness accounts of the *sati* that took place two years ago in Rajasthan? How would you compare and contrast it to the kinds of accounts that you talked about? In the few accounts that I read, there did not seem to be many attempts to stop it, nor were there many expressions of horror. It seemed as though both women and men thought that *sati* was not for the ordinary woman but for some kind of an exceptional woman.

MANI: You are referring to the burning of Roop Kanwar in Deorala, Rajasthan in September 1987? Firstly, I should clarify that *sati* in Rajasthan is located in a rather different history than *sati* in Bengal which is what I have been discussing here. *Sati* in Rajasthan is, for instance, more intimately tied to notions of valor and community honor. But to return to your question, I haven't had access to detailed eyewitness accounts of the kind I have examined here, but I, as well as many other feminists, have analyzed the debate on widow burning that developed in the wake of this incident. (I would refer you to the special issue of *Seminar* on *Sati,* to Rajeswari Sunder Rajan's piece in *Yale Journal of Criticism,* and mine in *Feminist Review.*) Our analysis has drawn on newspaper accounts, investigative reports by civil rights and feminist groups, and so on. As Rajeswari points out in her essay, one ironic consequence of the Indian government's outlawing of *sati* and its glorification (through the January 1988 legislation), would be to make eyewitness accounts of the kind I have looked at here *ipso facto* illegal, because to witness *sati* is necessarily to participate in an illegal event. As for the question of horror, yes, one did not encounter it to the same degree, but, in any case, I don't think horror functions as well as social critique since it tends to distance the horrified observer and make an absolute Other of the victim.

QUESTION: I traveled in India about eight or ten years ago. There was an outbreak of *sati* in Rajasthan at that time, and the press was following it quite carefully. One of the things that struck me was that the press seemed to be quite critical of that period of time when the British dominated India, and yet there seemed to be some grudging respect for the British for outlawing the practice. I wonder if you could comment on that.

MANI: Yes, the British abolition of *sati* is a kind of canonical event in dominant historiography, supposedly marking the passage of an East India Company administered by Orientalists enamored of things indigenous, to Anglicists representing a vigorously liberal, utilitarian tradition. My own attempt has been to show that the question is somewhat more complex, in that abolition of *sati* by the British was preceded by its legislation and that, for all the credit that has been conferred on the British for their humanitarian concerns, it is remarkable that the grounds for prohibition were not primarily that of *sati*'s cruelty to women, that there was a fundamental and persistent fascination with so-called voluntary *sati,* and that in crucial ways, women were actually marginal to the debate on widow burning. Bentick's famous 1829 *Minute on Sati,* for instance, does not contain a single mention of the widow. I want to make it absolutely clear, however, that my interest in a project of this kind is not in pointing an accusatory finger at the colonizer. My interest is rather in the ideological consequences of the *terms* of a certain discourse on women, society, and tradition for a range of discourses including Indian nationalism and feminism, Hindu fundamentalism, and Western representations.

QUESTION: First, I understand that the practice of *sati* was very restricted. Could you tell us how widespread it was? Second, how was it connected with Indian feminism? And finally, if it is true that most of these descriptions were by British narrators who were young civil servants, who came to India between the ages of twenty to twenty-five, might that explain the great emphasis on the beauty of burning widows?

MANI: Yes, *sati* was in the nineteenth century, and remains today, a minority practice. Between 1815–1828 when the British collected statistics, there were a little over eight thousand widows burnt. Needless to say, as soon as it was prohibited, it was assumed to have ceased to exist and no further statistics were collected. Since independence in 1947, there have been approximately forty reported incidents of widow burning in Rajasthan. The burning of Roop Kanwar in 1987 has made *sati* very much a live issue for Indian feminism even though feminists have always engaged the broader notions of women's self-negation and fidelity to husbands that are part and parcel of the ideology of *sati* though hardly restricted to it. As for whether the accent on the widow's beauty is related to the youth of the British civil servants . . . I have read literally hundreds of descriptions from Europeans of all ages and from all walks of life, and the image of the beautiful widow cuts across them. It seems to me to be related to the construction of the typical widow about to be burnt as young, nubile, and prepubescent, and the typical deceased husband as a much older if not elderly man. Interestingly, this construction of the widow as young flies in the face of the evidence we have from British records that over two-thirds of women who burnt between 1815–1828 were above 45 years of age. Beauty and youth, then, are not related to the age of the observer but become the tropes around which the observers' pathos is articulated.

MEAGHAN KRISTOFF: You mentioned that *sati* was performed among the higher castes, and I was just curious as to the role of class and if you were interested at all in a specific Marxist approach to that class distinction.

MANI: That's a really good question. I started off wanting to do a social history of widow burning but as I read through the materials it became clear that there was another very complicated story to be told about the emergence of a particular interpretive apparatus, the construction of tradition and so on. So that's what I've done. As I've already mentioned, widow burning is a predominantly high caste Hindu practice although there is some evidence of burning among lower caste, poorer communities. *Sati* is also a localized practice. In the early nineteenth century for instance, 63% of women who were burnt were burnt outside Calcutta City. A Marxist, more accurately materialist, approach to widow burning has related it to the introduction of private property by the British in the early nineteenth century. Under Dayabhaga law which prevailed in Bengal at the time, widows had access to the property of their husbands upon their death, a right that obviously acquires new significance with land becoming a commodity and with the increasing turnover of land in the wake of people unable to make revenue payments levied by the East India Company. Now while this is a viable narrative, *sati* in this period is undoubtedly related to these developments, it is a partial one—it cannot on its own explain the concentration of *sati* in certain districts. Furthermore, one wonders why, given women's lack of power in society, the right of widows was simply not ignored. Obviously, the cultural, the social, the historical, the familial, and the contingent combine in explaining widow burning at this time, but the picture is by no means clear.

QUESTION: How do you see the relationship between the first and second parts of your paper?

MANI: I guess in both my concern is that we take care to avoid globalizing the local. In the first section I am expressing a concern I share with others of the consequences of too quickly extending understandings of postmodernity that are rooted in particular socio-historical experiences, predominantly white and middle class. In the second I am anxious that we don't do the same with analysis of colonial texts, that we are at all times clear about the limits of our sources and of our analysis. Otherwise, we are at risk of granting colonialism more power than it achieved. It seems to me that a number of key questions about colonial discourse are yet to be decided. We have still, in my view, to grasp adequately the relation between the pre-colonial and colonial state, the scope of the latter and how its reach might have been differentiated by class, gender, geographical location. In this context, I have favored the local over the global in my own research, in that I see myself as identifying a discursive constellation, tracting it across a range of institutional and non-institutional sites in the context of the debate on *sati,* analyzing how it shapes representations of the practice, and its consequences for us as historians, activists, and so on. But it is only through a series of such local projects, globally informed, that we can begin to move to broader conclusions about the colonial or the postcolonial.

QUESTION: You have spoken in your paper about the concept of disjunction, and I am curious about how it applies to this paper itself. Do you feel that this paper is written specifically for the U.S. and, if so, how might it be different if it had been written in India?

MANI: The question of my own location has been something I have been compelled to think about because of the difficulties of being adequately local to the very different contexts of the U.S. and India today. For instance, if I had written this paper for an Indian anthology, the first section on cultural studies would have been replaced by one on the alarming spread of Hindu fundamentalism and its challenge for a genuinely secular and progressive scholarship. Fundamentalists and their "liberal" ideologues are rewriting history, positioning themselves as anti-imperialist and anti-modern whilst actively redeploying colonial discourse whether in support of widow burning or in denying the benefits of structural reform to the majority. You thus have a very complex situation which, while it certainly has its echoes in things happening here, requires interventions that are differently focused. I obviously have no easy way to resolve the situation except to keep reading and listening and to try to make sure that the things in my work that speak to the context of the U.S. are not, for example, counter-productive to the struggle of progressives in India. It's a very live issue for me and one that concerns me a great deal.

23

Body Narratives, Body Boundaries

Emily Martin

What can the political role of ethnography be in attempts to achieve social change? One of the uses to which ethnography in anthropology has been put in the last several years is the detection of "resistances," counter-hegemonic visions and practices. In Gramsci's (1971) terms, a social group may adopt, during " 'normal times'—that is when its conduct is not independent and autonomous but submissive and subordinate"—a conception of the world "which is not its own but is borrowed from another group": this it does for reasons of submission and subordination (p. 327). But at other times

> the social group in question may indeed have its own conception of the world, even
> if only embryonic; a conception which manifests itself in action, but occasionally and
> in flashes—when, that is, the group is acting as an organic totality. (p. 327)

Anthropological ethnographers have found many embryonic flashes of visions of social worlds that fly in the face of hegemonic conceptions. Most of this work has not focused on revolutionary moments in history, outside normal time, but instead on small moments within normal time that permit expressions of alternative consciousness. Some of these moments are at life crises: Chinese women sing laments at weddings and funerals that reveal acute understanding of the position of women in Chinese families and kinship structures, and bewail it (E. Johnson, 1988); others are at times of dramatic social transition, as when Malay women enter factory work (Ong, 1987), or Colombian peasants begin to work for wages on plantations (Taussig, 1980); still others occur at times of sickness, as among marginalized black peasant workers in rural South Africa (Comaroff, 1985).

Since intellectual communities are far from seamless wholes, however, it would be no surprise to find there have been protests from some quarters. A recent review summarizes: "Some theorists, impressed with the totalizing effects of official discourse, have suggested that subordinate groups are silenced altogether, either literally unequipped to speak in certain contexts or voluble but unable to articulate the alternate views that stem from their different structural positions in society" (Gal, 1989, p. 360). Some anthropologists have recently decried the "romanticism" in efforts to detect "resistance," arguing that there is a tendency to "read all forms of resistance as signs of the ineffectiveness of systems of power and of the resilience and creativity of the human spirit in its refusal to be dominated" (Abu-Loghud, 1990, p. 42). Instead, it is suggested, we should realize with Foucault that modern forms of power are not repressive, but productive. They do not just deny, prohibit, repress, and restrict; more importantly, they produce discourses, knowledge, pleasures, and goods. Since these powers extend from innumerable sources—education, health disciplines, science, entertainment, the state, the military—there is nowhere in society they can be escaped. Therefore, in Foucault's (1982) words, "resistance is never in a position of exteriority in relation to power" (p. 209), never outside the frame of this power's operation. The detection of resistance, then, is only good for one thing: "as a chemical catalyst so as to bring to light power relations, locate their position, find out their points of application and the methods used" (p. 211). This means that "we could continue to look for and consider nontrivial all sorts of resistance, but instead of taking these as signs of human freedom we will use them strategically to tell us more about forms of power and how people are caught up in them" (Abu-Loghud, 1990, a 42).

Outside of anthropology, in the world of books reviewed in the *New York Times Book Review* and excerpted in the *New Yorker,* and fashionable on the coffee tables of people like me and my friends, there is a similar current of thought, which also seeks to deny the possibility of breaking the boundary within which social thought and action are currently held. I have in mind the rather apocalyptic "End of . . ." publications: Fukuyama's (1989) "The End of History?," McKibbon's (1989) *The End of Nature,* and Hardison's (1989) *Disappearing Through the Skylight.* For this last, the chapter subtitles are: The Disappearance of Nature, The Disappearance of History, The Disappearance of Language, The Disappearance of Art, and The Disappearance of Man. I have found it disturbing to realize that these books share a profound denial of the possibilities of human agency to sustain the potential for fundamental social and cultural change. Fukuyama (1989) insists on "an unabashed victory of economic and political liberalism . . . the triumph of the West, of the Western *idea,* . . . in the total exhaustion of viable systematic alternatives to Western liberalism" (p. 3). We have reached "the end of history as such: that is, the end point of mankind's ideological evolution and the universalization of Western liberal democracy as the final form of human government" (p. 4). In the uniform sea of Western liberal/capitalist post-history there will only be "economic calculation, the endless solving of technical problems, environmental concerns, and the satisfaction of sophisticated consumer demands" (p. 18). What is denied here is the reality of fundamental differences among liberal democracies, as well as the possibility of the existence of or potential for viable alternatives in Eastern Europe, the Far East, Africa, Southeast Asia, or elsewhere.

Take another example: Bill McKibbon's (1989) prose poem about the degradation of the environment, the greenhouse effect, pollution, the depletion of the ozone layer, *The End of Nature.* There we learn that we are now living in a "post-natural" world, in which "every spot on earth is man-made and artificial" (p. 58). We have lost the world of Thoreau who could walk half an hour and come to a spot where man does not stand from one year's end to another (p. 60), because now there is no such spot. The book is filled with glowing reconstructions of the pristine natural beauty of the continent of North America which still existed several hundred years ago, all in terms of a "world that existed outside human history" (p. 52). This reconstruction contains scarcely a mention of human occupation, use, and alteration of the environment before the arrival of European colonists. What is denied here is human presence, vision, and action on the environment other than that brought by European settlers.

Finally, we come to Hardison's (1989) book, *Disappearing Through the Skylight,* about the end of almost everything. In particular he details the impending end of carbon-based man: "Carbon life is voracious. It consumes the resources it needs for survival. The price of human success has been deforestation, desertification, water pollution, extinction of species, ozone depletion, smog, and the Greenhouse Effect . . . He will not submit to being a part of the fabric of nature, so he may end like Samson by pulling the Temple down on his head" (p. 335). The end of this doomed species will be its replacement by silicon-based creatures, as the butterfly replaces the caterpillar . . . Silicon life will be bodiless, telepathic, immortal. The "dying animal to which carbon man is tied" will be replaced by pure intellect. This is no Donna Haraway-style (1991) cyborg, which she describes as a body with "prosthetic devices, intimate components, friendly selves, an aspect of our embodiment." Hardison's silicon creature (whose coming he extolls) will say, in the words of Yeats: "Once out of nature, I shall never take/My bodily form from any natural thing."

What is denied here? What is *not* denied! This vision denies the possibility of any form of human social life that is not voracious and destructive, it denies the body, it denies the death of the body and the coming into being of new bodies.

My own response to these intellectual currents is to strive even harder through ethnography (the anthropological study of culture) to try to break out of the "iron cage" of thought that seems to make a lot of us lack the imagination to think of other worlds that might exist and to deny the existence of other ways of living in the world that might have preceded or co-exist with the ones currently dominating the scene.

My own work looks at scientific knowledge as one purveyor of a view of the world from a particular vantage point. This knowledge is often able to masquerade as "natural fact," a powerful means by which its vision of hierarchical human relationships is learned and internalized. I am interested in imagery conveyed in various ways—scientific and otherwise—which depicts the body (in ever more fantastic magnification), and in how visual and print media used to convey scientific information to the public (ever more affordably) function within social processes. I have been doing participant observation in a biological research lab, participating as a volunteer in a community health education organization focused on HIV infection issues, and carrying out general fieldwork and interviews on health and work in three urban neighborhoods. Today I will focus on a particular incident that occurred in one of these urban neighborhoods, in which a group of young people watched a recent film about human reproduction called "The Miracle of Life." Before I describe that incident, let me introduce the kind of imagery and metaphors that occur throughout biology teaching materials used in textbooks as well as more popular publications, a lot of which is carried through into the film.

At a fundamental level, both male and female reproductive organs are metaphorically depicted in all major scientific textbooks as systems for the production of valuable things.[1] In the case of women, the monthly cycle is seen medically as preeminently designed to produce eggs, prepare a suitable place for them to be fertilized and grown, all, of course, to the end of making babies. Extolling production means that menstruation, which is seen as what occurs when an egg is not fertilized, carries with it an overlay of a productive system that has failed to be productive. Medically, menstruation is described as the "debris" of the uterine lining which is the result of necrosis or death of tissue. It also carries the idea of production gone awry, making products of no use, not to specification, unsalable, wasted, scrap. An illustration that accompanies a widely used medical text shows menstruation as a chaotic disintegration of the form, matching the many texts which describe it as: "ceasing," "dying," "losing," "denuding," and "expelling" (Guyton 1984, p. 624).[2] These are not neutral terms, but ones that convey failure and dissolution.

In contrast, processes in male reproductive physiology are evaluated quite differently. In one of the same texts that sees menstruation as failed production, we learn that, "The mechanisms which guide the *remarkable* cellular transformation from spermatid to mature sperm remain uncertain . . . Perhaps the most *amazing* characteristic of spermatogenesis is its *sheer magnitude*: the normal human male may manufacture several hundred million sperm per day" (Vander, Sherman, and Luciano, 1980, pp. 483–84, emphasis added). In the classic, *Medical Physiology,* edited by Vernon Mountcastle (1980), the comparison is explicit: "Whereas the female *sheds* only a single gamete each month, the seminiferous tubules *produce* hundreds of millions of sperm each day" (p. 1624, emphasis added). The female author of another text marvels at the length of the microscopic seminiferous tubules, which, if uncoiled and placed end to end, "would span almost one-third of a mile!" She comments, "In an adult male these structures produce millions of sperm cells each day" and wonders "How is this *feat* accomplished?" (Solomon, 1983, p. 678). None of these texts expresses such intense enthusiasm about any female processes, and it is surely no accident that the "remarkable" process of making sperm involves precisely what menstruation does not in the medical view: production of something deemed valuable.[3]

One could argue that menstruation should not be expected to elicit the same kind of response spermatogenesis does because it is not a biologically analogous process. The proper female analogy to spermatogenesis would be ovulation. Yet ovulation does not merit enthusiasm in these texts either. This could be partly because textbook descriptions stress that all the ovarian follicles containing ova are already present at birth. Far from being *produced* as sperm are, they seem merely to sit on the shelf, as it were, slowly degenerating and aging like overstocked inventory:

> At birth, normal human ovaries contain an estimated one million follicles [each], and no new ones appear after birth. Thus, in marked contrast to the male, the newborn female already has all the germ cells she will ever have. (Vander, Sherman and Luciano, 1985, pp. 567–68)

What is striking about this description is the "marked contrast" that is set up between male and female, the male who continuously produces fresh germ cells and the female who has stockpiled germ cells by birth and is faced with the continuous degeneration of this material. The same goes for the egg and the sperm themselves. Even though each contributes almost exactly half of the genetic stuff to the new individual in fertilization, it is astounding how different their roles seem and how "femininely" the egg behaves and how "masculinely" the sperm.

The egg is seen as large and passive. It does not *move* or *journey,* but passively "is transported," "is swept" (Guyton, 1984, p. 619; Mountcastle, 1980, p. 1609), or even, in a popular account, "drifts" (Miller and Pelham, 1984) along the fallopian tube. In utter contrast, sperm are small, "streamlined," and inevitably active. They "deliver" their genes to the egg, "activate the developmental program of the egg" (Alberts, et al., 1983, p. 796) and have a "velocity" which is always remarked on (Ganong, 1975, p. 322). Their tails are "strong" and efficiently powered (Alberts, et al., 1983, p. 796). Together with the forces of ejaculation, they can "propel the semen into the deepest recesses of the vagina" (Guyton, 1984, p. 615). For this they need "energy," "fuel" (Solomon, 1983, p. 683), so that with a "whiplashlike motion and strong lurches" (Vander, Sherman, and Luciano, 1985, p. 580) they can "burrow through the egg coat" (Alberts, et al., 1983, p. 796) and "penetrate" it.[4]

In our cultural tradition, passivity is a quintessential female attribute, activity a male one. So one might imagine there is some cultural overlay on how egg and sperm are seen. But there is more. The egg is hidden behind a protective barrier, the egg coat, sometimes called its "vestments," a term used for sacred, religious dress. In addition the egg is said to have a "corona," a crown (Solomon, 1983, p. 700), and is accompanied by "attendant cells" (Beldecos, et al., 1988, pp. 61–76). The egg is evidently special, holy, set apart and above. As such the egg could potentially play queen to the sperm as king. In actuality her passivity dominates her royalty, which means she must depend on sperm to rescue her. Sperm have a "mission" (Alberts, et al., 1983, p. 796), which is to "move through the female genital tract in quest of the ovum" (Guyton, 1984, p.

613). An extravagant popular book, *The Facts of Life,* co-authored by Jonathan Miller (1984), the producer of the BBC series, "The Body in Question," has it that the sperm carries out a "perilous journey" into the "warm darkness," where some fall away "exhausted," but other "survivors" "assault" the egg, the successful candidates "surrounding the prize" (p. 7). The journey is perilous in part because it takes place in the vagina, which is called a "hostile environment."

But the egg's journey is also perilous: "once released from the supportive environment of the ovary, an egg will die within hours unless rescued by a sperm" (Alberts, et al, 1983, p. 804). The way this is phrased stresses the fragility and dependency of the egg, even though it is acknowledged elsewhere in this very text that sperm also only live a few hours (p. 801).[5]

In one photograph from the *National Geographic,* sperm are "masters of subversion": "human sperm cells seek to penetrate an ovum. Foreigners in a hostile body, they employ several strategies to survive their mission . . ." (Jaret, 1986, p. 731). Sometimes the egg has her own defenses. In a "Far Side" cartoon, the egg is seen as a housewife besieged by clever sperm who try to get a foot inside the door. Sperm as postman says "Package for you to sign for, Ma'am." Sperm as phone repairman says "Need to check your lines, Ma'am," and sperm as insurance salesman says "Mind if I step inside?"

There is another way sperm can be made to loom in importance over the egg, despite their small size. The article in which an electron micrograph of sperm and an egg appeared is called "Portrait of a Sperm" (Nilsson, 1975). Of course, it is harder to photograph microscopic sperm than eggs, which are just large enough to see with the naked eye. But surely the use of the term "portrait," a term associated with the powerful and the wealthy, is significant. Eggs have only micrographs or pictures, not portraits.

As far as I know there is only one cultural representation in Western civilization of sperm as weak and timid instead of strong and powerful. This occurs in Woody Allen's movie, *Everything You ever Wanted to Know About Sex* *But Were Afraid to Ask.* Woody Allen, playing the part of a reluctant sperm inside a man's body, is afraid to go out into the darkness, afraid of contraceptive devices, and afraid of winding up on the ceiling if the man is masturbating. In biology texts, if there is an association between strong sperm and virility, it is never directly stated. But Allen makes explicit the link between weak sperm and the impotence of the man whose body he is in.

After getting to this point in my survey of scientific and popular materials, I looked extensively at very recent research coming out of labs investigating the sperm and the egg. To summarize briefly, the views I've just outlined have been overturned: scientists have found that the forward propulsive force of the sperm's tail is extremely weak, so that rather than strongly swimming forward with purpose, the sperm actually flail side to side, swim in circles, mill around. The current picture is that adhesive molecules on the surface of the egg capture the sperm and hold it fast; otherwise, its sideways motions would lead it to escape and swim away. (As an aside, nothing is simple: in this new research, the egg comes to be described as an engulfing female aggressor, dangerous and terrifying.)[6]

Nevertheless current scientific textbooks and journal articles continue to perpetuate the old stereotypes. An article from a recent issue of the journal *Cell* has the sperm making, not a heroic fight for his love, but an "existential decision" to penetrate her. "Sperm are cells with a limited behavioral repertoire, one that is directed toward fertilizing eggs. To execute the decision to abandon the haploid state, sperm swim to an egg and there acquire the ability to effect membrane fusion" (Shapiro, 1987, p. 293–94). Is this perhaps the corporate manager's version of the sperm's activities—*executing decisions* while fraught with dismay over difficult options, limited choices carrying very high risk?

Other recent scientific work also draws on virile images, but ones that are working class rather than executive. In research designed to help couples with sperm-related infertility, methods are being developed to force an opening in the zona, the outermost covering of the egg, and so permit the sperm to "penetrate" it. In "Zona Blasters: There's More Than One Way to Crack an Egg," a review article in *Science News,* we find an unrevised version of the saga of egg and sperm:

> The microscopic human egg floats in its fluid-filled shell. Suddenly, thousands of tiny sperm bombard it. Lashing their tails to power their entry, they bore into the shell, a tough glycoprotein coating known as the zona pellucida. One particularly vigorous sperm pierces the zona barrier, setting off a chemical reaction that shuts the others out. Then, if all goes well, the winning sperm fertilizes the egg and the miracle of human life ensues. (Fackelmann, 1990, p. 376)

But trouble arises, given this view, when "the sperm can't whip their tails hard enough to bore through the tough outer shell" (p. 376). To handle this cause of infertility, "scientists are now developing imaginative methods of cracking, blasting or drilling tiny passageways through the zona envelope" (p. 376). In line with this imagery, the cover of this issue of *Science News,* captioned "Sperm at Work," shows a cartoon of three sperm ferociously attacking an egg with a jackhammer, a pickaxe, and a sledgehammer.[7] The undertone of violence in both words and picture scarcely needs comment.

And the same goes for popular publications that purport to represent the latest scientific knowledge. In a recent issue of *Life Magazine,* the dynamic activities of sperm and the passive response of the egg are presented yet again. In "The First Days of Creation," we read, "Although few will finish, about 250 million sperm start the 5–7 inch journey from the vagina to the uterus and then to the fallopian tubes where an egg may be waiting" (Nilsson, 1990, p. 26). Two hours later, "like an eerie planet floating through space, a woman's egg or ovum . . . has been ejected by one of her ovaries into the fallopian tube. Over the next several hours sperm will begin beating their tails vigorously as they rotate like drill bits into the outer wall of the egg" (p. 28).

Other popular materials also do their part: the recent film *Look Who's Talking* begins with a simulation of a hugely magnified egg floating, drifting, gently bouncing along the fallopian tube of a woman who is in the midst of making love with a man. The soundtrack is "I Love You So" by the Chantals. Then we see, also hugely magnified, the man's sperm barreling down the tunnel of her vagina to the tune of "I Get Around" by the Beach Boys. The sperm are shouting and calling to each other like a gang of boys: "Come on, follow me, I know where I am, keep up, come on you kids, I've got the map." Then as the egg hoves into view, they shout, "This is it, yeah, this is definitely it, this is the place, Jackpot, right here, come on, dig in you kids." And when one sperm finally pushes hard enough to open a slit in the egg (a slit that looks remarkably like a vulva), that sperm (as his whole self is swallowed up) cries out, "Oh, oh, oh, I'm in!"

When I got to this point in my research, I was already wondering what social effects such vivid imagery might be having. I thought perhaps this imagery might encourage us to imagine that what results from the interaction of egg and sperm—a fertilized egg—is the result of intentional "human" action *at the cellular level.* In other words, whatever the intentions of the human couple, in this microscopic "culture," a cellular "bride" (or *"femme fatale"*) and a cellular "groom" (or her victim) make a cellular baby. Rosalind Petchesky (1987) makes the point that through visual representations such as sonograms, we are given "*images* of younger and younger, and tinier and tinier, fetuses being 'saved.' " This leads to "the point of viability being 'pushed back' *indefinitely*" (pp. 263–92). Endowing egg and sperm with intentional action, a key aspect of personhood in our culture, lays the foundation for the point of viability being pushed back to the moment of fertilization.

Why would this matter? Because endowing cells with personhood may play a part in the breaking down of boundaries between the self and the world, and a pushing back of the boundary of what constitutes the inviolable self.[8] In other words, whereas at an earlier time, the skin might have been regarded as the border of the individual self, now these microscopic cells are seen as tiny individual selves. This means that the "environment" of the egg and sperm, namely the human body, is fair game for invasion by medical scrutiny and intervention. It is not, of course, that the interior of our bodies was not the object of study and treatment until now. But we may be experiencing an intensification of those activities (made more potent by state support) which are understood as protecting the "rights," viability, or integrity of cellular entities.[9] It would not be that endowing cells with personhood by means of imagery in biology automatically *causes* intensification of initiatives in the legislature and elsewhere that enable protection of these new "persons." Rather, I am suggesting that this imagery may have a part in creating a general predisposition to think of the world in a certain way that can play an important role whenever legal and other initiatives do take place.

It is possible that in the 1990s what was the patient (or person) has itself begun to become *an environment* for a new core self, which exists at the cellular level. This change may be adding to our willingness to focus ever more attention on the internal structures of this tiny cellular self, namely its genes.[10] In turn, such a shift in attention may encourage us to permit dramatic changes in the "environment" of the genes in the name of maintaining their welfare.[11]

My thinking had gotten to this point, when, by one of the unpredictable twists of fieldwork, an unusual opportunity presented itself. It came about through John Marcellino, a largely self-educated man who is a community leader in the neighborhood he grew up in, a predominantly white neighborhood experiencing massive unemployment, a nearly 100% high school dropout rate, crime, health problems, and other adjuncts of persistent poverty. Several years ago, through John Marcellino's leadership and substantial community support, this neighborhood acquired—as a mortgage holder—a small rowhouse which it called the Community Survival Center. The Center is the location for a food coop; an alternative high school, where students who have dropped out of regular school can prepare for their high school equivalency degree; community meetings of various kinds; and liaisons with other groups they see as allies and as sharing the same conditions of life: residents of poor black urban neighborhoods, prisoners in Baltimore jails, and Native Americans in Baltimore or from other areas.

The group of high school students studying at the Center had just watched a videotape about human biology called "The Incredible Human Machine." John (as they call him) and the kids (as he calls them) were very excited about the video and full of talk about it. So, building on that interest, we arranged to bring another biology video, called "The Miracle of Life," to the Center. The class agreed that we would watch the video together, and then have a discussion, which we could tape record.

The video we took is made by Lennart Nilsson, one of the foremost purveyors of cell electron micrographs into popular media. It contains all the imagery I discussed a moment ago, the quest of the sperm for the egg, the thrust and penetration of the sperm, the hostile environment of the vagina which the sperm has to overcome, the passivity of the egg and the activity of the sperm, and so on. The film starts with a human couple in a swimming pool, and then moves inside the body. For 50 minutes,

only the activities of cells and internal organs are shown, in technicolor fiberoptic photography, in real-time movement, and, for cells, in huge magnification. We see the egg
released from the ovary and drifting down the fallopian tubes; we see sperm being
produced in the testis, traveling down the various male ducts, being ejaculated inside
the vagina. We then see the sperm struggling to travel up the vagina, through the cervix,
to reach the goal—the egg. We see successful fertilization, implantation, and the growth
of the fertilized egg in great detail into an embryo, through all the stages of pregnancy.
Finally, in a shocking shift of perspective, in the last 5 minutes of the film we see a
view of a woman in labor, from the perspective of the foot of her bed. She is undraped
and unshaved, her husband at her shoulder. She pushes strongly, and the baby's head
emerges, as often happens, purple, wet, slightly bloody, and covered with mucus and
white vernix. The mother pushes a couple more times and the baby slides out altogether.

What I want to focus on is the use John and the students made of this film,
remembering both my initial questions about the possibilities of envisioning other
worlds, and my worries about the ideological effects of biological images. At first I
thought my worries were entirely justified. During the movie John and the kids seemed
entranced with the imagery of cells. There were innumerable exclamations of wonder
and awe at this cell life. In contrast, the scene of the mother delivering her baby was
met with strongly expressed teenage revulsion, mock vomiting, exclamations of "Gross!,"
and shrieks of disgust and dismay.

But this was before the discussion following the film. In the discussion, John and
the students managed to analyze the implicit metaphors in the film, as well or better
than any ethnographer, and then lead the rest of the class to see their implications. First
John focused on the diversion in the film from the human environment to the environment of cells.

"Does it . . . change the way you might look at yourself or at other people?"

(the kids)—It kind of makes me feel bad for drinking and everything 'cause you
see all the good things and like the miracles that's going on inside your body: and it
kind of makes you feel bad for like messing it up when you drink, you know, all that
stuff.

(John) "That's what I was wondering, too . . . the only part that they tied in like
life to that, or like *the life we live* to that, is when they were talking about the testicles
in the man and heat, they talked about clothes, the environment and all that."

(the kids)—Make sure you don't wear tight jeans.—It *was* distorted.

(John) "Well I wish they could show . . . the woman: and all the stuff that a
woman goes through; they only showed, you know, how it affected the sperm. And you
know, like you say, if you drink here, or if, you, or like . . ."

(the kids)—drugs, drugs affect the baby.

(John) "You know, maybe, like cleaning out the house, all the poisons that you
have, you know, and when you clean your house and a woman breathes that in, how
does that affect it and that kind of stuff."

The film focuses on boundaries within the body; John focuses on boundaries
between the person and "the life we live." He continuously encourages the students to
state where they can exercise agency.

Then the group takes on directly the implications of seeing embryos in the round,
alive and moving at every stage of development.

(John) "How many people thought about abortion?"

(female student)—I did, cause I mean I never realized that the baby . . . has hands
and even other things at that time, at 8 weeks. And that kind of makes me feel bad, I
mean, but I guess it's somebody's own personal decision to make, but I personally don't

believe in it, especially now, I feel more stronger about it. John acknowledges her feelings but denies the film necessarily leads to this conclusion: (John) "But you felt that way before you watched this."

After some minutes of discussion, she agrees with him; She has her opinion but she had reached it independently of the film.

Next they tackle the metaphorical depiction of female—male relations in the guise of egg-sperm relations: During the movie itself, when the narrator described the hostile environment of the vagina, and showed how the woman's immune system tries to attack the sperm in the vagina, John blurted out "Just like our social studies!" Now, following up, he asks the class,

"Did it raise any questions for you, watching it?"

(the kids)—I never really knew they fought each other.—It was like revolutionary war.

"What made you think it was like a war?"

—Cause it said it in the movie, they started fighting . . . when the man's semen, the cells and everything, they went into the woman, the acids and stuff was killing it off and they all had to stick together so it wouldn't kill them.

(John) "But it really made it seem like you're invading. I mean didn't it give you that impression? I mean you're watching and it goes into the hostile environment, like very aggresssive, you know . . . like an invasion and you look at it and you go, damn, you know that's pretty serious. Because it isn't the way you think about . . . when you think about a baby you don't think about invasion, or it coming out of an invasion, you think about it coming together. At least that's the way I always thought about it."

(the kids)—Yeah you do, the boy and the girl meeting . . . —No, it seemed like the girl's egg was trying to hide from it or something . . .

(John) "Yeah, it was trying to hide. It had all these defense mechanisms it said, the girl's got one egg and the guy's got, you know, three million sperm going after it. You know attacking it, and she has all these defenses and it . . . really made it seem like the conception or the coming together was a hostile act but maybe a good thing comes out of it. It sure made it seem like they weren't friends."

John and the group see these metaphors, jolt them into consciousness and so rob them of their power to naturalize social conventions.

Later I ask John how it would have been to see the movie without sound.

"If you look at that *without* the voice, like if we watched it the first time without a voice or something and then the second time *with,* I think you'd probably tell a different story, than looking at it like an invading army . . . it seemed like there was this battalion, like T.V. or something, you know. A mission, like . . . here's this army and we're going after it and all this stuff, who's going to get through, who's going to catch the one, you know. But I think it would be different if you watched it without the sound."

In Foucault's (1980) analysis, resistance is usually held within the boundary of power. This is partly because he stresses how techniques of power such as the gaze are taken on by the subject: "a gaze which each individual under its weight will end by interiorizing to the point that he is his own overseer, each individual thus exercising this surveillance over, and against, himself" (p. 155). Such resistance as there is is like the resistance of copper wire to an electric current flowing through it, sometimes higher, sometimes lower, but always enabling the current to flow along.

Foucault has a point: the production and dissemination of these images has us thinking about the life of cells inside us, whether we will or no. But if we can, as Marx thought, erect a structure in imagination before we erect it in reality, we can erect an imaginary structure around something like this film and frame it differently, jarring it into another significance. This process amounts to redefining what counts as political, moving "science education" from the "exposition of natural facts" to revealing it as the imposition of a particular view of the world.

In *Outline of a Theory of Practice* Bourdieu (1977) chides anthropologists for imagining that members of a culture who have "practical mastery" of daily life operate as the ethnographer has to, by means of maps and rules.

> "Culture" is sometimes described as a *map;* it is the analogy which occurs to an outsider who has to find his way around in a foreign landscape and who compensates for his lack of practical mastery, the prerogative of the native, by the use of a model of all possible routes. (p. 2)

But although introducing this assumption into our description of a culture's daily life would be "pernicious," it would be equally pernicious to *miss* places, especially in stratified societies, where people deliberately introduce this kind of abstraction. Bourdieu describes the ethnographer this way:

> In taking up a point of view on the action, withdrawing from it in order to observe it from above and from a distance, he constitutes practical activity as an *object of observation and analysis, a representation.* (p. 2)

But what happened at the Community Survival Center, I would argue, is that the group viewed a particular example of scientific discourse about the body from a distance, constituted it as an object of observation, drew a map to guide a way relatively unharmed through it. In a sense they are and see themselves as "outsiders who have to find their way around a foreign landscape," the landscape of the scientific body.

"The same institutions that legitimate the political economic domination of one class or gender simultaneously and contradictorily create the space for the expression of opposing discourses" (Gal, 1989 p. 360). In the case I have discussed, such a space was created first by the mass and variety of the materials that are produced for the dissemination of scientific information, materials that can give people a language they can use to talk *about* scientific images, even as they disseminate them. It was created secondly by the community's ownership of a space set apart from state schools and dedicated to enabling collective organization for the survival of threatened communities, in which such talk could take place.

There is a danger that I have created working-class heroes in the form of John and his community, heroes invested with a liberal humanist subjectivity and agency, consciousness, reason, and freedom (O'Hanlon, 1988). I might be trying to invest these heroes with the guts to stand up in a kind of virile strength against the forces which make my coffee-table authors, writing about the end of everything, knuckle under, thus creating these heroes in the image of what is lacking in a part of the world close to me. As a political role for ethnography this would probably be better than silence in the face of intellectual publications that foster a sense of inevitability in the face of the forces of global capitalism.

In conclusion, the incident I have discussed shows how scientific knowledge of the body, its dissemination enabled by new technologies, comes into contact with diverse interests and sites of resistance which "fracture and constrain it even as it exerts its conforming power" (O'Hanlon, 1988 p. 223). With Rosalind O'Hanlon, we can take issue with the "Swiss cheese" theory of hegemony which assumes that resistance can only crawl through the holes left by the incomplete imposition of hegemony. Instead we can argue that "hegemony does not spring fully-formed into being to be followed by a resistance which must always operate within its pre-given confines" (p. 223). By tracing the markings of the processes by which resistance is built into the construction of the hegemonic, in places like the Community Survival Center, we can see that there are many coexisting and contending knowledges of the body.

NOTES

1. The textbooks I consulted for this paper are the main ones used in classes for undergraduate premedical students or medical students, or held on liberary reserve for these classes, over the past few years at The Johns Hopkins University. Although this does not represent a complete survey of all existing textbooks, it does include all of the most widely used and highly regarded texts at universities like Johns Hopkins.

2. Mary Ellman (1968, pp. 74–8) characterizes the feminine stereotype of formlessness.

3. For elaboration of these points, see Martin (1987).

4. All biology texts quoted above.

5. For a literary version of some of these themes, see Barth (1968).

6. For a description of this research and references to relevant publications, see Martin (1991).

7. For another version of this story see Leary (1990).

8. In these remarks I have been greatly helped by conversations with Barbara Duden.

9. Court-ordered restrictions on a pregnant woman's activities to protect her fetus, refusal of abortion, fetal surgery, and amniocentesis, are all various facets of this process (Arditti, Klein, and Minden [1984]; Goodman [1987]; Lewin [1987]; Irwin and Jordan [1987].

10. Evelyn Fox Keller (1987) discusses how emphasis on individualism operates in biology to hold attention on genetic structures.

11. To cite only one recently patented method, a man's sperm can be screened and then "washed" to remove all those sperm containing a gene complex encoding the human leukocyte antigens (HLA), which increase the susceptibility of the individual to certain diseases. This technique obviously profoundly affects and fragments the act of sexual intercourse for both men and women, replacing it with masturbation followed by chemical operations on the sperm and then artificial insemination (Bryant, 1987).

DISCUSSION: EMILY MARTIN

JULIAN HALLIDAY: Speaking of the attribution of subjectivity to a collection of cells reminded me of an image I've seen from the Victorian era, from right after the invention of the microscope. It's an image of a tiny sort of astronaut-like homunculus crouched at the top of a rocket in the shape of a sperm. I don't recall ever seeing an ovum represented in that way.

MARTIN: Well, going back even further in history there were seventeenth-century images of complete humans *in* sperm. The view of reproduction was that man's sperm contributed all the human substance to the developing baby and the woman's body was a kind of incubator. And there are pictures from Leeuwenhoek and others of homunculi, little creatures in the sperm. They'd look through microscopes, see complete creatures in the sperm and then draw pictures of these. I haven't found anything quite like that in contemporary biology, fortunately or unfortunately. Current biology focuses on the male characteristics of sperm, but does not make the claim that the sperm contain everything human.

QUESTION: Do you ever feel that you have to leave academia to accomplish your goals?

MARTIN: It's a problem I struggle with all the time. I could speak most easily about the research that I did over the last few years, that preceded what I talked about today, and preceded the work that I'm doing in connection with HIV infection. That research was about women's bodies as they're seen medically and how women themselves, women of different class, ethnic, racial identities, speak about events like menstruation, menopause, and so on. What that resulted in was a book written in a pretty angry tone, which was meant to speak both to my academic colleagues and to people who worked at other jobs all day and came home exhausted. I can't say that it always managed that, but now and then I hear about cases where it did: someone stopped me in the lobby this morning before the first session and said she'd given her copy of my book to a nurse, and the nurse read it and carried it with her always so that if she got into an argument with a doctor she could pull it out and show him where on the page it said what she was trying to say. I can't say that happens very often. But I guess that's my only hope. The only way I can stay sane, being an academic and living with these tensions, is through the hope that by doing what I have to do to stay in this business, that is publish, I can publish things that people can read, and that will make sense to them.

We inherit a lot of clear distinctions: academy vs. the world, pure research vs. applied research, and so on. When I do the work I'm doing now those distinctions don't hold up at all. I have a lot of trouble telling which is my academic work and which is not. Clearly there are some things that I do that aren't really academic work in the usual sense. I work as a volunteer here and there, I teach courses in the Community Center, and so on. Is that academic work or not? At the moment I'm doing it I am a volunteer. There aren't any two ways about it. But I'm also thinking about what's happening and eventually, sometime later, I might write something about it. The categories are misleading. I haven't yet got to a point where I can't stand my position, and I haven't quit academics, but I do think about it, because the tension between wanting to change the world somehow politically and standing back and talking about it, writing about it, which sometimes feels fruitless, and futile, is intense. I'm still managing to hold together a position that's satisfactory enough to me, one by doing research in this country, two by doing research on problems that I know have some social relevance, three by trying to write things I hope are accessible with publishers who won't price things unreachably high, and so on. There are niches within academia I think that move towards accommodation with these kinds of problems. There are a lot of anthropologists now trying to do work in these kinds of contexts, and when we get together we talk about how the old categories are just not up to what's happening. At the national anthropology meetings last year, I spoke with a colleague who's doing research on psychiatric walk-in clinics. The psychiatrist who was head of the clinic that she had done a year's research in had decided to go into anthropology and he was at the meetings, and he listened to her talk. There's another dimension of how the researcher and the "object of research" become in some cases part of the same institutional setting, part of the same body of talk. So, I think we're going to have to rethink a lot of things.

PAULA TREICHLER: I wonder if you could comment on the construction of medical images and the way that they construct particular kinds of realities, perhaps in terms of viruses, or Lennart Nilsson's ubiquitous photographs of the fetus.
MARTIN: Well, I can say something about the imagery problem, though I feel pretty tentative about it. One thing that happens in my research is that people talk about their immune systems. We ask, "what is an immune system, what is it like, what does it do," and so on. One interesting thing is that people find these to be well-formed questions. That is to say we have immune systems now. I don't think we had them very long ago, but now we certainly do. I can mention some of the things that come through these conversations about imagery and photographs of the sort that Nilsson produces. There

is a sense of loss of location in space. The question—where am I? —comes through very often. One thing we do is show people a micrograph of a macrophage eating an oil droplet in a lung or something like that. We tell them what it is and say, "What do you make of that? Have you ever seen anything like that before?" The great majority of people, say, "it looks like the moon!" or "outer space" or "space sharks" or "star wars" or "star trek" or something like that. They go on to express a sense of confusion about perspective. That's inside me, but it's outer space, in other words, it's something colossally huge but inside me. So where am I? People also react this way to some postmodern architectural forms. So one way that you could approach these images is to look at them as an example of architectural forms that are playing with a lot of the old sureties about perspective in space and also about placement in time.

ADAM LEIBOWITZ: How is AIDS presented, what symbolism is presented, to the kids growing up in the inner city of Baltimore right now and do you think it really gives them a handle on what really is going on?

MARTIN: There's no single answer for the whole city of Baltimore. I can answer in patches, maybe. The community survival center I described is concerned about what's called AIDS education. Their view of what's happened to their community is simple. It is that, say, six or seven years ago, when it became apparent to them what the dimensions of the epidemic were, they felt the community would be gone within five years. The fact that the community isn't gone, it's still there, it has survived, places them in a certain sort of position with respect to AIDS education. In other words they're quite skeptical about the claims of scientists. In their view, if the scientists had been right they would all be dead, or close to it. They're not, so they don't know why not. One has in hand brochures, handouts, booklets, things that are produced that don't always fit the particular situation of the people who want to know something. It's partly a problem of generalities. You have to write something down, and under limited material conditions you can only produce so many brochures, and often the information in them isn't sufficiently differentiated to meet up with many particular needs.

LEIBOWITZ: Did the kids think of the film in terms of, "Oh, no, here's another Star Wars invasion coming after us"? I mean that's basically what I was asking.

MARTIN: I can't answer the question now, but I might be able to in about a week or so. There's another one of these science education type films called "The Fighting Edge" which is more or less the equivalent of "The Miracle of Life" in style, in tone, in the level that it's pitched at, and the use of photography of a similar sort, and it's about the immune system. In this film the war within is carried out to the nth degree; the battleship and battle imagery is very much there. The group that I talked about has asked for a series of films. I asked them what they would like to see and they said they wanted to see one on the brain, one on the lungs (they want to see the effects of breathing the air on the lungs), and then I said how about one on the immune system and they said "fine." So, I'm planning to show them this film as a part of the regular course that they have and we'll see what they have to say about the immune system.

I can tell you one other thing. This guy John I talked about was looking at some micrographs of cells in which they're depicted as warriors in the battlefield of the body killing off the foreign "other." While this was going on, a person walked in the room, just a person from the community (in fact he had just got out of jail and he was coming around to see if he could find work), and John shoved these pictures at him and said, "Look at this! What's this?" And this innocent bystander, this guy who just walked in off the street, said he didn't know, and John used him really as a kind of model, as a person who just happened to be there, to show the other people in the room and me, that this material about cells was completely irrelevant to life, that was his point. And he kept pushing this poor guy who walked in to the point where he would have to say, "I don't know, I don't know!" But the point of the little drama was, it doesn't make any difference what these cells are doing, it's not what we want to know. So, it's an ongoing story. I can't say more than that right now.

JAN ZITA GROVER: When you were talking about the person who had just walked in off the street and couldn't make anything of this, it suddenly hit me that the formalism of the body is much like studying literature when I was going through school. Literature was about the formal relationships between things inside poems and stories. It left out all that is most significant about how we come to determine these meanings anyway, because it has nothing to do with where we're situated in our own lives. Showing those kinds of photomicrographs ignores the particular community, whether actual or one that we might constitute. It's just the same kind of deal.

QUESTION: It occurs to me that maybe there are representations of the egg and the sperm that can expose the absurdity of the anti-choice argument when taken to its logical extreme. I am thinking in particular of the scene in Monty Python's *The Meaning of Life,* when a Roman Catholic family, millions of kids all over the place, is singing, "Every sperm is sacred, every sperm is great, if a sperm is wasted, God gets quite irate." Have you seen any other such representations?

MARTIN: I don't know of any others, they may be out there. I actually oversimplified the situation in this talk because in fact scientific research on the sperm has just recently, in the last eighteen months or so, overturned the textbook view of the sperm on its quest, with lots of motility and directed action and so on, and the egg as only a passive thing. The new research has found that the egg is actually very active and does a whole lot of things and in fact captures the sperm. So I've been following the scientific research in one lab, and reading stuff from two other labs. My question was what will happen to the imagery? Well, what happened is that the egg has become (and I'm talking about scientific papers) an aggressive kind of vagina dentata, a predator. Spider images are used. She's like a horrible fearsome creature in the middle of a sticky web just lying there in a lair waiting for these poor hapless sperm to float by. And when one happens to bump up against her, Bang! she gets him. I thought that was very interesting because one big assumption is what will happen as scientific research proceeds and finds out more "truth" about nature, maybe these old stereotypes will disappear. Well, they don't disappear. In this case the relationship of the terms dominant-subordinate is reversed, but the female term is still seen very negatively. Then the corollary to that is what will happen to popular representations in books like *The Facts of Life*? I found one, by David Bodannis, called *The Body Book.* Anybody who sees this book on the shelf just has to turn to his section on the sperm and the egg. He's read all this recent scientific research and he's incorporated it into his popular accounts of the body. This egg, who remember has just now gotten her activity from science, is revealed as a homely girl with cold cream all over her face, her hair's still in rollers, waiting on the edge of the junior high school dance floor, ugly and malformed with not a single attractive thing about her. Meanwhile the sperm come up through the vagina, as if they were boys making their move on the junior high dance floor, and so on. I won't go on with it, it's a never-ending story.

DON HEDRICK: You suggested that the attribution of personhood to these elements of the body is essentially negative. But could there be cases in which the mystification might actually serve positive functions? It seems to be that there is a kind of residual scientism in everything that you're saying. A culmination is Bodywars, the most popular ride at EPCOT. In it, you're injected into the body and then something goes wrong and you're attacked by white blood cells and so on. At that moment the scientific and medical community which brought you there suddenly becomes irrelevant and other people have to take over.

MARTIN: I haven't been on the EPCOT Center ride yet, but I'm planning to go at the first possible opportunity. I don't know about the EPCOT Center ride but people do creative things with this imagery. It doesn't come with directions on how it's going to be used. And even with HIV, the immune system, and so on people do very creative things. One example is a man who has worked hard in his working-class community for better housing, and better health care and so on. He's a retired sea captain. He also read the magazine *Discover;* he had stacks of it in his house and articles about HIV and AIDS marked with their pages turned down. He gave us some of these to take home and read. Well, he had developed his own theory about HIV. Which was, everybody has HIV, *everyone,* but some people manifest it, and others don't. He meant this to be a kind of progressive view of the body, that if we all have it then it can't be used to discriminate against some of us and it can't be used to deny health care, housing, schooling, and so on to some of us. That's just one example, but people are very creative with these things. The trouble is there is no link between particular instances of creativity and the formal institutionalized books, articles, educational materials, and representations that find their way into schoolrooms and classrooms and on posters and so on. The problem is, how do we get these isolated instances into a more public format?

24

"1968": Periodizing Politics and Identity

Kobena Mercer

Identity has become a keyword in contemporary politics. Like any other keyword, it bears not one unitary meaning but a range of competing definitions and uses as different actors invest different meanings in one and the same sign. So, even if we are not sure about what "identity" really is, we can say that it acts as an essentially contested concept (see Gallie, 1963).[1] In this sense, whatever it is, identity becomes an issue when it is in crisis.

In political terms, identities are in crisis because traditional structures of membership and belonging inscribed in relations of class, party, and nation-state have been called into question. After more than ten years of Thatcherism, the political identity of the left in Britain has been thrown into crisis by the radical transformations associated with the New Right. Indeed, as a metaphor for the opposition between progressive and reactionary forces, the figurative meaning of the left/right dichotomy has been totally reversed: over the past decade the right has faced the future as an agent of radical historical change, while the left—and what used to be called the New Left—has experienced a crisis of agency that has left it disaggregated and fragmented: fading away into the past, like a forgotten memory of something that happened a long time ago. The vocabulary of left, right, and center is no longer adequate to the terrain of post-consensus politics.

In intellectual terms, the prevailing name for this predicament has been "post-modernism." Just as the traditional assumptions and attitudes of the postwar left have been thrown into question, a whole generation of postwar intellectuals have experienced an identity crisis as philosophies of Marxism and modernism have begun to lose their oppositional or adversarial aura. The loss of faith in the idea of a cultural avant-garde parallels the crisis of credibility in political notions of the vanguard party. What results is a mood of mourning and melancholia, or else an attitude of cynical indifference that seeks a disavowal of the past, as the predominant voices in postmodern criticism have emphasized an accent of narcissistic pathos by which the loss of authority and identity on the part of a tiny minority of privileged intellectuals is generalized and universalized as something that everybody is supposedly worried about.

Values and beliefs that were once held to be universal and transcendental have indeed been relativized and historicized; but far from being the end of the world, this predicament has brought a whole range of experiences and identities into view for the first time.

The relativization of the oppositional aura of Marxism and modernism actually enables us to appreciate the diversity of social and political agency among actors whose antagonistic practices have also contributed to the sense of fragmentation and plurality that is said to characterize the postmodern condition. Over the past decade, developments in black politics, in lesbian and gay communities, among women and numerous feminist movements, and across a range of struggles around social justice, nuclear power, and ecology have pluralized the domain of political antagonism. There is no satisfactory common noun that designates what these so-called "new social movements" represent and it's my impression that "identity" is currently invoked as a way of acknowledging the transformations in public and private life associated with the historical presence of new social actors.[2]

But, like the New Left or the New Right, the new social movements are not so "new" anymore: which is to say that, at the level of theory, it is no longer possible to map the terrain in terms of simple binary oppositions. It is here that we encounter the impoverished condition of cultural studies in that its ability to theorize questions of identity and difference is limited by the all-too-familiar "race, class, gender" mantra, which is really only a weak version of liberal multiculturalism. Insofar as contemporary enthusiasm for "identity" replays previous debates on what used to be called "consciousness" in the 1960s or "subjectivity" in the 1970s, the challenge is to go beyond the atomistic and essentialist logic of "identity politics" in which differences are dealt with only one-at-a-time and which therefore ignores the conflicts and contradictions that arise in the relations *within* and *between* the various movements, agents, and actors in contemporary forms of democratic antagonism.

In this sense, the challenge of radical pluralism has a double sense of urgency. As Dick Hebdige (1987a) has shown, one way of clarifying what is at stake in postmodernism is to point out that the prefix "post" simply means the noun it predicates is perceived as "past."[3] The cultural forms of postmodernism problematize perceptions of the past by creating an ironic sense of distance between "then" and "now." Through the pervasive mode retro/nostalgia/recycling aesthetic, the sixties and seventies are effectively historicized and periodized in much the same way as historians treat the twenties or forties. Following this path, Lawrence Grossberg (1988a) has argued that popular memory is a key site of postmodern politics, as popular consent for the policies and program of the New Right is not imposed from above, but rather draws from below on the mood of disillusionment and disenchantment with the utopian ideals of the 1960s.[4] The ideological onslaught against the myth of the "swinging sixties" has been a key theme of neo-liberal hegemony both in Britain and the United States: neo-conservatism hegemonizes our ability to imagine the future by identifying its adversaries with the past. The selective erasure of the recent past serves to disarticulate not only the postwar vocabulary of social democracy, but the rhetorical vocabularies of the various "liberation" movements within the New Left and the new social movements that once defined themselves in opposition to it.

The erasure of the recent past plays an important role in clearing the ground for the reconstruction of collective identities once grounded in systemic relations of class, party, and nation-state. Thus, in Britain, we have seen the neo–conservative remythification of the imperial past as Victorian values and Raj nostalgia movies, like Royal Weddings and the Falklands war, invoke a scenario of "regressive modernization" in which the nation and its people are invited to travel back to the future through the revival and recycling of images from the lost age of Empire—"it's great to be Great again," as the 1987 Tory election manifesto put it.[5] In this version of the past, entirely fabricated to answer the crises of national identity in the present, sources of democratic antagonism and opposition within the postwar period are written out of the account, as it is precisely the denial of difference that unifies "Little England" and the miserable combination of racism, nationalism, and populism that underpins its dominant versions of who does and who does not belong.

What makes matters worse is the legitimation provided by ex-leftist intellectuals eager to repudiate the oppositional fantasies of the past (Peter Fuller would be a good example), or more importantly, the inability of the left to produce a more pluralistic account of the past which recognizes the diversity of movements and actors implicated in the democratic revolutions of the 1960s. In this more general situation, what is in danger of disappearing is the desire for a dialogue about the common ground that used to articulate shared interests across the New Left and the new social actors.

Considering the recent historiography produced in Europe and the United States as part of the anniversary of "1968" in 1988, the predominant tone was one of nostalgia for the good old days when the good old boys could act out their heroic identities as student revolutionaries. As Michele Wallace (1989) has pointed out, the passion of remembrance invoked in most of these accounts effectively "whitewashed" the diverse range of democratic struggles around race, gender, ethnicity, and sexuality that also contributed to the moment of rupture against the consensual "center."[6] In my view, what is at stake in contemporary representations of 1968 is not just the question of who is excluded and who is included in the story, but the way in which organic connections between the New Left and the new social actors are subject to a process of selective erasure and active forgetting.

Alternatively, the challenge of radical pluralism demands a relational and dialogic response which brings us to a perspectival view of what antagonistic movements have in common, namely that *no one has a monopoly on oppositional identity.* The new social movements structured around race, gender, and sexuality are neither inherently progressive or reactionary: which is to say that just like the old social movements they are subject to what Claude Lefort (1986) describes as "the political indeterminacy of democracy." Just like everyday people, women, black people, lesbian and gay people, and people who worry about social justice, nuclear power, or ecology can be interpellated into positions on the right as much as they can be articulated into positions on the left. As antagonistic elements in ideological struggle, political identities have no necessary belonging on either side of the great divide between left and right. Even if such either/ or metaphors are inadequate, the point is that once we recognize the indeterminacy and ambivalence that inhabits the construction of every social identity—to use the vocabulary with which Ernesto Laclau and Chantal Mouffe (1985) have opened up this domain of analysis—we encounter the downside of difference, which could be called *the challenge of sameness.*

Different actors appropriate and articulate different meanings out of the same system of signs; or, to put it another way around, in Raymond Williams's (1976) vocabulary, the meaning of the keywords that signify the things that really matter—such as culture, community, justice, equality, or democracy—are never finally fixed in closed dictionary definitions, but constantly subject to antagonistic efforts of articulation as different subjects seek to hegemonize discourses which support their versions of each signified over alternative versions proposed by their adversaries and opponents. If we take the metaphor of language games seriously, i.e., literally, we recognize that, like any game with winners and losers, what matters most are the moves, strategies, and tactics by which opponents play the game.

Speaking from the specificity of postcolonial Britain, what was important about the "redefinition" of black identity that became generalized in the early 1980s was the construction of an identity made out of differences. When various peoples—of Asian, African, and Caribbean descent—interpellated themselves and each other as /black/ they invoked a collective identity predicated on political and not biological similarities. In other words, the naturalized connotations of the term /black/ were disarticulated out of the dominant codes of racial discourse, and rearticulated as signs of alliance and solidarity among dispersed groups of people sharing common historical experiences of British racism. The empowering effect of the transformed metaphor, which brought a new form of democratic subjectivity and agency into being, did not arise out of a binary reversal or a closed anti-white sensibility, but out of the inclusive character of Afro-Asian alliances which thus engendered a pluralistic sense of "imagined community."

No one has a monopoly or exclusive authorship over the signs they share in common: rather, elements from the same system of signs are constantly subject to antagonistic modes of appropriation and articulation. What was important and empowering about the redefinition of black identity in British society in the 1980s was that it showed that identities are not found but *made;* that they are not just there, waiting to be discovered in the vocabulary of Nature, but that they have to be culturally and politically *constructed* through political antagonism and cultural struggle. If this applies to "us" it also applies to those who are "not us" because, in the shared space that constitutes our common home, the dominant rearticulation of collective identities in Thatcherite Britain—with its exclusionary boundaries that have restructured the relations between state and society—is nothing if not thoroughly arbitrary and conventional, contingent and constructed in character.

The challenge of sameness entails the recognition that we share the same planet, even if we live in different worlds. We inhabit a discursive universe with a finite number of symbolic resources which can nevertheless be appropriated and articulated into a potentially infinite number of representations. Identities and differences are constructed out of a common stock of signs, and it is through the combination and substitution of these shared elements that antagonism becomes representable as such.

By taking this analytic approach, my aim is to open up an archaeological rereading of 1968 which starts from the recognition that the New Right, the New Left, and the new social movements inhabited a shared discursive universe within which the same signs produced radically different effects of meaning and value as they were subject to different modes of articulation and appropriation. As someone who was eight years old at the time I should emphasize that my aim is not so much to "articulate the past the way it really was," but to "seize hold of a memory as it flashes up at a moment of danger," in Walter Benjamin's (1973b [1940]) phrase: that is, a "memory" which I encountered, in 1976 or 1981, entirely in representations: in books, conversations, films, records, television programs (p. 257).

In this historical inquiry I will explore the privileged metaphor of race as an element of central importance to the New Left, the New Right, and the new social movements alike precisely on account of its metaphorical character as a multi-accentual signifier. The purpose of privileging representations of race in this way is not to make foundationalist claims about who was central and who was marginal to the popular-democratic revolutions of the postwar period, but to open a genealogical analysis of the contingent character of the *imaginary forms of identification* in what Laclau refers to as "the democratic imaginary" (see Laclau and Mouffe, 1985, chap. 4).

Struggles Over the Sign

I want first to contextualize the redefinition of black British identity in more depth, before mapping out the broader significance of race within the postwar democratic imaginary in Western societies.

The important point about the rearticulation of /black/was its polyvocal quality, as different connotations were inscribed within the shared semantic space of the same

signifier. The recoding of its biological signified into a political one thus vividly demonstrates Volosinov's (1973 [1929]) conception of the "social multi-accentuality of the
sign" in which

> every living sign has two faces, like Janus. Any current curse word can become a
> word of praise, any current truth must inevitably sound to many people as the greatest
> lie. This inner dialectical quality of the sign comes out fully in the open only in
> times of social crises or revolutionary changes. In the ordinary conditions of life, the
> contradiction embedded in every ideological sign cannot fully emerge because . . . an
> established dominant ideology . . . always tries, as it were, to stabilize the dialectical
> flux. (pp. 23–24)

Drawing on this model, Stuart Hall (1982) differentiates two strategies of articulation
involved in black struggles over the sign:

> Sometimes, the class struggle in language occurred between two different terms: the
> struggle, for example, to replace the term "immigrant" with the term "black." But
> often the struggle took the form of a different accenting of the same term: e.g., the
> process by which the derogatory colour "black" became the enhanced value "Black"
> (as in "Black is Beautiful"). In the latter case, the struggle was not over the term
> itself but over its connotative meanings . . . the same term . . . belonged in both the
> vocabularies of the oppressed and the oppressors. What was being struggled over was
> not the class belongingness of the term, but the inflexion it could be given, its
> connotative field of reference. (pp. 78–79)

For over four centuries in Western civilization, the sign /black/ had nothing but negative
connotations, as it was structured by the closure of an absolute symbolic division between
what was white and what was not-white. The primordial metaphor of classical racism,
in which opposite poles on the spectrum of light—black/white—stand in for and thereby
represent what Fanon called the "morphological equation" of racial superiority and
inferiority, can thus be redescribed in Laclau's (1980) terms as operating on the basis
of a logic of equivalence, A:non–A, in contrast to a logic of difference, A:B.

Throughout the modern period, the semiotic stability of this nodal system in racist
ideology has been undermined and thrown into a state of dialectical flux as a result of
the reappropriation and rearticulation of signs brought about by subaltern subjects themselves. It is precisely around the symbolic displacements of the "proper name" that we
can see the historical formation of new modes of democratic agency. In the United
States, this is seen most clearly in the recoding of the proper name—Negro, Colored,
Black, Afro-American, and more recently, African-American—each of which reinflect
the connotational value of a given vocabulary in renaming a collective subjectivity in
each historical period.

In Britain, a similar process underpins what Black Audio Film Collective called
"the war of naming the problem."[7] This metaphor describes the war-of-position that
turns on the displacement of previous ideological categories, most importantly /im-
migrant/ and /ethnic minority/, both of which articulate the postcolonial problematic
of membership and belonging inscribed in official definitions of subjecthood and citizenship in postwar Britian. During the 1950s and 60s, when race relations were constructed as a domain of social problems and state intervention, the connotations of the
term /immigrant/ lay in its ideological *othering* of citizens who had every legal and
formal right to equality. Paradoxically, it was precisely because of its de-racialized content
at the level of denotation that the connotations of /immigrant/ were saturated with
specifically "racial" connotations to designate the non-belonging of Afro-Asian citizens—

which was the political goal of the immigration and nationality legislation that has redefined constitutional definitions of who is and who is not a British citizen.

Similarly, the term /ethnic minorities/, associated with the social democracy in the sixties and seventies, connotes the black subject as a minor, an abject childlike figure necessary for the legitimation of paternalistic ideologies of assimilation and integration that underpinned the strategy of multiculturalism. A member of a "minority" is literally a minor, a subject who is *in-fans,* without a voice, debarred from access to democratic rights to representation: a subject who does not have the right-to-speak and who is therefore spoken-for by the state and its "representatives." Throughout the sixties and seventies, both of these terms were contested by the construction of a politics of Afro-Asian resistance, out of which the term /black community/ arose, itself partially out of a reappropriation of the categories of "community relations" by which the state sought to render race relations manageable and governable within the framework of social democratic consensus.

The recoding of /black/, which simply became generalized in the 1980s, did not arrive out of the blue therefore, but out of a set of determinate historical conditions in which new forms of cultural antagonism and political agency were constructed. In this sense, the range of activities brought to bear on "black representation"—and the diversification of blackness as such a key theme across the artistic practices over the last decade—can be described in bell hooks's (1989) terms as a process of finding a voice:

> As a metaphor for self-transformation . . . [the idea of finding one's voice] . . . has been especially relevant for groups of women who have previously never had a public voice, women who are speaking and writing for the first time, including many women of color. Feminist focus on finding a voice may sound clichéd at times . . . However, for women within oppressed groups . . . coming to voice is an act of resistance. Speaking becomes both a way to engage in active self-transformation and a rite of passage where one moves from being object to being subject. Only as subjects can we speak. (p. 12)

As a theory of the speaking subject, the metaphor of "coming to voice," by which the objects of racist ideologies become subjects and agents of historical change, enables us to approach the analysis of subject-formation in the broadest possible sense—in terms of democracy as a struggle over relations of representation. On this view, black struggles over access to the means of representation in the public sphere, in cultural and political institutions alike, require an analysis that is not exclusively centered on individualizing or psychologizing theories of subjectivity, but which acknowledge the contingent social and historical conditions in which new forms of collectivity and community are also brought into being as agents and subjects in the public sphere.

By adopting such a broader, anti-essentialist approach to the discursive analysis of subjectivity it becomes possible to develop Chantal Mouffe's (1988c) insight that

> the progressive character of a struggle does not depend on its place of origin . . . but rather on its link with other struggles. The longer the chain of equivalences set up between the defense of the rights of one group and those of other groups, the deeper will be the democratization process and the more difficult it will be to neutralize certain struggles or make them serve the ends of the Right. The concept of solidarity can be used to form such a chain of democratic equivalences. (p. 100)

On this view, I would argue that signifiers of race came to act as an important influence on the articulation of a radical democratic chain of equivalences in the postwar period. The concept of solidarity encoded around representations of race empowered not only black peoples but subordinate subjects within white society itself. The migration of racial signifiers suggests that it was precisely because of their metaphorical character that the signifying practice of black struggles became universalized in the tactics and strategies of new subjects and agents of democratic antagonism.

Speaking for the Subject

Cornel West (1989) offers a model for periodizing the postwar conjuncture in terms of three fundamental historical coordinates that concern, "the aftermath and legacy of the age of Europe, the precarious yet still prominent power of the United States, and the protracted struggles of Third World peoples (here and abroad)" (p. 87). Above all, the moral and political significance of the two overarching events of the modern age—the Jewish Holocaust in Nazi Germany and the use of the atom bomb in the destruction of Hiroshima and Nagasaki—can only indicate the profound importance of the changed conditions of ideological struggles around race and ethnicity in the postwar period.

I would locate in this context the historical rupture or break from a classical to a modern regime of truth with regards to the representation and signification of race. In its earlier formations, during the periods of slavery, colonialism, and imperialism, the black/white metaphor at the center of racist ideologies was characterized by its relative stability and was naturalized by the hegemony of a Eurocentric world-system. In the modern period, by contrast, its transcendental signified was de-biologized, as it were, and the fixity of the primordial racial metaphor was thrown into a state of dialectical flux. It was in this context that the metaphorical character of "race" was recognized in the human and social sciences. It was precisely because of the recognition of the meaninglessness of race that the signifier itself became the site for the making and remaking of meanings. I turn first therefore to the way in which black struggles subverted the signification of difference through strategies that operated "in and against" the same symbolic codes that had once circumscribed their subjection and oppression.

Frantz Fanon's (1980) brief essay, "West Indians and Africans," written in 1955, shows how contradictory meanings intersected across the semantic space of the same term /Negro/. "In 1939," he wrote, "no West Indian in the West Indies proclaimed himself to be a Negro," as the Caribbean subject identified with the dominant position of the European subject: "As we see, the positions were clear-cut: on the one hand, the African; on the other, the European and the West Indian. The West Indian was a black man, but the Negro was in Africa" (p. 21). After the war, however, these positions were reversed: "In 1945 [the West Indian] discovered himself to be not only black but a Negro and it was in the direction of distant Africa that he was henceforth to put out his feelers."

What brought about the change? Fanon says it was the German occupation of Martinique in which "the West Indian" saw the subordination of his French colonial masters at the hands of fellow Europeans. Insofar as this undermined the naturalized authority of the Other, and the binary system of colonial racism in which it was based, it opened the space for the dissemination of Negritude as a counter-hegemonic ideology based on an imaginary and symbolic strategy of inversion and reversal that would revalorize elements of African origin that had been previously devalorized in relation to elements of European origin. In this sense, the poetics of identity textualized by Aimé Césaire (1972 [1955]), served to formalize the oppositional logic of binary reversal that articulated the more general "strategic essentialism" of black cultural nationalism that developed within the African diaspora in the 1940s and 50s.

Here, in the context of the widening Pan-African movement, the logic of reversal and inversion associated with earlier forms of black cultural nationalism (in the Garveyite movements of the 1920s, for example) were displaced in favor of an inclusive and expansive form of "national liberation," whose discursive strategies were described by Richard Wright (1958) in his report of the Bandung Conference of 1955. Within the geopolitical metaphor of first, second, and third worlds, the anti-imperialist struggles in Africa and Asia appropriated the Western form of nation-state to unify previously disparate regional, traditional, or "tribal" loyalties and identities. In this respect, like the strategy of reversal in cultural nationalism, the mimetic reproduction of Western forms of nation-state was deeply contradictory, because although it empowered subordinate subjects in the name of national-popular sovereignty, it did so within the matrix of relations that remained within the binary system inherited from Western imperialism, now redefined in the articulated hierarchy between metropolitan center and dependent periphery.

On the other hand, however, insofar as these different struggles passed through the mediation of the West it was precisely this shared system of relations that brought about the transnational dispersal of new forms of democratic agency associated with Gandhi's role in the movement for Indian independence. Notwithstanding the specific cultural and religious traditions in which Gandhi's doctrine of non-violent protest was developed, the central point is that it not only influenced the anti-colonial movements for national liberation in Asia and Africa, but was taken up by movements at the metropolitan center that had no necessary relation to the post-imperial periphery. In the United States, non-violence was taken up by the Civil Rights movement, but in Britain it was taken up by the Campaign for Nuclear Disarment (CND) which was *not* specifically defined by its racial or ethnic character.[8]

In relation to the black Civil Rights movement of the 1950s, it was this widening of the chain of democratic equivalences—by which strategies such as non-violent protest were metaphorically transferred from one struggle to another—that underlines Mouffe's point about the progressive character of democratic struggles. In this sense, the solidarity between these different struggles is best understood not in naturalistic terms, as the spontaneous expression of aspirations to justice and equality, but in terms of the construction of a wider system of alliances and equivalences that strengthened the new forms of democratic agency. On this view, in contrast to the strategies of appropriation and rearticulation in cultural nationalism based on inversion and reversal, the progressive character of the Civil Rights movement involved a strategy for the rearticulation of black identity around the subversive logic of the demand for "equality."

Within the conditions of a developed capitalist society, the demand for "equality" can be seen as the effect of a "contradictory interpellation." Institutional forms of racism meant that black Americans could not become what they were—American citizens— because their access to democratic rights to equality was denied by racism. Race was overdetermined as a symbol of democratic antagonism because social democracy placed the values of equality and justice at the center of public life and yet denied black peoples' access to them. As historical accounts have emphasized, the equal participation of black Americans in the two world wars that were fought in Europe exacerbated mass movements for racial equality, whether in the 1920s or in the 1940s and 50s, as black subjects were interpellated as equal in one set of discourses and yet repositioned as unequal in others.

In this sense, such contradictory interpellation can be seen as a decisive factor in relation to the politics of race in postcolonial Britain. Like the equal participation of the colonies in the war, which gave further momentum to the demand for independence and self-determination, black settlers in postwar Britain were interpellated as equal citizens before the law, but in the labor market, in housing, education, and state welfare, and in politics, racism denied the possibility of such equality. The historical formation of /community/ as a site of survival and empowerment must be seen in relational terms of power and resistance and not as the spontaneous expression of an innate desire for solidarity. As C. L. R. James (1982) has commented, during the era of the "color-bar" in the forties and fifties such solidarity between, say, Africans and West Indians simply wasn't there. So, if the "black community" was not always already there but something that had to be constructed, what did people use to construct it with?

In no small measure, they used the representations encountered in the everyday forms of mass culture—newspapers, radio, cinema, television, literature, music—as it was the commodification of social relations associated with the overdevelopment of postwar capitalism that paradoxically *enabled* the transnational movement and migration of racial metaphors. Moreover, if such mediated representations were important for black subjects, who appropriated empowering identifications, they were also important for white subjects as well. I therefore want to turn to the other side of these struggles over the sign to look at how the strategies of inversion and reversal based on binary opposition, and the strategies of equivalence and ambivalence based on equality, reconstituted antagonistic identities in white society itself.

Mysteries of the Ethnic Signifier

The elements of periodization mapped out by Cornel West resonate with those offered in Andreas Huyssen's (1986a) account of the cultural development of "postmoderism," which backdates the "break" with modernity to the postwar period of the 1950s and 60s. In his description of the migration of the modernist avant-garde from Europe to the United States, Huyssen also describes the gradual displacement of the hierarchy between "high" culture and "popular" culture. It was in this context of displacement, in the literary bohemia of the "underground" and in vernacular youth subcultures of the time, that we see the appropriation and articulation of black signs as an iconic element in the cultural expression of oppositional identities within white society, one that came into the open between 1956 and 1966.

Here, the very concept of "identification" is problematized in the figure of "the White Negro," who appeared not only in the pages of *Dissent* in Norman Mailer's (1964) article of 1957 and among the beatniks and be-bop freaks, but in Elvis Presley's hips and Mick Jagger's lips and across the surface of postwar youth culture. The enigma of the White Negro raises the question: *What is it about whiteness that made them want to be black?* To the extent that the constitutive identifications of white subjectivity have not yet been construed as an object of theoretical analysis, the point of the question is simply to try and clarify the ambivalence that arises when white subjects appropriate signs from the other side of the "morphological equation."

On the one hand, there is a mode of appropriation that results in a form of *imitation,* based on a mimetic strategy of self-representation through which the white subject identifies with the de-valorized term of the black/white metaphor. In the iconic figure of the "nigger minstrel," in which white actors are blacked-up to become other than what they are, there is a complex psychic economy in the masquerade of white ethnicity. Alternatively, within high cultural traditions such as Romanticism in European art, the logic of reversal that over-valorizes an identification with racial otherness is also profoundly expressive of a dis-affiliation from dominant self-images, a kind of strategic self-othering. As Arthur Rimbaud (1965) put it in "A Season in Hell" in 1873, "I am a beast, a Negro. You are false Negroes, you maniacs, fierce, miserly. I am entering the true kingdom of the Children of Ham" (p. 202). In this sense, from noble savages to painterly primitives, the trope of the White Negro encodes an antagonistic subject-position on the part of the white subject in relation to the normative codes of his or her own society.

Thus, on the other hand, the question of political appropriations that result in forms of democratic *alliance,* entails analysis of the way white subjects dis-identify with the positions ascribed to them in racist ideologies. It may not be possible to develop such an analysis here, but it is important to note the alliances sought by the New Left, which emerged in Britain and the United States, as a political subculture and as an intellectual counterculture, precisely within this period between 1956 and 1966.

In this respect, the construction of popular-democratic alliances in the Civil Rights movement under Martin Luther King Jr's charismatic leadership (culminating in the "I Have a Dream" speech in Washington in 1963), opened onto similar transracial identifications among postwar youth implicated in collective dis-affiliation from the "American Dream" through mass protest against the war in Vietnam. In place of a chronological history, I merely want to draw out three privileged points between 1964 and 1968 in which new forms of antagonism were overdetermined by the ambivalence of the ethnic signifier.

First, the radical reconstruction of black subjectivity inscribed in the transformation of the proper name, from /Negro/ to /Black/, can be seen as an expression of widening forms of counter-hegemonic struggle in which the liberal goal of equality was displaced in favor of the radical democratic goal of freedom. Urban insurrections, religious and cultural nationalism, and student movements contributed to a situation in which the demand for legal or social equality was deepened into an existential affirmation of negated subjectivity—precisely that which was signified under erasure as simply "X" in Malcolm Little's (see 1966) symbolic renaming. At the level of the imaginary and symbolic dimension of popular-democratic antagonism, what Manning Marable describes as the "second reconstruction" must be seen also as the turning point in the subjective reconstruction of black consciousness and black identity. The process of "coming to voice" which transformed the objects of racist ideology into subjects empowered by their own sense of agency was inscribed in the dialectical flux of slogans such as Black is Beautiful and Black Power, signs that were characterized by their radically polyvocal and multiaccentual quality (see Marable, 1984).

What made /Black Power/ such a volatile metaphor was its political indeterminacy: it meant different things to different people in different discourses. It appeared in the discourse of the right, where even Richard Nixon endorsed it as a form of black enterprise, as much as the discourses of the left or the liberal center, whose enthusiasm for radical "mau-mau chic" was parodied by Tom Wolfe (1969).

The emergence of the Black Panther Party in 1966 played an important role in articulating the indeterminacy of /Black Power/ into progressive positions on the left, and as such played a pivotal role in influencing the direction of popular-democratic antagonism across both white and black society. The "revolutionary nationalism" advocated by the Black Panthers emphasized a theory of oppression answered by an identificatory link with the armed struggles and guerrilla tactics of anti-imperialist movements in the third world. This imaginary equivalence was underlined by the aura of their highly visible oppositional appearance, which differentiated the Panthers from other strands in black politics (see Newton, 1973; and Foner, 1970).

In this respect, the political positions of the Black Panthers had an empowering effect in extending the chain of radical democratic equivalences to more and more social groups precisely through their dramatic visibility in the public sphere. At the level of political discourse, it was this system of equivalences that generated women's liberation and gay liberation out of analogies with the goals, and methods, of black liberation, which were themselves based on an analogy with third world struggles for national liberation. The ten-point platform of the Black Panther Party, articulated by Huey P. Newton and Bobby Seale in 1966, formed a discursive framework through which the women's movement and the gay movement displaced the demand for reform and "equality" in favor of the wider goal of revolution and "liberation." The ten-point charter of demands of the Women's Liberation Movement (1968) and the Gay Liberation Front (1969) were based on a metaphorical transfer of the terms for the liberation of one group into the terms for the liberation of others and it was on the basis of such imagined equivalences that the connotative yield of slogans such as Black Power and Black Pride was appropriated to empower movements around gender and sexuality. Black pride acted as metonymic leverage for the expression of "gay pride" just as notions of "brotherhood" and "community" in black political discourse influenced the assertions of "global sisterhood" or "sisterhood is strength."[9]

If this form of solidarity depended on analogy, which implies an identification based on equivalence, there was also another form of identification, inscribed in the more ambiguous appropriation of black expressive culture, which culminated at one point in the Woodstock Festival in 1969. As a counter-cultural event and as a commodity spectacle, it constituted its audience as members of a separate, generationally defined, "imagined community" as the predominantly white, middle-class youth who went though they constituted a "nation within a nation"—the Woodstock Nation. On the day it was over, Jimi Hendrix performed the "Star Spangled Banner," or, rather, his sublime deconstruction of this icon of national identity gave voice to an antagonism that questioned its own conditions of representability.

Insofar as it is possible to represent the ambivalence of white identities theoretically, one might contrast the forms of identification based on imitation to those based on alliances that created new forms of political solidarity. At its liminal "far-out" degree, some of the versions of white identity produced in the counter-culture were based on an almost parodic imitation of black subjectivity, such as when the anarchist John Sinclair (1971) formed the short-lived White Panther Party in 1969 and managed a rock group which he thought would inspire the revolutionary consciousness of "lumpen" urban youth in Detroit.

On the other hand, I would like to recall Jean Genet's (1989) wild and adventurous story of being smuggled over the Canadian border by David Hilliard and other members of the Black Panther Party, in May 1968, to give a speech at Yale University in defense of Bobby Seale. Rather than act out imitative fantasies, Genet participated as an equal member of this "elective community," as he did among the fedayyin and the Palestinian freedom fighters in whose communities he lived between 1969 and 1972. What intrigues me about the way this wretched orphaned homosexual thief was adopted into these "imagined communities" is the ambivalent intermixing of eroticism in the political desire for solidarity and "community." The libidinal dimension is certainly there in Normal Mailer's White Negro who went into black culture in search of sex, speed, and psychosis; but in Genet's case it leads to a radically different subject-position which does not attempt to master or assimilate difference but which speaks from a position of equality as part of a shared struggle to decolonize inherited models of subjectivity.

As merely an other amongst others, Genet was able to recognize the way in which black struggles were remaking history: "In white America the Blacks are the characters in which history is written. They are the ink that gives the white page its meaning" (1989, p. 213). Genet adds, "[The Black Panther Party] built the black race on a white America that was splitting," and it was precisely this process of polarization that split the field of political antagonism in 1968. As Stuart Hall (1978) describes it, "It is when the great consensus of the 50s and early 60s comes apart, when the 'politics of the centre' dissolves and reveals the contradictions and social antagonisms which are gathering beneath" (p. 28).

This splitting engendered a new set of "frontier-effects" in the representation of political antagonism, most notably between "the people," unified as a counter-hegemonic bloc, against "the state."[10] In the United States, the election of Richard Nixon on a "law and order" platform consolidated the repressive response of the central state to the escalation of ungovernability. But the populist slogan of "Power to the People" was inherently ambivalent, as it did not belong exclusively to the left. In Britain, popular discontent with consensus found another form of populist expression: in the public response to the anti-immigration speeches made by Enoch Powell in April 1968. Through these speeches a marginal Conservative politician dramatized the crisis of the center by producing a form of discourse which helped polarize the multi-accentual connotations condensed around the metaphor of race.

The Reversible Connecting Factor

The historical importance of "Powellism" lies less in the story of an individual politician and more in the ideological transformations which his discourse made possible. In this sense, the discourse of Powellism had a dual significance: on the one hand, the issue of immigration provided symbolic leverage for the broader articulation of neo-liberal anti-statism, and on the other, the discursive combinations of populism and nationalism that Powell performed in speaking on immigration displaced the old biologizing language of racism, whose "morphological equation" of superiority and inferiority was associated with Nazi ideology, in favor of a culturalist vocabulary that depended on a binary system of identities and differences. In other words, Enoch Powell fully recognized that there are no such things as "races," which is to say that he contributed to the authorship of the new racism by entering into the semantic universe of liberal multiculturalism and reappropriating the concept of ethnicity into an anti-democratic discourse of right-wing populism.[11]

As Powell[12] put it in November 1968, referring to his earlier intervention:

> The reaction to that speech revealed a deep and dangerous gulf in the nation ... I do not mean between the indigenous population and the immigrants ... Nor do I mean the gulf between those who do, and those who do not, know from personal experience the impact and reality of immigration ... I mean the gulf between the overwhelming majority of people throughout the country on the one side, and on the other side, a tiny minority, with almost a monopoly hold on the channels of communication, who ... will resort to any device or extremity to blind both themselves and others. (p. 300)

The "conspiracy theory" expressed here already acknowledges the populist rupture created by the April speech; moreover, the splitting which Powell reveals is not the antagonism between whites and blacks but the antagonism between "the people" as silent majority against the media and the "establishment" which thus represent "the state." Through this bipolar division, the discourse set in motion a system of equivalences predicated on a textual strategy of binary reversal, which culminated in the "Enemies Within" speech in 1970.

This text marked a crucial turning point in the popularization of a New Right perspective in British politics. In it, Powell depicts the nation under attack from a series of enemies, thereby linking the "anarchy" of student demonstrations, the "civil war" in Northern Ireland, and the image of the "United States engulfed in fire and fighting." The signifying chain is underpinned by the central issue in the conspiracy: "The exploitation of what is called 'race' is a common factor which links the operations of the enemy on several different fronts.' "[13] It is through this equivalence that Powell's conspiracy theory posits the reversibility of racial metaphor as the liminal site of a crisis of national identity—"The public are literally made to say that black is white." In relation to immigration, the strategy of reversal proposed "repatriation" as the narrative solution to the problem of citizens who had the right of settlement: while in relation to race relations, it proposed "reverse discrimination," and the suffering of the silent (white) majorities, to undermine the consensual goal of "integration."

Insofar as the whole system turned on a coherent theory of national identity, the antagonistic logic of binary reversal was based not on genetic or essentialist notions of racial difference, but on the *cultural* construction of Little England as a domain of ethnic homogeneity, a unified and monocultural "imagined community." Enoch Powell's enunciative modalities in his rhetoric of race and nation merely reiterated what Rudyard Kipling meant when he wrote:

All the people like us are We/And every one else is They.

By drawing on such textual resources Powellism encoded a racist version of English cultural identity, not in the illegitimate language of biologizing racism, but through literary and rhetorical moves that enabled the dissemination of its discourse across the political spectrum, to the point where it became gradually instituted in commonsense and state policies.

In this sense, Enoch Powell's most revealing speeches are those made between 1961 and 1964 in which he sought to come to terms with the crisis of British national identity in the postcolonial period by de-mystifying the ideology of Empire itself. By showing that the British Empire was the product of culturally constructed "myths" invented in the 1880s, he would clear the space for the self-conscious construction of new "myths" in the 1960s. Powell's conception of myth—"The greatest task of the statesman is to offer his people good myths and save them from harmful myths; and I make no apology if Plato happens to have said just that in *The Republic*"—was grounded in a reflective theory in which he held that, "The life of nations, no less than that of men, is lived largely in the imagination."[14]

It may be difficult for cultural studies to grasp, but Enoch Powell's political practice in the de-mythification and re-mythification of English ethnicity in the 1960s was fully theorized in a relational logic that is not incompatible with that which underpins the concept of "myth" in Antonio Gramsci or Claude Levi-Strauss (1963):

> ... all history is myth. It is a pattern which men weave out of the materials of the past. The moment a fact enters history it becomes mythical, because it has been taken and fitted into its place in a set of ordered relationships which is the creation of the human mind and not otherwise present in nature.

To the extent that Powell was able to act on this theory in 1968, as the myth-prince of the New Conservatism, we could say that it was the New Right, and not the New Left nor the new social movements, that got hold of what the Situationists used to call "the reversible connecting factor." This was a term coined by Guy Debord in his theory of "detournement" or the bricolage of bits and pieces found in the streets.[15] Enoch Powell's bricolage of racism, nationalism, and populism was based on a similar textual strategy.

"The liberation of the imagination is the precondition of revolution," or so the Surrealists used to say in the 1920s. When the heroic protagonists of "Paris May '68" adopted similar slogans—Let the Imagination Seize Power—they might have known that their opponents and adversaries, the enemies of freedom and democracy, were perfectly capable of doing more or less the same thing. But, by virtue of the narcissistic conceit in this historical self-image, the left—what's left of it—still cannot bring itself to think that its enemies are any more capable than it is when dealing with the imaginary and symbolic dimensions of hegemonic politics.

To the extent that cultural studies remains within the attitudes, assumptions, and institutions created in the wake of that moment in 1968, I can't see how it will now and in the future get very far in negotiating a commitment to theory around this area of cultural and political difficulty, without letting go of some of those identifications and hanging on to some of the others.

NOTES

1. The question of identity addressed in this paper develops out of themes discussed in my Ph.D. dissertation, *Powellism: Race, Politics and Discourse,* University of London, Goldsmiths' College, 1990 and in "Welcome to the Jungle: Identity and Diversity in Postmodern Politics" (1990a).

2. Throughout this paper I have settled on Alain Touraine's term "new social movements," elaborated in Alain Touraine, *The Voice and the Eye: An Analysis of Social Movements* (1981) and Alain Touraine, *The Return of the Actor: Social Theory in Post-Industrial Society* (1988).

3. See also, Dick Hebdige, "Staking out the Posts," in (1988a), *Hiding in the Light.*

4. On the revision of the 1960s in popular culture, see John Savage, "Do You Know How to Pony? The Messianic Intensity of the Sixties" (1989).

5. On "regressive modernization" see Stuart Hall, "Gramsci and Us," in (1988b), *The Hard Road to Renewal: Thatcherism and the Crisis of the Left.*

6. Some of the recent texts at issue here include, David Caute, *The Year of the Barricades: A Journey Through 1968* (1988); Todd Gitlin, *The Sixties: Years of Hope, Days of Rage* (1989); and Sohnya Sayres, Anders Stephenson, Stanley Aronowitz, Fredric Jameson (eds), *The Sixties Without Apology* (1984). Alternatively, a wider and much more inclusive perspective is offered by George Katsiaficas, *The Imagination of the New Left: A Global Analysis of 1968* (1987).

7. From *Handsworth Songs,* directed by John Akomfrah, Black Audio Film Collective, London, 1985.

8. On CND and the British New Left, see contributions by Stuart Hall, Michael Barratt Brown, and Peter Worsley in Oxford University Socialist Discussion Group (ed.), *Out of Apathy: Voices of the New Left 30 Years On* (1989).

9. See various contributions to Peter Stansill and David Zane Mairowitz (eds.) *BAMN (By Any Means Necessary): Outlaw Manifestos and Ephemere, 1965–1970,* 1971; Robin Morgan (ed.), *Sisterhood* (1970); and Aubrey Walter (ed.), *Come Together: The Years of Gay Liberation, 1970–1973* (1980).

10. The concept of "frontier effects" initially discussed in relation to populism in Ernesto Laclau, *Politics and Ideology in Marxist Theory* (1977) is subsequently developed in Ernesto Laclau and Chantal Mouffe, *Hegemony and Socialist Strategy* (1985).

11. On Powell's role in the renewal of English nationalism and in the authorship of the new racism see Tom Nairn, "English Nationalism: The Case of Enoch Powell," in (1981) *The Break-Up of Britain: Crisis and Neo-Nationalism;* and Martin Barker, *The New Racism* (1982).

12. Enoch Powell, speech at Eastbourne, November 16, 1968, in *Freedom and Reality* (1969), p. 300.

13. Enoch Powell, speech at Northfields, June 13, 1970, in John Wood (ed.), *Enoch Powell and the 1970 Election* (1970), p. 107.

14. Enoch Powell, speech at Trinity College, Dublin, November 13, 1964, in *Freedom and Reality* (1969), p. 325.

15. The concept of the "reversible connecting factor" runs across the work of the Situationist International and is discussed by Guy Debord in "Detournement as negation and prelude" (1981); and in Greil Marcus, *Lipstick Traces: A Secret History of the Twentieth Century* (1989).

DISCUSSION: KOBENA MERCER

QUESTION: When you talked about the blurring of the distinction between left and right, or even its collapse, I thought about some direct action groups in the United States who have received some bizarre public perceptions. I'm thinking of organizations like ACT UP, PETA, and others which people in this conference might consider "politically correct," being perceived as both violent and anti-establishment. Yet, on the other hand, an organization like Randall Terry's Operation Rescue has been blockading abortion clinics and intervening in arguably violent ways against women who are seeking abortions. How do you think the collapse of the left/right distinction mediates the public's perception of what I see as groups like ACT UP and PETA, whose actions are directed against institutions and discourses, as opposed to Operation Rescue, whose actions seem directed at bodies? How do you think the breakdown of the perception of violence works in this context?

MERCER: Although I'm not familiar with all the groups you mention, such as PETA, I think it might be useful to distinguish between the way in which media representations of direct action might tend to blur the left/right distinction with regards to groups such as ACT UP or Operation Rescue, and the question of how the New Right has been able to appropriate tactics and strategies initially developed by new social movements or the New Left. In the first case, it would seem that when any political activity crosses the threshold of violence it becomes defined in media representations as an illegitimate form of protest, beyond the pale of consensus. Even so, however, I suspect that the left/right distinction has not yet totally broken down. Whereas ACT UP actions are clearly depicted as disruptive not only because they are directed against government policies but also precisely because they are enacted by "marginals," and led by gay men, and hence defined as all the more threatening and in need of containment, the activities of Operation Rescue seem to be framed more as a moral or evangelical crusade to "protect the rights of the unborn child," as they put it, and thus its somewhat dramatic methods of protest become merely the new expression of an anti-abortion discourse which has been traditionally associated with the moral agenda of the right.

On the other hand, on the question of protest strategies, I think it was precisely as a result of the success and impact of feminism during the sixties and seventies, in its assertion of women's right to choose, that the reactive agenda of the New Right took shape by invoking a countervailing set of rights on the part of the "unborn child." The important point here is not that the left/right distinction collapses, but that pro-choice and anti-abortion arguments compete with one another within a shared discourse of rights. Relatedly, I think what makes the New Right "new," or at least distinguishes it from earlier forms of political conservatism, is its ability to intervene in the language of democratic rights advocated by the left and appropriate it and recodify it in order to restrict and impose closure on the extension of democracy. In the paper, I mentioned Enoch Powell and the way in which his contribution to the "new racism" in Britain took the form of a defense of English cultural identity which he saw being threatened by the presence of "immigrants." Just as black struggles in the United States emphasized a distinct culture and identity to undermine the consensual project of assimilation and integration, aspects of the new racism have been organized by the attempt to defend "white" culture and identity in the face of its disappearance or disintegration in multiculturalism. In this sense, antagonists not only share the same language, but the same strategies—one thinks of the way in which white parents organized sit-ins and boycotts against the desegregation of public schools in Boston during the 1970s, in which a populist, racist backlash against the progressive gains of the Civil Rights movement was articulated by an appropriation of methods which originated precisely in the Civil Rights movement itself. The problem then is not the collapse of the left/right metaphor as a distinction between progressive and reactionary politics, but that the binary frontier or boundary between them is not totally closed or fixed and that it is the partial or incomplete character of any political identity that enables these appropriations to be made from either side of the oppositional divide.

QUESTION: I enjoyed your paper and found myself reconstructing in my own mind all the things that happened in the sixties. I wasn't eight years old at the time and yet I found your paper made sense of the connections and dynamics of the period. However, I sensed that what you were trying to do was conceive of history as a series of semiotic transformations that were expressed in binary oppositions leading from black/white to women/men and so on. While I think you've positioned the history of Afro-American struggle quite well, and given it a centrality that it's lacked in other accounts, I think that in the process you have over-centered it. This may have some bearing on the problems of race and identity you address *vis-à-vis* postwar history in England. But it is important to say that the black struggle in the United States in the sixties was not the only struggle, nor the only metaphor of struggle. Your paper seems to get at the question of myth at a deep level in U.S. history, but the notion that "black" is the only basis for otherness, and hence identity, is the ideology of the history of the United States, not its reality, which consists of a series of erasures and othering of many ethnic and racial identities. One thinks of the Indian question in the Americas as a whole, the Native American question, the Chicano question, and other movements that played a part in the changes brought about in the sixties. There were also many other social movements prior to the sixties—it doesn't just start with Norman Mailer or people like him. We have to see the modeling of one social movement upon another and examine their interconnections. Unfortunately, I felt you tended to obliterate or reduce some of these other concerns to this one otherness which was centered on the black struggles of the sixties alone.

MERCER: You've touched on some important questions about history and historiography, which I can respond to by clarifying two points about the aim and purpose of the paper. First, I was not trying to tell the history of the United States in its entirely, nor was I attempting to narrate everything that happened in the sixties as a whole. More modestly, I focused on the centrality of race in the articulation of new popular-democratic subject-positions during this period, mainly to highlight the historical mutability of political identities. In this way, against an essentialist conception of black identity, I wanted to demonstrate the relevance of poststructuralist theories concerning the discursive character of the construction of any political identity. It is precisely the metaphorical character of the black/white polarity, not simply as a sign of difference and identity but a sign of antagonism and oppositionality appropriated out of one discourse and rearticulated into another, that reveals the importance of language, discourse, and representation as the medium through which the material realities of "race" are lived, one way or another. I did indeed privilege such metaphorical representations of race, not to exclude or ignore the historical importance of other struggles around identity and ethnicity in American history, but as an epistemological or heuristic device with which to open up a space for thinking about the historical and material effects of imaginary and symbolic relations of identification as relations that empower or disempower people as agents of change and which are not necessarily reducible to a base/ superstructure model of explanation. Through the specificity of black struggles, I wanted to provide a grounded context for what Laclau calls the "democratic imaginary," and from there to historicize what psychoanalytic theory describes as imaginary relations of identification, in order to examine the vicissitudes of political identity and imagined community among the New Left, the New Right, and the new social movements.

For this reason, I really did mean it when I reiterated Benjamin's phrase that the point is not to articulate the past the way it really was but to "seize hold of a memory as it flashes up at a moment of danger." My aim was not so much a factual documentation of the substantive history of each and every political movement that contributed to the democratic revolutions of the sixties, but to find a way into the relational complex of the symbolic and imaginary connections in which political subjectivity is constituted, the "political unconscious" as it were in which democratic dreams and desires are figured out. This is also the domain in which different "memories" of the sixties are located in contemporary politics as an underpinning of some of our contemporary identities. If, as Stuart Hall has suggested, identities concern the way we position ourselves in the narratives of the past, my concern was to retell the story of what happened in the sixties in such a way that problematizes the mythical narrative of "1968" in the discourse of the contemporary left, and indeed in the discourse of cultural studies itself. The problem with the way that certain leftist intellectuals position themselves at the center of the mythic narrative of "Paris, May 1968" is that they construct an identity or a position that doesn't seem to recognize that this historical moment was equally important for their counterparts and adversaries on the New Right. Their heroic self-image thus inevitably entails the failure to recognize the vicissitudes of political identity and the way in which democratic antagonism can be hegemonized in favor of the right, which it has been, as much as in favor of the left.

I mentioned my age therefore only to signal a generational difference, as someone who has benefited from some of the changes brought about by the New Left and new social movements, but who also recognizes that the old myth of "1968" has very little appeal to anyone who grew up in the seventies and eighties. It probably seemed a bit arrogant on my part to propose a revisionist history which decentered some of the movements, such as the student movement, which are usually the key dramatis personae in our received narratives of "1968." Perhaps the inadvertent effect was to trample underfoot some of the memories that are a constitutive part of some of our contemporary identities. But at the same time, by placing it within quotation marks, I wanted to draw attention to my own inscription in the myth, as a beneficiary of intellectual projects, including cultural studies, which crystallized in that moment, as well as draw attention to the need to "seize hold" of a memory in danger of disappearing as a result of the revisionist narratives of the New Right. In this sense, I privileged black struggles into a central place in the democratic imaginary, not simply because of the appropriations which enabled new forms of black British identity, but because its metaphorical character brings to light the dissemination of signs across the field of democratic antagonism, and hence its role in extending the chain of equivalences to more and more areas of social life—in struggles around gender, sexuality, ethnicity—thus helping to construct a new social subject, the collective subject of new popular democratic antagonism.

In raising the issue of historiography, your question touches on a problem of writing, which is to say that when narrating events of the past, one seems to imply a linear, irreversible, causal sequence in which one thing leads to another, simply by virtue of the aorist tense. In this respect, though, I would only emphasize that there is no proper ending to the story and that it did not make any truth claims for itself as being the only story or the whole story. Rather, like an archaeology in Foucault's sense, the narration is shaped by a range of pragmatic imperatives that bear on the question of identity in contemporary politics: the paper was not an attempt to set the record straight, so much as an investigation into the genealogy of "identity" as a central problem in postmodern politics. I therefore wonder whether I didn't go far enough into the dimension of "myth"—in the sense that Gramsci defines it as the creation of a "concrete phantasy which acts upon a dispersed and shattered people to arouse and organize its collective will"—because it seems to me that what the current crisis of the left demands are precisely stories and narratives about postmodern forms of political struggle that would help to renew the struggle for a popular and democratic socialism. Insofar as those who once identified themselves as part of the New Left and the new social movements now constitute a "dispersed and shattered people," as it were, perhaps we ought to be thinking about historiographies which enable us to re-mythify socialism or create a new "myth" of socialism which would be adequate to our needs now and in the future.

TONY BENNETT: Thanks for your answer to that question, Kobena, as it clarified a lot for me. But is also caused a problem because the theoretical underpinning which you drew upon from Mouffe and Laclau would suggest something different. When you say that what you point to is a limited history of the production of imaginary subject-positions, and not the relations between that and other social processes in political society as a whole, that's fine. But for Mouffe and Laclau, that limit defines the very terrain of the social itself. So I wanted to ask you about the theoretical underpinning and why you drew upon it because it seems to me that if what you have examined are the rhetorical aspects of the production and organization of subject-positions, then you also have to say something about the limited sphere of effectivity of these rhetorical strategies. As I see it, the problem is that if you rely on Mouffe and Laclau, I don't think you can do that at all.

MERCER: That sounds a bit tendentious. Can you tell me why?

BENNETT: Because for Mouffe and Laclau the construction of imaginary positions through discursive articulations constitutes the sphere of the social *tout court.* Hence, for them, the social has no positivity independently of the construction of relational identities and subject-positions through different articulatory practices.

MERCER: Thanks. At first I wasn't sure what your question was asking for—that I should take responsibility, lock stock and barrel, for the theory of society implicit in the general claims made by Mouffe and Laclau or whether I myself was making general claims about the nature of society by not fully discussing the limits of the articulatory practices through which black identities have been reconstructed in political discourse.

With regards to the theoretical underpinning of my paper, I would say that I turned to aspects of Mouffe and Laclau's work not to set it up as yet another "master theory" or disciplinary paradigm, underneath which one inscribes one's intellectual loyalty, subservience, and subjection—after all, apart from the actual deaths of most of our master-thinkers, the good thing about postmodernism is the end of the "universal intellectual" who thought "he" had an answer for everything, and thus hopefully the end of all that moral masochism and rivalrous posturing in the intellectual culture of the left which had to do with whether or not one had the "correct" interpretation of Marx, Lenin, or Trotsky. But rather I wanted to use some of their insights to discuss certain problems in the articulatory practices of the present, problems which arise precisely when diverse social movements *do not* articulate in the name of socialism but instead produce numerous conflicts in the interstices between the fragments which have not yet been adequately theorized.

The work of Mouffe and Laclau is often organized at a rather frustrating level of generality and theoretical abstraction, but I was struck by its immediate relevance for an understanding of race and ethnicity. For example, they conceptualize Gramsci's "war of maneuver" in discursive terms as a logic of equivalence based on the binary opposition of A:non–A, which finds an immediate correlation not only in the classical, biologizing discourses of racism, based on the binary of white:not-white, but in the rhetoric of a certain contemporary bureaucratic discourse in which black people and other ethnic minorities are grouped together under the designation "non-whites." Say it loud, I'm "non-white" and proud? No, it doesn't quite work as the sign of an empowered identity because its non-substitutability with the term "black" reveals the extent to which it functions as an ascribed category in de-racialized racial discourse. On the other hand, one can see immediately how articulatory practices which have constructed "black" as an empowering sign of political identity shared among Asian, Caribbean, and African peoples in Britain, operate more along the lines of a "war of position," which Mouffe and Laclau characterize as a logic of difference, which depends not on the exclusionary either/or logic of a binary opposition but on the inclusive both/and logic of a hegemonic, or in this case counter-hegemonic, articulation. What appealed to me about the vocabulary of Mouffe and Laclau was its relevance for a discursive analysis of "race," and I suppose I wanted to bring the lofty and abstract character of their work down to earth by showing its worldly resonance in the historically specific context of the dissemination of black signs across the postmodern democratic imaginary.

With regards to your point about the limits of the effectivity of discursive and rhetorical strategies, I would reiterate that my goal was not a substantive history of everything that happened in the sixties, and for this reason the separation, in your question, between imaginary subject-positions and "other social processes in political society as a whole"—which suggests the distinction between discursive and non-discursive practices that Mouffe and Laclau dispute—is somewhat beside the point. If my aim was a totalized account of the effects of imaginary identifications in the material conditions of the society as a whole, I would have offered a sociology, rather than a genealogy, of 1968. In any case, by touching on the issues of reversibility and reappropriation in the discourse of Enoch Powell, I did at least indicate that the limitations of certain articulatory practices lie in the very principle that makes them empowering— the fact that signs have no necessary belonging in any one discourse, which is something political activists on the left and in the social movements still have difficulty recognizing.

In this respect I am less concerned to defend the general philosophical validity of Mouffe and Laclau's theory of society, than to suggest that as an attempt to address the genealogy of certain problems in and of the present, I wanted to argue that cultural studies itself does not as yet really know how imaginary relations of identification actually work in the construction of political agency and subjectivity. If we think about the rhetoric in which we ourselves attempt to recognize the plurality and diversity of actors and identities at play in contemporary politics, then it seems to me that cultural studies often colludes with the very problem of the rhetoric of "identity politics," in the pejorative sense, by simply repeating the race, class, gender mantra as if the serial acknowledgment of the various sources of identity was sufficient for an understanding of how different identities get articulated into a common project, or don't. So the problem lies more with the effective limitations of the current rhetorical strategies in which our own identities, as actors within the collective subject of democratic antagonism, are articulated.

In this sense, what I was concerned to show were the limitations of a rhetoric which seeks to guarantee or regulate a "politically correct" identity on the part of the left today. What tends to happen in the rhetoric of being ideologically "right on" and "politically correct" is the reproduction of the untheorized assumption, inherited from the mythology of 1968, that all the different fragments will somehow link up around a common agenda. This completely ignores how new social actors—women, black people, lesbian and gay people, youth—have been recruited in support of the project of the New Right, just like the old social actors whose identities were organized by discourses of class, party, and nation-state. There is also the problem of the limits of rhetorical strategy on the part of the new movements themselves, when the untheorized notion of a "hierarchy of oppressions" leads to the divisive and competitive logic of seeking to establish who is more oppressed than whom. Strangely enough, by implying a certain virtue in "victimization," such rhetoric comes full circle with the discourse of victimology so successfully orchestrated on the right by figures such as Powell who saw the long-suffering "silent majorities" as the victims of the official ideology of multiculturalism. To the extent that cultural studies remains captive to a certain self-image which neatly counterposes "us," the good guys on the New Left and among the new social movements, to "them," the bad guys on the New Right, it fails to recognize the limited effectivity of the rhetorical strategies which reproduce such disarticulatory practices.

TERESA EBERT: I was particularly interested in your attempt to retheorize race as a struggle over significations, since I have tried to do something similar in terms of gender. However, I found your perspective quite partial because when we examine the struggle over the signifier in terms of a politics of resistance, we have to look at the way that race or gender is always articulated as signifieds within a particular regime of exploitation. If this is a question of political struggle, then we have to look at the way that the dominant regime of exploitation always reappropriates reconstructions of race or gender because this is used to serve the purpose of exploitation. What we have to look for are the consequences of this recuperation for continual oppression and not just how signs are elements in the possibility of resistance. I found that this issue of the way signifiers of struggle are constantly reappropriated by the regime of oppression and exploitation was largely missing in your analysis.

MERCER: I'm not convinced or absolutely certain that it is inevitable that the discourses of social movements will always be recuperated by the right. I raised the issue of the reversibility of signs first articulated in black struggles, which were then rearticulated in the discourse of the new racism, not to suggest a teleology but to indicate how the form of resistance on the part of the dominant regime of oppression, as you call it, itself changes as a result of its reappropriation of such signs—which is why the culturalist discourse of the "new racism" differs from the biologizing precepts of the old racism, and articulates itself not around the old binary of superior/inferior but around the pairing of identity/difference, which is what democratic struggles around racial justice and equality are predicated on too.

EBERT: I'm not talking about left or right, that is a local and specific opposition. In relation to gender, which I have theorized more, the question of patriarchy entails that we cannot situate analysis only in the local and specific, but that we constantly have to try to theorize the relation of local struggles over gender or race to the broader struggle over exploitation. Patriarchy invests itself in constantly resecuring and stabilizing gender by naturalizing it as a sign which can't be localized in terms of left or right, so we have to look at that ongoing regime of oppression in terms of which power relations are articulated.

MERCER: Your point is well taken. But perhaps I can respond by saying that one of the challenges of the contemporary crisis of the social movements and of the left in general is to find a vocabulary in which to examine the interdependence between multiple elements of race, gender, class, and so on, without recourse to an either/or logic, which would play off one element against the others, without recourse to a notion of an unchanging hierarchy of oppressions, and without recourse to a base/superstructure determinism. So rather than deciding in advance what is local and what is universal, the challenge is to theorize the articulations which occur in the historically specific spaces and relations among and between diverse elements. In this respect the old left/ right metaphor still seems indispensable as a way of characterizing the reactionary or progressive direction and movement of those articulations.

What discourse theory offers is the possibility of describing such articulations precisely in terms of the construction of antagonistic subject-positions, which I tried to show by looking at the way in which the signs of black struggle were disseminated or distributed along an expanding chain of equivalence which contributed to the rupture against postwar consensus—as a result of the appropriation of such signs among the women's movement, the gay liberation movement, and in the United States, the Chicano and Native American movements. But precisely because of their polyvocal character as signs, they were also successfully appropriated by those, like Richard Nixon or Enoch Powell, who sought to limit and forestall the movement of this chain of equivalences, which they did by exploiting the reversibility and indeterminacy inherent in any multi-accentual sign. So on the issue of recuperation, rather than presume that it is an inevitable outcome of economic determinations, one has to recognize the specificity of political struggle, which like a game, does not have a predetermined outcome but nevertheless has outcomes in which one side wins and one side loses. If one thinks about the way in which, despite many gains, the new social movements and New Left have historically lost out to the New Right in the post-'68 conjuncture, discourse theory might provide access to an account of how this happened which does not either repudiate the utopian aspirations of those movements or erase a sense of agency by capitulating to the com-monsense terms for understanding the recent past that have been established by the ascendency of the New Right.

I might add that the need to think in terms of multiple determinations is made particularly acute in relation to what seems to be the "end of communism" in the Soviet Union and Eastern Europe right now. Certainly, economic crises have contributed to the policy of glasnost and perestroika, but there is also the specificity of political struggles around collective identity and imagined community which have been expressed by the resurgence of nationalism and ethnicity, with particular emphases on regional and local specificities. Although such movements have entailed reactionary tendencies, there is also the way in which the attempt to reconstitute sovereign national and ethnic identities is precisely the form in which democratic aspirations are articulated. No one can predict the outcomes of these struggles, whether in terms of the ongoing regime of exploitation and economic production or in terms of an inevitable recuperation of democratic tend-encies in favor of reactionary government. The challenge is precisely to refuse the search for ultimate answers or mono-causal explanations by taking the specificity of political antagonism into account.

STEVE FAGIN: I guess this question is situated within Kobena Mercer's talk as opposed to against it. In the beginning you talked about links that bond people as articulations which would allow for a type of movement which would be less easily recuperable. Later you talked about Genet's relation to the fedayyin in Palestinian struggles and right before that you talked about how peoples' hypocritical denial or disavowal of sexual relations between black and white somehow problematizes the political alliances they were trying to put together. Then you used the example of Genet to say that this underlined his clarity as a sexual dissident and his obsessiveness in relation to masochism. You said his inclusive awareness of differences allowed him to then form an egalitarian political front. Would you care to amplify on this issue or comment on the very complicated sexual relation between Genet and the fedayyin?

MERCER: Well, I really don't think I said as much as that, did I? More modestly, in the pairing of Mailer and Genet, I was simply offering a contrast between two subject-positions among white male identities on the part of the New Left which can be seen to be structured by a certain imaginary identification with blackness. Its purpose was not to pitch one against the other, by setting up Genet as the good guy and Mailer as the bad guy, but to raise the question of how the sexual investments that entered into their political identifications could lead to subject-positions that tended to go one way rather than another. Quite simply, whereas Mailer's "white negro" is clearly positioned in antagonism to the square society of postwar consensus, his subsequent arguments with feminists and feminism reveal the way in which a certain heterosexist masculinism, in his fantasmatic identification with the black as outsider, entailed a set of limits on how far he would extend the chain of radical democratic equivalence. In the case of Genet, on the other hand, the sexualization of difference is also problematic, as you suggest: one has the sense that, as far as a homosexual fascination with the symbols of phallic power is concerned, Genet's love for the the Black Panthers or Palestinian freedom fighters might even be equivalent to his admiration for the Nazi soldiers who occupied Paris in the 1940s. By reducing the two to exemplary figures of contradictory tendencies, I didn't mean to imply some essential difference between gay or straight sexual identities, as subtended by interracial indentifications, but to point to the complexity of the multiple determinants of the identities that formed, and gave form to, the New Left and new social movements.

In fact, on the question of race and masculinity, the question which seems to me more puzzling in relation to Genet is the political identification and desire on the part of the Black Panthers who invited him to the United States and "adopted" him as a spokesperson for Bobby Seale. Was there a sexual dynamic at play there as well? This bears on the question of recuperation in the sense that the gender politics of black liberation in the 1960s also entailed a reappropriation and revalorization of certain models of masculinity, which did not have particularly progressive consequences for black women or black gay men. Here, the more relevant contrast would be between figures such as Eldridge Cleaver and Amiri Baraka, whose rhetoric of homophobia sought to stabilize a model of black masculinity based on its opposition not only to "the man" but also to the "enemy within," and the rhetoric of Huey Newton, who sought to imagine some kind of alliance between black struggles and the struggles of lesbian and gay people. These questions are still very much with us, they are part of the present rather than the past, to the extent that we do not have a critical vocabulary for mapping the kind of complexity of imaginary identifications and dis-identifications that take place on the borderlines of differences grounded in race, gender, ethnicity, and sexuality.

LATA MANI: I wanted to say that I really enjoyed your paper and how it complicated, like the paper we heard from John Tagg and Marcos Sanchez-Tranquilino, our path through the sixties and seventies in a way that was specifically not ethnocentric. My question concerns your notion of solidarity being enabled through a chain of democratic equivalences. I was wondering how you would distinguish the outcomes of certain equivalences, or more specifically, of certain analogies which have not worked out that well. One thinks about the rhetoric of woman as the "last colony" in certain discourses of second wave feminism. Do you have a notion of specificity that would enable an understanding of the problem of these sorts of unsuccessful equivalence?

MERCER: Your question, like Tony Bennett's, is important because it points to the determinate historical conditions under which different discursive and representational strategies encounter the limits of their effectivity. Or rather, we should say, the limits of the progressive and emancipatory potential of certain strategies are thrown into relief when our adversaries articulate them to close down or redirect the chain of democratic equivalences.

In answer to your question, I can think of two specific instances in which the progressive potential of analogies has turned instead into a disaster area. In relation to feminism, as you mention, analogies between race and gender have been problematic because such notions of women as "the colonized," which Monique Wittig advocated, or the notion that "woman is the nigger of the world," to cite John Lennon, may exert a powerful influence in mobilizing a class of social actors, yet all too often end up being articulated in an either/or logic that has a divisive effect. One might say that racism and sexism share many similarities as ideologies, but to say that the oppression of women is the same as the oppression of black people is to cancel out of the equation the specific forms of oppression experienced by black women. In other words, such analogies tend to reduce and flatten out the combined and uneven articulation of relations of oppression by implying that they are simply identical, a logic which thereby inadvertently replicates analogies already established in the master codes of discourse on race and gender, such as the notion of feminity, like racial otherness, as a "dark continent."

However, the specific example I immediately thought of as a bad analogy which has arisen out of the politics of feminism concerns the rhetoric of the anti-pornography movement. Here, we have seen the emergence of a very unhappy alliance between a certain discourse of radical feminism and the anti-obscenity discourse of moral majorities on the New Right. When different actors demand the same sort of thing—censorship—for different reasons, one has an equivalence, not necessarily an identification, in which otherwise opposing elements come together around a shared objective. Moreover, if one thinks about how radical feminist anti-porn arguments have been appropriated by the right, in the legislation of the Meese Commission in the mid-1980s and in the Jesse Helms campaign played out across the Robert Mapplethorpe/NEA controversy more recently, one can see how an analogy based on a highly reductive theory of representation (which assumes that images actively cause certain harms and dangers) forms the point at which this previously "unthinkable" alliance or equivalence is generated.

The second instance of bad equivalence that comes to mind concerns race specifically. During the 1970s, with the extension of the concept of democratic rights to more areas of social life, one of the arguments of the animal rights movement, or indeed the "animal liberation" movement, was to extend the category of rights to non-human life on the grounds that animals are enslaved and exploited "just like" blacks were enslaved and exploited. The problem here is that the progressive potential of such rhetoric, which contests the limits of traditional notions of rights, depends on a reinscription of the racist assumption that black people were non-human or at best bestial in nature. In a curious way, one sees the return of this paradox in the contemporary rhetoric which depicts black men, or rather the specific ways in which black males are systematically disadvantaged as a distinct group identity within the urban underclass, as an "endangered species." While this draws attention to the way in which power relations of race, class, and gender combine to inscribe the over-representation of black men in statistics on mortality and morbidity rates, unemployment and crime, it does so at the cost of depicting black males as victims and nothing but victims. It not only cancels out the issue of agency, or the complex question of how oppressive relations are "internalized" in self-defeating and life-threatening ways, but as rhetoric implies a figurative solution which itself resembles elements of racist ideology. In relation to animals, an "endangered species" is to be protected by wildlife reservations patroled by the state: the closest human counterpart to such a solution, which the rhetoric of the "black male as endangered species" implies, is that of the Native American reservation or the apartheid system of separate homelands or "bantustans" in South Africa. Arguably, neither of these examples provides a "thinkable" solution for the oppression lived by underclass black males in societies such as the United States. Once we accept the political ambivalence of analogies, we need to recognize that the chain of democratic equivalences is open to articulations on the right as well as the left. Because this is something that cultural studies does not yet fully recognize, I think one way forward in future research lies precisely in empirical studies which speak to the issue of specificity you've raised.

QUESTION: In this discussion you have continually emphasized the limitations of cultural studies, whether as an academic discipline or as an intellectual project, and at the same time you have emphasized the need to historicize the question of identity in contemporary politics. My question concerns both of these issues, namely what do you see as the relationship between cultural studies and the politics of the university, or more specifically, the relationship between cultural studies as practised in Britain and the way it is being taken up by universities in the United States? Relatedly, what do you see as the relationship between cultural studies and the politics of multiculturalism, which has now become such an important and contentious issue in public policy?

MERCER: Yes, I agree that both issues are related. First of all, I think it is precisely the distinction between cultural studies as an intellectual project or as an academic genre that seems to be at stake in its transatlantic migration from Britain to the United States. The situation is contradictory because, on the one hand, when people talk about "British Cultural Studies" they often seem to be involved in the construction of a new mythology which implies a unitary and homogenous field of endeavor, which is certainly not the case in Britain itself. More to the point, one might say that what seems to be entailed by such mythology, as cultural studies is imported and "incorporated" into the humanities in the United States, is the construction of its institutional respectability as an academic discipline, complete with master-paradigms, master-theorists, and a canon of master-texts, which paradoxically erases the necessary and organic connections between the intellectual and the political that people like Richard Hoggart, Raymond Williams, E. P. Thompson, and Stuart Hall were involved in at the moment of its formation in the 1950s. On the other hand, though, the process of transatlantic translation seems to generate some productive contradictions and tensions that concern the internationalization or globalization of knowledge and thus open up cultural studies to questions of national specificity, cultural diversity, and so forth. In this respect, I think it's not for nothing that issues of race, ethnicity, and national identity are coming into the foreground of cultural studies right now, as they arise precisely from the reconfiguration of global and local boundaries at issue in the uncertainty of the so-called "new world order." In this sense, multiculturalism in its broadest sense, as the dilemma of living with difference, is really the decisive issue that cultural studies has to address in terms of the political project that it once represented. What I mean to suggest is that I think the way in which cultural studies theorizes multiculture may decide whether it deepens and extends the critical project that began in the fifties or whether it merely becomes just another item on the shopping list of the postmodern consumer and merely another option for business as usual in academia.

I think one of the key factors in the new degree of interest in cultural studies in the US has to do precisely with the crisis of the humanities, which has given rise to important debates about the cultural diversity of the canon and core curriculum. And this is the site around which neo-conservatives have launched various attacks on "multiculturalism." Here I think two important issues need to be borne in mind. First, that the authority and legitimacy of what is regarded as canonical in the arts and humanities has been called into question, and thrown into crisis, not just by cultural studies but by the new social movements as a whole. While the articulation of the political and the intellectual in the development of cultural studies in Britain can be seen to be organically linked to the first phase of the New Left in 1956 and its subsequent phases in 1968, parallel developments in the United States gave rise to women's studies, black studies, and ethnic studies during the 1970s. One of the dangers, it seems to me, in the mythologization of "British Cultural Studies" is that a certain kind of "import-substitution" would lead to the erasure and forgetting of the political impetus underlying the intellectual projects that black studies, women's studies, or lesbian and gay studies represents as a challenge to the exclusionary practices of the humanities. Or to put it another way, the problem is not only the familiar one of "incorporation," whereby each of these sites of intellectual practice is forced to compete within the institutional and administrative framework of the university, but the problem of maintaining some sort of dialogue between people on the inside and those on the outside of such institutions. While such dialogues are certainly in effect, if one thinks of the mediated form in which numerous artistic and cultural practices, from black British filmmaking to ACT UP's visual graphics, actively translate cultural theories into cultural politics, the pressures of institutionalization play upon certain tendencies, conflicts, and antagonisms between the various social movements, which are now played out in terms of a competitive dynamic between different "disciplines."

This brings me to the second point, which is that some of the worst aspects of the discourse of the social movements have been successfully translated into the academic world precisely in the way in which competitive relations are legitimated in terms of the rhetoric of being "politically correct." In a situation where black studies, womens studies, and cultural studies have to compete for scarce resources, such as jobs, one often sees a replication of the spectacle in which rival protagonists argue for their claims in terms of privileging one form of oppression over others, at the expense of an engagement in an analysis of their interdependency. It strikes me that such developments have been a considerable benefit to the New Right's counterattack on the diversification of the humanities, which sees multiculturalism as a "tribalization" of knowledge. However weak as a defense of monoculturalism, neo-conservative attacks nevertheless work on a kernel of truth when they point out that the moralism entailed by competing demands for "political correctness" leads to a censorious attitude of closure on debates about racism, sexism, and homophobia. The recourse to proscriptive interventions on the part of some "progressive" campuses, which forbid the expression of racist, sexist, or homophobic speech for example, does not strike me as being the most effective way of engaging with the conflicts that real diversity engenders within academia as much as in society at large. For their part, disciplines such as black studies and women's studies all too often play into this scenario because the desire to be "politically correct" constantly defers an interrogation of the downside of diversity, namely the pluralization of antagonism which it engenders.

One final point on multiculturalism concerns the possibility of a comparative reading of its inscription in official public policy in Britain and the United States. Whereas in Britain, the term emerged as part of a managerial strategy on the part of social democracy in the late 1960s in which cultural difference, or "ethnicity," was invoked as a means of fragmenting the emergence of a collective black identity, in the United States in the 1980s, against the background of neo-conservative hegemony, its connotations suggest a breakdown in the management of ethnic pluralism and draw attention to the question of possible alliances and coalitions between various groups. Its progressive potential is underlined by the way in which lesbian and gay identities are now recognized as an integral component in policies on cultural diversity. Thus on the other hand, from a British perspective, it becomes necessary to reinflect the term in order to think about the kinds of conflict which underline the fragility of the reconstruction of black identity which I discussed. In the wake of the Salman Rushdie affair, the whole issue of black identity as an identity made up of alliances among Asians and Afro-Caribbeans is definitely up for grabs. One cannot assume that the political forms of solidarity and identification will remain, because the Rushdie affair has not only brought to light key divisions within the British Muslim communities, but has thrown up the question of minority conservatism as a key issue that needs to be addressed in terms of sources of resistance to diversity and multiculturalism. Paradoxically, the political strength of fundamentalist tendencies within British Muslim communities, where the growing demand for separate Islamic schools, for instance, clearly entails the rejection of multiculturalism, was itself nurtured by the official discourse of multiculturalism, which gave certain "community leaders" an authoritative voice on the grounds that they were the authentic representatives, and interpreters, of their culture and constituency.

The emergence of prominent Afro-American conservatives during the Reagan years, such as Thomas Sowell and Glen Loury, underlines the need to examine critically the way in which the New Right has formed new kinds of alliances with certain tendencies in minority communities—an issue which, for many black intellectuals on the left, has been more or less "unthinkable" up to now, or at least an issue which has been censored out of the agenda. The downside of difference implicit in what I called "the challenge of sameness" does not imply a return to nice, cozy, consensual liberalism which assumed that underneath we're all the same: it implies a break with the social democratic version of cultural pluralism and an engagement with a radical democratic conception of diversity which begins from the recognition of the ambivalence of every antagonism and from the assumption that if identities have no necessary belonging on either side of the left/right divide then as "politically correct" progressives we are all more or less capable of forming identifications with our Other in the domain of political conservatism. The problem is that, as our Other, "they" are not out there, they are also in here, perhaps in this very room as well.

25

"On the Beach"

Meaghan Morris

This essay is different from my conference paper ("Money and Real Estate: The Limits of Cultural Studies"). That paper was about some problems that have arisen for me in studying the nexus of tourism and property speculation in Australia. Here, I look at broader debates which make it possible for such problems to arise. Whether my way of doing this also involves a shift from the "concrete" and the "social" to the "abstract" and "theoretical" (terms which I take to entail an often unrecognized degree of relativity as to their value for different academic cultures) is a problem that I shall address.

People often edit their conference papers after the event, but in this case I can't mask the signs of reconstruction. It was only after thinking about the difficulties that I had with the original paper (and the discussion which followed) that I began to be able to articulate what my argument was about. After spending several years on a study of how large-scale processes of economic restructuring can impact on the most intimate aspects of life in quite specific Australian communities, I originally had no intention of giving a paper on "speech," "writing," and "cultural difference." I now think that *is* what I was doing: perhaps a problem of enunciation (including ways of hearing as well as speaking) will unavoidably be at stake at an international gathering, if the "inter-" has any significance; perhaps our speech really is, as psychoanalysis would have it, more lucid than our intentions. Ten years ago I wrote an essay about enunciation and the historiography of white male nationality in Australia, called "Catatonia." I'm not sure that, whatever my topic, I'm not still working on that essay almost every time that I speak (Morris and Freadman 1981).

Whatever the reasons, the fact is that I experienced such resistance to addressing the topic of "Cultural Studies Now and in the Future" at a transatlantic conference in the United States that I found myself giving a paper that didn't—and couldn't—cohere. That situation has not fundamentally changed. To ask myself "why?" then becomes a practical way of addressing the topic. Not being a nationalist, I don't blame the American academic context. Not being an exponent of "global culture" either (a notion that seems to me an optimistic euphemism for the gentler forms of Northern neo-imperialism), I think that in order to talk about a "future" for my work I need to take some account of the present, and thus the *past,* of the cultural studies I actually practice in Australia (which is not the same thing as taking account of "Australian Cultural Studies").

The "future" in academic papers is in fact very often the immediate "past." It is a rhetorical fiction for wrapping up a completed piece of work, and for signifying engagement with a community of readers. This is a *polite* and civic fiction; I have to ask myself why, on this occasion, I found it harder to sustain.

One reason is that I am reluctant to see the small area of work that concerns me as having a predictable and logical relationship to the future of a discipline. This is partly a matter of placement; as a free-lance writer, I do not create practical "futures" in the form of curriculum proposals or research programs. I can envisage "a" future (in the short term) for my work, and I gain directions from reading other people. But I cannot think "the future" in a limited way as intrinsic to cultural studies.

This is a disadvantage, because my next difficulty is then the anxiety and uncertainty investing for me the very idea of the future. I start to think about the *big* future; nothing mediates between the fate of the world, and my personal concerns; this is a version of what Victor Burgin (1990) calls "paranoiac space." But then, this paranoia is not sustainable either; it is not the way things are for me in my ordinary working life.

There *are* "civic" mediations that constrain and direct my thinking, structuring what I do, and what I "look forward" to doing. But they are not *institutionally* coherent: some happen in the academy in Australia, and in different subject areas; some through the media; some through contacts in other countries, and by reading, in an erratic way, the work of many people whom I shall never meet. This situation does not lend itself easily to a *developmental* vision, not because it shatters "the subject" in space, but because it does not allow the fiction of a singular *temporality.* This fiction has been important in the past to the idea of a "project"; a group moves slowly from one "phase" to another in debate; the subject of a project can describe itself as "beyond" this argument, or that concern. This cannot happen in a mixed sort of space; something passionately important *there* is no longer, or not yet, or will never be, quite so vital *here;* in mixed space, one inhabits not just many "positions," but multiple *times.*

So what follows is a speculative rather than a programmatic paper about several problems with a future in my present, and it is a response to the conference rather than a simulacrum of what I wish I'd said.

I

On the Beach: A Bicentennial Poem
          2
               —after Juan Davila

     astonished
     trade union delegates
     watch a man behead a chicken
     in Martin Place—isn't there
     a poem about this
     & the shimmering ideal
     of just walking down the street?
                    not being religious
     we bet on how many full circles
     the headless chook will complete
     & won't this do for a formal
     model of Australia, not
              too far-fetched, not too cute?
     John Forbes, *The Stunned Mullet* (1988)

On an Australian beach on a hot summer day people doze in the sun or shoot the breakers like Hawaiian princes on pre-missionary Waikiki. The symbol is too far fetched for Australian taste. The image of Australia is of a man in an open-necked shirt solemnly enjoying an ice-cream. His kiddy is beside him.
Donald Horne, *The Lucky Country* (1964)

Some images die hard. By the mid-1960s—when it was still possible for a white social critic unself-consciously to compare postcolonial Australians to "pre-missionary" Hawaiians, then fix as the image of the nation a portrait of "a man" with child—the habit of keeping (and killing) chickens was beginning to disappear from the everyday domestic life of most less-than-princely Australians. Today, Donald Horne's "symbols" seem as remote and quaint as the cock crows that can sometimes still be heard in the middle of inner-city Sydney. Yet today, a problem of nationality can still be framed as a scene of white, male Ordinariness; still today, a subject in a state of confusion may dispassionately be described as "running round like a headless chook."

I have an interest in certain modes of persistence at work in mediated cultures (narrative, rhetorical, generic "modes," which I also take more broadly to be *practices* of change),[1] and in this paper I want to frame an account of some of my own problems and confusions about doing cultural studies by reading back and forth between two quite different texts about that historic national Ordinary.

In the process, the relations I construct between a passage of *The Lucky Country* and a poem published a quarter of a century later may be far-fetched, but not altogether forced. Both texts are *generically* marked as beach scenes (although it is important that "Martin Place" in Sydney is a downtown pedestrian mall). Both imagine "Australia" as a womanless, colorless space: "Hawaiian" for Horne in 1964 means "suntanned," and if a group of trade union delegates in 1988 might well be as mixed as a crowd on the beach, gender and race are unmarked by Forbes as they were excluded by Horne. But both texts offer little allegories of Democracy: each composes a model and then deals critically with it (Horne by correcting himself, Forbes by faking questions), and it is important that what Horne finds "too far fetched" about his own simile is not really its exoticism (still less the displacement of "Aboriginal" that "Hawaiian" effects and represses) but the romantic anachronism, *"princes."* This is the political figure that he replaces with "a man in an open-necked shirt"; this is the kind of *rhetorical* extravagance that John Forbes's poem, more sardonically, aspires to avoid. Both texts, then, are concerned with "taste," and with limits and limitations in a dominant—not marginal—popular aesthetic.

Both *The Lucky Country* and *"2—after Juan Davila"* are also involved in social *narratives* of foundation—and here I must elaborate some differences between them.

Published during the Bicentenary of the British invasion of Kamay (Botany Bay), *The Stunned Mullet & Other Poems* (Forbes, 1988) could easily be described as a "critique" of the national myths of white Australian culture. It may be more precise to think of it as a collection of puzzling little scenes—domestic, political, artistic, and economic as well as historical—connecting up in a discourse on a vast, multimedia public enterprise of narration. Monumental national histories appeared to mark the Bicentenary; media organizations funded reenactments, mini-series, documentaries galore; communities and individuals created a boom in diverse forms of family, local, regional, and ethnic history: in a way, *The Stunned Mullet* is a survival guide for living in the midst of *all that speech.*

Literally a fish knocked semi-conscious (the title poem begins "lips bruised blue/ from the impact of the shore"), "The Stunned Mullet" is a phrase alluding to a vernacular myth about speech and stupefaction. It usually occurs in the simile *"like* a stunned mullet"; an unflattering description of the appearance of someone else, or of oneself positioned as other, in a story. It means to be struck "dumb" (in every sense) by some little shock of history—to fall right out of ordinary speech. This is an experience of liminality, but a modest one: it isn't tragic, like Lyotard's *"différend,"* or heroic, like Deleuzian "stammering"; it is not a question of incommensurability between discourses, nor of using a major language in a revolutionary minor mode, but just a matter of momentarily *losing* it (and nothing of major significance is expected to follow from this; it is not a "subversive" moment, but an interruptive one). In Forbes's book, however, the mullet aspires to eloquence; the poems "form words you applaud/ because, after all, a fish is speaking."

"2—*after Juan Davila*" is from *On The Beach: A Bicentennial Poem,* a sequence of six texts in which the white male Anglo/Celtic poet succeeds in failing his national "vocation" to speak in honor of the occasion (the first line of "1" is, "Your vocation calls").[2] He works through various "models" of Australia and of a Laureate enunciative posture—taken from pop-historical images, paintings, tourist spectacles, TV shows, incidents in the street—and only in the last poem ("6") is a "blank, cut-up sense of what your vocation is going to be" glimpsed as *emergent* in the half-light of a beach pub lounge, an originary space "where you first dreamt up/ this model of the Ocean/ & watched it slide, slowly at first/ down the beach & into the surf." The cultural landscape of *On The Beach* is, like colonial history, neither womanless nor "white"; the *scene* considered by poem "2" is, and I will return to it later.

If John Forbes's text is troubled about a white male poet's public role at a festival of origins, Professor Donald Horne is comfortably regarded by many Australians as an ideal model of a "public intellectual"—and *The Lucky Country* (1964) is now being canonized by some as a founding text of cultural studies. In retrospect, it seems to present itself as such ("I came back from a trip to the Far East early in 1963 and decided that Australia was worth a book" [Horne, 1964, p. 13],[3] and while *Money Made Us* (1976) in fact gave more emphasis to what we now call cultural practices ("systems of honour, rhetoric, life-styles, cults, entertainments etc."[p. 6)], *The Lucky Country*'s success at analyzing these in a best-selling *social* critique of institutions and protocols of conduct has made it an influential work long after the society it criticized has disappeared. The phrase "the lucky country" passed into everyday language (losing the biting irony that Horne himself intended, and which "Lucky Country," a scathing song by Midnight Oil, naively later restored).

Yet I know few people (to be honest, no one) now poring over *The Lucky Country* with the same intensity that others accord to rereading Raymond Williams's *Culture and Society*. Horne's *practice* is made "canonical," rather than his theses: seeing "culture" as a field of action, he has worked as a mainstream tabloid journalist; a powerful newspaper and magazine editor; a literary autobiographer, essayist, and novelist; a historian; an academic; and, in recent years, as a prominent cultural policy-maker. Of course, Horne did not "found" the possibility of his own practice; something about Australian society made his model of action both practicable and influential, and he is not the only eminent intellectual to operate in this way. But *The Lucky Country* as a myth of origins for Cultural Studies 1990 is not an arbitrary choice; part of its interest now is that it was written as a critical document for a better *future* in which "it might be of interest to know what the huge continent was like in those early days in the nineteen sixties before it was peopled from all over Asia."

Forbes's poem and Horne's book do not have the same kind of relationship to foundation narratives (*On The Beach* is about one such narrative, *The Lucky Country* is a pretext for another), any more than they have a common posture about the terms of their own participation in Australian public life. Horne is an affirmative and canny populist (or a "middlebrow" in the special sense that Andrew Ross has given that term[4]); reading a Forbes poem is like sharing the secret thoughts of an edgy, sceptical citizen whom populist discourse addresses, and sometimes claims to represent.

At the same time, it would be a mistake to exaggerate these differences. Both writers are inventors of imaginary countries; both work in the "future perfect," in Jane Gallop's (1985) sense (see pp. 74–92). Both men are also masters of one of the dominant registers of public rhetoric in Australia, "irony"—a term which in an American context may not convey either the wide range of emotional modulations which this register is used to create, or the historical density of popular suspicion towards discourses of belief and identity that it can commonly assume—and both could plausibly be described as working within a "great tradition" of cultural criticism. So rather than resolve their differences formally as an opposition, I want to accept the tension between them as *productive*. Like the debate in cultural studies in Australia over "policy" and "aesthetics" (a model of which I shall also derive by reading Horne and Forbes), this tension in fact creates a space in which I can place my work.

It's tempting to say, *the* space. I'm well aware that the methodological refusal to choose which I've just performed also resonates for me with broader and deeper influences: I see myself as a rhetorical critic, *The Stunned Mullet* as a model text; I too idealize Donald Horne's practice, and *The Lucky Country* was one of the great revelations of my early adolescence—the "origin" (it would be easy to say) of a desire that was later to become my interest in cultural studies.

But I do mean "*a* space." I use these texts here to create what Deleuze and Guattari (1987) call a *home*. In their sense of the term, "home does not pre-exist"; it is the product of an effort "to organize a *limited space*" (p. 311, my emphasis), and the limit involved is not a figure of containment but of provisional (or "working") definition. This kind of home is always made of mixed components, and the interior space it creates is a filter or a *sieve* rather than a sealed-in consistency; it is not a place of origin, but an "aspect" of a process which it enables ("as though the circle tended on its own to open onto a future, as a function of the working forces it shelters") but does not precede—and so it is not an enclosure, but a way of going outside.

II

Why put forward *The Lucky Country* (in however cagey a manner) as a text of comparable historical importance to that of *Culture and Society* for "others"? If this is a gesture of reactive nationalism, or even just a shorthand way of insisting on the complex historical parameters of specific conditions for action, then any one of a number of institutionally honored texts might conceivably serve the same purpose—Phillips's *The Australian Tradition: Studies in a Colonial Culture* (1958), Russel Ward's *The Australian Legend* (1958), the essays of Ian Turner, or even the conservative symposium edited by Peter Coleman, *Australian Civilization* (1962). I could probably justify my choice—only Horne's text unequivocally looks forward to that ambiguous ideology of State that we now call "multiculturalism"[5]—but it is the purpose that I want to consider.

At an international conference held recently in Sydney, there was a discussion about why so many people working in quite different contexts had all begun "inventing histories" for cultural studies—often by reifying quite dispersed fields ("Birmingham," "Frankfurt," "Radical Nationalism") or by (de)sanctifying the works of various founding *fathers* ("Williams," "Gramsci," "Horne," "Innis"). Those who stressed the idea of "invention" felt that, whatever the dangers of myth-making this kind of history entailed, it was an important way in which new projects in cultural studies, and "new" subjects of history, could polemically be defined; for others, it ran the risk of reproducing the worst idealist forms of the History of Ideas, or of substituting History of Theory for empirical studies of culture, or else of performing relentlessly Oedipal disavowals of the most useful work of the past.

It was left to Dipesh Chakrabarty—a professional historian—to suggest that the real problem may be that the genre in which "histories" are being invented for cultural studies often leads people into positing a *single* origin for their practice—something which those same people would never do in any other context.[6]

Thinking about my own sporadic impulses to claim some looming historical precedent authorizing me to speak, it occurred to me that for the Eurocentered tradition of cultural studies from which I *do* speak, this genre has a name—the family romance. The family romance is a type of fantasy in which the subject "imagines that his (sic) relationship to his parents has been modified," usually for the better; for example, that he is adopted or illegitimate, and that his father was actually a prince (perhaps a "Hawaiian prince") (Laplanche and Pontalis, 1973,. pp. 160–161). In other words, the family romance is a way of "inventing history" that allows us not only to change but to *improve* upon the received and socially sanctioned versions of our beginnings.

The cultural pressure exerted by this genre (which adults rarely practice consciously but which lingers on as a symptomatic archaism) may possibly be felt in the common assumption that any history involving masculine proper names is *necessarily* obsessed with "paternity" and "filiation." In fact, you can write a history of power relations without having a thing about "ancestry." The cultural *temptation* of the family romance can certainly be read, however, in attempts to do this by installing a local hero *in the place of* the founding figures already promoted by powerful interests elsewhere; it is not uncommon to hear that Donald Horne, for example, always practiced cultural studies in "everything but name." The subsequent move to *name* the "real" (new, improved) Father is not peculiar to intellectuals inventing histories for peripheral national cultures: it is precisely how Frank Lentricchia frames much of his reading of Kenneth Burke against Paul de Man in *Criticism and Social Change,* and it is a strategy that Terry Eagleton uses regularly to redeem for England and Marxism selected aspects of poststructuralist critical theory.

Why is this temptation so tempting? In *Roman des origines et origines du roman—* an essentialist study projecting the structure of a Freudian myth on to the history of the European novel—Marthe Robert suggests that for children, the family romance is a response to "a moment of grave crisis" at the end of the idyll of infancy when social experience brings deflating intimations that other people exist: glorious plenitude gives way to unflattering comparisons, and the glow of eternity is replaced by the "murky reality of time" (M. Robert, 1972, pp. 44–50). Telling "foundling" stories is a way of coping by denying the logic of this experience; the family romance is a conservative as well as a nostalgic genre because it allows the child "to mature while refusing to progress." The discovery of sexuality then turns it into an active defense against difference: once uncertain *paternity,* rather than "parentage," becomes the object of imaginative work, a new opposition between the feminine (the child's "intimate and trivial" world) and the masculine ("distant and noble") then opens up the possibility of "romanesque" adventure.

In spite of the problems with this account (in which "the child" is really an allegory of certain aspects of imperialism), it has some resonance with the dilemmas of practicing cultural studies in an international frame, though strictly a resonance only: a discipline (if this is in fact what cultural studies has become) is not a personality. But for practitioners, some of whom remember cultural studies as a "project" on a much more intimate scale, the family-romantic genre can indeed provide a defense against the "difference" introduced by even a limited degree of internationalization—a process that not only brings to bear certain "global" market pressures, but also brings into *contact* groups who may inhabit the same nation but never ordinarily meet. "Cultural Studies Now and In The Future" was not the only conference in recent years to create a landscape of astonishment like a John Forbes poem, where bizarre non-encounters between incommensurable identities are made meaningful only by an effort to *do* something with the startling fact that they can occupy the same space.

I feel at home in a John Forbes landscape, and yet I want to ask whether there is always something wrong with a defensive response to its tensions. I find the family romance tempting at times: it *works,* transnationally, as a shorthand or metonymic way of claiming a difference to be constructed; precisely because of its currency, I can more easily envisage using it to present a critical reading of *The Lucky Country* than I could face embarking, in an American context, on a study (with every second word requiring an elaborate gloss, or leading into labyrinths of explanation where I might be the first to lose sight of the point of my beginning) of the intricate debates of Australian social criticism in the 1950s and 1960s—and the struggles for political and institutional power in which these were enmeshed. Maps of "history" differ, too: "Cultural Studies Now and In The Future" was the first occasion since about 1958 on which I heard someone other than an elderly Anglo refer to Australia with perfect simplicity as a "British" country.

Yet without some reference to those distant struggles *then*—without the bitter battles over mass non-"British" immigration that helped to double the population, without the slow dying of the White Australia Policy, without the re-emergence of demands for Aboriginal citizenship rights, without the conflict between parents with a fading allegiance to Britain or Ireland, and children born, like myself, under the constraints and cultural incentives of the American Alliance, without the class, ethnic, and religious Cold War between proponents of Rome and Moscow that tore the Labor Party apart while critics from all sides attacked the culture being created (in fibro or red brick houses each on a quarter acre block, perhaps a chookyard still down the back) by the rurally based affluence of the suburban working class—it is hard to make sense of the political context of cultural studies in an altered Australia *now.* General invocations of class-race-gender as "global" universals are not, in the end, transnationally sufficient for much more than making gestures of good will.

Then again, Graeme Turner has pointed out that there can be good reasons for defensiveness in an *economic* landscape of "internationalization." In material conditions where only one publisher (Allen & Unwin) and one journal *(Continuum)* now survive in the field in Australia, the word "international" comes to work in cultural studies as it does in the film and record industries—as a euphemism for a process of streamlining work to be "interesting" to American and European audiences (according to a commercial judgment of what those interests are). "Imperialism" is at once too strong and too vague as a name for this process; our governments gladly espouse it as an economic "export" strategy for the arts as well as research, and it is consistent with the broader drift of national policy-making in Australia as in other countries. It is also a *new* development insofar as it no longer blocks the circulation of some Australian work as "too specific" for readers elsewhere. Instead, it moves to influence what we should be producing *here.*

For those who maintain an activist view of their practice this is a troubling tendency, especially for work on gender, race, and class: after all, this is the "internationalism" that gave us Tina Turner instead of Justine Saunders as Queen of the Outback in *Mad Max Beyond Thunderdome,* and which may foster the "strategic" adoption in cultural studies of saleable rhetorics with tenuous links indeed to Australian social conditions (British assumptions about class have played this role in the past, American constructions of "identity" may do so more strongly in future). The interesting question for the future, then, is how to act in this situation without inventing a nostalgia for an unchanging, introverted (and imaginary) "national" culture.

There are two corollaries of this shift in the *realpolitik* of cultural studies. One is that the text/ethnography debate has actually intensified a drift *away* from the "concrete" values that ethnographers like to invoke; as Graeme Turner (1989) remarks, in practice "the current unfashionableness of historicized textual readings of specific instances of Australian media production has resulted in a net reduction of useful work on Australian texts, . . . practices and . . . ideological formations" (p. 7). The other is that a particular *kind* of "Theory" is privileged; working from a core of American and European references, liberally employing metonyms of wider debates ("difference," "pleasure," "subversion") that will signify the text's cross-cultural intelligibility, it may do its real work obliquely, drifting casually in and out of de-historicized "local" contexts. Other practices are then pushed for *methodological* reasons into the dead zone of the "*too* specific," or else are obliged to make a home in more cosmopolitan disciplines—History, Comparative Literature, Cinema Studies, "English."

Since these pressures on intellectual production do not evenly apply to Australian society at large, their first consequence for cultural studies is "a real danger of becoming academically entrenched but socially and politically irrelevant." It is not that the academy poses a threat to some pristine radicality, but rather that the conditions in which academics now operate will shape their work in particular, and in this case limiting, ways. These are the conditions in which a defensive response to "difference" (in fact, economic inequalities and power imbalances) can be quite reasonable, and in which a project of inventing history by creating an alternative myth of origins for cultural studies "in one country" can sometimes seem to be a locally empowering option.

However the trouble with the family romance is precisely, as Chakrabarty points out, its structural need to inscribe an emblematic *singularity*— "one" country, therefore one *origin*— as the source of its cultural authority. I have mentioned only the Anglo/ Celtic masculine possibilities so dear to nationalist thinking; it would theoretically be possible to produce "alternative" alternatives, foregrounding figures suppressed by our once dominant radical tradition but crucial to feminist, Koori, and immigrant constructions of Australian history. It is unlikely, however, that even separatist versions of such histories could effectively be written in the form of family romance (and so this is not the context to offer some examples). For only from a position of violent nostalgia for an imaginary "British" country pre-dating World War Two is it possible to ignore the plurality and mixity of origins that constitutes "Australia."

In the repertoire of canonical images of Australia there is a famous painting by Charles Meere called *Australian Beach Pattern*. It is a family scene, and while it models its images of strong, healthy, carefree Ordinary Australians in 1940 on the heroic postures of European Classicism rather than tourist dreams of a vanished Hawaii, it is also an allegory of Democracy. The value of analyzing the forms in which cultural histories have been composed was emphasized in a 1988 photograph by Anne Zahalka, which "redid" *Australian Beach Pattern* by substituting for its figures representatives of all the peoples that have long inhabited Australia (and enjoyed themselves at the beach). With this simple gesture, something usually unremarked about Meere's painting became apparent (see Dutton, 1985, pp. 84–85). His noble, athletic Australians in 1940 were not "European" gods and goddesses. They were *Aryan*.

III

One of the most genuinely "popular" forms of cultural studies in Australia is the kind of myth analysis that favors making paradigms of national cultural *topoi*. Books about national culture are often criticized for essentialism, and for nostalgic sentimentality. They are also often best-sellers, and are very widely read.

In this kind of cultural studies, "the beach" has figured often enough to earn a disclaimer in an essay prefacing a recent book in the genre by a British immigrant, Stephen Knight's *The Selling of the Australian Mind* (1990). Knight's tale of arrival and culture shock begins with two other such *topoi*, "the airport" and "the pub," but he quickly removes from his frame of future reference "those obvious things like sport, the beach, the car, the clothes, tourist sites and sounds"; his themes will be derived from his own urban middle-class life "in the business of education and literature" (pp. 1–11). His book is an alternative to the pub-beach-barbecue paradigm most recently explored by a text which Knight does not mention, *Myths of Oz* by John Fiske, Bob Hodge, and Graeme Turner (1987).

Knight's essays are delightful and persuasive. Instead of rehearsing the given features of a "lifestyle" ideology, he organizes his studies of places and practices around *problems* that are commonly discussed in the mainstream media: the "determinedly secular" ethos of Australian society; the deep refusal of patriotism that sometimes prompts governments to sponsor corrective campaigns; the politics of literacy; the greed of the 1980s; "the growing confrontation with race, history, possession and power." In this way, Knight treats critical activity as an *aspect* of the culture that he criticizes, and as a part of the everyday lives of the public whom he addresses. This allows him to overcome that anxiety of critical "position" endemic to topical myth analysis, which Barthes described in *Mythologies* (1972a) as an agonized alienation but which is now more often resolved by an act of identification between the critic and "the people."

Knight is not content, however, to exclude those things that play no part in his own experience. He dismisses sport-beach-car-clothes-tourism as, in his view, *superficial* (without "much significance in the deep-laid realities of life in this country"), and as *external*— "part of a carapace of materialism which any vertebrate structure of analysis and culture needs to crack open for the life inside." His mistrust of materialism aligns him here with past critics of Australian hedonism like Ronald Conway (*The Great Australian Stupor*, 1971; *Land of the Long Weekend*, 1978)—although he does not share their conservatism—and it leads him to ignore the constructive projects of the 1960s which, like *The Lucky Country*, sought to analyze (rather than celebrate) popular materialism as the *basis* for a new democratic model of social and political "life" (see also M. Clark, 1963). It also makes his book a polemic against *Myths of Oz*, which presents the beach as both "a national institution" and a myth complex enough not only to negotiate "the deep biblical opposition between land and sea, or the basic anthropological one between culture and nature," but to offer, via "the politics of pleasure" and "overflowing meanings," the possibility of "subversive" surf (Fiske, Hodge, and Turner, 1987, pp. 71–72).

I have no great sympathy for the idea that going surfing is *subversive*. Yet I think there is a problem with dismissing "obvious things" if we take them to be, as Knight does, *inessential*. I must admit to a bias here: the beach for me has always been a "deeplaid," and thus ambiguous, reality of life; my own disinterest in subcultures is probably due to a youth spent admiring my boyfriends' surfboards in an era when girls didn't ride; but when I read Knight's dedication, "For Margaret, who kept me here," I realize that were I to make such a tribute I could say, most sincerely, "For the beach." So I am shocked by Knight's judgment, and I want to argue with it; had he spent more time at the beach, he might have learned something about spirituality in our "secular" society (many Australians, I think, are pantheists), and so something more about the lack of patriotic feeling for anything much besides sport. But even as I think these things, I am more uneasy with the myth-*making* mode I slip into than I am with Knight's view of the beach. This is the usual problem with myth analyses when they are (as they were not by Barthes) unified by a strict thematics, like "subculture," or "nation": personal observation soon becomes imperious generalization.

My real problem with Knight's surface/essence, outside/inside metaphysic of cultural "significance" is the question that it begs. Why *is* the beach now such an "obvious thing"? For whom is it obvious, and how? It is plausible to say that the pop-cultural myth of the beach has a fragile importance indeed for other orders of Australian reality; a historian (for whom "the beach," via *Myths of Oz,* meant "cultural studies") once told me irritably that "most Australians don't go to the beach," and for him this simply proved that "people in cultural studies don't do any research." But we still do have to account for its massive, obsessive inscription: tourism, fashion, softdrink, and sanitary napkin commercials aside, a vast anthology could be compiled of beach scenes from literature, cinema, photography, painting, theater, television drama and documentary, newspapers, and magazines. How is this without "significance"?

In fact, *Myths of Oz* shares with *The Selling of the Australian Mind* the view that there is something misleading about the beach as promoted by the culture industries. For Knight, it belongs with many other things to a postwar ideology of consumerism which did "special damage" in a country where "the ideology of the collective" had been so strong; "it was an overthrow of the material poverty of most of previous Australian life and of the systems of public self-help, which in this austere environment had emerged earlier than in the rest of the world." So the "obvious" beach is at odds with historic *social* values which may still live on under the carapace of materialism. For Fiske, Hodge, and Turner, media images "colonize" the surf by imposing upon it the meanings of a "culturally dominant class"; for them the mediated or "suburban" beach is at odds with the resistant force of the subcultural or "surfing" beach—its "closeness to *nature.*" For them, the mythic Nature promoted by the media is different from the surfing "natural" ("physical sensation, and . . . the pleasure that this produces"). In other words, both texts oppose an image to a deeper (Knight) or other (Fiske, et al.) *reality.* Cultural studies is then a means of gaining access to that reality.

Epistemological issues aside, there is a complicated problem here about the relation between cultural studies and history, and how self-reflexive we need to be about considering that relation. I suspect that however we may construct or denigrate the beach as a mythic signifier, a sensual/spiritual experience, or a complex ethnographic object (surfers, "materialism," men eating ice-creams with their children), we certainly do not do so now from a space "outside" a history in which discourse about real and imaginary beaches has an intense significance for Australian *intellectuals*—especially those for whom the popular is an object of study and a condition of everyday living. This is a history which in fact has a great deal to do with that "growing confrontation with race, history, possession and power," thus with the position from which "we" speak, and Knight's text, at least, is aware of this; the title of his prefatory essay and the subtitle of his book is "From *First Fleet* to Third Mercedes" (emphasis mine).

It is not tautological or precious here to speak of history confronting history. Most traditional narrative accounts of Australia always began at the beach: until the 1970s white historians regularly assumed that only when the convicts arrived on "the fatal shore" did time and "history proper" begin in "the timeless land." One of the most important histories we have of the Enlightenment, Bernard Smith's *European Vision and the South Pacific 1768–1850,* is lavishly supplied with beach scenes—traces of a scientific and artistic struggle to confront the radically different, and to convert it into "the other." It probably isn't abusive to speak of a *primal* scene: sexuality and violence are often at stake when people wonder about "first contact" between the Eora and the British, or what happened that first night on the beach, when, after months at sea, female convicts were released from their separate ships to share a borderless prison with male convicts, sailors, soldiers; as Paul Carter (1987) points out in *The Road to Botany Bay,* the most chaste of narrative historians will always write these "scenes" as though there was someone else *there,* looking on.[7]

It was in "confrontation" with this kind of history that Eric Willmot (1987a) observed in *Australia: The Last Experiment* (the 1986 Boyer Lectures for ABC Radio) that Botany Bay 1788 is not necessarily the best "marker" of beginnings for a "poly-generic society" (pp. 32–33). His fourth lecture ("Lucky Country Dreaming") suggests that only in Arnhem Land in 1802 was a scene set "for all the actors of Modern Australia." Willmot's scene is not a fantasy of guilty or anxious presence. He speaks simply of history as a book, and of a page with Aboriginal Australians "looking out to sea," a Macassan ship returning "for the season's fishing," and a British ship appearing for the first time in the bay. The Macassans, coming and going for centuries in the cosmopolitan North, were always ignored by an Anglo imaginary mesmerized by its own "fatal" shore; only when they are re-presented do "the Europeans, the Asians and the Australians all meet on the shores of the Southland." This reminder that at least three peoples could always have occupied a given *historical* space "from the beginning" does not deny tragedy, violence, and conflict; it does try to change what the history of that space may be in the future.

My point is certainly not that we cannot write about beach culture without taking all this on board, although I do think that there are often involuntary resonances when people imagine the beach in Australia to offer utopian potential for a naturally natural "nature." My point is that Willmot's use of the beach as simultaneously a positive cultural value and a historical image which is *already* involved in the critical debates and political conflicts of contemporary Australia may point to a more complex project for cultural studies than the elaboration of paradigmatically "given" (sub)cultural or "national" topics—without denying the value of these, or indeed their cultural power.

In this spirit, it may be more useful to think of the beach as a chronotope rather than as a *topos* or myth. Bakhtin's (1981) famous "unit of analysis" based on variable time-space ratios can carry its own essentialist charge, but it does allow us to deal with the density and volatility of cultural reference systems without *either* bringing an impossible totality relentlessly to bear on every single occasion (each stray beach postcard a telling symptom of imperialism) *or* creating those spatialized paradigms of "popular" practice which so idealize and purify an atomized present (sport/beach/car) that they may function as defensive guarantees of perfect historical innocence. The beauty of the concept of chronotope is to enable us to think about the cultural interdependence of spatial and temporal categories in terms of *variable* relations.[8]

One of the most powerful beach scenes I know works directly on "the beach" in this way. In my reading, it also explains why the beach may be one of the deepest-laid "realities of life" in Australia, one in terms of which the danger of dissociating the pleasures of popular culture from the political conflicts of history—as well as a desire to do so—is lived in the everyday.

Mudrooroo Narogin Nyoongah's "Beached Party"—an occasional text for Australia Day (January 26) 1991—could be called an elegy.[9] It is certainly a mourning poem, but only in the first few lines is there a distinction between the present of the oration ("We all, all of us must have a beginning, a birth day") and the historic past ("I, we died a thousand, thousand,/ When Governor Phillip carried to terror nullus/ His ill cargo: 'I suffer, suffer—/ Why exile me here?' "). These lines already complicate the relations between a universal human "we," an Aboriginal "I, we," and a cited white "I": the rest of the poem shifts and stretches those relations back and forth in a crowded, flickering time-space rather like a party, where nothing so neat as a "split" subjectivity is sustained, where the mood swings wildly between benevolence, sarcasm, pity, and sorrow, and where the pasts and presents of radically different temporalities spill and crash into each other.

The beached party is a mess, but it isn't chaotic. There is a logic that holds together the "cliche" present of staged political consensus and national reconciliation, the "eternal" present of TV, tourism, beach holidays, and real estate sales, and the recurring present of Aboriginal mourning, just as there is a logic able to blur but not efface the differences between the Koori, Australian, human identities all assumed by Nyoongah's text. You could call it Modernity, the legacy of Enlightenment, or even just one of those contradictions abounding in popular culture. You could also call it "the environment," or "the hole in the ozone layer." Toward the end of the poem, the party scene clears for a "historical re-enactment" that is also (for "I, we") the present reality of a sacrificial scene: Governor Phillip holds "the shattered body of a Koori in his white arms slowly turning brown," while "I finger the scars of my sorrows and smile at the droppings of my tears," holding the boat steady as Phillip proffers his gifts; then as the musket speaks, "our new nation in mourning each and every year on this date" can salute the birth of its future under the deadly mid-summer sun:

> As indifferent skins blister with cancerous growths
> And my voice whispers a hopeful, happy birthday, Australia
> While daubing sunscreen cream over the worst lesions
> > of my past.

On the beach (a tag made famous by a novel and a film about the end of the world at the ends of the earth in Australia) is an old expression meaning *beached*: shipwrecked, destitute, bankrupt, abandoned, washed up. "On the beach" is also the name of a framework culturally available for addressing "the state of the nation" (also the world, the human condition, public affairs, perhaps an intimate, even trivial, situation). This is why John Forbes can set part of his *On the Beach* in a crowded city street, and why Mudrooroo Nyoongah's "Beached Party" has glimpses of the wood-chipping industry and struggles over foreign investment. In Marxian criticism, such an address is often assumed to be *essentially* essentialist, as well as pessimistic, and there can be good reason for this; if Nyoongah's black mourner/celebrant in anti-UV cream defines, in more ways than one, a new kind of historical subject, Forbes's bystanders casually gambling on the outcome of a certainty as though its grimness does not concern them are ancestral figures from an old legend of white working-class "character"—hard, cynical, soulless—largely invented, in fascination, by intellectuals.

Yet "on the beach" is one of those phrases that can undermine itself: simply because it is used by someone who still lives to tell a tale, it may refute its own declaration of a pathetic or hopeless finality. Projected as a narrative framework, this kind of enunciative irony generates stories of encounter rather than closure, in time as well as in space. This is how Mudrooroo Nyoongah's appropriation of the "fatal shore" mode of Australia Day meditation involves the global human future in a recurring Koori past; this is also why John Forbes's *On the Beach* implies that the answer to the question of its own small urban scenario—"won't this do for a formal model of Australia?"—will eventually have to be, "no."

IV

A comic cultural encounter is already going on in John Forbes's street scene. We don't need to know exactly what it is in order to know that it is happening; something is marked by the effort of memory in the middle of the text—"isn't there a poem about this & the shimmering ideal of just walking down the street?"—and by the coding of the poem as a formal imitation, "after Juan Davila."

There *is* another poem about this, or something like "this"—a famous poem by Les Murray (1990) called "An Absolutely Ordinary Rainbow." It is not about trade union delegates watching a man behead a chicken in the street (in Australia, just possibly a religious rite, probably an attempt at Art, but certainly a social transgression). It is about an epiphany transfiguring an anonymous man in Martin Place with a fit of cosmic weeping. His weeping brings the city to a halt; when it is over, "he simply walks" through the crowd and away (pp. 23–24). Les Murray is a Catholic, a celebrated poet (almost a *de facto* Laureate), and a conservative populist thinker in the straight, male, Irish/Australian tradition; his collection of *Poems 1961–1983* is called *The Vernacular Republic.*

Juan Davila is a Chilean/Australian gay artist, and Forbes's text is a tribute to his work (especially his 1982/83 history painting *Fable of Australian Art,* the first panel of which includes a blank canvas marked "A Republic for Australia"). In the past, Davila has used a lot of "transfigured" Catholic iconography to study sexual and cultural difference in the political economy of modernism. Some of his work in the 1980s combined the (sometimes transvestite, often male) Pietà together with defaced Art History "signature" scenes, comic-book characters, pop icons, and figures from Tom of Finland pornography in readings of psychoanalysis; his paintings have sometimes been seized on the request of fundamentalist Christian groups. In 1982 his *Stupid As A Painter* (involving Michelangelo's Pietà in a narrative called "Kiss of Spider-woman") incurred charges of obscenity, a rare event in Australia; in 1988, his image *Bivouac* for a book of critical essays about the Bicentenary was censored by the publisher lest its treatment of Governor Phillip prompt charges of lese-majesty (rarer still).[10]

While the media may frame him as inverting ordinary values, Davila is not beheading chickens to shock our sacred institutions, and his art is not being framed by Forbes as a "transgression" of Les Murray's. Writing "after Juan Davila" is precisely a matter of "framing" itself: the metonymic flipping over of an image ("behead a chicken"/"headless chook") from one context to another in which its first meaning is not "negated" but transformed in such a way that all the relationships resulting are *questioned.* The principle is familiar enough to contemporary critical theory; what I may need to stress here is that this questioning comes to bear not on, say, Catholic religious beliefs (Murray's poem is just a vague trace in Forbes's) but on "the shimmering ideal of just walking down the street"—that sacred, secular value of the Absolutely Ordinary.

This is a complicated question. Davila's work in part belongs to a broad critical movement created internationally over at least the past twenty years by people challenging the sexual, racial, ethnic, and class exclusions and defacements that constitute the Ordinary. In that sense, it is inscribed in opposition to Les Murray's aesthetics (although this poem is the only instance I know of direct contact between them). The relationship of Forbes's poem to "An Absolutely Ordinary Rainbow" is a little more involved: there is a bit of "Murray" in "Forbes" (the wry turn in the phrase *"not being religious"* echoes the spirit as well as the syntax of Murray's marvelous last line about the weeper after his epiphany: *"Evading believers,* he hurries off down Pitt Street"); and while the ideal of beatified ordinariness is treated ruthlessly indeed, an aura still hangs there, *"shimmering."*

This is not surprising; what "shimmers" is a powerful mirage. For at least a century in Australia since the heyday of Henry Lawson, theologians of social democracy have seen the (white male working-class) Ordinary as the luminous truth of the Popular that shines through the Everyday. Critics of that democracy from D. H. Lawrence (1968) in his 1923 novel *Kangaroo* ("this place is meant for all one dead level sort of people" [p. 82]) to Donald Horne (1964) in *The Lucky Country* ("A society whose predecessors pioneered a whole continent now appears to shun anything that is at all out of the ordinary. The trouble is that, by Australian standards, almost everything that is now important is out of the ordinary" [p. 24]) have reified the Ordinary as a crippling normalization—almost a repressive *regime.* But as these two quotations suggest, the recurring critique of the Ordinary as a political culture (Lawrence accurately predicted the form that fascism here would take) and as a social philosophy (Horne predicted Australia's economic decline in an age of new technology) has not always required thinking through those exclusions on which it depends.

I suspect that my future work in cultural studies will have something to learn from these not quite resolved encounters. There are always gaps and "incommensurables" in play between the materials of cultural critique, and it may be in working with those that critical affect is most at stake. What often interests me now is a gap between historic discourses on Australian culture (almost a second language for me, so foreign can they seem) and the transnational critical and political discourses—feminism, Marxism, poststructuralism—that have worked for me as a composite mother tongue. Both are used in public culture today, the former much more widely than the latter; the work most useful to me now in cultural studies increasingly mixes them up. So I am also aware of a gap between the Australian institutional *conditions* that Graeme Turner has discussed, and the institutional *assumptions* that often mark transnational criticism (absolutist distributions of the relation of theory to practice, "local" methodology debates—text *vs.* ethnos, the literary *vs.* the popular—raised to the status of global human dilemmas). These experiences are productive: "gaps" do not conceal an elusive truth for the critic to pursue, but they do help to define the *social* conditions for inventing a critical practice.

This is not a rarefied issue. Practical problems are at stake about the politics of cultural studies in a particular social formation. In recent years, for example, we have had some discussion of the problems that follow from what Turner (reflecting back on *Myths of Oz*) calls the "*theoretical* weakness . . . of wheeling in British subcultural theory to analyze mainstream Australian popular culture" (1991, my emphasis). Not quite so much attention has yet been paid to the problems that follow from wheeling in the abstract aesthetic vocabulary of European modernism to theorize in Australia what that modernism (as Marshall Berman [1982] has shown) has always taken to be "the practice of everyday life"—and which was historically invested here with once radical, now reactionary, *nationalist* populist values. In 1990, students graduating from high schools throughout New South Wales took an English exam containing a question that I quote from memory; " 'Les Murray makes the ordinary extraordinary and the extraordinary ordinary': Discuss."

This is also not exactly a "specific" Australian issue. If there is a local irony about learning the principle of "making strange" as part of a basic training in the Great Australian Ordinary, there is a broader irony about the reluctance widespread in cultural studies to question rigorously the aesthetic inheritance of frameworks now used to analyze popular culture—a reluctance that can be most intense in schools of media study that wouldn't for the world get involved in any talk of "art" or "literature" or in overly "theoretical" speculation.[11] Yet Ian Hunter (1988a) in *Culture and Government* has shown, for example, just how powerful an unscrutinized Leavisite pedagogy of mutual recognition through the text ("this *is* so, isn't it?") has remained for a cultural studies that claims not only to discard canons, but to go "beyond" texts to study *practices.*

V

The point of Ian Hunter's questioning, like Juan Davila's, is not to reveal a historic complicity that requires denunciation, but to ask what follows in *practice* from certain "shimmering" ideals, and what might also follow from working in a different way. I want to give an example of a problem I have with an ideal of my own that I would like to pursue in future, and which Hunter's work has helped me to clarify—without, however, providing me with a solution I can accept. It arises in a two-way "gap" (for want of a better word) between the history of the Ordinary in Australian social criticism, and the concept of the everyday in French philosophy. This gap, as usual, is material as well as conceptual: the "everyday" is already a complex and well-defined problem for a huge archive of texts; the history of the Ordinary exists only as a scattering of documents put together by "everyday knowhow." My terms, necessarily, are caught up in the problem that they would try to define. I can only gesture at my problem, and say why I think it matters.

Fortunately, an American critic provides me with an oblique but sound way of beginning. In "An Ontology of Everyday Distraction," Margaret Morse (1990) criticizes the anachronism of transferring to the study of U.S. consumer culture today the model of everyday "praxis as enunciation" developed by Michel de Certeau (1984) in *The Practice of Everyday Life.* This model is only one version, I think, of one of the most powerful "modernist" themes regularly assumed by cultural studies, the "excess" of process over structure. It is not arbitrary or inconsequential that Henri Lefebvre (1984) began *Everyday Life in the Modern World* with a few dense pages in praise of James Joyce's *Ulysses,* and the "great river of Heraclitean becoming" in which, for Lefebvre, Joyce had redeemed the urban and linguistic quotidian that it helped bring into discourse (pp. 1–6).

Like most critics following on from Lefebvre's work, de Certeau wanted to transcend the limits of a "critique of graphic representations" that merely looks "from the shores of legibility toward an inaccessible beyond." In the "beyond" of those limits there had to be a way to read social practices directly, yet not naively (de Certeau, 1984, p. 47). So in "Walking in the City," de Certeau proposed to "access" that beyond with his model of the pedestrian speech act. Walking could be considered as *"a space of enunciation";* "walking is to the urban system what the speech act is to language *[langue]* or to the statements uttered *[énoncés proférés].*" With this dodgy urban/spatial projection of a linguistic/temporal concept, that "shimmering ideal of just walking down the street" became a model of popular practice—and critical process—in administered societies.

In one form or another this, along with the closely related strategy/tactics distinction, has been one of the most influential models for cultural studies in recent years.[12] Morse wonders, however, whether de Certeau could ever have imagined, "as he wrote on walking as an evasive strategy of self-empowerment, that there would one day be video cassettes that demonstrate how to 'power' walk." She suggests that "praxis as enunciation" has dubious value as a "vision of liberation" once processes for gaining access to a beyond (in her terms, an *elsewhere*) have been fully "designed into the geometries of everyday life" with malls, freeways, and television, and now that de Certeau's "figurative practices of enunciation ('making do,' 'walking in the city,' or 'reading as poaching') are *modeled in representation itself*" (Morse, 1990, p. 195). In this particular time-space economy (that Morse calls "everyday distraction") designer process blocks, rather than exceeds, a process/structure dynamic; there is no "escape" in designer escape, or to put it another way, nothing exceeds like designer excess.

Now, in an abstract and quite fundamental way, I doubt that I could think without a concept of enunciative praxis (and while I recognize the environment Morse describes, it is still for me a tourist experience—someone else's elsewhere—and not a state of everyday life). De Certeau did not think praxis *only* as enunciation, a term which functions in his texts as an allegory of, and an adjunct to, other kinds of social action. But as Morse points out, de Certeau often does translate enunciation as *evasion,* and this is the problem; at these moments of his text, the "fugitive" nature of the speech act concerns him more than its cohesive, dialogic, or referential powers. In these moments, his work looks forward to a cultural studies that celebrates "resistance" as a programmed feature of capitalist culture, rather than towards that process (cohesive, dialogic, referential) by which, as Morse puts it in her own wise vision of criticism's role in social change, "alternative values and their constituencies have labored to *mark themselves* in discourse" (p. 215).[13]

The evasive/enunciative model of the everyday, moreover, was not unique or original to Michel de Certeau. It is already at work in Lefebvre's *Everyday Life in the Modern World,* and the most extended elaboration of it that I know is in Maurice Blanchot's (1987) wonderful essay on "the man in the street" from 1959, "Everyday Speech." Writing about Lefebvre's earlier *Critique de la vie quotidienne* (1946/1959), Blanchot sets out with miraculous brevity all the elements for a theoretical myth of the Evasive Everyday. In the intricate dialectic of his text (which owes little to Lefebvre's historical materialism), these elements are held together by one refrain: *"The everyday escapes."* "That is its definition": it escapes all "forms or structures," all "means of communication," all "dialectical recovery," all "authority, whether it be political, moral or religious," all division between true and false. It is pure process in excess, and it is always—like "the man in the street"—*potentially* political. For this reason the structural "other" to the excess of everyday speech is (as it was for Lefebvre) a double figure: the philosopher, the man of "metalanguage" in Lefebvre's phrase, and the *bureaucrat*— the "man of government"—in Blanchot's. For de Certeau, too, the "pedestrian speaker" confronted and evaded a twin: on the one hand, the cultural theorist; on the other, the urban *planner.*

This is an intense discourse of desire, and it could be analyzed historically in terms of philosophical debates about the question of "the other" in postwar France. Among the texts still used in cultural studies today, the symbolic bearer of evasive everydayness shifts easily from Blanchot's "man in the street," to "the woman in the home" (Lefebvre), to de Certeau's walker—of whom the *mythic* expression in his text is "Man Friday on the beach." In each case, this bearer is marked as discursively other to "metalanguage"—as female literalness (Lefebvre), as popular rumor, a discourse "without a subject" (Blanchot), or as a "savage" trace of orality in writing (de Certeau)—while the subject marking it as such shifts between "the philosopher" in Lefebvre's formal dialogues, the speculative thinker who also lives in the everyday (Blanchot), and the professional scholar in a research institution (de Certeau).

This recurring inscription of the historic subject of metalanguage—indeed, of cultural studies—as a white European middle–class male ("Robinson Crusoe" in de Certeau's terms) helps to explain why Wlad Godzich (1986) can argue persuasively in his preface to de Certeau's *Heterologies* that "this other *which forces discourses to take the meandering appearance that they have* is not a magical or a transcendental entity; it is the discourse's mode of relation to its own historicity in the moment of its utterance" (p. xx, my emphasis). This is also why the "critique of everyday life" is a discourse of critical involvement, and this is also why this involvement has to take the form of an enunciative praxis.

The interesting thing for me, however, is that for *all* these texts, this process does not extend to involvement with the one figure who in fact remains, for all three writers, quite unredeemably "other"—the bureaucrat. Prior to any instance of enunciative praxis, the subject of metalanguage is already split, by this discourse, between theoretical and "administrative" functions, process and structure: the latter terms are negatively valued, and the semantic attribute "political" migrates towards the former.

Here I must mark a first gap in my discourse, and between the materials I work with. I turn, once more, to Donald Horne's "man in an open-necked shirt." He doesn't say much as he enjoys his ice-cream on the beach (according to legend, he is enunciatively "laconic"); in spite of his setting, he is much closer to Blanchot's man in the street than he is to de Certeau's Man Friday, who still hovers in his memory as some sort of exotic prince; he is totally oblivious to the woman in the home. In a way, he fits the series. But he isn't at all evasive: his only everyday praxis is a modest material consumption, and he dislikes symbolic excesses ("too far-fetched"). He is the Ordinary Australian: retired now, worried about his pension and the Asians taking over the country; even his old trade union mates have just wasted rank and file money on a 20-page liftout for *Cleo,* that yuppie female fashion magazine. In his prime, he aroused few philosophers to discourse (that would *really* be a bit much). But he was, and he still is, an object of intense desire for many a man of government.

On the other side of this gap, in *Culture and Government,* and an associated essay on "Setting Limits to Culture," Ian Hunter (1988a, b) gives a rare defense of a "bureaucratic" practice. Hunter's critical object is not the Everyday, but Culture in the emergence of English literary education. Nevertheless, his harsh account of "the gigantic ethical pincers of the dialectic" in British cultural studies has a direct bearing on the French tradition. Hunter argues that cultural studies has underestimated its debt, via Marxism, to Romantic aesthetics, to Schiller and Hegel, and in so doing it has misrecognized its place in a history of criticism deployed in schools as an exemplary *ethical* practice, aimed at "forming the self." While cultural studies may claim to offer a materialist analysis of culture, and to politicize the critical process, the dialectic really functions as a virtuoso technique of "ethical athleticism"—in fact, as "a technique for *withdrawing* from the discursive and institutional spheres in which cultural attributes are actually specified and formulated" (Hunter, 1988b, p. 110). Such spheres are primarily administrative and bureaucratic; these are the spheres of the "properly" political.

In its developed form, this argument (like the related work of Tony Bennett and other theorists of policy) raises some awkward questions about the "critique of everyday life." Its vulnerability to Hunter's polemic only begins with the way it has so often defined its own processes as well as its objects as *necessarily* "evasive," even as precluded *by definition* from occupying those "spheres" of planning and administration. In the light of Hunter's history, critical "praxis as enunciation" can appear as a sign of ethical consent to the political *status quo.* It confirms the disquiets of my own experience, by showing how and *why* the Romantic inheritance in cultural studies works to create a "fraught space" of ethical grandiloquence, in which massive, world-historical problems are debated on such a level of generality that they cannot possibly be solved, and posed in ways which do not, will not and cannot ever connect to agencies by which actual social futures may be given a "definite shape." In the name of politics, this praxis enunciates a spiral from, as Tony Bennett puts it, "big debate to big debate": always swinging between activist desire and angst about its own effects, it has the form of precisely the doomed circularity that is known in everyday language as running round like a headless chook.

I have deep reservations about this thesis. Yet one of many things that attracts me to it is its compatibility both with recent feminist work that rethinks "praxis as enunciation" precisely through a pre-Kantian concept of ethics as, in Moira Gatens's (1991) phrase, "crucially concerned with the specificity of one's embodiment" (p. 85), and with the value that radical pedagogies have always attached—both in and out of school—to a "virtuoso" *collective* praxis aimed precisely at "(re)forming the self." Rather than dismissing these, Hunter's argument simply cautions some "ethical modesty" about what they can achieve. But then I am not sure what is to be gained by de-politicizing as "ethical" whole areas of intellectual practice where people are already confronting relations and structures of power; whether "culture" in media societies can be considered "rare" in the sense that Hunter assumes; whether any "self" can be so singular and orderly that its functions are neatly separable, ethics here, politics there; and whether enunciation in a discourse-*administered* class society can ever be restricted to an "ethical" technique.

Now I want to look back across that gap, where uncanny memories are stirring with no scholarly justification. In some of our debates about policy and aesthetics, the thematics of process re-presents itself in a strangely inverted form; cultural theorists identifying more closely with trade union delegates than with poets or painters or pop stars are defending administrative agencies against a presumed "semiotic" excess; this time, we aesthetes are astonished (are they talking about "transgression"?), but not surprised—even when one or two start hailing as the object of their desire, that ordinary soul, "the Citizen."[14] After all, there is a text about this, and the shimmering ideal of just getting on with the job; it's a utopian vision (from *The Lucky Country,* but many other texts have seen it too), in which the white male Ordinary Australian is dreaming a better future for his (br)others:

> The pragmatic, sceptical Australian can walk through the rhetoric of Asia like a blind man avoiding bullets. There they are, out there in Asia, advising on pest control, credit policies, irrigation, language teaching, some of the thousand and one little things that help civilizations survive the radiations of their own bombast . . . Their ability not to generalize, simply to get on with the job can open the hearts of practical-minded Asians. (Horne, 1964, p. 229)

Policy theorists would not say this, or would not use such rhetoric to say this, today. But this rhetoric, and this theory of rhetoric—along with the erasures, desires, and projections that this text inscribes—is part of their history, and of the history of the cultural studies that we practice in Australia today.

It is part of *my* history, not least (if not only) because I do cultural studies in a society where the dominant *political* discourse still sees "rhetoric" as an exotic bombast avoided by the ordinary (everyday life + government); and I do this using a theoretical discourse that wants to find in the "everyday" a rhetorical escape from the *metalinguistic* (philosophy + government). The former will not admit of any difference in discourse, and that, in a sense, is its politics; the latter does find it hard, I think, to make a political difference.

VI

I want to conclude with an informal description of the immediate context for my own view of cultural studies now and in the future.

My work will continue to be influenced more by concepts of everyday life than by debates about "popular" culture. This is partly a result of the way that feminism leads me to think about practice: I am less interested in music or TV than I am in how these cut across and organize the various time/spaces in which the labor, as well as the pleasure, of everyday living is carried out by Australian women. This is why I do not think of "tourist sites and sounds" as insignificant, like Stephen Knight, but nor do I think of them *primarily,* like *Myths of Oz,* as settings for reading the popular in terms of signifying practice (although I am an ardent reader). I think of them in the first place as political combat zones.

Take a tussle over a hypothetical tourist resort on a beach in the 1980s. It is a site where Aboriginal land claimants, Japanese or Malaysian developers, white racists, entrepreneurs of many ethnicities who will be pro-Japanese but may be anti-Aboriginal, environmentalists, surfers, and a broader community mixed in every respect and divided about development, will all have to fight, unequally, over a space where the "deep biblical opposition between land and sea" is administered by a Labor government committed to sustainable development, while trying to stave off bankruptcy. I say "hypothetical" to keep things simple: in reality, there will be Aboriginal supporters of development, racists who are not "white" racists, deep ecologists confronting Green-vote power brokers. . . .

In this context, "culture" is one medium of a power struggle in which most participants, at some stage or another, will passionately invoke on their own behalf the interests of "Ordinary Australians."

This struggle is represented in the everyday as profoundly economic. Most public discussions of "culture" in the past decade in Australia—whether on chat shows, in newspapers, or in pubs—have not been directly to do with TV or poetry or surfing. They have been about the impact of the deregulation of much of the economy on our social structure and ethical systems; about the Uruguay Round of the GATT talks, on which our economic welfare (and the underpinning of the culture *industries,* as well as consumption) depends; about the emergent division of the world into three rival trading empires with no clear place for "us," but a logic leading to the possibility of war between major capitalist powers; about the fragility of the global banking system, and of the Japanese property market on which much of it depends; about the conflict between national-economic, global-environmental, and local "quality of life" imperatives.

These are all terrifying "futures" which are happening to us now as media images, even as acts of media terrorism.

At the same time, "culture" now is an export industry, thought more in relation to debt management than to concepts of a "whole way of life." In the past, the administration of our English departments relegated almost all Australian literature to the unstudied field of the "popular." Today, English departments teach all forms of international popular culture, while "Australian Literature" (including criticism and theory) is a funding category conceptually on a par with opera, rock music, restoring old trade union banners, and financing Aboriginal arts.

In the field of this insistently economic representation of "culture," it is one of the concerns of cultural studies to open up this field to the experiences, and the critical expressions, of gender, race, and class. Like the teaching professions, policy-makers in Australia are comparatively well attuned to such expressions. The media are not.

In fact, the Australian media over the past few years have created the impression that what Ian Hunter calls "administrative intellectuals" are now deeply involved in constructing the everyday lives of Ordinary Australians as something like an evasive object.

During the 1980s, the word "culture" began to be used in a rather peculiar sense. In 1990, a week after the worst company crashes in Australian history ended a decade of financial mismanagement and "de-regulated" corporate crime, a groveling TV current affairs show host asked Rupert Murdoch (back home to shut down a couple of newspapers) what "we" could do to save "our" economy. The mighty multinationalist replied, "Oh you know—change the culture."

The host *did* know what he meant (although he nudged Murdoch to clarify that you can't have greenies wrecking the economy "to save some fish or wombats or something"). What Murdoch "meant" was a cliche: a 1980s media commonplace that Australia's biggest problem is the lazy, hedonist, uncompetitive, beach-bound, lotus-eating ethos of the Ordinary people. In fact, by the end of the decade, corporate leaders, bureaucrats, politicians, and opinion-makers were starting to sound like Maoists:

Changing the culture is not a quick process in something as old and as large as ARC.

A cultural shift must be made while there is still time. . . .

Professor [Helen] Hughes . . . said Australians had relied on the "lucky country" attitude for too long . . . "We have got to cultivate an export culture."

We are, nearly all of us, bludgers. That is the reason the country is in a mess and it will not get out of that mess until the national bludging culture has been reversed. [A bludger is a lazy, parasitic person.]

These slogans are from, respectively, a chief executive of Smorgon ARC, Australia's largest producer of concrete reinforcing steel; a past president of the Business Council of Australia introducing a planned "debt conference"; a financial journalist reviewing a speech by an academic economist; an editor of the *Australian Financial Review* in his other role as columnist in the nation's biggest-selling Sunday tabloid.[15]

In this context, "changing the culture" means "more work for less money." But it is assumed—at least in fantasy—that this will also mean changing the minutiae of conduct at the workplace ("work practices") and the values and expectations of home and family life, liberalizing attitudes to gender and race, increasing class consciousness (making inequality more acceptable), and in the end, changing the meaning of the enduring myths of history. During the 1980s, those discourses of desire known as government reports were *promoted in the media* as part of a doctrine of "changing the culture"—culture being taken to be malleable, or "calculable," in Hunter's and Bennett's sense. These are complex and ambiguous developments. A good example of the "desire" factor is the Garnaut Report, *Australia and the North-East Asian Ascendency,* which recommended as part of a single strategy the removal of all tariffs by the year 2000 and compulsory teaching of "an Asian Language" (ideally, Japanese) in all Australian primary schools. What it did not consider was how a partially dismantled state education system might be able to achieve this.

The distinction between popular culture and everyday life becomes tenuous indeed in the mediated policy field. Some people still fear that cultural studies will "aestheticize" politics. But what cultural studies has to confront is rather the aestheticization of "politics" as part of a modern process of government. For example, an image on the front page of the *Sydney Morning Herald* in 1988, captioned "The Band That Makes You Bop": four figures framed in cliche rock-promo style, half-vanishing in the shadows as they try to look tough and sexy. "BoP" is a pun on "Bop"—Balance of Payments. The stars are accountants—clerks who prepare the monthly statement on our balance of payments crisis—and the text is a human interest story. The logic of aestheticization is followed right through to modernist self-reference and postmodern obsolescence: by 1990, a cartoon has huge boulders hitting zombies on the head, BOP!—as the Treasurer says to the Prime Minister, "they get anaesthetized after a while."

It is an article of faith in cultural studies that (most) people are not zombies. You could say that "changing the culture" is a myth already being appropriated and revised in a resistant spirit by the people at whom it is directed. A few nights after Rupert Murdoch did his bit for national salvation, an airport fire brigade chief talked on the same show about disaster stress, and the therapy he'd needed after cleaning up a fatal accident. He said he was interested in "changing our work culture"; by "our," he meant men—making it all right for men to admit to emotional distress and seek help to do something about it. This, I think, is *"subversive"*: not perhaps in relation to a political economy that now needs workers to be more "flexible" than in the past, but in relation to the political myth of the Ordinary, past and present, in Australian everyday life—and the attacks that some of its *virtues* are now, in the name of "economy," sustaining.

By "changing the culture," this man meant something *ethical* in Ian Hunter's sense. It seems to me that administrative/political, aesthetic/ethical modes of practice may not so easily, or even usefully, be distinguished once "everyday life" has become— in the name of "culture"—an object of bureaucratic fantasy, policy desire, and media hype, as well as a subject of seemingly unlimited cultural production. However it is certainly not useful either to pose problems as though in studying "the everyday" one is always directly involved in a mortal combat with the history of Western philosophy.

In this context, I would like to think of cultural studies as a discipline capable of thinking the relations between local, regional, national, and international frames of action and experience (using these terms in a sense that must be based in a politics of gender, race, and class). There could be two consequences of this. First, projects in cultural studies in Australia could be oriented less towards the big debates galvanizing the discipline worldwide, and more towards the "ethical" and policy issues being debated in public media in the contexts that we take to concern us. For example, the Garnaut Report might provide a better starting point for discussing, say, "elitism" in Australia than the burden of the Literary in Britain or the United States. Second, I would like to see cultural studies more informed than it has been in the past—in my vicinity—by debates in political economy and in geopolitics.

But I will work in this direction myself, as I have in the past, as a textual critic, rather than as an amateur social scientist. The question of mediation—materially distinct from the policy process itself—is ignored by most policy polemics. Yet in my opinion, it is at least as appropriate for cultural studies to concern itself with this as it is to aspire to intervene directly in bureaucratic and business spheres. Recognizing that the media instance of the policy process may have a certain "autonomy," randomness, productivity, and "citizen input," can make it more difficult to mobilize the oppositions between "politics" and "aesthetics" that have marked this debate so far.

For this reason, among the reference points for my own work now are Eric Michaels's work on Warlpiri television; Tom O'Regan on the "space-binding" functions of new communications policy; Sneja Gunew on critical multiculturalism, migrant women's writing, and feminist critical theory; Stephen Muecke on Aboriginal story-telling and postmodern travel writing; Yuki Tanaka on the Japanese "political-construction" (as opposed to "military-industrial") complex; and Helen Grace on the folklore of finance capitalism and its modes of masculinity.[16] With perhaps little else in common, these projects are all engaged in some way with contesting *images* of policy: not simply images of what "policy" is or ought to be, but with its failures and absurdities; with how people live with its operations and unforeseen consequences, and then with multiple mediations and refractions of their own responses; with how they formulate initiatives of their own; with how all this living "exceeds" (to wheel in a useful term) the demands and the desires of the policy imaginary. So they are all concerned with culture and government in a very broad sense. They also define a framework from which we can ask why, at the end of a decade when Labor governments in Australia have supervised the shrinking of the State, *policy* has acquired for us the importance that it has.

For this reason, too, my favorite "founding text" for my own version of cultural studies is Sylvia Lawson's (1983) great critical biography of a nineteenth-century white male populist magazine editor, *The Archibald Paradox: A Strange Case of Authorship.* A theorization of media work as political practice, it is also one of the most subtle accounts we have of the dilemmas of a "colonial" intellectual (to use the term appropriate to Archibald's time)—and of the paradoxical conditions of his political effectivity. More broadly, it is a major reading of the 1890s: the very period in Australian cultural history which saw, partly thanks to Archibald, the apotheosis of the Ordinary in all its sexist, racist, social democratic glory; the very period which saw, partly thanks to the *Bulletin,* the formalization of an aesthetic doctrine forbidding the "too far-fetched"; and also the very period in our economic and political history which is figuring in our media now as the "model," if not the source, for our problems in the present.

Lawson's is a major reading, because it makes these legends problematic: she shows the radicalism and the idealism mixed up with the worst of the Ordinary; she shows the complexity produced as well as repressed by stereotypes in popular cultural thinking; obliquely, her work shows us why the posing of white male Ordinariness today as an object of cultural "restructuring" may involve, paradoxically, an attack on some social values that may well be, like the uncompetitive and unpatriotic beach, worth defending. In this way, *The Archibald Paradox* for me is an exemplary history of the present.

Fortunately, it would be too far-fetched for anyone romantically to claim Sylvia Lawson as their new, improved Father—academic, journalist, fiction writer, filmmaker, and policy-lobbyist that she is. One reason is that her achievement in *The Archibald Paradox* was already to show that there never was anything "singular" (and certainly nothing perfect) about the period supposed to be at the "origin" of modern Australian culture; we do not look back at the mythic white male 1890s from the plurality and mixity of our society today; that mixity was there, from the beginning.

John Forbes reminds us that knowing this can be a modest survival guide for living with *all that speech* as it circulates endlessly in paranoid space. His imagery, like everyday speech, can sometimes sound violent, a bit brutal and inhuman—all those stunned mullets and headless chooks, mute victims of a history that mistook itself for a war between Man and Nature. So too his discovery of the truth about the stunned mullet when it comes up for air after its burst of eloquence may seem "inhuman" or "impersonal"; in fact, it's rather tender and optimistic:

> up close
> the scales are false
> in fact a cunning mechanical contrivance,
> like Bob Hawke's hair—
> they glitter, exposed to the atmosphere
> instead of dying, being alloy not flesh
> *The Stunned Mullet.*

NOTES

1. This argument is developed in my "Panorama: The Live, the Dead and the Living" (1988b), and "Metamorphoses at Sydney Tower" (1990a).

2. Forbes (1988), pp. 15-20. "Anglo/Celtic" designates the dominant ethnic group in Australian society, "white" being too vague for the purpose. Since "Irish" Australians (traditionally between a quarter and a third of the population) regarded themselves until the 1950s as ethnically distinct from the "English" who starved or transported them out to Australia, "Anglo/Celtic" came back into the language as a polemical way for immigrants from non-English speaking

backgrounds to say that things had changed. Its use is now uncontentious. "British-Australian" refers to a person of any ethnicity who has recently migrated as a consenting adult from Britain.

3. Recently retired as chair of the Australia Council, Horne was invited to inaugurate the national Australian Cultural Studies Conference at the University of Western Sydney in December 1990.

4. Andrew Ross, *No Respect: Intellectuals and Popular Culture* (1989a), pp. 15–41, and *Strange Weather* (forthcoming). One difference between Australian and American middlebrow culture as Ross describes it may be that the former has not historically been subject either to successful patrician or effective left-wing backlash.

5. This term refers to a bi-partisan political agreement (that has held since the 1960s) against racial discrimination in Australian immigration policy, and to a cultural policy that from the early 1970s replaced the "assimilation" and "integration" of immigrant people. Since Australia is a post-colonial, not a post-imperial, nation, "multiculturalism" is not used (as it can be in Britain) as a euphemism for existing race relations; it refers to the decentering impact of some 74 new "languages" on the old colonial mix. However it can be used to deny the unique status of Koori (Aboriginal) people; in this case, it can be racially offensive as well hypocritical, since Aborigines suffer the most social discrimination. Multiculturalism is also supposed to accompany an economic and social philosophy of *state-fostered* equal opportunity. It is not a "melting pot" ideal, but (in theory) an affirmation of limited difference. In this paper, I refer to the work of people questioning the limitations of multiculturalism in practice as "critical multiculturalism."

See Stephen Castles, Mary Kalantzis, Bill Cope, and Michael Morrissey, *Mistaken Identity: Multiculturalism and the Demise of Nationalism in Australia* (1988), and Sneja Gunew (1990), "Denaturalizing cultural nationalism: multicultural readings of 'Australia'."

6. Discussion session on "Australian Cultural Studies: Past, Present and Future," University of Western Sydney, Nepean, December 1990.

7. See Robert Hughes, *The Fatal Shore* (1987); Eleanor Dark, *The Timeless Land* (1941); Bernard Smith, *European Vision and The South Pacific 1768–1850* (1960); Paul Carter, *The Road to Botany Bay* (1987). Alternative histories of this question are by Henry Reynolds, in *The Other Side of the Frontier: Aboriginal Resistance to the European Invasion of Australia* (1982), and *The Law of the Land* (1987); Anne Summers, *Damned Whores and God's Police: The Colonization of Women in Australia* (1975), and Eric Willmot, *Pemelwuy: The Rainbow Warrior* (1987b).

8. As chronotope, the beach in Australia can be very sinister. On the beach as a locus for apocalyptic thinking, see my "Fate and the Family Sedan" (1989).

9. Mudrooroo Nyoongah, "Beached Party," *Sydney Morning Herald,* January 19, 1991. The poem was commissioned as an occasional piece for Australia Day as part of the Sydney Writers' Festival, and the manuscript is to be donated to the Mitchell Library archive. Mudrooroo Nyoongah has also published novels and criticism under the names Mudrooroo Narogin, and Colin Johnson.

10. See Juan Davila and Paul Foss, *The Mutilated Pietà* (1985), and *Juan Davila: Hysterical Tears,* ed. Paul Taylor (1985). *Bivouac* is printed in *Island in the Stream,* ed. Paul Foss (1988), p. 110.

11. On the contradictions of this attitude in ethnographic Cultural Studies, see Virginia Nightingale (1989), "What's 'ethnographic' about ethnographic audience research."

12. My criticism of the strategy/tactics distinction is developed in "Banality in Cultural Studies" (1990a) and in "Great Moments in Social Climbing: King Kong and The Human Fly" (forthcoming).

13. For a useful modification of de Certeau's model, see Susan Ruddick (1990), "Heterotopias of the Homeless: Strategies and Tactics of Placemaking in Los Angeles."

14. The issue of citizenship is debated between Stuart Cunningham and Elizabeth Jacka, "Cultural Studies in the Light of the Policy Process—A Curate's Egg?," Australian Studies Conference, University of Western Sydney, Nepean 1990, papers forthcoming.

15. "Swan steels ARC for competition," *Sunday Telegraph,* November 28, 1989; "Coming to grips with the debt crisis," *Australian Financial Review,* November 20, 1989; "Poor performance 'shooting Aust [sic] in the head'," *Australian Financial Review,* October 26, 1989. Peter Robinson, "Fair go, we're all bludgers," *Sun-Herald,* June 18, 1989.

16. See, for example, Eric Michaels, *For a Cultural Future: Francis Jupurrurla Makes TV at Yuendumu* (1987); Tom O'Regan, "Towards a High Communication Policy," (1988/89); Sneja Gunew, "Home and Away: Nostalgia in Australian (Migrant) Writing" (1988); Stephen Muecke, "No Road: (Vague Directions for the Study of Tourism)," (1990); Krim Benterrak, Stephen Muecke and Paddy Roe, *Reading the Country* (1984); Yuki Tanaka, "The Japanese Political-Construction Complex," (1990); *The MFP [Multi Function Polis] Debate,* ed. Ross E. Mouer and Yoshio Sugimoto (1990).

DISCUSSION: Meaghan Morris

NOTE: These questions were addressed to the paper that Meaghan Morris presented at the conference, not to the rather different paper she has since written and published here. Some of the questions thus address issues not directly covered in the paper itself.

GREG COX: I'm interested in the type of internationalism or concern about the globe as a whole that you would want to affirm and what sort of practice you see capable of addressing it.

MORRIS: I think I'd be foolish to pretend to be able to answer that question easily. "The globe" is so vast, and most of us know so little about what goes on in most of it anyway, one feels that any reply is unsatisfactory and yet that anyone who doesn't face up to the question is fudging their responsibilities. To be caught between the two is depressing and disabling. I think part of the peril that global capitalism poses to us now is a terrorism of scale that gets right inside our emotional sense of what it means to think and to act. There's terror of a system so enormous, so complex and apparently out of control, certainly on any level at which most people can think about practice, and yet also a terror about time—a sense of urgency that you feel you have to act now even though it seems impossible. It's easy to mock this paralyzed feeling, but I think it's a crucial political factor today, at least in my own society.

But I can try to respond to your concern about internationalism by pointing to a strategy that for me doesn't work in practice, which is rejecting a politics of difference the way David Harvey (1989) does in *The Condition of Postmodernity,* a book which is influencing many people's thinking at the moment. Harvey says that the problem with difference-based movements is that their field of action is local—"place"—while the awesome form of capitalism emerging now operates at a universalizing level, "space." He gives a strong description of how this capitalism is carving up the world anew, and then he claims that only a return to some form of international working-class movement and to Marxist "meta-theory" can hope to oppose it.

Leaving aside the issue of "meta-theory" (which I think is a fantasy about theory's power, not a description of what Marxism actually is or needs to be), I have two problems with this. One is that he gives us no practical idea at all of how such a movement could come into play in the radically uneven and unequal world his own theory describes, and frankly I don't think he ever can. Here I'd agree with Ian Hunter, that this kind of Big Dialectic actually works to ensure that our idea of future society has no definite shape, and so it's really a way of withdrawing from the sites where change can be negotiated. The second problem is to do with Harvey's place/space opposition. Because he tends to universalize an old European model of place (small communities with long memories living in the same areas for ages) he thinks that "local" movements, and *therefore,* he assumes, a politics of difference, usually veer towards a nostalgia for tradition, to valorizing myth, to an aesthetics of blood and fatherland . . . in other words, via Heidegger, towards fascism. And he thinks this tendency continues into postmodernism. So, to fight global capitalism in practice, we should get back to some versions of the kind of workers' internationalism that under high modernism opposed (and failed against, I might add) reactionary nationalism in Europe.

I know that this "veer" is a real possibility now in Eastern Europe and other places. But it doesn't follow for the societies emerging from, or like modern Australia, entirely produced by, the massive "forced" movement and mixing and clashing of peoples that capitalism unleashes one way or another, and which may lead people to struggle to create a sense of place and memory in very complicated ways. Harvey's logic can't make sense of the terms of struggle in Australia around Aboriginal Land Rights, and it can't explain how a couple of hundred thousand Kooris have managed to make those struggles un-ignorable now by anyone dealing at the level of national economic policy, with the mining and tourist industries, along with its "global" implications, like environmental policy, and how they've done this by mixing and inventing new traditions as well as preserving old ones. That "Heideggerian" sense of place may not even be a good explanation of current forms of reactionary nationalism, and it is absolutely not, in my understanding, an underpinning of a radical politics of difference, where people have to engage in dialogue and make alliances in a process which *includes* conflictual experience and incommensurable positions, rather than externalizing them in some myth of an Enemy Alien.

That's why I think these politics are not marginal or divisive, but probably the best guide we have so far to what an international practice might mean. I can give a more positive example. Abe David and Ted Wheelwright in their book *The Third Wave: Australia and Asian Capitalism* give a really grim account of the exploitative and environmentally catastrophic non-society emerging round the Pacific Rim, trying to make Australians understand that we might only fit into it as minders of a huge quarry and tourist resort. They use similar economic arguments to Harvey's, and they seem to come to the same conclusion when they say the only hope is to strengthen links with the working-class movements in the *region*. But the more modest scope of their claim makes a difference; if one is to act nationally and *regionally* while thinking internationally in the Pacific Rim today, there are gulfs of language as well as of political, social, and cultural "tradition" to be negotiated, chasms of ignorance and indifference, gruesome histories of imperialism and racism to be confronted, and the consequences of Australian and American unions' past complicity in the destruction of Japanese and Korean labor movements to be faced. In other words—there's no way that a politics of difference can possibly be *avoided*.

But you can see things beginning to happen; Australian socialists working more frequently with Japanese critics of Japanese capitalism, artists and media workers doing projects with people in Thailand, Taiwan, the Philippines . . . These are small things, but I don't think that we're likely to have much purchase on "the globe as a whole" if we keep on dismissing all the efforts at international practice actually happening in our vicinity as unequal to the greater task. For academics in cultural studies, I think access to these can occur through work in pedagogy, in the media and culture industries which have an "internationalizing" force of their own, and in policy studies. On a theoretical level, I also think we can't develop an international practice until we break down those local/global, national/international frameworks by at least confronting the fact of regionalism in the world today, like the emergence of trade blocs in forms that are not only changing the political and "cultural" alignments of nations but could lead to universalized food warfare as well as the famines we have already, or the changes in international banking that could lead the right kind of crash on the Japanese property market to trigger global economic chaos. These issues, to my mind, need to be considered much more sensibly in cultural studies.

PAUL GILROY: You said that Eurocentrism wasn't a political sin. Could you comment on the difference between it being a political sin and it being a political error, particularly for certain kinds of intellectuals in the overdeveloped countries of the world?

BHABHA: I think the interrogation of Eurocentric practices and concepts is clearly the problematic of what we should do. And I think that the important issue is to take the Eurocentric focus and by decentering it, actually open up a whole number of issues which start from a number of other traditions which have defined themselves both in opposition to Eurocentric positions and in tension and contention with them. So I think it is important to elaborate other starting points and other destinations which would set up very different concepts of historicity, community, temporality, and cultural value generally.

MORRIS: I have a real problem with the rhetoric of political error and correctness. I start to lose a sense of reality when people use those terms. Perhaps it's just in the Australian context I'm working in, the bottom line is really a question-mark, a sense that nobody knows very clearly what is going on or what is likely to happen, even at the very "local" level of politics, in the next few years. So that to try to legitimate one's own strategy in terms of other people's "error" implies a certainty or an analytical confidence about the present that in a way elides part of the *problem* of politics, and especially cultural politics, now. So for me to say that Eurocentrism is not just a "political sin" is really to say that we can't take for granted that we always know what to say about the traditional objects of leftist criticism in current conditions. I wouldn't have any problem whatsoever in saying that I think David Harvey is wrong. I simply meant that the *terms* "political error"/"political correctness" congeal with a whole way of presenting politics that makes people crack up laughing or fall asleep. That's quite different from disclaiming the activity of producing partisan arguments, which is what I do all the time.

GILROY: Could I just ask what the difference is in saying David Harvey is wrong and saying Eurocentrism is wrong?

MORRIS: Perhaps because "David Harvey" and "Eurocentrism" are different kinds of objects. I don't *practice* "David Harvey," but I can, knowingly or unknowingly, practice Eurocentrism. But even then if I say "David Harvey is wrong," I need not only to make an argument about why that's the case, but to have a specific context of dialogue that will influence my sense of why it *matters* that it's the case. If I just truncate the process by saying "this is politically incorrect," that possibility is gone, that's it, it's all over.

I don't see why this is so important.

GILROY: There's a difference between an epistemological question and political correctness. I mean in the distinction between sin and error I wasn't trying to make it a matter of political correctness, I was trying to challenge the fact that you were saying Eurocentrism wasn't a political sin, that it was an ethical question. You chose the word sin carefully, presumably. The word sin is a religious word, it has certain connotations.

MORRIS: I'm sorry, to me it's not a religious word and it really didn't occur to me it could be taken that way. To me, a "sin" is more like a style lapse. I don't mean to be cynical; that's how I use the word in the everyday Australian idiom I was also using at that point in my presentation. I'm not sure if that's due to the relentlessly secular assumptions of Australian public life, or to a nonchalance about "sin" in the particular Irish-Australian political culture I grew up in.

There's a misunderstanding here. I certainly do *not* think that Eurocentrism is "ethical," not political. On the contrary: what I actually said when I gave the paper was that an analysis of Eurocentrism in the basic texts of cultural studies matters "not because Eurocentrism is a political *sin* . . . but because it is a *politically limiting* thing, a barrier to political perspectives in cultural studies." In other words—it's a big mistake. Since in your terms, as I now understand them, I'd already *said* it was a political error, I thought you must be challenging my use of words.

This exchange makes me realize that I haven't been explicit enough about why "Eurocentrism" should worry me at a rudimentary level at a conference like this. It's a restlessness I have, rather than a position I can expound, and maybe it came through in my speech rather than in the text of my paper. I'm restless about the map of cultural studies being constructed at this conference, about what's not *on* that map, rather than what is. We've talked about local and global relations in a world where Japan, South Korea, Hong Kong, Taiwan, Singapore, or Indonesia simply don't exist, certainly not as *forces* in emergent structures of world power. The one time I heard somebody mention the Pacific Rim, it turned out to be a way of talking about relations between North and Central and South America—another way of staying on the American land mass, not a way of crossing the ocean. I'm not making a plea for inclusiveness, it's just that certain globalizing structures have potential, if "only" on the economic level, to affect people's lives everywhere in the future, and they aren't "centered" now in quite the same old *doubled* way (UK/USA, or USA/USSR), that traditional critiques of Eurocentrism sometimes Eurocentrically assume. To ignore this seems to me to be a political error.

IAIN CHAMBERS: It seems to me that the concept of the other operates in two different perspectives. You talk about the concept of the other and the pathos of distance it reproduced in Eurocentric philosophy. I think that's often right, particularly in terms of Heidegger and his concept of the sameness of being, which has been rather beautifully criticized by Levinas in *Totality and Infinity*. On the other hand, in the work of Homi Bhabha, the question of otherness also represents the sign of excess, which is not excess in terms of an alternative essentialism, but excess as something that cannot be reduced to a unique logic or rationalism, for example a Eurocentric discourse. You seem to refuse to take on board what Homi Bhabha was talking about in terms of the excess, those who are sentenced by history, written into history or written out of history, that sense of otherness which represents the incommensurable differences which we're trying to address.

MORRIS: I agree about the two positions too, except that I want to clarify that my object was not "Eurocentrism," but in a much more limited way a particular model which is taken very widely in cultural studies to work in a wide range of situations where I don't think it does work, and can even be disabling.

I agree that it's absolutely necessary to make the move which Homi Bhabha talked about of starting out from other traditions which have defined themselves against Eurocentrism or which have been struggling with it. I personally find the way Homi does that exemplary. It's just that I also think that the classical "Other" stuff is coming back in a quite raw form in cultural studies, and needs to be dealt with. I don't think there's a developmental relation between the two kinds of activity, unfortunately; the second kind doesn't eliminate the necessity for the first. I wish it did.

But the next part of your question—about liquidating the other and refusing to take on excess—raises some tricky problems for me. I have to be honest and say that there's a point at which my interest in the *philosophical* issue of "the other" runs out, partly because I don't have the training, in German philosophy especially, to follow the arguments very far. I can't do much with *Totality and Infinity* simply because I don't understand it, although I do get glimmers from the work of Elizabeth Grosz and feminists working on Irigaray. But at the moment I am very invested in some quite specific problems in Australian cultural history, and I am finding the frameworks of European philosophy, including the developments you mention, less and less useful or inspiring in an immediate way. So I suppose the real question for me is why that should be so.

I think it's partly to do with meta-language. It's not that I want to liquidate a concept of the other, and I doubt that you could anyway, but I probably do want to liquidate from my own discourse some fairly top-heavy ways of *talking about* the issue. It's not that I think Australian history is outside "excess"—on the contrary, if you consider how the place started out as a gulag for "excess" victims of the Industrial Revolution and went through genocide and ethocide and gynocide to pioneer hyper-discreet forms of apartheid and race management through genetic engineering, then Australia is something of a case study in what it means to be sentenced by history. But the vocabulary of critical theory can *sometimes* be an obstacle to actually doing the work involved in bringing different concepts of historicity into play, because it is so very remote both from the dominant Anglo/Celtic male vernacular, and all the other traditions of difference which have been contesting it for a very long time. That's not always true; someone like Sneja Gunew makes it work in relation to migrant writing, by emphasizing the non-British "Europeaness" suppressed in Australian culture, and Eric Michaels, Stephen Muecke, and Mudrooroo Narogin make it work in different ways for Aboriginal cultural politics. But they're also all very much about creating hybrid kinds of discourse, with a high degree of accessibility to particular groups—bureaucrats and teachers in some cases, as well as specific communities.

There's something I find quite hard to express here, almost an incommensurable difference between Australia and Europe or the United States, which is how *thin* the academic context of theoretical work really is, and on the other hand, how close the worlds of policy and media can be if you make the effort. It's to do with living in a small society. You have to think carefully about who you're writing for, and what works on different occasions. I am violently opposed to "everyday language" anti-intellectualism, and the idea that theory is about confirming what you already know. But in my own work, I am less willing to inscribe signs of theoretical-ness, which are really signs of audience, and also of the past of a generation of critics, than I might have been five years ago, or to frame what I'm doing in a codified way. I think a lot of work in cultural studies now massively overworks values like "difference," "incommensurability," and "excess," turning them into almost subcultural signs-of-theory without really putting them to work in a useful or enlightening way. I don't use them much unless I have to, although I do work in connection with the critical tradition those terms are used to valorize. Sometimes this leads people to assume I'm naive and offer me reading lists, but so be it.

All that said, I think you're right to suggest I'm often inclined to make a polemical kind of straight political criticism, even knowing its limitations. Maybe that reflects the positioning of my own ethnicity in Australian society, which has gone within my lifetime from being socially and economically marginal to being politically dominant with the loathsome Hawke Labor government. But whatever the reason, I feel very strongly that we have not finished with the Eurocentric discourse of sameness in its most basic and violent forms, and I am a bit skeptical about the practical effectiveness of taking it as read or as already bypassed somehow.

SCOTT COOPER: What is gained by seeing your work as cultural studies? One could see studies like this in literary study, in film and television study, in communications. Are all of these things today cultural study?

MORRIS: That's an interesting question. I don't have a deep personal identification with cultural studies as a discipline, which may be why I mentioned it so much. To tell you the truth, until very recently I thought of it in a narrow way as "Birmingham stuff," and I wasn't very sympathetic to that, especially the consumption-as-"resistance" line that developed in the mid-1980s. It's only recently that I can see my own work too as part of cultural studies, with events like this conference where connections are made to work that does influence me, like postcolonial criticism and the sort of politics of living that Douglas Crimp is involved with around representation. I think you need some identification in the first place in order to worry about what would be "lost" if you called your work something else.

For my own part, I have always wanted to do Australian cultural *history,* since right back when I was a student in the early 1970s. No institution in Sydney at that time had a place for what I wanted to do, especially since I was really excited by the critical theories I was learning in the French department, not the English department. For all sorts of reasons, there's still very little *written* about culture in Australian history; you don't have all these weighty indigenous schools of criticism, just lots of stuff coming now from all over the world, or left behind from colonialism, to make up a context together with all the Australian writing and thinking that was never "taught" when I was at school. So I had that wide-eyed sense of mystery about Australian history, as I still do, and I found that the work of, especially, Foucault and Deleuze when I mixed it up with feminism gave me a framework to think about cultural history in a realistic way. The realism matters, I think: Australians who took up poststructuralism in the 1970s did so because it seemed to be describing the world we lived in, not as a way to renovate literary criticism. Even today, Australian students who learn to think of "deconstruction" as a radical mode of political good sense can get a shock when they first come up against what Americans make out of it.

So when I could not work in our universities twenty years ago, I left formal academic study and did it not "on my own," because I had lots of people to talk with, but informally, supporting myself in other ways. And it has been amazing to watch the changes in how institutions define my sort of work over the years, the shifts in which departments invite you to speak and so on. A long time ago it used to be "semiotics," then "philosophy," then it was "film theory," then it was "art theory," and now it's "cultural studies" and I've even had contacts recently with "Australian Studies" and "English." So this experience makes me a bit skeptical about the seriousness of what is really at stake in the names of disciplines, you know.

So from that perspective, I probably have a fairly basic view of the issue you raise. I think first that cultural studies is going to be in the future whatever a collection of institutions say it is at any given time. I also think there is a tradition coming particularly from British work that allows us to say that cultural studies as a practice is necessarily an activist project of interrogating the relations between culture, politics, and economy in a way that constantly questions the purpose of its own practices—and so is open to non-"disciplinary" pressures and demands. I'm not sure that any of the other disciplines you mentioned really *necessitate* that.

26

Feminism, Psychoanalysis, and the Study of Popular Culture

Constance Penley

My paper is about some of the possible relations that can be forged among the three terms in the title of my talk, that is, feminism, psychoanalysis, and the study of popular culture. I am going to be proposing at least one way those terms might productively be brought together by describing my involvement in, and study of, a female fandom, called "slash" fandom, that is an intriguing spin-off of the large and lively *Star Trek* fandom.

Let me start off with a theoretical polemic. The way that I am trying to address the issues that have arisen for me in looking at this particular female fandom is a response to a tendency that disturbs me in recent feminist studies of popular culture. The tendency is to dismiss or bypass the work on subjectivity and sexual difference developed over the last fifteen years in feminist film theory. This dismissive or evasive move is typically accompanied by a call to adopt models considered more appropriate to the study of popular forms like the romance, the melodrama, the soap opera, or the sit-com. Almost automatically, it seems, theorists of women and popular culture are turning to Nancy Chodorow's (1978) object relations model of female subjectivity to describe how women read, view, and otherwise consume the artifacts of mass-produced culture. They see Chodorow's model as superior, first of all, because she focuses almost exclusively on *female* subjectivity, an emphasis seen to be wanting in the Freudian and Lacanian models that have been so influential in feminist film theory. Her account is also deemed to be better in that her idea of subject formation allows an easier theoretical move from the social to the psychical, and vice versa, since her psychoanalytic categories are already quite sociologized (for example, the way she recasts the process of unconscious identification into a kind of more or less conscious role modeling). And finally, Chodorow's ideas are taken up in the belief that she offers a more *optimistic* account of subjectivity: if the social and the psychical are not so far apart, this holds out the hope that it might be possible to reform the psyche through reforming the social (as seen in her belief, for example, that requiring men to share the work of nurturing children will produce a change in the basic configuration of the Oedipus complex).

But when Chodorow's model of female subjectivity is taken up to describe how women encounter popular culture, what results, I think, is a reduced account of female viewing, reading, or consuming because of her emphasis on *regression* as a specifically feminine mode of identification. For example, in Janice Radway's (1984) *Reading the Romance: Women, Patriarchy, and Popular Literature,* she argues, borrowing from Chodorow, that romance novels "work" to the extent that they successfully induce the reader imaginatively to regress, through identification with the heroine, to a pre-Oedipal moment of being nurtured and absolutely taken care of, a privilege typically denied adult women in this culture because they have the sole responsibility for nurturing. Or, to

479

take another example, Tania Modleski, in *Loving with a Vengeance: Mass-Produced Fantasies for Women*, (1984) claims that female viewers have such close identifications with soap opera characters because the shows stimulate the kind of psychological fusion that occurs between mothers and daughters in our culture, an inability to see oneself as separate that allows the female viewer to be easily sutured into the soap opera world. In both these otherwise useful and stimulating studies (and, indeed, Janice Radway's work was the inspiration for my own) female identification is seen to occur by means of a regressive pre-Oedipal fantasy.[1]

Although I already had my doubts about reducing the account of female fantasy in popular culture to a fantasy of pre-Oedipal regression, it was my work with and on slash fandom that finally convinced me of the limitations of that account. But, as I said, I already had my doubts, and those doubts were based on my understanding of the psychoanalytic idea of *fantasy,* with its ability to describe how the subject participates in and restages a scenario in which crucial questions about desire, knowledge, and identity can be posed, and in which the subject can hold a number of identificatory positions.[2] Adopting the Freudian and Lacanian description of fantasy allows one to account for multiple (if contradictory) subject positions, but it also ensures that one give a strict attention to the relation of desire and law, that is, to the subject of the symbolic as well as the imaginary. Only this more complex account of identification and sexual difference in fantasy could help me to describe what goes on in the reading and writing of the fan stories, given what seems to be the multiple possibilities of identification and numerous pleasures found there that do not seem to originate in the time and space of the pre-Oedipal.

I will get back to these claims later, but now I need to describe the fandom itself and the work that it produces, a unique hybrid genre of romance, pornography, and utopian science fiction.

In 1988 I was invited to a convention sponsored by a group called WHIPS, which, very disappointingly, only stands for Women of Houston in Publishing. I was invited to the convention because, for two years, I had been ordering through the mail a multitude of fan publications that go under the rubric "slash lit," which was the subject of the convention. If you look at Figure 1, you will see a copy of a page taken from a publication called *Datazine,* which comes out six times a year and lists most of the currently available amateur fan magazines, or fanzines as they are called, or, more often, just zines. On this page you will see advertisements for fanzines on *Battlestar Galactica* (BG), *Star Trek* (ST), *Miami Vice* (MV), a general media letter and discussion fanzine called *Comlink* (M [Media]), and three fanzines with the code K/S printed in the left margin. A code designation with a slash in it refers to any fanzine that features stories, poems, or drawings that take as their premise an explicitly sexual relationship between two of the main male characters. A K/S zine, then, is a *Star Trek* fan publication, but one in which all the material printed there concerns a romantic, sexual relationship between Captain James T. Kirk of the USS Enterprise and his first officer, Mr. Spock. As you can see from Figures 2–3 the artwork found in these zines is both romantic and explicit, which should give you an idea of the flavor of the stories and poems. Much of the work is so explicit, in fact, that if you wanted to send off for any of these zines you would be required to accompany your payment with a written statement declaring that you are over 18. Other media male relationships have also been slashed in the fanzines, and these you would find listed under other codes, for example, S/S for Simon and Simon, S/H, for Starsky and Hutch, H/Mc for Hardcastle and McCormick, or M/V for *Miami Vice*'s Crockett and Tubbs, although the best recent *Miami Vice* slash story put Crockett and Castillo together to great effect. The first slash zines though were

≡NOW≡IN≡PRINT≡≡≡≡≡≡≡12≡

BG   THE BATTLE OF MOLUKAI   **$11.00FC**
What led to the devastating battle that destroyed a great empire and annihilated an entire Colonial fleet? This novel is the history of the Fifth Colonial Fleet, led by the legendary Commander Cain of the Battlestar PEGASUS.
All checks must be payable to Joy Harrison.
OSIRIS PUBLICATIONS, 8928 N. Olcott Ave., Morton Grove, IL 60053

ST   A BEACH TO WALK ON   **$16.00**
A novella by Dolly Weissberg. A story about how Janice Rand again saw the Captain and Spock and remembered how long ago she had loved him, and married him, lost him and how their lives progressed from there. Over 70 pgs., in zine format.
Dolly Weissberg, Riverview Aprt. 7718 High Water G-2, N. Port Richey, FL 34655-2815

MV   BERNAY'S CAFE   **$2.50**
A HOT Miami Vice letter zine. If you like Vice come join the crowd that keeps you up on all the latest things about Miami Vice. Going on Issue #12. Back issues are available for same price.
Noel Silva, 674 Clarinada Ave., Daly City, CA 94015

ST   BEYOND THE FARTHEST STAR   **SEE BELOW**
#2-$6.00 PPD. Orion Press' X-rated, "no slash" Star Trek zine returns with a second issue! Includes "Questions about Maltz" by Endres, "All That Glitters"--a Spock/Christine story by Baker, "Southern Comfort"--a McCoy story by McInnis, and "Power Failure"--a Kirk tale. Also works by Summers, Cesari, and more. 70 pgs.
#1-$6.75. Features adult-oriented, erotic, action-adventure ST fiction from mary Cress and Chris Hamann, Beth Holland, Randall Landers, Linda Marcusky, and Esther Lemay. See Kirk captured because of his "reputation". See the ship go crazy as revealing pictures of the stalwart commander of the ENTERPRISE start popping up everywhere. Also Spock-Christine and Valkris-Torg. Definitely not for the the weak-hearted. Plenty of explicit, steamy scenes, nudity (art by Rick Endres). Age statement required (obviously). 70 pgs.
Bill Hupe, 6273 Balfour, Lansing, MI 48911

K/S   A COLLECTION OF DREAMS   **$14.00 US CAN $20.00 OS AIR**
Short stories, poetry & art set in the DREAMS OF THE SLEEPERS universe. Includes the short-story DAYBREAK, which is the prologue to the third DOTS novel (DAYBREAK, DREAM COME TRUE). Works by: Crouch, Solten, Hood, Tessman, Donovan, Jaeger, Feyrer, Whild, Soto, Dragon, Chiya Foulard, A.F. Black.
PON FARR PRESS, PO Box 1323, Poway, CA 92064-0014

M   COMLINK   **SEE BELOW**
#29, 31, 32 - $2.00 EACH; $7/4 ISSUES FC. The media discussion zine, published 4-5 times per year. Each issue contains letters on various media subjects (comics, movies, fandom), class-ads, (free with a current sub), and occasional articles. #32 is current (Oct 87), #31 (8-87) looks at 30 years of Hanna-Barbera animation.
Checks payable to Allyson M. Dyar.
Allyson M. Dyar, 40-A Cecil Ln., Montgomery, AL 36109-2872

K/S   COMMAND DECISION: THE UNEXPECTED BEGINNING $19.25 US $21.50 CAN $28.00 EUR
An explicit ST novel of adventure, intrigue, love, friendship and self-discovery, by C. Smythe; art by TACS; Poetry by Fine. Nominated for two Surak Awards. (Not an A.U. or Mirror story). 300+ pgs; offset; spiral bound. SASE for detailed flyer. Age statement required. Published by J.H. Publications, the LAST few copies of this novel have been turned over to Kaleidos Publications for handling. Only orders from Kaleidos Publ. can be honored.
KALEIDOS PUBLICATION, 19 Engle St., Tenafly, NJ 07670

K/S   CONSORT 2   **$16.00 PPD**
Consort 2 features material by Barr, Bush, Lansing, Lewis, Poste, Resch, Solten, Laoang, Lovett, TACS, TSC, and more. 272 pgs; K/S; age statement required.
REPREHENSIBLE PRESS, RFD #2 Box 1250, Lisbon Falls, ME 04252

FIGURE 1.   A page from *Datazine* listing fan publications for sale.

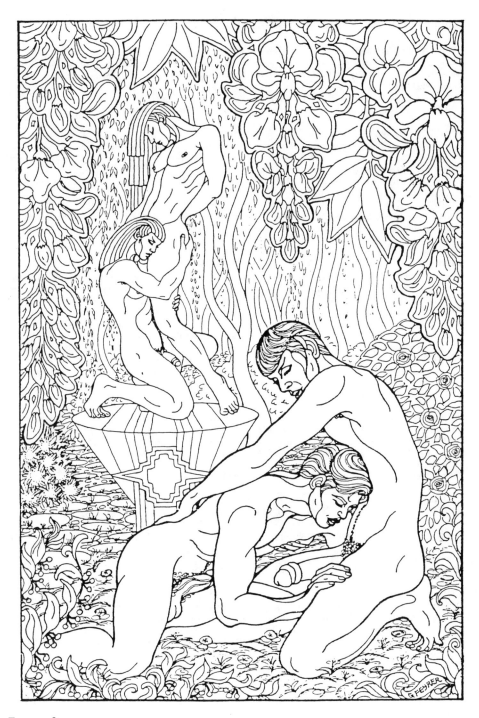

FIGURE 2.

K/S (they date from about 1976 or 1977) and they still represent the majority of slash publishing.

What is, however, perhaps most astonishing about all of this is that the fandom is almost 100% female, although an editorial in a recent issue of the K/S zine *First Time* proudly announced that it included the long promised story by a male writer. The editor went on to say, "Now be nice, ladies, send loc's [letters of comment] and let him know what you think. He can take it!" And, as another exception; at the second slash convention I attended, in June of 1989 in San Diego, for the first time two men had a real presence there, two gay men who had been sending their stories to a *Blake's 7* slash zine edited by women, who were then encouraged and helped by the women to start their own zine. So the almost completely female and heterosexual composition of the fandom may be breaking up slightly in some interesting ways.

The K/S fans write, edit, and publish hundreds of stories and poems in the zines, produce a great deal of artwork, which can sell for hundreds of dollars at slash convention art auctions, and also publish separate novels. It is truly a cottage industry, done mostly in their own homes (or sometimes at work), all made a great deal easier, of course, by the advent of desktop publishing and cheap photocopying. Most of the zines and novels are spiral bound, often with varnished, strikingly illustrated covers, and contain many other graphics and drawings. The level of editorial professionalism is very high. The zines and novels are beautifully produced and skillfully edited by amateurs who have trained themselves and each other.

The slash convention in Houston, the fourth of its kind, was called IDICon IV. All fan conventions are referred to by the fans as cons and given a significant prefix. The IDIC, I-D-I-C, in the name IDICon IV is the acronym for the Vulcan philosophy of Infinite Diversity in Infinite Combination, an idea that has become this fandom's watchword. (In the K/S letterzine, *On the Double,* a publication devoted to printing letters of comment on all aspects of the fandom, writers will often sign off with either "Yours in slash" or "Yours in IDIC.") Even before I went to the convention, I knew a bit about the fandom, other than what I had been able to glean from reading the zines and letterzines, through an incisive and informative essay on K/S zines by Patricia Frazer Lamb and Diana Veith (1986). Their essay, entitled "Romantic Myth, Transcendence, and *Star Trek* Zines," appeared in 1986 in the only good collection I have ever seen on science fiction and sexuality, a book called *Erotic Universe.* In addition, I had read the only other substantive article that has been written on the K/S zines, a rave appreciation of them by science fiction writer Joanna Russ (1985) that appeared in a 1985 collection of her essays. I already knew then from these two essays that this was an almost all-female fandom, and had also been able to get an idea of the extent of the production and the number of fans involved: there are probably not more than 500 active, core fans, although they publish a tremendous amount, which is disseminated beyond the core group through mail order and convention sales of the zines, borrowing, and even photocopying, although this latter practice is frowned upon if the zine is still "in print," that is, still being sold and circulated.

But many of my questions were still unanswered, and I went to the convention looking for more answers, as well as more zines to add to my ever-growing collection. Among my questions were these: What reasons did the fans give for writing their erotic fantasies across the bodies of two men —and why these particular men? What was the sexual orientation of the fans—straight, lesbian, or some of each? What was their relation to gay politics, given that the focus of their writing was a same sex couple? Did they see themselves as writing renovated romances or more satisfying female pornography? (The Lamb and Veith article claimed the K/S fans were trying to rewrite the romance along less sexist lines, the Joanna Russ essay insisted that they were attempting to write better pornography than is usually available to women.) How did their slash activity, which clearly consumes many hours and days of their lives spent in reading, writing, editing, and publishing, fit into their work schedules and domestic lives? Was the fandom as racially mixed as *Star Trek* fandom is? What was their class makeup? Why were female media couples never slashed—for example, why were there no Cagney and Lacey stories in the zines? Given their insistence on their amateur status, their claim that this is a hobby and nothing more, what was their relation to professionalism, especially since they seem to set such high standards for themselves as writers, editors, and publishers, and given the growing phenomenon of so many of them becoming professional writers, some of them taking their own and other's stories and de-slashing them, heterosexualizing them for commercial publication, as, for example, official *Star Trek* novels? What was their relation to feminism? And finally, what cannot be said in K/S writing; what are its self-imposed or unconscious taboos? But a more personal and ethical question was, where did I fit in to all this?—was I going to the conference as a fan, even perhaps a potential writer of K/S stories, a voyeur of a fascinating subculture, or a feminist academic and critic? I certainly liked the stories well enough, and in fact K/S was the first pornographic writing that I had ever really responded to, which made me remember that as a girl, while I had read and enjoyed Nancy Drew, I had really gotten off on the Hardy Boys, Tom Swift, and Tarzan of the Apes. (However, it never occurred to me, as an adolescent reader, to put any of these men together in erotic scenarios, although friends have reported doing so, especially Tonto and the Lone Ranger—and this is before reading Leslie Fiedler!) So I was certainly a fan of K/S but even while I was enjoying reading the stories, I kept coming across things I just had to take notes on. Given that all of my intellectual and political work has been on women and media, I could not help also responding to the slash phenomenon as one of the most radical and intriguing female appropriations of a popular culture product that I had ever seen. It begged to be analyzed and theorized because so much could be learned from it about how women, and people, resist, negotiate, and adapt to their own desires this overwhelming media environment that we all inhabit. So I decided finally that I was all three, a fan, a feminist critic, and perhaps inescapably a voyeur, keeping in mind, however, that voyeurism is an interesting position in itself, since the voyeur is always far more implicated in the scene than the fantasy of observation at a distance acknowledges.

Obviously, I was not able to find answers to all of my questions in the three days and four nights I spent at the convention in Houston, or the ones I attended in 1989 and 1990 in San Diego, and even of those that I did, I would not have time to tell you all of them now. What I want then to focus on in the time I have left are some of the issues that came up that offer the greatest *challenge* to a feminist analysis of women and popular culture.

I think it is important to point out, though, right from the beginning, that everything that was a question for me, from issues of genre—is K/S romance or pornography?— to the sexual orientation of the K/Sers, to the role of their fan activity in their daily lives, is in fact verbalized and contested by the fans themselves. It is a highly self-reflexive and self-critical fandom; their intellectual and political interests and anxieties are apparent in far more than merely symptomatic ways. *They* want to know why they are so drawn to fandom and why they love reading and writing erotic stories about two men together. *They* are curious about the sexual makeup of the fandom; for example, the number of lesbians, in what is admittedly a mostly heterosexual fandom, and the nature of their interest in K/S, has been debated in two recent issues of *On the Double,* by both lesbian and straight fans; and at the last convention in San Diego there was, for the first time, a hugely well-attended panel on gay lifestyles made up of lesbian and gay fan writers and artists. The fans are also asking themselves if the AIDS crisis is having or should have an effect on what they are writing, whether, for example, Kirk and Spock should be shown practicing safer sex. These questions and others like them are made into panel topics at the conventions, along with other more practical panels, of course, like one that was a brainstorming session on how to go about slashing *Star Trek: The Next Generation,* the new TV series. So I do not feel so much as if I am *analyzing* the women in this fandom, as thinking along with them. Several fans are also now quite interested in what I am doing (they refer to me as one of the "academic fans," of which there is a handful), and are giving me a great deal of help in my thinking about fan culture. The fans are, of course, wary of having their activity revealed to the outside world—to the "mundanes" as the fans call non-fans. There are very good reasons for this, with the most immediate and practical one being that we live in a time when "obscenity" and "homoeroticism" have been conflated in the minds of many people, following the urgings of bigots like Jesse Helms, and jobs and lives are on the line. So too, the part of me that is a fan is as ambivalent as other fans about public, even "academic," scrutiny of our pleasures. I describe the attitude as ambivalence rather than rejection only because I know how rightfully proud the slash fans are of their own creativity as writers, artists, and publishers. Insofar then as they want and deserve recognition for their work, this desire conflicts with their wish to remain unknown. Just as there is a strong code of ethics for writing *within* fan culture (which has been discussed in great detail by Henry Jenkins [1991]), so too there will have to be a complex negotiation around the ethics of writing *about* fan culture, especially slash fandom since it is potentially vulnerable not only to the guardians of morality but the keepers of copyright.

To give you a sense of what slash stories are like, I will briefly describe to you a fairly typical one that contains many of the most common motifs. It is "The Ring of Soshern" by a fan writer whose name or even pseudonym I cannot give. Most fans write under pseudonyms, and the choices of pseudonyms (fans often have more than one) reveal an extraordinary sense of play and humor. But those pseudonyms cannot be reproduced here; some of them have become so associated with the real author, that it would be like revealing the identity of the author. I thus use only the names or pseudonyms of authors I have been able to contact and who have given me permission.

"The Ring of Soshern" was probably written before 1976, making it one of the earliest K/S stories. Photocopies of the manuscript circulated very privately, and it is a highly revered and imitated story. In recognition of its status as a classic it was finally published in 1987 in *Alien Brothers,* a new anthology series with very high production values and controversial cash prizes.

In the story Kirk and Spock beam down to a previously unexplored planet to investigate some mysterious sensor readings. Through a miscalculation the Enterprise gets caught in an ion storm and must leave them behind to try to flee it. Kirk and Spock are left deserted on the planet, not knowing when the ship will be able to return for them, for there will be much damage from the ion storm that Scotty will have to fix first. Over the next days Kirk and Spock have to deal with dangerous plants, dinosaur-like creatures, and even some shaggy humanoids. They each in turn get wounded and must be tenderly ministered to by the other. But the real crisis comes when Spock begins to go into *pon farr.* Although Spock is only half-Vulcan, he still goes into the heat suffered every seven years by all Vulcan males. He will go into a blood fever, become violent, and finally die if he does not mate. And he cannot mate with just anyone; it must be someone with whom he is already empathically bonded. (Up to this point the author is not making it up: perhaps the most famous *Star Trek* episode, "Amok Time," written by Theodore Sturgeon, depicts Spock going into *pon farr* and being returned to Vulcan by Kirk and Dr. McCoy so that he can undergo the mating ritual and save his life.) Kirk realizes that there is a bond of love between him and Spock because of all the years they have worked together, all the times they have saved each other's lives, and their deep respect and affection for one another. Kirk goes to Spock, who at first refuses his offer but then his blood fever takes him over and he has no choice. Not only does their sexual act save Spock's life, it makes Kirk realize that he does not just love Spock, he is *in* love with Spock. Spock too realizes his love for the captain and they spend all their remaining days on the planet exploring both the planet and each other's bodies.

Although they are worried about the fate of the Enterprise and its crew, they are very perturbed one day to hear Scotty's voice on the long-dead communicator announcing that they can be beamed up immediately. They return to the ship, not knowing what will happen to their new relationship. Surely Dr. McCoy, who has by now realized that it was the infallible Spock who miscalculated the location of the ion storm because he was mentally and physically incapacitated by the onset of *pon farr,* will know that Spock would not be alive now unless *someone* had mated with him. The story ends with Kirk and Spock, each in his own quarters, bleakly contemplating all the obstacles to continuing their erotic relationship, but Spock makes the brave decision to go to Kirk's quarters anyway, and the last line of the story has Spock looking into Kirk's eyes and closing the door behind him.

While "The Ring of Soshern" has several sex scenes in it, the sex is described fairly abstractly and is a great deal tamer than that found in the thousands of stories that came after. Over the years several conventions have become established. For example, Spock does want to have sex even when not in the throes of *pon farr,* which allows many more narrative occasions for erotic couplings. Although there were some pretty exotic descriptions of his half-alien genitalia in early stories (in Janet Alyx's novel *The Matchmaker,* for example, Spock's penis is hidden behind a furry mound that becomes tumescent and unfolds like petals from which his emerald green penis unfurls like a stamen—it sounds like a Judy Chicago Dinner plate with a penis!), the conventions for describing his penis are fairly settled now: it is green of course, because of the green Vulcan blood that flows in his veins, it is double-ridged, and somewhat larger than a human one.

Once conventions become established though, the writer then has the delightful problem of having to come up with variations inside those conventional limits. One conference workshop I attended was entirely devoted to brainstorming new ways to describe Kirk's solid, golden, blond body and the Vulcan's taut, lissome, pale green one. The writers, however, voiced their concern that they might have exhausted all the possible descriptions. As one participant remarked, to the appreciative laughter of everyone present, how many ways are there to describe a green cock after you have used up "his green, throbbing member," "his quivering jade tower," and so on?!

One question that is often debated in this fandom is whether Kirk and Spock are in fact having homosexual sex, whether they are homosexual. The solution to this, or rather solutions, because there are more than one, has a great many implications for issues of genre, identification, and fantasy. One answer to whether they are having homosexual sex or not is a practical one. In Joanna Russ's (1985) essay on K/S, called "Pornography by Women, for Women, with Love," she points out that in some of the early stories the women writers do not seem to be quite sure of the details of gay male sexuality. Some of the betraying details include, she says, characters leaping into anal intercourse with a blithe lack of lubrication that makes it clear the authors are thinking of vaginal penetration, both men approaching orgasm with a speeded-up intensity of pelvic thrusting, and multiple orgasms. However, I have found what Russ calls "betraying details" in many recent stories too. Since it would not be difficult to do a minimum amount of research or reading on male physiology and gay male sex (and the fans in fact do so, consulting books like *The Joy of Gay Sex* and gay beefcake magazines), this suggests that the women writing the stories do not want Kirk and Spock to be homosexual. And it is true that some of the authors try to write their stories so that somehow the two men are lovers without being homosexual. Here is a good example of this premise in a story called "Homecoming," which also appeared in *Alien Brothers*. This passage reports Kirk's thoughts:

> Until that moment five years ago—almost two years before Spock left for Gol and Kirk accepted the Admiralty—Kirk had never had any inclination toward a same sex relationship. He's never wanted any man until Spock. Hadn't wanted one after. Perhaps it was exactly what he'd finally concluded: some forms of love defy, transcend all barriers, all differences or similarities.

In such a way, then, the whole issue of object choice or sexual orientation gets resolved in an idea of *cosmic destiny:* the two men are somehow meant for each other and homosexuality has nothing to do with it.

Russ says that another sure sign that Kirk and Spock are not intended to be homosexual is that in these stories one finds no depiction of a gay subculture, no awareness of being derogated, no friends or family, absolutely no gay friends, and no gay politics. Now, I have not done enough reading across the entire range of K/S to be able to speak authoritatively about historical shifts of perspective in this female fan writing, but I have come across recent stories that do, in contrast to Russ's claim, seem to be trying to incorporate elements of contemporary gay life, stories, for example, about the difficulty of coming out to one's parents, as when Spock must tell Amanda, his human mother, and Sarek, his Vulcan father, that he and Jim have bonded forever. Another story, "He Who Loves Last," in the zine *As I Do Thee* #11, tells of Kirk and Spock's troubles when, having temporarily set up housekeeping on the planet Timoran, Spock has an affair with one member of a gay couple who are their next-door neighbors. And there are other such stories, for example, "Love with the Proper Vulcan," in *Off Duty* #1, in which Kirk goes to another human captain who has a male Vulcan lover for advice on how to start a relationship with Spock, while Spock is meanwhile consulting the other captain's Vulcan first officer on how to get things going with Kirk.

Therefore, even though I agree with Russ that there is a tendency in this literature to put these two men together sexually but still, improbably, maintain that they are heterosexual, I do find emerging a kind of political self-consciousness about that scenario and a new willingness to let them be gay.[3] I will predict though that this slight recent trend toward homosexualizing Kirk and Spock will not grow substantially, and the reason does not entirely have to do with homophobia. Of course there must be some element of homophobia in the wish to keep them heterosexual, although it would distress the K/S writers a great deal to think that they might be harboring homophobic thoughts. They see their adherence to the philosophy of IDIC, Infinite Diversity in Infinite Combination, as somehow putting them above the crude intolerance, xenophobia, and homophobia they abhor in the society around them. I would argue that the reason Kirk and Spock are heterosexualized in these stories is that it allows another kind of Infinite Diversity in Infinite Combination that the writers and readers seem to desire, and here I am starting to talk about identification and fantasy. Some of the stories, as I have said, do depict Kirk and Spock as homosexual, and clearly the pleasure is in imagining what two men, two gay men, do together sexually. Some of the fans defend this by saying that men, after all, have had their pornography about lesbians all these years, now it's our turn (after saying this, however, they usually acknowledge that it is not simply reversible). But what is served, at the level of *fantasy,* by having them together sexually but not somehow being homosexual? I think it allows a much greater range of identification and desire for the women: in the fantasy one can *be* Kirk or Spock (a possible phallic identification) and also still *have* (as sexual objects) either or both of them since, as heterosexuals, they are not *un*available to women. If, in the psychoanalytic description of fantasy, its two poles are being and having, in the slash universe this binary opposition remains but is not held to be divided along gender lines.

My aim is not to construct this female phallic identification or this active adoption of men as sexual objects in fantasy as a privileged or "progressive" position. Rather, I want to show that the range and diversity of identifications and object relations can be much greater than is currently being recognized in feminist studies of women and popular culture. Once shown, it will then be possible to give a fuller and more complex account of what women *do* with popular culture, how it gives them pleasure, and how it can be consciously and unconsciously reworked to give them *more* pleasure, at both a social and psychical level.

I think I need to backtrack a little bit to explain why women would want to *be* Kirk or Spock. I have no theoretical problem with the idea of women identifying with

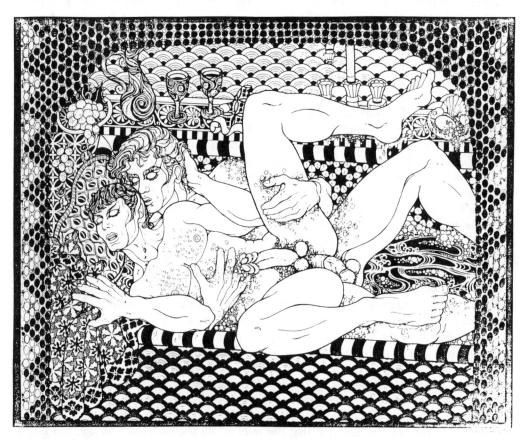

FIGURE 3.

men in fantasy or in fiction. Such an account of cross-gender identification and the claim that one can, no matter what one's gender, identify with either the man or the woman, or the entire scene itself, or the fictional place of the one who looks on to the scene, has been made possible through the shift in feminist film theory from a model based on voyeurism and fetishism, with its often fixed positions that are gendered from the very beginning, to a model based on the psychoanalytic account of fantasy. If we believe that the subject, at the level of the unconscious, is bisexual, then a great variety and range of identifications are possible, even and above all across gender boundaries.[4] But I am not so much concerned with arguing that women can identify with men, because I think that has already been proven, but why these women are identifying with these fictional men. Why Kirk and Spock? As I mentioned before, even though what the fans call "the slash premise"—that the two men are really in love and sexually involved—can be found in other shows, like *Simon and Simon* and *Starsky and Hutch,* for instance, the Kirk/Spock stories came first and still dominate slash writing. We must turn, I think, to the *Star Trek* universe to see what might have spawned such strong identifications.

Although I do not have exact figures, I think from what I have read and heard in the fandom that almost all of the K/Sers were originally involved in *Star Trek* fandom, and many still are. Fan testimonials to K/S are repeatedly put this way: "I couldn't believe it when I found K/S, it was as if it was what I'd always been looking for in *Star Trek* fandom but was missing." It is important, in trying to describe the possibility of identification with Kirk and Spock, to understand the identification with the entire *Star Trek* universe. To be involved in *Star Trek* fandom, one must have a full working knowledge of what is called "the canon universe," that is, the 78 TV episodes (plus the pilot), the five films, and to some extent the *Star Trek* universe as it has been expanded in the official *Star Trek* novels, and in the *Star Trek* magazines, both professional and fan. One goes to conventions, where one buys *Star Trek* paraphernalia: meets the actors from both the old TV series and the new one, *Star Trek: The Next Generation;* participates in auctions, trivia contests, and costumed reenactments of favorite scenes. If the fan has a modem, she or he can join in the ongoing *Star Trek* electronic conference. It is a complete world, and very often referred to by the fans as a family. And crucially here, in trying to understand women's involvement in the larger world of science fiction writing and fandom, it is thought of in terms of Before *Star Trek* and After *Star Trek*. Marion Zimmer Bradley (1985) has said that, yes, Ursula LeGuin's winning both the Hugo and the Nebula for *The Left Hand of Darkness* was important for breaking up what had been an almost totally male field, as was the appearance of Joanna Russ's *The Female Man,* but what really changed everything for women's involvement in science fiction was *Star Trek.* And it is widely acknowledged that *Star Trek* fandom was really begun and kept alive by women (see, e.g., Trimble, 1983). But as loyal as the women fans of *Star Trek* have been, they have always been vocal about their disappointment with the women characters. There is a great deal of affection for the characters Lt. Uhura, the communications officer, Nurse Chapel, and Yeoman Rand, for example, but there is bitter disappointment that these women of the twenty-third century are still behind the switchboard, at the doctor's side, or in miniskirts serving coffee to the men. And it has not gotten a whole lot better on *Star Trek: The Next Generation.* It was, then, in large part, the women fans' abiding *love* for the *Star Trek* universe, which at an important moment in the late sixties made at least a gesture toward sexual equality—there are, after all women both on the bridge and off who perform important duties—and their disappointment—everything they felt was missing from *Star Trek*— that pushed them to begin elaborating on the *Star Trek* universe, to move it imaginatively toward what *they* wanted: a better romance formula, and compelling pornography for women. They could only do so, however, through the characters they loved, respected, identified with, and lusted after, the men, not the women of *Star Trek.*

But as we know, identification in fantasy does not just go through character. The subject can also identify with the entire scene, or the narrative itself. One important aspect of this fandom, which I am only just beginning to understand and can only comment on here very briefly, is the love the fans have for the social and political values represented by the *Star Trek* universe. In *Star Trek,* especially the television series, one can see, almost as if frozen in amber, a perfect representation of Kennedy-era liberalism, which the fans equate with producer Gene Roddenberry's version of it, the philosophy of IDIC—the militarist adventurism of both the Kennedy era and *Star Trek* not seeming to be a contradiction for the fans. The fans feel as if they are part of that universe, want it to *be* our universe, and write thousands of stories trying at least to create it on paper and in the mind—that is their utopia, with a few modern additions of course, like a more sustained attention to sexual and racial equality, freedom of sexual preference, and global ecology, often expressed in a New Age-inspired language more suited for describing inner space than outer space.

Now that I have laid out something of the strength and force of the fan investment in the *Star Trek* universe and in these two characters, an investment that manifests itself through both identification and desire, I think it is possible to begin to show how K/S works as romance and as pornography, how it edges toward something that might be characterized as romantic pornography.

It is the essay by Patricia Lamb and Diana Veith (1986) that I have already cited that puts forth the most persuasive argument for K/S as renovated romance, a renovation that takes care of what fans and feminist critics have seen as some of the more troubling aspects of the romance formula. Lamb and Veith argue that the characters of Kirk and Spock offer the possibility of a transcendent mystical union, but this time based on a relationship of radical equality, not the usual erotics of dominance and submission found in the typical romance formula, in which dominance and submission are invariably the respective roles of male and female. The two authors even construct a chart to demonstrate that the K/S writers are only mildly extrapolating from the television show's characterizations of Kirk and Spock as equally androgynous. They see Kirk, for example, to be coded as "feminine" in that he is shorter, physically weaker, emotional, intuitive, and sensual, but "masculine" insofar as he, as Captain, is undisputed leader, the initiator of action, the sexually promiscuous one, and usually the seducer. Spock, on the other hand, is coded as "feminine" in that he is the "alien" or "other," follows Kirk loyally, and is a virgin before marriage and expects to be absolutely monogamous after marriage. His masculine characteristics include his being taller, more powerful, logical, rational, controlled, and reticent about divulging personal matters. Thus, even though Kirk and Spock have to overcome the usual obstacles of the romance formula—their love is forbidden, it must be kept a secret, neither lover can take the initiative, each constantly mistakes or doubts the reciprocity of the other's desire—when they do get together, they do so as a couple in which love and work can be shared. Their passionate lifetime union is only an extension of the friendship and loyalty they have always felt for each other while working as Captain and first officer on the bridge of the Enterprise. Lamb and Veith's answer, then, to the question of why the slashers write their romances about two men, is that we still live in a patriarchal culture, and it is thus still not possible to imagine two women passionately in love with one another who go out and save the galaxy once a week.

I agree with Lamb and Veith's argument, although I think it helps us more to understand the sociological question of "why Kirk and Spock?" than the perhaps more psychical question of "why two men?" To grasp why the erotic charge is always depicted as occurring between two men and why it takes place in a scenario in which women can fantasmatically participate but are, finally, radically excluded, we would also have to turn, I think, to descriptions of our culture that emphasize its homosocial organization, along the lines that Eve Sedgwick (1985), among others, has suggested to us.

I would also put more emphasis than Lamb and Veith do on the fans' identification with the whole *Star Trek* universe, not just the characters. But, finally, my main criticism of their work (which I otherwise find invaluable) is that their focus on K/S as romance slights the pornographic force of these stories. Just as K/S redoes romance, so too it constructs new versions of female pornography. One ingenious way that it redoes pornography is that it attempts to resolve the vexed issue of S & M, an issue that still bitterly divides feminists. There is a lot of S & M in these stories. However, through neatly borrowing a familiar science fiction device, the K/Sers are able to have their S & M, while firmly siding with those who believe that whatever you do in your fantasy life is fine, because it is fundamentally separate from what you do in daily life. This is how it works: rarely will a scene of rape, torture, or bondage take place in the regular K/S universe. But, through the science fiction device of the alternate or mirror universe, the evil Spock can find himself working for the Orion slave traders and a degraded Kirk will be the handsome blond slave brought to him in chains to be put through various sexual initiations before being shipped off to the brothels of Omicron Pi. But after all this is over, a fortuitous time warp occurs that flips the two men back into the parallel universe where everything is normal. (Again, as with *pon farr* stories, the narrative premise is taken from a *Star Trek* episode, here the Hugo-nominated "Mirror, Mirror.")

Some fans show a strongly psychoanalytic understanding of the relation of the unconscious to everyday life. In several alternate universe stories I have read, the Kirk and Spock of the original time line have flashbacks to, or at least nagging memories of, their evil mirror counterparts, as if to acknowledge that even though fantasy and "reality" are separate, that does not mean that there is *no* relation.

There is clearly much more to be said about the ingenious ways the K/S fans are reshaping both romance and pornography to their own desiring ends. But I need to begin to move toward a conclusion and I want to do so by mentioning some aspects of the fandom that I find troubling. It is probably been obvious to you from my tone here that I am, for the most part, completely ga-ga over this fandom. It indeed represents the most radical and intriguing female appropriation of a mass-produced cultural product that I have ever seen. A friend of mine told me that I wasn't really a fan of *Star Trek*, I was a fan of this fandom, and I think there is a great deal of truth in that.[5] But here, for example, is one thing that troubles me about the fandom: I cannot tell you how many times during the three slash conventions I have attended that I heard the phrase, "I'm not a feminist but . . . ." The fans, who from everything else they said on individual issues—from reproductive rights to equal pay for women—appeared to be liberal to left, could not speak of themselves as feminists, could not speak from a feminist position. One reason that immediately springs to mind is that, insofar as the women fans see themselves as readers and writers of pornography, they do not feel accepted by a feminism that is popularly perceived as moralistically anti-pornography. (I am referring here, of course, to the great success of the Women Against Pornography movement in fostering the now widely held notion that pornography's only function and purpose is to victimize women.)

But beyond that, I think that there is also the class issue. Most of the fans are either working class or "subprofessional" (I use the term "subprofessional" to designate the kinds of jobs that, if men held them, they would be thought of as professional jobs, but because women hold them and are paid so little, they are not quite considered professional). The fans who also work outside the house, either part-time or full-time, are secretaries, clerks, librarians, daycare workers, social workers, schoolteachers, and nurses; one of the fans at the most recent convention claimed that 40% of the fans were nurses, mostly in intensive care units. Feminists, on the other hand, seem to be perceived by the fans as middle-class professionals and therefore not like them. All of this is not to say that I did not hear feminist *sentiments* strongly, frequently, and humorously voiced by the fans, but rarely from the position of being a feminist. Instead, the affiliation is to fandom. I found out participants' occupations and class background only incidentally; one is not asked, on first being introduced, "What do you do?," but "How long have you been in fandom?"

A very telling event was one conference workshop I attended devoted to dysfunctional families. The workshop was put together from the perception that many fans come from so-called dysfunctional families and in fact turn to fandom for the kind of unconditional acceptance one gets (supposedly) only from one's family. The two moderators of the workshop had chosen to focus it specifically on the problems of adult children of alcoholics, taking parental alcoholism and the children's response to it as a model for all forms of abuse and victimization. We were asked to read together and comment on the ACOA list of 14 characteristics adult "children of alcoholics seem to have in common due to having been brought up in an alcoholic household." They included statements like, "We became isolated and afraid of people and authority figures." "We became approval seekers and lost our identity in the process." "We are frightened by angry people and any personal criticism." "We have an overdeveloped sense of responsibility, and it is easier for us to be concerned with others than ourselves." Now I think it was when we got to no. 10 that I finally spoke up to ask whether these descriptions weren't almost identical to those of the behavior of women in our culture because of their unequal treatment. One of the moderators energetically responded, "Yes," but then immediately offered a disclaimer. "Yes, women are generally devalued, but I don't want to say anything too global." She didn't want to say anything "too global," I think, because she might have been appearing to make a feminist statement.

There are many lessons in all of this for feminism and the study of popular culture. We would indeed love to take this fandom as an exemplary case of female appropriation of, resistance to, and negotiation with mass-produced culture. And we would also like to be able to use a discussion of K/S to help dislodge the still rigid positions in the feminist sexuality debates around fantasy, pornography, and S & M. But if we are to do so it must be within the recognition that the slashers do not feel they can express their desires for a better, sexually liberated, and more egalitarian world through feminism; they do not feel they can speak as feminists, they do not feel that feminism speaks for them. Fandom, the various popular ideologies of abuse and self-help, and New Age philosophies are seen as far more relevant to their needs and desires than what they perceive as a middle-class feminism that disdains popular culture and believes that pornography degrades women.

My final question, then, is to contemporary feminism and its work on popular culture: are we ready, like the slash fans, "to explore strange new worlds . . . to boldly go where no one has gone before?"

Notes

1. Another, and more recent, example of this tendency I am pointing to would be Jackie Byars's (1988) "Gazes/Voices/Power: Expanding Psychoanalysis for Feminist Film and Television

Theory." Just as Modleski tries to construct the female spectator's pre-Oedipal regression as *ultimately* positive (from her victimized position the woman enacts a revenge fantasy in and through the mass-culture text), Byars, after arguing for the pre-Oedipality of the female spectator, also tries to show that this conservative, compensatory position is finally active and positive. She does so by bringing in Carol Gilligan's theories to argue that this *different* spectator (that is, different from the male spectator) is a *better* one: caring, responsive, and connected rather than distant, voyeuristic, and sadistic. This conceptual move, which establishes the pre-Oedipal as the origin and the limit of female subjectivity but then attempts to give that position a positive value, ultimately reduces and essentializes the account of female subjectivity, in one case making woman always-already a victim (revenge is the tactic of the victim) and in the other conceiving of woman as having a profoundly different nature from those who manage the world, which would seem to be a dangerous conclusion.

2. The now classic psychoanalytic account of fantasy to which my own description is indebted is found in Jean Laplanche and J.-B. Pontalis (1968), "Fantasy and the Origins of Sexuality." Particularly important for my approach to describing female media fan culture and its artistic products are the following conclusions of Laplanche and Pontalis:

1. Fantasy has nothing to do with an opposition between "reality" and "illusion" but rather interjects a third term—psychical reality—that structures both;

2. Fantasy is not the object of desire but its setting;

3. Fantasy is a story for the subject, a story that attempts to answer certain basic or "primal" questions about the origin of the individual, the origin of sexuality, and the origin of the difference between the sexes (other questions can be posed and "answered" in fantasy but these are the most basic ones);

4. Sexuality is detached from any natural object; to start existing as sexuality, it must begin in fantasy;

5. Although the subject is always present in the fantasy, she or he may be there in a number of positions or in a de-subjectivized form, that is, "in the very syntax" of the fantasy sequence;

6. There is no separation between conscious and unconscious fantasies but rather a profound relationship and continuity between the various fantasy scenarios—"the stage setting of desire"—ranging from the daydream to the fantasies that can be recovered or reconstructed only in an analytic investigation;

7. A psychoanalytic account of fantasy must necessarily show the dialectic relationship between fantasy productions, the underlying structures, and the reality of the scene.

To which must be added the Lacanian emphasis on the non-reciprocity between subject and object, as described in his formula for fantasy: $\$\lozenge a$ (the subject is barred from the desire of or for *objet petit a*); in other words, the subject is structured by that which is lacking to it.

3. Fan friends who are involved in *Professionals* fandom (stories based on the lives of the two male leads of a sophisticated, action-oriented, British secret agent show) say that the PROS writers explicitly depict the two men as a gay couple living in homophobic Thatcherist Britain. I have also noticed that the male characters in *Blake's 7* fan fiction seem to be more forthrightly depicted as gay. The differences here—that the characters can be more or less or not at all gay—demonstrate that there is not a single, monolithic fantasy of gender or sexual orientation in fan writing but a number of positions and possibilities. These positions can, however, be in conflict; they are not merely multiple and dispersed. For example, even though most K/S writers never set out to write explicitly gay characters but rather men who can share love and work in an egalitarian way (and indeed for their project of refashioning heterosexual masculinity—which I argue elsewhere—they *need* Kirk and Spock not to be gay [see Penley, 1991]), they have in fact written characters who could be reasonably taken to be homosexual, and thus eventually have to face the question (asked by themselves and other fans) of why they are reluctant to let these two men who are joined erotically and emotionally be gay. This questioning has led, I believe, to the beginnings of a fan debate around homophobia in our culture, its causes and consequences. That this debate should be taking place in what might seem an improbable location—female media fan culture, many of whose members must maintain an exceptionally conventional demeanor because

of their jobs and domestic situations—is heartening during this time of severe backlash against any sexual role or orientation repressively deemed to be "non-standard."

4. For examples of recent work using the psychoanalytic account of fantasy to describe desire and identification in film see Elisabeth Lyon (1988), "The Cinema of Lol V. Stein"; Janet Bergstrom (1988), "Enunciation and Sexual Difference"; Elizabeth Cowie (1990), "Fantasia"; Constance Penley, "Feminism, Film Theory, and the Bachelor Machines," in (1989), *The Future of an Illusion: Film, Feminism, and Psychoanalysis;* and the essays in *Fantasy and the Cinema,* ed. James Donald (1989).

5. I now know, since attending a slash convention panel on "How did you get into slash [fandom]?" that my position as a fan of the fandom rather than a fan of *Star Trek* is not unusual. Although many of the women fans came to slash after years of involvement in *Star Trek* fandom, many others came to love and appreciate *Star Trek* only through the version of it elaborated in slash fan culture. There are a very few who claim to have little or no interest in *Star Trek* itself, although at least a bit of indulgent affection for it seems to be necessary to the enjoyment of the slash version.

DISCUSSION: CONSTANCE PENLEY

ED BRUNER: Would you elaborate on the use of pseudonyms or real names by the people at these conventions?

PENLEY: The fact that most fans use a pseudonym, and often more than one, is highly significant in that it shows how much the fans value being able to inhabit a social space in which one can adopt a fictional identity or even a number of fictional identities. I'm sorry that I can't reproduce some of those pseudonyms here (for reasons of confidentiality that I mentioned in my paper) because they would show evidence of a good deal of humor and imagination in their construction. There is, of course, a tradition in women's writing of women using pseudonyms and more often than not using male names. That, however, is rarely the case in slash fandom—I've come across almost no pseudonyms that are male. If I had to characterize the kinds of pseudonyms, I'd say they range from names that are based on well-known fantasy or story book characters, therefore a lot of Celtic-sounding names, or names that are "Vulcanized," if I can put it that way: if I were to write a slash story I might choose, for example, to write under "T'Penley," after a famous Vulcan matriarch, T'Pau. One prolific and popular slash author whose pseudonym I do have permission to mention goes under the name Alexis Fegan Black, which sounds very much like a romance author's name. One finds quite a few ana-grammatized names and others made up out of sexual puns, the more outrageous the better. Or an author might choose to write under the name of a character of her own creation from an earlier story.

I want to emphasize, however, that fans use pseudonyms not just for the joyful and imaginative expression of alternative and shifting identities. They also have some-thing to hide: It's one thing for your co-workers, domestic partners, or children to know you're a "Trekkie," it's another to know you're a producer of pornography with gay overtones. It's important to see both sides of the fan use of names that are not their own.

JANICE RADWAY: How would you distinguish your vision of this new approach to popular culture—through attention to desire and pleasure and the multiplicity of subject positions—from other feminist work on popular culture?

PENLEY: I see my approach as "new" only insofar as I'm insisting on the importance of not dismissing from the feminist study of popular culture the ideas about subjectivity and sexual difference developed over the last fifteen years in feminist film theory. As I said in my paper, I was struck by the fact that feminist scholars working on popular forms such as the romance novel or the soap opera seem to think that the Freudian and Lacanian accounts of desire and identification are either not relevant (most popular culture researchers that I know utterly reject psychoanalysis) or that a more "sociologized" version of psychoanalysis is preferable. In my paper I emphasized the advantages of using a "properly" psychoanalytic description of desire and identification when one is trying to account for subject positions beyond those located in the time and space of the pre-Oedipal. But using the psychoanalytic account of fantasy can help us to do much more than demonstrate the fact that the subject positions of women consumers of popular culture can be multiple and shifting, which was all I was able to do in this paper. It can also help us to understand that desire is as much a real issue here as satisfaction: the slash fans have not written thousands of stories, poems, and novels, produced all those erotic drawings and made all those videos simply because it was satisfying to do so, although the pleasure of the activity is obviously very important. Psychoanalysis tells us that wherever there's repetition we need to look beyond the pleasure principle—to something that is not leading to satisfaction, to something that is lacking. And fantasy is precisely the staging of that desire and a fictional attempt to answer the questions that it poses, to do something about that lack. (Here, of course, I'm borrowing from the now classic account of fantasy in Laplanche and Pontalis's [1968] "Fantasy and the Origins of Sexuality," which has been so influential in feminist film theory.) Every slash story, I would argue, is an attempt to paper over a basic lack: the fact that "there is no sexual relation" (as Lacan so bluntly put it), that the sexes are fundamentally antagonistic. Every slash story, drawing, and video tries to show how there could be a sexual relation: it is up to us (meaning feminists studying popular culture) to deal with the fact that the women fans can imagine a sexual relation only if it involves a childless couple made up of two men, who never have to cook or scrub the tub, and who live three hundred years in the future. I would also argue that *Star Trek* fandom in general is an attempt to resolve another lack, that of a social relation. *Trek* fan culture is structured around the same void that structures American culture generally, and its desire too is that fundamental antagonisms, like class and race, not exist.

JOHN FISKE: Contrasting your essay with Kaplan's and Glover's, I'd like to focus on whether the agency of culture is ascribed to the text and the critic or the fan. You directed our attention to the active fan who might be seen as an extreme version of a much more normal popular reader. You implicitly then redefined the text as a cultural resource rather than as a cultural agent, and located the agency in the fans and readers, rather than in the text. As a critic you explicitly aligned yourself with the fans, learnt from, experienced their productive reading practices. You allowed yourself no privileged insight into the original text. I'd be interested in whether you agree with this description.
PENLEY: I can't go along with your attempt to pit my somewhat ethnographic approach against Cora Kaplan and David Glover's more textual method of analysis. As Cora and David have just said, the readings they presented today are only part of an overall project that includes an attempt to account for readers' responses to these new detective novels. And part of what I didn't present today is precisely my textual interpretations of the slash stories. I don't think that any of us on this panel would want to say that one approach is more "correct" than another or that the study of popular culture could do without one approach or the other. It seems to me that the strongest work in this field is the kind that attempts to mix a number of strategically chosen methods of analysis. As I said in my paper, Janice Radway's work on romance novels and their readers inspired my own work, and it was precisely because her book includes literary critical readings, ethnographic study, psychoanalytical interpretations, and industry

analysis. She addresses all the different sites of "agency," both conscious and unconscious, textual, individual, and social.

I also think you're seeing only one side of my project when you characterize me as having aligned myself with the fans, experiencing and learning from their reading practices. And following from that, you describe my position as one that deliberately claims no distance and thus no privileged insight into the fandom or its productions. Yes, I have learned a great deal from the fans about the strength of the popular will to transform the products of mass-produced culture and some remarkable ways in which this can be done, but at least as much of my knowledge comes from the understanding of my distance from the fans, from seeing where I don't fit in at all. In my paper I talked about my difficulty with the fact that so many of the fans refuse to think of themselves as feminists, whereas for me that is an absolutely necessary identity. But yet another kind of distance or difference is that of class. It's not just that as a professional intellectual I've been able to leap a class, economically and culturally, but that I typically think and write differently from the fans because of my professional training. Fans who have read my work on slash culture agree to a suprising degree with my interpretations, but they often express discomfort with my way of presenting those interpretations. In fact, they have more difficulty with what they call my tendency to "intellectualize" than they do with my being an avowed feminist. For example, they object to any attempt on my part to offer a generalization: if I describe the fans as mostly working class and "subprofessional," they will point out to me that this fan or another has a Ph.D. or is a professional; if I claim that most fans won't call themselves feminists, they will remind me of one or more who will. They don't feel that I have gotten it right unless I account for the individuality of each and every fan, but to write critically one must be able to generalize, see patterns, recognize tendencies, construct interpretive grids, and so on, which necessarily is going to leave out some details and privilege others. So, yes, I am learning from the fans, but much of what I learn comes from recognizing and acknowledging the distance between us.

BILL MILLER: You mentioned that those in fandom are self-reflective and self-critical. Do they also exercise self-parody? Do they do what they do sometimes with tongue-in-cheek? Would the videos have elicited from a group of them the same laughter it elicited from this group?

PENLEY: I'm glad you brought that up because it allows me to say in a very direct way that this fan culture provides a space not only for women to express their erotic fantasies but also to be funny, and I mean *very* funny. The level of wit and self-parody found in the fan culture and its products is astonishing only if you haven't experienced it yourself. I've been at fan convention panel discussions or video shows where the people in the room (including me) begged to stop because our sides were hurting too much to go on. It's for this reason—to try to get across the role and importance of humor in the fan culture—that I made the difficult decision to present my paper in the way that I did. It gets a lot of laughs, as do the videos that I showed. But eliciting laughter can be risky because I don't want you to be laughing *at* the fans; I want you to be laughing in appreciation of their outrageous talent for transforming the media universe, making it work for their own ends. Because isn't that precisely what *we* are supposed to be doing, *we* meaning cultural studies scholars who want to do more than just study mass-produced culture, but change it? [Note added after the conference: I invited local slash fans that I knew to come to my talk. They told me afterwards that they agreed for the most part with my analyses, and liked my not-too-academic mode of presenting, but they felt strongly that the people in the audience were laughing at the fans from a distant and superior position. They also felt that there was some sexual anxiety in the laughter because people were simply nervous about the same-sex erotic images and stories they were being told about and shown. I accept the fans' impression of the audience response but put it in the context of their profound disdain for professional intellectuals and their perceived aims. They dislike their values almost as much as those of journalists, whom they consider to be at the very bottom of the food chain.]

NANCY CARAWAY: I was wondering whether this is a completely white world that you're describing? And I'm wondering why the racial politics of this fandom community was implicit and not more explicit?

PENLEY: Slash fandom, like the larger *Star Trek* fandom is quite racially mixed, at least from what I have seen at conventions. It's important to remember that *Star Trek,* when it was broadcast from 1968–1971, was considered very bold and controversial for its attempt to have a racially and sexually mixed crew, and in one episode had the first interracial kiss seen on television, which a few stations in the South refused to show. The reason I didn't make the issue of race more explicit in my paper was because I've discovered that it's a huge and complicated one that I'm going to have to give a lot of attention to in my thinking about the fan culture, and I simply didn't feel that I could do it justice here. So, many thanks for your question, which will allow me to say a few things about it. The fans for the most part seem to think of themselves as liberals, although in their extreme emphasis on individualism and individual rights, I would rather characterize them as libertarians. But insofar as they see themselves as having liberal values, understood, of course, through the Vulcan version—Infinite Diversity in Infinite Combination—they think of themselves as progressive on matters of race because they are committed to tolerance for all differences. However, race is talked about very little in the fandom, even though Kirk and Spock, for example, are an interracial (or, I guess, interspecies) couple and even though Spock comes from a mixed background (Terran mother and Vulcan father), and many of the stories depict each man's difficulty in understanding the other's difference. Also, I was struck recently by the absence of any mention of race on an exhaustive questionnaire I received in the mail, "Who *Are* Star Trek Fans: A Survey," circulated by a *Star Trek* fan group in Connecticut. Fans are asked to answer a myriad of questions about their age, sex, marital status, education, occupation, income, religious and political affiliations, volunteerism or activism, hobbies, reading, TV viewing, "Trexpertise" and involvement in fandom, but nothing about their race. Is this a puzzling repression or a sign that anti-racism is absolutely taken for granted in fan culture? I don't know yet. What I do know is that in the fan stories racial difference is dealt with in a way very typical to American literature and film. Spock's racial "otherness" is never coded as black or African-American (in opposition to Kirk's white identity); instead Vulcan culture is rewritten by the fans along the lines of either Native American culture or, less frequently, Asian culture. The relation between blacks and whites, always so fraught in the U.S., thus gets turned into the more romantizable difference between reds and whites, or is exotically Orientalized. I would argue that racial difference gets talked about all the time in the fan stories, but the specific question of black/white difference and black/white relations gets repressed almost entirely or displaced onto other kinds of racial differences.

ROSALIND BRUNT: I wanted to ask you to say more about the intense scrutiny of masculinity in this culture. I must say I was incredibly moved by those videos, my laughter was a laughter of recognition. I think those are my fantasies too. And the fact that they are straight men reminded me very much of romance, and the way in which, in romance, aggressive brutal men are suddenly transformed into moody, intense, emotional men.

PENLEY: You're right to point to the fans' concern with masculinity, which seems to follow necessarily from their attempt to fictionally create the possibility of a sexual relation. And you're also right to remind us that the intense scrutiny of masculinity is central to the romance formula. The more I read and think about the Kirk and Spock of these stories, the more I think that Lamb and Veith's description of them as "androgynous" isn't quite accurate. Kirk and Spock *have* to be male in the stories because the project here, if I can make a terrible pun, is precisely the attempt to "retool" masculinity. First you start with a man from the future, because the ones now are fairly hopeless, then you try to come up with a man who is sensitive and nurturing without being wimpy, decisive and intelligent without being macho, and able to combine love and work without jealousy or rivalry. And then, by putting the two men together, you add the ability to acknowledge and act upon one's own sexual desires even when they are not the socially normative ones.

I think there's another reason why the slash characters have to be male, and this has to do with the fans' rejection of the female body. The fans do indeed reject the female body as a terrain of fantasy or utopian thinking, but the female body they are rejecting is the body of the woman as it has been constituted in this culture: a body that is a legal, moral, and religious battleground; a body seen as murderously dangerous to the fetus it may house; a body held to painfully higher standards of beauty than the male body. One feminist theorist told me that she felt it somehow "inauthentic" that these women would choose to write their sexual and social fantasies across male bodies, but from what position could one say to them that they have no right to refuse these bodies that have been imposed on them?

One final bit of "retooling" that I'd like to mention because I think it's really brilliant can be seen in the fans' love of *pon farr* stories, in which, you'll remember, Spock goes into heat, is overcome by the blood fever, and so on. These stories are so popular that a new fanzine has appeared, called *Fever,* that publishes only *pon farr* stories. I think the fans love these stories because they delight in the idea of a man at the mercy of a hormonal cycle, and indeed, they often give Spock the symptoms of PMS just before he goes into his blood fever. Another nice touch, in some stories, is that Kirk, because he is empathically bonded with his Vulcan mate, experiences the same symptoms, and doesn't have to be *told* how badly Spock is feeling, he already knows. What we have here, I think, is a playful and transgressive leveling of the biological playing field.

HENRY JENKINS: It's not clear to me, having displaced the Chodorow/Radway model at the beginning of your paper, which you do acknowledge was designed at least to make some connections between psychoanalysis and the social, how you fit the social and cultural explanations back into psychoanalysis. And to follow up on that, I had some observations from a more social and cultural perspective about the question of pseudonyms, which I think have to be understood in two sets of social contexts. One is the relationship of the fan to what fans choose to call "the mundane world": they choose this identity in specific opposition to everyday life. Here they can adapt an identity fundamentally different from that that they are forced to assume as wives, mothers, lowly paid office workers, nurses, librarians, and so forth. The second is the context of larger fan culture where this play with identity is important both because slash is opposed to the dominant interpretive norms of a lot of other fans. The issue crops up rather poignantly in the fact that many non-slash fans have been naming names, revealing the identity of slash writers to stars, to producers, etc., duplicating the structures of "outing" of gay society itself (e.g., of choosing to come out of the closet, having your name revealed against your will, and the threat or power that comes through masking your identity within a specific fan culture). Both of these questions require a theory of social and cultural relations to be integrated into some theory of psychoanalytic fantasy identity in order to get a fuller sense of the importance of adapting a pseudonym, or the importance of slash within its original community.

PENLEY: In the abstract, I think that all of us can appreciate your cautionary note about the need to integrate a theory of social and cultural relations into a psychoanalytic account of identity or fantasy in fan culture. I'm not sure who you're cautioning, however, since very few of those who study popular culture would allow *any* role for psychoanalytic interpretation, so it's hardly a matter of adding social considerations to psychoanalytic interpretations. I would obviously argue it from the other direction: that you can't do this kind of ethnographic work without some psychoanalytic understanding of desire, identification, fantasy, and subjectivity. The ethnographic findings will, in their turn, shape and challenge the psychoanalytic account. If I appear to be privileging or starting from the side of psychoanalysis, it's only because it's been done so little that it seems to stand out. Finally, I don't see why we can't provide, simultaneously and giving equal weight to each, an account of what the fans say and do (the ethnographic emphasis on everyday activity and popular logic) and what fans don't say and do (the psychoanalytic emphasis on the repressed and the taboo).

DONNA HARAWAY: I'd like you to address what I hear as a very interesting tension between popular culture, on the one hand, and political and social movements on the other. I'm thinking of the kinds of connection and disconnection in the last twenty-five years, and the ways that new social movement theory and psychoanalytic theories of different kinds of social agencies and subjectivities are in tension with the very differently socially located popular culture movements like fandom and social movements such as those of the non-violent direct action movements.

PENLEY: I don't think there's much similarity between the kinds of popular groups such as the fandom I've described today and organized groups on the left. But I think the old New Left could learn a lot from the fans' activities, just as it is learning (I hope) from the forms of organization and action of groups like ACT UP, Gran Fury, or the Guerrilla Girls, which combine old yippie notions of transgressive fun with a postmodern acceptance of the need to use rather than refuse the media to achieve their sexual-political ends. What I was trying to insist on in my paper was the necessity of learning from the popular, which involves a great deal more than discovering and celebrating popular moments of transgression or resistance.

NORMAN DENZIN: Could you speak some more about these ACOA women and these women taking on the characteristics of Adult Children of Alcoholics, taking a kind of pathological state into a new form of the popular? Is there a politics, a bio-politics of a sort, an inner protest here, which is not political in the traditional sense of the left, but is espousing a new form of subjectivity which is really counter to what we've seen before?

PENLEY: When I first came across the fans' use of the ACOA program in the workshop I described, it shook up my strong preconceptions about such programs. I had always been very distrustful of the ideology of the addiction and self-help groups, which seem to encourage religious and highly individualistic ways of thinking that lead to social and political disempowerment. But through seeing the ways the fans were using the precepts of these programs (and sometimes, I might add, not exactly in the ways they were intended to be used) to carry on a popular debate about their sexuality, their identity, and their everyday lives, it made me rethink my initial rejection. What also helped me to look beyond the ideology of the programs to actual uses made of them were the fierce debates going on at the same time in gay and lesbian communities about the role and value of these programs that have become so immensely popular with gays and lesbians. There too I encountered strong claims about the benefits of these programs, which address people's everyday pleasures, pains, and needs in ways a left or feminist discourse has not been able to do. While still retaining the doubts I've already mentioned, I now think it important that feminists and socialists try to learn more about the way, as Norm says, there is a kind of politics of inner protest here that is not political in a traditional left sense but nonetheless extremely important to recognize.

LIDIA CURTI: I was a bit uneasy about your automatically describing the pre-Oedipal trace as a regressive trace. I think there has been some work done, especially in France, but in Italy as well, about looking into this as a sort of complex ritual.

PENLEY: Thanks for giving me a chance to clarify what must have sounded like a polemic against the pre-Oedipal. I'm only against reducing all accounts of female subjectivity to a pre-Oedipal position, which I pointed to as a marked tendency in much recent feminist writing on women and popular culture. I think that any analysis of desire and identification at work in the popular response to mass-produced culture must take the possibility of regression to the pre-Oedipal into account. Mass-produced fantasies to a very great degree play on and produce the desire to return to the mother's body, to fuse with it, to enter a world without distinctions or differences. But this is not the *only* desire that structures those fantasies—that was my point. One can want completion but one can also desire lack. It's also important to remember that "regression" is not something negative in the psychoanalytic understanding of it. It signifies a direction, not a failing.

ED BRUNER: Shouldn't a proper ethnography include more testimonial from informants?

PENLEY: I don't want to claim that I'm doing a proper ethnography. I know for sure I'm not a proper ethnographer. In my finished project I'm including as much original material and actual fan speech as possible, but I'm not attempting to present an exhaustive "study" of the fandom. I'm not interested in uncovering and describing yet another "subculture" for the sake of adding it to a now almost canonical group of subcultures (punks, girl gangs, working-class lads, and so on). It was probably obvious from my paper that I'm more interested in writing about the way my encounter with slash fandom shaped or changed much of my own thinking on a range of issues, including women and pornography; popular pleasure and popular logic; the social and psychical role of fantasy; the popular reception of feminism; and the relative determinations of sex, class, and race. I want to understand slash fandom, then, not "exhaustively," but only insofar as I and we (as cultural studies researchers and activists) can learn from the fans' practices something of how people might empower themselves in relation to the mass-mediated culture we all inhabit.

27

Technologizing the Self: A Future Anterior for Cultural Studies

Elspeth Probyn

A central problematic that has emerged from postmodernist debates is, of course, that of representation. From one side of the argument, Baudrillard's denial of the possibility of representation deeply challenges many of cultural studies' assumptions, theoretical and commonsensical, about the task of speaking; of who speaks for whom, and why. As Baudrillard bluntly puts it, the death of a representable social field is, or should be, the death of sociological theory. It is a death contained within social theory, one that is closer to suicide than anything else: "The hypothesis of the death of the social is also that of its own death" (1982, pp. 9–10). In Gayatri Spivak's (1988) reformulation of representation as the doubled project of *Vertretung* and *Darstellung,* there is also a rather bleak outlook for the social theorist. The critic as "proxy" is dislodged; his position undermined by the absence, or the indifference, of any constituency: in Spivak's words, "the choice of and the need for "heroes," paternal proxies, agents of power—*Vertretung*" (p. 279) can no longer sustain a radical practice of interpretation.

Now, it would be comforting to be able to state that this injunction against proxies only applies to male theorists, to middle-aged lefty heroes. Unfortunately, this is not the case and, at the expense of alienating myself, it's been a while since they were seriously considered as the proxy for anyone—least of all by themselves. However, the project of representing women has been a condition of possibility for feminism and continues to provide the underlying epistemological basis for the articulation of feminisms. Quite simply, it continues to be the ground upon and from which many feminists and feminisms speak. However, this ground, or rather, the representation of women as its horizon, is not undermined only by theoretical decrees, it is increasingly attacked by the "public"—men and women alike.

The problematic of representation is not confined to the pages of critical journals. It can be felt generally as a kind of "bored yet hyper" cynicism in a climate marked by a certain *m'en foutisme,* a couldn't-care-less-ism. Canadians, in our banal way, carry on with our daily lives and shrug at our national representative Brian Mulroney—who himself seems to care less that in the last several years his popularity has remained at 15% in opinion polls. But this mood of indifference was abruptly shattered last December when a young man, Marc Lépine, shot and killed fourteen women engineering students at the University of Montreal because they were, to use his word, feminists. Suddenly, the question of representation became an urgent public matter: did newspapers have the right to publish front-page photographs of a dead woman, covered in blood and slumped in a cafeteria chair? And then, more heatedly, attention turned to what right feminists had to speak of this tragedy. In fact, feminists were doubly hit. Lépine clearly stated at the moment of the shooting and in a letter that he wanted to kill feminists; separating the men from the women, he shouted "je hais les féministes." Later, however, much was made of the fact that these poor young women had protested that they weren't feminists; they were bright, articulate women who wanted good jobs as engineers—they didn't hate men. In the search to comprehend how such a thing could happen in Canada, one interpretation held quite amazing sway: the man (and sometimes the woman) on the street agreed with the expert on the screen that feminism made men scared; that in taking jobs away from men, feminists were responsible for this state of affairs. That they were supposedly "responsible" was clear, but who they were responsible to was less so. There was also a backlash against feminists who spoke about the massacre, who "recuperated" the killing for their own cause.

Not surprisingly, many feminists took their own anger and grief as a discursive point of departure. As two of my colleagues wrote of the massacre: "This gesture was aimed against each one of us and against us all . . . fear, anger, fear, pain, fear, sadness invades us" (Juteau and Laurin-Frenette, 1990 p. 206). The awful recognition, that *shock* of recognition of where we are as women, the terrible feeling as the very space of the university, of the streets, is rearranged in fear, brought forward another tone. There was no way to avoid a sexed interpretation, there was no way of not speaking as a woman and as a feminist. Nevertheless, this spontaneous move to speak of and to a collectivity of women was, in turn, represented as a speaking position founded upon the dead bodies of fourteen young women.

Here the neat distinction between *Darstellung* and *Vertretung* threatens to implode. I cannot represent this situation except from my position as a feminist and yet many were the times that I stood in front of my class unable to speak of the killings, unable to say the word "feminism" for fear of reviving memories of the dead in students who had perhaps lost friends, for fear of encouraging another Lépine, for fear of being told by nice young women that it was my fault. Silenced by all these factors, silenced by a young generation of "I'm not a feminist, but," power becomes palpable but doesn't seem to be in anyone's hands. Who am I to speak to them and for them? What good is my political commitment if it can't convey some comfort, if it can't carry my convictions that, somehow, life has got to be better, more equal and just, more joyous and fun, than this.

Perhaps unfairly, this event reminds me of some of the debates within cultural studies over identity and difference and who gets to speak from where and for whom. The tone of these debates is also bloody, if less immediately tragic. Indeed, many North American academic conferences are increasingly mired in the banalities of an identity crisis, in the accompanying viciousness of a breakdown of certain forms of representation. Paranoia tends to produce rather strident and worried cries of identification as speakers and audience members loudly enlist in one ethnic, sexual, and gender encampment or another. The most evoked and phatic phrase of cultural studies, the one that Kobena Mercer (1990a) refers to as "the all-too-familiar mantra of race, gender, ethnicity, sexuality" (p. 58), is stretched to the limit. However, when it is deployed within a field of fraught fidelities, the idea of forming articulations among these differences gets lost in the move to claim allegiance, to get in on the star-coded politics of identity.

Of course, this wrangling over difference is not a purely North American phenomenon. The recent collection of essays edited by Jonathan Rutherford, *Identity, Community, Culture, Difference* (1990) is an exemplar of British debates. While there are many important interventions here, the tenor is one of agonesis, if not downright antagonism. If one makes up new rules as one goes along, the temptation to trash existing rules is too great to overcome. Among the many targets, the left and "white" feminism are the most severely trounced for having erected a "hierarchy" of difference. Thus, Pratibha

Parmar argues that white feminism's articulation of the politics of identity has "given rise to a self-righteous assertion that if one inhabits a certain identity this gives one the legitimate and moral right to guilt-trip others into particular ways of behaving" (1990, p. 107). According to Andrea Stuart (1990), by the early 1980s, "Being a feminist had come to say more about what you didn't do—eat meat, fuck men, wear make-up—than what you did do" (p. 32). Located at the end of the collection, the voice of Stuart Hall (1990b) intervenes to argue for a theorization of identity that would be

> constituted, not outside but within representation ... not as a second-hand mirror held up to reflect what already exists, but as that form of representation which is able to constitute us as new kinds of subjects, and thereby enable us to discover places from which to speak. (pp. 236–37)

While most of the authors cite, refer, and defer to Hall, it is interesting to note the ways in which "Identity" emerges as an articulation of a rather static and rhetorical use of difference; difference as a second-hand image of various theoretical battles within feminism and the left. While Hall's mode of speaking the modalities of the self are known either through "live" or textual encounters, the care with which he speaks is not often emulated. Rather, the joust of debate tends to cut, not into the real, but into actual people taken as representatives of various theoretical positions. It's as if in the late twentieth century, with the fragmentation of populist causes and political programs, the project of *Vertretung* has given way to a rather vicious game of issues and individuals elbowing each other out of the way, each crying, "he's passé," "listen to *me*," "she's a white straight femocrat," "hear *my* difference."

At this point in the game, at this socio-cultural and theoretical conjuncture, it might be beneficial to remember Jane Gallop's (1988) articulation of "the necessarily double and ... urgent questions of feminism: not merely who am I? But who is the other woman?" (p. 177). The first part of this equation, the question of who am I?, has already generated a small industry as theorists turn to themselves, their own difference, trying to explicate the world metonymically from their own. From Valerie Walkerdine's (1986) analysis of herself as Tinkerbell, and Carolyn Steedman's (1986) autoanalysis, to John Fiske's (1990) semiotics of his living room, the autobiographical is back. While this resurgence of the personal is understandable, given the fraught times in which we live, it often seems more like a reflex than a calculated theoretical move. Simply put, the casual, or the heartfelt, insertion of the writer's autobiography cannot be taken as a panacea for cultural studies' various woes. As Lawrence Grossberg (1988) has argued, "this merely reincribes, not only the privileged place of experience, but the privileged place of the author's experience" (p. 67). His point is well taken. In arguing for the positivity of experience and the possibilities of using the self in theory, I'll emphasize that we must articulate the question "who am I?" *and* the question of "who is she?" My elaboration of theoretical selves is therefore not a reinscription of authorial centrality; rather, it is put forward as a potential move beyond the current crisis of representation; a movement through the impasse of (in)difference. In emphasizing the urgency of the construction of enunciatory selves, I want to suggest that, as Hall states, it is within alternative forms of representation we may be able to construct new places from which to speak. I'll argue here that our "selves" constitute an obvious place from which to rework the ways in which we go about "representing." However, let me quickly add that this sense of the self is not necessarily the entity we sit at home with or go to conferences as. It is these parts of ourselves but it is also necessarily more. I am proposing a set of enunciatory strategies that seek to transform the boundaries of discourse, a mode of speaking which may work over the limitations of our mundane individual existences.

In a sense, this is to go beyond Foucault's Gaelic shrug of "what matter who speaks?" in order to conceive of a mode of speaking one's difference that does change matters both personal and social/theoretical. In other words, there is here a possibility of putting the experiences of our selves, of our differences, to work within cultural studies and thence to those small spheres in which our voices may be able to reach, to touch, and to change. The question then, as Jeffrey Weeks (1990) puts it, is how to construct "a language of politics that is able to speak to difference and uncertainty within a framework of common principles?" (p. 98). My additional question focuses on the ways of making that language matter.

This language would be dependent on being able to care about another's difference; to go somehow from one's own experience to another's, and in the doubledness of this alterity reinvest "the process of community" with some sort of care. In the best of all possible worlds, this language would entail similar operations as those of Foucault's (1988) "technologies of the self," which

> permit individuals to effect by their own means or with the help of others a certain number of operations on their bodies and souls, thoughts, conduct, and a way of being, so as to transform themselves. . . . (p. 18)

This necessity of caring is a crucial part of the theoretical tradition of cultural studies, one that is too often overlooked. Indeed, Raymond Williams gave us some of the keywords and feeling necessary to elaborate a political language of caring. In an interview shortly before his death, Williams remarked upon the general pervasiveness of what I would call a lack of "the care of the self":

> The suppression of tenderness and emotional response, the willingness to admit what isn't weakness—one's feelings in and through another; all this is a repression not only of women's experience but of something much more general. (1989e, p. 319)

Here, then, in Williams's inimitable voice, is something along the lines of issues I want to raise: we can hear intimations of the possibility of reworking the project of representation in ways that can include, and even be grounded in, tenderness and the centrality of theorizing through one's feeling *in and through another*. Included in Williams's "resources of hope" we find joyfulness, pleasure of the local (the sight of the Black Mountains guarding the Welsh border), and the deep necessity to theorize through the experiences of ourselves and of others in order to forge agendas beyond those which seek to restrain our individual and community lives. In the very ordinariness of these experiences we find "a ratifying sense of movement and the necessary sense of direction" (1965, p. 60).

In a more immediate time and space, Joseph Bristow (1989) raises this crucial question: "If the personal is political, can it also be pleasurable?" (p. 62). Living with the ideological, economic, and personal devastations of AIDS, gay and lesbian communities, perhaps not surprisingly, are returning to the pleasures of identities. Perhaps not surprising, but nonetheless incredibly courageous given the present history of pain. Bristow's article raises the stakes of the seriousness of pleasure. Quoting Christopher Isherwood's observation that "You can't camp about something you don't take seriously. You're not making fun of it; you're making fun out of it" (p. 71), Bristow takes as his point of departure into theory the practices of "camp." He articulates camp's positivity as a challenge:

> the resilience of its critical pleasures . . . can provide a starting-point for the left to consider how to enjoy the serious issue of establishing a political identity as a strategic

form of empowerment, and yet not lapse into an essentializing rhetoric of authenticity. (pp. 71–72)

Of course, one of camp's most obvious and serious pleasures is precisely the way in which any truth becomes yet another conceit to be played with. Viewed through the perspective of camp we can begin to consider the artificiality as well as the political necessity of reconstructing a self outside of the dictates of sincerity. Quite simply we need a theory and a practice of speaking the self which does not condense back into a narrow tale of origins or the petty politeness of good intentions. We need a "wild" theory of the self, a radical practice of enunciation where the truth of the *I* is indifferent but where difference is created in the tension, the movement, between a *she* and an *I*. Theorizing with camp is, of necessity, a sexually marked practice (even if the sexes are never still). As Richard Dyer (1986) argues, "camp is a characteristically gay way of handling the values, images and products of the dominant culture . . . an ambivalent making fun out of the serious and respectable" (p. 178). Camp then plays havoc in a situation where one is marked by an integral difference and thus endowed with the singular right to speak within difference. Against the respectable tones of academic debate "anyone can be read as camp," but it is more difficult "to be inward with camp" (pp. 178–79). The question then becomes one of speaking oneself without reifying the self, of putting one's self to work discursively without taking oneself too seriously. The stakes involved in this deeply serious game of identity are too high to allow for discursive or physical situations wherein "hierarchies of identities in which women, determined to prove their worthiness within the movement (and therefore to assert their right both to speak and to be heard) competed against each other over the nature and extent of their oppressions" (Stuart, 1990, p. 38). The point then is to theorize our differences and put them to work not as adjectives to "oppression" but rather as constituting an image-repertoire of conjunctural selves to be spoken.

Simply put, we need to consider the work of the self, to refigure identity and difference as images that enable alternative articulations of the non-discursive to the discursive which then play back again into the non-discursive. Michèle Le Doeuff argues that "images are not, properly speaking, 'what I think,' but rather 'what I think with,' or again, 'that by which what I think is able to define itself' " (cited in Morris, 1988c, p. 83). She refigures the ways in which these images can also be made to work outside of the text as an "operative viewpoint" into the relations of the "real" (Le Doeuff, 1979, p. 55). Speaking the self within a representational scene (inserting the self into the text) is therefore an act of inserting an appropriate image in order to articulate levels within the textual context. Its work there is important, and in one instance it is a fully discursive entity with no necessary connection to "me." However, this image of the self is then rendered into viewpoint, refracted from the text in order to focus upon the "relations of the real." As Morris states, "Le Doeuff passes from a concept of images as 'located' in relation to a given discourse (as *lodged* 'outside,' 'at home,' 'elsewhere') to a functional analysis of what they do—the 'faire' of images in discourse" (1988c, p. 83). Thus, we can analyze the work of the image as it cuts across discursive and non-discursive areas. At one point, the image of the self may be quite uninteresting as it quietly lodges inside, a non-discursive and rather mute entity. However, at another point the self as a motivated image is located in relation to a given discourse in such a way as to provoke and destabilize its authority. Images of selves trouble as they are put into spheres where they don't "belong." For instance, the spoken image of a "lipstick lesbian" can disturb both radical feminists and leftist male professors; it "bothers" fixed notions of the articulations of sexuality, gender, and politics. As a personal aside, one of the more rewarding comments that I have received after giving a paper was from a male member of the audience who found that a certain image of myself had made him "nervous." While this response was not intended as a compliment, it suggests how images of the self can work successfully to annoy, to enervate discursive fixities and extra-discursive expectations. It is in this nervous movement that we can construct alternative enunciative positions. As Morris states, "the question that [Le Doeuff] poses of possible places for speech, places other than those prescribed by the Outside/Inside alternative, is an operational question for feminism" (1988c, p. 76).

The "faire" of Le Doeuff's concept of the image allows us to reconsider the use of the self as an image within discourses of identity. This is to conceptualize the self as that "in which the writer thinks himself and thinks his relation to the Other" (Le Doeuff, cited in Morris, 1988c, p. 84). Deployed as a speaking position, the self can be used "to construct questions and modes of analysis from the 'patch' of reality under consideration" (Le Doeuff, 1989, pp. 105–6). This is to emphasize that the work *(le faire)* of this self, taken as a discursive point of departure, is to refigure the patch of reality from which it is taken. As an image "lodged" in specific conjunctures, it is a condition of possibility for the rearticulation of the discourses in which it finds itself. Articulating the political and gendered "here" from which it is spoken, it is a declension of what Le Doeuff calls "the process by which a localized discovery can overthrow the philosopher's palace of idea" (1981/82, p. 62). As an enunciatory artifice, this use of the self breaks with the "notion of some absolute, integral self," "a fully closed narrative of the self" which, as Hall points out, obstructs the theorizing of new identities (Hall cited in Parmar, 1990, pp. 107–8).

To draw further attention to the *construction* of the self, I'll add that it is a *tactical* rhetoric. Michel de Certeau's (1984) distinction between strategies and tactics reminds us that tactics have no particular place of belonging; they are "calculated actions determined by the absence of a proper locus" (p. 38). A self, deployed tactically in theoretical constructs, is neither innocent nor transcendent, it does not seek to represent an essence; rather, it can introduce into the text "the rhetoric, the conceits, the tricks of the everyday" (cited in Silverstone, 1989, p. 82). "I" am entered as a conceit into the representational scene; this self can then be made to move in various ways, circumventing the affirmation of the authenticity of a full and integral "I"dentity. It is a device which insists that modes of speaking cannot be tied down to the supposed truth of an outside referent, that the spaces mobilized cannot be known in advance. Meaghan Morris (1990a) captures the potential movements of the personal in her discussion of the work of anecdotes. She portrays their movement as "oriented futuristically towards the construction of a precise, local, and *discursive* context, of which the anecdote then functions as a *mise en abîme*" (p. 7).

This is then to begin to remake the concept of the self in its full analytic reach. Refusing the authority of the arbiters of authenticity who insist on fixing the real moments of the real me, this self must be active. Its work is at two registers. At an epistemological level, a self is used to reveal certain bases of knowledge; and at an ontological level selves reveal their affectivity of *being* in the world. This is, then, to put the self into play within the work of theoretical writing, which is, after all, a major part of what we do. Implicating images of our selves in theoretical contexts may allow for articulations grounded in the knowledge of the non-necessity of their conjunctures. This serious and perhaps pleasurable ludic movement of the self in discourse may go some way to addressing Bristow's (1989) two crucial imperatives: "The first of these is to do with language-use in the strategic voicing of identities. The second relates to the pleasures of acceding to and living an identity" (p. 64). This is a direct challenge to academic criticism which, as Bristow reminds us, "finds it necessary to suppress the personal in its tone and style" (p. 73). Such a challenge is not necessarily easy nor safe. Tenure committees, after all, do read one's articles and colleagues may be in the audience when you speak your identities.

Against these strictures, however, are more and more instances of individuals putting their selves on the line. Recently, at the International Communications Association conference, during an extremely straight (both mainstream and heterosexual) session, Larry Gross (1990) spoke with passion and humor about the need to be "out" about where one speaks from. In his case, his declared speaking position as a gay man is fully part of his academic work. His sexual identity is brought into play within his theoretical orientation. This is not autobiography for its own sake, nor solely the politics of "coming out"; rather, it is an articulation of identities (sexual and theoretical) at work within a specific context. Moreover, what struck me then, as now, is the way in which some gay and lesbian academics speak out, and put their selves to work; that they take the risk of losing their jobs or being snubbed by colleagues, while heterosexuals (the ones with ideology on their side) stand silently by. Surely in this era in which Madonna and Sandra dance on the ruins of straightforward heterosexuality, questions can be asked of this "silent" norm. Questions aimed at what Richard Dyer (1990) calls heterosexuality's "anxieties of the fluidity of sex-categories"; questions about the incompleteness, the descriptive and affective insufficiency, of the heterosexual apparatus. Questions like: Why am I heterosexual? Am I? What does it mean (to me and to her)? As I deal with these questions, I always seem to come up with a reassuring (or, easy) answer couched in the terms of structural overdetermination. But the more I think about it, the more ridiculous that sounds. I don't subscribe to a notion of strict determination in my theorizing so why should I accept its reassurances in my life and my sexual identity? Moreover, a number of contradictions mark this identity and contest the ideology of fixed heterosexuality: from my inseparable high-school girlfriend ("the lezzies of Llandrindod Wells Grammar School"), to my mother's constant injunction "not to get married but to get a good job," to my formative years in the seventies gay disco scene where I was a proud "fag-hag," to my investment in theorizing and representing sexuality as essentially fluid.

While the practice and content of my self-disclosure may be quite banal, it is about time that we dismantle the taken-for-grantedness of heterosexuality within positions of enunciation. This is not to reinscribe heterosexuality with even more centrality, but to deconstruct it as the norm against which "exotic" differences are measured. Nor is this to discourse endlessly on our various self-fabrications, but to be clear about where we are speaking from; to use the personal as a point of departure. It is to dislodge the ideology by which, unless stated, the world is spoken as heterosexual. In going against the idea of sexuality as a "zero-sum game" wherein your preference somehow takes away from mine, we should start asking the type of questions that Rosi Braidotti (1989) raises: "What are the links and the possible tensions between my "being-a-feminist" and my "being-a-woman," between politics and a sense of self, between subjectivity and identity, between sexuality as an institution and also as one of the pillars for one's sense of self?" (p. 94). Living and speaking these tensions is one way of technologizing and working over our senses of the self; it is a starting point in the deconstruction of the fixity of categories. Discursively, this entails dislodging some rather entrenched dichotomies: those of heterosexuality/homosexuality, feeling/thinking, I/thou, and discourse/the "real," to name but a few. As Jane Tompkins bluntly states:

> The public-private dichotomy, which is to say the public-private *hierarchy,* is a founding condition of female oppression. I say to hell with it . . . I think people are scared

to talk about themselves, that they haven't got the guts to do it. . . . Sometimes, when a writer introduces some personal bit of story into an essay, I can hardly contain my pleasure. (cited in Bristow, 1989, p. 74)

Implicating one's self does indeed take guts. It is not a necessarily easy thing to do nor is it only done for one's own pleasure. Many years ago, Richard Hoggart (1963) wrote of the difficulties of finding the right "tone" for the autobiographical, of resisting the "socio-cultural mood . . . and the tones of voice it calls out in writers" (p. 73). It seems increasingly clear to me that the current socio-cultural mood requires a more caring tone. Lest there be any confusion, a concern with care does not subscribe to George Bush's "kinder, gentler America"; it is, however, to struggle to be able to speak of, and to claim, this vital site. As the left continues to attack itself from within, a growing public discourse of "new traditionalism" actively articulates care and community to the New Right. Reagan's worry that "*they're* going to steal our symbols and slogans: words like community and the family" (Moyers, 1989) is, as yet, unfounded. Transparent as it may seem, and as selective as their "caring" is, the right's reclaiming of "fundamental" values constitutes an appealing platform. But it is not too late to work towards a mode of thinking and speaking wherein, as June Jordan states, we would "try to measure each other on the basis of what we do for each other rather than on the basis of who we are" (cited in Parmar, 1990, p. 112).

In learning to speak this language we might consider the possibilities of thinking in other tenses and speaking in a different grammatical mood. As my dictionary reminds me, a "mood" is also "a distinction of form of a verb to express whether its action or state is conceived as fact or in some other manner." A different mood may help us express a political language grounded in what we can do for each other. Of course, the history of theoretical language is marked by mood changes. Braidotti reminds us that the dominant tense or mood of feminist theory in the 1960s and 1970s was that of the future; it conveyed "a deep sense of determination, of certainty about the course of history" (1989, p. 103). She proposes as a tense more complementary to the current historical moment, the conditional present. Braidotti defines this enunciatory stance as "beyond the logic of ideology and teleological progress. Akin to dreamtime, it is the tense of open potentiality and consequently of desire in the sense of a web of interconnected conditions of possibility" (p. 103).

It expresses the potential for articulating "wishes" to "facts," of turning wishes into *des faits accomplis*. It is a subjunctive voice and direction *(voix/voie)* secured in the conditional present of accomplishment; it is speaking the politics of an "as if." It is in this mood that I hear Week's hopeful definition of sexual identities as "what we want to be and could be" (cited in Bristow, 1989, p. 61). Similarly, Braidotti locates her feminist critical speaking stance in a sexual identity that "far from being prescriptive in an essentialist-deterministic way . . . opens up a field of possible 'becoming' providing . . . a symbolic bond among women *qua* female sexed beings" (1989, p. 102).

Nowhere is the conditional present, the enunciative establishment of a web of interconnected possibilities, more needed than in speaking about, to, and with AIDS. It is here that one already hears its resonances. In his introduction to *Taking Liberties: AIDS and Cultural Politics,* Simon Watney (1989) articulates a simple but vital requirement in the fight against AIDS. As he puts it, "this . . . means winning people over to a new, ineradicable sense of their worth and dignity as human beings" (p. 54). This fight for the dignity and for the care of the self can clearly be seen in what David Edgar describes as the ways in which AIDS "has brought into stark relief what many in the gay constituency knew already (particularly those who lived in gay communities), that a kinship based on shared nature and a consequent shared oppression can be as mutually sustaining as that of the family, and in many ways more binding and less conditional" (cited in Watney, 1989, p. 26).

This accent on a "common ground of enunciation" confirms a will to speak in caring tones; to act, in Braidotti's (1989) words, "as if the subjectivity of all was at stake in the enunciative patterns of each one." This is not to say that one represents all; rather, that in technologizing one's self, one necessarily works on and for the selves of others as well. This type of commitment to reworking the self can also be seen, for example, in projects like the Lesbian Herstory Archives which is dedicated to lesbians now and, as Joan Nestle (1990) puts it, "to a new generation of rememberers." It is a project which articulates past and future in the present: "Our will to remember is our will to change the world, to continually reconstruct the words 'woman,' 'lesbian' and 'gender' so they reflect the complex creations which we call our lives" (p. 93). Like Issac Julien's beautiful film, *Looking for Langston,* this is a task of reclaiming and reinflecting history for the conditional present. These reconstructions, these operations upon the representations of a lesbian or gay self, allow for the possibility of articulating and living creations of identity differently. These practices illustrate what Hall calls the ways in which "cultural identity . . . is a matter of 'becoming' as well as of 'being'. It belongs to the future as much as to the past" (Hall, 1990b, p. 111).

It is in these contexts, in the ways in which the gay community lives with AIDS (from the perseverance of individuals to the organized practices of ACT UP and Queer Nation), and in the projects of speaking gay and lesbian identities and histories within a climate of increasing homophobia, that I can most clearly hear Foucault's (1988) insistence on the positivity of the self. Before he himself died of AIDS, he wrote:

> Perhaps I've insisted too much on the technology of domination and power. I am more and more interested in the interaction between oneself and others and in the technologies of individual domination, the history of how an individual works upon himself, in the technology of the self.

Conversely, it is to those individuals smug in their imagined security of "normality," or caught in what Watney (1989) describes as the "sheer *loneliness*" of the vision of the ideal family," that I want to shout GET A LIFE, DO SOMETHING WITH YOUR SELF. It is to them, perhaps to all of us, at one point or another, and to the ideological stains in us, that Foucault (1985) can be seen to be addressing here:

> What would be the value of the passion for knowledge if it resulted only in a certain amount of knowledgeableness and not, in one way or another and to the extent possible, in the knower's straying afield of himself? There are times in life when the question of knowing if one can think differently than one thinks, and perceive differently than one sees, is absolutely necessary if one is to go on looking and reflecting at all.

Central to the technologies of the self is an attention to the passion of knowledge, a passion which does not reify knowing but rather entails a probability that one occasionally will lose oneself, only to find it in another place, caught up with other knowledge and people, in the reflection of another angle and perspective. The radical potential of the technologies of the self offers a theory and a practice of the arts and politics of existence, a way of actualizing 'oneself' as the opening perspective: "the self as possibility." Foucault's self is not an *a priori;* it is not given but rather made through an involvement in the practice of life. Like *living* with AIDS, "it is not given but is to be created . . . it isn't a substance but a form" (Foucault cited in Schmid, 1989).

The possibilities of Foucault's theory of the care of the self are many; in conclusion, I will note only its importance for a politics of identity in cultural studies. As in Le

Doeuff's "operative reasoning," Foucault offers us more than a theory of positionality, of meaning in difference; rather, his entire work elaborates the necessity of theorizing the positivity of the ground from which we speak. Moreover, with the care of the self, he urges us to realize the theoretical and affective richness of involving the self. Both Le Doeuff's theory of the work of the image and Foucault's "technologies of the self" connect with and, perhaps, extend a theory of articulation. Used in relation to the construction of identities, this is to emphasize that identity is only useful when put to work (as June Jordan asks us, "what is your identity for?" [cited in Parmar, 1990, p. 111]). We should also remember that Hall's (1986b) definition foregrounds the *work* of "articulation":

> An articulation is thus the form of the connection that *can* make a unity of two different elements, under certain conditions. It is a linkage which is not necessary, determined, absolute and essential for all time. You have to ask, under what circumstances *can* a connection be forged or made?

The image of the self can therefore be theorized as the articulation of different elements, as a practice formulated in the demands of the moment. Forged under certain circumstances, this self has no necessary essential substance; it undermines "the idea of universal necessities in human existence" (Foucault, 1988, p. 11). As Foucault (1989) argues, "the 'care of the self' is understood as experience and also as a technique which elaborates and transforms this experience" (p. 134).

The positivity of the self lies in the epistemological conditions of "how the experience and the knowledge of the self, and the knowledge that gets formed of the self . . . is defined, valorized, requested, imposed" (p. 133).

Foucault grounds his theory of the self in the historical and present configurations of desires and sexual practices. The last two volumes of *The History of Sexuality* are explicitly located in an investigation of homosexual love, a point often overlooked in straight academic appropriations of Foucault. Moreover, this investigation clearly demonstrates that practices of sexual identity are never stable. As a technique, the care of the self articulates the different modalities of identity and the experience of living through them. Thus, it is "a matter of analyzing . . . the *problematizations* through which being offers itself to be, necessarily, thought—and the *practices* on the basis of which these problematizations are formed" (p. 11). Gilles Deleuze (1986) uses the metaphor of *le pli* (which variously translates as both "pleat" and "fold") to describe the doubled operations of Foucault's theory of the self: the inside and the outside; the ontological and the epistemological: the practice and the problematization. Thus we have the possibility of thinking, using, and feeling a self. It is, however, serious work; it is "always a real activity and not just an attitude" (Foucault, 1988, p 24). It is an analytic tool fashioned from our lives, grounded in the fact that "being occupied with oneself and political activities are linked" (p. 26). Moreover, articulated in the practices of taking care of the self, caring for the community, sexual practices, "the self is something to write about, a theme or object (subject) of writing activity" (p. 27). The self is not an end in itself; rather, it is the opening of a perspective, one which allows us to conceive of transforming our selves and our communities "in order to attain a certain state of happiness, purity, wisdom, perfection, or immortality" (p. 18). We may not immediately get there, but we can technologize our selves as a point of departure.

The stakes in using a self go beyond the mere construction of a theoretical position of difference; they entail a political realization that a necessary moment in continuing to theorize is the articulation of where we speak from. Debates on identity and difference can only move forward if we overcome the antimonies involved in the construction of hierarchies. Instead of standing on our differences and wearing our identities as slogans we need to put the images of our selves to work epistemologically and ontologically. The absurdly simple proposition of taking care of the self requires some careful thought, a change of stance, and a modulation of tone and mood. As Braidotti (1989) puts it, "the personal is not only political, it is also the theoretical" (p. 95). This means that taking care of the self cannot be an unmediated practice: speaking from the heart and shooting from the hip may feel good but they may, as theoretical modes of enunciation, reinscribe certain ideological positions. Moreover, to advocate the care of the self as a place to speak from is not an injunction for everyone to bare their souls. This is not a plan for mandatory "outing." It is, however, to suggest a mode of going about theorizing; it is to engage in a "tense of open potentiality," to speak and activate the possibility of social and personal transformation. This mode cannot speak a static present; thinking in the "as if" throws us forward, not into the securities of a definite future but into the practicalities of getting from here to there. Operating in a "conditional present" or a "future anterior" is one way of continually reminding ourselves that identities are always constructed, lived, and enunciated within what Althusser (1970b) called the "backwardness, forwardness, survivals and unevennesses of development which *co-exist* in the structure of the real historical present: the present of the *conjuncture*" (p. 106). The conceit of the images of our selves, working in the momentary tense of "as if" carries with it the imperative of an "optimism of the will." As Dick Hebdige (1985) puts it, "we have to go on making connections, to *bear* our witness and to *feel* the times we're living through" (p. 39). This is, then, to go beyond discrete positions of difference and to refuse the crisis mode of representation. It is to make the sound of our identities count as we work to construct communities of caring, to technologize and transform ourselves in the care of others. Quite simply, this is the past and future of cultural studies that we must speak in the present.

28

Mail-Order Culture and Its Critics: The Book-of-the-Month Club, Commodification and Consumption, and the Problem of Cultural Authority

Janice Radway

In 1956, a nearly 1200-page typed transcript of oral history interviews conducted with the officials of the Book-of-the-Month Club was deposited in the Oral History Research Office of Columbia University. The editors of the transcripts noted in their introduction that the project had been undertaken upon a single premise. "The premise," they observed, "is that the Book-of-the-Month Club has had, and in all likelihood will continue to have, a very considerable impact upon the cultural life of the American people of the Twentieth Century." [1] They continued, "we leave it to others to evaluate that impact, for our function is not to interpret material but simply to collect what appears to be worth collecting. We do submit that such an impact exists, and that its existence is incontestable."

Although the historians connected with the Columbia project were clearly envisioning interpretive assessments like the one I will give today, the business of evaluating the impact of the Book-of-the-Month Club actually began almost immediately after the Club's incorporation was first announced in the pages of *Publishers' Weekly* in 1926. Indeed, the Book-of-the-Month Club was one of the most thoroughly debated American cultural institutions of the first half of the twentieth century. So controversial was it that many pages of commentary were devoted to it in the most prominent literary monthlies. Dwight MacDonald's (1953) now famous denunciation of it as the quintessential middlebrow institution in his essay, "A Theory of Mass Culture," was only a late entry in a familiar debate. Part of common parlance through the thirties, forties, and fifties, the name itself was borrowed repeatedly to sell everything from underwear to fruit and the Club's customers were satirized in numerous magazine cartoons. It is easy enough to assent, then, to the Columbia historians' claim, especially since it can be shown that the Book-of-the-Month Club distributed more than one hundred million books in the first 25 years of its existence.[2] It is harder to specify, however, the exact nature of the impact the Club had just as it is difficult to say precisely why the institution generated such controversy and heated debate within literary and cultural circles.

What I want to suggest today is that to understand both the cultural impact of the Book-of-the-Month Club and the nature of the controversy it generated, it is necessary to look carefully at the character of the ideological challenges embodied in Harry Scherman's decision to unite the world of culture and books with that of advertising and mail-order sales in what he claimed to be simply a book distribution scheme. Although Scherman only applied to the activity of bookselling techniques already developed elsewhere to secure the mass consumption of innumerable other commodities, it was his irreverent willingness to use these to commodify the very idea of culture itself that insured the rebuke of the cultural community. In wedding cultural production to mass distribution, and more particularly to mass consumption, Scherman was challenging some of his culture's most fundamental ideological assumptions about the character of culture, education, literature, art, and criticism. Those assumptions were made evident not only in the various critiques of the Book-of-the-Month Club, but also in the Club's own publicity and public relations material, most of which was written by Scherman himself with a clear eye to defending the operation against the charge that the Club was usurping the individual's right to choose cultural fare.

A close look at the terms of the discourse used both by the Book-of-the-Month Club's critics and by its officials suggests that the rights-based language of bourgeois liberalism structured the debate about culture in the early decades of this century. Ironically, it did so at a critical moment when the continued expansion of a consumer economy was profoundly challenging the continued applicability and efficacy of this older way of understanding the social world as a contractual and contracting group of autonomous individuals. Despite new ideological pressures to rethink audiences, crowds, and the mass, a liberal approach to art continued to dominate cultural debate. Consequently, mass cultural consumption was generally conceived as an undifferentiated process of indiscriminate and, above all, passive absorption. Indeed, the Book-of-the-Month Club's critics all conceptualized consumption in diametric opposition to the individuated, autonomous, rational, and willed choice of the educated individual.[3] This language, we will shortly see, was as deeply gendered as it was politically inflected.

Although my initial object will be to describe the character of the Book-of-the-Month Club's innovations and achievements, I also want to explore further the nature of the debate it spawned about the status and function of cultural production, consumption, and use. Such an exploration is worthwhile, I think, because the terms used in the twenties and thirties specifically to disparage the Club were also the terms that governed the larger culture critique as it developed in response to the rise of mass-mediated entertainments. Because I believe these terms tend to structure our thoughts about mass culture even now, despite recent efforts to rethink the ideological assumptions dictating their use, I want to employ the debate about the Book-of-the-Month Club to reopen discussion of the mass culture critique, particularly with respect to the way gender figures so centrally within it. Ultimately, I want to suggest that we need a more complex understanding of the gendered nature of the assumptions about subjectivity that govern contemporary theories of cultural production, consumption, and use. We need such an understanding, I believe, if we are to engage as academics and intellectuals in less self-serving ways with mass-mediated culture in order to think of it productively and strategically as a technology that might more effectively be used for progressive political ends.

The discussion of the mass culture critique has recently been advanced significantly by Andreas Huyssen (1986b; see also Modleski, 1986a) in his important book, *After the Great Divide*. There, Huyssen develops the argument that mass culture was ideologically demonized by its critics in the early years of this century as "woman." However, because he argues the claim in the context of his prior interest in the consequences of a *post-modernist* remapping of the high culture/low culture dichotomy, he tends to repress discussion of the full range of social and political issues at stake in the historical construction of "the Great Divide." As a result, it seems to me, although he clearly wants to reopen the question of what sort of position the contemporary cultural critic ought to take with respect to mass culture, he seems to fall back into the very dichotomy he wishes to explode by failing to examine fully the issues at stake in the construction of the divide. For this reason, I think, he deals unsatisfactorily with the fraught issues of evaluation and judgment. Unexamined quality distinctions creep back into Huyssen's discussion. I would add here that I don't think he is alone in this fate. These distinctions are astonishingly resilient in a good deal of cultural studies work, despite our best intentions to rethink them.

Early in his introduction, which attempts to deconstruct the usual dismissal of mass culture, Huyssen reassures his potentially uneasy reader, "The point of my argument . . . will not be to deny the quality differences between a successful work of art and cultural trash." He continues encouragingly, "To make quality distinctions remains an important task for the critic, and I will not fall into the mindless pluralism of anything goes" (1986a, p. ix). It is the matter-of-fact, common sense nature of Huyssen's assertion about the cultural critic's proper activity that I want to foreground and call into question today. In fact, in this curious admission made about three pages into his introduction, Huyssen inexplicably recuperates the basis of the conceptual distinction his whole book attempts to historicize and thereby to rethink. Although he acknowledges almost immediately that "to reduce all cultural criticism to the problem of quality is a symptom of the anxiety of contamination," his previous aside suggests that at some level he continues to assume that there are clear differences between successful art and cultural trash, *real* differences which are not produced by any anxiety. Huyssen does not explicitly state that these "quality" differences are aesthetic, but his use of the terms "successful" and "trash" implies such a distinction. Thus he can comfortably suggest that the issue of quality can be side-stepped in favor of his more "theoretical and historical" attempt to rethink "the Great Divide."

The interesting question, it seems to me, is why this recuperation of a qualitative hierarchy? Why is it so difficult for even as sophisticated a cultural critic as Huyssen to avoid engaging in the cartographic activity that has produced and reproduced the "Great Divide" over the course of this century? Why does he assume that he need not include the very notion of quality itself in his historical and theoretical deconstruction of the binary opposition between the high and the low? Is it possible that his political critique does not fully displace the social division cum aesthetic divide he wants to analyze but, in fact, simply recodes it, thereby perpetuating it inadvertently?

I think a look at the nature of the conflict over the Book-of-the-Month Club may help to remind us once again that in the book club wars specifically, and within the mass culture critique more generally, what has appeared as intellectual warfare over aesthetic issues has actually been a dispute over the exercise of cultural authority. Although we ritually repeat this observation within cultural studies scholarship, I am not yet convinced that we have thought critically enough about the implications of such an assertion with respect to our own daily practice as cultural critics. Indeed I am afraid that even now, as we attempt to treat the question of mass production and consumption more carefully, we fall repeatedly into the same trap that opened up for our predecessors. I worry that we do not yet think clearly enough about the fact that mass culture and the middlebrow are concrete and specific challenges to our own authority as cultural custodians. Familiar evaluative assessment of mass entertainment as a form calling only for passive response repeatedly recurs, I believe, because our day-to-day praxis as academic intellectuals is itself predicated on a gendered notion of the subject and because the legitimacy of our authority depends significantly on our continuing ability to naturalize *that* subject as the norm in opposition to others. Significantly, the subject we continue to naturalize in our critical activity is not unrelated to that authorized by critics of the Book-of-the-Month Club.

We will see very shortly that the Book-of-the-Month Club's critics focused attention on the activities of their cultural competitors by demonizing them furiously as authoritarian and disgustingly effeminate. They thereby repressed the fact that what most frightened them was that the Book-of-the-Month Club and other agencies like it betokened a significant threat to their own authority. They were incapable of addressing this issue directly because they conceptualized the problem within ideologically loaded and profoundly limited terms. Since they conceived of true cultural debate and evaluation as activities engaged in only by autonomous and rational individuals—in opposition to the interested and dictatorial pronouncements of authoritarian agencies like the Book-of-the-Month Club—they necessarily erased the fact that they themselves were interested and in fact wished to and did exert cultural authority over others. Thus they could not think clearly about why the masses they so feared might turn to their competitors for guidance in cultural matters. They could not see that in maintaining their lofty, apparently disinterested pose, they were also speaking a dominant discourse that predicated the individuated male subject as the fundamental cultural norm, a discourse that might not appeal to groups of people denied the material and social conditions conducive to the realization of that identity and the values associated with it

I want to venture the suggestion that despite our recent best efforts, little may have changed over the course of this century and that even in many recent postmodern attempts to remap the cultural divide, this norm reasserts itself inadvertently as the enabling condition of cultural criticism itself, of the academic exercise of analysis, and of the cultural activity Pierre Bourdieu (1984) has so aptly named "distinction." We must go further, I think, in recognizing that our discussions of mass culture continue to be located within structures, institutions, and practices of cultural authority, themselves predicated on a profoundly gendered and therefore patriarchal norm. Were we to think more clearly about the consequences of this, we might be able to understand more fully why the activity of cultural criticism is itself anathema to populations that take profound pleasure in the business of cultural consumption. Even the politicized discourse of cultural studies, which tries hard to dispense with aesthetic distinctions in favor of political discriminations among forms, hitches its critical narrative to the notion of a highly rational, independent *political* actor capable of seeing the difference between the blandishments of self-indulgent pleasure and the authentic, utopian work of "real popular culture."

Although I do not wish to suggest that we ought to stop worrying and learn to love consumption, I do feel we need to recognize that our confessed wariness about some forms of popular culture continues to encode the familiar assumption that consumption involves passive ingestion and that ingestion itself is suspiciously easy, if not infantile and grotesque.[4] And this assumption, clearly, rests on a whole host of assumptions about gender which are as limiting as they are enabling. Were we able to interrogate more thoughtfully our still naturalized assumption that cultural criticism is a self-evidently valuable activity and that at the heart of that activity is the activity of discriminating and dividing, always in the service of the distinctive and the singular, we might be able to think the processes of consumption differently. Indeed we might begin to understand that the conceptual opposition between consumption and criticism is itself a historically contingent construction that conceals the fact that all consumption involves criticism and that criticism is itself wholly dependent on previous consumption. Were we able to think consumption differently as a process figuring integration, engulfing, the loss of boundaries, dependency, and collaboration, we might better be able to re-conceive the apparatuses of mass distribution and mass consumption as technologies with an enormous capacity for mobilizing new political communities. Were we able to acknowledge more fully the ways in which we, too, are implicated in the commodification of culture as producers and consumers, we might be able to sustain more rigorous thought about the process of community-building, a process no longer directed by us as the knowing, politically correct avant-garde, but one that includes us as co-opted but nonetheless struggling participants. Were we able to acknowledge this, we might better be able to imagine ourselves more effectively breaching the walls of the academy in order to imagine many more forms of articulation. We can't afford to be complacent about the structure of the university and the limited opportunities for articulation that it offers us. The fact that we haven't discussed our own teaching except informally at this conference suggests that we continue to devalue even this form of intersubjective articulation most closely associated with the academy. The debate about middlebrow culture can be useful to us, I believe, because that debate explicitly foregrounded the question of what authorities would control cultural dissemination, evaluation, and use in the modern era.

Together with two partners, Robert Haas and Maxwell Sackheim, Harry Scherman created the Book-of-the-Month Club in 1926.[5] The account he gave to the Columbia historians of the Club's founding suggests that Scherman himself saw it principally as an interesting financial venture. Although he regularly justified the Club's activities publicly by focusing on its cultural mission to distribute good books to people who otherwise would not acquire them, in the narrative he spun for the oral history project he stressed the financial and technical problems of designing a book distribution operation that would sell new books rather than sets of classics by mail. Although Scherman was deeply interested in books and culture throughout his life, his Columbia narrative suggests that he thought of himself principally as an advertising man and of the club as a marketing innovation. For Scherman, culture was an important component of life, but it did not define his existence. Indeed, after recounting to the interviewer that as a child he "had a bent towards reading," that he was "quite a voracious reader,"[6] he rushed to reassure him additionally that "I wasn't what you might call the scholastic, ingrown type at all. I had a good, rounded bringing-up and a very happy one" (vol. 1, p. 3).

Scherman's 1956 repetition of the notion of a well-rounded education, a concept which had dominated debate about progressivism and pedagogy in the twenties and the thirties, suggests that he had been schooled to believe that culture and learning might somehow be incompatible with the hard realities of everyday American life. Maladjusted eggheads, many Americans suspected, were fit only for the isolation of the library and could not cope with the American century of business. Of course, the obverse view of this conceptual separation of learning and culture from the world of everyday self-interest and business specified that culture could only be tainted by association with activities designed to market mundane products like toothpaste, mouthwash, and soap. What is perhaps most interesting about Scherman's narrative is that it suggests that he spent his entire life trying to bring these conceptually distinct spheres together. He saw no reason why books had to be the prized possessions of only a few. Nor did he agree with most of his critics that the wedding of culture and commerce led only to the tainting and degradation of the cultural sphere, which ought more properly to remain unsullied by any contact with the dirt and self-interest associated with money.

Scherman's first venture into the mass production and mass distribution of books resulted in the creation of the Little Leather Library with booksellers Charles and Albert Boni. Loosely patterned after the Haldeman Julius books of the previous century, the Little Leather Library was created when the Bonis noticed that a cigarette company was giving away a pocket volume of Shakespeare with a package of cigarettes. Thinking that this demonstrated popular interest in the classics, they designed a small, leather-bound dummy of *Romeo and Juliet* to be sold for twenty-five cents, much below the regular hard bound price of two to three dollars. They intended to piggy-back the sale of the book onto the sale of another commodity widely distributed among the American population. When the Whitman Candy Company of Philadelphia placed an order for 15,000 such volumes, Scherman and his partners had to scramble to scrape up the capital to produce the books. They managed the task and launched their enterprise as one that marketed a whole series of titles, all of them in the public domain because, as Scherman noted to his interviewers, they couldn't afford to pay royalties. Spurred on by high candy sales and apparent demand for cheap copies of the classics, the partners then began to market their books through bookstores, drugstores, and in Woolworths. To their great surprise, the Little Leather Library did better in Woolworths than in any other outlet. What this meant to Scherman was that a very large audience for quality books lay untapped in the American marketplace. He therefore decided to bypass both book dealers and Woolworths by marketing the books directly through the mail.

In this new scheme, Scherman and his partners relied on a combination of publication advertising and direct circularizing to reach people who might never set foot in a bookstore. To do this, Scherman created what he thought to be a new selling technique—he included a sample leather cover in the initial mailing. This cover was supplemented by a short letter that asked "How much do you think thirty classics with this kind of binding and this size would sell for? Make your guess and then open the enclosed, sealed envelope" (vol. 1, p. 31). The appeal suggests that the audience that eventually bought 30 to 40 million copies of Little Leather Library books was interested not only in economy but also in the idea of a library of classics, clearly a concept associated with education and social respectability. That the cover also seemed to prompt sales suggests as well that the audience was additionally attracted to the possibility of owning an elegant and tasteful object. Indeed it seems clear that what Scherman was selling was less a series of individual and ephemeral books to read than a collection of potentially permanent, respected, almost sacred objects, a set of things to own.

Some of the remarks Scherman made to the Columbia interviewers as he attempted to explain how the Little Leather Library metamorphosed into the Book-of-the-Month Club suggest that he was well aware of this. He noted, in fact, that it was generally thought impossible to sell books other than sets of classics by mail. He observed, however, that at the J. Walter Thompson advertising agency, he had found that "we could sell types of books which it had never been thought possible to sell by mail—Conrad, Oscar Wilde, and so on" (vol. 1, p. 33). He continued with the crucial detail, "They were sets and expensive sets." Since Scherman himself would later term these books "furniture books" (vol. 3, p. 169), it seems clear that he understood that people bought the book sets not necessarily because they wanted to read them but rather because they wished to own them. What the act of owning such expensive sets must have meant is difficult to say with any certainty but surely it must have been bound up with the possibility of constructing an image of the purchaser as a cultured, educated individual. Such books were perhaps the perfect embodiment of what Bourdieu has called "cultural capital"— a kind of verbal real estate.

It is fairly clear, however, that the Little Leather Library and other related book distribution schemes worked because the idea of the literary classic was well-established in American culture. The classic was a classic because its claim to legitimacy and worth was already established by accepted authorities and it was therefore understood to have, first, a particular use-value, and then, later with its entry into the marketplace, a specific exchange-value. Precious as a potential moral and spiritual guide, the classic gained its conceptual weight from its association with the clergy, the university, and the school. It was considered worth owning because it possessed "universal" human wisdom and could be called upon in time of need for advice and guidance. Because such books were *already* understood to have this particular use, enterprising men like Scherman could commodify the idea of the classic by embodying it within the object his publicity was selling, that is, the elegant *set* of revered volumes worthy of a place of honor in the home. In effect, Scherman prompted multiple acts of purchase by exchanging the culturally valuable notion of "the classic" with a physical object, in this case, the set of books. By gathering individual volumes into a set, Scherman was able to market them both as classics and as a library and thus to mobilize and to use class-based desires for his own purposes.

It was only when Scherman worked out some of the complexity of this process for himself, albeit in a somewhat different language and form, that he was able to solve the problem of marketing new books by mail. As he told the Columbia interviewers, one of the ideas he and his partners regularly discussed as a way to maintain sales at the Little Leather Library was that of selling newly published fiction by mail. The principal problem with such a scheme, he observed, was that it was financially unfeasible since the high cost of direct mail advertising would have to be charged against a single book, thus making profits almost nil. In fact, however, Scherman's narration of the way the corporation's thinking evolved suggests that he understood that the limitations were not financial ones alone. He followed his first observation about the prohibitive cost of advertising single books with these rather more complex comments:

> Now, we had known as part of our established experience that you could sell individual books which might be called "use books," like *Power of Will* or *American Gardening*, things of that kind where there would be a broad market. If you put your ad in the right place or had the right list you could probably sell it successfully by mail. . . . I mean, you could sell individual books of that kind which had a broad use, but you couldn't sell the new fiction, or new non-fiction books about which the general public knew nothing. (vol. 1, p. 37)

Although Scherman was obviously concerned about developing a mass audience cheaply, his remarks also point to an awareness that in the United States of the 1920s a new piece of fiction was simply not a "use book." While it is difficult to reconstruct Scherman's thinking completely, these comments suggest that he understood that most Americans did not have a general use-category within which to place new fiction. In other words, while they understood that gardening books and self-help volumes had clear functions and concrete applications, as did the older classics—an understanding that enabled advertisers to write appropriate appeals for them—individual volumes of new fiction, each ostensibly different from the next, were not easily or automatically grouped into a conceptual category with its own culturally determined value.

The question of how to think about new fiction was in fact raised again and again in the pages of the literary monthlies of the 1920s in articles worrying about the validity and worth of something called "pleasure reading." Pleasure reading, it would seem, was reconstructed at this time, now not as a morally corrupt, entirely wasteful activity, but as a relaxing, self-enhancing pastime that might lead to the creation of "the book habit." Innumerable commentators in *Publishers' Weekly,* the *Nation,* the *New Republic,* and other like magazines labored industriously to establish a positive connection between fiction reading and pleasure. Again, the obvious question is "why?" Why were so many column inches devoted to articles like "The Book Habit" or "The Humboldt State College Plan for Recreational Reading" (Robinson, 1926; Graves, 1926)?

The residual ambivalence with which the category was treated is the best clue we have to the fears that underwrote this discourse. Despite their obvious intention to associate reading with fun, the authors of articles like these continued to stumble over the question of what a new work of fiction was useful for. No matter how hard they tried to privilege enjoyment and pleasure, these champions of the book returned again and again to its association with education and edification. Although they repeatedly extolled the pleasures induced by reading, they also revealed significant discomfort in severing too cleanly the connection between books, education, and work when they equivocated in particular about the qualitative virtues of pulp fiction, adventure tales, and best-sellers. None of them could recommend these books without reservation. Fiction, then, was increasingly associated with the promotion of pleasure, but the pleasure constructed in this discourse was a pleasure with a difference. It was a pleasure that also fostered edification and uplift.

The distinction was established, of course, by implicit reference to more suspect pleasures, those fostering only enjoyment and fun. The relevant referents here were the pleasures of the ear and the gaze, those prompted by radio and the movies. These activities solicited the interest and participation of the American working classes, many of them newly arrived, clearly different, and wholly unassimilated. The discourse of pleasure reading, then, was a social discourse about particular populations as much as it was a cultural discourse about books. In hailing the upwardly mobile, largely white middle-class population addressed by the magazines for which they wrote, these writers not only helped to construct a particular function or use-value for new fiction but also thereby offered to their readers a strategy for distinguishing themselves from those alien others who were made content by simple and simple-minded fun. Harry Scherman soon learned how to exploit both this discourse about pleasure reading and the social fears that warranted it.

Indeed Scherman recognized quickly that if he was to sell new books by mail, he would not only have to spread the advertising and solicitation costs across a number of volumes, but he would also have to sell the idea of a series of books by giving that series a comprehensive use and application for the potential customer. As Scherman reasoned, customers bought sets of classics because they were assured of their value and knew what to do with them. New books, on the other hand, possessed neither evident authority and worth nor perceptible function. Thus he faced the problem of how to characterize the new books he wished to sell. As he explained it

> That was the genesis of the Book-of-the-Month Club. Somebody had to take a group of books. It couldn't be immediate, because people were not buying groups of books immediately; therefore they had to buy over a period of time. It therefore had to be something like a subscription. On whose authority, then? You had to set up some kind of authority so that the subscriber would feel there was some reason for buying a group of books, so that he'd know he wasn't buying a pig in a poke, and also that he wasn't buying books which were suspect. (vol. 1, p. 38)

Scherman understood, finally, that he not only had to authorize the books he wanted to sell but that he had to authorize them specifically as a group. That is, in designing his advertising appeal, he knew he had to conceptualize the set of unknown and different books to be bought in the future as a single cultural commodity with a clear function and use.

Given the ongoing instability and volatility of the as-yet semantically and normatively unsecured concept of pleasure reading, it should not be surprising to learn that Scherman accomplished these tasks by wedding this discourse about pleasure to the older discourse surrounding the classic. He did so by establishing a selection committee of "eminent experts" who were deputized initially to pick "the best book published each month." What he did, then, was to commodify culture and authority further by exchanging these concepts not with a set of classics but with the promise that these new books, because they were the best, were assured of becoming classics. The prior status of the individuals he chose as experts in the field of letters broadly defined enabled Scherman to confer metonymically the same status and value on the books they chose. In consciously mobilizing the phrase, "the best," Scherman clearly evoked Matthew Arnold's famous pedagogical dictum as well as the cultural value and function of "the classic." Thus the Book-of-the-Month Club was founded upon the class discourse of cultural privilege even as it sought to distribute books to a population hitherto inadequately integrated into literary culture. Ironically, we will shortly see that in his zeal to solve a marketing problem, by poaching on earlier formations of literary authority in order to confer value and use on the commodity he wished to sell, Scherman foregrounded, even exposed, the structure and function of literary authority too prominently. This move brought the Book-of-the-Month Club into direct conflict with the more traditional guardians of the cultural realm whose interests were better served by suppressing or denying the existence of that literary authority itself.

To be sure, when the Book-of-the-Month Club was first announced to the trade in February 1926, *Publishers' Weekly* noted only that the monthly selection was to be chosen by what it called "an unusual committee of critics and authors" (Anonymous, 1926). However, this announcement would be the last to employ such an understated term as "unusual" to describe the Club's selection committee, for that committee soon became the focal point of the controversy generated by the Club. As Joan Shelley Rubin (1985) has demonstrated, the committee itself was composed of already well-known celebrities. Foremost among these and the chair of the committee was Henry Seidel Canby, a Yale English professor and recently appointed editor of the *Saturday Review of Literature.* He was joined by the author and educator, Dorothy Canfield Fisher, by the literary columnist, Christopher Morley, by Heywood Broun, the literary and drama editor of the *New York Tribune,* and finally by William Allen White, the owner and editor of the *Emporia Gazette.* Each of the committee members, then, except perhaps Fisher, was associated with a well-thought-of but nonetheless fairly broad-based print publication. Neither isolated in the literary academy nor identified with the minority defense of literary modernism, these critics could therefore be plausibly presented by Scherman as representative of a cross-section of the American population. Indeed he evoked the discourse of representative democracy by repeatedly calling his group of experts a committee (only later would they be referred to as "judges") and by stressing their individual differences through the inclusion of small, singular portraits in all of his early advertising. Rarely photographed as a group for club publicity, the committee members were arrayed individually before potential subscribers as unique individuals with their own interests, idiosyncrasies, and tastes, and, of course, pleasures.

Despite Scherman's first, fumbling efforts to evoke the discourse of democracy and liberal humanism, the Book-of-the-Month Club was soon roundly attacked for its usurpation of the individual's right to choose his or her own reading matter. These attacks on the Club, however, actually only contributed to a debate that had already been joined about the forces of standardization in the modern world. Standardization, in fact, was a code word for mass production, mass distribution, and mass consumption. It was portrayed repeatedly as an evil specter spreading its cloak of uniformity over a once vitally differentiated population, producing as a consequence uniform automatons open to coercion by others. In the context of what became known as the book club wars, the specter of standardization was thought to rest in committees who claimed for themselves the right to recommend or to select books for others. Their chief crime was their attack on the business of individual discrimination.[7]

In objecting to both prize and selection committees, the book club critics were objecting to any external formalization of the structure of literary authority. They managed this by demonizing those committees through the use of a recurrent and particular language. What the book club critics did was to represent them metaphorically as coercive authorities, that is, as invaders, dictators, and policemen. In doing so, they differentiated themselves from club officials by portraying their own activities as the disinterested work of representative public officials who sought only to insure that "the best" might naturally rise to its appropriate position. Since our time is brief and I have analyzed this language in some depth in an earlier paper entitled, "The Scandal of the Middlebrow," I can only hope to map out the basic parameters of the discourse here.

Essentially, what the book club critics did again and again was to set up an opposition between book club members and non-members. Members were represented as passive dopes in the thrall of nefarious authorities, whereas non-members were portrayed as thoughtful and independent individuals fully in charge of their own book choices. In constructing such a schema, the critics were thereby denying the efficacy of their own advisory activities as well as those of bookstore owners, clerks, and librarians. Rarely did they object to the actual selections made by club officials. Rather, they decried the fact that those officials had arrogated to themselves the role of advisor and judge to large *groups* of consumers. Thus they objected to the centralization of an authority that they believed would otherwise remain dispersed and therefore open to uncoerced, "free" assessment by individuals.

Clearly, then, the book club debate was a response to the reorganization of the culture industries produced by vast changes in capital concentration in the years, 1880 to 1920. What was at issue was the growing ability of organizations to assemble vast audiences as the target for general address. As a consequence, the debate furthered American discussion of the effects of the process of massification. By accusing the book clubs of usurping the power and prerogatives that formerly belonged to individuals, the book club critics suggested that organizations like Scherman's threatened to destroy the process of rational inquiry and the public sphere in which that activity ought properly to take place. The hegemonic power of this discourse about freely deliberating individuals was so strong that it dictated even Harry Scherman's responses to his critics. Indeed, in the many defenses he wrote of the Book-of-the-Month Club, Scherman always attempted to show how carefully the club had attempted to preserve the possibility of individual choice. Thus his defenses hinged on the strategic repetition of words like "will," "volition," "agency, "and even "the inalienable right to choose." Like his critics, Scherman was unwilling to give up the illusion that individual choice in cultural matters was independent, entirely rational, and uninfluenced by external factors.

We need to ask at this point why both the critics of the Book-of-the-Month Club and its own officials labored so feverishly to assert that cultural production, dissemination, and use remained individual activities unaffected by the interests or influence of others. What fears warranted this endless rhetorical reconstruction of a public sphere of cultural activity where fully autonomous, wholly individuated, free human subjects exercised their rationality and agency by selecting the cultural fare that best suited their taste? What exactly were the Club's critics so afraid of when they sneered at it as a wholly middlebrow institution? The dominant metaphors controlling this critical discourse, it seems to me, provide the answers to this question.

Clearly, in insisting that true cultural choice had always to be individual, the Club's critics and its management were alike refusing to come to terms with the fact that the new media industries and mass market agencies such as the Club were assembling mass audiences open to easy address by anyone capable of securing the technology of production and distribution. Like earlier critics of popular culture who always deliberately distinguished themselves from the noisy, unruly ungovernable mob, the critics of the Book-of-the-Month Club were constructing themselves as disinterested, wholly rational individuals by opposing themselves to Scherman and his selection committee who were accused of degrading culture by offering it incautiously and indiscrimately to the wrong people. The people's body the critics labored to repress, however, was not so much the carnivalesque body discussed by Peter Stallybrass and Allon White (1986) after Bahktin, but the live, militarized body of the mass assembled by fascism and bolshevism on the Continent and by labor unions and people's parties in the United States. The fear that warranted the insistence on the rationality of cultural activity and the active suppression of the workings of interest and authority upon it was a social fear that new technologies and the exigencies of the political environment might unite to produce a demanding mass or mob bent on wresting control from the genteel elite who recognized true culture when they saw it. Small wonder, then, that in this rhetoric, the term, "democracy," was repeatedly disarticulated from its association with groups or with the common people and articulated anew to the notion of a smaller, rational, elite body of unique individuals.

Because the book club critics were apparently so alarmed by the sudden social resurgence of the masses as a threatening mob, they resisted any impulse to admit to their discursive presence on the cultural scene. Ironically, to manage this, they also had to repress all knowledge of the leadership they wished to and did exert and to deny the existence of the very machinery through which that authority was wielded. As a consequence, they ruled out the possibility from the outset that they might seize these new, powerful technologies in order to use them for their own purposes. Individualized and individuated, intellectual critique, then, in the early years of this century, was specifically constructed in opposition to media production, distribution, and use, a process portrayed always as undifferentiated, muddled, and coercive.

The Book-of-the-Month Club, it would seem, was objectionable to a logic that remained through and through fundamentally bourgeois in its construction. The Club was scandalous both because it managed to expose what was necessarily repressed in order to construct the autonomous self-regulating individual and because it muddied distinctions that were essential to the maintenance of the resulting conceptions of rationality, independence, and will. On the one hand, the Book-of-the-Month Club displayed—even celebrated—the function of critical authority and it thereby externalized a process that was otherwise conceived as internal to the individual who, in arriving at independent judgment, was thought to be exercising only universal reason. The club suggested by its very existence that in fact judgment was neither independent nor autonomous but predicated on the exercise of quite specific and identifiable power. The metaphors of autocracy and dictatorship that demonized the Book-of-the-Month Club thus expressed critics' fears that the familiar rational culture of independent individuals was under concerted attack both by political enemies and by the abstract processes of standardization and industrialization.

What we see then in this struggle over the appropriate way to disseminate culture is a clash between class fractions over the right to direct the struggle between American liberal ideology on the one hand and a new social formation made possible by the processes of massification on the other. Both parties to the dispute—the critics of the book clubs who saw them as agencies usurping the rights and prerogatives of individuals to direct their own cultural activities—and the club management, which claimed only to be making choice more convenient and effective for its members—both parties to the dispute—resorted to the rights-based language of bourgeois liberalism in order to insist that readers could still operate as autonomous, fully individuated, and self-regulating citizens. Indeed, it is striking that while both the Club's critics and its own management could articulately demonstrate how an economy of interests determined and made contingent the cultural selections proffered by their opponents, thus constraining readers' choices, neither side was willing to recognize that such contingency and positionality dictated its own operations as well. In effect, both sides in the dispute resolutely refused to acknowledge that they were making claims to cultural authority simply by recommending books to others, no matter how those recommendations were disseminated.

What this suggests is that the controversy over the Book-of-the-Month Club developed as an instance of an intra-class dispute over who precisely would stake the claim to cultural authority even while denying that was what was being done. At issue was whether cultural selection would continue to be the province of the urban Protestant elite of the Northeastern cities who controlled most of the respected literary journals or the newly arrived immigrant entrepreneurs like Scherman who were beginning to dominate the culture industry. Both sides sought to justify their claim to such authority not by demonstrating their particular facility at or preparation for cultural leadership but rather by suggesting that they did not constrain the inherent natural rights of the already-autonomous individual to exercise his faculties on his own.[8]

I want to point out that I have used the gendered pronoun, "his," deliberately here because the discourse generated both by the Book-of-the-Month Club's critics and by its officials was profoundly gendered in its construction. That is, it rhetorically constructed the autonomous individual not only in opposition to an undifferentiated mass represented as passively docile in the face of militarized domination, but also in opposition to an organically simple mass that was naturally grotesque. As frequently as the discourse branded the Book-of-the-Month Club anathema to the cause of democracy and the fate of the individual, so too did it metaphorically connect the Club with the organic lack of differentiation associated with the feminine and the maternal. By associating the Club again and again with forced feeding, pabulum, and indiscriminate consumption, the Club's critics were once again unconsciously evoking traces of the scandalous, grotesque body and its earthy, material nature believed capable of engulfing everything from below.

In the following passage, for example, the author of "Books on the Belt" slid easily from ambiguous images of authority to evocations of food associated with the surveillance of mothers. "Have you had your book this month?," he queried. "If not, some club, league, guild, society, cabal, academy, mail-order house, or synod of presbyters has missed a chance. . . . For books are being made as accessible as milk on the stoop in this land of higher salesmanship, as compulsory as spinach. Thanks to the book clubs" (Whipple, 1929, p. 182). This articulation of authoritarian agencies with mothers was made even clearer in a letter written to the *Saturday Review* specifically criticizing the book clubs. The letter writer protested, "I am forced to accept Big Ben as a roomy, forced to partake of canned soups, radio, movies, and censorship, but I'll be consigned if I am going to have my books ladled out to me by literary cooks regardless of their professed or actual standing as critics, reviewers, or blurbsmiths. No literary goose-stepping for me" ("The Bookseller," 1927). After further detailing his criticism of the book clubs' selections as a "pig in a poke, all picked, packed, trimmed, deodorized," the letter writer concluded that he would stick with bookstores. He added finally and triumphantly, "[n]o literary wet nurses for me."

As Stallybrass and White have shown, the grotesque body has traditionally been figured as a "subject of pleasure in the process of exchange, never closed off from either its social or ecosystemic context" (1986, p. 22). Hence, the constant references to feeding, to nursing, to mothers, and to pigs. These passages suggest that the early book club critics resorted to familiar strategies. Indeed their descriptions remained fixated on the processes of exchange at the heart of the book club operation, the processes of distribution and, in particular, consumption. Most frequently, they elaborated upon this exchange as a process dominated by the indiscriminate distribution of pabulum and the passive consumption of an undigested mass. These distant echoes of maternal force and infantile regression betokened the critics' unconscious worry about the threatening resurgence of social and material forces that posed a challenge to the survival of the separate, elevated, purified, rational, bourgeois body. What they seemed to fear now was both the grotesque body of the smothering female, an image made perhaps newly frightening by the recent successes of the women's movement, and the grotesque body of the mass duly regimented, militarized, standardized, and assembled for assault, a body incarnated in the labor movement, in bolshevism, and in fascism. The Club's transgression was precisely its assertion of its authoritative role and therefore its denial of the absolute autonomy of the self-regulating individual. Paradoxically, the Club's presence suggested to its critics that real "Culture" was endangered by high, authoritarian forces on the one hand as well as by the denizens of a demi-monde devoted to promiscuous, wanton revelling in mere entertainment on the other. In fact, it may have been an alliance between the two that was most deeply feared. This, I think, was the particular scandal of the middlebrow.

What this combative discourse about the book clubs reveals finally is the extent to which the fast-changing processes of mass production and mass consumption were conceptually predicated on historically contingent definitions of the subject even as late as the 1930s. One might even be tempted to say that they still are. The act of mobilizing technologies capable of reaching millions of people was both stigmatized and defended within a discursive framework that took the autonomous, individuated, independent subject to be the irreducible political and cultural agent of a social formation. Conceived always as a fully intentional, self-directing individual with naturally endowed rights to exercise those faculties, the approved cultural actor in the discourse about the book clubs was one who differentiated himself from a mass conceived as militarily subdued and passively feminine. The very definition of the individual used to gauge the consequences of massification was thus thoroughly bourgeois and wholly patriarchal in construction. Anything producing repetitive or serial connection between large numbers of persons was demonized either as coercive or as smotheringly maternal. Coercive cultural authorities were presented as militaristic forces annihilating the right to self-determination of otherwise free individuals. Indiscriminate, effeminate agencies were implicitly criticized for the regressive, infantile pleasure they took in entertainment and were pictured as insufficiently respective of the responsible adult who would otherwise engage responsibly in the disciplined labor of cultural discrimination.

The appearance of new technologies for mass production, distribution, and consumption was consequently narrated as a tale of declension rather than of possibility, at least within the cultural sphere. This ensured, of course, that those participating most fully in this discourse would never seriously address the question of how these technologies might be used to hail large numbers of individuals differently so as to gather them into the kind of political communities they envisioned. Because the notion of individuation functioned as the primary and fundamental norm, any process producing merging, the breaking of boundaries, or the easy exchange of cultural material between persons was stigmatized as destructive of the social fabric.

The question I want to raise, in closing, then, about the dominant discourse on consumption is intimately bound up with this predication of the individuated male subject as the fundamental cultural norm, a norm I'm not sure we have learned how to dispense with fully. Were this not the source of all our cultural calibrations and the practices grounded upon them—were we better able to remember that all individuals are both socially and culturally dependent—would we be able to evaluate the consequences of mass distribution and mass consumption differently? Were we able to dispense with such patriarchal self-construction, perhaps to evaluate integration, connection, merging, and dependency differently—that is, as forces tending toward the fostering of community—would we be able to acknowledge that the technologies of mass production, distribution, and use are not *necessarily* evil but simply tools which can be mobilized by and in the service of different communities? Could we recognize this, would we more effectively be able to disarticulate these technologies from their control by the authorities and institutions of capitalism? Would a less patriarchal discourse prompt us to ask more troublesome and difficult questions about the now-naturalized structure and mission of the university and its crucial connection to the business of cultural criticism, which is to say, the process of producing and reproducing essential distinctions? The school, after all, as Allon White (1983) has so acerbically shown, is the dominant institution in our society charged with the social reproduction of seriousness and with the demarcation and production of a crucial difference between dirty, unruly, dependent children and the autonomous, individuated adult. And, as he notes further, "Seriousness always has more to do with power than with content. The authority to designate what is to be taken seriously (and the authority to enforce reverential solemnity in certain contexts) is a way of creating and maintaining power" (p. 9).

An examination of school architecture, of course, tells us a lot about what has traditionally been dismissed by Western, patriarchal culture as unworthy of serious recognition. White points out, "The provision of playgrounds in school puts games, exuberant bodies, scatology, sexual exploration, dirt, jokes and pleasure in an open enclave where they cannot contaminate the realm of 'pure' knowledge" (p.12). Hence, the electrifying effect produced by those mysterious and subversive guitar riffs that momentarily silenced Homi Bhabha the other night. Forced outside the schoolroom door are "nonsense rhymes, tongue-twisters and tales that never end, riddles, jeers, crooked answers, tricks, tricksters and embarrassers, greedy-guts, Lazybones, Fatties, Lankies and improper songs" (p.13), all things which foreground connection, intertwining, blurred distinctions, corporeality and food. What White calls "the primary law of double exclusion" (p.12) is therefore at the very heart of the schooling enterprise. Children are taught not only to sit still in individual seats for certain subjects but instructed more generally that "where knowledge is, play is not; where play is, knowledge is not" (p.12).

The distinction between work and play, knowledge and ignorance, culture and entertainment, therefore, is not something incidental to the structure of the school and the university and therefore easily dispensed with. It is in fact the distinction that calls the whole enterprise into being, the distinction that creates the authority to dispel so-called ignorance in the first place. No wonder we find it so difficult to dispense with the binary distinction between high and low culture, to rethink the Great Divide. The talk of "quality" thus recurs as the figure or trope of our role as cultural missionaries, of our participation in the hegemonic business of constructing the serious even when we present ourselves as critical intellectuals challenging the domination of bourgeois capitalists. In fact, we too may only be engaged in an intra-class dispute over the right to dictate the particular contents of the serious and the silly, of the specific placement of the boundary between the high and the low. Are we so sure our conceptions of the political are not simply remapped onto this prior distinction between the serious and the playful, the high and the low? I worry that we still do not put to the question the necessity of making such distinctions in the first place, of discriminating the child from the man.

The question I want to pose finally is this. What would it mean to organize education not about individuation, autonomy, and power, but about a recognition of and respect for the inevitability of dependency, interdependency, collaboration, for the persistence of childish interests and pleasures within the business of adult life? What would our daily practice look like? Would discrimination, distinction, and criticism figure so centrally in our activity? Can we afford to take what we do for granted? Can criticism and pedagogy be organized on another model that might lead to newer, more broadly based forms of social articulation? If we didn't valorize distinction, discrimination, and work so confidently in our day-to-day practice, would consumption, entertainment, and pleasure look so suspect? If *they* didn't, would we better be able to recognize and to act upon our *identity* with those who have no qualms about indulging in the polymorphous pleasures of the ear, the gaze, and the body? Would a less patriarchal discourse prompt us to raise the question of cultural authority more openly by enabling us to avoid demonizing any and all groups in favor of independent, self-regulating individuals represented most prominently and conveniently by our rational selves?

These are exceedingly difficult questions and of course I do not have simple answers to any of them. But before I turn them over to you for debate and disagreement, I want to anticipate two important objections to my claims here. I do not mean to romanticize childhood or dependency in my remarks. I am not suggesting that the experience, knowledge, and judgment of the adult cannot get us a little further down the road, to paraphrase Stuart Hall. Obviously, they can. But what I am urging is a more dialectical recognition of the fact that the child always haunts us, as Peter Stallybrass and bell hooks have so clearly shown at this conference, and that that haunting need not be feared and therefore repressed by the policing of the childish pleasures of the polymorphous, dependent body. As intellectuals, we need to think more clearly about the way in which the pleasure we take in words, in verbal display, in speech, are very like the pleasures people take in the rituals, practices, and play associated with popular *and* mass culture. We need to think more clearly about how we *are* those people.

I am also not saying that there is some essential and therefore necessary connection between rationality, thought, analysis, and gender. If there were, I could not stand before you today asking you to think about the constructed and enforced division between the rational and the corporeal. Rather, what I am saying is that rationality and analysis — *as we know them*—are tools fashioned and forged in a patriarchal society organized by a phallic divide granting those tools and agency to some and not to others. Those tools have a history, then, that requires refashioning. My point is that those tools have historically been used to do some things and not others, that is, they have been used to discriminate and to divide more than they have been used to link, to collaborate, to join. The immodesty of so many academic practices and spaces, it seems to me, is the legacy of these articulations. Our agenda, I think, is to scale them down, to rethink them, to modestly join in collaboration with all those intellectuals outside the academy who struggle to understand and to remake their lives in conditions not of their own making.

Notes

I would like to acknowledge the work of two of my former graduate students who have had an enormous impact on the remarks in this paper. As my research assistant, Barry Shank unearthed the historical material from which I quote here. This paper quite literally could not have been written without his help. Gerry O'Sullivan first introduced me to the work of Allon White, work which has affected me profoundly. It was Gerry who gave me my now tattered copy of "The Dismal Sacred Word," an article I find myself returning to again and again.

I would also like to acknowledge the work and struggles of my feminist foremothers and sisters. Without their earlier persistence and success at "breaking in," as Stuart Hall put it yesterday, I could not be standing here before you today. It is their theft of the masters' tools and their efforts to reforge them—so as to say the unsayable—which has enabled my speech today. If my remarks express concern about those tools and the resistance they offer to such reforging, it is because I have been taught by people like Audre Lorde that the masters' tools may not be *enough* to dismantle and rebuild the masters' house. Yet we cannot afford *not* to steal them. The remarks I will make today arise from my worry that we have not yet adequately learned how to disarticulate the tools of the patriarchy from the misogynist hands and hierarchical practices to which they have been historically allied.

1. Introduction, Book-of-the-Month Club Oral History transcript, 1955, Columbia Oral History Collection (Butler Library, Columbia University, New York City). Quoted with permission of the Book-of-the-Month Club and the Trustees of Columbia University.

2. Supplement to the *Book-of-the-Month Club News*, April 1949, p. 1.

3. For a full discussion of the terms of this critical discourse about the Book-of-the-Month Club, see my article, "The Scandal of the Middlebrow: The Book-of-the-Month Club, Class Fracture, and the Cultural Authority" (1990). The present essay is meant to build on the analysis in this earlier piece by showing how the defense of the cultural choices of the autonomous individual was specifically gendered.

4. For a fuller discussion of the consequences of the consumption metaphor, see my "Reading is not Eating: Mass-Produced Literature and the Theoretical, Methodological and Political Consequences of a Metaphor" (1986).

5. Details about the creation of the Book-of-the-Month Club are drawn from the interviews in the Columbia Oral History collection and from Charles Lee (1958), *The Hidden Public: The Story of the Book-of-the-Month Club*.

6. Scherman interview, Columbia Oral History Collection, vol. 1, p. 1. Volume and page numbers follow later quotations.

7. For a more complete discussion of this, see Radway (1990).

8. The nature of this intra-class dispute is discussed more fully in Radway (1990).

DISCUSSION: Janice Radway

SANDRA BRAMAN: I would have been more comfortable if you had placed your discussion more solidly in the history of the commodification of the book that goes back to the serialization of Dickens and so on. Regarding the place of gender in that history I felt that you took an elitist approach because the appreciation of the book as an object may be an aesthetic appreciation as well as a commodity form of appreciation. There are a number of art forms involved in the production of the book: e.g., fine printing, etching and binding, in addition to the literary content. At least grant all of the people who enjoy them that aesthetic pleasure, and that includes women. And women have also played an important role in printing in U.S. history, especially in the colonial period. Also you could almost make the counter-argument that it was feminine interest in the novel and in fine literature that led to its great success in the 1920s. Finally, I disagree with your statement that there was not already pleasure in the novel that was very sophisticated, that was mass, and that was heavily feminine. Production of cheap novels was emancipation for women who had very little time, very little money, but who found great pleasure in the reading. How else do you understand somebody like Fanny Hurst in the 1920s, who had a mass audience and wrote about very ordinary women's lives—a servant in the South, a woman trying to be an entrepreneur in the

Midwest and so on? It was those women whose lives she was writing about who were reading them.

RADWAY: I would say that your first point concerning the question of my elitist position with respect to the book as object is a useful correction and I would accept it. This is evidence, I think, for the way in which these unexamined value distinctions recur inadvertently in virtually all of our discourse about books. It's extremely difficult to think our way out of this logic. In response to your second question about my discussion of pleasure reading, I would stress that I'm not saying that various populations didn't have uses for novels or that they didn't take pleasure in them. Nor am I saying that there wasn't a connection between women and fiction, and that it wasn't elaborate. What I am saying is that in the dominant discourse of the cultural authorities, this was not elaborately developed or well understood. Perhaps the distinction I draw between the actual political practices of populations and the dominant discourse about those populations is not as clear as it might be. The only other thing I might add is that perhaps this paper makes my attitude towards the Book-of-the-Month Club sound wholly critical. In fact it's not. One of the things I'm most interested in and which I have not dealt with here at all, is the Book-of-the-Month Club's championing of women's literature. Dorothy Canfield Fisher was extremely powerful at the Book-of-the-Month Club and the Book-of-the-Month Club was instrumental in disseminating books by Willa Cather, Josephine Herbst, and believe it or not, Gertrude Stein.

MICHAEL BERUBE: As you point out elsewhere, the mid-thirties is a very odd time in book publishing. The market had shrunk about tenfold, and yet it saw the first blockbusters. Was there a point in the thirties or sometime after when the Book-of-the-Month Club was spoken of not as coercive massification, but as a means for preventing the loss of caste, as a means of maintaining and distinguishing readers from an undifferentiated mass in the midst of economic instability?

RADWAY: No. The discourse was almost entirely critical. There were some defenses of the Book-of-the-Month Club, often by people associated with it. Clifton Fadiman, for instance. One of the most positive ones I know of was written by Malcolm Cowley. Cowley was interested in the question of distribution and the dissemination of culture to the larger mass population. He believed the Club might be confounding the distinction between the learned and the unwashed. Later on, the aesthetic issue became more prominent and more critics objected to the "trash" disseminated by the Book-of-the-Month Club. In Dwight MacDonald's famous essay, "Mass Cult and Mid-Cult," the Book-of-the-Month Club figures as the epitome of what he called "mid-cult."

BILL BUXTON: In terms of the agenda for critical theory, to what extent do you think meetings such as this, which are actually contributing to the commodification of critical discourse, are at odds with our own critical impulses? Perhaps you could indicate what sorts of other possibilities there might be for disseminating our knowledge?

RADWAY: I'm not suggesting that there's any *necessary* correlation between the exercise of power and particular forms of academic discourse, although I do feel that we haven't very effectively disarticulated these two things. I would agree that the lecture format, which is enshrined in the University, in our classrooms, and even in this format, is very problematic. But I worry that we personalize these issues too easily. What we have to understand, I think, is that we too are held by institutionalized practices and discourses. This isn't always easy or pleasant. During the discussions that have taken place here about the conference, I thought to myself—and crassly, I might add—"I'm glad I didn't organize this; I'm free of the criticism." Then I realized with horror that that was ridiculous! I'm as guilty with respect to this sort of format as anyone else, and I certainly could have thought more self-consciously about my continued participation, and written, and asked, are there ways that we can possibly open this up? But I didn't. Nor do I now have simple answers. Many others, including feminist pedagogical theorists, have been working on this issue as have people in various kinds of workers movements and people associated with institutions like the Open University. I think there are more democratic practices. They are not simply superstructural, they can make differences. I think it has to do with opening up discussions, thinking about smaller sessions, juxtaposing smaller sessions with bigger sessions. I realize it's very difficult. Everybody wants to hear some of the people here and I think that ought to be facilitated. We could have thought less hierarchically about integrating our students into this, and not so informally, but more formally. Those are the sorts of things I think we need to discuss. I would also say that the whole structure of the University needs to be questioned and openly discussed. We still isolate the discussion of pedagogy in schools of education. It seems to me that all of us have got to take on the question ourselves.

ANITA SHETH: Could you comment on the paradox of taking an anti-academic stand within the academy?

RADWAY: The reason I continue to stay in the academy is that I don't think we can afford simply to walk out. I think Constance Penley's comment was an appropriate one: We can't simply give up on the academy. If we do, there are other people ready to make it an even purer space of domination. I would say, then, that we have to struggle constantly. I'm often frustrated with my own inability to rethink these standard practices. I think it's important that various people have noted the connection between practices of print production and domination, and we haven't managed to push very far with them. So if I have erased my own precursors and those thinking about those issues, that's a mistake.

CORA KAPLAN: It seems to me, curiously, that in the academy, certainly within English, the legitimation of feminism and of feminist criticism is often used to exclude and further marginalize not only questions of race but the actual bodies of others. There is a metonymy that goes through race, through gender, through the black woman which delegitimates certain kinds of voices or gives them only marginal time within those institutions. So I don't think it's just a question of reversing patriarchy, but of actually taking all those things, that very difficult not only double position (as Michele Wallace described it) but triple and sometimes quadruple position as a point of criticism, entry, and struggle around pedagogy.

RADWAY: Your critique is pointed and accurate. I think that I have as much trouble as anybody else at thinking two of these processes together. As you were talking I was thinking, you're right, how then can I rethink what I'm doing and try and take that into account? And I immediately thought well, clearly I can parallel or widen the historical context, place what the Book-of-the-Month Club was doing in the context of other struggles and other practices. And then I immediately thought, with a disheartening sort of "Oh, my God, that means an even longer book!" And then I realized, "but that's the problem." The problem arises with the definition of my project as manageable, as something I can accomplish in a book that will be published; I can finish it in a space of five or six years so people don't constantly keep asking me when that book will come out. It speaks to the structure of our practice once again, to the way books are published, to the way we are expected to have only a certain number of years between projects. Those constraints help to reduce the complexity of what we take on. So I accept your criticism, but I am also painfully aware of what taking on these multiple variables means in our attempt to contest and confound all of the practices that contain us.

ELSPETH PROBYN: I want to ask about television in the classroom because it is something that unites teachers and students, allowing a younger generation of women to forge relations with feminist theory. I was thinking about how important Oprah Winfrey is, or has been, in raising questions about, e.g., the representation of black women or the ways in which *thirtysomething* represents sexual preference. And I was wondering whether you would comment on the positivities in Foucault's sense, of what Oprah allows to be said.

RADWAY: I agree that television is an empowering artifact and discourse for people much younger than we. It's something that ought to move not only into the University but into high schools and grade schools as well. Something occurred to me a moment ago in response to the earlier questions about rethinking pedagogy. One thing that goes on at Duke, as elitist as it is, is that undergraduates teach house courses themselves in their dorms. They are entirely responsible for these courses. They think up the subjects, they teach them, and people go and end up in long discussions. TV figures centrally in many of those courses. Why not harness that energy and activity by getting those undergraduates not only to teach each other but to go into high schools and grade schools? No one is teaching my seven-year-old daughter how to think about TV critically except her mother, and that's clearly problematic.

LIDIA CURTI: During my research on TV serial texts and their consumption, I still seem to come up a lot against the problem of differentiating the bad and the good. While I think the problem of the good and the bad is primarily an aesthetic question as it touches on the reasons why we like something or don't like it, on the quality of pleasure, on which way they intersect with formal languages, etc., it also intersects with the problems of gender, race, class, nationality. For instance, the good and bad often are defined in relation to who watches what. Usually a "good" show is watched by certain groups who are able to present their case for the quality of the show, and vice versa. There is very interesting work that could be done on the reception of certain fictions by various ethnic minorities within a dominant culture. So I was wondering whether you had any suggestions as to how to go about differentiating without falling into the same categories?

RADWAY: I can only repeat what I've already said. I'm not really sure we can escape the process of discriminating between good and bad. We can attempt to make it much more self-conscious; we can problematize it. And we can, I hope, try to recognize that there are other systems for discriminating good and bad and set them in dialogue.

29

New Age Technoculture

Andrew Ross

Not long after moving to the United States from Britain, I visited a dentist to inquire about my first symptoms of gum decay. In an attempt to allay my anxiety, the dentist told me that it wasn't my gums that I should be worried about. "Look at it this way," she said. "It's not your gums that are decaying, it's your body that's decaying." She was, I suppose, appealing to the knowledge I was supposed to have about the irreversibly entropic nature of my body, here showing the "natural" signs of advancing age. But I was unaccustomed to meeting dentists who didn't simply fetishize the contents of my mouth, and her advice, even if it was offered tongue-in-cheek, did give me cause for alarm. Having recently moved from a society where responsibility for the upkeep of my teeth had always been seen as the obligation of the welfare state, this dentist's implicit suggestion that bodily maintenance was now my own economic, even moral, responsibility took on ominous overtones for me. Although my dentist was not a holistic practitioner, she had made reference to a holistic idea about the interdependence of bodily functions. In retrospect, I realized that a more serious holist would not have placed any such emphasis on the entropic process. More recently, I have discovered that a wide range of alternative psychotherapies promote techniques, usually involving hypnosis, which claim to redirect the body's energies to heal tooth and gum decay, and thereby partly reverse the entropic process.

Many holistic health practices are unequivocally in the business of *reversing* entropy. In contrast to the paternalistic diktat of the health professional, holistic therapies have set up shop on the basis of faith in the body's self-healing faculties. There, the health professional's obscurantism is often replaced by an apparent voluntarism based on the assumption that "we are participating, however unconsciously, in the process of disease," and that "we can choose health instead" (Ferguson, 1980, p.257). The AIDS crisis, for example, far from being seen as the result of criminal mismanagement, on the part of politicians, bureaucrats, drug companies, and physicians, is viewed in certain New Age circles as the result of negative thinking: it is not the virus that makes us ill, it is our negative overreaction to the virus that causes the illness. It is no small irony to see, in the thick of AIDS activists' demonstrations and protests, New Age banners proclaiming "The Healing is Happening," commingling with more militant slogans that castigate the "genocidal" effects of government health policies, while proclaiming that "Health Care is a Right." There is no doubt that some PWAs have turned to holistic remedies more out of desperation than because of any philosophical opposition to drugs as such. Nonetheless, the holistic spirit of looking after oneself in one's own environment seems to be at odds (but not irrevocably so) with activists' demands that medicine be redefined as a social process in which the people most affected should have the right to participate at all levels: decisions about government policy and funding, pharmaceutical development and testing, and inexpensive access to care and treatment.

The story about my dentist's pseudo-holistic humor hints at the increasing penetration of the medical establishment by the ideas and values of holistic health culture. By the late eighties, holistic values had at least one foot in the door of many major institutional centers of Western medicine. For many healers, this move was a potentially fatal one, heralding the absorption of a minority culture which had hitherto enjoyed its own non-institutionalized freedoms. Others are more enthusiastic about the prospect of a semi-professionalized challenge to the mechanistic foundations of biomedicine. If extrasomatic factors pertaining to holistic, as well as environmental and psychosocial, medicine are to transform the dominant picture of disease causation, then paradigmatic treatment of the diseased body ought to include the concept of the environmentally "sick person." In addition, then, to the challenge of the insurgents' *alternative* model of health, a more contestatory challenge would be needed in the form of a thoroughgoing foundational critique.[1]

These contests in the medical field are one leading feature of the growth of New Age thought and practice as a social movement in its own right. In the pages that follow, I will be trying to explain and describe the platform of "rationality" that the New Age movement, however inchoate, has come to present as an alternative, though not necessarily oppositional, to the dominant paradigms of scientific and technological rationality. The fierce independence of the New Age community is increasingly compromised by the evangelical desire to move beyond its marginal status in the legitimate scientific world. Consequently, the claim to an *alternative* worldview, distinct from orthodox rationalism, increasingly rests upon arguments that this claim is nonetheless unjustly *excluded* from or suppressed by the dominant scientific paradigm. A certain degree of common cause is thus established with those within the legitimate scientific community whose work is locally contestatory and is thus marginalized or suppressed. Ultimately, some part of the holists' desire lies in the hope that rationalist science, no matter how fundamentally impaired by its materialist premises, will be able to prove the legitimacy of New Age claims about, say, the electro-vitalist basis of human life. As a result, the shape and language of holists' claims about alternative scientific knowledge are mediated through appeals to the rationalist language and experimental procedures of the dominant paradigm. Contestation, as I have suggested, would be impossible otherwise. But it is here that we can see the tension within a social movement founded on an *alternative* scientific culture, distinct from dominant values, that is increasingly obliged to wage *oppositional* claims lucidly obedient to the language and terms set by the legitimate culture. Therein lies a story about the contradictions of New Age culture as it exists today, but it may also be a story about the evolutionary structure of all such social movements which display a slow evolution from marginal, utopian origins to mainstream encounters with professionalization and institutionalization.

Perhaps there is nothing more to be observed here than the old Marxist lesson that a dominant culture has the power to engender an opposition in its own image. I would have to say that it is a good introductory lesson, quite applicable to many of the features of the New Age movement as they exist today. By New Age, I am referring to that exotic subculture whose cultural practices and beliefs have attracted tens of millions in the West, and increasingly large numbers in the Soviet Union, where alternative, metaphysical voices have begun to appear daily on television screens in a culture that has made a state religion of science and technology for the collective good. It is a useful lesson to bear in mind if we want to trace the swollen flood of philosophies and practices with a rich and diverse historical heritage that emerged in a relatively coherent form in the wake of the sixties' counterculture, and underwent a sea-change as they developed their own institutions and networks in the seventies and eighties, often within an entrepreneurial milieu love-sick with the romance of the technological sublime. But there are other, more complex lessons that I wish to draw from the widespread influence of New Age ideas in our culture: lessons, for example, about the crisis of science and technologism; the crisis of "nature"; and the crisis of materialist individualism. While most New Age practices today are still seen as restricted to a minority culture, the influence of their ethical principles is quite mainstream and middle class, permeating suburban life and corporate philosophy alike. One need only tune into popular TV talk shows like the *Oprah Winfrey Show* to hear the language of "growth" and "potential" in full flow. To understand the logic of New Age's language of individualism is crucial for anyone who wants to understand the ideological shape of North American culture today.

New Age individualism, with its overriding appeals to personal growth, draws upon a long history of decentralized minority traditions in Western culture: for example, the Christian esoteric tradition, with its various Gnostic sects and heresies; or the Transcendentalist, Spiritualist, and self-help movements of the last two centuries, each preserved in non-institutional ways in avant-garde or bohemian circles (or jealously guarded by masonic and aristocratic cliques), while occasionally exercising a broad political appeal to larger constituencies in revolutionary or reformist historical moments. For many centuries, those traditions of radical individualism have been influenced by the more established Oriental social philosophies of the Asian and Aryuvedic medical traditions. All of these influences, grounded in naturalistic, holistic, and pantheistic sciences, have been systematically displaced and repressed by Western empiricism.

Notwithstanding these important histories, however, any explanation of the currency of the social movement based on New Age individualism must address the more recent socio-historical conditions in which appeals to "personal growth" have taken root. In this respect, we might consider the New Age discourse about "growth" as a response to widespread anxieties about the official Western ideology of growth and development that have been generated, primarily by ecological concerns, in recent years. In the pages that follow, my aim is to draw some lessons from the study of alternative cultures like the New Age movement, and to show how the "solutions" and new wisdoms about "limits to growth" offered by such a culture at once contest and reinforce dominant values about human and technological growth and development.

New Age rationality, as I briefly describe it here, can be seen as a countercultural formation in an age of technocratic crisis. This crisis appears at a time when the official legitimacy accorded to technology-worship has guaranteed it the status of a new civil religion in North America, perhaps the only possible millenialist home that remains for official versions of the emptied-out American dream. Yet it is also a time when faith in modern science's founding sacraments—its claims to unimpeachable objectivity, axiomatic certitude, and autonomy from the prejudices of power—is rapidly disintegrating under the pressure not only of demythologizing critics and activists within the priesthood, but also from the thoroughgoing historical critiques of scientism waged by feminists and ecologists with one foot in the door, and from public disaffection with science's starring role in the grisly drama of global degradation.

The New Age community considers itself to be the renegade home of a truly radical alternative to the authority enjoyed by scientific positivism's high priests. While the science establishment is ritually vilified by New Agers as elitist, left-brainist, and inhumane, it would be a mistake, however, to assume that the spirit or the name of science is *persona non grata* in New Age circles; rather, what we find are all the signs of a love-and-hate affair. The preeminence of science in our knowledge hierarchy is echoed and emulated, to some extent, by all cultures subordinate to it, even when their identity is marked as alternative. This applies even to the most occult sectors of the New Age community which share a worldview as logically consistent in its own way as the rationalist explanation of the natural world offered by modern science. Holists who subscribe to a cosmology of dynamic forces and energies may not share the mechanistic world-picture of separable causes and effects, but they do share an everyday world in which rationalist assumptions are dominant; therefore, any attempt to promulgate their claims must make its persuasive mark in a culture saturated with these assumptions.

The Demarcation Debate

A long history lies behind the anxious intimacy of New Age metaphysics with scientific thought. Practitioners of the occult who subscribed to the ancient Hermetic tradition, and who were hit hard by the Reformation's anti-supernaturalism, ultimately leaped to embrace science as one of their primary vehicles for a critique of orthodox Christianity. For centuries, this embrace of science helped the heretic traditions to survive. Many of the health and parapsychological cults of today are the direct descendants of the heretical, science-loving, metaphysical movements of the eighteenth- and nineteenth-century, like Magnetism, Mesmerism, Spiritualism, Swedenborgism, and Theosophy, or the more unapologetic medical sects of Phrenology, Hydropathy, Vitalism, Chronothermalism, and other non-allopathic remedies. Not only were these practices grounded in the principles of empirical science and inductive reasoning, they were also caught up in the fabric of the reform movements of the time, and consequently appealed to a broad and popular social constituency. By the time of the Flexner Report in 1912, the American Medical Association had succeeded in outlawing many of the pseudo-scientific practices but not before the medical establishment had incorporated some of the lessons of the alternative, reformist, and healing practices, and not before some of its early redbaiters had articulated the clear link between "pseudo-scientific" trends and the specters of socialism and feminism. As the editors of the *Boston Medical and Surgical Journal* complained: the medical practitioners who were currently "running after this hydropathic mummery" were last year "full of transcendentalism, the year before of homeopathy, the years before of animal magnetism, Grahamism, phrenology. Next year, they will be Fourierites, communists, George Sandists, etc." (quoted in Wrobel, 1978, p. 13).

A similar kind of story might be told about the role of alchemy at the time of the formation of modern science. Inheritor of the ancient Hermetic quest for a universal specific—a magic elixir, powder, potion, or touchstone that prolonged life and cured all ills—alchemy was *the* medieval science of matter, suffused with the ideology of animism, but very much in cahoots with the industrial logic of mining, dyeing, glass manufacture, and medicinal preparation. The displacement of animism by mechanism, and the subscription of new artisanal groups to laissez-faire market principles that openly challenged the secretive trade knowledge harbored by the older craft guild system, sounded the death-knell of the alchemists' power. Alchemy was increasingly cast as heretical by a Reformation dressed up in its rationalist Sunday best, and survived only in obscurantist groups or in politically radical circles like the leveling sects of the English Commonwealth (Hill 1972). As Morris Berman (1981) has argued, however, it would be a mistake to think that the mechanistic worldview of the new science simply excluded or excommunicated the Hermetic tradition (in fact, it was driven underground) as illegitimate, demonizing it as a cover for quacksalving charlatans. Rather, the foundational components of magic—the capacity to alter, transform, and thereby dominate nature—became central, albeit in a distilled and extracted form, to a mechanist worldview bent on systematically governing the natural world (pp. 89–90). Alchemy, after all, was nothing more than a method for transmuting nature into energy, and few could deny that this has become one of the technological projects, with a vengeance, of modern science. The alchemists' dreamy pursuit of Nature's truth was no less shared by Galileo or Newton (a closet occultist himself). By their time, mechanistic science had recycled many elements of the magician's enterprise and relocated the early research laboratory of his kitchen to larger institutional spaces, equally in the secular service of earthly powers. As the governing premises of animism were displaced by the new materialism, the science/pseudo-science border, ever shifting, was accordingly redefined. The esoteric sciences, now subordinate rather than dominant, were obliged to incorporate a shell of inductive reasoning in order to wage their claims, just as they would learn to survive under cover of rationalism's long and unholy war against the established churches.

The sound and fury generated today not only by the flourishing of holistic health and occult metaphysics (often self-styled as the new alchemies) but also by the revived fundamentalist agenda of creationism demonstrate that the demarcation debate about "false" and "true" science is not one whose significance lies only in some parochial past, safely relegated to a period of science's infancy. On the contrary, histories of the sort that I have only briefly sketched show that any such demarcation is *always* historically specific, determined by the cultural and ideological circumstances of its day, and thus by the particular ideological claims that "science" and "scientists" make for themselves in a particular time and place. Moreover, the border between scientific cultures is not only semi-permeable, it is rigorously patrolled in the institutionalized interests of power, and increasingly so, ever since the modern laboratory itself became a model of power, and ever since corporate capitalism started to bet its future on the magical elixir of basic patents.

In this respect, it is perhaps worth drawing an analogy between the demarcation lines in science and the borders between hierarchical taste cultures—high, middlebrow, and popular—that cultural critics and other experts involved in the business of culture have long had the vocational function of supervising. In both cases, we find the same need for experts to police the borders with their criteria of inclusion and exclusion. In the wake of Karl Popper's influential work, for example, falsifiability is often put forward as a criterion for evaluating scientific authenticity, and thus for distinguishing between the truly scientific and the pseudo-scientific. But such a yardstick is no more objectively adequate and no less mythical a criterion than appeals to, say, aesthetic complexity have been in the history of cultural criticism. Falsifiability is a self-referential concept in science, inasmuch as it appeals to those normative codes of science that favor objective authentification of evidence by a supposedly dispassionate observer. In the same way, "aesthetic complexity" only makes sense as a criterion of demarcation inasmuch as it refers to assumptions about the supposed objectivity of categories like the "aesthetic," refereed by institutionally accredited judges of taste.

I do not want to insist on a literal interpretation of this analogy, but it is an analogy that informs my own thinking as a cultural critic about some of the points I want to make in this chapter. A more exhaustive treatment would take account of the local qualifying differences between the realm of cultural taste and that of science, but it would run up, finally, against the stand-off between the empiricist's claim that non-context-dependent beliefs exist and that they can be true, and the culturalist's claim that beliefs are only socially accepted as true. Ultimately, the power of science rests upon making and maintaining that distinction, and we ought to recognize that science's anxiety about authenticating its belief in truths is, in the truly Foucauldian sense, a question of power. Consequently, it is not such a great leap from seeing that categories of taste are also categories of power employed to exclude the unwanted to seeing that the power of scientific ideology rests upon its unwillingness to question the role of the powerful institutions or sponsors whose interests are not only heavily mortgaged in the demarcation debate, but who are also well served by the hireling scientists who referee it. Cultural critics have, for some time now, been faced with the task of exposing similar vested institutional interests in the debates about class, gender, race, and sexual preference that touch upon the demarcations between taste cultures, and I see no ultimate reason for us to abandon our hard-earned skepticism when we confront science.

For my purposes here, the analogy with taste cultures helps make sense of certain "middlebrow" elements of New Age philosophy and culture when compared with the "highbrow" status of the official scientific cultures and the lowbrow gadget-fetishism of popular science. For the components of New Age culture are both middlebrow *and* alternative, a composite that can probably be found in any counterculture that has found some kind of breathing space, however marginal, within the dominant culture. On the one hand, the devotion to alternative, non-rationalist belief systems places New Age thought outside the hierarchical structure of cultural capital observed by the legitimate scientific culture. On the other hand, the New Age commitment to transforming science into a more humanistic and holistic enterprise involves taking on, to some degree, the structure of deference to authority that governs the institutional system of rationalist cultural capital. As a middlebrow scientific culture, New Age wants to be fiercely self-determining, but the path to establishing that authority leads through the obstacle course of accreditation that underpins scientific authority and marks non-institutionalized opinions as illegitimate.

If the components of New Age culture are a complex fusion of the alternative and the middlebrow, then critical precedents for describing such a culture are not so easy to find. The middlebrow, or what used to be so termed, remains one of the largest challenges for cultural studies, a field in which so many have leapt with alacrity to the analysis of popular cultures, uncovering elements of "resistance" that are comfortably remote from the levels of cultural capital more appropriate to the critiques of intellectuals. By contrast, the more contiguous field of middlebrow culture, when it is not passionately denigrated, is thought to be stale, flat, and unprofitable, its politics unremarkable, and its pretensions devoid of the edge that comes with the everyday alienation, as at least one version of populist cultural studies would put it, endured by the popular classes.[2] I know, for example, that many of my fellow intellectuals think of New Age as the lowest of the low, and cringe on contact with evidence of its influence on their daily environments, while these same people can be passionately devoted to analyzing and talking about the cultural politics of TV soap opera. I do not want to distance myself from this habit, for I am as much a "victim," if you like, of this, essentially intellectual, tendency. It is a symptom of the logic of cultural capital that the culturally wealthy can afford the kind of downward mobility which sanctions their devotion to the popular, while they police the cultural order by deriding the sub-legitimate middlebrow as only they can. The challenge for intellectuals, clearly, is to help create a more democratic cultural politics that would not be hamstrung by this logic.

Like most fellow intellectuals I know who grew up in the heady wake of the 1960s counterculture, our experience with holistic friends, acquaintances, and also, in my case at least, an ex-spouse with New Age devotions, has been touched by a shared passion for the utopian, experimental cultures that survive to some degree in the New Age community. However, the history of our political and intellectual training has made us "outsiders," for the most part, in relation to this community, with whom we might share a commitment to forging social and cultural alternatives, and with whom we often share the field of grassroots activism. It should be clear, for example, from the marks of tone, style, and critical distance, that I am neither speaking from the New Age community nor on its behalf. But neither am I primarily interested in speaking *against* the New Age belief systems and their political implications. My position is more that of a speculative critic who thinks and feels that there are political lessons to be drawn from the shape and development of New Age culture. Consequently, a large part of my interest here lies in discussing not only the self-coherent logic that governs New Age (however eclectic its cultural range) as a movement, but also the major lines of conflict and contestation that have developed around the New Age community's challenge to established institutions of science and religion.

The disadvantage of this polemical position is that it neglects the more exhaustive, or deep, "ethnographic" study of cultural communities that has produced some of the most exciting developments in recent cultural studies. Although my research has involved little in the way of "field work," it does draw upon an extensive immersion in the literatures produced by and around the New Age community: a broad spectrum from the established book classics to the more eclectic flood of magazines, pamphlets, and newsletters that has poured daily into my mailbox over the last few years. The traditional function of the polemical critic lies in making *interventions*, in using his or her position as an intellectual to enter into the more general public debate about the shape of cultural politics. There are many reasons to be critical of this tradition: it has reproduced elitist access to media and intellectual opinion; it has often fallen prey to the voice and style that signifies a remoteness from the lived experience of culture; it has renounced the official authority that comes with exhaustive academic scholarship, just as surely as it has lacked the organic authority derived from involvement with active cultural communities. If public intellectuals today are learning these lessons in self-criticism, then the tradition of cultural studies is one of our best resources, for its strengths lie in learning how to respect the lived experiences of cultures other than the intellectual, and to draw out, rather than preach about or against, their political implications. But if the practice of cultural studies is to preserve its activist direction, then it cannot afford to give up a public voice that goes beyond the relativism of respectfully recognizing and appreciating all cultural differences equally. The problem with such relativism is that it tends to lose sight of the way in which cultural differences are themselves always a function of power; these differences, in other words, are never equivalent, and always unequal. The game of assessing the differences between cultures is not just a game of words, in which the stronger rhetoric wins; a great deal of material power is exercised through the existence of these unequal differences. Consequently, we cannot afford to relinquish the authority, derived from institutions and professions, that can be put to good use in contesting the official policing of cultural politics.

In science, probably more than in culture, there remains the challenge of providing, as Donna Haraway (1991) puts it, "better accounts of the world," that will be publicly accountable and of some service to progressive interests. To keep that obligation in mind is to resist many critical temptations in describing scientific cultures: the temptation to explain scientific claims as merely epiphenomenal effects of vested material and institutional interests; or, alternately, to try to separate the wheat from the chaff, and isolate particular scientific claims, if any, that can be said to be truthful and thus immune to the contagions of power; the temptation to collapse all competing knowledge claims into a relativistic picture of warring subcultures; or, alternately, to romanticize those subcultures that are deemed "illegitimate" as havens of resistance. If the rallying-cry for a "science for the people" is still to stand for something that resembles an objective vision of the social good, then it depends on salvaging workable strategies from the vertiginous relativism that often results from extreme culturalist analyses of science's day-to-day workings. Such strategies, which will need to be locally relevant and not generally self-affirming, can no longer afford to appeal simply to optimistic or progressive versions of technocratic radicalism, in which a socially minded elite leads the way forward. They must also be addressed to the desire for personal responsibility and control that will allow non-experts to make sense of the role of science in their everyday dealings with the social and physical world.

I do not believe that New Age culture has produced anything like a more consistently accurate account of the world than rationalist science. Rather, in its own eclectic and self-fashioned way, New Age has assumed a virtuoso, experimental role in reconstructing a humanistic *personality* for science—science with a human face, a kinder, gentler science, as it were. This appeal to personalism is deeply rooted in popular distrust of authority and the desire for self-control; it cannot be dismissed as a "petty-bourgeois" obsession. But the need to acknowledge the personalist appeal coexists with the need to properly socialize this concept of individualism, to show how self-responsibility can only be achieved by transforming social institutions that govern our identity in the natural world. In its embattled attempts to practice a science pirated and reappropriated from the experts, the New Age community feeds off the popular desire for more democratic control of information and resources. Because of its embattled position, however, the New Age community is also driven into the position of defending the moral purity of an *alternative* scientific culture, which draws upon philosophical traditions, whether "Oriental" or archaic, that are not part of our socialized landscape in the West, and that consequently have much less purchase on people's commonplace thoughts and desires. All too often, the result is to dream us back to the pre-scientific, and to the alchemists' kitchen, which, for all its charm, is a rather claustrophobic place for us to be in the 1990s.

Non-Social Nature

At the center of New Age culture lies a set of governing principles about the use of "appropriate technology" for the goal of personal transformation. The concept of appropriate technology was pioneered by the economist E. F. Schumacher to describe the advocacy of small-scale intermediate technologies for developing countries, whose cultures are threatened by the introduction of large-scale Western technologies. Although the term is not widely used in holistic circles to describe healing techniques, I find it quite relevant since it carries reminders about the lessons of postcolonial dependency that are usually glossed over in the philosophies of New Age Orientalism, or the New Age patronage of traditional, archaic cultures.

In holistic terms, the inherent life-energy of the body is self-sufficient. The body, or the body-mind-spirit continuum, therefore contains its own appropriate technology that does not require the intervention of external technological mediation to fulfill its own healing or evolutionary potential: left to its devices, the body always knows what's best. The Faustian mistake of modern science in making a pact with *externalized* technology must be avoided at all costs, even if it means demonizing what might, under controlled circumstances, be liberating. The object, as Berman has suggested of the alchemists, is not necessarily to make gold, but to become golden.

At least one of the operative images here is that of the body as a kind of electrical capacitor, an image continuous with nineteenth-century vitalism, as opposed to the more orthodox mechanist notion that organic matter, far from harboring an *elan vital*, is no different in its capacity to conduct energy than non-organic matter.[3] In general, however, the body's system of energy flow and harmony is not perceived simply as physical; it is the combined effect of the spiritual, social, and natural environments inhabited by the individual.[4] Alongside the archaic and the Oriental, there are also more postmodern images—the attempt, for example, to introduce elements of the cybernetical body familiar from modern molecular biology: the body must also be intelligent. Life energy is also, then, a conduit for carrying information, and in the words of one advocate, the mind and body communicate "as a data cable carries transmitted information between two computers" (Patten and Patten, 1988, p. 159).

The New Age, as it is conventionally presented, stands breathlessly on the brink of a collective leap in evolution—a major upgrade for the species as a whole. How to accelerate this evolutionary leap without violating the "natural" way of things (it is no longer apposite to speak of the "laws of nature")? This is the question directly posed to technology itself, the noisy vehicle of science's ideas of progress. How "external" do technologies have to be to fall outside of the orbit of the "natural"? And how is consensus reached on drawing the line of demarcation?

In addressing these questions, New Age practitioners have placed their evolutionary faith in what are commonly known as the "psychotechnologies." These extend from the biofeedback machines, at the hardware margin of the spectrum, to shamanic and magical techniques at the visionary end. It is a vast and accommodating spectrum, however, stretching across the whole range of holistic therapies, bodywork disciplines, paranormal activities, and alternative religious practices. Even a selective list of the numerous holistic psychotechnologies would include reflexology, rebirthing, creative visualization, aromatherapy, flotation, acupressure, actualism, naturopathy, Bach Flower therapy, holotropic breath therapy, numerology, herbology, connective tissue therapy and deep tissue bodywork, personology, iridology, muscle therapy, Touch for Health, polar energetics, Neo-Reichian release, orthobionomy, biomagnetics, flotation, Reiki, mentastics, chakra therapy, past life regression therapy, magnetotherapy, kinesiology, Rolfing, colon healing, stress management, ecstasy breathing, craniosacral therapy, body tuning and vibrational medicine, quantum healing, polarity therapy, chelation therapy, phototherapy, neurolinguistic programming, the Trager approach, Aston Patterning, the Alexander technique, the Radiance technique, the Rubenfield Synergy method, hakomi, ohashiatsu, Jin-Shin Do.

The broad community of holistic practitioners ranges from private healers operating within confidential networks to fully licensed, professionalized practitioners operating within the restraints of community or state standards.[5] While training is important, the underlying principle is an amateurist one—everyone has the potential to become the engineer/architect/designer of his or her own environment. Reskilling oneself in the arts of the psychotechnologies can be seen as a way of reappropriating, from the experts, folk skills that were once everyday knowledge. The revival of traditional medicines in countries like India and China where rational, cosmopolitan medicine was already well established, has demonstrated that nine-tenths of what we think of as "medicine" is within the hands of the non-professional. The flourishing of interest in non-cosmopolitan medicine is also inspired by social critiques of the medicalization of health (Illich, 1976). Biomedicine, "of all industries, the most wasteful, polluting, and pathogenic" (Gortz, 1980, p. 152), has been held responsible for an explosion in iatrogenic illness—structural generation of diseases by institutional medicine (poisoning, infection, and unnecessary surgery in hospitals, which is the site of most accidents)—and the general appropriation of people's bodies by professionals dependent on megatechnology.

In recent years, the legitimacy of medical professionals has further eroded as popular consciousness absorbs the more general social critique of biomedicine's "inhumanity," and lack of caring for the patient. In a profession where the orthodox faith in the (large) technology fix has often led to consequences "worse than the disease," the multitude of alternative health therapies have had greatest impact. The professionals' bad attitude is often characterized in the following way: biomedicine sees and treats the body as a functional machine that occasionally breaks down, and for whose dysfunctions a physical cause and remedy can always be found by the repairman, the doctor. In addition, bio-medicine is seen to have "failed" in its treatment of chronic, degenerative diseases, like cancer and cardiovascular illnesses, primarily caused by social and environmental con-ditions, and its miracle drugs have often proven to generate further problems in their side-effects and consequences. The scandal of the AIDS crisis and the particular social forms taken by this virus have exposed the extent to which medicine is a fully political process, saturated by homophobic, sexist, and racist prejudice. In general, biomedicine's role in contributing to the health of a population is actually rather small when compared to social and environmental conditions, and it is precisely because of its neglect of these social and environmental factors that its closed, mechanistic model of the body as a system of efficient causality has come to be seen as inadequate.

If orthodox biomedicine treats the body as if the mind were not there, then the body-mind-spirit continuum that is central to the New Age concept of health appeals directly to transcendentalist codes of self-reliance. The physical is the least important part of holistic treatment since it is seen primarily as a symptom of disturbances in the individual's spiritual and social environments. The patient is asked to make a "com-mitment" to his or her health, and the cure involves a good deal of self-analysis for which the healer acts as a catalyst in restoring the natural balance of the body-mind-spirit's economy of energies.

More often than not, however, the argument for holism is reduced to the idea that health must be actively pursued by a person and not simply underwritten by a bureaucratic commonweal. What is left begging is any question of a socialized health care system that can properly accommodate holistic healing practices. It takes little political ingenuity to see that this philosophy of alternative medicine transforms the business of health into an entirely privatized affair, decoupled from the welfare state, and hostile to any notion of intervention on the part of social agencies. This is partly a consequence of the fierce independence of the holistic community, and partly the result of the *sub rosa* legal conditions under which many of its practitioners are obliged to operate. For the holistic healers, concepts like the "individual," and the "body," along with the cultural beliefs that support these concepts, *mean* something quite different from equivalent concepts as defined in orthodox biomedicine and in the atomistic individualism of liberal ideology at large. But these practices, and the particular shape of the philosophy of health to which they subscribe, have not evolved in a social vacuum, immune to the general ideology.

In many respects, the holistic picture of the body-mind-spirit as an efficiency state of equilibrium tends to reflect or express the ideology of the "natural," self-regulating organism of the free market economy that has again come to prevail during the last two decades, over the troubled Keynesian body of liberal social democracy. Logical flaws in the bureaucratic technology of "external" statist solutions have brought the welfare house down; now, all responsibility falls upon the more "natural" economy of individ-ualism. To drive this point home, I suppose we could say that what we saw under Reaganism and Thatcherism was the revival of a "homeopathic" economics, where the principle of supply-side investment acts as a kind of biofeedback input, a trickle-down stimulant for accelerating the dynamic health of the free market system as a whole.

The new "insurgent" therapies reflect this recent ideological reformation just as surely as they trade on the popular suspicion and resentment of the institutions of allopathic medicine. Only a diehard rationalist would be surprised to find that an alternative health paradigm appealing to personal values and self-responsibility has won over significant portions of popular consciousness in recent years, and has partially redefined the given wisdom, or common sense, about our bodily and spiritual relation to the natural world. But the insurgents are often just as blind to the incipient conservative meanings attached in the culture at large to the philosophy of individual responsibility which they have espoused. In the eighties, conservative forms of populism were quite successful in collapsing the perception that individuals *count* into the laissez-faire principle of self-reliance as the foundation of the social good.

In her book, *The Whole Truth* (1989), an incisive critique of the alternative health movement, Rosalind Coward sums up the reductive effects of the new social philosophies centered upon the individual body:

> This new concern with the body is a place where people can express dissatisfaction with contemporary society *and* feel they are doing something personally to resist the encroachments of that society. Indeed, so strong is the sense of social criticism in this health movement that many adherents proclaim that they are the adherents of a quiet social revolution. Yet the journey to this social revolution is rarely a journey towards social rebellion but more often an inner journey, a journey of personal transformation. The quest for natural health has come to be the focus of a new morality where the individual is encouraged to exercise personal control over disease. And the principal route to this control is a "changed consciousness" and changed lifestyle. With this emphasis on changing consciousness have come all the fantasies and projections associated with religious morality, fantasies of wholeness, of integration and of the individual as origin of everything good or bad in their life. And with these fantasies there has mushroomed the industry of "humanistic psychotherapies" emphasizing the role of the individual will-power in making changes (p. 197)

Coward goes on to argue that health has displaced sexuality as the new privileged discourse of bodily truth and inner essence. Health has become the new moralizing category for power to exercise its hegemonic oppositions. Bad health is a sign of the moral failing that only recently was attributed to repressed sexuality. As Coward points out, this new good health doctrine recycles many of the Christian dualist elements of a doctrine of salvation, in which the thirst for self-purification reappears unassuaged. The perpetual, paranoid maintenance of a cleansed, purified body, immune to all sorts of external "pollution," tends to feed into a social philosophy saturated with the historical barbarism of the politics of quarantine, natural selection, and social apartheid.

A similar argument about the displacement of "sexuality" by "health" could be addressed to the metaphysical holism of the body as conceived by the alternative therapies. The holistic body bears little resemblance to the fragmented body favored by, say, psychoanalytically oriented poststructuralist thought, although both philosophies are equally critical of the ego-centered Cartesian humanist tradition. In contrast to the fractured life of the poststructuralist body, shot through with the disordering effects of the unconscious, the healthy New Age body is an efficient, smoothly circulating system of energies, resonating, on a higher plane, with the natural frequencies of the global/ astral body itself. The post-Freudian explanation of bodily "nature" is one that includes the troublesome, contingent narrative of a psychosexual history, inseparable from the narratives of socialization. By contrast, the New Age body, inasmuch as it is aligned with "nature's ways," is quite ahistorical; it is therefore immune, and often strictly opposed, to any conception of "nature" as a social construct.

The view that "nature" is a final arbiter of human behavior is quite central to the whole range of psychotechnologies. To take an example from the non-metaphysical health fringe, I will cite a few of the arguments presented in a critique of the "modern toilet," which accompanies promotional literature for "The Welles Step," manufactured by Welles Enterprises of San Diego. The Welles Step, a plainly fashioned pedestal or stool that allows people to squat while sitting on the lavatory, is promoted by appealing to nature: "People were intended to squat. They squatted throughout history. With this posture the abdominal wall and bowel are supported as we bear down. This is nature's way." In his advertisement, the manufacturer promises to remedy "incomplete elimination," kinked bowels and fecal stagnation, the entry of toxins into the bloodstream, hemorrhoids, varicose veins, and diseased colons and bodies. All of these claims answer directly to the holistic model of a smoothly circulating bodily system, where the cleanliness of the colon, in particular, is a major reference point.

In a technical paper by Dr. Welles, entitled "The Hidden Crime of the Porcelain Throne," the author explicates his medical discovery of the "ileocecal valve," which regulates the flow of digestive contents from the small into the large intestine. Midway through the paper—a narrative report on his research findings—Dr. Welles announces: "I then came to suspect the Western toilet as a causative factor in the all too commonly dysfunctional state of the ileocecal valve found in my patients." The appearance of the epithet "Western" is like the mark of Satan for the holistic health community, which systematically conceives of us as victims rather than beneficiaries of specifically Western technology. What follows almost inevitably, in Dr. Welles's paper, is an appeal to the wisdom of the older, squatting (non-Western) civilizations, punctuated by further elaboration of his research findings.

I am no authority on the digestive system, and so I cannot report on the validity of Dr. Welles's medical theories. I can however point to what is clearly missing from his analysis—any description of the historical or ideological conditions under which immaculately white porcelain toilet technology was developed to demarcate squatting from non-squatting populations, and thereby create, if you will, an international division of excremental labor.[6] The vestiges of this division are still clearly evident in European cultures stratified along North/South, and internal class, lines, and in postcolonial cultures where imported Western toilet technology still exercises its inscrutable power over squatters. Welles's only gesture in this direction is his observation that although the modern toilet was "well suited to the sedentary Westerner," it was created "with absolute disregard for the anatomy of the human body." On the latter point of anatomy, I am, again, not qualified to say whether he is correct, but the former point leaves begging the question of Western "upright" sedentariness, with all of its connotations of moral and racial superiority. Notwithstanding Dr. Welles's moral resentment, technologies are seldom developed simply with human, anatomical functionalism in mind. Their architecture embodies existing values—heavily socialized, heavily politicized—in a particular culture at a particular historical moment. The highly technological concept of a "correct" or "natural" human posture is itself a culturally relative idea for which no universal norm can be assumed.

There is, of course, no reason to expect a medical entrepreneur like Dr. Welles to include the social history of the "Western toilet" in his brief account, although one would think, at first hand, that any reference to this history might add to the overall critique of "Western" technology. What it would add, however, is a dimension that would take it out of the orbit of a critique founded on the appeals to "nature's way." Nature's way does not include the social; if it did, the philosophical opposition upon which holistic thought depends would collapse. If Nature's authority were to rest upon such a social critique of science and technology, then nature's own "technologies" might be subject to the same critical scrutiny, exposing their own ideological underpinnings.

In this respect, the alternative, holistic concept of nature mirrors modern science's own desperate attempts to conceal its "hidden crimes."

In any final analysis, the holistic opposition between "nature" and "technology" is quite groundless. Technologies are social processes of organization, in one form or another, and the sacralized passing of a healer's hands over the body of a patient is just as much a technological process as the demonized use of external hardware like CAT scans or electroencephalograph machines. For all its philosophical coherence, the New Age community's imposition of *limits* to the categories of nature and technology may be as arbitrary as the process by which the gatekeepers of science go about demarcating science from pseudo-science. But "arbitrary" is obviously not the right word here. The demarcation line that New Age draws between "good" holistic nature and "bad" scientific culture is far from arbitrary, because it always reflects a particular state of power relations. Just as the demarcation line, drawn from above, between science and pseudo-science reflects vested interests on the part of powerful institutions in the world of science, so too the line, drawn from below, between "nature" and "technology" expresses a critique, however mediated and paranoid, of technologism on the part of disempowered non-experts, scientific autodidacts, technological free spirits—call them what you will.

New Age Politics

It is now time to draw together some of the political observations I have made about New Age culture in the course of this paper. Just as I have insisted that New Age challenges to scientific rationality bear the impress of legitimate structures of rationality, however transformed, so too it would be unwise to evaluate the politics of the New Age movement in the abstract, as a freestanding platform with an autonomous viewpoint on society. Just as one is likely to find in New Age culture some of the best and the worst ideas about science and technology, the same holds true for the political ideas to be found in the community. My own affiliations are to cultural and political communities that do not always respond sympathetically to New Age cultural practices, and so I will only propose to represent the claims of New Age politics inasmuch as they speak to a political (mostly socialist) sensibility which, in the New Age mind, has long been superseded, but ought, in my opinion, to be able to extend an interested critique. In spite of its sheer diversity and apparent tolerance for all manner of esoteric practices and disciplines, I have nevertheless assumed that New Age culture is the product of a highly structured community of interests, strengthened by the moralistic nature of its vanguardist resolve. In the absence of any central institutional forum, its networking communities and the internal debates about the direction of the New Age movement (quite explicit in the pages of prominent magazines like *New Age*) take on the function of regulating the codes that hold the disparate range of practices and disciplines together.

By far the articulate majority of New Agers are economically comfortable white folks; one prominent publication, the *Llewellyn Times,* claims that 70% of New Agers are of "Celtic" descent. But there is no tidy class constituency to speak of; audiences range from office workers to business executives, and from technicians to intellectuals. Prominent New Age ideologues are nonetheless inclined to present the whole community as a decentralized avant-garde, with a theory of global human transformations, and with the desire, like all vanguards, to initiate people into the cause of making a radical break with history. Like all vanguards, the responsibility for the Aquarian revolution lies in a creative minority, while the conditions for a revolutionary transformation only require a sufficient number of consciousness-changing individuals. As Marilyn Ferguson (1980) puts it, this minority is "a conspiracy without a political doctrine. Without a manifesto. With conspirators who seek power only to disperse it. . . . Broader than reform, deeper than revolution, this benign conspiracy for a new human agenda has triggered the most rapid cultural alignment in history" (p. 23). As a vanguard group, their inability to hasten the fulfillment of their goals is often rationalized as "popular" resistance to change on the part of conservative, change-fearing masses. On the other hand, New Age recruitism is tempered by the native tradition of appeals to voluntarism, a transformational appeal that the U.S. Army—"Be All That You Can Be"—has worked to a fine point in recent years.

Despite the appeals to the history of American transcendentalism and its various great awakenings, most of the transformational rhetoric of New Age comes from the 1960s counterculture, and it is there that any narrative of the history of New Age politics is obliged to begin. There already exists a dominant media narrative about "the sixties" that involves New Age, and that recounts the falling off of radicalism, and the absorption, recuperation, commodification, or yuppification of countercultural politics. It is a narrative that recounts how promises of postscarcity that once encouraged a glut of cultural transgressions now sanction the culture of yuppie gluttony; how a liberatory revolution in individual rights became a privatized cult of self-interest; how the feminist watchword, "the personal is the political," became inverted in the course of becoming "the political is the personal"; how the bohemian rejection of materialism became an acceptance of corporate transmaterialism; how the radical otherness of Eastern spirituality was distilled into a radical Protestantism, fully aligned with the American work ethic; how the medium of personal transformation evolved from outlawed psychedelia to corporate hi-technology; how the collectivist experiments in cooperative community living became experiments in small-scale entrepreneurship; how radical libertarianism became neo-liberalism; how the concept of consciousness-raising groups became a seminar model for executive corporate philosophy; how the hunger for collectivism was taken up in the concept of social networking, a parody of the idea of participatory democracy; how respect for Schumacher's small-scale economics turned into enthusiasm for John Naisbitt's "megatrends"; how Blakean innocence became social mystification; and how the semiotic gestures of disaffiliation from a dominant culture became incorporated in the business of marketing lifestyles.

This is, by now, a familiar story, told by the media and partially accepted by large sectors of society. It is often accompanied by the testimony of prominent New Left apostates, among whom Jerry Rubin usually figures as the most likely suspect to be quoted as favoring changes in consciousness over changes in social structure. It is presented as a story about the maturing of a generation, who have inevitably made their peace with capitalism. But it is also a narrative favored by strong patrician voices on the left, where the tradition of cultural despair and pessimism runs deep, and where the burden of that tradition weighs too heavily upon younger generations. For the left, it is a narrative of decline. A narrative which we cannot afford, since its only reward lies in prizing the past, or, alternately, in seeing the "excesses" of sixties "irrationalism" as an infantile disorder which led inevitably to excesses of self-interest in the decades that followed—similar in form, then, to the conservative "I told you so" narrative. The conventional antidotes offered by this narrative are, respectively, collectively mobilizing nostalgia, or a responsible patrician call for self-restraint, deference to public interest, and heroic affirmation of traditional reason. Neither antidote speaks very persuasively to the changed cultural landscape since the 1960s, or to the rise of new utopian social movements centered around ecology, gender, minority rights, and sexual preference. Above all, neither addresses the symptoms of failure in leftist thinking that New Left subjectivism sought to address; the failure of collectivist thinking to account for the importance of "private" or personal acts in people's everyday lives, and, consequently, the failure to effectively persuade people to abandon an individualist for a collectivist identity.

The rise of Thatcherism and Reaganism was due, in large part, to the ability of the New Right to give reactionary form and shape to the focus on individual responsibility that emerged from the crisis of political paternalism in the sixties. Appeals to individual consumerism and guarantees of the autonomous right to choose were successful in channeling and containing the desires for individual citizenship that were liberated under the concept of participatory democracy. In the cultural vacuum created by the absence of a leftist alternative of progressive individualism, alternative cultures such as the New Age movement evolved in the 1970s. New Age took to heart the sixties languages of personal and everyday life transformation, grafting them onto the grammar of self-determination that eschewed the materialism of acquisitive self-interest espoused by the New Right, while offering a weak vocabulary of social responsibility somewhat removed from the politics of class, race, gender, and sexual preference waged by the post-sixties left.

It is in New Age, then, that we can find at least one version, however troubled, and however incipiently conservative, of a politics of subjectivity that has not been entirely subsumed by the New Right's picture of individualism, aggressively protective of its privatized will to consume. Nor can this culture of self-development be entirely collapsed into the orgiastic picture of "narcissism" offered by conservative left patricians like Christopher Lasch, Daniel Bell, and Russell Jacoby; or into the class "error" of petty-bourgeois self-interest offered by the unreconstructed left. If New Age politics exists, then it does start by taking politics personally. If there is a secular end to this process of personal transformation, then it depends upon the naive assumption that changing the self will change the world, an equation that might point to the lack of any available non-materialist language for linking subjectivity with larger social or structural change. If, on the other hand, the end result of New Age exercises in personal transformation invariably lies in mysticism, then we are obliged to consider how and why the personal desires set in motion there cannot be consummated in everyday social life. Without any alternative (left) politics of social individualism, it is no surprise to find that people will opt for spiritualist solutions for the problems encountered in a materialistic culture. This is surely one of the lessons to be drawn from the worldwide revival of religious fundamentalism as well as the flood of non-institutional cults, old and new, that have poured into the respective vacuums created by the bankrupt cultures of state socialist, capitalist, and scientific materialism.

In this respect, New Age politics might be seen not as a wayward, pathological creature of the New Left's imagination, but as a political innocent in candid, questioning dialogue with the unclaimed mainstream territory of progressive, rather than atomistic, individualism. Indeed, if we were to examine some of the social and political threads that run through the aery fabric of New Age thinking, we would find much that resonates with necessary conditions for a left version of progressive individualism. Generally speaking, New Age addresses and calls upon its adherents as active participants, with a measure of control over their everyday lives, and not as passive subjects, even victims, of larger, objective forces. The New Age "person" is also, in many respects, an individual whose personal growth is indissociable from the environment, a link fleshed out in a variety of ecotopian stories and romances. So, too, the small-scale imperative of the New Age's cooperative communitarianism brings with it a host of potentially critical positions: against big, centralized bureaucracies; against big, transnational business conglomerates; against large-scale, and environmentally destructive, technologies; against the imperialist claims made on the basis of strong nationalism; and against monolithic institutions, in education, industry, religion, and the nuclear family. The focus on self-empowerment might be extended to include forms of local self-government and citizen diplomacy, worker self-management, job-sharing, family role-sharing, reproductive self-determination, children's rights, and health care rights. Last but not least, the pervasive influence, on mainstream consciousness, of the dietary and nutritional emphasis of holistic thought and practice has had an enormous impact on public health.[7]

Above all, New Age consciousness, whose activist roots lie in a deep, mystical affinity with nature, has played an important role in shaping the social and cultural activism of the ecology movement, increasingly divided between the philosophies of deep ecology and social ecology. Neither side, however, seems to want to claim New Age as an official ally. Deep ecologists denigrate New Age's evolutionary devotions to growth as a technocratic strategy for using the earth as an expendable resource, citing the image of "Spaceship Earth" as an example of New Agers' technohumanist contempt for a planet, which, once exhausted, will then be left behind (Devall and Sessions, 1985, pp. 6,141). Social ecologists, on the other hand, equate New Age influence with the mystical nature cults, wiccan goddesses and all, that have saturated the eco-feminist and deep ecology constituencies of the movement with an atavistic taste for supernaturalism (Bookchin, 1990). From this perspective, New Age thought is seen as a dangerously anti-social element, exhausting the rationalist reserves needed to reconstruct a free society living in non-dominating balance with the natural world.

There are lessons to be drawn from both of these critiques. On the one hand, the commitment of New Age humanism to unlimited, personal growth, by whatever appropriate technological means, is a principle that excludes the more organic view of co-existence with the natural world. I find the latter critique more persuasive, however. New Age shares deep ecology's championing of voluntary simplicity and its religious opposition between "nature" and "society/technology." This construction of nature as a social vaccuum distances us from any direct engagement with the actual social forces that command vast power in our everyday lives through their organization of technology and bureaucracy. One of the inevitable effects of this retreat is to encourage Arcadian fantasies of pre-industrialist life resourcefully embellished with many of the philosophical contents of a post-industrialist wardrobe. To advocate, as a reformist program, massively cleansing the techno-material world in the interests of social purity is to cast a blind eye on the enormous human costs involved, for example, in de-industrialization, especially in the developing countries of the world. Conceived as a social program, this would require a large measure of equal access to technology and thus to control over the development of more democratic, ecological technologies.

Similar critiques apply to New Age individualism. When personal consciousness is the single determining factor in social change, then all social problems, including the specters raised by racism, imperialism, sexism, and homophobia, are seen as the result of personal failures and shortcomings. Individual consciousness becomes the source, rather than a major site of socially oppressive structures, and the opportunities for a radical humanism are lost. A radical politics of personalism stands to learn a good deal from the deeply felt response of New Age humanism to large-scale technological organization, especially those organizations of political rationality whose explanatory social models exclude the politics of everyday life and subjectivity. But a radical humanism can hardly afford to jettison its social critiques of the institutions and ideologies of unfreedom in favor of an individual voluntarism that quarantines the human or individual from the social.

Since I have warned against seeing "New Age politics" as a free-standing agenda, there remains the obligation to try to understand how and why the limitations of New Age politics are set in the ways that I have tried to describe. It would be patronizing and recruitist to explain these limits by lamenting the absence of a credibly persuasive left alternative that might draw out and extend into a coherent philosophy of social individualism the more critical features of New Age personalism. Such an explanation undervalues, if it does not altogether ignore, the powerful desire for self-respect, self-determination, and utopian experimentalism that lies behind the development of an alternative cultural community like the New Age movement. This desire, inspired by a deep hunger for community, provides such a culture with a coherent *raison d'être* in the first place, and surely saves it from being a disorganized set of psycho-social impulses. It is this desire that enables the New Age movement to present the aspect of a relatively coherent challenge to medical, scientific, and religious orthodoxies. And yet it is the same desire for self-coherence that distances New Age thinking from thoroughgoing social critiques of the institutions that house these same orthodoxies. Therein lies both the fate and the strength of self-coherent countercultures which try to live out aspects of utopian futures in the present, making histories, as always, under conditions not entirely of their own choosing.

One of the undeniable strengths of cultural studies has lain in its willingness to explain the political significance of such countercultures. Their practices offer less articulate, less pure, and less overtly political kinds of cultural critique than the left has traditionally felt comfortable endorsing. More articulate critiques of science than those offered by New Age certainly do exist and flourish: in medicine, the still thriving alternatives offered by the women's healthcare movement, and, most recently, the struggle of activists and PWAs in the AIDS community to redefine the praxis of medical research by using their own bodies as socialized laboratories. I am sure that most readers could cite any number of activist movements around issues of science and technology: nuclear technologies, biotechnologies, pesticides, toxic biohazards, animal rights, and so on. When it comes to political evaluation of New Age culture, we are on less secure ground and therefore miss some of the more familiar landmarks for recognizing social and political criticism. At the beginning of a decade which will surely witness a whole range of political appeals to different notions of "nature," and different interpretations of (limits to) "growth," New Age definitions of these categories can serve both as a caveat to and a stimulus for our efforts to shape a green cultural criticism and politics.

With the need for a green future in mind, I want to conclude by suggesting that New Age culture can also be seen as a particular version of the arguments raised in the debates about postmodernism. For in New Age we can see an expression of one of our most urgent political horizons—the need to be able to go on speaking about growth—human and/or social—while recognizing the need to acknowledge finite ecological limits to technological growth and development. In this respect, New Age is a response, if you like, to the so-called Enlightenment "project of modernity" that was, and still is, bound up with the imperatives of growth and development. In principle, New Age proposes a continuation of this project, but in the name of a different human rationality. This proposal has something in common with social theorists like Jürgen Habermas (1983a), who speak of the "incomplete project of modernity," and who want to renew the foundational principles of Enlightenment rationality, ever distorted by capitalist forms of instrumental reason and techno-rationality. New Age ideas of "rationality" may be as distant from Habermas's ideal of communicative rationality as they are from poststructuralists' emphasis on "difference," but each is a dissenting response to dominant forms of Western rationality; each is a symptom of the crisis of technical rationality that "postmodernism," in its many forms, has come to address.

The most crucial aspect of the postmodernism debate, and perhaps the least discussed, is its bearing upon the ecological questions of growth and development. In this respect, there may be a concluding lesson to be drawn from the New Age movement. The New Age community itself comprises a sizable population who believe that there ought to exist limits to the authority of science and to technological growth. The community shares a fiercely moral attachment to the idea of setting external limits, while at the same time it is devoted to limitless "internal" development. What we must remember, however, especially in the years of green politics and activism ahead, is that there is a difference between saying that limits *ought* to exist, and saying that we ought to recognize the existence of limits. The first, the New Age formulation, rests upon an absolute philosophical imperative, and appeals to an absolute and thoroughly unsocialized view of nature. The second is the formulation that I recommend—it rests its case on the evidence that limits to growth may be socially desirable, and can be shown to be so. Such limits cannot be dictated; they must be freely chosen, without falling back on appeals to Nature's perennial wisdom, and without forsaking the differentiated goals of social growth for the purely individualistic or universal goals of human growth.

NOTES

1. For an attempt at a foundational critique, see Laurence Foss and Kenneth Rothenberg, *The Second Medical Revolution: From Biomedicine to Infomedicine* (1988).

2. See Meaghan Morris, "Banality in Cultural Studies" (1990a), for a critique of this tendency in cultural studies.

3. For a modern medical attempt to reintroduce the case for vitalism, see Robert O. Becker and Gary Selden, *The Body Electric: Electromagnetism and the Foundation of Life* (1985).

4. Rosalind Coward has suggested that the focus of holistic therapies on "energy" also reflects the general form of industrial ideology's reliance on concepts of productivity and efficiency: "When it is applied to the body, energy appears as a metaphor for the kinds of productive relations which individuals have to an advanced industrial society" (1989, p. 57). This tendency is even more evident in many of the New Age interests in fringe science; the obsession with the work of forgotten or neglected scientist-inventors like Nicolas Tesla; or the dedicated amateur research devoted to producing more efficient techniques of energy production, driven on by a neo-alchemical pursuit of "free energy," or perpetual motion machines. See, for example, *The Journal of Borderland Research,* published by Borderland Sciences Research Foundation, PO Box 429, Garberville, CA 95440; or the infolios produced by *Rex Research,* PO Box 1258, Berkeley, CA 94701.

5. See J. A. English-Hueck's (1990) ethnographic study of the holistic practitioners in Paraiso, California: *Health in the New Age: A Study in California Holistic Practices.*

6. See, for example, *Clean and Decent* by Lawrence Wright (1980) and Witold Rybcznsky, *Home: A Short History of an Idea* (1986), pp. 78–79.

7. The most adequate example of an attempt to offer a systematic overview of New Age politics is Mark Satin, *New Age Politics: Healing, Self and Society* (1979).

DISCUSSION: ANDREW ROSS

JAN ZITA GROVER: It appears to me that identifying the notions of alternative health community and New Age health projects leaves less latitude for what goes on in alternative health communities than does in fact go on. I've worked the last few years at San Francisco General Hospital which has an alternative health clinic. It just closed, but it was a clinic that was funded by the county and city and did provide alternative therapies and holistic preventive health programs for over a period of four years. I also think that there's more of a continuity than I heard in your talk between certain feminist health projects and alternative healing communities and/or New Age projects. In fact, although there is a vernacular model of oppositional health projects like botanic medicine that goes all the way back to the early nineteenth century, I think that the immediate precedent for a lot of what's gone on in alternative health projects in the seventies and eighties was the resurgence of midwifery, the repudiation of pregnancy as a pathologic condition, and the women's self-help model.

ROSS: Yes, I think that's probably right, and I'm glad that you've pointed this out. Although one important difference is that the non-holistic alternative health movements tend to be more politically articulate—founded on political principles, rather than philosophical ones. The gray area seems to be where both movements—holistic and non-holistic—are obliged to become fully professionalized, whether for the purposes of survival, or, for more evangelistic reasons, when they want to actually change the shape and structure of dominant medical practices. It's at that point that the commitment to being "alternative," for both communities, raises similar problems.

PATTY LATHER: Could you please speak to the relation of postmodernism to your analysis, and to what you referred to as the vertigo of extreme relativism?

ROSS: I'm quite skeptical about the "anything goes" spirit that is often the prevailing climate of relativism around postmodernism. As I indicated at the end of my paper, I also think that New Age culture can be seen as a symptom of some of the concerns that have engaged people in the postmodernism debate, especially in the notion of a disarticulation between these two elements of the so-called "project of modernity"— social growth on the one hand, and technological growth on the other. It's a disarticulation that is often referred to by political realists as "not throwing the baby out with the bathwater." More generally, however, I think there are ways here of beginning to think of situating ecological questions within the context of the postmodernism debate— something which, to my knowledge, has only just begun. To do that involves bringing a *materialist* element to bear upon the debate about "limits." Much of the postmodernist debate has been devoted to grappling with the philosophical or cultural limits to the grand narratives of the Enlightenment. If you think about ecological questions in this light, however, then you are talking about "real" physical, or material, limits to our resources for encouraging social growth. And postmodernism, as we know, has been loath to address the "real," except to announce its banishment. To add an ecological discourse to this debate is going to change a lot of the terms of this debate. For one thing, we ought to have some new, clean bathwater, before we wastefully throw out the old.

HOMI BHABHA: I don't know very much about New Age culture. I come from one sort of old country, and another older one, both of them rather decrepit. I know something about the squatting position. And it also prevents piles. And it is efficient. But I do not recognize this kind of holistic body, this naturalism, maybe as much as I should. And I wonder whether you would say something about the differences or the cultural specificities of the New Age take on this issue *vis-à-vis* the New Times take, where I think there is a very different notion of the place of the natural, or nature.

ROSS: Well, much of what I've said, I think, about individualism is more or less directly in agreement with the kinds of ideas that have been presented in Britain as New Times. And reading certain issues of *Marxism Today* these days is not so far away from reading some of the more politically conscious of the New Age journals. We ought to bear in mind, however, that questions about citizenship and social individualism that are at the center of the New Times agenda have a somewhat different meaning in North America.

Obviously, there's a much longer and deeper history of constitutional rights pertaining to citizenship in this part of the world than in Britain. Libertarianism, for example, has been one of the strengths of the left (as well as of the right) over here, in contesting the various contracts between the individual and the state. I suppose I would make the same kind of caveat about the influence of New Age naturalism. Take Rosalind Coward's fascinating book, *The Whole Truth,* which is primarily a critique of holistic health in the British context. Any comparative account of the differences between the British and the North American movements would have to address different national factors and influences. In the North American case—the awesome economic power of a professionalist body like the American Medical Association (next to the military, medicine is the largest recipient of legal profit in the United States); the historical role of "snake-oil" entrepreneurialism in frontier culture; and the persistence of revivalist, millenialist, and utopian elements in North American religious culture, which exert a powerful political pressure upon social movements at particular times. In the British case—the hegemonic presence of a welfare state, and all of the social functions that are paternalistically adopted by such a system; and the history of the royal family's influential fondness for homeopathic medicine, reinforced by the aristocracy's dislike for modernity in general. This is speculative, but I think there may be grounds for assuming that, historically, the British cults of Nature are more socially stratified than North American cults of Nature.

FRED PFEIL: My question comes out of my own activist politics, and the fact that I live in the Northwest, where New Age philosophies are alive and well. It reflects my own sense of disjunction here: do we have something to learn from these centered, moral, naturalized discourses? Is there something that we *can* take from them, or are they only historical symptoms that can be read?

ROSS: At this point, Fred, I would appeal to what I think is one of the strengths of cultural studies in helping to resolve that sense of "disjunction" that you mention, and that all of us in one way must have felt, between the world of theory and the world of practice. Cultural studies, as a discipline, has been an activist discipline, and let's hope that it remains so. For the most part, however, it has not taken, as its object, the culture of activist groups. Rather, it has been involved in looking at the protopolitical expressions of subcultures and countercultures that are not always politically articulate. In this respect, it has been useful in showing the kind of dialectical links that do exist between the utopian experimentalism of these groups—often deeply saturated by all sorts of naturalistic mystifications—and the world of organized political thought. A lot of time and energy were wasted in the sixties, for example, by the New Left dismissing countercultural groups as apolitical. I don't think that this sort of dismissal is so prevalent today thanks, in some part, to a lot of work that has been done in cultural studies. On the other hand, the category of the activist is often glossed over in the work we do on negotiating the divide between the "intellectual" and the "popular," and I think that this ought to be rectified. As you say, it is in the world of the activist—a very specific temporality that is different from the temporality of the intellectual and the temporality of the popular—that we find an articulate level of political consciousness co-existing with inspirational beliefs in naturalism and so on and so forth. We ought to be more aware of this, even in doing cultural studies, especially in doing cultural studies.

HENRY GIROUX: I want to focus on your point that New Age philosophy exists in a strangely curious dialectical relationship with modernity. At one level it attacks its notions of fragmentation, growth, and progress, but at the same time, it supports a principle very central to modernity—consensus. How can a radical politics of difference be developed from the kinds of possibilities that New Age philosophies suggest without sliding into a politics that completely rejects modernism *en toto*? How do we reconcile the affirmation of certain aspects of modernity with a politics of difference that might deepen its possibilities rather than appropriate its worst dimensions?

ROSS: That's a difficult question, but perhaps I can go about answering it by saying one or two things about the role of countercultures. It's perhaps true of all countercultures that they do have this dialectical relationship with the dominant culture, the dominant social values of "modernity," in this case. The counterculture takes the promises of the dominant culture to the letter; it says, let's imagine that the promises of the dominant culture are actually realizable, and then let's see if we can actually live them out for real. In this respect, the counterculture shares the spirit of the dominant culture. The socialist countercultures in the first half of this century promised more production and more maximized growth in a way that the dominant culture, fettered by the regulatory restraints of capitalism, could not do. The sixties counterculture took the dominant promise of a postscarcity society seriously, and tried to live as if it were true. On the other hand, the dominant culture uses the counterculture as a kind of corrective, uses it to say the kinds of things that it cannot say itself, and to stimulate changes within its own structure and shape. That, perhaps, is another way of talking about the process of "appropriation" which doesn't necessarily feed into left despair. Each are, to some extent, dependent on the other. Now I'm not saying that we should be comfortable with that kind of dependency, but rather that we should exploit it wherever possible. In the case of your question, I suppose that would mean recognizing that the roots of "consensus" are already there to some extent, in the way in which countercultural politics often models itself on pursuing and realizing ideals and values that the dominant culture is supposed to be espousing but obviously isn't—liberties, democratic rights, protections of minorities, and so on. And, on the other hand, using whatever privileges the countercultural voice enjoys in our society to correct the dominant culture's view of what a politics of difference is.

LATA MANI: There are obviously different kinds of histories that come together from different places, from different social and political and historical locations, that converge in a critique of the unified subject. Some of this critique has come precisely from people of color, who are resisting a certain kind of authenticity that's being demanded from them, particularly radical lesbians of color. And it seems to me that a rather odd thing happens when you tell the history of cultural studies, or we tell the history of certain kinds of theoretical developments, which is that the whole thing is made to be a kind of disembodied "race for theory," to use Barbara Christian's term, and I use it with the pun that she intends on it. What can we say so that notions of fragmentation are not entirely co-opted within a highly theoretical discourse? I'm constantly struck by the fact that some of these interventions actually come from marginalized groups in society, and yet those marginalized groups in society are frequently pointed out as holding on to something organic, which is not to say that certain organicists or naturalists or even proto-essentialist arguments aren't being made by parts of communities of color. How do we tell the story so that we can keep the tension between the fact that the concept of differences comes both from within certain philosophical self-questioning *and* from real human beings in real active political struggles who are pointing to their fragmentation, even while other folks in the quest of nationhood might push for that similarity and to make a case for themselves as a people?

ROSS: I'll try to take a concrete example in responding to your very important comments, and perhaps begin by asking why black Americans have not been more active in environmental politics in this country. Notwithstanding the racist hiring practices of many leading environmental organizations, there seem to be other reasons one can point to. One of those reasons has to do with the way in which "nature" has been defined in the public mind. For many people, the dominant Sierra Club idea of nature as trees, rivers, and wildlife does not include the sense of everyday living environments for the majority of the population, especially the inner-city populations who have least access to this kind of green world. A broader, more socialized definition of "nature" and the "environment" includes lead poisoning in homes, nutrient-deficient diets, industrial health and safety, pernicious urban planning, gentrification, homelessness, and many other urban ills that are usually thought of as social rather than environmental problems. They are all aspects of "nature" that are not usually included in the dominant purview of green-identified issues. In addition, many people of color in inner-city areas tend not to be major producers of pollution, or major consumers of energy. Consequently, they don't think of themselves as part of the problem, and aren't encouraged to think of themselves as part of the solution. Ecology, as a result, is often seen as a white, middle-class issue, when, in fact, the victims—those on the hazardous frontline—are precisely the inner-city populations. The same argument is often made about middle-class feminism, when in fact it is actually working-class women who have most to gain from the assertion of women's rights. On the other hand, the discourse of victimage and survivalism that often takes these people as its object is a patronizing one, since it sees their problems and struggles as the "authentic" or "essential" ones, precisely because they are not middle class. This is somehow reinforced, I think, by the lingering racist assumptions that identify people of color with nature itself. The general point I'm trying to make, which is related to what I think you had in mind in your question, is that these problems I've mentioned all depend on how you go about defining "nature," whether in an essentialist, universalist, class, or racial analysis. It's a keyword for the nineties.

QUESTION: It seems to me that many of the roots of New Age medicine have more to do with nineteenth-century bourgeois commitments, historically connected through the continuity of those movements in Southern California, than they have to do with medicine shows and snake oil salesmen, and those kinds of things, that could legitimately be considered populist. And it seems to me that the class basis for New Age is fairly evident: these are people who have a great degree of cultural capital, and to a large extent represent normative rather than countercultural values in U.S. society.

ROSS: It's true that the most visible end of the New Age community—the practitioners, the patients, the workshop participants—tends to be quite well-heeled, even in terms of cultural capital. Then, again, all countercultures are middle class, that's one of the things that distinguishes them from working-class subcultures. And one of the things I've tried to describe is the mixture of middlebrow and countercultural elements in the New Age movement. But the class borders are very indistinct if you consider that New Age philosophies and values permeate executive boardrooms and popular TV talk show audiences alike. That's when the question of what is normative and what is not is open to debate. In addition, one could compare New Age with the social constituency of, say, the fundamentalist religious culture in the South. Susan Harding has shown that, contrary to dominant assumptions, the fundamentalist movement is not at all solidly working class—the opium of the masses, as it were—and that the class constituency is much wider. In the world of cultural capital, however, it seems to me that there is more of an overt class war at stake. From the point of view of the scientific establishment, both New Age and fundamentalist creationism are presented as movements that are going to pull us back to the Dark Ages. The real threat there, it seems to me, is not at all the threat of the Dark Ages, but rather the influential success of these movements in challenging the authority of scientific intellectuals. You can see this quite clearly in the activities of CSICOP, the Committee for Scientific Investigation into Claims of the Paranormal—this was set up in the late seventies to debunk, in the most boringly positivist way, the claims of New Agers and creationists. It functions like a protective militia for the scientific profession.

DONNA HARAWAY: As you spoke, I was also thinking of the popular physiology of the nineteenth-century mechanics institutes, mainly in England, and the degree to which it is not true that all of the movements that Andrew was naming were entirely bourgeois. The importance of popular physiology in working-class British culture is an important issue. I think, in a parallel way, of Judy Stacey's ethnographic work among some of the working-class women in Silicon Valley. Stacey's work touches on beliefs about health and religion. And while it would be wrong to characterize their beliefs as "New Age," because of the class ring to that label, there are edges in common. It's hard to draw clear boundaries. If we insist on a strict definition of "New Age," it might have a narrow class base, but if we think more broadly in terms of the diverse and overlapping cultural formations that are in opposition to the scientistic and technoscience cults of modernism, then we have a much messier and richer issue around class.

JENNIFER SLACK: I'm concerned that in using the term "New Age" you seem to have reduced this to a relatively homogeneous movement. I see it far more complexly than that. And I think that it's very important to acknowledge that not only are the boundaries of that movement contested, but that within groups that consider themselves New Age there are significant and relevant debates. To put this another way, you don't sound like a fan, and I am reminded of what Donna Haraway said earlier: that she never undertakes the criticism of that to which she is not vulnerable. I would like to ask about the degree to which you are vulnerable. What kind of relationship do you have personally with this complex movement that operates under the aegis of the New Age?

ROSS: I'm grateful to you for pointing out that the whole spectrum of New Age practices is much more disparate than I have had time to cover in this talk. For the sake of polemical efficiency, I certainly assumed a coherence to the New Age movement that any larger, and more ethnographic, study would probably contest. There are reasons for this, however, some of which I have tried to suggest, and some of which you invoke when you say that I don't "sound like a fan." Some of the most exciting work being done in cultural studies, as you know, is ethnographic, and positions the critic in some respects as a "fan." Constitutionally, I know that I lack the patience to do that kind of ethnography, and so I wouldn't be very good at it. On the other hand, I'm wary of giving up certain privileges that we have struggled to enjoy as polemical critics—the capacity to use our hard-earned public voices to intervene and to contest the shape of public thinking about countercultural communities and practices. While there is *everything* to be learned from ethnographic work that devotes itself to entering into the "deep" structural context in which subcultures and alternative communities have developed, I think that there are also some dangers involved in that kind of submersion. We often cede too much ground in submerging our own voices, ground that will be occupied by other, less sympathetic voices. The other question is whether the position of the "intellectual as fan" is going to be erected as a new kind of credentialism within cultural studies. I'm sort of sympathetic to this, but I wouldn't like to see this position harden into a moralistic criterion for doing cultural studies. On the question of vulnerability, I can try to assure you, for what it's worth, that I have had quite a long history of personal relations with people—friends, acquaintances, an ex-spouse—in the

New Age community. In general, however, I don't believe that anyone undertakes any kind of cultural study—chooses an object for such a study—that one is not personally invested in. All such research is deeply autobiographical—how could it not be? But you see, I'm a Scot, from a very repressive culture. And let me assure you that I didn't come here to bury New Age, nor to praise it.

ANDREW PAINTER: It seems to me that, at one level, both orthodox science and pseudo-science are based in some conception of science. Isn't this, at some level, the same situation facing cultural studies? Aren't we caught up in the same game of having to base our own claims to authority on science? Is there any more ammunition we have than simply saying it's all political?

ROSS: We might mention CSICOP again, and their journal, the *Skeptical Inquirer;* it's interesting that one of their governing assumptions, as a member, Carl Sagan, has put it, is one that used to circulate in the fifties debates about mass culture. And that is, that there's a Gresham's Law of science that says that bad science, if it proliferates, drives out good science. This was something that also used to be said of popular culture—if we had a cultural diet that was good for people then the popular hunger for trash would disappear. Sagan's view is that if science were properly explained to a non-expert audience, then there would be no pseudo-science. This strikes me as a naive position, since science—the ideological discourse of an expert elite—can no more be "explained" outside of the context of an expert audience than "high" culture can be explained to a non-expert audience. Cultural studies, it seems to me, has come a long way toward repealing Gresham's Law, at least in the intellectual community. But the real issue here is that scientists, like cultural intellectuals, have to share their lives with non-experts who both respect and resent the experts' authority to judge the rationality of popular science or popular culture. That's not to say that we ought to give up our authority to speak. But we ought to take time to learn more about how the "common sense" about science or culture is constructed. That's what ought to distinguish us from Sagan's hectoring paternalism. The alternative, of course, that you are asking for, is to actually do science— look at what the PWA community has achieved in doing science for themselves—and to do culture—look at the alternative media movement in this country.

WILL STRAW: Would you be willing to claim that the ongoing and sort of perpetually renewed preference of cultural theorists for theories which stress fragmentation, multiplicity, and so on is itself a response to a particular level of cultural capital? And to get back to what Lata Mani was asking, if this is the case, if a certain level of cultural capital will almost inevitably favor these sorts of theories, then the embracing within that theory of certain kinds of alterity and difference may not be seen simply as the success of certain political claims but also a move on the part of a certain academic community to perpetuate or consolidate its power or its particular view of things. What do you think?

ROSS: Yes, you are reaffirming what I have come across in this particular study of New Age culture. That there is a world of difference between the sort of holistic, or completist, sense of identity espoused in New Age, and the sort of fragmentary identity that intellectual fractions in this society have become accustomed to talking about. Even though both worldviews are equally critical of the Cartesian tradition, it's quite bewildering to move between them. And I agree that the liberatory fantasies of many postmodern theorists—perhaps they are indeed fantasies about escaping the class identity of the intellectual—have little in common with the utopian fantasies of groups with less cultural capital—fantasies that are solidly tied to the hunger for completion, or self-transcendence. So, then, ought we to consider that these respective fantasies are also responses to given class positions, at least in the terms of cultural capital—the certainty of a secure identity for intellectuals, on the one hand, and the uncertainty of unhappy identities for non-intellectuals, on the other? Both fantasies, then, can be seen as resistant compensations of some kind. A somewhat different analysis might be required for economic class identities, however, because it's there that you can see how capitalist culture profits, at all levels of society, from exploiting the sense of rootlessness, or mobile, partial identities, on the one hand, and utopian appeals to security on the other. Both appeals co-exist more often. In that kind of analysis, it's much more difficult to separate these respective views of identity across a hierarchy of class locations, and so it's more difficult to blame intellectuals for all of the pernicious things that we think and do.

30

The Pachuco's Flayed Hide: Mobility, Identity, and Buenas Garras

MARCOS SANCHEZ-TRANQUILINO AND JOHN TAGG

I

Founded on the disciplines of archaeology and natural history, both inherited from the classical age, the museum was a discredited institution from its very inception. And the history of museology is a history of all the various attempts to deny the heterogeneity of the museum, to reduce it to a homogeneous system or series.

Through reproductive technology postmodernist art dispenses with the aura. The fiction of the creating subject gives way to the frank confiscation, quotation, excerptation, accumulation and repetition of already existing images. Notions of originality, authenticity and presence, essential to the ordered discourse of the museum, are undermined.
Douglas Crimp (1983, pp. 49, 53)[1]

There is an irony here—if you are in a position to enjoy it: those who never made it till now arrive to find the Museum in ruins (though not before ASCO have signed it with their *placas*). But it gets worse. They arrive to find their Identity already gone, their Culture in fragments, their Nationhood dispersed, and their Monuments reduced to canonical rubble. The site they were to occupy is nothing but a razed discursive plane. Welcome to the New Art History. There is room for everyone and a place for none.

A victory like this might invite cynicism. At the very moment that the counter-mobilizations of dominated cultures come to challenge their exclusion from the privileged representations and institutions of the National Cultural Heritage, there ceases to be an occupiable space in which to celebrate their "coming of age." It is not just that the precious, airless vaults of Serious Art have *exploded*, as the differences and particularities that once were obstacles to inclusion have been transformed into the means of new and more flexible forms of accumulation. Nor is it just that, in the process, museums have willingly relativized themselves, eagerly colonizing the market opportunities of diversity and enthusiastically embracing a new division of labor: social history for museums of daily life or folk and "ethnic" art; vivid dioramic displays for museums of ethnography; and a wealth of spectacle, contextualization, and exhaustive cataloguing for the international circuit of major metropolitan museums of Art. This much might be dismissed as the "spectacular reification"[2] of a service economy culture and stoically resisted in the name of an authentic presence and expression. The problem is that the grounds of this resistance have also *imploded* and the consequences for history, theory, and practice have not been welcome.

As long as the Museum could be conceived as an Ideological State Apparatus (see Althusser, 1971b) and art history as an ideological expression, then it was possible to imagine another place, another consciousness, the expression of another center: an ex-cluded but emergent and oppositional culture. The Universal Survey Museum (See Dun-can and Wallach, 1980) and a complicit conception of art history as the narrative un-folding of a universal cultural expression could be counterposed to oppositional art histories, as counter-narratives of the coming to consciousness of dominated but defiant peoples. The effectivity of this opposition depended, however, on preserving intact a conception of the constitutive subject and a logic of representation as expression or reflection that compelled such oppositional art histories to cling to the imaginary body of their Other, even as they struggled to turn it on its head. Now, with the undermining of these categories and logics, both sides seem to have been flung out or sucked into a gravity-less space—a space without familiar coordinates.

In such a space, art history can no longer be stabilized around that familiar strategic mixture of connoisseurship, iconography, artistic biography, and the study of periods and movements; but this is not because of the exposure of their functional implication in the power of the state or because of the revelation, beneath the "one-sided, immediate unity" of their analyses, of a denied but determinant social basis. Such forms of soci-ological explanation have themselves been caught in the internal collapse of the discipline they claim to critique, as a new impetus in critical theory and cultural practice has invaded art history's structural categories, its narrative voice, its institutional security, and even its object of study. To see this itself as symptomatic of a "cultural logic" of "Late Capitalist" commodification would merely be circular: what is at issue is the "logic" of symptomatic expression and the privileged knowledge on which it depends (cf. Jameson, 1984). Appeals to experience or determinant interests similarly beg the question, but such appeals are no more a precondition of action than is a map of the imagined totality (Jameson, 1984, pp. 89–92).[3] What is unraveling now is the discursive formation of a discipline—the conjunctural effects of its practices, institutions, technol-ogies, and strategies of explanation. It is precisely this unraveling that opens up spaces for new kinds of questioning and intervention so that, if the deconstruction of art historical narratives of expression and identity conflicts with ideas of the cultural self-assertion of dominated groups previously excluded from the space of the active subject of culture and heritage, then what we need to ask is whether this conflict need be disabling or defeating. Are there other models of identity and cultural struggle?

It is time to return to cases. What is left of "resistance and affirmation" for the subjects of *el Movimiento,* the Chicano civil rights movement, or of its cultural wing? At the end of this dry road stands a familiar figure. *Ese,* Louie: "un vato de atolle," posing in Bogart-tough role, with his own imaginary music, in his dark topcoat and tailor-made drapes: "his smile as deadly as his vaisas!" "Legs Louie Diamond": switching the codes of fetishism on the street (Montoya, 1970).

II

Coats cannot be exchanged for coats . . .
Karl Marx (1977, p. 132)

Xipe Totec, Our Lord of the Flayed Hide, changes his skin.
Carlos Fuentes (1968, p. 371)

It should be explained that "Louie" is the protagonist of a historically pivotal poem by José Montoya, to whom we shall have cause to return later. Louie is a small town *pachuco:* a stylish Mexican-American youth from the margins, who began to assert his ambivalent place in Californian society in the years following the end of the Second World War. Most significantly for us, he did this in part by wearing a Zoot Suit, and it is the effects of this suit's meanings that we are going to pursue. For, while Marx has told us that "coats cannot be exchanged for coats," Louie changed his coat and, like the great Aztec God *Xipe Totec,* Our Lord of the Flayed Hide, in putting on a new skin, he put on a new identity. But this identity has a strange history in the challenge it posed, not only to the codes of respectable American and Mexican society, but also—subsequently—to the codes of cultural history.

In 1973, Arturo Madrid-Barela, finding that literary portraits of the *pachuco* paradoxically "shed more light on his interpreters than on the subject," called on scholars "to begin the long, laborious process of peeling back the layers of falsehood and fantasy that obscure [the *pachuco's*] true history" (pp. 57, 31). The problem, Madrid-Barela knew, was one of visibility: the visibility for which *pachuco* and *pachuca* dressed, and were beaten and imprisoned. The question is whether this can be grasped in terms of paring, illuminating, clarifying, or exposing a "true history," free of the mythmakers' "distortions" (p. 32), outside the conditions of historical narration. As Bruce-Novoa (1987) has written in the context of the debate on representations of Chicano history and cultural production:

> As more and more emphasis is placed on the discursive process of the creation of a text of cultural past, the possibility of returning to a belief in a monological history invested with the status of truth fades. (p. 42)

The peeling of history implies the trace of the knife and the hand. Whose *vaisa* holds the *fila?* What is the arc of the cut? As Bruce-Novoa has argued, it was the continued closure of institutions of national culture to Chicanos that provoked a shift in the 1960s to a strategy of cultural nationalism, constructed out of the totalization of "communal memory and tradition" as a new truth with which to challenge "dominant history" as false or, at best, partial and distorted (pp. 41–42). The mythologizing and the coupled demythologizing of *pachuco* culture were outgrowths of attempts to fix such truth in narrative historiographical forms that assimilated themselves to the expressive structure of cultural nationalism. At the same time, this logic of cultural nationalism fixed the identity of writer and written—historian and object—in a cultural affinity that, paradoxically, had to transcend historicity. What was suppressed, whether tactically or not, was the play of difference that was the very field of emergence of the *pachuco's* game. The *pachuco* could then be "recovered" as the proto-subject of national regeneration, in a nationalist narration grounded on the notion of an essential ethnic identity that *expresses* itself in cultural form.

Yet a troubling residuum remained: the enigmatic problem of the *pachuco's* Mexicanness or Americanness, bequeathed by Octavio Paz to all subsequent commentators. It has been, however, the essentializing narrative itself that has made this trouble and produced the enigma of the *pachuco.* Desertion from both Mexican and American cultures and insubordinate difference were, for wartime superpatriots, the marks of the *pachuco's* treason. Seven years later, Paz looked back with lofty patrician disdain at the scowling, self-destructive "sinister clown" as existential casualty:

> His whole being is sheer negative impulse, a tangle of contradictions, an enigma. Even his very name is enigmatic: *pachuco,* a word of uncertain derivation, saying nothing and saying everything. (1961, p. 14)[4]

The puzzle of the *pachuco* as failure of identity was premised on a conception of subjectivity as given, unitary, and constitutive, and on a logic of culture as the expression of this constitutive subject. But these are the same assumptions that we encounter in later subcultural studies, which see in the Zoot Suit "the product of a particular social context" (Cosgrove, 1988, [1984], p. 5) and "a shared set of experiences" (p. 8): a ritual form through which "resistance can find natural and unconscious expression" (p. 20). The structure of explanation is the same, which may account for why, as late as 1984, Stuart Cosgrove could still believe that Paz's description of the *pachuco's* delinquency and ambivalence could provide "a framework in which the Zoot Suit can be understood" (pp. 5–6).

And what of the notion of *pachuco* and *pachuca* culture as a *subculture—sub*ordinated yet again? How could this be compatible with the recognition that it had no "parent," that it was neither the child of North America, nor the orphan of Mexico? Derivation and dominance, as Paz vaguely sensed, were what it put at issue. And just as it spoke a double offense to both institutionally solidified national cultures and their violent securities of identity, so it has gone on offending the protocols of cultural histories—dominant or alternative—because they do not speak its *language.*

By contrast, *el pachuco* and *la pachuca* insisted on the textures of language—on *el Caló, el tacuche, los plaqueazos;* on their intransigence to monolingual readings—even while they insolently appropriated the "stinking badges" of the cultures they moved through. To Paz's apparent annoyance, they refused to "return to the dress of [their] forebears" (1961, p. 16); and what a bizarre imagining that conjures up. Instead, they got into the dress codes of white male status and normality, playing with the images of an Anglo popular culture's own masculine "outsiders"—the Southern dandy, the Western gambler, the *modern* urban gangster. They did not therefore negate "the very principles" of North American fashion, as Paz tells us (p. 15), but subsumed them in their own rhythms, arenas, and exchanges, thereby exposing the limits of Paz's presumed subject of modernity, comfort, practicality, and convenience. Such a strategy repudiated *sub*ordination in a hierarchy of national cultures. It was neither "inside" nor "outside": it ruptured their structures of Otherness, at least for a moment, at least for the best times of the week.

Pachuco culture was an assemblage, built from machines for which they never read the manuals. It was a cultural *affirmation* not by nostalgic return to an imaginary original wholeness and past, but by appropriation, transgression, reassemblage, breaking and restructuring the laws of language: in the speech of *Caló* and *pochismos,*[5] but also in the languages of the body, gesture, hair, tattoos, dress, and dance; and in the languages of space, the city, the *barrio,* the street. Paz was offended and saw only negativity: a grotesque and anarchic language that said nothing and everything: a failure of memory or assimilation. The refusal to choose made no sense. The aggressive visibility only exacerbated the lack of cultural presence. The *pachuco* was an indecipherable mythology. (The *pachuca*— the Black Widow—could not even be thought.) And so it goes on. Tragic, heroic, delinquent, or grotesque, without a clear identity and location, the *pachuco* is a scandal of civilized meaning. In the name of national dignity, for Madrid-Barela in 1973 as for the white uniformed servicemen in the streets of East Los Angeles exactly thirty years earlier, he must be stripped, peeled, skinned, down to a raw and naked truth (cf. Mazón, 1984).

Why do they want the *pachuco* naked? Why do they want his clothes? The *pachuco's tacuche:* the padded, finger-length coat with wide lapels; the narrow-brimmed lid or hat; the draped pants with reat-pleats, ballooning to the knee then narrowing tightly at the ankle; the looping chain; the double-soled shoes, good for dancing "El Pachuco" and "La Pachuquilla" to Lalo Guerrero and his "Trio Imperial" (G. Barker, 1950, p. 39). And the *pachuca*—different from but not other to the male—in the same drape coat, straight black skirt or narrow slacks, flat black shoes or "zombie slippers," and beehive hairdo, piled high and decorated, often with razor blades.[6] They knew what they were putting on. Like the Filipinos in Los Angeles and the black youth of Georgia and Harlem, with whom *pachucos* and *pachucas* exchanged style cues.[7] And beyond this, without necessary connection, like those other fascinating delinquents of the "Africas" and "jungles" of great, industrialized cities: the "flash" costermongers of Mayhew's (1851) London,[8] the Northern Scuttlers and their Molls (see Roberts, 1971), the Bowery Boys and Gals of mid-nineteenth-century New York City,[9] or the *sapeurs* and *sapeuses* of present-day Kinshasa, with their immodest flashing of labels and their exuberant chanting songs of French, Italian, and Japanese designers' names (M. MacIntyre, 1989).

The clothes made meanings with their bodies. They made them hateful and desirable. They made them visible. But, worse than that, they made them readable in a way that had to be denied. This is not to suggest that there was ever a fixed and final reading attached to the clothes, outside a specific moment, framework, and intervention, or that the space of identity they described was ever homogeneous or resolved. (Transgressive or not, the suit of clothes torn from the back of the Zoot Suiter by rioters in Harlem and East Los Angeles in 1943 could appear again on the backs of the working-class, London Teds who fomented the "Race Riots" of Notting Hill in 1958.) The point is that the meanings were *not* unreadable to the cultures they inflamed. You couldn't miss a Zoot Suit or a Pompadour in the street. But not only there. They stood out in a discursive space the *pachuco* and *pachuca* extended around them: a third space, between the dualities of rural and urban, Eastside and Westside, Mexican and American, and, arguably, feminine and masculine. Not pure negation. Not *mestizo*—half and half—but an even greater *mestizaje* (Cf. Anzaldúa, 1987, p. 5). A new space: a new field of identity.

On either side of this refusal of Otherness and "this stubborn desire to be different" (Paz, 1961, p. 15), the dominant Anglo and estranged Mexican cultures each refused to recognize this new space and continued to blame the *pachuco's* corruption on the contamination of the other. Displaced from both, *pachucos* and *pachucas* sought to make an identity as mobile as the space of the street they inhabited; mobile, yet legible, at least to those who shared the code and could read the *placas* emblazoned throughout the *barrio*. As a space of mobility without guarantees, the street articulated a new economy of identity and power. It was a polity marked out, but also made legible, in emphatic and constantly overpainted *plaqueazos* that served as a check on the local abuse of power in the street by their public declaration of an always shifting pattern of relations, as territories, cohorts, friends, and lovers were gained and lost. Yet this writing was always on others' walls. The space of the streets was always staked out in advance: the routes and boundaries laid down by city planners and patrolled by city police, social workers, and ethno-linguists; the fixed grid for regulating movement and dissent; the commercial strips for commodity display and consumption; the passages and barriers to and from the *colonia* or *barrio*; never an equal space for the housed and the homeless, or for men and women, even when, in prurient indignation, the Los Angeles newspapers crowed that "Zooter Girls" were fighting with knives and brass knuckles alongside the men (see Montoya, 1977).

The field was one they neither owned nor controlled. And if the path they cut across it was a path of resistance, what they made was not a track to something lost or excluded, but a path of interference: a resistance to reading—for which they paid a heavy price. And the resistance has not stopped. It frustrates Madrid-Barela's (1973) call for "social and economic documentation" that will dispel the *pachuco's* "mythic dimensions" and expose the "construct of fact and fiction" (pp. 58, 31). Madrid-Barela will have no truck with "the empty posturings of brown power or the middle-class accommodations of ethnic politics," but what he offers in their place is a reduction to a duality that insists on a choice *pachucos* and *pachucas* had already subverted.

This is not to deny that *pachucas* and *pachucos* operated on historical and political grounds: that they negotiated changing conditions of urban working-class life, family structure, and employment; or that they found their opportunity in the emerging patterns of a new cross-national and intercultural economy, as war work brought a relative affluence and changed patterns of labor and consumption. It is not to deny that they were touched by the desire for the beyond of an impossible integration, by that sad optimism and nostalgia for the future which is the pathos of modernism. It is to suggest that their interlingual strategy of identity and resistance was a strategy of the border and will not accommodate to the old homilies and historiographies, and that the consequences of this have not been engaged. Octavio Romano (1969), for example, decides that: *"The Pachuco movement was one of the few truly separatist movements in American History."* Yet, undoing his own assertion, he goes on:

> Even then, it was singularly unique among separatist movements in that it did not seek or even attempt a return to roots and origins. The Pachuco indulged in a self-separation from history, created his own reality as he went along even to the extent of creating his own language. (Quoted in Bruce-Novoa, 1982, p. 219)

For those who wore the Zoot Suit, it was not a question of discovering beneath the structures of domination an innate individual and collective identity that could be safeguarded and cultivated until the political moment destined for its emergence. *Pachuco* culture was a survival strategy not of purity, of saying *less,* but rather of saying *more,* of saying too much, with the wrong accent and intonation, of mixing the metaphors, making illegal crossings, and continually transforming language so that its effects might never be wholly assimilable to an essential ethnicity, to a "social ecology" of delinquency, or to the spectacle of multiculturalism and commodified diversity.[10]

III

It is the secret fantasy of every bato **in or out of the** Chicanada **to put on a Zoot Suit and play the Myth** más chucote que la chingada.
Luis Valdez[11]

In 1970, José Montoya buried El Louie. In 1977, he dug him up again to take his pulse. His aim was to combat a loss of cultural memory at a time when *el Movimiento,* the Chicano civil rights movement, seemed to be entering a less militant phase. In his documentary exhibition and publication, *Pachuco Art: A Historical Update,* which grew out of the Royal Chicano Air Force's *Barrio* Art Program in Sacramento, Montoya sought to do this through collective remembering, infusing the imagery and symbolism of the *pachuco* into contemporary Chicano art and *barrio* life, inverting the stereotype of negation and marginalization, and instilling pride in a new generation of *Chicanitos.* Against the embrassed forgetfulness of conservatives and the moralizing denial of leftists, Montoya ensured that the *pachuco* would push his defiant foot forward and fix his stare again, reinvented and reinvested as the prototype of Chicano cultural resistance: "the first Chicano freedom-fighters of the Chicano movement" (1977, p. 1).

The paradox, however, was that the *pachuco,* who never looked back or stood still, should be absorbed into a mythology of the past as a means of making sense of present grounds of struggle in terms of an assertion of an essential national identity and cultural expression. The effect was to be underlined in the following year by the popular success of Luis Valdez's play *Zoot Suit* and the image of Ignacio Gómez's poster, with its monumental and phallicized figure, legs triumphantly astride the diminutive projection of *El Lay's* City Hall. The "enigma" had taken on a new and unambiguous dignity of presence, though Montoya seemed to know the *pachuco* remained a troubling if necessary space of absence in this discourse. (El Louie was always already gone; buried from the start: "Hoy enterraron al Louie."[12] Buried in a textuality, one might say, with which he had known how to play. In all events, gone—as the very spur to his resurrection in words of remembering.[13])

What is at issue in this resurrection of the *pachuco* in the late 1970s is not the displacement of militancy by nostalgia. It is the representation of that militancy through the articulation of the *pachuco* into the politics of identity of a *nationalist* movement. The problems here are the problems of all nationalisms through which, as Tom Nairn (1981) has put it, "societies try to propel themselves forward to certain kinds of goals (industralization, prosperity, equality with other peoples, etc.) *by a certain sort of regression*—by looking inwards, drawing more deeply upon their indigenous resources, resurrecting past folk-heroes and myths about themselves and so on" (p. 348). Nationalisms work through such *differentiae* because they have to, caught as they are in the conflicts of *modernity* and *modernization,* in conditions of uneven development that, within the spaces of colonialist domination, may yield no resources but the geographical, ethnological, and cultural peculiarities of a region which, in the rhetorics of nationalism, become the indices of origins, roots, hidden histories and shared heritages. Yet, however successful it may be in articulating a populist culture of identity, "all nationalism," Nairn says, "is both healthy and morbid" (p. 347).

Whatever momentum of re-identification and re-territorialization nationalisms make possible, they always turn on their own strategy of terror: their own interiorization of a center, their own essentializing of a dominant frame of differentiation, their own pograms and expulsions. Whatever the tactical value of their reactive inversions, nationalist discourses remain prisoner to the very terms and structures they seek to reverse, mirroring their fixities and exclusions. But the attachment is also deeper and its effects more pervasive and unconscious, as nationalisms are fractured by the drive of a desire for the very Other they constitute, denigrate, and expel, yet to which they continue to attribute enormous powers.

The crisis of coherence and the instability of such nationalist formations are not, then, only a function of accelerating multinational exchange or globalized communications and travel. They mark an internal crisis, and a crisis, we have been arguing, that the *pachuco* and *pachuca* knowingly provoked. There is a deep contradiction, therefore, in their assimilation, alongside the *conquistador* and Aztec noble, to the discourse of essential identity and expressive culture; just as there is something highly significant in the fact that this assimilation was primarily negotiated around the monumentalized figure of the male, largely to the exclusion of the *pachuca*.[14] The transgressive nature of their mutual practice could not be recognized.

Yet, we should be careful ourselves not to be reductive here. The Chicano nationalist movement that began in the 1960s was centrally an anti-racist, civil rights movement that rejected all previous identities and defined Mexican-Americans as a regionally diversified, multicultural and mixed race people from whom would arise *La Nueva Raza* (cf. Muñoz, 1989, pp. 15–16). Nevertheless, its attempt to shape a politics of unification and nationhood on the basis of the "reclamation" of an indigenous, non-white, family-based identity and culture—"a Bronze People with a Bronze Culture"[15]— suppressed differences and conflicts in the historically antagonistic elements it sought to merge and remained haunted by a duality of assimilation and secession that the *pachuca* and *pachuco* had already gone beyond.

There is another sense, however, in which the rediscovery of *pachuco* culture was rightfully central. If the term "Chicano," itself taken over from *pachuco* vocabulary (G. Barker, 1950, p. 41),[16] can be understood as an assertion not of a lost origin but of a simultaneity and multiplicity of identities, then the question of cultural retrieval may be posed as one of engaging not the *imagery*, but the *strategy* of the *pachuco* and *pachuca*; a strategy, that is, not of fixed difference, but of the transformation of languages and spaces of operation to evade both invisibility and assimilation. From this point of view, the re-engagement of the past might lead not to a litany and iconography of masculinist heroics, but to the mode of operation of a group such as ASCO, founded in 1972 by *"veteranos"* of the sixties' car clubs and "blowouts" of East Los Angeles's Garfield High: Harry Gamboa Jr., Gronk, Willie Herrón, and Patssi Valdez.[17]

ASCO: nausea, disgust, repulsion: their audience's response, but also their own reaction to themselves, to an American social environment of poverty, racism, sexism, and militarism, and to what Gamboa (1987) has described as "the frenzied fiasco of depersonalized survival in the urban environment" (p. 22). Like the *pachuco* and *pachuca*, ASCO did not depend on establishing a continuist historical tradition through which the imaginary securities of the past might guarantee the resistance of the present. Nor did they seek to avoid what Kobena Mercer (1987) has called "skirmishes of appropriation and commodification played out around the semiotic economy of the ethnic signifier" (p. 49). ASCO risked the streets and found in the accelerating commodity theater and political battleground of Whittier Boulevard the material and characteristic exaggerations from which they could make their performance work.

Their response to Chicano displacement, denial, and subjugation did not, however, stay in the *barrio*. It spilled over into the Anglo Westside and its prospering network of institutions for marketing and promoting a quasi-official "modern" art culture. In 1972, ASCO "signed" or vandalized the Los Angeles County Museum of Art with their *plaqueazos*, claiming the building, the entire eclectic collection, its *mainstreams* and organizing historiographical narratives for their "art." The "work" lasted a day before it disappeared, like Siqueiros's mural in Olvera Street, behind a coat of official whitewash. But a significant territory had been breached. As Jean Baudrillard (1981) has argued, in the absence of any transcendent system from which works of art may be said to derive, it is the signature—sign of the subject-creator in name—that secures authenticity and the code on which the integrity of meaning of the oeuvre and the system of consumption founded upon it both depend:

> the slightest attack upon this sign which is both authentic and accepted, unmotivated and codified, is felt as a profound attack upon the cultural system itself. . . . (p. 106)

But ASCO's was a calligraphic gesture that, at the same time, mocked itself: marking, in the gap between *signature* and *placa*, its own impossibility, at the site of an institution that had already marked their work and that of contemporary Chicano artists as Other, "outside."

ASCO marked, resigned, but refused to occupy the spaces, genres, and languages disposed in advance "for Chicanos." Gronk and Herrón might work, on and off, for years on the *Black and White Mural* in the Estrada Courts Housing Project, but on another occasion—as on Christmas Eve 1974—it would be enough for Gronk to tape Patssi Valdez and Humberto Sandoval to a liquor store wall to constitute an *Instant Mural*. Yet the tapes could never hold them. Like the *pachucos y pachucas*, ASCO saw the spaces of cultural barrioization as spaces of transformation and borders as lines to be erased.[18] They seemed at odds, therefore, not only with the agencies of a dominant Anglo culture, but also with those Chicano artists and historians whose sense of cultural identity sprang from the fountainhead of nationalist cultural metaphors—pre-Columbian themes, the iconography of the Mexican Revolution, and the relics of the imagery of an adapted Roman Catholicism—rather than from the exhilaration of cultural cross-dressing. For ASCO, the space of this nationalist strategy and its attendant historiography were in ruins; but this was not disabling.

As Stuart Hall has remarked:

> The past is not waiting for us back there to recoup our identities against. It is always retold, rediscovered, reinvented. It has to be narrativized. We go to our own pasts through history, through memory, through desire, not as a literal fact.[19]

What we begin to make out is another narration of identity, another resistance. One that asserts a difference, yet cannot be absorbed into the pleasures of a global marketing culture. One that locates its different voice, yet will not take a stand on the unmoving ground of a defensive fundamentalism. One that speaks its location as more than local, yet makes no claim to universality for its viewpoint or language. One that knows the border and crosses the line.

This is not a new story. It is not one that had to wait for the theorization of the "global postmodern." As we began to hear it, it drifted into *El Lay* with the *pachucos* from El Paso, Texas. Not from Utopia or from Paris, but from "ol' E.P.T." and the border with Juárez. A voice from the borderlands; though the border, as we know, was not always there. Should we find this a surprise: that this uncertain, in-between space should be the arena of a new formation of identity? Gloria Anzaldúa (1987) would remind us:

> Borders are set up to define the places that are safe and unsafe, to distinguish *us* from *them*. A border is a dividing line, a narrow strip along a steep edge. A borderland is a vague and undetermined place created by the emotional residue of an unnatural boundary. It is in a constant state of transition. The prohibited and forbidden are its inhabitants. *Los atravesados* live here: the squint-eyed, the perverse, the queer, the troublesome, the mongrel, the mulato, the half-breed, the half dead; in short, those who cross over, pass over, or go through the confines of the "normal." (p. 3)

NOTES

1. It should be understood from what follows that the ruining of the Museum can only be understood as a rhetorical inflation of a specific and conditional crisis, comparable to Baudrillard's equally hyperbolic, and only apparently opposite, assertion that: "The museum, instead of being circumscribed in geometrical location, is now everywhere, like a dimension of life itself" (Baudrillard, 1983b, pp. 15–16).

2. The term comes from Hal Foster (1989), "Wild Signs: The Breakup of the Sign in Seventies' Art."

3. Cf. also: Fredric Jameson (1988), "Cognitive Mapping," and Anders Stephanson (1987), "Regarding Postmodernism—A Conversation with Fredric Jameson."

4. For a more extended analysis of this essay, see: Marcos Sanchez-Tranquilino (1987), "Mano A Mano: An Essay on the Representation of the Zoot Suit and Its Misrepresentation by Octavio Paz."

5. *Pochismos* or *Anglicismos* are translated and Hispanicized English words taken over into southwestern interlingual slang. *Caló* draws on Southwestern Spanish, regional dialect, Mexican slang, and words that have changed little in form and meaning from Spanish Gypsy slang of the fifteenth century; but it is also a language of constant innovation, kept in restrictive usage by frequent and rapid changes of content through the invention of new terms. See: George Carpenter Barker (1950), *Pachuco: An American-Spanish Argot and Its Social Functions in Tucson, Arizona*. See also, Raphael Jesús Gonzales (1967), "Pachuco: the Birth of a Creole Language."

6. See, for example, Beatrice Griffith (1948), *American Me,* p. 47.

7. Cf., Cosgrove (1988 [1984]); Ralph H. Turner and Samuel J. Surace (1972), "Zoot-Suiters and Mexicans"; Steve Chibnall (1985), "Whistle and Zoot: The Changing Meaning of a Suit of Clothes"; and Kobena Mercer (1987), "Black Hair/Style Politics."

8. See Henry Mayhew (1851), *London Labour and the London Poor.* vol. 1, *The London Street Folk,* pp. 4–61, especially "Language of Costermongers," pp. 23–24, and "Of the Dress of Costermongers," pp. 51–52. See also, Dick Hebdige (1988b), "Hiding in the Light: Youth Surveillance and Display."

9. See Christine Stansell (1987), *City of Women: Sex and Class in New York, 1789–1860.* See also: Alvin F. Harlow (1931), *Old Bowery Days: The Chronicles of a Famous Street;* and Lloyd Morris (1951), *Incredible New York: High Life and Low Life of the Last Hundred Years.* Contemporary accounts and journalism include: George C. Foster (1850), *New York by Gas-Light;* Abram C. Dayton (1882), *Last Days of Knickerbocker Life in New York;* and George Ellington (1869), *The Women of New York, Or the Underworld of the Great City.*

10. The emergence of "youth" as a psycho-social category linked to the notion that the city was divided and organized into distinct "ecological" areas, each with its own "world," was developed by the Chicago School of Social Ecology from the late 1920s on: see R. E. Park & R. D. McKenzie (eds.) (1967), *The City;* and R. E. Faris (1967), *Chicago Sociology: 1920–1932.* For an application of this model to research on Chicano youth gang members and *pintos* (prison inmates), see Joan W. Moore (1978), *Homeboys: Gangs, Drugs, and Prison in the Barrios of Los Angeles.*

On the question of cultural innovation and the diversification of commodity production and marketing, see, e.g., Mercer (1987). Nevertheless, even if, as Mercer argues, the Zoot Suit was absorbed into the "Bold Look" of mainstream 1949 "menswear," what was repressed in this incorporation? And what repressed meanings returned to weigh "like a nightmare" on the backs of the wearers?

In other respects, and aside from his continued attachment to subcultural theory, our analysis comes close to Mercer's notion of the "creolization" of inter-cultural forms and his analysis of black dress and hair styles in the 1940s as encoding "a refusal of passivity by way of a creolizing accentuation and subtle inflection of given elements, codes and conventions" (Mercer, 1987, p. 47).

11. Luis Valdez, *Zoot Suit: An American Play, 1978.* Although Valdez's historic play has never been published, this line is often quoted in discussions: see Jorge A. Huerta (1982), "The Ultimate Pachuco: Zoot Suit," in *Chicano Theater: Themes and Forms.* For timely Chicana feminist analyses of *Zoot Suit* and Chicano theatre, see Yolanda Broyles Gonzáles (1989), "Toward a Re-Vision of Chicano Theatre History: The Women of El Teatro Campesino" and Yvonne Yarbro-Bejarano (1986), "The Female Subject in Chicano Theatre: Sexuality, 'Race,' and Class."

12. The opening line of Montoya (1970), "El Louie."

13. In George Barker's (1950) classic study of *pachuco* argot, for example, "Luey" is one of Barker's informants and *dramatis personae* in the imaginary *pachuco* dialogue in which, as in Montoya's poem, "Luey" stages a fight with "Goat": pp. 34–35. Montoya insisted that La Chiva actually existed, though reminded by Bruce-Novoa that *la chiva* is slang for heroin and an occasional euphemism for La Chingada: The Fucked One—Death. Cf. Bruce-Novoa (1982), pp. 14–25.

14. There are important exceptions, however, in the work of Judy Baca and Isabel Castro and, indeed, of José Montoya himself.

15. *El Plan Espiritual de Aztlán,* National Chicano Youth Liberation Conference, Denver, Colorado, 1969. Perhaps the tensions of this nationalism are most poignantly gathered in the notion of "our *Mestizo* Nation." See Rudolfo A. Anaya and Francisco Lomeli (eds.) (1989), *Aztlán: Essays on the Chicano Homeland,* pp. 1–5.

16. The simultaneity of identities signified by the term "Chicano" is what characterizes "American" identity when that identity is not reduced to a mythical Anglo-European paradigm: see Marcos Sanchez-Tranquilino (1990), *"Murales del Movimiento:* Chicano Murals and the Discourses of Art and Americanization."

17. Members of the group had earlier distinguished themselves as "jetters": Chicano high school students who differentiated themselves from contemporary *cholos* and Anglos through a fashion code based not on exaggeration, but on sardonic and elegant understatement. The "blo-

wouts" were the 1968 walkouts of students from the high schools of East Los Angeles, protesting both the Vietnam War and the discriminatory conditions and lack of resources of their segregated education.

18. Gronk announced that he would be erasing the border in 1980. See: Harry Gamboa Jr. (1980), "Gronk: Off-The-Wall Artist."

19. Stuart Hall, "Old and New Ethnicities," unedited transcription of the second of two lectures given in conjunction with the Third Annual Symposium on "Current Debates in Art History," *Culture, Globalization and the World-System: Contemporary Conditions for the Representation of Identity*, organized by Anthony King, Department of Art and Art History, SUNY Binghamton, March 14, 1989, p. 28.

Glossary

atravesados	those who cross over or are crossed over.
barrio	Chicano urban neighborhood.
Caló	argot of the Mexican underworld and *pachucos*, which can be traced back to the Gypsies of Spain who referred to their language as *Caló*; thought to have been brought to Mexico by bullfighters.
chucote	abbreviation of *pachucote*.
colonia	Chicano rural neighborhood.
ese	say, hey; guy; him; you.
fila	a type of knife *(pachuco;* from *filero:* colloquial Mexican).
garras	clothes *(pachuco;* from New Mexican dialect: rags), e.g., "buenas garras": fine clothes.
pachuco, pachuca	(originally) man, woman from El Paso *(El Pachuco)*.
placa	Chicano "graffiti" signature or emblem.
plaqueazo	Chicano public "graffiti" badge or emblem.
pochismos	or "Anglicismos" are of two main types: English words that have been made into Spanish nouns or verbs through Hispanicization or changes in spelling or pronunciation (e.g. *birria*—beer); and English or American slang expressions that have been translated into Spanish (e.g. *pegarle*—to beat it).
tacuche	suit *(pachuco:* Zoot Suit).
vaisa	hand *(pachuco:* Zoot Suit).
vato de atolle	a man of high integrity and strong character.
veterano	*pachuco* or veteran of the so-called Los Angeles "Zoot-Suit Riots" of 1943; more generally, a veteran youth gang member, a long-time *barrio* resident, or a Chicano elder.

DISCUSSION: MARCOS SANCHEZ-TRANQUILINO AND JOHN TAGG

STEVE FAGIN: I'd like to ask you about the consequences of the history you describe: first, the debate between the sort of anarchistic, youthful gestures of ASCO, and the way it was engaged in a more grass roots politics within neighborhoods. And second, that it led very strongly into an alternative art community outside of major museums in Los Angeles, particularly the institution LACE grew out of their intervention. So, I think in a way there's been too much emphasis on the confrontational and not so much the tactical. And I think that it's the tactical in a way that has served over the last ten years to be ongoing.

SANCHEZ-TRANQUILINO: It was not our intent to emphasize ASCO's confrontational stance over their tactical deployment in relation to their unique position *vis-à-vis* the mainstream or alternative art world. Indeed, their most effective public spectacles represented a balance between their (often) confrontational means and tactical ends. In the Chicano art community, ASCO were considered firebrands because no one in that community was making the kind of highly theatrical and seemingly spontaneous cultural interventions that called for, among other things, the very questioning of how Chicanos were constructing their nationalist identities. By using themselves, their bodies, as the basis for their innovative performances, ASCO brought the politics of Chicano representation into confrontation with the historical conditions of the *barrio* that restricted representation of Chicanos to that of the Other. As for LACE, what can we say for an institution that may have benefited from the participation of certain ASCO members as instrumental in its creation in the not art-trendy working-class section of Los Angeles fifteen plus years ago, but which now has no Chicanos on its staff? I mean, it goes to show that we need to question the methods and objectives of "alternative art institutions" as much as those of the mainstream.

FRED PFEIL: I want to challenge your assertion that this kind of transgressiveness, this kind of life on the border and these cultural practices on the border, can't be picked up by global marketing culture. I think late capitalist culture is precisely in love with border crossings and with transgressiveness and with unstable and fluctuating identities. I'm not recommending that we fall back into a certain kind of nostalgic nationalism, or notions of unified identity. I just mean to suggest that we don't want to fetishize this particular strategy as The Way Out.

TAGG: I agree, but I'm not sure which of us is fetishizing it. We didn't propose hybridization, in this paper, as a general strategy; nor did we say that, as a particular strategy, it could not be recuperated or absorbed into a cultural production dominated by marketing values. Indeed, Kobena Mercer, in his essay "Black Hair/Style Politics," has shown that, in fact, the Zoot Suit was, to some extent, absorbed into Anglo-American mainstream fashion, as in the 1949 "Bold Look" for men. Yet, the first Zoot Suits were custom-made, in every sense, and broke all wartime regulations on the use of cloth, as well as regulations on the meaning of race. More crucially, their later commodification did not displace the question of their *meaning* and the subjectivities they inscribed. What had to be *repressed* in the suit in the course of that marketing? Or, on the other hand, and more troublingly, what *persisted?* What disavowed meanings weighed like a nightmare on the backs of the wearers as they went to their business meetings in the Bold Look? These questions complicate the issue of the Zoot Suit's absorption into processes of commodification. They make us question whether absorption is simply recuperation. (And, to backtrack to the first question, talking specifically about ASCO, I might add that they have certainly not been unproblematically absorbed into a burgeoning Los Angeles art economy, with the possible exception of Gronk.)

DONNA HARAWAY: I'd like to ask a question about the use of Anzaldúa and the quote from *Borderlands/La Frontera,* and especially in view of a kind of comparison between ASCO, the *Pachuca,* and Anzaldúa in relationship to the different strategies of *mestizaje.* I heard a talk by Rosaura Sánchez, who completely distanced Anzaldúa because of her importance in many kinds of circuits, including those of women's studies publishing, and some of the commodity circuits of contemporary institutionalized feminisms that take Anzaldúa out of the community of working-class Chicanos and Chicanas and insert her in a circulation that Sánchez wanted to argue was really very hostile. She also criticized her for the particular reappropriation of Aztlán, and the remythification in the particular ways that she figures *la mestiza*. I was very interested in the particular way that you used Alzaldúa's quote from *Borderlands* to insist that none of these practices allowed a strategy of *mestizaje* that essentialized any kind of remythified racial origin. Instead they figure kinds of contradictions that don't readily either assimilate or articulate but have some chance of a politics of articulation—but it would be a politics that would require work, inside and outside. They're politics of provocation that name identity through a kind of relentless contradiction. And I guess I'm asking how you address figures, contemporary figures like Anzaldúa in relationship to a comparison of the strategies of the *pachuca* and ASCO?

SANCHEZ-TRANQUILINO: Only recently did I start reading Gloria Anzaldúa and felt immediately that her "new *mestiza*" provided an important way of thinking a new space, a third space such as that suggested by ASCO's tactics as well as that of the *Pachuco*. Her interpretation goes beyond the traditional concept of *mestizaje*. For Anzaldúa, that concept cannot ever again be thought of as a simple mixing of blood or cultures, but rather that what has always been in effect has been a mixing of identities many times over—beyond the old dualities be they gender, historical, economic, or cultural, etc. It is difficult to compare Anzaldúa in relationship to the strategies of the *pachuca* and ASCO because, in fact, she does *look back* to *Aztlán* for a necessary reappropriation of that concept in the construction of a contemporary *mestiza* identity (albeit broader) whereas, ostensibly, ASCO and *pachucos* of the 1940s only *looked forward*. However, the effectivity of *her* interventions require that, in fact, she do exactly this. Her terrain is different from theirs. Anzaldúa needs to look back with us and reappropriate this space, especially now that it has become entrenched in a highly academicized realm that was originally constructed by Chicano men and that continues to be elaborated and dominated by them.

TAGG: I'm just going to say thank you for that contribution because, having left the platform, I no longer have to answer any of these questions or to be the Master Voice. But, I'd add that Donna Haraway's remarks do articulate very precisely a distinction we very much wanted to make on the question of cultural nationalism and the politics of identity. I think it is also very important to say that the reference to Anzaldúa was chosen very, very specifically. There is a whole literature here that I did not know until I started learning while working on this paper and the closing reference to Anzaldúa was chosen, in preference to other theorizations of "border crossings," precisely to foreground this material. I guess the answer to the question that came at the end of your long analysis would be, quite simply, "Yes." We share your reading of Anzaldúa's *Borderlands/La Frontera*. But here—in this voice of hesitancy—is also the recognition of my, our, need to read the materials of this "other" debate, before putting myself in a position of being able to comment with authority on a literature that was only opened up for me in the writing of this paper. This hesitancy is, then, the mark of a beginning and I remember Lata Mani's comment last night that, whether we know it or not, the body of theoretical work that we have to address—not only writing, but also other kinds of cultural interventions—is not only coming out of the centers of Paris or Birmingham, or New York or London. And this is the point we made for ourselves in the final quote that opens on another project.

MARK ZIMMERMAN: The *Pachuco* revival in 1970–71 seems to me to be tied up with the question of the historical sources of what the first established wave of Chicano intellectuals was all about. That is to say the question has to do, I believe, with: who are our forebears, what are our roots in our past, and how do we explain the kinds of otherness which developed in our communities without resorting to a negative analysis that Octavio Paz resorted to? And there was a kind of essential attractiveness in this negativity, as every member of the *Pachucada* wanted to put on the Zoot Suit. Nevertheless, it's also, I think, in some ways the last stand of the male centeredness of the Chicano movement. It's the last effort to have that absolutely phallic image of the Zoot Suiter as the prime representation of *la Raza,* and to tie the whole orientation of Chicano nationalism to that extreme image of male defiance which not only resists the cops because it's the state, but also resists the coming down of the maleness of the Chicano male as he's beaten around in the barrio. But of course you cannot over-romanticize the image and I think your presentation does not escape that romanticism. The *Pachuca* was a victim of the *Pachuco;* anybody who looks at that history will understand the internal victimization within the group. And I would assume that the whole development of feminism in the second wave of Chicano culture and Chicano discourse needs a more firmly rooted development, and maybe that's what the question was about, in *Borderlands* and other recent texts. It would seem to me that there was a kind of negation of the possibility of the *Pachuco* being really a forerunner of the Chicano movement and a search for a wider set of roots towards explaining some of the more progressive tendencies that could be found and built upon in the Chicano community. I don't believe that you'll find too many people who will look to the *Pachuco* as a prime or central source to that. That was the criticism of Luis Valdez's play almost from the beginning. That would be my problem, I guess, with the ultimate drift of the paper as a kind of a mythification of another kind of otherness. Even though you raised doubts about it I don't think you really brought the full weight of feminism and feminist critique to bear on the image.

SANCHEZ-TRANQUILINO: It's true that the issues between men and women in the Chicano community, and especially in the Chicano art community, have pointed to uneven participation. Early nationalist (and idealistic) objectives towards achieving political unity often led to conscious exclusion of women's participation in leadership capacities. At other times, their exclusion seemed unconscious; more a product of "traditional" cultural/familial values. It is, however, important that a distinction be made between *developments* in Chicana feminist politics and *developments* by Chicanas who make art. While Chicana artists are by definition politicized and cannot really be separated from Chicana feminists, as cultural practitioners they nevertheless seem to surge as a group at about the same time that Montoya's "Louie" is being resurrected and reburied in the mid-seventies. To us, that is a significant development that must be further investigated because while the *Pachuco* is being affirmed symbolically by the play "ZOOT SUIT" as the urban prototype of Chicano defiance, it is the Chicana artists who are developing the broader current interventions in the arts. This is particularly apparent in the field of Chicana literature where someone such as Yolanda Broyles Gonzáles has begun to provide a feminist revision of the history of El Teatro Campesino and the contributions women in that company made to its historical development. One remarkable suggestion by Broyles Gonzáles's work, which is based heavily on women's oral histories, is that Luis Valdez's sister, Socorro, was oftentimes the actor who initiated and developed the male roles. You're right, we didn't deal with the Chicana feminist critique in this oral presentation, but we do in another version of this paper. However, even then, it isn't the central thesis.

TAGG: It's an interesting story that none of the male actors in the company wished at first to play the roles of the *Pachucos.* It certainly opens up the question about the supposed masculinism of the Zoot Suiters at the time and about the volatility of their transgressive spectacle of race, class, and, also, gender identity. In the paper, we also tried to make a distinction between two moments: between 1943 and 1977, when the

Pachuco was being reinvested and reinvented. This distinction is clear if you look at the accounts of the street culture of 1943, in which *Pachucas* were as active as the men, wearing the same drapes. I think that the anecdote about the male actors' reluctance to play the part of the *Pachucos* in the late 1970s perhaps also suggests that, even thirty-five years later, the Zoot Suiter's positionality was not so unambiguous—not so uncomplicatedly male-marketed—as you're suggesting. And what we do make of the anger and desire of those white servicemen who couldn't wait to get to East L.A. to lay their hands on the bodies of those "Mexicans," to strip them naked and even urinate on them. I don't see the meaning of this as straightforward, nor does it suggest that the Zoot Suiters were being seen in unconflicted gender terms, that as being as unproblematic a place. On the other hand, in the second moment we described, I think the Gomez poster, for example, does precisely try to rewrite the place of the *Pachuco* as phallic; but here's a historical difference we might pursue.

31

Ethics and Cultural Studies

Jennifer Daryl Slack and Laurie Anne Whitt

Theorists and practitioners of divergent disciplines have increasingly committed themselves to addressing the ethical aspects of their work over the past few decades. A similar concern has recently emerged within cultural studies (Hebdige, 1985, 1987a; Williamson, 1986). A growing number of cultural theorists[1] have begun to recognize that the ethical issues raised by or implicit in their research deserve critical attention and analysis. As in other disciplines, the ethical issues that arise are unique—overdetermined by the specific conditions within which they arise. For cultural studies, it is the recent engagement with postmodernism that has brought questions of ethics to the surface and prompted debates over the constitution of the subject and the problems and possibilities of a politics.

The problems of politics and a related ethics demand our attention, not only for theoretical reasons, but for political ones as well.[2] In the face of the developing political and ethical influence of the New Right, cultural studies must be able to rise to the challenge of providing a critique and a basis for intervention.[3] Furthermore, given the growing appreciation of the nature, scope and implications of ecological interdependence, cultural studies must respond to the political and ethical challenges which that recognition poses. Both of these tasks—intervening to counter the oppressive forces of the New Right and of the well-entrenched ecological indifference of late capitalism—require a sustained analysis and critique of the ethical assumptions from which cultural studies has operated and continues to operate.

This paper attempts to make explicit the dominant ethical assumptions that inform the research of cultural theorists, assumptions shaped largely by cultural studies' Marxist-humanist origins. We then chart the changes in these fundamental ethical commitments which emerge as cultural studies has responded to new theoretical and political conditions—most notably to structuralism, feminism, and postmodernism. The engagement with postmodernism is particularly significant precisely because postmodernism works to undercut the possibility of ethics and so to vitiate any effective interventionist project which cultural theorists might undertake. Ironically, it is just this concern for the impossibility of an ethics in postmodernism that has made the assessment of ethics and cultural studies so crucial and so urgently sought.

In generating this critique, we draw substantially on the conceptual resources of moral philosophy and, in particular, on material developed in contemporary debates over the adequacy of traditional ethics. Much of this has been initiated by recent work in environmental ethics, which has drawn attention to and questioned several of the largely implicit foundational assumptions on which much of ethics has been based.[4] Specifically, environmental ethicists have challenged the anthropocentric and atomistic nature of traditional moral theories. According to anthropocentrism, humans alone have moral standing; moral atomism is the belief that individuals and only individuals have moral standing.[5] As critics of anthropocentrism, environmental ethicists have argued for the recognition of the intrinsic value (and so the moral standing) of other-than-human entities. Many, moreover, are also critics of moral atomism, arguing for holism—the view that ultimate value is located in ecosystems rather than in the individuals who comprise them. The ecosystem replaces the individual as the fundamental moral datum, or unit of moral analysis, in terms of which we do our thinking about what is morally right and wrong.[6]

Our intent, in the discussion that follows, is to demonstrate that the anthropocentrism characteristic of the history of cultural studies is an inadequate and morally dubious construct, and to invite cultural theorists to rethink the normative bases of their theory and practice in terms of a non-anthropocentric alternative: an ecoculturalist perspective which acknowledges ecological interdependence and offers a basis for intervening to resist the instrumental reduction of the ecosystem, including both its human and non-human constituents. We maintain that to do so is consistent with the project of cultural studies and in many respects represents an extension rather than a rejection of its normative commitments. It is also a move for which cultural studies has been well prepared, given the persistent and dynamic tension throughout its history between atomism and holism (or in terms more commonly used in cultural studies, between individuals and the totality in which the individual is immersed). Moreover, the extension we suggest would open up the terrain for cultural studies to describe and intervene in one of the most pressing political, economic, and cultural issues of the late twentieth century: the relations between the human and other-than-human world.

NORMATIVE ASSUMPTIONS

That there are strong normative commitments at work in cultural studies becomes readily apparent with a little reflection on the nature of the project in which cultural theorists are engaged. According to a recent account of this project,

> Cultural Studies is concerned with describing and intervening in the ways discourses are produced within, inserted into and operate in the relations between people's everyday lives and the structures of the social formation so as to reproduce, resist and transform the existing structures of power. (Grossberg, 1988a p. 22)

Cultural theorists, consciously and emphatically, aim not merely to describe or explain contemporary cultural and social practices, but to change them, and more pointedly, to transform existing structures of power. The interventionist commitment is avowed and straightforward.[7] Not so straightforward perhaps is the destination. What lies at the end of such intervention? What kind of society inspires and motivates the project? In a somewhat "utopian" way, cultural studies carries with it a vision of a better, more just society. When the precise nature of this just society is discussed at all, it remains somewhat elusive.[8] More commonly, however, there is no explicit treatment of the nature of the just society, only an underlying assumption that it is a goal. A careful examination of those assumptions would undoubtedly reveal different—perhaps even contradictory—notions of what the just society would be, but that is outside the scope of our present argument.

While the exact nature of the destination is elusive, it is much easier to be confident about what is being moved away from. The project of cultural studies is grounded on a moral and political critique of late capitalism, and more generally of oppressive cultural and social formations. The dual commitment to description and intervention that characterizes cultural studies has assured that studies have described cultural sites where intervention is deemed to be either needed or actively taking place—for example, in the identification of *sites of resistance*. The identification of these sites as the objects of analysis, and the very designation of them as sites of *resistance*, involves basic ethical commitments which are themselves seldom acknowledged explicitly. Cultural studies advocates for the disenfranchised and has served as a voice for those individuals and groups who are variously seen as subjugated, silenced, repressed, oppressed, and discriminated against. It speaks not just for those "here," but for those "there," that is, for those anywhere without a voice in the dominant discourse and without a place in the dominant political and economic hierarchy.[9]

Such normative commitments direct research and practice that work to resist the treatment of individuals and groups as mere instruments, tools, or means to another's ends (be that "other" a system or an individual). It is the instrumental reduction of intrinsically valuable beings which is opposed, and which lies at the heart of the cultural theorists' critique of late capitalism. In short, the normative assumptions which have appeared to course their way (in however subterranean a manner) through the history of cultural studies may be described as follows: 1) that human beings—whether as a species or as individuals—are intrinsically valuable and enjoy moral standing, which must be respected and reflected in how they are treated; and 2) that oppressive social and political formations are objectionable and to be resisted to the extent that they are indifferent to this.[10]

These normative commitments are condensed in cultural studies' attention to processes of "empowerment." Although the term "empowerment" in its explicitly theorized form is relatively new, what it represents in terms of the motivations of cultural theory is not. Empowerment is the enablement of possibility. As Grossberg (1987a) defines it, empowerment is "the enablement of particular practices, that is ... the conditions of possibility that enable a particular practice or statement to exist in a specific social context and that enable people to live their lives in different ways" (p. 95). Cultural theorists recognize that even when people are not actively engaged in political struggles for power, they continue to make history in conditions that are not entirely of their own making. In other words, people are never entirely subordinated; there are always ways in which their practice is enabling, creative—opening up possibilities. Grossberg (1988b) emphasizes these two aspects of empowerment:

> Most cultural criticism focuses on culture's critical relation (negativity) to the dominant positions and ideologies. Politics becomes defined as resistance to or emancipation from an assumed reality; politics is measured by difference. But empowerment can also be positive; celebration, however much it ignores relations of domination, can be enabling. Opposition may be constituted by living, even momentarily, within alternative practices, structures, and spaces, even though they may take no notice of their relationship to existing systems of power. (p. 170)

To "disempower" a person or group has, then, two aspects: 1) to subordinate them in hierarchical relations of power and 2) to deny the inherent ability to construct alternative practices, structures, and spaces, despite degrees of subordination. The distinction is important to acknowledge for, besides resisting relations of subordination in structures of dominance, cultural theory resists the reduction of individuals and groups—even in how they are described—to the status of mere tool or instrument for another's (or a structure's) end.

The theoretical ground where these ethical commitments have been worked out is in the dynamic tension between the individual and the social (or totality), a tension in evidence throughout the history of cultural studies. This tension can be understood as the product of divergent views as to what constitutes the appropriate theoretical and empirical focus of cultural studies. Are cultural theorists concerned primarily with the ways in which individuals are inserted into social positions and their social, political, and cultural identities constructed? Or are they concerned primarily with the social, cultural, political, economic formations themselves, and in particular with the analysis of ideology, power, or hegemony in such formations? To the degree to which this question has been resolved in cultural studies, the answer appears to be "yes" to both— we have been and must continue to do both if we are to theorize adequately.

Martin Allor (1984; 1989) has drawn our attention to this issue of alternative problem orientation in cultural theorizing and of the need to see cultural studies as a research tradition whose scope is such that it requires and benefits from the existence of such theoretical diversity. Allor (1989) argues that cultural studies' very mode of inquiry has opened up two sets of questions that operate in different registers: 1) questions regarding "the ways in which the individual is inserted into social positions" and 2) questions regarding "the relations between social institutions and the more discursive levels of analysis of culture, semiosis, or ideology" (p. 1). The "culture" in cultural studies is the theoretical site where this tension between divergent problem contexts is worked out. As Allor states, culture "has come to designate a problematic of mediation which attempts to link, in an immanent system of analysis, practices of subject formation and the analysis of power or hegemony in the social formation" (p. 1). It is in this vacillation between what Allor (1984; 1989) has labeled the "sociological" and "productivist" pulls within cultural studies that we will trace the shifting historical commitments to different loci of value (or units of moral analysis) as cultural studies has gone on theorizing.

Although these normative assumptions and accompanying theoretical tensions can be traced throughout the evolution of cultural studies, they articulate differently in the various moments of that history given different theoretical exchanges and political and economic realities. These changes are reflected in the "slide" of the locus of value between individuals and the totality (the structure or the social formation). In the "culturalist" moment, the locus of intrinsic value resides primarily in the individual. In the "structuralist" moment, it shifts more to the totality (the structure or social formation). Finally, with postmodernism, the possibility of the locus of value residing in either subjects or structures is challenged.

Ethical Assumptions in Early Cultural Studies: Marxism, Humanism, and the Individual

In the earliest cultural studies, individuals are the locus of intrinsic value. Moreover, individual members of the working class (or the working class conceived of as an aggregate of individuals) are also the locus of moral value.[11] Greatly influenced by Marxist humanism, the early cultural theorists set out to "rescue" that group of individuals which had been disenfranchised and treated instrumentally in capitalist modes of production and were therefore denied their intrinsic identity, worth, and dignity. E. P. Thompson is particularly explicit about this interventionist strategy. He writes in the preface to *The Making of the English Working Class* (1966):

> I am seeking to rescue the poor stockinger, the Luddite cropper, the "obsolete" hand-loom weaver, the "utopian" artisan, and even the deluded follower of Joanna Southcott, from the enormous condescension of posterity. Their crafts and traditions may

have been dying. Their hostility to the new industrialism may have been backward-looking. Their communitarian ideals may have been fantasies. Their insurrectionary conspiracies may have been foolhardy. But they lived through these times of acute social disturbance, and we did not. Their aspirations were valid in terms of their own experience; and, if they were casualties of history, they remain, condemned in their own lives, as casualties. (p. 13)

Thompson recognizes the intrinsic value of those individuals who make up the working class and denies the appropriateness of a purely consequentialist assessment of their actions: "Our only criterion of judgment should not be whether or not a man's (sic) actions are justified in the light of subsequent evolution" (p. 13). For Thompson, the members of the working class should be treated, instead, as ends in themselves—both in political hierarchies and by theorists and historians. They are also the locus of moral value. One aspect of this project is forward-looking: in drawing attention to their moral worth we might find models to help us move toward the very ideals those individuals had struggled to realize:

> [I]t was a time in which the plebeian movement placed an exceptionally high valuation upon egalitarian and democratic values. . . . Causes which were lost in England might, in Asia or Africa, yet be won. (p. 13)

In another seminal work, *The Uses of Literacy* (1970), Richard Hoggart rails against the commercial popular culture that undermines the intrinsic value of the members of the working class (by eroding their culture) and effectively disempowers them. He describes mass-produced popular culture as "trivial entertainments" (p. 276) that "make it harder for people without an intellectual bent to become wise in their own way" (p. 276), and that "make their audience less likely to arrive at a wisdom derived from an inner, felt discrimination in their sense of people and their attitude to experience" (p. 277). While he is less influenced than Thompson by the Marxist sense of the working class subjugated economically by the capitalist class, Hoggart sees the "force of the assault" (p. 281) as one which disenfranchises the class and transforms it into a mass by stripping it of its unique identity. The process he fears is one in which the commercial culture reduces the members of the working class to instrumental standing—as consumers—in commercial relations of production. He writes, "we are moving towards the creation of a mass culture" in which "the remnants of what was at least in parts an urban culture 'of the people' are being destroyed," a culture which "is in some important ways less healthy than the often crude culture it is replacing" (pp. 23–24). And he fears that

> If the active minority continue to allow themselves too exclusively to think of immediate political and economic objectives, the pass will be sold, culturally, behind their backs. (p. 264)

However, for Hoggart, as with Thompson, the goal is also forward-looking. Hoggart clearly hopes that by describing in minute detail the culture of the working class (as *The Uses of Literacy* does) as well as the assault of commercial culture, we will begin to appreciate—and presumably work to preserve—the intrinsic value of members of the working class. After recognizing their intrinsic value, we are then expected to address the question of how to accomplish the task of preservation against the onslaught. This would include, Hoggart suggests, "questions about direct action in the present situation: for instance, as to the extent and nature of permissible official interference with cultural matters in a democracy" (p. 281).

Raymond Williams, perhaps the most acclaimed of the early cultural theorists, is particularly committed to the descriptive task of documenting the creative power of individuals to interpret their common experience and thereby change it. Williams (1958), in contrasting conceptions of culture and society, prioritizes culture, by which he means "a whole way of life, not only as a scale of integrity, but as a mode of interpreting all our common experience, and, in this new interpretation, changing it" (p. 18). Williams's emphasis is thus largely on individuals' inherent abilities to construct their own experience even though they do not originally find themselves in conditions of their own making. By prioritizing the creative process of individuals, Williams gives weight to the issue of the non-instrumental reduction of human beings rather than to the struggles of resistance in relations of power.

Williams is taken to task for this emphasis by E. P. Thompson (1961) in his review of *The Long Revolution*. Thompson calls for the emphasis on class conflict in a definition of culture as a "whole way of struggle" as opposed to Williams's "whole way of life." In terms of their ethical commitments, the difference between their positions is primarily a matter of the weight they give to—on the one hand—resisting the subordination of human beings in hierarchical relations of power and—on the other hand—celebrating the intrinsic, non-instrumental conception of those human beings. Williams's position is evident in his argument against using the term "mass" to describe individuals:

> If our purpose is art, education, the giving of information or opinion, our interpretation will be in terms of the rational and interested being. If, on the other hand, our purpose is manipulation—the persuasion of a large number of people to act, feel, think, know, in certain ways—the convenient formula will be that of the masses. (1958, p. 292)

Williams is also decidedly activist in his anti-instrumentalist orientation to the work of cultural description. In *The Long Revolution* (1965), Williams locates his theorizing squarely in the midst of a long, democratic revolution. He takes as his principal criterion that "people should govern themselves (the methods by which they do so being less important than this central fact) . . . and make their own decisions, without concession of this right to any particular group, nationality or class." With that as a measure, "it is evident," he continues, "that the democratic revolution is still at a very early stage" (p. 10). Both *Culture and Society* (1958) and *The Long Revolution* (1965) sustain a plea for a "participating democracy" in which the "individual is in fact the general process of our humanity" and in which "no one of us, and no group, is in a position to understand, let alone seek to control" (1965, p. 118).

As this brief treatment of Thompson, Hoggart, and Williams suggests, the ethical commitment most evident in these studies is that of resistance and opposition to the instrumental reduction of the human. Further, these early studies can be characterized as atomistic. Even when discussion proceeds in terms of the working class, the urban working class, or the people, these groups acquire their status as groups in a process whereby the whole (or totality) is conceived as an aggregate, the sum of individual, atomistic parts. Nowhere is this clearer than in Williams's description of the community of process, where the additive and collective process of individual experience and creativity make up the whole (which he calls culture):

> The individual creative description is part of the general process which creates conventions and institutions, through which the meanings that are valued by the community are shared and made active. This is the true significance of our modern definition of culture, which insists on this community of process. (1965, p. 55)

Thompson (1966) also betrays the commitment to atomism in his description of how a class comes into being:

And class happens when some men (sic), as a result of common experiences (inherited or shared), feel and articulate the identity of their interests as between themselves, and as against other men whose interests are different from (and usually opposed to) theirs. The class experience is largely determined by the productive relations into which men are born—or enter involuntarily. Class consciousness is the way in which these experiences are handled in cultural terms: embodied in traditions, value-systems, ideas, and institutional forms. (8–10)

As the above examples illustrate, the atomistic commitment is not unqualified. Even though in Williams the creative actor seems to be the exemplar of intrinsic worth and in Thompson what matters is what people (i.e., individuals) feel, experience, and share, both betray a counter (but less determining) tendency to consider that other register: the influence of structure on the individual. We deem the tendency still minor because the individual, not the structure, is clearly originary. In Williams, the community shares and activates what originates with the creative individual. In Thompson, class experience is only "largely" determined by the conditions within which one finds oneself; and class is only constructed when people share their common experiences.

Thus, in this early period of the development of cultural studies, the ethical commitment to the disenfranchised is directed largely to the working class as a group of atomistic individuals recognized as possessing intrinsic, non-instrumental value. The members of the working class are treated almost as a privileged subspecies within the human species, by virtue of their intrinsic value, subordinated status, and comparative moral worth. While in Williams the long revolution would bring democracy to all, it is still clearly the underclasses that have been disenfranchised and instrumentally reduced and thus deserve most attention.

In addition, we must draw attention to an obvious yet critical point: that the locus of value resides wholly in the *human* individual who is a member of the oppressed class. There is no consideration of the intrinsic value or moral standing of the non-human: either in terms of animals or the non-sentient environment. As will be evident, this silience persists, even as cultural studies differentiates the groups of individuals deserving particular ethical consideration and even as it shifts the locus of intrinsic value from the individual to the structures within which individuals are constructed.

From Class to Subculture, Gender, and Race: The Differentiation of the Locus of Value

If, as we suggest above, it is possible to characterize the working class as a sort of subspecies of the human species, then it is possible to characterize the next relevant theoretical move in cultural studies having ethical implications as one which recognizes the intrinsic worth of *other* human subspecies, differentiated according to different criteria (notably, subculture, gender, and race). Additionally, in redirecting the identification of the locus of value, or the unit of moral analysis, toward these "subspecies," a theoretical gap widens between the commitment to the celebration of the intrinsic value of individuals, individual experience and expression, and the commitment to resisting the oppressive social and political formations that exert domination over those individuals.

As cultural theorists became more "practiced" at analyzing cultural groups, "the working class," "class," or "the people" could not adequately account for the various identities of individuals or groups. Moreover, the differentiation of the working class, given conditions of increased affluence, the development of mass culture, and the emergence of new modes of consumption (e.g., "styles"), seemed to necessitate the separate treatment of various "subcultures" (Clark, et al, 1976). It is not that class disappears as a unit of analysis. On the contrary, class is still the lens through which the theorist understands the semiotic meaning of subcultural resistance. Subcultures are, however, considered to be doubly articulated: on the one hand they are manifestations of the need to express autonomy from their parent (working-class) culture; on the other hand they are maintaining their parent culture's opposition to the dominant culture. It was even found that often the forms of resistance enacted by working-class youths against the dominant and parent cultures assured that they would end up tied to the subordinated occupational roles that would keep them in their subordinated, working-class status (Willis, 1977).

The varieties of subcultural theorizing illustrate the commitment to the intrinsic worth of members of working-class subcultures. This is evident in the studies of groups and social behavior considered by the dominant culture to be "deviant." Cultural theorists dignify the subcultures and their members as, by their very nature, engaged in the fundamental work of any culture: the semiotic process of constructing meaning. Phil Cohen explains, for example, that

> Mods, rockers, skinheads, crombies, all represent in their different ways, an attempt to retrieve some of the socially cohesive elements destroyed in the parent culture, and to combine these with elements selected from other class fractions, symbolizing one or other of the options confronted. (quoted in Hall and Jefferson, 1976, p. 32)

In the process of the celebration of the intrinsic worth of groups otherwise vilified, there begins a subtle slide away from the concern for the working class as being disenfranchised politically toward the celebration of various "styles" of semiotic resistance to the "styles" of the parent and dominant cultures (Hall and Jefferson, 1976). In what is perhaps the most widely read of the subcultural studies, Dick Hebige's *Subculture* (1979), there is a significant move toward locating value in the semiotic struggle for possession of the sign, a move that is, as we will see, exacerbated in postmodernism. He explains the nature of the struggle thus:

> The struggle between different discourses, different definitions and meanings within ideology is therefore always, at the same time, a struggle within signification: a struggle for possession of the sign which extends to even the most mundane areas of everyday life. (p. 17)

The forms of resistance thus slide to the expressly semiotic; Hebdige uses Eco's phrase "semiotic guerrilla warfare" to describe forms of youth culture resistance (p. 105). To be empowered is to be "other," to be read as different by making the sign your own. What it means to be disenfranchised shifts accordingly: to be disempowered is to be "conventional," that is, to lose possession of the sign. Hebdige, not unlike Hoggart, insists on the intrinsic identity, worth, and dignity of those individuals who remain authentic, which is to say, uncorrupted by commercial mass culture. *Subculture* is as much a celebration of the authentic moments in postwar youth subcultures as it is an epitaph of their inevitable passing:

> Youth cultural styles may begin by issuing symbolic challenges, but they must inevitably end by establishing new sets of conventions; by creating new commodities, new industries or rejuvenating old ones (think of the boost punk must have given haberdashery!). (p. 96)

While Hebdige's approach represents a distinctive reorientation with respect to the locus of value in cultural studies, an even more fundamental reorientation emerges in the critique of those studies. Angela McRobbie's (1981) feminist critique of subcultural studies disrupted the rather orderly process of differentiation of the working class into component parts by asserting that gender is a significant and different organizing principle. McRobbie acknowledges that an important part of the subcultural literature has been "the ascription of a sense of dignity and purpose, an integrity and a rationale, to that section of youth commonly labeled 'animals' in the popular media" (p. 115). But she criticizes the subcultural theorists for not noticing a significant silence their work reproduces, specifically, that the very subcultures and subcultural styles they reveled in often reproduced the oppression of women and girls.

The feminist critique of subcultures draws attention to the fact that gender and gender discrimination cut across classes and subcultures. Thus, one cannot assume a simple homology between the working class (or working-class subcultures), social and political oppression, and the denial of intrinsic value. The disempowerment and instrumentalist reduction of women must be assessed and resisted wherever it is found. The problem for cultural studies becomes, not replacing gender oppression for class oppression as the basis of moral critique, but determining how gender *articulates to* class oppression as the basis of moral critique (Barrett, 1980).

Stuart Hall (1980b) takes a similar position regarding race. While he asserts that "racial structures cannot be understood adequately outside the framework of quite specific sets of economic relations," the problem is to explain "how the two are theoretically connected" (p. 308). Hall begins to develop his principle of articulation, in which different extra-economic social factors such as race are understood to play crucial roles in the reproduction of social formations and thereby in the reproduction of relations of dominance and subordination.

The process of differentiating the site of the working class as the focus of ethical concern is consequently disrupted in this subculturalist moment in cultural studies; the focus shifts to the articulation of a series of alternative ways of characterizing human beings and human experience—for example, class, gender, and race.[12] The theoretical diversity insisted on by the recognition of the effective roles of various articulating principles reflects an appreciation that class oppression is but one of many forms that disempowerment and the denial of intrinsic value may take. With this appreciation comes a growing commitment to emphasize the various respects in which such disempowerment and instrumentalist "rendering" of human beings remains partial and incomplete. The very nature of its incompleteness suggests that the theorist can intervene most effectively by encouraging the recognition and celebration of the many forms that resistance can assume.

While this recognition that the instrumentalist rendering of individuals is partial and incomplete opens up various sites of resistance and opposition, it also poses new problems for the cultural theorists who remain committed to resisting and transforming oppressive power structures which reach beyond single principles such as gender, race, and class. The challenge becomes to theorize the connections between gender, race, class, etc., that is, to analyze and critique the ways in which they are articulated. Recognizing that cultural studies cannot adequately ground its interventionist strategy by appealing to a *single* principle (class, gender, or race), cultural theorists begin to shift their concern to the articulating principles that *connect* gender, race, and class, principles in which relations of subordination and domination are entailed. Stuart Hall (1980b) explains:

> The unity formed by this combination or articulation, is always, necessarily, a "complex structure": a structure in which things are related, as much through their differences as through their similarities. This requires that the mechanisms which connect dissimilar features must be shown—since no "necessary correspondence" or expressive homology can be assumed as given. It also means—since the combination

> is a structure (an articulated combination) and not a random association—that there will be structured relations between the parts, i.e., relations of dominance and subordination. (p. 325)

It should be obvious that cultural theory is in some respects sliding here into its more "productivist" position. The fundamental moral datum becomes a unity of "structured relations" within which individuals are dominant and subordinant in various registers. This turn toward the structure (the unity or the totality) as the moral datum is heavily influenced by structuralism—in particular by the work of Claude Lévi-Strauss and Louis Althusser.

The Influence of Structuralism: The Move to the System as The Unit of Moral Analysis

Before the engagement with structuralism, the fundamental moral datum in cultural studies was the atomistically conceived individual who, in and through communication and common experience, joins with other individuals to become members of cultural or subcultural aggregates. The concomitant normative assumption during what Stuart Hall (1980a) designates as the "culturalist" moment of cultural studies is framed in terms of resistance and opposition to the instrumental reduction of human beings— severally and collectively[13]—by oppressive forces. While the concept of a totality (a system, a whole) not reducible to the sum of its parts is operative in early cultural studies, that totality is not originary. In speaking of the culturalist construal of the totality, Hall (1980a) says that such theorists

> have a particular way of understanding the totality—though it is with a small "t", concrete and historically determinate, uneven in its correspondences. They understand it "expressively." And since they constantly inflect the more traditional analysis towards the experiential level, or read the other structures and relations downwards from the vantage point of how they are "lived," they are properly (even if not adequately or fully) characterized as "culturalist" in their emphasis. (p. 64)

In his pivotal article, "Cultural Studies: Two Paradigms," Hall (1980a) contrasts the culturalist moment in cultural studies with the structuralisms that were increasingly challenging its formulations. Of particular importance to us here is the move from the grounding of culturalism in individual experience to the grounding of structuralism in a holistically conceived structure:

> Whereas, in "culturalism," experience was the ground—the terrain of "the lived"— where consciousness and conditions intersected, structuralism insisted that "experience" could not, by definition, be the ground of anything, since one could only "live" and experience one's conditions *in and through* the categories, classifications and frameworks of the culture. These categories, however, did not arise from or in experience: rather, experience was their "effect." The culturalists had defined the forms of consciousness and culture as collective. But they had stopped far short of the radical proposition that, in culture and in language, the subject was "spoken by" the categories of culture in which he/she thought, rather than "speaking them." These categories were, however, not merely collective rather than individual productions: they were *unconscious* structures. (p. 66)

Structuralism offers the radical proposition that individuals (and individual experiences) are "effects" rather than intrinsically valuable entities whose moral standing must be recognized and respected. In Althusser's (1970a; 1971a) "theoretical anti-humanism," it is unquestionably the structure that must be thought of as the primary moral datum, a structure which has the power to exert domination over human subjects who are, themselves, constituted in and by that structure. The subject (understood as that which is subjected by the structure) is "reproduced" in the process of living as it must: in ideology. Ideology and "ideological state apparatuses" might be morally assessed; but insofar as subjects merely reproduce the structure, there is no way that we can directly assess them. In its most extreme manifestations, structuralism reduces individuals to a purely instrumental status, from which they can never escape: even those who would "use ideology purely as a means of action, as a tool, find that they have been caught by it, implicated by it, just when they are using it and believe to be absolute masters of it" (Althusser, 1970a, p. 234).

The generative aspects of the cultural studies' engagement with structuralism derive from the latter's emphasis on the determinate conditions within which people make history and on the insistence of the complex interdependence of the totality ("a complexly structured whole"). Structuralism challenges the culturalist commitment to atomism. There are no essentially independent, atomistic individuals that *could* come together to form aggregates. There are only subjects who are "spoken" by the structure, and so no locus of value is *possible* other than a holistically construed structure.

Not suprisingly, cultural studies does not slide entirely into this position. At the extreme, structuralism's functionalist portrayal of subjects as wholly disempowered, their value definitively and unalterably reduced to the instrumental, leaves the cultural theorist's interventionist strategy an exercise in quixotic futility. Structuralism thereby also appears to acquiesce to the hegemony of the power structures that are in place, rather than to seek to transform them. As Hall (1980a, p. 70) points out, by lodging struggle "wholly at the level of 'the structure,' " there is *no* role for conscious ("subjective") processes on the part of individuals. This prompted an increased unease over the object of analysis in cultural theory, which in turn led to more pronounced divergence between culturalist-and structuralist-influenced studies, with some (like Hall) traversing the center.[14]

In some respects the move toward totality brings cultural studies into greater conceptual rapport with the holistic commitments of certain contemporary theories of environmental ethics. The latter are, however, grounded on the mutual interdependence of individuals within a totality, a concept which acknowledges the very effectivity of the individual that structuralism denies. Moreover, in structuralism, the understanding of totality is an anthropocentric one, confined to that of a *human* social totality. The effectivity and moral standing of the other-than-human fails to be addressed.

The Challenge from Postmodernisms: The Loss of Criteria For Moral Judgment

Before a settlement between cultural studies and structuralism had time to be worked out, and specifically before the concept of totality as a "unity which is constructed through the differences between, rather than the homology of, practices" (Hall, 1980a) could be worked out, cultural studies was running full tilt with (and against) various postmodernisms.[15] As various authors (Grossberg, 1986a; Chen, 1989) argue, there are both commonalities and differences between these traditions.

Although no clearly identifiable theoretical perspective has settled out as yet in the space between these two traditions, their commonalities suggest that this is likely to occur, while their differences suggest that it must. Some of these commonalities and differences have a significant bearing on our project here. Of particular importance is the shared assumption that people "are not passively manipulated, colonized zombies of the system, but rather, the actively struggling site of a politics in, if not of, everyday life" (Grossberg, 1986a, p. 72). Although the conception of that politics differs markedly, both perspectives are similarly committed to the belief that "the truth of theory can only be defined by its ability to intervene into, to give us a different and perhaps better ability to come to grips with, the relations that constitute its context" (Grossberg, 1986a, p. 72). Both, then, would seem to share an interventionist moment as well as a sense of the intrinsic value of human beings. However, it is crucial to recognize that there are several tendencies in postmodern theorizing that differ rather dramatically from cultural studies and have serious and disturbing implications for a politics and ethics. Three of these differences are identified by Hebdige (1986) as taking the form of "negations": of totalization, teleology, and utopia.

In rejecting teleology, postmodern theorists reject the idea of decidable origins or causes and with this, of directedness toward an end. As Hebdige points out, this is "sometimes evoked explicitly against the precepts of historical materialism: 'mode of production,' 'determination,' etc." (p. 84). But it is also used in arguing for the disappearance of the signified in relation to the signifier. It is Baudrillard's "simulacrum" or Lyotard's "sensorium" that comes to characterize the world: where the "unreal," "hyperreal," or "surface" is all that is (and therefore all that *matters*). There is no originary power in either the individual or the structure. Indeed, there really is no structure in the structuralist sense, merely fragments which may or may not be drawn into an ephemeral configuration. There is only power within discourse. "There is," as Hebdige puts it, "no space left to struggle over, to struggle from (or . . . to struggle towards)" (p. 86).

Having no space to struggle towards follows from (if we may be so bold as to point out the homology) postmodernism's anti-teleological position. With no ground from which to make judgment, how can one evision a structure or situation (utopia) in which power is held accountable and exercised according to some "acceptable" criteria? Postmodernists expressly reject the value and possibility of criteria for assessing the exercise of power, contending that any such criteria would be foundational.[16] Lyotard, in *Just Gaming* (Lyotard and Thebaud, 1985) acknowledges that we do and must judge, but insists that we "judge without criteria" (p. 14). He continues:

> We are dealing with judgments that are not regulated by categories. History itself provides no help in their formulation, at least not on the spot. For it to do so, one would have to presuppose that history proceeds by concepts, dialectically. Whereas it guides us only after the fact. . . . I judge. But if I am asked by what criteria do I judge, I will have no answer to give. (pp. 14–15)

The ability to judge is, for Lyotard, not a matter of the observance of non-arbitrary criteria. Rather, it is dependent on the power of the constitutive imagination that has the "power to invent criteria" (p. 17).

With power understood in a merely local sense, as in Foucault's (1980) microphysics of power, and the constitutive imagination as the only force behind the invention of moral criteria, postmodernism leaves us normatively adrift, thereby vitiating the possibility of a politics and an ethics that can motivate the interventionist moment of cultural studies. In a rather remarkable document, "The Bottom Line on Planet One," Hebdige (1987a) plays out the dilemma of human beings who try to live in or theorize such a world. We draw from it at some length to illustrate the depth of the challenge.

Hebdige imagines a mythical (postmodern) world where there is no subject behind appearances, no meaning, no history, and no classes. There is only the endless parade of simulacra. The "I" is illusion, the subject ceases to exist, and with it all judgment, values, meaning, politics, and subject-object oppositions. The implications for ethics in such a world are clear:

> [T]he People of the Post have set out to undermine the validity of the distinction between for instance, good and bad, legitimate and illegitimate, style and substance by challenging the authority of any distinction which is not alert to its own partial and provisional status and aware, too, of its own impermanence. This then is the project of the Post: to replace the dominant (Platonic) regime of meaning—that is, representation—by a radical anti-system which promotes the articulation of difference as an end in itself. (p. 43)

There can be no ethics that is not merely illusion and elusion, nor any recognition of the intrinsic value of human or other-than-human beings. The only end in itself is the ceaseless production and celebration of a radically relativized Difference.

Having posed this "Second World," however, Hebdige points out that no matter how diligently we may theorize it or attempt to live in it (in art, for example), the world of the Now, that "other" world (the "First" world, Planet One), the world of the subject, of judgment, of representation of the somethings beneath the appearances asserts itself. As he puts it,

> [W]ords like "love" and "hate" and "faith" and "history," "pain" and "joy," "passion" and "compassion"—the depth words drawn up like ghosts from a different dimension will always come back in the 11th hour to haunt the Second World and those who try to live there in the Now. This is not just pious sentiment. *It is, quite simply, in the very nature of the human project that those words and what they stand for will never go away.* (p. 48) (our emphasis)

Hebdige concludes by disassociating his own position from the "flat" surfaces of the Post. And he does this, we would like to point out, by appropriating as a metaphor for "depth" the round Earth:

> I shall go on reminding myself that this earth is round not flat, that there will never be an end to judgement, that the ghosts will go on gathering at the bitter line which separates truth from lies, justice from injustice, Chile, Biafra and all the other avoidable disasters from all of us, whose order is built upon their chaos. And that, I suppose, is the bottom line on Planet 1. (p. 48)

As Hebdige suggests, while we may visit or tour the Post, we cannot, we do not inhabit it. Rather, we move in and out of it as dominant regimes of truth (in this case Planet One) assert the unity of the subject beneath appearances (see also, Hebdige, 1985). The problem for cultural studies has been to incorporate the significance of sliding signifiers and disappearing signifieds without asserting that meaning no longer exists, without giving up a politics, without lapsing into a radical moral relativism, without abandoning the interventionist commitment which has motivated the research of cultural theorists. We submit that it is vital that cultural studies not ignore—but strive to explain—the relations of force that account for the reassertion of unity, the unity of the subject and the possibility of judgment, and that this can be done without giving up what structuralism has taught us to appreciate—difference—and what postmodernism has taught us to recognize—the effectivity of surfaces. We must find a way to theorize and judge in that elusive "unity in difference."

Hebdige also suggests that postmodernism attacks totalization. It is antagonistic to "those discourses which set out to address a transcendental Subject, to define an essential human nature, to prescribe a global human destiny or to proscribe (sic?) collective human goals" (1986, p. 81). In the desire to avoid those "humanist," "essentializing," "moralizing," "classical" positions, cultural theorists influenced by postmodernism have gone to great lengths to avoid discussing human nature, judgment, or even the concept of totality. The price paid has been serious. As Judith Williamson (1986) and Meaghan Morris (1990a) have argued, cultural theory has reveled in the celebration of the popular without articulating those practices to larger political positions. Consequently a tendency in contemporary cultural studies has been to abandon the commitment to struggle against oppressive social and political formations and to find and celebrate essentially semiotic "resistance" in virtually any manifestation of popular culture (for examples, see Williamson, 1986).

We respond to this trend with critical unease. If cultural studies abandons that terrain, it will be unable to articulate its project to the disempowered, to provide an alternative to the political and ethical domination of the New Right, to respond to the environmental devastation that threatens the very existence of *this* planet and its inhabitants, or to develop an understanding of the intrinsic value of the other-than-human. Again, we require a concept of totality that has been carefully thought through in terms of a "unity in difference." In such a totality, the subject need not be Transcendental, human nature need not be Essentialized, a global human Destiny need not be prescribed, and, certainly, collective human goals need not be proscribed. Totality does not in and of itself demand this.

What we would like to begin to argue, in the remainder of this paper, is that by engaging the debates developing in environmental ethics, cultural studies might enrich its conception of totality, remain faithful to—and extend the scope of—its normative interventionist commitments, and, finally, reinstate the value and possibility of an ethics and a politics. By addressing *this* planet and the effectivity of the human in it, we may be able to move beyond, and even to integrate, the "depths" and "surfaces" of Planets One *and* Two.

Toward an Ecocultural Alternative

We shall have to recognize that the fragmentations and dispersals that we're living through today require a new kind of integration and synthesis. We shall have to go beyond our bodies, beyond the pursuit of pleasure for its own sake and learn to cultivate instead a responsible yearning: a yearning out towards something more and something better than this and this place now. (Hebdige, 1985 p. 38)

We have argued that life in the Post is purchased at the cost of the possibility of an ethics and a compelling politics. The mesmerization with the play of surfaces, the enclosure within self-reflexive and self-distancing discourses, and the celebration of a radically relativized, iconized Difference threaten to vitiate the interventionist project in which cultural studies is engaged. There is evidence of a growing concern among cultural theorists, some of whom are struggling to speak about realms beyond the reach of representation, to move beyond the confines of the Post. Grossberg (1986a, p. 73), for example, argues that "discourses may not only have contradictory effects within the ideological, but . . . those ideological effects may themselves be placed within complex networks of other sorts of effects." And elsewhere:

> If not every meaning is a representation, and not every text has representational effects, it may also be true that texts may have effects other than meaning-effects, and meanings themselves may be involved in relations other than representational. That is, the connection between a particular cultural practice and its actual effects may be a complex multiplicity of lines or articulations. (Grossberg 1987b, pp. 36–37)

To articulate those connections *in discourse* is a characteristically *human* social struggle. As Stuart Hall (1986b) explains:

> An articulation is thus the form of the connection that *can* make a unity of two different elements, under certain conditions. It is a linkage which is not necessary, determined, absolute and essential for all time. You have to ask, under what circumstances *can* a connection be forged or made? So the so-called "unity" of a discourse is really the articulation of different, distinct elements which can be rearticulated in different ways because they have no necessary "belongingness." The unity which matters is a linkage between that articulated discourse and the social forces with which it can, under certain historical conditions, but need not necessarily, be connected. (p. 53)

The "distinct elements" may have "no necessary belongingness" in discourse. But there is at least one realm beyond discourse—the biotic—in which there *is* a necessary belongingness, an interconnectedness or interdependence which cultural studies must seek to articulate *to* and *within* its discourse. To understand the nature of that belongingness and to forge an ecocultural alternative, we might draw on conceptual resources currently being developed within environmental ethics.

With the rapid maturation of ecological science in this century there has come a pronounced change in the way in which biological reality is conceived. The model of an ecosystem[17] provides an ecological description of the natural environment based on the priority of integrated, differentiated wholes over their component parts, of relations over discrete, individual objects that are related. Expressly designed to serve as the field theory of modern biology, this model has altered our understanding of the natural environment. The natural environment is now seen as "more fluid and integrally patterned and less substantive and discrete than it had been previously represented ... An individual organism ... is, as it were, a momentary configuration, a local perturbation, in an energy flux or field" (Callicott, 1989, pp. 108–9). As biophysicist Harold Morowitz (1972) has described it, "viewed from the point of view of modern [ecology], each living thing is a dissipative structure, that is, it does not endure in and of itself but only as a result of the continual flow of energy in the system" (p. 156).

Theorizing in cultural studies might find constructs such as these fruitful and generative. An ecologically informed appreciation of the natural environment displaces atomism with a holism that acknowledges and respects the integrity of its constituent individuals. Such individuals are not discrete, independent entities bound by merely external relations. They are moments "in the biospherical net of intrinsic relations" (Naess, 1973 p. 98), internally related and vitally interdependent formations, "summations" of their "historically, adaptive relationship[s] to the environment" (Callicott, 1989, p. 110). The conception of one individual "necessarily involves the conception of others and so on, until the entire system is, in principle, implicated" (Callicott, 1989, p. 110). The totality or unity of things, ecologically portrayed, is not substantive and essential. Rather, the ecosphere "is a *structured, differentiated* whole. The multiplicity ... of living organisms ... retain, ultimately, their peculiar, if ephemeral, characters and identities. But they are systemically integrated and mutually defining. The wholes revealed by ecology ... are unified, not blankly unitary "(Callicott, 1989, p. 111). What is uniquely human (as well as other-than-human) can then be recognized and respected, including what is of particular concern to us here—that characteristic mode of human being in which life is conducted in discursive conditions not of our own making. These discursive conditions or articulations can assert interconnectedness (interdependence) or deny it. But on the level of the biotic, no denial of interdependence can conjure it out of existence, or succeed in making it "go away."

Ecological science, as we have seen, offers a theoretical model that embraces a holism while recognizing and respecting the integrity, uniqueness, and value of the constituent individuals whose relations of interdependence overdetermine the whole. It is crucial to appreciate this point. The interconnected nature of individuals within such a whole implies that the fate and well-being of each is not only bound up with, but has implications for, that of each of the others; the "other" is, in this sense then, never completely "other." The degree to which the constituent individuals are impacted by what happens to one—or several—among them, depends in large part on the types of relations which bind them to the affected individual(s). Moreover, an equally crucial point is that these relations or bonds—typically used to describe and differentiate (biotic) community membership—are not static or temporally fixed. An ecosystem is the site of evolving communities which must be diachronically appraised. The individuals participating in such communities play different and changing roles; at times their contributions may seem marginal, at other times central. If our ability to "fix" their synchronic importance to the well-being of the whole with any degree of confidence is currently questionable, it seems out of the question to suppose we can confidently assess their diachronic worth. The moral of this is a "preservative" one—to err on the side of caution whenever confronted with an issue of securing or enhancing the existence and well-being of participant individuals, that is, to respect their integrity and actual or potential worth.

We have emphasized these implications of the ecological model for a reason. Certain forms of environmental philosophy have been criticized—by those supportive of environmentalism as well as by those not—for either openly embracing or uneasily courting misanthropy, for threatening an environmental facism in which decisions regarding the continued existence and well-being of (human) individuals (and indeed of *homo sapiens*) are justified purely in terms of the contribution—positive or negative—of such individuals to the health and integrity of the ecosystem. We share the evident concern of philosophers like Tom Regan, William Aiken, and Baird Callicott to distance themselves from positions and implications such as these:

> Like political fascism, where "the good of the State" supercedes "the good of the individual," what holism gives us is a fascist understanding of the environment. (Regan, 1983, p. 372)

> [I]t would be difficult to defend saving humans at all. In fact massive human die backs would be good. Is it our duty to cause them? Is it our species' duty, relative to the whole, to eliminate 90 percent of our numbers? . . . This extreme eco-holism may not prescribe mass genocide or species suicide but it comes close. (Aiken, 1984, p. 269)

> The extent of misanthropy in modern environmentalism . . . may be taken as a measure of the degree to which it is biocentric. Edward Abbey in his enormously popular *Desert Solitaire* bluntly states that he would sooner shoot a man than a snake. (Callicott, 1989, p. 27)

Such positions amount in effect to an instrumentalist reduction of individuals, which become mere means to a holistic ends. It is important to realize, however, that not all forms of environmental holism are consistent with—much less do they endorse—such obviously unacceptable consequences. In fact, the metaphysical and ethical implications of the ecological model just sketched contradict the fascistic scenario. In his defense and sustained elaboration of Aldo Leopold's land ethic, Callicott has repeatedly emphasized this. Stressing the dangers of an "untempered holistic environmental ethic" and acknowledging "Leopold's narrative drift away from attention to *members* of the biotic community to the biotic *community per se*" (Callicott, 1986, pp. 409–410), he contends that "Leopold never intended the land ethic to have either inhumane or antihumanitarian implications or consequences . . . [these] would constitute a *reductio ad absurdum* of the whole land ethic enterprise and entrench and reinforce our current human chauvinism and moral alienation from nature." (Callicott, 1989, p. 92).

Callicott argues forcefully that the charge that such consequences follow from the land ethic reveals more about the theoretical presuppositions of the critics than it does about the land ethic which, he maintains, "is heir to a line of moral analysis different from that institutionalized in contemporary moral philosophy" (Callicott, 1989 p. 92). Drawing on Mary Midgley's concept of the nested community, Callicott (1989) demonstrates that the holism characteristic of the land ethic is a refined or "tempered" one:

> [O]ur recognition of the biotic community and our immersion in it does not imply that we do not also remain members of the human community . . . or that we are relieved of the attendant and correlative moral responsibilities of that membership, among them to respect universal human rights and uphold the principles of individual human worth and dignity. (p. 93)

As individuals we are embedded in numerous concentric communities, and in each of these we enter into and are bound by different sets of relations to other individuals—human and non-human—which carry with them attendant moral responsibilities.[18] The recognition that we are also part of the biotic community does not thereby override or cancel our membership in and responsibilities to these other communities: "Prior moral sensibilities and obligations attendant upon and correlative to prior strata of social involvement remain operative and preemptive" (Callicott, 1989, p. 93):

> Therefore, just as the existence of a global human community with its humanitarian ethic does not submerge and override smaller, more primitive human communities and their moral codes, neither does the newly discovered existence of a global biotic community and its land ethic submerge and override the global human community and its humanitarian ethics. To seriously propose, then, that to preserve the integrity, beauty, and stability of the biotic community we ought summarily to eliminate 90 percent of the current human population is . . . morally skewed. (Callicott, 1986, p. 411)

While Callicott's contributions to the elaboration of a viable land ethic have been extensive, there remains much to be done in the way of refinement and specification. We have hoped here to introduce cultural theorists to the general outlines of an environmental philosophy that seems amenable to the project of an ecoculturalism, and to which they may have a good deal to contribute. For example, in order to avoid an environmental fascism as well as to understand why it is that the left has been so ineffectual in affecting the moral basis of late capitalism, cultural theorists might benefit greatly by exploring the concept of nested communities. No group of theorists is more sensitive to the fascistic tendencies in the realization of "community" or to the multiple articulations of communities to which we all belong than cultural theorists. Thus, no group is more equipped to enter into this discourse to assure that the notion of nested communities be critically examined and articulated to an anti-fascist project. Furthermore, because we suspect that a conception of differing moral commitments at least partially modeled on that of a nested community is part of what gives the New Right some of its effectivity in popular morality, the task is all the more pressing.

What an ecoculturalist theoretical perspective suggests for cultural studies is an appreciation of the significance and of the sense in which human beings, and the social and political formations in which we are immersed, are *implicated*— in the etymological sense of being enfolded, involved, or engaged—in the environment (be it wilderness, rural, or urban). We are "implicated in and implied by" (Callicott, 1989, p. 101) the terrestrial environment, and are at once responsive to and responsible for our divergent ways of adapting ourselves to this habitat. Our effectivity as inhabitants must be addressed by cultural theorists. We must consider what can be learned from the recognition that among those "conditions not of our own making" is the fact that we are situated in a biotic community, a society of plants, animals, fluids, minerals, and gases. As the ecologist and environmentalist, Aldo Leopold (1949) has put it: "That land yields a cultural harvest is a fact long known but latterly often forgotten" (pp. viii, ix).

Another distinctive aspect of an ecocultural approach to cultural studies is the abandonment of anthropocentrism. In some ways, this might seem a rather more difficult proposal for cultural theorists to endorse, as it requires addressing issues that are quite new to cultural studies. In other ways, however, the proposed task is quite simple. It invites cultural theorists to expand the scope of their interventionist project, to extend their concern for instrumentally reduced and socially subjugated subjects beyond the exclusively human to the other-than-human, to intervene for the land (understood in Leopold's (1949, p. 204) inclusive sense, as embracing soils, waters, plants, and animals). We have argued that cultural studies has, throughout its history, been anthropocentric, and that there are new sites of resistance whose identification and description it is vital for us to address—sites for which new strategies of intervention must be forged and implemented. The implications of no longer seeing ourselves as masters of nature, but as members of a biotic community, have yet to be explored.

As we write this paper, we have been struck by the pressing importance, the final urgency of this task. The implications of biotic interdependence have asserted themselves repeatedly in contemporary discourses developing around the devastation of the environment: the recent events in the Amazon which have drawn a complex cast of peoples— rubber tappers, Indian tribal groups, rubber barons, ranchers, landowners, environmentalists, and first and third world politicians—into a struggle over the fate of the rain forest; the tragic consequences of oil exploration and development in the Arctic with the wreck of the Exxon *Valdez,* and the potential for similar environmental exploitation in the Arctic National Wildlife Refuge; an Oprah Winfrey program devoted to discussing the consequences of the "trade off" between jobs and chemical pollution in what is now called "cancer alley" along the Mississippi River from Baton Rouge to New Orleans; the designation as a Superfund cleanup site of Torch Lake outside our doors— necessitated by the dumping of copper mining slag nearly 100 years ago; the recent debates in *Zeta* and *The Nation* over whether or not the promotion of recycling merely aids in the smoother operation of capitalism and the eventual devastation of the environment. The evidence of the importance of this issue is staggering. But where is cultural studies if not struggling to extricate itself from the infinite loop of the representations of discourse on discourse?

Theoretical and empirical studies undertaken by cultural theorists responding to the challenge of developing a non-anthropocentric, holistic cultural theory will differ from previous efforts in a number of ways. The most obvious difference is that in analyzing a particular cultural phenomenon, we must also consider the way that the other-than-human articulates to it. This is what Gail Valaskakis (1989) comes close to in her analysis of the Chippewa's relationship to spearfishing in the Northwoods of Wisconsin. We say "close" in that Valaskakis points to the silences in the anthropological treatment of the relationship between Indians and spearfishing—silences that begin to open up the kinds of questions we propose here. We appeal to theorists to answer these heretofore unasked questions:

No one has asked about the confirmation of walking to hunt in woodlands ceded by the thumbprints of our grandfathers, or our romanticized image of Lac du Flambeau's "People of the Torch," stitched in ambiguity to Strawberry Island and Medicine Rock, Bert Sky and the Midewiwin. No one has asked about the impact of accidental deaths, of fighting, or family living in the city, the beer cans rusting in the water at Boy Scout Beach, or the traditional heritage of Flambeau's Christian churches. No one has asked about the maze of tribal membership and politics, the empowerment of inter-tribal process, or the social act of spearing with a formerly feuding cousin. No one has asked about the purpose represented in fifty years of the fish hatchery, or the practices through which "Flambeau currently is the center of winter spearing," or of the 33 out of 79 Wisconsin carvers in a book on fish decoys who are Flambeau Indians. . . . No one has asked about the *heritage*, experienced and imagined, Flambeau and foreign, tentative and transforming, from which we act. No one has asked who we are or what it signifies to hunt and spear through treaty rights. (Valaskakis, 1989, p. 16)

We *are* asking now. And we need to hear and wrestle with the answers: to understand the rich social, cultural, and political implications of the Flambeau engagement with the land; to appreciate the full importance and impact of this exercise of treaty rights within the existing power structures of the dominant culture; to intervene in and resist the oppressive, racist, and increasingly violent forces within the dominant culture agitating at the boat landings and demanding the abrogation of treaty rights;[19] finally to understand and intervene in the way in which the human social environment articulates to the other-than-human everywhere in order to rearticulate those relationships in noninstrumental and non-subjugated ways. Cultural theorists must analyze and reassess our commitments to profit, efficiency, progress, pleasure, and the popular with a sense of how they articulate to the other-than-human world.

Consequently, we also call for the study of the ways in which different cultures and different cultural groups relate and have related to the other-than-human world. One particularly fruitful way to understand these differences is to study indigenous cultures and their relations to the land in their various stages of engagement with colonizing cultures. Such research can enhance our sense of the varied possibilities for human relationships to the other-than-human world, and how these relationships may be altered by changes in social and political formations.[20] This is made tellingly evident in the emergence of the recent analytic methodology of "indigenism," grounded upon an appreciation of the significance of addressing the global dimension of an indigenous "Fourth" or "Host" World on the planet (inhabited by a diverse range of peoples).[21] According to this notion, the modern, industrialized world (or industrializing) States of the First, Second, and Third Worlds are seen as sitting squarely atop the "Host World" (Jaimes, 1987, p. 12). Annette Jaimes (1987) points out that the indigenous inhabitants of this Host World have two main things in common: 1) non-disruptive ways of relating to the habitat "at least to the extent that they allow for the perpetual coexistence of human and other organic life (a matter radically different from the environmental *pathos* of the other three worlds)," and 2) the shared experience of having been "conquered, colonized and ultimately encapsulated within one or another modern nation-state" (pp. 12–13).

We anticipate the reluctance of cultural theorists to enter this ecoculturalist terrain based on a fear that to reorient cultural studies thus would be to change its project. In response to such wariness, we urge reflection on the following points. Tolerance of diversity and the attendant proliferation of theoretical perspectives is essential—intellectually and politically—to the project in which cultural studies has been engaged. Moreover, given the contemporary concern for, and discussion of, environmental issues, together with cultural studies' commitment to describe, as well as to intervene in existing social and political formations, *failure* to develop an ecoculturalist perspective would seem to require explanation and defense. Finally, cultural studies has always initially resisted the challenges to rethink its project that have arisen—repeatedly—from outside its current modes of discourse. Yet, consistently and determinedly, it has remained a project committed to rethinking its project. This is what has kept cultural studies vibrant, alive, and responsive to the changing world we inhabit. And we hasten to add that if cultural studies does not enter this terrain, the New Right can be relied on to exploit both it and our hesitancy. Based on its already well-entrenched position in social, political, and ethical struggles, the New Right will likely try to impose a global environmental fascism, in which the mechanism of the marketplace alone would be allowed to settle the ethical question of how we should treat this planet and its inhabitants.[22] The stakes could not be any greater.

NOTES

1. We use the term "cultural theorist" to designate the practitioners of cultural studies, although not all cultural theorists do cultural studies.

2. Clarification of the nature of the distinction between politics and ethics is beyond the scope of this paper. We are concerned here with the ethical assumptions that inform cultural studies. We view ethical assumptions as informing politics, but we are not suggesting that politics can be reduced to ethics.

3. See Grossberg (1988a) and Stuart Hall (1983).

4. Other contemporary challenges to the dominant ethical tradition have arisen from feminism (see Gilligan [1982]), as well as from critics of analytic methodology (see MacIntyre [1984] and Bernard Williams [1985]). For an overview of traditional ethics see Rachels (1986), Frankena (1973), and Frankena and Granrose (1974).

5. To say that something has moral standing is not to attribute positive or negative moral worth to it, that is, to contend that it is morally good or bad. It simply indicates that the well-being or interests of the entity or entities in question must be positively weighed in deciding what it is morally permissible to do. If something does not have moral standing (because it is of merely instrumental value) then it will figure in our moral decision-making at best indirectly—that is, insofar as our treatment of it will affect the interests or well-being of those (intrinsically valuable) beings who do have moral standing. For qualification and elaboration, as well as for a useful introduction to the range of ethical concerns in environmental ethics, see Regan (1984) and VanDeVeer and Pierce (1986).

6. Influential arguments for the recognition of the moral standing of animals have been advanced by Midgley (1983), Regan (1983), and Singer (1975). The most notable advocate of holism is Callicott (1989). Feminists have also entered into these debates (see Warren [1987] and Zimmerman [1987]).

7. The dual commitment to description and intervention is evident even where the object of study has been defined differently. Compare, for example, R. Johnson (1986–1987) and Grossberg (1987a).

8. Such is the case, for example, with Raymond Williams's *The Long Revolution* (1965), in which the ideal democratic community is one based on a continual process of the production (i.e., communication) of shared values. It is difficult to imagine what such a community would look like and how it would operate in anything other than idealistic and abstract terms.

9. Of course this raises all the current arguments about whether one can or should speak for the other (see Spivak [1988] and Valaskakis [1988; 1989]).

10. The distinction between intrinsic and instrumental—or extrinsic—value is a fundamental one in moral philosophy. Things are valued extrinsically or instrumentally if they are valued as a means to an end. They are valued intrinsically if they are valued as ends in themselves, and not as mere means or instruments to some ends. Certain things are typically regarded as having no

more than instrumental value—money for instance. Happiness, health, life itself, peace, justice, and so forth are among things typically valued intrinsically, just for being the kinds of things they are and not because they are means to something else that we value.

Usually we value other human beings in both senses. What is important, according to the position expressed here, is that human beings not be treated as though they possessed *merely* instrumental value—for example, as no more than generators of surplus value. They must be recognized and respected as self-determining agents, entitled to determine their own destiny—however much they are also historically situated as well as politically, culturally, and socially "expressed" beings. Coercion and manipulation are classic examples of the instrumental reduction of intrinsically valuable beings, but more subtle hegemonic processes can accomplish instrumental reduction just as effectively—potentially more effectively (see Gramsci [1971]; see also S. Hall's [1986a] discussion of Gramsci).

11. By this we mean that they are regarded as having positive moral worth and as being worthy of emulation, especially as compared to the alternative presented by the bourgeois class.

12. Stuart Hall (1980b) argues for the use of race as an articulating principle. McRobbie (1981, p. 121) suggests the use of populism, leisure, and pleasure as articulating principles in relation to class, sex, and race.

13. However, as we have seen, this collective—the working class—is conceived as an aggregate of individuals.

14. The "structuralist" version is most evident in what has come to be called "screen theory," that is, the dominant theoretical orientation of articles published in *Screen* from about 1974 to 1980. E. P. Thompson's (1978) tirade against Althusser can be characterized as a "culturalist" backlash. Stuart Hall's (1983; 1985a) continued development of articulation theory theorizes a space between culturalism and structuralism.

15. See Chen (1989), Grossberg (1986a), Grossberg (1988a), Hebdige (1986), and Ross (1988b) for considerations of the varieties of, and relations between, postmodernism and cultural studies.

16. It is not clear that such criteria *must* be "foundational." Moreover, there is a difference between having doubts about the epistemological grounding of such criteria and denying their existence, which postmodernists often overlook—apparently supposing that the first implies the second.

17. The term "ecosystem" was first used in 1935 by Arthur Tansley, an ecologist at Oxford University.

18. Each of these, according to Callicott (1989, p. 55), "has a different structure and therefore different moral requirements." The "mixed" community is contained within the biotic community and includes pets and domestic animals. Members (human and animal) of our immediate family lie at the center, after which follow social groups, cities, townships, countries, the human community, and the biotic community. Cultural studies could certainly contribute to the understanding of the different ways that communities are constituted. The recent work in cultural studies on the "nomadic subject" might be helpful here. See, for example, Radway (1988) and Grossberg (1988c).

19. Members of groups such as PARR (Protect America's Rights and Resources) and Stop Treaty Abuse have turned out annually to throw stones and shout racial epithets at Ojibwe spearfishers in Wisconsin, bearing placards that proclaim "Save a Fish—Spear an Indian" and "Timber Niggers." During the 1989 season, explosives were found planted at one landing. Those interested in following this issue may wish to consult *News from Indian Country: The Journal,* a newspaper published on the Lac Courte Oreilles Reservation and *The Masinaigan,* the official publication of the Great Lakes Indian Fish and Wildlife Commission.

20. Works such as Chatwin's *The Songlines* (1987) can sensitize us to the need to explore these issues systematically.

21. As Annette Jaimes (1987) has noted, this range includes the Indians of North and South America, the Innuits and Samis of the Arctic Circle, the Maori of New Zealand and Koori of Australia, the Karins and Katchins of Burma, the Kurds of Persia, the Bedouins of the Sahara and onward, the Zulus and Bantus of southern Africa and many others.

22. For example, a recent (May 21, 1989) article in *The Milwaukee Journal,* titled "Environment Has a Price," discusses legislation currently being drafted by the White House which "would allow companies to buy and sell the right to pollute and thus let the market decide the cheapest way to contain smokestack emissions that cause acid rain."

32

Shakespeare, the Individual, and the Text[1]

PETER STALLYBRASS

In a famous passage of what has been his most influential essay, Louis Althusser (1971a) writes: "Ideology interpellates individuals as subjects" (p.160). That is, the function of ideology in Althusser's account is the positioning of the subject who is called upon ("hey, you there!") and who, in responding, cannot but occupy a space that has already been relationally defined. Etymologically, a subject is that which has been thrown under. In his *Dictionary*, Dr. Johnson draws upon an array of authorities to define the active verb, "to subject": "to put under (Pope)"; "to reduce to submission (Dryden)," "to enslave; to make obnoxious (Locke)"; "to make subservient (Milton)." And for the substantive, "the subject," Johnson's first definition is "one who lives under the dominion of another: opposed to *governour* (Shakespeare)." Within the extensive philosophical and psychoanalytical meditations upon the subject, it is usual to think of the subject within the subject/object dyad. What Althusser emphasizes, like Dr. Johnson, is the *political* trajectory of the word. To be a subject is to be subjected, to be under the dominion of a governor. For Johnson, both for historical and cultural reasons, such subjection is normal. His own dictionary suggests the hesitancy with which the bourgeois notion of the free political individual would challenge the monarchical subject. In Britain, that challenge has never been more than half-hearted. In France, as in the U.S., one is a citizen; in Britain, to my shame and anger, one is still a subject (see P. Smith, 1988, pp. xxxiii–xxxv). The rhetorical force of Althusser's formulation depends, of course, upon his insistence that "the individual," the imagined center of free consciousness and independent judgment, is still subjected, positioned within relations of domination and subordination. Yet Althusser's synchronic formulation masks a curious diachronic reversal. It would surely be more exact to say that within a capitalist mode of production, ideology interpellated, not the individual as a subject, but the *subject* as an *individual*. For the individual is not the simple given of bourgeois social formations. On the contrary, he/she is a laborious construction in the political defeat of absolutism, when political freedom is gained at the expense of the occlusion of economic dependence. To put it crudely: historically the subject *precedes* the individual.

My paper is an attempt to understand the significance of that order of precedence. In other words, it is an unfashionable exploration of origins. But my question is not primarily "When did the modern individual emerge?" but rather when and how was the specific signifier "individual" deployed in England in the seventeenth century, and how do our modern concepts of the individual meet resistance in the very places where we would expect them to be most applicable?

There are two particularly useful starting points for any inquiry into the "individual": the Oxford English Dictionary and Raymond Williams's *Keywords* (1976). Let me begin by quoting Williams's suggestive opening to his remarks on the individual:

> Individual originally meant indivisible. That now sounds like a paradox. "Individual"
> stresses a distinction from others; "indivisible" a necessary connection. The devel-
> opment of the modern meaning from the original meaning is a record in language
> of an extraordinary social and political history. (p. 133)

Perhaps the first point to note is the *absence* of the word "individual," even as meaning indivisible, until relatively late. Despite the variety of words in medieval Latin suggestive of "society" *(societas, communitas, corpus, universitas, multitudo, congregatio, collectio, coetus, collegium),* there was no word equivalent to "individual." The nearest term was probably *persona singularis,* although this was pretty much a technical scholastic term. A person was *civis,* a member of the *civitas,* one was *fidelis,* a member of the church; one was not an individual. Even stranger, perhaps, for us is the first recorded use of "individual," as an adjective, in c. 1425: "to the glorie of the hye and indyvyduall Trynyte" (OED A1). In this context, individual suggests not merely indivisibility but indivisibility among what one would normally assume, outside a theological context, to be different elements. "Individual" here implies a relation between parts, even though that relation is such that the division into parts is impossible. The trinity, although three in number, is one in substance.

After 1425, the OED does not record any new use of the term until 1597, when it records Hooker's use of the adverb, "individually": "How should that subsist solitarily by it selfe which hath no substance, but individually the very same whereby others subsist with it." Here again, "individually" seems to mean "indivisibly." Indeed, Hooker's very point is the impossibility of individual existence in the modern sense. For this passage, like the previous one, is about the Trinity, and thus about a relation between parts. As Hooker puts it, "The Persons of the Godhead, by reason of the unity of their substance, do as necessarily remain one within another, as they are of necessity to be distinguished one from another . . . And sith they all are but one God in number, one indivisible essence or substance, their distinction cannot possibly admit separation" (V. 1vi. 2). But that's it for the fifteenth and sixteenth centuries: one example of "individual" as an adjective, one example of the adverb "individually." And then in the seventeenth century there's an extraordinary explosion of the term: "dividual" recorded in 1598; four more main definitions of "individual" as an adjective in the early seventeenth century (1605, 1613, 1623, 1646), and no new definitions at all after that; four main definitions of "individual" as a substantive, all from the seventeenth century (1605, 1626, 1627, 1655); three definitions of "individuality" (1614, 1645, 1658), and only two new headings after that; two definitions of "individualize" (1637, 1656) and only one later heading; three new definitions of "individually" (1624, 1641, 1660), and none after that. The only important new developments of the term given in the dictionary are "individualism" (1835), "individualist" (1840), "individualistic" (1874).

Of course, the principles of categorization of the O.E.D. are questionable. Why, for instance are the biological (1776) and the botanical and zoological (1859) definitions of the "individual" included only under subheadings? Do some of the categories construct a spurious continuity between the seventeenth century and the moment of the dictionary's production? As David Kastan has suggested, does the O.E.D. pay sufficient attention to legal records? Still, two remarkable features of the term "individual" are apparent: first, the concept is an extremely specialized theological one prior to the seventeenth century; second, during the course of the seventeenth century, the meanings of the concept seem to be *inverted:* from meaning an indistinguishable relation between parts, the "individual" comes to signify the separation of the part from the whole and, indeed, the possibility of contemplating a person in and of her or him self. But what I hope to show is that the relation between these two significations is less a temporal one of gradual evolution than an active struggle over definition. If we refuse, for a moment, to read the history of the term from the perspective of the victorious definition, one peculiar fact is apparent: namely, that with the exception of the specifically Trinitarian use of the term, the uses of "individual" suggesting indivisibility and those suggesting divisibility emerge *together*.

The O.E.D. gives the first instance of "individual" as a substantive, meaning "a single object or thing," as 1605; it gives the first use of the substantive to mean the *inseparabilty* of two things as 1627. Or take the definition of the individual as "a single human being, as opposed to Society, the Family, etc." The O.E.D. gives the first example of this meaning in 1626; its second, which I quote, is from 1641: "Peace . . . is the very supporter of Individualls, Families, Churches, Commonwealths." On the other hand, the first use of the phrase "individual society" (i.e., a society that is indivisible) is, as far as I know, by Milton in his 1645 divorce tract, *Tetrachordon* (Milton, 1931, p. 107). "Individual," in other words, is used simultaneously in the seventeenth century in nearly opposite ways.

But I want to approach this problem indirectly, and I shall do so by looking at an author who, if the concordances are to be believed, never once uses the word "individual." I mean Shakespeare. The absence is, perhaps, not surprising. He did not have much to say about the Trinity, and the new meanings of "individual," either as a separate entity or as an inseparable relation, were only being forged in the first decades of the seventeenth century, just as Shakespeare was ceasing to write. And yet, by the nineteenth century, and even before, Shakespeare was taken to be the very definer of individuality through his dramatic characters. That makes it all the more curious that the one example of the word "individual" in a text bearing Shakespeare's name is not only unrecorded in the concordances, but was erased by textual scholars from 1750 on. (I am deeply indebted to Jeff Masten both for drawing my attention to this, and for sharing his research on the topic with me.) Emilia, recalling her past friendship with Flavina, argues that "the true love tweene Mayde, and mayde, may be/ More then in sex individuall." The passage is from *The Two Noble Kinsmen,* printed in 1634 with a title page that declares it was "presented at the Blackfriers by the Kings Majesties servants, with great applause: Written by the memorable Worthies of their time; Mr. John Fletcher, and Mr. William Shakspeare. Gent."

I will return to the question of emendation in a moment. But we may note first that the question that scholars have asked even prior to emendation is the question of who wrote the passage. Failing any simple answer to that question, the play was usually excluded from the canon of Shakespeare's works. It first appeared in a collected edition of Shakespeare at the end of Charles Knight's *Pictorial Edition* (1839–41), where it is included amongst the doubtful plays. It also appeared in William Gilmore Simms's *A Supplement to the Plays of William Shakespeare* (n.d.) and in C. F. Tucker Brooke's *The Shakespeare Apocrypha* (1908). Alexander Dyce, who at first denied Shakespeare any hand in the play, included it in his edition of *The Works of Beaumont and Fletcher* (1854) but he later changed his mind and scrupulously edited it for his edition of *The Works of William Shakespeare* (1876).

The dominant editorial problem of *The Two Noble Kinsmen,* then, has been the problem of *individual authorship.* As Margreta de Grazia has brilliantly demonstrated, it was not until Edmund Malone's edition of 1790 that the modern notion of Shakespeare as an "individual author" was constructed (de Grazia, 1990b). Here, for the first time, was the full apparatus of documentary biography, comparison and analyses of the portraits, plays arranged in chronological rather than generic order, an obsessive concern to differentiate the "authentic" Shakespeare from any corruptions or collaborations. And, as de Grazia also shows, it was this individualizing endeavour which spawned as its corollary the first serious attempts to forge specimens of Shakespeare's handwriting, authenticating documents, early emendations, and testimonies of his life. The more rigorous the attempt to raise the individual author above the imagined contaminations of history, the more plausible and convincing forgeries were absorbed into the text and the textual apparatus. The whole function of Malone's enterprise, we might say, was to undo the conditions of theatrical writing in Renaissance England and to replace them with an exact notion of authorial ownership.

It is for that very reason that Malone is so important. For he illuminates with peculiar force the connections as they emerged between authorship and individuality. The individuality of the text came in turn to rest upon the individuality of the author. It was suddenly of crucial importance that *Shakespeare* was the author: or Bacon, or Oxford, or Southampton. Yet Malone was also the most important founder of modern textual scholarship. He knew an immense amount about the conditions of the theater, book publishing and book selling, and so on; he cared about documentary evidence. But, like most modern editors, he saw the evidence as the shadowy trace of the authorial origin which he pursued. That is, he saw the documents as corrupt traces which needed to be reinscribed in accordance with the author's "intentions," and so, in a sense, he didn't *see* the documents at all. For what "Shakespeare's" early texts suggest—and now we need to put Shakespeare in quotes—is precisely the absence of individual authorship, if we mean by "individual" "peculiar to a single person" (O.E.D. 5) and "distinguished from others by attributes of its own" (O.E.D. 4). I want, indeed, to suggest the there is a close connection between the ability to imagine the individual in its modern shape and the ability to imagine the author.

How and when, then, is Shakespeare's authorship constructed? Prior to 1600, of eight first quartos now attributed to Shakespeare, only one bears his name, and even then in a peculiarly ambiguous fashion. In 1598, "A Pleasant Conceited Comedie called Loves labors lost" was printed, "newly corrected and augmented by W. Shakespere." The play was reprinted in the first Folio and has been generally accepted as Shakespeare's. And yet the title page makes no claim for Shakespeare's authorship. Rather, it suggests his role as a refashioner of other's material: he is not "author," but correcter and augmenter. And even these roles take secondary place, both in terms of the layout and the size of typeface, to an occasion of the play's performance: "As it was presented before her Highnes this last Christmas." In none of the other early quartos is Shakespeare's name even mentioned.

We may note what *is* worthy of mention. First, and invariably, the place of publication, the name of the printer, and where the book shall be sold. Second, the name of the acting company, which occurs in five of the eight quartos, sometimes proclaiming that it was "sundrie times" acted, sometimes emphasizing that it was played "publiquely," sometimes assuring the reader that the play met "with great applause." Third, in three quartos, including the only two apart from *Love's Labor's Lost* which do not mention the acting company, an extension of the play's title to describe particular actions in the play. Indeed, in these cases the plays can scarcely be said to have "individual titles" even, since there is no clear way, either typographical or grammatical, to distinguish title from description. What is now called *3 Henry VI* has on the quarto title page: "The true Tragedie of Richard Duke of Yorke, and the death of good King Henrie the Sixt, with the whole contention betweene the two Houses Lancaster and Yorke." The modern title, following the Folio published after Shakespeare's death, selects out of this array the name of Henry VI, despite the fact that the "Tragedie" is claimed as being that of Richard, Duke of York. In fact, this occlusion of the "Tragedie" is no more arbitrary than its usual privileging in modern texts, since "tragedy" has little honorific value in these title pages. Look, for instance, at the title page of what is now called *2 Henry VI.* "The First part of the Contention betwixt the two famous Houses of Yorke and Lancaster, with the death of the good Duke Humphrey: And the banishment and death of the Duke of Suffolke, and the Tragicall end of the proud Cardinall of Winchester, with the notable Rebellion of Jack Cade: And the Duke of Yorkes first claime unto the Crowne." Here, "tragedy" makes a belated appearance in reference to the cardinal, and it is subordinated to the "contention" of houses and to the "deaths" of two dukes. We can see, then, that the notion of an "individual" author, and even at times of a specific title, are absent from the early quartos. What is emphasized instead is the apparatus of printing and selling and the performance of the text by a particular acting company.

The assumption, in other words, that "the authority of a text derives from the author" is, as Stephen Orgel (1981) says, "almost never true" in the case of Renaissance dramatic texts. The early quarto title pages reflect the fact that, and I quote Orgel again,

> a play was a collaborative process, with the author by no means at the center of the collaboration. The company commissioned the play, usually stipulated the subject, often provided the plot, often parcelled it out, scene by scene, to several playwrights. The text thus produced was a working model, which the company then revised as seemed appropriate. The author had little or no say in these revisions: the text belonged to the company, and the authority represented by the text—I am talking about the *performing* text—is that of the company, the owners, not that of the playwright, the author. (p. 3)

Collaboration, then, both in the broad and the narrow sense, was the norm rather than the exception. In Renaissance terms, there's nothing *peculiar* about *The Two Noble Kinsmen;* on the contrary, what needs explaining is the emergence of Shakespeare as individual author.

If that emergence was largely the work of eighteenth- and nineteenth-century editors, though, there were important preconditions for their taking Shakespeare as the very model of the "individual author." Because he was in the unusual position of being an actor and a shareholder in his own company, he had an unusually full role in the collaborative process: he would have economic interests in the choosing of a topic, in the theatrical revisions, and so on. And many of the works on which he collaborated were undoubtedly successful, which may account for the appearance of his name on the title pages of 10 out of 11 of the first quartos published between 1600 and the publication of the first Folio in 1623. The author's name is still usually subordinated, both in terms of layout and in terms of type-size, to the acting company. The one notable exception is the 1608 *King Lear,* where the title page blazons the dramatist's name:

M. William Shak-speare:
HIS
True Chronicle Historie of the life and
death of King LEAR and his three
Daughters

This might be taken as evidence that either the author or the printer recognized this as a masterwork. If that was the case, it would be a particularly damaging fact against my argument. But the probable explanation of the *Lear* title page has little to do with the sudden arrival of the "author" in his most heroic form. More mundanely, the printer needed to sell *this* play without it being mistaken for the *Leir* which had been published just three years previously in 1605, with a title page that declared:

THE
True Chronicle Hi-
story of King Leir, and his three
daughters, Gonorill, Ragan,
and Cordella.

(Note that both *Leir* and the quarto *Lear* are "true chronicle histories," unlike the folio *Lear* which is a tragedy.)

The *Lear* title page remained a rather extraordinary aberration. In the quarto of *Troilus and Cressida,* published the following year, the name "William Shakespeare" is set in the smallest type on the whole page, as if to deflate any grand pretensions to authorship. But there could be no deflation because there were no pretensions. These title pages sometimes declare a writer, a correcter, an augmenter; they do not declare an author.

The *problem* of the *The Two Noble Kinsmen* only emerges as such when authorship becomes the determining category. Undoubtedly, the first Folio had much to do with that, establishing as it did both a notion of the author (although a very different one from Malone's) and of his canon. In that canon, *The Two Noble Kinsmen* was not included. It was later added to the canon (or rather, to some versions of the canon) only after the probable collaboration between Shakespeare and Fletcher had been undone, and specific portions of the play assigned to each author. The techniques they used to make their distinctions were surprisingly sophisticated, depending upon the quantification of particular metrical effects supposedly peculiar to each author (Fletcher making frequent use of end-stopped lines and lines with "double endings"), and those techniques are still the main basis of differentiation in Eugene Waith's Oxford edition (1989), the play's most recent edition. From the nineteenth century, most editors assigned almost the whole of the first and the last acts to Shakespeare. "Sex individual" thus belonged to "Shakespeare."

What followed was the employment of the second kind of editorial skill: the determining of what Shakespeare *really* wrote, which could only be deciphered beneath the corrupt text in front of the editor. And now "sex individual" disappears again. Let me quote first the Quarto passage at some length, followed by its "correction":

> her affections (pretty
> Though happely, her careles, were, I followed
> For my most serious decking, had mine eare
> Stolne some new aire, or at adventure humd on
> From misicall Coynadge, why it was a note
> Whereon her spirits would sojourne (rather dwell on)
> And sing it in her slumbers; This rehearsall
> (Which fury-innocent wots well) comes in
> Like old Importments bastard, has this end,
> That the true love tweene Mayde, and mayde, may be
> More then in sex individuall. (1. 3, p. 14)

Now here's the 1989 Oxford version:

> her affections—pretty,
> Though happily her careless wear—I followed
> For my most serious decking; had mine ear
> Stol'n some new air, or at adventure hummed one

From musical coinage, why, it was a note
Whereon her spirits would sojourn—rather dwell on—
And sing it in her slumbers. This rehearsal—
Which seely innocence wots well, comes in
Like old importment's bastard—has this end
That the true love 'tween maid and maid may be
More than in sex dividual. (1.3.72–82)

"Sex dividual" is only one of many changes that Waith has made and before looking at that I shall look at some of his other emendations. Let me begin with what is perhaps the most striking emendation. What are we to make of the extraordinary rewriting of "fury-innocent" as "seely innocence"? Here, it seems, we have the long-standing tradition of editorial emendation with a vengeance. The emendation is the more interesting because it has nothing to do with the particular virtues and vices of Waith's edition. It was Charles Lamb in *Specimens of English Dramatic Poets* who first emended "fury-innocent" to "every innocent" and the great majority of editors have followed Lamb. The change from "fury" to "every" would have required the mistran-scription of a single letter if, as was common, the spelling of the manuscript was "eury." But Waith has this to say: "Lamb's emendation makes sense of the incomprehensible "fury-innocent," though, as the Oxford editor says, "it is difficult to explain how an initial *e* could have been read as an *f*." The Oxford edition, then, transforms "fury-innocent" into "seely innocence" on the "assumption of the easier misreading of "sely" (a common spelling of "seely") as "fury," confusion of long *s* with *f*, *e* with *u*, and *l* with *r* being fairly common. If the manuscript read "innocenc," the final *c* could have been taken for a *t*. Thus, from Lamb's changing of a single letter, we have moved to the invention of *four* new letters. O brave new world, where inventions arise so fast and freely! But why did Lamb make the emendation in the first place? Because, we are told, "fury-innocent" is incomprehensible. Now Lamb, at least, could plead that he did not have the use of the (indispensable, however problematic) O.E.D. There, we find the first definition of "fury" as "fierce passion, disorder or tumult of mind approaching madness." The fact that the word is used *especially* of anger or rage does not mean that it is used *exclusively* so. And, indeed, any Renaissance scholar who is aware of the influence of Plato will be familiar with the concepts of poetic fury and the fury of love. Do we need to recall that in 1591, John Harington had translated *Orlando Furioso*? Orlando is *furioso*, not "furious" in the modern sense but mad with love. Certainly, Emilia is not *angry*. But she is describing her passionate love for Flavina. "Fury-innocent": Emilia's love for Flavina is an innocent passion. What is "incomprehensible" here?

But having eliminated passion from "fury-innocent" the editors *reintroduce* it in the very next line. Emilia's "rehearsall" (as innocent passion knows well) "comes in/ Like old Importments bastard." Waith's reading takes "importment," which usually means "significance," in the sense of the French *emportement*, "passion." The return of the repressed. Passion reappears in French disguise. Now I have no quarrel with this ingenious reading. I *do* quarrel with the erasure of "significance." For if the rehearsal of Emilia's tale is the illegitimate progeny of her passion, it also displaces the passion's significance. Love and grief are now *staged*.

Yet this emendation has perhaps less to tell us about the immense gap between our presuppositions about the authorial work and the Renaissance text that confronts us than changes that appear more minor. My point is not to criticize a particular editor nor, indeed, to reject the practice of modernization which may perhaps be a practical necessity. What I now want to suggest, though, is that modernization as all editors have practiced it depends upon a notion of the *individual word* that is quite foreign to most early seventeenth-century texts. In such texts, where there is no standardized orthography or prescribed definition, words bleed into each other, so that there is no simple rule whereby one can tell one word from another.

Paradoxically, the very notion of the pun, and the supposition of Shakespeare's fondness for them, has obscured the orthographic conditions of writing, as Margreta de Grazia has finely demonstrated (1990a). For the notion of a pun suggests a specific disorder in a field of order. It is not surprising, then, that the word "pun" came into use as orthography was being standardized. Its first use recorded by the O.E.D. is in 1662, and most of the early uses are derogatory. In 1670 Eachard inquired "whether or no punning . . . might not be very conveniently omitted"; and in *The Dunciad,* Pope notoriously quoted a "great Critick" as saying "he that would pun would pick a Pocket" (1.63, note). But even when puns have been praised, as they increasingly have in recent years (witness, for instance, Jonathan Culler's [1988] fascinating collection, *On Puns*), they have usually been localized so as to occlude the more general conditions of writing in the Renaissance.

I can perhaps clarify those conditions, and illuminate the problem of defining the "individual word" by looking at the passage above. Apart from the obvious changes, there are also several smaller ones duly noted by the editor. Emilia, having "stol'n some new air," "hummed one," in Waith's reading. In the Quarto, Emilia "humd on." Is Waith justified in his emendation? But the problem, I suggest, is that when an orthography is unfixed, it is at times hard to *even know* when an emendation is being made. For a modern editor, the word is either "on" or "one." In the early seventeenth century, the spellings could be used interchangeably. It was certainly occasional for "on" to be written "one," but one still finds many instances of it up to the mid-seventeenth century. Bernard Beckerman (1989) for instance, notes the opening direction for the Plot for *The Seven Deadly Sins,* which reads: "A tent being plast *one* the stage for Henry the sixt he in it A sleepe," p. 116). And in *The Miseries of Inforst Mariage* (1607), a young man is praised by his guardian as "*one* whom older looke upon, as *one* a booke" (B2v). Similarly, in the *Staffordshire Quarter Sessions Rolls,* an accused man is said to have "ridde *one* a bay mare" (Burne, 1933, p. 243). Before the standardization of orthography, there was an extraordinary variety of forms for what we would now spell "one": "an," "en," "ane," "on," "oon," "owne," "won," "wone," "woon," "wan," and so on. "One" was not one but many. Most of those many were already obsolete by the seventeenth century and others were beginning to be marginalized as dialect forms. And yet, there was no one local habitation for "one." In 1648, Gage writes of its being about "on or two of the clocke"—the particular orthographical form which Waith turns into a problem.

Let me take a more extended example of the adventures of "one" from George Puttenham's *The Arte of English Poesie* (1589 [1970]). Puttenham, exemplifying the rhetorical figure of *Traductio,* or the Translator" gives his own version of a passage from Persius:

> Thou weenest thy wit nought worth if other weet it not
> As wel as thou thy selfe, but o thing well I wot,
> Who so in earnest weenes, he doth in mine advise,
> Shew himselfe witlesse, or more wittie than wise.

> Here ye see how in the former rime this word life is translaced into live, living, lively, livelode: and in the latter rime this word wit is translated into weete, weene, wotte, witlesse, witty and wise: which all come from one originall. (pp. 213–14)

What Puttenham means by translacing is a running play with the morphological forms of a single etymological root; yet his passage is also a kind of orthographical translacing:

"o"/"one"; "weet"/"weete"; "wot"/"wotte"; "witty"/"wittie"; "translaced"/"translated." The very concept of "one originall" with which Puttenham concludes is opened up by the orthographical play. The task of Redcrosse Knight in *The Faerie Queene* was to distinguish Una from Duessa. But how is one to do this when a text like Puttenham's bifurcates Una into "o" and "one"? It is perhaps only in Latin, a prestige language fantasized as stable, that Spenser can imagine "Una" as "one." "Una" is always "una"; "one" is not always "one." In *The Faerie Queene,* a Latinate fantasy of fixed meaning is forced to submit to the orthographic play of the vernacular. This play of language is perhaps the more unsettling for us, though, in that it does not, like the pun, seem to have any settled semantic implications. It disturbs *our* notions of sense without suggesting any alternative. The orthographical conditions of Renaissance writing leave the modern editor with impossible decisions, for either to emend or not to emend is still to translate into our orthography. "Hummed on"/"hummed one": either reading resolves in the modern text what cannot be resolved in the Renaissance text. Either fixes the shape of an individual word which did not exist in the early seventeenth century. And even a fascimile does not solve the problem, because for the modern reader *one* spelling will appear as the dominant form with the other spellings appearing as deviations from a given norm. In the Renaissance text, no such norm is given. Then, words bled into each other.

Some other examples of modern editorial "correction" may further suggest the magnitude of the labor by which a Renaissance book is transformed into a modern text. In the passage above, Waith transcribes "happely" as "happily," and yet, being a conscientious editor, he notes that one might also transcribe the word as "haply" ("by chance"). What he does not note (no doubt because it would be laborious to do it for line after line of the play) is that "haply" and "happily" were both frequently written "happely," with, as the O.E.D. notes, definite semantic effects: namely, that to meet haply might be assumed, without evidence to the contrary, to meet happily. One might also note Waith's emendation of "were" to "wear." As far as I know, there are no other examples in the Shakespearean canon of "wear" printed as "were," and yet *The Canterbury Tales,* the source for the play, almost invariably have "were" where a modernizer would write "wear." On the other hand, we also find in the Renaissance "wear" where a modernizer would write "were": "Item wheare theare *weare* certen swyne stollen by a boye . . ." (Burne, 1933, p. 103).

In my analysis of these editorial emendations, I do not wish to advocate one particular reading over another. Rather, I want to suggest the inadequacy of our own terms (pun, word-play, and so on) to examine the constant *conflation of signifiers* that characterizes Renaissance texts. I am also arguing that, as the Shakespearean "author" is a backwards projection, so too is the notion of the "individual words" which for the modern editor constitute an authentic text.

Let me try to summarize my argument so far. We have still to examine the range of meanings of "individual" in the seventeenth century, but what we have suggested is that precisely those areas where a modern editor attempts to establish the elementary units of textual organization—the individual author, the individual word—the Renaissance dramatic text is most resistant. Instead of a single author, we have a network of collaborative relations, normally between two or more writers, between writers and acting companies, between acting companies and printers, between compositors and proofreaders, between printers and censors. There is no single moment of the "individual text" which is why so many of the plays we read come to us in a variety of forms depending upon different collaborative relations: whether an earlier play has been rewritten for a later performance (often by new writers), whether the actors have partially or radically transformed the script, whether a writer has added new scenes for the printed copy, whether a text has been censored. Hence, perhaps, the difficulty—or should we rather say the absurdity?—which the modern notion of the "individual" would present to a Renaissance dramatist.

Yet, as we have noted, the word occurs in *The Two Noble Kinsmen,* in a play that is named as collaborative and where, therefore, the individual "ownership" of the word, even if ownership could be said to belong to the writer, cannot be determined. What are we to make of the word and how are we to explain the fact that the great majority of editors have followed Thomas Seward's 1750 emendation of "individual" to "dividual" in his *The Works of Mr. Francis Beaumont and Mr. John Fletcher?* The most striking aspect of this emendation is the total failure of editors to establish what they think the problem is. That is, they take for granted that "individual" in this context must mean "a separate indivisible entity," and that therefore it must be wrong since the presumed sense of the passage is that Emilia is praising the love between women, between maid and maid, between herself and Flavina, over the love between man and woman. I am in no disagreement with this as *one* possible reading. Emilia's interlocutor, Hippolyta, certainly seems to read Emilia's speech in that way. Hippolyta responds:

> Y'are out of breath
> And this high speeded-pace, is but to say
> That you shall never (like the Maide Flavina)
> Love any that's calld Man. (1.3, p. 14)

"Individuall," then, needs emendation if "sex individuall" means a *single* sex because the whole point of Emilia's speech is to praise the love of a single sex over the love between women and men.

But does "sex individuall" mean a single sex? The first definition of "individual" in that kind of sense is given in the O.E.D. as 1613, the probable date of the play. So that is a further argument for emendation, although not one that has previously been used. *If* we are to retain "individuall sex" in the sense of separate sex, then not only is it impossible to make sense of the passage, but we would also have to suppose that the word was being used in this way for one of the first times ever. By no means an impossibility, of course, but unlikely. On the other hand, the emendation to "dividual" seems even more improbable. When we look up the word in the O.E.D., we find this very passage (i.e., the 1750 emendation) as the second source for the word, a source supposedly dating from 1613. The O.E.D. is its usual honest self. It *notes* that the word "dividual" is an emendation but it *still* relies upon that emendation as one of its earliest authorities for the word. How do we know that the emendation to "dividual" is possible? Because the O.E.D. shows the possibility. How does the O.E.D. show the possibility? By appealing to the emendation.

Let us return, then, to "individuall." What else could it mean? We have already noted the trinitarian meaning, the sense of the indivisibility of the three persons of the godhead. Now that, of course, is an implausible definition in this context. Yet it seems to me the most suggestive in that it points toward "individuall sex" not as meaning one particular sex but rather the indivisibility of the sexes. And, in fact, it is precisely in this sense of the indivisibility of the sexes that the word "individual" recurs throughout the seventeenth century, at the very same time as the word is coming to be defined in the opposite sense of a separate element. In *The English Dictionarie* (1623), Henry Cockerham defines "individuall" as "not to be parted, as man and wife," but it is in Milton that this sense of individual as the indivisible relation of man and woman finds its apotheosis. When Eve flees from Adam, he says:

> to give thee being I lent
> Out of my side to thee, nearest my heart
> Substantial Life, to have thee by my side
> Henceforth an *individual* solace dear. (IV. 483–486)

And when in "On Time" Milton writes of "an individual kiss," the dominant meaning seems to be of an inseparable kiss rather than a single one: "Then long Eternity shall greet our bliss/ With an *individual* kiss." But paradoxically, it is in the divorce tracts, to which I will return, that he plays at length upon the sense of "individual" as suggesting the indivisibility of husband and wife, and in *Tetrachordon* he calls marriage "an *individual society*" (Milton, 1931, p. 107).

In this sense, "sex individuall" would mean not a single sex, but the indivisibility of sexes, male and female. It would be another way of describing what Milton calls "individual society." One possible antithesis for this meaning of "individual" would be the unrelated "viduall," meaning "widowed." As for the connection between the unity of indissoluble parts in the trinity and in marriage, it was perhaps suggested by the fact that in the marriage ceremony, the man puts the wedding ring upon "the fowerth finger of the womans left hande" in "the name of the father, and of the sonne, and of the holy goste." The analogy between the trinity and marriage is explicitly drawn by William Heale in *An Apologie for Women,* published in 1609. Heale, writing of the relation between Adam and Eve and God, argues: "As their Creator is devided in the trinitie of persons, yet still remaineth one only God in essence: so these his creatures were distinguished in the duality of persons, yet stil should they abide as only *Individuum* in nature" (Heale, 1609, p. 59). Here, the Latin term *(individuum)* is used in its technical theological sense, to assert the inseparability of Adam and Eve, despite the fact that they, like God, are divided into "persons." Indeed, to maintain Adam and Eve as *individuum,* Heale emphasizes a non-hierarchical view of marriage. The wife is not, he argues, a domestic clog but an equal partner:

> the name of a wife is a name of dignity. The law stiles her thy familiar friend: thine equal associate: the Mistresse of thy house: to speake at once, the same person and *Individuum* (as it were) togither with thee. (p. 48)

Yet the *strain* of imagining marriage through the language of trinitarian inseparability is apparent in this passage: the Latin term *individuum* is still employed and the concept is further estranged by the parenthetical "as it were."

It is the more surprising, then, that Heale not only *does* anglicize the concept, but also that he does so without any specific reference to the trinity. He writes of the division and re-memberment of Adam and Eve:

> no sooner were these of one divided into two, and made distinct and personal: but streight waie againe they were of two contracted into one, and made the same and Individuall. (p. 56)

Here, the inseparability of father, son, and holy ghost has been fully absorbed into the vernacular in the inseparability of Adam and Eve. It is the latter who are "one," "the same and Individuall." Yet no sooner is the term anglicized than it becomes possible to read it in antithetical ways. Could we not read the phrase "the same and Individuall" as suggesting that Adam and Eve are one and yet *separate,* individuated (individual taking on its "modern" meaning)? In a trinitarian context, such a reading would be impossible, because of the clear distinctions which were drawn between the three *persons* of the trinity and the *individuality* (-inseparability) of those three persons. In Heale's writing, though, "person" has already split into antithetical meanings. In the first and third passages I have quoted, "person" is used in its trinitarian sense to emphasize *separation:* "divided into two," Adam and Eve are "distinct" and *"personal";* they are "distinguished in the duality of *persons*" (my emphases). But in the second quotation, "person" is used to inscribe the *in*separability of Adam and Eve: they are "the same *person.*" In this latter instance, "person" is transformed from the opposite of "individual" into a synonym for it. And as "person" slides, it becomes difficult to stabilize "individual." While retaining its etymological meaning of inseparability, it begins to suggest separability; while meaning the merging of two into the same, it begins to imply the splitting of the same into two.

Thus, even in its earliest vernacular uses outside a strictly theological discourse, "individual" can be read in antithetical ways. This returns us to my argument at the beginning of the chapter: that, in the seventeenth century, it is not so much that the meanings of "individual" are inverted over time (the sense of separate entity displacing the sense of indivisibility) as that "individuality" is a site of synchronic conflict—a conflict which has, of course, diachronic consequences. That conflict of unity and division was perhaps already implied in the curious formulation of Genesis 1.27: "So God created man in his own image, in the image of God created he *him;* male and female created he *them*" (my emphasis).

But it has to be said that it is precisely "individuality," in either of the antithetical senses of the term, which is undone in *The Two Noble Kinsmen.* The plot of *The Two Noble Kinsmen,* like the plot of *A Midsummer Night's Dream,* shows that whatever the "individuality" of friendship, the love between man and woman is not "individual." Indeed, it is individual *neither* in the sense of being indivisible *nor* in the sense of being about two distinctive "individuals." In *The Two Noble Kinsmen,* a reworking of Chaucer's *Knight's Tale,* Palamon and Arcite, the dearest of friends, become rivals for the love of Emilia. When Theseus asks her to choose between them, she cannot. In the ensuing trial by combat, Arcite defeats Palamon and claims Emilia as his wife, but he immediately meets with a fatal riding accident, and Emilia is married off, by Arcite's dying wish, to Palamon. In other words, marriage, far from being "individual" (=indivisible), is immediately divided, and the husbands, far from being "individual" (=distinguished from others by attributes of their own), are interchangeable. And in the subplot, the Jailor's Daughter falls in love with Palamon, but after going mad, is persuaded that her previous, anonymous "Wooer" is really Palamon. So again the love between man and woman is defined by the substitutability of male lovers. Similarly, in *A Midsummer Night's Dream,* which, like *The Two Noble Kinsmen,* is presided over by the Amazon Queen, Hippolyta, and her betrothed, Theseus, Oberon's love potion makes Hermia and Helena interchangeable to their lovers, Lysander and Demetrius, while Titania's love-object, the changeling boy, is interchangeable with Bottom.

Yet the conjuncture of indivisibility and the distinctiveness of the entities who compose that indivisibility recurs in both plays. One might say, though, that whereas in Locke's view, the distinctiveness of the individual is guranteed by the individual's freedom from external determination, distinctiveness in these dramatic texts emerges from the social relations of twinning and twining. And if this distinctiveness is thus incompatible with bourgeois individuality, it is also incompatible with the Renaissance notion of the subject in that it does not depend upon priority and subordination. "Individuality," in this sense, is the province of a mimetic identification to be found more often in the friendship between woman and woman or man and man than in marriage. In her own narrative, Emilia becomes herself through imitating Flavina, just as Flavina becomes herself through imitating Emilia:

> what she lik'd,
> Was then of me approov'd, what not condemd
> No more arraignement, the flowre that I would plucke
> And put betweene my breasts, oh (then but beginning
> To swell about the blossome) she would long
> Till shee had such another, and commit it
> To the like innocent Cradle, where Phenix like
> They dide in perfume. (1.3.64–71)

Of course, the very language which Emilia uses (the cradle, the phoenix, the plucked flower) conjures up the antithesis of the innocence she proclaims. The plucked flower, indeed, is to be literalized at the end of the play when Emilia, praying to the goddess of chastity, is shown, as the stage direction puts it, "a Rose Tree, having one Rose upon it" which "fals from the Tree" (V. 1. 162, 168). And Emilia is self-conscious of the way in which her description of her friendship transforms or even displaces it. Her "rehearsall" to Hippolyta "comes in like old importments bastard," as, in other words, the illegitimate progeny of its previous meaning or significance. The indivisibility of friend and friend emerges only in the shadow of its loss: the death of Flavina; the prefiguring of marriage.

It is in friendship, then, not in marriage that the "individuality" applied to the Trinity is reimagined. For in marriage, in *The Two Noble Kinsmen* as in *A Midsummer Night's Dream,* questions of precedence, hierarchy, and enforced mimesis return with a vengeance. Both plays are framed by the subordination of the Queen of the Amazons to Theseus. As the second queen puts it in *The Two Noble Kinsmen:*

> Honoured Hypolita
> Most dreaded Amazonian, that ha'st slaine
> The Sith-tuskd-Bore; that with thy Arme as strong
> As it is white, wast neere to make the male
> To thy Sex captive; but that this thy Lord
> Borne to uphold Creation, in that honour
> First nature stilde it in, shrunke thee into
> The bownd thou wast ore-flowing; at once subduing
> Thy force, and thy affection. (1.1.77–85)

Marriage is here imagined not as the twinning or twining of friendship but as the subjugation of wife to husband, the restoration of "Creation's" supposed orderings. And, as Pat Parker (1987) finely notes of *A Midsummer Night's Dream:*

> this marriage play not only concludes by bringing an Amazon and an unruly Titania to their proper subjection to their husbands as "head" (a restoration of the proper order of 1 Corinthians: "Neither was the man created for the woman; but the woman for the man"), but, in its joining of right "Jack" to "Jill," corrects an earlier Amazonian and finally unlawful union of woman to woman, the "union in partition" of Helena and Hermia which improperly echoes the ceremony of marriage in its exclusion of "men." (p. 124)

Pat Parker further shows that the hierarchical joining of man and wife both mirrors and is mirrored by the correct rhetorical deployment of language, as in Richard Sherry's *Treatise of Schemes and Tropes* where Sherry insists upon the "naturall order" of "men & women, daye and night, easte and weste, rather than backwards" (Parker, 1987, p. 112).

To Sherry's list we might add father and son. And that suggests, I believe, one aspect of the problematic history of the concept of the "individual." For if we suppose, as I do, that the notions of the individual both as indivisible and as separate are constructed through the dismantling of the trinitarian "individual," the new concepts reproduced the contradictory sense of the trinity itself. I do not mean the paradox of three-in-one but the contradiction between a notion of three inseparable elements in which there was no priority and the language of father and son which was determined by priority and authority. There are perhaps few more extreme assertions of the pecedence of father to child than in *A Midsummer Night's Dream* where Egeus argues that Hermia "is mine, I may dispose of her" and is seconded by Theseus who claims that Hermia is "but as a forme in wax,/ By [her father] imprinted, and within his power,/ To leave the figure, or disfigure it." Here the father is, in the fullest sense, the author; and this author (unlike the Renaissance dramatist) controls the process of printing. The figuring and the disfiguring is his alone.

Yet it is the father's or husband's control of female sexuality which is undone by Emilia's praise of "sex individuall." In returning to that phrase for a final time, I do not wish to offer a single reading but rather to suggest the cultural parameters within which we can make sense of Emilia's use of "individuall." Certainly, given the ways in which "individual" is used specifically to refer to the conjunction of man and woman in marriage, Emilia could be seen as praising the love between maid and maid as a greater love, a more indivisible love, than the "sex individuall" (the indivisibility of genders) in marriage. But this interpretation does not exhaust the possibilities. Let me just suggest two others. We could read the extolling of "love tweene Mayde, and mayde" as being "[m]ore then in sex individuall" as the praise of the mutual love of women which transcends the identity of their gender ("individual" would here take on the opposite meaning of "single"). In this sense, Emilia would be suggesting that their love depended upon *more* than the fact that they were both women. On the other hand, we could read the lines in just the *opposite* way, if we take "sex individuall" to refer to that crucial Renaissance figure, the hermaphrodite. In that case, the gender of the two women would be of central import, since it would be that which defined them as superior to the intermixing of genders in an androgyne often imagined in the Renaissance as defining the ideal of love. (On this, as on the formation of "identity" and "individuality" in the seventeenth century, see Jim Swan's [1985] "Difference and Silence: John Milton and the Question of Gender," to which I am indebted throughout this paper.) On such a reading, Emilia would be reversing Marvell's fantasy that "Two Paradises' twere in one/ To live in Paradise alone." The single androgyne, though, would be displaced not by the joining of woman and man but by that of woman and woman.

However we read "sex individuall," I hope to have shown two things: first, that the phrase does not need emendation (or that no coherent case for emendation has yet been made); second, that in the "Shakespearean" context, "individual," whatever its range of possible meanings, suggests a *relation* (of part to whole, of part to part, of member to body, of body to body) not a separate entity. There is a crucial corollary to this. Namely, that "every single character in Shakespear is "*not*" as much an Individual, as those in Life itself" (Pope, quoted in Cloud [1988]). Against Pope, and innumerable later commentators, I want to make the claim that Shakespeare was not in the business of producing individuals (this might be called the weaker claim) *and,* the stronger claim, that "individuals," in Pope's sense, were not being produced "in Life itself" in early seventeenth-century England. It would take another paper to show what *were* being produced before the English Revolution. "Subjects," we might say, but it would take much labor and analysis to show just how complex and unstable such "beings" were.

Here, I want to pursue the weaker claim and to show that Shakespeare did not produce "individuals" in Pope's sense but something more interesting: shifting relations of power and desire which form and transform the person, in a process of naming, unnaming, and renaming. As Random Cloud has brilliantly shown, even those lists of *dramatis personae,* later affixed to Shakespeare's work, suggest an "individuality" that is not to be found in most early quartos and folios. Cloud (also sometimes known as McLeod) notes that in nearly all modern editions of *All's Well, That Ends Well* the editors introduce us, in their lists of *dramatis personae,* to "Countess of Rossillion, mother to Bertram." In the first folio, there is no such person; rather, there are five different speech tags for what we now take to be a single role: Mother, Countess, Old Countess, Lady, and Old Lady. Each title suggests a different *relation:* in terms of the family, in terms of political hierarchy, in terms of age, in terms of gender. If "the Countess of Rossillion" is an extreme case of the non-oneness of one, it is certainly not an isolated example. The first quarto of *The Second Part of Henrie the Fourth* has an equally striking array of names for the "individuals" whom we now confidently (or perhaps less so after the Oxford Shakespeare) name Falstaff and Doll: Falstaffe, John, Sir John, Old. (for "Old-castle"); Doll Tere-sheet, Dorothy, Doll, Whoore. There is no "substance" ("the individual") in which these "accidents" inhere. The "accidents" (contingencies, occasions, conflicting interpellations) *are* the "substance."

This is nowhere more fully dramatized than in *Coriolanus*. Coriolanus, of course, fantasizes that he can "stand/As if a man were Author of himself, & knew no other kin." But not only is he forced to acknowledge his relational identity to mother and child; his own name, in the folio text, is shown as undergoing profound mutations. We first encounter the name "Caius Martius" and, in the speech tags, "Martius.," "Mart.," or "Mar." But then to "Martius Caius" is added "Coriolanus" and the speech tags change to "Coriol.," "Corio.," or "Cor." And it is the name which is crucially at stake when Aufidius accuses Martius/Coriolanus of treason at the end of the play:

> *Corio.* Traitor? How now?
> *Auf.* I Traitor, *Martius.*
> *Corio.* Martius?
> *Auf.* I *Martius, Caius Martius:* Do'st thou thinke
> Ile grace thee with that Robbery, thy stolne name
> *Coriolanus in Corioles?*

One would expect the text to resolve the question of naming in favor of "Coriolanus." After all, even Aufidius, who instigates Coriolanus's death, concludes "Yet he shall have a Noble Memory." What would that memory consist in if not his name, "Coriolanus," the testament to his military triumphs? But what follows Aufidius's concluding line is a stage direction which reads: *"Exeunt bearing the Body of Martius. A dead March Sounded."* And so the play concludes with the unnaming of Coriolanus, not by Aufidius but by. . . whom? Shakespeare, the "prompter" (if such a creature existed), an actor, a scribe, a compositor? We do not know. What we can know, though, if we look at the practices of particular Renaissance books rather than at a hypothetical authorial manuscript is the textual workings that establish the instability of any name.

Dramatic texts, of course, tend to foreground this instability by reminding us of the etymological derivation of the "person" from the Latin *persona*—a mask. I want to insist, though, that the instability which I am describing is not a transhistorical feature of "drama" but a specific effect of historical textual practices. Ironically, the most "authoritative" of Renaissance books—the divine revelations of the supposedly one true Author—were subject to at least some of the same instabilities. Take, for instance, the rendering of the Acts of the Apostles 7:44–45 in the Bishops' Bible (1568): "Our fathers had the tabernacle of witnesse in the wildernesse . . . which also our fathers that came after, brought in with Jesus into the possession of the Gentiles . . . ." Or note the version of Hebrews 4: 8: "yf Jesus had geven them rest, then would he not afterwarde have spoken of another day." There is a marginal gloss to the Hebrews verse which notes, "By Jesus, is meant Josuah." There is no such gloss for the verses from Acts. A modern scholar, commenting upon the same "confusion" in the Authorized translation (1611), complains: "it is particularly unhelpful to have Joshua twice referred to as "Jesus" in the New Testament" (Bruce, 1961, p. 98). In fact, the early translators are following their sources, whereas modern editorial procedures demand an emendation so as to separate out Jesus/Joshua.

At the same time, the multiplicity of Biblical translations had the effect of destabilizing the authenticity of the Author. The so-called Authorized version, dedicated to James I and partly organized by him, admits to the variants which replace the transcendent Word with material words. The translators criticize Pope Sixtus V's declaration that no variant readings should be allowed and argue that "[t]hey that are wise, had rather have their judgements at libertie in differences of readings, then to be captivated to one, when it might be the other" (Anon., 1611, p. 29). How, for instance, could one reconcile the Geneva Bible (1560), translated from the Hebrew and the Greek with the addition of radical Protestant glosses, with the Douai Bible (N.T. 1582; O.T. 1609–10), translated from the Latin Vulgate with Catholic glosses? More strikingly perhaps, how could one reconcile the Authorized version with itself? In 1611, there were three folio editions of the Authorized translation. The first was soon known as "the HE edition," because it rendered the end of Ruth 3: 15 as "and he went into the city"; the other two editions were known as "the SHE editions," because they translated the "same" passage as "and she went into the city." This is not necessarily a question of a misprint, since the Hebrew manuscripts are themselves divided between "he" and "she." Perhaps we should say that the very notion of "the same passage" mystifies the conditions of textual production and transmission. Given the conditions of setting by hand, the "same" translation was to undergo further transformations: the "Wicked Bible" of 1631, where the seventh commandment is "Thou shalt commit adultery" (Exodus 20: 14) and what I like to think of as the Compositors' Bible where Psalm 119: 161 reads "Printers [for "princes"] have persecuted me without a cause" (Bruce, 1961, p. 109). There was, as Stephanie Jed (1989) has remarked, a long history of noting the dangers of the scribal transmission of the Latin Vulgate: the danger that *correctores* would become *corruptores,* that "the 'slightest graphic alteration' could potentially wreak great havoc on the meaning of The Text." Examples of potentially threatening errors include the transcription of *voluntatem* ("will") as *voluptatem* ("pleasure") or *potens* ("power") as *potans* ("drinking") (pp. 34–35).

Instability was inscribed in the material means of reproduction. Not only are the names "within" the text unstable, but there is, in an important sense, no "text." I have in front of me Charlton Hinman's (1968) wonderful facsimile of Shakespeare's first Folio. But what is this a fascimile *of*? Not, as Hinman is the first to acknowledge, of any single Renaissance book. Hinman's first Folio is, indeed, an idealized reconstruction, dependent on no less than *thirty* copies of the first Folio (pp., xxiii) (I draw my point from Margreta de Grazia [1990b]). The way in which "corrections" were done while the edition was being printed, combined with the fact that "corrected" and "uncorrected" forms were randomly bound together means that, as Hinman notes, "no two copies will be found textually identical throughout" (p. xix). Even what we mean by a "text," then, is constructed by the erasure of the conditions of the Renaissance book: conditions that established the uniqueness of every book in the same moment that they displaced the individual text.

Let me put my argument as crudely and controversially as possible: in what we now call "Shakespeare," no individual author, no individual word, no individual, in the modern sense. Just the signifier, "individuall," at a particular moment where it looks so impossible to us that it has been consistently emended. But what if we now turn to Milton? Have we not entered an entirely new world? We might, indeed, imagine John Milton as himself the author of the author, giving material reality to the metaphor of the writer's absolute control. Let us posit a crude set of binary oppositions between the collaborative process of *The Two Noble Kinsmen* in 1613 and the individual authorship of *Paradise Lost: A Poem in Twelve Books* in 1674. Before, writing as a composite process, involving many hands; after, the individual author's control of every stage of the process. Before patronage; after, the market economy. Before, the shifting orthography in which word bleeds into word; after, the standardized orthography of the individual word. Before, subjecthood, subjection, and the body of the state; after, individuality, republicanism, and the social contract. Before marital hierarchy and indivisibility; after marital choice and divorce. Crude as these oppositions are, they still seem to me suggestive, even when wrong. It is, perhaps, strange to compare Milton with Shakespeare when his more obvious literary precursors in England were the "laureate poets" (to quote Richard Helgerson's phrase), Spenser and Jonson. Yet it's worth nothing that Spenser does not appear on the title page of *The Faerie Queene*. He is consigned to the dedication where the eternity of his labors is said to live with the eternity of the fame of the monarch, whose "most humble servant" he is. Flattery, perhaps, yet all the more revealing for that of the literary relations of production. The 1674 *Paradise Lost,* on the contrary, declares that it is by "The Author John Milton," and although, like some of the Shakespearean quartos, it has been "revised and augmented," these changes have been carried out, we are told, by "the same Author."

Yet if Milton fantasized authorship as emanating from a single source, the early textual history of his epic bears the marks of the extent to which the name of the author was given over into other hands. It was in the year of his death that the twelve-book *Paradise Lost* appeared, as the possibility of personal control slipped irrevocably out of his hands. But seven years before, in 1667, *Paradise Lost: A Poem in Ten Books* had been published. And within two years, the same poem had been given three different title pages. On the first, the poem is "by John Milton" in relatively small capitals; on the second "The Author" appears for the first time as the designation of the poet, but this coincides with the reduction of the author's name to two initials, J. M. On the third title page is printed "The Author" and underneath in large capitals "John Milton." Paradoxically, the two earlier title pages declare that they are "Licensed and Entred according to Order," whereas the arrival of "the author John Milton" is simultaneous with the disappearance from the title page of the rival authority of the stationers and censors. There is no clear reason for these transformations. One suggestion is that it was the very name of the author, a known advocate of regicide, which delegitimated the poem, and that the printer in consequence erased his name on the second title page. But whatever the reason for the change, it suggests the extent to which both the proper name of the writer and his status as author were out of his own control.

At the same time, Milton's blindness necessitated the delegation of writing to others. The manuscript of *Paradise Lost* was taken down by dictation by more than one amanuensis. The manuscript was then copied by a professional amanuensis, and this copy was in turn emended by "at least five different correctors" (Moyles, 1985, p. 18). What does seem certain by comparing the manuscript with the first edition is that a still relatively unstandardized orthography was partially standardized by the printer, Samuel Simmons. It was the printer, not Milton, who changed the ampersand to "and," eliminated some double consonants ("mortall"/"mortal"), and cut many of the final silent *e*'s ("losse"/"loss") (p. 20). Thus, standardization emerges outside the control of the author.

If I emphasize the heterogeneity of the published Milton, though, it is not because I believe that he writes within the same problematic as the dramatists in the early seventeenth century. On the contrary, Milton both acted in and was acted upon by the English revolution where, for the first time, the word "individual" is explicitly used to displace the implication of subjection in the subject. Despite the fact that Milton self-consciously used the word to mean "indivisible," he wrote in full knowledge of the emergence of a new signification. For the more radical of the Levellers, it was the free individual, a quite new political concept, who would overthrow kings and priests.

Ironically, this free individual was theorized from within the constraints of Newgate prison. In 1646, the Leveller, Richard Overton, imprisoned by Cromwell, wrote *An arrow against all tyrants*. It begins:

> To every Individuall in nature is given an individual property by nature, not to be invaded or usurped by any: for every one as he is himselfe, so he hath a selfe propriety, else could he not be himselfe, and on this no second may presume to deprive any of, without manifest violation and affront to the very principles of nature, and of the Rules of equity and justice between man and man; mine and thine cannot be, except this be; No man hath power over my rights and liberties, and I over no mans; I may be but an Individuall, enjoy my selfe, and my selfe propriety, and may write my selfe no more than my selfe. . . . (pp. 3–4)

They are lines which, a century later, would be a commonplace. But for Overton, they were an attempt to level the politics of aristocratic enclosure into the commons of political and economic rights. For everyone to have property in themselves was, as Overton put it, to turn each man into "a King, Priest and Prophet in his owne naturall circuite and compasse." The language of the "individual" as proprietor of himself was, at this moment, the language not only of regicide but of a radical critique of Cromwell's gentry republicanism. It was Cromwell, not the monarch, who had imprisoned Overton.

And yet, the radical notion of the separate individual had its cost: the reduction of the political subject, language, the author to independent atoms which preceded all social relations. The cost was the invention of an entity which, as Marx observed, has tended within bourgeois social formations to become both abstract and empty: the individual.

NOTES

1. I am indebted throughout this talk to the work of and conversations with Random Cloud (also known as Randy McLeod), Margreta de Grazia, David Kastan, and Jeff Masten.

DISCUSSION: PETER STALLYBRASS

TERRY COMITO: I wonder what relations, if any, you see between cultural studies and the new historicism.

STALLYBRASS: I've never thought of myself as a new historicist; I've thought of myself as working within a British Marxist tradition. Obviously I've been incredibly influenced by the work of people like Stephen Greenblatt. And one of the things that I find disquieting, although I engaged in it myself some time ago, is trying to make sharp distinctions between new historicism and Marxism. There are real differences, and I think they shouldn't be ironed out. It's a productive and interesting debate. My own interest at the moment is less in people who are called either Marxist or new historicist. I'm interested in what has been relegated to antiquarians, to the field of people who write books which only six people read, which are about spelling in Shakespeare. I'm very interested at the moment in spelling because I think that the question of spelling has a lot to do with the notion of the individual word. What does it mean to talk about an individual word if you don't have a standardized orthography? This kind of textual scholarship has a tremendous history at the University of Pennsylvania, and through the efforts of the librarians there, there are even material conditions, one might say, that make available that kind of work. So I'm partly trying to understand what late nineteenth-century editors were up to, both for good and for bad.

LARRY SCANLON: My question is about the explanatory power that the term "individual" retains in your own account. By getting rid of it in this almost global way, you left the impression that the only alternative is a collectivity that is neither individuated nor separate. And I point to two examples. You said that in medieval Latin, there are no terms for person or for individual. But there are terms which are more individuated or have to do with separating groups more than simply *civis*. Moreover, you focus on Shakespeare as an author who is not an individual. But certainly there are, in other genres, clear examples of marking the names of authors. Chaucer would be the most obvious; very quickly after his death he gets designated as an auctor, as an authority, and retains that through the Renaissance. And I think that would be the case for someone like Spenser as well. What are you going to use now that you've got rid of the term individual?

STALLYBRASS: I hear two different questions. The first one is a philological question. My sense is that auctor is always used about the dead. In other words, auctors are formed through death. You're always looking back to an auctor, but auctors don't ever exist in the present moment. The second question was about getting rid of the individual. The point of quoting Richard Overton at the end was to mark a moment of what I call political crisis in the paper. The political crisis results because there are two different things I want to do. One involves the notion of collaboration and the extent to which work is collaborative. There is a temptation, which I certainly have, to sentimetalize that. I don't want to say that collective work is necessarily unhierarchical. If you take the printer's shop as an example of collaborative work, it is both hierarchical and sexist. It's the hierarchy of masters, journeymen, and then apprentices. There's a sense in which I want to celebrate collaboration in the moment before the individual, but I would have to look more seriously at the question of subjection. I also wanted to end with Richard Overton to suggest that I don't have an essential position about the possibilities of the use of the individual. Quite clearly, there are all sorts of political groups at the moment who need to use that term. There's a whole range of ways in which various groups are still finding the radical potential within that term. I don't want to just say the individual is something that you can't touch. My suspicion is that it's something that will be used, will have particular dangers attached to it. And in the context of the United States, the dangers seem to be all too manifest. It's incredible to have a society which emphasizes the notion of democratic freedom in voting while having one of the lowest turn-outs at the polls. Why do people not vote? The interpellation of subjects as individuals has not worked, I would say, in the United States.

ELSPETH PROBYN: Do you find Foucault's discussion of the technologies of the self, of the care of the self, grounded in the homosexual practices of Greek antiquity, useful?
STALLYBRASS: I have found Foucault's work immensely useful in addressing questions of sexual politics. I also think it has very serious limitations and dangers precisely around

sexual politics. We need to examine the relationship between the homosexual and the homosocial, and the relationship between certain formations of masculinity that are simultaneously misogynist and homophobic. One thing I do think is interesting in Foucault is his way of understanding individuation as often a violent, enforced process. One aspect, it's not the only aspect, of individuation involves the attempt—quite literally the notion of the census—to produce the enumeration of population.

DONNA HARAWAY: To comment on the question that was just made. I think both of the theories of compulsory heterosexuality and Jan Grover's work on what counts as the general population make clear the ways that gay/lesbian people are not counted as proper individuals. The question I wanted to ask was actually about the intersection between your paper and Emily Martin's in relationship to the modes of production of what counts as an individual, modes that involve disaggregations and reductions and condensations. In many late twentieth-century contexts, the production of the book of man reified in advance in such a way as to erase the processes by which we determine what is to count as an adequate individual in, e.g., pharmaceutical practice, medical practice, legal practice, the same processes allow entities like the fetus, the replicon, the codon, the genome, as well as corporate individuals, to count as legal individuals. It is precisely the same situation you're talking about in the history of literary studies: the actual social processes of multiply collaborating people in all sorts of hierarchical and horizontal relationality are erased from the process of what will count as a property-bearing substance.

STALLYBRASS: I found Emily's paper enormously rich and suggestive. The problem might be how one deals with the vast range of collaborative networks in which we are all engaged, on the one hand; and on the other hand the extent to which to be deprived of legal individuality is something that, in this society, is often devastating.

HARAWAY: Particularly in the human rights context.

STALLYBRASS: Yes, particularly in the human rights context, but also in the context of a whole range of areas where one can't simply dump the individual. Though that's not what I'm trying to think about for the moment. What I'm trying to think about, you might say, is what it means to be haunted, to be inhabited by other people, to be composed by those people who have worked with us, worked upon us, who have transformed us. And so a lot of what my present work is about is the desire to be haunted. The desire that those who are lost should still be with us, in some sense.

33

Culture, Cultural Studies, and the Historians

Carolyn Steedman

This paper is about the idea of "culture" itself; about cultural studies in Britain now, and in the recent past; and about the connection of both of these to the practice and writing of history. The account I give (the story I tell) will be partly institutional in focus, to do with forms of school-based and higher education in Britain since the last war; and it will also be text-based. Here, I follow a historiographical tradition laid down by British cultural studies itself (a historiography that this Conference has often evoked): histories of cultural studies, written by its practitioners, usually organize themselves in a particular way, rendering up *their* own account in terms of the books—always three key-texts: Richard Hoggart's *The Uses of Literacy,* 1957; Raymond Williams's *Culture and Society,* 1958; and E. P. Thompson's *The Making of the English Working Class,* 1963.

To make this observation is to use the most compelling device in the historian's rhetorical repertoire: the historian can always, in this manner, present a plot that seemingly *had* to be shaped in a particular way, according to what the documents used for its composition authorized, or what they forbade: can always present herself as the invisible servant of her material, merely uncovering what already lies there, waiting to be told. It is as well that readers are alerted to the fact that the historian is able in this way to appropriate to herself the most massive authority as a narrator. And of course, I have not innocently followed these histories of British cultural studies along their textual path; rather, have chosen to do so, so that I am enabled to say something about text-based studies of history, within cultural studies, and without; and about the text as a historical reality, not simply a representation of an alterior reality, but also constituting a reality, in and of itself.

As I complete this prolegomenon, I should make two other points. First, I *am* one of those who the definite article in my title so rudely excludes, one of them: "the historians"; and as one of them I know that there is nothing deader and colder than old history. We can read Gibbon, or Thierry, or Michelet for the elegance of their prose, in order to observe their rhetorical structures of explanation and persuasion, in order perhaps, to see in Gibbon's work the very mark of that late eighteenth-century historical purpose: philosophy teaching by example; or in Michelet, watch the Romantic historian insert himself in the text in order to convey that great distance that separates the living from the dead (Pomata, 1989, p. 9). But we cannot read any of it as we read the new secondary source published last week, as an account that informs about its overt subject matter. The life of the written history is not very long; the written history is the most unstable of written forms. The historical component of the trinity of texts that formed British cultural studies —*The Making of the English Working Class*— is in its transitional stage now, between being a quarry of information about class formation, the actual meeting of actual men under cover of darkness on moors six miles beyond Huddersfield, and the language they used in consciousness of their making a new political world—to being (among all these other things, which it still, of course, remains) an epic telling of a history that we watch with wonder and pity, that is also now, in our reading, about *us,* and our lost past. Too much has happened for this to operate as a simple historical source; there are too many new items of information—about what women were doing, at that moment, back in Huddersfield, about all the men who were not present at their own class formation, all those who did not "specially want it to happen . . ." (Auden, 1966, p. 123); about recent events in Eastern Europe; about all our lost socialisms.

This is to say that history is the most impermanent of written forms: it is only ever an account that will last a while. The very practice of historical work, the uncovering of new facts, the endless reordering of the immense detail that makes the historian's map of the past, performs this act of narrative destabilization, on a daily basis. The written history does, of course, reach narrative closure all the time, for manuscripts have to be delivered to publishers and papers given; but that is only its formal closure. Soon, the written history rejoins—has to rejoin—the insistent, tireless, repetitive beat of a cognitive form that has no end. The written history is a story that can only be told by the implicit understanding that *things are not over,* that the story isn't finished, can never be finished, for some new item of information may alter the account that has been given. In this way, history breaks the most ordinary and accepted narrative rule, and in this way also, the written history is not just *about* time, doesn't just *describe* time, or take *time as its setting;* rather, it embeds time in its narrative structure. And it really doesn't matter how much historians may know this, or not know this; know or do not know that at the center of the written history is the invitation to acknowledge its temporariness and impermanence. It may matter however, when text-based historical knowledge is removed from the narrative and cognitive frame of historical practice, and used within another field.

It has been observed before what can happen to the written history in these circumstances: it loses its impermanence (and the potential irony, that derives from its impermanence). The historical item (the bit of written history) taken out of its narrative setting in order to explain something else (an event, a development, a structure), is stabilized, made a building block for a different structure of explanation. This has been observed for the main part, in the use of the written history within sociological explanation. It is probably the case that within British cultural studies, formed and shaped within undergraduate degrees in Polytechnics and Universities (and dramatically historical as a pedagogy in comparison with cultural studies in the U.S., as far as I can tell), that history meets the same fate as it has within sociology.

That was the prolegomenon. Now I shall proceed for a few minutes by way of illustrative anecdote: I spent a strange year, this last academic year. In the hours of gloomy reflection accompanying the reading I did for this Conference, it occurred to me that I passed it doing nothing more than producing long, elaborate, historical foot-notes to Raymond Williams's accounts of "culture" in his *Culture and Society, Keywords,* and *Marxism and Literature.* I published a book, which is a description of the use and development of nineteenth-century cultural theory within British socialism, and the reorganization of its key components around the the figure of the child and the idea of childhood, in the period 1890–1920 (Steedman, 1990). I was thus able at the end of the book, and with some satisfaction, to suggest that William's radical philology is missing something: that an explosion of growth studies from the middle years of the century and a consequent theorization of those social subjects—children—who demonstrate growth (who *embody* growth), within many forms of writing (from the novel to neurological physiology), may align a late nineteenth-century understanding of "culture" with an older one, with that earlier meaning that Williams outlines in *Keywords*, of the actual material improvement and cultivation of bodies and minds in society (Williams, 1976 p. 87). There are those blank pages at the end of the 1983 edition of *Keywords,* the sign, as Williams wrote, "that the inquiry remains open"; but my notes of contribution are three hundred pages long ... (In order, as a good Freudian, to deal with my very deep anxieties about what I might *really* be up to, I tell a joke to myself about this obsessive footnoting of Williams: I have invented an all-girl backing group of the very early sixties: the Rayettes, who accompany Raymond's now disembodied voice ...). My other footnote to William's work of the last academic year 1989–1990 has been planning, with a colleague, a new undergraduate option course at the University of Warwick, where I teach. The course is called "Learning Culture," and takes as its central preoccupations first, a history of subjectivity (a history of the kinds of subjectivity that people have felt obliged to construct for themselves over the last three hundred years or so); and second, the connection of subjectivity to the idea of culture; and third, the organization of both of these around women, particularly, in a wide variety of texts, around the figure of the teacher. Again and again, we have returned to those passages in *Marxism and Literature* (1977), where Williams describes first, "the notion of 'civilising,' as bringing men within a social organisation ... ," then the way in which the aim of "civilisation" was expressed in the adjective " 'civil,' as orderly, educated, or polite...." We have returned to the pages that tell how " 'civilisation' and 'culture' ... were ... in the late eighteenth century, interchangable terms," how their eventual divergence came through the attack on "civilisation" as superficial, on all things "artificial" as distinct from those in a "natural" state (pp. 11–20).

We have returned the students to those texts (which Williams does not mention) in which the ideas he works with were actually carved out: to Locke's *Thoughts Concerning Education,* and his *Two Treatises on Government;* to Rousseau's *Emile,* and to other strange hybrids of the eighteenth century which have not achieved their canonical status: to conduct books, household and educational and etiquette manuals, chap-books, folk and fairy-tales. We have tried hard to make the students see that the attack on artificiality through into the nineteenth century, was indeed, as Williams claims, "the basis of one important alternative sense of 'culture'—as a process of 'inner' or 'spiritual' as distinct from 'external' development." We have expressed our astonishment (there is the teaching of response as much as there is of content) at this description of an actual historical process that is inexplicable without some knowledge of the history of women and children in European society, but that never, ever mentions women and children. "The primary effect of this alternative sense of the term 'culture,' " says Williams, "was to associate it with religion, art, *the family and personal life....*" In those five words, we have said, is occluded a whole history: of women and children in English society, between about 1680 and the middle of this century. But without the history, Williams still manages to say that through these processes, "culture" came to be related to "the 'inner life' in its most accessible, secular forms; came to be related to 'subjectivity,' to 'the imagination.' " At points like these, and because there is simply nothing else to be done at the moment, in our present state of knowledge, we have boldly followed Nancy Armstrong (1987), in asserting out of the pages of her *Desire and Domestic Fiction* that the first bourgeois individual was not "economic man" but rather "domestic woman," and that she—this figure, born of the conduct books, educational manuals and (maybe, above all, from Samuel Richardson's pen)—was the first to possess a subjectivity: a consciousness of depth and space within, a sensibility, an interiority.

One of my worries about all of this is of course, the edgy but certain knowledge that writing footnotes to Raymond Williams (being a Rayette) is not at all what a girl ought to be doing with her life. A more serious worry, is my very strong suspicion that Raymond Williams was probably right. What I mean by the problem of his probably being right is this: in *Marxism and Literature,* in *Keywords,* and in his many other discussions of "culture," it is impossible to tell if Williams is giving us an account that has been abstracted away from the history that informs it, or whether it has been constructed in some other manner. I can put the problem in another way: it is quite possible (indeed, I have spent since October 1989 doing this) to insert (re-insert?) the history—*Some Thoughts Concerning Education,* its authorship, its readership, a sociology of the gendered reader of the first half of the eighteenth century, a history of the family and childcare, the many imitations of Locke, the startling appearance of this particular text of Locke in the very last part of Richardson's *Pamela*— to put all of this and more into William's account, and still end up with the same one. I can turn the problem around, talk in the future tense, and say that in the same way, it is quite possible to draw up a program of reading and archive research that will track down the historicized subjectivity, locate it first in the feminine; then move on, see Freud at the end of the last century, as one of the first to theorize human inwardness, interiority: the lost past within each one of us—which he did by using the many nineteenth-century rewritings of the child-figure that were available to him from sources as diverse as neurological physiology and realist fiction: to see Freud writing a theory of history in his account of repression and childhood sexuality (Roth, 1987). It would (it will) take some years to do the historical work (and I have to do it, otherwise I will not, in my terms, know it) but in 1995 it will still be possible to extract from the detail that will by then have been amassed the schema that Williams published in 1977, in *Marxism and Literature,* and probably in the same words (though I think that by 1995 the words "woman" and "child" will be there too; and so, I guess, the account might be most profoundly changed).

Patient friends and colleagues to whom I have confessed this worry, have not been able to understand what I'm bothering my head about; or have told me that there is anyway "the connectedness of everything" to explain Williams's rightness: that because everything is joined up to everything else, it really does not signify that Raymond Williams may never have read *Some Thoughts Concerning Education,* because the ideas it contains (which are expressed in schematic form in his accounts of culture) would be available from the very historical air he breathed, the moment he set to write about the late seventeenth century (and this holds even though he might not have known he was writing about the late seventeenth century).

On the question of the connectedness of everything, I have brooded a lot on the latest issue of *New Literary History,* where Carolyn Porter (1990) writes about what might happen "After the New Historicism." In order to expose the underlying *formalism* of a critical practice that purports to be *historical,* she comments on the tendency of the new historicists to deploy "riveting anecdotes" in their explorations of texts and contexts. This anecdotal technique she claims, reflects a principle of arbitrary connectedness, by which it is assumed that any one aspect of a society is related to any other. This is what Dominick LaCapra (1985), in different manner, and being rude about social historians rather than literary historicists, has called their trance-like reliance on the concept of culture in their work, where everything connects to everything else and "culture" is the primordial reality in which all historical actors have their being, do their thing, share discourses, worldviews, "languages" where everyone (I repeat the joke because I enjoy it so much) "is a mentalité case"; and where it is not possible to write the exception:

to write about the thing, event, relationship, entity, that does not connect with anything else (pp. 46, 51, 71–94).

The social historian's reliance on the notion of "culture" as the bottom line, the real historical reality, has, of course its own (rather short) history, and can be seen in the academy's elevation of nineteenth-century historians like Burkhardt and de Tocqueville to canonical status in the post-Second World War period. What Burkhardt's history did was to put together the disparate and fragmented elements of social life under the heading of cultural coherence. I know from experience that his work provided the first alluring figure of cultural totality in many undergraduate history courses of the early 1960s in Britain; and Carl Schorske (1990), writing in the same issue of *NLH* as Carolyn Porter, tells me that this attention to nineteenth-century texts of cultural history started earlier here, in the USA of the 1950s (pp. 414–15). He says of Burkhardt's and de Tocqueville's writing, that "time did not stop" in it, "but it was . . . slowed down. Not transformation but cultural coherence became the focus of attention." For LaCapra this particular concept of "culture"—"the culture concept"—shatters chronology and dissolves the very ordinance of time.

Cultural studies in Britain has intersected with these questions of culture, the culture concept, history, and time. I want to consider some of these intersections now, intersections that actually reveal (in a historical sense) a more general social and institutional shaping of history and historical knowledge in Britain, over the last thirty years. The following account shows British cultural studies shaped by teachers and taught, by their particular educational histories and their purchase on different forms of historical knowledge, quite as much as a shaping by theoretical questions. I shall start where I started before, by considering cultural studies' writing of its own history.

Cultural studies in Britain is extremely nervous of what Richard Johnson (1986–1987) has called "codification of methods or knowledges," and of attempts at institutionalization (p. 38). Alan O'Connor (1989) in his interpretation of the British field for academics in the United States, calls it a practice, a cultural form, an intellectual tradition (never, ever, a discipline). Tony Dunn (1986) starts out by refusing any position for cultural studies at all, by celebrating its polymorphic perversity: "Cultural studies," he wrote in 1986 "is a whirling and quiescent and swaying mobile which continuously repositions any participating subject. Cultural Studies is a project whose realization— absolute integrity through fragmentation and disassembly—is forever deferred" (p. 71). They all *start* like that, but within a few paragraphs are well into that most conventional claim for disciplinary orthodoxy—the writing of their own history (Johnson, 1986; Johnson, 1981; S. Hall, 1980a). (What they are also doing, the historiographically informed observer notes, is defining themselves, finding themselves, through an act of consciousness-raising: telling their own story, reaping all the social and psychic benefits of autobiography and oral history.)

The story goes like this: sprung from native texts, the account of its evolution propelled by key theoretical moments (the existence of the Communist Party Historians Group, from 1946–1956; Perry Anderson's editorship of *New Left Review* from 1962 onwards), institutionally established at the Centre in Birmingham, cultural studies is "interrupted by the arrival on the intellectual scene of the 'structuralisms' " (S. Hall, 1980a, p. 40). This historical account of the early period, and of later accommodations made to Continental theory, is available from many secondary sources (and indeed, from accounts given at this Conference), and I do not intend to rehearse it for you here. I want instead to explore some of the history that is missing from the account so far, by making some observations about forms of teaching and learning that have been embodied in the cultural studies degrees institutionalized at British Polytechnics (to a far lesser extent, at British Universities), and about the connection of this educational practice in higher education with "the culture concept" in schools. I suspect that "the culture concept" in England has much to do with the organization of historical knowledge for young children and adolescents in the British school system, at least since the 1950s; and I want to suggest too, that organization of historical knowledge in British cultural studies has been about questions of education, a question of accommodation to constituencies of learners and the allure of certain models of teacher-student relationship that higher education saw operating in the schools, in the 1970s. Moreover, the teaching force in cultural studies has had its own relationship to historical knowledge orientated by the economics of a historical education, and by the cost of historical research.

I want to deal with the schools, but I shan't start there. Rather, I shall begin at the other end, with the practice of history in university-based cultural studies—on the M.A. program at Birmingham—from the late 1960s onwards. When Alan O'Connor (1989) tells North American audiences that "the characteristic cultural form of cultural studies is a certain kind of collectively produced book," and that "the best examples of English cultural studies are all of this kind . . . ," he is describing work done at the Birmingham Centre, and work that was, at least on a reading of the texts produced out of it and various descriptions of their production available, inimical to the conventional practices of historical research. The Centre's Popular Memory Group, on its own account, spent a good deal of time wrestling with history's empiricism and resistance to "Theory" (Popular Memory Group 1982). What the historian must do with this account, in the historian's prosaic and deflationary way, is point out that the educational form within which they did their wrestling is actually inimical to conventional historical practice, particularly to the processes of archive research. Group practice is collective; archive research involves the lone historian, taking part in an undemocratic practice. Archive research is expensive, of time and of money, and not something that a group of people can practically do, anyway. Within this educational form, it is not surprising to find historical work at the Centre based on the analysis of text. The *kind* of text generally used (government documents and fictions) does deserve some comment, as do the structuralist models of reading that were a major influence on their analysis. The use of structuralist linguistics, and the notion of "discourse" itself (which had among its enticements a ready critique of empiricism) dictated a particular choice of texts for the purposes of historical analysis.

Government reports, printed and widely distributed in the nineteenth century, are the most readily available of British historical documents; fictions (prose fictions) from the past get put on reading lists everywhere because they are available in mass-produced paperbacks; and every person growing up literate in twentieth-century Britain has massive experience of reading continuous fictional prose, brings to it a most sophisticated (though unarticulated) repertoire of reading techniques. These are good (and necessary) reasons for concentrating on these particular kinds of texts; but if there really is no "connectedness of everything" (if there were this connectedness, then the Report of a Commission of Inquiry would give access to the same primordial whole of reality as a cookery book, and one bit of writing does as well as another) then a textual reading of the nineteenth century that omits other forms of writing (poetry, for instance, and an understanding of the meaning of different poetic forms to different audiences) is going to produce a very odd account. The model of language available in these textual approaches was, as well, quite inadequate to the task in hand, first, making no distiction between spoken and written language; and second, having no recognition of language as a form of cognition and a process of development, that is actively acquired by human beings in a social and psychological process; and third, also being without a range of strategies for analyzing the literary form as a negotiated form, wrought, used, written, read, abandoned within specific societies. (All of this must be seen as a pointer to future and necessary work, rather than as a digression). The structuralist model of language was quite inadequate for the historical task it was set. History's most urgent need is indeed, for an adequate model of both spoken and written language; and whether this model is developed within historical studies or by students of cultural studies working on the past, does not seem to me to matter half as much as the fact that it might be done.

There are many accounts of curriculum change in systems of national education by which to interpret the particular use of texts and choice of methodology that I have been discussing. In Britain, the establishment of English literature as the foundation of a national system of education between 1880 and 1920 was also the getting of education on the cheap, for each child already had his or her own resource in the possession of the English language, and a long and expensive linguistic training of teachers was unnecessary (Baldick, 1983; Doyle, 1989) Practical Criticism in the Universities in Britain after 1930 (for which each undergradute had a resource in his own sensibility) and New Criticism in the US—its capacity, in Porter's words, "to provide a pedagogically functional solution to the problems posed by the numbers and kinds of new college students poured into the American academy by the G.I. Bill after World War Two" (Porter, 1990)—are only two recent examples of the reorganization of education in terms of cheapness and practicality, and around accessible texts. A historical education in Britain was never as expensive as a linguistic one, but the patient laying down of a fantastically detailed historical map over the ten years before a student entered higher education at the age of 18, demands a teaching force in the schools that is able to do the laying down: the amount of history taught in British society has steadily diminished over the last thirty years—a point to which I shall return in a moment.

The cheapness and practicality of text-based historical inquiry could also be seen as a theoretical propriety. The academy observed the last great flowering of English progressive education in the schools in the 1970s, and in some cases, certainly within cultural studies, tried to take that flowering as its own. This flowering was seen to take place in both the English departments of secondary schools, and in the practice of integrated topic work in many primary schools. The breaking down of barriers between teachers and taught, common involvement in a common project, a text or groups of texts making inquirers of them all—all of this was most movingly described throughout the 1970s, particularly in the journal of the National Association of the Teaching of English, and in the journals *Teaching London Kids* and *The English Magazine.*

This is to suggest what the influence of pedagogical forms on the organization of historical knowledge in the early days of British cultural studies might have been. I would make suggestions as well, about the practice of history (which could also be called the disappearance of history) in the primary school and in the lower forms of the secondary school as exercising a particular shaping force. Here, I have to rely on government publications (those most easily obtained of historical documents) and the series of reports by Her Majesty's Inspectors of Schools, which chart the virtual disappearance of history as a subject taught to children, its integration into topic and project work, and the abandonment of the cognitive form of the chronology, from the the late 1960s onwards. Particular theories of the child-mind and application of Piagetian psychology, dictated that children should "discover" the past through a study of its artifacts (Clothes, Houses, Food) and through their identification and empathy with people living in the past. Was "the culture concept" as used by historians, and in some of the models for acquiring historical knowledge within cultural studies, actually invented in the schools, between about 1955 and 1975? In Britain, we do not even have a social and cultural history of education that allows us to think that this might be a question.

Recently, the focus of cultural studies has moved from Masters teaching to the undergraduate degree (it is taught to undergraduates at nine British polytechnics and at two universities, one of them Birmingham University, which now has a Department, not a Centre, and which has offered an honors and a joint honors degree for the last two years). If the history of history in cultural studies is to be written, it will involve taking account of the institutional setting yet again, the particular alignment of humanities subjects under departmental reorganization in the Polytechnics, and the need of historians for students to teach. At the same time, those historians are bound to do less history, as recession (which recession?—all our recessions) imposes constraints of time as well as money on conventional historical practice. Existing history courses and options have fitted into many new cultural studies degrees in the Polytechnics, and we need to ask particular questions of them, about the interface of different knowledges, brought together in undergraduate teaching. Super-ordinate to all these reorganizations of pedagogy and the uses of historical knowledge within a particular society over a span of some thirty years, is a paradigm shift observable across all academic culture (and in the commonplace and secular world of which the academy is a part) in the way in which, since the 1950s, "one discipline after another in the human sciences (has) cut its ties to history, strengthened its autonomy with theory, and produced its meanings without that pervasive historical perspective that in the 19th century had permeated the self-understanding of almost every branch of learning" (Schorske, 1990, p. 416). The discipline of history itself has taken part in this general flight from the historical: in the abandonment of time in favor of "the culture concept"; or in favor of what Raymond Williams (1976) noted in *Keywords* when he wrote of a specific twentieth-century form of the term "history" as a tale of "accidents, unforeseen events, frustration of conscious purpose . . . an argument especially against hope" (p. 147).

It is in this particular historical moment—to be intensely parochial for a moment— that British cultural studies needs to think about what it will *do* with history, and what kind of historical thinking it will ask its students to perform. It has no choice, I think, but to *have* history, for by my reckoning, very soon more history (historical topics, history options) will be taught to undergraduates taking interdisciplinary degree courses than to those doing history in the conventional manner, in Polytechnics and Universities. And this will be—strange conjunction—in a dehistoricized intellectual world in which— as soon as the new National Curriculum in history becomes operative, *all* children in the society (including that very small percentage of 18-year-olds who enter higher education in the UK) will be taught exactly the same set of historical knowledges, from the age of five to sixteen.

Then, after the parochialism, I was going to be polite, for I wanted to be polite, as a guest of the Conference and of cultural studies. It was going to be a politeness that would be, in its turn, a response to the politeness that historians often experience: for there is a common and accommodating reflection that is found in many moments of disciplinary niceness—and those took place here, at the Conference, quite as much as anywhere else—where they will tell you this: that any rigorous theoretical form or mode of inquiry needs a historical perspective, a proper historicity. So, knowing that this would be said, and wanting to be polite, I was going to say something like this:

If British cultural studies really does operate in the "reflexive and even self-conscious mood" that Richard Johnson claims for it (Johnson, 1986–1987, p. 38) then it seems to me that it just might, in these times, be able achieve what history cannot; for the history of a pedagogical practice and educational forms (in Britain at least) puts cultural studies in a position to do its own historiography (to deconstruct itself?) as it goes along.

But I came to understand that I was thinking about a British situation, a situation of enforced cross-disciplinarity, in times of economic hardship for the academy. Instead, after those Conference days I would ask—politely—a series of questions: Why does cultural studies *want* history? What does wanting it mean? What new acts of transference will items from the past help cultural studies—or make it—perform? How will it be done? How taught? Will there be any room for detailed historical work; or are students of cultural studies bound to rely on great schematic and secondary sweeps through time? Will there be any room for the historical case-study in its pedagogy? What good is it all to you, anyway? Perhaps no good at all . . . .

W. H. Auden had a conversation with Clio, sometime in the 1930s, in his "Homage to Clio"; or rather, not a conversation at all, for the blank-faced girl said nothing back to him. He watched her watch the the world's alteration, unique disaster, *longue durée*, everything, all of it, and commented: "You had nothing to say and did not, one could see/Observe where you were, Muse of the unique /Historical fact" (Auden, 1966, p. 309). What all our students will need is an understanding that the texts and documents that they use for historical study are themselves historical facts, not just repositories of facts . . . and that the past that the texts and sources configure is not carved in stone simply because texts and sources go on being used as representatives of a real historical reality. They need to grasp its impermanence even as they read it, and write it. "Observe where you are . . ."; but that is the historian's instruction to herself, as much as a suggestion made to you.

DISCUSSION: Carolyn Steedman

QUESTION: Just as you traced cultural studies' work to the forms of pedagogical practice that current cultural studies workers were exposed to, would it be fair to trace your own criticisms of cultural studies to a theory of language that you were exposed to, a theory of language that in a way made its work invisible?
STEEDMAN: I can't claim to have traced the form of cultural studies to the particular educational biographies of its practitioners because I'm simply not in a position to do that. I can't write a history of cultural studies. And *of course* I received an education that presented me with a particular theory of language, that did indeed make its own work invisible. I'm still a victim of that theory, as we all are of one education; and at the same time believe I have seen through it. As this is universally the case with all the theories that all of us live by, all I can finally say is "So what?"

BILL BUXTON: In terms of your own work, do you see history as a way of becoming involved in radical interventions? And more generally, do you think that history and cultural history would play a role in this kind of project?
STEEDMAN: Is the History Workshop in England what you mean? The whole project of returning people's history to them, the whole enterprise of oral history and worker/ writer groups in Britain, and that complex of radical interventions through questions of popular memory and the popular past? Well, I was shaped and formed by those enterprises, but now I think I'm more interested in questions of what the projects of radical and socialist history, with their notion of a particular kind of practice or idea of intervention, can't do and can't perform. Raymond Williams, in an interview with Stephen Heath, talked about a very common and unexamined impulse on the part of the radical historians in Britain: the idea that somewhere out there, back there, there

was a radical constituency, and one simply had to go out and find it and make connections between it and the present, and a great many of our problems would be over. And he commented on the falsity of that extraordinarily romantic quest. I suppose I'm more interested now in what history doesn't perform for people.

MEAGHAN MORRIS: I'd like to take up Carolyn's very provocative question, "Why do you want history?" in the positive spirit that I think it was put to us. I think at a cultural studies conference somebody—and I'm prepared to play the part—should answer that question as an avowed textualist, postmodernist, poststructuralist, and really, a raging formalist. I'd like to answer it by way of trying to explain why I circulate work that is categorized by the above litany in the United States, and in Australia as cultural history. There's something very important at stake in that and that's something to do precisely with Australia's location in the history that Catherine Hall outlined. There has been in cultural studies for some years a discourse on the death of history. The notion has something to do with changes in mass media, commodification, and so on, which have shifted culture in such a way that, once upon a time, there was a thing called "real history" and now there's something else. It's a very powerful discourse which, no matter how hard you criticize it, doesn't go away. And of course it circulates in my country too. It is an even more poisonous discourse in my country than the most raging forms of American idealist deconstruction, at the same time that this discourse on the death of history is circulating something else that is happening in the popular. There has emerged a passion for history across a range of popular cultural activities I couldn't even begin to list. The focus is often around a theme called amnesia. In the seventies it was very common for people to say, "Australia is an amnesiac society." How could we have forgotten what happened to Aboriginal people? Why did America make fictions about their frontier history and we just did not know about ours? Then, of course, a generation of Aboriginal intellectuals and activists said, "Whose amnesia? We didn't forget." Then satellite technology allowed for a set of political actions around the status of history to circulate as popular culture between white people, Aboriginal people, and immigrant peoples. It produced a huge genre, called by the media and lived by people as, Historical Miniseries. Necessarily, all these developments coalesced around the Australian Bicentennial in 1988. In the convergence of these two things—an academic idea in cultural studies that history is dead because of the media and an enormously complicated set of developments not only in the popular but in otherwise very antagonistic political debates—history becomes the name of the space in which a politics of the relationship between those two things is possible. And that's why I'm simultaneously a formalist—because I think you can't think the novelty of things that happen in the popular without confronting them—and why I call it history—because in the culture I live in history is the name of the space where we define what matters. That's an answer to Carolyn's question. And I think if we all answered it we would produce an absolutely fantastic collective discourse.

34

Bandits, Heroes, the Honest, and the Misled: Exploring the Politics of Representation in the Hungarian Uprising of 1956*

Anna Szemere

Because the theoretical framework of cultural studies has developed in Western Europe and North America, it is perhaps natural that its primary focus has been advanced capitalist society. Additionally, because of the presence and impact of anthropology on this multidisciplinary inquiry into cultures and—not unrelated to this—the political pull of the so-called third world, cultural studies has had a lot to say about the dominated or colonized "Other" as well, focusing on the cultural interaction between capitalist and traditional societies. Yet those societies which until quite recently have been the site of "existing socialism" have been left virtually unexplored by cultural studies. I have wondered whether this apparent lack of interest might be due to Western leftists' ambivalence towards these societies: are they perceived as sites of a compromised, abused, and now defeated utopia? Could there have been a fear that a critical stance towards these political systems (while they were still socialist) would threaten the distinctive political edge of cultural studies and Western leftism *vis-à-vis* the dominant discourse on socialism in their own society? Whatever inhibitions have rendered the so-called second world as a virtually blank space, it is obvious that cultural studies research on this part of the world is important and that researchers in Eastern and Central Europe can make fundamental contributions. This essay is a beginning.

The Hungarian revolution of 1956 is an event of special significance not only for Hungarians, who have recently elevated it to the rank of a national holiday, but also for the Western socialist and communist movements. In Stuart Hall's talk at this conference, "1956 Budapest" marked the beginning of the disintegration of Marxist theory and of a crisis within the international Labor movement. In the contemporary Hungarian historical consciousness the predominant meaning of the revolt is somewhat differently inflected. Rather than signifying crisis and breach, it enjoys moral approval as an act of resistance and defiance against an oppressive tyrannical order. The present essay attempts to capture the initial discursive construction of the uprising in the public political domain—specifically, through a close analysis of Hungarian Radio broadcasts.

From 1956 to 1989

The timeliness of a close investigation of the Hungarian national uprising of 1956 is made evident by its recent official reevaluation. It does not seem unnatural that a new regime, which came to power as a result of free elections early this year (in April 1990), would rewrite national history and its special events. The reassessment of 1956, however, had been initiated a year before by Imre Pozsgay, an eminent reformist within the Hungarian Socialist Workers' Party (at the time a state party). To the astonishment of many of his comrades, Mr. Pozsgay proposed characterizing the events of 1956 as a "national uprising." In thus dismissing the official label of "counterrevolution," Pozsgay directly challenged the political views, sentiments, and interests of an ever shrinking minority of communists who, even inside the Communist Party, had been rapidly losing political control.

A set of significant events inevitably followed from the renaming of what in colloquial speech had been merely referred to as "fifty-six." The oppositional parties demanded that October 23rd, the initial day of the uprising, be commemorated as a red-letter day (paid holiday) and replace the enforced celebration of an earlier October Revolution, the one which had brought about the first socialist society in Russia in 1917. The leading figure of the 1956 events, Prime Minister Imre Nagy, was rehabilitated. A communist leader whose political orientation would classify him as a reformist today, Nagy was pushed aside in the early 1950s Rákosi era with the less benign label "re-visionist" and even excluded temporarily from the Communist Party.[1] As the revolution of 1956 commenced, however, there was massive pressure to appoint him Head of the Government. He enjoyed the support not only of the revolutionary crowds but also of the Hungarian and even the Soviet Communist Parties (Kopácsi, 1986). Nevertheless, two years after the defeat of the revolt, Nagy was imprisoned and executed under pressure from predominantly rank and file participants, and buried in an unmarked mass prison grave.

In her study of the political culture of the French revolution, Lynn Hunt (1984 pp.34–38) discusses its successive states in terms of theatrical genres. She has argued that comedy was followed by romance, which eventually grew into tragedy. Analogously, I would suggest that the Hungarian uprising enacted the script of a tragedy. More particularly, the circumstances and the mode of Imre Nagy and his comrades' execution revived a theme known from ancient Greek tragedies. Sophocles's *Antigone* may come to one's mind, a play in which the tyrant Kreon forbids the protagonist to bury her brother, a victim of Kreon's lust for power.[2]

No wonder that during the thirty-two years of the Kádár regime (1956–1988), the name of Prime Minister Imre Nagy was rarely mentioned, and the facts of his undignified death were known only to a small, politically active minority. But when doctrinaire communist control over definition was removed, a bewildering multiplicity of previously muted or suppressed voices came to be heard through the mass media and the printed word. In the spring of 1989 the streets of Budapest were flooded by books—exhibited on temporary newsstands—dedicated to this subject and other events of 1956. The releases included other "classics"—previously on index—and more recent writings: local and foreign publications; memoirs and archival materials; facsimile reissues of contemporary newspapers; and so forth.[3] Imre Nagy and the politicans closest to him thus became publicly recognized national heroes, a process culminating in an elaborate funeral ceremony where the several hundred victims of the post-revolutionary terror were individually commemorated.

That definitions of the 1956 revolt fundamentally shaped the new political system is indicated by the choice of the date October 23 and of the name, the Republic of Hungary. Substituting for the denomination People's Republic, a shorthand term for proletarian dictatorship, the new name signifies the restoration of pluralist democracy abandoned in 1948.

This acknowledgment of the events of 1956 is of great symbolic significance not only in shattering the old socio-political system but in establishing and cementing the new one in its wake. As the rivalry between the major new parties grew into nasty confrontations, particularly during the election campaigns, it became imperative to emphasize images and events evoking a sense of unity and bond between political forces as diverse as Christian Democrats and Radical Liberals, Reform Communists and Peasant Smallholders. The memory of the revolt proved sufficiently powerful in the Hungarian collective consciousness to serve such a purpose. As a headline of a local daily newspaper recently announced, "1956 is the grounding of our future."

The contrast between the concepts of "revolution" and "counterrevolution" as definitions of the nature of the 1956 revolt not only signifies opposing political interests, ideologies, and sentiments but also stands for competing narrative accounts of what actually took place between October 23rd and November 4th of that year. The conspiracy theory, which János Kádár resorted to in an attempt to legitimize his Soviet-backed power, persisted in official political publications even as recently as 1986. Thus, for example, János Berecz's book (1986), issued on the occasion of the thirtieth anniversary of the event, attributes the uprising predominantly to an organized conspiracy of internal and external enemies comprised of local fascist elements and Western imperialists; in contrast, most "unofficial" accounts emphasize the spontaneous character of the revolt. During the Kádár era the validity of the "conspiracy-theory" could not be overtly challenged. Yet on the level of language, an implicit debate and negotiation over the words "fifty-six" had been going on a long time.[4] As a result, both adversaries and supporters of the revolt tended to avoid explicit definitions. In the official domain the more neutral phrase "tragic events of '56" gradually replaced the term "counterrevolution" with its connotations of violent retaliation and betrayal. In other sites of public discourse, the term "uprising" gained legitimacy. Imre Pozsgay's proposal of "popular uprising," cautiously acknowledging a rightful cause, aimed at creating an alliance between relatively reform-minded communists who had nevertheless refused to call the events of '56 a freedom fight, and those diverse, increasingly visible political groups who had been struggling for the revolt's sanctification.

The debate over the name and the meaning of the October events started before the revolt was put down. Indeed, from the very first sign of civil unrest, the contest of diverse political forces for the definition of the participants' political goals and actions was apparent. This contest was not merely running parallel to or reflecting the events. The interpretations and reinterpretations of what was taking place were integral and directly relevant to the political process as a whole.

In attaching special significance to revolutionary rhetoric, I am drawing on Lynn Hunt's discussion of the political culture of the French revolution. Hunt is interested "in the logic of political action as it was expressed symbolically," in the ways people "put the Revolution and themselves as revolutionaries into images and gestures" (1984, p. 14). She does not see symbolic practices, including rhetoric, as epiphenomenal to non-linguistically constituted realities but views them as practices that shape actors' consciousness and their resulting intentions, interests, and activities. This methodology shares its basic assumptions with constitutive theories of human activity in treating language as an active political force (see Mehan, et al., 1990); the specific relevance of Hunt's study for my present investigation lies in her application of poststructuralist theories to revolutionary discourse. Hunt contends that the very concepts of modern politics and ideology were forged by French revolutionaries in the sense that they "managed to invest these concepts with extraordinary emotional and symbolic significance" (pp. 2–3).

I will argue that public discourse in modern non-democratic and non-pluralistic political contexts—exemplified by any unitary language, whether revolutionary or totalitarian—follows distinctive rules. First of all, the relative significance of discursive practices *vis-à-vis* non-linguistic/non-symbolic ones is greatly enhanced. In other words, representation assumes a disproportionate amount of autonomy in relation to social praxis. As Hunt observes, "the crumbling of the French state let loose a deluge of words," making talk the "order of the day" (pp. 19–20). However, as François Furet emphasizes, "speech substitutes itself for the power" and "the semiotic circuit is the absolute master of politics." This is explained by the disruption of what he considers "the normal relationship between society and politics." Therefore, according to the logic of this argument, "politics becomes a struggle for the right to speak on behalf of the Nation. Language becomes an expression of power, and power is expressed by the right to speak for people" (quoted by Hunt, 1984, p. 23).

The French revolution has, in my view, established a double-faced tradition. In its struggle against royal tyranny and its fervor to establish civil rights and bourgeois freedoms, the revolution showed its liberatory democratic face. On the other hand, as the process of radicalization moved—to borrow Hunt's metaphors—from comedy and romance toward tragedy, a distinctly different face, an increasingly oppressive one, made itself visible. With its paranoid obsession about detecting conspiracy, with its elevation of denunciation to a civil duty, and with its repeated rewriting of history, the Terror laid the grounds for twentieth-century totalitarian political systems.

In admitting their indebtedness to the French example, revolutionary movements tacitly identify with its liberationist face. Hungarians acted so in 1848 for the first time, struggling for bourgeois democracy and national sovereignty. In 1956, because some of the most crucial of those nineteenth century demands had not been met (civil rights) or became topical once again (national sovereignty), the French revolution once again became an empowering model to follow. The inclusion of the "Marseillaise" in the revolutionary musical repertory indicated how the liberationist ethos of that tradition helped shape a new collective consciousness.

A close analysis of Hungarian radio broadcasts identifies two modes of discourse that constitute as well as articulate the two facets of the revolutionary tradition: a liberationist/democratic one and an oppressive/terrorist one. Ironically, in Hungary of the mid-1950s, the liberationist efforts—as part of the broader process of de-Stalinization throughout Eastern Europe—were directed at transforming a system that perceived itself as revolutionary: hence the controversy over whether the revolt was to be designated as revolutionary or counterrevolutionary. The spokesmen of the Stalinist regime were bound to speak the language of terror, even under the radically changed circumstances of the uprising. Instead of passive or compliant acceptance, typical for a time of uncontested domination, their rhetoric was now received as provocative and prompted violent forms of resistance as well as opposing accounts of reality.

The revolutionary voices spoke diverse dialects of what I call "liberationist" language. Although feeding on national historical traditions of liberation movements, the unity of this discourse was extremely precarious, for it was based on very different understandings of democracy, freedom, and "Hungarianness." The relative strength of this popular alliance was ensured and enhanced by its anti-Soviet theme—dramatically foregrounded throughout the course of the events—because of the initial intervention of the Red Army, its unceasing presence, and the threat of a total invasion. It is important to note, however, that individual voices representing particular social groups, political forces, or institutions cannot be neatly distributed between "liberationist" and "terrorist." First, as I have tried to point out, both modes of discourse were totalizing in their claim to represent the whole nation. In both, dichotomous value systems and a black-and-white worldview dominated their meaning-constructions. Certain inflections of the national theme, which had started as part of a liberationist discourse, increasingly assumed elements of terrorist rhetoric. Speakers of the Stalinist status quo, on the other hand, attempted to coopt the "liberator's" nationalistic rhetoric. It follows that liberationist and terrorist modes of expression were not fixed with particular ideologies. The diverse articulations and elaborations of central concepts and themes, such as national independence and unity or the democratic renewal of socialism, involve incessantly changing accents, value emphases, and refractions of meanings.

Additionally, acts of genuine conversion were also the order of the day, resulting in extremely dynamic formations and reformations of what may be called discursive alliances. What themes and issues defined the formation and rearticulation of discursive alliances? How were particular political goals translated into revolutionary rhetoric? How did the revolution create its own myth and what kind of myths did it feed on? Before attempting to answer these questions, I need to discuss the special role of the Hungarian Radio as a preeminent site of public political struggle during the revolt.

Radio, Action, and Discourse

During the 1950s in Hungary, radio was the only electronic mass medium and, as a state monopoly, it functioned primarily as a political institution. Therefore, the struggle for control of Hungarian Radio was both symbolically and strategically important. Horkheimer and Adorno (1972, pp. 159) note the importance of the mass media for totalitarian systems. They argue that the wireless was as instrumental to the National Socialists' cause in Nazi Germany as the printing press was to the Reformation. The liberationist struggle to abolish the Stalinist monopoly of this medium took on a tragic dimension, however, since it was an incident around the Radio building on October 23rd that served as a spark, turning the students' peaceful and disciplined demonstration into an armed confrontation. The students marched to the Radio building in the hope that their demands would be broadcast. Instead, they found themselves intimidated by the Secret Police (Kopácsi, 1986). Ironically, their demands included civil rights issues such as the freedom of speech (Fabó, 1957, p. 12).

It took another week for the rioters to liberate the Radio, which eliminated the Communist Party's power of censorship. But they also expelled all Stalinist voices from the Radio as well. Attempts were made to establish guidelines for a new democratic broadcast policy (Nagy, 1984). Radio Kossuth marked its renewal by inserting the distinctive "free" into its name.

From the start, radio assumed a direct and active political role, unusual in times of peace and order. Because of the constant changes at the top echelons of the Communist Party and the Government, Hungarian Radio served as a loudspeaker for the leaders to address the "people out there." These speeches and various "public notices"—threats, promises, warnings—had a special urgency, since their intent was clearly to intervene in the armed fights. In a sense, the Radio belonged to the community of the nation—not because it was to be used by anyone or everyone, but because it addressed people as members of a collective rather than as casual listeners. From time to time, in order to address the fighters directly and immediately, listeners were requested to place their sets out in the windows. This act spatially reinforced a specific communicational arrangement whereby atomized individual households or families, the typical contexts for radio use, were roughly made into one space. In this sense, the radio may have helped shape a new kind of collectivity with a special force, seen in such recurring metaphors for the nation as "family" or a "wounded body" or the description of the armed clashes as "fratricide."

Despite its preeminent role, the Radio did not represent the public discourse of the revolt in its entirety. The most extremist voices speaking the brutal language of revenge and lynching, anti-Semitism and chauvinism, did not make it to the studio. Certainly, some accounts exaggerated the presence of right-wing extremism. Nonetheless, the repeated appeals by respectable personalities calling on the public to preserve their sobriety and to renounce lynch-law indicates the existence of a revolutionary underworld (Fabó, 1957).

Discursive Alliances and the Revolutionary Process

This afternoon an enormous youth demonstration took place in our capital. Perhaps you Hungarians living abroad will be surprised to hear this piece of news. We, the witnesses of this wonderful ferment, having manifested itself in passionate assemblies and newspaper articles over the past few weeks, have been expecting it to happen. (Fabó, 1957, p. 15)

This enthusiastic and sympathetic radio account went on to describe the youth's symbolic evocation of the War of Independence of 1848 by reference to their songs, national banners, and emblems. The announcer further recounted their demands, which addressed a range of political and economic issues. This was located in the context of the democratic movement of the past few years which has attempted to "purify" the "sacred ideals of socialism" from the "sins" attributed to the Hungarian leaders of the Communist Party. The emergence of this voice was significant in that it conveyed the political and moral concerns and passions of the university students and intellectuals, the initiators of the revolution. In identifying himself with the demonstrators, the radio reporter assumed the historically informed rhetoric of the revolution and emphasized its central symbols and metaphors in statements like "Budapest is celebrating a new March 15th in the October spring."[5]

The report was aired on Radio Freedom, a state-run station airing programs for Hungarians abroad. Half an hour later, the First Secretary of the Communist Party (named the Hungarian Workers' Party and abbreviated HWP), Erno Gerö delivered a speech denouncing the youth movement as "poisoned by chauvinism" and "reactionary." Similarly, he condemned their call for pluralism and civil rights as bourgeois rather than socialist democracy (Fabó, pp. 16–18).

These two voices set the tone for the confrontation and negotiation taking place between two discursive alliances during the initial stage of the uprising: one comprised predominantly of socialist reformist "liberators" empowered by a particular reading of national history; the other representing the Stalinist ruling elite. The latter's tone altered radically, first as Stalinists and subsequently as communists in general recognized that they were losing ground. Months prior to the outbreak of the revolt, a relative tolerance for different, though not openly contesting voices, characterized the Radio's broadcast policy (Scarlett, 1980, p. 31). It is worth nothing that the youth demonstration itself was officially approved by the Minister of the Interior. Nevertheless, until they were removed, the Radio Party leadership had exercised overall control in setting the agenda and providing the definitive interpretations for the actual situation. The representation of active political forces was often distorted and censorship was common. The chronicling of the events blatantly contradicted many observers' and participants' experiences. Alternative accounts, which I will discuss later, surfaced only after successive changes had taken place in the composition of the Party administration and the Government.

My distinction between the liberationist and the terrorist modes of language is based on their contrasting attempts to make sense of what was actually happening, as well as on their different style and rhetoric. These differences are manifested in three closely interrelated areas of debate: (a) the definitions of the actions and the identity of the actors (their socio-political status, interests, and intentions); (b) the general moral/cultural frame underlying the fight between opposing political forces for the meaning of such quasi-religious notions as "honesty," "sin," "sacredness," "pollution," and "purification of patriotism"; and (c) the "national issue," where differing constructions of patriotism and forms of national historical consciousness were set against one another.

Who were the revolutionary actors and in what activities were they involved? The struggle between the "liberationists" and the Stalinist rulers over this question began even before the demonstration had turned into a bloody conflict. What the radio report described as "wonderful ferment" (Fabó, p. 15) was referred to by the Party Secretary Gerö as "evil nationalist poisoning" (Fabó, p. 18). The two texts suggested incompatible concepts of national history and identity. The reporter drew on the ethos of 1848 to promote a sense of unity through reviving and reliving history.[6] In contrast, Gerö implicitly identified Hungarian history with that of its Communist movement, which had represented a rather inconsequential political force until the end of World War Two:

> We communists are Hungarian patriots. We were patriots in the prisons of Horthy-fascism during the hard decades of illegality. (Fabó, p. 17)[7]

Both voices foregrounded youth as the center of the present movement. While the reporter projected an image of them modeled after the legendary revolutionary youth of 1848, celebrated by successive generations, Gerö claimed that these young people were merely acting under the influence of certain inimical forces. The sinister abstractness of the phrase "enemies of our people" (Fabó, p. 17) contrasted curiously with the radio report's empirical everyday concreteness in depicting the actual adherents to the call for social and political change. Speakers of totalitarian and terrorist discourse typically employ abstract sociological categories or labels to refer to social subjects ("working class," "peasantry," "intelligentsia," "imperialists," "enemy of the people"). As opposed to this, the reporter substituted a spontaneous classification for the established, one that was based upon demographic, occupational, and situational roles. This had the overall effect of articulating and, at the same time, promoting an emerging collective identity. Naming the actors as "young workers, pedestrians, soldiers, old people, high school students, conductors," the reporter suggested a diversity in a developing unity of action (Fabó, p. 16).

The following morning the Hungarian Cabinet announced to radio listeners that "fascist reactionary elements" had launched an armed attack against "our public buildings" and "our armed forces" (Fabó p. 21). The voice of the Ministry of the Interior spoke about "looting counterrevolutionary groups." Many more notices reported on the outbreak of the revolt in a similarly terrorist manner. Significantly, the act of taking up arms against the establishment earned the insurgents not only the nastiest political label available in the existing vocabulary ("fascists"), but also the stigma of being little more than ordinary criminals. "Counterrevolutionary bandits," "hordes," etc., were accused of murdering "ordinary citizens, soldiers and secret policemen" (Fabó p. 22). Through this minor manipulation of facts—arranging the classes of victims in a particular order—the official voice suggested that the fighters were mindless killers. Additionally, the defeat of the "counterrevolution" was declared to be the sacred goal of the nation and "every honest Hungarian worker" was summoned to condemn the "bloody ravage."

This mode of criminalizing political adversaries and commanding unconditional loyalty on a moral basis remained a decisive feature of terrorist discourse, despite its subsequent readjustments.

October 24th witnessed important personnel changes in the State and Party apparatus. Imre Nagy was made Prime Minister and other previously silenced and persecuted Party leaders appointed to the Central Committee. Nagy proclaimed the institution of summary justice for the fighters, but the deadline for amnesty for those willing to lay down their arms had to be repeatedly extended.

Radio listeners were requested to place their sets in the windows so that fighters could be called on directly to end the shootings. This was a remarkable turn in that revolutionaries, up to then stigmatized as criminals and enemies, came to be acknowledged and addressed as members of the *body social*. From that moment on, Hungarian Radio was exploited by the power elite as a major tool for negotiation with the insurgents.

Rather than calming down, the fighting became ever more intense. The intervention of the Soviet Red Army troops, unexpected and incomprehensible even for some members of the ruling elite, prompted many to take sides with the revolutionaries, including entire units of the Budapest Police and the Army (Kopácsi, 1986). Official public notices displayed the results of pressure forcing them to describe elements of the insurgents as something other than "counterrevolutionary," such as "drifting and misled young people." This ideological concession was compelled by the Party and Government's immediate need to influence the armed masses and to persuade them to surrender.

Imre Nagy's speech later during the day added a respectable voice of support to the uprising. First, his informal and inclusive mode of address made no distinction between the fighters and the general public: "People of Budapest" was meant to include the insurgents as part of the city's community. Second, while rhetorically constructing this unity, he claimed to be part of it rather than distancing himself as a leader. Third, for the first time, the complexities of the situation were addressed by distinguishing between three groups of revolutionaries: the young "peaceful demonstrators," the "good-willed workers," and some unspecified "hostile elements." Although this description of the workers was somewhat condescending, Nagy no longer used the omniscient terrorist language of the Party elite. Lastly, the Prime Minister refused to condemn the revolt by labeling it; he simply referred to it as the "fight."

This speech marked a shift and redefined the Stalinist rulers' agenda. Despite his call for reconciliation and peace, Nagy's idea of restoring order was proposed as a means rather than an end in itself. He saw it as a precondition of carrying out what he called "our sacred national program" of democratization in every domain of the political and economic life, a program he had proposed as early as 1953. By removing the sacred overtones from the Party's objective of restoring order, the Prime Minister made a political as well as a moral commitment for social change. A believer in peaceful reforms, Nagy regarded the armed confrontation as a *moral* threat:

> . . . we must not allow that blood to pollute our sacred national program. (Fabó, p. 23)

The Communist Party's hard-liners used various discursive strategies to enhance their communicative efficacy and regain control. Firstly, they appropriated certain elements from Nagy's speech, for example, in making a clear distinction between the students' demonstration and the activities of hostile forces who were persistently designated as "robbers," "murderers," and "counterrevolutionary bandits" (Fabó, pp. 24–29).

Second, they coopted a nationalist style of rhetoric removed from the cause of sovereignty. The Hungarian Popular Front, a mouthpiece of the Party, for example, crowded its text with the adjective "Hungarian" ("shed Hungarian blood," "Hungarian future") to make its appeal as broad as possible. It subverted itself, however, because of the contradiction in both the right-wing fascistic connotations of its phrasings and the left-wing extremism carried by two elements of the text: the brutal, derogatory language decrying the "provocateurs" and the dehistoricized concept of national identity. As exemplified by Gerö's speech, this mode of dehistoricized discourse assumed that the existence of the country was entirely a communist accomplishment.[8] By confusing the interests and history of the Hungarian people with those of the Party, the insurgents were constructed as a threat, not to the regime but to the survival of the nation as a whole (Fabó, p. 34).

Third, the Party created (and controlled) pseudo-autonomous organizations targeted at specific segments of the population. The rhetoric of the National Council of Hungarian Women represented perhaps the most militant and aggressive version of terrorist speech (Fabó p. 24). Apart from indiscriminately labeling the fighters as "murderous provocateurs," "slanderers," and "liars," the short notice was packed with threats and commands. Like the appeals of the Popular Front, this rhetoric was also bound to fail. The very idea of calling on women to keep relatives from joining street battles was based on an assumption of women's "natural" domesticity and instinctive rejection of violence. The militant tone undermined the effectiveness of such a strategy, which was, by the way, out of line with the communist ideology of women's emancipation. The National Peace Council issued a similar notice appealing to women's traditional roles and attitudes, but now in a more sentimental tone:

> Wives, mothers, Hungarian women! . . . Wives, mothers! You must know what the blessings of peace are. Help so that the bloodshed will be ended . . . (Fabó, p. 25).

A fourth discursive strategy on the part of the Radio Party leadership consisted in broadcasting a host of telegrams reportedly received from workers' collectives and student committees. These texts displayed a striking uniformity in content and style. The recurring motifs included the condemnation of the "counterrevolutionary provocation"; greetings for the newly elected Central Committee of the HWP and the Prime Minister; the approval of his program of renewal; and lastly, the assurance of the State and Party leaders of the collective's loyalty and trust for them. It would be difficult to identify the authors of these telegrams. Interestingly, they were aired immediately after a Party official's call to "every honest worker" to "condemn the bloody ravage of the counter-revolutionary gangs." This can leave little doubt about the existence of a script, which was followed, presumably by low-level Party committees, on behalf of particular communities excluded from the process. Fiction was thus translated by the Party into the desired consensus, into a simulacrum of political representation. Broadcasting these telegrams epitomized how much the world of public discourse had been detached from the world of experiential realities, even as it invaded it. The terrorist politics of representation tended to reduce people to passive characters, if not puppets, of a very real script, written by distant authors, according to inscrutable rules.

This voluntaristic political practice—one which deliberately confuses a desired state of affairs with the actual one—is seldom effective in molding people's perceptions and judgments of reality, but it is definitely self-defeating when discourse is not monopolized by one speaker. The credibility of the telegrams was seriously undermined by more balanced accounts. In one of these, the Journalists' National Association argued for a massive working-class participation in the revolt. Rather than assuming that the insurgents had been "misled," the journalists claimed that their struggle was "just and perfectly justified" (Fabó, p. 31). With this reading of the uprising, however, the Association's aim was to make a more powerful case against the perceived minority of "hostile provocateurs" who were disrupting the revolutionary process. At this point, the Stalinist and the "liberationist" speakers did not merely compete for the discursive control of the situation; they also shared some common goals resulting from their fear about the potential consequences of the fighting and about the potential power of the right-wing forces. Puting an end to the fighting was seen by both groups as the most important immediate goal. The appointment of Imre Nagy and the formation of a new Government must have felt like a disturbing concession for the Stalinist elite and an encouraging prospect for the intellectuals and students. On the other hand, the masses of workers, especially in the countryside, were less trustful and tended to see Nagy as "just another Communist" who could only deserve credit by ridding his Government of its predominantly compromised personnel and shaking off Soviet domination. Therefore, the discursive construction of Imre Nagy by "terrorist" and "liberationist" speakers alike as a wise ruler capable of restoring order expressed a shared interest of both major sides having access to the Radio. The two political forces had different motivations for supporting him: the Stalinist elite for strategic reasons; the democratic reformers genuinely believed him to be a trustworthy leader. Transferring the leading role of administration to Nagy, however, involved shifting the center of power from the Party to the Government. In fact, this was compelled by the Party's acute crisis of legitimation. The unpopular First Secretary Gerö resigned (and escaped to the Soviet Union) to be replaced by János Kádár, who attempted a cautious departure from the Stalinist agenda.

Purity, Unity, and the Rhetoric of the National Democratic Revolution

On October 25th the general tone of the Radio abruptly changed. At this point, the Radio seemed to move into the very center of the revolutionary process. The communique announcing Kádár's appointment to the post of First Secretary was repeatedly broadcast and followed by a call for all "Hungarians" to celebrate, display national flags, etc. They were summoned back to their homes and workplaces from street demonstrations. Reports were subsequently aired on people's ecstatic mood as they were hooraying, kissing, and embracing in the streets. The National Anthem and the "Marseillaise" were played. Broadcasters created the impression that the revolt had arrived at a turning point, if not at victory.

Without relying on other sources, it is difficult to judge how much these reports were edited and orchestrated, or how much they accurately reflected people's mood. In either case, the program served to introduce and accentuate Kádár's and Nagy's upcoming speeches. Keen to adjust himself to the "liberationist" or "national democratic" mode of rhetoric, by now the dominant one, the First Secretary of the Party seemed desperate to formulate a differentiated and balanced account of the past few days' events. Attempting to abandon the overall derogatory tone of his predecessor while at the same time expressing his serious reservations about the politics of the movement as a whole, he seemed to be dancing on a tightrope:

> The demonstration—honest as to *most* of its *goals*—in which *part* of our youth was involved; a demonstration starting out peacefully degenerated, in a matter of hours, into an armed revolt against the state power of the People's Democracy—according to the intentions of counterrevolutionary elements, enemies of our people. (Fabó, p. 56, italics added)

For Kádár, the People's Democracy, that is, the monopolistic Party rule "remains and must remain sacred." To support this claim, he gave a new twist to the notion of "liberation" as it was being used by those supporting Imre Nagy. Kádár saw the socialist dictatorship as the guarantee of freedom from the "old yoke," a popular communist metaphor for the semi-feudal capitalist system characterizing Hungary before the Second World War.

On the other side, the Prime Minister shifted the accent from the counterrevolutionary elements to the workers and justified their participation by contextualizing it:

> A small number of counterrevolutionary instigators launched an armed attack against the order of our People's Democracy. They enjoyed the partial support of the workers of Budapest, who had been desperate over the prevailing conditions in our country. This desperation was aggravated by the severe political and economic mistakes committed in the past, the redemption of which should be an imperative both regarding the country's situation and the general wish of the people. (Fabó, p. 56)

This portrait of the process not only invalidated the Communist Party's "theory of deception," which had denied any coherence or meaning to the mass activities, it also established a causal relation between the destructive political practices of the regime and the revolution. The crucial moment of the speech, however, was Nagy's promise to start negotiations with the Soviet Union on the withdrawal of their troops from Hungarian territories. Embracing the theme of independence, which eventuated in his declaration of Hungary's neutrality at the United Nations, earned Imre Nagy a genuine mass following. This manifested itself in his ability to terminate the combat by the last days of October.

With the Stalinist voices suppressed, the Radio reflected, as well as helped shape, a democratically organized national unity across the multiplicity of voices now demanding to be heard. A host of new grass-roots organizations erupted nationwide, such as workers' councils, various national and youth guards, committees, etc. Political parties, churches, and professional associations, silenced and banned since the communist takeover in 1948, re-emerged to welcome and influence the revolutionary proceedings according to their widely differing political visions. Organs up to then controlled by the Stalinists like the Radio itself or the Communist Party's daily, the *Szabad Nép* (Free People), aligned themselves with the country's new leaders. Purges began to replace compromised figures holding key positions.

The revolution started to weave its own myth from a variety of sources. It drew on the national historical mythology, but also on the day-to-day expressions of international solidarity. On the negative side, it also gained strength from an acute sense of being threatened and from the painful awareness of lost lives sacrificed in the fighting. Although endangered by its own excesses (purges, lynch-law, anti-Semitism), the uprising was acquiring a certain tragic dignity. Many of those initially protesting against the Stalinist/terrorist misrepresentation of the revolt were now concerned to retain and discursively elaborate this sense of dignity, or, in their own words, the "purity of the revolution."

This process of naming and renaming remained central throughout the twelve days of the uprising. At this stage redefinitions were vital to the moral dignity and political self-perception of the revolutionary participants. It was a kind of meta-discourse discrediting the claims made by the spokesmen of the defeated regime in earlier broadcasts. Reinscribing the "story" by challenging the crude or condescending descriptions had a number of motives. First, it may have been an instinctive gesture of self-defense. People had been conditioned during the Rákosi-era to fear imposed political labels ("kulak," "imperialist agent," etc.) because of their often fatal consequences. Attributing counterrevolutionary intentions to anyone implied a death sentence—which actually happened on a mass scale during the post-revolutionary terror. Additionally, people must have felt a genuine desire to restore the disturbed relations between their experiential sense of truth and the official representations. Such labels and categories were connected with particular, in many cases fabricated, narratives. The editorial of *Szabad Nép* (October 28th) read on the Radio provided the first passionate and eloquent defense of the insurgents and their cause:

> We disagree with those globally evaluating the events of the past few days as a counterrevolutionary and fascistic *coup* attempt. . . . The uprising started with the rallies of the college youth. Yet it would be a grave mistake to view them as expressions of merely a youth movement. The young people of Budapest articulated the sentiments and noble passions to be found in the hearts of the people as a whole. At last, we must recognize that in our country a great national democratic movement has evolved embracing and uniting the whole nation . . . . Especially later in the afternoon, some dissonant voices joined the demonstration whose demands no longer related to socialist democracy. It must be noted that at this stage, a number of students undertook to convince the blinded and the extremist elements that the struggle was being carried for socialist democracy and not against the social order. (Fabó, p. 89).

By voicing the participants' viewpoints and motives, marginalized up to then, the author suggested a narrative of the proceedings of the first day dissimilar from the "terrorist" accounts. With respect to the explosive moment of the revolution, the journalist emphasized the role of the First Secretary Gerö's speech, which, in its total unresponsiveness to the revolutionary demands, caused considerable public disappointment. A new aspect of the "story" was thus uncovered: the Party leaders' responsibility for letting the demonstration grow into armed clashes:

> By then the street atmosphere had been extremely tense. At various points of the city shootings began. Let me add that even during the second and third days protesters marched in front of public buildings with slogans such as "Independence! Freedom! We are no fascists!" (Fabó, p. 89)

The indiscriminate imposition of the "fascist" label in "terrorist" speech—even though in some cases derived from a genuine dread—had created a sense of hideous threat. Simultaneous charges of petty burglary had framed the insurgents in an equally dishonoring tone, mocking and despising them. In order to defend the revolutionary actors from such accusations, the journalist recalled the sight of untouched goods behind broken shop windows: a favored and lasting image signifying '56 as a "moral revolution."

Certain words and metaphors, increasingly solemn and religion-based, such as "purity," "blood," "brotherhood," "sanctity," "sin," "sacrifice," "conversion," "resurrection," etc., flooded the public rhetoric. In the discursive construction of the youth as leaders of the democratic movement and fighters, even martyrs of the uprising, it was a short road from "purity" and "honesty" to "sanctity." The ideology of democratic renewal found a "natural" symbol in them. Onto this "natural" symbolism, an historical one relating to 1848 and its celebrated youth was grafted. As the writer Gyula Hay stated, this was the revolution of the young and those "young in spirit" (Fabó, p. 57). In its repeated calls to end the fighting, the Government also appealed to the preciousness of young lives. Reformers emphasized the need to save lives for the future to carry out the program of democratization. The nationalist argument was built upon the idea that Hungary as a small nation could not afford to waste her young in what was experienced as a "fratricide."

Rhetoric notwithstanding, the confrontations lasted and many died. The tragic sense of lost lives became essential in the evolving myth of the revolution. And as the metaphor of "family" for nation grew prevalent (even implicitly in the form of addressing the public as "my Hungarian brothers"), Biblical images of blood sacrifice—Christ and first-born sons—were evoked as well. The exalted atmosphere in which the young were glorified as heroes and saints of the uprising is tellingly illustrated by a piece of writing authored and read out by the ex-Stalinist poet Zoltán Zelk; in his tortured cry he implored them to be granted absolution from his sins and to be allowed a communion with them (Fabó, p. 131).

The grief over the death of young people also prompted the rise of anti-communist terrorist voices calling for revenge. Such speeches, some of them occasioned by the Memorial Day funerals (commemorated in Hungary on November 1st), oddly mirrored— that is, echoed with reversed meanings—the Stalinist discourse with its name-calling and brutal language.[9] The revolution created new alliances and dissolved old ones. A great number of communists abandoned the old faith in the Party, ever more intensely denounced as the "evil" and "sinful" Rákosi/Gerö clique. The new leaders' legitimacy depended on what was seen as their "honesty" and "true Hungarianness."

The construction of Imre Nagy and, to a lesser degree, of János Kádár as trust-worthy leaders is of interest, not only for the role of rhetoric in soliciting popular support, but also for the odd convergence of ethical and ethnic purity in public speech. As early as 1953, Nagy had started to build his credibility as the focus of the democratic movement. He was exluded temporarily from the Party as a "right-wing revisionist." Kádár had been jailed for some time during the early 1950s. The autobiographic moment of being victimized by the Rákosi regime had a key function in generating trust and loyalty for both leaders. In general, persecution provided the moral capital for many of the newly appointed directors and secretaries in diverse political and cultural institutions.

Obviously, the recurrent use of phrases like "true Hungarian" or "true patriot" communicated two things about the persons they described: on one level it denoted moral integrity and a commitment to serve national interests against the Soviet Union; on another, it coded ethnicity and, in the given context, Hungarianness was invested with a special value in itself. Any attempt to illuminate the complexities of this context, involving the relationship between ethnicity and political ideologies in twentieth-century Hungarian history, would lead me too far from my topic. Yet it is fair to say that a disproportionate number of Jews had served in the highest positions of the Communist Party. Therefore they were distrusted by certain groups of ethnic Hungarians. It was assumed that they were imported by Soviet communism, since most prominent leaders had been exiled in the Soviet Union during the 1930s. Indeed, they helped establish socialism in Hungary on the Stalinist model, backed by the Soviet military presence. This historical fact proved to be sufficient for the survival, and even the reinvigoration of anti-Semitism, an inherited component of ardent nationalism since the early twentieth century. The perception of Jews as aliens and agents of an alien power had barely been affected by other facts; e.g., a number of Jews were important opponents and/or victims of the Rákosi regime, including followers of Imre Nagy (Judt, 1990). While the Radio provided no overt anti-Semitic (or chauvinist) propaganda during the uprising, it re-mained within the double entendre of nationalist rhetoric.

Besides or maybe due to his "true Hungarianness," understood in his complete identification with a particular historical and cultural tradition, Imre Nagy was able to command a distinctive style of speech. He addressed his public without the typical restraint and remoteness of other communist leaders. He spoke the language of a his-torically grounded romantic nationalism, although without any recognizable anti-Semitic overtones. It is in his speeches that the interrelatedness of the three key issues can be seen most clearly: the self-definition of the revolutionary acts and actors; the ethos of the uprising (the "moral" theme); and the historically located concept of national unity (the "national" theme). In his speech of October 28th, these themes cohered into something close to a "master script" of the revolution.

The Prime Minister started off by setting up a three-layered temporal framework: the events of the "past week" were placed in the perspective of the "past decade," and he embedded all of this in the context of "our one-thousand-year-old history," viewed as a series of tragic blows. Thus a sense of continuity with the past was established; the past was portrayed as a site and sequence of negative historical experience. The uprising, seen to be unprecedented in its severity, appeared as both a disruption and a tragic climax of Hungary's history. The evocation of the idea of the one-thousand-year-old Hungrary carried a great emotional weight, for it had been deeply ingrained in people's minds by pre-communist hegemonic ideologies. It conveyed a "structure of feeling" vital to a tragic-heroic sense of national identity. Although the phrase had been overused and abused in conservative rhetoric, in the given context it was bound to resonate with the actual sentiments of diverse constituencies:

> During the last week murderous events followed one another with tragic speed. It is the fatal consequences of the past decade's horrendous faults and sins that have surfaced in these misadventures which we are now witnessing and in which we are partici- pating. In the course of our one-thousand-year-old history our Fate has not spared our people from trials and tribulations. Yet a shock comparable to this one has never befallen to our country . . . . (Fabó, p. 93)

Following this introduction, his denunciation of the views that had constructed the uprising as a counterrevolution sounded particularly sharp and emphatic. While ac- knowledging the presence of some criminal and reactionary forces (note his distinction!), Nagy asserted that in the fighting a "national democratic movement" had developed "with elementary force," one "encompassing and uniting our whole people." He ex- plicitly established the Party rulers' moral and political responsibility, not only in the growth of a democratic oppositional movement, but in the actual explosive outbreak of the revolt. In appreciating the national unity produced by the revolutionary acts, Nagy reinforced the historically based sense of collectivity to which he initially appealed. In this manner, he managed discursively to create the foundations of legitimacy for his new "independent and socialist Government," proclaimed to serve as a "genuine expres- sion of the people's will."

Along with his radical political moves and gestures—the declaration of Hungary's neutrality, the institution of the multi-party system, the dissolution of the Secret Police (AVH), the encouragement of active workers' councils, etc.—Imre Nagy's communi- cational skills may have had a profound effect on the growing cult surrounding him. Even during his lifetime, he was often placed on a pedestal elevated to the status of a prophet:

> He was the man who, harrassed and stained, has always persisted with the Hungarian people's demands; even when the country's situation became truly severe, he assumed responsibility to lead the nation out of the catastrophe. (Fabó, p. 118)

As is well known, Imre Nagy eventually lost control over the course of events. On November 4th the Soviet authorities arrested him together with his Cabinet. Simulta- neously, Kádár announced the establishment of the Hungarian Workers' and Peasants' Government. Historians may only speculate on the extent to which the utopia of an independent socialist democracy could have been upheld had the revolution survived. Yet despite its precarious political unity and its recognizable shift from a socialist dem- ocratic towards a more conservative nationalist discourse, the revolution succeeded in creating an identity of its own. I have attempted to show how this identity was linguistically shaped by the acts of redefining the very nature of the events and by producing and celebrating its heroes: its charismatic leader Imre Nagy and its martyrs, the youth.

Conclusion

The purpose of this paper was to investigate the discursive construction of the Hungarian revolt of '56 through the interaction and confrontation of diverse political forces made available by broadcast Radio during the twelve days of the uprising. I was primarily interested in the process by which two distinct types of rhetoric—"terrorist" and "liberationist"—attempted to take and keep control over the definition of the situation, that is, of the revolt itself.

The struggle was initially constrained by the institutional arrangements characterizing totalitarian political systems. Although this system had some cracks in it when the revolt broke out, public speech was barely open to contestation, not unlike the unitary belief system which it articulated and attempted to shape. The discursive space of public life, the official domain, was considerably detached from the non-public or non-official sphere, as well as from social praxis. Most of the official accounts of the proceedings of the revolution (including reports on people's responses to them) were voluntaristic and arbitrary; that is, they were constructed according to the dictates of pre-existing scripts or immediate tactical needs. Representation was typically perceived by the public as misrepresentation. Furthermore, this domain grew beyond its own "normal" boundaries, not solely to mold or even to overshadow but eventually to substitute itself for the world of everyday experience.

In my analysis I have sought to point to the inflexibility and crudeness of the terrorist language. Those employing this language were not prepared to defend its validity when questioned by the opposition's own accounts of the revolt. They were not prepared to integrate perspectives other than their own. That is why various elements taken over from the opposition were so easily identifiable as coopted: they accorded with neither the basic ideological assumptions nor with the style of rhetoric typical of the Stalinists' scripts.

The revolt of '56 may be regarded as a complex intertwined system of discourse and action. Paradoxically, the struggle to dominate representation was far too essential to have stayed within the confines of verbal contestation. Thus it is not coincidental that the insurgents' program demanded that speech be liberated. In other words, a principal of the uprising was to restore a "normal" interactive relationship between public and private discursive spaces, between representational practices and experience. The "liberationist" voices, by virtue of their very presence, challenged the legitimacy of the *whole system* of public political discourse. This is exemplified by such symbolic acts as the renaming of the Radio Station or by announcing on October 28th that "Today the papers already write the truth" (Fabó, 1957).

Because the right of free speech did not already exist, much of the debate over the meaning of the events assumed the form of a meta-discourse: retrospectively, "liberationists" discredited the claims made by the Stalinist speakers who had been silenced by then. I contend that this was primarily a counter-discourse in that it tended to mirror the terrorist language. In reinscribing the uprising, the insurgents employed the same moral and quasi-religious vocabulary as the Stalinist ruling elite. In fact, the debate involved a struggle to relocate the "sacred center" of the social system from the Party to the Nation (represented by the Government), and to invest notions of "honesty," "sin," "stain," "brotherhood," and "patriotism" with new oppositional meaning.

The concept of patriotism leads to questions about the uses and meanings of history in the revolutionary practices of signification. Most interesting is the mode in which the cause of self-determination was linked to the celebration of the national past, and to the reliving of a particular chapter of it, the Independence War of 1848. As Martha Lampland (1986) has suggested, the insurgents spoke the nineteenth-century language of their predecessors and revived a whole symbolic system (names, emblems, cockades, forms of manifesto, etc.) attached to that revolution. Everyday language spontaneously incorporated full verses from the romantic revolutionary poet Sándor Petöfi's poems, as if the past were projected onto the present. There may be a number of possible explanations for this phenomenon. It may be viewed as a protest against the Stalinist practices which systematically dehistoricized and emaciated the Hungarian national identity.[10] On the other hand, the degree to which people embraced the tradition of 1848 also speaks to the political culture of Hungarian society of the time. In the mid-1950s there was no other language available except that of the past. Just as the political issues raised by 1848 (civil rights, independence) had not been properly settled over the one hundred years that followed, their re-emergence carried the rhetoric in which they had originally been voiced into the present. The importance of this phenomenon is difficult to over-estimate in the light of contemporary analogous developments in Eastern Europe, following the collapse of the communist governments (Judt, 1990). Because these countries have had very weak or no liberal parliamentary traditions whatsoever, at present they also find themselves lacking the appropriate language of modern pluralist politics. As Tony Judt has observed:

> All they could look back to—and herein lies the problem—is exactly what they're now getting: nationalist rhetoric, a strong emphasis on the identity of the nation and religion. (p. 14)

The revolution of '56 also drew on national rhetoric embedded in the oppositional or dominant ideologies of different regimes over the past two centuries. For the "last" available movement combining demands of democracy and independence, the insurgents needed to reach as far back as 1848. And this also explains why the French revolution—mediated by the events of 1848, with its strong emphasis on a unitary language invested with high moral passion—proved such an empowering example to follow. France at the end of the eighteenth century was similar to twentieth-century Eastern European societies in one sense, namely that they all lacked a "Whig science of politics" on which to base democratic institutions and practices (Hunt, 1984, p. 43). Without understanding this similarity (and other related ones, such as the lack of a solid bourgeois class [B. Moore, 1966]), it would be difficult to account for the impact of the the French Revolution on a society located in radically different historical times.

In further research on this subject it would be interesting to explore the tension within the liberationist discourse, a tension arising from its commitment to bourgeois democratic values on the one hand, and the emotionally infused nationalist rhetoric burdened with conservative authoritarianism on the other. That this was sensed by many witnesses of the uprising as a real threat to its original goals is indicated by the fact that even a non-liberal writer such as László Németh voiced his anxiety, a mere three days before the Soviet tanks had invaded Budapest:

> The day before the revolution had broken out, I moved to the countryside with the resolution that I would only be concerned with working on my unpublished manuscripts. After the days of awful anxiety, I only had one night to struggle with my joy. Since then I have merely been feeling the pressure of responsibility, which must be a concern of every intellectual today. I still had seen no more than what the radio

and the events in the countryside had allowed me to see, but then already I clearly perceived the danger, the immediate threat that the nation, in her sacred impulse, responding only to her emotions, would commit something irredeemable. And looking ahead a little, I was worried that, while the fighters' attention was focused on the withdrawal of the Soviet troops, others expecting the return of their old glory would elbow their ways to the new positions, thus turning the revolution into a counterrevolution . . . . (Fabó, p. 249)

NOTES

*I wish to express my thanks to Hugh Mehan, Akos Rona-Tas, and Martha Lampland for their insightful suggestions and comments on the drafts of this paper.

1. Mátyás Rákosi was the leader of the Communist Party from 1941 to 1956. On returning to Hungary from Soviet exile, he became Secretary General of the HCP. He was State Minister (1945–49) and Deputy Prime Minister (1952–53). In 1953 he ceded the premiership to Imre Nagy but remained First Secretary until July 1956 when he emigrated to the USSR. In 1962 he was expelled from the Hungarian Communist Party for his political crimes (Kádár, 1985, p. 156).

2. Having finished the draft of this paper, I came across a publication containing Ferenc Fejtö's speech commemorating the 30th anniversary of the execution of Imre Nagy and his fellow martyrs, and inaugurating their symbolic memorial in Père Lachaise, Paris, June 16, 1988. Fejtö, the emigré writer and President of the Hungarian League of Human Rights, also referred to the ancient Greek literary parable in his speech entitled: "Our Kreons violated the laws" (Tobias, 1989, p. 529).

3. To name a few of the most significant publications: Bill Lomax; *1956—Hungary* (London, 1976); *United Nations Report of the Special Committee on the Problem of Hungary,* General Assembly, Official Records: 11th Session (New York, 1957); *A forradalom hangja* (The Voice of the Revolution), Radio Broadcasts of Hungary between October 23–November 9, 1956, in *Századveg Füzetek* 3 (Budapest, 1989); 1956—*A forradalom sajtoja* (The Press during the Revolution). Assembled and introduced by E. Nagy (Gyromagny, 1984); Ag *igazság* a *Nagy Imre ügyben* (The Truth in the Imre Nagy Case). Re-issue of first edition Brussels, 1959, in Századvég Füzetek 2 (Budapest, 1989).

4. The history of designating the '56 events in official and colloquial speech was briefly but perceptively remarked on by György Csepeli in his lecture "The Twilight of State Socialism in Hungary" given at the University of California, San Diego, April 1990.

5. March 15th was the day when the War of the Independence and Freedom commenced in 1848.

6. For a fine analysis of the attribution of meaning to past actions in the "making" of history, see Lampland (1986).

7. Miklós Horthy was the Regent of Hungary (1920–44). Although he allowed a certain freedom to parliamentary forms, the system was essentially authoritarian (e.g. Horthy banned leftist parties). In 1944 he ceded power to the fascist Arrow Cross Party.

8. For a discussion of the historical roots of such communist assumptions in Eastern Europe, see Judt (1990).

9. In line with the more right-wing attitudes prevailing in the countryside, the radio stations in the provincial towns showed more openness to anti-communist "terrorist" propaganda than those in Budapest.

10. The Rákosi regime did not entirely dispense with Hungarian history and culture. It is more appropriate to say that Stalinist politics was ambivalent and abusive towards this heritage. In the arts, for example, indigenous folklore forms were used to convey "socialist" ideological contents, thus ruling out modernist cultural influences. As regards history and the appreciation of the revolution of 1848, the latter was canonized as part of the "progressive tradition," yet March 15th was erased as a national holiday. This ambivalence may be explained with the rulers' apprehension about the obvious potential of March 15th to articulate national resistance.

35

"It Works for Me": British Cultural Studies, Australian Cultural Studies, Australian Film

GRAEME TURNER

In Australia, as in the U.S.A., the influence of British cultural studies has been profound. Most of us are aware that, as it establishes itself ever more securely within the academy, and as it becomes increasingly comfortable in its relations with the disciplines it originally interrogated, British cultural studies is in danger of becoming a pedagogic rather than a critical or political enterprise. British cultural studies has always fought against such an eventuality, consistently rejecting suggestions that it was a new and discrete discipline, an evolving orthodoxy within the humanities or social sciences. Motivated, at least in part, by a critique of the disciplines, cultural studies has been reluctant to become one. One can understand why cultural studies, having worked so hard to discredit an elderly universalism within the humanities, should be wary of simply appearing to replace it with something a little more robust and youthful.

But there *is* a universalizing momentum building up through the export and development of British cultural studies, and its installation as an orthodoxy seems almost inevitable. While I believe this highlights a theoretical problem within cultural studies as a whole, in this paper I want to consider some particular questions raised by this movement, questions about the cultural specificity of British cultural studies and its usefulness within other political or national contexts—in this case, Australia.

My starting point is Ken Ruthven's (1989) article on *Keywords,* published in a special issue of the Australian journal, *Southern Review,* in memory of Raymond Williams. In it, Ruthven criticizes the implicit universality of Williams's *Keywords* project, reminding us that "the very act of identifying" such key words is "the product of interpretive processes in the service of an ideological position" which is itself historically and culturally specific (p. 118). While Williams himself is unlikely to have denied this, the wide dissemination of Williams's books, and his status as a major intellectual figure in cultures he never visited or probably never thought about, has conferred onto Williams's project an implied universality. Among the consequences of the canonization of Williams's book(s) within Australian literary and cultural studies, Ruthven argues, is the "ironic" co-option of *Keywords* "in the suppression of Australian 'difference.' " Only a comparable, but more explicitly motivated, study of Australian "keywords" might recover that difference.

It seems to me that such arguments are appearing with greater frequency now. Postcolonial theory within literary studies in Australia and elsewhere constitutes itself through its critique of the often unacknowledged national positions from which the theoretical orthodoxies speak; in the U.S.A., similar arguments have caught my attention on a number of occasions in the last year, the most recent being Andrew Ross's (1989a) caution about the cultural and political specificity of British cultural studies in *No Respect* (pp. 7, 233). The privileging of class over gender or race in early British cultural studies, the Anglocentricity of much work on (and resulting assumptions about) ideologies of nationalism or the social function of subcultures, have been noted by cultural studies' friends as well as its enemies (e.g., Schwartz, 1989). Cultural studies' continuing relation to the moralist/elitist "culture and civilization" tradition customarily represented by the ghostly figures of the Leavises, has a genuinely recondite feel in the U.S.A., I am told, although this is less true of Australia where it released a burst of contagion in English departments during the 1960s. Criticism of the subcultures research identified with Hebdige, Chambers, and, to a lesser extent, Paul Willis also raises the question of the relation between cultural theory and the specific historical conditions which produce it. Examples of such criticism have focused on the romantic treatment of urban subcultures and of popular culture in general—a romanticism seen to derive in part from the common experiences researchers recognize in the subjects of their research (See Born, 1987). This problem is not confined to such relatively early work in the tradition. The temptation to identify sufficiently strongly with "the people" to see within the practices of their everyday lives an intrinsic subversiveness, is a hotly contested feature of a wide range of work in cultural studies now—particularly the work of John Fiske, itself a hybrid of British, Australian, and American theoretical traditions. In all these instances, the critique of what is now a dominant set of theories and practices suggests they are more culture-bound than they themselves acknowledge.

It has been said that one of the distinctive features of the British appropriations of European structuralist and poststructuralist theory is their applied character (Harland, 1987, p. 4): so much of the theoretical labor in this tradition occurs while dealing with particular, if still resonant, research tasks. David Morley's work on television audiences, or Paul Willis's on youth subcultures, are examples. In such applications, the practical value of theoretical principles is made abundantly clear; what is less clear is the difference between the work of theoretical clarification and the subject matter through which it is developed. Key studies in which important theoretical moves are made are often primarily known through their subject matter: Morley's contribution is, as it were, his *Nationwide* studies, not his testing of the encoding/decoding process; Hebdige's work is on punk and reggae rather than a semiotics of cultural style. Serving the twin objectives of producing applied research dealing with specified materials or processes, and the development through this process of a set of theoretical principles or methodological protocols, the research becomes separated from its own history as its relation to its subject matter is naturalized, universalized.

And yet, British cultural studies is also resolutely parochial. The consistently English (rather than Scottish or Welsh, for instance) perspective employed within British cultural studies, most often goes without acknowledgment or apology. Among the many works examining the making of British histories, Patrick Wright's *On Living in an Old Country* (1985) is remarkable for, at least, his explicit acknowledgment of the particular *kind* of national history he is dealing with, and of the specific rather than merely representative ways in which the nation is called up through its histories. Within media studies, one meets the assumption that the structural and textual features of British television are in the same relation to those of the rest of the world as BBC English is to other versions of spoken English: they are the standard around which the rest of the world provides variants. In so many discussions of news or current affairs in the seventies, the inquiry into the signifying practices of the British media is assumed to be an inquiry into the signifying practices of the media in general. At its worst, British media studies incorporates other media systems into the general argument as variants, their constitutive political and social histories ignored in a way that the British context would never be.

What is being described here is, to some extent at least, a simple Anglocentrism. Just as Britian is the only nation not to put its name on its postage stamp—since they invented it, presumably, only the subsequent users need to nominate themselves—there is a consistent pattern of ex-nomination in the applied British cultural studies. It is *Popular Culture: The Metropolitan Experience,* not *English Popular Cultures;* it is *Television: Technology and Cultural Form,* not *Television in Britain;* and so on. British cultural studies speaks unapologetically from the centers of Britain and Europe, both of them locations where the perspective from the margins is rarely considered. Indeed, Eurocentrism has lately begun to deny itself in a novel way, bidding for the ideological purity that comes with subordination, marginalization, without, of course, needing to accept the power-lessness that denies the genuinely subordinated any satisfaction in such a position. David Morley and Ien Ang's (1989) introduction to their issue of *Cultural Studies* employs such a maneuver: "Europe itself," they say, now occupies "a marginal place in the developed world" (p. 133). (Any discourse that can call itself the developed world is far from being marginal.) Within an otherwise worthwhile argument for the recognition of the "con-text-dependence" of cultural studies, suggesting that the "place and relevance" of cul-tural studies has to "be related to the specific character of local forms of political and intellectual discourse on culture" (p. 136), Morley and Ang reveal that, from where they stand, some contexts require less attention than others. They report on the export of cultural studies to such farflung places as Canada and Australia, producing unproblematic if "ironic echoes" of the "original map of British imperialism's conquests." In Australia, we are told on the authority of a letter to the pages of *Screen* magazine, Australian cultural studies is complicated by "strange-new-world factors" such as the "inordinate number of left academics wandering round Australia, but talking about Birmingham" (Morley and Ang, 1989, p. 136). This tells us rather less than we would like about "the specific character of local [Australian] forms of political and intellectual discourse on culture" (which, in fact, are not dominated by Birmingham). Many such "discourses," in fact, are available in published form—even in the source of the imperial "echo"—for the authors to have consulted themselves. That they didn't bother, makes it clear that there is at least one place which is more marginal than Europe, and that there are limits to cultural studies' sensitivity to difference.[1]

It is this insensitivity to differences between, rather than within, cultures which may be the most pervasive disease working away at contemporary practice in cultural studies. Jim Bee's (1989) review of John Fiske's *Television Culture* registers his disquiet, not only at the theory of resistance and pleasure contained within the book, but at its deliberate homogenizing of television texts and audiences across cultural and political borders. While on the one hand *Television Culture* argues against the notion of the homogeneous audience, on the other hand it assumes that *"Miami Vice* will be empow-ering whenever and wherever people find it pleasurable" (p. 358). The lack of any conjunctural analysis, locating the articulation of formal and symbolic structures within social processes, practices, and institutions, makes *Television Culture* less than typical of contemporary British cultural studies; more representative is its homogenizing account of television which internationalizes it not only as a technology but as a set of social practices of production and reception. Excised from such an account are the very dif-ferences cultural studies set out to recover. Music video, in particular, has suffered from an overly textual criticism; its disarticulation from the industries which produce it and the audiences which consume it has turned the form into a second *nouvelle vague* for some critics. At its most worrying, television analysis within the British tradition is in danger of simultaneously championing certain versions of British television production (Channel 4) as the (paradoxical) representatives of "the people" and of "minorities"—

a view that insists on the maintenance of difference; while also instituting a blithe internationalism which obliterates differences, assuming commonality across cultures and social structures rather than interrogating the means through which that commonality is constructed.

Australian intellectual traditions have been directly affected by their British counterparts since the beginning, so it is not surprising that Australian cultural studies should bear the traces of all this. In Australia, the cultural studies project has had to find space for itself within existing disciplinary boundaries—working within a strong tradition of left-conservative history, for instance, or within the critical and nationalist movements within literary studies, or the new interest in film and media studies which was reinforced by the revival of the national film industry—or look for a home within the eclectic and cautiously multidisciplinary field of Australian studies. Cultural studies' penetration into these areas has been assisted by its theoretical and temporal coincidence with new accounts of "the national character" in history, literary studies, and film. Consequently, Australian cultural studies has so far concentrated very closely on local texts, institutions, and constitutive discourses while drawing its major theoretical categories and protocols from Europe, particularly from Britain. Internalized through the practice of analysis and argument, this theoretical influence—inserted into the already complex cultural relations between Britain and Australia—has proved particularly productive; but it has also proved to be very difficult to separate off and interrogate. Subsequently, it is only quite recently that I, for one, have felt the pressing need to review the relevance of the assumptions behind the theories and practice of British cultural studies: to ask, if it works for them will it, to quote TV's Hunter, "work for me"? Often the answer turns out to be "no."

To elaborate a little further on this. It is probably unexceptionable to see E. P. Thompson's *The Making of The English Working Class* as one of the constitutive texts in British cultural studies; it opens the way for a new "history from below" which recovers the stories of social formations, of popular cultural movements, of non-institutional and subordinated groups and places them against the large-scale administrative, institutional, and constitutional narratives of traditional histories. This was not merely an empirical retrieval, though; also recovered were the resistant, oppositional politics of these subordinated social movements. White Australian histories—as distinct from imperial or colonial histories—have, in a sense, *always* been histories "from below": accounts of a subordinated (that is, a colonized) people, and of their construction of social groups and identities within an extremely repressive and authoritarian social and administrative structure. The whole of Australian social history has been reconstructed through a series of determining oppositions which defined an essential Australianness as the subordinated, the repressed, and the resistant: it is a history which throws convicts against the jailers, prospectors against the diggings police, free settlers against squatters, the Digger against the British officers, and so on. Such structural oppositions located the formation of an Australian identity in the battle between the foreign and the local, the boss and the worker, the authorities and their subjects—a battle always lost by the local, the worker, or the subject. This binary pattern, and its characteristic resolution in the suppression of the national character, has been hailed as constitutive not only of an Australian history but also of an Australian cultural identity.

The binary habit dies hard in Australian cultural questions precisely because they are questions about a postcolonial definition of the nation which is directly provoked by the domination of the colonial power. The postcolonial nation does not simply establish its difference. It defines itself against the imperial Other, distinguishing between two mutually exclusive values. The clearer the distinction, the more categoric the construction of Otherness, the clearer the case for national identity. Within Australian history, the Other has mostly been Britain. (This may perhaps explain why so many Australian cultural critics—myself included—have internalized Britain's high culture/low culture split so strongly, felt such an affinity for the anti-Leavisite tradition of British cultural studies, and thus absorbed its assumptions so uncritically.)

Accordingly, then, when the writers of an Australian history make their most successful bid to control the definitions of the Australian character in the 1950s, theirs is not a mission of recovery; rather, it is an act of revelation. Their version of the Australian is immediately hailed, recognized, and installed as the dominant articulation of the national identity. Russell Ward's *Australian Legend* (1958) inverts the Barthesian process and turns myth into history, its images and ideologies empirically authorized as the definers of the national character. Ward's work of cultural definition revives and confirms, by and large, regressive attributes: sexism, xenophoboia, anti-intellectualism, a populist nationalism, a simple identification between urban and rural working classes, and a sentimental egalitarianism that never quite extends to a commitment to democratic principles. In fact, the characteristics of Paul Willis's (1977) subordinated "counterschool culture" in *Learning to Labour* are strikingly similar to those of Ward's Australian character. There is, however, a crucial, structural, difference: instead of recognizing an embattled and material subordination, Ward celebrates the ideological dominance of a conservative, masculinist, nationalist, anti-authoritarian ethos which honors manual labor, is sceptical of the intellect, and which proudly sees itself as essentially working class. In much of the British work on subcultures, of which Willis's work is representative, and within many of the histories from below, there is an investment in the subcultures examined which celebrates the resistance of the subordinated, the challenges they offer to dominant ideological formations. Attempts to draw similar political significances from within Australian ideological formations are complicated by the fact that it is the *dominant* which mobilizes nationalist mythologies of resistance and subordination. It is all too easy to become complicit with this strategy; as Tony Bennett (1988b) has noted in a review of *Myths of Oz*, a book I co-authored, the "mythologist" can become the "myth-maker."

A key difference between Australian and British theoretical practice is relevant here. Within Australian cultural criticism it has become conventional to construct aspects of Australian life as distinctive—not of a class or of a subculture but of the nation. As Tony Bennett, again, has pointed out in his review:

> This foregrounds an important difference between the European contexts from which Fiske, Hodge and Turner derive most of their theories and the Australian situation to and in which they are applied. Definitions of the distinctiveness of English culture, for example, are so massively mortgaged to bourgeois conceptions of the nation that the self-respecting leftwing critic would rarely regard this ground as worth struggling for—although the situation is different in Scotland and Wales. In these cases, as in Australia, the fact that definitions of the national culture are, in part, shaped through the process of their emergence in opposition to the dominance of imported cultures lend such questions a political pertinence which, in other contexts, would be lacking. (1988b, p. 34)

The "national" within Australia is, of course, largely the captive of similarly bourgeois dominant constructions. That is not the whole story, however; the idea of the nation also contains another, more radical, political potential which is probably unthinkable within the British context. The definition of national identity serves slightly different functions for a nation constructing itself out of a colonial past; different from those which it might serve for a nation attempting to recover an imperial past. This does not only apply to Australia; Laura Mulvey (1986) has acknowledged a similar relevance within Canada:

> The question of Canadian identity is political in the most direct sense of the word, and it brings the political together with the cultural and ideological immediately and inevitably. For the Canada delineated by multinationals, international finance, U.S. economic and political imperialism, national identity is a point of resistance, defining the border fortifications against exterior colonial penetration. Here nationalism can perform the political function familiar in Third World countries. (p. 10)

(The strain in producing such a perception from a European center is visible in the reference to the third world and in the simplification of a unitary Canadian identity.) Australia, of course, offers a less clear-cut case of continuing colonization; the consequence of this, however, is that it is increasingly difficult to understand the ideological alignments around versions of Australian nationalism through their simple identification with either progressive or regressive effects or through their allegiance to the left or right of the political spectrum. Nationalism can be inscribed into an extraordinary range of political and cultural positions.

If Ruthven was to have his *Australian Keywords*, certainly the longest entry would be for the category of "the nation." Australia was settled by Europeans when European nationalism was just beginning, and when the partnership between the ideologies of nationalism, production and colonial capitalism, and social democracy were being forged. Colonial and (later) postcolonial Australia found itself locked into a world increasingly defined by competing nationalisms, a world in which difference had to be given a national character. At the turn of the twentieth century, nationalism was a clear ideological choice for many Australian intellectuals although it was a more pragmatic choice for its politicians, intent on removing restrictions on trade between the various colonial centers. Australians faced what Sylvia Lawson (1983) refers to as the colonial paradox:

> To know enough of the metropolitan world, colonials must, in limited ways at least, move and think internationally; to resist it strongly enough for the colony to cease to be colonial and become its own place, they must become nationalists. (p. ix)

The curious thing about Australian nationalism is not only its varied political potential; it is also the narrow range of images and iconography through which it has signified itself: imagery which locates an essential and distinctive national character in the landscape, in the social structures of the bush, and in a masculinist/socialist pioneering ethic.[2] Initially these images "belonged," as it were, to the left—or at least to the mixture of racism, sexism, xenophobia, nationalism, rural trade unionism, and international socialism which fed into the foundation of the Labour Party at the end of the nineteenth century. Since Federation (1901), however, this same repertoire of images of the nation has operated as movable but indispensable signifiers of any new hegemonic formation. They are now called up by whoever wants to invoke an essential Australian spirit: as an alibi for the appeal to a "fair go for families" within a Liberal Party election strategy (which actually narrowed the definition of the family to exclude single parents and the unemployed and thus justify a cut in welfare spending); or within a beer commercial incorporating the holy trinity of men, sport, and beer.

These images do not go uncontested, of course, but any discourse which seeks to oppose "the national"—to install the "international" or the "European" or even the "Asian"—must deal with a colonial history that categorically attributes such discourses to the regimes of the imperial Other. There are strategies around this problem; proponents of an aggressive development capitalism have inserted notions of progress and prosperity into the depiction of the nation by connecting the myths of the pioneers with the signifiers of industrialization. There is a Eurocentric conservative discourse which is vigorously anti-populist, anti-mass culture, anti-nationalist, but which defends its version of "culture and civilization," much as the British did, through attacks on strategic targets (Australian vernacular writing, television, popular feature films) rather than through a comprehensive cultural and social agenda. Paradoxically, those voices from the conservative right which defend the maintenance of sophisticated standards in the arts and which remind Australians of the values of the European Metropolitan Centers, can find themselves in unison with progressive left-wing intellectuals calling for the protection of the avant-garde or the experimental in all areas of cultural production.[3]

Within any one field of cultural production, cultural analysts are faced with an intricate set of alliances around the idea of the nation—a left historically connected with, but in many cases antipathetic to, a radical populist nationalism, and a right historically antipathetic to nationalism but accommodated to it through a censorious rhetoric which polices "cultural standards" and which privileges the elite over the popular, the international over the national, the universal over the international. If we move into a specific area, the Australian film and television industry, it is not difficult to demonstrate how substantive and how ideologically complex a role has been played by specific definitions of the nation and thus of the national film industry over the last twenty years, the years of the revival (or, as some would have it, the renaissance) of the local industry.

It is now widely acknowledged that the funding decisions which produced the revival of the Australian film industry in the 1970s were sufficiently coherent to amount to a conservative hegemony. Against the competing claims of other kinds of film genres (such as the radical nationalist "ocker films"), conservative definitions of Australian cultural standards were defended through the privileging of the period drama, the Euro-colonial history which collapsed distinctions between the colony and its inhabitants in a cultural *bildungsroman*. For the state-funding bodies which almost singlehandedly determined the character of the industry in these early days, film served a semiotic rather than a commercial function—representing the nation at home and overseas. Films which did not represent the nation in acceptable ways were thus of little interest: contemporary and critical films were eschewed, as well as frankly generic films working—however effectively—within a Hollywood tradition. The first *Mad Max* (1979) film, for example, was a casualty of this narrow range of aesthetic and generic preferences.

The problem, as this example no doubt suggests, is that film does not only represent the nation; it also entertains it. Film may be a culture industry, but it *is* an industry and eventually the state determinations of its character were undermined by measures aimed at enhancing its commercial viability. In the early 1980s, changes to the funding structure attracted private, non-government investors to the industry. This produced a boom in film and television production; also the range of styles, subjects and genres broadened significantly. In this instance, private investment proved more flexible, more liberal, and more adventurous than the state-funding bodies—partly, perhaps, because the cultural function of each film was no longer a central consideration in all cases.

From many points of view, however, this expansion was worrying. The industry itself was, and still is, torn between one view which held that private money and mass marketing offered the route to survival, and the alternative view that while this route may spell financial survival it will defeat the cultural objectives of the Australian film industry—of telling Australian stories for Australian audiences. As Dermody and Jacka (1987, pp. 197–98) point out, within the mainstream Australian film industry there are two, almost entirely discrete discourses: Industry 1, as they call it, is socially concerned, searching for an Australian identity, leftish in its politics, middle class, suspicious of the marketplace and thus in favor of government intervention, arty, and committed to combatting cultural imperialism; Industry 2 is more interested in entertainment than national identity, and is generally internationalist, populist, working class, free marketeer, and unperturbed by cultural imperialism. Signs of Australianness are comfortably accommodated within both discourses—Industry 2 has the working-class, pragmatic, anti-aesthetic ideologies of the dominant masculine Australian culture, while Industry 1 is strongly nationalist in its social and aesthetic objectives.[4]

The divisions in the production industry have their counterparts in the wider film culture—the critics, reviewers, and audiences. Again, the local reception of Australian films is shot through with arguments over the cultural function of the national industry. The highbrow establishment critics have been pleased by those films which elided (that is, transcended) their "Australianness" by working within the conventions of European art film, or those which offered a mythologized, colonialist version of Australian history and culture. There have been fewer and fewer of such films, though; increasingly, those films which achieve popular success are panned by the highbrow reviewers: *Mad Max, The Man From Snowy River 1 and 2, Crocodile Dundee 1 and 2, Young Einstein,* and most recently, *Delinquents,* are all examples of this. What these films represent is a move towards more clearly generic productions; that is, features which are more recognizably within a Hollyood commercial, rather than a European art film, tradition. This development has angered critics on both sides of the nationalist fence, but for reasons which are still contained within nationalist arguments. Genre films are criticized as a sellout to Hollywood and a retreat from the enterprise of making distinctively Australian films; critics and producers alike see them as regrettable concessions to the lowest common denominator in mass entertainment, bleeding limited funding away from more adventurous, progressive, or avant-garde projects. This may sound like a straightforward high culture/low culture argument but it is not quite that simple. Defending the genre films does not necessarily entail establishing their aesthetic quality. Indeed, for those of us working within cultural studies and film studies in Australia, dealing with the films *at all* requires a degree of subtlety. In criticizing them, one does not want to support the elitism and internationalism of either the right or the left; yet, in supporting them, one does not want simply to recycle the dominant discourses of a strident, chauvinistic nationalism.

One illustrative argument has aggressively defended the move into the mainstream as a necessary and constitutive strategy for the national film industry on nationalist, commercial, *and* textual grounds. Recent work has suggested that while certain Australian films and television miniseries may have taken on American generic conventions, they have given them an Australian inflection.[5] Such an argument differentiates itself from other nationalist positions through its distinctly postcolonial ring, defining the films' strategy as one of appropriation not of accommodation, as if the American genres were being colonized to Australian ends—naturalizing, rather than raucously foregounding, Australian subjects, locations, and stories. This position has worked to isolate that section of the film culture which is most similar to the British culture and civilization tradition, which deplores the genre films and wonders why we can't just make things like *Brideshead Revisited.* Finally, the argument is representative of Australian cultural studies inscription of a nationalist politics in both the production strategies it supports and the aesthetic ideologies it resists.

We could peel back further layers, but this should be sufficient to indicate the pervasiveness of the idea of the nation, how specific and contested it is as a category, within Australian cultural debates. The differences between the Australian and the British formation hardly need enumerating, but it is these differences which recommend caution in the application of British theoretical influences.

As a means of extending this argument, I want to conclude by recounting an instance where the adoption of European cultural theory to the Australian context has produced a quite remarkable set of propositions. The example emerges from arguments around the problem of Australian content in Australian television and film. In most Western capitalist countries (other than the USA) there are regulatory mechanisms aimed at preserving some proportion of local material on television and, less frequently, in cinemas. In Australia, the local content debates have largely been resolved in favor of a nationalist and paternalist model of cultural stewardship where the jobs of Australian media workers and an Australian cultural "identity" are protected by a prescribed proportion of Australian content which the networks are required to screen each year. Inscribed into this requirement is a set of aesthetic assumptions which insist that some forms of television production—drama, primarily—are more essential to our national identity than others—such as sport. The requirement is an imposition, of course. Since male sports are so tightly articulated to the discourses of national identity, they appear on TV no matter what; drama, however, its place in the Australian character less assured, survives as a consequence of government intervention. Nevertheless, within a culture subject to successive waves of cultural imperialism—from Britain, the USA, and Japan— the need to keep Australian subjects, ideas, and voices on our screens attracts support from across the political spectrum. The highbrow right sees it as a way of policing standards and insisting that ballet earns higher points than football, while the nationalist left sees it as a means of resisting American cultural domination, of limiting the powers of an institutionally agglomerated but industrially diversified clique of media owners, and of supporting an indigenous popular culture.

However, and notwithstanding the support of this left populism, the Australian content regulations do express a fear of and distaste for popular culture; what they police is not only cultural imperialism but also the excesses of mass culture. It would be easy to see the regulations as an anti-democratic, anti-populist strategy sheltering under the nationalist alibi of an Australianized media. This is just how John Docker sees them in his unpublished monograph, *Popular Culture versus the State: An argument against Australian content regulations for television.*

What is interesting about Docker's argument and its repercussions, is the strength of its theoretical pedigree—its grounding in European theories of transgression and the popular—and the reception it has met from those who might share his theoretical influences but who have entirely opposite views on their specific application to the issue of state intervention in the Australian media. Docker's argument is built upon relatively conventional notions drawn from the cultural studies of the last few years. His work privileges the audience over the producer of the television text; he deploys Bakhtinian notions of the carnivalesque in order to attribute an intrinsically resistant politics to popular cultural formations; and he allows a high culture/low culture split to dominate the institutional politics he formulates as a simple binary division. Docker's objective is a critique of the elite paternalism of the existing regulatory system in Australia, and a defense of the open market as an alternative. Not surprisingly, the document was incorporated into a FACTS (Federation of Australian Commercial Television Stations) submission to the Australian Broadcasting Tribunal (the chief regulatory body) in support of an argument for the abolition of all Australian content requirements. To many of Docker's peers working in cultural studies in Australia, this was a scandalous sellout, his enlistment only giving aid and comfort to the enemies of the Australian production industry and of the Australian audience.

And yet, Docker's argument too has its nationalist dimension. He collapses the history of the Australian Broadcasting Commission into that of the Reithian BBC, clearly the initial model for its design, as if there were *no* cultural or historical gaps between the two. This enables Docker to generate post-Leavisite anxieties about the kind of high culture ethic which was institutionalized through government intervention in Britain and which, he claims, has been exported without modification to Australia. State intervention thus becomes identified with a specifically British ideological project, and so it seems reasonable to suggest we will better protect the Australian public by rejecting it. Docker is also a populist. Where the state is elite and conservative, the popular is democratic and transgressive, and so the regulation of the cultural economy should be left to the people themselves. The paternalistic supervisory regime instituted by the regulations is, he argues, intrinsically objectionable and actually impedes the open and balanced negotiation that would otherwise occur between the TV networks and the national-popular.

Histories of the Australian media certainly raise empirical doubts about Docker's proposition, and there are many theoretical and political objections to be made as well. I am aware that this libertarian argument is more at home in the USA, which is the agent rather than the victim of the cultural and economic imperialism state intervention is intended to ameliorate; I was caught by the enunciation of such a principle as one of the ground rules for cultural criticism in *No Respect,* for instance. But it is definitely an unconventional view to come from within Australian cultural studies; and, presumably, it would be a bizarre view to come from the left in the deregulated climate of Thatcher's Britain. To see commercial TV as serving a transgressive definition of the popular *and* the commercial ends of the market, without acknowledging their competing interests, is far from being a familiar left position in either country.

However, I would argue that Docker's view is directly licensed by recent theoretical trends within British cultural studies. The recovery of the audience, the new understandings of the strategies of resistance audiences employ, and the invocation of such strategies within definitions of popular culture, have all been important, corrective developments within British cultural studies. Their export to the USA, however, to a context where the notion of the popular occupies a very different place within dominant cultural definitions, seems to have exacerbated an already significant expansion in the cultural optimism such explanations generate—an optimism that is ultimately about capitalism and its toleration of resistance. The appropriation of de Certeau's work, and the development of John Fiske's line on the popular in the last three years, are symptomatic of this developing theoretical asymmetry in favor of resistance and against containment. Seen in this way, Docker might be regarded as a continuation of a theoretical tradition rather than an aberration; it is only the conclusions produced through his theoretical practice which are idiosyncratic.

This paper has been about the cultural specificity of theory, and it is of course itself speaking from a particular position. I have particular concerns about the effects of British cultural studies on Australian cultural studies; I am concerned that its ultimate effect may well be to turn our attention away from where we live in order that we might speak globally—thereby minimizing the differences that got us into this area in the first place. Without doubt, this is part of a larger problem for Australian cultural politics, that of being on the margins of the "developed world" while being continually drawn towards "the centre." As I have argued elsewhere (Turner, 1989), while one does not want to remain marginal, pushing one's way into the center often carries the penalty of the submersion of difference, the denial of contradictions, the glossing over of oppositions. This is also, however, a problem for cultural studies as a whole; after all, the universalizing process I have just described is one cultural studies should be uncovering, not reproducing.

My aim has been to stress the need to acknowledge that even theory has to have some historical location, specific contexts within which it works to particular ends. The dominance of British models is not intrinsically dangerous unless we take it for granted but, so far, I think we have failed to interrogate the nature and effects of that dominance. More comparative work of the kind I have hinted at in this paper might help to make such an interrogation possible: how do we begin to understand, for example, the industrialized cultures of a Westernized Asia—Korea, Taiwan, Hong Kong—with the tools currently available? As long as cultural studies resists the challenge of more comparative studies, there will be little provocation to revise the British models so that they "work" for the margins as well as the centers. Cultural studies has a lot to gain from the margins, and it should do its best to investigate the ways in which their specific conditions demand the modification of explanations generated elsewhere. At the very least, such an expansion of the cultural studies project provides a hedge against the development of a new universalism.

NOTES

1. I should add that the center's claim to marginality is not only advanced from European centers; *Cultural Studies* has also published a piece recently by Cohen (1989) describing the colonization of American popular culture by such European intellectuals as Eco and Baudrillard as a marginalization of American culture.

2. See my *National Fictions: Literature, Film, and the Construction of Australian Narrative* (1986) for discussion of this.

3. *Screen* theory, for instance, found and still finds its strongest proponents amongst Anglocentric, anti-nationalist cosmopolitans, not among the hard-core nationalists of the Labour left.

4. In 1988, the government dealt with these contradictions by installing a new and even more contradictory funding structure. It downgraded the tax concessions which had attracted investors so that they would no longer serve that function; and to compensate they installed a new state-funded institution which would operate as a commercial lending bank to filmmakers— but only to top up budgets already primarily filled with private money. This new institution, the Film Finance Corporation, attempts to speak the language of both Industry 1 and Industry 2: it professes to support only commercial projects but it also accepts the cultural responsibility of supporting distinctively Australian films. It is too soon to tell just which discourse will prevail.

5. Eg. Stuart Cunningham, "Hollywood Genres, Australian Movies" (1985). Cunningham takes this argument further in "Textual Innovation in the Miniseries."

DISCUSSION: GRAEME TURNER

ALAN O'CONNOR: I really want to challenge the kind of selective tradition of cultural studies that you've presented this morning. It seems to me to leave out those British books that are very specifically British and make no claim whatsoever to a universal generality, books like *There Ain't No Black in the Union Jack,* or *Unpopular Education* or *Policing the Crisis* or *The Empire Strikes Back.* I'm also wondering about the entire rhetorical strategy in your talk because in the United States the usual kind of rejection of British cultural studies as being inappropriate for this society is in fact a hidden rejection of its Marxism and its radicalism.

TURNER: What my paper presented was certainly not a comprehensive account of British cultural studies; rather, it was an explicit attempt to describe a received, strategically partial, idea of British cultural studies, and the specific function of that received idea within Australian cultural studies. And so, yes, it was selective—intentionally and importantly so. The second part of your question, however, implies that behind my "rhetorical strategy" lies a rejection of the politics of British cultural studies—its Marxism. I am aware of arguments that accuse American appropriations of cultural studies of such a motivation, and I am not in a position yet to assess the justice of such accounts. But I do think it is necessary to strongly refute the suggestion in relation to my paper here, and to Australian cultural studies generally. Indeed, I think the reason why British cultural studies has been extremely powerful in Australia is precisely because of its Marxism. Due to the history I have just sketched out in my paper, the left tradition in cultural criticism in Australia has often been associated with quite regressive and conservative positions—this is certainly true of the left in traditional disciplines such as history. What cultural studies, and British cultural studies in particular, has done is to provide a way for the New Left to discredit the Old Left without simply lining up with another breed of conservatives on the right. And so my intention is very far from an attempt to discredit British cultural studies for its politics—it is its politics which has been of most use. Of course, I'm not authorized to speak on behalf of Australian cultural studies, and I still have much to learn about what is being done in America, but my view is that there is a very precise difference between the way in which the Marxism of cultural studies has become part of our work in Australia, and the way in which it becomes part of the work here.

MEAGHAN MORRIS: I wonder whether part of the problem of the circulation of British cultural studies as you describe it is not what you were able to discuss here but rather its interaction with the dreaded tradition in Australian historiography of men, sport, and beer. What is really eloquent in the kind of critique you gave is, I'm afraid I have to say, the absolute invisibility of twenty years of feminist criticism of media, film theory, art, and Australian culture and its more recent intersection with a whole range of debates around Aboriginal studies, Pacific studies and so on. I think it's a problem of how theories circulate. I think that the world that has called itself cultural studies in Australia just has not been reading work that is seen as Sydney art theory or Melbourne film theory, work that just has not got into this very closed space of the Oedipal debate with Britain. The last time I can remember Britain as a real influence was when I was seven years old and we had our last Empire Day bonfire. And since then, the whole problem of Britishness has not posed itself very acutely in my immediate environment. Finally, in your position, questions of high culture/low culture, elite/popular, only pertain to programs on TV, to the problematic of consumption and so on. But this ignores the fact that, for most of this decade, there's been a deafening public debate around Asian immigration, the restructuring of higher education, the production of new elites in Australian culture, discrimination between what kinds of immigrants from Asia do "we" want, business immigration versus family reunion, which involves creating new hierarchies of elitism between different kinds of categorization of ethnic immigration to Australia and so on. It seems to me that it's in this space that Australian cultural studies, if it's to give itself any political aspirations at all, has to start defining itself. Isn't it time that we actually got on to the positive definition of the contemporary present which doesn't have a lot to do with blokes, beer, and Britain?

TURNER: First, I should say that I don't believe I have rendered your work invisible but would see it, too, implicated in the problems I describe—although certainly less so than, as you suggest, my own work has been. Secondly, I don't agree that the relation with Britain is simply a nostalgic hangover, despite what you say about your own memories. One doesn't have to remain with "men, sport, and beer" in order to see the enormous cultural and political power still exercised through the colonial relation: I can think of such recent events as the *Spycatcher* trials, or the Maralinga Royal Commissions

into British atomic tests in Australia, or of economic structures such as those that constrain the publishing and distribution of Australian books, which encourage me to persist
in still seeing the colonial/postcolonial relationship as a crucial one. All of that said, I
would certainly agree that what I am describing is from some perspectives a little
particular. Indeed, as I think my paper suggests, part of what I am doing is responding
to critiques, such as yours, of the "men, beer, and Britain" accent in *Myths of Oz*. That
is, I am trying to work through what is both a general and a personal (and perhaps
you're right, a male) problem of trying to understand the ways in which British paradigms have distorted approaches to Australian cultural studies. I am arguing that this
is a problem for Australian cultural studies in general. Your comment, though, that we
have tended to think in very narrow terms about what "Australian cultural studies"
might be, and that this narrowness may in itself be the crucial factor in the problematics
I am interested in, is one that I would want to consider further. Certainly you are
absolutely right about the major debates going on in Australia that what is called cultural
studies has left untouched while it considered problems of national identity and national
character. I want to think a little more about your remarks.

QUESTION: I had a comment on the concept of the nation-state in the postcolonial
society which you've been using. I'd really like to problematize that a little more. I
personally find a lot of disparity between the whole post colonial spectrum. So the
appropriation and usefulness of British cultural studies in national context is going to
differ throughout the postcolonial spectrum. And if British studies can become parochial,
so can Australian cultural studies become parochial.

TURNER: I hope I wasn't suggesting that the postcolonial spectrum represented "a
unity." If I have given that impression, I can correct it. I am interested in talking about
cultural differences in this discussion—and that includes differences between cultures as
well as differences within them. And although I am not saying that Australia exemplifies
the problem of the postcolonial nation-state, I *am* saying that the problems of Australia
are those of a postcolonial nation-state. Some of our problems we share with other
countries, some we don't. And so I wouldn't generalize from our position to that of
Canada, or to postcolonial Asian countries. What the "postcolonial" describes is a structural asymmetry, an arrangement of power, but the actual workings of that structure,
or the effects of that power, are clearly various and diverse.

GILBERT RODMAN: I agree that we need to look at what's coming out of Britain
as culturally specific, but it seemed to me that you placed too much blame on the British
side of it and not on scholars in the U.S. or Australia who read that work and then
don't acknowledge or critique it as culturally specific.

TURNER: I agree that there is little point or justice in blaming (say) Raymond Williams,
and something to be said for castigating those who fall so readily in line behind the
British intellectual tradition. But I wouldn't want to follow that principle too compre-
hensively. The influence has been useful, and now does not seem too late a moment to
begin interrogating this usefulness. So, I am not (and can't afford to be) at all scornful
of our enlistment in the tradition I have described. Furthermore, I am wary of accepting
a position which might imply that one does not blame those who have the power to
naturalize their view of the world for exercising that power. I am always more inclined
to blame the agent than the victim.

QUESTION: I was just wondering, in response to Meaghan Morris's question, how the
question of Asian immigrants and Australian racism fits into your Australian cultural
studies? So how does this fit into this tradition of left and right notions of national
character that you've been talking about, and does Australian cultural studies treat this?

TURNER: Not nearly enough in my view. Firstly, there are not enough of those of us who work in institutions who are prepared to take public positions on such issues. And secondly, as Meaghan Morris has already said, the compartmentalization of cultural studies has separated it off from such work as there is and focused itself perhaps too fetishistically on notions of white (masculine) Australian identity. Some traditions of work on immigration and the conditions of the migrant have failed to offer more than another essentialized version of Australian-ness—that is particularly so within Australian literary studies. Also, it must be admitted, that both the left and the right in Australia have a racist history. The New Left finds itself attacking, for instance, an old guard in the Labour Party who once defended a White Australia policy. So what happens is we end up attacking the Old Left for a range of outdated assumptions, but we don't seem to have progressed much beyond that in applying the new positions to the things that are most important. I guess what you're saying is similar to what Meaghan said before, and that there's an awful lot of work yet to be done in these areas.

MORRIS: Can't we count all the publications produced, for example, by the Center for Multicultural Studies at Woollongong—multiculturalism meaning in Australia something quite different from what it means in Britain—as cultural studies? In other words, can't we right now expand the definition of cultural studies to include the work of immigrants and people involved in the anti-racist campaigns and the struggles around the reports on the structure of Asian immigration? Rather than saying, "we're not doing it," can't we link up with the other people who have been doing it?

TURNER: At the risk of again too narrowly defining the enterprise of cultural studies, I'm afraid I do see differences between cultural studies and the work you describe. Also, I have severe reservations about the category of multiculturalism. There is a sense in which it has worked like an ideology and has been instrumental in providing alibis for a range of government policies—particularly in regard to Aboriginal communities and their administrations—that I would want to attack rather than incorporate. Because I don't see multiculturalism as an unproblematic category I'm cautious about enlisting work carried on under its heading.

36

Negative Images: Towards a Black Feminist Cultural Criticism

MICHELE WALLACE

American mass media rolled the camera away from Black life and the quantity of print on the subject became too small to read. As a result, the number of books published by and about Black people has been negligible since the beginning of the decade. For this reason alone, Michele Wallace's *Black Macho and The Myth of The Superwoman* is ready-made for commercial exploitation. Its destiny, so far, has been further assured by nearly unprecedented promotion and publicity.
June Jordan, "Black History as Myth," (1981)

Phillis Wheatley has for far too long suffered from the spurious attacks of black and white critics alike for being the original *rara avis* of a school of so-called mockingbird poets, whose use and imitation of received European and American literary conventions has been regarded, simply put, as a corruption itself of a "purer" black expression, privileged somehow in black artistic forms such as the blues, signifying, the spirituals and the Afro-American dance. Can we, as critics, escape a "mockingbird" relation to "theory," one destined to be derivative, often to the point of parody? Can we, moreover, escape the racism of so many critical theorists, from Hume and Kant through the Southern Agrarians and the Frankfurt School?
Henry Louis Gates, Jr., "Authority, (White) Power and the (Black) Critic; It's All Greek to Me," (1987a)

It is useless to argue with the point of view that sees every successful and controversial black female publication as a monolithic conspiracy to undo the race. I am even ready to concede that the participation of black women (and black men) in American cultural production and reproduction, from TV to literary criticism, shows signs of some regrettable trends. While I am enjoying the increasing visibility of blacks on TV and in films as much as anybody else, I feel compelled to remember the downside: material conditions are not changing for the masses of blacks. Moreover, it may even be that the economic and political victimization of the urban and rural black poor in the U.S. and worldwide is somehow exacerbated by the deeply flawed and inadequate representations of "race" currently sponsored by both blacks and non-blacks in both "high" and "low" culture.

I think, however, that this dilemma is best confronted in the form of an ongoing critical dialectic, and not in the form of censorship and foregone conclusions. The possibility that something I've written, or will write, might be part of the problem makes me interested in the problem in general. Because black feminism all but entirely lacks an analytical and/or self-critical sphere (such as the complex network of conference-journal-and-book production which generally supports the speculations of white, and often "minority" or "third world" male scholars and intellectuals), I would like to take this opportunity to write about how my view of black feminism has evolved under the pressure of the criticism of *Black Macho* and in the light of black feminism's increasingly public presence within literature, film, and television.

It is necessary to realize that the voices of black feminism in the U.S. emerge today from a long tradition of the structural "silence" of women of color within the sphere of the production of knowledge worldwide. Rarely addressed by mainstream or radical feminism or by anyone, this "silence" has doomed to failure most efforts to change the black woman's status and/or condition within society. There is presently a further danger that in the proliferation of black female images on TV, in music videos and, to a lesser extent, in film, we are witnessing merely a postmodern variation on this phenomenon of black female "silence."

I think it is imperative that we begin to develop a radical black feminist perspective. It may build upon the work of Trinh Minh-ha, Gayatri Spivak, Hazel Carby, bell hooks, and Hortense Spillers in that it will examine the interplay of "gender," "race," and class in Anglo-American and Afro-American culture as they may shape the "production" of knowledge, the structure, content, and "circulation" of the "text," as well as the "audience" of consumption (R. Johnson, 1986–87).

It is crucial that a diagnostic focus on how "black" and "white" culture progresses or regresses on issues of race, class, gender, and sexuality should not preclude that much delayed "close reading" or textual analysis of black feminist creativity, particularly in mass culture where it is most neglected. Such textual analysis might begin in a lot of places but I am particularly interested in the foregrounding and contrasting of psychoanalytic and ethnographic perspectives on the "other." As the two sides of a Western modernist regression/progression on "race" and "sexuality," they need to be reunited in discussions of postcolonial "minority" discourse, which is where I would place black feminist cultural production.

In particular, I would emphasize Claude Lévi-Strauss's (1977b) notion of "myth" in his work with "primitive" people of color and Roland Barthes's (1972b) notion of "myth" in his reading of contemporary mass culture, precisely because they both emerge out of modernism's frustration with "history" as a linear and ideological narrative. Also, both interpretations seem still influential in determining contemporary "political" definitions (in postmodernism and cultural studies) of incorrect thinking.

In a recent essay called "Mythology and History: An Afrocentric Perspective of the World," Amon Saba Saakana (1988) talks about the juxtaposition of "myth" and "history" in terms of Western science rationalizing the murder of Native Americans and the enslavement and colonization of Africans and Asians. In Saakana's account, European and British imperialism in the seventeenth and eighteenth centuries was inevitably accompanied by the development of "history," as a form of narrative discourse considered by the Enlightenment as infinitely superior to "myth," which then was made to stand in for all other approaches to the past. Although the roots of Greek culture in Egyptian and Ethiopian cultures were once recognized as African, these roots were then denied and effaced, even as "civilization" became the polite word for "the ability to define, through power of conquest, the control of knowledge, and the framing of meanings."

A priority continues to be given to "history" over "myth" in even the most sophisticated cases of cultural critique as it forms the basis for a much preferred "historical consciousness" of the kind conventionally necessary to leftist and/or Marxist intellectual production in the West.

To be more specific, I am less interested in the way that Barthes's and Lévi-Strauss's uses of "myth" are customarily read as colorblind in a secondary process of signification than I am in the distinctions that are being made by these authors between two different kinds of "readings" of culture on the part of distinct categories of the population of the world. The "masses" in Barthes's *Mythologies* and "primitive" non-white peoples in Lévi-Strauss's *Tristes Tropiques* and *The Savage Mind* (the bulk of the postcolonial non-white populations in Europe and the Americas of today could be seen as a combination of the two) are presumed to be less literate, less "historical" in their thinking and, therefore, less knowledgeable than that white, male, educated elite who is always in the know.

Beginning with the work of Zora Neale Hurston as anthropologist under Franz Boas at Columbia, the Afro-American literary tradition acquires its present character as the writing down, or the translation of a predominantly oral, or mythic tradition previously sealed off from mainstream white American culture, not only by economic and political disenfranchisement, but also by its enclosure in a system that Barthes and Lévi-Strauss will later bracket as "myth," and which Trinh Minh-ha (1989) has lately called "separate development." It is how people who lack the broader, more "universal" knowledge of the scholar and the historian think about, or fail to think about "History."

Even as Hurston, Lévi-Strauss, and Afro-American literary critic Henry Louis Gates, Jr. insist that the formulations of "myth" or the "oral tradition" are just as good, just as complex and rigorous, this focus emphasizes the comparative inadequacy of black culture. For it is always in the terms of the dominant critical discourse that the alternative mythic practice is being described and named, not the other way around. Nor does the reversal of the terms of interpretation, so that "myth" or the "oral tradition" reads "History" (as Toni Morrison attempts to do in *Beloved,* for instance), do anything but further mystify the grossly unequal relation between the two discourses.

Psychoanalytic readings, too, will need to be revised in terms of race in order to interpret the complex priority quite typically given to "family," or its aberrations, in fictional texts by Afro-American women especially. That the development of the Afro-American family bears a necessarily problematic relationship to the Oedipal myth, and that that relationship might potentially reveal much about issues of orality vs. literacy vs. "silence" in Afro-American culture is borne out by the narrative choices of Afro-American writers beginning with Ralph Ellison's *Invisible Man* (1952) where folk artist Trueblood's "incest" is used to bring together psychoanalytical (familial-sexual) and anthropological (ethnographic-racial) notions of "taboo."[1]

If the "close reading" of Afro-American literature or culture is thus attempted by black feminists, it becomes impossible not to draw upon the relationship of the text to other texts that proceed and surround it in a web of signification and "history," as Barthes reads Balzac in *S/Z* but with "race," class, and gender included this time, instead of excluded and effaced. Yet, the "close reading" should not be employed as the automatic first move but rather as the subsequent stage of an institutional, theoretical, and political critique which leaves key textual issues unresolved. If after one has demystified issues of production as well as how and where the audience receives or views the text, there is still a "text" remaining, then the "close reading" can and should be employed as a means of further investigation and analysis.

The point, finally, is not only to write such cultural criticism but also to promulgate "cultural reading" as an act of resistance. Whereas most people concerned with political repression in the U.S. seem to view such an analysis of culture as a low priority, particularly when that analysis asks questions about "race" and "gender" as well as class, I can't any longer imagine how one manages, as a black woman, to get through a single day of television, film, advertising, magazines, and newspapers, without interpretation and analysis. For instance, I can't imagine getting through the recent presidential election process in the U.S. without employing some mode of interpretation, for the subject of "black women" or "women of color" never came up even as she might be considered the object, along with her children, of some of the most repressive policies in both the Democratic and the Republican Parties. So where and how do we then read ourselves into events? As blacks who are not men and women who are not white, it simply wasn't safe to accept any representation of the candidates, either in television news, in the televised debates, or in the newspapers and magazines, or on the "left" or the "right" without the thinking for oneself that involves "interpretation," that is without bringing some other information gathered from elsewhere to bear upon the "official" information so freely and repetitively given.

By contrast, consider some recent instances in which mass culture addresses the black woman in an attempt to mainstream "black feminism." You will remember that most of us became familiar with the name Oprah Winfrey when she appeared in the role of Sofia in the movie *The Color Purple,* which was adapted from the black feminist novel by the author Alice Walker, but which became, under the guidance and supervision of Hollywood director Steven Spielberg, a sentimental tale which had little to do with "black feminism," or rather little to do with changing the status and condition of black women as a group. As the most successful daytime television talkshow host the networks have ever seen and as the first black female to ever own a prosperous TV and film production company, Oprah Winfrey is buying up all the "black feminist" literature she can lay her hands on. Not only does she own *Beloved* by Toni Morrison, and *Their Eyes Were Watching God* by Zora Neale Hurston (with Quincy Jones), her production of *The Women of Brewster Place* (the novel was by Gloria Naylor), starring herself in the lead role, recently aired on network television.

For the Sunday and Monday that the miniseries was on, network viewers could witness the contrast of a bubbly, carefree Oprah on her daytime talk show versus a downtrodden, unhappy Oprah playing "Mattie Michaels" at night. Fat, old, and poor, Mattie demonstrated the murky immutability of black female life as "it really is," even as she was the exact opposite of the daytime Oprah who has all the answers to such problems as domestic violence, marital strife, mental illness, and other such forms of social "immorality" and disorder. Don't worry, be "rich," the talkshow Oprah seems to say via her "Valley Girl" speech, her straightened hair in a different hairstyle on every other show, her elegant couture wardrobe, her much celebrated weight loss, her meteoric industry success.

On the other hand, the television version of *Women of Brewster Place* is about a collection of black women who live on a dead end urban street. It is their "choice" of men that dooms them to remain there. For instance, Mattie Michaels, Oprah's character, begins the show by mortgaging her house in order to post bail for her "no good" son. Of course, he runs off to avoid trial. Mattie loses the house and ends up in a slum apartment on Brewster Place. While Mattie's son was not exactly her "choice" in the way that one might choose a lover, it was her "choice," the drama leads us to believe, as a teenager to have sex with the "no good" boy who got her pregnant, and it was her "choice" to "spoil" the son by allowing him to sleep in bed with her because he was "afraid of the dark." Whether or not Mattie had also chosen the racism of whites and the poverty of blacks, without which this television drama would make no sense, is a question rendered irrelevant by this story's ideological presupposition, which is that any black woman may freely choose to follow the example of the daytime or the nighttime Oprah.

When Mattie and her friends start to take down that wall blocking off Brewster Place with their bare hands in the rain one night toward the end of the second and final installment of the miniseries, as part of the audience, my attention was not focused on the relationship these women have to the "real world," which is presumably beyond the wall. My attention was focused on their relationship to the discourse of network nighttime television, which was as further confirmation of television's currently deplorable record on black female characterization. Black women play two kinds of parts: tragic chippies and weeping mothers. If a black female actress can't or won't cry, she can forget about working in TV drama. What this means, quite simply, is that black women are turned into an unspeakable, unknowable "other" by nighttime network television.[2]

Before television can be about the politics of real life, it must confront television's own inner politics, and, quite predictably, despite her superficially "feminist" agenda which was reported in the pages of *TV Guide* in a story titled "There's Oprah, Jackee, Robin Givens—and a Break Men May Not Deserve,"[3] Winfrey's *Women of Brewster Place* has left that picture unchanged. For this reason, the melodramatic, maudlin portrayal of lesbianism and the flat, stereotypical portrayal of black men, despite the effort to provide in casting and script "a break men may not deserve," seem to me only symptomatic of this production's larger failure to address the underlying problems of television's discourse.[4]

In 1986, in response to the controversy in the "black community" over "negative images" of black men in the movie *The Color Purple*, I was asked by an organization of third world women graduate students at The University of California in Berkeley to speak on the issue of black feminist intellectual responsibility. The organizer of this conference, Carrie Mae Weems (now a well-known artist in New York), asked me because she saw parallels in the promotion of my book *Black Macho and The Myth of The Superwoman* as a *Ms.* magazine cover in 1979 and the translation of Alice Walker's novel *The Color Purple* into a successful movie. Both Alice Walker and I had somehow been used by the white power structure to hurt the image of blacks, or as she put it in her letter to me:

> Michele Wallace experienced a blacklash after the publication of your *Black Macho and The Myth of The Superwoman*. Some folks felt that your analysis seemed to validate, for whites, the negative and stereotypic views of Black men held by whites; you were thus "used" by the media, and the white Feminist Movement. Does a book like *The Color Purple* operate in a similar way?

In 1979, a large number of black critics in *The Black Scholar,* among them a few black feminists, had linked *Black Macho* with Ntozake Shange's *For Colored Girls Who Have Considered Suicide When The Rainbow Is Enuf,* which became a successful Broadway show, in order to make the same kind of argument.[5] The commercially profitable Broadway show, Hollywood movie, or "best-selling" book[6] issuing from mostly lily white theater, film, and book industries, which rarely provide a hospitable environment for "black talent," was and is as much the rub as the idea of black women criticizing black men in permanent and public ways. The problem reached critical mass in regard to *Black Macho,* also in 1979, when the book was reviewed in the *Sunday New York Times* by black feminist poet and essayist June Jordan (1981), who characterized its production as part of a massive media conspiracy to deny the historical significance of the Civil Rights Movement.

At Berkeley in 1986, in my first concerted effort to respond to such criticisms, I did not try to defend my version of "history" against such attacks, especially since the views of people who actually participated in the Civil Rights Movement in the South were clearly more reliable and authoritative. Instead, I made a blanket defense of black feminist creativity as inherently subversive of a racist and exclusionary status quo. The point was to go beyond an argument about "facts" to a general observation about how rarely black women participate in the production of "fact" and "history." Therefore, when they make any move to do so, it is potentially subversive of a repressive status quo.

I used a black w/hole as a metaphor—a hole in space which appears empty but is actually intensely full—to portray a black feminist creativity that appeared to authorize a "negative" view of the black community but was, in fact, thereby engaged in reformulating black female subjectivity as the product of a complex structure of American (U.S.) inequality. By black feminist creativity, I meant all public creative acts inaugurated by black women, primarily because I never questioned until recently the intrinsic "feminism" or progressive politics of black female expression, or, moreover, the power of feminist thought to transform society in a way beneficial to all.

In the process, I advocated a more dialectical and less paranoid interpretation of cultural hegemony which, somewhat randomly, drew upon the insights of Hegel, Gramsci, Raymond Williams, Kenneth Burke, and Fredric Jameson. In particular, hegemony, as Raymond Williams defined and employed it, together with Jameson's notion of a "political unconscious," helped to explain how cultural production represented a complex process which is not fundamentally altered by any single cultural event. The individual act of writing a book, regardless of whether Shange or Walker or I was the author, was less significant than the absence of published black female critical voices, the void we wrote into and could never hope to fill.

Since then, I've become more concerned about incorporating the methodologies (not necessarily exhaustively) of Marxist cultural criticism, structuralism, psychoanalysis, deconstruction and postmodernism in the development of a critical practice designed to grapple with the complexities of racial/sexual politics as a constellation of increasingly global issues. I am firmly convinced that if black feminism, or the feminism of women of color, is going to thrive on any level as a cultural analysis, it cannot continue to ignore the way that Freud, Marx, Saussure, Nietzsche, Lévi-Strauss, Lacan, Derrida, and Foucault have forever altered the credibility of obvious truth, "common sense," or any unitary conception of reality. Moreover, there are many feminists who are practicing cultural studies, postmodernist, deconstructive, and psychoanalytic criticism who can contribute to our formulations if we read them against the grain. Since the concerns and issues of women of color are so often not included in prevailing definitions of "reality," any analysis which suggests that "reality," or "knowledge," is not simply given but rather produced, seems to me particularly welcome.

Yet this theoretically engaged stance of black feminist cultural theory which I advocate challenges some more cautious and skeptical tendencies within African-American literary theory. Such theorists emphasize that the canonical texts of the West have never included anything but the most derogatory perception of "blackness." As preeminent Afro-American literary critic Henry Louis Gates (1987a) puts it, the question is whether we as theorists can "escape a 'mockingbird' relation to 'theory.' " Is our use of theory "destined to be derivative, often to the point of parody," as he worries? Can we, "escape the racism of so many critical theorists, from Hume and Kant through the Southern Agrarians and the Frankfurt School?" (p. 35).

Throughout Gates's critical work, there is an ongoing preoccupation with the idea that a black person will appear ridiculous in the act of adopting the white man's critical discourses. In his introduction to the anthology *"Race," Writing, and Difference* (1986) while he argues that racial categories are essentially mythological and pernicious, he makes it just as clear that the Afro-American writer and critic is in the uncomfortable position of claiming an intellectual heritage designed to make it impossible for him (never mind her) to write a single word. In *Figures in Black* (1987b), his first book-length study, Gates invokes the Afro-American folk figure of the Signifying Monkey in order to describe the modern black critic's necessarily subversive and problematic relationship to Western critical approaches. Just as blacks have "imitated" white Western languages, literatures, religions, music, dance, dress, and family life, but with a critical, "signifyin'" difference, so shall Afro-American literary criticism steal the meat from the sandwich but leave the white bread untouched (pp. xxx–xxxi, 235–236).

Yet for some black critics of deconstructive and postmodern approaches, it's as though white people had come up with critical theory precisely in order to avoid the question that the persistence of racial inequality poses to the epoch. From an "Afrocentric" perspective, current trends in critical theory look mighty like an exercise in self-absorption designed to reconsolidate the canon of Western Masters (not just Milton and Shakespeare but Hegel, Marx, and Freud, too!), thus trivializing the analysis of any aspect of Afro-American or African diasporic cultural development.

But Gates often fails, I think, in the effort to portray Afro-American writing as a "minority" literature hotly engaged in an antagonistic dialogue with a majority "white" culture in order to transcend and/or transform it. This failure becomes particularly unfortunate in regard to contemporary Afro-American literature by women. Having encountered considerable commercial success and publicity, this literature calls into question, even more than women's books or black books in general, conventional academic notions of a canonical literary tradition, as well as art world concepts of an elite "avant-garde," as inconsistent with mass appeal.

Any "close reading" of these texts disassociated from their cultural and political context is only adequate to the task of a superficial and temporary canonization. However "close" that reading may be, it won't provide much information about how literature by black women alternately conspires with and rebels against our present cultural and political arrangements. In feminist terms, it is just as important to have a way of talking about *The Color Purple*'s impact on how racism or sexism is perceived in contemporary culture, as it is to talk about *The Color Purple* as a symbolic (literary) resolution of racism's concrete irresolvability.

Gates began to venture into the field of such a cultural problematic when he wrote recently,

> And, if only for the record, let me state clearly here that only a black person alienated from black language-use could fail to understand that we have been deconstructing white people's languages and discourse since that dreadful day in 1619 when we were marched off the boat in Virginia. Derrida did not invent deconstruction, *we* did! That is what the blues and signifying are all about. Ours must be a signifying, vernacular criticism, related to other critical theories, yet indelibly black, a critical theory of our own. (1987a, p. 38)

But a continuation of his own discussion here of the social and political roots of what might be called a nascent Afro-American "deconstruction" and/or "postmodernism" only becomes viable in the context of a broader reading of culture as a complex network of patterns and processes which coordinate the influence of "high" and "low" art, vernacular expression, and mass culture in a newly variegated field of contemporary mainstream cultural hegemony. Instead, Gates's primary intention seems to be to delineate an Afro-American literary tradition, which makes sense in terms of consolidating the status of Afro-American studies, but in another sense which I am almost certain that Gates does not intend, it is most unfortunate. In his role as pre-eminent literary critical token—the only black scholar in the humanities really being taken seriously by the mainstream at the moment—it is almost as if to have Gates write about a particular aspect of black culture is to canonize it on the spot.

Raymond Williams's discussion of the hegemonic impulses toward nationalism and an exclusionary elitism embedded in the concept of literary "traditions" remains relevant here. But the process bears particular watching in this case because of the potential danger of metamorphosizing contemporary political texts into dead, historical monuments in order to enshrine them. That is to say, to pre-select, praise, and revere a subset of Afro-American literature (to be designated the canon) is a process totally antithetical to that of becoming critically engaged by the questions an Afro-American literature (either inside or outside of the canon) is designed to pose to its contemporary political and social context.

So what is a black feminist to say about the fact that Henry Louis Gates, Jr. is not only the editor of the first Norton Anthology of Afro-American Literature but also the editor of an extensive Oxford series of re-publications of black women writers? He is singlehandedly reshaping, codifying, and consolidating the entire field of Afro-American studies, including black feminist studies.

While Gates is, no doubt, well intentioned in his efforts to recognize and acknowledge the contributions of black women writers, the *New York Times Book Review* presentation of his recent essay "Whose Canon Is It, Anyway?" (1989) seems to me to alter the stakes as he demonstrates a kind of ability to define black feminist inquiry for the dominant discourse in a manner as yet unavailable to black feminist critics. The results, so far, are inevitably patriarchal. Having established himself as the father of Afro-American studies, with the help of the *NYTBR* he now proposes to become the phallic mother of a newly depoliticized, mainstreamed, and commodified black feminist literary criticism.

There's a clue to this agenda in the anecdote that introduces this essay's black feminist catharsis: At four, Gates was supposed to perform in church the speech "Jesus was a boy like me/And like him I want to be," but he couldn't remember it to save his life so his mother, from the back of the church, stood up and said it for him in "her strong compelling cadences." Everybody in the church laughed. While Gates proposes this anecdote as an example of his symbiotic relationship with his mother, and thereby his love for her, rather it seems a story which justifies, as revenge for this humiliating incident, his appropriation of black female subjectivity or "voice." The hostile twist is embedded in the lines, themselves, for there was never any question of his mother being a "boy" anything like "Jesus."

Whereas she is powerless to appropriate his "voice" in any meaningful sense, he is perfectly free to speak for her and the rest of us besides. " . . . learning to speak in the voice of the black mother," Gates ends his article ominously, "is perhaps the ultimate challenge of producing a discourse of the Other" (1989, p. 45). Not only is it impossible for anybody to speak in anybody else's voice, such a project tends to further consolidate the lethal global presupposition (which is unconscious) in the dominant discourse that women of color or black women generally are incapable of describing, much less analyzing the world, themselves, or their place within the world.

In every case, public statements of black feminism have been controversial in their relationship to an idealized and utopian black feminism which, nevertheless, remains almost entirely unarticulated and untheorized. It is almost as if black feminism were only called upon to deny all attempts to attach its name to an agenda. Yet I have not abandoned the notion that black feminist creativity is inherently (potentially) subversive of a partiarchal hegemony, as well as of a racist and exclusionary white cultural hegemony.

Let me focus briefly upon the external limitations placed upon a black feminist vision by a society that feeds upon and subsumes all resistance and critique, even as it is broadcasting its open-mindedness via the massive proliferation of the "mechanical reproduction" of representation, interpretation, and analysis in the form of TV, film, and print journalism. Again and again, when the negative space of the woman of color meets the Age of Mechanical Reproduction or, worse yet, Baudrillard's "simulations," the resulting affect is a "strong black woman" floating above our heads like one of the cartoon characters in a Macy's Christmas Parade, a form larger than life and yet a deformation powerless to speak. This is not so because any black woman anywhere ever meant to come before the American public without a message, but because the culture routinely and automatically denies her the opportunity of producing autonomous or productive meanings.

The genesis of *The Color Purple* as bestselling novel, then blockbuster movie, seems to me to provide an excellent example of a text initially proposing a complex rereading of Afro-American history and Afro-American literature, which becomes something else entirely in the process of its own success. Finally, the overwhelming urgency of form associated with mass appeal—a Spielberg movie as compelling as *E.T.*, and for all the same reasons—seemed to supercede all other considerations. None of this means that I do not endorse the black feminist voice in such a production nor does it mean I didn't "enjoy" *The Color Purple* on some level. It only means that I now better understand that the feminist project, which is actually part of the same scheme as that production of knowledge that trivialized the "silence" of women of color in the first place, needs profound and multiple acts of revision. It is not enough merely to address the dilemma posed by the black female condition in the U.S. or the world as an object of misery and pathos. Black feminism must insist upon a critical oppositional representation of the black female subject.

While black feminism remains largely undeveloped in terms of its program, "black feminism" can no longer be regarded as the same mystery that it was in 1976 when *For Colored Girls* was first produced. Although I may be disappointed about its public progress, I can no longer deny that some manifestations of black feminism have entered the public arena. Moreover, in retrospect, the movie *The Color Purple* seems to have initiated this second stage in the process of black feminism's public articulation.

In 1987, Toni Morrison published the novel *Beloved* to a very warm critical mass media and book industry reception. While there were no commensurate changes in the status or condition of black women in general, there was nothing remotely "marginal" about Morrison's success. Our enemies persist in pointing out that black women writers are now enjoying a certain vogue as publishable authors and as topics of literary critical speculation.

The key event may be the Oxford series of re-issues of books by black women writers, the key figure Gates, and the key idea that every book black women have ever written should be in print. As for the status of black feminist interpretation, all of which now springs from the largesses of the "mother" of them all, Gates himself, the fortunes of a small number of black female academic literary critics are rising.

While I am not suggesting that this movement to canonize black women writers is reactionary, it does seem as though the participants take for granted that the revision of a once all-white, all-male canon is as progressive as anybody needs to get. Perhaps they are right, for this task is far from safely accomplished, but it seems to me that one must also consider whether relations of power in higher education or relations of representation in the production of knowledge are significantly altered by any of this. When I see "black feminism" being touted by the safest of all possible "spokesmen" on the cover of the safest of all cultural venues—the *New York Times Book Review*—I say the time has arrived to start asking such questions.

Moreover, Gates's academic feminist ventriloquism may be just the sideshow. It is mass media that promises to offer the main attraction, that always seems to determine our image, our absence of critical voice: as in a silent movie, we are always pictures without words, or music without lyrics.

Two names tell the story thus far: Whoopi Goldberg and Oprah Winfrey, both of whom first became widely known as actors in *The Color Purple*. The reputation of each in its own way unsettles previous conceptions of black feminism as inherently a process of collective black female empowerment. This realization is on the same terms as the realization that various landmarks in white female success or black male success have not essentially transformed the brutal overall inequality of the status quo in regard to "women and blacks." A black feminist critique must now provide us with a means of investigating and articulating the multiple dimensions of ideological space that define the relationship of a Whoopi Goldberg or an Oprah Winfrey to *The Color Purple* and a black feminist "ideal" now hopelessly compromised by concrete substantiation. Nor can we continue to fail to forge a way to comment upon the successes of Grace Jones, Aretha Franklin, Tina Turner, Diane Carroll, Diana Ross, or any black female artist or performer whose image functions as cultural icon, and thus as battering ram to all our other cultural and political aspirations.

In line with a frustratingly general notion of "black liberation" as it would manifest itself in mass culture ("the revolution will not be televized"), we still credit and discredit black feminist creativity according to a mechanical concept of "negative" versus "positive" images on the theory that such an evaluation will indicate who is doing more or less for the race, or for the "cause," as it is sometimes vaguely but appropriately called.

But three years since my trip to Berkeley and the movie release of *The Color Purple*, I am beginning to wonder whether the binary opposition of negative and positive images has any relationship at all to what Jesse Jackson called "the real world" at the National Democratic Convention this summer, the world of poverty and despair in this country and the "third world," which is black and brown and "homeless," which cannot "speak for itself," and which one delegate to the convention, a farmer from Kansas, called a "constituency of pain."

What I am calling into question is the idea that black feminism (or any program) should assume, uncritically, its ability to speak *for* black women, most of whom are poor and "silenced" by inadequate education, health care, housing, and lack of public access. Not because I think that black feminism should have nothing to do with representing the black woman who cannot speak for herself but because the problem of silence, and the shortcomings inherent in any representation of the silenced, need to be acknowledged as a central problematic in an oppositional black feminist process.

NOTES

1. I am also borrowing here, in part, from Houston Baker's (1989) reading of Trueblood in *Blues, Ideology, and Afro-American Literature*, pp. 172–88.

2. This situation is changing as a middle-class black woman, usually as "wife of" a black male lead, as on Bill Cosby's Show, *The Heat of The Night*, or the new show *Men*, becomes more visible. Yet I would argue that there is little connection between these bourgeois simulations of

the "white woman" and the signifier "black woman" as it is understood by the rest of television, particularly the news shows and documentaries.

    3. *TV Guide,* March 18–29, cover and pp. 4–8.

    4. These matters have been thoroughly addressed elsewhere, for instance in M. Gurevitch, T. Bennett, J. Curran, J. Woollacott (eds.) *Culture, Society and The Media* (1982); Donald Lazere, (ed.) *American Media and Mass Culture* (1987); Mark Crispin Miller, *Boxed In* (1988); Brian Wallis and Cynthia Schneider (eds.), *Global Television* (1989).

    5. See Robert Staples, "The Myth of Black Macho: A Response to Angry Black Feminists" (1979); and "The Black Scholar Reader Forum: Black Male/Female Relationships" (1979).

    6. The only best-seller list *Black Macho* made it onto was the *Washington Post's* but it was widely perceived as a "best-seller."

DISCUSSION: MICHELE WALLACE

STUART HALL: Listening to you this morning, it struck me for the first time how similar the reaction and the response to *Black Macho* was to the response and reaction in the United Kingdom to the film *My Beautiful Laundrette* by Stephen Frears and Hanif Kureishi. On exactly the same grounds. I can't go into it, but those of you who know the film will know that that film transgressed on every possible grounds: A film by an Asian scriptwriter that didn't make all Asians look all right, which has at its center a gay relationship between an Asian boy and a white boy. You see the point. I don't say that at all to undermine the specificity of the feminist point and the question of gender but to invite you to comment on the particular jeopardy of the double discrimination, when you're advancing not just on one but on two fronts, on the black front and on the feminist front at the same time, or on the black front and the question of sexual politics at the same time. Because an area of double jeopardy is not only specific to those who are trying to do work on that double front; it also raises the question of a form of critical intervention which doesn't operate according to a politics of simple reversal, which I take it is what you were talking about in your attack on the attempt to elaborate a black canon in the place of an erstwhile white canon. You addressed the difficulties of a more positional kind of criticism which involves the politics of a criticism where there's no guarantees that you will always like the fiction or the films or the position taken by the people from your own community. Such a political criticism advances by establishing its own position as it goes because it can't rest on a set of pre-given guarantees as to what is politically correct criticism.

WALLACE: What I wanted to take up, in part, in this paper was the whole idea of doubles as a way of describing this business of double jeopardy. What I'm finally left with is the doubles, themselves, as an operating principle apart from their particular content, whether that may be, for instance, class, race, or gender, or even something slightly less analyzable like old age, physical disability, or mental illness. There is something problematic from the point of view of analytical description about oppressions which double up.

    I see a relationship to Douglas Crimp's paper on AIDS which was an illustration of one kind of confusion that can result when two or more problems of oppression which have very different contingencies and specificities happen in the same space. What struck me about Crimp's analysis of a PBS documentary on AIDS is that the documentary crew was unable to deal with a homeless black bisexual male with AIDS in the same way that they had dealt with other non-black subjects who had AIDS. Their complicity in various official means of social control became evident. For instance, they considered informing on him to the authorities because he told them that he was having unsafe sex. Meanwhile, what happens to their ability to describe his particular experience of

AIDS? And, moreover, what does it say about their so-called objectivity, that their pristine modes of interpretation and analysis fall apart when confronted with a subject who is poor, black, and has AIDS (after all the condition of the majority of people with AIDS)? Of course, it is easier for them to deal with the ideal subject—a white middle-class male who happens to have AIDS because it allows them to focus on a single problem at a time. But this is not how problems generally occur. They generally occur in clusters— black and poor, gay and Asian, Puerto Rican and female, Mexican and mentally ill, etc.

On the other hand, the kind of analysis in black feminism which argues, commonsensically, that being female and black and poor and/or lesbian occurs in "nature" and therefore analysis of the oppression of such "doubles" should occur naturally as well doesn't really work for me. It's ironic that you compare the success of *Black Macho and the Myth of the Superwoman* to the success of *My Beautiful Laundrette* in Britain because I find myself often invoking homophobia and representations of gay people within mass and/or "high" culture in order to borrow the combination of critical analysis and gay activism represented by the work associated with ACT UP for proposing a new way of approaching the problems of women of color.

It is absolutely a function of the logic of hegemonic domination that it is more convenient to invoke a single mode of alterity at a time. Feminist description and analysis has run into this problem quite a lot. When you try to invoke more than one kind of oppression, particularly if one or both kinds have been underdescribed, the effort can even backfire. And I'm only just beginning to realize the implications of the fact that it's not just the double of being black and female but the double of being Native American and female, the double of being gay and poor, all the doubles. Obviously most problematic is having to actually live with double jeopardy. But could it be that part of that difficulty has precisely to do with the problem of representation?

But what concerns me is that representations of double jeopardy should enable and empower the person inside the experience to analyze that experience and to analyze his or her relationship to the dominant discourse. That it is not automatically the case that people who have the experience of double jeopardy are most qualified to describe it seems the opposite of the way it should naturally be. But in fact if you are trying to talk about a mode of cultural practice that you yourself are engaged in as a participant, there is an alienating effect—and a feeling of committing an act of betrayal as well— from the moment you begin to describe it to the outsider. What I am saying is that if you are personally engaged through experience with this double jeopardy, it makes it all the more difficult to talk about, especially in terms of cultural studies, than if you're not. This seems to me potentially dangerous.

QUESTION: Can you tell us from your experience how we can generate an ethics of criticism within our communities? Can we learn from the pain and the difficulty that has happened to you?

WALLACE: There are a lot of casualties over the years, not just me and not just Black women. One of the things I want to say is that on the horizon here is the model of this conference itself. I think it's important not to think of this as an ideal model which we can then impose upon others. I think that Cary was right in saying that this conference is a part of other processes. My only specific recommendation is that within the academic practices of cultural studies, a great range of cultural workers engaged in *contemporary* cultural production should be included, listened to, and encouraged to use various cultural studies approaches and formulas in a speculative manner. We need the participation of people who are on the frontlines, in that sense, either struggling with the conflicts of "high" culture in various institutions or pop culture in the marketplace, like the people who did *My Beautiful Laundrette* or the many filmmakers who inhabit the margins between the mainstream and the avant-grade. It is from such emergent practices that change will always come.

It seems to me that one should be engaged with people who are confronting contemporary problems of representation on the border of politics, on the borders of mass and high culture. Again Crimp's paper, in which he compared visual representations of AIDS in an exhibition of photos at the Museum of Modern Art and representations of AIDS on *Frontline* on PBS, occurs to me as a good example of the benefit that can be drawn from juxtaposing that which has been overanalyzed with that which has suffered from too little analysis. Such a juxtaposition comes out of a current cultural situation that is really open-ended—nobody knows the answer. It is not a discussion in which one can determine the politically correct response beforehand. So the finality and closure of academic description is not only inappropriate but inadvisable. And there are so many people out there trying to do this kind of work who feel very unconnected from and alienated by cultural studies. I think this is a shame.

BELL HOOKS: When *Black Macho* came out, we didn't know one another. When *Ain't I a Woman* came out, and I suffered the same pain and censorship, we didn't know one another. So one of the things that I think people of color have to do is to create a kind of solidarity, so that we can constitute some critical space for one another in which we can both affirm and critique in a helpful way. I was thinking about the question of what is our responsibility as people of color when we write outside our communities about underclass people or about things that are held sacred by our communities. For example, my parents feel very angry about my work, and angered about what I say about them in *Talking Back*. Take for example the fact that you and I seem to be making gender-based criticisms of Spike Lee. Recently, black people accused me of being down on Spike Lee. But I'm not. I'm interested in Spike Lee and I want to respect his work by thinking about it critically and analytically. That requires us to set up a framework that can distinguish between critiquing a work by African-Americans, as an African-American critic, for other African-Americans, and trashing it. That distinction has to be made clear.

JANICE RADWAY: Could I address the issue of ethics? What has occurred to me as the result of doing ethnography, particularly of an elite, is that there are ways of using our knowledge of and understanding of unconscious determinations to good effect. I think we can work hard at depersonalizing these issues, acknowledging good will on the part of those we criticize but recognizing that institutionalized discourses and practices hold all of us. Then, in our criticism, we can target those discourses and practices while acknowledging the better intentions of those with whom we disagree. I think it is important to implicate ourselves in these processes, to acknowledge that we too are held by discourses. I must recognize that there are unconscious determinants of my thoughts, determinants I simply can't uncover myself. I have to rely on my collaborators, my interlocutors, to uncover them for me.

WALLACE: My conclusion, which is not really a conclusion but part of the process of my work, is simply that it is not really possible for me to unproblematically and uncritically speak for the people who are excluded. Even though I stand on the borders of such excluded people consistently and threaten to fall over into them at any particular moment, in any particular space. My commitment, in this paper, is to speak about and near such issues of marginality and locations of exclusion. I am also concerned about not effectively combining issues of "race" and gender. Attempting to combine critiques without conflating them into hierarchical relationships causes a consistent tension between feminism and other kinds of critiques, between the critiques of "race" and what cultural studies understands to be its central problematic around Marxist or post-Marxist interpretations of culture. These tensions or collisions, which have provided the most interesting moments in this conference (the moments in which analysis breaks down and debate begins), are to be fought for in terms of the challenge they pose to current trends in critical discourse. The problem with current trends in critical discourse, to be specific, is that they somehow engage with these tensions in a way that is unreadable, sometimes incredibly boring, sometimes aimed exclusively at a hyper-educated audience. For me at least that's the challenge of my own critical practice.

DAVE MITCHELL: Could you talk a little about the relationship and role, if you see any, for black men and white men in feminist criticism?

WALLACE: I think of feminism as functioning on at least three different horizons simultaneously. Some people see them as stages that we progress through and that we should move through these stages and leave the other stages behind. But I think that all three stages remain engaging and important to maintain simultaneously or one at a time or two at a time.

The first stage is the idea of the equality of women, and although people are constantly leaving it behind, it seems to me that it really cannot be left behind, particularly for women of color, particularly for black women. There continues to be a practical level at which that point has to be engaged with again and again. The second level involves the discussion of difference and I think that there's a whole series of feminisms around the discussion of difference, either racial or ethnic, that needs to be consistently engaged with. Of course, struggles around "race" and ethnicity function at both level 1 and 2 as well.

And then there's the third level, which describes the kind of engagement that feminists have been involved in at this conference. It doesn't necessarily always appear under the name of feminism. It is where we can then join, at least hypothetically, with other kinds of cultural criticism. It is the level at which we like to think that maybe one can translate things from one set of terminologies to another or at least speak across terminologies or from one location in cultural production or critique to another. And I think that it's an ideal utopian moment in which, of course, men—black, white, and brown—are as free to engage in feminist discourse as anybody else. At the level at which the essentialism of "race" or "gender" is hypothetically banished, difference is no longer the only critical issue. This possibility is precisely the point of struggling with and imagining that third position, even if it can't ever be realized in a practical sense, at least it hasn't been. But for me it is much more important that we are aware that it is possible to think about moving toward such a position because it will enable the development of progressive intellectuals of color.

But it isn't me as one of the two black women who have spoken at this conference who has the power to determine whether or not feminism on the left will allow men to speak. Even as I say that it will and it can, it is important to remember that black feminists have never spoken for (white) feminism. Rather it has always been the other way around—white feminism speaking for black feminism. This can even be the case when a black feminist is speaking.

SANDRA BASGALL: Women have always had to find voice within the cracks in the fabric of society, and we here, to a certain extent, are privileged because we do have voice. How do we find ways to give voice to people that don't have a way to find those cracks within society? How do we give them voice other than doing it ourselves, even though the representation may not be entirely accurate? Yet it begins to make people think.

WALLACE: Well, I think possibly the only way to actually give voice is to give voice. But what I would like to emphasize is that we can constitute the cracks or the border or the margins as a position in discourse. I mean that the "cracks" that Stuart Hall spoke about cannot only be a location but a process that is worth being maintained, that feminism can be a process that subverts the consolidation of everybody's comfort of taking a final position. This is the way I think of feminism, as a kind of deconstruction. So perhaps what I mean by giving voice is this process of deconstruction in which you deny yourself voice in various ways both analytically and literally thus actually leaving a void (I'm thinking of the classroom here) to be filled by those who wouldn't ordinarily speak.

It's the idea of feminism coming through the window that Stuart talked about that I want to see continued as a feminist position that can be filled in different ways by people who don't yet have a voice. And by voice, I actually mean authority or the power to define experience. Such a feminist position would give voice to the degree that that is possible. I'm not sure that you can give "voice," as in I give this to you, like a pair of earrings. But what I think you can do is allow it and leave space for it to happen.

What I was thinking about was the discussion following Janice Radway's paper, when somebody brought up Fanny Hurst and the popularity of her work. I don't really know much about Fanny Hurst except what Zora Neale Hurston said about her in her autobiography *Dust Tracks on the Road*. Zora Neale Hurston worked as her maid. Hurston's popularity as a writer fluctuated in her lifetime so much so that she ended up working as a maid near the end of her life, after which she died penniless in a nursing home.

One point I'm trying to make here is that I don't think mainstream popularity necessarily works the same way for black authors or female black authors (or Native American or Latino authors for that matter). Given this, what do general observations about best-selling books and mainstream success that don't talk about "race" and ethnicity really mean?

The second point is that the way to allow this voice about Hurston working as Hurst's maid to occur is not necessarily to always have to assimilate and integrate all the fragmentary voices to arrive at a kind of supervoice. Maybe the best way to modify what was said about Hurst is not necessarily to incorporate the observation about Hurston, which could be better made, by the way, in Hurston's discourse than in any academic discourse, but rather to provide the opportunity within the classroom or within the conference or whatever, for the possibility of that kind of dissonance to occur.

JANICE RADWAY: I would also suggest that we have to enlarge our notion of voice. In fact, there are people "out there" who have voices. They speak in languages and practices that we don't ordinarily try to hear. The problem is our ability to hear different speech. The issue is that they're already speaking—with actions, with fury, with anger, and we don't know how to hear them yet. The problem is really with our listening practices.

WALLACE: Absolutely, I agree. But of course, when I talk about people who are denied "voice," individual practices of speaking is only one level of it. I am also referring to the denial of voice at collective and institutional levels. You might say that that "silence" or lack of "voice" is culturally and/or socially constructed. As such, this void or chasm is not necessarily affected by the actual number of voices that may be attempting to speak from such communities, or even the desire of those of us who may be listening to "hear" them. I suspect that the missing component in making some change in this situation will have to involve some fundamental restructuring of knowledge production.

QUESTION: I would like to say that it is important for conferences like this to re-examine the role of their institutions in other countries, e.g., India. In such countries the dissemination of American culture, even intellectual and academic culture, is debated. Unfortunately, there is no reciprocity in this situation and our voices, particularly given the troubled business of translation, are simply not heard here. I think that institutions like the USIS, the Ford Foundation, and so on flood us with information about America. Perhaps we should think about whether these institutions can be conduits for our work to reach you. This is something you must do, not something that we are asking for. It is something which I feel you must demand and create a space for within cultural studies. We already have heard your voices over and over again.

ELSPETH PROBYN: I want to ask about television in the classroom because it is something that unites teachers and students, allowing a younger generation of women to forge relations with feminist theory. I was thinking about how important Oprah Winfrey is, or has been, in raising questions about, e.g., the representation of black women or the ways in which *thirtysomething* represents sexual preference. And I was wondering whether you would comment on the positivities, in Foucault's sense, of what Oprah allows to be said.

WALLACE: I like watching television but I don't enjoy watching the Oprah Winfrey show for the most part. I don't know exactly why that is. I'm still trying to figure it out. And it may simply be a matter of some proprietary claim on her or what I think she ought to be doing because she's a black woman. But my interventionist strategy is really grounded in my own relationship to academic institutions, which is, I think, still somewhat marginal although less and less so every year. But I still feel as though I don't really have an academic home in terms of discipline and this conference has really underscored that for me. In my case, having an academic home may be a necessary precondition for being able to provide new cultural space for marginalized voices, not just my own. Whether American cultural studies is going to be my academic home remains to be seen. But if it is I can already anticipate a lot of problems. I don't think it will be a comfortable fit any more than English or journalism or writing fiction has been. I've already had the experience of being in a department that sees itself as left of the center (American studies at SUNY Buffalo) where you are constantly engaged in critiquing both the mainstream and the so-called "left," whether you want to or not. Being institutionally situated on the left can be problematic, especially if you're black because you must deal with the racism of the "left" and the "right" more or less simultaneously.

So right now my strategy remains one of intervening in the practices of others from the margins of their discourse. I will leave this conference feeling as though it is the only viable position for me. I was really fascinated by Cornel West's argument for the necessity of engaging with marginalized cultures and the culture of everyday life. I agree. On the other hand, as a black feminist who feels grounded in a variety of marginal communities, I insist upon leaving myself room for a critical perspective on such matters, as well as the status quo. I will never be the dispassionate politically correct ethnographer mainly because I feel entirely too implicated in the cultural practices of the marginal and the everyday.

QUESTION: I'm from a department of Film and Television where we have both film and television production and film and television critical studies. Most of the students want to succeed in the business of Hollywood film and television. However, many of them are sympathetic to the kinds of issues and sensitivities and politics that we're talking about here. But they find the critical categories of cultural studies too restrictive. In the end, the two areas are completely separate, there's no communication, there's a lot of animosity. My feeling is that, to some extent, cultural studies has failed to address that kind of question. Do you have any thoughts on that?

WALLACE: I was thinking of the mutual exclusivity between the critical engagement with and the concrete reception of television itself. What I was thinking about the people who are planning to go into it is, it seems to me that what they're going to encounter in mainstream television in the U.S. is going to be this overwhelming structure, or structuration, which consists not only of television's brand of hegemony, but also the relationship of everything on television to everything else—the "flow." The more striking the difference of the new thing you've managed to do on television, the more the difference will be undermined by "the flow." Even the exceptions to the rules prove the rules. In other words, in trying to imagine something that will somehow break with current cultural hegemony or transform it, we are blocked by what Jameson called "the ideology of form." In the case of network television in the U.S. we're talking about fairly obvious things like having 3 minute commercial breaks every 12 minutes.

So even though I like television, especially the commercials which are often the most formally innovative, I have a tendency to feel that it's absolutely necessary to teach people to read it critically and to reinforce all those practices by which ordinary people don't quite concentrate on watching TV, or they talk back to the TV screen and so forth. So part of the critical reading that we can teach, and that young people who watch TV can teach us, is to always resist the unnegotiated reading. I also feel as well that one has to pursue the possibility of going beyond existing structures, beyond PBS and cable. For instance, there are a lot of "video artists" who are doing work that contests current TV practices. The reform of television is absolutely crucial, for the impact of mainstream TV practices is global. As such, I tend to feel as though it is central to both what's going well and going badly in everyday life among people of color in the U.S. and elsewhere.

QUESTION: What I want to know is how we can use feminism as a tool to help unteach the messages that have been set about the black woman as artifact, as a tradition, as an archetype, as a Mammy, as a Temptress, as incompetent: these are the messages that are coming across in popular culture. How can we then teach the things that are not only going on with black women but also with black men? I'm more concerned with black men who are being denied the right to sing Motown songs while dressed up as raisins than I am with what some prominent black women are doing with them in their novels.

WALLACE: Well, I don't know. But your question reminded me of what it is about Oprah that I'm interested in that is blocking my being able to really deal with her as the host of this show. She's getting ready to become a major producer of black feminist texts in the broadest sense. She already has her own production company, she produces her own show. When she starts to produce the film versions of *Beloved* or of *Their Eyes Were Watching God,* I want my cultural criticism to be ready to address the possibility that they may not be too different from *The Color Purple.* Many people still see Oprah Winfrey, Bill Cosby, and Eddie Murphy as visible celebrities when, in fact, what is most important about their phenomenal successes is that they have become producers. White performers often become directors and producers. It happens more rarely with black performers and even more rarely with black female performers. Debbie Allen, who used to be on *Fame* and acted as its choreographer, now directs *A Different World,* which is produced by Bill Cosby. But Oprah will really be the first powerful black female TV and film producer. As a cultural critic, I would like to be able to talk about why this is happening and whether or not it means any change in the status of women of color in the world. On one level, for the first stage of feminism or black feminism, it will be a momentous advance for black women that one of us will finally have entered this sphere of cultural production. What else will it mean?

LIDIA CURTI: During my research on TV serial texts and their consumption, I seemed to come up a lot against the problem of differentiating the bad and the good. While I think the problem of the good and the bad is primarily an aesthetic question, as it touches on the reasons why we like something or don't like it, on the quality of pleasure, on which way they intersect with formal languages, etc., it also intersects with the problems of gender, race, class, nationality. For instance, the good and bad often are defined in relation to who watches what. Usually a "good" show is watched by certain groups who are able to present their case for the quality of the show. There is very interesting work that could be done on the reception of certain fictions by various ethnic minorities within a dominant culture.

WALLACE: I find that as a teacher I'm getting less and less interested in what's good or bad. I'm sure a lot of people find that on a practical level from day to day in the classroom if one measures what is "good" or "bad" by the pleasure it gives, viewing the pleasure as a correlate of the aesthetic, you'll find that such matters are largely determined by education, class (previous exposure), socio-economic background, gender, sexual preference, cultural context, and, in some cases, personal psychological issues. My point here is that "the good" and "the bad" don't remain the same. They aren't universal, consistent, or even singular. They are historically variable. This doesn't mean there isn't any point in talking about aesthetic quality. It just means that aesthetic quality becomes another variable in a discussion of relative variables.

37

Spectacular Action:
Rambo and the Popular Pleasures of Pain*

WILLIAM WARNER

> After the shoving around America took in the world of the 70s . . . finally the
> giant said, "Wait a minute, I'm big and strong, but I haven't done anything that's
> *that* atrocious."
> Sylvester Stallone, in interview (*Newsweek;* October 23, 1985, p. 62)

> Boy, I'm glad I saw *Rambo* last night. Now I'll know what to do next time.
> President Ronald Reagan, July 1985, before welcoming freed hostages from the
> TWA flight held in Lebanon (*Sunday London Times,* July 7, 1985)

How is it that American film audiences in the late seventies and early eighties found
pleasure in entering the World of the Hero—a bracing new cinematic realm of extravagant courage and literal violence where modern skepticism of the hero could be magically suspended? How does one understand the relationship between these new detours
in the history of pleasure, the developing technology of the action film, and ideologically
fraught debates about "America's position in the world"? What articulations of culture
and film technique made the production and consumption of the hero's spectacular action
one of the most characteristic impulses of a decade? Among those films constructed
around a new literalization of the heroic—from *Star Wars* (1977) to *Robocop* (1987), from
Excalibur (1981) to *Aliens* (1986)—no films caused a greater scandal to critics than *First
Blood* (1982) and *Rambo: First Blood Part II* (1985). Here the action-adventure genre
seemed to strive for a preposterously direct political address. The story of John Rambo,
and the film's refiguration of the Vietnam War, not only develop an interpretation of
America's Vietnam defeat as a betrayal of the soldier by his nation, it also indulges an
openly compensatory scenario. For many critics the popularity of Rambo seemed to
involve an inflection of taste and style in entertainment which, by the way it exalted
America over her adversaries, produced a fictional analogue to Reagan's strident nationalism and military buildup. Executed with a deadly seriousness of posture, these films
seemed to beg for the deflating critical mockery they received. But rebukes offered by
a broad spectrum of critics to this "return of the hero" did little to check this swerve
in popular taste. For critics and commentators, the most vexing scandal of these films
was the fact that they were consumed by vast numbers, with evident pleasure. If there
were ever to be an instance of the "bad popular," Rambo seemed to be it.

In this essay I will interpret the popularity of the Rambo films by exploring the
following thesis. In the late seventies and early eighties the rise of the hero film offered
audiences a pleasurable way to work upon an insistent historical problem—the perceived

decline of American power both in relation to other nations, as well as a recent, fondly remembered past. When this issue is given particularly explicit political inflection in the Rambo films, the critical condemnation of *Rambo* as Reaganism-in-film diagnosed the films' wishful and tendentious reinterpretation of the Vietnam War. But this critique obscured several aspects of Rambo's successful address to its popular audience. The appeal of these films depends upon subjecting hero and audience to a certain masochistic scenario—the pleasure of intensely felt pain, and crippling incapacity, as it is written into the action, and onto the body of the hero. Secondly, each film supports the natural virtue of the hero through a display of technology's magic. Finally, each film wins the audience an anti-therapeutic relief from confining subjectivity by releasing it into a vertiginous cinematic experience of spectacular action. It is precisely what most offended critics about the Rambo films—their implausible blending of fantasy and "history"— that gives these films special usefulness for reading the switch point between politics and entertainment, between debate in the public sphere about "the state of the nation" and the pleasures of summer action on the silver screen.

Remembering Vietnam, Rescuing America

The Rambo films are shaped to intervene in what might be called "the Vietnam Debate": that broad and dispersed interpretive joust, or conversation in culture, about the meaning of the Vietnam War, especially as this, the "first war America ever lost," seemed from the vantage point of the early eighties to mark the beginning of the decline in American power. This "debate" was given new impetus and focus by the Iran Hostage Crisis (1979–1980) and Ronald Reagan's election (1980). The many different forms of cultural work on and around Vietnam and the vet in the early 1980s suggest that the war's trauma was far from dissipated, its wound still open and in need of the kind of suturing that can only be done with words and representations.[1]

How did *First Blood* and *Rambo* intervene in the "Vietnam Debate"? The Rambo films are founded upon the assumption that a beloved object was lost in Vietnam—men who died, American honor, and, with the war, America's position of post-World War II pre-eminence. How might film scenarios be devised that would redress this loss? First there must be an interpretation of the war's losses that allows rage to be justified, locates blame in a restricted way, and devises some plausible action that will afford a new chance to recover what has been lost. Rambo is the ordinary Vietnam vet who, in his self-doubts and potential greatness, personifies America. He is justified in his rage, because America's fighting men have been in various ways betrayed—they were never allowed to fight to win; they were not supported at home; as returned vets they were called "Babykillers." Who is responsible for the loss of American honor? Blame is located in those liberal bureaucrats, and thin-blooded Americans who have wasted American strength, and squandered America's proper position of priority in the world. It is they who are also responsible for a suppression of "the fact" that there are still POWs alive in Vietnam. The Rambo films' magical solution to the riddle of American decline hinges upon a new remembering of war and nation: how one remembers "the War" turns out to have everything to do with how one can re-member American strength. One must join and heal by finding and returning the lost "parts" of the nation. But in such a "rescue mission" the question of who is essential and expendable comes to the fore. When asked by his Vietnamese female guide Co Bao, why he, Rambo, was chosen for this mission, Rambo explains his presence on the mission by saying that, for those in power, he is "expendable." When pressed by Co Bao to explain this word, Rambo describes someone invited to a party, who fails to come, and is never missed. Later in the film, when they are parting, her loving rejoinder is: "Rambo, you are *not* expendable." And this is the crux of the film's explicit discursive project: not only to reclaim the American vet as not expendable, but further, to discover that what Rambo is and represents (pride, strength, will) is precisely that which is most indispensable for America today.

The scenario of the rescue mission allows America and Rambo one more chance in Vietnam. The rescue mission is a central feature of major Vietnam War films like *Deerhunter* (1978) and *Apocalypse Now* (1979). But while these two films, and *Platoon* (1986), make Vietnam the site for a moral test, and the "return" an action fraught with soul-searching and liberal guilt, *Rambo* follows a very different path. *First Blood*'s account of John Rambo's unfair persecution by a small town in the Pacific Northwest, and his delayed but explosive war against the town and its sheriff, allow the negative ideas about the Vietnam vet (as haunted, "crazy," a social cripple) to be assumed and transvalued, until they become sources of his uncanny strength. When *First Blood* turned out to be one of the surprise film hits of 1982, having as Stallone put it, "triggered long-suppressed emotions," Stallone and James Cameron developed a script which would take Rambo back to Vietnam for the sort of rescue mission that *Uncommon Valor* (1983) and Chuck Norris's *Missing in Action* (1984) used with such popular success. Inserted in this rescue scenario, John Rambo loses most of his internal paralysis, and his fighting ability, no longer a dangerous anachronism, becomes useful to the nation.

The familiarity and tenacity of the idea of living MIAs should not obscure what is odd and symptomatic about this notion. Neither the clandestine efforts of Texas billionaire H. Ross Perot, nor the congressional fact-finding mission sent to Vietnam at the beginning of the Carter administration succeeded in finding *even one* of the 2,500 MIAs. Nor have any shown up since. Instead, the idea that there are American POWs still alive in Vietnam must be understood as a popular fiction, only slightly less fantastic than belief in UFOs. This fiction expresses a will to believe that there are betrayed American soldiers still alive, still suffering, awaiting rescue. To refuse to believe in these lost American souls is to become complicit in the theft of American strength. In *Rambo*, the MIAs that Rambo locates and rescues are withered, diseased, and fading. Closer to the gaunt denizens of a TB ward than the robust bands who execute the prison escapes in World War II films, these POWs are the visual antithesis to Rambo's muscled vigor. While Rambo provides the resolve and fire power for escape, they provide the unambiguous moral vindication for the mission of their rescuer. Together, as agent and alibis of the rescue, they provide the mysterious supplements needed to complete the puzzle of American strength. By film's end, the history of American failure in Vietnam seems to be overwritten by a fable of America's restored greatness.

By the time *Rambo* was released in June of 1985, reconsiderations of the Vietnam War had become entangled with a debate about America's proper posture in the world. The vehement critical condemnation of *Rambo* made the film's central male character one of the condensation points for the struggle of interpretations around the Vietnam War, Reaganism, and the question of American strength. Some critics disputed the outlandish reversals of fact necessary to fabricate Rambo's story. Tom O'Brien points out one: it was the Vietcong, not Americans, who fought like Rambo, using "primitive technology and expertise in jungle warfare"—"American methodology was hi-tech and high altitude" (*Commonweal,* June 21, 1985). But for liberal critics the distortion of history was more pervasive: *Rambo* converted what should be the object of regret and lessons learned into the site for a certain nostalgic revisionary heroism—a memory of the band of brothers now gone. What *Rambo* contests is a settled liberal interpretation of the war as "tragic" and "unjust." By glorifying battle in Vietnam, *Rambo* renews the old debate about the war, but on a puzzling new ground of popular culture, where it is not exactly the war, but "Rambo," as figure of the Vietnam vet, who is vindicated. Prospectively, *Rambo*'s popularity, as it seems to justify Reagan's aggressive policy in Central America in the early eighties, may be a menacing harbinger of new foreign military adventures. Marxist and feminist criticism has focused upon the pathology of Rambo's aggressive individualism, his compensatory masculinity, and the fascist resonances of the film's association of Rambo with nature.[2]

For the broad spectrum of critics to the left of Reagan, the phenomenon of Rambo's popularity evidences the profound gulf which had opened between them and audiences ready for blatantly heroic fare with a strong Reaganite cast. The films seemed to construct a subject position—one which is Western, white, and male—which hails spectators to an ethos for being in the world which, echoing Stuart Hall's description of Thatcherism, might be called "Reaganism": it values isolated self-assertion, competitive zeal, chauvinist Americanism, and the use of force.[3] By reading Rambo as a filmic expression of Reaganism, an approach used repeatedly by film critics and cultural and political commentators and even at moments by Ronald Reagan and Sylvester Stallone themselves, film hero and President become each other's latent cultural truth. This reading uses the popularity of Reaganism to gloss, explain, and (for many commentators) discredit the popularity of Rambo. In a complementary fashion, Rambo becomes the dream-fantasy in film, the "truth" of Reaganism, now blatantly exposed as in various ways mendacious. This double critique of Rambo and Reagan had a paradoxical effect within the political culture of the mid-1980s: it helped Rambo become a generally recognized cultural icon. It is this critical condemnation of Rambo, almost as much as the film itself, as both unfold around certain contested cultural terms (Vietnam, the vet, patriotism, America's proper role in the world), which allows Rambo to emerge as a cultural icon in the mid-1980s. Thus Rambo as a cultural icon includes the idealized filmic projection, and its scathing critique, condensed in one image. Even for those who refused to become consumers of these films, Rambo, as an icon of the masculine, the primitive, and the heroic, becomes the site of a (bad) truth about American culture in the eighties. The political-allegorical reading of Rambo not only filters the film's audience of left intellectuals and academics, it also obscures, by pathologizing, the sources of the film's popularity. The Rambo films—organized as they are around the experience of American failure—produce their pleasures . . . through pain.

The Pleasures of Pains; or
Unsutured Scars on a White Male Body

Rambo is one of a series of films of the late seventies and early eighties which took up an old theme of American film and culture—the individual's struggle against an unjust system—and gave that scenario a distinct new turn. The protagonist did not challenge the system by teaming up with an ambiguous woman to solve a crime (as in *film noir*), or organizing the good ranchers against the Boss who owns the whole town (as in some Westerns). Now the System—sometimes a state, sometimes a corporation—is given extraordinary new powers of surveillance and control of the individual. The protagonist, almost entirely cut off from others, endures the most insidious forms of manipulation and pain, reaches into the primordial levels of the self, and emerges as a hero with powers sufficient to fight the System to the point of its catastrophe. In *Rollerball* (1975), *Alien* (1979), *Bladerunner* (1982), *Aliens* (1986), and *Robocop* (1987) the hero becomes the culture's last chance to save the personal and the human from engulfment in a perverse system of manipulative consumer gratification and corporate control. The hero arrives to cleanse this dystopic system by destroying it.

Rambo, like many hero films of the early eighties, develops a version of the fable of self and system which dichotomizes fictional space into two positions. The self, often associated with nature and the erotic, becomes the locus for the expression of every positive human value, most especially "freedom." Opposite the self is the System, which in its colorless, mechanical operations, is anathematized as a faceless monster using its insidious powers to bend all human effort to its own service. In their consideration of *Rollerball* (1975), Ryan and Kellner (1988) find this dichotomizing to be the film's essential ideological gesture, by which "no middle ground is allowed . . . anything that departs from the ideal of pure individual freedom (corporations, but also socialism) is by implication lumped under domination" (p. 256). But before we dub this narrative scenario "ideological," and thus in some sense simply false, it is worth attempting to understand the popular appeal of this fable of self and system in films and political culture of the late seventies and early eighties. Such a fiction no doubt has deep roots in American populist paranoia about global conspiracy. But the popular appeal of this fable may also express legitimate disenchantment with an aspect of the modern world that Foucault's work has exhaustively detailed—the diffuseness of power as it inheres in the bureaucracies and discursive formations of modern systems for shaping power and knowledge.[4] Rambo becomes the populist warrior fighting those systems. Thus his climactic act in *Rambo* is the machine-gunning of the "wolf-den" computer systems used to guide his reconnaissance operation. By destroying, or interrupting, the operation of the system, the audience is left at the end of a film with a freeze frame image of Rambo as a nuclear subject, a self etched against a landscape where no supporting social network seems necessary.

In the Rambo films the exchanges of self and system are given the insistently Oedipal configuration of a struggle between overbearing fathers and a defiant son. But here the "father's" authority is linked to the state, and even the "son's" rebellion finds ways to reassert US military pre-eminence in Asia. Thus, when Col. Trautman enters in *First Blood* his first words to Teasle are, "God didn't make Rambo; . . . I made him . . . I recruited him, I trained him, I commanded him for three years in Vietnam. I say that makes him mine." Rambo's public dimension means that those film tropes that are revived from Westerns—both the rugged individualism of the cowboy, the stealth and life in nature of the Indian—are now articulated with the most centralized activity of the modern state, the fighting of war.

Within this fictive restaging of America's Vietnam involvements, the plot suspense of *Rambo* pivots upon a personal drama, meant to allegorize the struggle of every modern person who would remember their freedom: a contest between the system's agenda for the self and the self's attempt to manipulate the system to his own ends. Upon arrival at base camp in Thailand, Rambo is instructed to avoid "the blood and guts routine," to let "technology do most of the work," and "try to forget the war." In these ways Rambo is programmed by Murdock and Trautman as an instrument in the sophisticated war-fighting apparatus. But this process is complicated by two countermovements to Rambo's ostensible mission. Rambo has a personal agenda: the will to remember—"If I'm alive, [the war's] still alive isn't it?"; he assumes responsibility for America's "missing in action" and invites the heroic test in hopes that this time "we get to win." But so too does the system have another agenda than the announced one. Murdock has secretly planned the mission so Rambo will not find and rescue, but instead will confirm the absence of living MIAs.

While the explicit ideological address of the Rambo films helps win their "reality effect," the moral alibi for their consuming violence comes from the display of the hero's suffering. Within the films, two ideas are developed about loss in Vietnam. Both emphasize the cruel sadistic sources of this pain and loss: "we were unfairly beaten in Vietnam, and experienced loss"; "others were responsible for that loss, and they should now be punished." Between these two ideas—one about the past and one about the future, but each emphasizing that blame and punishment lies elsewhere—there is a third idea which is never allowed to reach consciousness in the Rambo films, but nonetheless motivates and informs the narrative diegesis: "I am responsible for the losses (in Vietnam), and I should be beaten." Rambo's unconscious guilt leads him to accept masochistic positions which bring pain and humiliation as punishment for failure. Thus Rambo's adventures start in both films with an act which invites pain. After he is given a ride out of town from Sheriff Teasle, Rambo turns back into town, where he is arrested, tortured, escapes, etc. In *Rambo,* after weighing the advantages of prison ("[I've] seen worse"; "In here I know where I stand"), Rambo accepts the mission although Trautman has warned him that the "risk factor is very high." Rambo's unconscious guilt for failing in Vietnam is deflected away from consciousness, but it motivates that defiant and risky behavior which repeatedly throws Rambo into the position to receive punishment for failing. The Rambo films also encourage audience guilt for American failure to remain unconscious; in place of guilt, Rambo models an alternative posture for Americans—that of being wronged and righteous.

How might one explain Rambo's rage against the self? Because of the discrepancy between a valued ideal of himself (I'm a winner, the best, on top . . .) and what "the war" made him (. . . a loser, no longer the best, in decline), Rambo suffers anxiety, and a withering self-judgment. Within the theoretical framework of psychoanalysis, Freud (1963b) postulates that the self's judgment against the self develops when the ego comes under the attack of the superego. The superego confronts the self with ego-ideals—monuments to that epoch when the father and mother were objects of libidinal attachment—which now transmit certain qualities of the early parents: "their power, their severity, their tendency to watch over and to punish. . . . The superego . . . can become harsh, cruel and inexorable against the ego which is in its charge" (pp. 197–98). In *First Blood* and *Rambo,* pain becomes the occasion for pleasure through an encounter with figures of "the father"—but not the mother (more on this below). In each film that father is bifurcated into "good" and "bad" fathers, so each becomes emblematic of public aspects of America. In both films Colonel Trautman is that "good father," who knows, loves, and believes in Rambo. He not only claims the role as Rambo's "maker," he also insists he's "the closest thing to family" Rambo has. Trautman embodies those old-fashioned American qualities of selfless loyalty and service expressed in the Special Forces "Baker Troop" Trautman led. Crisp and noble in his appearance and manner, Colonel Trautman's formality and precision of address articulates the military with an expression of moral authority.

Opposite Colonel Trautman in both films are the bad fathers—each a symptomatic embodiment of what America has become after the catastrophe of Vietnam. Rambo's opponent in *First Blood* is Sheriff Teasle, a descendant of the corrupt redneck sheriffs of sixties film and culture. Sloppy and imprecise in his swagger, Teasle wears a genial smirk as he surveys "his town," guarding its peace with patriarchal presumption. After giving Rambo an unrequested ride out of town ("we don't want people like you around here"), he offers "friendly advice" ("get a hair cut," "take a bath," "get rid of that army jacket"), and then drives off with a final, ironic, "Have a nice day." When Rambo, here positioned rather paradoxically as both vet and longhaired hippy, disobeys, Teasle becomes livid. Teasle's persecution of Rambo is intensely personal, even demonic: "I wanted to kill that kid . . . so much I could taste it." By contrast Murdock, who runs Rambo's mission into Vietnam from Thailand, and then orders the extraction helicopter to desert him, has none of Teasle's animus toward Rambo. As the calculating, and entirely cynical bureaucrat, he has no military discipline: he sweats like a pig, constantly complains of the heat, and even drinks out of a glass. As the duplicitous organization man, Murdock combines an absence of moral principle with a streak of sadism. To Murdock the lost POWs are described not as "men" but "ghosts," and when Rambo violates his orders by rescuing a POW, he becomes expendable.

Although both films stage a struggle between "good" and "bad" fathers on how to "handle" John Rambo, there is enough evidence of the complicity between these rival fathers to suggest that they are in fact two sides of one father. In *First Blood,* Trautman is willing to talk to Rambo by radio, though he knows this will help Teasle get a "fix" on Rambo's forest hideaway. After Rambo's apparent "death," they share a drink and some tough manly talk at the country western bar in town. In *Rambo,* Murdock deflects Trautman's indignation at the betrayal of Rambo at the pickup point by accusing him of suspecting the mission's secret goal all along: "Don't act so innocent, Colonel. You had your suspicions, and if you suspected then, you're sort of an accessory, aren't you?"

Both fathers provide a rich vein of pain to gratify the hero's masochism. Trautman's demand that "Johnny" be good allows Rambo to be "bad," to transgress Trautman's injunctions to "give yourself in" and "forget the war." When Rambo is tortured in Teasle's prison, when Murdock aborts the pickup, and so leaves Rambo to suffer Oriental and Russian tortures, Teasle and Murdock have provided the occasions for the most literal bodily pain. These physical tortures are explicitly presented as a repetition of wounds still unsutured from his prison camp tortures during the war. Thus, at four points in Rambo's brutal processing at the police station in *First Blood,* there are crosscut flashbacks to scenes of Rambo's torture in Vietnam: slop is thrown down into his cage/cell, he is hoisted up and hung crucifix-style, then cut in the side with an enormous knife. Suspended before the spectator's eye, the vulnerability and sensitivity of Rambo's body gets added emphasis from a soundtrack which allows us to hear every ugh, grunt, moan, and scream that comes from Rambo. *Rambo* magnifies the scenes of Rambo's torture so they become outlandish in their extremity—Rambo deserted by his own rescue helicopter, Rambo suspended in a pool of leech-infested slime, Rambo upon an electric rack, Rambo being tortured with his own knife (Figure 1). In these scenes, every possible filmic device—vivid colors, extreme close-up, abrupt sounds, caricatured villains—is used to overcome the distance between Rambo's body and those who administer his suffering. The torture scenes produce the effect of a perfect complementarity of positions, with the relay of gazes closing the S and M circuit.

The hallucinatory vividness of Rambo's torture results from the elaboration of a social and political allegory which is always also intrapsychic and fantasmatic. The persecuting other emerges as much from within as outside the self; the other is always an agent of the father. Because they are shaped by the remorseless demands of an (introjected) father, Rambo's denuding, humiliation, and repeated "castration" become the occasions for a masochistic pleasure that "leans up against," and is nourished by the other's sadistic pleasure. Later in the action, when Rambo controls the instruments of power, the other's pain will augment Rambo's pleasure.

What is the rhetoric of this spectacle—and its intended effect upon the audience—as shaped by Rambo's masochistic role, and the film's representation of that role? The narrative interpolates the audience on the "side" of Rambo—the masochist/victim/

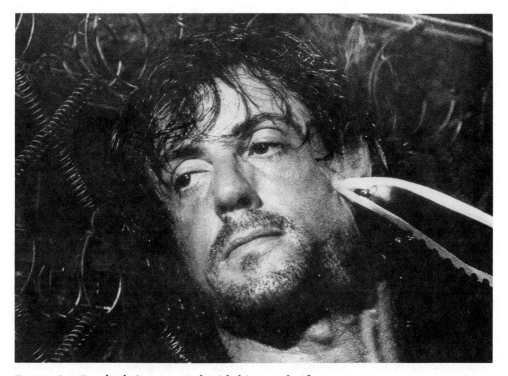

FIGURE 1. Rambo being tortured with his own knife.

hero—but the camera also implicates us in the sadistic position, watching Rambo from the position of his tormenters. Compelled to oscillate between these two positions, the display of Rambo's sufferings seems calculated to produce in its audience a certain disturbing proximity and fascinated unease. In an essay entitled "Masochism and Male Subjectivity," Kaja Silverman (1988) speculates upon the power of the "male masochist's" "self-exposure" to unsettle, by laying bare, the violence which undergirds the social contract. The passage helps us explicate several registers of Rambo's "complaint" to the audience:

> [The male masochist] acts out in an insistent and exaggerated way the basic conditions of cultural subjectivity, conditions that are normally disavowed; he loudly proclaims that his meaning comes to him from the Other, prostrates himself before the Gaze even as he solicits it, exhibits his castration for all to see, and revels in the sacrificial basis of the social contract. The male masochist magnifies the losses and division upon which cultural identity is based, refusing to be sutured or recompensed. In short, he radiates a negativity inimical to the social order. (p. 51)

By assuming the position of the male masochist, by assenting to his own torture, Rambo provokes the social judgment that he is somehow "crazy." Crippled with this "madness"—an anger and insanity that scandalizes the social order—the tortured hero escapes to the forest alone and comparatively weak; but he returns with astonishing strength.

What allows this reversal in Rambo's position? In reflecting upon his chances to survive his mission, Rambo intones to his guide Co Bao, "To survive war, you've got to become war." For the masochist hero "becoming war" means bringing the war that rages inside out, and changing the direction and object of his aggression from self to other, so he can assume the sadistic position. "Becoming war," Rambo can prevail in the chase (which guarantees the hero's freedom), the hunt (where hunter becomes the hunted), and in those duels with a demonized other (which certifies the hero's greater virtue). But "becoming war" means more: it means Rambo becomes a kind of terrorist— as destructively cataclysmic to the whole established order as a terrorist might dream of being. In *First Blood* Rambo spreads catastrophe from town members to the whole town: citizens scatter as he escapes the prison; his victory over the police in the forest results in the establishing of a "base camp" on the forest's edge with the familiar elements of disaster—ambulances and newsmen, helicopters and the national guard. Finally, after he blows up a huge gasoline depot upon his return to town, we watch the blaze reflected on the shocked faces of the police station personnel. Sheriff Teasle announces a "police emergency" of the sort reminiscent of the disaster films of the 1950s. In *Rambo* there is an even more relentless, and still more implausible, expansion of disaster: from the Vietnamese soldiers he immolates in the brush, to those he blows up on the bridge; to the prisoner camp he destroys and liberates; and finally, in Rambo's return to base camp and its computer center. Every battle generates larger and larger explosions, and each explosion is shot in such a way that Rambo seems to turn his enemies, as if by magic, into nothing. These explosions figure the catastrophe Rambo would control and deliver to some more quiet end. Just as the scenes of torture demonstrated a fantasmatic exaggeration of self-punishment, so these scenes of destruction realize a child's fantasy of total control, of effortless mastery of every conceivable impediment to the self.

In both films the final cascade of spectacular action achieves its "liberation effect" by oscillating from a passive, "feminine" masochistic position to an active, "masculine" sadistic one. Now Rambo can channel all his righteous, vengeful fury into an attack upon the enemy. Rambo's triumph climaxes with Rambo's (symbolic) "killing" of the bad father. As if the spell of the S and M double-bind were suddenly broken, Rambo goes from being a murderous destroyer to a tearful confessor of sorrows. In *First Blood* the silent hero suddenly speaks—of his memories of the war, of his sense of being wronged, of his present failures. In this intensification of the subject position of the hero, the audience is positioned with Trautman as the receiver of the hero's direct address. This final therapeutic exchange attempts to suture a certain ideological meaning to Rambo's actions. Rambo's violence is motivated by America's betrayal of the memory of the men of Baker Troop, now gone, or the demand for love founded in patriotism that closes *Rambo*: "We just want our country to love us, as much as we love it." But there is an excessiveness, an unreserved expenditure about these final spectacles of violence which cannot be contained or alibied by the hero's final speech.

The Manichean division of the Rambo films between polarities of self and system, son and father depends upon a suppression of the woman. This marginalizing of the woman is more than a question of topic (stories of war and male physical prowess) or film genre (the action-adventure films' address to a male audience). As we have seen, the film constructs itself through a set of reversible exchanges between sadistic and masochistic positions, where both positions are coded as male. In this homoerotic bonding between Rambo and his opponents there is strong identification across lines of race and nation. Thus while interrogating Rambo on the rack, the Russian Col. Podovsk says, "To me, you are a comrade similar to myself just opposed by a matter of fate." What is "missing in (this) action," or at least severely displaced, is the woman, the mother, the sister. The woman's position is suppressed because it is not the site of guilt, anger, or masochistic pleasure. But precisely because she is *not* the locus of these ambivalent feelings, it is she who must be recruited to offer indispensable support to the narrative of the male hero. Thus it is Co Bao, the only female character in the two Rambo films, who can step in, from outside the male-male dyad, to save Rambo. Functioning in the role of the "good native," Co Bao is the Vietnamese guide who meets Rambo in the jungle, and leads him to the prison camp. Rambo is guarded from any initial sentimental entanglements with this sisterly fellow orphan of the war by the sheer resolve with which he pursues his mission. But after she returns to the prison camp, disguised as a whore, and makes possible Rambo's escape, he thanks her. Co Bao acts on her dream of "going to America" with a request: "You take me with you, Rambo?" He agrees, and kisses her. She smiles and says, "You make good choice, Rambo," then steps into a hail of bullets (Figure 2). Rambo's kiss is fatal, because any special entanglement with another, especially a woman, would imperil his isolation, and complicate rather than motivate a subject position able to orchestrate the spectacular action of the film's finale. But in this final battle, Rambo carries a trace of the (erased) female role—in the form of Co Bao's green jade "lucky charm."

Spectacular Action, or the Hero and the Machine

When *Rambo* turned out to be a popular success in the early summer of 1985, that popularity was attributed by a broad range of critics to the excellence of its technological development of the action-adventure genre. For liberal critics the effectiveness of its bracing and inventive spectacularizing of action—conceived as a separable feature of film style—made the film's ideology all the more dangerously seductive. But I do not think one should disengage ideology and cinematic form. My study of the Rambo films and their various forms of appeal for their audience suggests an important symbiosis between

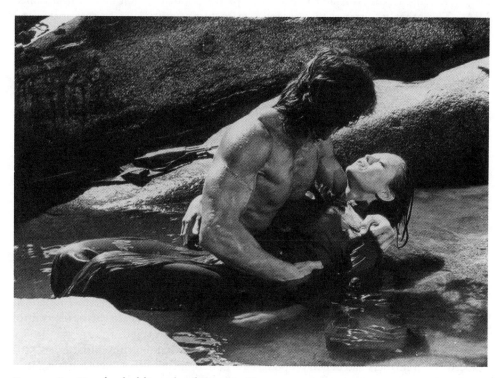

FIGURE 2. Rambo holding the dying Co Bao.

ideology and technology in the development of the action-adventure film in the late seventies and early eighties.

In his essays upon the development of deep focus cinematography in the 1940s, Jean-Louis Comolli (1980) insists that changes in film practice do not result from an inevitable development of technology, nor from the inventive genius of certain film artists who fashion newly available technologies to their ideas. Instead, Comolli brings the history of film into relationship with a broader and more heterogenous factor—the mobile cultural history of the film audience. In his account of film mimesis, certain techniques of filmmaking become ways, at particular historical junctures, for the spectator to both encourage the analogy between the film image and the realized spectacle, and then disavow what is arbitrary and mendacious in that analogy:

> The spectacle is always a game, requiring the spectator's participation not as "passive," as "alienated" consumers, but as players, accomplices, masters of the game even if they are also what is at stake. . . . Different in this to ideological and political representations, spectatorial representations declare their existence as simulacrum and, on the contractual basis, invite the spectator to *use* the simulacrum to fool him or herself. Never "passive," the spectator works. But that work is not only a work of deciphering, reading, elaboration of signs. . . . it is to maintain—if the spectacle, its play makes it possible—the mechanism of disavowal at its highest level of intensity. (p. 140)

What are the ideological interpellations, the pleasurable recognitions, which allowed spectators to disavow the rather blatantly fictional analogy between Rambo and the Vietnam vet, between Rambo's return to Vietnam and that war the country experienced for over a decade, between Rambo's victories and America's failures? In this essay, I have been tracing two actions and effects of the Rambo films. One might be described as diegetic: "refight" the War and win by way of the popular fiction of still imprisoned MIAs. The other is intrapsychic: accept a masochistic position of torture, pain, and humiliation as punishment for loss; then, through a sudden reversal, achieve the pleasures of a sadistic position of utter mastery. But there is a third "action" of the Rambo films as well: the move from an embodied, bound, limited subjectivity to a subject position which is abstract, disembodied, general, empty, and therefore open. In this third action, *Rambo* becomes the site of moving spectacle itself. Here, awash in sensation, the diegetic serves as stage set, the intrapsychic as mental set for a series of increasingly big production numbers, each louder, brighter, and busier than the last. This third and ultimately final action and effect of the Rambo films might be represented as a perverse detour away from any "real" political or psychic object, where "repression . . . is, at bottom, an attempt at flight" (Freud, 1958, p. 133). It certainly leaves behind the haggle about vets as well as the "drag" of the Oedipal configuration, with its doubled and divided paternity. The sheer intensity of explosions, motion, and illusory sound around (you are there) the filmic presence allows the audience to disavow, by seeming to pass beyond, the implausibility of the film's founding analogies. The seat in the theater, in a film designed to profit from the current technological difference between TV and cinema, becomes like the seat in an electronic—auditory, visual, kinesthetic—roller coaster. This is the Rambo film's final gift to its audience: a victorious helicopter ride home to base camp becomes, like Luke Skywalker's defeat of the Death Star in *Star Wars,* an emblem of liberation. On this ride everything depends upon the mobility of the hero, his control of his own visibility, and his ability to destroy anything that stands in his way.

How do the Rambo films arrive at this final ride? Rambo's instantiation as "superhero" both furthers and depends upon a new development of the cinematic apparatus. Rambo's heroic invincibility allows a spectator to pass through the cascades of violence, the vertiginous motion, the catastrophic explosions of the films' *finales*. The new American hero motivates the development of film practices which, taken together, produce a new film style: wide-screen and Dolby sound; special effects, stunt-routines, and aerial photography; and, perhaps most crucially, editing techniques where rapid multiple cuts become a cinematic analogue to the represented action, and a variety of tricks are used to startle. The ensemble of these techniques allows these films to develop, market, and sell a cinematic experience of excitement, motion, and literal violence.

Rambo's function—as the subject position which carries its spectator through this spectacular action—depends upon sustaining a contradictory relation to the machine. We have noted the way the Rambo films exalt the hero as natural instrument over the machine as technological instrument of a nefarious system. In both films he escapes danger by moving, in an exhilarating regress, deeper and deeper into nature. Rich green forests and thick jungles do not impede but rather frame his swift passage. Rambo's magically sustaining relation to nature restores power and makes possible his triumphant return. This valuation of nature over the machine mobilizes a whole series of affiliated oppositions: feeling over calculation, body over things, innocent nakedness over uniform dress, virtue over corruption, and so on. Since all that Rambo opposes comes to be characterized as anti-nature, these films demonize technology. But although Rambo repeatedly subverts or surpasses the machine from the side of nature, the forest, instinct, and the mind, he is also aligned with the machine. Continually relying upon machines (motorcycles and trucks, helicopters and guns), the action sequences give Rambo's action a repetitively mechanical aspect, and Trautman calls Rambo "a pure fighting machine." In an earlier draft of the film script this phrase was different: Trautman tells Murdock, "After his last tour in Nam, Rambo came back more of a machine than a man." When Rambo's body is unfurled in shiny nakedness, a fetishized disrobing of muscle and pistons, it stands for a natural machine, a mechanical human. "Rambo," the character and film-image, is always already on the way to becoming the robot-like action figure that sold so well in the Christmas season. The ambiguity of Rambo's relationship to the machine gets emphasis in the montage sequence in which he prepares for his mission. A series of cross-cuts show Rambo sharpening his knife, the plane being prepared, Rambo loading bullets, a technician scanning a screen, Rambo sheathing his knife, a jet engine firing, and so on. This sequence fetishizes two bodies of power: the technical body of modern weaponry and Rambo's natural body, armed. The editing represents these two bodies as both opposed and complementary.

Rambo's double relationship to technology—as its opponent, and as its highest realization—gains expression in the ambiguous double function of Rambo's knife. As too primitive and lowly to be a high-tech weapon, this comically enlarged signifier of potency becomes Rambo's Excalibur—a magic fighting instrument which denotes his invulnerability. But this is no ordinary knife. Because it has a compass, it can direct him; a needle and thread in its butt allow him to suture his own wounds; its specially serrated edge can cut barbed wire; and because it is always at his side, it is a weapon of last resort which repeatedly saves him. In defeat, it is taken from him and wielded against him by his tormentors (Figure 1). He retrieves it while escaping from both police station and prison camp. Rambo's knife is the technological supplement, the inscription of civilized technique and tool-making within the body of the natural warrior. It is the one indispensable object that allows him to confront his enemies naked. Without this tool he could not be the natural hero that defeats the high-tech weaponry arrayed against him.

Rambo's ambiguous relationship to the machine is not a simple contradiction. It points to the constitutive relationship between "Rambo" and the cinematic apparatus which supports spectacular action that can never be simply "his." The basic two-part shift in the action we traced above through both films—from masochistic to sadistic positions—depends upon a corresponding shift in the function of the camera: from what might be called a hostile or sadistic camera, to a camera which displays the hero's power magically. In the early scenes of *First Blood,* the camera objectifies Rambo in two ways: we watch from Rambo's perspective as various hostile agents attack him; we also watch from the persecutor's side, as Rambo receives the abuse hurled at him from "our" position. An oscillation between both these uses of the camera are at work during Rambo's processing in the cell block. Thus for example, the camera pans down the fire hose in the police station to Rambo's naked writhing body; later we watch as a razor is brought in extreme close-up toward Rambo's face (the spectator's position). In both films the "sadistic" camera isolates, fixes, and arrests Rambo. Under its eye he is incapable of agency or motion. Once Rambo flashes into motion, once he escapes to forest or jungle, a new relationship between hero and camera, and, through the camera, to audience, prevails. The hunt sequences in natural settings draw the cinematic apparatus into the wake of Rambo's ingenuity and skill: Rambo seems to emerge from nature, overthrowing his opponents, by controlling his visibility. When the police track Rambo through the gloomy Northwestern forest, each is shot full length, isolated and anxious. Suddenly the underbrush at a policeman's feet moves up . . . becoming brush tied to Rambo's back, who now swiftly stabs his pursuer. Later, a low angle shot pans upward as another policeman passes the black silhouette of a tall tree stump . . . which becomes Rambo jumping down on his prey. In these moments, camera work and editing operate in complicity with Rambo to allow him to emerge from nature with a suddenness and surprise which assure victory. In *Rambo* we are shown a Russian pursuer frozen in a stealthy position against a large indistinct mud-bank, . . . when suddenly there is a rack focus from the Russian's face to the mud-bank, in which we see a single blinking eye. Rambo's arm emerges out of the mud-bank to take down his astonished pursuer (Figure 3).

When Rambo engages in a more open battle, the cinematic apparatus gives him the fabled power to return from death. When his mine-shaft is blown up, or his boat explodes, after a huge canister is dropped on him, or his copter takes a huge blast . . . ; in all these moments, Rambo's life is charmed—not only by his heroic position as it is defined in the script, but most especially by what the film shows and conceals. Momentarily enveloped by catastrophe, Rambo emerges repeatedly, etched in silhouette against a wall of fire which cannot consume him (Figure 4). It is only through the operation of this intricate cinematic machine that Rambo, the natural hero, the hero-as-nature can disavow two machines that enable him: within the film narrative, the state's military apparatus, and "beneath" the film, the cinematic one. In other words, Rambo's "naturalness" helps obscure the cinematic support which produces Rambo's mastery of the spectacular action that unfolds about him, and realizes so much of the cinematic pleasure for the film's spectator.

As the "superhero" becomes the positional standpoint for vertiginous, accelerating action, "he" becomes empty of content. These films may begin developing the protagonist's singular, embodied, memory-fraught subject position, and this motivates the "action" of the film's finale; but as subject and spectator enter into vertiginous cinematic motion, there is a rupture with any link to a specific narrative problem or figured human subjectivity. This is why Comolli's game metaphor is so useful for understanding the popularity of the action-adventure films like *First Blood* and *Rambo.* The Rambo films "work" for American teenagers and children who have little or no knowledge or interest in its Reaganist statement. *Rambo*'s spectacular action seems, too, to have worked in

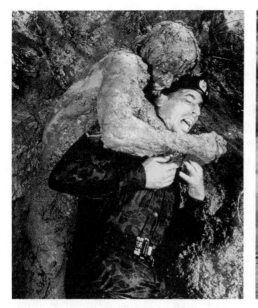 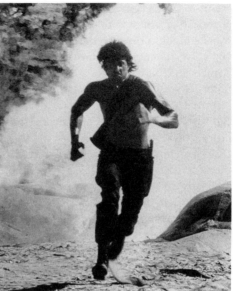

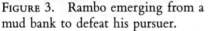

FIGURE 3.   Rambo emerging from a
mud bank to defeat his pursuer.

FIGURE 4.   Rambo eluding the
explosion that would engulf him.

tandem with its heroic masculinity in making it extraordinarily popular from Iceland
to Yugoslavia to Lebanon.[5] Within the initial context or problem the films develop—of
anxiety about American loss (of strength, of the pleasures of mastery, of pre-eminence)—
the solution is the audience's acceptance of our "natural" place in a machine—the cinematic action-adventure illusion of being in flight, in the cockpit of a helicopter, turning
all adversaries, as if by magic, into nothing. This is the final reward for the film's
masochistic heroism, its technological, *non*-psychic way of turning pain into pleasure,
so pain becomes nothing more than the prelude to the vivid illusion of motion.

In this essay I have carried out three critical passes in an effort to understand how the
different actions of the Rambo films succeed in working with—thinking and disavowing,
representing and revising, evading and playing with—a sense of American decline and
failure. This is done first with a revisionary political fantasy; then, through a morally
charged drama of masochistic suffering, and justified vengeance; and finally, through
the rhythm of a spectacular game ride that allows a "forgetting" of politics, affect, and
any confining subject position. Rambo's "success" in working out the cultural problem
of American decline depends in part upon the articulation together of these three partially
contradictory "actions"—one political/ideological, the second psychological, the third
techno-cinematic. But the tensions between different strata of the Rambo films is not
merely the result of a "divided subject," the overdetermination of these film texts, or
the constitutive tensions between the conceptual and metaphorical terms (like "masculinity," "America," "betrayal," or "rescue") used to suture together differences—
though these all play a part in unsettling the cohesion of the Rambo films they weave.
My tri-part reading also suggests that these popular films are opened in meaning by the
way they "touch" culture at different sites, where cultural work and struggle goes
forward on common ideas, in different and competing ways.

Here are some examples of the ways the Rambo films intersect with their cultural
moments. *Rambo* offers a model and film analogue for Reagan administration media-

events in Grenada and Libya—where swift televisual military action was used to confirm American greatness with comparatively little cost to this country. When the Iran/Contra scandal brought the activities of Oliver North to light, there was a strong sense of "déjà vu." Over twenty columnists and political commentators drew the analogy between Rambo and North, each a "lone wolf" working within, and against the system to restore a squandered American greatness. Viewers of the Rambo films would not be surprised when President Reagan declared that "Ollie North is a real American hero." But the Rambo films did not become a prelude to American intervention in Nicaragua; instead they were used as a way to diagnose and contest American imperial claims in Latin America. When *First Blood* was at the top of the movie charts in November 1982, the nation dedicated a Vietnam Veterans Memorial which offered a dramatically different, markedly anti-heroic way to remember the Vietnam vet. Finally, coming as they did, between *Atari* and *Nintendo*, the Rambo films offered an analogue to the video game.

How is one to assess the cultural tendency of the Rambo films' representation of a male hero who is also somehow a victim? In the contest for social sway and political attention, representations of suffering produce a purchase on the national memory, media attention, and even the budget. Thus Rambo's histrionic display of his own suffering, no less than the "feminized masculinity" that Christopher Newfield (1989) describes, may be a kind of masquerade of weakness designed to assert the new (and all too old) prerogatives of the white American male. But the very extremity of Rambo's macho self-assertion may have another cultural tendency. Like the subversive effects of the fifties hyper femininity of Marilyn Monroe that Andrew Ross (1989a) describes in *No Respect*, the Rambo films may be part of a cultural fictionalizing of male macho that discredits any literal unreflected assumption of masculinity (p. 161). If to pose as ultra male comes to be understood as "acting like a Rambo," then it cannot any longer be what it might have seemed at one time—"being a (real) man."

After the Rambo films, the superhero has lived on, but has been inflected in new ways. In order to sustain the superhero as a plausible vehicle for entertainment pleasure, various changes have been worked: making heroism an adolescent fantasy and the effect of a piece of machinery *(Top Gun)*; making the superhero an ordinary guy inside a high tech body *(Robocop)*; placing the superhero in a narrative and film style derived from the comics *(Batman* and *Dick Tracy)*. There have been other, more subtly inflected ways to appropriate Rambo-style heroism. When *Aliens* appeared the year after *Rambo*, critics bemoaned the fact that the subtlety of the female lead character of Ridley Scott's 1979 film *Alien*— Ripley, science officer of the Nostromo, played by Sigourney Weaver—had apparently been transformed in imitation of Rambo. I suspect this simplifies the matter. When Ripley takes over leadership of the mission's struggle to survive the onslaught of the "aliens," Hicks, the head military officer, offers to "introduce [her] to a close personal friend of mine," his "M-41A 10mm pulse-rifle with a 30mm pump-action grenade launcher." After learning how to use the "pulse-rifle" she "indicates a stout TUBE underneath the slender pulse-rifle barrel. RIPLEY: What's this? HICKS: Well, that's the grenade launcher . . . you probably don't want to mess with that. RIPLEY: Look, you started this. Now show me everything. I can handle myself." Nothing seemed more risible about the Rambo films, posters, and studio stills than the hero's gloomy muscle-flexed posture while holding (a hugely enlarged) phallus (Figure 5). A studio still of Sigourney Weaver, shot during the filming of *Aliens,* suggests the pleasure she takes in the scandal of a woman's assumption of the Rambo-like weapon (Figure 6). This image may also suggest that by imitating Rambo with a difference—a tilted head, reposed hands, and an ironic smile—it might be possible to modify by displacing what

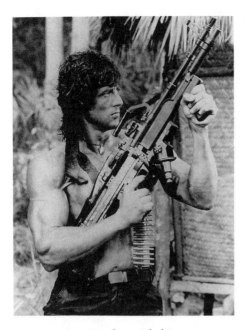

FIGURE 5. Rambo with his gun.

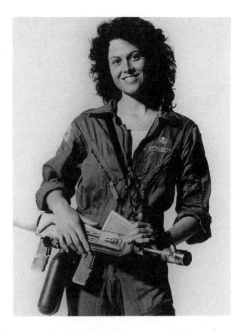

FIGURE 6. Ripley (Sigourney Weaver) of *Aliens* with her gun.

has been everywhere at issue with Rambo, Reaganism, and the fabulous cures for American strength—the somber metaphysics of the phallus.

NOTES

*Editors' Note Warner's essay was written before the 1991 war in the Persian Gulf. Readers may note, however, the ways in which widespread popular support for the war among the American public parallels the multiple sources of popularity Warner identifies for the Rambo films: military, ideological, emotional, historical, cinematic, and technological. This is not, of course, to suggest that the war should be seen as a spectacle or an entertainment but rather that the war, like the Rambo films, touched deep wellsprings of emotion and represented, as Warner puts it, a complex blending of fantasy and history.

1. For a description of the cultural strife expressed around the planning and construction of the Vietnam Veterans Memorial see *The Vietnam Veterans Memorial: To Heal a Nation,* Jan C. Scruggs and Joel L. Swerdlow (1985), pp. 82–83.

2. For a spectrum of critical condemnation see, Stanley Kauffmann, *New Republic,* July 1, 1985, p.16; Michael Musto, "Bloody Awful," *Saturday Review,* July/August 1985, pp. 81–82; and Pauline Kael, *New Yorker,* p. 117. Marxist and feminist readings may be found in J. Hoberman (1988), "The Fascist Guns in the West"; Michael Ryan and Douglas Kellner (1988), *Camera Politica: The Politics and Ideology of Contemporary Hollywood Film;* p. 215; and Lee Edwards (1988), "The Labors of Psyche."

3. Throughout this essay I have relied upon Stuart Hall's important essays on "Thatcherism" to conceptualize "Reaganism." While this essay develops a brief working definition of Reaganism and the role of popular culture in its effective circulation, I have not attempted a systematic differentiation of these Anglo-American ideological siblings. See Hall (1979; 1985b; 1987a). For a bibliography of Stuart Hall's publications see Hall (1986c.)

4. For a discussion of the popular resistance to "technobureaucratic privilege and arrogance" see Andrew Ross's (1989a), *No Respect,* p. 231.

5. The archieves of the Academy of Motion Pictures chronicled *Rambo*'s popularity: one-seventh of Iceland's population saw the film in its first week; in Lebanon, *Rambo* was the most popular film in the country's history; in Yugoslavia, *Rambo* was the most popular film video rental.

6. The quotation from the screenplay of *Aliens* comes from the "Script City" version of the screenplay.

38

The Postmodern Crisis
of the Black Intellectuals

CORNEL WEST

I would like to dedicate my brief presentation to the memory of one of the towering artists and great cultural workers of our time. I'm talking about none other than Sarah Vaughan, who was buried just yesterday in Newark, New Jersey. In fact I debated whether I would come yesterday or whether I should go to the Mt. Zion Baptist Church that helped produce one of the most subtle and nuanced voices of intelligence, insight, and pleasure-giving ever produced by this country and working within, of course, the great art form produced by working-class people in this century, namely jazz.

I want to reflect briefly on the postmodern crisis of the black intellectual. And I must say that I actually did write a paper, but I decided it became relatively obsolete after this afternoon. So I thought that I would just attempt to speak directly.

The Postmodern Crisis: What do I mean by the "postmodern crisis" and what does it have to do with intellectuals of African descent at this particular historical and cultural moment? Well, actually I think it has to do with the fact that we are struggling with the vocation of political intellectuals, or what it means to be a political intellectual at the moment. Is it any longer a credible notion? And this is a very important question for me because though I could be self-deceived I understand myself to be first and foremost an intellectual freedom fighter. So the academy is only one terrain among many others.

So it might be the case that the very idea of being a political intellectual is antiquated and outdated; and that's the challenge. That's why the discourse about cultural studies for me is not first and foremost a question of area or discipline, but rather I understand it as the initial slogan used by a group of political intellectuals in Britain at a particular time attempting to bring to bear their own analytical tools, their moral and political vision and their sense of sacrifice, of giving their energy and time in order to fundamentally change Britain. And so Raymond Williams, Stuart Hall, and the host of others become not only sources of inspiration or simply models to imitate or emulate: no, what they become are exemplars of how they could keep the notion of being a political intellectual on the left alive in a world of shrinking options and alternatives for leftists. And that's in part what we're dealing with today, it seems to me.

And so when I talk about the postmodern crisis it has to do with the issue of the vocation of being a political intellectual. It's reflected on the one hand, of course, on the right, by Allan Bloom; and on the not-so-left by Russell Jacoby. I think that's one of the reasons Foucault and Said are so attractive to so many of us. It's not just the acuity of their analyses. I think Homi Bhabha is right; I think Foucault is indispensable, but his Eurocentrism and his Francocentrism stares at you on every page. That's called parochialism; no matter how sophisticated and subtle and nuanced it is, it's still parochialism, especially in the light of the call for Atlanticism, internationalism, and hybridity that Paul Gilroy and a whole host of others have talked about. But what Foucault and Said do speak to directly is the possibility of doing intellectual work in a world full of so much social misery and loss of social hope that we can justify ourselves as being significant in contributing to struggle. Because none of us can actually justify our pursuit of the life of the mind on sheer hedonistic grounds—because we like it, because it gives pleasure. It goes hand in hand with the hedonism promoted by the culture of consumption, of the postmodern culture of late capital society anyway. There's nothing wrong with acknowledging that there's a hedonistic dimension to pursuing the life of the mind. But that's not all there is; there's got to be some moral and political grounds to this vocation. Thus the issue of vocation becomes very important indeed.

Why the term "postmodern"? The term postmodern becomes useful—though in many ways it does obscure and obfuscate—precisely because it helps us situate a new kind of culture being created in the midst of the restructuring of the capitalist international order. In that sense, Jameson is right. You may disagree with his laundry lists, he may misread particular cultural phenomena, but he's right in terms of understanding postmodernism not just as a set of styles and forms but as a cultural dominant of a restructured international capitalist order with its automation, robotization, computerization, its de-skilling of the working class, its re-skilling of the working class, and creating space for people like us: an expanding professional managerial strata. We must situate the academy within this context of the postmodern crisis, given this restructuring of capitalism as we understand it. This is one of the reasons why I forever defend the insights, just as I criticize the blindnesses, of what was once called the classical sociological tradition, of Marx, Weber, Simmel, Lukács, Du Bois, and others. Blinding, why? Because there's very little talk about race, gender, very little talk about sexual orientation and anti-homophobic theoretical formulations, not just anti-homophobic moral gestures. But they're crucial because, when Simmel talks about objectification in *The Philosophy of Money* in 1900, he's talking about the degree to which there is an eclipse not simply of subjectivity but an eclipse of agency in which people no longer feel they can make a difference, so they view themselves as objects in the world. This is a very important cultural phenomenon; it's the first attempt, not even on the left as I understand it but on the left liberal side of the ideological spectrum, to provide a phenomenological description of the lived experience in capitalist society. This is, in part, what cultural studies ought to be about. Where are our phenomenologies of lived experience in advanced capitalist society? Jean-Christophe Agnew's book *Worlds Apart,* which some of you may have read, is an attempt to do that, as a mode of historical reconstruction. Simmel's legacy is one crucial element of cultural studies.

The second key element is provided by Weber, of course, and he must not be downplayed. In some sense Foucault is a rich footnote to Weber. The extension of disciplinary order is in fact a certain twist of the extension of the iron cage, but at the level of micro-institutional practices. Why is Weber important? Because bureaucratization remains central in our lives. The ideologies of professionalism, of managerial perspectives, are part and parcel of the expansion of those institutions whose impersonal rules and regulations constitute deferential identities and subjectivities for us; that's what bureaucracy is about. All you need to do is to look at your university to see that. I just read a report in the *Chronicle of Higher Education,* that cites a 46 percent increase in the ranks of non-teaching professionals in our universities; that's a phenomenon Weber helps us recognize. But the larger point is that the analytical tools that are now necessary are part and parcel of this tradition, though it is a tradition that has its blindnesses. Just as we need Weber, we need Marx; among other things his concept of commodification is indispensible. I'm just finishing a text now on the continuing and considerable relevance of Marxist theory after Eastern Europe. Marxism remains important in part because it theorized commodification, and the process of commodification, especially in the form of big capital, especially in the form of oligopolies and monopolies, remains fundamental if we are to have any clue about how to talk about culture.

Herbert Schiller just wrote a book called *Culture Incorporated: The Corporate Takeover of Public Expression*. It's a kind of economistic Marxism, but a dose of vulgar Marxism is often necessary to keep us sober and "on the ground" in these days of cultural textualism. I don't advise stopping there, but he's got useful figures on corporate control within the most crucial forms of public expression, from the 32,248 "public" malls, which are not public in any sense—despite being among the few spots of public space left in late capitalist society—but in fact are private property where the right to hand out political leaflets is denied, to his study of the American Library Association—the transformation of knowledge into a salable commodity as opposed to a social good; and why in New York City at this very moment libraries are only open four days a week. And they talk about black kids and brown kids not wanting to read. What are the objective conditions as well as the subjective conditions that folk used to talk about twenty, thirty years ago? Commodification. That is not, of course, a kind of catechistic retelling of Marx; it's an attempt to update where Capital is and what's it doing and to what degree it is a source of so much social misery in the world.

These three processes for me become useful in trying to talk about the postmodern crisis because it has something to do with the fact that large numbers of people in the world, especially in American society, don't believe that they make a difference. Especially in the black community; that's what the meaninglessness and the hopelessness and the state of siege that is raging is in part about: the collapsing of structures of meaning, and the collapsing of structures of feeling such that hopelessness becomes the conclusion and walking nihilism becomes the enactment of it. How do you preserve agency? How do they think agency can be preserved given the resources available to them? And by resources I don't mean only financial and economic ones, I also mean cultural and existential ones as well—self-worth, self-regard, self-esteem, self-affirmation. Fundamental issues, if there's going to be any politics at all. And hence we see the decline in popular mobilization and the decline of political participation and the decomposition more and more of the institutions of old civil society, especially of old black civil society in the context of our shattered families and neighborhoods, and voluntary associations, with the market-driven mass media as the only means in which a person becomes socialized. I think, in fact, one way of reading rap music is as an attempt by certain highly talented cultural artists to socialize a generation in the light of the shattered institutions of black civil society; the families no longer do it, the schools can't do it. "How do I relate to other people? Tell me." And so they listen to Salt-N-Pepa who provide some moral guidelines as to how to relate to other people. They used to get it in Sunday School thirty years ago.

What does this have to do with black intellectuals? Much to do. Why? Because so much of American intellectual life, of course, now has been monopolized by the academy. I think this is a very, very sad affair but there's no way out. So that academicist forms of expression regarding intellectual work have become hegemonic. There is no doubt that one does indeed have to learn the language and learn the jargon in order to gain some sort of legitimacy, so that one can be heard by the main- and male-stream. There's no way around it unless we are able to sustain subcultures on the margins, but it's very difficult to do so because there are very few economic resources to sustain them. Unfortunately, almost every major intellectual today has to have something to do with the academy out of default, unless of course you're Gore Vidal who can go off to live in Italy off his money—God bless him! It's the only way to survive, though more and more move into journalism and mass media, becoming intellectual cultural workers outside the academy, but nonetheless forever feeding off the academy. And hence the kind of intra-class struggles that go on between journalists and academicians, struggles that I think are likely to escalate.

But there are other important points to note in talking about the academy. We know it's not only a place where there's tremendous competition for status and prestige, but that humanistic intellectuals are actually losing this competition. We know we're being marginalized *vis-à-vis* the technical intelligentsia. More and more we feel that what we have to offer has very little to do with the crucial role that science and technology play in advanced capitalist society. Even our legitimating role is being cut back. So many feel as if they can let humanist intellectuals do what they want to do as long as they speak only to each other; it seems they have very little linkage anyway to anything that actually makes a difference, other than the sustaining of their own careers. This is not my view; it's just a cynical view from the vantage point of a highly placed bureaucrat. Yet we also know that the academy has remained a major means by which working-class people have experienced upward social mobility. In that sense it's very different from the history of British university education, very different indeed. And in fact, I think for some of us the academy is a subculture of escape—and I'm not using escapism in a pejorative sense—but as an escape from the rampant anti-intellectualism in this country, the fear of critical sensibilities, democratic sensibilities, that is deeply ensconced within the parochialism and provincialism of the very people whom we often invoke. And we recognize that the academy is a crucial terrain for struggle. This distinction between the academy and the world, of course, must be called into question. There are many crucial fields of forces and operations of power, and they criss-cross every institution in this society. There's no escape.

If you think you can go from the academy to the labor movement, to the church, or to some activist movement and not have similar fields of forces and operations of power at work, you simply have an academicist understanding of the academy. There's no escape. But that doesn't mean that the academy's a privileged site either. Not at all. The kind of work we've heard in the last day and a half ought to have taught us it is no privileged site whatsoever. But it also behooves us to think about the degree to which the waning of public spheres in this society tends to displace politics into the few spheres where there is in fact some public discussion—spheres like the academy. Hence so much of academic politics is a displacement of the relative absence of serious politics within the larger "public" spheres where serious resources are being produced, distributed, and consumed. And so much of academic politics—in terms of the level of what's at stake— seems to be exorbitant in a country in which our actual politics are comical. No real public sphere: we know about the theatricalization of our politics and the packaged character of our candidates and so forth.

Those political energies become rechanneled in the academic context in our attempt to talk about pedagogy. I think this is a lesson that we can learn from John Dewey. Dewey actually became preoccupied with pedagogy after he moved to Chicago in 1894. He moved the year of the Pullman Strike, and he concluded (it's one of the reasons he was silent on the Pullman Strike) that labor could never win in America in a direct confrontation; thus he had to engage in his own kind of politics, cultural politics. A cultural politics that would highlight the role of education in providing new perspectives, critical alternative orientations to lead toward what he thought for awhile would be a serious confrontation of capital and labor. John Dewey was a Democratic

Socialist for sixty-five years. He concluded that the political left based on class struggle could never win, so cultural politics became his major terrain for contestation out of pessimism about the American left. This deep pessimism about the American left ever winning, even imagining the American left winning, deeply affected John Dewey's politics. We can take some clues from this, not from the pessimism, but from the struggle with it. Hence the crucial role of pedagogy, but we also need to keep open the notion that pedagogy can never be all there is, that there must be some grass-roots organization and mobilization if there's ever going to be serious left politics in America.

Let me say a word about the role of cultural studies in the postmodern crisis as it relates to black intellectuals, especially like myself. Because it seems to me that what we need first is to read very closely the kind of narratives and tales that have been told about cultural studies by Stuart Hall and others within the British context. The traveling of cultural studies to the United States must be met with a critical reception—and by critical what I mean is an appropriation of the best: acknowledging where the blindnesses were, while discussing to what degree British cultural studies can be related to the U.S. context.

We did not do that with deconstruction and you have seen the results. It's true: the promiscuous formalism in which every text can be turned against itself in order to show the degree to which every ground can be undermined, including the very ground that is put forward to undermine it, and so on and so forth. There's still power there, though I won't go into the positive moments in deconstruction, since I'm highlighting the degree to which there was an uncritical reception. This is also true for Michel Foucault. Foucault cannot be understood without understanding his early years in the communist party, his polemics against the French left, the degree to which Marx's culture was so deeply influential on the Left Bank, and Foucault's own attempts to create new left space in relation to those various tendencies and elements. That's what a critical reception of Foucault, or anybody from anywhere, is about. We can learn much, to be sure, but not without knowing our own intellectual history or without considering how the U.S. context will receive these texts. This is the question. Who, for example, reads Thorstein Veblen's *Theory of the Leisure Class* in talking about cultural studies in the USA? Go back and take a look at Paul Sweezy's essay on Thorstein Veblen in the 1952 *Socialism and American Life* volume that Princeton University put out. Why did Paul Sweezy, the leading Marxist intellectual at the time, think Veblen was a crucial figure in terms of our cultural realities and in the light of his Marxist theory? I'm not saying he's right, but look at the dialogue—there is a tradition of very important left cultural reflection that can provide a site upon which cross-intellectual fertilization with the best of Williams and Hall and Rowbotham and others can take place in the U.S. context. We could say the same about Du Bois; we could say the same about Charlotte Perkins Gilman; we could say the same about F. O. Matthiessen. One can work one's way through U.S. intellectual history by tracking the contributions of progressive thinkers.

Now part of the problem is going to be the degree to which American studies— given its own history as told by Kermit Vanderbilt in his recent text *American Literature and the Academy,* or Richard Ruland's earlier book on the recovery of American litera- ture—either welcomes or resists this interchange. The history of American studies is in some ways parallel with cultural studies in Britain. But the major objects of attack in the U.S. were not left Leavisite perspectives, or even Eliot's elitism, but rather New Criticism and its different ideological trajectory. Yet it also is certain American Marxisms: the Marxism of Granville Hicks, of V. F. Calverton, and other American Marxists at- tempting to create their own left American cultural studies in the thirties and the forties. Of course I'm being quite fragmentary, but I'm trying to give you a sense of how we can tease out a dialogue between the British and U.S. traditions within the U.S. context. It's not a matter of Americanism in the life of the mind. America indeed has something to contribute without our succumbing to atavistic patriotism in intellectual matters. We're talking about trying to keep our eye on analytical tools that have, in fact, been put forward and in some ways sharpened by intellectuals on the American terrain who should have been in contact with what was going on in the late fifties and sixties and seventies in Britain. But we must not commit the same mistake by looking to see what's new, while forgetting about this American tradition. This is precisely how theory actually leads one astray in ways that Stuart was talking about.

Stuart mentioned today the degree to which there was, in fact, a Marxist moment in cultural studies in Britain, and then critical breakthroughs with feminism and race. I think Douglas Crimp was correct to say we need to highlight the homophobic moment as well. But in the United States it is very, very different. As Richard Slotkin, Michael Rogin, and others have stressed, the U.S. begins with the dispossession of Native American lands. And the continuing racial encounter is there from the very beginning, with Mexican peoples and African peoples. America starts in part with the expansion of European empire and these racial encounters. The country commits civil suicide over the issue in the 1860s. By describing this as a starting point, I don't necessarily mean to privilege it exclusively; I simply mean it has a lot of weight and gravity in any story that you tell. How can the reception of cultural studies in the United States not put race—not at the center (we're not making claims for center and margins)—but give it a tremendous weight and gravity if we're going to understand the internal dynamics of U.S. culture? There's no escape. It's a different history than the formation of the British Empire with its attempt to relegate race to the periphery and resist its intrusions within the metropole. Yes, race is there in Britain, as we all know, but with very different histories, different developments. And similarly so in terms of gender. And, of course, when we look at the academic interventions what do we see? In '69 there was a movement for Afro-American studies. It was not a Marxist moment because there were very few Marxists around in '67–'68 in black America. Ten years earlier they'd all been thrown in jail and deported, so there's discontinuity in terms of the Marxist trajectory in this country. They are radical, oppositional; some are subversive. How do we understand the moment of the intervention of Afro-American studies in the academy? Let's read that history next to the intervention of cultural studies in Britain.

Women's studies offers a comparable picture. Where are all the Marxist women's studies people in 1968–69? There aren't too many, certainly not a tradition that's developed. But they went back and recovered a radical tradition, a long rich tradition of feminist thought and praxis in the United States. Let's read the intervention of that particular construction and creation over against the construction and creation of cultural studies in Britain and talk about how interfertilization at this moment can create deeper insight and enable more effective praxis.

I want to say a word about how this relates to popular culture, because we know what happens—especially after 1945 in this country—is by means of the classic Fordist formula of mass consumption creating mass production. We can recall the creation not only of the first mass culture but the creation of a mass middle class, or least a mass working class with a bourgeois identity that understood itself as middle class. So popular culture, mass culture, becomes fundamental for the creation of American culture after 1945. And postmodernism and its attempts to undermine the division between high and low culture has much to do with the fact that it's a profoundly American phenomenon, one dealing with the pervasiveness of popular culture (given U.S. economic hegemony in Latin America and in Europe with the Marshall Plan). And so that popular

culture, Hollywood, music, film, radio, becomes fundamental. If you're going to understand what is going on in American culture, given this distinctive development that
is different than any other capitalist nation at that time, given its world hegemonic status,
you must come to terms with popular culture. Of course there's also the matter of
understanding the degree to which you've been shaped by it. When I talk about Sarah
Vaughan—and I could talk about Baby Face or Marvin Gaye or a host of others—I'm
talking about people who help keep me alive. I'm not just talking about some ornamental
or decorative cultural object of investigation! These are people who make a difference
in your life. James Brown makes a difference in my life, that's a fact. That doesn't mean
he's the only one, but the point is that when we talk about popular culture we're talking
about its materiality at the level of producing and sustaining human bodies. Or at least
at times convincing that body not to end its vitality and vibrancy, not to kill oneself.
That's in part what culture does; it convinces you not to kill yourself, at least for a
while. Which means that, of course, it's breaking down in parts of American society,
as suicide rates suggest. But I'm getting way off the track. The important point is that
popular culture mediated by mass commodification becomes crucial in the U.S. context.
It's very different in other places around the world.

And this leads me, of course, to religion. We could trot out facts: 97% of Americans
believe in God, 75% believe Jesus Christ is the Son of God, and we say, "Oh, God have
mercy, I've struggled up here and we've got all of these fundamentalists out here." Why
is that so? What is it about religion as a cultural phenomenon in this distinctive capitalist
nation that makes it so crucial? This is a crucial question, especially if you're an activist,
because you'll be bumping up against all these folks who have all these strange beliefs,
from your point of view. This is very important. This is something that the communists
who were looking to Europe in the 1930s and 40s could never understand when they
went into the black community. They would say, "Paul Robeson, intelligent man that
you are, your brother is a bishop in the A.M.E. Church, you're the son of a preacher,
and you still have such a respect for the black church, but you're too intelligent for
that." "Kiss my so and so, I'm the product of a rich tradition," Paul would say. I'm
trying to use a concrete example to give you a sense of the degree to which we have
got to attempt to understand what goes on in a complex phenomenon in this country:
Namely, all of the various religious sects and groups and cults and denominations and
temples and synagogues and all the other forms of association through which folk come
together. How do we understand them, especially as potential for broad progressive and
oppositional praxis? These are fundamental questions. It's very different in Britain, where
the working class rejected religion a long time ago.

What does this have to do with black intellectuals? A great deal. Why? Because
I still follow Gramsci's injunction to know more and preserve the links in broader civil
society. Stuart said it with insight today: by knowing more it means you've got to be
rooted within subcultures and subgroupings and traditions, intellectual and political, and
yet also be conversant with the best of what's going on in the academy—which means
you sleep less, because you have to know more. But you know more not in order simply
to know more, though it is a lot of fun, but you know more in order to make your
links better. So when you're rooted in the broader institutions in civil society, whatever
they are and in whatever role—the trade unions, the mass media as a cultural worker,
or in musical production or video production, or a preacher, or what have you—you
have the roots required for what you have to say to bring some insight, and yet your
insight can be informed by the very folk whom you're talking to, because they have a
wisdom to bring. And it provides the context for struggle, so that bonds of trust can be
generated that will sustain you when the police come after you, as courageous Michael

McGee may discover in a few weeks in Milwaukee, God bless him. I like his spirit of resistance no matter what you think about his tactics. There's too much death going on, he says, somebody else got to die too. There's something about that moral ground. I have trouble with this, but I also resonate with his sense of desperation because I've also seen too much death, too much despair. That's the kind of spirit of resistance you need, but that's the challenge of a kind of linkage that must be forged in order to rechannel that kind of energy into a more effective and efficacious progressive project.

That's what the aim is; that's what the project is all about. And that's going to be the challenge for black intellectuals in particular, as well as for progressive intellectuals in general. I hope that we can overcome the virtual *de facto* segregation in the life of the mind in this country, for we have yet actually to create contexts in which black intellectuals, brown intellectuals, red intellectuals, white intellectuals, feminist intellectuals, genuinely struggle with each other. There are very few contexts for that. Prince's band is more interracial than most of the intellectual dialogue that goes on in America. That's a requisite, that's a precondition for the emergence of the kind of thing that Jackson and others have envisioned, namely a Rainbow politics, which is the only means by which fundamental social change is going to come about. It may not be Jesse who leads the coalition, but we know it's got to be some multiracial coalition, an alliance, and that might not be strong enough in and of itself; it might all get crushed. Capital's powerful but we must take a chance, take a risk. But there has to be some intellectual coming together, not closing of ranks but coming together, before there can in fact be possibilities for this kind of flowering and flourishing. Not because intellectuals will lead, but rather because there must indeed be a role for theory if we are to understand the circumstances against which we're struggling and if there are going to be visionaries who have the courage to lead it. And there will be leaders. They may not come from us, probably not, but come from a host of various sources. But they must have tools available, and we can contribute to that. Hence, there is a role, there is a function, there is a possible vocation for cultural studies in the academy, no matter how overwhelming the odds.

DISCUSSION: Paul Gilroy, bell hooks, Cornel West

QUESTION: I want to ask about commodification. In the past when we used the word, we were saying that there's something bad about it. It seems now that there's some uncertainty about that. I wonder whether you think that in the current period we have to give in to this idea that markets are necessary—or can we rehabilitate the vision that markets could be done away with?

CORNEL WEST: That's a very complicated question because commodification, as initially used by Marx in the "Fetishism of Commodities" chapter had to do with the transformations of relations of human beings into relations of things. For Marx it had to do with a certain relation of domination, of workers selling their labor power, their energy and time and so forth, to employers. The market was the primary force for objectifying people. Simmel argued that was not just the market; there are a whole host of other forces that were doing this kind of objectification. By the time you get to Lukács you have something different, in many ways more profound, partly because he read Simmel and Weber. In that crucial chapter in *History and Class Consciousness,* which I still think is necessary reading for any serious left cultural thinker, he has a very new understanding of commodification as a cultural phenomenon, linked to market forces, that has to do with how subjects are constituted. You are asking about how one goes about arranging economies in light of present day alternatives. Command economies had commodification and objectification under Stalin. Were there markets? Of course there were markets. The problem was who regulated them—the bureaucratic class. We could go on and tell a long story. So when we talk about markets these days, especially given all the kinds of fetishizing and idolizing that are going on in the markets these days, we've got to raise the question of what are the conditions under which market operations take place. Do I believe that markets are inescapable for the economy? Yes I do. The best explanation of this, I think, is Alex Nove's book *The Economics of Feasible Socialism.* Why? Because democratic ideals can in fact be promoted only if we can sustain levels of productivity. But that's a different kind of discussion, that's a discussion about how you arrange economic affairs. And about sustained levels of productivity so that you don't have a lack of commodities in a society which falsely claims that they don't have commodification, which is one of the results of the low productivity of the command economies, and so on. I think it's important that one unpack and tease these various levels out in talking about it.

PAUL GILROY: I hear in your question an echo of a deeper question about Marxism itself and about what I would want to call the productivism of Marxism and about whether or not Marxism can survive the productivism being extracted. And for me here the issue is really a question of growth, and how we can move towards a political vision which, in asserting this link between sustainability and justice, actually says that the overdeveloped countries must give up that growth.

QUESTION: You seem reluctant to talk about deconstructive thinking. Why are you not willing to say how can we appropriate this in the same way we're trying to appropriate British cultural studies, Marx, Weber, etc.?

WEST: In another essay (published in *Out There: Marginalization and Contemporary Cultures*) I argue that there's something quite positive about deconstruction, having to do with keeping track of the rhetorical operations of power and binary oppositions. And this can provide new openings, and it has been quite powerful in relation to race, gender, sexual orientation, and so forth. The problem is that it too easily becomes linked to an austere epistemic skepticism. And that austere epistemic skepticism makes it very difficult to make the links between rhetorical powers, military powers, political powers, social powers, and other kinds of powers. I see this also in Foucault. Foucault doesn't tell us anything about the nation-state, he doesn't tell us anything about nation-states bumping up against each other. But you can't tell a history of the modern world without telling a history of nation-states bumping up against each other, like August 1914. These are serious silences about macro-structural operations, about which Foucault has very little to say, and Derrida has hardly anything to say. So when it comes to issues of the materiality of linguistic practices, Derrida and Foucault are very important. This is what Stuart Hall described in his paper. Marx doesn't talk about the materiality of language at the level of perspicacity and acuity that Derrida and Foucault do. Marx throws it out in *The German Ideology* but it's flat, it's wooden, he doesn't follow up on it. So that there is a crucial set of insights that come from deconstruction. But what I'm really fighting, as you can imagine, is the American reception. That's what makes my blood boil. And the reason it actually boils is this: I said that one crucial element of the restructuring of this society in which we live is the expansion of the Professional Managerial Class or strata, and we're a part of it. That means that we're getting a lot of resources that other people are not getting. And some of them are your cousins and my cousins, they're working-class people. They're poor people. Collapsing educational systems, and we get these lectureships and fellowships that are proliferating all the time. I'm in Italy this month, next month I'm in New Brunswick and then California. Where's all the money that *we* get coming from? How come that money is not going to some of the failing educational systems, in Chicago and New York and Houston? I'm not trying to be ugly here; what I'm saying is that we're part of the restructuring, we're part of the new class. And we have to be self-critical; this is what critical self-inventory is all about in a Gramscian sense. So the question is how do we fight as progressives and co-opted? And at the same time how do we understand the degree to which the larger structural institutional forces that help enable some of our activities might actually be siphoning off a whole host of resources from other people who need it badly? And that's a much larger discussion about educational policy on various levels of elementary school, secondary school, community colleges, state colleges, and in elite institutions. But we have to be aware of those kinds of discussions and dialogues, it seems to me. It's not that what I'm saying is necessarily true, but we need to talk about this in a serious kind of way.

BELL HOOKS: I want to ask how, in the U.S., cultural studies can avoid simply reproducing a more sophisticated group of people who are interpreting the experience of the "other" under the guise of identifying themselves as comrades and allies.
WEST: As the humanities as a whole is being marginalized, *vis-à-vis* the technical intelligentsia, cultural studies becomes one of the rubrics used to justify what I think is a highly salutary development, namely interdisciplinary studies in colleges and universities. But it differs from one place to another. Here in Champaign-Urbana you have persons who were exposed to cultural studies when I think it was at its height in terms of vitality and vibrancy. I'm not saying that things are dead now, but I think that the Birmingham school in many ways provided such an exciting context in which issues of vocation, of being political intellectuals, of struggles over the Marxist traditions, struggles over the feminist challenge, struggles over race were going on. The legacy is still alive but it was at its height, I think, and people like Larry Grossberg at this particular place were part of that. So that they're able to bring that experience to bear upon their own institutional context and remain in contact with Stuart Hall and others in Britain as they have continued to work, have made this place very different than a lot of other places who just are starting their cultural studies projects right now. At different institutions, they're going to have to deal with levels of professionalization and specialization that are very different than what has been established here at the Unit for Criticism and Interpretive Theory. Look at CUNY, there's a tremendous advantage where you've got Stanley Aronowitz and a host of others who are also in contact with and producing some of the best critical theory being done at the time. That's going to be very different than some other places. So one would have to make assessments in light of each and every place.
GILROY: I want to caution Cornel against that enthusiasm for some inevitably reified memory of what was going on at Birmingham. I mean I feel a bit like the way Miles Davis feels about the definition of musical authenticity in which he got trapped, when he said he was there and actually it wasn't like that.
WEST: I like to think that it was, though.
GILROY: Well, maybe as an imaginary, it's OK.
WEST: Sure. But you'd say that about my religion too, wouldn't you?
GILROY: Yes, I would. The point is that the answer to bell's question depends not on anything which is intrinsic to cultural studies, but on factors which are external to it. There are no guarantees in any heuristic idea of cultural studies. If people can struggle to rescue something from it which enables them to face three ways at once and to hold

on to some notion of themselves as interventionist scholars, then great. But if cultural studies becomes a fetter on that, then I imagine cultural studies will have to be left in the distance. And I think that's what Stuart called the moment of danger, but it's likely to be longer than a moment.

QUESTION: I'm struck by the fact that there are more people of African descent from London here than there are from the United States. I'm wondering if the importation of the Birmingham model and its representatives, however useful, might inadvertently silence both an indigenous African-American tradition and living, practicing African-American activist scholars in the United States today?

HOOKS: I think that Paul Gilroy touched on that in his paper by saying that part of our oppositionality as peoples of African descent, globally, has to involve countering that impulse by being just as engaged in the work of Paul Gilroy, Stuart Hall, etc., as other groups of people. I think that's just beginning to happen in African-American intellectual thought right now. Where do we look to for our references, as African-American intellectuals? Who are we reading? Who are we teaching our students to read? I don't think, in a white supremacist context, we can counter the fact that people might want to play off black British intellectuals against black intellectuals in the U.S. I think our best opposition to that is the kind of collective solidarity that comes through global awareness of our connections.

GILROY: Yes, I agree with that. I think there's a lot more work that has to be done in making those links something vital. When you look at the nineteenth–century material, it's impossible not to be struck by the fact that they were closer to each other than we are. Considering the space-time distanciation of the world, that's an extraordinary thing to appreciate.

WEST: Let me just say a quick word about the silencing of Afro-American intellectuals in this country. I think that there is an intellectual and social chasm between large numbers of persons in Afro-American Studies programs and persons in interdisciplinary studies, or cultural studies. Now why does this chasm exist, that's a much longer story that has to do with what particular schools of thinking have shaped significant numbers of Afro-American scholars who are in Afro-American studies programs *vis-à-vis* the kinds of developments that have been going on in literary criticism and cultural studies and so forth. There is this *de facto* segregation, when we actually look at what some of the dynamics have been in a variety of different institutions, between black scholars and left intellectuals.

GILROY: Isn't that a consequence of the fact that reification and institutionalization aren't only problems of cultural studies? I mean I almost feel like I want to shift it slightly back the other way and say that these are issues which are intrinsic to the nature of the academy. Cultural studies doesn't have a monopoly on that difficulty.

WEST: Yes, but you sound a bit too Marxist on this one now. It cuts deeper than that. It's not just a matter of reification and commodification, specialization and bureaucratization, and so forth. It has to do with the very deep racist legacy in which black persons, black intellectuals are guilty before being proven innocent, in terms of perceiving them capable of intellectual partnership, capable of being part of a serious conversation. I think that traverses the processes that Paul is talking about. And so it makes it very difficult indeed, and it's part of the larger struggle against the racist legacy in this country as it's manifested in this case.

HOOKS: We can think about this in terms of the construction of film criticism and the lack of black people doing film criticism. Look at how Spike Lee has been constructed in popular culture as if there were no other popular black filmmakers ever. Most of us continue, never seeing, never hearing of Oscar Micheaux, who made 38 films between 1918 and 1938. When we think about "the insurrection of subjugated knowledges," we have to think about where those subjugated knowledges are going to surface if the very construction of popular culture is such that it says to people that black filmmaking begins with Spike Lee. And so when I have black students who want to be filmmakers, I ask them if they've thought about how much we need people to write about film. How much we need to go back and talk about Oscar Micheaux's vision, as a person who saw himself as making films for black people that would deal with the complexity of their lives. We have more complex representations in Micheaux's films than in most films we can see right now by black filmmakers, particularly in terms of his representations of black females, because he wasn't trying to reach a cross-over audience; there was no such thing as a cross-over audience.

ITTY ABRAHAM: I would like you to comment on a kind of black nationalist rhetoric in which it seems that the removal or reduction of oppression for African-Americans can only come at the cost of the oppression of other minorities.

WEST: The historical records show that the progress of people of African descent in this country tends to go hand in hand with the unleashing of new opportunities for large numbers of people far outside the black community, from women to peoples of color, to the handicapped, to the elderly, and so forth. I think you are talking about a certain kind of rhetoric of desperation that comes from certain black nationalist corners, given what they perceive to be a zero sum game. And therefore, when they see that progress is not being made, they assume that some other group is making it. And that is an expression of frustration, but it is far removed from the historical record. I think that distinction must be made and all of what I have said is not only an attempt to expand that historical record but to insure that the struggles of the people of African descent go hand in hand with struggles of people of color and working people and people of good will across the board. That doesn't mean that we're going to sidestep this struggle over the crumbs that often occurs among peoples of color; it doesn't mean that we're going to eliminate the resentment and envy and jealousy that some people might have for other peoples of color who seem to be moving rather quickly up the social ladder. That's a cultural phenomenon, it's there. At the normative level, of course, I find myself very much in agreement with what I perceive the historical record to be: black progressive movement going hand in hand with other progress. But this does not occur easily.

QUESTION: This, too, is a question about the interrelationship of forms of oppression. You made reference to rap as a cultural resource providing moral guidance. What is the nature of that guidance and how do we theorize it?

HOOKS: I think we have to talk about the production of rap, as well as about what rap is listened to by whom. Because in fact there are black men who are doing feminist raps, anti-rape raps. But we have to talk about the kind of African-American culture that is being produced for a cross-over audience. Take, for example, a production like *House Party,* which we know to be homophobic and misogynist. Now is this because "black culture" is homophobic and misogynist in some more intense form, or is it in fact that when racist white spectators go to the cinema one of the things that makes that cinema more enjoyable is if there are certain kinds of things that can be hooked into, including certain kinds of stereotypes about black people, i.e., that black people are more homophobic than other groups in this society? Black people are homophobic and xenophobic, but not necessarily more so than other groups of people in this society. We have to keep that in mind, too, when we talk about rap. Because it's a minority of rap people who are doing the sorts of things that are getting a lot of attention, including misogyny, homophobia, and anti-Semitism. And so we have to ask, why are people focusing so much on those forms of rap? Why do we not read about black men who are doing anti-rape rap? Because that's not as interesting!

WEST: I think it is very important to say that rap is not monolithic, homogeneous, that there are a whole host of different kinds of raps. I invoked Salt-N-Pepa just as an instance of a certain way of responding to black patriarchal practices and the black male predatory lust towards black women's bodies. And they have certain ways of black women's bodies responding to that. Moreover, there are dominant forms among these various forms of rap, and they're highly problematic in terms of moral guidance. But it's not as if they could actually go to other sources and find significantly less patriarchal guidelines. If they go to church, they're going to find patriarchal guidelines; if they go to some other institutions of black civil society, they're going to find it too. So it's not as if U.S. society is overflowing with sources of anti-patriarchal values and practices. But there are some sources there and some of these rap musicians are trying to provide them, but the ones who do it are not dominant.

WAN-LING WEE: I wonder why discussions of race and class in Britain never discuss the Chinese in Britain?

GILROY: I don't know the answer to that question. I think it's probably got to do with who owns and manages and controls the spaces in which such discussions appear and the particular definition of race politics that they want to trade in. I really don't know how to account for it beyond that. I think when we talk about the question of race in Britain, you have to appreciate that the numbers of people involved are actually tiny by comparison to the numbers of people involved in this society's minority ethnic groups. I don't see in the development of those particular political spaces any attempt to address the diversity and the differences which exist within those minority ethnic communities in our country. Also, these discussions are often involved with a very specific political project which has to do with a particularly economistic definition of Marxism and the attempt to advance that within a very familiar pattern of political organization. The reason that those other experiences aren't addressed or recorded as having any significance is because they're perceived to be peripheral to where the real action is supposedly identified. And it's hard to imagine where the forces that could shift that parochialism will emerge from. Presumably from within those communities themselves at some later stage. I don't mean to sound complacent about it, but I do want to say to you that those kinds of publishing are probably much more peripheral than you imagine to the lived reality of the experiences, not just of Chinese people, but of the very ethnic groups in whose name the kind of authority to speak is actually derived.

CONSTANCE PENLEY: I appreciated your exhortation that pedagogy is not enough. Of course it's not enough. But the way you couched that exhortation built upon a polemical separation between politics and what goes on in the university. You claim that an academic discourse in politics is just a displacement from wider politics, what goes on "out there." I've heard this stated several times throughout the conference; Henry Giroux always makes reference to the ivory tower, the academy; Janet Wolff said that it was crucial that cultural studies not be off in its own isolated enclave; Jan Zita Grover said that she didn't know what went on in terms of activism within the university and implied that she didn't think much did. I think that a lot goes on there. Pedagogy goes on there. For most of us, that's our political practice. And we're doing more than just canon-bashing. When I look around at what's going on at universities around the country, I see people trying to get issues of sex, class, race, and anti-homophobia made into a public discourse. I see a new move to eliminate the military, and fraternities, and the CIA from campus. There's a lot of work that's being waged against the increasing corporatization of the universities. People are working all the time to increase the number of women and minorities among the students and the faculty. There are still divestment struggles going on all across America. I think we might want to look at our need to imagine that we are working in a place that is without politics.

WEST: I think you picked up a tension in my presentation, I won't call it a contradiction (I like Stuart Hall's term, though I get it from Paul Tillich). As you recall, I said that this distinction between the academy and the world had to be called into question because all we had were fields of forces and operations of power. If you take that line, you and I are on the same wavelength, because the same powers that work in the academy work elsewhere, and the struggles that you talk about are oppositional in the same way in other contexts. I would say over and over again that the academy's a crucial site. On the other hand, in my own attempt to move from context to context, we have to recognize that there's still a level of privilege in the academy that makes it very different from other sites in civil society. And that level of privilege cannot be overlooked even as we agree with what you say. The university is a crucial site but a different site. It has its own kinds of privileges that do promote, sometimes, an insularity, and a parochialism, in the name of being cosmopolitan. And it's this other side that might lead you to infer that somehow I might be part of this cast of voices that seems to be trashing the academy, which I do not want to do at all. But I'm not sure I want to lose the tension, either. I think I'm going to go to the grave with that tension.

GILROY: Isn't the point about cultural studies that it helps you preserve the tension and work with the tension, which is not to say that the tension does not need tuning?

HOOKS: If this conference had been called "Feminist Cultural Criticism: Now and in the Future," a lot of people would be talking about the kind of political agency that is produced in and extends beyond our classrooms. There would not be this sense of separation between the classroom and some outside, because what we so overwhelmingly see is the continuity between them as people come to critical consciousness in the feminist classroom. The dynamic and momentum of cultural studies that most excites me is that it has helped me to teach many marginalized groups the joy of theory and theory-making, and how it is linked to a political practice. Part of what keeps me in the academy is seeing it as a field of contestation; it is in the context of a liberatory feminist pedagogy that I see enormous kinds of change, the kinds of education for critical consciousness that moves out beyond the academy precisely because the issues of race and gender touch people in how they live in their everyday life. And I think that's part of the joy of the kind of work many of us are doing.

ARLENE TORRES: I am concerned about the use of the term "subculture." What does it mean, and what does it say about African-Americans, Chicanos, Puerto Ricans, Asian-Americans, and Native Americans, considering that most of us have been largely absent from this conference?

WEST: When I talk about subculture I mean primarily just me and my partners trying to keep alive a particular left project in my neighborhood. I mean the black intellectuals, let's say, in parts of New York City, who come together every other week to try to stay sane. I mean that little small subculture that helps keep you going, discussing the issues, doing what you do next in terms of your project. What that group that talks through you thinks about police brutality, what you think about what's going on in Milwaukee: That keeps that kind of dialogue going. It also provides deep emotional networks of support and so on. That's what I meant by using that term to talk about a crisis of black intellectuals. I'm not talking about a deeper methodological issue about the culture of Chicanos, or the culture of Chinese or Asians and so forth. I agree with you that at that deeper level one has to contest the use of such a term.

DONNA HARAWAY: I grew up in a town in Colorado where I thought the Atlantic Ocean began somewhere in Kansas and that anything that happened East of Kansas City counted as the East Coast. And I know Cornel grew up in California, but I think maybe you've been in the East too long. Paul's Atlanticist reformulation of African heritage, African culture, and African-Americans reformulated a lot of issues for me. But it's a California statement I want to make. It has to do with seeing the world in relationship to Latin America, Central America, Mexico, living in conquest territory so that it almost seems like Quebec is part of California rather than part of the world you're talking about. It's the sense of the Pacific. I think of Bernice Johnson Reagon's speech on coalition politics which took place at a West Coast women's music festival and is an absolutely canonical text in U.S. feminism and in the constructions of the category, "women of color," but also of a feminist cultural politics and a vision of a new world cultural politics. None of this is caught by the tendency to build the world as black/white and America/Britain, with a little bit of Australia and Canada thrown in. This particular global mapping leaves out these really crucial questions.

GILROY: I didn't want to push the thing about the Atlantic too far for many of those reasons. I suppose for me what was important about trying to do that was that I feel that most of the decisive political battles are actually going to be registered at that intermediate level, between the local and the global. And I wanted to actually try and illustrate what it might mean to put some concepts in there in a very provisional way. And I hope it didn't sound as if the Atlantic was supposed to exhaust that; that was just an instance. I think we've got to try if we want to face the future instead of looking back over our shoulders. We've got to try and be a bit more imaginative about what those intermediate identities, concepts, localities, loyalties, are going to be. And I think we need a new topography and I think that maybe, I'm not even sure about it, the Atlantic thing might be part of that.

QUESTION: I was particularly taken with Cornel West's engaging comments concerning the intellectual life of the mind. I have some concern about the *de facto* segregation of the life of the mind. I don't know if you have any kind of recipe for making the mind more culturally plural, but I certainly would feel a lot better leaving this conference if you would share such with us. When I start to think about the classroom which attempts to teach cultural studies with attention to race, as you so desire, I try to imagine who indeed will teach in that classroom, and how we can be sure that that person will not abrogate the responsibility to all of the constituents who come into that classroom. And furthermore I wonder to whom the constituency will address itself once it leaves the classroom, once it has graduated and goes out. Because I have great fear when I look around this room, and I really do wonder about the number of African-American men and women who will take their places to teach cultural studies. I think about the violence of one-year appointments and two-year appointments, and I hear this rumor that there is a lack of blacks with Ph.D.'s and I know of blacks with Ph.D.'s who don't have appointments at all. These kinds of things are disturbing when you are talking about the crisis of the black intellectual. I'm particularly wondering about why you chose not to address issues of safety, feeling safe as being a reason for not speaking, a reason for not teaching as the very basis for silence. I wondered that you did not address the very real problem of the fact that there is violence in the classroom. And when one does go through the very harrowing experience of attaining the credentials needed to enter the academy, one black person walks into the classroom, the white students break into tears and rush out. These are very real issues for those of us who sit on the other side of the desk. And I wonder, could you tell us something to help us to have hope?

WEST: I think what you've said is quite real. I was just touching the surface of this issue when I talked about gaining cultural resources. How do you build up a context in which self-confidence can be acquired? In which you are able to conceive of yourself, not only as being part of the conversation, but as being taken seriously? The idea of taking black people seriously in the life of the mind is a very new notion for white people, so they have to get used to it. Now, it's true that among white progressives it's a bit more distributed than among the larger white society, but they suffer from the disease too. So the question is how you create conditions that will facilitate taking black people seriously in the life of the mind. Which means giving them the benefit of being wrong; we can't be right all the time, or we're not being taken seriously. Which means they also have the benefit of being right, and you can be wrong, and so forth. Now, we could just call that human interaction, but the idea of human interaction across races is a new notion in Western Civilization at some levels, especially at the level of practice, as Ghandi noted quite aptly. So the question is, on this individual level, how do we insure the possibility of this kind of human interaction? I think one way of doing that is by creating very substantive links with colleagues who you are sure are in touch with your humanity and you are in touch with theirs, in affairs of the life of the mind. That's very important. I'm speaking personally now. When I think back on my own formation, what was it that sustained the intellectual part; I had a lot of the other parts on different axes, but the intellectual part had to do with being part of a network that was involved in that kind of critical exchange in which one's voice is a serious voice. That's very important. And one finds it among a small group usually—sometimes it might be just one or two—and one hopes that it's across racial lines, not always, but one hopes. At that very individual level, that's one way of sustaining hope. The problem is that many of our students don't experience that, and hence the life of the mind becomes something that's completely alien; it's a white thing, it's nothing to do with what I'm about, and they move in other directions. And of course, they still will pursue the life of the mind in their own way, but it will be linked to a very very different kind of project, owing in part to not experiencing that kind of human interaction with teacher, with peer, with friend, with colleague, whatever it is. I think that's one way of doing it. More importantly it has to do with the larger picture: race relations in America. As they deteriorate it will be reflected and refracted in the universities and colleges and so forth. And even in California, Donna, Farrakhan will draw thirty-five thousand people, which is to say it's still part of a black/white discourse. You can talk about the multicolored, the multiracial, and so forth, but a certain black nationalist rhetoric that is still operating in a binary oppositional discourse is still quite powerful in Los Angeles and Oakland. So that those deep resonances are there, and the question becomes, how does one understand that kind of black nationalism as a way of affirming one's sense of self-worth? But then, how does one rechannel it in such a way that the multiracial and multicultural character of California in its actual population becomes reflected in one's left politics in the black community? And that's a struggle that we have all the time. I recognize that the issue of identity, positive identity, self-affirmation, and holding at bay self-doubt and self-contempt and self-hatred, is an indispensable element for people of African descent. This is the great lesson of Garvey. You can disagree with Garvey's politics but his cultural insights are profound. And that's one of the means by which students can feel empowered to take the life of the mind seriously in all of its various forms as they move towards the kind of progressive multiracial vision that Donna, myself, and others have talked about.

39

Excess and Inhibition:
Interdisciplinarity in the Study of Art

JANET WOLFF

In the introduction to a recent posthumously published book of Raymond Williams's essays, the editor commends what he calls "the steady strength" of Williams's work over many decades. In a rather strange compliment, he points out that the most persistent conjunction in the titles of Williams's books has been "and" (Pinkney, 1989, p. 8). *Culture and Society, Marxism and Literature, Politics and Letters:* the present volume could have maintained the tradition with the title *Politics and Modernism,* instead of its actual title of *The Politics of Modernism.* The irony of this endorsement is that Williams was one of the few people writing in critical cultural studies who did not succumb to the dangers of that misleadingly innocent conjunction. One of my intentions in this paper, despite my own title, is to address the question "What is wrong with the word 'and'?"

By now it is no great revelation to point to the transformation in the study of culture and the arts which has taken place over the past fifteen or twenty years. The social history of art and the so-called "new art history" have challenged an older art historical practice (and its institutions), which unreflexively recorded "great artists," "great works," and important art movements. Although this challenge has hardly revolutionized the establishment (as popular histories, like the recent public TV program *Art of the Western World,* make clear), its impact has been significant. At the same time, social science disciplines, which for decades have ignored the arts, have begun to develop a body of work which analyzes culture. Here I will only talk about the sociology of art (though there are also sub-disciplines in the economics of art and the political economy of art). And lastly, the interdisciplinary project of cultural studies (often inspired by the early work of Raymond Williams, amongst others) has engaged in the investigation of the interrelations of the arts, popular culture, lived cultures, and social structures. For reasons which I want to explore here, each of these projects has failed to produce an adequate theory or method for the study of art. This is partly because of the intense specialization within disciplines and of the exaggerated separation between them. It is also the result of what I believe to be distortions in the practice of those disciplines, and I shall say something about their origin and effects.

Whatever we may think of Raymond Williams's work on culture, in the case of art history and sociology the conjunction "and" is often both a reason for and a symptom of this failure to develop an adequate theory. An art history which believes, in some vague way, that cultural works are social products can indicate this in courses and publications with the title "Art and Society." Often, the "society" which appears is a kind of painted backdrop, referred to only as a tableau of social groups and their practices, which are said to inform the works, or as a series of events which in some unexamined way are believed to transform them. An extreme version of this approach is Frances

Rust's (1969) book on dance and society. (It is true that her title is *Dance in Society,* but I think the preposition functions here in an identical way to the conjunction "and.") Frances Rust traces the history of social dance in England, from the Middle Ages to the 1960s. She makes sure to begin each chapter with a few social facts, a one-paragraph summary of the economics and the politics of the age. The dance is then "explained" by reference to the social. She is confident in assuming the most straightforward relationships between dance and society, and generous with her attributions of causality.

> There can be little doubt that the gay and lively dances of the Elizabethan period were a reflection of the adventurous and joyous spirit of the age. (p. 51)

> It is . . . possible to see in the harmony, grace and stylization of the minuet a reflection of certain facets of early eighteenth-century life. (p. 64)

On the success of the polka in the nineteenth century:

> People were ready to transfer their enthusiasm from the romantic waltz to a dance more in keeping with the quickening tempo of social change. (pp. 74–75)

And, most dramatically of all,

> In France, there is no doubt that the French Revolution killed the minuet. (p. 70)

Her sociology is primitive and, more importantly for a dance historian, she operates with a mechanistic notion of the relationship between cultural form and social process. On the one hand we have the "social facts"; on the other, we have the changing styles of dance, which can be explained as a cultural response to such things as industrialization, revolution, changes in sex roles, and so on. Her use of the word "reflection" is the key to her theoretical assumptions. This has traditionally operated as a shortcut to any real sociology of the arts, either in the service of a crude determinism (earlier forms of Marxist criticism were sometimes guilty of this, or (as in the case of Rust's study) as a way of avoiding any analysis of the actual relationship between culture and society. But "reflection" is no longer a notion which theories of representation will allow. Cultural forms, like dance, do not just directly represent the social in some unmediated way. Rather, they *re*-present it in the codes and processes of signification—the language of dance. Moreover, far from reflecting the already-given social world, dance and other cultural forms participate in the production *of* that world. This is something I will come back to a little later.

This kind of facile sociologizing is not uncommon in art history, particularly in popular texts. The sociology of the arts, on more secure ground with its analysis of the social, employs the conjunction "and" in the service of a reverse kind of reductionism, invading the arena of culture and the arts with even less respect for its subject matter. Paul Spencer's (1985) introduction to the collection of anthropological essays, *Society and the Dance,* is interested only in ascertaining the "seven functions" of dance in societies: dance as a safety valve, dance as an organ of social control, the educational role of dance, dance as ritual drama, and so on. A new collection, republishing key essays in the sociology of art and entitled *Art and Society,* confirms the inability of sociologists to take art seriously and to address questions of representation. Of the section of the book which deals specifically with "art and society," the editors say: "These papers clarify the way in which art can be used as an instrument to some further end such as to sway people to support a cause." (Foster and Blau, 1989, p. 19). In general, their intention is clear, as is their indifference to the nature of their very subject matter: "We are interested in the uses to which art is put, whether it be to enhance ideas, products or events. We use art to measure social phenomena . . . We are interested in describing the artist, the patron, the critic and the public. All of this is important in reminding us of the influence of social organization on art. Even though the connection is seldom clear in our studies, by implication we learn something about the distinctiveness of art when compared to other cultural artifacts" (p. 17).

But the "distinctiveness of art" is surely crucial to any sociology of art. In any case, here we have a reversal of the mechanistic approach of art and dance historians. On this view, the focus is either on the ways in which the social process (ideas, events, institutions) "influences" art, or on the ways in which art is "used" in the social process. In neither case is the specificity of art allowed, nor the mutually constitutive nature of the relationship between the cultural and the social acknowledged or explored.

So we are confronted with arts disciplines which allude to "the social" without any theory of society or any knowledge (other than superficial and commonsensical) about actual societies, and with a sociology which revels in a philistinism that it attempts to justify as methodological objectivity. As Raymond Williams (1989c) has put it, in a lecture on the uses of cultural theory: "What at last came through, theoretically, in the significant new keywords of 'culture' and 'society,' was the now familiar model: of the arts on the one hand, the social structure on the other, with the assumption of significant relations between them" (p. 165). The question is: What are those significant relations, and how might we conceptualize them?

T. J. Clark's (1982) essays of 1973 and 1974 on the "social history of art" are often cited as a key moment in the development of the "new art history."

> I am not interested in the notion of works of art "reflecting" ideologies, social relations, or history. Equally, I do not want to talk about history as "background" to the work of art—as something which is essentially absent from the work of art and its production, but which occasionally puts in an appearance. . . . Lastly, I do not want the social history of art to depend on intuitive analogies between form and ideological content—on saying, for example, that the lack of compositional focus in Courbet's *Burial at Ornans* is an expression of the painter's egalitarianism, or that Manet's fragmented composition in the extraordinary *View of the Paris World's Fair (1867)* is a visual equivalent of human alienation in industrial society. (p. 250)

His program is to explain "the connecting links between artistic form, the available systems of visual representation, the current theories of art, other ideologies, social classes, and more general historical structures and processes." (p. 252). Included in this would be the more narrowly empirical aspects of a social history of art: "patronage, sales, criticism, public opinion" (p. 251). Now this is an excellent and comprehensive project for a social history of art. Unfortunately, it has rarely been pursued. The social history of art and the "new art history," radical developments though they are in the context of traditional history and criticism, are almost invariably critical readings of *texts.* The best of them do not succumb to the "art and society" model. Instead they explore in sophisticated and fascinating ways the encoding of the social and the political in the visual. But what has been abandoned here is the commitment to social history—to the analysis of those social processes and institutions in which art is produced and consumed, and of the social relations which both inform and are constituted by those texts.

A collection of essays, presenting and celebrating the "new art history," gives the game away in its first paragraphs: "When an article analyzes the images of women in paintings rather than the qualities of the brushwork, or when a gallery lecturer ignores the sheen of the Virgin Mary's robe for the Church's use of religious art in the Counter-Reformation, the new art history is casting its shadow" (Rees and Borzello, 1986, p. 2). In other words, the new art history deals with rereadings of texts, with the decoding of images in relation to social, political, and ideological meanings. This is, of course, a very worthwhile project. It exposes the myth of aesthetic autonomy, and insists on the recognition of paintings as social products, bearing the trace of their origins in relations of power and inequality. My criticism is that it remains at the level of textuality. The social is only there *in* the text. Stephen Bann's contribution to the same collection confirms this interpretation, in stressing the new developments which pay attention to representation itself, linking word and image, exploring the "craft of seeing" (in Rees and Borzello, 1986, pp. 25–29). He refers to the journal *Representations* as a model of this work. But the journal, as its title makes clear, prioritizes text over social process (though some of the articles which have appeared in its pages do, it is true, attempt a more sociological analysis of literary and other texts).

I think it is worth noting that the "critical criticism" of literary studies has undergone the same deflection from a more ambitious project. Literary criticism, too, has had its share of "literature and society" books. But since the early 1970s we have had the far more exciting prospect of an approach which exposed the institutional and ideological biases of the literary canon, exploded the myth of transcendently "great" literature, and began to look at texts in terms of their social production, systems of signification, and possibilities of interpretation. Terry Eagleton's model for the study of literature, outlined in his 1976 book *Criticism and Ideology,* combined the analysis of the text itself with the investigation of contemporary institutions and ideologies of literature, mediation through the author, and the wider social and political contexts which enable and inform the work. But here too it turned out we had a project with no empirical follow-up. I would argue that most work in critical criticism has persisted in giving priority to text over social relations. Eagleton's own work since 1976 has reverted to theories of textuality, apart from his short study of Richardson in *The Rape of Clarissa,* which did attempt to relate the novel and its meanings to the literary relations of production in which Richardson was involved. Meanwhile, as in the areas of dance and art history, *sociologists* of literature have produced studies of the social production of books, like the weighty volume by Lewis Coser (1982) and colleagues, entitled *Books: The Culture and Commerce of Publishing,* which examines the publishing industry, the role of agents and editors, and so on, without ever entertaining the necessity of discussing what these books are actually *about.*

In art history and sociology, then, we have two parallel traditions, and two bodies of work, both ostensibly addressing the same question (the sociological study of culture), but each with its own particular exclusion—an exclusion, I would argue, which is ultimately damaging. The "excess" and "inhibition" of my title refer to the excess of textuality in literary and art studies, and the inhibition with regard to the text on the part of most sociologists. Both sides have their reasons (other, that is, than disciplinary blindness) for this strangely distorted perspective, and it is worth considering these for a moment before I try to assess the prospects for a different approach.

Sociologists have been quite explicit about the need to avoid any engagement with questions of content. The development of a sociology of art in the United States over the past couple of decades has clearly been a case of sociology applying its existing tools and methods to a new area of study. (I should emphasize, however, that the sociology of the arts in other countries, including Britain, is far less narrowly intra-disciplinary, reflecting the different nature of sociology itself in the two countries.) About three years ago, the American Sociological Association founded a new section, on the Sociology of Culture. Already, that section, with over 500 members, is the fourth largest within the organization. Courses and publications in the area of the sociology of the arts have also been proliferating. But much of the work is disappointingly limited, and its hostility to theory (endemic to much U.S. sociology) has produced an unexciting (and often plainly mistaken) series of empirical studies. Mainstream sociology identifies the social institutions within its various areas of specialization—the factory in industrial sociology, the school in the sociology of education, the bureaucracy in the sociology of organizations—and investigates the social relations and processes within them. In the newly colonized area of culture, it therefore results in an approach which lights on particular institutions of cultural production (publishing houses, museums, opera companies, recording studios, and so on), and proceeds to analyze their internal operations: hierarchies of power, decision-making processes, conflicts of personnel, professional and bureaucratic ideologies, and other social relations. In the "production of culture" approach, it hardly matters what the product is. It is a given: the real interest is in the processes in which it is produced.

This neutrality and agnosticism with regard to the subject of study is in fact thought to be a virtue by a sociology which is still infected by the ideology of positivism. There are two reasons for this: first, a commitment to value-neutrality (because discussing the text could implicate the social scientist in questions of aesthetics, and hence overstep the divide between science and value); and secondly, a misguided belief in the inviolable boundary between the disciplines (the belief that social science studies process, while humanities disciplines study texts). But the problem isn't just that this produces an unfortunately limited account on the part of sociologists. More seriously, a refusal to engage with the text, rather than guaranteeing any kind of objectivity, actually confirms and reinforces traditional aesthetic hierarchies. An example of this ingenuous collusion with conservative forms of thought is a recent book by Diana Crane (*The Transformation of the Avant-Garde* [1987]), which sets out to explore the social circumstances of a variety of art movements in New York since the Second World War. The book is full of fascinating and valuable information on the role of galleries, critics, and museums, but it never turns a sociological eye on the way in which the very categories of "Abstract Expressionism," "Minimalism," and "Pop Art" are constituted. One consequence of this is that the absence of women artists from this contemporary canon cannot be addressed, since the social processes of exclusion which produced an all-male category are out of bounds in an approach which takes over those categories from an uncritical art history. In addition, since the method precludes discussion of actual paintings, the relationship between representation, ideology, and social process is obscured. Crane's explanation of her approach to texts is not reassuring, as she justifies the limited method of her minimal interest in the paintings.

> Systematic analysis of visual materials by social scientists has rarely been done and few guidelines exist for a sociological examination of aesthetic and expressive content in art objects. I based my analysis on two approaches: a content analysis of themes contained in representative works by these artists and analysis of statements concerning the content of these works that appeared in critical writings and in interviews with and statements by the artists themselves. (p. 148)

But her study is constrained, not by the current limitations of an empiricist content analysis, but by a misconception of the nature of representation and, hence, a failure to understand how images may be interpreted.

The problem is that mainstream sociology, confidently indifferent if not hostile to developments in theory, is unable to acknowledge the constitutive role of culture and representation *in* social relations. Work in the "production of culture" mode, in its relentless sociologizing, takes a naively realist view of cultural institutions and products, and in the process both produces a seriously distorted study of art and participates in an epistemologically discredited account of society. The social world cannot be conceptualized as having some independent existence, but rather has to be understood as a provisionally stable and constantly reconstituted complex of discourses, processes, and institutions.

This weakness of sociology is, however, the strength of critical studies in the humanities. But here the argument is reversed. Poststructuralist theory and discourse theory, in demonstrating the discursive nature of the social, operate as license to *deny* the social. In the case of criticism in the pre-theoretical mode, this exclusion is the product of either accident or arrogance. Traditional criticism persists in refusing the relevance to art of the extra-aesthetic; and primitive sociology of art ("The French Revolution killed the minuet" school of thought) collapses the social into a series of haphazardly chosen moments and events. But critical criticism has serious and important reasons for insisting on the primacy of discourse, and hence on the focus on the text at the expense of the extra-textual. In particular, we might consider a weaker and a stronger version of this argument.

The feminist art historian, Griselda Pollock, published an article in 1977 entitled "What's wrong with images of women?" This piece has been reprinted several times, most recently in a book of essays on femininity in the visual arts (Betterton, 1987). Ironically, in each case a mistake in the printing of the title has undermined the argument of the article. The phrase "images of women" was intended to be inside quotation marks, and their omission in publication produced a very different question—one, indeed, which Pollock was concerned in that article to prove illegitimate. The title as printed asks "What's wrong with the *actual* images of women in circulation?" But Pollock is asking the question "What's wrong with the very *notion* of 'images of women?' "

It was (and in some circles still is) common for feminist art historians and literary critics to reread texts in order to expose and dismantle stereotypes and dominant forms of representation of women in a patriarchal culture; reading lists in women's studies courses are full of such texts, which do address the question of what is wrong with images of women—that is, with the ways in which women are represented. But this type of critique is premised on the assumption that on the one hand we have "women," and on the other hand we have (distorted, partial, inaccurate) "images" of them. Poststructuralist theories have demolished this opposition, and Griselda Pollock is objecting to the very notion that there can *be* in this uncomplicated way, "images of women." Representation is central to the constitution of the category of "woman." It is for this reason that feminist work in the past ten years or so has been preoccupied with the cultural formation of gendered identities. What is wrong with "images of women" is that the notion obscures the constitutive role *of* images ("women" do not somehow pre-exist representation), and that culture is thus still perceived in terms of earlier reflection theories of art. The work of Lynda Nead (1987, 1989) on nineteenth-century painting in England has made clear the construction of notions of femininity and domesticity in the Victorian period. She argues, for example, that the image of the "fallen woman," rather than simply reflecting and reinforcing dominant ideologies of gender, actually participated in a discourse of sexuality (including a discourse of the forbidden and repressed) which actively produced those ideologies and social relations.

I have called this the weaker version of the argument—an argument on behalf of what is referred to as "the materiality of the text," indicating that texts and representation have their own levels of operation and effectivity, and are not mere reflections or responses. It is "weaker" in the sense that in insisting on the complex interplay of representation and social relations it still allows both the existence of each of these levels, and the epistemological possibility of access to each. Social reality, mediated and constituted though it is seen to be by culture and representation, is still social reality. The "stronger" version of discourse theory denies either the independent existence of, or access to, the "real." This is where I would want to talk about "excess" in the study of culture. This approach, I believe, blocks the necessary collaboration between sociology and critical studies.

The basis of this account is in the more radical versions of hermeneutics, poststructuralist theory, and theories of language, which conclude from the undeniable fact that we only experience and know the world *through* language that there *is* no world outside language and discourse (or, at the very least, that if there is then it is unknowable). This is at issue in the debate between Gadamer and Habermas, (Gadamer, 1980; Habermas, 1980), with regard to the possibility of a critical theory of society. Given that interaction and communication form the fundamental basis of knowledge, essential to social experience, can we still talk about "systematically distorted communication," whose distortion results from *non*-linguistic social inequalities? Gadamer's insistence on the "universality of the hermeneutic" renders any discussion of such inequalities extremely problematic. Against Habermas, he argues: "From the hermeneutical standpoint, rightly understood, it is absolutely absurd to regard the concrete factors of work and politics as outside the scope of hermeneutics" (Gadamer, 1976, p. 31). And, more categorically, "Reality does not happen 'behind the back' of language: it happens rather behind the backs of those who live in the subjective opinion that they have understood "the world" (or can no longer understand it); that is, reality happens precisely *within* language" (p. 35). Habermas, on the other hand, wants to explore the *limits* of hermeneutic understanding, as well as the constitution of language itself in social relations of work and domination. The issue is not whether or not we can "get outside" language, but whether there are social facts which are *non*-linguistic.

The linguistic turn of hermeneutics is paralleled by developments in semiotics and poststructuralist theory, which have also stressed the fundamentally discursive nature of the social world. (I will have to risk generalization here, despite the philosophical and theoretical differences within this body of work: Barthesian theories of the sign, Foucauldian discourse theory, Lacanian psychoanalysis, and the varieties of "postmodern theory.") Economic, social, and political realities are reconceptualized as discursive entities, constituted (and always in process of *re*-constitution) by language and systems of representation. Critics of this position insist that there *are* real structures and entities (classes, subjects, social inequalities) which are not reducible to discourse. Discourse theory responds to this kind of criticism by pointing out that the categories of class, sex, and race are themselves cultural constructions, not pre-existing entities. But this commitment to the primacy of the discursive cannot account for the continuities and solidities in social life and political conflict, nor for the ways in which social divisions and inequalities *do* influence and determine the course of events.

The implication of discourse theory for the sociological study of art is not simply that the focus is restricted to the literary or visual text while "the social" is exiled from the account. It is also that the social itself *becomes* text. The dual limitation of much recent work in critical studies is that either it reads the social *through* the text, or, in addressing the social outside the text, it does so in terms of textuality. The position I want to defend here is an unreconstructed (though not, I hope, uninformed) dialectical realism, in which the cultural constitution of social subjects, social groups, and the social world is fully acknowledged, and at the same time the persistence, effects, and power of particular subjects, processes, and institutions is recognized. As Allen Hunter (1988) has said, in a recent critique of the work of Ernesto Laclau and Chantal Mouffe, "Their focus on the constitutive or constructive moment is important, undercutting essentialism, determinism, and holism; but *in itself* (as opposed to the predilections of those who theorize it) this position argues neither against the existence of constituted totalities nor against the greater power, durability, and reproducibility of some forms of social activity over others." That is to say, class, work, power, and other social phenomena operate at the limits of discourse, and "play a role in constructing knowledge and meaning" (p. 892).

Radical discourse theories, in rejecting naive realism and essentialism, and in recognizing the ultimate fluidity and cultural constitution of social groups and institutions, take the unjustified epistemological step of abandoning all forms of realism and of denying any categories of solidity or determinism. In addition to the philosophical critique of this new idealism, a number of authors have defended a limited realism on pragmatic or political grounds. This has been a crucial issue for feminist theory and for the critique of racism. Susan Bordo (1989) and Denise Riley (1988) have both argued that, important though it is to recognize the shifting historical construction of the category "women," and at the same time to engage in a critique of the false universality of patriarchal thought, nevertheless a feminist politics requires the provisional identification of women's experience, and a focus in the category "women." As Riley puts it, "I'd argue that it is compatible to suggest that 'women' don't exist—while maintaining a politics of before as if they existed"—since the world behaves as if they unambiguously did" (p. 112). Marnia Lazreg (1988) has made a similar point about the problems of excessive deconstruction for Algerian women, when she argues that "what is needed is a phenomenology of women's lived experience to explode the constraining power of categories" (p. 95). Arbitrary though the cultural categories of gender and race are, the fact is that they constitute the lived experience, the basis of prejudice and inequality, and the possibility for political organization. The permanently evanescent categories of poststructuralist theory preclude the possibility of mobilization and political action (a point also made by Allen Hunter against Laclau and Mouffe).

I have been arguing that the necessary project for the study of art is an approach which integrates textual analysis with the sociological investigation of institutions of cultural production and of those social and political processes and relations in which this takes place. I have therefore argued against, on the one hand, a sociology which is unprepared to discuss representation, and on the other hand, a critical practice which either ignores or denies the social. Inasmuch as these limitations are the product of narrow professionalism and discipline protectionism, current developments in the interdisciplinary area of cultural studies have begun to provide an escape from this impasse. In Britain, as Raymond Williams (1989b, 1989c) has shown, cultural studies originated in adult education, outside the academy, and developed in response to the specific interests and lives of those taking the classes. The more systematic expansion of cultural studies, beginning with the foundation of the Birmingham Centre for Contemporary Cultural Studies in 1964, combined an institutional location within literary studies with a central interest in *lived* cultures, and with a commitment to historical and social analysis (Hall, 1980c). (The last Director of the Centre was a social historian; the present Chair of the newly constituted Department of Cultural Studies is a sociologist.) Since then, the collaboration across disciplines by literary scholars, art historians, sociologists, and social historians, as well as those working in film and media studies, has produced a growing number of cultural studies departments and degree programs in Britain, as well as series of texts and studies which employ theory (including poststructuralist theories) in the context of social-historical analysis. Journals like *Theory, Culture & Society,* and *New*

Formations, and the Cultural Politics series of half a dozen publishers participate in this enterprise. It is my impression that the same kind of cross-disciplinary collaboration has been less easy in the U.S., for reasons which I think have a great deal to do with disciplinary formations and institutional constraints. Nevertheless, it is exciting to see so many centers and programs in cultural studies and similar humanities projects taking shape. Of course the label of "cultural studies" does not guarantee real interdisciplinarity: I have seen the term used to describe programs whose main claim to interdisciplinarity has been an interest in inter-*textuality.* Rather than exploring the interrelations of text and social process, they investigate the connections between, for example, the literary and the visual, or between the aesthetic and other areas of discourse (political, philosophical, medical). For those committed to the social-historical study of culture, though, there are certain problems which they are bound to confront in challenging existing discipline boundaries.

In the first place, we should not underestimate the continuing institutional and ideological power of the established disciplines. Stuart Hall (1980c) recounts the obstacles encountered at Birmingham when the Centre was first established: "It was proposed that since we were not equipped to undertake proper sociological investigation, we should analyze the texts by methods of cultural reading, and then the social scientists might be recruited to test our (soft) hypotheses by the appropriate (hard) scientific methods" (p. 22). He also tells that the opening of the Centre "was greeted by a letter from two social scientists who issued a sort of warning: if Cultural Studies overstepped its proper limits and took on the study of contemporary society (not just its texts), without proper scientific (that is quasi-scientific) controls, it would provoke reprisals for illegitimately crossing the territorial boundary" (p. 21). Setting up centers and new programs involves institutional power, financial and other resources, and academic and political debates, and many of those of us who have been involved in such projects are well aware of the resistance which can be encountered in this.

Secondly, it has been suggested that cultural studies *needs* to exist and thrive in a marginal space, and that as soon as it is institutionalized (and thus, in a sense, becomes a new discipline), its intellectual motivation—its commitment to critique—is fatally compromised. (see Giroux, et al., 1984). If this were true, there would clearly be a real dilemma for those attempting to establish cultural studies in institutions of higher education. But I do not believe that setting up cultural studies centers and departments is itself counter-productive. If formal establishment entailed loss of the initial critical spirit, then of course that would undermine the whole exercise. But there is no reason why this should occur. The inevitable involvement of a new cultural studies department in the compromise and participation involved in its very existence within an institution of higher education is, of course, problematic—though I do not see why it should undercut the entire project. A rather different danger is that the removal of critical cultural studies into a self-contained program leaves the more traditional disciplines to their old practices, and ghettoizes what had once been, however obscurely, a constantly nagging voice from within. This is a replay of old arguments about entryism versus specialization, dilution versus marginalization. It has consequences not just for those traditional disciplines, which may remain unchallenged, but also for the practice of cultural studies. I am convinced that any critical practice *must* exist in constant and close contact with those cultural forms it is interrogating, if it is not to become abstract and self-indulgent. In 1986, Raymond Williams (1989b) reflected on the new problems of an increasingly institutionalized cultural studies.

> I do wonder about the course where at least the teachers—and I would say also the students—have not themselves encountered the problems of the whole development

of naturalist and realist drama, of social-problem drama, or of certain kinds of serial form in the nineteenth century. . . . In the very effort to define a clearer subject, to establish a discipline, to bring order into the work—all of which are laudable ambitions—the real problem of the project as a whole, which is that people's questions are not answered by the existing distribution of the educational curriculum, can be forgotten (pp. 159–160)

What is the point of critical studies, if we have forgotten what we are criticizing? This question, of the continuing confrontation between critical cultural studies and traditional humanities disciplines, needs to be addressed.

Finally, the institutionalization of cultural studies raises the question of the politics of critique. Lawrence Grossberg (1988a) has argued that cultural studies has increasingly lost its connection with the political. The "scandal" of cultural studies, he maintains, is that "it cannot talk about the increasingly important connections between . . . political struggles and popular tastes" (pp. 6–7). This objection, made by others too, is connected with the institutionalization (and consequent respectability and inward-lookingness) of much work in this field. Henry Giroux and colleagues (1984) have argued that those involved in cultural studies need to engage with the "public sphere," and not restrict their activities to the ivory tower community of the academy. Raymond Williams (1989b) himself came to see the future of cultural studies entirely outside the academy, with groups like those sixteen-to-eighteen-year-olds in Britain who have increasingly been excluded from mainstream education by Tory policies. This comes full circle, with a return to the origins of cultural studies, over thirty years earlier, in extra-mural classes and workers' education. (pp. 160–161).

I have no conclusions to offer about the ideal location of cultural studies, or on the desirability of pursuing Williams's radical project. I do think there is both the space and the need for interdisciplinary cultural studies within the academy, with the complex mission I have tried to outline here. Its first target is the still-dominant humanist tradition of art and literary studies. Its next objective must be to develop an approach which avoids the excess of textual studies and the inhibition of sociologies of art, in a critical analysis of the interrelations of power, inequalities, institutions, and representation. In these endeavors, it would do well to pay heed to the warnings I have referred to, of the dangers, limitations, and perversions of cultural studies. I am optimistic that a practice which is born out of, and motivated by, critical, self-reflexive methods will not make the mistake of abandoning those methods and lapsing into new forms of conservative thought.

I want to end with an example which warns us against too hasty assumptions about the various approaches to art history which I have discussed. Earlier, I spoke somewhat dismissively about the TV program, *Art of the Western World*. And it is true that for the most part this series adopted quite uncritically the categories of mainstream art history— periods, movements, influences, and Great Artists. Despite the benefit of one or two more critical scholars in its list of credits (Linda Nochlin, for example), the programs dutifully started with the Classical Age, and guided us through the Middle Ages, the Romanesque, Gothic, to the Renaissance, the Baroque, Rococo, Neoclassicism and Romanticism (this program entitled "An Age of Reason; an Age of Passion"), then Impressionism and Post-Impressionism, and the broadly titled "Into the 20th Century." This reproducing of given categories was a sure sign that the series would not incorporate critical studies which have demonstrated the ideological and political nature of those terms, the social circumstances of their production and critical reception, and the processes of exclusion which went into their formation. This was indeed the case. Not only that: in the early programs at least, there was more than a hint of that teleological perspective which makes it clear that all those people in the past were trying their hardest to become *us*. The Greeks are described as "moving towards realism" (as well as towards democracy); in the eleventh century, we discover, "Europe turned the corner" (from unreason to reason). History is reread through the prejudices and perspective of twentieth-century liberal thought.

While I was working on an earlier version of this paper, I watched the program on Impressionism and Post-Impressionism. I switched on without much enthusiasm, already knowing the kind of account we would get. (The TV Guide announced that "A Fresh View: Impressionism and Post-Impressionism" would cover works by Courbet, Manet, Degas, Renoir, Pissarro, Monet, Seurat.) I also had in mind the excellent article by Fred Orton and Griselda Pollock (1980) written on the occasion of the major Royal Academy exhibition *Post-Impressionism* in London in 1979–1980, and published in the journal *Art History*. This essay convincingly deconstructs the very term, demonstrating its construction in the ideologies and practices of art criticism and art history, and exposing the total lack of coherence of the styles and artists grouped together under this label. And here was yet another television program operating with the same discredited categories.

And then, about halfway through the program, Pollock herself was suddenly on the screen, presenting in a charming and suitably televisual manner a radical reading of paintings by Seurat, Van Gogh, Signac. She suggested that the social and economic contradictions of late nineteenth-century France could be "read" in the representation in their works of the city as distant prospect, troubling the edges of the rural landscape or suburban leisure zone.[1] She went on to discuss the women artists, Mary Cassatt and Suzanne Valadon, contrasting the style and themes of their work with that of contemporary male artists, and suggesting that this difference alerts us to the sexual politics involved in the formation of modernism. She concluded by indicting the "sexual tourism" of Gauguin, Manet, and others, making it clear that the male avant-garde artists have, as she said, "staked their claims as ambitious modernists on the bodies of women." These startling interventions were embedded in a longer discourse, in which she discussed the paintings, the lives of the painters, the changes in style, and so on, but nevertheless they were clearly made. When the series "host," Michael Wood, came back to summarize all this for us, I thought for a moment that he had been converted to the new art history. He said: "There is no such thing as objective art history. There are only the interpretations of art historians." It seemed that the series itself had suddenly become self-reflexive, and at this late stage taken on the critical perspective. However, it turned out that what he meant was that the work of the Post-Impressionists has been assessed in different ways by different commentators—some liked it, some didn't. No radical revision of approach, and we were all set to proceed to Cubism, Expressionism, and Futurism the following week.

But this small example of entryism suggests to me that the *intra*-disciplinary project is still very much worth pursuing. Without making any unwarranted assumptions about TV spectators and their viewing practices, or about the actual impact of new ideas, I do want to argue strongly against exiling critical cultural studies to its own separate enclave. The case of this television program also reminds us to look for the contradictions and spaces within areas which can too easily be written off as traditional, mainstream, or conservative. I think we are now in an excellent position to pursue the study of culture within disciplines and on the margins of disciplines, as well as in the newly cleared space of interdisciplinary studies. Without excess or inhibition, we should be able to contribute to the essential intellectual and political task of a critical sociology of art.

NOTES

1. In this she drew on some work we had done together, with Caroline Arscott, a few years ago, on representations of the city in nineteenth-century English painting (Arscott, Pollock, and Wolff, 1988).

DISCUSSION: JANET WOLFF

QUESTION: What are the struggles involved in trying to do a cultural studies program? How effective is it? How effective is it for the kind of goals that Stuart Hall was talking about? It seems to me these involved real struggles, and perhaps they are effective in some cases and not in others.

WOLFF: One difference between Stuart Hall's talk and mine, I think, was that he was centrally interested in the question of politics in cultural studies, and I only alluded to it. I was mainly interested in reviewing some issues involved in developing an adequate analytic model, or an adequate cultural studies. But I'm not sure about whether you are asking me to answer the question Stuart posed, which was about the effectivity of cultural politics, or the politics of cultural studies; or whether you are asking how we put into operation the positive aspect of my negative project. In other words, having criticized a series of approaches, what would be an adequate cultural studies?

QUESTION: I was thinking more of the second question. But it seems to me to be a problem if we separate the two. For example I remember at the University of California at Berkeley there were programs in interdisciplinary study which were clearly being identified by the administration as pockets of radical activity continuing into the seventies and which they were determined to get rid of. So there was real politics tied to the issue of interdisciplinarity.

WOLFF: One thing I would say by way of answer is that there was one point on which I probably disagreed with Stuart. He argued that (as I think he put it) "textuality isn't enough." I agree with this, of course. But his argument at that point seemed to be that "textuality isn't enough because we also need politics." Well, I wouldn't differentiate so clearly between textuality and politics. I think you can have a textual politics, a politics of the text. Douglas Crimp's talk was, amongst other things, centrally about that. So I don't think in discussions about textuality, about representation, and about engagement in the politics of representation we are somehow denying "real" politics. This *is* an arena of political activity. What *I* meant by saying textuality isn't enough was in terms of my particular concerns in this paper: namely, how do we do cultural studies, and how do we go about cultural analysis and cultural critique? In saying that textuality wasn't enough, I wanted to stress that there are extra-textual conditions, social relations, inequalities (though these are, of course, also discursively produced and mediated), and that these need to be recognized and incorporated into a model of cultural analysis.

ANITA SHETH: I agree with you that embedded in textuality are social relations. It depends on what we take the text to be, and whether we go inside the text to look at social relations. I'm wondering what happened to that missing dimension, referring back to your discussion of discourse analysis. What about the conversation analysts like Goffman and Garfinkel, Schegloff and Gail Jefferson, who look at textuality, and look directly at social relations as they are constructed and constituted in people's talk?

WOLFF: That is a really interesting question. Ethnomethodological studies, or what is sometimes called conversation analysis, does, as you say, look at how people speak and at the way in which they construct the world in which they speak. But I think of that as a very different kind of enterprise from the theories of representation that have been developed in literary studies, film studies, and in the visual arts in the last ten years. And although it's right to say that they emphasize the constructed and constitutive role of language, they are, in one sense, still, in their own way, very positivistic. They are not concerned with the way in which language operates as ideology, or the ways in which forms of representation—literary, visual, and other—construct gender, for example, and construct the categories of "femininity" and "masculinity." I don't think this can be done within the framework of ethnomethodological studies in sociology. With regards to your other point: I think you were suggesting that some sociologists of culture do use approaches which are not just the "production of culture" model which I have criticized, and, of course, that is true. One of the things I have wondered about, though, is the possibility of incorporating work from other disciplines in a cultural studies project. Partly the problem is that of professionalization, and of the exclusionary practice of the professions. Partly it is about the difficulty of attaining such wide-ranging competence oneself. One solution is cross-disciplinary collaboration with others, and I have been involved in such a project myself. But some have argued that there is no real problem, and that there is no need to try to develop some comprehensive account—that as long as the limits of each framework are recognized, then there is no reason not to work from *within* a discipline.

COLIN SPARKS: You seem to be suggesting that there's something in the production of art, the political economy of broadcasting for example, which will give you the politics of representation of a text. I'm not convinced that's possible.

WOLFF: No, nor would I be if this produced some kind of reductionist account whereby all you need to do is look at the political economy of the media, or perhaps the professional organization of media institutions, and then "read off" the text. That isn't at all what I am advocating. What I *am* saying is that it's a mistake, and a distortion, to separate an emphasis on the text on the one hand (as in some of the work of the Glasgow Media Group, for example) and on political economy of the media on the other (as in the work of Garnham, Murdock, and others). In order to understand the text, you need to analyze its social, political, and economic relations—but *not* because these are somehow reflected in the text. They are mediated, amongst other things, through professional hierarchies, ideologies, activities, and so on, of the media institutions. I am not arguing for an explanation of the text in terms of political economy, but rather for some way of working towards a recognition of both these arenas and the way in which they operate, and the contexts in which that text is produced. I don't think that has to be a reductionist account, of the kind you suggest.

40

Post-Marxism and Cultural Studies: A Post-script

Angela McRobbie

The word crisis is one which appears with alarming regularity in the discourses of cultural studies. In this collection of papers Lidia Curti uses it to refer not just to the ever-increasing marginality of intellectuals from political life, but to the collapse of many of the intellectual frames of reference which have fueled the development of cultural studies. From structuralism to poststructuralism, from Marxism to feminism, there has, she argues, been an erosion of belief, a decline in the centrality of "strong narratives," a turning away from binary relations in favor of what Derrida describes as "an indefinite series of differences."

But there are additional difficulties strewn in the path of cultural studies which might make panic a more appropriate word to describe its current condition. Marxism, a major point of reference for the whole cultural studies project in the U.K., has been undermined not just from the viewpoint of the postmodern critics who attack its teleological propositions, its meta-narrative status, its essentialism, economism, Eurocentrism, and its place within the whole Enlightenment project, but also, of course, as a result of the events in Eastern Europe, with the discrediting of much of the socialist project and with the bewildering changes in the Soviet Union which leave the Western critic at a loss as to what is now meant by right- or left-wing politics.

As I have argued elsewhere (1991), the kind of Marxism which cultural studies can retain in these very different circumstances is as yet unclear. What does seem certain is that the return to a pre-postmodern Marxism as marked out by critics like Fredric Jameson (1984) and David Harvey (1989) is untenable because the terms of that return are predicated on prioritizing economic relations and economic determinations over cultural and political relations by positioning these latter in a mechanical and reflectionist role. The debate about the future of Marxism in cultural studies has not yet taken place. Instead the great debate around modernity and postmodernity has quite conveniently leapt in and filled that space. Stuart Hall in his contribution to this collection begins to open up such a dialogue. Of course in one sense he is right, that Marxism was one problematic among many in the history of British cultural studies. For the likes of Raymond Williams and E. P. Thompson and, indeed, Richard Hoggart it was not just a problematic but a real problem. All three writers have displayed a difficult and unresolved relationship to Marxism.

Nonetheless it would be wrong to underestimate the extent to which neo-Marxist theory informed a good deal of cultural analysis in the ten-year period between 1975 and 1985. Admittedly, both the culturalist and the structuralist paradigms described by Stuart Hall (1980a) as at that time informing the field of cultural studies drew on traditions well beyond that of Marxism. Yet a touchstone in both paradigms remained the early Marx of the *1844 Manuscripts* as a critical influence on culturalism, and the later scientific Marxism of *Capital* as read by Althusser as a form of structuralist neo-Marxism. The absolute pre-eminence of Gramsci's (neo-Marxist) notion of hegemony gave a tighter political focus to the field in the conjunctural analyses developed by Stuart Hall (et al. 1979) in another seminal text, *Policing the Crisis,* and on his later work on Thatcherism. The complexities and historical specificities of the means by which consent is secured have, by drawing on Gramsci, enabled us to understand the force and political effectiveness of the Thatcher years, the success of the New Right and equally the lack of success on the part of the left even to begin to compete with this ideological radicalism.

But in these papers the place of Gramsci is no longer so certain. Lidia Curti discusses Bill Schwartz's description of his work as the "last bulwark of totalizing theory" and while Stuart Hall recognizes Gramsci's contribution to an understanding of the formation of social blocs and ensembles and class relations as well as the need for alliances and solidarities, it is Gramsci's "displacement of Marxism" which is now emphasized. Also problematized is the role of the organic intellectual and the politics of knowledge inscribed in that role. In the era of post-Marxism who will be leading whom? If the notion of a unified class whose historic role was that of agency and emancipation disappears, then what role is now to be allocated to the organic intellectual? On whose behalf is he or she acting?

It is not just textuality, difference, identity politics, and Derrida's insistence on the relational and unfixed nature of meaning (the "floating signifier"), nor is it the "interruptions" of feminism and race which have wrought the crisis of Marxism in cultural studies. Stuart Hall is quite right to remind us that from the start cultural studies emerged as a form of radical inquiry which went against reductionism and economism, which went against the base and superstructure metaphor, and which resisted the notion of false consciousness. However, no matter how far removed cultural theory became from political economy, for example, it did, nonetheless, retain a sense of political urgency.

But what has now gone, with Marxism, and partly in response to the political bewilderment and disempowerment of the left, is that sense of urgency. This has not been helped by the way in which postmodernism has been construed in the U.K., as either playful or conservative. The deferral of meaning in Derridean deconstruction has not necessarily helped matters in this respect. Intellectually, deconstruction is dazzling. Politically, it is enabling. But in the name of deconstruction there can also be produced a series of tasteful and elegant forays into the field of culture, dipping into it in the absence of the need to be constrained by materialism (a requirement or obligation which itself would be subject to deconstruction), or held to account by a political agenda. Hall reminds us that deconstruction can "formalize out of existence the critical questions of power, history, and politics."

What is significant in this collection is that where there remains a political urgency, as there does in the field of race (and also in feminism and in the battle against AIDS), then that elegance does not become merely skillful, that simultaneous pursuit and deferral of meaning does not become totally formalized. I am not, therefore, talking about the kind of deconstruction practiced by Gayatri Spivak (in McRobbie, 1985) who uses it as a tool of conceptual interrogation which ensures political vigilance and who also talks about the "strategic use of essentialism." Nor am I casting aspersions on the kind of deconstruction found in the writing of Homi Bhabha. When he talks in this volume about "affective writing" and when he encourages us to "think outside the certainty of the sententious," he remains within both theory and politics. Rephrasing Lacan, he wants us to understand politics as "structured like a language." It, too, is relational, deferred, and continually within what Chantal Mouffe describes as a wider "chain of equivalences" (Laclau and Mouffe, 1985).

Deconstruction and the move away from binary oppositions, including those of absolute beginnings and absolute endings can here be seen as opening up a new way of conceptualizing the political field and creating a new set of methods for cultural studies. This is manifest in all the contributions on race, and most forcibly in Kobena Mercer's analysis of race as a major signifier across the postwar years on both sides of the Atlantic. Likewise, Paul Gilroy shows how, far from being on the outside of political meaning and cultural formation, race has been right in there, at the heart of English debates on what is meant by national culture, and on the nature and value of European culture and European aesthetics. Gilroy skillfully connects nineteenth-century debates with the formative moments of cultural studies. He parts company with that aspect of Gramscian Marxism which considered the political potential of the "national popular." Nationalism has meant repudiation and exclusion, the drawing up of borders and boundaries which keep out, but which by virtue of their very existence, also define a population negatively, and so keep them within, but in relations of exclusion and subordination. Gilroy invents a transnational perspective, the black Atlantic world, as a better way of conceptualizing the space of black political and cultural dissent.

In all of the papers cited above, theoretical developments combine with a sense of political urgency bringing to cultural studies what we might still expect of it, a mode of study which is engaged and which seeks not the truth, but knowledge and understanding as a practical and material means of communicating with and helping to empower subordinate social groups and movements. Theory need not always lead so directly to politics. But what has worried me recently in cultural studies is when the theoretical detours become literary and textual excursions and when I begin to lose a sense of why the object of study is constituted as the object of study in the first place. Why do it? What is the point? Who is it for? On my first reading of many of the papers I was gripped by panic. Where have I been for the last five years? Much of this kind of cultural studies does not at all tally with what I teach, with what I find useful in understanding the everyday world and everyday culture around me. I was struck by a number of absences. Cultural policy is addressed in only one of the papers included in the volume (Bennett's). Likewise, "lived experience" and the culture of everyday life is considered only by John Fiske. There is relatively little direct engagement with the role of cultural intellectuals in the U.K., in the U.S.A., in the new Europe, or, indeed, in any of the emergent global socio-political formations of the 1990s.

And yet this is our very own terrain. As part of the '68-educated radical professionals, our everyday lives at work, especially in teaching and in education, but also at home and in the community, comprise of endless political interventions conducted at every level, from simple acts of communication and pedagogy to high level policy-making decisions. Postmodernity has not stopped us from functioning in this hyperactive way. The totalizing field of Marxist theory may have been discredited, but it has not meant the end of politics. Academics working in media studies, cultural studies, and in sociology have found ample opportunity to become involved in educational and cultural policy-making. This in itself is evidence of the impact which work in these fields has had outside as well as inside the academy.

This intense intellectual and political activity finds only a partial expression in the book. Maybe because in being asked to think exclusively about the future of cultural studies all of those external questions, which have fed into it and sustained it, fade into the background. The multi-disciplinarity is shaken off (evident in the decline of a sociological presence, found in only two contributions, one by Simon Frith and the other by Janet Wolff), and a much purer and less colorful discipline emerges. At the very moment at which cultural studies begins to gain institutional recognition, it seems that it is not only shorn of its interdisciplinary character, but its foundations are shaken by the critique of Marxism and by the decentering of class relations which in the early years gave cultural studies much of its distinctive identity.

What remains is a sophisticated but virtually unrecognizable mode of inquiry. Why unrecognizable? Because, in my view, cultural studies was always messy. Characterized by intense internal theoretical conflict, it was also a messy amalgam of sociology, social history, and literature, rewritten as it were into the language of contemporary culture. Not only did these disciplines feed into and sustain cultural studies (many of us got jobs teaching sociology after all), but they also came in for heavy criticism from within cultural studies. In the first instance it was part of the cultural studies project to subject sociology, history, and literature to critique, then later these same subject areas as well as cultural studies itself were shown to be heavily Anglocentric and blind to the perspective of the colonial or postcolonial subject.

The ferocity of this critique has, ironically, brought back to cultural studies what has been missing from it, the notion of it being a contested terrain of study. Not only contested but also resistant to disciplinary purity. Precisely because it is so embedded in contemporary social and political processes, because, for example, the recent changes in Europe affect how we think about culture, because class diminishes as a site of identification before our very eyes, cultural studies must continue to argue against its incorporation into what is conventionally recognized as a "subject area." For cultural studies to survive it cannot afford to lose this disciplinary looseness, this feeling that, like other radical areas of inquiry, such as psychoanalysis, its authors are making it up as they go along.

Contingency, Historicity, and Identity

I haven't rejected Marxism. Something different has occurred. It is Marxism that has broken up and I believe I am holding on to its best fragments. (Laclau, 1990)

I want to draw the preceding section together with the critique which follows by exploring in more detail what the meaning of post-Marxism might be for cultural studies. So far I have ascertained that, apart from the continuing centrality of "textuality," there is a hesitancy about where the theoretical future of the field might lie. There is no shortage of critical terms or political ideas, but to grasp them and their potential it seems we have to dig beneath the surface. For example, Kobena Mercer's contribution refers to the idea of the "democratic antagonism." It also draws on and makes use of other key terms found in recent work by Ernesto Laclau and Chantal Mouffe (1985). However, the emphasis in Kobena's piece is, of course, on his own chosen object of study, the place of race as a "floating signifier" in postwar political and cultural discourse, and so this underlying theoretical frame of reference remains cryptic or assumed rather than fully explicated. Like several other contributors, Kobena also rejects any notion of a binary relation (signifier/signified) as having a validity in the analysis of cultural meaning. Instead, he talks about relations of equivalence. In addition, there is the question of identity and identity politics which runs right through a number of papers, especially those which deal with race. But what exactly is meant by identity? Is it a term which implies the psychic processes of aquiring identity as theorized by Lacan? Is it a term which somehow suggests the political shift away from class? Or does class identity constitute one among many identities of equal validity in the struggle for a pluralist radical democracy? Through what processes has identity in cultural studies come to replace the more psychoanalytic notion of the subject?

In a recent interview, Ernesto Laclau (1990) explains that his is not a rejection of Marxism *tout court* so much as a process of moving on beyond the theoretical vocabulary of the various Marxisms and neo-Marxisms. It is no longer useful to retain the word Marxism to characterize the current mode of inquiry. Post-Marxism suggests taking the radical political project further, and at the same time using what has been called the crisis of Marxism as an opportunity to go back and deconstruct, in Derridean terms, the Marxist canon.

What is Laclau's starting point? That the emancipation of society through the agency of one united class no longer stands as a model for understanding or anticipating social change. That class struggle is not inevitable; that this was a theoretically flawed argument based on the misapplication of the Hegelian concept of "contradiction" to the processes of capital accumulation and the wage labor relation; that antagonism is not inherent to capital, but based around external, contigent, and historical processes. It is, therefore, the conditions outside capital which contribute to social antagonisms— the inability of the worker, for example, to participate in the broader society as a consumer. The "constitutive outside" is therefore necessary in what Laclau calls antagonism.

We are, therefore, entering a very different kind of socio-political universe from that understood by Marxism. "What we find is not an interaction or determination between fully constituted areas of the social, but a field of relational semi-identities in which 'political,' 'ideological,' and 'economic' elements will enter into unstable relations of imbrication without ever managing to constitute themselves as separate objects" (Laclau, 1990). This begs several questions. What of the subject? What are the mechanics of identification? Laclau seems to be drawing on Lacan and extending his psychoanalytic vocabulary to incorporate a more socio-political perspective. Full identity is never achieved, just as the subject of Lacan is defined through lack. Identity requires acts of identification, and this, in turn, implies agency and process. The social subject can take responsibility for his or her own history, though not to achieve "fullness." It is this incompleteness which creates the "social imaginary," which, in turn, is the sphere of representation. "The imaginary is a horizon . . . as modes of representation of the very form of fullness, they are located beyond the precariousness and dislocations typical of the world of objects" (Laclau, 1990).

Incompleteness, fragmentation, and the pluralities of emergent identities need not mean loss of political capacity. Instead, they can point the way to new forms of struggle; they can create conditions which are "more difficult to manipulate and control." As the subject of social control disperses, the strategies of social control are, in a sense, thrown off guard. This means that techniques of evasion can be more easily realized. What de Certeau (1984) would call "ruses" can, for Laclau, mean an avoidance of the "dictatorship by market, state, or direct producers."

There is a certain obsfucation about the actual processes of acquiring identity in Laclau's recent work which remains unresolved. He is on more solid ground in his critique of Gramsci. Following his abandonment of Marx's reliance on the notion of a fundamental class, which bears within it emancipatory capacities as inherent and therefore "outside political struggle," Laclau extends this argument to key elements in Gramsci's writing. While the great value of Gramsci's thinking is that it brings Marxist theories down to the level of "concrete social contexts," the very notion of hegemony depends, nonetheless, on a "privileged" class which, by necessity will emerge, and which will be led to a dominant position by those organic intellectuals whose role it is to "know ... the underlying movement of history." It is this logic of necessity which, argues Laclau, binds Gramsci to an essentially authoritarian notion of leadership. For a more democratic conception of social change to emerge, a logic of contingency would need to be prevail. When contingency is combined with equivalence and when no social group is granted a privileged place as an emancipatory agent, then a form of relational hegemony can extend the sequence of democratic antagonisms through a series of social displacements. Laclau gives as an example the trade union organization set up in a neighborhood and able to stretch its interests to engage with gay struggles and to thus let slip the centrality of class from the trade union identity. When this happens then a hegemonic center can be said to exist. "The radicality of a conflict depends on the extent to which the differences are re-articulated in chains of equivalence."

What we have to expect is not the growing simplification of the class structure as predicted by Marx, nor the inevitability of a universal class subject emerging, but rather the development of a multiplicity of partial and fragmented identities, each with its own role to play in the pursuit of radical democracy. The collapse of Marxism need not be construed as signaling the end of socialist politics; indeed the beginning of a new era, where the opportunities for a pluralist democracy are strengthened rather than weakened, is now within reach. What is inconceivable, however, is a society without conflict, a harmonious entity like that post-revolutionary utopia envisaged by Marx. This is impossible because "power is the condition for society to be possible."

It would seem, then, that if Laclau is correct we have little option but to work within the confines of the contingent and historically specific processes which are con- stitutive of our positioning and of our identities. There is no longer a pressure to rank identities in some kind of grand universal order of ascending political importance, since the road to radical democracy lies both in the incommensurability of such struggles and also in the possibility of forming chains of connection and articulation across different interest groups. Laclau's analysis remains focused around the political. Radical democracy suggests an alternative to capital, but, we are reminded, democratic freedom need not imply greater state intervention in public life; it might involve less. Likewise, the free market offers opportunities for new emergent identities and, besides which, capital in the homogenous absolutist way in which we on the left have tended to refer to it, is itself a more fractured and fragile entity.

Laclau's recent writings raise a number of questions of key importance to cultural intellectuals. In one sense he is providing the theoretical underpinning for what has already happened in cultural studies, the evidence of which can be seen in these papers. There is a greater degree of openness in most of the contributions than would have been the case some years ago, when the pressure to bring the chosen object of study firmly into the conceptual landmarks, provided first by Althusser and then by Gramsci, imposed on cultural studies a degree of rigidity. This new discursiveness allows or permits a speculative "writerly" approach, the dangers of which I have already outlined, but the advantages of which can be seen in the broader, reflective, and insightful mode which the absence of the tyranny of theory, as it was once understood, makes possible. This is most evident in Lidia Curti's commentary on soap opera as a mode of continually articulating the practices of identification and the anxieties around identity. She draws attention to the staple of narrative strategies in soap, the sudden loss of memory prompt- ing the question "Who am I?" The adopted child's search for the real mother or father in a bid once again to find out who s/he is. The split identity of the heroine who is mysteriously replaced by a double. The close-ups, as women viewers lose themselves in the subjects whose innermost feelings they identify with. All of these acts comprise of forms of self-interrogation about who I am and how I want to be, or how I expect to be.

What remains underdeveloped in Laclau's analysis is the place and role of culture, in the process of "building a new left" (the title of one of the pieces). When this question was put to him, Laclau agreed that hegemony was indeed a type of articulation working through culture and not just in the field of politics (Laclau, 1990). It is also in culture that identity is most thoroughly shaped, and it is the task of culture in the post-Marxist period to "transform the forms of identification and the construction of subjectivity that exist in our civilization." But the direction of the movement that this process must now take is not toward some universal subjectivity but toward an identity which maintains the "dignity of the specific." It is his commitment to the historically specific which allows Laclau not to be specific. He cannot spell out the practices of, or the mechanics of, identity formation, for the very reason that they are, like their subjects, produced within particular social and historical conditions. This permits a consistently high level of abstraction in his political philosophy. But the work of transformation which is implicit in his analysis is exactly concurrent with the kind of critical work found in the contributions on race in this volume.

Ghosts, AIDS, and Moby Dick

Bell hooks in her article in this volume, "Representing Whiteness in the Black Imagination," describes the way in which black people who did not live in the "bush of ghosts" represented white people and whiteness in their own everyday experience and in black popular culture. These white ghosts combined the strange with the terrible. From the child's point of view white people were a source of terror. Hooks remembers her own trips across town to get to her grandmother's house in a predominantly white neighborhood. Her image of whites as potentially violent, with the capacity to terrorize her, was drawn partly from their stares of hate as she passed by. As a child, she had to learn that in order to be safe she must recognize "the power of whiteness, even to fear it and to avoid encountering it." Living in a black neighborhood, her only experience of white men was the insurance salesmen who "terrorized by economic exploitation." This constant fear is something white people learn about "secondhand," but it is formative in the development of black identity, and it accompanies black people as they move through different states, countries, and social situations. The suspicious glances of the airport immigration officers staring down at her passport are not so different from the antagonistic stares of the white people looking at the young bell hooks from their porches as she ran toward the safety of her grandmother's house.

The experience of *travel* in the formation of black identity remains a critical example in the history of racial subordination, but as Paul Gilroy argues in his contribution, it is also something which can be turned to political advantage in the reconceptualization of the world map to create a transnationalism expressive of the historical mobility of black people. The aim is not to achieve a black oneness, an absolute ethnicity, but rather to allow a plurality of black identities to emerge. The specificities of black settlement in any one place will produce a particularly nuanced identity. But this co-exists with the reality of the dislocated map, the articulations across and beyond the barriers and boundaries set by the nation-states. Thus there are set in place, in Laclau's terms, the conditions for a much longer chain of equivalences which preclude reductionism or essentialism and which give rise to both a common and uncommon culture emerging. This is not simply cultural diversity in the liberal sense. As Homi Bhabha argues in his paper, such a notion slides too easily into ideas of difference as reflective of tolerance.

What is really at stake is the nature and form of the relationships which bind these differences together and from which they accrue their meaning. It is in relation to each other that identity is formed. If meaning is relational, so too is identity.

Kobena Mercer understands the new politics of identity as partly emerging from a deep rupture within the traditional sites of consciousness, including those of class, party, nation, and state. It is not enough, however, to fill the theoretical gap opened up by this social de-alignment by acknowledging or citing what he calls the cultural studies "mantra" of race, sex, and class identities. When sex and race are mechanistically added to class there is a tendency to slide back into seeing them as intact and absolute categories, which is, of course, exactly what Mercer, Gilroy, and, some years previously, a number of feminist theorists including Denise Riley (1988) have argued they are not.

Mercer also suggests that the New Right has been much more successful than the left at mobilizing around the "signifiers" of identity by forging radical meanings onto the pre-existing meanings of race. These are political struggles over the "multi-accentuality" of the sign.[1] If representation remains a site of power and regulation as well as a source of identity, then cultural academics working in the fields of representation have a critical job to do in attempting to recast these terms by inflecting new meanings and by prizing apart and disentangling old ones—as, for example, Kobena Mercer himself does in his invoking of the place of race in the events of 1968, in the hippy underground and the counterculture, and even in the notion of the Woodstock nation. As he shows, racial signifiers were not just adopted by white youth, but were constructive in creating the actual subcultural discourses of those sectors of postwar white youth who "disidentified with racism." Black expressive culture provided a language for the new social movements which emerged in the early 1970s; black pride re-emerged as gay pride; and black liberation struggles helped create "gay lib" and, indeed, "women's lib."

In the last ten years it has been the right which has managed most successfully to intervene and shape the "imaginary and symbolic dimensions of hegemonic politics" (Mercer, this volume). The importance of the fields of the symbolic and the imaginary should not be underestimated. These are also, of course, the fields of culture and of the mass media. How might they be more successfully re-inflected or cathected by the left, by black intellectuals, by feminists? If there was a simple answer to this question then we would not spend so much time worrying about it. But the power of representation, the seduction of received rhetoric, the ease with which the self dissolves into the image on the screen, the appeal of easy pleasures and the occasional desire to relinquish responsibility, gives to the ever-ready radical right a clear advantage over and above the political and material advantages they already have at their disposal. With these adversaries in mind, Stuart Hall reminds us of the difference between academic and intellectual work. He urges intellectual modesty and, at the same time, insists on the urgency of politics on the intellectual agenda of cultural studies. This is like saying: "Look here, as marginal intellectuals there is not a great deal which we can do, so let's not kid ourselves. On the other hand, the critical attention which we can pay to the field of dominant culture and to the world of representation, and the extent to which we can show how meanings are constructed and how they are neither inevitable or natural or God-given, is an important task. What is more, it is increasingly in culture that politics itself is constructed as a discourse; it is here that popular assent in a democratic society is sought. While we should not overestimate our social effectivity, neither should we wallow in our own marginality and leave the field of forging cultural meanings to those who already take it as their preordained right."

In his essay Stuart Hall considers the disparity between the intense political activity which has emerged around AIDS and the too-leisurely mode of the deconstructive voice in cultural studies. His fear is also that the dominant language through which AIDS is understood will eventually spell the death of desire itself. This threat is at the very heart of Douglas Crimp's important contribution to this volume, because what he shows is how intent the media and the powers of representation are to de-sexualize the gay community in the light of AIDS. This strategy has been pursued with relentless force, with great brutality, and with a callous disregard for people's privacy and for their suffering. The value of Crimp's study is as follows: first, it charts with historical specificity the unfolding and developmental chain of images and narratives through which the U.S. media interprets and makes sense of AIDS for the general public (i.e., for white middle-class heterosexuals); second, it shows how in the guise of sensitivity and realism the liberal arts, and in particular the work of one art photographer, Nicholas Nixon, merely reinforces the pathologization of the gay community; third, it records the views of the art critics who, with only one exception, William Olander, the Curator of New York's New Museum of Contemporary Arts, congratulate the photographer for managing to get his subjects, many of them in advanced states of illness, to "hold nothing back." What, in contrast, Olander and Crimp see in the pictures is loneliness, lack of help and community, no sign of work or activity, no names and no identities.

In a particularly exploitative and sensationalized piece of reportage, one that Crimp describes, PBS TV tracks down a disadvantaged young gay black AIDS sufferer as he is moved on from town to town by family and by local authorities anxious to get rid of him. The media portray him, poor and still hustling, as a kind of sexual terrorist, a walking time bomb. He, in his misery and like so many other millions of would-be TV celebrities, revels momentarily in this brief moment of fame and notoriety. Crimp ends his piece with a discussion of an independently produced videotape titled "Danny." The filmmaker, Stashu Kybartas, who is documenting Danny's experience of AIDS, breaks the rules which have implicitly established themselves around the treatment of this subject in the arts and the visual media by attributing to Danny, despite his skin lesions, an active sexuality to which he himself is drawn. As Crimp points out, Danny is "nevertheless still fully sexualized."

Nothing could be further apart from this erotic moment recorded on the voice-over ("It was suddenly very quiet in the studio, and my heart was beating fast") described by Crimp than the current "phobic" representations of sexual desire found in the commercial cinema. Fear of AIDS has created a structural problem about how to represent sex in a visual medium which, since the late 1960s, has depended on what might be called a never-ending stream of promiscuous narratives. While, at one level, heterosexual culture has defined itself as safely removed from the immediate threat of AIDS, at a much deeper level there is a recognition of how wrong this is. Through a tangled web of anxieties there emerges a set of narrative solutions: monogamy replaces promiscuity, the baby replaces the penis, the couple at home replaces the singles bar, *parenthood* becomes a subject worthy of narrative investigation. In last year's surprise blockbuster, *Ghost,* we find race and sex brought together as critical "floating signifiers" in contemporary urban discourse. *Ghost* might be seen, then, as one of those moments in popular culture where there is a vast overinvestment of meaning. Its popularity is partly dependent on its ability as a cinematic narrative to transcend and overcome social fears and anxieties within the framework of comedy and entertainment. While it has been condemned by critics like Judith Williamson (1990) writing in *The Guardian* as particularly pernicious in its use of moral absolutes (good people who die go to heaven in a cloud of light, bad people are dragged by screaming hags downwards to hell), it is precisely the assertion of absolutes in what is a much murkier and unclear landscape of contemporary urban society which adds to its appeal.

Ghost is a modern fairy-tale/horror film predicated on a supernatural device which allows a young white man, mugged to death on the streets of Manhattan while his girlfriend looks on helplessly, to return to earth as an invisible observer/protector. Race is a necessary counterpoint to the narrative. The yuppie couple are just settling into their loft apartment when tragedy strikes. Their environment is middle class and "cultured." She is a potter, he works on Wall Street. They are surrounded by art objects; they go out one evening to the theater; they are confronted by a non-white assailant and the young man, Sam, dies in a violent struggle.

The young mixed-race audience in the Holloway cinema where I saw the film holds its breath, puzzled. Is it possible that a blockbuster movie made in 1990 could conceivably rely on such negative stereotypes for its narrative action? But wait a minute. Sigh of relief. The narrative slowly unfolds. Their assailant is Hispanic. And he is set up by the white yuppie business partner of the dead man. For some complicated reason the business partner has to get rid of Sam in order to complete the fraudulent dealings he has gotten involved with as a means of paying off his cocaine debts. Thus he hires José. As a ghost, Sam manages to establish contact with a black woman, Oda Mae Brown (played by Whoopi Goldberg), who makes a living as a medium. Only through her can Sam alert his girlfriend Molly to the danger she is in as the owner of a vital computer code left among his personal belongings. The humor and fun in the film derive partly through the culture clash between Sam and Oda Mae. This is expressed in language and in the contrast between sophisticated white consumer culture and black folk culture and superstition. The partnership which emerges in the end is, however, between the two unpartnered women. Mixed-race female friendship triumphs, presenting itself both as a narrative solution (in the light of the death of the male lover) and as a metaphoric bonding process which overcomes the problem of urban race conflict and the threat to whites posed by the poor black underclass.

What is counterposed in the film is black and white urban culture. *Ghost* is a mixed-race "women's film" as viewed from a white perspective. Blacks are poor but not, as it originally seems, criminalized and angry. Black and white cultures are geographically separate, coming together only under extremely unusual circumstances. Oda Mae Brown rarely goes uptown and overdresses for the occasion. Molly hardly moves out of her loft for the duration of the film. Apart from José there are no other significant non-white male figures, and it is, therefore, a black woman who takes on the role of the racial "other." She can survive living in poverty without resorting to either drugs or crime, and she is able to turn her personal talents, including her wit and good humor, to her advantage by working as a medium.

Oda Mae is given no particular sexual identity. Sex in *Ghost* is wholly focused around the glamorous couple Sam and Molly (played by Patrick Swayze and Demi Moore). Their love ends tragically in Sam's premature death. In what has become one of the most celebrated sex scenes in recent cinematic history, sex-in-love in *Ghost* is celebrated symbolically as an erotic exchange of bodily fluids. The sex scene lasts for the entire duration of the classic pop song by the Righteous Brothers, "Unchained Melody" (subsequently re-released as a chart-topping single). It begins with Molly at her potter's wheel. She is sculpting a clay piece which increasingly takes on phallic proportions. She molds and caresses the emergent penis/pot. The clay suddenly melts and crumbles and she starts again. It is a comic moment of detumescence. Then she is joined by Sam and the rising clay becomes part of their sexual foreplay. It collapses again and this time the soft liquid clay takes on an erotic charge of its own. Both partners begin to play with it, letting it run through their fingers, smearing it onto their hands, and rubbing it onto each other's bodies. Eventually, towards the end of the scene, the clay is left aside as the couple moves towards "real sex."

In this scene of highly romanticized sex between a monogamous young couple, sex is so safe that it is able to incorporate into its momentum the metonymic equivalent of unsafe sex. It acts as a riposte to those who would urge the universal adoption of safe sex. The exchange of body fluids is made safe, as long as it takes place within the monogamous partnership. It is the erotic moment.

I was encouraged to see this film by my fourteen-year-old daughter who had already seen it several times. She came to see it with me again and warned me that there was a "naughty" scene in it. But, she added afterwards, "it was very nice, wasn't it, because they really loved each other." The "naughtiness" was the "sight" of the erect penis as a flesh colored clay form, Demi's active sexual pleasure in caressing this penis/pot, and finally the couple's shared pleasure in touching each other's bodies with the soft running clay.

The centrality of this scene in the film represents a defiant statement about sex and eroticism in the 1990s. There is no question of using a condom, there are no questions about each partner's sexual past. There is no need for the new vigilance around sex. The running clay has a literary precedent, in Melville's classic novel *Moby Dick,* when the sperm and fluid remains of the trawl of fish are discovered as a source of strong erotic charge by the narrator who immerses his hands in the cloudy semen-like discharges and finds himself losing his whole sense of being. In the novel, the scene acts as a centerpoint. Sex is about lubrication, dissolution, and the polymorphously perverse infantile pleasures of smearing, touching, and rubbing.

Why conclude this post-script to the book with such an example of the power of popular culture to encode popular anxieties into the language of desire and social conformity, and to treat race from the assumed viewpoint of the white spectator (the popular audience) as a gendered category, an urban experience, and a folk culture? The answer to this question must be that my sketchy account of the film and its audience reflects a number of themes which have informed this paper. Race is a floating signifier in *Ghost* rather than an absolute category. It travels across the city which is, at one level, racially divided, but at another, through the currency of drugs and, then, through the forces of good, connected. *Ghost* also shows how deeply internalized the fear of AIDS has been and how at a symbolic level even heterosexual monogamy (in the context of physical beauty, youth, wealth, and cultural capital) is threatened by a malevolent external force. Sam, after all, dies in horrible and unexpected circumstances. Finally, *Ghost* addresses and gives a place to new emergent identities. Its women, one black and funny, the other white and an artist, are the survivors. They embody integrity, good sense, and racial goodwill. Their single status at the end of the film also says something significant about changes in sexual culture and even about the possibility of sexual abstinence. In popular culture today it is possible to envisage a future not predicated on sex.

What remains problematic in this new terrain of cultural studies where identity plays such an important role is the actual process of identity acquisition. It is unclear as to how this important process is actually being conceptualized. On the one hand, it is fluid, never completely secured and continually being remade, reconstructed afresh. On the other hand, it only exists in relation to what it is not, to the other identities which are its "other." Identity is not the "bourgeois" individual, nor is it the personality, the unique person, but neither is it the psychoanalytic subject. As it is used in current cultural discourse it implies a combative sense of self, but one which makes sense in terms of a broader overarching category, such as race or sexuality or, indeed, class. Identity, therefore, is predicated on social identity, on social groups or populations with some sense of a shared experience and history. And yet it is also a category doomed to dispersal and to fragmentation, committed to anti-essentialism, to anti-absolutism.

Identity could be seen as dragging cultural studies into the 1990s by acting as a kind of guide to how people see themselves, not as class subjects, not as psychoanalytic subjects, not as subjects of ideology, not as textual subjects, but as active agents whose sense of self is projected onto and expressed in an expansive range of cultural practices, including texts, images, and commodities. If this is the case, then the problem in cultural studies today, and witnessed in the overall tone of the conference papers (and elsewhere, in the UK "New Times" debate, for example), is the absence of reference to real existing identities in the ethnographic sense. The identities being discussed, and I am as guilty of this myself as anybody else, are textual or discursive identities. The site of identity formation in cultural studies remains implicitly in and through cultural commodities and texts rather than in and through the cultural practices of everyday life. This, then, is where I want to end, with a plea for identity ethnography in cultural studies, with a plea for carrying out interactive research on groups and individuals who are more than just audiences for texts. In this sense, I an with John Fiske in his desire to find the right theoretical vocabulary to understand everyday life in its fleeting, fluid, and volatile formations. Looking at it this way, identity becomes submerged into and virtually indistinguishable from everyday life in all its contingency and with all its historical specificity. For it to re–emerge at the other end, it is necessary that we somehow move away from the binary opposition which still haunts cultural studies, that is, the distinction between text and lived experience, between media and reality, between culture and society. What is now required is a methodology, a new paradigm for conceptualizing identity-in-culture, an ethnographic approach which takes as its starting point the relational interactive quality of everyday life and which brings a renewed rigor to this kind of work by integrating into it a keen sense of history and contingency.

Notes

1. A phrase borrowed from Volosinov/Bahktin and used by Stuart Hall and Kobena Mercer in their contributions to this volume.

References

A. A. VV. (1987) *Diotima—Il pensiero della differenza sessuale.* Milano: La Tartaruga.

Abu-Loghud, Lila (1986) *Veiled Sentiments: Honor and Poetry in Bedouin Society.* Berkeley: U. of Calif. Press.

Abu-Loghud, L. (1990) "The romance of resistance: Tracing transformations of power through Bedouin women." *American Ethnologist,* 17, pp. 41–55.

Adorno, Theodor W. (1976) *Introduction to the Sociology of Music.* Trans. E. B. Ashton. New York: Continuum.

Ahmad, Aijaz (1987) "Jameson's rhetoric of otherness and the 'National Allegory.'" *Social Text,* 17, pp. 3–25.

Ahmad, A. (1989) " 'Third world literature' and the national ideology." *Journal of Arts and Ideas,* 17–18, June, pp. 117–135.

Aiken, William (1984) "Ethical issues in agriculture." In T. Regan (ed) (1984), pp. 247–288.

Alarcon, Norma (1990) "The theoretical subject(s) of *This Bridge Called My Back* and Anglo American Feminism." In G. Anzaldúa (ed) (1990), pp. 356–369.

Alberts, Bruce et al (1983) *Molecular Biology of the Cell.* New York: Garland.

Allor, Martin (1984) *Cinema, Culture, and the Social Formation: Ideology and Critical Practice.* Unpublished dissertation. U. of Illinois at Urbana-Champaign.

Allor, M. (1989) "In private practices: Rearticulating the subject/audience nexus." *Discours Social/Social Discourse,* 2 (1–2), pp. 1–7.

Alloula, Malek (1986) *The Colonial Harem.* Minneapolis: U. of Minn. Press.

Alonso, W. (ed) (1987) *Population in an Interacting World.* Cambridge: Harvard U. Press.

Althusser, Louis (1970a) *For Marx.* Trans. Ben Brewster. New York: Random House.

Althusser, L. (1970b) "The object of *Capital.* In L. Althusser and E. Balibar *Reading Capital.* Trans. B. Brewster. London: NLB.

Althusser, L. (1971a) *Lenin and Philosophy and Other Essays.* Trans. B. Brewster. New York: Monthly Review.

Althusser, L. (1971b) "Ideology and ideological state apparatuses (Notes towards an investigation)." In L. Althusser (1971a), pp. 121–173.

Anaya, Rudolfo A. and Francisco Lomeli (eds) (1989) *Aztlán: Essays on the Chicano Homeland.* Albuquerque: Academia/El Norte Publications.

Anderson, Benedict (1983) *Imagined Communities: Reflections on the Origin and Spread of Nationalism.* London: Verso.

Anderson, Perry (1984) "Modernity and revolution." *New Left Review* (144), pp. 96–113.

Ang, Ien (1985) *Watching Dallas.* New York: Methuen.

Anon. (1611 [1967]) *The English Bible* (the "Authorized" translation). New York: AMS Press.

Anon. (1607) *Miseries of Inforst Mariage.* London.

Anon. (1926) "Buy a book a month." *Publisher's Weekly,* (Feb. 13), p. 519.

Anzaldúa, Gloria (1987) *Borderlands, La Frontera: The New Mestiza.* San Francisco: Spinsters/Aunt Lute.

Anzaldúa, G. (ed) (1990) *Making Face, Making Soul: Haciendo Caras.* San Francisco: Aunt Lute.

Appadurai, Arjun (1988) "Putting hierarchy in its place." *Cultural Anthropology,* 3(1), pp. 36–49.

Appadurai, A. (1990) "Disjuncture and difference in the global cultural economy." *Public Culture,* 2(2), pp. 1–24.

Arac, Jonathan (ed) (1986) *Postmodernism and Politics.* Minneapolis: U. of Minnesota Press.

Arditti, Rita, Renata Klein and Shelley Minden (1984) *Test Tube Women.* London: Pandora Press.

Arena-DeRosa, James (1990) "Indigenous leaders host U.S. environmentalists in the Amazon." *Oxfam America News,* Summer/Fall, pp. 1–2.

Armstrong, Nancy (1987) *Desire and Domestic Fiction: A Political History of the Novel.* New York: Oxford U. Press.

Arnold, Matthew (1965) [1883]) *Culture and Anarchy.* R. H. Super (ed). Ann Arbor: U. of Michigan Press.

Aronowitz, Stanley and Henry Giroux (1991) *Postmodern Education: Politics, Culture, and Social Criticism.* Minneapolis: U. of Minn. Press.

Arscott, Carolyn, Griselda Pollock and Janet Wolff (1988) "The partial view: The visual representation of the early nineteenth-century industrial city." In J. Wolff and J. Seed (eds) (1988).

Asad, Talal (ed) (1973; rpt. 1979) *Anthropology and the Colonial Encounter.* New York: Humanities Press.

Atkins, Robert (1988) "Nicholas Nixon." *7 Days,* 5 Oct.

Auden, W. H. (1966) *Collected Shorter Poems, 1927–1957.* London: Faber & Faber.

Austin, Regina (1989) "Sapphire bound!" *Wisconsin Law Review,* Fall, pp. 539–578.

Bailey, P. (ed) (1986) *Music Hall: The Business of Pleasure.* Milton Keynes: Open U. Press.

Baker, Houston (1989) *Blues, Ideology, and Afro-American Literature.* Chicago: U. of Chicago Press.

Bakhtin, Mikhail (1981) *The Dialogic Imagination.* Austin: U. of Texas Press.

Bakhtin, M. (1984) *Rabelais and His World.* Bloomington: Indiana U. Press.

Baldick, Chris (1983) *The Social Mission of English Criticism.* Oxford: Clarendon Press.

Baldwin, James (1955; rpt. 1984) *Notes of a Native Son.* Boston: Beacon Press.

Baldwin, T. W. (1944) *William Shakespeare's small Latine and lesse Greeke.* Urbana: U. of Illinois Press.

Ballard, J. G. (1981) "J. G. Ballard." In A. Burns and C. Sugnet (eds) *The Imagination on Trial.* London: Allison & Busby.

Ballard, J. G. (1988) *Running Wild.* London: Century Hutchinson.

Balsamo, Anne and Paula A. Treichler (1990) "Feminist Cultural Studies: Questions for the 1990s." *Women and Language,* 13(1), pp. 3–6.

Balsamo, Anne (1991) "Feminism and cultural studies." *Journal of the Midwest Modern Language Association,* 24(1), pp. 50–73.

Baransky, Z. and B. Lumley (eds) (1990) *Culture and Conflict in Post-War Italy: Essays in Popular and Mass Culture.* London: Macmillan.

Barinaga, Marcia (1990) "A muted victory for the biotech industry." *Science,* 249 (20 July).

Barker, Francis (1984) *The Tremulous Private Body.* New York: Methuen.

Barker, George (1950) *Pachuco: An American-Spanish argot and its social functions in Tucson, Arizona.* Social Science Bulletin no. 18, U. of Arizona Bulletin, 21(1).

Barker, Martin (1982) *The New Racism.* London: Junction Books.

Barrett, Michele (1980) *Women's Oppression Today: Problems in Marxist Feminist Analysis.* London: Verso.

Barringer, F. (1991) "Ancient tribes that didn't vanish, they just moved." *New York Times,* 23 Oct., pp. C1, C6.

Barth, John (1968) *Lost in the Funhouse.* Garden City, N.Y.: Doubleday.

Barthes, Roland (1972a) *Mythologies.* Trans. A. Lavers. London: Cape.

Barthes, R. (1972b [1957]) "Myth today." In R. Barthes (1972a), pp. 109–159.

Barthes, R. (1975) *The Pleasure of the Text.* New York: Hill and Wang.

Barthes, R. (1980) *Barthes par Roland Barthes.* Paris: Editions du Seuil.

Bateson, Mary Catherine and Richard Goldsby (1988) *Thinking AIDS: The Social Response to the Biological Threat.* Reading, MA: Addison-Wesley.

Battouta, Ibn (1972) *Travels of Ibn Battouta, AD 1325–1354.* C. Detremery, B. Sanguinetti and H. Gibbs (eds). Nendeln: Kraus Reprint.

Baudrillard, Jean (1981) "Gesture and signature: Semiurgy in contemporary art." *For a Critique of the Political Economy of the Sign.* Trans. C. Levin. St. Louis, MO: Telos Press, pp. 102–111.

Baudrillard, J. (1982) *A L'Ombre des Majorités Silencieuses ou la fin du Social.* Paris: Editions Denoel/Gunthier.

Baudrillard, J. (1983a) *Les stratégies fatales.* Paris: Editions Grasset & Pasquelle.

Baudrillard, J. (1983b) "The precession of simulacra." *Simulations.* Trans. P. Foss and P. Patton. New York: Semiotext(e), pp. 1–79.

Baudrillard, J. (1989) *America.* New York: Verso.

Bayton, Mavis (1990) "How women become musicians." In S. Frith and A. Goodwin (eds) (1990), pp. 238–257.

Becker, Robert and Gary Selden (1985) *The Body Electric: Electromagnetism and the Foundation of Life.* New York: William Morrow.

Beckerman, Bernard (1989) "Theatrical plots and Elizabethan stage practice." In W. Elton and W. Long (eds) *Shakespeare and Dramatic Tradition: Essays in Honor of S. F. Johnson.* Newark: U. of Delaware Press, pp. 109–124.

Bee, Jim (1989) "First citizen of the semiotic democracy." *Cultural Studies,* 3(3), pp. 353–359.

Beldecos, A. et al (1988) "The importance of feminist critique for contemporary cell biology." *Hypatia,* 3, pp. 61–76.

Benjamin, Jessica (1986) "A desire of one's own: Psychoanalytic feminism and intersubjective space." In T. de Lauretis (ed) (1986).

Benjamin, Walter (1973a) *Understanding Brecht.* London: New Left Books.

Benjamin, W. (1973b) "Theses on the Philosophy of History." *Illuminations.* London: Fontana.

Benmayor, Rita, Ana Juarbe, Celia Alvarez, and Blanca Vasquez (1987) "Stories to live by: Continuity and change in three generations of Puerto Rican women." Working paper. New York: Centro de Estudios Puertorriquenos, Hunter College.

Bennett, Tony (1988a) "The exhibitionary complex." *New Formations,* 4, pp. 73–102.

Bennett, T. (1988b) "Ozmosis: Looking at Australian popular culture." *Australian Left Review,* April/May.

Bennett, T. (1990a) *Outside Literature.* London: Routledge.

Bennett, T. (1990b) "The political rationality of the museum." *Continuum.*

Bennett, T. and Janet Woollacott (1987) *Bond and Beyond: The Political Career of a Popular Hero.* New York: Methuen.

Benterrak, Krim, S. Muecke and P. Roe (1984) *Reading the Country.* Fremantle: Fremantle Arts Centre Press.

Berecz, János (1986) *1956—Counterrevolution in Hungary: Words and Weapons.* Budapest: Akadémiai.

Bergstrom, Janet (1988) "Enunciation and sexual difference." In C. Penley (ed.) (1988).

Berland, Jody (1988) "Locating listening: Popular music, technological space, Canadian mediation." *Cultural Studies,* 2(3), pp. 343–358.

Berland, J. (1990a) "Radio space and industrial time: music formats, local narratives and technological mediation." *Popular Music,* 9(2), pp. 179–192.

Berland, J. (1990b) "Towards creative anachronism: radio, the state, and sound government." *Public 4: Sound.* Toronto.

Berland, J. (1991) "Sound, image and social space: Rock video and social reconstruction." In S. Frith, A. Goodwin and L. Grossberg (eds) (1991). Revised from (1986) "Sound, image and social space." *Journal of Communication Inquiry,* 10(1), pp. 34–47.

Berman, Marshall (1982) *All That is Solid Melts into Air: The Experience of Modernity.* New York: Simon and Schuster.

Berman, Morris (1981) *The Reenchantment of the World.* Ithaca: Cornell U. Press.

Bernal, Martin (1987) *Black Athena, vol. 1, The Fabrication of Ancient Greece, 1785–1985.* London: Free Association Books.

Betterton, Rosemary (ed) (1987) *Looking On: Images of Femininity in the Visual Arts and Media.* London: Pandora Press.

Bhabha, Homi (1983) "The other question—The stereotype and colonial discourse." *Screen,* 24(6), pp. 18–36.

Bhabha, H. (1990) "DissemiNation: Time, narrative, and the margins of the modern nation." In H. Bhabha (ed) *Nation and Narration.* London: Routledge.

Bingham, Sallie (1989) *Passion and Prejudice.* New York: Knopf.

Bird, Elizabeth (1987) "The social construction of nature: Theoretical approaches to the history of environmental problems." *Environmental Review,* 11(4), pp. 255–264.

Bisseret, Noelle (1979) *Education, Class Language, and Ideology.* London: Routledge.

Blackburn, Robin (1988) *The Overthrow of Colonial Slavery.* London: Verso.

Blackett, R. (1975) "In search of international support for African colonisation. Martin Delany's visit to England, 1860." *Canadian Journal of History,* 10(3), pp. 307–324.

Blackmur, R. P. (1957) "D. H. Lawrence and expressive form." *Form and Value in Modern Poetry.* New York: Doubleday, pp. 253–268.

"The Black scholar reader forum: Black male/female relationships." (1979) *The Black Scholar,* May/June, pp. 14–67.

Blanchot, Maurice (1987) "Everyday speech." *Yale French Studies,* 73, pp. 12–20.

Bleicher, Josef (ed) (1980) *Contemporary Hermeneutics.* London: Routledge.

Bloom, Lisa (1990) "Gender on ice: Ideological voyages of polar expeditions." PhD Dissertation. History of Consciousness Program, U. of Calif., Santa Cruz.

Bobo, Jacqueline (1988) " 'The Color Purple': Black women as cultural readers." In E. Deirdre Pribram (ed) *Female Spectators: Looking at Film and Television.* London: Verso.

Boime, Albert (1990) *The Art of Exclusion: Representing Blacks in the Nineteenth Century.* London: Thames and Hudson.

Bookchin, Murray (1990) *Remaking Society: Pathways to a Green Future.* Boston: South End Press.

"Bookseller, The" (1927) *The Saturday Review of Literature,* (Feb. 19), p. 598. Unsigned letter.

Boon, James A. (1990) *Affinities and Extremes.* Chicago: U. of Chicago Press.

Bordo, Susan (1989) "Feminism, postmodernism and gender–scepticism." In L. Nicholson (ed.) (1990), pp. 133–156.

Born, Georgina (1987) "Modern music culture: On shock, pop and synthesis." *New Formations,* 1(2), pp. 51–78.

Bourdieu, Pierre (1977) *Outline of a Theory of Practice.* Trans. R. Nice. Cambridge: Cambridge U. Press.

Bourdieu, P. (1984) *Distinction: A Social Critique of the Judgement of Taste.* Trans. R. Nice. Cambridge, MA: Harvard U. Press.

Bradley, Marion Zimmer (1985) "Responsibilities and temptations of women science fiction writers." In Jane Weedman (ed) *Women World-walkers: New Dimensions of Science Fiction and Fantasy.* Lubbock, TX: Texas Tech Press.

Braidotti, Rosa (1987) "Commento alla relazione di Adriana Cavarero." In M. Marcuzzo and A. Rossi Doria (eds) (1987).

Braidotti, R. (1989) "The politics of ontological difference." In T. Brennan (ed) *Between Feminism and Psychoanalysis.* London: Routledge.

Brantlinger, Patrick (1990) *Crusoe's Footprints: Cultural Studies in Britain and America.* New York: Routledge.

Brecht, Bertholdt (1964) *Brecht on Theatre.* Trans. J. Willett (ed). New York: Hill and Wang.

Bridges, George W. (1968 [1828]) *The Annals of Jamaica,* 2 vol. Frank Cass (reprint).

Briggs, Asa (1960) *The Rise of Entertainment as an Industry.* Adelaide: Fischer Lectures.

Bristow, Joseph (1989) "Being gay: Politics, identity, pleasure." *New Formations,* 9, pp. 61–82.

Brodkey, Linda (1990) "Towards a feminist rhetoric of difference." Unpublished paper. U. of Texas, Austin. 24pp.

Brody, Hugh (1982) *Maps and Dreams.* New York: Pantheon.

Brown, Karen M. (1991) *Mama Lola: A Vodou Priestess in Brooklyn.* Berkeley: U. of Calif. Press.

Brown, Peter (1978) *The Making of Late Antiquity.* Cambridge, MA: Harvard U. Press.

Broyles Gonzáles, Yolanda (1989) "Toward a re-vision of Chicano theater history: The women of El Teatro Campesino." In *Making a Spectacle: Feminist Essays on Contemporary Women's Theatre.* Ann Arbor: U. of Michigan Press, pp. 209–239.

Bruce, F. (1961) *The English Bible: A History of Translations.* Oxford: Oxford U. Press.

Bruce-Novoa, Juan (1975) "The space of Chicano literature." In Ortego and Conde (eds) *De Colores,* 1(4), pp. 22–44.

Bruce-Novoa, J. (1982) *Chicano Poetry: A response to chaos.* Austin: U. of Texas Press.

Bruce-Novoa, J. (1987) "History as content, history as act: The Chicano novel." *Aztlán,* 18(1).

Brunsdon, Charlotte and David Morley (1978) *Everyday Television "Nationwide."* London: British Film Institute.

Brunt, Rosalind and M. Jordin (1987) "The politics of 'bias': How television audiences view current affairs." In J. Hawthorn (ed) *Propaganda, Persuasion and Polemic.* London: E. Arnold.

Bryan, C. (1987) *The National Geographic Society: 100 Years of Adventure and Discovery.* New York: Abrams.

Bryant, Bernard (1987) Antibody method for lowering risk of susceptibility to HLA-associated diseases in future human generations. U.S. Patent No. 4,643,967 (17 Feb).

Budd, Mike, Robert Entman and Clay Steinman (1990) "The affirmative character of U.S. cultural studies." *Critical Studies in Mass Communication,* 7, pp. 169–184.

Burchell, William F. (1849) *Memoir of Thomas Burchell, 22 years a Missionary in Jamaica.* London: Benjamin L. Green.

Burgin, Victor (1990) "Paranoiac space." *New Formations,* 12, Winter, pp. 61–75.

Burkhardt, Jacob (1960 [1860]) *Civilization of the Renaissance in Italy.* New York: New American Library.

Burne, S. A. H. (1933) *Staffordshire Quarter Sessions Rolls,* vol. 3, Kendal, pp. 1594–1597.

Buxton, Charles (ed) (1848) *The Memoirs of Sir Thomas Fowell Buxton.* John Murray.

Byars, Jackie (1988) "Gazes/voices/power: Expanding psychoanalysis for feminist film and television theory." In E. Deirdre Pribram (ed) *Female Spectators: Looking at Film and Television.* London: Verso, pp. 110–131.

Cahill, Jack (1985) "Culture shock: How U.S. business put the squeeze on culture." *Toronto Star,* 23 Nov., BI, p.6.

Callicott, Baird (1986) "The search for an environmental ethic." In T. Regan (ed) *Matters of Life and Death.* New York: Random House, pp.381–424.

Callicott, B. (1989) *In Defense of the Land Ethic: Essays in Environmental Philosophy.* New York: SUNY.

Canclini, N. (1988) "Culture and power: The state of research." *Media, Culture and Society,* 10(4), pp.467–497.

Candler, John (1840–1841) *Extracts from the Journal of John Candler whilst Travelling in Jamaica,* 2 parts. London: Henry and Darton.

Carby, Hazel (1987) *Reconstructing Womanhood.* Oxford: Oxford U. Press.

Carby, H. (1990) "The politics of difference." *Ms: The World of Women,* Sept./Oct., pp.84–85.

Carey, James (1975) "Canadian communication theory." In G. Robinson and D. Theall (eds) *Studies in Canadian Communication.* Montreal: McGill U. Studies in Communications.

Carey, J. (1989) *Communication as Culture: Essays on Media and Society.* Boston: Unwin Hyman.

Carey, William (1792) *An Enquiry into the Obligations of Christians to use Means for the Conversion of the Heathens.* Leicester. Quoted in E. Daniel Potts (1967).

Carter, Paul (1987) *The Road to Botany Bay.* London & Boston: Faber and Faber.

Casteñeda, Shular and S. Ybarra-Frausto (eds) (1972) *Literatura Chicana: Texto y Contexto.* Englewood Cliffs, NJ: Prentice Hall.

Castles, Stephen, Mary Kalantzis, Bill Cope and Michael Morrissey (1988) *Mistaken Identity: Multiculturalism and the Demise of Nationalism in Australia.* Sydney: Pluto Press.

Caute, David (1988) *The Year of the Barricades: A Journey Through 1968.* London: Andre Deutsch.

Cavarero, A. (1987) "L'elaborazione filosofica della differenza sessuale." In M. Marcuzzo and A. Rossi Doria (eds) (1987).

Centre for Contemporary Cultural Studies (1982a) *Making Histories: Studies in History-Writing and Politics.* London: Hutchinson.

Centre for Contemporary Cultural Studies (1982b) *The Empire Strikes Back: Race and Racism in 70s Britain.* London: Hutchinson.

Centre for Contemporary Cultural Studies Education Group (1981) *Unpopular Education: Schooling and Social Democracy in England since 1944.* London: Hutchinson.

Césaire, Aimé (1972 [1955]) *Discourse on Colonialism.* New York: Monthly Review Press.

Chabram, Angie (1990) "Chicana/o studies as oppositional ethnography." *Cultural Studies,* 4(3), pp.228–247.

Chabram, A. and Rosa Linda Fregoso (eds) (1990) "Chicana/o cultural representations: Reframing alternative critical discourses." *Cultural Studies,* 4(3), pp.203–212.

Cham, M. and C. Andrade-Watkins (eds) (1988) *Blackframes: Critical Perspectives on Black Independent Cinema.* Cambridge: MIT Press.

Chambers, Iain, John Clarke, Ian Connell, Lidia Curti, Stuart Hall, and Tony Jefferson (1977) "Marxism and culture" [reply to Rosalind Coward]. *Screen* 18, pp.109–119.

Chambers, Iain (1986) *Popular Culture: The Metropolitan Experience.* New York: Methuen.

Chambers, I. (1990) *Border Dialogues: Journeys in Postmodernity.* New York: Routledge.

Chandler, Raymond (1942) "Letter to Alfred Knopf." In F. MacShane (ed) (1981) *Selected Letters.* New York: Columbia U. Press.

Chandler, R. (1944) "The simple art of murder." In (1980) *Pearls Are a Nuisance.* London: Pan Books.

Chandler, R. (1973) *Raymond Chandler Speaking.* D. Gardiner and K. Walker (eds). Harmondsworth: Penguin.

Chatterjee, Partha (1986) *Nationalist Thought in the Colonial World: A Derivative Discourse?* London: Zed Press.

Chatwin, Bruce (1987) *The Songlines.* Harmondsworth: Penguin.

Chen, Kuan-Hsing (1989) " 'If I'm not me, who are you?' Or collapsing the war zone between postmodernism and cultural studies." Paper delivered at the International Communications Association Conference, 25–29 May.

Cherryholmes, Cleo (1988) *Power and Criticism: Poststructural Investigations in Education.* New York: Teachers College Press.

Chibnall, Steve (1985) "Whistle and zoot: The changing meaning of a suit of clothes." *History Workshop Journal,* 20, pp. 56–81.

Chodorow, Nancy (1978) *The Reproduction of Mothering: Psychoanalysis and the Sociology of Gender.* Berkeley: U. of Calif. Press.

Chytry, J. (1989) *The Aesthetic State: A Quest in Modern German Thought.* Berkeley: U. of Calif. Press.

Clark, John, W. Dendy and J. Phillippo (1865) *The Voice of Jubilee: A narrative of the Baptist Mission, Jamaica.* London: John Snow.

Clark, Manning (1963) "The ruins of the ideologies." In I. Turner (ed) (1968) *The Australian Dream.* Melbourne: Sun Books.

Clark, T. J. (1982) "On the social history of art." In F. Frascina and C. Harrison (eds) *Modern Art and Modernism.* London: Harper & Row.

Clarke, John (1869) *Memorials of Baptist Missionaries in Jamaica, including a sketch of early religious instructors in Jamaica.* London: Yates and Alexander.

Clarke, John and Chas Critcher (1985) *The Devil Makes Work: Leisure in Capitalist Britain.* Urbana: U. of Illinois Press.

Clarke, J., Chas Critcher and Richard Johnson (1979) *Working Class Culture: Studies in History and Theory.* New York: St. Martin's.

Clarke, J., Stuart Hall, Tony Jefferson and Brian Roberts (1976) "Subcultures, cultures and class: A theoretical overview." In S. Hall and T. Jefferson (eds) (1976), pp.9–74.

Clifford, James (1981) "On ethnographic surrealism." *Comparative Studies in Society and History,* 23, pp.539–564.

Clifford, J. (1986) "On ethnographic allegory." In J. Clifford and G. Marcus (eds) (1986), pp.98–121.

Clifford, J. (1988) *The Predicament of Culture: Twentieth Century Ethnography, Literature, and Art.* Cambridge, MA: Harvard U. Press.

Clifford, J. (1990a) "Notes on (Field) notes." In R. Sanjek (ed) (1990), pp.47–69.

Clifford, J. (1990b) *"Documents:* A decomposition." In S. Stitch (ed) (1990).

Clifford, J. and Vivek Dhareshwar (eds) (1989) *Traveling Theory, Traveling Theorists, Inscriptions,* 5.

Clifford, J. and George Marcus (eds) (1986) *Writing Culture: The Poetics and Politics of Ethnography.* Berkeley: U. of Calif. Press.

Cloud, Random (1988) [see Randy McLeod] "What is the bastard's name?" Unpublished mss.

Cockerham, Henry (1623) *The English Dictionarie.* London.

Cohen, Ed (1989) "The 'hyperreal' vs. the 'really real': If European intellectuals stop making sense of American culture can we still dance?" *Cultural Studies,* 3(1), pp. 25–37.

Cohen, Robin (1987) *The New Helots: Migrants in the International Division of Labour.* Aldershot: Gower Publishing.

Cohen, Sara (1987) "Society and culture in the making of rock music in Liverpool." Unpublished Ph.D. Thesis. Oxford U.

Cohn, C. (1987) "Sex and death in the rational world of defense intellectuals." *Signs,* 12(4), pp. 687–718.

Coleman, Peter (1962) *Australian Civilization.* Melbourne: U. of Melbourne Press.

Collins, Jim (1989) *Uncommon Cultures: Popular Culture and Post-Modernism.* New York: Routledge.

Colls, Robert and Phillip Dodd (eds) (1987) *Englishness: Politics and Culture 1880–1920.* London: Croom Helm.

Comaroff, Jean (1985) *Body and Power, Spirit of Resistance.* Urbana: U. of Illinois Press.

Comolli, J.-L. (1980) "Machines of the visible." In T. de Lauretis and S. Heath (eds) *The Cinematic Apparatus.* New York: St. Martin's Press, pp. 121–142.

Conrad, Joseph (1957) *Victory.* Garden City: Doubleday.

Correa, Viola (1970) "La nueva chicana." Poem in The Chicana Caucus Papers.

Corr, H. and L. Jamieson (eds) (1990) *The Politics of Everyday Life: Continuity and Change in Work, Labour and the Family.* London: Macmillan.

Coser, Lewis, C. Kadushin and W. Powell (1982) *Books: The Culture and Commerce of Publishing.* New York: Basic Books.

Cosgrove, Stuart (1988[1984]) "The zoot suit and style warfare." In A. McRobbie (ed) *Zoot Suits and Second-Hand Dresses: An Anthology of Fashion and Music.* Boston: Unwin Hyman, pp. 3–22.

Cota-Cárdenas, Margarita (1980) "Manifestación tardía." *La Palabra,* 2(2).

Cotera, Martha. (1978) "La loca de la raza cósmica." *Comadre,* Spring (2).

Cotera, M. (1980) "Feminism: The Chicana and the Anglo versions." In M. Melville (ed) *Twice a Minority.* St. Louis: Mosby, pp.217–234.

Counter, S. Allen (1988) "The Henson family." *National Geographic,* Sept., pp. 423–429.

Coward, Rosalind (1977) "Class, 'culture' and the social formation." *Screen,* 18(1), pp. 75–105.

Coward, R. (1986) "Come back Miss Ellie: On character and narrative in soap operas." *Critical Quarterly,* 28 (1&2), pp. 171–178.

Coward, R. (1989) *The Whole Truth: The Myth of Alternative Health.* London: Faber & Faber.

Cowie, Elizabeth (1990) "Fantasia." In P. Adams and E. Cowie (eds) *The Woman in Question.* Cambridge, MA: MIT Press.

Cox, Rev. F. A. (1842) *History of the Baptist Missionary Society from 1792–1842,* 2 vol. London: T. Ward and Co.

Crane, Diana (1987) *The Transformation of the Avant-Garde: The New York Art World 1940–1985.* Chicago: U. of Chicago Press.

Craton, Michael (1982) "Slave Culture, resistance and the achievement of emancipation in the British West Indies 1783–1838." In J. Walvin (ed) (1982).

Crawley, Patrick (1986) "The Canadian difference in media: Or, why Harold Innis' strategy for culture is more relevant today than ever before." *Cinema Canada,* June, pp. 19–23.

Crenshaw, Kimberle (1989) "Demarginalizing the intersection of race and sex: A Black feminist critique of Antidiscrimination doctrine, feminist theory and antiracist politics." *The U. of Chicago Legal Forum,* pp. 139–167.

Crimp, Douglas (1983) "On the museum's ruins." In H. Foster (ed) *The Anti-Aesthetic: Essays on Postmodern Culture.* Port Townsend, WA: Bay Press, pp. 43–56.

Crimp, D. (ed) (1988) *AIDS: Cultural Analysis/Cultural Activism.* Cambridge, MA: MIT Press.

Crimp, D. and A. Rolston (1990) *AIDSDEMOGRAPHICS.* Seattle: Bay Press.

Crocombe, R. G. and Marjorie Crocombe (1968) *The Works of Ta'unga: Records of a Polynesian Traveller in the South Seas, 1833–1896.* Canberra: A.N.U. Press.

Crowley, Tony (1989) *Standard English and the Politics of Language.* Urbana: U. of Illinois Press.

Crump, Jeremy (1986) "Provincial music hall: Promoters and public in Leicester, 1863–1929." In P. Bailey (ed) (1986).

Cubitt, Sean (1989) "Introduction: Over the borderlines." *Screen,* 30(4), pp. 2–9.

Culler, Jonathan (ed) (1988) *On Puns: The Foundation of Letters.* Oxford: Basil Blackwell.

Cunningham, Stuart (1985) "Hollywood genres, Australian movies." In A. Moran and T. O'Regan (eds) *An Australia Film Reader.* Sydney: Currency.

Cunningham, S. (1989) "Textual innovation in the miniseries." In J. Tulloch and G. Turner (eds) *Australian Television: Programs, Pleasures, and Politics.* Sydney: Allen and Unwin, pp. 39–51.

Curti, Lidia (1988) "Genre and gender." *Cultural Studies,* 2(2), pp. 152–167.

Curti, L. (1990) "Imported utopias." In Z. Baransky and B. Lumley (eds) (1990).

Curtin, Philip D. (1955) *Two Jamaicas: The Role of Ideas in a Tropical Colony 1830–1865.* Cambridge, MA: Harvard U. Press.

Czitrom, Daniel (1982) *Media and the American Mind: From Morse to McLuhan.* Chapel Hill: U. of North Carolina Press.

Dark, Eleanor (1941) *The Timeless Land.* Sydney: Collins.

Das, Veena (1989) "Subaltern as perspective." In R. Guha (ed) (1982/9) (vol. 6).

Davidoff, Leonore (1979) "Class and gender in Victorian England." *Feminist Studies,* 5.

Davidoff, L. (1990) " 'Adam spoke first and named the orders of the world': Masculine and feminine domains in history and sociology." In H. Corr and L. Jamieson (eds) (1990).

Davidoff, L. and Catherine Hall (1987) *Family Fortunes: Men and Women of the English Middle Class 1780–1850.* London: Hutchinson.

Davies, K., J. Dickey and Teresa Stratford (1987) *Out of Focus: Writings on Women and the Media.* London: The Women's Press.

Davila, Juan and Paul Foss (1985) *The Mutilated Pietà.* Sydney: Artspace.

Davis, David Brion (1975) *The Problem of Slavery in the Age of Revolution 1770–1823*. Ithaca: Cornell U. Press.

Dayton, Abram (1882) *Last Days of Knickerbocker Life in New York*. New York: G. W. Harlan.

Debord, Guy (1981) "Detournement as negation and prelude." In K. Knabb (ed) *Situationist International Anthology*. Berkeley: Bureau of Public Secrets, pp. 55–56.

de Certeau, Michel (1984) *The Practice of Everyday Life*. Berkeley: U. of Calif. Press.

de Grazia, Margreta (1988) "The essential Shakespeare and the material book." *Textual Practice*, 2, pp. 69–86.

de Grazia, M. (1990a) "Homonyms before and after lexical standardization." *Deutsche Shakespeare—Gesellschaft West*, pp. 143–156.

de Grazia, M. (1990b) *Shakespeare Verbatim*. Oxford: Oxford U. Press.

Delany, Martin (1970) *Blake; or, the Huts of America*. Boston: Beacon Press.

de la Torre, Adela, and Beatriz Pesquera (eds) (1982) *Building with our Hands*. Berkeley: U. of Calif. Press.

de Lauretis, Teresa (1984) *Alice Doesn't*. Bloomington: Indiana U. Press.

de Lauretis, T. (ed) (1986) *Feminist Studies/Critical Studies*. Bloomington: Indiana U. Press.

de Lauretis, T. (1987) *Technologies of Gender: Essays on Theory, Film, and Fiction*. Bloomington: Indiana U. Press.

de Lauretis, T. (1989) "The essence of the triangle or, taking the risk of essentialism seriously: Feminist theory in Italy, the U.S., and Britain." *Difference*, 1(1), pp. 3–37.

Deleuze, Gilles (1986) *Foucault*. Paris: Les Editions de Minuit.

Deleuze, G. and Félix Guattari (1987) *A Thousand Plateaus*. Trans. Brian Massumi. Minneapolis: U. of Minn. Press.

Demographic Review Secretariat (1989) *Charting Canada's Future*. Ottawa: Health and Welfare, Canada.

Dening, Greg (1980) *Islands and Beaches: Discourse on a Silent Land: Marquesas, 1774–1880*. Honolulu: U. Press of Hawaii.

Dermody, S. and E. Jacka (1987) *The Screening of Australia: Volume One—Anatomy of a Film Industry*. Sydney: Currency.

Derrida, Jacques (1976) *Of Grammatology*. Trans. G. Spivak. Baltimore: Johns Hopkins U. Press.

Derrida, J. (1987) "Women in the beehive: A seminar." In A. Jardine and P. Smith (eds) (1987), pp. 189–203.

de Tocqueville, Alexis (1966[1856]) *L'Ancien Regime et la Revolution*. London: Collins.

Devall, Bill and George Sessions (1985) *Deep Ecology: Living as if Nature Mattered*. Layton, UT: Gibbs Smith.

Dhareshwar, Vivek (1989a) "Toward a narrative epistemology of the postcolonial predicament." *Inscriptions*, 5, pp. 135–157.

Dhareshwar, V. (1989b) "Self-fashioning, colonial habitus and double exclusion: V. S. Naipaul's *The Mimic Men*." *Criticism*, 31(1), pp. 75–102.

Doane, Mary Ann (1987) "The 'Woman's Film'—Possession and address." In C. Gledhill (ed) (1987), pp. 283–298.

Donald, James (ed) (1989) *Fantasy and the Cinema*. London: BFI Publishing.

Donzelot, Jacques (1979) *The Policing of Families*. London: Hutchinson.

Douglas, Mary (1966) *Purity and Danger: An Analysis of the Concepts of Pollution and Taboo*. London: Routledge.

Douglass, Frederick (1962) *Life and Times*. London: Macmillan.

Doyle, Brian (1989) *English and Englishness*. London: Routledge.

Du Bois, W. E. B. (1975) *Dark Princess*. London: Krause International.

Duncan, Carol and Allan Wallach (1980) "The universal survey museum." *Art History*, 3(4), pp. 448–469.

Dunn, Tony (1986) "The evolution of cultural studies." In D. Punter (ed) (1986), pp. 71–91.

Dutton, Geoffrey (1985) *Sun, Sea, Surf and Sand—The Myth of the Beach*. Oxford and Melbourne: Oxford U. Press.

Dworkin, Andrea (1987) *Intercourse*. New York: Macmillan.

Dyer, Richard (1986) *Heavenly Bodies: Film Stars and Society*. New York: St. Martin's Press.

Dyer, R. (1988) "White." *Screen*, 29(4), pp. 44–65.

Dyer, R. (1990) "More than meets the eye: The sad young man stereotype." Paper presented at the International Communications Association Annual Conference, Dublin.

Eagleton, Terry (1984) *The Function of Criticism*. London: Verso.

Eagleton, T. (1985) "Capitalism, modernism and post-modernism." *New Left Review*, 152, pp. 60–71.

Eagleton, T. (1990) *The Ideology of the Aesthetic*. Oxford: Basil Blackwell.

Edwards, Lee (1988) "The labors of Psyche." *Aperture*, 110, pp. 48–55.

Eickelman, Dale and James Piscatori (eds) (1990) *Muslim Travelers: Pilgrimage, Migration, and the Religious Imagination*. Berkeley: U. of Calif. Press.

Eimerl, Sarel and Irven Devore (1965) *The Primates*. New York: Time, Inc.

Elias, Norbert (1978) *The History of Manners*. New York: Urizen Books.

Elias, N. (1982) *State Formation and Civilization*. Oxford: Basil Blackwell.

Ellington, George (1869) *The Women of New York, Or the Underworld of the Great City*. New York: Arno Press.

Ellis, John (1982) *Visible Fictions: Cinema, Television, Video*. London: Routledge.

Ellis, Kate et al (eds) (1988) *Caught Looking: Feminism, Pornography, and Censorship*. Seattle: The Real Comet Press.

Ellison, Ralph (1952) *Invisible Man*. New York: Random House.

Ellman, Mary (1968) *Thinking About Women*. New York: Harcourt.

English-Hueck, J. A. (1990) *Health in the New Age: A Study in California Holistic Practices*. Albuquerque: U. of New Mexico Press.

Enloe, Cynthia (1990) *Bananas, Beaches, and Bases*. Berkeley: U. of Calif. Press.

"Environment has its price" (1989) *The Milwaukee Journal*, 21 May, p. A6.

Epstein, Barbara (1991) *Title*. Berkeley: U. of Calif. Press.

Erdman, David V. (1977) *Blake Prophet Against Empire*. Princeton: Princeton U. Press.

Estrella, Sara (c. 1972) "Yo soy la chicana de Aztlán." *Hijas de Cuahtemoc*. Long Beach.

Fabian, Johannes (1983) *Time and the Other*. New York: Columbia U. Press.

Fabian, J. (1986) *Language and Colonial Power*. New York: Cambridge U. Press.

Fabó, L. (ed) (1957) *1956—A magyar forradalon és szabadságharc a hazai rádióadások tükrében* (The Hungarian Revolution and Freedom War as Reflected by the Local Radio Broadcastings). San Francisco: Hidfo.

Fackelmann, Kathy A. (1990) "Zona Blasters." *Science News*, 138(24), pp. 376–379.

Fanon, Frantz (1965) *The Wretched of the Earth*. New York: Grove Press.

Fanon, F. (1967) *Black Skin, White Masks*. New York: Grove Press.

Fanon, F. (1980[1955]) "West Indians and Africans." *Toward The African Revolution.* London: Writers and Readers.

Faris, Robert (1967) *Chicago Sociology: 1920–1932.* Chicago: U. of Chicago Press.

"Fauci gets softer on activists" (1990) *Science,* 249, p. 244.

Fee, Elizabeth and Daniel M. Fox (eds) (1988) *AIDS: The Burdens of History.* Berkeley: U. of Calif. Press.

Fejtö, Ferenc (1989) "Kreonjaink áthágták a törvényeket (Our Kreons violated the laws)." In A. Tóbiás (ed) *In Memoriam Nagy Imre.* Budapest: Szabad Tér.

Felski, Rita (1989) "Feminism, postmodernism, and the critique of modernity." *Cultural Critique,* 13, pp. 33–56.

Ferguson, Marilyn (1980) *The Aquarian Conspiracy: Personal and Social Transformation in the 1980s.* Los Angeles: J. P. Tarcher.

Ferguson, Russell, Martha Gever, Trinh T. Minh-ha and Cornel West (eds) (1990) *Out There: Marginalization and Contemporary Cultures.* Cambridge, MA: MIT Press.

Ferraris, M. (1983) *Tracce.* Milan: Multhipla.

Finnegan, Ruth (1989) *Hidden Musicians.* Cambridge: Cambridge U. Press.

Fischer, Hans-Dietrich (1979) "Entertainment: An underestimated central function of communication." In H.-D. Fischer and S. Melnick (eds) *Entertainment: A Cross-Cultural Examination.* New York: Hastings House.

Fischer, Michael and Mehdi Abedi (1990) *Debating Muslims.* Madison: U. of Wisconsin Press.

Fiske, John (1987a) *Television Culture.* New York: Routledge.

Fiske, J. (1987b) "British cultural studies and television." In R. Allen (ed) *Channels of Discourse: Television and Contemporary Criticism.* Chapel Hill: U. of North Carolina Press.

Fiske, J. (1989a) *Understanding Popular Culture.* Boston: Unwin Hyman.

Fiske, J. (1989b) *Reading the Popular.* Boston: Unwin Hyman.

Fiske, J. (1990) "Ethnosemiotics: Some personal and theoretical reflections." *Cultural Studies,* 4(1), pp. 85–99.

Fiske, J., B. Hodge and G. Turner (1987) *Myths of Oz: Reading Australian Popular Culture.* Sydney, London, Boston: Allen & Unwin.

Flores, Francisca (1971) "Editorial." *Regeneración,* 1(10).

Flores, Juan and George Yudice (1990) "Living Borders/Buscando America." *Social Text,* 24, pp. 57–84.

Foner, Phillip (ed) (1970) *The Black Panthers Speak.* Philadelphia: Lippincott.

Forbes, John (1988) *The Stunned Mullet & Other Poems.* Sydney: Hale & Iremonger.

Foss, Laurence and Kenneth Rothenberg (1988) *The Second Medical Revolution: From Biomedicine to Infomedicine.* Boston: Shambala.

Foss, Paul (ed) (1988) *Island in the Stream: Myth of Place in Australian Culture.* Sydney: Pluto Press.

Foster, Arnold W. and J. Blau (eds) (1989) *Art and Society: Readings in the Sociology of the Arts.* Albany: SUNY Press.

Foster, George (1850) *New York by Gas-Light.* New York: Dewitt & Davenport.

Foster, Hal (1983) *Post-modern Culture.* London: Pluto Press.

Foster, H. (1989) "Wild signs: The breakup of the sign in seventies' art." In J. Tagg (ed) (1989), pp. 69–85.

Foucault, Michel (1970) *The Order of Things: An Archaeology of the Human Sciences.* New York: Random House.

Foucault, M. (1972a) *The Archaeology of Knowledge and the Discourse on Language.* New York: Pantheon.

Foucault, M. (1972b) "The discourse on language." In M. Foucault (1972a), pp. 215–237.

Foucault, M. (1979) "On governmentality." *I&C*, 6, pp. 5–22.

Foucault, M. (1980) *Power/Knowledge: Selected Interviews and other Writings: 1972–1977*. C. Gordon (ed). Trans. C. Gordon, L. Marshall, J. Mepham, K. Soper. New York: Pantheon.

Foucault, M. (1981) "Questions of method: An interview with Michel Foucault." *I&C*, 8, pp. 3–14.

Foucault, M. (1982) "Afterword." In H. Dreyfus and P. Rabinow *Michel Foucault: Beyond Structuralism and Hermeneutics*. Chicago: U. of Chicago Press, pp. 208–226.

Foucault, M. (1984) "What is enlightenment?" In P. Rabinow (ed) *The Foucault Reader*. New York: Pantheon Books.

Foucault, M. (1985) *The Use of Pleasure*. Harmondsworth: Penguin.

Foucault, M. (1986) *The Care of the Self*. New York: Pantheon Books.

Foucault, M. (1988) "The political technology of individuals." In L. Martin, H. Gutman, and P. Hutton (eds) *Technologies of the Self: A Seminar with Michel Foucault*. London: Tavistock.

Foucault, M. (1989) *Résumé des Cours: 1970–1982*. Paris: Julliard.

Fourmile, H. (1989) "Aboriginal heritage legislation and self-determination." *Australian-Canadian Studies*, 7 (1–2).

Frankena, William (1973) *Ethics*, 2nd ed. Englewood Cliffs, NJ: Prentice Hall.

Frankena, W. and J. Granrose (eds) (1974) *Introductory Readings in Ethics*. Englewood Cliffs, NJ: Prentice Hall.

Frankenberg, Ruth (forthcoming) *White Women, Race Matters: The Social Construction of Whiteness*. Berkeley: U. of Calif. Press.

Franklin, Sarah (1988) "Life Story: The gene as fetish object on TV." *Science as Culture*, 3, pp. 92–100.

Freud, Sigmund (1917) "Mourning and melancholia." In Freud, *Collected Papers* (vol. 4) New York: Basic Books.

Freud, S. (1958) *Dictionary of Psychoanalysis*. N. Fodor and F. Gaynor (eds). Greenwich, Conn.: Fawcett Publications.

Freud, S. (1963a) *Jokes and Their Relation to the Unconscious*. New York: Norton.

Freud, S. (1963b) "The economic problem of masochism." In P. Reiff (ed) *General Psychological Theory*. New York: Collier, pp. 190–201.

Frith, Simon (1987) "The aesthetics of popular music." In R. Leppart and S. McClary (eds) *Music and Society*. Cambridge: Cambridge U. Press, pp. 133–150.

Frith, S. (1988) *Music for Pleasure: Essays in the Sociology of Pop*. New York: Routledge.

Frith, S. and Andrew Goodwin (eds) (1990) *On Record: Rock, Pop and the Written Word*. New York: Pantheon.

Frith, S., Andrew Goodwin, and Lawrence Grossberg (eds) (1991) *Sound and Vision: The Music Television Reader*. Boston: Unwin and Hyman.

Frye, Northrop (1957) *Anatomy of Criticism: Four Essays*. Princeton: Princeton U. Press.

Fryer, Peter (1984) *Staying Power*. London: Pluto Press.

Fuentes, Carlos (1968) *A Change of Skin*. Trans. S. Hileman. New York: Farrar, Straus & Giroux.

Fukuyama, Francis (1989) "The end of history?" *The National Interest*, 16, pp. 3–18.

Fusini, N. (1987) "Commento alla relazione di Silvia Vegetti Finzi." In M. Marcuzzo and A. Rossi Doria (1987).

Fuss, Diana (1989a) *Essentially Speaking: Feminism, Nature and Difference*. New York: Routledge.

Fuss, D. (1989b) "Lesbian and Gay theory: The question of identity politics." In D. Fuss (1989a).

Gadamer, Hans-Georg (1976) "On the scope and function of hermeneutical reflection." In *Philosophical Hermeneutics*. Berkeley: U. of Calif. Press.

Gadamer, H.-G. (1980) "The universality of the hermeneutical problem." In J. Bleicher (ed) (1980).

Gal, Susan (1989) "Language and political economy." *Annual Reviews of Anthropology*, 18, pp. 345–367.

Galassi, Peter (1988) "Introduction." In *Nicholas Nixon: Pictures of People*. New York: Museum of Modern Art.

Gallagher, B. and A. Wilson (1987) "Sex and the politics of identity: An interview with Michel Foucault." In M. Thompson (ed) *Gay Spirit: Myth and Meaning*. New York: St. Martin's Press.

Gallie, William B. (1963) "Essentially contested concepts." In M. Black (ed) *The Importance of Language*. New York: Prentice Hall.

Gallop, Jane (1985) *Reading Lacan*. Ithaca: Cornell U. Press.

Gallop, J. (1988) *Thinking Through the Body*. New York: Columbia U. Press.

Gamboa, Jr., Harry (1980) "Gronk: Off-the-wall artist." *Neworld Magazine*, 6(4), pp. 33–43.

Gamboa, Jr., H. (1987) "The Chicano/a artist inside and outside the mainstream." *Journal of the Los Angeles Institute of Contemporary Art*, Winter.

Gamman, Lorraine and M. Marshment (eds) (1988) *The Female Gaze: Women as Viewers of Popular Culture*. London: Verso.

Gandoulou, Justin-Daniel (1984) *Entre Paris et Bacongo*. Paris: Centre Georges Pompidou, C.C.I.

Ganong, William (1975) *Review of Medical Physiology*, 7th ed. Los Altos, CA: Lange Medical Publications.

García, Alma (1990) "The development of chicana feminist discourse." In V. Ruiz and E. Dubois (eds) *Unequal Sisters*. London: Routledge, pp. 421–435.

Gatens, Moira (1991) "Corporeal representation in/and the body politic." In R. Diprose and R. Ferrell (eds) *Cartographies: Poststructuralism and the Mapping of Bodies and Spaces*. Sydney: Allen & Unwin.

Gates, Jr., Henry L. (1986) "Introduction." *"Race," Writing, and Difference*. Chicago: U. of Chicago Press, pp. 2–13.

Gates, Jr., H. (1987a) "Authority, (White) power and the (Black) critic; It's all greek to me." *Cultural Critique*, 7, pp. 19–46.

Gates, Jr., H. (1987b) *Figures in Black: Words, Signs, and the "Racial" Self*. New York: Oxford U. Press.

Gates, Jr., H. (1988) *The Signifying Monkey: A Theory of Afro-American Literary Criticism*. New York: Oxford U. Press.

Gates, Jr., H. (1989) "Whose canon is it, anyway?" *The New York Times Book Review*, Feb. 26.

Gay, E. Jane (1981) *With the Nez Perce: Alice Fletcher in the field, 1889–1892*. F. Hoxie and J. Mark (eds). Lincoln: U. of Nebraska Press.

Genet, Jean (1989) *Prisoner of Love*. London: Picador.

Gibson, William (1986) *Neuromancer*. New York: Ace.

Gilligan, Carol (1982) *In a Different Voice*. Cambridge, MA: Harvard U. Press.

Gilman, Sander (1982) *On Blackness Without Blacks*. London: G. K. Hall & Co.

Gilroy, Paul (1987) *There Ain't No Black in the Union Jack: The Cultural Politics of Race and Nation.* London: Hutchinson.

Gilroy, P. (1990a) "Art of darkness, Black art and the problem of belonging to England." *Third Text,* 10, pp. 45–52.

Gilroy, P. (1990b) "Climbing the racial mountain—An interview with Isaac Julien." *Mediamatic,* 4(4).

Gilroy, P. (forthcoming) "Richard Wright and the metaphysics of modernity." Introduction to R. Wright, *The Outsider.* London: Chatto.

Giroux, Henry (1988a) *Schooling and the Struggle for Public Life.* Minneapolis: U. of Minn. Press.

Giroux, H. (1988b) *Teachers as Intellectuals.* New York: Bergin and Garvey Press.

Giroux, H. (forthcoming, a) "Postmodernism as border pedagogy: Redefining the boundaries of race and ethnicity." In H. Giroux (ed) *Postmodernism, Feminism, and Cultural Politics: Redrawing the Boundaries of Educational Discourse.* Albany: SUNY Press.

Giroux, H. (forthcoming, b) "Rethinking the boundaries of educational discourse: Modernism, postmodernism, and feminism." *College Literature.*

Giroux, H., D. Shumway, P. Smith and J. Sosnoski (1984) "The need for cultural studies: Resisting intellectuals and oppositional public spheres." *Dalhousie Review,* 64(2), pp. 472–486.

Giroux, H. and R. Simon (eds) (1989) *Popular Culture, Schooling, and Everyday Life.* New York: Bergin and Garvey Press.

Gitlin, Todd (1989) *The Sixties: Years of Hope, Days of Rage.* New York: Pantheon.

Gledhill, C. (ed) (1987) *Home is Where the Heart Is: Studies in Melodrama and the Woman's Film.* London: BFI.

Glissant, Edouard (1981) *Le Discours Antillais.* Paris: Editions du Seuil.

Godzich, Wlad (1986) "Foreword: The further possibility of knowledge." In M. de Certeau *Heterologies: Discourse on the Other.* Trans. B. Massumi. Minneapolis: U. of Minn. Press.

Goldberg, Michael and J. Mercer (1986) *The Myth of the North American City: Continentalism Challenged.* Vancouver: U. of British Columbia Press.

Golub, Edward (1987) *Immunology: A Synthesis.* Sunderland, MA: Sinauer.

Gomez, A. (1975) "La Chicana." *Women Struggle,* p. 9.

Gonzalez, Rodolpho (1967) *I am Joaquin.* Denver: El Gallo.

Goodall, Jane (1971) *In the Shadow of Man.* Boston: Houghton Mifflin.

Goodman, Ellen (1987) "Whose right to life?" *The Sun,* Baltimore, MD, 17 Nov.

Gorz, André (1980) *Ecology as Politics.* Trans. P. Vigderman and J. Cloud. Boston: South End Press.

Gramsci, Antonio (1971) *Selections from the Prison Notebooks.* Trans. Q. Hoare and G. N. Smith (eds). London: Lawrence and Wishart.

Grasmuck, Sherri and Patricia Pessar (1991) *Between Two Islands: Dominican International Migration.* Berkeley: U. of Calif. Press.

Graves, C. Edward (1926) "The Humboldt College Plan of Recreational Reading." *Publisher's Weekly,* 24 July, pp. 244–248.

Green, Andre (1987) *On Private Madness.* New York: International Universities Press.

Green, Martin (1980) *Dreams of Adventure, Deeds of Empire.* London: Routledge.

Green, William A. (1976) *British Slave Emancipation: The Sugar Colonies and the Great Experiment 1830–1865.* Oxford: Oxford U. Press.

Greer, Germaine (1971) *The Female Eunuch.* London: Paladin.

Greimas, A. J. (1966) *Sémantique Structurale.* Paris: Larousse.

Griffith, Beatrice (1948) *American Me.* Boston: Houghton Mifflin.

Gross, Larry (1990) "Gender, identity and the view from the margin: Gay still means happy." Paper presented at the International Communications Association Annual Conference, Dublin.

Grossberg, Lawrence (1986a) "History, politics and postmodernism: Stuart Hall and cultural studies." *Journal of Communication Inquiry,* 10(2), pp. 61–77.

Grossberg, L. (1986b) "Teaching the Popular." In C. Nelson (ed) (1986), pp. 177–200.

Grossberg, L. (1987a) "Critical theory and the politics of empirical research." In M. Gurevitch and M. Levy (eds) *Mass Communication Review Yearbook,* vol. 6. London: Sage, pp. 86–106.

Grossberg, L. (1987b) "The in-difference of television." *Screen,* 2(8), pp. 28–45.

Grossberg, L. (1988a) (with) T. Fry, A. Curthoys and P. Patton *It's a Sin: Essays on Postmodernism, Politics and Culture.* Sydney: Power Publication.

Grossberg, L. (1988b) "Putting the pop back into postmodernism." In A. Ross (ed) (1988a), pp. 167–90.

Grossberg, L. (1988c) "Wandering audiences, nomadic critics." *Cultural Studies,* 2(3), pp. 377–391.

Grossberg, L. (1989a) "The context of audiences and the politics of difference." *Australian Journal of Communication,* 16, pp. 13–35.

Grossberg, L. (1989b) "The formations of cultural studies: An American in Birmingham." *Strategies,* 2, pp. 114–149.

Grossberg, L. (1989c) "The circulation of cultural studies." *Critical Studies in Mass Communication,* 6(4), pp. 413–420.

Grossberg, L. (1990) "Is there rock after punk?" In S. Frith and A. Goodwin (eds) (1990), pp. 111–123.

Grosz, Elizabeth (1989) *Sexual Subversions: Three French Feminists.* Sydney: Allen & Unwin.

Grundberg, Andy (1988) "Nicholas Nixon seeks a path to the heart." *New York Times,* 11 Sept., p. H37.

Guha, Ranajit (ed) (1982/9) *Subaltern Studies.* vols. 1–6. Delhi: Oxford U. Press.

Guha, R. (1982) "On some aspects of the historiography of colonial India." In R. Guha (ed.) (vol. 1), pp. 1–8.

Guha, R. (1989) "Dominance without hegemony and its historiography." In R. Guha (ed.) (vol. 6), pp. 210–309.

Guillory, J. (1969) "The pro-slavery arguments of S. A. Cartwright." *Louisiana History,* 9.

Gunew, Sneja (1988) "Home and away: Nostalgia in Australian (migrant) writing." In P. Foss (ed) (1988), pp. 35–46.

Gunew, S. (1990) "Denaturalizing cultural nationalism: Multicultural readings of 'Australia.' " In H. Bhabha (ed) *Nation and Narration.* New York: Routledge, pp. 99–120.

Gurevitch, Michael, Tony Bennett, James Curran, and Janet Woollacott (eds) (1982) *Culture, Society and the Media.* London: Methuen.

Gurney, Joseph J. (1840) *A winter in the West Indies described in familiar letters to Henry Clay of Kentucky.* London: John Murray.

Guyton, Arthur C. (1984) *Physiology of the Human Body,* 6th ed. Philadelphia: Saunders College Publishing.

Habermas, Jürgen (1980) "The hermeneutic claim to universality." In J. Bleicher (ed) (1980).

Habermas, J. (1983a) "Modernity—An incomplete project?" In H. Foster (ed) *The Anti-Aesthetic: Essays on Postmodern Culture.* Port Townsend, WA: Bay Press, pp. 3–15.

Habermas, J. (1983b) "Introduction." *Observations on "The Spiritual Situation of the Age."* Trans. A. Buchwalter. Cambridge, MA: MIT Press.

Hacker, Sally (1989) *Pleasure, Power, and Technology: Some Tales of Gender, Engineering, and the Cooperative Workplace.* Boston: Unwin Hyman.

Hall, Catherine (1989) "The economy of intellectual prestige: Thomas Carlyle, John Stuart Mill and the case of Governor Eyre." *Cultural Critique,* 12, pp. 167–196.

Hall, Douglas (1959) *Free Jamaica 1836–1865.* New Haven: Yale U. Press.

Hall, Stuart (1974) "Marx's notes on method: A 'reading' of the 1857 Introduction." *Working Papers in Cultural Study,* 6, pp. 132–171.

Hall, S. (1977) "Culture, the media and the 'ideological effect.' " In J. Curran et al, *Mass Communication and Society.* London: E. Arnold.

Hall, S. (1978) "Racism and reaction." In *Five Views of Multiracial Britain.* London: Commission for Racial Equality.

Hall, S. (1979) "The great moving right show." *Marxism Today,* Jan., pp. 14–20.

Hall, S. (1980a) "Cultural studies: Two paradigms." *Media, Culture and Society,* 2, pp. 57–72. Also (1986) In R. Collins et al (eds) *Media Culture and Society: A Critical Reader.* London: Sage, pp. 33–48.

Hall, S. (1980b) "Race, articulation and societies structured in dominance." In UNESCO, *Sociological Theories: Race and Colonialism.* Paris: UNESCO, pp. 305–345.

Hall, S. (1980c) "Cultural studies and the Centre: Some problematics and problems." In S. Hall et al (eds) *Culture, Media, Language.* London: Hutchinson—CCCS, pp. 15–47.

Hall, S. (1980d) "The hinterland of science." In The Centre for Contemporary Cultural Studies, *On Ideology.* London: Hutchinson.

Hall, S. (1980e) "Encoding and decoding." In S. Hall et al (eds) *Culture, Media, Language.* London: Hutchinson.

Hall, S. (1981) "Notes on deconstructing 'the popular.' " In R. Samuel (ed) *People's History and Socialist Theory.* London: Routledge, pp. 227–239.

Hall, S. (1982) "The rediscovery of 'ideology': Return of the repressed in media studies." In M. Gurevitch, T. Bennett, J. Curran, and J. Woollacott (1982), pp. 56–90.

Hall, S. (1983) "The problem of ideology—Marxism without guarantees." In B. Matthews (ed) *Marx 100 Years On.* London: Lawrence and Wishart, pp. 57–86.

Hall, S. (1985a) "Signification, representation, ideology: Althusser and the post-structuralist debates." *Critical Studies in Mass Communication,* 2(2), pp. 91–114.

Hall, S. (1985b) "Authoritarian populism: A reply to Jessop et al." *New Left Review,* 151, pp. 115–124.

Hall, S. (1985c) "Religious Ideology and Social Movement in Jamaica." In R. Bobcock and K. Thompson (eds) *Religion and Ideology.* Manchester: Manchester U. Press.

Hall, S. (1986a) "Gramsci's relevance for the study of race and ethnicity." *Journal of Communication Inquiry,* 10(2), pp. 5–27.

Hall, S. (1986b) "On postmodernism and articulation: An interview with Stuart Hall." L. Grossberg (ed). *Journal of Communication Inquiry,* 10(2), pp. 45–60.

Hall, S. (1986c) "A working bibliography. *Journal of Communication Inquiry,* 10(2), pp. 125–129.

Hall, S. (1987a) "The toad in the garden: Thatcherism among the theorists," and "Stuart Hall: Question and answer." In C. Nelson and L. Grossberg (eds) (1988), pp. 35–73.

Hall, S. (1987b) "Minimal selves." In *The Real Me: Postmodernism and the Question of Identity*. London: ICA, pp. 44–46.

Hall, S. (1988a) "New ethnicities." *Black Film, British Cinema*. ICA Documents, 7, pp. 27–31.

Hall, S. (1988b) *The Hard Road to Renewal*. London: Verso.

Hall, S. (1989) "Cultural identity and cinematographic representation." *Frame Works*, 36, pp. 68–81.

Hall, S. (1990a) "The emergence of cultural studies and the crisis of the humanities." *October*, 53, pp. 11–90.

Hall, S. (1990b) "Cultural identity and diaspora. In J. Rutherford (ed) (1990), pp. 222–237.

Hall, S., Chas Critcher, Tony Jefferson, John Clarke and Brian Roberts (1979) *Policing the Crisis: Mugging, the State, and Law and Order*. London: Macmillan.

Hall, S. and Fredric Jameson (1990) "Clinging to the wreckage: A conversation." *Marxism Today*, Sept. pp. 28–31.

Hall, S. and Tony Jefferson (eds) (1976) *Resistance Through Rituals: Youth Subcultures in Post War Britain*. London: Hutchinson.

Hall, S. with Lawrence Grossberg and Jennifer Daryl Slack (forthcoming) *Cultural Studies*. London: Macmillan.

Halloran, J. (ed) (1970) *The Effects of Television*. London: Panther.

Halsell, Grace (1969) *Soul Sister*. New York: World Publishing Co.

Hamer, Phillip M. (1935a) "British Consuls and the Negro Seamen's Acts 1850–1860." *Journal of Southern History*, 1, pp. 138–168.

Hamer, P. (1935b) "Great Britain, the United States and the Negro Seamen's Acts." *Journal of Southern History*, 1, pp. 3–28.

Handler, Richard (1987) *Nationalism and the Politics of Culture in Quebec*. Madison: U. of Wisconsin Press.

Hansberry, Lorraine (1969) *To Be Young, Gifted, and Black*. Englewood Cliffs, N.J.: Prentice Hall.

Harasym, Sarah (ed) (1990) [see G. Spivak, 1990]

Haraway, Donna (1988) "Situated knowledge." *Feminist Studies*, 14(3), pp. 575–599.

Haraway, D. (1989a) *Primate Visions: Gender, Race, and Nature in the World of Modern Science*. New York: Routledge.

Haraway, D. (1989b) "Technics, erotics, vision, touch: Fantasies of the designer body." Talk presented at the meetings of the Society for the History of Technology, 13 Oct.

Haraway, D. (1991) *Simians, Cyborgs, and Women: The Reinvention of Nature*. New York: Routledge.

Hardison, O. (1989) *Disappearing Through the Skylight*. New York: Viking.

Harland, Richard (1987) *Superstructuralism*. London: Routledge.

Harlow, Alvin (1931) *Old Bowery Days: The Chronicles of a Famous Street*. New York: D. Appleton & Co.

Harris, Angela (1990) "Race and essentialism in feminist legal theory." *Stanford Law Review*, 42.

Hartouni, Valerie (1991) "Containing women: Reproductive discourse in the 1980s." In C. Penley and A. Ross (eds) (1991).

Harvey, David (1978) "The urban process under capitalism." *International Journal of Urban and Regional Research*, 2, pp. 101–131.

Harvey, D. (1985) "The geopolitics of capitalism." In Gregory and Urry (eds) *Social Relations and Spatial Structures*. London: Methuen.

Harvey, D. (1989) *The Condition of Postmodernity.* Oxford: Blackwell.

Hayles, N. Katherine (1990) *Chaos Bound: Orderly Disorder in Contemporary Literature and Science.* Ithaca: Cornell U. Press, pp. 265–295.

Hawkes, Terence (1977) *Structuralism and Semiotics.* Berkeley: U. of Calif. Press.

Heale, William (1609) *An Apologie for Women.* London.

Heath, Stephen (1982) *The Sexual Fix.* London: Macmillan.

Hebdige, Dick (1979) *Subculture: The Meaning of Style.* New York: Routledge.

Hebdige, D. (1985) "Some sons and their fathers: An essay with photographs." *Ten-8,* 17, pp. 30–39.

Hebdige, D. (1986) "Postmodernism and 'The Other Side.'" *Journal of Communication Inquiry,* 10(2), pp. 78–98.

Hebdige, D. (1987a) "The bottom line on planet one: Squaring up to the face." *Ten-8,* 19, pp. 40–49.

Hebdige, D. (1987b) "Digging for Britain: An excavation in 7 parts." In *The British Edge.* Boston: Institute of Contemporary Arts.

Hebdige, D. (1988a) *Hiding in the Light: On Images and Things.* London: Routledge.

Hebdige, D. (1988b) "Hiding in the light: Youth surveillance and display." In D. Hebdige (1988a), pp. 17–36.

Hecht, Susanna and Alexander Cockburn (1989) *The Fate of the Forest: Developers, Destroyers, and Defenders of the Amazon.* New York: Verso.

Helms, Mary (1988) *Ulysses' Sail: An Ethnographic Odyssey of Power, Knowledge, and Geographical Distance.* Princeton: Princeton U. Press.

Hennion, Antoine (1990) "The production of success: An antimusicology of the pop song." In S. Frith and A. Goodwin (eds) (1990).

Hennis, W. (1988) *Max Weber: Essays in Reconstruction.* London: Allen & Unwin.

Henriques, Julian, W. Hollway, C. Urwin, C. Venn and V. Walkerdine (1984) *Changing the Subject: Psychology, Social Regulation, and Subjectivity.* New York: Methuen.

Hernández, Ester (1976) "La guadalupe militante." *La Razon Meztiza II,* [special edition], Summer.

Higgins, G. (1987) *Outlaws.* London: Andre Deutsch.

Hill, Christopher (1972) *The World Turned Upside Down.* New York: Viking.

Hindess, Barry (1986) "Interests in political analysis." In J. Law (ed) *Power, Action and Belief.* London: Routledge and Kegan Paul. And (1987) *Politics and Class Analysis.* Oxford: Basil Blackwell.

Hindess, B. (1988) unpublished seminar paper given at the Sociology Department, U. of Queensland.

Hinman, C. (1968) *The First Folio of Shakespeare.* New York: Norton.

Hinton, John H. (1847) *Memoir of William Knibb, Missionary in Jamaica.* London: Houlston and Stoneman.

Hoberman, J. (1988) "The fascist guns in the west." *Aperture,* 110, pp. 64–69.

Hobsbawm, Eric (1979) "The historians' group of the communist party" In M. Cornforth (ed) *Essays in Honour of A. L. Morton.* London: Humanities Press.

Hobson, Dorothy (1982) *Crossroads: The Drama of a Soap Opera.* London: Methuen.

Hoggart, Richard (1963) "A Question of tone: Some problems in autobiographical writing." *The Critical Quarterly,* 5(1), pp. 73–90.

Hoggart, R. (1969) "Contemporary Cultural Studies." C.C.C.S. Occasional Paper.

Hoggart, R. (1958; rpt. 1970) *The Uses of Literacy.* New York: Oxford U. Press.

Hoggart, R. (1972) *On Culture and Communication.* New York: Oxford U. Press.

Hohendahl, Peter (1982) *The Institution of Criticism.* Ithaca: Cornell U. Press.

hooks, bell (1989) *Talking Back.* Boston: South End Press.

hooks, b. (1990) *Yearning: Race, Gender, and Cultural Politics.* Boston: South End Press.

Horkheimer, Max and Theodore Adorno (1972) *Dialectic of Enlightenment.* Trans. J. Cumming. New York: Herder and Herder.

Horne, Donald (1964) *The Lucky Country.* Ringwood and Harmondsworth: Penguin.

Horne, D. (1976) *Money Made Us.* Ringwood and Harmondsworth: Penguin.

Hubbard, Ruth (1990) "Technology and childbearing." In *The Politics of Women's Biology.* New Brunswick, NJ: Rutgers U. Press.

Huerta, Jorge (1982) "The ultimate Pachuco: Zoot suit." *Chicano Theater: Themes and Forms.* Ypsilanti, MI: Bilingual Press/Editorial Bilingue, pp. 174–185.

Hughes, Robert (1987) *The Fatal Shore.* London: Collins Harvill.

Hunt, Lynn (1984) *Politics, Culture, and Class in the French Revolution.* Berkeley: U. of Calif. Press.

Hunter, Allen (1988) "Post-marxism and the new social movements." *Theory and Society,* 17, pp. 885–900.

Hunter, Ian (1988a) *Culture and Government: The Emergence of Literary Education.* London: Macmillan.

Hunter, I. (1988b) "Setting limits to culture." *New Formations,* 4, Spring, pp. 103–124.

Huther, Jürgen (1979) "Comments in the functional change of television viewing as a leisure pursuit." In H. Fischer and S. Melnik (eds) *Entertainment: A Cross-Cultural Examination.* New York: Hastings House.

Huyssen, Andreas (1986a) *After the Great Divide: Modernism, Mass Culture and Postmodernism.* London: Macmillan.

Huyssen, A. (1986b) "Mass culture as woman: Modernism's other." In A. Huyssen (1986a) and T. Modleski (1986b).

Huyssen, A. (1990) "Mapping the postmodern." In L. Nicholson (ed) (1990), pp. 234–277.

Illich, Ivan (1976) *Medical Nemesis: The Expropriation of Health.* New York: Pantheon.

Innis, Harold (1950) *Empire and Communications.* Oxford: Oxford U. Press.

Institute of Contemporary Arts (1987) *Identity: The Real Me.* London.

Institute of Contemporary Arts (1988) *Black Film, British Cinema.* London.

"Introduction." (1955) Book-of-the-Month Club Oral History Transcript, Columbia Oral History Collection. New York: Butler Library, Columbia U.

Irigaray, Luce (1974) *Spéculum de l'autre femme.* Paris: Minuit. (1985) *Speculum of the Other Woman.* Trans. G. Gill. Ithaca: Cornell U. Press.

Irigaray, L. (1978) *Ce sexe qui n'est pas un sexe.* Paris: Les Editions de Minuit.

Irigaray, L. (1985) *Etique de la différence sexuelle.* Paris: Les Editions de Minuit.

Irwin, Susan and Brigitte Jordan (1987) "Knowledge, practice and power: Court ordered cesarean sections." *Medical Anthropology Quarterly,* 3, pp. 319–334.

Itabari, Njer (1990) *Every Goodbye Ain't Gone.* New York: Random House.

Iyer, Pico (1988) *Video Night in Kathmandu: And Other Reports from the Not-So-Far East.* New York: Vintage.

Jacobus, Mary (1982) "Is there a woman in this text?" *New Literary History,* 14, pp. 117–141.

Jaimes, Annette (1987) "American Indian studies: Towards an indigenous model." *American Indian Culture and Research Journal,* 11(3), pp. 1–16.

James, C. L. R. (1981) *Notes on Dialectics.* London: Allison and Busby.

James, C. L. R. (1982) "Africans and Afro-Carribeans." *Ten–8,* 16, pp. 54–55.

James, C. L. R. (1984) *Beyond a Boundary.* New York: Pantheon.

Jameson, Fredric (1972) *The Prison-House of Language.* Princeton: Princeton U. Press.

Jameson, F. (1984) "Postmodernism, Or the cultural logic of late capitalism." *New Left Review,* 146, pp. 53–92.

Jameson, F. (1988) "Cognitive mapping." In C. Nelson and L. Grossberg (eds) (1988), pp. 347–357.

Jardine, Alice and Paul Smith (eds) (1987) *Men in Feminism.* London: Methuen.

Jaret, Peter (1986) "Our immune system: The wars within." *National Geographic,* 169(6), pp. 701–735.

Jasny, Barbara and Daniel Koshland, Jr. (eds) (1990) *Biological Systems.* Washington, D.C.: AAAS Books.

Jed, Stephanie (1989) *Chaste Thinking: The Rape of Lucretia and the Birth of Humanism.* Bloomington: Indiana U. Press.

Jenkins, Henry (1991) "*Star Trek* rerun, reread, rewritten: Fan writing as textual poaching." In C. Penley, E. Lyon, L. Spigel and J. Bergstrom (eds) *Close Encounters: Film, Feminism, and Science Fiction.* Minneapolis: U. of Minn. Press, pp. 170–203.

Jerne, N. (1985) "The generative grammar of the immune system." *Science,* 229, pp. 1057–1059.

Jesus González, Raphael (1967) "Pachuco: The birth of a creole language." *Arizona Quarterly,* 23(4), pp. 343–356.

John, Mary E. (1989) "Postcolonial feminists in the intellectual field: Anthropologists *and* native informants?" In J. Clifford and V. Dhareshwar (eds) (1989), pp. 49–73.

John, M. E. (1990) "Discrepant dislocations: Feminism, theory, and the post-colonial condition." Qualifying Essay, History of Consciousness Board. U. of Calif., Santa Cruz.

Johns, W. (1816) *A Collection of Facts and Opinions Relative to the Burning of Widows.* Birmingham.

Johnson, Elizabeth (1988) "Grieving for the dead, grieving for the living: Funeral laments of Hakka Women." In J. Watson and E. Rawski (eds) *Death Ritual in Late Imperial and Modern China.* Berkeley: U. of Calif. Press, pp. 135–163.

Johnson, Richard (1981) "Against absolutism." In R. Samuel (ed) *People's History and Socialist Theory.* London: Routledge, pp. 386–395.

Johnson, R. (1986) "The story so far: And further transformations?" In D. Punter (1986), pp. 277–313.

Johnson, R. (1986/7) "What is cultural studies anyway?" *Social Text,* 16, pp. 38–80.

Johnson, R. et al (1982) *Making Histories: Studies in History-Writing and Politics.* London: Hutchinson.

Jones, Simon (1988) *Black Culture, White Youth.* London: Macmillan.

Jordan, June (1981) "Black history as myth." In *Civil Wars.* Boston: Beacon Press, pp. 163–168.

Jordan, J. (1989) "Waiting for a taxi," *The Progressive,* June p. 16.

Jordin, M. and Rosalind Brunt (1988) "Constituting the television audience: A problem of method." In P. Drummond and R. Patterson (eds) *Television and Its Audiences, International Research Perspectives.* London: British Film Institute.

Judt, Tony (1990) "The unmastered future: What prospects for Eastern Europe?" *Tikkun,* 5(2), pp. 11–18.

Juteau, D. and N. Laurin-Frenette (1990) "Une sociologie de l'horreur: 'See no evil, hear no evil, speak no evil.' " *Sociologie et Sociétés,* 22(1).

Kádár, János (1985) *Selected Speeches and Interviews.* New York: Pergamon Press.

Kane, Joe (1989) *Running the Amazon.* New York: Knopf.

Kaplan, Caren (1986) "The poetics of displacement in Alicia Dujoune Ortiz's *Buenos Aires.*" *Discourse,* 8, pp. 84–100.

Kaplan, C. (forthcoming) *Questions of Travel: Postmodernism and the Poetics of Displacement.* Mss.

Katsiaficas, George (1987) *The Imagination of the New Left: A Global Analysis of 1968.* Boston: South End Press.

Kealy, Edward (1990) "From craft to art: The case of sound mixers and popular music." In S. Frith and A. Goodwin (eds) (1990). And (1979) *Sociology of Work and Occupations,* 6(1), pp. 3–29.

Keller, Evelyn Fox (1987) "Reproduction and the central project of evolutionary theory." *Biology and Philosophy,* 2, pp. 383–396.

Keller, E. (1990) "From secrets of life to secrets of death." In M. Jacobus, E. Fox Keller and S. Shuttleworth (eds) *Body/Politics: Women and the Discourse of Science.* New York: Routledge, pp. 177–191.

Kilgour, Maggie (1990) *From Communion to Cannibalism: An Anatomy of Metaphors of Incorporation.* Princeton: Princeton U. Press.

Kincaid, Jamaica (1988) *A Small Place.* New York: Farrar, Straus, Giroux.

King, Katie (1986) "The situation of lesbianism as feminism's magical sign: Contests for meaning and the U.S. women's movement, 1968–1972." *Communication,* 9(1), pp. 65–91.

King, K. (1990) "A Feminist apparatus of literary production." *Text,* 5 pp. 91–103.

King, K. (in progress) *Conversations: Some Travels of Theory in U.S. Feminism.* Women's Studies, U. of Maryland at College Park.

Kipnis, Laura (1986) "Refunctioning reconsidered: Toward a left popular culture." In C. MacCabe (ed) *High Culture/Low Theory.* New York: St. Martin's Press, pp. 29–31.

Klein, Jeffrey (1978) "Born against porn." *Mother Jones,* Feb./Mar., p. 18.

Knapland, Paul (1953) *James Stephen and the British Colonial System 1813–1847.* Madison: U. of Wisconsin Press.

Knibb, William (1832) "Speech at a public meeting of the friends of Christian mission." London: S. Bagster.

Knibb, W. (1833) "Speech on the immediate abolition of British colonial slavery." Newcastle: J. Blackwell and Co.

Knibb, W. (1842) "Jamaica." Speech to the BMS. London: G. and J. Dyer.

Knight, Stephen (1990) *The Selling of the Australian Mind: From First Fleet to Third Mercedes.* Port Melbourne, Australia: William Heinemann.

Kopácsi, Sándor (1986) *In the Name of the Working Class: The Inside Story of the Hungarian Revolution.* Trans. D. and J. Stoffman. Toronto: Lester and Orpen Dennys.

Koundoura, Maria (1989) "Naming Gayatri Spivak." *Stanford Humanities Review,* 1(1), pp. 91–95.

Krassner, Paul (1984) "Is this the real message of pornography?" *Harpers,* Nov., p. 35.

Kristeva, Julia (1979) *Eretica dell'amore.* Torino: LaRosa.

Kroker, Arthur (1984) *Technology and the Canadian Mind: Innis/McLuhan/Grant.* Montreal: New World Perspectives.

Krupnik, Mark (ed) (1983) *Displacement, Derrida and After.* Bloomington: Indiana U. Press.

Lacan, Jacques (1988) *The Seminars of Jacques Lacan.* New York: W. W. Norton.

LaCapra, Dominick (1985) *History and Criticism.* Ithaca: Cornell U. Press.

Laclau, Ernesto (1977) *Politics and Ideology in Marxist Theory.* London: New Left Books.

Laclau, E. (1980) "Populist rupture and discourse." *Screen Education,* 34, Spring.

Laclau, E. (1990) *New Reflections on the Revolutions of Our Time.* London: Verso.

Laclau, E. and Chantal Mouffe (1985) *Hegemony and Socialist Strategy: Towards a Radical Democratic Politics.* London: Verso.

Lamb, Patricia F. and Diana Veith (1986) "Romantic myth, transcendence, and *Star Trek* zines." In D. Palumbo (ed) *Erotic Universe: Sexuality and Fantastic Literature.* New York: Greenwood Press, pp. 235–256.

Lampland, Martha (1986) "The politics of poetry in Hungary: Historical consciousness and the revolution of 1956." Paper presented on the panel "The Ideological Constitution of Histories." American Anthropological Association, Dec. 1986.

Langan, Mary and Bill Schwarz (eds) (1985) *Crisis in the British State 1880–1930.* London: Hutchinson.

Laplanche, Jean and J. B. Pontalis (1968) "Fantasy and the origins of sexuality." *The International Journal of Psycho-Analysis,* 49.

Laplanche, J. and J. B. Pontalis (1973) *The Language of Psychoanalysis.* New York: Norton.

Lash, S. and S. Whimster (1987) *Max Weber, Rationality and Modernity.* London: Allen & Unwin.

Latimer, Dan (1984) "Jameson and postmodernism." *New Left Review,* 148, pp. 116–128.

Latour, Bruno (1987) *Science in Action: How to Follow Scientists and Engineers Through Society.* Cambridge, MA: Harvard U. Press.

Latour, B. (1990) "Postmodern? No, simply *A*modern! Steps towards an anthropology of science." *Studies in the History and Philosophy of Science,* 21(1), pp. 145–171.

Latour, B. (forthcoming, a) "One more turn after the social turn ... Easing science studies into the non-modern world." In E. McMullin (ed) *The Social Dimension of Science.*

Latour, B. (forthcoming, b) "Where are the missing masses? Sociology of a few mundane artifacts." In Bijker and Law (eds) *Constructing Networks and Systems.* Cambridge, MA: MIT Press.

Lave, Jean (1988) *Cognition in Practice.* Cambridge: Cambridge U. Press.

Lavie, Smadar (1990) *The Poetics of Military Occupation: Mzeina Allegories of Bedouin Identity under Israeli and Egyptian Rule.* Berkeley: U. of Calif. Press.

Lawrence, D. H. (1968) *Kangaroo.* Harmondsworth: Penguin.

Lawson, Sylvia (1983) *The Archibald Paradox.* Ringwood: Penguin.

Lazere, Donald (ed) (1987) *American Media and Mass Culture.* Berkeley: U. of Calif. Press.

Lazreg, Marnia (1988) "Feminism and difference: The perils of writing as a woman on women in Algeria." *Feminist Studies,* 14(1), pp. 81–108.

Leal, Odina Fachel (1990) "Popular taste and erudite repertoire: The place and space of television in Brazil." *Cultural Studies,* 4(1), pp. 19–29.

Leal, O. and R. Oliver (1988) "Class interpretations of a soap opera narrative: The case of the Brazilian novella *Summer Sun.*" *Theory, Culture and Society,* 5, pp. 81–89.

Leary, Warren (1990) "New focus on sperm brings fertility successes." *New York Times,* 13 Sept., B11.

Leavis, F. R. (1969) *English in Our Time and the University.* London: Chatto & Windus.

Le Doeuff, Michele (1979) "Operative reasoning: Simone de Beauvoir and existentialism." *I&C,* 6, pp. 47–58.

Le Doeuff, M. (1981/2) "Pierre Roussel's Chiasmas." *I&C,* 9, pp. 39–70.

Le Doeuff, M. (1989) *L'étude et le rouet.* Paris: Editions du Seuil.

Lee, Charles (1958) *The Hidden Public: The Story of the Book-of-the-Month Club.* Garden City, NY: Doubleday.

Lefebvre, Henri (1979) "Space: Social Product and use value." In J. W. Freiberg (ed) *Critical Sociology.* New York: Irvington Publishers.

Lefebvre, H. (1983) "Theses on modernism." In Buchloh, Guilbaut and Solkin (eds) *Modernism and Modernity.* Halifax: Press of the Novia Scotia College of Art and Design.

Lefebvre, H. (1984) *Everyday Life in the Modern World.* Trans. S. Rabinovitch. New Brunswick: Transaction Books.

Lefort, Claude (1986) *The Political Forms of Modern Democracy.* Oxford: Polity Press.

Legge, Gordon (1989) *The Shoe.* Edinburgh: Polygon.

Leonard, Elmore (1988) *Freaky Deaky.* New York: Arbor House.

Leopold, Aldo (1949) *A Sand County Almanac.* New York: Oxford U. Press.

Lesage, Julia (1987) "Artful racism, artful rape: Griffith's *Broken Blossoms.*" In C. Gledhill (ed) (1987).

Levine, S. (1972) "Art values, institutions and culture." *American Quarterly,* 24(2), pp. 131–165.

Lévi-Strauss, Claude (1963) *Structural Anthropology.* New York: Basic Books.

Lévi-Strauss, C. (1977a[1955]) *Tristes Tropiques.* New York: Washington Square Press.

Lévi-Strauss, C. (1977b) "A writing lesson." In Lévi-Strauss (1977a), pp. 331–343.

Lewin, Tamar (1987) "Courts acting to force care of the unborn." *New York Times,* 23 Nov., A1, B10.

Linebaugh, Peter (1982) "All the atlantic mountains shook." *Labour/Le Travailleur,* 10.

Linebaugh, P. and Marcus Rediker (1990) "The many headed hydra: Sailors, slaves and the atlantic working class in the eighteenth century." *Journal of Historical Sociology,* 3(3), pp. 225–352.

Locke, John (1989[1693]) *Some Thoughts Concerning Education.* J. W. and J. S. Yolton (eds). Oxford: Clarendon Press.

López, Phyllis (1978) "La chicana." *Comadre,* Spring (2).

Lord, Albert (1960) *The Singer of Tales.* Cambridge, MA: MIT Press.

Lorde, Audre (1984) *Sister Outsider.* Freedom, CA: The Crossing Press.

Lorenzana, Noemi (1974) "Hijas de Aztlán." *De Colores,* 1(3), pp. 39–43.

Lukács, Georg (1977) "Realism in the balance." In E. Bloch et al. *Aesthetics and Politics.* London: New Left Books, pp. 28–59.

Lynch, Michael (1985) *Art and Artifact in Laboratory Science: A Study of Shop Work and Shop Talk in a Research Laboratory.* London: Routledge.

Lyon, Elizabeth (1988) "The cinema of Lol V. Stein." In C. Penley (ed) (1988).

Lyotard, Jean-Francois and J. Thebaud (1985) *Just Gaming.* Trans. W. Godzich. Minneapolis: U. of Minn. Press.

MacCallman, Iain (1986) "Anti-slavery and ultra radicalism in early nineteenth century England: The case of Robert Wedderburn." *Slavery and Abolition,* 7.

MacDonald, Dwight (1953) "A theory of mass culture." *Diogenes,* 3, pp. 1–17.

Macdonell, Diane (1986) *Theories of Discourse.* London: Blackwell.

MacIntyre, Alasdaire (1984) *After Virtue,* 2nd ed. Notre Dame: Notre Dame.

MacIntyre, Michael (1989) "Hot couture." *The Face,* 2(14), pp. 84–89.

Madrid-Barela, Arturo (1973) "In search of the authentic pachuco: An interpretive essay." *Aztlán,* 4(1).

Mailer, Norman (1964) "The white negro." In *Advertisements for Myself.* New York: Andre Deutsch.

Malinowski, Bronislaw (1922) *Argonauts of the Western Pacific*. New York: Dutton.

Mani, Lata (1987) "Contentious traditions: The debate on *sati* in colonial India." *Cultural Critique*, 7, pp. 152–153.

Mani, L. (1990) "Multiple mediations: Feminist scholarship in the age of multi-national reception." *Feminist Review*, 35, pp. 32–38.

Mani, L. (forthcoming) *Contentious Traditions: The Debate on Sati in Colonial India, 1780–1833*. Berkeley: U. of Calif. Press.

Marable, Manning (1984) *Race, Reform and Rebellion: The Second Reconstruction of Black America, 1945–1982*. London: Macmillan

Marcus, George (1986) "Contemporary problems of ethnography in the modern world system." In J. Clifford and G. Marcus (eds) (1986), pp. 165–193.

Marcus, G. and Michael Fischer (1986) *Anthropology as Cultural Critique: An Experimental Moment in the Human Sciences*. Chicago: U. of Chicago Press.

Marcus, Greil (1989) *Lipstick Traces: A Secret History of the Twentieth Century*. Cambridge, MA: Harvard U. Press.

Marcuzzo, M. and Rossi Doria, A. (eds) (1987) *Alla ricerca delle donne: studi femministi in Italia*. Torino: Rosenberg & Sellier.

Margulis, Lynn and Dorian Sagan (1986) *Origins of Sex: Three Billion Years of Genetic Recombination*. New Haven: Yale U. Press.

Martin, Emily (1987) *The Woman in the Body: A Cultural Analysis of Reproduction*. Boston: Beacon Press.

Martin, E. (1991) "The egg and the sperm: How science has constructed a romance based on stereotypical male-female roles." *Signs: Journal of Women in Culture and Society*, 16, pp. 1–18.

Marx, Karl (1968[1859]) "Preface to a contribution to the critique of political economy." In *Marx and Engels Selected Works*. London: Lawrence and Wishart.

Marx, K. (1977) *Capital: A Critique of Political Economy*, vol.1. Trans. B. Fowkes. New York: Vintage Books.

Massey, Doreen (1984) *Spatial Divisions of Labour: Social Structures and the Geography of Production*. London: Macmillan.

Mattelart, Armand, Xavier Delcourt and Michelle Mattelart (1984) *International Image Markets: In Search of An Alternative Perspective*. London: Comedia.

Matthaeli, Julie and Teresa Amott (1990) "Race, gender, work: The history of Asian and Asian American women." *Race and Class*, 31(3), pp. 61–80.

Mayhew, Henry (1851) *London Labour and the London Poor, vol. 1, The London Street Folk*. London: Frank Cass & Co.

Mazón, Mauricio (1984) *The Zoot-Suit Riots: The Psychology of Symbolic Annihilation*. Austin: U. of Texas Press.

McKibbon, Bill (1989) *The End of Nature*. New York: Random House.

McLeod, Randy [See Cloud, Random]

McLuhan, Marshall (1964) *Understanding Media: The Extensions of Man*. New York: Signet Books.

McRobbie, Angela (1981) "Settling accounts with subcultures: A feminist critique." In T. Bennett, G. Martin, C. Mercer and J. Woollacott (eds) *Culture, Ideology and Social Process: A Reader*. London: Batsford Academic and Education Ltd., pp. 113–123. Rpt. in S. Frith and A. Goodwin (eds) (1990), pp. 66–80.

McRobbie, A. (1985) "Strategies of vigilance: An interview with Gayatri Chakravorty Spivak." *Block*, 10, pp. 5–9.

McRobbie, A. (1986) "Postmodernism and popular culture." *Postmodernism*. London: ICA, pp. 54–58.

McRobbie, A. (1991) "New times in cultural studies." *New Formations,* Spring, pp. 1–17.

Medina, José (1970) "The chicano has emerged from indohispanic roots." Drawing in P. Ortego (1973), p. 217.

Mehan, Hugh, Charles Nathanson and James Skelly (1990) "Nuclear discourse in the 1980s: The unravelling conventions of the cold war." *Discourse and Society.*

Mellencamp, Patricia (ed) (1990) *The Logics of Television.* Bloomington: Indiana U. Press, pp. 193–221.

Memmi, Albert (1965) *The Colonizer and the Colonized.* Boston: Beacon Press.

Mercer, Colin (1988) "Entertainment, or the policing of virtue." *New Formations,* 4, pp. 51–71.

Mercer, Kobena (1987) "Black Hair/Style Politics." *New Formations,* 3, pp. 33–54.

Mercer, K. (1988) "Diaspora culture and the dialogic imagination." In M. Cham and C. Andrade-Watkins (eds) (1988), pp. 50–61.

Mercer, K. (1990a) "Welcome to the jungle: Identity and diversity in postmodern politics." In J. Rutherford (1990), pp. 43–71.

Mercer, K. (1990b) *Powellism: Race, Politics and Discourse.* PhD dissertation. U. of London, Goldsmith's College.

Michaels, Eric (1987) *For a Cultural Future: Francis Jupurrurla Makes TV at Yuendumu.* Sydney: Artspace.

Middleditch, T. (1840) *The youthful female missionary: A memoir of Mary Ann Hutchins, wife of the Rev. John Hutchins, Baptist missionary, Savanna-la-mar, Jamaica; And daughter of the Rev. T. Middleditch of Ipswitch; Compiled chiefly from her own correspondence by her father.* London: G. Wightman and Hamilton Adams.

Middleton, Dorothy (1982) *Victorian Lady Travellers.* Chicago: Academy.

Midgley, Clare (1989) "Women and the anti-slavery movement 1780s-1860s." Ph.D. dissertation, U. of Kent.

Midgely, Mary (1983) *Animals and Why They Matter.* Athens, GA: U. of Georgia Press.

Miller, Jonathan and David Pelham (1984) *The Facts of Life.* New York: Viking Penguin.

Miller, Mark Crispin (1988) *Boxed In.* Chicago: Northwestern U. Press.

Miller, Neil (1989) "The compassionate eye." *Boston Globe Magazine,* 29 Jan., p. 36.

Miller, Nancy K. (ed) (1986) *The Poetics of Gender.* New York: Columbia U. Press.

Miller, Peter and Nikolas Rose (1990) "Governing economic life." *Economy and Society,* 19, pp. 1–31.

Mills, Sara (1990) "Discourses of Difference." *Cultural Studies,* 4(2), pp. 128–140.

Mills, S. (forthcoming) *Unexplored Continent: British Women's Travel Writing.* London: Routledge.

Minh-ha, Trinh T. (1986/7a) "Difference: A special third world women's issue." *Discourse,* 8, pp. 11–37.

Minh-ha, T. (ed) (1986/7b) *She, The Inappropriated Other. Discourse,* 8.

Minh-ha, T. (1989) *Woman, Native, Other: Writing Post-coloniality and Feminism.* Bloomington: Indiana U. Press.

Minson, Jeffrey (1989) "Men and manners: Kantian humanism, rhetoric and the history of ethics." *Economy and Society,* 18, pp. 191–220.

Mintz, Sidney (1974) *Caribbean Transformations.* Chicago: Aldine.

Modleski, Tania (1984) *Loving with a Vengeance.* London: Methuen.

Modleski, T. (1986a) "Femininity as mas(s)querade: A feminist approach to mass culture." In C. McCabe (ed) (1986) *High Theory, Low Culture: Analyzing Popular Television and Film.* New York: St. Martin's Press, pp. 37–52.

Modleski, T. (ed) (1986b) *Studies in Entertainment: Critical Approaches to Mass Culture.* Bloomington: Indiana U. Press.

Mohanty, Chandra (1988) "Under western eyes: Feminist scholarship and colonial discourses." *Feminist Review,* 30, Autumn, pp. 60–88.

Mohanty, Satya (1989) "Us and them: On the philosophical basis of political criticism." *Yale Journal of Criticism,* 2(2), pp. 1–31.

Montoya, José (1970) "El Louie." *Rascatripas,* vol 2. Oakland, CA. Republished in L. Valdez and S. Steiner (eds) (1972) *Aztlán, An Anthology of Mexican American Literature.* New York: Random House, pp. 333–337.

Montoya, J. (1977) *Pachuco Art: A Historical Update.* Sacramento: RCAF.

Moore, Jr., Barrington (1966) *Social Origins of Dictatorship and Democracy: Lord and Peasant in the Making of the Modern World.* Boston: Beacon Press.

Moore, Joan (1978) *Homeboys: Gangs, Drugs, and Prison in the Barrios of Los Angeles.* Philadelphia: Temple U. Press.

Moraga, Cherríe (1986) "From a long line of vendidas: Chicanas feminism." In T. de Lauretis (ed) (1986), pp. 173–190.

Morgan, Robin (ed) (1970) *Sisterhood.* New York: Pantheon.

Morley, David (1980) *The "Nationwide" Audience.* London: BFI.

Morley, David and Ien Ang (1989) "Mayonnaisse culture and other European follies." *Cultural Studies,* 3(2), pp.133–144.

Morowitz, Harold (1972) "Biology as a cosmological science." *Main Currents in Modern Thought,* 28.

Morris, Lloyd (1951) *Incredible New York: High Life and Low Life of the Last Hundred Years.* New York: Random House.

Morris, Meaghan (1988a) "At Henry Parkes Motel." *Cultural Studies,* 2(1), pp. 1–47.

Morris, M. (1988b) "Panorama: The live, the dead and the living." In P. Foss (ed) (1988), pp. 160–187.

Morris, M. (1988c) "Operative reasoning: Reading Michele Le Doeuff." In *The Pirate's Fiancée: Feminism, Reading, Postmodernism.* London: Verso, pp. 71–102.

Morris, M. (1989) "Fate and the family sedan." *East-West Film Journal,* 4(1), pp. 113–134.

Morris, M. (1990a) "Banality in cultural studies." In P. Mellencamp (ed) (1990), pp. 14–43. And (1988) *Block 14,* Autumn. And (1988) *Discourse,* 10(2), pp. 3–29.

Morris, M. (1990b) "Metamorphoses at Sydney Tower." *New Formations,* 11, Summer, pp. 5–18.

Morris, M. (forthcoming) "Great moments in social climbing: King Kong and the Human Fly." In B. Colominia (ed) *Sexuality and Space.* New York: DIA.

Morris, M. and A. Freedman (1981) "Import rhetoric: Semiotics in/and Australia" (Part One, "Catatonia"). In P. Botsman, C. Burns and P. Hutchings (eds) *The Foreign Bodies Papers.* Sydney: Local Consumption Publications, pp. 122–139.

Morrison, Toni (1987) *Beloved.* New York: Knopf.

Morse, Margaret (1990) "An ontology of everyday distraction: The freeway, the mall, and television." In P. Mellencamp (ed) (1990), pp. 193–221.

Mosco, Vincent (1990) "Towards a transnational world information order: The Canada-U.S. free trade agreement." *Canadian Journal of Communications,* 15(2), pp. 46–53.

Mouer, Ross and Yoshio Sugimoto (eds) (1990) *The MFP [Multi Function Polis] Debate.* Melbourne: La Trobe U. Press.

Mouffe, Chantal (1988a) "The civics lesson." *The New Statesman and Society,* 7 Oct., p. 28.

Mouffe, C. (1988b) "Radical democracy: Modern or postmodern." In A. Ross (ed) (1988a), pp. 31–45.

Mouffe, C. (1988c) "Hegemony and new political subjects: Toward a new concept of Democracy." In C. Nelson and L. Grossberg (eds) (1988).

Mountcastle, Vernon B. (1980) *Medical Physiology,* vol. 2, 14th ed. London: The C. V. Mosby Co.

Moyers, Bill (1989) *Bill Moyers: The Public Mind.* PBS, Nov.

Moyles, R. G. (1985) *The Text of Paradise Lost: A Study in Editorial Procedure.* Toronto: U. of Toronto Press.

Muecke, Stephen (1990) "No road: (Vague directions for the study of tourism.)" *Meanjin,* 49(3), pp. 402–409.

Mulvey, Laura (1986) "Magnificent obsession." *Parachute 42,* 6(12).

Mulvey, L. (1989) *Visual and Other Pleasures.* London: Macmillan.

Muñoz, Jr., C. (1989) *Youth, Identity, Power: The Chicano Movement.* New York: Verso.

Murray, Les (1990) *The Vernacular Republic: Poems 1961–1983.*Sydney: Angus & Robertson.

Naess, Arne (1973) "The shallow and the deep, long-range ecology movement: A summary." *Inquiry,* 16.

Nagy, E. (ed) (1984) *1956—A forradalon sajtója* (The Press of the Revolution). Giromagny: Ernest Nagy.

Naipaul, V. S. (1976) *Mimic Men.* Harmondsworth: Penguin.

Nairn, Tom (1981) "The modern Janus." *In The Break-Up of Britain: Crisis and Neo-Nationalism,* 2nd enlarged ed. London: Verso.

Nead, Lynn (1987) "The Magdalen in modern times: The mythology of the fallen woman in Pre-Raphaelite painting." In R. Betterton (ed) (1987), pp. 73–92.

Nead, Lynda (1989) *Myths of Sexuality: Representations of Women in Victorian Britain.* London: Blackwell.

Nelson, Cary (ed) (1986) *Theory in the Classroom.* Urbana: U. of Illinois Press.

Nelson, C. (1987) "Men, feminism: The materiality of discourse." In A. Jardine and P. Smith (eds) (1987), pp. 153–172, 278.

Nelson, C. (1989) *Repression and Recovery: Modern American Poetry and the Politics of Cultural Memory, 1910–1945.* Madison: U. of Wisconsin Press.

Nelson, C. (1991) "Always already cultural studies: Two conferences and a manifesto." *Journal of the Midwest Modern Language Association,* 24(1), pp. 24–38.

Nelson, C. and Lawrence Grossberg (eds) (1988) *Marxism and the Interpretation of Culture.* Urbana: U. of Illinois Press.

Nelson, Joyce (1987) *The Perfect Machine: TV in the Nuclear Age.* Toronto: Between the Lines.

Nestle, Joan (1990) "The will to remember: The Lesbian Herstory Archives of New York." *Feminist Review,* 34, pp. 86–99.

Newfield, Christopher (1989) "The politics of male suffering: Masochism and hegemony in the American Renaissance." *Differences,* 1(3), pp. 55–87.

Newton, Huey P. (1973) *Revolutionary Suicide.* London: Wildwood House.

Nicholson, Linda J. (ed) (1990) *Feminism/Postmodernism.* New York: Routledge.

Nieto-Gómez, Anna (1976) "La chicana." *Women Struggle,* 9.

Nightingale, Virginia (1989) "What's 'ethnographic' about ethnographic audience research." *Australian Journal of Communication,* 16, pp. 50–63.

Nilsson, Lennart (1975) "A portrait of the sperm." In *The Functional Anatomy of the Spermatozoan.* B. Afzelius (ed). New York: Pergamon, pp. 79–82.

Nilsson, L. (1977) *A Child is Born*. New York: Dell.

Nilsson, L. (1987) *The Body Victorious: The Illustrated Story of Our Immune System and Other Defenses of the Human Body*. New York: Delacourt.

Nilsson, L. (1990) "The first days of creation." *Life*, 13(10), pp.26–43.

Noske, Barbara (1989) *Humans and Other Animals: Beyond the Boundaries of Anthropology*. London: Pluto Press.

O'Connor, Alan (1989) "The problem of American cultural studies." *Critical Studies in Mass Communication*, 6, pp. 405–413.

Oestreich, Gerhard (1982) *Neostoicism and the Early Modern State*. Cambridge: Cambridge U. Press.

O'Hanlon, Rosalind (1988) "Recovering the subject: Subaltern studies and histories of resistance in colonial South Asia." *Modern Asian Studies*, 22(1), pp. 189–224.

Olander, William (1988) " 'I undertook this project as a personal exploration of the human components of an *Alarming Situation*' 3 Vignettes (2)." *New Observations*, 61, Oct.

Ong, Aihwa (1987) *Spirits of Resistance and Capitalist Discipline*. Albany: SUNY Press.

O'Regan, Tom (1988/9) "Towards a high communication policy." *Continuum*, 2(1).

Orgel, Stephen (1981) "What is a text?" *Research Opportunities in Renaissance Drama*, 24, pp. 3–6.

Ortego, Phillip D. (ed) (1973) *We Are Chicanos*. New York: Washington Square Press.

Orton, Fred and Griselda Pollock (1980) "Les données Bretonnantes: La prairie de représentation." *Art History*, 3(3), pp. 314–344.

Overton, Richard (1646) *An Arrow Against Our Tyrants*. London.

Owens, Craig (1985) "The discourse of others: Feminists and postmodernism." In H. Foster (ed) *The Anti-Aesthetic*. Port Townsend, WA: Bay Press.

Oxford University Socialist Discussion Group (ed) (1989) *Out of Apathy: Voices of the New Left 30 Years On*. London: Verso.

Paredes, Américo (1982 [1958]) *With His Pistol in His Hand*. Austin: U. of Texas Press.

Park, Robert and R. McKenzie (eds) (1967) *The City*. Chicago: U. of Chicago Press.

Parker, Patricia (1987) *Literary Fat Ladies: Rhetoric, Gender, Property*. London: Methuen.

Parker, R. and G. Pollock (1983) *Old Mistresses: Women, Art and Ideology*. London: Routledge.

Parkin, F. (1972) *Class Inequality and Political Order*. London: Paladin

Parmar, Pratibha (1989) "Other kinds of dreams." *Feminist Review* 31, Spring, pp. 55–66.

Parmar, P. (1990) "Black feminism: The politics of articulation." In J. Rutherford (ed) (1990), pp. 101–126.

Parry, Benita (1987) "Problems in current theories of colonial discourse." *Oxford Literary Review*, 9 (1–2), pp. 27–58.

Patai, Daphne (1988) "Who's calling whom subaltern?" *Women and Language*. 11(2), pp. 23–26.

Patrick, Lannie (1989) "Global economy, global communication: The Canada-U.S. free trade agreement." In M. Raboy and P. Bruck (eds) *Communication: For and Against Democracy*. Montreal: Black Rose Books.

Patten, Leslie with Terry Patten (1988) *Biocircuits: Amazing New Tools for Energy Health*. Tiburon, CA: H. J. Kramer.

Patterson, Orlando (1987) "The emerging west atlantic system: Migration, culture, and underdevelopment in the United States and the Circum-Caribbean region." In W. Alonso (ed) (1987), pp. 227–260.

Payne, E. A. (1933) *Freedom in Jamaica*. London: Carey Press.

Paz, Octavio (1961) "The pachuco and other extremes." *The Labyrinth of Solitude*. Trans. L. Kemp, Y. Milos and R. Belash. New York: Grove Press.

Peers, Frank (1969) *The Politics of Canadian Broadcasting, 1920–1951*. Toronto: U. of Toronto Press.

Penley, Constance (ed) (1988) *Feminism and Film Theory*. New York and London: Routledge and BFI Publishing.

Penley, C. (1989) *The Future of an Illusion: Film, Feminism, and Psychoanalysis*. Minneapolis: U. of Minn. Press.

Penley, C. (1991) "Brownian motion: Women, tactics and technology." In C. Penley and A. Ross (eds) (1991).

Penley, C. and Andrew Ross (eds) (1991) *Technoculture*. Minneapolis: U. of Minn. Press.

Petchesky, Rosalind (1987) "Fetal images: The power of visual culture in the politics of reproduction." *Feminist Studies*, 13(2), pp. 263–292.

Phillip, D. (1980) " 'A new engine of power and authority': The institutionalization of law enforcement in England; 1780–1830." In V. A. Gatrell (ed) *Crime and The Law*. London: Europa Publications.

Phillippo, James M. (1843) *Jamaica: Its Past and Present State*. London: John Snow.

Phillips, Arthur Angell (1958) *The Australian Tradition: Studies in a Colonial Culture*. Melbourne: U. of Melbourne Press.

Pinkney, Tony (1989) "Editor's introduction: Modernism and cultural theory." In R. Williams (1989a).

Plank, William (1989) "Ape and *Ecriture*: The chimpanzee as post-structuralist." Paper presented at the meetings of the Society for Literature and Science, Ann Arbor, MI, 21–24 Sept.

Playfair, J. (1984) *Immunology at a Glance*, 3rd ed. Oxford: Blackwell.

Policar, Alain (1990) "Racism and its mirror images." *Telos*, 83, pp. 99–108.

Pollock, Griselda (1977) "What's wrong with images of women?" *Screen Education*, 24.

Pomata, Gianna (1989) "Versions of narrative: Overt and covert narrators in nineteenth century historiography." *History Workshop*, 27, pp. 1–17.

Popular Memory Group (1982) "Popular memory: Theory, politics, method." In R. Johnson et al (1982), pp. 205–252.

Porter, Carolyn (1990) "History and literature: After the new historicism." *New Literary History*, 21(2), pp. 253–272.

Porter, G. (1988) "Putting your house in order: Representations of women and domestic life." In Lumley (ed) *The Museum Time-Machine: Putting Cultures on Display*. London: Routledge.

Potts, E. Daniel (1967) *British Baptist Missionaries in India, 1793–1837*. Cambridge: Cambridge U. Press.

Poulantzas, Nicos (1978) *State, Power, Socialism*. London: Verso.

Powell, Enoch (1969) *Freedom and Reality*. Farnham: Elliot Right Way Books.

Pratt, Mary Louise (forthcoming) *Imperial Eyes: Studies in Travel Writing and Transculturation*. London: Routledge.

Punter, David (ed) (1986) *Introduction to Contemporary Cultural Studies*. London: Longman.

Puttenham, George (1589[1970]) *The Arte of English Poesie*. Kent, OH: Kent State U. Press.

Rachels, James (1986) *The Elements of Moral Philosophy*. New York: Random House.

Radway, Janice A. (1984) *Reading the Romance: Women, Patriarchy, and Popular Literature*. Chapel Hill: U. of North Carolina Press.

Radway, J. (1986a) "Reading is not eating: Mass produced literature and the theoretical, methodological and political consequences of a metaphor." *Book Research Quarterly*, 2, pp. 7–29.

Radway, J. (1986b) "Identifying ideological seams: Mass culture, analytical method, and political practice." *Communication*, 9(1), pp. 93–123.

Radway, J. (1988) "Reception study: Ethnography and the problems of dispersed audiences and nomadic subjects." *Cultural Studies*, 2(3), pp. 359–367.

Radway, J. (1990) "The scandal of the middlebrow: The Book-of-the-Month Club, class fracture, and cultural authority." *South Atlantic Quarterly*, Fall, pp. 703–737.

Rajan, Rajeswari Sunder (1990) "The subject of *sati*: Pain and death in the contemporary discourse on *sati*." *Yale Journal of Criticism*, 3(2), pp. 1–23.

Rakow, Lana F. (1986) "Feminist approaches to popular culture: Giving patriarchy its due." *Communication*, 9(1), pp. 19–41.

Rasy, Elisabetta (1978) *La lingua della nutrice*. Roma: Edizioni delle Donne.

Rediker, Marcus (1987) *Between the Devil and the Deep Blue Sea: Merchant Seamen, Pirates, and the Anglo-American Maritime World. 1700–1750*. Cambridge: Cambridge U. Press.

Reed, Sally and Craig Sautter (1990) "Children of poverty: The status of 12 million young Americans." *Phi Delta Kappan*, June, pp. 1–13.

Rees, A. and F. Borzello (eds) (1986) *The New Art History*. London: Camden Press.

Regan, Tom (1983) *The Case for Animal Rights*. Berkeley: U. of Calif. Press.

Regan, T. (ed) (1984) *Earthbound: New Introductory Essays in Environmental Ethics*. New York: Random House.

Rella, Franco (1989) "Ho tanta nostalgia di Brecht e Lukács." *Mercurio: La Republica*, 10 June.

Rendon, Armando B. (1972) *The Chicano Manifesto*. New York: Collier.

Revkin, Andrew (1990) *The Burning Season*. New York: Houghton Mifflin.

Reynolds, Henry (1982) *The Other Side of the Frontier: Aboriginal Resistance to the European Invasion of Australia*. Ringwood and Harmondsworth: Penguin.

Reynolds, H. (1987) *The Law of the Land*. Ringwood and Harmondsworth: Penguin.

Rice, C. Duncan (1982) "The missionary context of the anti-slavery movement." In J. Walvin (ed) (1982).

Rich, Adrienne (1986) "Notes toward a politics of location." *Blood, Bread and Poetry: Selected Prose, 1979–1985*. New York: Norton.

Rich, B. Ruby (1986) "Anti-porn: Soft issue, hard world." In C. Brunsdon (ed) *Films for Women*. London: BFI, pp. 31–43.

Richardson, Samuel (1980[1740]) *Pamela: Or, Virtue Rewarded*. Harmondsworth: Penguin.

Riley, Denise (1988) *"Am I That Name?" Feminism and the Category of "Women" in History*. Minneapolis: U. of Minn. Press.

Rimbaud, Arthur (1965[1873]) "A season in hell." In W. Fowlie (ed) *Illuminations: Complete Works of Arthur Rimbaud*. Chicago: U. of Chicago Press.

Ripley, C. Peter (ed) (1986) *The Black Abolitionist Papers, vol.2, Canada 1830–1865*. Chapel Hill: U. of North Carolina Press.

Robert, Marthe (1972) *Roman des origines et origines du roman*. Paris: Gallimard.

Roberts, R. (1971) *The Classic Slum*. Manchester: Manchester U. Press.

Robinson, Ted (1926) "The book habit: An inquiry in four parts." *Publisher's Quarterly*, 8, 15 May and 5 June, pp. 1530–1531, 1593–1594, 1840–1842.

Rodríguez, Raquel (1978) "Yo soy mujer." *Comadre*, 18.

Romano, Octavio (1969) "The historical and intellectual presence of Mexican-Americans." *El Grito,* 2(2).

Romano, O. (1970) *El Espejo—The Mirror.* Berkeley: Quinto Sol.

Rorty, Richard (1989) *Contingency, Irony, and Solidarity.* New York: Cambridge U. Press.

Rosaldo, Renato (1989) *Culture and Truth: The Remaking of Social Analysis.* Boston: Beacon Press.

Rose, Jacqueline (1986) *Sexuality in the Field of Vision.* London: Verso.

Rosing, Helmut (1984) "Listening behavior and musical preferences in the age of 'transmitted music.' " *Popular Music,* 5: Continuity and Change, pp. 119–149.

Ross, Andrew (ed) (1988a) *Universal Abandon? The Politics of Post-modernism.* Minneapolis: U. of Minn. Press.

Ross, A. (1988b) "Introduction." To A. Ross (ed) (1988a), pp. vii–xviii.

Ross, A. (1989a) *No Respect: Intellectuals and Popular Culture.* London: Routledge.

Ross, A. (1989b) "The popularity of pornography." In A. Ross (1989a), pp. 171–208.

Roth, Michael S. (1987) *Psychoanalysis as History: Negation and Freedom in Freud.* Ithaca: Cornell U. Press.

Rothenberg, Paula (1990) "The construction, deconstruction, and reconstruction of difference." *Hypatia,* 5(1), pp. 42–58.

Rötzer, F. (1990) "Virtuelle Katastrophen." *Kunstforum,* Jan.-Feb. [Interview with Jean Baudrillard].

Rouse, Irving (1986) *Migrations in Prehistory.* New Haven: Yale U. Press.

Rubin, Gayle (1984) "Thinking sex: Notes for a radical theory of the politics of sexuality." In C. Vance (ed) (1984), pp. 267–319.

Rubin, Joan Shelley (1985) "Self, culture, and self-culture in modern America: The early history of the Book-of-the-Month Club." *The Journal of American History,* 71, pp. 782–806.

Ruddick, Susan (1990) "Heterotopias of the homeless: Strategies and tactics of place-making in Los Angeles." *Strategies,* 3, pp. 184–201.

Rushdie, Salman (1988) *The Satanic Verses.* London: Viking Penguin.

Russ, Joanna (1985) "Pornography for women, by women, with love." *Magic Mommas, Trembling Sisters, Puritans and Perverts: Feminist Essays.* Trumansburg, NY: Crossing Press.

Russell, Mary (1986) *The Blessings of a Good Thick Skirt.* London: Collins.

Rust, Frances (1969) *Dance in Society.* London: Routledge.

Rutherford, Jonathan (ed) (1990) *Identity, Community, Culture, Difference.* London: Lawrence & Wishart.

Ruthven, Ken (1989) "Unlocking ideologies: 'Key-Words' as a trope." *Southern Review,* 25(1).

Ryan, Michael and Douglas Kellner (1988) *Camera Politica: The Politics and Ideology of Contemporary Hollywood Film.* Bloomington: Indiana U. Press.

Saakana, Amon Saba (1988) "Mythology and history: An afrocentric perspective of the world." *Third Text,* 3/4, pp. 143–150.

Said, Edward (1978) *Orientalism.* New York: Random House. (1985) Harmondsworth: Penguin.

Said, E. (1983) *The World, The Text, and the Critic.* Cambridge: Harvard U. Press.

Salazar, Claudia (ed) (1989) *Third World Feminism,* special issue of *Women and Language,* 11(2).

Sánchez, Luis Rafael (1984) "The airbus." Trans. D. Velez. *Village Voice,* 24 Jan., pp. 39–43.

Sánchez, Margarita V. (1973) "Escape." In P. Ortego (ed) (1973).

Sanchez-Tranquilino, Marcos (1987) "Mano a mano: An essay on the representation of the Zoot suit and its misrepresentation by Octavio Paz." *Journal of the Los Angeles Institute of Contemporary Art,* Winter, pp. 34–42.

Sanchez-Tranquilino, M. (1990) "*Murales del movimiento:* Chicano murals and the discourses of art and Americanization." In E. Cockroft and H. Barnet-Sanchez (eds) *Signs from the Heart: California Chicano Murals.* Venice, CA: Social and Public Art Resource Center, pp. 85–101.

Sandoval, Chela (1990) "Feminism and racism." In G. Anzaldúa (ed) (1990), pp. 55–71.

Sandoval, C. (forthcoming) "U.S. Third World Feminism: Towards a theory and method of oppositional consciousness in the postmodern world." *Genders.*

Sangari, Kum Kum (1987) "The politics of the possible." *Cultural Critique,* 7, pp. 157–186.

Sangari, K. (1989) "Introduction: Representations in history." *Journal of Arts and Ideas,* 17–18 June, p. 5.

Sangari, K. and Sudesh Vaid (eds) (1989) *Recasting Women: Essays in Colonial History.* Delhi: Kali.

Sanjek, R. (ed) (1990) *Fieldnotes: The Makings of Anthropology.* Ithaca: Cornell U. Press.

Satin, Mark (1979) *New Age Politics: Healing, Self and Society.* New York: Delta.

Savage, Jon (1989) "Do you know how to pony? The messianic intensity of the sixties." In A. McRobbie (ed) *Zoot Suits and Second Hand Dresses: An Anthology of Fashion and Music.* London: Macmillan.

Savage, J. (1990) "Tainted love: The influence of male homosexuality and sexual divergence on pop music and culture since the war." In A. Tomlinson (ed) *Consumption, Identity, and Style.* London: Comedia/Routledge, pp.153–171.

Sayers, Dorothy L. (1929) "The omnibus of crime." In R. Winks (ed) (1980) *Detective Fiction: A Collection of Critical Essays.* Englewood Cliffs, NJ: Prentice Hall.

Sayre, Ann (1975) *Rosalind Franklin and DNA.* New York: Norton.

Sayres, Sohnya, Anders Stephenson, Stanley Aronowitz, Fredric Jameson (eds) (1984) *The Sixties without Apology.* Minneapolis: U. of Minnesota Press.

Scarlett, Dora (1980) "Window onto Hungary." In B. Lommax (ed) *Eye-Witness in Hungary: The Soviet Invasion of 1956.* Nottingham: Spokesman.

Schiller, Frederick (1968) *On the Aesthetic Education of Man.* Trans. E. Wilkinson and L. Willoughby (eds). Oxford: The Clarendon Press.

Schiller, Herb (1989) *Culture Inc.: The Corporate Takeover of Public Expression.* New York: Oxford U. Press.

Schmitt, Carl (1986) *Political Romanticism.* Trans. G. Oakes. Cambridge, MA: MIT Press.

Schorske, Carl (1990) "History and the study of culture." *New Literary History,* 21(2), pp. 407–420.

Schwartz, Bill (1985) "Gramsci goes to Disneyland: Postmodernism and the popular." *Anglistica* (Naples), 28(3).

Schwartz, B. (1989) "Popular culture: The long march." *Cultural Studies,* 3(2), pp. 250–254.

Scruggs, Jan C. and Joel L. Swerdlow (1985) *The Vietnam Veterans Memorial: To Heal a Nation.* New York: Harper and Row.

Sedgwick, Eve Kosofsky (1985) *Between Men: English Literature and Male Homosocial Desire.* New York: Columbia U. Press.

Sekula, Allan (1984) "Dismantling modernism, reinventing documentary (Notes on the politics of representation)." *Photography Against the Grain.* Halifax: Press of the Nova Scotia College of Art and Design.

Semmel, Bernard (1976) *Jamaican Blood and the Victorian Conscience.* London: Greenwood Press.

Shaftesbury, Anthony, (The Third) Earl of (1900) *The Life, Unpublished Letters and Philosophical Regimen of Anthony, Earl of Shaftesbury.* B. Rand (ed). London: Swan Sonnenchein.

Shaftesbury, A., Earl of (n.d.) *Characteristics (Of Men, Manners, Opinions, Times).* G. Hemmerich and W. Benda (ed. in 2 vols.). Berlin: Fromann-Holzboog.

Shakespeare, William (1981) *Shakespeare's Plays in Quarto.* M. Allen and K. Muir (eds). Berkeley: U. of Calif. Press.

Shakespeare, W. and John Fletcher (1989) *The Two Noble Kinsmen.* E. Waith (ed). Oxford: Oxford U. Press.

Shapiro, Bennett M. (1987) "The existential decision of a sperm." *Cell,* 49, pp. 293–294.

Sharma, Arvind (1979) "Suttee: A study in Western reactions." In A. Sharma (ed) *Threshold of Hindu-Buddhist Studies.* Calcutta. pp. 83–111.

Shiach, Morag (1989) *Discourse on Popular Culture.* Cambridge: Polity Press.

Silverman, Kaja (1988) "Masochism and male subjectivity." *Camera Obscura,* 17, pp. 31–68.

Silverstone, Roger (1989) " 'Let us then return to the murmuring of everyday life': A note on Michel de Certeau, television and everyday life." *Theory and Society,* 6.

Sinclair, John (1971) "White panther party manifesto." In P. Stansill and D. Mairowitz (eds) (1971).

Singer, Peter (1975) *Animal Liberation: A New Ethics for Our Treatment of Animals.* New York: The New York Review.

Slater, P. (1977) *Origin and Significance of the Frankfurt School.* London: Routledge.

Small, Albion (1909) *The Cameralists: The Pioneers of German Social Polity.* Chicago: U. of Chicago Press.

Smith, Bernard (1960) *European Vision and the South Pacific 1768–1850.* Oxford: Oxford U. Press.

Smith, Paul (1988) *Discerning the Subject.* Minneapolis: U. of Minn. Press.

Smith, William Gardner (1953) Interview with Richard Wright. *Ebony,* 8 July, pp. 32–42.

Snitow, Ann, Christine Stansell and Sharon Thompson (eds) (1983) *Powers of Desire: The Politics of Sexuality.* New York: Monthly Review Press.

Sofia, Zoe (1984) "Exterminating fetuses: Abortion, disarmament, and the sexo-semiotics of extraterrestrialism." *Diacritics,* 14(2), pp. 47–59.

Soja, Edward W. (1985) "The spatiality of social life: Towards a transformative re-theorization." In D. Gregory and J. Urry (eds) *Social Relations and Spatial Structures.* London: Macmillan.

Soja, E. W. (1989) *Postmodern Geographies: The Reassertion of Space in Critical Social Theory.* New York: Verso.

Sokolowski, Thomas (1988a) "Preface." *Rosalind Solomon: Portraits in the Time of AIDS.* New York: Grey Art Gallery and Study Center, New York U.

Sokolowski, T. (1988b) "Looking in a mirror." *Rosalind Solomon: Portraits in the Time of AIDS.* New York: Grey Gallery and Study Center, New York U.

Solomon, Eldra Pearl (1983) *Human Anatomy and Physiology.* New York: CBS College Publishing.

Spencer, Paul (ed) (1985) *Society and the Dance.* Cambridge: Cambridge U. Press.

Spigel, Lynn (1988) "Installing the television set: Popular discourses on Television and domestic space, 1948–1955." *Camera Obscura,* 16, pp. 11–46.

Spivak, Gayatri C. (1983) "Displacement and the discourse of woman." In M. Krupnik (ed) (1983).

Spivak, G. C. (1985) "The Rani of Sirmur." In F. Barker, et al (eds) *Europe and Its Others*. Colchester: U. of Essex.

Spivak, G. C. (1987) *In Other Worlds: Essays in Cultural Politics*. London and New York: Methuen.

Spivak, G. C. (1988) "Can the subaltern speak?" In C. Nelson and L. Grossberg (eds) (1988) pp. 271–313.

Spivak, G. C. (1990) *The Post-Colonial Critic: Interviews, Strategies, Dialogues*. S. Harasym (ed). New York: Routledge.

Stacey, Jackie (1988) "Desperately seeking difference." In L. Gamman and M. Marshment (eds) (1988).

Stallybrass, Peter and Allon White (1986) *The Politics and Poetics of Transgression*. Ithaca: Cornell U. Press.

Stansell, Christine (1987) *City of Women: Sex and Class in New York, 1789–1860*. Urbana: U. of Illinois Press.

Stansill, Peter and David Mairowitz (eds) (1971) *BAMN (By Any Means Necessary): Outlaw Manifestos and Ephemera, 1965–1970*. Harmondsworth: Penguin.

Staples, Robert (1979) "The myth of Black Macho: A response to angry Black feminists." *The Black Scholar*, Mar./Apr., pp. 24–33.

Steedman, Carolyn (1984) "Battleground." *History Workshop Journal*, 17, pp. 102–112.

Steedman, C. (1986) *Landscape for a Good Woman: A Story of Two Lives*. London: Virago.

Steedman, C. (1990) *Childhood, Culture, and Class in Britain: Margaret McMillan, 1860–1931*. London: Virago Press. New Brunswick: Rutgers U. Press.

Stephanson, Anders (1987) "Regarding postmodernism—A conversation with Fredric Jameson." *Social Text*, 17, pp. 29–54.

Sterling, Dorothy (1971) *The Making of an Afro-American: Martin Robinson Delany 1812–1885*. Garden City, NY: Doubleday.

Stimpson, Catherine (1986) "Gertrude Stein and the transposition of gender." In N. Miller (ed) (1986).

Stitch, S. (ed) (1990) *Anxious Visions: Surrealist Art*. New York: Abbeville Press.

Strathern, Marilyn (1988) *The Gender of the Gift*. Berkeley: U. of Calif. Press.

Strum, S. (1987) *Almost Home: A Journey into the World of Baboons*. New York: Random House.

Stuart, Andrea (1990) "Feminism: Dead or alive?" In J. Rutherford (ed) (1990), pp. 28–42.

Sturge, Joseph and Thomas Harvey (1838) *The West Indies in 1837 being the journal of a visit to Antigua, Montserrat, Dominica, St. Lucia, Barbadoes, and Jamaica; undertaken for the purpose of ascertaining the actual condition of the negro population of those islands*. London: Hamilton Adams and Co.

Summers, Anne (1975) *Damned Whores and God's Police: The Colonization of Women in Australia*. Ringwood and Harmondsworth: Penguin.

Swan, Jim (1985) "Difference and silence: John Milton and the question of gender." In S. Garner, C. Kahane and M. Spenghether (eds) *(M)other Tongue: Essays in Feminist Psychoanalytic Interpretation*. Ithaca: Cornell U. Press.

Szasz, Thomas (1971) "An historical note on the use of medical diagnosis as justificatory rhetoric." *American Journal of Psychotherapy*, 25.

Tagg, John (ed) (1989) *The Cultural Politics of "Postmodernism."* Binghamton: SUNY at Binghamton.

Taguieff, Pierre-André (1990) "The new cultural racism in France." *Telos*, 83, pp. 109–122.

Tanaka, Yuki (1990) "The Japanese political-construction complex." In P. James (ed) *Technocratic Dreaming: Of Very Fast Trains and Japanese Designer Cities*. Melbourne: Left Book Club, pp. 71–77.

Taussig, Michael (1980) *The Devil and Commodity Fetishism in South America*. Chapel Hill: U. of North Carolina Press.

Taussig, M. (1987) *Shamanism, Colonialism, and the Wild Man: A Study in Terror and Healing*. Chicago: U. of Chicago Press.

Taylor, Charles (1985) *Philosphical Papers*. New York: Cambridge U. Press.

Taylor, Helen (1989) *Scarlett's Women*. London: Virago.

Taylor, L. and R. Mullan (1986) *Uninvited Guests*. London: Chatto and Windus.

Taylor, Paul (ed) (1985) *Juan Davila: Hysterical Tears*. Melbourne: Greenhouse.

El Teatro Campesino (1967) "Los vendidos." In Teatro Campesino (eds) (1971) *Actos*. Fresno: Cucaracha Press, pp. 35–49.

Temperley, Howard (1972) *British Antislavery 1833–1870*. London: Longman.

Terry, Jennifer (1989) "The body invaded: medical surveillance of women as reproducers." *Socialist Review*, 19(3), pp. 13–43.

Thiong'o, Ngugi Wa (1986) *Decolonizing the Mind: The Politics of Language in African Literature*. Portsmouth, NH: Heineman.

Thompson, E. P. (1961) Review of *The Long Revolution*. *New Left Review*, 9, pp. 24–33, and 10, pp. 34–39.

Thompson, E. P. (1963; rpt. 1966) *The Making of the English Working Class*. New York: Vintage.

Thompson, E. P. (1978) *The Poverty of Theory & Other Essays*. London: Merlin Press.

Thompson, Jemima (1841) *Memoirs of British female missionaries with a survey of the condition of women in heathen countries*. London: William Smith.

Timmerman, Col. Frederick (1987) "Future warriors." *Military Review*, Sept., pp. 44–55.

Tompkins, Jane (ed) (1980) *Reader Response Criticism*. Baltimore: Johns Hopkins U. Press.

Touraine, Alain (1981) *The Voice and the Eye: An Analysis of Social Movements*. Cambridge: Cambridge U. Press.

Touraine, A. (1988) *The Return of the Actor: Social Theory in Post-Industrial Society*. Minneapolis: U. of Minnesota Press.

Traweek, Sharon (1988) *Beam Times and Life Times: The World of High Energy Physicists*. Cambridge, MA: Harvard U. Press.

Treichler, Paula A. and Ellen Wartella (1986) "Interventions: Feminist theory and communication studies."*Communication*, 9(1), pp. 1–18.

Treichler, Paula A. (1988) "AIDS, homophobia, and biomedical discourse: An epidemic of signification." In D. Crimp (ed) (1988).

Treichler, P. (1989) "AIDS and HIV infection in the third world: A first world chronicle." In P. Mariani and B. Kruger (eds) *Remaking History*. New York: Dia Arts Foundation, pp. 31–86.

Treichler, P. (1990) "Feminism, medicine, and the meaning of childbirth." In M. Jacobus, E. Keller and S. Shuttleworth (eds) *Body/Politics: Women and the Discourses of Science*. New York: Routledge.

Tribe, K. (ed) (1989) *Reading Weber*. London: Routledge.

Trimble, Bjo (1983) *On the Good Ship Enterprise: My 15 Years with Star Trek*. Norfolk/Virginia Beach, VA: Donning Company.

Trujillo, Marcela L. (1978) "The terminology of machismo." *De Colores,* 4(3), pp. 34–42.

Turner, Graeme (1986) *National Fictions: Literature, Film, and the Construction of Australian Narrative.* Sydney: Allen and Unwin.

Turner, G. (1989) "Dilemmas of cultural critique." *Australian Journal of Communication,* 16.

Turner, G. (1990) *British Cultural Studies: An Introduction.* Boston: Unwin Hyman.

Turner, G. (1991) "Return to Oz: Populism, the academy, and the future of Australian Studies." *Meanjin,* 50, Autumn.

Turner, Mary (1982) *Slaves and Missionaries: The Disintegration of Jamaica Slave Society, 1787–1834.* Urbana: U. of Illinois Press.

Turner, Ralph and Samuel Surace (1972) "Zoot-suiters and mexicans." In R. Daniels and S. Olm (eds) *Racism in California: A Reader in the History of Oppression.* New York: Macmillan, pp. 210–219.

Turner, T. (1990) "Visual media, cultural politics, and anthropological practice: Some implications of recent uses of film and video among the Kaiapo of Brazil." *Commission on Visual Anthropology Review,* Spring.

Tuve, Rosemund (1947) *Elizabethan and Metaphysical Imagery: Renaissance Poetics and Twentieth Century Critics.* Chicago: U. of Chicago Press.

Tyrrell, Alex (1987) *Joseph Sturge and the Moral Radical Party in Early Victorian Britain.* London: Christopher Helm.

Underhill, Edward B. (1881) *Life of James Mursell Phillippo, Missionary in Jamaica.* London: Yates and Alexander.

Valaskakis, Gail (1988) "The Chippewa and the other: Living the heritage of Lac Du Flambeau." *Cultural Studies,* 2(3), pp. 267–293.

Valaskakis, G. (1989) "Partners in heritage: Living the tradition of spring spearing." *Journal of Communication Inquiry,* 13(2), pp. 12–17.

Vance, Carole (ed) (1984) *Pleasure and Danger.* Boston: Routledge.

Vander, Arthur, James Sherman and Dorothy Luciano (1980) *Human Physiology: The Mechanics of Body Function,* 3rd ed. New York: McGraw Hill.

Vander, A., J. Sherman and D. Luciano (1985) *Human Physiology: The Mechanics of Body Function,* 4th ed. New York: McGraw Hill.

VanDeVeer, Donald and Christine Pierce (1986) *People, Penguins, and Plastic Trees: Basic Issues in Environmental Ethics.* Belmont, CA: Wadsworth.

Van Vogt, A. E. (1974 [1948]) *Players of Null–A.* New York: Berkeley Books.

Varley, John (1979) *Titan.* New York: Berkeley Books.

Varley, J. (1986) "Press enter." In *Blue Champagne.* New York: Berkeley Books.

Vasconcelos, José (1979 [1925]) *La Raza Cósmica.* Trans. D. Jaen. Los Angeles: Calif. State U.

Vattimo, Gianni (1985) *La fine della modernità.* Milan: Garzanti. (1988) *The End of Modernity.* Oxford: Polity Press.

Vidal, Gore (1983) *Duluth.* New York: Ballantine Books.

Vidal, Mirta (1971) "New voices of La Raza: Chicanas speak out." *International Socialist Review,* 32, pp. 31–33.

Villanueva, Tino (1970) "Chicano is an act of defiance." In P. Ortego (ed) (1973).

Virillo, Paul and Sylvere Lotringer (1983) *Pure War.* New York: Semiotext(e).

Volonisov, V. N. (1973 [1929]) *Marxism and the Philosophy of Language.* Cambridge: Harvard U. Press.

Waith, Eugene [see Shakespeare, W.]

Walkerdine, Valerie (1986) "Video replay: Families, films and fantasy." In V. Burgin, J. Donald and C. Kaplan (eds) *Formations of Fantasy*. London: Methuen.

Wallace, Michele (1989) "Reading 1968 and the great American whitewash." In B. Kruger and P. Mariani (eds) *Remaking History*. Seattle, WA: Bay Press, pp. 97–109.

Wallace, M. (1990) *Invisibility Blues: From Pop to Theory*. London: Verso.

Wallis, Brian and Cynthia Schneider (eds) (1989) *Global Television*. Cambridge, MA: MIT and Wedge.

Walter, Aubrey (ed) (1980) *Come Together: The Years of Gay Liberation, 1970–1973*. London: Gay Men's Press.

Walvin, James (ed) (1982) *Slavery and British Society 1776–1846*. London: Macmillan.

Ward, Russell (1958) *The Australian Legend*. Melbourne: OUP.

Ward, William (1822) *View of the History, Literature, and Mythology of the Hindoos,* vol. 3. London.

Warner, William (1989) "Treating me like an object: Reading Catharine MacKinnon's Feminism." In L. Kauffman (ed) *Feminism and Institutions: Dialogues on Feminist Theory*. Cambridge: Basil Blackwell.

Warren, Karen J. (1987) "Feminism and ecology: Making connections." *Environmental Ethics,* 9, pp. 3–20.

Watney, Simon (1989) "Taking liberties: An introduction." In E. Carter and S. Watney (eds) *Taking Liberties: AIDS and Cultural Politics*. London: Serpent's Tail.

Waugh, P. (1989) *Feminine Fictions: Revisiting the Postmodern*. New York: Routledge.

Weaver, Kenneth (1961) "Countdown for space." *National Geographic,* 119(5), pp. 702–734.

Weber, Max (1930) *The Protestant Ethic and the Spirit of Capitalism*. Trans. T. Parsons. London: Allen & Unwin.

Wedderburn, R. (1824) *The Horrors of Slavery; Exemplified in the Life and History of the Rev. Robert Wedderburn*. London.

Weedon, Chris (1987) *Feminist Practice and Poststructuralist Theory*. Oxford: Blackwell.

Weeks, Jeffrey (1990) "The value of difference." In J. Rutherford (ed) (1990), pp. 88–100.

Wenzel, S. (1985) "Poets, preachers, and the plight of the literary critics." *Speculum,* 60, pp. 343–351.

Wersky, Gary (1978) *The Invisible College: The Collective Biography of British Socialist Scientists in the 1930s*. London: Allen Lane.

West, Cornel (1988) "An interview with Cornel West." In A. Ross (ed) (1988a), pp. 269–286.

West, C. (1989) "Black culture and postmodernism." In B. Kruger and P. Mariani (eds) *Remaking History*. Seattle: Bay Press, pp. 87–96.

West, C. (1990a) *The American Evasion of Philosophy*. Madison: U. of Wisconsin Press.

West, C. (1990b) "The new cultural politics of difference." *October,* 53, pp. 93–108.

Whipple, Leon (1929) "Books on the belt." *The Nation,* 128, p. 182.

White, Allon (1983) "The dismal sacred word: Academic language and the social reproduction of seriousness." *Journal of Literature, Teaching, Politics,* 2, pp. 4–15.

Williams, Bernard (1985) *Ethics and the Limits of Philosophy*. Cambridge, MA: Harvard U. Press.

Williams, Brett (1988) *Upscaling Downtown: Stalled Gentrification in Washington, D.C.* Ithaca: Cornell U. Press.

Williams, Linda (1987) " 'Something else besides a mother': Stella Dallas and the maternal melodrama." In C. Gledhill (ed) (1987).

Williams, L. (1989) *Hard Core: Power, Pleasure and the Frenzy of the Visible.* Berkeley: U. of Calif. Press.

Williams, Raymond (1958) *Culture and Society 1780–1950.* London: Chatto and Windus. (1963) Harmondsworth: Penguin.

Williams, R. (1961; rpt. 1965) *The Long Revolution.* London: Penguin.

Williams, R. (1975) *Television: Technology and Cultural Form.* New York: Schocken Books.

Williams, R. (1976) *Keywords.* London: Fontana.

Williams, R. (1977) *Marxism and Literature.* Oxford: Oxford U. Press.

Williams, R. (1979) *Politics and Letters.* London: Verso.

Williams, R. (1981) *Culture.* London: Fontana.

Williams, R. (1989a) *The Politics of Modernism: Against the New Conformists.* London: Verso.

Williams, R. (1989b) "The future of cultural studies." In R. Williams (1989a), pp. 151–162.

Williams, R. (1989c) "The uses of cultural theory." In R. Williams (1989a), pp. 163–177.

Williams, R. (1989d) "Adult education and social change." *What I Came to Say.* London: Hutchinson-Radus, pp. 157–166.

Williams, R. (1989e) *Resources of Hope: Culture, Democracy, Socialism.* R. Gable (ed). London: Verso.

Williamson, Judith (1986) "The problems of being popular." *New Socialist,* Sept., pp. 14–15.

Williamson, J. (1990) "Arts Diary." *The Guardian,* Oct.

Willis, Paul (1977) *Learning to Labour: How Working Class Kids Get Working Class Jobs.* New York: Columbia U. Press.

Willis, P. (1980) "Introduction to ethnography at the Centre." In S. Hall et al (eds) *Culture, Media, Language.* London: Hutchinson.

Willis, P. (1990) "The golden age." In S. Frith and A. Goodwin (eds) (1990), pp. 43–55.

Willmot, Eric (1987a) *Australia: The Last Experiment.* Sydney: ABC Enterprises.

Willmot, E. (1987b) *Pemelwuy: The Rainbow Warrior.* Sydney: Weldons.

Wilmot, S. (1982) "The peacemakers: Baptist missionaries and ex-slaves in West Jamaica." *Jamaican Historical Review,* 13, pp. 42–48.

Winant, Howard (1990) "Gayatri Spivak and the politics of the subaltern." *Socialist Review,* 20, pp. 89–91.

Winship, Janice (1987) *Inside Women's Magazines.* London: Pandora.

Winzen, Peter (1981) "Treitschke's influence on the rise of imperialist and anti-British nationalism in Germany." In P. Kennedy and A. Nicholls (eds) *Nationalist and Racialist Movements in Britain and Germany Before 1914.* London: Macmillan.

Wittig, Monique (1986) "The mark of gender." In N. Miller (ed) (1986).

Wolf, Eric (1982) *Europe and the People Without History.* Berkeley: U. of Calif. Press.

Wolfe, Tom (1969) *Mau Mau and the Radical Chic.* New York: Wildwood House.

Wolff, Janet and John Seed (eds) (1988) *The Culture of Capital: Art, Power and the Nineteenth-Century Middle Class.* Manchester: Manchester U. Press.

Women's Studies Group, Centre for Contemporary Cultural Studies (1978) *Women Take Issue: Aspects of Women's Subordination.* London: Hutchinson.

Wood, John (ed) (1970) *Enoch Powell and the 1970 Election.* Farnham: Elliot Right Way Books.

Workman, Gillian (1974) "Thomas Carlyle and the Governor Eyre controversy." *Victorian Studies,* 18(1), pp. 77–102.

Wright, Lawrence (1980) *Clean and Decent.* Harmondsworth: Penguin.

Wright, Patrick (1985) *On Living in an Old Country.* London: Verso.

Wright, Richard (1958) *The Color Curtain.* New York: Collins.

Wrobel, Arthur (ed) (1978) *Pseudo-Science and Society in Nineteenth-Century America.* Lexington: U. of Kentucky Press.

X, Malcolm (1966) *The Autobiography of Malcolm X.* Harmondsworth: Penguin.

Yarbro-Bejarano, Yvonne (1986) "The female subject in Chicano theatre: Sexuality, 'race,' and class." *Theatre Journal,* 38(4), pp. 389–407.

Yarbro-Bejarano, Y. (forthcoming) "Gloria Anzaldúa's *Borderlands/La Frontera:* Cultural studies, 'difference,' and the non-unitary subject." In M. Garcia and E. McCracken (eds) *Cultural Studies: New Critical Directions.*

Yates, Frances (1964) *Giordano Bruno and the Hermetic Tradition.* London: Routledge.

Zimmer, Carl (1990) "Tech in the jungle." *Discover,* Aug., p. 42.

Zimmerman, Michael (1987) "Feminism, deep ecology, and environmental ethics." *Environmental Ethics,* 9, pp. 21–44.

Contributors' Notes

Lawrence Grossberg
Lawrence Grossberg teaches in the department of Speech Communications at the University of Illinois at Urbana-Champaign. He is the author of *It's a Sin: Essays on Postmodernity, Politics, and Culture* and *We Gotta Get Out of This Place: Pop, Politics, and Postmodernity*. He has co-edited numerous volumes, including *Marxism and the Interpretation of Culture*, and is co-editor of the journal *Cultural Studies*.

Cary Nelson
Cary Nelson is Jubilee Professor of Liberal Arts and Sciences, Professor of English, and founding director of the Unit for Criticism and Interpretive Theory at the University of Illinois at Urbana-Champaign. He is the author of *The Incarnate Word: Literature as Verbal Space; Our Last First Poets: Vision and History in Contemporary American Poetry*, and, most recently, *Repression and Recovery: Modern American Poetry and the Politics of Cultural Memory, 1910–1945*. He is the editor of *Theory in the Classroom* and the co-editor of several books, including *Marxism and the Interpretation of Culture* and *Edwin Rolfe*.

Paula A. Treichler
Paula A. Treichler holds joint appointments in the College of Medicine, the Institute for Communications Research, and Women's Studies at the University of Illinois at Urbana-Champaign. She is the co-author of *A Feminist Dictionary* and of *Language, Gender, and Professional Writing: Theoretical Approaches and Guidelines for Nonsexist Usage*. She is the co-editor of *For Alma Mater: Theory and Practice in Feminist Scholarship*. She is presently completing *AIDS and Culture: An Epidemic of Signification* and a book on language and women's literature.

Homi Bhabha
Homi K. Bhabha teaches English at the University of Sussex. He is the editor of *Nation and Narration*, and publishes widely on postcolonial discourses.

Tony Bennett
Tony Bennett is Associate Professor at Griffith University (Brisbane, Australia) where he is Dean of Humanities and Director of the Institute for Cultural Policy Studies. He is the editor of *Popular Culture and Social Relations* (with Kobena Mercer and Janet Woollacott), *Popular Television and Film* (with Boyd-Bowman, et al.), *Culture, Ideology and Social Process* (with Martin, et al.), and *Popular Fiction: Technology, Ideology, Production, Reading*. He is the co-author of *Bond and Beyond: The Political Career of a Popular Hero* (with J. Woollacott) and the author of *Formalism and Marxism* and *Outside Literature*. His forthcoming *Show and Tell: The Museum, the Fair and the Exhibition* is a study of the museum as a structure of power.

Jody Berland
Jody Berland teaches Communications at Concordia University in Montreal. She has published numerous essays on music and technology, radio, television, video, and

cultural policies. She is currently writing an historical analysis of the culture of weather, and editing a collection on Canadian culture and cultural studies.

Rosalind Brunt

Rosalind Brunt is Director of the Centre for Popular Culture and Principal Lecturer in Communication Studies at the Sheffield City Polytechnic in England. She has co-edited *Feminism, Culture and Politics* and *Silver Linings: Some Strategies for the Eighties.* She is on the editorial board of *Marxism Today* and on the executive committees of the British Association for Cultural Studies and the Association for Media Film and Television Studies in Higher Education.

Angie Chabram-Dernersesian

Angie Chabram-Dernersesian is an activist Chicana scholar born in Monterey, California. Chabram-Dernersesian earned her B.A. at UC Berkeley, and her M.A. and Ph.D. at UC San Diego (1986) and is currently teaching at the University of California at Davis and is a member of MALCS (Active Women in Letters and Social Change). Author of articles in the areas of feminism, ethnography, and criticism, she has recently co-edited a special volume of *Cultural Studies* on Chicana/o cultural representations which includes her essay "Chicana/o Studies as Oppositional Ethnography."

James Clifford

James Clifford is Professor in the History of Consciousness Program, University of California, Santa Cruz. He is co-editor of *Writing Culture: The Politics and Poetics of Ethnography* and author of *The Predicament of Culture.*

Douglas Crimp

Douglas Crimp, an art critic and AIDS activist, was coeditor of *October* for thirteen years and currently teaches gay and lesbian studies at Sarah Lawrence College. He is the author of *AIDS Demo Graphics* (with Adam Rolston), editor of *AIDS: Cultural Analysis/Cultural Activism,* and coeditor of *How Do I Look? Queer Film and Video.* A collection of his essays entitled *On the Museum's Ruins* is forthcoming.

Lidia Curti

Lidia Curti teaches English and cultural studies at the Istituto Universitario Orientale, Naples. She studied at the Centre for Contemporary Cultural Studies (Birmingham) and translated Richard Hoggart's *The Uses of Literacy* into Italian. She is the author of a book on Shakespeare in avant-grade theater, is on the editorial board of *New Formations* (London), and has published various essays on contemporary culture and feminism. She is presently preparing a book on *Genre and Gender* for Macmillan.

John Fiske

John Fiske is Professor of Communication at the University of Wisconsin. His books include *Reading Television* (with John Hartley), *Television Culture, Reading the Popular,* and *Understanding Popular Culture.*

Simon Frith

Simon Frith is Professor and Research Director of the John Logie Baird Centre and Head of the English Department at Strathclyde University. His books include *The Sociology of Rock, Sound Effects, Art into Pop,* and *Music for Pleasure.* He has written music criticism for the *Sunday Times* (London), the *Observer, Scotland on Sunday,* and the *Village Voice.* He has recently edited three collections—*Facing the Music, World Music, Politics and Social Change,* and *On Record: The Pop and Rock Reader* (with A. Goodwin). He chairs the International Association for the Study of Popular Music.

Paul Gilroy

Paul Gilroy is Lecturer in Sociology at the University of Essex. He is the author of *There Ain't No Black in the Union Jack.*

Henry Giroux

Henry Giroux is Waterbury Chair in Secondary Education at Pennsylvania State University. His most recent book is *Border Crossings: Cultural Workers and the Politics of Education.*

David Glover

David Glover teaches in Eugene Lang College at the New School for Social Research. He is the author of *The Sociology of the Mass Media* and *The Sociology of Knowledge.* His current book is called *Mastering Mystery: The Sexual Politics of Crime Fiction* (with Cora Kaplan), and he is also working on *The 'Mechanical' and the 'Artistic': Popular Fiction and the Crisis of Liberalism,* a study of British popular culture in the inter-war years.

Jan Zita Grover

Jan Zita Grover edits *Artpaper* in Minneapolis. Her articles on AIDS have appeared in such journals as *Afterimage, Christianity & Crisis, In These Times, Jump Cut, October,* and *The Women's Review of Books.*

Catherine Hall

Catherine Hall is Senior Lecturer in Cultural Studies, Polytechnic of East London. She is co-author of *Family Fortunes: Men and Women of the English Middle Class, 1780–1850,* and is on the collective of *Feminist Review.*

Stuart Hall

Stuart Hall, Professor of Sociology at the Open University, was for a decade director of the Centre for Contemporary Cultural Studies in Birmingham. He has co-edited many volumes including *Culture, Media, Language, Resistance Through Rituals,* and most recently, *New Times.* He has co-authored *Policing The Crisis* and recently published *The Hard Road to Renewal: Thatcherism and the Crisis of the Left.*

Donna Haraway

Donna Haraway works in the History of Consciousness Program at the University of California at Santa Cruz, where she teaches feminist theory, science studies, and women's studies. She is the author of *Crystals, Fabrics, and Fields: Metaphors of Organicism in Twentieth-Century Developmental Biology; Primate Visions: Gender, Race, and Nature in the World of Modern Science;* and *Simians, Cyborgs and Women: The Reinvention of Nature.*

bell hooks

bell hooks teaches at Oberlin College. Her books include *Ain't I a Woman; Talking Back;* and *Yearning: Race, Gender, and Cultural Politics.*

Ian Hunter

Ian Hunter teaches in the Division of Humanities at Griffith University (Brisbane, Australia). His book *Culture and Government: The Emergence of Literary Education* has recently been published by Macmillan. A second book, co-authored with David Saunders and Dugald Willamson, *On Pornography: Literature, Sexuality, and Obscenity Law,* is currently in press.

Cora Kaplan

Cora Kaplan teaches English at Rutgers University. Her work is collected in *Sea Changes: Essays on Culture and Feminism.* She is currently working on two books, *"Giant*

Propensities": *Race, Gender, and Nation in Jane Eyre,* and *Mastering Mystery: The Sexual Politics of Crime Fiction* (with David Glover).

Laura Kipnis

Laura Kipnis is a video artist and critic who teaches in the Department of Radio, TV, and Film at Northwestern University. A collection of her video scripts and essays titled *Symptoms* will be published by the University of Minnesota Press.

Lata Mani

Lata Mani is Assistant Professor of Women's Studies at the University of California, Davis. She is a historian whose research interests include feminist theory and colonial and contemporary discourses on women and culture. She is currently completing a manuscript on nineteenth-century British colonial, missionary, and indigenous discourses on widow burning, to be published by the University of California Press.

Emily Martin

Emily Martin is Professor of Anthropology at Johns Hopkins University. Her books include *The Woman in the Body: A Cultural Analysis of Reproduction; The Cult of the Dead in a Chinese Village; The Anthropology of Taiwanese Society;* and *Chinese Ritual and Politics.*

Angela McRobbie

Angela McRobbie is Seminar Lecturer in Sociology at Ealing College, London. She is editor of *Zoot Suits and Second-Hand Dresses: An Anthology of Fashion and Music,* and author of *Feminism and Youth Culture: From Jackie to Just Seventeen* and *On Gender, Culture, and Criticism.*

Kobena Mercer

Kobena Mercer grew up in Ghana and England, and received a B.A. in Fine Art from St. Martins School of Art and a Ph.D. in Sociology from University of London, Goldsmiths' College. He has published widely on the cultural politics of race, identity, and representation, edited *Black Film/British Cinema* for the Institute of Contemporary Arts, London, co-edited *Screen's* "Last 'Special Issue' on Race?" and is anthologized in *Photography/Politics: Two, The Media Reader,* and *Out There: Marginalization and Contemporary Cultures.* Formerly at the British Film Institute, he is currently Assistant Professor in the Art History and History of Consciousness programs at the University of California, Santa Cruz.

Meaghan Morris

Meaghan Morris is a freelance writer in Sydney, Australia. Her essays are collected in *The Pirate's Fiancée: Feminism, Reading, Postmodernism.* She is currently completing a book about history on television, *The Live, the Dead, and the Living,* and a book about Australian women's cultural practices in capitalist spaces, *Upward Mobility.*

Constance Penley

Constance Penley teaches film at the University of California at Santa Barbara, and edits *Camera Obscura.* Her books include *The Future of an Illusion: Film, Feminism, and Psychoanalysis* and the edited collection *Feminism and Film Theory.*

Elspeth Probyn

Elspeth Probyn teaches in the Sociology Department at the University of Montreal. She has published widely in feminism, cultural studies, and postmodernism. Her forthcoming book (Routledge) explores questions of subjectivity and experience in feminist theory.

Janice Radway

Janice Radway teaches in the Program in Literature at Duke University. She is author of *Reading the Romance*, and is currently completing a cultural analysis of the Book-of-the-Month Club. She is past editor of *American Quarterly* and new co-editor of *Cultural Studies*.

Andrew Ross

Andrew Ross teaches English at Princeton University. His books include *Strange Weather: Culture, Science, and Technology in the Age of Limits* and *No Respect: Intellectuals and Popular Culture*. He is also editor of *Universal Abandon?*, the co-editor (with Constance Penley) of *Technoculture*, and a member of the *Social Text* editorial collective.

Marcos Sanchez-Tranquilino

Marcos Sanchez-Tranquilino was a founding consultant, co-project coordinator, and National Selection Committee member for the national and historical exhibition, "Chicano Art: Resistance and Affirmation, 1965–85." He was a principal archivist for the California Chicano Mural Slide Archive at the Social and Public Art Resource Center (SPARC) in Venice, California, and has written, lectured, and published on the subject of Chicano art history and theory.

Jennifer Daryl Slack

Jennifer Daryl Slack teaches in Humanities at Michigan Technological University. She is the author of *Communications Technologies and Society*.

Peter Stallybrass

Peter Stallybrass is Professor of Comparative Literature and Literary Theory at the University of Pennsylvania. He published *The Politics and Poetics of Transgression* (with Allon White). He is currently working on *Embodied Politics: Enclosure and Transgression in Early Modern England*, and editing *Staging the Renaissance: Studies in Elizabethan and Jacobean Drama* (with David Kastan).

Carolyn Steedman

Carolyn Steedman is Senior Lecturer in Arts Education at the University of Warwick, England. Her works include *Landscape for a Good Woman, Childhood, Culture, and Class in Britain: Margaret McMillan, 1860–1931, Policing the Victorian Community, The Tidy House*, and *The Radical Soldier's Tale*. She is currently (1990–1991) Senior Simon Research Fellow at the University of Manchester, working on a history of subjectivity and interiority in the period 1780–1930.

Anna Szemere

Anna Szemere is a Research Fellow at the Hungarian Academy of Sciences, Budapest. Her field of interest involves the sociology of culture and issues of political culture. She has published numerous articles and chapters with a focus on popular culture, music, and youth. She is Advisory Editor to the journal *Popular Music*. She currently lives and works in San Diego, California.

John Tagg

John Tagg is Associate Professor of Art History at SUNY Binghamton. He is author of *The Burden of Representation: Essays on Photographies and Histories* and *Grounds of Dispute: Art History, Cultural Politics, and the Discursive Field*, and the editor of *The Cultural Politics of "Postmodernism"* and of Max Raphael's *Proudhon, Marx, Picasso: Three Essays on the Sociology of Art*.

Graeme Turner

Graeme Turner is Associate Professor in the Department of English, University of Queensland, Australia. He is the author of *National Fictions: Literature, Film and the Construction of Australian Narrative, Film as Social Practice,* and *British Cultural Studies: An Introduction.* He is co-author (with John Fiske and Bob Hodge) of *Myths of Oz: Reading Australian Popular Culture,* and co-editor (with John Tullock) of *Australian Television: Programs, Pleasures, and Politics.* He was one of the founding editors of the *Australian Journal of Cultural Studies* and of its successor, *Cultural Studies.*

Michele Wallace

Michele Wallace, Assistant Professor of English at the City College of New York, teaches Afro-American literature and literary criticism, and black feminist theory. She is the author of *Black Macho and The Myth of The Superwoman* and *Invisibility Blues: From Pop to Theory.* She is currently working on a book project called "The Problem of The Visual in Afro-American Culture."

William Warner

William Warner teaches in the English Department at SUNY Buffalo. He is the author of *Reading Clarissa: The Struggles of Interpretation* and *Chance and the Text of Experience: Freud, Nietzsche, and Shakespeare's Hamlet.*

Cornel West

Cornel West is Professor of Religion and Director of Afro-American Studies at Princeton University. His most recent books are *The American Evasion of Philosophy, Breakin' Bread: Insurgent Black Intellectual Life* (with bell hooks), and *The Ethical Dimensions of Marxist Thought. Prophetic Criticism* is forthcoming.

Laurie Anne Whitt

Laurie Anne Whitt teaches in Humanities at Michigan Technological University.

Janet Wolff

Janet Wolff is Professor of Art History and Comparative Arts at the University of Rochester. Her most recent book is *Feminine Sentences: Essays on Women and Culture.* She is also the author of *The Social Production of Art* and *Aesthetics and the Sociology of Art,* and editor, with John Seed, of *The Culture of Capital: Art, Power, and the Nineteenth-Century Middle Class.*

Index